UNIVERSITY OF EVANSVILLE
HARLAXTON COLL
HARLAXTON M
GRANTHAM

HARLAXTON COLL

15190

57/DAV

D1634178

A HISTORY OF
THE METHODIST CHURCH
IN GREAT BRITAIN

VOLUME FOUR

UNIVERSITY OF EVANSVILLE
HARLAXTON COLLEGE LIBRARY
HARLAXTON MANOR
GRANTHAM, LINCS.

General Editors

RUPERT DAVIES

A. RAYMOND GEORGE

GORDON RUPP

A History of
THE
METHODIST
CHURCH
in Great Britain

———◦⊙◦———

VOLUME FOUR

UNIVERSITY OF EVANSVILLE
HARLAXTON COLLEGE LIBRARY
HARLAXTON MANOR
GRANTHAM, LINCS.

LONDON
EPWORTH PRESS

015190

© *Epworth Press 1988*

First published 1988
by Epworth Press
All rights reserved
No part of this publication
may be reproduced, stored in a
retrieval system, or
transmitted, in any form or by
any means, electronic, mechanical,
photocopying, recording or
otherwise, without the prior
permission of Epworth Press

Enquiries should be addressed to
The Epworth Press
Room 195
1 Central Buildings
Westminster
London SW1H 9NR

Typeset by Gloucester Typesetting Services
and printed in Great Britain by
Richard Clay (The Chaucer Press) Plc
Bungay, Suffolk

British Library Cataloguing in Publication Data

A history of the Methodist Church in Great
Britain.
Vol. 4
1. Methodist Church (Great Britain) –
History
287'.5'09

ISBN 0-7162-0444-4

CONTENTS

PREFACE

With this volume the publication of *A History of the Methodist Church in Great Britain* comes to its appointed end. The project of writing it was initiated by the Methodist Conference of 1953, and the lapse of time since then has made it possible to include at appropriate points the results of the continuing research into the origins and nature of Methodism; but 'the chances and changes of this mortal life', which are bound to impinge on the progress of so complex an enterprise, together with the heavy involvement of all of the contributors in ecclesiastical, ecumenical and academic affairs, have made this period much longer than the General Editors would have wished.

The promise was made in the earlier Prefaces that the *History* would be completed by a volume which would include a collection of the primary documents which are needed for the further study of Methodist history, and a bibliography to cover the whole work. The General Editors commissioned Mr (now Dr) John A. Vickers, then Principal Lecturer in Religious Studies at the Bognor Regis College of Education, to assemble the documents; and Dr Clive D. Field, Assistant Librarian, and now also Head of the Audio-Visual and Publications Department in the John Rylands University Library of Manchester, to compile and select the bibliography. The General Editors have had the light task of exercising general supervision, making occasional suggestions, and giving final approval to the comprehensive and judicious work done by these two scholars; and therefore they are able warmly to commend this volume to everyone, Methodist or not, who wishes to pursue in depth the study of Methodism within the context of the Church Catholic of which it is an abiding part.

The Methodist Churches of the world are now looking forward to the celebration in 1988 of the 250th anniversary of John Wesley's evangelical conversion. We hope that this *History* in all its parts will serve as a spiritual and intellectual preparation for the proper commemoration of that momentous event.

We are very grateful to successive editors of the Epworth Press for their help and patience during the fulfilment of the long-laid plans of the History of Methodism Committee of the Methodist Conference.

December 1986   RUPERT E. DAVIES
                                                        A. RAYMOND GEORGE
                                                        E. GORDON RUPP

As this volume was being finally prepared for the printers, we learned that our colleague, Gordon Rupp, had died. We place on record our deep admiration for the scholarly enthusiasm which has inspired and sustained us throughout the execution of this enterprise, for his wise advice and careful attention at each succeeding stage, and for the wide-ranging historical learning which informed all his judgments.

                                                                R.E.D.
                                                                A.R.G.

LIST OF ILLUSTRATIONS

ACKNOWLEDGEMENTS

We are grateful to the following for their consent to the inclusion of unpublished material in this volume:

In the United Kingdom
The British Library, Department of Manuscripts
Humberside County Council
Lambeth Palace Library
The Methodist Archives Centre, John Rylands University Library of
    Manchester
The Methodist Church Overseas Division
The New Room, Bristol
Wesley College, Bristol

In the United States of America
Drew University, Madison, NJ
Duke University, Durham, NC
Emory University, Atlanta, GA
Garrett-Evangelical Theological Seminary, Evanston, Ill
Southern Methodist University, Dallas, TX
Wesley Theological Seminary, Washington DC

And to the Rev. Dr Frank Baker, Dr A. J. Hayes, Mr G. E. Milburn, Miss Janet Robb, Mr E. A. Rose

ABBREVIATIONS

————o⊙o————

BC	Bible Christian
CMHA	Cornish Methodist Historical Association
CWJ	*The Journal of the Rev. Charles Wesley M.A.*, edited by Thomas Jackson, 2 vols, 1849
DNB	*Dictionary of National Biography*
EMP	*Lives of the Early Methodist Preachers, chiefly written by themselves*, edited by Thomas Jackson, 4th edition, 6 vols., 1871–2
Hayes and Gowland	*Scottish Methodism in the early Victorian Period*, edited by A. J. Hayes and D. A. Gowland, 1981
HMGB	*A History of the Methodist Church in Great Britain*, Vols. 1–3, 1965, 1978, 1983
JWJ	*The Journal of John Wesley*, standard edition, edited by Nehemiah Curnock, 8 vols., 1909–16
JWL	*The Letters of John Wesley*, standard edition, edited by John Telford, 8 vols., 1931
JWW	*The Works of John Wesley*, 3rd edition, edited by Thomas Jackson, 14 vols., 1829–31
MA	Methodist Archives Centre, The John Rylands University Library of Manchester
MCOD	Methodist Church Overseas Division
Minutes	*Minutes of the Methodist/Wesleyan Methodist Conferences*[1]
MNC	Methodist New Connexion
Oxford *Letters*	*Oxford Edition of the Works of John Wesley*, Vols. 25 and 26, *Letters I and II*, edited by Frank Baker, 1980, 1982
Petty, *History*	*The History of the Primitive Methodist Connexion from its origin to the Conference of 1859*, by John Petty, 1860
PM	Primitive Methodist
PW	*The Poetical Works of John and Charles Wesley*, edited by George Osborn, 13 vols., 1868–72
Sermons	*Bicentennial Edition of the Works of John Wesley*, Vols. 1–4, *Sermons*, edited by Albert C. Outler, 1984–87

[1] Wherever no other Methodist denomination is specified, the reference is to Wesleyan Methodism.

Sidelights	*Sidelights on the Conflicts of Methodism during the second quarter of the nineteenth century, 1827–1852*, by Benjamin Gregory, 1898
Smith, *History*	*History of Wesleyan Methodism* by George Smith, 2nd edition, 3 vols., 1859–61
SMU	Southern Methodist University, Dallas, Texas
UMC	United Methodist Church
WHS	*Proceedings of the Wesley Historical Society*, 1897ff
WM	Wesleyan Methodist

NOTE

Various American universities and seminaries are referred to by name only at the head of some of the documents. Their full addresses are to be found in the Acknowledgements, p. xi.

PART ONE

Documents and Source Material

INTRODUCTORY NOTE

The collection of source material presented here is designed to supplement the three-volume *History of the Methodist Church in Great Britain*, but also to stand in its own right. From the wealth of material available, limitations of space permit only a representative selection, but one which, I hope, will throw light on many different aspects of British Methodism and serve as a pointer to what has been left out. (The vast resources of Methodist periodicals and newspapers, for example, remain largely untapped.) Inevitably, some items are familiar or are readily available elsewhere; but wherever possible I have given preference to the unknown and the unpublished. In doing so, I have drawn on a wide variety of manuscript sources, including American collections not easily accessible to the British-based student.

The extracts are chronologically rather than thematically arranged, with only occasional exceptions, where it seemed convenient to group two or more related items together. The juxtaposition of roughly contemporary documents may, often inadvertently, bring their significance into sharper focus.

Within the imposed limitations, an attempt has been made to strike a series of balances: between the eighteenth century and later periods (despite an inevitable bias in favour of the former), the connexional and the local, official policy and grassroots deviations, organisation and spirituality, controversy and piety, high Wesleyan and Radical Methodist, and so on. Impressions and verdicts on Methodism from outside the Methodist fold provide alternative perspectives, whether Anglican, dissenting or secular. But beyond this it has not here been possible to give any of the wider social and cultural background without which the rise and development of Methodism cannot be understood.

Some topics, such as the development of Methodist architecture and the vast field of overseas missions, have only a token representation. Others are excluded altogether by editorial policy: notably, Calvinistic Methodism, which played a significant part in the Evangelical Revival but has never been part of the British Methodist Church or its antecedents, and the period since 1932.

Many of the extracts have been abbreviated, not only to economise on space, but in the hope that this will send the serious student back to the originals, for which, in the end, there is no substitute. Whether in either selecting or abbreviating I have distorted the evidence must be for others to judge. The source of each extract is indicated. Ellipses are always marked, except where they occur at the beginning or end of an extract. In the case of letters, opening and closing courtesies are normally omitted. Punctuation and spelling have been to some extent modernised, except where this might diminish the impact of the original. Editorial comment is kept to a minimum, since the background to the documents is provided by Volumes 1–3 of the *History* or by such standard works of reference as the *Encyclopaedia of World Methodism*. Notes indicated by an asterisk are part of the original extract. Notes indicated by a number have been added by the present editor.

A few items are reproduced in facsimile. Rather than attempt a full range of statistics, only a few statistical tables are included, with no implied claim as to their reliability or significance. For those who enjoy playing statistical games, the full annual membership figures for all branches of Methodism have been made available by Currie, Gilbert and Horsley.[1]

The gathering of this harvest has taken place in many different libraries and repositories on both sides of the Atlantic, and I gladly acknowledge the courtesy and helpfulness of the many librarians and archivists involved. The collection also owes much to what I have learned from others, both from their books and from personal contacts and friendships over the years. My first resource has always been the documentation to the various chapters in Volumes 1–3. But in the case of such special topics as the non-Wesleyan branches, Irish Methodism, and overseas missions, I am indebted to the advice of specialists in those fields. It would be a lengthy and hazardous task to attempt an exhaustive catalogue of my indebtedness, but I am grateful for it all. If this volume had a dedication, it would certainly be to Charles and Betty Young of Durham N.C., whose long-standing friendship and generous hospitality made it possible for so much of the work to be done on the Duke University campus.

John A. Vickers

---

[1] Robert Currie, Alan Gilbert and Lee Horsley, *Churches and Churchgoers: Patterns of Church Growth in the British Isles since 1700*, 1977.

1. To the Death of John Wesley

The 'Oxford Methodists'

(John Gambold, letter 'to a friend: Wrote about the time when Mr. Wesley was in America', printed in the *Methodist Magazine*, March 1798, pp. 117–21, 168–72)

Gambold came under the influence of the Wesleys while a student at Christ Church. He became vicar of Stanton Harcourt, near Oxford, but later joined the Moravians.

About the middle of March, 1730, I became acquainted with Mr. Charles Wesley, of Christ Church. I was just then come up from the country, and had made a resolution to find out some persons of religion to keep company with, or else to instill something of it into those I knew already ... One day an old acquaintance entertained me with some reflections on the whimsical Mr. Wesley, his preciseness and pious extravagancies. Tho' I had lived with him four years in the same college, yet so unable was I to take notice of anything that passed, that I knew nothing of his character; but upon hearing this, I suspected he might be a good Christian. I therefore went to his room, and without any ceremony desired the benefit of his conversation. I had so large a share of it thenceforth, that hardly a day passed, while I was at college, but we were together once, if not oftener.

After some time he introduced me to his brother John, of Lincoln College. 'For,' said he, 'he is somewhat older than I, and can resolve your doubts better.' This, as I found afterwards, was a thing which he was deeply sensible of; for I never observed any person have a more real deference for another, than he constantly had for his brother ... Indeed, he followed his brother entirely. Could I describe one of them, I should describe both: And therefore I shall say no more of Charles, but that he was a man made for friendship; who by his cheerfulness and vivacity would refresh his friend's heart; with attentive consideration would enter into and settle all his concerns; so far as he was able, would do anything for him great or small; and by a habit of mutual openness and freedom, leave no room for misunderstanding.

The Wesleys were already talked of for some religious practices, which were first occasioned by Mr. Morgan, of Christchurch.[1] He being a young man of excellent disposition, took all opportunities to make his companions in love with a good life, to create in them a reverence for the public worship, to tell them of their faults with a sweetness and simplicity that disarmed the worst tempers. He delighted much in works of charity; he kept several children at school, and when he found beggars in the street, he would bring them into his chambers, and talk to them. Many such things he did; and being acquainted with these two brothers, he invited them to join with him; and proposed that they should meet frequently to encourage one another, and have some scheme to proceed by in their daily employments. About half a year after I got among them, Mr. Morgan died: His calm and resigned behaviour, hardly curbing in a confident joy in God, wrought very much upon me; tho' when I had an opportunity to observe him, he was under a lingering distemper.

From these combined friends began a little Society (tho' all such names they also declined); for several others from time to time fell in, most of them only to be improved by their serious and useful discourse; and some few espousing all their resolutions and their whole way of life. Mr. John Wesley was always the chief manager, for which he was very fit. For he had not only more learning and experience than the rest, but he was blest with such activity as to be always gaining ground, and such steadiness that he lost none: What proposals he made to any were sure to charm them, because he was so much in earnest; nor could they afterwards slight them, because they saw him always the same. What supported this uniform vigour was the care he took to consider well of every affair before he engaged in it, making all his decisions in the fear of God, without passion, humour, or self-confidence: for tho' he had naturally a very clear apprehension, yet his exact prudence depended more on humility and singleness of heart. To this I may add, that he had, I think, something of authority in his countenance; tho' as he did not want address, he could soften his manner, and point it as occasion required. Yet he never assumed anything to himself above his companions; any of them might speak their mind, and their words were as strictly regarded by him as his were by them.

It was their custom to meet most evenings either at his chamber or one of the others, where after some prayers (the chief subject of which was charity) they ate their supper together and he read some book. But the chief business was to review what each had done that day, in pursuance of their common design, and to consult what steps were to be taken next.

Their undertaking included these several particulars: to converse with young students, to visit the prisons, to instruct some poor families, to take care of a school and a parish work-house. They took great pains with the younger members of the University to rescue them from bad company and encourage them in a sober studious life. If they had some influence with any such, they would get them to breakfast, and over a dish of tea endeavour to fasten some good hint upon them; they would bring them acquainted with other well disposed young men; they would help them in those parts of learning which they stuck at; they would close with their best sentiments, drive on their convictions, give them rules of piety, when they would receive them, and watch over them with great tenderness. Some or other of them went to the Castle every day, and another most commonly to Bocardo; whoever came to the Castle was to read in the chapel to as many prisoners as would attend, and to talk apart to the man or men whom he had taken particularly in charge . . . In order to release those who were confined for small debts and were battered by their affliction (and likewise to purchase books, physic, and other necessaries), they raised a little fund, to which many of their acquaintance contributed quarterly. They had prayers at the Castle most Wednesdays and Fridays, a sermon on Sunday, and the sacrament once a month.

When they undertook any poor family, they saw them at least once a week, sometimes gave them money, admonished them of their vices, read to them, and examined their children. The school was, I think, of Mr. Wesley's own setting up; however he paid the Mistress, and clothed some, if not all of the children. When they went thither, they enquired how each child behaved, saw their work (for some could knit or spin), heard them read, heard them their prayers or their catechism, and explained part of it. In the same manner they taught the children in the Work-house, and read to the old people as they did to the prisoners.

Tho' some other practises of Mr. Wesley and his friends were much blamed, as their fasting on Wednesday and Friday, after the custom of the Primitive Church; their coming on those Sundays when there was no sacrament at their own Colleges to receive it at Christ Church (which they thought, being the Cathedral, might properly be resorted to by any within the Diocese), yet nothing was so much disliked as these charitable employments. . . .

Because he required such a regulation of our studies as might devote them all to God, [Wesley] has been cried out upon as one that discouraged learning. Far from that; – the first thing he struck at in young men was that indolence which would not submit to close thinking. Nor was he against reading much, especially at first; because then the mind ought to fill itself with materials, and try everything that looks bright and perfect, tho' afterwards, in the coolness of a mortified heart, and the simplicity of one that knows God, many of them will be forgot and superseded.

He earnestly recommended to them a method and order in all their actions. After their morning devotions (which were at a fixed and early hour, from 5 to 6 being the time, morning as well as evening; and upon the point of early rising, he told them the well spending of the day would very much depend) he advised them to determine with themselves what they were to do all parts of the day. By such foresight they should at every

hour's end, not be in doubt how to dispose of themselves; and by bringing themselves under the necessity of such a plan, they might correct
the impotence of a mind that had been used to live by humour and
chance, and prepare it by degrees to bear the other restraints of a holy
life.

The next thing was to put them upon keeping the fasts, visiting poor
people, and coming to the weekly sacrament; not only to subdue the
body, increase charity, and obtain divine grace; but (as he expressed it)
to cut off their retreat to the world. He judged that if they did these things,
men would cast out their names as evil, and by the impossibility of keeping fair any longer with the world, oblige them to take their whole refuge
in Christianity. But those whose resolutions he thought would not bear
this test, he left to gather strength by their secret exercises.

It was his earnest care to introduce them to the treasures of wisdom
and hope in the Holy Scriptures; to teach them not only to endure that
Book (for which, I fear, all before their conversion, especially scholars,
have not a particular relish but a particular loathing), but to form themselves by it, and to fly to it as the great antidote against the darkness of
this world. For some years past he and his friends read the New Testament together at evening. After every portion of it, having heard the
conjectures the rest had to offer, he made his observations on the phrase,
design, and difficult places; one or two wrote these down from his
mouth.

Because the more thoroughly we know the diseases of our souls, the
more we will undergo to purchase their health, and attend more seriously
on the Great Physician, he laid much stress upon self-examination. He
taught them (besides what occurs in his Collection of Prayers) to take
account of their actions in a very exact manner, by writing a constant
Diary; in this they noted down in cyphers, once if not oftener in the day,
what chiefly their employments had been in several parts of it, and how
they had performed each. . . .

Then, to keep in their minds an awful sense of God's presence, with
a constant dependence on his help, he advised them to Ejaculatory
Prayers. The use of this naturally accompanies self-examination; for the
soul, distressed at her own deformity, treachery and darkness, will have
continually something to beg, to complain of, or at least to spread and
expose before the eyes of God. . . .

The last means he recommended was Meditation. It is a great benefit
to a man to detain himself, not for a moment, but for a considerable
while, in a deep attention to divine things . . . Some acquaintance with
God is certainly attained by it, if not in the way of reasoning and distinct
conceptions, yet at least by the slight which is put upon all than man
can think or do, and by boldly lifting up a naked helpless heart to receive

the stamp of eternal truth. Their usual time of meditating was the hour next before dinner.

---

[1] William Morgan, son of a distinguished Dublin citizen and one of the four original 'Oxford Methodists', introduced the 'Holy Club' to sick-visiting and other benevolent activities. His tragically early death was at first blamed on his association with the Methodists, but his father soon afterwards entrusted his second son, Richard, to Wesley's care.

Charles Wesley's 'Conversion'

(*CWJ*, I, 90–5)

THE DAY OF PENTECOST

Sunday, May 21st, 1738. I waked in hope and expectation of His coming. At nine my brother and some friends came, and sang an hymn to the Holy Ghost. My comfort and hope were hereby increased. In about half-an-hour they went: I betook myself to prayer; the substance as follows:—'O Jesus, thou hast said, "I will come unto you;" thou hast said, "I will send the Comforter unto you;" thou hast said, "My Father and I will come unto you, and make our abode with you." Thou art God who canst not lie; I wholly rely upon thy most true promise: accomplish it in thy time and manner.' Having said this, I was composing myself to sleep, in quietness and peace, when I heard one come in (Mrs. Musgrave, I thought, by the voice) and say, 'In the name of Jesus of Nazareth, arise, and believe, and thou shalt be healed of all thy infirmities.' I wondered how it should enter into her head to speak in that manner. The words struck me to the heart. I sighed, and said within myself, 'O that Christ would but speak thus to me!' I lay musing and trembling: then thought, 'But what if it should be Him? I will send at least to see.' I rang, and, Mrs. Turner coming, I desired her to send up Mrs. Musgrave. She went down, and, returning, said, 'Mrs. Musgrave had not been here.' My heart sunk within me at the word, and I hoped it might be Christ indeed. However, I sent her down again to inquire, and felt in the meantime a strange palpitation of heart. I said, yet feared to say, 'I believe, I believe!' She came up again and said, 'It was I, a weak, sinful creature, spoke; but the words were Christ's: he commanded me to say them, and so constrained me that I could not forbear.' . . .

I now found myself at peace with God, and rejoiced in hope of loving Christ. My temper for the rest of the day was, mistrust of my own great, but before unknown, weakness. I saw that by faith I stood; by the continual support of faith, which kept me from falling, though of myself I am ever sinking into sin. I went to bed still sensible of my own weakness, (I humbly hope to be more and more so,) yet confident of Christ's protection.

Monday, May 22nd. Under his protection I waked next morning, and rejoiced in reading the 107th Psalm, so nobly describing what God had done for my soul. I fell asleep again, and waked out of a dream that I was fighting with two devils; had one under my feet; the other faced me some time, but faded, and sunk, and vanished away, upon my telling him I belonged to Christ.

To-day I saw him chiefly as my King, and found him in his power: but saw little of the love of Christ crucified, or of my sins past: though more, I humbly hope, of my own weakness and his strength. I had many evil thoughts darted into my mind, but I rejected them immediately (yet not I). At noon I rose, continually fainting, nevertheless upheld. I was greatly strengthened by Isaiah xliii., which God directed me to. 'But now thus saith the Lord that created thee, O Jacob, and he that formed three, O Israel, Fear not: for I have redeemed thee, I have called thee by thy name; thou art mine. When thou passest through the waters, I will be with thee; and through the rivers, they shall not overflow thee: when thou walkest through the fire, thou shalt not be burned; neither shall the flame kindle upon thee. For I am the Lord thy God, the Holy One of Israel, thy Saviour.'

My brother coming, we joined in intercession for him. In the midst of prayer, I almost believed the Holy Ghost was coming upon him. In the evening we sang and prayed again. I found myself very weak in body, but thought I ought to pray for my friends, being the only Priest among them. I kneeled down, and was immediately strengthened, both mind and body. The enemy did not lose such an opportunity of tempting me to pride: but, God be praised, my strength did I ascribe unto Him. I was often since assisted to pray readily and earnestly, without a form. Not unto me, O Lord, not unto me, but to thy name be the glory! . . .

It was morning before I could get to sleep. Many motions of pride arose, and were continually beaten down by Christ my King. The devil also tempted me to impatience through pain; but God turned it into an occasion of resignation.

Tuesday, May 23rd. I waked under the protection of Christ, and gave myself up, soul and body, to him. At nine I began an hymn upon my conversion, but was persuaded to break off, for fear of pride. Mr. Bray coming, encouraged me to proceed in spite of Satan. I prayed Christ to stand by me, and finished the hymn. Upon my afterwards showing it to Mr. Bray, the devil threw in a fiery dart, suggesting, that it was wrong, and I had displeased God. My heart sunk within me; when, casting my eye upon a Prayer-book, I met with an answer for him. 'Why boastest thou thyself, thou tyrant, that thou canst do mischief?' Upon this, I clearly discerned it was a device of the enemy to keep back glory from God. And it is most usual with him to preach humility, when speaking will endanger his kingdom, or do honour to Christ. Least of all would he have us tell what things God has done for our souls, so tenderly does he guard us from pride. But God has showed me, he can defend me from it, while speaking for him. In his name therefore, and through his strength, I will perform my vows unto the Lord, of not hiding his righteousness within my heart, if it should ever please him to plant it there.

Throughout this day he has kept up in me a constant sense of my own weakness. At night I was tempted to think the reason of my believing before others was, my sincerity. I rejected the thought with horror, and remained more than conqueror, through Him that loved me.

Wednesday, May 24th. Being to receive the sacrament to-day, I was assaulted by the fear of my old accustomed deadness; but soon recovered my confidence in Christ, that he would give me so much sense of his love now, as he saw good for me. I received without any sensible devotion, much as I used to be, only that I was afterwards perfectly calm and satisfied, without doubt, fear, or scruple.

We passed the afternoon in prayer, singing, and conference. For one half hour I was with Miss Delamotte; now unconvinced, and full of dispute. I bore my testimony with plainness and confidence, declaring what God had done for my soul. Not hurt, but strengthened hereby . . .

From her I went to Miss Claggetts; young women of a better and more childlike spirit, who calmly and confidently looked for the promises. I was farther comforted by an excellent letter from my namesake in Georgia, persecuted for Christ's sake; on the highest step, I trust, of the legal state.

At eight I prayed by myself for love; with some feeling, and assurance of feeling more. Towards ten, my brother was brought in triumph by a troop of our friends, and declared, 'I believe.' We sang the hymn with great joy, and parted with prayer. At midnight I gave myself up to Christ; assured I was safe, sleeping or waking. Had continual experience of his power to overrule all temptation; and confessed, with joy and surprise, that he was able to do exceeding abundantly for me, above what I can ask or think.

Charles Wesley's 'Conversion Hymn'

(*Hymns and Sacred Poems*, 1739, pp. 103–4; *PW*, I, 91–3)

Entitled 'Christ the Friend of Sinners', this is most probably the hymn referred to in Charles' *Journal* above.

1 Where shall my wond'ring Soul begin?
    How shall I All to Heaven aspire?
A Slave redeem'd from Death and Sin,
    A Brand pluck'd from Eternal Fire,
How shall I equal Triumphs raise,
And sing my great Deliverer's Praise!

2 O how shall I the Goodness tell,
    Father, which Thou to me hast show'd,
That I, a Child of Wrath, and Hell,
    I should be call'd a Child of GOD!
Should know, should feel my Sins forgiven,
Blest with this Antepast of Heaven!

3 And shall I slight my Father's Love,
    Or basely fear his Gifts to own?
Unmindful of his Favours prove?
    Shall I the hallow'd Cross to shun
Refuse his Righteousness t'impart
By hiding it within my Heart?

4 No – tho' the Antient Dragon rage
    And call forth all his Hosts to War,
Tho' Earth's self-righteous Sons engage;
    Them, and their God alike I dare:
JESUS the Sinner's Friend proclaim,
JESUS, to Sinners still the same.

5 Outcasts of Men, to You I call,
    Harlots and Publicans, and Thieves!
He spreads his Arms t'embrace you all;
    Sinners alone his Grace receives:
No Need of Him the Righteous have,
He came the Lost to seek and save!

6 Come all ye *Magdalens* in Lust,
    Ye Ruffians fell in Murders old;
Repent, and live: despair and trust!
    JESUS for you to Death was sold;
Tho' Hell protest, and Earth repine,
He died for Crimes like Yours – and Mine.

7 Come O my guilty Brethren come,
   Groaning beneath your Load of Sin!
His bleeding Heart shall make you room,
   His open Side shall take you in.
He calls you Now, invites you home –
Come, O my guilty Brethren, come!

8 For you the purple Current flow'd
   In Pardons from his wounded Side:
Languish'd for you th'Eternal GOD,
   For you the Prince of Glory dy'd.
Believe: and all your Guilt's forgiven,
Only Believe – and yours is Heaven.

John Wesley's 'Conversion'

(*JWJ*, I, 465–77)

What occurred on Wednesday the 24th [May, 1738], I think best to relate at large, after premising what may make it the better understood. Let him that cannot receive it ask of the Father of lights that He would give more light to him and me.

1. I believe, till I was about ten years old I had not sinned away that 'washing of the Holy Ghost' which was given me in baptism; having been strictly educated and carefully taught that I could only be saved 'by universal obedience, by keeping all the commandments of God'; in the meaning of which I was diligently instructed. And those instructions, so far as they respected outward duties and sins, I gladly received and often thought of. But all that was said to me of inward obedience or holiness I neither understood nor remembered. So that I was indeed as ignorant of the true meaning of the law as I was of the gospel of Christ.

2. The next six or seven years were spent at school; where, outward restraints being removed, I was much more negligent than before, even of outward duties, and almost continually guilty of outward sins, which I knew to be such, though they were not scandalous in the eye of the world. However, I still read the Scriptures, and said my prayers morning and evening. And what I now hoped to be saved by, was, (1) not being so bad as other people; (2) having still a kindness for religion; and (3) reading the Bible, going to church, and saying my prayers.

3. Being removed to the University for five years, I still said my prayers both in public and in private, and read, with the Scriptures,

several other books of religion, especially comments on the New Testament. Yet I had not all this while so much as a notion of inward holiness; nay, went on habitually, and for the most part very contentedly, in some or other known sin: indeed, with some intermission and short struggles, especially before and after the Holy Communion, which I was obliged to receive thrice a year. I cannot well tell what I hoped to be saved by now, when I was continually sinning against that little light I had; unless by those transient fits of what many divines taught me to call repentance.

4. When I was about twenty-two, my father pressed me to enter into holy orders. At the same time, the providence of God directing me to Kempis's *Christian Pattern*, I began to see, that true religion was seated in the heart, and that God's law extended to all our thoughts as well as words and actions. I was, however, very angry at Kempis for being too strict; though I read him only in Dean Stanhope's translation. Yet I had frequently much sensible comfort in reading him, such as I was an utter stranger to before; and meeting likewise with a religious friend, which I never had till now, I began to alter the whole form of my conversation, and to set in earnest upon a new life. I set apart an hour or two a day for religious retirement. I communicated every week. I watched against all sin, whether in word or deed. I began to aim at, and pray for, inward holiness. So that now, 'doing so much, and living so good a life,' I doubted not but I was a good Christian.

5. Removing soon after to another College, I executed a resolution which I was before convinced was of the utmost importance, – shaking off at once all my trifling acquaintance. I began to see more and more the value of time. I applied myself closer to study. I watched more carefully against actual sins; I advised others to be religious, according to that scheme of religion by which I modelled my own life. But meeting now with Mr. Law's *Christian Perfection* and *Serious Call*, although I was much offended at many parts of both, yet they convinced me more than ever of the exceeding height and breadth and depth of the law of God. The light flowed in so mightily upon my soul, that everything appeared in a new view. I cried to God for help, and resolved not to prolong the time of obeying Him as I had never done before. And by my continued endeavour to keep His whole law, inward and outward, to the utmost of my power, I was persuaded that I should be accepted of Him, and that I was even then in a state of salvation.

6. In 1730 I began visiting the prisons; assisting the poor and sick in town; and doing what other good I could, by my presence or my little fortune, to the bodies and souls of all men. To this end I abridged myself of all superfluities, and many that are called necessaries of life. I soon became a by-word for so doing, and I rejoiced that my name was cast out as evil. The next spring I began observing the Wednesday and Friday

Fasts, commonly observed in the ancient Church; tasting no food till three in the afternoon. And now I knew not how to go any further. I diligently strove against all sin. I omitted no sort of self-denial which I thought lawful; I carefully used, both in public and in private, all the means of grace at all opportunities. I omitted no occasion of doing good; I for that reason suffered evil. And all this I knew to be nothing, unless as it was directed towards inward holiness. Accordingly this, the image of God, was what I aimed at in all, by doing His will, not my own. Yet when, after continuing some years in this course, I apprehended myself to be near death, I could not find that all this gave me any comfort or any assurance of acceptance with God. At this I was then not a little surprised; not imagining I had been all this time building on the sand, nor considering that 'other foundation can no man lay than that which is laid' by God, 'even Christ Jesus.'

7. Soon after, a contemplative man convinced me still more than I was convinced before, that outward works are nothing, being alone; and in several conversations instructed me how to pursue inward holiness, or a union of the soul with God. But even of his instructions (though I then received them as the words of God) I cannot but now observe (1) that he spoke so incautiously against trusting in outward works, that he discouraged me from doing them at all; (2) that he recommended (as it were, to supply what was wanting in them) *mental prayer*, and the like exercises, as the most effectual means of purifying the soul and uniting it with God. Now these were, in truth, as much my own works as visiting the sick or clothing the naked; and the union with God thus pursued was as really my own righteousness as any I had before pursued under another name.

8. In this refined way of trusting to my own works and my own righteousness (so zealously inculcated by the Mystic writers), I dragged on heavily, finding no comfort or help therein till the time of my leaving England. On shipboard, however, I was again active in outward works; where it pleased God of His free mercy to give me twenty-six of the Moravian brethren for companions, who endeavoured to show me 'a more excellent way'. But I understood it not at first. I was too learned and too wise. So that it seemed foolishness unto me. And I continued preaching, and following after, and trusting in, that righteousness whereby no flesh can be justified.

9. All the time I was at Savannah I was thus beating the air. Being ignorant of the righteousness of Christ, which, by a living faith in Him, bringeth salvation 'to every one that believeth', I sought to establish my own righteousness; and so laboured in the fire all my days. I was now properly 'under the law'; I knew that 'the law' of God was 'spiritual; I consented to it that it was good.' Yea, 'I delighted in it, after the inner man.' Yet was I 'carnal, sold under sin.' Every day was I constrained to

cry out, 'What I do, I allow not: for what I would, I do not; but what
I hate, that I do. To will is' indeed 'present with me: but how to perform
that which is good, I find not. For the good which I would, I do not;
but the evil which I would not, that I do. I find a law, that when I would
do good, evil is present with me': even 'the law in my members, warring
against the law of my mind, and still 'bringing me into captivity to the
law of sin.'

10. In this vile, abject state of bondage to sin, I was indeed fighting
continually, but not conquering. Before, I had willingly served sin: now
it was unwillingly; but still I served it. I fell, and rose, and fell again.
Sometimes I was overcome, and in heaviness: sometimes I overcame,
and was in joy. For as in the former state I had some foretastes of the
terrors of the law; so had I in this, of the comforts of the gospel. During
this whole struggle between nature and grace, which had now continued above ten years, I had many remarkable returns to prayer, especially when I was in trouble; I had many sensible comforts, which are
indeed no other than short anticipations of the life of faith. But I was
still 'under the law,' not 'under grace' (the state most who are called
Christians are content to live and die in); for I was only striving with,
not freed from, sin. Neither had I the witness of the Spirit with my spirit,
and indeed could not; for I 'sought it not by faith, but as it were by the
works of the law.'

11. In my return to England, January 1738, being in imminent danger
of death, and very uneasy on that account, I was strongly convinced that
the cause of that uneasiness was unbelief; and that the gaining a true,
living faith was the 'one thing needful' for me. But still I fixed not this
faith on its right object: I meant only faith in God, not faith in or through
Christ. Again, I knew not that I was wholly void of this faith; but only
thought I had not enough of it. So that when Peter Böhler, whom God
prepared for me as soon as I came to London, affirmed of true faith in
Christ (which is but one) that it had those two fruits inseparably attending it, 'dominion over sin and constant peace from a sense of forgiveness,'
I was quite amazed, and looked upon it as a new gospel. If this was so, it
was clear I had not faith. But I was not willing to be convinced of this.
Therefore I disputed with all my might, and laboured to prove that
faith might be where these were not: for all the scriptures relating to
this I had been long since taught to construe away; and to call all Presbyterians who spoke otherwise. Besides, I well saw no one could, in the
nature of things, have such a sense of forgiveness, and not *feel* it. But
I felt it not. If, then, there was no faith without this, all my pretensions
to faith dropped at once.

12. When I met Peter Böhler again, he consented to put the dispute
upon the issue which I desired, namely, Scripture and experience. I first
consulted the Scripture. But when I set aside the glosses of men, and

simply considered the words of God, comparing them together, endeavouring to illustrate the obscure by the plainer passages, I found they all made against me, and was forced to retreat to my last hold, 'that experience would never agree with the *literal interpretation* of those scriptures. Nor could I therefore allow it to be true, till I found some living witnesses of it.' He replied, he could show me such at any time; if I desired it, the next day. And accordingly the next day he came again with three others, all of whom testified, of their own personal experience, that a true living faith in Christ is inseparable from a sense of pardon for all past and freedom from all present sins. They added with one mouth that this faith was the gift, the free gift of God; and that he would surely bestow it upon every soul who earnestly and perseveringly sought it. I was now throughly convinced; and, by the grace of God, I resolved to seek it unto the end, (1) By absolutely renouncing all dependence, in whole or in part, upon *my own* works or righteousness; on which I had really grounded my hope of salvation, though I knew it not, from my youth up; (2) by adding to the constant use of all the other means of grace, continual prayer for this very thing, justifying, saving faith, a full reliance on the blood of Christ shed for *me*; a trust in Him, as *my* Christ, as *my* sole justification, sanctification, and redemption.

13. I continued thus to seek it (though with strange indifference, dullness, and coldness, and unusually frequent relapses into sin) till Wednesday, May 24. I think it was about five this morning, that I opened my Testament on those words, Τὰ μέγιστα ἡμῖν καὶ τίμια ἐπαγγέλματα δεδώρηται, ἵνα γένησθε θείας κοινωνοὶ φύσεως. 'There are given unto us exceeding great and precious promises, even that ye should be partakers of the divine nature' (2 Pet. i. 4). Just as I went out, I opened it again on those words, 'Thou art not far from the kingdom of God.' In the afternoon I was asked to go to St. Paul's. The anthem was, 'Out of the deep have I called unto Thee, O Lord: Lord, hear my voice. O let Thine ears consider well the voice of my complaint. If Thou, Lord, wilt be extreme to mark what is done amiss, O Lord, who may abide it? For there is mercy with Thee; therefore shalt Thou be feared. O Israel, trust in the Lord: for with the Lord there is mercy, and with Him is plenteous redemption. And He shall redeem Israel from all his sins.'

14. In the evening I went very unwillingly to a society in Aldersgate Street, where one was reading Luther's preface to the *Epistle to the Romans*. About a quarter before nine, while he was describing the change which God works in the heart through faith in Christ, I felt my heart strangely warmed. I felt I did trust in Christ, Christ alone for salvation; and an assurance was given me that He had taken away *my* sins, even *mine*, and saved *me* from the law of sin and death.

15. I began to pray with all my might for those who had in a more especial manner despitefully used me and persecuted me. I then testified

openly to all there what I now first felt in my heart. But it was not long before the enemy suggested, 'This cannot be faith; for where is thy joy?' Then was I taught that peace and victory over sin are essential to faith in the Captain of our salvation; but that, as to the transports of joy that usually attend the beginning of it, especially in those who have mourned deeply, God sometimes giveth, sometimes withholdeth them, according to the counsels of His own will.

16. After my return home, I was much buffeted with temptations; but cried out, and they fled away. They returned again and again. I as often lifted up my eyes, and He 'sent me help from His holy place.' And herein I found the difference between this and my former state chiefly consisted. I was striving, yea, fighting with all my might under the laws, as well as under grace. But then I was sometimes, if not often, conquered; now, I was always conqueror.

'Salvation by Faith'

A sermon preached by John Wesley before Oxford University in the University Church of St Mary the Virgin on June 18, 1738, and placed at the head of his collected sermons. (*Sermons* I, 117–30)

' *By grace are ye saved through faith.*' Eph. ii. 8.

1. All the blessings which God hath bestowed upon man, are of his mere grace, bounty, or favour; his free, undeserved favour; favour altogether undeserved; man having no claim to the least of his mercies. It was free grace that 'formed man of the dust of the ground, and breathed into him a living soul,' and stamped on that soul the image of God, and 'put all things under his feet.' The same free grace continues to us, at this day, life, and breath, and all things. For there is nothing we are, or have, or do, which can deserve the least thing at God's hand. 'All our works, thou, O God! hast wrought in us.' These, therefore, are so many more instances of free mercy: And whatever righteousness may be found in man, this is also the gift of God. . . .

I.4. What faith is it then through which we are saved? It may be answered, First, in general, it is a faith in Christ: Christ, and God through Christ, are the proper objects of it. Herein, therefore, it is sufficiently, absolutely distinguished from the faith either of ancient or modern Heathens. And from the faith of a devil it is fully distinguished by this, – it is not barely a speculative, rational thing, a cold, lifeless assent, a train of ideas in the head; but also a disposition of the heart. For thus saith the

Scripture, 'With the heart man believeth unto righteousness;' and, 'If thou shalt confess with thy mouth the Lord Jesus, and shalt believe with thy heart, that God hath raised him from the dead, thou shalt be saved.'

II. What salvation it is, which is through this faith, is the Second thing to be considered.

1. And, First, whatsoever else it imply, it is a present salvation. It is something attainable, yea, actually attained, on earth, by those who are partakers of this faith. For thus saith the Apostle to the believers at Ephesus, and in them to the believers of all ages, not, *Ye shall be* (though that also is true), but, '*Ye are saved* through faith.'

2. *Ye are saved* (to comprise all in one word) from sin. This is the salvation which is through faith. This is that great salvation foretold by the angel, before God brought his First-begotten into the world: 'Thou shalt call his name JESUS: For he shall save his people from their sins.' And neither here, nor in other parts of holy writ, is there any limitation or restriction. All his people, or, as it is elsewhere expressed, 'all that believe in him,' he will save from all their sins; from original and actual, past and present sin, 'of the flesh and of the spirit'. Through faith that is in him, they are saved both from the guilt and from the power of it.

3. First. From the guilt of all past sin: For, whereas all the world is guilty before God, insomuch that should he 'be extreme to mark what is done amiss, there is none that could abide it;' and whereas, 'by the law is' only 'the knowledge of sin', but no deliverance from it, so that, 'by fulfilling the deeds of the law, no flesh can be justified in his sight;' now 'the righteousness of God, which is by faith of Jesus Christ, is manifested unto all that believe.' Now 'they are justified freely by his grace, through the redemption that is in Jesus Christ.' 'Him God hath set forth to be a propitiation through faith in his blood, to declare his righteousness for (or by) the remission of the sins that are past.' Now hath Christ taken away 'the curse of the law, being made a curse for us.' He hath 'blotted out the handwriting that was against us, taking it out of the way, nailing it to his cross.' 'There is, therefore, no condemnation now, to them which' believe 'in Christ Jesus.'

4. And being saved from guilt, they are saved from fear. Not indeed from a filial fear of offending; but from all servile fear; from that fear which hath torment; from fear of punishment; from fear of the wrath of God, whom they now no longer regard as a severe Master, but as an indulgent Father. 'They have not received again the spirit of bondage, but the Spirit of adoption, whereby they cry, Abba, Father: The Spirit itself also bearing witness with their spirits, that they are the children of God.' They are also saved from the fear, though not from the possibility,

of falling away from the grace of God, and coming short of the great and precious promises. Thus have they 'peace with God through our Lord Jesus Christ. They rejoice in hope of the glory of God. And the love of God is shed abroad in their hearts, through the Holy Ghost which is given unto them.' And hereby they are persuaded (though perhaps not at all times, nor with the same fulness of persuasion) that 'neither death, nor life, nor things present, nor things to come, nor height, nor depth, nor any other creature, shall be able to separate them from the love of God, which is in Christ Jesus our Lord.'

5. Again, through his faith they are saved from the power of sin, as well as from the guilt of it. So the Apostle declares, 'Ye know that he was manifested to take away our sins; and in him is no sin. Whosoever abideth in him, sinneth not.' (1 John iii. 5, &c.) Again, 'little children, let no man deceive you. He that committeth sin is of the devil. Whosoever believeth, is born of God. And whosoever is born of God doth not commit sin, for his seed remaineth in him: And he cannot sin, because he is born of God.' Once more, 'We know that whosoever is born of God sinneth not: But he that is begotten of God, keepeth himself, and that wicked one toucheth him not.' (1 John v. 18.)

6. He that is, by faith, born of God, sinneth not (1) By any habitual sin; for all habitual sin is sin reigning: But sin cannot reign in any that believeth. Nor (2) by any wilful sin; for his will, while he abideth in the faith, is utterly set against all sin, and abhorreth it as deadly poison. Nor (3) by any sinful desire; for he continually desireth the holy and perfect will of God; and any tendency to an unholy desire, he, by the grace of God, stifleth in the birth. Nor (4) doth he sin by infirmities, whether in act, word, or thought; for his infirmities have no concurrence of his will; and without this they are not properly sins. Thus, 'he that is born of God doth not commit sin': And though he cannot say, he hath not sinned, yet now 'he sinneth not'.

7. This then is the salvation which is through faith, even in the present world: A salvation from sin, and the consequences of sin, both often expressed in the word *justification*; which, taken in the largest sense, implies a deliverance from guilt and punishment, by the atonement of Christ actually applied to the soul of the sinner now believing on him, and a deliverance from the power of sin, through Christ *formed in his heart*. So that he who is thus justified, or saved by faith, is indeed *born again*. He is *born again of the Spirit* unto a new life, which 'is hid with Christ in God'. And as a new-born babe he gladly receives the ἄδολον, '*sincere* milk of the word, and grows thereby', going on in the might of the Lord his God, from faith to faith, from grace to grace, until, at length, he come unto 'a perfect man, unto the measure of the stature of the fulness of Christ'. . . .

8. At this time, more especially, will we speak, that 'by grace are ye saved through faith': Because, never was the maintaining this doctrine more seasonable than it is at this day. Nothing but this can effectually prevent the increase of the Romish delusion among us. It is endless to attack, one by one, all the errors of that Church. But salvation by faith strikes at the root, and all fall at once where this is established. It was this doctrine, which our Church justly calls *the strong rock and foundation of the Christian religion*, that first drove Popery out of these kingdoms; and it is this alone can keep it out. Nothing but this can give a check to that immorality which hath 'overspread the land as a flood'. Can you empty the great deep, drop by drop? Then you may reform us by dissuasives from particular vices. But let the 'righteousness which is of God by faith'' be brought in, and so shall its proud waves be stayed. Nothing but this can stop the mouths of those who 'glory in their shame, and openly deny the Lord that bought them'. They can talk as sublimely of the law, as he that hath it written, by God, in his heart. To hear them speak on this head might incline one to think they were not far from the kingdom of God: But take them out of the law into the gospel; begin with the righteousness of faith; with Christ, 'the end of the law to every one that believeth'; and those who but now appeared almost, if not altogether Christians, stand confessed the sons of perdition; as far from life and salvation (God be merciful unto them!) as the depth of hell from the height of heaven.

Rules of the Band Societies
drawn up December 25, 1738

(*JWW*, VIII, 272–4)

The design of our meeting is, to obey that command of God, 'Confess your faults one to another, and pray one for another, that ye may be healed.'

To this end, we intend:—

1. To meet once a week, at the least.

2. To come punctually at the hour appointed, without some extraordinary reason.

3. To begin (those of us who are present) exactly at the hour, with singing or prayer.

4. To speak each of us in order, freely and plainly, the true state of our souls, with the faults we have committed in thought, word, or deed, and the temptations we have felt, since our last meeting.

5. To end every meeting with prayer, suited to the state of each person present.

6. To desire some person among us to speak his own state first, and then to ask the rest, in order, as many and as searching questions as may be, concerning their state, sins, and temptations.

Some of the questions proposed to every one before he is admitted among us may be to this effect:—

1. Have you the forgiveness of your sins?

2. Have you peace with God, through our Lord Jesus Christ?

3. Have you the witness of God's Spirit with your spirit, that you are a child of God?

4. Is the love of God shed abroad in your heart?

5. Has no sin, inward or outward, dominion over you?

6. Do you desire to be told of your faults?

7. Do you desire to be told of all your faults, and that plain and home?

8. Do you desire that every one of us should tell you, from time to time, whatsoever is in his heart concerning you?

9. Consider! Do you desire we should tell you whatsoever we think, whatsoever we fear, whatsoever we hear, concerning you?

10. Do you desire that, in doing this, we should come as close as possible, that we should cut to the quick, and search your heart to the bottom?

11. Is it your desire and design to be on this, and all other occasions, entirely open, so as to speak everything that is in your heart without exception, without disguise, and without reserve?

Any of the preceding questions may be asked as often as occasion offers; the four following at every meeting:—

1. What known sins have you committed since our last meeting?

2. What temptations have you met with?

3. How were you delivered?

4. What have you thought, said, or done, of which you doubt whether it be sin or not?

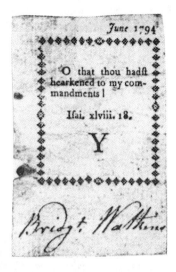

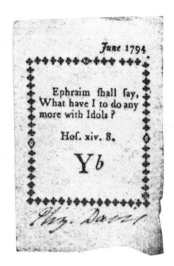

Wesley introduced 'bands' (small intimate groups with strict rules of life) in 1738, and 'classes' (somewhat larger groups, with slightly less stringent rules) in 1742. 'Band-tickets' began to be distributed each quarter in 1741, or a little later, and 'class-tickets' in 1750, also each quarter. As the classes overtook the bands in importance, the two kinds of ticket came to be distinguishable only by the letter 'b' on the band-ticket. Each member of a Methodist society received either a band-ticket and a class-ticket, or just a class-ticket.

Tensions in a London Parish

(Islington Vestry minutes, printed in Leonard Hale, *Highbury Methodism*, 1924)

The parish of Islington, just north of the City of London, had at the time of the revival an evangelical vicar, the Rev. George Stonehouse, who welcomed the Wesleys and Whitefield to his pulpit.

April 29, 1739: Resolved, that it appears to this Vestry that the Rev. Mr. Stonehouse is the real occasion of the frequent disturbances in this Church and Churchyard, by his introducing strangers to preach in this Church, particularly Mr. Charles Wesley, Mr. Whitfield [sic], and other unlicensed persons, by encouraging and promising to stand by and indemnify them in their preaching and without producing their licences as the Canon directs.

May 6, 1739: It having been agreed to refer all matters in difference between Mr. Stonehouse and this parish to ten gentlemen of the said parish, five of whom were nominated by Mr. Stonehouse, and five by the parish, it has been concluded by the said ten gentlemen that the Rev. Mr. Stonehouse shall absolutely refuse the granting of his pulpit to Mr. John Wesley, Mr. Charles Wesley and Mr. George Whitefield, and that those gentlemen shall not officiate any more for him in the parish Church or Churchyard, in any part of the duty whatever.

[Endorsed by the Vicar:] I do hereby ratifie and confirm the above agreement. George Stonehouse.

[The Vicar continued to allow Methodist gatherings in the vicarage, with the result that a further entry appears in the Vestry Minutes:]

August 19, 1739: Complaint being made to this Vestry of several irregular practices of the Vicar of this parish, particularly of his holding illegal assemblies at the Vicarage house . . . it is ordered, *nem. con.*, and agreed that a representation be made thereof to the Bishop of the diocese, and that the same be in the words following, i.e. Notwithstanding his being an ordained priest of the Church of England, and Vicar of the said parish, whereby he hath a right to officiate in the said parish Church as often as he pleases, so that he need not be destitute of a convenient place for performing the same in a decent and orderly manner, [he] hath nevertheless taken upon himself to hold illegal assemblies once a week and oftener in his own and other private houses, and there publish, preach and expound to a numerous audience contrary to law.

September 11, 1739: Resolved, *nem. con.*, that it is the opinion of this Vestry that Mr. John Westley Hall is not duly qualified to preach in this diocese, and that Mr. Dennis be desired from time to time to sit in the pew in which the pulpit stairs stand, and to prevent the said Mr. Hall, or any other unqualified minister, from preaching.

[Two months later another petition to the Bishop prayed him not to license Westley Hall as curate of the parish, on the ground that he 'has rendered himself disagreeable by being a common field preacher and a holder of assemblies in private houses in an unlawful manner'. Stonehouse resigned the living early in 1740.]

Wesley's Bristol Ministry

(*JWJ*, II, 167–73, 184–5, 194–8, 201–2)

In the spring of 1739 Wesley spent over two months in and around Bristol, during the course of which several important developments took place.

Saturday, [March] 31. In the evening I reached Bristol, and met Mr. Whitefield there. I could scarce reconcile myself at first to this strange way of preaching in the fields, of which he set me an example on Sunday; having been all my life (till very lately) so tenacious of every point relating to decency and order, that I should have thought the saving of souls almost a sin if it had not been done in a church.

April 1, Sunday. In the evening, Mr. Whitefield being gone, I begun expounding our Lord's Sermon on the Mount (one pretty remarkable precedent of field-preaching, though I suppose there were churches at that time also) to a little society which was accustomed to meet once or twice a week in Nicholas Street.

Monday 2. At four in the afternoon I submitted to be more vile, and proclaimed in the highways the glad tidings of salvation, speaking from a little eminence in a ground adjoining to the city, to about three thousand people. The scripture on which I spoke was this (is it possible anyone should be ignorant that it is fulfilled in every true minister of Christ?), 'The Spirit of the Lord is upon Me, because He hath anointed Me to preach the gospel to the poor . . .'

Thursday, 26. While I was preaching at Newgate on these words, 'He that believeth hath everlasting life,' I was insensibly led, without any previous design, to declare strongly and explicitly that God willeth 'all men to be' thus 'saved'; and to pray that, 'if this were not the truth of God, He would not suffer the blind to go out of the way; but, if it were, He would bear witness to His word.' Immediately one, and another, and another sunk to the earth; they dropped on every side as thunderstruck. One of them cried aloud. We besought God in her behalf, and He turned her heaviness into joy. A second being in the same agony, we called upon God for her also; and He spoke peace unto her soul. In the evening I was again pressed in spirit to declare that 'Christ gave Himself a ransom for all.' And almost before we called upon Him to set His seal, He answered. One was so wounded by the sword of the Spirit that you would have imagined she could not live a moment. But immediately His abundant kindness was showed, and she loudly sang of His righteousness.

Friday, 27. All Newgate rang with the cries of those whom the word of God cut to the heart; two of whom were in a moment filled with joy, to the astonishment of those that beheld them . . .

Wednesday, [May] 9. We took possession of a piece of ground, near St. James's churchyard, in the Horsefair, where it was designed to build a room, large enough to contain both the societies of Nicholas and Baldwin Streets, and such of their acquaintance as might desire to be present with them, at such times as the Scripture was expounded. And on Saturday the 12th the first stone was laid, with the voice of praise and thanksgiving.

I had not at first the least apprehension or design of being personally engaged, either in the expense of this work or in the direction of it:

having appointed eleven feoffees,[1] on whom I supposed these burdens would fall of course. But I quickly found my mistake; first with regard to the expense: for the whole undertaking must have stood still had not I immediately taken upon myself the payment of all the workmen; so that, before I knew where I was, I had contracted a debt of more than a hundred and fifty pounds. And this I was to discharge how I could; the subscriptions of both societies not amounting to one quarter of the sum. And as to the direction of the work, I presently received letters from my friends in London, Mr. Whitefield in particular, backed with a message from one just come from thence, that neither he nor they would have anything to do with the building, neither contribute anything towards it, unless I would instantly discharge all feoffees and do everything in my own name. Many reasons they gave for this; but one was enough, viz. 'that such feoffees always would have it in their power to control me; and, if I preached not as they liked, to turn me out of the room I had built.' I accordingly yielded to their advice, and, calling all the feoffees together, cancelled (no man opposing) the instrument made before, and took the whole management into my own hands ...

Sunday, 20. ... During this whole time I was almost continually asked, either by those who purposely came to Bristol to inquire concerning this strange work, or by my old or new correspondents, 'How can these things be?' And innumerable cautions were given me (generally grounded on gross misrepresentations of things), not to regard visions or dreams, or to fancy people had remission of sins because of their cries, or tears, or bare outward professions. To one[2] who had many times written to me on this head, the sum of my answer was as follows:

The question between us turns chiefly, if not wholly, on matter of fact. You deny that God does now work these effects; at least, that He works them in this manner. I affirm both; because I have heard these things with my own ears, and have seen them with my eyes. I have seen (as far as a thing of this kind can be seen) very many persons changed in a moment from the spirit of fear, horror, despair, to the spirit of love, joy, and peace; and from sinful desire, till then reigning over them, to a pure desire of doing the will of God. These are matters of fact, whereof I have been, and almost daily am, an eye or ear witness. What I have to say touching visions or dreams, is this: I know several persons in whom this great change was wrought in a dream, or during a strong representation to the eye of their mind, of Christ either on the cross, or in glory. This is the fact; let any judge of it as they please. And that such a change was then wrought appears (not from their shedding tears only, or falling into fits, or crying out: these are not the fruits, as you seem to suppose, whereby I judge, but) from the whole tenor of their life, till then many ways wicked; from that time holy, just, and good.

I will show you him that was a lion till then, and is now a lamb; him that was a drunkard, and is now exemplarily sober; the whoremonger that was, who now abhors the very 'garment spotted by the flesh'. These are my living arguments for what I assert – viz. 'That God does now, as aforetime, give remission of sins, and the gift of the Holy Ghost, even to us and to our children; yea, and that always suddenly, as far as I have known, and often in dreams or in the visions of God.' If it be not so, I am found a false witness before God. For these things I *do*, and His grace *will*, testify.

¹ A legal equivalent of 'trustees', i.e. those holding property for charitable or other public purposes.
² His older brother, Samuel.

John Wesley and Bishop Butler

(Henry Moore, *Life of Wesley*, 1824, I, 463–5)

Wesley had two conversations with Joseph Butler, Bishop of Bristol, on 16th and 18th August, 1739. This account of the second was found by Moore among his papers. (*JWJ*, II, 256–7)

BISHOP. Why, Sir, our faith itself is a good work, it is a virtuous temper of mind.
MR. WESLEY. My Lord, whatever faith is, our church asserts, we are justified by faith alone. But how it can be called a good work, I see not: It is the gift of God; and a gift that pre-supposes nothing in us, but sin and misery.
B. How, Sir! Then you make God a tyrannical Being, if he justifies some without any goodness in them preceding, and does not justify all. If these are not justified on account of some moral goodness in them, why are not those justified too?
W. Because, my Lord, they *'resist his Spirit'*; because *'they will not come to him that they may have life'*; because they suffer him not to *'work in them both to will and to do'*. They cannot be *saved*, because they will not *believe*.
B. Sir, what do you mean by faith?
W. My Lord; by justifying faith I mean, a conviction wrought in a man by the Holy Ghost, that Christ hath loved *him*, and given himself for *him*, and that, through Christ, *his* sins are forgiven.
B. I believe some good men have this, but not all. But how do you prove this to be the justifying faith taught by our church?

W. My Lord, from her Homily on Salvation, where she describes it thus; '*A sure trust and confidence which a man hath in God, that through the merits of Christ his sins are forgiven, and he reconciled to the favour of God.*'

B. Why, Sir, this is quite another thing.

W. My Lord, I conceive it to be the very same.

B. Mr. Wesley, I will deal plainly with you. I once thought you, and Mr. Whitefield, well-meaning men; but I cannot think so now. For I have heard more of you: matters of fact, Sir. And Mr. Whitefield says in his Journal, 'There are promises still to be fulfilled in me.' Sir, the pretending to extraordinary revelations and gifts of the Holy Ghost, is a horrid thing, a very horrid thing!

W. My Lord, for what Mr. Whitefield says, Mr. Whitefield, and not I, is accountable. I pretend to no *extraordinary* revelations, or gifts of the Holy Ghost: None but what every Christian may receive, and ought to expect and pray for. But I do not wonder your Lordship has heard facts asserted, which, if true, would prove the contrary: Nor do I wonder, that your Lordship, believing them true, should alter the opinion you once had of me. A quarter of an hour I spent with your Lordship before, and about an hour now: And perhaps you have never conversed one other hour with any one who spake in my favour. But how many with those who spake on the other side! So that your Lordship could not but think as you do. – But pray, my Lord, what are those facts you have heard?

B. I hear you administer the sacrament in your societies.

W. My Lord, I never did yet, and I believe never shall.

B. I hear too, that many people fall into fits in your societies, and that you pray over them.

W. I do so, my Lord, when any shew by strong cries and tears, that their soul is in deep anguish; I frequently pray to God, to deliver them from it, and our prayer is often heard in that hour.

B. Very extraordinary indeed! Well, Sir, since you ask my advice, I will give it you very freely. You have no business here. You are not commissioned to preach in this diocese. Therefore, I advise you to go hence.

W. My Lord, my business on earth is, to do what good I can. Wherever, therefore, I think I can do most good, there must I stay, so long as I think so. At present I think I can do most good here; therefore, here I stay. As to my preaching here, a dispensation of the Gospel is committed to me, and woe is me if I preach not the Gospel, wherever I am in the habitable world. Your Lordship knows, being ordained a Priest, by the commission I then received, I am a Priest of the church universal: And being ordained as Fellow of a College, I was not limited to any particular cure, but have an indeterminate commission to preach the word of God, in any part of the Church of England. I do not therefore conceive, that, in preaching here by this commission, I break any human law. When I am convinced I do, then it will be time to ask, 'Shall I obey God or man?' But if I should be convinced in the meanwhile, that I could advance the glory of God, and the salvation of souls in any other place, more than in Bristol; in that hour, by God's help, I will go hence; which till then I may not do.

Itinerant Preaching

(Oxford *Letters*, I, 677, 692–3)

James Hervey to John Wesley, August 21, 1739 (answering Wesley's letter of August 4)

Hervey had known Wesley while he was a student at Lincoln College, Oxford. At the time of this correspondence he was serving as curate at Bideford, Devon. He is remembered mainly for his once popular *Meditations among the Tombs*.

You ask what I am doing in my present situation. I answer, The same that Basil and Nazianzen did in the wilderness: studying the Scriptures, furnishing my mind with saving knowledge, and fitting a poor deacon for the service of Christ's Church . . .

At present, had I the strongest inclination, I have no manner of ability to bestir myself in the way you propose. I be a thundering Boanerges? – I lift up my voice to the whole world, and make the canopy of the skies ring? Never, dear sir, never could you have made choice of so improper a person, so vastly unequal to the task.

Besides, I freely own I cannot approve of itinerant preaching. I think it is repugnant to the apostolical as well as English constitution. I find Timothy settled at Ephesus, Titus stationed at Crete, and other of our Captain's commanders assigned to their particular posts. These labourers (and industrious labourers they were) did not think it necessary or expedient to travel from this county to that, with words of exhortation in their mouths, but chose to lay out their pastoral vigilance upon the flock consigned to their care. Thus would I humbly advise my dear Mr. Wesley to act. Be content to imitate those primitive and only not inspired preachers. Fix in some parish, visit carefully your people, let every individual be the object of your compassionate zeal, in a word be a living Ouranius.[1] O what good might this do to the cause of Christianity! How might neighbouring ministers follow the unexceptionable example, and from inveighing against my good friend, as they now unanimously do, honour him and tread in his steps!

John Wesley to Hervey, October 25, 1739

Though Basil and Nazianzen were good men, I know a better, Jesus of Nazareth. And were I now to prepare myself for the service of his church, I would do it by following his example, 'going about doing good', temporal or spiritual, as of the small 'ability which God giveth'.

After his example, as well as by his commission, which man cannot take away, 'while I have time I do good unto all men', knowing the night cometh, when no man can work. The manner wherein I do this (as confidently as it has been asserted), is contrary to no law that I know, either of church or state. Though if it were, I would still act as I do; for I am to obey God rather than man. A dispensation of the gospel is committed to me, and woe is me if I preach not the gospel.

'But you would have me preach it in a parish.' What parish, my brother? I have none at all. Nor I believe ever shall. Must I therefore bury my talent in the earth? Then am I a wicked, unprofitable servant.

The constitution of the apostolical church is as much for our preaching everywhere as the example of the apostles. The travels of Timothy are recorded in the Acts. Nor do I believe either *he or Titus or any Christian minister was confined to any one place till the love of Christians waxed cold*.

But indeed I could not serve (as they term it) a cure now. I have tried, and know it is impracticable to observe the laws of the English Church in any parish in England. I observed them in my parish of Savannah, till I was obliged to fly for my life. Mr. Stonehouse[2] is now persecuted on every side for observing them; and the good bishop, instead of defending his presbyter, is at the head of his persecutors.

Set the matter in another light, and it comes to a short issue. I everywhere see God's people perishing for lack of knowledge. I have power (through God) to save their souls from death. Shall I use it, or shall I let them perish – 'because they are not of my parish'?

[1] Ouranius: a pious and faithful country priest in William Law's *Serious Call*.

[2] The Rev. George Stonehouse, vicar of St Mary's, Islington (see above, pp. 25–6). In *A Farther Appeal to Men of Reason and Religion*, II, 32, Wesley refers to an action brought by a gentleman against Stonehouse for repelling him from the Lord's table. In 1746, however, Wesley was obliged to correct some of his facts in a letter to the *London Magazine*.

'Social Holiness'

(Preface to *Hymns and Sacred Poems* by John and Charles Wesley, 1739; *JWW*, XIV, 334)

Directly opposite to this [the teaching of the mystics] is the gospel of Christ. Solitary religion is not to be found there. 'Holy solitaries' is a phrase no more consistent with the gospel than holy adulterers. The gospel of Christ knows of no religion, but social; no holiness but social holiness. 'Faith working by love' is the length and breadth and depth and height of Christian perfection. 'This commandment have we from Christ, that he who loves God, love his brother also'; and that we manifest our love 'by doing good unto all men; especially to them that are of the household of faith'. And in truth, whosoever loveth his brethren, not in word only, but as Christ loved him, cannot but be 'zealous of good works'. He feels in his soul a burning, restless desire of spending and being spent for them. 'My Father', will he say, 'worketh hitherto, and I work.' And at all possible opportunities he is, like his Master, 'going about doing good'.

The Wesleys at Kingswood

(*JWJ*, II, 322–3)

Wesley is quoting a letter which he seems to have sent to several people, perhaps as part of his appeal for funds for the school for colliers' children which had been initiated by Whitefield before he left for Georgia.

Tuesday, November 27, 1739. I writ Mr. D. (according to his request) a short account of what had been done in Kingswood, and of our present undertaking there. The account was as follows:

Few persons have lived long in the West of England who have not heard of the colliers of Kingswood: a people famous, from the beginning hitherto, for neither fearing God nor regarding man; so ignorant of the things of God that they seemed but one remove from the beasts that perish; and therefore utterly without desire of instruction, as well as without the means of it.

Many last winter used tauntingly to say of Mr. Whitefield, 'If he will convert heathens, why does not he go to the colliers of Kingswood?' In spring he did so. And as there were thousands who resorted to no place of public worship, he went after them into their own wilderness, 'to seek and save that which was lost.' When he was called away, others went into 'the highways and hedges, to compel them to come in.' And, by the grace of God, their labour was not in vain. The scene is already changed. Kingswood does not now, as a year ago, resound with cursing and blasphemy. It is no more filled with drunkenness and uncleanness, and the idle diversions that naturally lead thereto. It is no longer full of wars and fightings, of clamour and bitterness, of wrath and envyings. Peace and love are there. Great numbers of the people are mild, gentle, and easy to be entreated. They 'do not cry, neither strive', and hardly is their 'voice heard in the streets'; or, indeed, in their own wood, unless when they are at their usual evening diversion, singing praise unto God their Saviour.

That their children, too, might know the things that make for their peace, it was some time since proposed to build a house in Kingswood; and, after many foreseen and unforeseen difficulties, in June last the foundation was laid. The ground made choice of was in the middle of the wood, between the London and Bath roads, not far from that called Two-Mile-Hill, about three measured miles from Bristol.

Here a large room was begun for the school, having four small rooms at either end for the schoolmasters (and, perhaps, if it should please God, some poor children) to lodge in. Two persons are ready to teach, so soon as the house is fit to receive them, the shell of which is nearly finished; so that it is hoped the whole will be completed in spring, or early in the summer. [It is proposed, in the usual hours of the day, to teach chiefly the poorer children to read, write, and cast accounts; but more especially (by God's assistance) to 'know God, and Jesus Christ, whom He hath sent.' The older people, being not so proper to be mixed with children (for we expect scholars of all ages, some of them grey-headed) will be taught in the inner rooms, either early in the morning, or late at night, so that their work may not be hindered.][1]

---

[1] The words in square brackets were omitted from the *Journal*, but appear in a copy of the letter sent to Thomas Price of Cardiff (Oxford *Letters*, I, 701–2).

A visit by Charles Wesley

(*CWJ*, I, 243, 245)

Sunday, June 29th [1740]. I found the spirit of the colliers before I began to speak. Then my mouth was opened to declare the promise of sanctification in Ezekiel. I gave the sacrament to about eighty colliers; exhorted the last-baptized; met the men-Leaders; preached to the usual congregation at Rose-green; and returned without strength to the Horsefair . . .

Sunday, July 20th. Our poor colliers being repelled from the Lord's table, by most of the Bristol Ministers, I exhorted them, notwithstanding, to continue daily with one accord in the temple; where the wickedest administrator can neither spoil the prayers, nor poison the sacrament. *These* poor sinners *have* ears to hear.

'Free Grace'

A sermon preached by John Wesley at Bristol in the year 1739

(Sermon CXXVIII, *JWW*, VII, 373–86; *Sermons* III, 542–63)

TO THE READER

Nothing but the strongest conviction, not only that what is here advanced is 'the truth as it is in Jesus', but also that I am indispensably obliged to declare this truth to all the world, could have induced me openly to oppose the sentiments of those whom I esteem for their work's sake: At whose feet may I be found in the day of the Lord Jesus!

Should any believe it his duty to reply hereto, I have only one request to make, – Let whatsoever you do, be done in charity, in love, and in the spirit of meekness. Let your very disputing show that you have 'put on, as the elect of God, bowels of mercies, gentleness, longsuffering'; that even according to this time it may be said, 'See how these Christians love one another!'

ADVERTISEMENT

Whereas a pamphlet, entitled, 'Free Grace Indeed', has been published against this Sermon; this is to inform the publisher, that I cannot answer his tract till he appears to be more in earnest. For I dare not speak of 'the deep things of God' in the spirit of a prize-fighter or a stage-player.

'*He that spared not his own Son, but delivered him up for us all, how shall he not with him also freely give us all things?*' Romans viii. 32.

1. How freely does God love the world! While we were yet sinners, 'Christ died for the ungodly.' While we were 'dead in sin', God 'spared not his own Son, but delivered him up for us all.' And how freely with him does he 'give us all things!' Verily, FREE GRACE is all in all! . . .

4. But is it free FOR ALL, as well as IN ALL? To this some have answered, 'No: It is free only for those whom God hath ordained to life; and they

are but a little flock. The greater part of mankind God hath ordained to death; and it is not free for them. Them God hateth; and, therefore, before they were born, decreed they should die eternally. And this he absolutely decreed; because so was his good pleasure; because it was his sovereign will. Accordingly, they are born for this, – to be destroyed body and soul in hell. And they grow up under the irrevocable curse of God, without any possibility of redemption; for what grace God gives, he gives only for this, to increase, not prevent, their damnation.'. . .

9. Call it therefore by whatever name you please, election, preterition, predestination, or reprobation, it comes in the end to the same thing. The sense of all is plainly this, – by virtue of an eternal, unchangeable, irresistible decree of God, one part of mankind are infallibly saved, and the rest infallibly damned; it being impossible that any of the former should be damned, or that any of the latter should be saved.

10. But if this be so, then is all preaching vain. It is needless to them that are elected; for they, whether with preaching or without, will infallibly be saved. Therefore, the end of preaching – to save souls – is void with regard to them; and it is useless to them that are not elected, for they cannot possibly be saved: They, whether with preaching or without, will infallibly be damned. The end of preaching is therefore void with regard to them likewise; so that in either case our preaching is vain, as your hearing is also vain.

11. This, then, is a plain proof that the doctrine of predestination is not a doctrine of God, because it makes void the ordinance of God; and God is not divided against himself. A second is, that it directly tends to destroy that holiness which is the end of all the ordinances of God. I do not say, none who hold it are holy (for God is of tender mercy to those who are unavoidably entangled in errors of any kind); but that the doctrine itself, – that every man is either elected or not elected from eternity, and that the one must inevitably be saved, and the other inevitably damned, – has a manifest tendency to destroy holiness in general; for it wholly takes away those first motives to follow after it, so frequently proposed in Scripture, the hope of future reward and fear of punishment, the hope of heaven and fear of hell. That these shall go away into everlasting punishment, and those into life eternal, is no motive to him to struggle for life who believes his lot is cast already; it is not reasonable for him so to do, if he thinks he is unalterably adjudged either to life or death. You will say, 'But he knows not whether it is life or death.' What then? – this helps not the matter; for if a sick man knows that he must unavoidably die, or unavoidably recover, though he knows not which, it is unreasonable for him to take any physic at all. He might justly say (and so I have heard some speak, both in bodily sickness and in spiritual), 'If I am ordained to life, I shall live; if to death, I shall die; so I need not

trouble myself about it.' So directly does this doctrine tend to shut the very gate of holiness in general, – to hinder unholy men from ever approaching thereto, or striving to enter in thereat.

12. As directly does this doctrine tend to destroy several particular branches of holiness. Such are meekness and love, – love, I mean, of our enemies, – of the evil and unthankful. I say not, that none who hold it have meekness and love (for as is the power of God, so is his mercy); but that it naturally tends to inspire, or increase, a sharpness or eagerness of temper, which is quite contrary to the meekness of Christ; as then especially appears, when they are opposed on this head. And it as naturally inspires contempt or coldness towards those whom we suppose outcasts from God. 'O but', you say, 'I suppose no particular man a reprobate.' You mean you would not if you could help it: But you cannot help sometimes applying your general doctrine to particular persons: The enemy of souls will apply it for you. You know how often he has done so. But you rejected the thought with abhorrence. True; as soon as you could; but how did it sour and sharpen your spirit in the mean time! You well know it was not the spirit of love which you then felt towards that poor sinner, whom you supposed or suspected, whether you would or no, to have been hated of God from eternity.

13. Thirdly. This doctrine tends to destoy the comfort of religion, the happiness of Christianity. This is evident as to all those who believe themselves to be reprobated, or who only suspect or fear it. All the great and precious promises are lost to them; they afford them no ray of comfort: For they are not the elect of God; therefore they have neither lot nor portion in them. This is an effectual bar to their finding any comfort or happiness, even in that religion whose ways are designed to be 'ways of pleasantness, and all her paths peace'. . . .

17. Again: How uncomfortable a thought is this, that thousands and millions of men, without any preceding offence or fault of theirs, were unchangeably doomed to everlasting burnings! How peculiarly uncomfortable must it be to those who have put on Christ! to those who, being filled with bowels of mercy, tenderness, and compassion, could even 'wish themselves accursed for their brethren's sake!'

18. Fourthly. This uncomfortable doctrine directly tends to destroy our zeal for good works. And this it does, First, as it naturally tends (according to what was observed before) to destroy our love to the greater part of mankind, namely, the evil and unthankful. For whatever lessens our love, must so far lessen our desire to do them good. This it does, Secondly, as it cuts off one of the strongest motives to all acts of bodily mercy, such as feeding the hungry, clothing the naked, and the like, – viz., the hope of saving their souls from death. For what avails it to relieve their temporal wants, who are just dropping into eternal fire?

'Well; but run and snatch them as brands out of the fire.' Nay, this you suppose impossible. They were appointed thereunto, you say, from eternity, before they had done either good or evil. You believe it is the will of God they should die. And 'who hath resisted his will?' But you say you do not know whether these are elected or not. What then? If you know they are the one or the other, – that they are either elected or not elected, – all your labour is void and vain. In either case, your advice, reproof, or exhortation is as needless and useless as our preaching. It is needless to them that are elected; for they will infallibly be saved without it. It is useless to them that are not elected; for with or without it they will infallibly be damned; therefore you cannot consistently with your principles take any pains about their salvation. Consequently, those principles directly tend to destroy your zeal for good works; for all good works; but particularly for the greatest of all, the saving of souls from death.

19. But, Fifthly, this doctrine not only tends to destroy Christian holiness, happiness, and good works, but hath also a direct and manifest tendency to overthrow the whole Christian Revelation. The point which the wisest of the modern unbelievers most industriously labour to prove, is, that the Christian Revelation is not necessary. They well know, could they once show this, the conclusion would be too plain to be denied, 'If it be not necessary, it is not true.' Now, this fundamental point you give up. For supposing that eternal, unchangeable decree, one part of mankind must be saved, though the Christian Revelation were not in being, and the other part of mankind must be damned, notwithstanding that Revelation. And what would an infidel desire more? You allow him all he asks. In making the gospel thus unnecessary to all sorts of men, you give up the whole Christian cause. 'O tell it not in Gath! Publish it not in the streets of Askelon! lest the daughters of the uncircumcised rejoice'; lest the sons of unbelief triumph! . . .

26. This is the blasphemy clearly contained in *the horrible decree of* predestination! And here I fix my foot. On this I join issue with every assertor of it. You represent God as worse than the devil; more false, more cruel, more unjust. But you say you will prove it by Scripture. Hold! What will you prove by Scripture? that God is worse than the devil? It cannot be. Whatever that Scripture proves, it never can prove this; whatever its true meaning be, this cannot be its true meaning. Do you ask, 'What is its true meaning then?' If I say, 'I know not', you have gained nothing; for there are many scriptures the true sense whereof neither you nor I shall know till death is swallowed up in victory. But this I know, better it were to say it had no sense at all, than to say it had such a sense as this. It cannot mean, whatever it mean besides, that the God of truth is a liar. Let it mean what it will, it cannot mean that the

Judge of all the world is unjust. No scripture can mean that God is not love, or that his mercy is not over all his works; that is, whatever it prove beside, no scripture can prove predestination.

George Whitefield to John Wesley; Bethesda in Georgia, December 24, 1740

(*George Whitefield's Journals*, 1960, pp. 573–88)

Whitefield had pleaded with Wesley not to publish his sermon on the issue which divided the two wings of the Revival.

I must next observe, that as you have been unhappy in printing at all, upon such an *imaginary warrant*,[1] so you have been as unhappy in the choice of your text. Honoured Sir, how could it enter into your head, to chuse a text to disprove the doctrine of election, out of the 8th of the Romans, where this doctrine is so plainly asserted, that once talking with a Quaker upon this subject, he had no other way of evading the force of the Apostle's assertion than by saying, 'I believe Paul was in the wrong.'

Indeed, honoured Sir, it is plain, beyond all contradiction, that St. Paul, through the whole eighth of the Romans, is speaking of the privileges of those only who are really in Christ. And let any unprejudiced person read what goes before, and what follows your text, and he must confess the word 'all' only signifies those that are in Christ; and the latter part of the text plainly proves what, I find, dear Mr. Wesley will, by no means, grant, I mean the *final perseverance* of the children of God. 'He that spared not his own Son, but delivered him up for us all (i.e. all Saints), how shall he not with him also freely give us all things.' Grace, in particular, to enable us to persevere, and every thing else necessary to carry us home to our Father's heavenly kingdom . . .

But passing by . . . your equivocal definition of the word *grace*, and your false definition of the word *free*, and that I may be as short as possible, I frankly acknowledge, I believe the doctrine of reprobation, in this view, that God intends to give saving grace, through Jesus Christ, only to a certain number, and that the rest of mankind, after the fall of Adam, being justly left of God to continue in sin, will at last suffer that eternal death, which is its proper wages.

This is the established doctrine of scripture, and acknowledged as such in the 17th article of the church of England, as Bishop Burnet himself confesses; yet dear Mr. Wesley absolutely denies it.

Thirdly, says your sermon, 'This doctrine tends to destroy the comforts of religion, the happiness of Christianity. This is evident as to all those who believe themselves to be reprobate, or only suspect or fear it; all the great and precious promises are lost to them; they afford them no ray of comfort.'

In answer to this, let me observe, that none living, especially none who are desirous of salvation, can know that they are not of the number of God's elect. None, but the unconverted, can have any just reason, so much as to fear it. And would dear Mr. Wesley give comfort, or dare you apply the precious promises of the gospel, being children's bread, to men in a natural state, while they continue so? God forbid! What if the doctrine of election and reprobation does put some upon doubting? So does that of regeneration. But, is not this doubting a good means to make their calling and their election sure? This is one reason among many others, why I admire the doctrine of election, and am convinced that it should have a place in gospel ministrations, and should be insisted on with faithfulness and care. It has a natural tendency to rouse the soul out of its carnal security. And therefore many carnal men cry out against it. Whereas universal redemption is a notion sadly adapted to keep the soul in its lethargic sleepy condition, and therefore so many natural men admire and applaud it. . . .

Says the dear Mr. Wesley, 'How uncomfortable a thought is this, that thousands and millions of men, without any preceding offence or fault of theirs, were unchangeably doomed to everlasting burnings?'

But who ever asserted [this]? Do not they who believe God's doom-ing men to everlasting burnings, also believe, that God looked upon them as men fallen in Adam? And that the decree which ordained the punishment, first regarded the crime by which it was deserved? How then are they doomed without any preceding fault? Surely Mr. Wesley will own God's justice, in imputing Adam's sin to his posterity; and also, that after Adam fell, and his posterity in him, God might justly have passed them *all* by, without sending his own Son to be a saviour for any one. Unless you heartily agree to both these points, you do not believe original sin aright. If you do own them, then you must acknow-ledge the doctrine of election and reprobation to be highly just and reasonable . . .

Further, you say, 'This doctrine makes revelation contradict itself.' For instance, say you, 'The assertors of this doctrine interpret that text of scripture, Jacob have I loved, but Esau have I hated, as implying that God, in a literal sense, hated Esau and all the reprobates from eternity!' And, when considered as fallen in Adam, were they not the objects of his hatred? And might not God, of his own good pleasure, love or shew mercy to Jacob and the elect, and yet at the same time do the re-probate no wrong? But you say, 'God is love.' And cannot God be love, unless he shews the same mercy to all? . . . As the sovereign Lord of all, who is debtor to none, he has a right to do what he will with his own, and to dispense his favours to what objects he sees fit, merely at his pleasure. And his supreme right herein, is clearly, and strongly asserted in those passages of scripture, where he says, 'I will have mercy on whom I will have mercy, and have compassion on whom I will have compassion,' Rom. ix. 15; Exod. xxxiii. 19. . . .

Dear Sir, for Jesus Christ's sake, consider how you dishonour God by denying election. You plainly make salvation depend not on God's *free-grace*, but on man's *free-will*; and if thus, it is more than probable, Jesus Christ would not have had the satisfaction of seeing the fruit of his death in the eternal salvation of one soul. Our preaching would then be in vain, and all invitations for people to believe in him, would also be in vain.

But blessed be God, our Lord knew for whom he died. There was an eternal compact between the Father and the Son. A certain number was then given him, as the purchase and reward of his obedience and death. For these he prayed, John xvii, and not for the world. For these, and these only, he is now interceding, and with their salvation he will be fully satisfied . . .

Dear, dear Sir, O be not offended! For Christ's sake be not rash! Give yourself to reading. Study the covenant of grace. Down with your carnal reasoning. Be a little child; and then, instead of pawning your salvation, as you have done in a late hymn book,[2] if the doctrine of *universal redemption* be not true; instead of talking of *sinless perfection*, as you have done in the preface to that hymn book, and making man's salvation to depend on his own *free-will*, as you have in this sermon; you will compose an hymn in praise of sovereign distinguishing love.[3] You will caution believers against striving to work a perfection out of their own hearts, and print another sermon the reverse of this, and entitle it free-grace *indeed*. Free, not because free to all; but free, because God may withhold or give it to whom and when he pleases.

---

[1] The reference is to Wesley's casting lots to determine whether or not to publish the sermon. Whitefield had reservations about this early Methodist practice. (Arnold Dallimore, *George Whitefield*, Vol. 1, 1970, pp. 592–3)

[2] *Hymns and Sacred Poems*, 1739. The preface does not actually use the term 'sinless perfection', but there is much stress on 'holiness of heart as well as holiness of life'.

[3] Cf. Charles Wesley's lines in his *Hymns on God's Everlasting Love*, 1741:

> Thy undistinguishing regard
> Was cast on Adam's fallen race;
> For all Thou hast in Christ prepared
> Sufficient, sovereign, saving grace.

Charles Wesley in South Wales

(*CWJ*, I, 254–62)

Friday, October 31st [1740]. The time for my going to Wales is now come. To-day Captain Philips challenged me; said he came to fetch me; and Mr. Wells invited me to preach in his churches. . . .

Thursday, November 6th. At six I took boat for Cardiff, and at six in the evening landed on Welsh ground with the voice of praise and thanksgiving. Mr. Wells, who invited me over, waited to give me the first greeting. From his house we went to the Society, where God opened my mouth to call, 'Ho, every one that thirsteth, come ye to the waters.' They received the word with all readiness. I lodged at Mr. Glascot's.

Friday, November 7th. I rode with Mr. Williams to St. Andrew's, a little town four Welsh miles from Cardiff. Mr. Wells was not afraid to trust me in his pulpit. I was greatly assisted to invite many poor sinners to come weary and heavy laden to Christ. They gladly received my saying. Mr. Hodges desired me to preach next Tuesday in his church at Wenvo. I returned to Cardiff rejoicing; and expounded 1 John i., to the conviction, I hope, of many.

Saturday, November 8th. I had an opportunity to moderate the spirits of some who were greatly exasperated against Howel Harris, for preaching predestination among them.

After church I waited with Mr. Wells on the sick Minister; who was extremely civil, invited me to dinner, and to preach in his pulpit morning and evening.

I spent the day in singing and close conference ,with some who would fain persuade themselves they had faith, without forgiveness. My Master, I trust, will soon persuade them that they have both together.

Sunday, November 9th. At six I explained the legal state, from Rom. vii. I read prayers, and preached to a large congregation, 'All have sinned and come short of the glory of God.' I administered the sacrament to many strangers. I read prayers in the afternoon, baptized a child, and preached both law and Gospel with great plainness. My hearers were surprisingly patient. Only one went out. I continued my discourse till it was dark; and had much comfort in having delivered my message.

The scripture to be expounded at night was, 1 John ii.: 'If any man sin, we have an advocate with the Father,' &c. God opened my mouth to declare the truth of his everlasting love to all mankind. At the same time he enlarged my heart to its opposers. I took the occasion to speak of Howel Harris; bore such a testimony of him as he deserves; and mildly upbraided them for their ingratitude toward the greatest benefactor their country ever had. We all expressed our love by joining in hearty prayer for him.

Monday, November 10th. I set out for St. Nicholas; called at Llandaff on the then officiating Minister, to ask the pulpit. He referred me to the Chapter; but I do not mean to trouble them. The church at St. Nicholas, also, was shut against me; but we met at a neighbouring house, Mr. Deer's, where I offered Christ to all sinners, with much freedom and power . . .

I sent a messenger to Howel Harris, with the following letter:—

'My dearest Friend and Brother, – In the name of Jesus Christ I beseech you, if you have his glory and the good of souls at heart, come immediately, and meet me here. I trust we shall never be two in time or eternity. O my brother, I am grieved that Satan should get a moment's advantage over us; and am ready to lay my neck under your feet for Christ's sake. If your heart is as my heart, hasten, in the name of our dear Lord, to your second self,

C. WESLEY.'

Sunday, November 16th. Mr. Williams informed me that many had bound themselves with a curse to make a disturbance in the church, and not suffer me to preach. Then the Clerk told me I was not to preach in the afternoon. I answered, I had not expected to preach there in the morning, or, indeed, a second time.

The Psalms began, 'O God, the Heathen are come into thine inheritance; thy holy temple have they defiled.' The Second Lesson was very animating, being John viii; that earnest contention of our Lord with the Pharisees.

My text was, 'If God be for us, who can be against us?' I began abruptly with the opposers, and defied them in the name of the Lord Jesus. The Spirit of power was with me; but I soon perceived him as the Spirit of love; and besought those unhappy sinners to be reconciled unto God. Their master durst not hazard their staying any longer; but, in the midst of my discourse, hurried them out of church.

I went on convincing and entreating the Pharisees to submit to the righteousness of God. Never was my mouth and heart more enlarged. Upon my repeating, 'It pleased God by the foolishness of preaching to save all them that believe,' a gentleman rose, and turned his back on the Gospel of his salvation. I called after him in vain; then earnestly prayed for him and the rest, the Spirit helping my infirmity. . . .

Tuesday, November 18th. I preached at St. Bride's, 'Thou shalt call his name Jesus,' &c. Here, too, I cast my net to catch the fisher. We were setting out from the public-house, when God brought Howel Harris to us. All misunderstandings vanished at sight of each other, and our hearts were knit together as at the beginning. We sang an hymn of triumph. God had prepared his heart for this meeting. At the sacrament he had found the spirit of martyrdom falling upon him, and immediately I was brought to his remembrance. His heart overflowed with love, and he thought we were going hand in hand to the stake.

Before the Society, several were with me, desiring me, now I had gotten him, to reprove him openly. Some wanted me to preach against lay-preaching; some against predestination, &c. In my discourse on Isai. xl., a gentleman, who had come thither on purpose, interrupted me, by desiring I would now speak to Mr. Harris, since I was sent for to disprove his errors, and Mr. Wells, an experienced Clergyman, sat by to moderate between us. God gave me immediate recollection. I smiled at Satan's impudence; but turned aside the question with mildness, and thanks to the proposer. In vain he urged me to enter the lists with my friend. I quashed all farther importunity by declaring, 'I am unwilling to speak of my brother Howel Harris, because, when I begin, I know not how to leave off; and should say so much good of him, as some of you could not bear.' The gentleman, disappointed of his hope, immediately departed.

After this victory over Satan, I proceeded with double power, addressing myself particularly to the ladies, whose company we were favoured with because there was no play to-night. I showed them they were no better than common harlots, if they outwardly differed from them through pride, not virtue. The Lord open their hearts to receive my hard saying.

The Captain giving me notice that he should sail the next day, I determined to spend the night in taking leave. We supped at the friendly Mr. Wells's, and then called at Captain Philips's. Between ten and eleven, just as I was going, Satan began to show his wrath at the many sore disappointments he has met with this very day. He could not set the children of God against each other, and was therefore forced to make use of his own. The Physician, who had gone out of church on Sunday, stirred up by his companions, and unusually heated with wine, came and demanded satisfaction of me for calling him Pharisee. I said, 'I was ready to acknowledge my mistake, if he would assure me he had gone out of church to visit his patients.' He replied, 'He had gone out because he disliked my discourse.' 'Then, Sir,' said I, 'I cannot ask pardon for telling you the truth.' 'But you must for calling me a Pharisee.' 'I still insist you are a Pharisee, and cannot endure sound doctrine. My commission is, to show you your sins; and I shall make no apology for so doing, to you or any man living. You are a damned sinner by nature, and a Pharisee, like me: and this testimony I should bear before rulers and Kings. You are a rebel against God, and must bow your stiff neck to Him before you can be forgiven.' 'How do you know my heart?' 'My heart showeth me the wickedness of the ungodly.' 'Sir, I am as good a Christian as yourself.' 'You are no Christian at all, unless you have received the Holy Ghost.' 'How do you prove that you have the Holy Ghost?' 'By searching your heart, and showing you that you are a Pharisee.' Here he lifted up his cane, and struck me. Mrs. Philips intercepted and broke the blow; F. Farley tripped up his heels; and the company rushed in between. My soul was immediately filled with the calm, recollected boldness of faith. There was a great outcry among the women. Several of them he struck, and hurt, and raged like one possessed, till the men forced him out, and shut the door.

Soon after, it was broken open by a Justice, and the Bailiff, or head-Magistrate. The latter began expostulating with me upon the affront offered the Doctor; and said, 'As it was a public injury, I ought to make him public satisfaction.' I answered, 'Mr. Bailiff, I honour you for your office' sake; but was you yourself, or His Majesty King George, among my hearers, I should tell you both that you are by nature damned sinners. In the church, while preaching, I have no superior but God; and shall not ask man leave to show him his sins. – As a ruler, it is your duty to be a terror to evil-doers, but a praise to them that do well.' Upon my thus speaking, he became exceeding civil; assured me of his good-will, and that he had come to prevent my being insulted; and none should touch an hair of my head . . .

About four, Mr. Wells, &c., attended me to the vessel. I laid me down, and slept, and took my rest; for it is thou, Lord, only, that makest me dwell in safety.

Thursday, November 20th. By five this morning, He who blest our going out, blest our coming in to Bristol.

The Exercise of Discipline

JWJ, II, 517; III, 68–71, 491)

December 9, 1741. [Bristol] God humbled us in the evening by the loss of more than thirty of our little company, whom I was obliged to exclude, as no longer adorning the gospel of Christ. I believed it best openly to declare both their names and the reasons why they were excluded. We then cried unto God that this might be for their edification and not for destruction.

March 6, 1743. [Newcastle] I read over in the society the rules which all our members are to observe; and desired every one seriously to consider whether he was willing to conform thereto or no. . . .

Saturday 12. I concluded my second course of visiting, in which I inquired particularly into . . . the number of those who were separated from us, and the reason and occasion of it . . . I observed the number of those who had left the society since December 30 was seventy-six:

Fourteen of these (chiefly Dissenters) said they left it because otherwise their ministers would not give them the sacrament.

Nine more, because their husbands or wives were not willing they should stay in it.

Twelve, because their parents were not willing.

Five, because their master and mistress would not let them come.

Seven, because their acquaintance persuaded them to leave it.

Five, because people said such bad things of the society.

Nine, because they would not be laughed at.

Three, because they would not lose the poor's allowance.

Three more, because they could not spare time to come.

Two, because it was too far off.

One, because she was afraid of falling into fits.

One, because people were so rude in the street.

Two, because Thomas Naisbit was in the society.

One, because he would not turn his back on his baptism.

One, because we were mere Church of England men. And,

One, because it was time enough to serve God yet.

The number of those who were expelled the society was sixty-four:

Two for cursing and swearing.

Two for habitual Sabbath-breaking.

Seventeen for drunkenness.

Two for retailing spirituous liquors.

Three for quarrelling and brawling.

One for beating his wife.

Three for habitual, wilful lying.

Four for railing and evil-speaking.

One for idleness and laziness. And,

Nine-and-twenty for lightness and carelessness.

August 17, 1750. Through all Cornwall I find the societies have suffered great loss from want of discipline. Wisely said the ancients, 'The soul and body make a man; the Spirit and discipline make a Christian.'

The continuing struggle: Wesley's correspondence, 1762–1782

(*JWL*, IV, 169; V, 204, 208; VI, 208, 238; VII, 101)

January 25, 1762: to Matthew Lowes

You do well to be exact in discipline. Disorderly walkers will give us neither credit nor strength. Let us have just as many members as walk by one rule.

October 13, 1770: to Christopher Hopper, at Bradford

You are quite right. If a man preach like an angel, he will do little good without exact discipline.

November 18, 1770: to Mrs. Woodhouse, at Owston Ferry, Lincs

It always gives me pleasure to hear from you, and to know that your soul prospers; so does the work of God in various places, and I hope in Lincolnshire. It certainly will if Mr. Ellis is exact in discipline. It is sure none is a member of a *Methodist* Society that has not a ticket. This is a necessary thing; but it is only a small one. The great point is to conform to the Bible *method* of salvation – to have the mind which was in Christ, and to walk as Christ walked. I hope all your three preachers insist upon this, which is the very essence of Christian perfection.

February 22, 1776: to Joseph Benson, at Newcastle

We must threaten no longer, but perform. In November last I told the London Society, 'Our rule is to meet a class once a week, not once in two or three. I now give you warning: I will give tickets to none in February but those that have done this.' I have stood to my word. Go you and do likewise wherever you visit the classes. Begin, if need be, at Newcastle, and go on at Sunderland. Promises to meet are now out of date. Those that have not met seven times in the quarter exclude. Read their names in the Society, and inform them all you will the next quarter exclude all that have not met twelve times – that is, unless they were hindered by distance, sickness, or by some unavoidable business.

And I pray without fear or favour remove the leaders, whether of classes or bands, who do not watch over the souls committed to their care 'as those that must give account'.

November 7, 1776: to Joseph Benson, at Newcastle

Not only the Assistant, but every preacher is concerned to see all our Rules observed. I desire Brother Rhodes will give no tickets either to those who have not constantly met their classes or to any that do not solemnly promise to deal in stolen goods no more. He and you together may put a stop to this crying sin.

January 18, 1782: to John Valton, at Manchester

I cannot allow John Sellars to be any longer a leader; and if he will lead the class, whether I will or no, I require you to put him out of our Society. If twenty of his class will leave the Society too, they must. The first loss is the best. Better forty members should be lost than our discipline lost. They are no Methodists that will bear no restraints.

Whitefield at Moorfields

(George Whitefield, *Works*, 1771, I, 384–6)

Letter to Mr. L——; London, May 11, 1742. See also the following letter, May 15, 1742, for an account of similar scenes at Marylebone.

With this, I send you a few out of the many notes I have received from persons, who were convicted, converted, or comforted in *Moorfields*, during the late holidays. For many weeks, I found my heart much pressed to determine to venture to preach there at this season, when, if ever, Satan's children keep up their annual rendezvous. I must inform you, that *Moorfields* is a large, spacious place, given, as I have been told, by one *Madame Moore*, on purpose for all sorts of people to divert themselves in. For many years past, from one end to the other, booths of all kinds have been erected for mountebanks, players, puppet shows, and such like. With a heart bleeding with compassion for so many thousands led captive by the devil at his will, on *Whit-Monday*, at six o'clock in the morning, attended by a large congregation of praying people, I ventured to lift up a standard amongst them in the name of Jesus of *Nazareth*. Perhaps there were about ten thousand in waiting, not for me, but for Satan's instruments to amuse them. Glad was I to find, that I had for once as it were got the start of the devil. I mounted my field pulpit, almost all flocked immediately around it. I preached on these words, 'As *Moses* lifted up the serpent in the wilderness, so shall the son of man be lifted up, &c.' They gazed, they listened, they wept; and I believe that many felt themselves stung with deep conviction for their past sins. All was hushed and solemn. Being thus encouraged, I ventured out again at noon; but what a scene! The fields, the whole fields seemed, in a bad sense of the word, all white, ready not for the Redeemer's, but Beelzebub's harvest. All his agents were in full motion, drummers, trumpeters, merry andrews, masters of puppet shows, exhibiters of wild beasts, players, &c. &c. all busy entertaining their respective auditories. I suppose there could not be less than twenty or thirty thousand people. My pulpit was fixed on the opposite side, and immediately, to their great mortification, they found the number of their attendants sadly lessened. Judging that like saint *Paul*, I should now be called as it were to fight with beasts at *Ephesus*, I preached from these words: 'Great is *Diana* of the *Ephesians*.' You may easily guess, that there was some noise among the craftsmen, and that I was honoured with having a few stones, dirt, rotten eggs and pieces of dead cats thrown at me, whilst engaged in calling them from their favourite but lying vanities. My soul was indeed among lions; but far the greatest part of my congregation, which was very large, seemed for a while to be turned into lambs. This encouraged me to give notice, that I would preach again at six o'clock in the evening. I came, I saw, but what – thousands and thousands more than before if possible, still more deeply engaged in their unhappy diversions; but some thousands amongst them waiting as earnestly to hear the gospel. This Satan could not brook. One of his choicest servants was exhibiting, trumpeting on a large stage; but as soon as the people saw me in my black robes and my pulpit, I think all to a man left him and ran to me. For a while I was enabled to lift up my voice like a trumpet, and many heard the joyful sound. God's people kept praying, and the enemy's agents made a kind of a roaring at some distance from our camp. At length they approached nearer, and the merry andrew, (attended by others, who complained that they had taken many pounds less that day on account of my preaching) got upon a man's shoulders, and advancing near the pulpit attempted to slash me with a long heavy whip several times, but always with the violence of his motion tumbled down. Soon afterwards, they got a recruiting serjeant with his drum, &c. to pass through the congregation. I gave the word of command, and ordered that way might be made for the king's officer. The ranks opened, while all marched quietly through, and then closed again. Finding those efforts to fail, a large body quite on the opposite side assembled together, and having got a large pole for their standard, advanced towards us with steady and formidable steps, till they came very near the skirts of our hearing, praying, and almost undaunted congregation. I saw, gave warning, and prayed to the captain of our salvation for present support and deliverance. He heard and answered; for just as they approached us with looks full of resentment, I know not by what accident, they quarrelled among themselves, threw down their staff and went their way, leaving however many of their company behind, who before we had done, I trust were brought over to join the besieged party. I think I continued in praying, preaching and singing, (for the noise was too great at times to preach) about three hours. We then retired to the tabernacle, with my pockets full of notes from persons brought under concern, and read them amidst the praises and spiritual acclamations of thousands, who joined with the holy angels in rejoicing that so many sinners were snatched, in such an unexpected, unlikely place and manner, out of the very jaws of the devil. This was the beginning of the tabernacle society. – Three hundred and fifty awakened souls were received in one day, and I believe the number of notes exceeded a thousand . . .

The Character of a Methodist

(First published 1742; *JWW*, VIII, 339–47)

Not as though I had already attained

TO THE READER

1. Since the name first came abroad into the world, many have been at a loss to know what a Methodist is; what are the principles and the practice of those who are commonly called by that name; and what the distinguishing marks of this sect, 'which is everywhere spoken against.'

2. And it being generally believed, that I was able to give the clearest account of these things (as having been one of the first to whom that name was given, and the person by whom the rest were supposed to be directed), I have been called upon, in all manner of ways, and with the utmost earnestness, so to do. I yield at last to the continued importunity both of friends and enemies; and do now give the clearest account I can, in the presence of the Lord and Judge of heaven and earth, of the principles and practice whereby those who are called Methodists are distinguished from other men.

3. I say those who are called Methodists; for, let it be well observed, that this is not a name which they take to themselves, but one fixed upon them by way of reproach, without their approbation or consent. It was first given to three or four young men at Oxford, by a student of Christ Church; either in allusion to the ancient sect of Physicians so called, from their teaching, that almost all diseases might be cured by a specific *method* of diet and exercise, or from their observing a more regular *method* of study and behaviour than was usual with those of their age and station.

4. I should rejoice (so little ambitious am I to be at the head of any sect or party) if the very name might never be mentioned more, but be buried in eternal oblivion. But if that cannot be, at least let those who will use it, know the meaning of the word they use. Let us not always be fighting in the dark. Come, and let us look one another in the face. And perhaps some of you who hate what I am *called*, may love what I *am* by the grace of God; or rather, what 'I follow after, if that I may apprehend that for which also I am apprehended of Christ Jesus.'

THE CHARACTER OF A METHODIST

1. The distinguishing marks of a Methodist are not his opinions of any sort. His assenting to this or that scheme of religion, his embracing any particular set of notions, his espousing the judgment of one man or of

another, are all quite wide of the point. Whosoever, therefore, imagines that a Methodist is a man of such or such an opinion, is grossly ignorant of the whole affair; he mistakes the truth totally. We believe, indeed, that 'all Scripture is given by the inspiration of God'; and herein we are distinguished from Jews, Turks, and Infidels. We believe the written word of God to be the only and sufficient rule both of Christian faith and practice; and herein we are fundamentally distinguished from those from those of the Romish Church. We believe Christ to be the eternal, supreme God; and herein we are distinguished from the Socinians and Arians. But as to all opinions which do not strike at the root of Christianity, we think and let think. So that whatsoever they are, whether right or wrong, they are no distinguishing marks of a Methodist.

2. Neither are words or phrases of any sort. We do not place our religion, or any part of it, in being attached to any peculiar mode of speaking, any quaint or uncommon set of expressions. The most obvious, easy, common words, wherein our meaning can be conveyed, we prefer before others, both on ordinary occasions, and when we speak of the things of God. We never, therefore, willingly or designedly, deviate from the most usual way of speaking; unless when we express scripture truths in scripture words, which, we presume, no Christian will condemn. Neither do we affect to use any particular expressions of Scripture more frequently than others, unless they are such as are more frequently used by the inspired writers themselves. So that it is as gross an error, to place the marks of a Methodist in his words, as in opinions of any sort.

3. Nor do we desire to be distinguished by actions, customs, or usages, of an indifferent nature. Our religion does not lie in doing what God has not enjoined, or abstaining from what he hath not forbidden. It does not lie in the form of our apparel, in the posture of our body, or the covering of our heads; nor yet in abstaining from marriage, or from meats and drinks, which are all good if received with thanksgiving. Therefore, neither will any man, who knows whereof he affirms, fix the mark of a Methodist here, – in any actions or customs purely indifferent, undetermined by the word of God.

4. Nor, lastly, is he distinguished by laying the whole stress of religion on any single part of it. If you say, 'Yes, he is; for he thinks "we are saved by faith alone",' I answer, You do not understand the terms. By salvation he means holiness of heart and life. And this he affirms to spring from true faith alone. Can even a nominal Christian deny it? Is this placing a part of religion for the whole? 'Do we then make void the law through faith? God forbid! Yea, we establish the law.' We do not place the whole of religion (as too many do, God knoweth) either in doing no harm, or in doing good, or in using the ordinances of God. No, not in all of them together; wherein we know by experience a man

may labour many years, and at the end have no religion at all, no more than he had at the beginning. Much less in any one of these; or, it may be, in a scrap of one of them: Like her who fancies herself a virtuous woman, only because she is not a prostitute; or him who dreams he is an honest man, merely because he does not rob or steal. May the Lord God of my fathers preserve me from such a poor, starved religion as this! Were this the mark of a Methodist, I would sooner choose to be a sincere Jew, Turk, or Pagan.

5. 'What then is the mark? Who is a Methodist, according to your own account?' I answer: A Methodist is one who has 'the love of God shed abroad in his heart by the Holy Ghost given unto him'; one who 'loves the Lord his God with all his heart, and with all his soul, and with all his mind, and with all his strength.' God is the joy of his heart, and the desire of his soul; which is constantly crying out, 'Whom have I in heaven but thee? and there is none upon earth that I desire beside thee! My God and my all! Thou art the strength of my heart, and my portion for ever!'

6. He is therefore happy in God, yea, always happy, as having in him 'a well of water springing up into everlasting life', and overflowing his soul with peace and joy. 'Perfect love' having now 'cast out fear', he 'rejoices evermore'. He 'rejoices in the Lord always', even 'in God his Saviour'; and in the Father, 'through our Lord Jesus Christ, by whom he hath now received the atonement'. 'Having' found 'redemption through his blood, the forgiveness of his sins', he cannot but rejoice, whenever he looks back on the horrible pit out of which he is delivered; when he sees 'all his transgressions blotted out as a cloud, and his iniquities as a thick cloud'. He cannot but rejoice, whenever he looks on the state wherein he now is; 'being justified freely, and having peace with God through our Lord Jesus Christ' . . .

7. And he who hath this hope, thus 'full of immortality, in everything giveth thanks'; as knowing that this (whatsoever it is) 'is the will of God in Christ Jesus concerning him.' From him, therefore, he cheerfully receives all, saying, 'Good is the will of the Lord;' and whether the Lord giveth or taketh away, equally 'blessing the name of the Lord'. For he hath 'learned, in whatsoever state he is, therewith to be content.' He knoweth 'both how to be abased and how to abound'. . . .

8. For indeed he 'prays without ceasing'. It is given him 'always to pray, and not to faint'. Not that he is always in the house of prayer; though he neglects no opportunity of being there. Neither is he always on his knees, although he often is, or on his face, before the Lord his God. Nor yet is he always crying aloud to God, or calling upon him in words: For many times 'the Spirit maketh intercession for him with groans that cannot be uttered.' But at all times the language of his heart

is this: 'Thou brightness of the eternal glory, unto thee is my heart, though without a voice, and my silence speaketh unto thee.' And this is true prayer, and this alone. But his heart is ever lifted up to God, at all times and in all places. In this he is never hindered, much less interrupted, by any person or thing. In retirement or company, in leisure, business, or conversation, his heart is ever with the Lord. Whether he lie down or rise up, God is in all his thoughts; he walks with God continually, having the loving eye of his mind still fixed upon him, and everywhere 'seeing Him that is invisible'.

9. And while he thus always exercises his love to God, by praying without ceasing, rejoicing evermore, and in everthing giving thanks, this commandment is written in his heart, 'That he who loveth God, love his brother also.' And he accordingly loves his neighbour as himself; he loves every man as his own soul. His heart is full of love to all mankind, to every child of 'the Father of the spirits of all flesh'. That a man is not personally known to him, is no bar to his love; no, nor that he is known to be such as he approves not, that he repays hatred for his good-will. For he 'loves his enemies'; yea, and the enemies of God, 'the evil and the unthankful'. And if it be not in his power to 'do good to them that hate him', yet he ceases not to pray for them, though they continue to spurn his love, and still 'despitefully use him and persecute him'.

10. For he is 'pure in heart'. The love of God has purified his heart from all revengeful passions, from envy, malice, and wrath, from every unkind temper or malign affection. It hath cleansed him from pride and haughtiness of spirit, whereof alone cometh contention. And he hath now 'put on bowels of mercies, kindness, humbleness of mind, meekness, longsuffering.' So that he 'forbears and forgives, if he had a quarrel against any; even as God in Christ hath forgiven him.' And indeed all possible ground for contention, on his part, is utterly cut off. For none can take from him what he desires; seeing he 'loves not the world, nor' any of 'the things of the world'; being now 'crucified to the world, and the world crucified to him'; being dead to all that is in the world, both to 'the lust of the flesh, the lust of the eye, and the pride of life'. For 'all his desire is unto God, and to the remembrance of his name.'

11. Agreeable to this his own desire, is the one design of his life, namely, 'not to do his own will, but the will of Him that sent him.' His one intention at all times and in all things is, not to please himself, but Him whom his soul loveth. He has a single eye. And because 'his eye is single, his whole body is full of light.' Indeed, where the loving eye of the soul is continually fixed upon God, there can be no darkness at all, 'but the whole is light; as when the bright shining of a candle doth enlighten the house.' God then reigns alone. All that is in the soul is holiness to the Lord. There is not a motion in his heart, but is according

to His will. Every thought that arises points to Him, and is in obedience to the law of Christ.

12. And the tree is known by its fruits. For as he loves God, so he keeps his commandments; not only some, or most of them, but all, from the least to the greatest. He is not content to 'keep the whole law, and offend in one point;' but has, in all points, 'a conscience void offence towards God and towards man'. Whatever God has forbidden, he avoids; whatever God hath enjoined, he doeth; and that whether it be little or great, hard or easy, joyous or grievous to the flesh. He 'runs the way of God's commandments', now he hath set his heart at liberty. It is his glory so to do; it is his daily crown of rejoicing, 'to do the will of God on earth, as it is done in heaven'; knowing it is the highest privilege of 'the angels of God, of those that excel in strength, to fulfil his commandments, and hearken to the voice of his word'.

13. All the commandments of God he accordingly keeps, and that with all his might. For his obedience is in proportion to his love, the source from whence it flows. And therefore, loving God with all his heart, he serves him with all his strength. He continually presents his soul and body a living sacrifice, holy, acceptable to God; entirely and without reserve devoting himself, all he has, and all he is, to his glory. All the talents he has received, he constantly employs according to his Master's will; every power and faculty of his soul, every member of his body. . . .

15. Nor do the customs of the world at all hinder his 'running the race that is set before him'. He knows that vice does not lose its nature, though it becomes ever so fashionable; and remembers, that 'every man is to give an account of himself to God.' He cannot, therefore, 'follow' even 'a multitude to do evil'. He cannot 'fare sumptuously every day', or 'make provision for the flesh to fulfil the lusts thereof'. He cannot 'lay up treasures upon earth', any more than he can take fire into his bosom. He cannot 'adorn himself', on any pretence, 'with gold or costly apparel'. He cannot join in or countenance any diversion which has the least tendency to vice of any kind. He cannot 'speak evil' of his neighbour, any more than he can lie either for God or man. He cannot utter an unkind word of any one; for love keeps the door of his lips. He cannot speak 'idle words'; 'no corrupt communication' ever 'comes out of his mouth', as is all that 'which is' not 'good to the use of edifying', not 'fit to minister grace to the hearers'. But 'whatsoever things are pure, whatsoever things are lovely, whatsoever things are' justly 'of good reports', he thinks, and speaks, and acts, 'adorning the Gospel of our Lord Jesus Christ in all things'.

16. Lastly. As he has time, he 'does good unto all men'; unto neighbours and strangers, friends and enemies: And that in every possible

kind; not only to their bodies, by 'feeding the hungry, clothing the naked, visiting those that are sick or in prison'; but much more does he labour to do good to their souls, as of the ability which God giveth; to awaken those that sleep in death; to bring those who are awakened to the atoning blood, that, 'being justified by faith, they may have peace with God'; and to provoke those who have peace with God to abound more in love and in good works. And he is willing to 'spend and be spent herein', even 'to be offered up on the sacrifice and service of their faith', so they may 'all come unto the measure of the stature of the fulness of Christ.'

17. These are the principles and practices of our sect; these are the marks of a true Methodist. By these alone do those who are in derision so called, desire to be distinguished from other men. If any man say, 'Why, these are only the common fundamental principles of Christianity!' thou hast said; so I mean; this is the very truth; I know they are no other; and I would to God both thou and all men knew, that I, and all who follow my judgment, do vehemently refuse to be distinguished from other men, by any but the common principles of Christianity, – the plain, old Christianity that I teach, renouncing and detesting all other marks of distinction. And whosoever is what I preach (let him be called what he will, for names change not the nature of things), he is a Christian, not in name only, but in heart and in life. He is inwardly and outwardly conformed to the will of God, as revealed in the written word. He thinks, speaks, and lives, according to the method laid down in the revelation of Jesus Christ. His soul is renewed after the image of God, in righteousness and in all true holiness. And having the mind that was in Christ, he so walks as Christ also walked.

18. By these marks, by these fruits of a living faith, do we labour to distinguish ourselves from the unbelieving world, from all those whose minds or lives are not according to the Gospel of Christ. But from real Christians, of whatsoever denomination they be, we earnestly desire not to be distinguished at all, not from any who sincerely follow after what they know they have not yet attained. No: 'Whosoever doeth the will of my Father which is in heaven, the same is my brother, and sister, and mother.' And I beseech you, brethren, by the mercies of God, that we be in no wise divided among ourselves. Is thy heart right, as my heart is with thine? I ask no farther question. If it be, give me thy hand. For opinions, or terms, let us not destroy the work of God. Dost thou love and serve God? It is enough. I give thee the right hand of fellowship. If there be any consolation in Christ, if any comfort of love, if any fellowship of the Spirit, if any bowels and mercies; let us strive together for the faith of the Gospel; walking worthy of the vocation wherewith we are called; with all lowliness and meekness, with long-suffering, forbearing one another in love, endeavouring to keep the unity of the Spirit

in the bond of peace; remembering, there is one body, and one Spirit, even as we are called with one hope of our calling; 'one Lord, one faith, one baptism; one God and Father of all, who is above all, and through all, and in you all'.

The Whole Armour of God: Ephesians vi

(*PW*, V, 40–44)

This poem by Charles Wesley was printed at the end of the first edition of *The Character of a Methodist* (1742).

> 1 Soldiers of CHRIST, arise,
>   And put your Armour on,
> Strong in the Strength which GOD supplies
>   Thro' his Eternal Son;
>   Strong in the LORD of Hosts,
>   And in his mighty Power,
> Who in the Strength of JESUS trusts
>   Is more than Conqueror.
>
> 2 Stand then in His great Might,
>   With all his Strength endu'd,
> And take, to arm you for the Fight,
>   The Panoply of GOD;
>   That having all Things done,
>   And all your Conflicts past,
> Ye may o'ercome thro' CHRIST alone,
>   And stand entire at last.
>
> 3 Stand then against your Foes,
>   In close and firm Array,
> Legions of wily Fiends oppose
>   Throughout the Evil Day;
>   But meet the Sons of Night,
>   But mock their vain Design,
> Arm'd in the Arms of Heavenly Light
>   And Righteousness Divine.

4　　Leave no Unguarded Place,
　　　No Weakness of the Soul,
　　Take every Virtue, every Grace,
　　　And fortify the Whole;
　　　Indissolubly join'd,
　　　To Battle all proceed,
　　But arm yourselves with all the Mind
　　　That was in CHRIST your Head.

5　　Let Truth the Girdle be
　　　That binds your Armour on,
　　In Faithful firm Sincerity
　　　To JESUS cleave alone;
　　　Let Faith and Love combine
　　　To guard your Valiant Breast,
　　The Plate be Righteousness Divine,
　　　Imputed and Imprest.

6　　Still let your Feet be shod,
　　　Ready His Will to do,
　　Ready in all the Ways of GOD
　　　His Glory to pursue:
　　　Ruin is spread beneath,
　　　The Gospel Greaves put on,
　　And safe thro' all the Snares of Death
　　　To Life eternal run.

7　　But above all, lay hold
　　　On FAITH's victorious Shield
　　Arm'd with that Adamant and Gold
　　　Be sure to win the Field;
　　　If Faith surround your Heart,
　　　Satan shall be subdu'd
　　Repell'd his ev'ry Fiery Dart,
　　　And quench'd with JESU's Blood.

8　　JESUS hath died for You!
　　　What can his Love withstand?
　　Believe; hold fast your Shield; and who
　　　Shall pluck you from His Hand?
　　　Believe that JESUS reigns,
　　　All Power to Him is giv'n,
　　Believe, 'till freed from Sin's Remains,
　　　Believe yourselves to Heaven.

9   Your Rock can never shake:
      Hither, He saith, come up!
The Helmet of Salvation take,
      The Confidence of Hope:
      Hope for His Perfect Love,
      Hope for His People's Rest,
Hope to sit down with CHRIST above
      And share the Marriage Feast.

10   Brandish in Faith 'till then
      The Spirit's two-edg'd Sword,
Hew all the Snares of Fiends and Men
      In Pieces with the Word;
      'TIS WRITTEN; This applied
      Baffles their Strength and Art;
Spirit and Soul with this divide,
      And Joints and Marrow part.

11   To keep your Armour bright
      Attend with constant Care,
Still walking in your Captain's Sight,
      And watching unto Prayer;
      Ready for all Alarms,
      Stedfastly set your Face,
And always exercise your Arms,
      And use your every Grace.

12   Pray, without ceasing pray,
      (Your Captain gives the Word)
His Summons chearfully obey,
      And call upon the LORD;
      To GOD your every Want
      In Instant Prayer display,
Pray always; pray, and never faint;
      Pray, without ceasing Pray.

13   In Fellowship; alone
      To GOD with Faith draw near,
Approach his Courts, besiege His Throne
      With all the Power of Prayer:
      Go to His Temple, go,
      Nor from His Altar move;
Let every House His Worship know,
      And every Heart His Love.

14   To GOD your Spirits dart,
     Your Souls in Words declare,
Or groan, to Him who reads the Heart,
     Th'unutterable Prayer.
     His Mercy now implore,
     And now shew forth His Praise,
In Shouts, or silent Awe adore
     His Miracles of Grace.

15   Pour out your Souls to GOD,
     And bow them with your Knees,
And spread your Hearts and Hands abroad
     And pray for *Sion*'s Peace;
     Your Guides and Brethren, bear
     For ever on your Mind;
Extend the Arms of mighty Prayer
     Ingrasping all Mankind.

16   From Strength to Strength go on,
     Wrestle, and fight, and pray,
Tread all the Powers of Darkness down,
     And win the well-fought Day;
     Still let the Spirit cry
     In all His Soldiers, 'Come'
Till CHRIST the LORD descends from High
     And takes the Conqu'rors Home.

The Nature, Design and General Rules of the United Societies
in London, Bristol, Kingswood, Newcastle upon Tyne, etc.

(*JWW*, VIII, 269–71)

These Rules were prompted by the 'lack of discipline' and 'even of common morality' which Wesley found on his northern tour in the spring of 1743 (see the extract from his *Journal*, pp. 45–6 above).

1. In the latter end of the year 1739, eight or ten persons came to me in London, who appeared to be deeply convinced of sin, and earnestly groaning for redemption. They desired (as did two or three more the next day) that I would spend some time with them in prayer, and advise

them how to flee from the wrath to come; which they saw continually hanging over their heads. That we might have more time for this great work, I appointed a day when they might all come together, which from thenceforward they did every week, namely, on Thursday, in the evening. To these, and as many more as desired to join with them (for their number increased daily), I gave those advices, from time to time, which I judged most needful for them; and we always concluded our meeting with prayer suited to their several necessities.

2. This was the rise of the United Society, first in London, and then in other places. Such a society is no other than 'a company of men having the form and seeking the power of godliness, united in order to pray together, to receive the word of exhortation, and to watch over one another in love, that they may help each other to work out their salvation'.

3. That it may the more easily be discerned, whether they are indeed working out their own salvation, each society is divided into smaller companies, called *classes*, according to their respective places of abode. There are about twelve persons in every class; one of whom is styled *the Leader*. It is his business, (1) To see each person in his class once a week at least, in order to inquire how their souls prosper; to advise, reprove, comfort, or exhort, as occasion may require; to receive what they are willing to give toward the relief of the poor. (2) To meet the Minister and the Stewards of the society once a week; in order to inform the Minister of any that are sick, or of any that walk disorderly, and will not be reproved; to pay to the Stewards what they have received of their several classes in the week preceding; and to show their account of what each person has contributed.

4. There is one only condition previously required in those who desire admission into these societies, – a desire 'to flee from the wrath to come, to be saved from their sins'. But, wherever this is really fixed in the soul, it will be shown by its fruits. It is therefore expected of all who continue therein, that they should continue to evidence their desire of salvation,

First, by doing no harm, by avoiding evil in every kind; especially that which is most generally practised: Such is, the taking the name of God in vain; the profaning the day of the Lord, either by doing ordinary work thereon, or by buying or selling; drunkenness, buying or selling spirituous liquors, or drinking them, unless in cases of extreme necessity; fighting, quarreling, brawling; brother going to law with brother; returning evil for evil, or railing for railing; the using many words in buying or selling; the buying or selling uncustomed goods; the giving or taking things on usury, that is, unlawful interest; uncharitable or unprofitable conversation, particularly speaking evil of Magistrates or of Ministers; doing to others as we would not they should do unto us;

doing what we know is not for the glory of God, as the 'putting on of gold or costly apparel'; the taking such diversions as cannot be used in the name of the Lord Jesus; the singing those songs, or reading those books, which do not tend to the knowledge or love of God; softness, and needless self-indulgence; laying up treasures upon earth; borrowing without a probability of paying; or taking up goods without a probability of paying for them.

5. It is expected of all who continue in these societies, that they should continue to evidence their desire of salvation,

Secondly, by doing good, by being, in every kind, merciful after their power; as they have opportunity, doing good of every possible sort, and as far as is possible, to all men; – to their bodies, of the ability which God giveth, by giving food to the hungry, by clothing the naked, by visiting or helping them that are sick, or in prison; – to their souls, by instructing, reproving, or exhorting all they have any intercourse with; trampling under foot that enthusiastic doctrine of devils, that 'we are not to do good unless our heart be free to it': By doing good especially to them that are of the household of faith, or groaning so to be; employing them preferably to others, buying one of another; helping each other in business; and so much the more, because the world will love its own, and them only: By all possible diligence and frugality, that the gospel be not blamed: By running with patience the race that is set before them, 'denying themselves, and taking up their cross daily'; submitting to bear the reproach of Christ, to be as the filth and off-scouring of the world; and looking that men should 'say all manner of evil of them falsely for the Lord's sake'.

6. It is expected of all who desire to continue in these societies, that they should continue to evidence their desire of salvation,

Thirdly, by attending upon all the ordinances of God. Such are, the public worship of God; the ministry of the word, either read or expounded; the supper of the Lord; family and private prayer; searching the Scriptures; and fasting, or abstinence.

7. These are the General Rules of our societies; all which we are taught of God to observe, even in his written word, the only rule, and the sufficient rule, both of our faith and practice. And all these, we know, his Spirit writes on every truly awakened heart. If there be any among us who observe them not, who habitually break any of them, let it be made known unto them who watch over that soul as they that must give an account. We will admonish him of the error of his ways; we will bear with him for a season: But then if he repent not, he hath no more place among us. We have delivered our own souls.

May 1, 1743   JOHN WESLEY,
                                                          CHARLES WESLEY

The Newcastle 'Orphan House'

Like the Foundery in London, this was not a chapel, but a multi-purpose building, housing a school for poor children, a clinic and living accommodation for the preachers, etc.

Rigours of the Itinerancy

John Nelson in Cornwall

(*EMP*, I, 73–6)

John Wesley first visited Cornwall in August and September 1743, with John Nelson and John Downes as his companions. This is Nelson's account of their travels and labours. Nelson was a stonemason by trade, but had been an itinerant preacher for about two years.

After I had laboured in Yorkshire awhile longer, Mr. John Wesley sent for me to London. But, by this time, I had almost worn out my clothes, and I did not know where the next should come from: my wife said, I was not fit to go anywhere as I was. I answered, 'I have worn them out in the Lord's work, and He will not let me want long.' Two days after, a tradesman in our parish, that did not belong to our Society, came to my house, and brought me a piece of blue cloth for a coat, and a piece of black cloth for a waistcoat and breeches: so I see the Lord is mindful of them that trust in Him.

As soon as I well could, I set out for London on foot; but one of my neighbours was going, and he took my place, and let me ride sometimes . . .

[After a few days in London, he set out to meet Wesley at Bristol.]

After tarrying a few days at Bristol, and preaching once at Bath, Mr. Wesley, Mr. Downs, and I set out for Cornwall. Mr. Downs and I had but one horse; so we rode by turns. Mr. Wesley preached at Taunton Cross and Exeter Castle, as we went. We generally set out before Mr. Wesley and Mr. Shepherd.

One day, having travelled twenty miles without baiting, we came to a village, and inquired for an inn; but the people told us there was none in the town, nor any on our road within twelve Cornish miles: then I said, 'Come, brother Downs, we must live by faith.' When we had stood awhile, I said, 'Let us go to yonder house, where the stone porch is, and ask for something;' so we did, and the woman said, 'We have bread, butter, and milk, and good hay for your horse.' When we had refreshed ourselves, I gave the woman a shilling; but she said, she did not desire anything. I said, 'I insist upon it.'

We got to Bodmin that night; but it was late before Mr. Wesley and Mr. Shepherd arrived, having lost the path on the twelve-mile common, and found the way again by the sound of the bells. The next day we got to Gwennap, and the day after to St. Ives. The following day I worked at my own business, and continued to work for several days.

When I had done my job of work, I went to St. Just, and preached at the cross to a large company of well-behaved people. Then I went to the Land's End, and preached the same evening. Next morning, which was Sunday, I came to Morva church: after service, I preached there, and in the evening at Zennor. . . .

One day we had been at St. Hilary Downs, and Mr. Wesley had preached from Ezekiel's vision of dry bones, and there was a shaking among the people as he preached. As we returned, Mr. Wesley stopped his horse to pick the blackberries, saying, 'Brother Nelson, we ought to be thankful that there are plenty of blackberries; for this is the best country I ever saw for getting a stomach, but the worst that ever I saw for getting food. Do the people think we can live by preaching?' I said, 'I know not what they may think; but one asked me to eat something as I came from St. Just, when I ate heartily of barley-bread and honey.' He said, 'You are well off: I had a thought of begging a crust of bread of the woman where I met the people at Morva, but forgot it till I had got some distance from the house.'

One Sunday, having been at the Land's-End in the morning, and at Morva at noon, I came to Zennor to preach at night, and got there before the afternoon service began. In the sermon, the minister said, 'Here is a people who hold that damnable Popish doctrine of justification by faith; therefore, I beg you not to hear them.' After the service was over, I went about two hundred yards from the church, and got upon a rock, where I began to sing a hymn; and I believe the whole congregation came to hear me. According to the light I had, I showed what was the faith of the Gospel, and what the faith of the Church of Rome.

I stayed a fortnight after Mr. Wesley was gone, and I found my soul was much blessed among the people.

Thomas Mitchell in Lincolnshire

(EMP, I, 248–50)

On Sunday, August 7th, [1751] I came to Wrangle, very early in the morning. I preached, as usual, at five. About six, two constables came, at the head of a large mob. They violently broke in upon the people, seized upon me, pulled me down, and took me to a public-house, where they kept me till four in the afternoon. Then one of the constables seemed to relent, and said, 'I will go to the minister, and inquire of him whether we may not now let the poor man go.' When he came back, he said, 'They were not to let him go yet.' So he took me out to the mob, who presently hurried me away, and threw me into a pool of standing water. It took me up to the neck. Several times I strove to get out, but they pitched me in again. They told me I must go through it seven times. I did so, and then they let me come out. When I had got upon dry ground, a man stood ready with a pot full of white paint. He painted me all over from head to foot; and then they carried me into a public-house again. Here I was kept, till they had put five more of our friends into the water. Then they came and took me out again, and carried me to a great pond, which was railed in on every side, being ten or twelve feet deep. Here, four men took me by my legs and arms, and swung me backward and forward. For a moment I felt the flesh shrink; but it was quickly gone. I gave myself up to the Lord, and was content His will should be done. They swung me two or three times, and then threw me as far as they could into the water. The fall and the water soon took away my senses, so that I felt nothing more. But some of them were not willing to have me drowned. So they watched till I came above water, and then, catching hold of my clothes with a long pole, made shift to drag me out.

17. I lay senseless for some time. When I came to myself, I saw only two men standing by me. One of them helped me up, and desired me to go with him. He brought me to a little house, where they quickly put me to bed. But I had not lain long, before the mob came again, pulled me out of bed, carried me into the street, and swore they would take away one of my limbs, if I would not promise to come there no more. I told them, 'I can promise no such thing.' But the man that had hold of me promised for me, and took me back into the house, and put me to bed again.

Some of the mob then went to the minister again, to know what they must do with me. He told them, 'You must take him out of the parish.' So they came and took me out of bed a second time. But I had no clothes to put on; my own being wet, and also covered with paint. But they put an old coat about me, took me about a mile, and set me upon a little hill. They then shouted three times, 'God save the king, and the devil take the preacher!'

18. Here they left me penniless and friendless: for no one durst come near me. And my strength was nearly gone; so that I had much ado to walk, or even to stand. But, from the beginning to the end, my mind was in perfect peace. I found no anger or resentment, but could heartily pray for my persecutors. But I knew not what to do, or where to go. Indeed, one of our friends lived three or four miles off. But I was so weak and ill, that it did not seem possible for me to get so far. However, I trusted in God, and set out; and at length I got to the house. The family did everything for me that was in their power: they got me clothes, and whatever else was needful. I rested four days with them, in which time my strength was tolerably restored.

Philip Doddridge: A Dissenting View

(*Diary and Correspondence*, IV, 253–5)

Doddridge was a leading figure in early eighteenth-century Dissent. He was on friendly terms with the Wesleys, but had reservations about some aspects of Methodism; in particular, what he called 'those extravagant reveries which have filled the mind of so many and brought so great a dishonour on the work of God' (letter to John Wesley, June 18, 1746).

Doddridge's correspondent, Richard Witton, was pastor of the Old Meeting, West Bromwich, and therefore close to the storm-centre in 1743.

Northampton, June 8, 1743.

Rev. and Dear Sir,

I am much concerned at the anxiety and disturbance which Mr. Wesley's coming into your neighbourhood has occasioned. You are pleased to ask my advice, and, therefore, I give it you as well as I can in this hasty moment, though I am sensible your own superior wisdom and experience render it unnecessary. I think the gentlest methods will be the most effectual: opposition will but give strength to the faction if it be attended with violence and heat. Should Mr. Wesley come hither, as perhaps he may, and excite such a flame among the weaker part of my hearers, I would appoint some stated season of meeting once a week, with a few steady and experienced brethren of the church, that an hour or two might be spent in prayer and consultation, as new incidents might arise within the sphere of our personal observation. I would endeavour, by Divine assistance, to renew my zeal in preaching the great truths of the Gospel, and in visiting and exhorting my hearers. I would, with great meekness and compassion, and yet with great solemnity, admonish the persons attacked by the contagion, and lay open before them, with all the mildness and strength I could, the absurd nature, and mischievous tendency of the views they had rashly entertained; and I would, as God enabled me, pray earnestly for them; and should, I hope, consider such a disagreeable scene as calling me to a more accurate survey of my heart, my life, and my ministry; to a renewed surrender of myself to my great Master, and a more solicitous care to maintain communion with him in every duty, and to do every thing in his name, with renewed and earnest prayers for guidance and success . . .

If dangerous errors were intermingled with the Gospel in their congregation (which I would sometimes attend, or get some prudent friend to do so), I would endeavour to establish the contrary truths, but would decline controversy as much as I could with a safe conscience. And if on the whole a few were drawn off from my ministry, I should hope that on my prosecuting my work with continued vigour and fidelity, that God, in whose hand are all hearts, would either bring them back in time, or raise up others to fill their places.

This, dear Sir, so far as I can at present judge, is the method I should incline to take, and I believe it is what you are taking yourself. I hope I shall be quickened to pray that it may succeed; and to hear that the cloud is blown over will give me great pleasure.

The First Methodist Conference

No printed Minutes were issued before 1749. Records of the first five Conferences have survived in manuscript. The following extracts are based on the text prepared for the Bicentennial Edition of Wesley's *Works*.

Monday, June 25th, 1744
The following persons being met at the Foundery: John Wesley, Charles Wesley, John Hodges, Henry Piers, Samuel Taylor, and John Meriton; after some time spent in prayer, the design of our meeting was proposed, namely, to consider:

1. What to teach;
2. How to teach, and
3. What to do, i.e. how to regulate our doctrine, discipline and practice.

But first it was inquired whether any of our lay brethren should be present at this Conference. And it was agreed to invite from time to time such of 'em as we should judge proper. It was then asked, Which of 'em shall we invite today? And the answer was: Thomas Richards, Thomas Maxfield, John Bennet, and John Downes, who were accordingly brought in. Then was read as follows:

It is desired
  That all things may be considered as in the immediate presence of God;
  That we may meet with a single eye, and as little children which have everything to learn;
  That every point may be examined from the foundation;
  That every person may speak freely whatever is in his heart; and
  That every question proposed may be fully debated, and bolted to the bran.[1]

The first preliminary question was then proposed, namely, How far does each of us agree to submit to the unanimous judgment of the rest?

It was answered, In speculative things each can only submit so far as his judgment shall be convinced: In every practical point so far as we can without wounding our several consciences.

To the second preliminary question, viz., How far should any of us mention to others what may be mentioned here? it was replied,

> Not one word which may be here spoken of persons should be mentioned elsewhere.
>
> Nothing at all, unless so far as we may be convinced the glory of God requires it.
>
> And from time to time we will consider on each head, Is it for the glory of God that what we have now spoken should be mentioned again?

[There followed a discussion on justifying faith.]

Q.17: Have we not then unawares leaned too much towards Calvinism?
A.   It seems that we have.
Q.18: Have we not leaned towards antinomianism?
A.   We are afraid we have.
Q.19: What is antinomianism?
A.   The doctrine which makes void the law through faith.
Q.20: What are the main pillars thereof?
A.   (1) That Christ abolished the moral law.

> (2) That therefore Christians are not obliged to observe it.
>
> (3) That one branch of Christian liberty is liberty from obeying the commandments of God.
>
> (4) That it is bondage to do a thing because it is commanded, or forbear it because it is forbidden.
>
> (5) That a believer is not obliged to use the ordinances of God, or to do good works.
>
> (6) That a preacher ought not to exhort to good works; not unbelievers because it is hurtful, not believers because it is needless . . .

[On Tuesday, the doctrine of sanctification was considered; and on Wednesday matters of discipline, especially their relations with the Church of England as defined in the 19th Article: 'the congregation of English believers in which the pure word of God is preached, and the sacraments duly administered'.]

Q.9:   Do we separate from the Church?
A.   We conceive not. We hold communion therewith for conscience' sake, by constantly attending both the Word preached, and the Sacraments administered therein.
Q.10: What then do they mean who say, You separate from the Church?
A.   We cannot certainly tell. Perhaps they have no determinate meaning; unless by the Church they mean *themselves*, i.e. that part

of the clergy who accuse us of preaching false doctrine. And it is sure we do herein separate from *them* by maintaining the doctrine which they deny.

Q.11: But do you not *weaken the Church*?

A.   Do not they that ask this by the Church mean themselves? We do not purposely weaken any man's hands, but accidentally we may thus far: they who come to know the truth by us will esteem such as deny it less than they did before. But the *Church*, in the proper sense, the congregation of English believers, we do not weaken at all.

Q.12: Do not you entail a schism on the Church? i.e., Is it not probable that your hearers after your death will be scattered into all sects and parties? Or that they will form themselves into a distinct sect?

A. (1) We are persuaded, the body of our hearers will even after our death remain in the Church, unless they be thrust out.

(2) We believe notwithstanding either that they will be thrust out, or that they will leaven the whole Church.

(3) We do, and will do, all we can to prevent those consequences which are supposed likely to happen after our death.

(4) But we cannot with good conscience neglect the present opportunity of saving souls while we live, for fear of consequences which may possibly or probably happen after we are dead.

On Thursday, June 28th,
were considered other points of discipline. The substance of the questions and answers were as follows:

Q.1: How are the people divided who desire to be under your care?

A.   Into the United Societies, the Bands, the Select Societies, and the Penitents.

Q.2: How do these differ from each other?

A.   The United Societies (which are the largest of all) consist of awakened persons. Part of these, who are supposed to have remission of sins, are more closely united in the Bands. Those of the Bands who seem to walk in the light of God compose the Select Societies. Those of them who have made shipwreck of the faith meet apart as penitents . . .

Q.10: Is field preaching unlawful?

A.   We do not conceive that it is contrary to any law, either of God or man. Yet (to avoid giving any needless offence) we never preach *without* doors when we can with any convenience preach *within*.

Q.11: Where should we endeavour to preach most?

A. (1) Where we can preach in the Church.

    (2) Where there is an open door, quiet and willing hearers.

    (3) Where there is the greatest increase of souls.

Q.12: What is the best way of spreading the gospel?

A.   To go a little and a little farther from London, Bristol, St. Ives, Newcastle, or any other Society. So a little leaven would spread with more effect and less noise, and help would always be at hand . . .

Friday, June 29th . . .

Q.2: What is the office of our Assistants?

A.   In the absence of the Minister to feed and guide, to teach and govern the flock.

    (1) To expound every morning and evening.

    (2) To meet the United Societies, the Bands, the Select Societies and the Penitents every week.

    (3) To visit the classes (London excepted) once a month.

    (4) To hear and decide all differences.

    (5) To put the disorderly back on trial, and to receive on trial for the Bands or Society.

    (6) To see that the Stewards, the Leaders, Schoolmasters, and Housekeepers faithfully discharge their several offices.

    (7) To meet the Stewards, and the Leaders of the Bands and Classes weekly, and overlook their accounts.

[For the Rules of an Assistant, see 1753, pp. 116–19 below.]

Q.7: What are the Rules of a Steward?

A. (1) Be frugal, save everything that can be saved honestly.

    (2) Spend no more than you receive. Contract no debt.

    (3) Do nothing rashly: let every design be thoroughly weighed before you begin to execute it.

    (4) Have no long accounts: pay everything within the week.

    (5) Give none that ask relief either an ill word or an ill look. Do not hurt 'em, if you cannot help 'em.

    (6) Expect no thanks from man.

    (7) Remember you are a servant of the Helper, not his *master*; therefore speak to him always as such.

---

[1] I.e., sifted thoroughly.

The Band-Societies

Directions given to the Band-Societies, December 25, 1744

(*JWW*, VIII, 273–4)

You are supposed to have the faith that 'overcometh the world'. To you, therefore, it is not grievous:—
    I. Carefully to abstain from doing evil; in particular:—
    1. Neither to buy nor sell anything at all on the Lord's day.
    2. To taste no spirituous liquor, no dram of any kind, unless prescribed by a Physician.
    3. To be at a word both in buying and selling.
    4. To pawn nothing, no, not to save life.
    5. Not to mention the fault of any behind his back, and to stop those short that do.
    6. To wear no needless ornaments, such as rings, ear-rings, necklaces, lace, ruffles.
    7. To use no needless self-indulgence, such as taking snuff or tobacco, unless prescribed by a Physician.

    II. Zealously to maintain good works; in particular:—
    1. To give alms of such things as you possess, and that to the uttermost of your power.
    2. To reprove all that sin in your sight, and that in love and meekness of wisdom.
    3. To be patterns of diligence and frugality, of self-denial, and taking up the cross daily.

    III. Constantly to attend on all the ordinances of God; in particular:—
    1. To be at church and at the Lord's table every week, and at every public meeting of the Bands.
    2. To attend the ministry of the word every morning, unless distance, business, or sickness prevent.
    3. To use private prayer every day; and family prayer, if you are at the head of a family.
    4. To read the Scriptures, and meditate therein, at every vacant hour. And, –
    5. To observe, as days of fasting or abstinence, all Fridays in the year.

Mr. Chas. Wesley's improvisation on seeing the Band Rules written by his brother John Wesley

(Adam Clarke papers, Duke University)

We heard a Romish founder say,
Cast not your sins but shoes away.
Another cries with whining note,
Strip off the buttons from your coat.
But our supreme Reformer cries,
Your wrists and elbows circumcise.

The Lord's Supper

(J. E. Rattenbury, *The Eucharistic Hymns of John and Charles Wesley*, 1948, pp. 182–3, 231–2)

Charles Wesley's *Hymns on the Lord's Supper* (1745) versified a treatise *On the Christian Sacrament and Sacrifice* by the Caroline Divine, Daniel Brevint and expresses the Wesleys' high doctrine of the sacrament.

Brevint, 'Concerning the Sacrament as it is a Means of Grace'

(Op. cit., Section IV)

It is Christ Himself, with His Body and Blood, once offered to God upon the Cross, and ever since standing before Him as slain, who fills His Church with the perfumes of His Sacrifice, whence faithful communicants return home with the first-fruits of salvation. Bread and wine can contribute no more to it than the rod of *Moses* or the oil of the apostles. But yet since it pleaseth Christ to work thereby, O my God, whensoever Thou shalt bid me *go and wash in* Jordan, I will go; and will no more doubt of being made clean from my sins, than if I had bathed in Thy Blood. And when thou sayest, *Go, take and eat this Bread* which I have blessed, I will doubt no more of being fed with the Bread of Life, than if I were eating Thy very Flesh.

This Victim having been offered up in the fulness of times, and in the midst of the world, which is Christ's great temple, and having been thence carried up to heaven, which is His sanctuary; from thence spreads salvation all around, as the burnt-offering did its smoke. And thus His Body and Blood have everywhere, but especially at this Sacrament, a true and real Presence. When He offered Himself upon earth, the vapour of His Atonement went up and darkened the very sun; and, by rending the great veil, it clearly showed He had made a way into heaven. And, since He is gone up, He sends down to earth the graces that spring continually both from His everlasting Sacrifice and from the continual intercession that attends it. So that we need not say, *Who will go up into heaven?* since, without either ascending or descending, this sacred Body of Jesus fills with atonement and blessing the remotest part of this temple.

Charles Wesley, 'The Holy Eucharist as it implies a Sacrifice'

(Op. cit., Section IV)

1 VICTIM DIVINE, Thy grace we claim
     While thus Thy precious death we
       show;
   Once offer'd up, a spotless Lamb,
     In Thy great temple here below,
   Thou didst for all mankind atone,
   And standest now before the throne.

2 Thou standest in the holiest place,
     As now for guilty sinners slain;
   Thy blood of sprinkling speaks, and
       prays,
     All-prevalent for helpless man;
   Thy blood is still our ransom found,
   And spreads salvation all around.

3 The smoke of Thy atonement here
     Darken'd the sun and rent the veil,
   Made the new way to heaven appear,
     And show'd the great Invisible;
   Well pleased in Thee our God look'd
       down,
   And call'd His rebels to a crown.

4 He still respects Thy sacrifice,
     Its savour sweet doth always please;
   The offering smokes through earth and
       skies,
     Diffusing life, and joy, and peace;
   To these Thy lower courts it comes,
   And fills them with divine perfumes.

5 We need not now go up to heaven,
     To bring the long-sought Saviour
       down;
   Thou art to all already given,
     Thou dost even now Thy banquet
       crown:
   To every faithful soul appear,
   And show Thy real presence here!

The Clergy and Methodism

(*JWJ*, III, 166–9; Oxford *Letters*, II, 125–7)

Wesley wrote from Newcastle upon Tyne on March 11, 1745, presumably to a clerical friend.

I have been drawing up this morning a short state of the case between the clergy and us; I leave you to make any such use of it as you believe will be to the glory of God.

1. About seven years since we began preaching inward, present salvation, as attainable by faith alone.

2. For preaching this doctrine we were forbidden to preach in the churches.

3. We then preached in private houses, as occasion offered; and when the houses could not contain the people, in the open air.

4. For this, many of the clergy preached or printed against us, as both heretics and schismatics.

5. Persons who were convinced of sin begged us to advise them more particularly how to flee from the wrath to come. We replied, if they would all come at one time (for they were numerous) we would endeavour it.

6. For this we were represented, both from the pulpit and the press (we have heard it with our ears, and seen it with our eyes), as introducing Popery, raising sedition, practising both against Church and State; and all manner of evil was publicly said both of us and those who were accustomed to meet with us.

7. Finding some truth herein, viz. that some of those who so met together walked disorderly, we immediately desired them not to come to us any more.

8. And the more steady were desired to overlook the rest, that we might know if they walked according to the gospel.

9. But now several of the bishops began to speak against us, either in conversation or in public.

10. On this encouragement, several of the clergy stirred up the people to treat us as outlaws or mad dogs.

11. The people did so, both in Staffordshire, Cornwall, and many other places.

12. And they do so still, wherever they are not restrained by their fear of the secular magistrate.

Thus the case stands at present. Now, what can we do, or what can you our brethren do, towards healing this breach? which is highly desirable, that we may withstand, with joint force, the still increasing flood of Popery, Deism, and immorality.

Desire of us anything we can do with a safe conscience, and we will do it immediately. Will you meet us here? Will you do what we desire of you, so far as you can with safe conscience?

Let us come to particulars. Do you desire us (1) To preach another, or to desist from preaching this, doctrine?

We think you do not desire it, as knowing we cannot do this with a safe conscience. Do you desire us (2) To desist from preaching in private houses, or in the open air? As things are now circumstanced, this would be the same as desiring us not to preach at all.

Do you desire us (3) To desist from advising those who now meet together for that purpose? Or, in other words, to dissolve our societies?

We cannot do this with a safe conscience; for we apprehend many souls would be lost thereby, and that God would require their blood at our hands.

Do you desire us (4) To advise them only one by one?

This is impossible because of their number.

Do you desire us (5) To suffer those who walk disorderly still to mix with the rest?

Neither can we do this with a safe conscience; because 'evil communications corrupt good manners.'

Do you desire us (6) To discharge those leaders of bands or classes (as we term them) who overlook the rest?

This is, in effect, to suffer the disorderly walkers still to mix with the rest, which we dare not do.

Do you desire us, lastly, to behave with reverence toward those who are overseers of the Church of God? And with tenderness both to the character and persons of our brethren, the inferior clergy?

By the grace of God, we can and will do this. Yea, our conscience beareth us witness that we have already laboured so to do, and that at all times and in all places.

If you ask what we desire of you to do, we answer: 1. We do not desire any one of you to let us preach in your church, either if you believe us to preach false doctrine, or if you have, upon any other ground, the least scruple of conscience concerning it. But we desire any who believes us to preach true doctrine, and has no scruple at all in this matter, may not be either publicly or privately discouraged from inviting us to preach in his church.

2. We do not desire that any one who thinks that we are heretics or schismatics, and that it is his duty to preach or print against us, as such, should refrain therefrom, so long as he thinks it is his duty. (Although in this case, the breach can never be healed.)

But we desire that none will pass such a sentence till he has calmly considered both sides of the question; that he would not condemn us unheard; but first read what we have written, and pray earnestly that God may direct him in the right way.

3. We do not desire any favour if either Popery, sedition, or immorality be proved against us.

But we desire you will not credit, without proof, any of those senseless tales that pass current with the vulgar: that if you do not credit them yourselves, you will not relate them to others (which we have known done); yea, that you will confute them, so far as ye have opportunity, and discountenance those who still retail them abroad.

4. We do not desire any preferment, favour, or recommendation, from those that are in authority, either in Church or State; but we desire:

(1) That if anything material be laid to our charge, we may be permitted to answer for ourselves. (2) That you would hinder your dependents from stirring up the rabble against us; who are certainly not the proper judges of these matters. And (3) That you would effectually suppress, and thoroughly discountenance, all riots and popular insurrections, which evidently strike at the foundation of all government, whether of Church or State.

Now these things you certainly can do, and that with a safe conscience. Therefore, till these things are done, the continuance of the breach is chargeable on you, and you only.

The Conference of 1745

(See note on p. 67)

Friday, August 2nd.

Q.17: Do not our Assistants preach too much of the wrath and too little of the love of God?

A.   We fear they have leaned to that extreme; and hence some of their hearers may have lost the joy of faith.

Q.18: Need we ever preach the terror of the Lord to those who know they are accepted of him?

A.   No. It is folly so to do. For love is to them the strongest of all motives.

Q.19: Do we ordinarily represent a justified state so great and happy as it is?

A.   Perhaps not. A believer walking in the light is inexpressibly great and happy. . . .

Q.22: Does not the truth of the gospel lie very near both to Calvinism and antinomianism?

A.   Indeed it does – as it were, within a hair's breath. So that 'tis altogether foolish and sinful, because we do not quite agree either with one or the other, to run from them as far as ever we can.

Q.23: Wherein may we come to the very edge of Calvinism?

A.(1) In ascribing all good to the free grace of God. (2) In denying all natural free will, and all power antecedent to grace; and (3) in excluding all merit from man, even for what he has or does by the grace of God.

Q.24: Wherein may we come to the very edge of antinomianism?

A.(1) In exalting the merits and love of Christ. (2) In rejoicing evermore.

About ten we began to speak of sanctification . . .

Q.10: In what manner should we preach entire sanctification?

A.   Scarce at all to those who are not pressing forward. To those who are, always by way of promise, always drawing rather than driving.

Q.11: How should we wait for the fulfilling of this promise?

A.   In universal obedience; in keeping all the commandments; in denying ourselves, and taking up our cross daily. These are the general means which God hath ordained for our receiving his sanctifying grace. The particular are prayer, searching the Scripture, communicating, and fasting.

On Saturday, Aug. 3rd,
were considered points of discipline. . . .

Q.5:   Is Episcopal, Presbyterian, or Independent church government most agreeable to reason?

A.   The plain origin of church government seems to be this. Christ sends forth a preacher of the gospel. Some who hear him repent and believe the gospel. They then desire him to watch over them, to build them up in the faith, and to guide their souls in the paths of righteousness. Here then is an independent congregation, subject to no pastor but their own, neither liable to be controlled in things spiritual by any other man or body of men whatsoever.

But soon after some from other parts, who are occasionally present while he speaks in the name of him that sent him, beseech him to come over and help them also. He complies. Knowing it to be the will of God he consents, yet not till he has conferred with the wisest and holiest of his congregation, and with their advice appointed one who has gifts and grace to watch over the flock till his return.

If it please God to raise another flock in the new place, before he leaves them he does the same thing, appointing one whom God has fitted for the work to watch over these souls also.

In like manner, in every place where it pleases God to gather a little flock by his word, he appoints one in his absence to take the oversight of the rest, and to assist them of the ability which God giveth. These are Deacons, or servants of the church, and look on the first pastor as their common father. And all these congregations regard him in the same light, and esteem him still as the shepherd of their souls.

These congregations are not strictly independent. They depend on one pastor, though not on each other.

As these congregations increase, and as the Deacons grow in years and grace, they need other subordinate Deacons or helpers; in respect of whom they may be called Presbyters, or Elders, as their father in the Lord may be called the Bishop, or Overseer of them all.

Q.6: Is mutual consent absolutely necessary between the pastor and his flock?

A. No question: I cannot guide any soul unless he consent to be guided by me. Neither can any soul force me to guide him, if I consent not . . .

Q.11: May we not make a trial, especially in in Wales and Cornwall, of preaching without forming any societies?[1]

A. It might be well; and by this means we may preach in every large town where a door is open.

[1] Cf. the Minutes of the 1748 Conference, June 2nd, Q.2, p. 91 below.

'Perceptible Inspiration'

(Oxford *Letters*, II, 183, 188–9, 202–3)

In his lengthy correspondence with 'John Smith' (a perceptive critic of early Methodism, once thought to be Thomas Secker, the future Archbishop), Wesley found an opponent worthy of his skill as a controversialist. The discussion ranged over a variety of topics, including the 'extraordinary revelations' to which Bishop Butler had earlier taken exception (pp. 29–31 above).

John Wesley to 'John Smith', December 30, 1745

We are at length come to the real state of the question between the Methodists (so called) and their opponents. Is there perceptible inspiration or is there not? Is there such a thing (if we divide the question into its parts) as faith producing peace and joy and love, and inward (as well as outward) holiness? Is that faith which is productive of these fruits wrought in us by the Holy Ghost, or not? And is he in whom they are wrought necessarily *conscious* of them, or is he not? These are the points on which I am ready to join issue with any serious and candid man.

'Smith' to Wesley, February 26, 1746

That there is inspiration, or the influence of the divine Spirit on the human spirit, is agreed by both parties; the whole of the question therefore turns upon the perceptibility of this inspiration. The question then is, does God's Spirit work perceptibly on our spirit by *direct testimony* (as you elsewhere call it), by such *perceivable impulses* and *dictates* as are as distinguishable from darkness (as the Quakers maintain), or does he imperceptibly influence our minds to goodness by gently and insensibly assisting our faculties, and biasing them aright? Here is the whole of the question. Now let us consider how you attempt to divide this question into its parts. 'Is there such a thing as faith producing peace and joy and love, etc.?' Yes, and producing a general good life into the bargain. 'Is that faith which is productive of these fruits wrought in us by the Holy Ghost or no?' Yes, as all other good things are wrought in us. 'Is he in whom they (the fruits) are wrought necessarily conscious of them (peace, joy, love, etc.) or is he not?' Yes, for he who perceives not *joy* has not *joy*; but what is this to perceptibility of *inspiration*? You would not venture to shift terms thus in a *physical* dissertation. Suppose we were disputing about *vegetation*. I maintain that it is a work so slow and gentle as to be altogether imperceptible. You on the contrary assert that it is *a work* as *perceptible* as the sun's light at noonday, for, say you, are not these *fruits*, these *apples*, *pears*, and *plums*, things plainly *perceptible*? Yes, indeed they are, but not one whit more perceptible than that you have now entirely *shifted* the question . . .

10. The question to be debated, then, is not whether the *fruits* of inspiration are things perceptible, but whether *the work* of inspiration itself be so; whether the work of God's Spirit in us be as easily distinguishable from the working of our own spirit as light is from darkness (as you have elsewhere asserted). If we are in the wrong, confute us by *argumentation*, but not by threatening us with our 'awaking in hell'. The profuse throwing about hell and damnation may have its effects on *weak minds*; it may terrify such into hasty and sudden converts; but on men of 'reason and religion', to whom you appeal, it will be apt to have a quite contrary effect. They well know that *that scheme* of religion bids fairest for the *true one* which breathes the largest and most extensive *Christian charity*.

Wesley to 'Smith', June 25, 1746

One point of doctrine remains. 'Is there any such thing as perceptible inspiration or not?' I asserted, there is, but at the same time subjoined, 'Be pleased to observe what we mean thereby: we mean that inspiration of God's Holy Spirit whereby he fills us' (every true believer) 'with righteousness and peace and joy, with love to him and all mankind. And we believe it cannot be, in the nature of things, that a man should be filled with this peace and joy and love by the inspiration of the Holy Ghost without *perceiving* it as clearly as he does the light of the sun.'

You reply, 'You have now entirely shifted the question.' I think not. You objected that I held perceptible inspiration. I answered, I do; but observe in what sense (otherwise I must recall my concession). I hold, God *inspires* every Christian with peace and joy and love, which are all *perceptible*. You reply, 'The question is not whether the *fruits* of inspiration are *perceptible*, but whether the *work* of inspiration itself be so.' This was not my question; nor did I till now understand that it was yours. If I had I should have returned a different answer, as I have elsewhere done already.

When one warmly objected, near two years ago, 'All reasonable Christians believe that the Holy Spirit works his graces in us in an imperceptible manner,' my answer was, 'You are here disproving, as you suppose, a proposition of mine. But are you sure you understand it? By the "operations" ' (*inspirations*, or *workings*) 'of the Spirit I do not mean the manner in which he operates, but the *graces* which he operates' (*inspires* or *works*) 'in a Christian.' If you ask, But do not you hold that 'Christian faith implies a direct, *perceptible* testimony of the Spirit, as distinguishable from the suggestion of fancy as light is distinguishable from darkness' (whereas we suppose he *imperceptibly* influences our minds), I answer, I do hold this. I suppose that every Christian believer, over and above that imperceptible influence, hath a direct perceptible testimony of the Spirit that he is a child of God . . .[1]

I would just add that I regard even faith itself not as an *end*, but as a *means* only. The end of the commandment is love – of every command, of the whole Christian dispensation. Let this love be attained, by whatever means, and I am content; I desire no more. All is well if we love the Lord our God with all our heart, and our neighbour as ourselves.

---

[1] On this point, cf. Wesley's *Farther Appeal*, 1745, Part I, V, 2–3.

Lay Preaching

(John Wesley, *A Farther Appeal to Men of Reason and Religion*, 1745, Part III, III. 14–17)

14. It pleased God by two or three ministers of the Church of England to call many sinners to repentance, who in several parts were undeniably turned from a course of sin to a course of holiness.

The ministers of the places where this was done ought to have received those ministers with open arms, and to have taken them who had just begun to serve God into their peculiar care; watching over them in tender love, lest they should fall back into the snare of the devil.

Instead of this, the greater part spoke of those ministers as if the devil, not God, had sent them. Some repelled them from the Lord's table; others stirred up the people against them, representing them, even in their public discourses, as fellows not fit to live – Papists, heretics, traitors, conspirators against their King and country.

And how did they watch over the sinners lately reformed? Even as a leopard watcheth over his prey. They drove some of them also from the Lord's table; to which till now they had no desire to approach. They preached all manner of evil concerning them, openly cursing them in the name of the Lord. They turned many out of their work; persuaded others to do so, too, and harassed them all manner of ways.

The event was that some were wearied out, and so turned back to their vomit again. And then these good pastors gloried over them, and endeavoured to shake others by their example.

15. When the ministers by whom God had helped them before came again to those places, great part of their work was to begin again – if it could be begun again. But the relapsers were often so hardened in sin that no impression could be made upon them.

What could they do in a case of so extreme necessity? Where so many souls lay at stake?

No clergyman would assist at all. The expedient that remained was to find someone among themselves who was upright of heart, and of sound judgment in the things of God, and to desire him to meet the rest as often as he could, in order to confirm them, as he was able, in the ways of God, either by reading to them, or by prayer, or by exhortation.

God immediately gave a blessing hereto. In several places, by means of these plain men, not only those who had already begun to run well were hindered from drawing back to perdition, but other sinners also from time to time were converted from the error of their ways.

This plain account of the whole proceeding I take to be the best defence of it. I know no Scripture which forbids making use of such help in a case of such necessity. And I praise God who has given even this help to those poor sheep when 'their own shepherds pitied them not'.

[16.] 'But does not the Scripture say, "No man taketh *this honour* to himself, but he that is called of God, as was Aaron"?' Nor do these. The 'honour' here mentioned is the priesthood. But they no more take upon them to be priests than to be kings. They take not upon them to administer the sacraments, an honour peculiar to the priests of God. Only according to their power they exhort their brethren to continue in the grace of God.

'But for these *laymen* to exhort at all is a violation of all *order*.'

What is this 'order' of which you speak? Will it serve instead of the knowledge and love of God? Will this order rescue those from the snare of the devil who are not taken captive at his will? Will it keep them who are escaped a little way from turning back into Egypt? If not, how should I answer it to God, if rather than violate I know not what order I should *sacrifice* thousands of souls thereto? I dare not do it. It is at the peril of my own soul.

Indeed if by 'order' were meant *true Christian discipline*, whereby all the living members of Christ are knit together in one, and all that are putrid and dead immediately cut off from the body; this order I reverence, for it is of God. But where is it to be found? In what diocese, in what town or parish, within England or Wales? Are you rector of a parish? Then let us go no farther. Does this order obtain there? Nothing less. Your parishioners are a rope of sand. As few (if any) of them are alive to God, so they have no connexion with each other, unless such as might be among Turks or heathens. Neither have *you* any power to cut off from that body, were it alive, the dead and putrid members. Perhaps you have no desire; but all are jumbled together, without any care or concern of yours.

It is plain, then, that what order is to be found is not among you who so loudly contend for it, but among that very people whom you continually blame for their violation and contempt of it. The little flock you condemn is united together in one body, by one Spirit; so that if 'one member suffers, all the members suffer with it; if one be honoured, all rejoice with it'. Nor does any dead member long remain; but as soon as the hope of recovering it is past, it is cut off.

[17.] Now suppose we were willing to relinquish our charge, and to give up this flock into *your* hands, would *you* observe the same order as we do now with them and the other souls under your care? You *dare* not; because you have respect of persons. You fear the faces of men. You *cannot*; because you have not 'overcome the world'. You are not above the desire of earthly things. And it is impossible you should ever have any *true order*, or exercise any *Christian discipline*, till you are wholly 'crucified to the world', till you desire nothing more but God.

Consider this matter, I entreat you, a little farther. Here are seven thousand persons (perhaps somewhat more) of whom I take care, watching over their souls as he that must give account. In order hereto it lies upon me (so I judge), at the peril of my own salvation, to know not only their names but their outward and inward states, their difficulties and dangers; otherwise how can I know either how to guide them aright, or to commend them to God in prayer? Now if I am willing to make these over to *you*, will *you* watch over them in the same manner? Will *you* take the same care (or as much more as you please) of each soul as I have hitherto done? Not such *curam animarum*[1] as you have taken these ten years in your own parish. Poor empty name! Has not your parish been in fact as much a *sinecure* to you as your prebend? O what an account have *you* to give to the great Shepherd and Bishop of souls!

[1] The care of souls.

Wesley's Irregularities

(Oxford *Letters*, II, 210, 213–14, 214–15)

'John Smith' to John Wesley, August 11, 1746

Whatever side of the question is for the present uppermost in your mind, that you are apt to push with such impetuosity and excess as unavoidably occasions the appearance of great variety (not to say inconsistency) of sentiment. . . .

Well, then, how shall we account for the considerable success of your itinerant ministry? It must be owned that you have a natural knack of persuasion, and that you speak with much awakening warmth and earnestness, that God has blessed you with a strength of constitution equal to the indefatigable industry of your mind. These natural abilities, then, without having recourse to anything supernatural or miraculous, might alone account for the measure of your success. Yet there is another thing which gives you more advantage, and occasions you to make more impression than all these put together, and that is the very irregularity and novelty of your manner. 'The *tinners, keelmen, colliers* and *harlots*', say you, 'never came near the church, nor had any desire or design so to do.' But when it was told them, There is a man preaching upon yonder mountain, they came in as great flocks to such a dispenser of divinity as they do to a *dispenser of physic who dances on a slack rope*. Such a doctor may by a stratagem have more patients, and consequently if he has equal skill may do more good than Dr. Mead, who confines himself to the unalarming and customary carriage of a chariot; yet since it is next to certain that the rules of the college once broken in upon, many unskilful persons will take upon them to get patients by the novelty of the slack rope, it is likewise next to certain that if we cast up the physic account at the end of any one century we shall find that surprise and novelty have done much more harm than good, and that it was upon the whole much better to go on in the slower but safer way of the college . . .

I fear you do not know every evil seed that may still lurk in your own breast. Are you sure there is no spark of vanity there? No love of singularity? No desire of distinction, *digito monstrari et dicier, hic est?*[1] At least turn your emulation into a right channel. God can make you as conspicuous in a regular as you are endeavouring to make yourself in this irregular way.

[1] Persius, *Satires*, l. 28: 'To be pointed out and have people say, "That's him!"' '

The Conference of 1746

(See note on p. 67)

On Wednesday, [May] 14th
were considered points relating to Discipline. . . .

Q.5:   In what view are we and our helpers to be considered?
A.   Perhaps as extraordinary messengers, designed of God to provoke others to jealousy.
Q.6:   Do you not insensibly slide into taking state upon yourselves? Or lording it over God's heritage?
A.(1) We are not conscious to ourselves that we do. (2) But there is a continual danger. Therefore, (3) we cannot be too jealous lest we should. And (4) we will thank anyone that shall warn us against it. . . .

Q.11: Why do we not use more form and solemnity in receiving a new labourer?
A.   We purposely decline it:
   (1) Because there is something of stateliness in it, whereas we would be little and inconsiderable;
   (2) Because we would not make haste. We desire barely to follow Providence, as it gradually opens to us. . . .

Q.14: In what light should your Assistants consider themselves?

A.   As learners rather than teachers; as young students at the university, for whom therefore a method of study is expedient in the highest degree.

Q.15: What method would you advise them to?

(1) Always to rise at 4 o'clock in the morning.

(2) From 4 to 5 in the morning, and from 5 to 6 in the evening, partly to use meditation and private prayer, partly to read the Scripture (two or three verses, or one or two chapters), partly some close practical book of divinity, in particular *The Life of God in the Soul of Man*, Kempis, *Christian Pattern*, *The Pilgrim's Progress*, Mr. Law's Tracts, Beveridge's *Private Thoughts*, Heylyn's *Devotional Tracts*, *The Life of Mr. Halyburton*, and Monsieur De Renty.

(3) From 6 in the morning (allowing one hour for breakfast) to 12, to read in order slowly, and with much prayer, Bp. Pearson on the *Creed*, Bp. Fell on the *Epistles*, Mr. Boehm's and Mr. Nalson's *Sermons*, Mr. Pascal's *Thoughts*, our other tracts and poems, Milton's *Paradise Lost*, Cave and Fleury's *Primitive Christianity*, and Mr. Echard's *Ecclesiastical History*. . . .

Thursday, May 15th

Q.1:   What is a sufficient call of providence to a new place, suppose Edinburgh or Dublin?

A. (1) An invitation from someone that is worthy, from a serious man, fearing God, who has a house to receive us.

(2) A probability of doing more good by going thither than by staying longer where we are.

Q.2:   Ought we not diligently to observe in what place God is pleased to pour out his spirit more abundantly?

A.   We ought, and at that time to send more labourers than usual into that part of the harvest, as at this time into Yorkshire and the country round about Coleford. . . .

Q.4:   How shall we guard more effectually against formality in public singing?

A. (1) By the careful choice of hymns proper for the congregation.

(2) In general try by choosing hymns of praise or prayer, rather than descriptive of particular states.

(3) By not singing too much together, seldom a whole hymn at one time, seldom more than five or six verses at once.

(4) By suiting the tunes to them;

(5) By stopping short often, and asking the people, 'Now do you know what you said last? Did it suit your case? Did you sing it as to God with the spirit and with the understanding also?'

Q.5:   Should we insist more on people's going to Church? Shall we set them the example at Bristol?

A.   We will make a trial of the effect of it, by going to St. James's every Wednesday and Friday. . . .

Q.7:   How are your Circuits now divided?

A.   Into seven. (1) London (which includes Surrey, Kent, Essex, Brentford, Egham, Windsor, Wycombe). (2) Bristol (which includes Somersetshire, Portland, Wiltshire, Oxfordshire, Gloucestershire). (3) Cornwall. (4) Evesham (which includes Shrewsbury, Leominster, Hereford, and from Stroud to Wednesbury). (5) Yorkshire (which includes Cheshire, Lancashire, Derbyshire, Nottinghamshire, Rutlandshire, Lincolnshire). (6) Newcastle. (7) Wales.

The Conference of 1747

(See note on p. 67)

[Wednesday, June 17th] About 10 (Mr. Perronet, vicar of Shoreham, being added) we began to consider points of discipline . . .

Q.4:   You profess to obey both the governors and rules of the Church, yet in many instances you do not obey them. How is this consistent? Upon what principles do you act while you sometimes obey and sometimes not?

A.   It is entirely consistent. We act at all times on one plain uniform principle: 'We will obey the rules and governors of the Church whenever we can consistently with our duty to God. Whenever we cannot, we quietly obey God rather than men.'

Q.5:   But why do you say you are thrust out of the churches? Has not every minister a right to dispose of his own church?

A.   He ought to have, but in fact he has not. A minister desires I should preach in his church, but the bishop forbids him. That bishop then injures him, and thrusts me out of that church.

Q.8:   Are the three orders of Bishops, Priests, and Deacons plainly described in the New Testament?

A.   We think they are, and believe they generally obtained in the churches of the apostolic age.

Q.9:   But are you assured that God designed the same plan should obtain in all churches throughout all ages?

A.   We are not assured of this, because we do not know that it is asserted in Holy Writ.

Q.10: If this plan were essential to a Christian church, what must become of all the foreign Reformed Churches?

A.   It would follow, they are no part of the Church of Christ – a consequence full of shocking absurdity . . .

Thursday, 18th

Q.1: Have we not limited field preaching too much?

A.   It seems we have. (1) Because our calling is to save that which is lost. Now we cannot expect the wanderers from God to seek us: it is our part to go and seek them. (2) Because we are more peculiarly called, by going out into the highways and hedges (which none will do if we do not) to compel them to come in (3) Because that reason against it is not good, 'The house will hold all that come.' The house may hold all that will come to the house, but not all that would come to the field. (4) Because we have found a greater blessing in field preaching than in any other preaching whatever. . . .

Q.12: Are there any smaller advices concerning preaching which it may be useful for [our Assistants] to observe?

A.   Perhaps these that follow: (1) Be sure to begin and end precisely at the time appointed. (2) Sing no hymns of your own composing. (3) Endeavour to be serious, weighty, and solemn in your whole deportment before the congregation. (4) Choose the plainest text you can. (5) Take care not to ramble from your text, but keep close to it, and make out what you undertake. (6) Always suit the subject to the audience. (7) Beware of allegorizing or spiritualizing too much. (8) Take care of anything awkward or affected, either in your gesture or pronunciation. (9) Tell each other if you observe anything of this kind.

Methodism in Redruth

(Lambeth Palace Library)

The Bishop of Exeter's *Enthusiasm of Methodists and Papists Compar'd* (1749) was one of the best known attacks on early Methodism. Vivian, one of the Bishop's informants, was curate to the rector of Redruth in 1747. His information was more accurate and his appraisal more judicious than most.

The Rev. Thomas Vivian to Bishop George Lavington; Redruth, August 27, 1747

My Lord,

... Your Lordship desir'd me to send an Account of the Methodists in this neighbourhood; but I have long been considering in what manner this can best be done. Should I write all I hear of them, it would be a confus'd Medley of Contradictions. I shall therefore confine myself to those things which I know to be fact.

When I first came to Redruth I sent for some of the principal persons among them & took all opportunities of asking questions of others. I found them all very free and open in declaring *what God had done for their souls; that he had let them see the sinful state they were in, and had recover'd them out of darkness into his marvellous light.* This is the manner they express themselves.

In order to form a better judgment of them, I generally took down Minutes of what they said; and had some thoughts of sending your Lordship an abstract of these, as the most effectual method of informing your Lordship of their sentiments. But this I thought would be too long and tedious for your Lordship to read, & have therefore omitted it. The following particulars your Lordship may depend upon.

With regard to their opinions.

1. They profess they can live without *committing* sin, though not without sin *remaining* in them. The former, they say, supposes a concurrence of the *will*. The latter is involuntary, and the remains of the *Old Man*.

2. *Their distinguishing principle*, & the only one wherein they say they differ from the rest of the Church is what they call *sensible justification*. Some declare *they are waiting for the promise which they see afar off.* Others that God *has* been gracious to them, given them remission of their sins, & such a sense of his love towards them as is always accompanied with great peace & sometimes with joy.

This comfortable sense of God's favour, they say, usually follows a great sorrowing under conviction of sin; and they receive it at once.

Their other notions are just the same as are found in Mr. Wesley's works.

With regard to their practice.

1. They are *to all appearance* persons of great sanctity of life, avoiding strictly not only gross sins but every approach to evil.

2. They never frequent any sports, revels, diversions, &c, & sigh and grieve to see others do so; calling them the *Devil's snares whereby he entraps unwary souls.*

3. Besides that which is spent in labour & sleep they pass their time usually in walking together, talking on religious subjects, reading, singing hymns, and praying.

4. They frequently affront people by reproving them for *singing idle songs*, talking of *worldly matters* in going or coming from Church, being angry, irregularly merry &c.

5. If they see any person drunk, swearing, or the like, they reprove him, and are apt to tell him he is in the way to Damnation.

6. They call each other *Brother & Sister*, seem to be linkt together in the strictest friendship, and make it an invariable rule to tell each other if they think or suspect anything to be amiss.

7. In their devotions they sometimes make use of the collects of the Church, but usually extempore prayer.

8. In their private devotions I'm told they have been sometimes overheard to make use of rapturous expressions, & seem'd to be in a kind of ecstasy.

9. In public prayer I hear they frequently shed tears especially in singing their hymns.

10. They are very constant attendants at Church & the Sacrament, & when there seem very attentive & much affected.

11. The dangers I apprehend them most liable to are spiritual pride, & presumption. Against these I take all opportunities to caution them, & they seem very thankful.

With regard to pride, some have confess'd to me this was the greatest enemy they had to struggle with. And as to presumption, they allow there have been some among them that *deceiv'd themselves* imagining they were in a state of grace when really they were not, as appear'd to others by their actions.

With regard to their discipline.

They very strictly follow those rules that are found in two pamphlets; one entitled *Rules of the United Societies*; the other *Rules of the Bands* . . . Every Friday is a fast-day when those that can meet & pray for all mankind, which they call the intercession . . .

There is one person in this parish who preaches sometimes, or (as he would rather call it) *exhorts*; whom I can by no means persuade to desist from so irregular & dangerous an undertaking. His arguments are that whosoever is gifted, & God blesses with success, must be effectually call'd to preach the Gospel.

When I represent to them the danger of making a schism, they say they cannot leave what they have experienc'd to be so great a means of grace, & declare the greatest abhorrence of separating from the Church. When I would enter farther into the irregularity of the thing, they refer me to Mr. Wesley's appeal.

This, My Lord, is the best account I can give you of these people, & as your Lordship will perceive, that amongst their irregularities there is something very commendable in them. This I endeavour to promote, & at the same time draw them off from everything that is irregular by the softest methods I am capable . . .

John Wesley in Ireland

(*JWJ*, III, 314; VII, 515–17)

First visit, 1747

Saturday 15 [Aug., Dublin]. – I stayed at home, and spoke to all that came; but I found scarce any Irish among them. At least ninety-nine in an hundred of the native Irish remain in the religion of their forefathers. The Protestants, whether in Dublin or elsewhere, are almost all transplanted lately from England. Nor is it any wonder that those who are born Papists generally live and die such, when the Protestants can find no better ways to convert them than Penal Laws and Acts of Parliament . . .

Monday 17. – I began examining the society, which I finished the next day. It contained about two hundred and four score members, many of whom appeared to be strong in faith. The people in general are of a more teachable spirit than in most parts of England; but, on that very account, they must be watched over with the more care, being equally susceptible of good and ill impressions.

Last visit, 1789

July 3, Friday. – Our little Conference began in Dublin, and ended Tuesday the 7th. On this I observe (1) I never had between forty and fifty such preachers together in Ireland before; all of them, we had reason to hope, alive to God, and earnestly devoted to His service; (2) I never saw such a number of preachers before, so unanimous in all points, particularly as to leaving the Church, which none of them had the least thought of. It is no wonder that there has been this year so large an increase of the society.

Sunday, 5. – I desired as many as chose it of our society to go to St. Patrick's, being the first Sunday in the month. The Dean preached a serious, useful sermon, and we had such a company of communicants as, I suppose, had scarce been seen there together for above a hundred years. Our house would not contain them that came in the evening, many of whom being little awakened, I preached on 'It is a fearful thing to fall into the hands of the living God.' On Monday and Tuesday we settled the rest of our business, and on Wednesday morning we parted in the same love that we met.

I had much satisfaction in this Conference, in which, conversing with between forty and fifty travelling preachers, I found such a body of men as I hardly believed could have been found together in Ireland; men of so sound experience, so deep piety, and so strong understanding. I am convinced they are no way inferior to the English Conference, except it be in number.

Friday the 10th we observed as a day of fasting and prayer, chiefly for the increase of the work of God. This was concluded with a very solemn watch-night, wherein the hearts of many were greatly comforted.

The Conference of 1748

(See note on p. 67)

Thursday, June 2, 1748 . . .

Q.2:   We are again pressed 'only to preach in as many places as we can, but not to form any societies'. Shall we follow this advice?

A.   By no means. We have made the trial already. We have preached for more than a year without forming societies in a large tracts of lands from Newcastle to Berwick-upon-Tweed; and almost all the seed has fallen by the wayside. There is scarce any fruit of it remaining.

Q.3:   But what particular inconvenience do you observe when people are not formed into societies?

A.   These among others: (1) The preacher cannot give proper exhortations and instructions to those who are convinced of sin unless he has opportunities of meeting them apart from the mixed, unawakened multitude. (2) They cannot watch over one another in love unless they are thus united together. Nor, (3), can the believers build up one another and bear one another's burthens.

Q.4:   Ought we not to have a longer time of probation for the rich before we admit them into our society?

A.   It seems not. But neither should we have a shorter. Let either rich or poor stay three months.

Q.5:   How shall we more effectually avoid respect of persons?

A.   Let us take care to visit the poor as the rich. (2). Let us strictly examine our hearts, whether we are not more willing to preach to the rich than to the poor. (3). We will speak to the poor at the chapel[1] as often as to the rich; to the latter on Wednesday, to the former on Friday.

---

[1] West Street Chapel, London, where this Conference was held.

A Plain Account of the People Called Methodists

(*JWW*, VIII, 248–68)

This account, contained in a letter to the Reverend Mr. Perronet, vicar of Shoreham in Kent, in the year 1748, is the most detailed account given by Wesley of the development of early Methodism and its organisation. Some sections are already covered by other writings such as *The Nature, Design, and General Rules of the United Societies* (pp. 59–61 above).

Reverend and Dear Sir,

1. Some time since, you desired an account of the whole economy of the people commonly called *Methodists*. And you received a true (as far as it went) but not a full, account. To supply what I think was wanting in that, I send you this account, that you may know, not only their practice on every head, but likewise the reasons whereon it is grounded, the occasion of every step they have taken, and the advantages reaped thereby.

2. But I must premise, that as they had not the least expectation, at first, of any thing like what has since followed, so they had no previous design or plan at all; but every thing arose just as the occasion offered. They saw or felt some impending or pressing evil, or some good end necessary to be pursued. And many times they fell unawares on the very thing which secured the good, or removed the evil. At other times, they consulted on the most probable means, following only common sense and Scripture: Though they generally found, in looking back, something in Christian antiquity likewise, very nearly parallel thereto.

I. 1. About ten years ago, my brother and I were desired to preach in many parts of London. We had no view herein, but, so far as we were able (and we knew God could work by whomsoever it pleased him), to convince those who would hear what true Christianity was, and to persuade them to embrace it.

2. The points we chiefly insisted upon were four: First, that orthodoxy, or right opinions, is, at best, but a very slender part of religion, if it can be allowed to be any part of it at all; that neither does religion consist in negatives, in bare harmlessness of any kind; nor merely in externals, in doing good, or using the means of grace, in works of piety (so called) or of charity; that it is nothing short of, or different from, 'the mind that was in Christ'; the image of God stamped upon the heart; inward righteousness, attended with the peace of God; and 'joy in the Holy Ghost'. Secondly, that the only way under heaven to this religion is, to 'repent and believe the gospel'; or (as the Apostle words it) 'repentance towards God, and faith in our Lord Jesus Christ'. Thirdly,

that by this faith, 'he that worketh not, but believeth on him that justi-
fieth the ungodly, is justified freely by his grace, through the redemption
which is in Jesus Christ.' And, Lastly, that 'being justified by faith', we
taste of heaven to which we are going; we are holy and happy; we tread
down sin and fear, and 'sit in heavenly places with Christ Jesus'.

3. Many of those who heard this began to cry out that we brought
'strange things to their ears'; that this was doctrine which they never
heard before, or at least never regarded. They 'searched the Scriptures,
whether these things were so', and acknowledged 'the truth as it is in
Jesus'. Their hearts also were influenced as well as their understandings,
and they determined to follow 'Jesus Christ, and him crucified'.

4. Immediately they were surrounded with difficulties; – all the world
rose up against them; neighbours, strangers, acquaintance, relations,
friends, began to cry out amain, 'Be not righteous overmuch; why
shouldest thou destroy thyself?' Let not 'much religion make thee mad'.

5. One, and another, and another came to us, asking what they should
do, being distressed on every side; as every one strove to weaken, and
none to strengthen, their hands in God. We advised them, 'Strengthen
you one another. Talk together as often as you can. And pray earnestly
with and for one another, that you may "endure to the end, and be
saved".' Against this advice we presumed there could be no objection;
as being grounded on the plainest reason, and on so many scriptures
both of the Old Testament and New, that it would be tedious to recite
them.

6. They said, 'But we want you likewise to talk with us often, to
direct and quicken us in our way, to give us the advices which you well
know we need, and to pray with us, as well as for us.' I asked, 'Which of
you desire this? Let me know your names and places of abode.' They did
so. But I soon found they were too many for me to talk with severally so
often as they wanted it. So I told them, 'If you will all of you come
together every Thursday, in the evening, I will gladly spend some time
with you in prayer, and give you the best advice I can.'

7. Thus arose, without any previous design on either side, what was
afterwards called *a Society*; a very innocent name, and very common in
London, for any number of people associating themselves together. The
thing proposed in their associating themselves together was obvious to
every one. They wanted to 'flee from the wrath to come', and to assist
each other in so doing. They therefore united themselves 'in order to
pray together, to receive the word of exhortation, and to watch over one
another in love, that they might help each other to work out their
salvation'.

8. There is one only condition previously required in those who
desire admission into this Society, – 'a desire to flee from the wrath to
come, to be saved from their sins'.

They now likewise agreed, that as many of them as had an opportunity would meet together every Friday, and spend the dinner hour in crying to God, both for each other, and for all mankind.

9. It quickly appeared, that their thus uniting together answered the end proposed therein. In a few months, the far greater part of those who had begun to 'fear God, and work righteousness', but were not united together, grew faint in their minds, and fell back into what they were before. Meanwhile the far greater part of those who were thus united together continued 'striving to enter in at the strait gate', and to 'lay hold on eternal life' . . .

11. But it was not long before an objection was made to this, which had not once entered into my thought:—'Is not this making a schism? Is not the joining these people together, gathering Churches out of Churches?'

It was easily answered, If you mean only gathering people out of buildings called churches, it is. But if you mean, dividing Christians from Christians, and so destroying Christian fellowship, it is not. For, (1) These were not Christians before they were thus joined. Most of them were barefaced Heathens. (2) Neither are they Christians, from whom you suppose them to be divided. You will not look me in the face and say they are. What! drunken Christians! cursing and swearing Christians! lying Christians! cheating Christians! If these are Christians at all, they are devil Christians, as the poor Malabarians term them. (3) Neither are they divided any more than they were before, even from these wretched devil Christians. They are as ready as ever to assist them, and to perform every office of real kindness towards them. (4) If it be said, 'But there are some true Christians in the parish, and you destroy the Christian fellowship between these and them;' I answer, That which never existed, cannot be destroyed. But the fellowship you speak of never existed. Therefore it cannot be destroyed. Which of those true Christians had any such fellowship with these? Who watched over them in love? Who marked their growth in grace? Who advised and exhorted them from time to time? Who prayed with them and for them, as they had need? This, and this alone, is Christian fellowship: But, alas! where is it to be found? Look east or west, north or south; name what parish you please: Is this Christian fellowship there? Rather, are not the bulk of the parishioners a mere rope of sand? What Christian connexion is there between them? What intercourse in spiritual things? What watching over each other's souls? What bearing of one another's burdens? What a mere jest is it then, to talk so gravely of destroying what never was! The real truth is just the reverse of this: We introduce Christian fellowship where it was utterly destroyed. And the fruits of it have been peace, joy, love, and zeal for every good word and work.

II. 1. But as much as we endeavoured to watch over each other, we soon found some who did not live the gospel. I do not know that any hypocrites were crept in; for indeed there was no temptation: But several grew cold, and gave way to the sins which had long easily beset them. We quickly perceived there were many ill consequences of suffering these to remain among us. It was dangerous to others; inasmuch as all sin is of an infectious nature. It brought such a scandal on their brethren as exposed them to what was not properly the reproach of Christ. It laid a stumbling-block in the way of others, and caused the truth to be evil spoken of.

2. We groaned under these inconveniences long, before a remedy could be found. The people were scattered so wide in all parts of the town, from Wapping to Westminster, that I could not easily see what the behaviour of each person in his own neighbourhood was: So that several disorderly walkers did much hurt before I was apprized of it.

3. At length, while we were thinking of quite another thing, we struck upon a method for which we have cause to bless God ever since. I was talking with several of the society in Bristol concerning the means of paying the debts there, when one stood up and said, 'Let every member of the society give a penny a week till all are paid.' Another answered, 'But many of them are poor, and cannot afford to do it.' 'Then,' said he, 'put eleven of the poorest with me; and if they can give anything, well: I will call on them weekly; and if they can give nothing, I will give for them as well as for myself. And each of you call on eleven of your neighbours weekly; receive what they give, and make up what is wanting.' It was done. In a while, some of these informed me, they found such and such an one did not live as he ought. It struck me immediately, 'This is the thing; the very thing we have wanted so long.' I called together all the Leaders of the classes (so we used to term them and their companies), and desired, that each would make a particular inquiry into the behaviour of those whom he saw weekly. They did so. Many disorderly walkers were detected. Some turned from the evil of their ways. Some were put away from us. Many saw it with fear, and rejoiced unto God with reverence.

6. At first they visited each person at his own house; but this was soon found not so expedient. And that on many accounts: (1) It took up more time than most of the Leaders had to spare. (2) Many persons lived with masters, mistresses, or relations, who would not suffer them to be thus visited. (3) At the houses of those who were not so averse, they often had no opportunity of speaking to them but in company. And this did not at all answer the end proposed, – of exhorting, comforting, or reproving. (4) It frequently happened that one affirmed what another denied. (5) Little misunderstandings and quarrels of various kinds frequently arose among relations or neighbours; effectually to remove

which, it was needful to see them all face to face. Upon all these considerations it was agreed, that those of each class should meet all together. And by this means, a more full inquiry was made into the
behaviour of every person. Those who could not be visited at home, or
no otherwise than in company, had the same advantage with others.
Advice or reproof was given as need required, quarrels made up, misunderstandings removed: And after an hour or two spent in this labour
of love, they concluded with prayer and thanksgiving.

7. It can scarce be conceived what advantages have been reaped from
this little prudential regulation. Many now happily experienced that
Christian fellowship of which they had not so much as an idea before.
They began to 'bear one another's burdens' and naturally to 'care for
each other'. As they had daily a more intimate acquaintance with, so
they had a more endeared affection for, each other. And 'speaking the
truth in love, they grew up into Him in all things, who is the Head, even
Christ; from whom the whole body, fitly joined together, and com-
pacted by that which every joint supplied, according to the effectual
working in the measure of every part, increased unto the edifying itself
in love.'

8. But notwithstanding all these advantages, many were at first
extremely averse to meeting thus. Some, viewing it in a wrong point of
light, not as a privilege (indeed an invaluable one), but rather a restraint, disliked it on that account, because they did not love to be
restrained in anything. Some were ashamed to speak before company.
Others honestly said, 'I do not know why; but I do not like it.' . . .

12. They spoke far more plausibly than these, who said, 'The thing
is well enough in itself. But the Leaders are insufficient for the work:
They have neither gifts nor graces for such an employment.' I answer,
(1) Yet such Leaders as they are, it is plain God has blessed their labour.
(2) If any of these is remarkably wanting in gifts or grace, he is soon
taken notice of and removed. (3) If you know any such, tell it to me, not
to others, and I will endeavour to exchange him for a better. (4) It may
be hoped they will all be better than they are, both by experience and
observation, and by the advices given them by the Minister every Tuesday night, and the prayers (then in particular) offered up for them.

III. 1. About this time, I was informed that several persons in Kingswood frequently met together at the school; and, when they could spare
the time, spent the greater part of the night in prayer, and praise, and
thanksgiving. Some advised me to put an end to this; but, upon weighing the thing thoroughly, and comparing it with the practice of the
ancient Christians, I could see no cause to forbid it. Rather, I believed it
might be made of more general use. So I sent them word, I designed to
watch with them on the Friday nearest the full moon, that we might have

light thither and back again. I gave public notice of this the Sunday before, and, withal, that I intended to preach; desiring they, and they only, would meet me there, who could do it without prejudice to their business or families. On Friday abundance of people came. I began preaching between eight and nine; and we continued till a little beyond the noon of night, singing, praying, and praising God.

2. This we have continued to do once a month ever since, in Bristol, London, and Newcastle, as well as Kingswood; and exceeding great are the blessings we have found therein: It has generally been an extremely solemn season; when the word of God sunk deep into the heart, even of those who till then knew him not. If it be said, 'This was only owing to the novelty of the thing (the circumstance which still draws such multitudes together at those seasons), or perhaps to the awful silence of the night,' I am not careful to answer in this matter. Be it so: However, the impression then made on many souls has never since been effaced. Now, allowing that God did make use either of the novelty or any other indifferent circumstance, in order to bring sinners to repentance, yet they are brought. And herein let us rejoice together. . . .

IV. 1. As the society increased, I found it required still greater care to separate the precious from the vile. In order to this, I determined, at least once in three months, to talk with every member myself, and to inquire at their own mouths, as well as of their Leaders and neighbours, whether they grew in grace and in the knowledge of our Lord Jesus Christ. At these seasons I likewise particularly inquire whether there be any misunderstanding or difference among them; that every hinderance of peace and brotherly love may be taken out of the way.

2. To each of those of whose seriousness and good conversation I found no reason to doubt, I gave a testimony under my own hand, by writing their name on a ticket prepared for that purpose; every ticket implying as strong a recommendation of the person to whom it was given as if I had wrote at length, 'I believe the bearer hereof to be one that fears God and works righteousness.'

3. Those who bore these tickets, . . . wherever they came, were acknowledged by their brethren, and received with all cheerfulness. These were likewise of use in other respects. By these it was easily distinguished, when the society were to meet apart, who were members of it, and who not. These also supplied us with a quiet and inoffensive method of removing any disorderly member. He has no new ticket at the the quarterly visitation (for so often the tickets are changed); and hereby it is immediately known that he is no longer of the community.

VI. 1. By the blessing of God upon their endeavours to help one another, many found the pearl of great price. Being justified by faith, they had 'peace with God, through our Lord Jesus Christ'. These felt a more tender affection than before, to those who were partakers of like precious faith; and hence arose such a confidence in each other, that they poured out their souls into each other's bosom. . . .

2. . . . And they were the more desirous of this, when they observed it was the express advice of an inspired writer: 'Confess your faults one to another, and pray one for another, that ye may be healed.'

3. In compliance with their desire, I divided them into smaller companies; putting the married or single men, and married or single women, together. . . .

5. In order to increase in them a grateful sense of all his mercies, I desired that, one evening in a quarter, all the men in band, on a second, all the women, would meet; and on a third, both men and women together; that we might together 'eat bread', as the ancient Christians did, 'with gladness and singleness of heart'. At these love-feasts (so we termed them, retaining the name, as well as the thing, which was in use from the beginning) our food is only a little plain cake and water. But we seldom return from them without being fed, not only with the 'meat which perisheth', but with 'that which endureth to everlasting life.' . . .

7. But it was soon objected to the bands (as to the classes before), 'These were not at first. There is no Scripture for them. These are man's works, man's building, man's invention.' I reply, as before, these are also prudential helps, grounded on reason and experience, in order to apply the general rules given in Scripture according to particular circumstances.

8. An objection much more boldly and frequently urged, is, that 'all these bands are mere Popery.' I hope I need not pass a harder censure on those (most of them at least) who affirm this, than that they talk of they know not what; they betray in themselves the most gross and shameful ignorance. Do not they yet know, that the only Popish confession is, the confession made by a single person to a Priest? – and this itself is in nowise condemned by our Church; nay, she recommends it in some cases. Whereas, that we practise is, the confession of several persons conjointly, not to a Priest, but to each other. Consequently, it has no analogy at all to Popish confession. But the truth is, this is a stale objection, which many people make against anything they do not like. It is all Popery out of hand.

VII. 1. And yet while most of these who were thus intimately joined together, went on daily from faith to faith; some fell from the faith, either all at once, by falling into known, wilful sin; or gradually, and almost insensibly, by giving way in what they called little things; by sins of omission, by yielding to heart-sins, or by not watching unto prayer. The exhortations and prayers used among the believers did no longer profit these. They wanted advice and instructions suited to their case; which as soon as I observed, I separated them from the rest, and desired them to meet me apart on Saturday evenings.

2. At this hour, all the hymns, exhortations, and prayers are adapted to their circumstances; being wholly suited to those who *did* see God, but have now lost sight of the light of his countenance; and who mourn after him, and refuse to be comforted till they know he has healed their backsliding.

3. By applying both the threats and promises of God to these real, not nominal, penitents, and by crying to God in their behalf, we endeavoured to bring them back to the great 'Shepherd and Bishop of their souls'; not by any of the fopperies of the Roman Church, although, in some measure, countenanced by antiquity. In prescribing hair-shirts, and bodily austerities, we durst not follow even the ancient Church; although we had unawares, both in dividing οἱ πιστοί, the believers, from the rest of the society, and in separating the penitents from them, and appointing a peculiar service for them.

VIII. 1. Many of these soon recovered the ground they had lost. Yea, they rose higher than before; being more watchful than ever, and more meek and lowly, as well as stronger in the faith that worketh by love. They now outran the greater part of their brethren, continually walking in the light of God, and having fellowship with the Father, and with his Son Jesus Christ.

2. I saw it might be useful to give some advices to all those who continued in the light of God's countenance, which the rest of their brethren did not want, and probably could not receive. So I desired a small number of such as appeared to be in this state, to spend an hour with me every Monday morning. My design was, not only to direct them how to press after perfection; to exercise their every grace, and improve every talent they had received; and to incite them to love one another more, and to watch more carefully over each other; but also to have a select company, to whom I might unbosom myself on all occasions, without reserve; and whom I could propose to all their brethren as a pattern of love, of holiness, and of good works.

3. They had no need of being incumbered with many rules; having the best rule of all in their hearts. No peculiar directions were therefore given to them, excepting only these three:—

First. Let nothing spoken in this society be spoken again. (Hereby we had the more full confidence in each other.)

Secondly. Every member agrees to submit to his Minister in all indifferent things.

Thirdly. Every member will bring, once a week, all he can spare toward a common stock.

4. Every one here has an equal liberty of speaking, there being none

greater or less than another. I could say freely to these, when they were met together, 'Ye may all prophesy one by one,' (taking that word in its lowest sense) 'that all may learn, and all may be comforted.' And I often found the advantage of such a free conversation and, and that 'in the multitude of counsellors there is safety.' Any who is inclined so to do is likewise encouraged to pour out his soul to God. And here especially we have found, that 'the effectual fervent prayer of a righteous man availeth much.'

IX. 1. This is the plainest and clearest account I can give of the people commonly called *Methodists*. It remains only to give you a short account of those who serve their brethren in love. These are Leaders of classes and bands (spoken of before), Assistants, Stewards, Visitors of the sick, and Schoolmasters.

[For the offices of Assistants and Stewards, see p. 70; also pp. 116–17 below.]

XI. 1. But it was not long before the Stewards found a great difficulty with regard to the sick. Some were ready to perish before they knew of their illness; and when they did know, it was not in their power (being persons generally employed in trade) to visit them so often as they desired.

2. When I was apprized of this, I laid the case at large before the whole society; showed how impossible it was for the Stewards to attend all that were sick in all parts of the town; desired the Leaders of classes would more carefully inquire, and more constantly inform them, who were sick; and asked, 'Who among you is willing, as well as able, to supply this lack of service?'

3. The next morning many willingly offered themselves. I chose six-and-forty of them, whom I judged to be of the most tender, loving spirit; divided the town into twenty-three parts, and desired two of them to visit the sick in each division.

4. It is the business of a Visitor of the sick,

To see every sick person within his district thrice a week. To inquire into the state of their souls, and to advise them as occasion may require. To inquire into their disorders, and procure advice for them. To relieve them, if they are in want. To do any thing for them, which he (or she) can do. To bring in his accounts weekly to the Stewards. . . .

6. We have ever since had great reason to praise God for his continued blessing on this undertaking. Many lives have been saved, many sicknesses healed, much pain and want prevented or removed. Many heavy hearts have been made glad, many mourners comforted: And the Visitors have found, from Him whom they serve, a present reward for all their labour. . . .

XIII. 1. But I had for some years observed many who, although not sick, were not able to provide for themselves, and had none who took care to provide for them: These were chiefly feeble, aged widows. I consulted with the Stewards, how they might be relieved. They all agreed, if we could keep them in one house, it would not only be far less expensive to us, but also far more comfortable for them. Indeed we had no money to begin; but we believed He would provide 'who defendeth the cause of the widow'. So we took a lease of two little houses near; we fitted them up, so as to be warm and clean. We took in as many widows as we had room for, and provided them with things needful for the body; toward the expense of which I set aside, first, the weekly contributions of the bands, and then all that was collected at the Lord's Supper. It is true, this does not suffice: So that we are considerably in debt, on this account also. But we are persuaded, it will not always be so; seeing 'the earth is the Lord's, and the fulness thereof.'

2. In this (commonly called The Poor House) we have now nine widows, one blind woman, two poor children, two upper-servants, a maid and a man. I might add, four or five Preachers; for I myself, as well as the other Preachers who are in town, diet with the poor, on the same food, and at the same table; and we rejoice herein, as a comfortable earnest of our eating bread together in our Father's kingdom.

3. I have blessed God for this house ever since it began; but lately much more than ever. I honour these widows; for they 'are widows indeed'. So that it is not in vain, that, without any design of so doing, we have copied after another of the institutions of the Apostolic age. I can now say to all the world, 'Come and see how these Christians love one another!'

XIV. 1. Another thing which had given me frequent concern was, the case of abundance of children. Some their parents could not afford to put to school: So they remained like 'a wild ass's colt'. Others were sent to school, and learned, at least, to read and write; but they learned all kind of vice at the same time: So that it had been better for them to have been without their knowledge, than to have bought it at so dear a price.

2. At length I determined to have them taught in my own house, that they might have an opportunity of learning to read, write, and cast accounts (if no more), without being under almost a necessity of learning Heathenism at the same time: And after several unsuccessful trials, I found two such Schoolmasters as I wanted; men of honesty and of sufficient knowledge, who had talents for, and their hearts in, the work.

3. They have now under their care near sixty children. The parents of some pay for their schooling; but the greater part, being very poor, do not; so that the expense is chiefly defrayed by voluntary contributions. We have of late clothed them too, as many as wanted. The rules of the school are these that follow:—

First. No child is admitted under six years of age. Secondly. All the children are to be present at the morning sermon. Thirdly. They are at school from six to twelve, and from one to five. Fourthly. They have no play-days. Fifthly. No child is to speak in school, but to the masters. Sixthly. The child who misses two days in one week, without leave, is excluded the school. . . .

5. A happy change was soon observed in the children, both with regard to their tempers and behaviours. They learned reading, writing, and arithmetic swiftly; and at the same time they were diligently instructed in the sound principles of religion, and earnestly exhorted to fear God, and work out their own salvation.

XV. 1. A year or two ago, I observed among many a distress of another kind. They frequently wanted, perhaps in order to carry on their business, a present supply of money. They scrupled to make use of a pawnbroker; but where to borrow it they knew not. I resolved to try if we could not find a remedy for this also. I went, in a few days, from one end of the town to the other, and exhorted those who had this world's goods, to assist their needy brethren. Fifty pounds were contributed. This was immediately lodged in the hands of two Stewards; who attended every Tuesday morning, in order to lend to those who wanted any small sum, not exceeding twenty shillings, to be repaid within three months.

2. It is almost incredible, but it manifestly appears from their accounts, that, with this inconsiderable sum, two hundred and fifty have been assisted, within the space of one year. Will not God put it into the heart of some lover of mankind to increase this little stock? If this is not 'lending unto the Lord', what is? O confer not with flesh and blood, but immediately

> 'Join hands with God, to make a poor man live!'

The Growth of Methodism

(*JWJ*, III, 360; IV, 54; VI, 167–8)

[3 July, 1748.] Mr. Hay, the rector, reading prayers, I had once more the comfort of receiving the Lord's Supper at Epworth. After the evening service I preached at the Cross again, to almost the whole town. I see plainly we have often judged amiss when we have measured the increase of the work of God, in this and other places, by the increase of the society only. The society here is not large; but God has wrought upon the whole place. Sabbath-breaking and drunkenness are no more seen in these streets; cursing and swearing are rarely heard. Wickedness hides its head already. Who knows but, by-and-by, God may utterly take it away?

Wednesday 28 [Feb. 1753.] – We rode to Bristol. I now looked over Mr. Prince's *Christian History*. What an amazing difference is there in the manner wherein God has carried on His work in England and in America! There, above a hundred of the established clergy, men of age and experience, and of the greatest note for sense and learning in those parts, are zealously engaged in the work. Here almost the whole body of the aged, experienced, learned clergy are zealously engaged against it; and few, but a handful of raw young men, engaged in it, without name, learning, or eminent sense. And yet by that large number of honourable men the work seldom flourished above six months at a time, and then followed a lamentable and general decay before the next revival of it; whereas that which God hath wrought by these despised instruments has continually increased for fifteen years together; and at whatever time it has declined in any one place, has more eminently flourished in others.[1]

Tuesday 5 [Aug. 1777.] – Our yearly Conference began. I now particularly inquired (as that report had been spread far and wide) of every Assistant, 'Have you reason to believe, from your own observation, that the Methodists are a fallen people? Is there a decay or an increase in the work of God where you have been? Are the societies in general more dead, or more alive to God, than they were some years ago?' The almost universal answer was, 'If we must "know them by their fruits", there is no decay in the work of God among the people in general. The societies are not dead to God; they are as much alive as they have been for many years. And we look on this report as a mere device of Satan, to make our hands hang down.'

'But how can this question be decided?' You, and you, can judge no farther than you see. You cannot judge of one part by another; of the people of London, suppose, by those of Bristol. And none but myself has an opportunity of seeing them throughout the three kingdoms.

But to come to a short issue. In most places the Methodists are still a poor, despised people, labouring under reproach, and many inconveniences; therefore, wherever the power of God is not, they decrease. By this, then, you may form a sure judgment. Do the Methodists in general decrease in number? Then they decrease in grace; they are a fallen, or, at least, a falling people. But they do not decrease in number; they continually increase; therefore they are not a fallen people.

[1] Cf. *JWJ*, IV, 122 (16 June 1755).

Kingswood School

(*JWW*, XIII, 249–54)

Published in 1749; reprinted in 1768, with minor variations and an additional section outlining the 'method ... observed by those who design to go through a course of academical learning', which Wesley claimed to be superior to the course at Oxford or Cambridge. See also his later, more defensive *Plain Account*, composed in 1768–9, but not published until 1781 (*JWW*, XIII, 255–67).

1. Our design is, with God's assistance, to train up children, in every branch of useful learning.

2. We teach none but boarders. These are taken in, being between the years of six and twelve, in order to be taught reading, writing, arithmetic, English, French, Latin, Greek, Hebrew; history, geography, chronology; rhetoric, logic, ethics; geometry, algebra, physics; music.

3. The School is to contain eight classes.

In the first class the children read the *Hornbook*, *Instructions for Children*, and *Lessons for Children*; and begin learning to write.

In the second class they read *The Manners of the Ancient Christians*, go on in writing, learn the *short* English Grammar, the *short* Latin Grammar, read *Praelectiones Pueriles*: translate them into *English*, and the *Instructions for Children* into *Latin*: part of which they transcribe and repeat.

In the third class they read Dr. Cave's *Primitive Christianity*, go on in writing, perfect themselves in the *English* and *Latin* grammar; read *Corderii Colloquia Selecta* and *Historiae Selectae*: translate *Historiae Selectae* into *English*, and *Lessons for Children* into *Latin*: part of which they transcribe and repeat.

In the fourth class they read *The Pilgrim's Progress*, perfect themselves in writing; learn Dilworth's *Arithmetic*: read Castalio's Kempis and Cornelius Nepos: translate *Castalio* into *English*, and *Manners of the Ancient Christians* into *Latin*: transcribe and repeat select portions of *Moral and Sacred Poems*.

In the fifth class they read *The Life of Mr. Haliburton*, perfect themselves in arithmetic; read Select *Dialogues* of Erasmus, Phaedrus and Sallust: translate *Erasmus* into *English*, and *Primitive Christianity* into *Latin*: transcribe and repeat select portions of *Moral and Sacred Poems*.

In the sixth class they read *The Life of Mr. De Renty* and Kennet's *Roman Antiquities*: they learn Randal's *Geography*: read Caesar, select parts of Terence and Velleius Paterculus: translate *Erasmus* into *English*, and *The Life of Mr. Haliburton* into *Latin*: transcribe and repeat select portions of *Sacred Hymns and Poems*.

In the seventh class they read Mr. Law's *Christian Perfection*, Marshal's *Mystery of Sanctification*, and Archbishop Potter's *Greek Antiquities*: they learn Bengelii *Introductio ad Chronologiam*, with Marshal's *Chronological Tables*: read Tully's *Offices*, and Virgil's *Aeneid*: translate Bengelius into *English*, and Mr. Law into *Latin*: learn (those who have a turn for it) to make verses, and the *Short Greek Grammar*: read the Epistles of St. John: transcribe and repeat select portions of Milton.

In the eighth class they read Mr. Law's *Serious Call*, and Lewis's *Hebrew Antiquities*: they learn to make themes and to declaim: learn Vossius's *Rhetoric*: read Tully's *Tusculan Questions*, and *Selecta ex Ovidio, Virgilio, Horatio, Juvenale, Persio, Martiale*: perfect themselves in the *Greek* grammar; read the *Gospels* and six books of Homer's *Iliad*: translate Tully into *English*, and Mr. Law into *Latin*: learn the *Short Hebrew Grammar*, and read *Genesis*: transcribe and repeat *Selecta ex Virgilio, Horatio, Juvenale*.

4. It is our particular desire, that all who are educated here, may be brought up in the fear of God: and at the utmost distance as from vice in general, so in particular from idleness and effeminacy. The children therefore of *tender* parents, so call'd, (who are indeed offering up their sons and their daughters unto devils) have no business here; for the rules will not be broken, in favour of any person whatsoever. Nor is any child receiv'd unless his parents agree, 1. that he shall observe all the rules of the house, and 2. that they will not take him from school, no, not a day, till they take him for good and all.

5. The general rules of the house are these:

First, the children rise at four, winter and summer, and spend the time till five in private: partly in reading, partly in singing, partly in self-examination or meditation (if capable of it) and partly in prayer. They at first use a short form (which is varied continually) and then pray in their own words.

Secondly, at five they attend the public service.[1] From six they work till breakfast. For as we have no play-days (the school being taught every day in the year but *Sunday*) so neither do we allow any time for play on any day. He that plays when he is a child, will play when he is a man.

On fair days they work, according to their strength in the garden; on rainy days in the house. Some of them also learn music: and some of the larger will be employed in *Philosophical Experiments*. But particular care is taken that they never work alone, but always in the presence of a master.

We have six masters in all; one for teaching *French*, two for reading and writing, and three for the ancient languages.

Thirdly, the school begins at seven, in which languages are taught 'till nine, and then writing, &c. 'till eleven. At eleven the children walk or work. At twelve they dine, and then work or sing 'till one. They diet thus:

Breakfast, milk-porridge and water-gruel, by turns:

Supper, bread and butter, and milk by turns:

Dinner, *Sunday*, cold roast beef:

        Monday, Hash'd meat and apple dumplings:

        Tuesday, Boil'd mutton:

        Wednesday, Vegetables and dumplings:

        Thursday, boil'd mutton or beef:

        Friday, vegetables and dumplings. And so in Lent:

        Saturday, bacon and greens, apple dumplings.

They drink water at meals, nothing between meals. On *Friday*, if healthy,[2] they fast till three in the afternoon. Experience shews, this is so far from impairing health, that it greatly conduces to it.

Fourthly, from one to four languages are taught, and then writing, &c. 'till five. At five begins the hour of private prayer. From six they walk or work 'till supper. A little before seven the public service begins. At eight they go to bed, the youngest first.

Fifthly, they lodge all in one room, in which a lamp burns all night. Every child lies by himself. A master lies at each end of the room. All their beds have mattresses on them, not feather-beds.

Sixthly: on *Sunday*, at six they dress and breakfast: at seven, learn hymns or poems: at eight attend the public service: at nine go to the parish church; at one dine and sing: at two attend the public service, and at four are privately instructed . . .

The price for the board and teaching of a child (including his books, pens, ink and paper) is fourteen pounds a year, while he is in the school: after he has gone thro' the school, twenty, and he is then to find his own books.

    FINIS

[1] 1768: 'at five they all meet together'.
[2] 'if healthy'; 1768: 'if they choose it'.

Vincent Perronet to Walter Sellon, February 24, 1752

(Ms at Drew University)

I believe my dear brother John Wesley wonders at the bad taste of those who seem not to be in raptures with Kingswood School. If there was no other objection but the want of good water upon the spot, it would be an insuperable objection to all wise men but himself and his brother.

'The True Church of Christ'

John Wesley to the Rev. Gilbert Boyce; Bandon, near Cork,
May 22, 1750

(Oxford *Letters*, II, 424–6)

Boyce was the Baptist pastor at Coningsby, Lincs, with whom Wesley stayed
in 1748. The following letter was a reply to one in which Boyce pressed
Wesley to substantiate his claim that the Church of England, or the Methodists, were closer than any other to the 'Scriptural plan' for the Church,
insisting that some of the differences between them went beyond matters of
'opinion'.

Dear sir

I do not think either the Church of England, or the people called
Methodists, or any other particular society under heaven, to be 'the true
Church of Christ', for that church is but one, and contains all the true
believers on earth. But I conceive every society of true believers to be a
branch of the one, true, Church of Christ.

'Tis no wonder that young and unlearned preachers use some improper expressions. I trust, upon friendly advice, they will lay them
aside. And as they grow in years they will increase in knowledge.

I have neither inclination nor time to draw the saw of controversy.
But a few little remarks I would make in order to our understanding and
(I hope) loving one another the better.

You think the mode of baptism is 'necessary to salvation'. I deny that
even baptism itself is so. If it were, every Quaker must be damned,
which I can in no wise believe.

I hold nothing to be (strictly speaking) necessary to salvation but the
mind which was in Christ. If I did not think you had a measure of this I
could only love you as an heathen man or a publican.

They who believe, with the faith working by love, are God's children.
I don't wonder that God permits (not causes) smaller evils among these,
when I observe far greater evils among them – for sin is an infinitely
greater evil than ignorance.

I do not conceive that unity in the outward modes of worship is *so*
necessary among the children of God that they cannot be children of
God without it – although I once thought it was.

I do make use (so far as I know) of the means of grace God has
ordained, *exactly* as God has ordained them. But here is your grand mistake. You think, my design is 'to form a church'. No. I have no such
design. It is not my design or desire that any who accept of my help
should leave the church of which they are now members. Were I converting Indians I would take every step St. Paul took. But I am not.

Therefore some of those steps I am not to take. Therefore I still join with the Church of England so far as I can, at the same time that I and my friends use several prudential helps which our Church neither enjoins nor forbids, as being in themselves of a purely indifferent nature.

What I affirm of the generality both of teachers and people in the Church of England I affirm of teachers and people of every denomination. I mean, so far as I have known them – and I have known not a few, both in Europe and America. I never saw an unmixed communion yet, unless (perhaps) among the Moravian Brethren, or the Methodists. Yet that God does bless us, even when we receive the Lord's Supper at St. Paul's, I can prove by numberless instances.

If I were in the Church of Rome I *would* conform to all her doctrines and practices, so far as they were not contrary to plain Scripture. And (according to the best of my judgment) I conform so far only to those of the Church of England.

I have largely explained myself in the third volume of *Sermons* touching the stress which I judge is to be laid on opinions. This likewise I have learned by dear experience. However, I thank God that I have learned it at any price.

I am not conscious of embracing any opinion or practice which is not agreeable to the Word of God. And I do believe the doctrines, worship, and discipline (so far as it goes) of the Church of England to be agreeable thereto.

I wish your zeal was better employed than in persuading men to be either dipped or sprinkled. I will employ mine, by the grace of God, in persuading them to love God with all their hearts, and their neighbour as themselves.

I cannot answer it to God to spend any part of that precious time, every hour of which I can employ in what directly tends to the promoting this love among men, in oppugning or defending this or that form of church government. I have 'proved all things' of that kind for more that twenty years: I now 'hold fast that which is good', that which, in my judgment, is not only not contrary to Scripture, but strictly agreeable thereto. But I, upon fixed principle, absolutely refuse to enter into a formal controversy upon the head. Herein I also am at a point. And if on this account you judge me to be a Papist or a Turk, I cannot help it.

I am throughly convinced that you do not speak from anger, but from a zeal for your own opinion and mode of worship. And it might be worthwhile for another man to dispute these points with you. But for me it is not. I am called to other work: not to make Church of England men, or Baptists, but Christians, men of faith and love. That God may fill you therewith is the prayer of, dear sir, your affectionate friend and brother,

JOHN WESLEY

A Conference at Shoreham

(L. Tyerman, *Life and Times of John Wesley*, 1870–71, II, 129–30)

One issue on which the Wesley brothers differed was the status, role and choice of lay itinerant preachers. This was the subject of their discussion at Shoreham, Kent, recorded in Charles Wesley's memorandum.

Mon. Nov. 25, 1751. At Shoreham, agreed with my brother (present Mr. Perronet) to receive or reject preachers. [Here follows a list of nine preachers, including James Wheatley, Michael Fenwick and William Darney, whom they agreed 'to lay aside'.]
With regard to the preachers we agree:

  1. That none shall be permitted to preach in any of our societies till he be examined both as to his grace and gifts; at least by the Assistant, who sending word to us, may by our answer admit him a Local Preacher.

  2. That such preacher be not immediately taken from his trade, but be exhorted to follow it with all diligence.

  3. That no person shall be received as a *Travelling* Preacher, or be taken from his trade, by either of us alone, but by both of us conjointly, giving him a note under both our hands.

  4. That neither of us will re-admit a *Travelling* Preacher laid aside without the consent of the other.

  5. That if we should ever disagree in our judgment, we will refer the matter to Mr. Perronet.

  6. That we will entirely be patterns of all we expect from every preacher, particularly of zeal, diligence, and punctuality in the work; by constantly preaching and meeting the society; by visiting yearly Ireland, Cornwall, and the north; and in general by superintending the whole work, and every branch of it, with all the strength which God shall give us. We agree to the above-written, till this day next year, in the presence of Mr. Perronet.

JOHN WESLEY
CHARLES WESLEY

'Gospel Preaching'

John Wesley to 'an Evangelical Layman'; London, Dec. 20, 1751

(Oxford *Letters*, II, 482–9)

I mean by 'preaching the gospel' preaching the love of God to sinners, preaching the life, death, resurrection, and the intercession of Christ, with all the blessings which in consequence thereof are freely given to true believers.

By 'preaching the law' I mean explaining and enforcing the commands of Christ, briefly comprised in the Sermon on the Mount.

Now it is certain, preaching the gospel to penitent sinners 'begets faith', that it 'sustains and increases spiritual life in true believers'.

Nay, sometimes it 'teaches and guides' them that believe; yea, and 'convinces them that believe not'.

So far all are agreed. But what is the stated means of 'feeding and comforting' believers? What is the means, as of 'begetting spiritual life' where it is not, so of 'sustaining and increasing' it where it is?

Here they divide. Some think, preaching the law only; others, preaching the gospel only. I think, neither the one nor the other, but duly mixing both, in every place, if not in every sermon.

I think the right method of preaching is this. At our first beginning to preach at any place, after a general declaration of the love of God to sinners, and his willingness that they should be saved, to preach the law in the strongest, the closest, the most searching manner possible, only intermixing the gospel here and there, and showing it, as it were, afar off.

After more and more persons are convinced of sin, we may mix more and more of the gospel, in order to 'beget faith', to raise into spiritual life those whom the law hath slain – but this is not to be done too hastily, neither. Therefore it is not expedient wholly to omit the law; not only because we may well suppose that many of our hearers are still unconvinced, but because otherwise there is danger that many who are convinced will heal their own wounds slightly: therefore it is only in private converse with a thoroughly convinced sinner that we should preach nothing but the gospel.

If, indeed, we could suppose a whole congregation to be thus convinced, we should need to preach only the gospel; and the same we might do if our whole congregation were supposed to be newly justified. But when these grow in grace, and in the knowledge of Christ, a wise builder would preach the law to them again, only taking particular care to place every part of it in a gospel light, as not only a command but a privilege also, as a branch of the glorious liberty of the sons of God. He would take equal care to remind them that this is not the cause but the fruit of their acceptance with God; that other cause, 'other foundation can no man lay, than that which is laid, even Jesus Christ'; that we are still forgiven and accepted only for the sake of what he hath done and suffered for us; and that all true obedience springs from love to him, grounded on his first loving us. He would labour, therefore, in preaching any part of the law, to keep the love of Christ continually before their eyes, that thence they might draw fresh life, vigour, and strength to run the way of his commandments.

Thus he would preach the law even to those who were pressing on to the mark. But to those who were careless or drawing back he would preach it in another manner, nearly as he did before they were convinced of sin. To those meanwhile who were earnest, but feeble-minded, he would preach the gospel chiefly, yet variously intermixing more or less of the law according to their various necessities . . .

Not that I would advise to preach the law without the gospel, any more than the gospel without the law. Undoubtedly both should be preached in their turns; yea, both at once, or both in one. All the conditional promises are instances of this: they are law and gospel mixed together.

According to this model I should advise every preacher continually to preach the law: the law grafted upon, tempered by, and animated with the spirit of the gospel. I advise him to declare, explain, and enforce every command of God. But meantime to declare in every sermon (and the more explicitly the better) that the first and great command to a Christian is, 'Believe in the Lord Jesus Christ;' that Christ is all in all, our 'wisdom, righteousness, sanctification, and redemption'; that all life, love, strength, are from him alone, and all freely given to us through faith. And it will ever be found that the law thus preached both enlightens and strengthens the soul; that it both nourishes and teaches; that it is the guide, 'food, medicine, and stay', of the believing soul.

Thus all the apostles built up believers: witness all the epistles of St. Paul, James, Peter, and John. And upon this plan all the Methodists first set out. In this manner not only my brother and I, but Mr Maxfield, Nelson, James Jones, Westell, and Reeves all preached at the beginning.

By this preaching it pleased God to work those mighty effects in London, Bristol, Kingswood, Yorkshire, and Newcastle. By means of this twenty-nine persons received remission of sins in one day at Bristol only, most of them while I was opening and enforcing in this manner our Lord's Sermon upon the Mount.

In this manner John Downes, John Bennet, John Haughton, and all the other Methodists preached till James Wheatley came among them, who never was clear – perhaps not sound – in the faith. According to his understanding was his preaching – an unconnected rhapsody of unmeaning words, like Sir John Suckling's

> Verses, smooth and soft as cream
> In which was neither depth nor stream.

Yet (to the utter reproach of the Methodist congregations) this man became a most popular preacher. He was admired more and more wherever he went, till he went over the second time into Ireland, and conversed more intimately than before with some of the Moravian preachers.

The consequence was that he leaned more and more both to their doctrine and manner of preaching. At first several of our preachers complained of this; but in the space of a few months (so incredible is the force of soft words) he by slow and imperceptible degrees brought almost all the preachers then in the kingdom to think and speak like himself.

These, returning to England, spread the contagion to some others of their brethren. But still the far greater part of the Methodist preachers thought and spoke as they had done from the beginning.

This is the plain fact. As to the fruit of this *new* manner of preaching (entirely new to the Methodists), speaking much of the promises, little of the commands (even to unbelievers, and still less to believers), you think it has done great good. I think it has done great harm ... The 'gospel preachers', so called, corrupt their hearers; they vitiate their taste, so that they cannot relish sound doctrine, and spoil their appetite, so that they cannot turn it into nourishment; they, as it were, feed them with sweetmeats till the genuine wine of the kingdom seems quite insipid to them. They give them cordial upon cordial, which make them all life and spirit for the present; but meantime their appetite is destroyed, so that they can neither retain nor digest the pure milk of the Word ...

This was the very case when I went last into the north. For some time before my coming John Downes had scarce been able to preach *at all* – the three others in the round were such as styled themselves 'gospel preachers'. When I came to review the societies, with great expectation of finding a vast increase, I found most of them lessened by one-third – one entirely broken up. That of Newcastle itself was less by an hundred members than when I visited it before. And of those that remained the far greater number in every place were cold, weary, heartless, dead. Such were the blessed effects of *this* 'gospel-preaching', of this *new* method of 'preaching Christ'!

On the other hand, when in my return I took an account of the societies in Yorkshire, chiefly under the care of John Nelson, one of the *old* way, in whose preaching you could find no life, no food, I found them all alive, strong, and vigorous of soul, believing, loving, and praising God their Saviour; and increased in number from eighteen or nineteen hundred to upwards of three thousand. These had been continually fed with that wholesome food which *you* could neither relish nor digest. From the beginning they had been taught both the law and the gospel: 'God loves *you*: therefore love and obey him. Christ died for *you*: therefore die to sin. Christ is risen: therefore rise in the image of God. Christ liveth evermore: therefore live to God, till you live with him in glory.'

So we preached; and so *you* believed. This is the scriptural way, the *Methodist* way, the true way. God grant we may never turn therefrom to the right hand or to the left!

The First Irish Conference

(Ms Minutes; copy supplied by Dr. Frank Baker)

The first Irish Conference was held at Limerick on August 14–15, 1752. Two manuscript records of it have survived: one by Jacob Rowell on which the following version is based; the other, with a few variants, by Philip Guier, one of those received as an itinerant at this Conference.

Q.1: What is the cause of the general decay of the societies in Ireland? Have they been taught any wrong doctrines? Or has there been want of discipline among them? Or have any of our preachers behaved amiss?

A. All these causes have concurred.

Q.2: What wrong doctrines have been taught?

A. Such as border on antinomianism and Calvinism . . .

With regard to Discipline

Q.1: Have not some of our preachers neglected some of the rules laid down in our former conference?

A. We are resolved, by the grace of God, to keep them for the time to come.

Q2.: If any Assistant neglect his duty, shall the nearest preacher endeavour to supply his neglect?

A. Yes; after he has lovingly told him of his fault, and, secondly, wrote to the next Assistant.

Q.3: What shall a steward or leader do who hears any wrong doctrine preached, or sees any rules broke, either by a preacher or Assistant?

A. Immediately tell the person of his fault, betwixt him and you alone.

Q.4: How shall we avoid speaking evil of each other?

A. (1) Be extremely wary of believing anything you hear before you have spoken to the party concerned.

   (2) Speak to him the first time you see him.

   (3) Till then, tell it to no person whatsoever . . .

Q.7: Should any set up for a preacher in any place without the approbation of an Assistant?

A. By no means. That has already been attended with ill consequences . . .

Q.9: Should the morning preaching be neglected in any place?

A. Of the two, it is better to neglect the evening . . .

Q.12: How shall we set an example to the people of decency in public worship?

A. (1) Let us constantly kneel during prayer; and stand both in singing, and while the text is repeating, etc. (2) Let us be serious and silent while service lasts, and when we are coming and going away.[1]

Q.13: Shall we permit any to be present at the public meeting of the bands who have not band-tickets?

A.   Certainly not. By that means we should make them cheap, and discourage them who are admitted.

Q.14: What if one forget his band or society ticket?

A.   He may come in once; but not if he forget it two times to gether. . .

With regard to the Behaviour of the Preachers

Q.1:   Is there any objection to the behaviour of Thomas Kead?

A.   He hath been charged with idleness and lightness; but we are convinced both these charges are false.

Q.2:   Have not several of the preachers spoke unkindly of each other?

A.   They have; and it has hurt the people extremely. But we hope it will be so no more.

Q.3:   Should we not preach more expressly and strongly on self-denial than we have hitherto done?

A.   By all means; in this kingdom more especially, where it is scarce mentioned or thought of.

Q.4:   Should we not recommend fasting by preaching it?

A.   We should, both frequently and strongly.

Q.5:   Ought we not to practice it ourselves?

A.   Undoubtedly we ought, especially on Friday, if health permit. Nay, we ought to be patterns not barely of temperance, but of abstemiousness of every kind.

Q.6:   What ought we to avoid next to luxury?

A.   Idleness; or it will destroy the whole work of God on the soul. And in order to this, let us spend one hour every day in private prayer.

---

[1] Guier's copy reads: (1) Let us constantly kneel at prayer; and stand during singing, and while the text is repeated. (2) Let us be *serious* and *silent* both while the service lasts, and while we are coming and going out.

Shortcomings of the Early Itinerants

(Diary of Thomas Butts of Bristol; ms at Duke University)

Butts was associated with the Wesleys c. 1744–59 and was one of John Wesley's first book stewards.

Sunday, Dec. 10, 1752. Am clearly convinced the want of study ruins half our preachers. Perhaps one reason of their unwillingness to improve themselves may arise from a misunderstanding of St. John's words: '*Ye have an unction from the Holy One &c* and the same anointing teacheth you all things.' True, but not without the use of all other Helps. No more than the Spirit sanctifies without prayer, or hearing the Word &c. Tis the grossest enthusiasm to think to attain the end without the means. Whoever thus vainly dreams is fitter for a place in Bedlam than to be a Preacher of the Gospel. Without making use of every improvement a man is no ways qualified for the Ministry. The mere emanations of his own mind are no ways adequate to such a work. Be his natural talents ever so great, he will stand in need of all assistance. The want of this 'tis makes their discourses so jejeune, trite & sapless; the same dull round notwithstanding the many different texts they speak from. A horse in a mill keeps going on, but tis the same dull track. So the Congregation may feed and feed, but it must be upon one dish still!

I think Mr. Wesley is highly to blame, in taking so many raw, young fellows from their trades; to a work they are as utterly unqualified for as for ministers of State! . . . Went to the Hall and heard one of our young Preachers. Somewhat better than the last. One great fault in their preaching is allegorising so much. They find wonders where never any was placed. The plain meaning of Scripture is cast aside, and their whims substituted in the room of it. If this is allowed, we shall have Scripture have as many meanings as there are pretended explainers!

The Conference of 1753

(See note on p. 67)

Q.4:   Have not some of us been led off from practical preaching by what was called preaching Christ?

A.   It may be we have. But we find by experience the most effectual way of preaching Christ is to preach him in all his offices, and to declare his law, as well as gospel both to believers and unbelievers.

Q.5: But if we are fully sanctified in this life, shall we then have any need of Christ?

A. Undoubtedly as much as ever: for the only foundation of all holiness is faith in him; a divine conviction that he died and now intercedes, and a divine confidence in God through him.

Q.6: Do we observe any evil which has lately prevailed among our societies?

A. Many of our members have lately married with unbelievers, even such as were wholly unawakened; and this has been attended with fatal consequences. Few of these have gained the unbelievers, wives or husbands. Generally they have themselves either had a grievous cross for life, or have entirely fallen back into the world . . .

Q.8: Do not sabbath-breaking, dram-drinking, evil-speaking, unprofitable conversation, lightness, and contracting debts without sufficient care to discharge them, prevail in many places? And what method can we take to remove these growing evils?

A. (1) Let us preach expressly and strongly on each of these heads. (2) Let the leaders closely examine their several classes, and exhort every single person to put away the accursed thing. (3) Let the preacher warn the society in every place that none who is hereafter guilty can remain with us. (4) In order to give them clearer views of these and all other branches of practical religion, let every preacher recommend to every society the reading our books preferably to any other; and when any new book is sent to any place, let him give notice in the public congregation.

The Twelve Rules of a Helper

These rules for Wesley's lay preachers originated in the minutes of the first Conference, but were reprinted in amended form in 1753. Words enclosed in square brackets in the 1744 version represent variations made in Wesley's hand to John Bennet's version of the Minutes.

1744	1753
Q. What are the Rules of an Assistant?	Q. What are the Rules of a Helper?
1. Be diligent, never be unemployed a moment, never be triflingly employed, [never while away time]	1. Be diligent, never be unemployed a moment, never be triflingly employed. Never while away time, nor

spend no more time at any
place than is strictly
necessary.

2. Be serious. Let your motto
be 'Holiness unto the Lord'.
Avoid all lightness as you
would avoid hell-fire, and
laughing as you would
cursing and swearing.

3. Touch no woman: be as
loving as you will, but
hold your hands off 'em.
Custom is nothing to us.

4. Believe evil of no one.
If you see it done, well:
else take heed how you
credit it. Put the best
construction on every thing.
You know the judge is always
allowed [supposed] to be
on the prisoner's side.

5. Speak evil of no one: else
your word especially would
eat as doth a canker. Keep
your thoughts within your
[own] breast, till you come
to the person concerned.

6. Tell everyone what you think
wrong in him, and that
plainly, and as soon as may
be, else it will fester in
your heart. Make all haste,
therefore, to cast the fire
out of your bosom.

7. Do nothing as a gentleman:
you have no more to do with
this character than with
that of a dancing master.
You are the servant of all
therefore.

spend more time at any place
than is strictly necessary.

2. Be serious. Let your motto
be 'Holiness to the Lord'.
Avoid all lightness, jesting,
and foolish talking.

3. Converse sparingly and
cautiously with women,
particularly with young
women.

4. Take no step towards
marriage without solemn
prayer to God, and
consulting with your
Brethren.

5. Believe evil of no one
unless fully proved: take
heed how you credit it.
Put the best construction
you can on everything. You
know the Judge is always
supposed to be on the
prisoner's side.

6. Speak evil of no one: else
your word, especially,
would eat as doth a canker.
Keep your thoughts within
your own breast till you
come to the person concerned.

7. Tell everyone what you
think wrong in him,
lovingly and plainly: and
as soon as may be, else it
will fester in your own
heart. Make all haste to
cast the fire out of your
bosom.

8. Do not affect the gentleman.
A Preacher of the Gospel is
the servant of all.

(Rules of a Helper: 2)

8. Be ashamed of nothing but sin: not of fetching wood, or drawing water, if time permit; not of cleaning your own shoes or your neighbour's.

9. Take no money of anyone. If they give you food when you are hungry, or clothes when you need them, it is good. But not silver or gold. Let there be no pretence to say, we grow rich by the Gospel.

10. Contract no debt without my knowledge.

11. Be punctual: do everything exactly at the time: and in general do not mend our rules, but keep them, not for wrath but for conscience sake.

12. Act in all things not according to your own will but as a son in the Gospel. As such, it it your part to employ your time in the manner which we direct: partly in visiting the flock from house to house (the sick in particular): partly in such a course of Reading, Meditation and Prayer, as we advise from time to time. Above all if you labour with us in our Lord's vineyard, it is needful you should do that part of the work [which]

9. Be ashamed of nothing but sin; no, not of cleaning your own shoes, when necessary.

10. Be punctual. Do everything exactly at the time. And do not mend our Rules, but keep them: and that for conscience' sake.

11. You have nothing to do but to save souls. Therefore spend and be spent in this work. And go always, not only to those who want you but to those who want you most.[1]

12. Act in all things, not according to your own will, but as a son in the Gospel, and in union with your Brethren. As such, it is your part to employ your time as our Rules direct: partly in preaching and visiting from house to house; partly in reading, meditation and prayer. Above all, if you labour with us in our Lord's vineyard, it is needful that you should do that part of the work which

we prescribe [direct] at those times and places which we judge most for His glory.

the Conference shall advise at those times and places which they shall judge most for His glory. Observe: It is not your business to preach so many times, and to take care merely of this or that Society, but to save as many souls as you can: to bring as many sinners as you possibly can to repentance: and, with all your power, to build them up in that holiness without which they cannot see the Lord. And remember, a Methodist Preacher is to mind every point, great and small, in Methodist Discipline. Therefore you will need all the grace and all the sense you have, and to have all your wits about you.

¹ This rule was added at the Conference of 1745.

Methodism and the Established Church

The question of separation from the Church of England came to a head in 1755. Charles Wesley was increasingly suspicious of the intentions of most of the itinerants and enlisted the support of clerical friends such as Walker of Truro and Walter Sellon of Ashby-de-la-Zouch in an effort to keep his brother loyal to the Church. The eventual outcome was the publication of *Reasons against a Separation from the Church of England* in 1758 (pp. 128–34 below).

Letters from Charles Wesley to the Rev. Walter Sellon

(Mss at Drew University)

Sellon was a protégé of the Countess of Huntingdon and vicar of Ashby-de-la-Zouch, Leics. He supported the Wesleys in the Calvinistic controversy of 1770.

Nov. 29, 1754

I have seen your honest friendly letter to C[harles] P[erronet], for which I thank you on behalf of myself and the Church of England.

You see through him & his fellows. Pride, cursed pride has perverted him & them; & unless the Lord interpose will destroy the Work of God & scatter us all as sheep upon the mountains.

In your fidelity to my old honoured Mother you are a man after my own heart. I always loved you, but never so much as now.

O pray on for the peace of Jerusalem. They shall prosper that love her. I know you wish her prosperity. You think upon her stones and it pityeth you to see her in the dust.

How unlike the spirit of poor Perronet & his associates! What a pity such spirits should have any influence over my brother! They are continually urging him to a separation, that is to pull down all he has built, to put a sword in our enemies' hands, to destroy the Work, scatter the flock, disgrace himself, & go out – like the snuff of a candle.

May I not desire it of you, as a debt you owe the Methodists & me, & the Church as well as him, to write him a full, close, plain transcript of your heart on the occasion. C.P. you know has taken upon him to administer the Sacrament for a month together to the preachers & twice to some of the people. Walsh & three others have followed his vile example. The consequence you see with open eyes. O that my brother did so too! Our worthy friend at Clifton could not but believe my brother had *laid on hands*, or they would not have dared to act thus. You have her thoughts in mine.

I have heard *your* sincerity called in question as if you ran with the hare & held with the hounds. I don't believe a word of it; as this letter proves. Only let me caution you not to communicate this to anyone.

Inclose, if you think proper, your letter to my brother in one to me, at Saml. Lloyd's Esqr in Devonshire Square. I shall not grudge double postage.

Write to my Lady also, that you may have her mind from herself.

You *must* make one at our Conference in Leeds, which will be in May. I give you timely notice.

Pray for us. I stand alone: as other preachers imagine. Nonetheless, the Lord stands by me. Fain would they thrust me out, that they may carry all before them.

The Lord Jesus bless & keep you unto that Day!

London, Dec. 14, 1754

Write again & spare not. My brother took no notice to me of your letter. Since the Melchizedechians have been taken in I have been excluded his Cabinet Counsel. They know me too well to trust him with me. He is come so far as to believe a separation quite lawful; only not yet expedient. They are indefatigable in urging him to go so far that he may not be able to retreat. He may *lay on hands*, say they without separating. I charge you keep it to yourself that *I stand in doubt of him*: which I tell you that you may pray for him the more earnestly, & write to him the more plainly.

In May our Conference is. You must be there, if alive.

Direct to my brother at the F[oundery]; to me at Sam. Lloyd's Esqr. in Devonshire Square.

We can hold it no longer (the Methodist preachers, I mean), but must quickly divide to the right or left, the Church or Meeting. God be praised for this, that Satan is dragged out to do his worst, while we are yet living to look him in the face.

I know none fitter for training up the young men in learning than yourself or J. Jones. We must, among us, get the sound preachers qualified for Orders . . .

London, Feb. 4, 1755

There is no danger of *my* countenancing them, but rather of my opposing them too fiercely. 'Tis pity a good cause should suffer by a warm advocate. If God gives me meekness, I shall at the Conference speak & not spare. Till then 'tis best the matter should sleep; or we should make the delinquents desperate, & their associates among the preachers hypocrites.

My brother purposely holds his peace, that he may come to the bottom of them. Your letters (& some others wrote with the same honesty) have had the due effect on him, & made him forget he was ever inclined to their party. He has spoken as strongly of late in behalf of the Church of England, as I could wish: and everywhere declares he never intends to leave her. This has made the Melchizedechians draw in their horns & drop their design. *Sed non ego credulus illis!*[1] We *must* know the heart of every preacher & give them their choice, of the Church or meeting. The wound can no longer be healed slightly. Those who are disposed to separate had best do it while we are yet alive.

It seems not so proper to shew my brother your last to me. Write to him again & urge it upon his conscience whether he is not bound to prevent a separation, both before & after his death? Whether in order to this, he should not take the utmost pains to settle the preachers, discharging those who are irreclaimable & never receiving another without this previous condition, 'that he will never leave the Church'?

He is writing an excellent treatise on the question, Whether it is expedient to separate from the C. of E.? Which he talks of printing.

Be very mild & loving in your next, lest he should still say, 'The Separatists shew a better spirit than their opposers.' You may *honestly suppose* him now of our mind.

I will answer for your admission to the Conference at Leeds in the beginning of May . . .

Is not Nich. Norton under the influence of Cha. Perronet? . . .

I am setting out for Bristol. Direct to me at the Horsefair.

Keep copies of yours to my Brother.

J. Jones will thank you for a title. W. Prior, I suppose you know, is ordained: without learning, interest or aught but Providence to recommend him . . .

The Lord of the harvest is thrusting out labourers in diverse places. Mr. Romain, Venn, Dodd, Jones & others here are much blest. Pray for them as well as us. The Lord be your strength.

¹ Virgil, *Eclogues* 9.34: 'I am not disposed to trust them.'

The Rev. Samuel Walker to John Wesley, Sept. 5, 1755

This letter has survived in several variant copies, including one at Emory University; see Oxford *Letters*, II, 582–6, and for Wesley's reply, ibid, 592–6.

I venture to say you must (1) Be determined in your own breast whether it be lawful to separate or no. (2) What is and what is not separation. (3) Supposing you determine it is not lawful, whether you have taken any steps towards it already. (4) If so, and separation be unlawful, whether you ought not prudently to put a stop to them. (5) In this view, what you are to do with the lay preachers. This I know is a tender point. But methinks it comes into the very heart of the question. For is it not likely that a handle hath been given from hence to press a separation? Perhaps some of the preachers may have been seeking it: doubtless there being such persons raised a desire of their being ordained in those of your people who contend for a separation. Now if the laws of the Church of England admit not such preachers, then herein is a step made in separation, and that whatever necessity there may be of them.

Put this together and may you not have cause to think, that either you will not be able to stop a separation, or must somehow or other stop these preachers? As long as they remain there is a beginning of separation, and that also which will continually keep the people in mind of it. I am only, you will be pleased to observe, stating the case, not offering any advice, which I would by no means presume to do in so nice a matter. If you say, I dare not separate from the Church, what will you do with the lay preachers? If you dare not lay aside the lay preachers, how will you prevent a separation in part begun already in them? You must needs come to some resolution of this point, and I pray God to direct you to that which may be most for his glory. That middle way you have trod of permitting, not appointing, them, puts the matter quite out of your hands and deprives you of all your influence. If you are persuaded that they are extraordinarily called, and that there is such a necessity as justifies a separation and departure from the laws of the Church in this particular, why should you not appoint them to preach and so keep them under your own direction? . . .

Remember, Sir, how needful it is something should be done in your lifetime. Is there not much cause to fear that otherwise there will be little peace afterwards? . . .

Now as to any expediency, the lawfulness of the separation supposed, that the Methodists separate, the enquiry is, To what end? Will it probably promote, or probably hinder, the interests of Christ's kingdom? I submit these enquiries to your consideration.

1. Will it be likely to make the Body of Methodists into more confirmed Christians? If it be said, 'Yes, for hereby they will not hear God's Word badly taught, nor be present at a slovenly performance of his worship, and will have the Word and worship in Gospel purity and simplicity;' it must be weighed on the other hand, how many will be hurt by dispute, how teachers sufficient in number or ability may be found for the several congregations, how discipline can be preserved so as that the Word and worship shall be done to edification. Whether the Methodists will not be more apt to decay, being then either left quietly alone or attacked, for their separation, not their practice as now, which will have an evident tendency to make them rest upon their separation &c. &c.

2. Will it render the Methodists more useful to others? There is not the least appearance of it: but just the contrary. Hereby Methodists will come insensibly to separate themselves from all conversation with others. Hereby others will be afraid of them; and few will come near them.

3. What effect will it probably have upon bystanders? (i) Upon those ministers who are zealous for the power of godliness? Will it not throw a prodigious objection in their way, and put it more out of their power to preserve the interests of religion by any schemes which are not common, particularly by Societies? This seems an important matter as many are raised up of this sort, and there is good hope of many more. (ii) Upon those who are coming near the truth? Can it be expected they will not stumble at it? (iii) Upon the Infidels and Socinians? Will they not be glad they are fairly rid of you? (iv) Upon every man in England who would do service? Will it not be a bar to him? (v) Upon every careless sinner? Will it not supply him with somewhat to defend himself?

On all these accounts a separation seems inexpedient. But on the other hand there is a strong expediency (i) That the Methodists should remain in the Church and that with the strictest observance possible of all the laws of it. The more regular they are, the readier access will they gain, and the more evidently will the difference appear where we should always endeavour to make it seen, in the power and practice of godliness. (ii) That if any of them depart, you, Sir, do not follow them, but declare publicly against it. Such a conduct in you would probably reconcile the hearts of multitudes to you, and those who should abide with you in the Church; while for my own part (and I dare believe I speak the general desire of the kingdom) I should make little account of the separatists.

Death of the Unconverted

(Ms diary of Thomas Illingworth, Duke University)

Illingworth was a weaver turned schoolteacher of Silsden and Yeadon, Yorks. The diary covers the years 1755–59 and ends as he was about to leave for London. Here is grassroots Methodism.

Friday, October 10, 1755: On Thursday night, just as we were beginning for the evening, a young woman came in and told us of a fatal accident that had happened that day. A young man as he went to the coalpit had his hat tied on with the Wantey.[1] The horse stumbling or falling he fell off and the horse ran away, dragging him after that so he was both hanged and almost beat in pieces. After she'd related the story she said, Misfortunes would happen. I said, Death was not always misfortune. She said, No, she hoped it was not to him. I asked her what reason she had to hope so. Well, she said, he was a quiet lad. I said that was only a natural qualification; did she ever hear that he was converted? She said, Nay, she did not think he was. I said what would she say if I should say, if he was not converted he was as surely in Hell as the Devil was. Some of them seemed astonished, but after reasoning a little with them they had nothing to say against it.

[1] Want[e]y: a rope or band used to fasten the pack on a pack-saddle or the load on the back of a horse.

The Doctrine of Assurance

Samuel Walker to Charles Wesley, August 16, 1756

(Ms at Emory University)

I could wish there might be a reconsideration of that matter respecting *assurance*. I take it, the way wherein your brother states faith, or the witness of the Spirit, to be unscriptural and unsafe. I have examined all he has said about it, but find no warrant of God's word, whereon it's built; especially, I am not satisfied with the proofs produced in the *Minutes of Conversation* &c. which seem to me directly to make against it. I do not quarrel at sensible feelings, they are proper in their place. But faith and feeling appear to me direct opposites, & feeling alone cannot be the witness of the Spirit. I don't say that people that make more of sensible feelings than I do are not right, or suppose there may not be a true work under them: but as the thing is stated, it seems to me dangerous and often uncomfortable. That we are justified by faith alone, or by the merits of Christ applied by faith, is as clear as the sun. But then what is that faith and the witness of the Spirit? I wish this matter might be reconsidered. I think there are many ill consequences arising from his manner of stating it. I fancy were this matter regulated the Methodists would be more useful, and in their classes more benefited. Believe me, dear Sir, I say not this from a spirit of opposition: but simply for the promoting the interests of true, vital Christianity among the Methodists and by them.

Sunday Worship

John Wesley to 'a Friend'; Truro, September 20, 1757

(*JWL*, III, 226–8)

Dear Sir, – The longer I am absent from London, and the more I attend the service of the Church in other places, the more I am convinced of the unspeakable advantage which the people called Methodists enjoy: I mean even with regard to public worship, particularly on the Lord's Day. The church where they assemble is not gay or splendid, which might be an hindrance on the one hand; nor sordid or dirty, which might give distaste on the other; but plain as well as clean. The persons who assemble there are not a gay, giddy crowd, who come chiefly to see and be seen; nor a company of goodly, formal, outside Christians, whose religion lies in a dull round of duties; but a people most of whom do, and the rest earnestly seek to, worship God in spirit and in truth. Accordingly they do not spend their time there in bowing and courtesying, or in staring about them, but in looking upward and looking inward, in hearkening to the voice of God, and pouring out their hearts before Him.

It is also no small advantage that the person who reads prayers, though not always the same, yet is always one who may be supposed to speak from his heart, one whose life is no reproach to his profession, and one who performs that solemn part of divine service, not in a careless, hurrying, slovenly manner, but seriously and slowly, as becomes him who is transacting so high an affair between God and man.

Nor are their solemn addresses to God interrupted either by the formal drawl of a parish clerk, the screaming of boys who bawl out what they neither feel nor understand, or the unseasonable and unmeaning impertinence of a voluntary on the organ. When it is seasonable to sing praise to God, they do it with the spirit and with the understanding also; not in the miserable, scandalous doggerel of Hopkins and Sternhold, but in psalms and hymns which are both sense and poetry, such as would sooner provoke a critic to turn Christian than a Christian to turn critic. What they sing is therefore a proper continuation of the spiritual and reasonable service; being selected for that end, not by a poor humdrum wretch who can scarce read what he drones out with such an air of importance, but by one who knows what he is about and how to connect the preceding with the following part of the service. Nor does he take just 'two staves,' but more or less, as may best raise the soul to God; especially when sung in well-composed and well-adapted tunes, not by an handful of wild, unawakened striplings, but by an whole serious congregation; and these not lolling at ease, or in the indecent posture of sitting, drawling out one word after another, but all standing before God, and praising Him lustily and with a good courage.

Nor is it a little advantage as to the next part of the service to hear a preacher whom you know to live as he speaks, speaking the genuine gospel of present salvation through faith, wrought in the heart by the Holy Ghost, declaring present, free, full justification, and enforcing every branch of inward and outward holiness. And this you hear done in the most clear, plain, simple, unaffected language, yet with an earnestness becoming the importance of the subject and with the demonstration of the Spirit.

With regard to the last and most awful part of divine service, the celebration of the Lord's Supper, although we cannot say that either the unworthiness of the minister or the unholiness of some of the communicants deprives the rest of a blessing from God, yet do they greatly lessen the comfort of receiving. But these discouragements are removed from you: you have proof that he who administers fears God; and you have no reason to believe that any of your fellow communicants walk unworthy of their profession. Add to this that the whole service is performed in a decent and solemn manner, is enlivened by hymns suitable to the occasion, and concluded with prayer that comes not out of feigned lips.

Surely, then, of all the people in Great Britain, the Methodists would be the most inexcusable, should they let any opportunity slip of attending that worship which has so many advantages, should they prefer any before it, or not continually improve by the advantages they enjoy! What can be pleaded for them, if they do not worship God in spirit and in truth, if they are still outward worshippers only, approaching God with their lips while their hearts are far from Him – yea, if, having known Him, they do not daily grow in grace and in the knowledge of our Lord Jesus Christ?

Smollett on Methodism, 1757

(Tobias Smollett, *History of England from the Revolution to the Death of George the Second*, new edition, with the author's last corrections and improvements, 1790, Vol. V, pp. 375–6)

The progress of reason, and free cultivation of the human mind, had not, however, entirely banished those ridiculous sects and schisms of which the kingdom had been formerly so productive. Imposture and fanaticism still hung upon the skirts of religion. Weak minds were seduced by the delusions of a superstition stiled Methodism, raised upon the affection of superior sanctity, and maintained by pretentions to divine illumination. Many thousands in the lower ranks of life were infected with this species of enthusiasm, by the unwearied endeavours of a few obscure preachers, such as Whit[e]field, and the two Wesleys, who propagated their doctrines to the most remote corners of the British dominions, and found means to lay the whole kingdom under contribution.

Reasons Against a Separation from the Church of England

(*JWW*, XIII, 193–200; *PW*, VI, 103)

This was John Wesley's considered verdict on the question of separation. It was written in the year 1758, towards the end of the decade in which it had been much debated. His brother's hymn was one of seven added to some editions of the *Reasons*.

I. Whether it be lawful or no (which itself may be disputed, being not so clear a point as some may imagine), it is by no means expedient, for us to separate from the established Church:—

(1) Because it would be a contradiction to the solemn and repeated declarations which we have made in all manner of ways, in preaching, in print, and in private conversation.

(2) Because (on this as well as on many other accounts) it would give huge occasion of offence to those who seek and desire occasion, to all the enemies of God and his truth.

(3) Because it would exceedingly prejudice against us many who fear, yea, who love, God, and thereby hinder their receiving so much, perhaps any farther, benefit from our preaching.

(4) Because it would hinder multitudes of those who neither love nor fear God from hearing us at all.

(5) Because it would occasion many hundreds, if not some thousands, of those who are now united with us, to separate from us; yea, and some of those who have a deep work of grace in their souls.

(6) Because it would be throwing balls of wild-fire among them that are now quiet in the land. We are now sweetly united together in love. We mostly think and speak the same thing. But this would occasion inconceivable strife and contention, between those who left, and those who remained in, the Church; as well as between those who left us, and those who remained with us; nay, and between those very persons who remained, as they were variously inclined one way or the other.

(7) Because, whereas controversy is now asleep, and we in great measure live peaceably with all men, so that we are strangely at leisure to spend our whole time and strength in enforcing plain, practical, vital religion, (O what would many of our forefathers have given, to have enjoyed so blessed a calm!) this would utterly banish peace from among us, and that without hope of its return. It would engage me, for one, in a thousand controversies, both in public and private; (for I should be in conscience obliged to give the reasons of my conduct, and to defend those reasons against all opposers;) and so take me off from those more

useful labours which might otherwise employ the short remainder of my life.

(8) Because to form the plan of a new church would require infinite time and care (which might be far more profitably bestowed), with much more wisdom and greater depth and extensiveness of thought than any of us are masters of.

(9) Because from some having barely entertained a distant thought of this, evil fruits have already followed; such as prejudice against the Clergy in general, and aptness to believe ill of them; contempt (not without a degree of bitterness) of Clergymen, as such; and a sharpness of language toward the whole order, utterly unbecoming either gentlemen or Christians.

(10) Because the experiment has been so frequently tried already, and the success never answered the expectation. God has since the Reformation raised up from time to time many witnesses of pure religion. If these lived and died (like John Arndt, Robert Bolton, and many others) in the churches to which they belonged, notwithstanding the wickedness which overflowed both the Teachers and people therein, they spread the leaven of true religion far and wide, and were more and more useful, till they went to paradise. But if, upon any provocation or consideration whatever, they separated, and founded distinct parties, their influence was more and more confined; they grew less and less useful to others, and generally lost the spirit of religion themselves in the spirit of controversy.

(11) Because we have melancholy instances of this, even now before our eyes. Many have in our memory left the Church, and formed themselves into distinct bodies. And certainly some of them from a real persuasion that they should do God more service. But have any separated themselves and prospered? Have they been either more holy, or more useful, than they were before?

(12) Because by such a separation we should not only throw away the peculiar glorying which God has given us, that we do and will suffer all things for our brethren's sake, though the more we love them, the less we be loved; but should act in direct contradiction to that very end for which we believe God hath raised us up. The chief design of His providence in sending us out is, undoubtedly, to quicken our brethren. And the first message of all our Preachers is, to the lost sheep of the Church of England. Now, would it not be a flat contradiction to this design, to separate from the Church? These things being considered, we cannot apprehend (whether it be lawful in itself or no) that it is lawful for us; were it only on this ground, that it is by no means expedient.

II. It has indeed been objected, that till we do separate, we cannot be a compact, united body.

It is true, we cannot till then be 'a compact, united body', if you mean by that expression, a body distinct from all others. And we have no desire so to be.

It has been objected, secondly, 'It is mere cowardice and fear of persecution which makes you desire to remain united with them.'

This cannot be proved. Let every one examine his own heart, and not judge his brother.

It is not probable. We never yet, for any persecution, when we were in the midst of it, either turned back from the work, or even slackened our pace.

But this is certain; that although persecution many times proves an unspeakable blessing to them that suffer it, yet we ought not wilfully to bring it upon ourselves. Nay, we ought to do whatever can lawfully be done, in order to prevent it. We ought to avoid it so far as we lawfully can; when persecuted in one city, to flee into another. If God should suffer a general persecution, who would be able to abide it we know not. Perhaps those who talk loudest might flee first. Remember the case of Dr. Pendleton.

III. Upon the whole, one cannot but observe how desirable it is, that all of us who are engaged in the same work should think and speak the same thing, be united in one judgment, and use one and the same language.

Do we not all now see ourselves, the Methodists (so called) in general, the Church and the Clergy, in a clear light?

We look upon ourselves, not as the authors or ringleaders of a particular sect or party; (it is the farthest thing from our thoughts;) but as messengers of God to those who are Christians in name, but Heathens in heart and in life, to call them back to that from which they are fallen, to real genuine Christianity. We are therefore debtors to all these, of whatever opinion or denomination; and are consequently to do all that in us lies, to please all for their good, to edification.

We look upon the Methodists (so called) in general, not as any particular party; (this would exceedingly obstruct the grand design, for which we conceive God has raised them up;) but as living witnesses, in and to every party, of that Christianity which we preach; which is hereby demonstrated to be a real thing, and visibly held out to all the world.

We look upon England as that part of the world, and the Church as that part of England, to which all we who are born and have been brought up therein, owe our first and chief regard. We feel in ourselves a strong στοργή, a kind of natural affection for our country, which we apprehend Christianity was never designed either to root out or to impair. We have a more peculiar concern for our brethren, for that part of our countrymen to whom we have been joined from our youth up, by ties of a religious as well as a civil nature. True it is, that they are, in general, 'without God in the world:' So much the more do our bowels yearn over them. They do lie 'in darkness and the shadow of death:' The more tender is our compassion for them. And when we have the fullest conviction of that complicated wickedness which covers them as a flood, then do we feel the most (and we desire to feel yet more) of that inexpressible emotion with which our blessed Lord beheld Jerusalem, and wept and lamented over it. Then are we the most willing 'to spend and to be spent' for them; yea, to 'lay down our lives for our brethren.'

We look upon the Clergy, not only as a part of these our brethren, but as that part whom God by His adorable providence has called to be watchmen over the rest, for whom therefore they are to give a strict account. If these then neglect their important charge, if they do not watch over them with all their power, they will be of all most miserable, and so are entitled to our deepest compassion. So that to feel, and much more to express, either contempt or bitterness towards them, betrays an utter ignorance of ourselves and of the spirit which we especially should be of.

Because this is a point of uncommon concern, let us consider it a little farther.

(1) The Clergy, wherever we are, are either friends to the truth, or neuters, or enemies to it.

If they are friends to it, certainly we should do everything, and omit everything we can with a safe conscience, in order to continue, and, if it be possible, increase, their good-will to it.

If they neither further nor hinder it, we should do all that in us lies, both for their sakes and for the sake of their several flocks, to give their neutrality the right turn, that it may change into love rather than hatred.

If they are enemies, still we should not despair of lessening, if not removing, their prejudice. We should try every means again and again; we should employ all our care, labour, prudence, joined with fervent prayer, to overcome evil with good, to melt their hardness into love.

It is true, that when any of these openly wrest the Scriptures, and deny the grand truths of the Gospel, we cannot but declare and defend, at convenient opportunities, the important truths which they deny. But in this case especially we have need of all gentleness and meekness of wisdom. Contempt, sharpness, bitterness, can do no good. 'The wrath of man worketh not the righteousness of God.' Harsh methods have been tried again and again (by two or three unsettled railers) at Wednesbury, St. Ives, Cork, Canterbury. And how did they succeed? They always occasioned numberless evils; often wholly stopped the course of the Gospel. Therefore, were it only on a prudential account, were conscience unconcerned therein, it should be a sacred rule to all our Preachers, – 'No contempt, no bitterness, to the Clergy.'

(2) Might it not be another (at least, prudential) rule for every Methodist Preacher, not to frequent any Dissenting meeting? (Though we blame none who have been always accustomed to it.) But if we do this, certainly our people will. Now, this is actually separating from the Church. If, therefore, it is (at least) not expedient to separate, neither is this expedient. Indeed, we may attend our assemblies, and the church too; because they are at different hours. But we cannot attend both the meeting and the church, because they are at the same hours.

If it be said, 'But at the church we are fed with chaff, whereas at the meeting we have wholesome food;' we answer, (i.) The prayers of the Church are not chaff; they are substantial food for any who are alive to God. (ii.) The Lord's Supper is not chaff, but pure and wholesome for all who receive it with upright hearts. Yea, (iii.) In almost all the sermons we hear there, we hear many great and important truths: And whoever has a spiritual discernment, may easily separate the chaff from the wheat therein. (iv.) How little is the case mended at the meeting! Either the Teachers are 'new light' men, denying the Lord that bought them, and overturning His Gospel from the very foundations; or they are Predestinarians, and so preach predestination and final perseverance, more or less. Now, whatever this may be to them who were educated therein, yet to those of our brethren who have lately embraced it, repeated experience shows it is not wholesome food; rather, to them it has the effect of deadly poison. In a short time it destroys all their zeal for God. They grow fond of opinions, and strife of words; they despise self-denial and the daily cross; and, to complete all, wholly separate from their brethren.

(3) Nor is it expedient for any Methodist Preacher to imitate the Dissenters in their manner of praying; either in his tone, – all particular tones both in prayer and preaching should be avoided with the utmost care; nor in his language, – all his words should be plain and simple, such as the lowest of his hearers both use and understand; or in the length of his prayer, which should not usually exceed four or five minutes, either before or after sermon. One might add, neither should we sing like them, in a slow, drawling manner: We sing swift, both because it saves time, and because it tends to awake and enliven the soul.

(4) If we continue in the Church, not by chance, or for want of thought, but upon solid and well-weighed reasons, then we should never speak contemptuously of the Church, or anything pertaining to it. In some sense it is the mother of us all, who have been brought up therein. We ought never to make her blemishes matter of diversion, but rather of solemn sorrow before God. We ought never to talk ludicrously of them; no, not at all, without clear necessity. Rather, we should conceal them, as far as ever we can, without bringing guilt upon our own conscience. And we should all use every rational and scriptural means,

to bring others to the same temper and behaviour. I say, 'all'; for if some of us are thus minded, and others of an opposite spirit and behaviour, this will breed a real schism among ourselves. It will of course divide us into two parties; each of which will be liable to perpetual jealousies, suspicions, and animosities against the other. Therefore, on this account likewise, it is expedient, in the highest degree, that we should be tender of the Church to which we belong.

(5) In order to secure this end, to cut off all jealousy and suspicion from our friends, and hope from our enemies, of our having any design to separate from the Church, it would be well for every Methodist Preacher, who has no scruple concerning it, to attend the service of the Church as often as conveniently he can. And the more we attend it, the more we love it, as constant experience shows. On the contrary, the longer we abstain from it, the less desire we have to attend it at all.

(6) Lastly. Whereas we are surrounded on every side by those who are equally enemies to us and to the Church of England; and whereas these are long practised in this war, and skilled in all the objections against it; while our brethren, on the other hand, are quite strangers to them all, and so, on a sudden, know not how to answer them; it is highly expedient for every Preacher to be provided with sound answers to those objections, and then to instruct the societies where he labours, how to defend themselves against those assaults. It would be therefore well for you carefully to read over the 'Preservative against unsettled Notions in Religion', together with 'Serious Thoughts concerning Perseverance', and 'Predestination calmly considered'. And when you are masters of them yourselves, it will be easy for you to recommend and explain them to our societies; that they may 'no more be tossed to and fro by every wind of doctrine;' but, being settled in one mind and one judgment by solid scriptural and rational arguments, 'may grow up in all things into Him who is our Head, even Jesus Christ.'

JOHN WESLEY

I think myself bound in duty to add my testimony to my brother's. His twelve reasons against our ever separating from the Church of England are mine also. I subscribe to them with all my heart. Only, with regard to the first, I am quite clear that it is neither expedient nor lawful for me to separate; and I never had the least inclination or temptation so to do. My affection for the Church is as strong as ever; and I clearly see my calling; which is, to live and to die in her communion. This, therefore, I am determined to do, the Lord being my Helper.

I have subjoined the Hymns for the Lay Preachers; still farther to secure this end, to cut off all jealousy and suspicion from our friends, or hope from our enemies, of our having any design of ever separating from the Church. I have no secret reserve, or distant thought of it. I never had. Would to God all the Methodist Preachers were, in this respect, like-minded with

CHARLES WESLEY.

HYMN IV

1 Master, at Thy command we rise,
 No prophets we, or prophets' sons,
Or mighty, or well-born, or wise;
 But quicken'd clods, but breathing stones,
Urged to cry out, constrain'd to call,
And tell mankind – He died for all!

2 We speak, because *they* hold their peace,
 Who *should* Thy dying love proclaim:
We *must* declare Thy righteousness,
 Thy truth, and power, and saving name,
Though the dumb ass with accent clear
Rebuke the silence of the seer.

3 But shall we e'er ourselves forget,
 And in our gifts and graces trust,
With wild contempt the prophets treat,
 Proudly against the branches boast,
Or dare the rulers vilify,
Or mock the priests of God most high?

4 *Let them alone*, Thy wisdom cries,
 If blind conductors of the blind!
Let them alone, our heart replies,
 And draws us to the work assign'd,
The work of publishing the word,
And seizing sinners for our Lord.

5 Here let us spend our utmost zeal,
 Here let us all our powers exert,
To testify Thy gracious will,
 Inform the world how kind Thou art,
And nothing know, desire, approve,
But Jesus – and Thy bleeding love.

Methodism in Shoreham, Kent, 1758

Vincent Perronet's answer to Archbishop Secker

(Lambeth Palace Library)

The Archbishop's questionnaire at his primary Visitation of the Canterbury diocese furnished an opportunity for a homily on the nature of Methodism.

There are no Dissenters, but one *Baptist* only. As to *Methodists* – there are five or six serious *Church*-people, of low rank, who, together with my own Family, are distinguished by that name.

I have for many years observed, my Lord, that when any persons have appeared deeply serious and earnestly solicitous about their salvation, they have received this name, by way of reproach, However, *such Methodists*, my Lord, and *such Methodism*, I shall always endeavour to encourage. Indeed, some years ago, there were many more joined in Society; but the Rules being too strict, they dropped off. For no *tippler*, no *card-player*, no *breaker* of any part of the *Sabbath*, or of any other *Divine Command*, can be a member of that Society. There is one, however, who has still the courage to refuse following his profession on the Lord's Day: though he has for many years lost the greatest part of his bread by it; and had a very large family when he first ventured upon it.

Thoughts on Christian Perfection

Reprinted in Wesley's *Plain Account of Christian Perfection*, 1766

(*JWW*, XI, 394–406)

19. At the Conference in the year 1759, perceiving some danger that a diversity of sentiments should insensibly steal in among us, we again largely considered this doctrine; and soon after I published 'Thoughts on Christian Perfection', prefaced with the following advertisement:—

The following tract is by no means designed to gratify the curiosity of any man. It is not intended to prove the doctrine at large, in opposition to those who explode and ridicule it; no, nor to answer the numerous objections against it, which may be raised even by serious men. All I intend here is, simply to declare what are my sentiments on this head; what Christian perfection does, according to my apprehension, include, and what it does not; and to add a few practical observations and directions relative to the subject.

As these thoughts were at first thrown together by way of question and answer, I let them continue in the same form. They are just the same that I have entertained for above twenty years.

QUESTION. What is Christian perfection?

ANSWER. The loving God with all our heart, mind, soul, and strength. This implies, that no wrong temper, none contrary to love, remains in the soul; and that all the thoughts, words, and actions, are governed by pure love.

Q. Do you affirm, that this perfection excludes all infirmities, ignorance, and mistake?

A. I continually affirm quite the contrary, and always have done so.

Q. But how can every thought, word, and work, be governed by pure love, and the man be subject at the same time to ignorance and mistake?

A. I see no contradiction here: 'A man may be filled with pure love, and still be liable to mistake.' Indeed I do not expect to be freed from actual mistakes, till this mortal puts on immortality. I believe this to be a natural consequence of the soul's dwelling in flesh and blood. For we cannot now think at all, but by the mediation of those bodily organs which have suffered equally with the rest of our frame. And hence we cannot avoid sometimes thinking wrong, till this corruptible shall have put on incorruption.

But we may carry this thought farther yet. A mistake in judgment may possibly occasion a mistake in practice. For instance: Mr. De Renty's mistake touching the nature of mortification, arising from prejudice of education, occasioned that practical mistake, his wearing an iron girdle. And a thousand such instances there may be, even in those who are in the highest state of grace. Yet, where every word and action springs from love, such a mistake is not properly a sin. However, it cannot bear the rigour of God's justice, but needs the atoning blood.

Q. What was the judgment of all our brethren who met at Bristol in August, 1758, on this head?

A. It was expressed in these words: (1) Every one may mistake as long as he lives. (2) A mistake in opinion may occasion a mistake in practice. (3) Every such mistake is a transgression of the perfect law. Therefore, (4) Every such mistake, were it not for the blood of atonement, would expose to eternal damnation. (5) It follows, that the most perfect have continual need of the merits of Christ, even for their actual transgressions, and may say for themselves, as well as for their brethren, 'Forgive us our trespasses.'

This easily accounts for what might otherwise seem to be utterly unaccountable; namely, that those who are not offended when we speak of the highest degree of love, yet will not hear of living without sin. The reason is, they know all men are liable to mistake, and that in practice as well as in judgment. But they do not know, or do not observe, that this is not sin, if love is the sole principle of action.

Q. But still, if they live without sin, does not this exclude the necessity of a Mediator? At least, is it not plain that they stand no longer in need of Christ in his priestly office?

A. Far from it. None feel their need of Christ like these; none so entirely depend upon him. For Christ does not give life to the soul separate from, but in and with, himself. Hence his words are equally true of all men, in whatsoever state of grace they are: 'As the branch cannot bear fruit of itself, except it abide in the vine; no more can ye, except ye abide in me: Without' (or separate from) 'me ye can do nothing.'

In every state we need Christ in the following respects: (1) Whatever grace we receive, it is a free gift from him. (2) We receive it as his purchase, merely in consideration of the price he paid. (3) We have this grace, not only from Christ, but in him. For our perfection is not like that of a tree, which flourishes by the sap derived from its own root, but, as was said before, like that of a branch which, united to the vine, bears fruit; but, severed from it, is dried up and withered. (4) All our blessings, temporal, spiritual, and eternal, depend on his intercession for us, which is one branch of his priestly office, whereof therefore we have always equal need. (5) The best of men still need Christ in his priestly office, to atone for their omissions, their short-comings, (as some not improperly speak,) their mistakes in judgment and practice, and their defects of various kinds. For these are all deviations from the perfect law, and consequently need an atonement. Yet that they are not properly sins, we apprehend may appear from the words of St. Paul, 'He that loveth, hath fulfilled the law; for love is the fulfilling of the law.' (Rom. xiii. 10.) Now, mistakes, and whatever infirmities necessarily flow from the corruptible state of the body, are noway contrary to love; nor therefore, in the Scripture sense, sin.

To explain myself a little farther on this head: (1) Not only sin, properly so called, (that is, a voluntary transgression of a known law,) but sin, improperly so called, (that is, an involuntary transgression of a divine law, known or unknown,) needs the atoning blood. (2) I believe there is no such perfection in this life as excludes these involuntary transgressions which I apprehend to be naturally consequent on the ignorance and mistakes inseparable from mortality. (3) Therefore *sinless perfection* is a phrase I never use, lest I should seem to contradict myself. (4) I believe, a person filled with the love of God is still liable to these involuntary transgressions. (5) Such transgressions you may call sins, if you please: I do not, for the reasons above-mentioned. . . .

Q. How shall we avoid setting perfection too high or too low?

A. By keeping to the Bible, and setting it just as high as the Scripture does. It is nothing higher and nothing lower than this, – the pure love of God and man; the loving God with all our heart and soul, and our neighbour as ourselves. It is love governing the heart and life, running through all our tempers, words, and actions.

Q. Suppose one had attained to this, would you advise him to speak of it?

A. At first perhaps he would scarce be able to refrain, the fire would be so hot within him; his desire to declare the loving-kindness of the Lord carrying him away like a torrent. But afterwards he might; and then it would be advisable, not to speak of it to them that know not God (it is most likely, it would only provoke them to contradict and blaspheme); nor to others, without some particular reason, without some good in view. And then he should have especial care to avoid all appearance of boasting; to speak with the deepest humility and reverence, giving all the glory to God.

Q. But would it not be better to be entirely silent, not to speak of it at all?

A. By silence, he might avoid many crosses, which will naturally and necessarily ensue, if he simply declare, even among believers, what God has wrought in his soul. If, therefore, such a one were to confer with flesh and blood, he would be entirely silent. But this could not be done with a clear conscience; for undoubtedly he ought to speak. Men do not light a candle to put it under a bushel; much less does the all-wise God. He does not raise such a monument of his power and love, to hide it from all mankind. Rather, he intends it as a general blessing to those who are simple of heart. He designs thereby, not barely the happiness of that individual person, but the animating and encouraging others to follow after the same blessing. His will is, 'that many shall see it' and rejoice, 'and put their trust in the Lord.' Nor does anything under heaven more quicken the desires of those who are justified, than to converse with those whom they believe to have experienced a still higher salvation. This places that salvation full in their view, and increases their hunger and thirst after it; an advantage which must have been entirely lost, had the person so saved buried himself in silence.

Q. But is there no way to prevent these crosses which usually fall on those who speak of being thus saved?

A. It seems they cannot be prevented altogether, while so much of nature remains even in believers. But something might be done, if the Preacher in every place would, (1) Talk freely with all who speak thus; and, (2) Labour to prevent the unjust or unkind treatment of those in favour of whom there is reasonable proof.

Q. What is reasonable proof? How may we certainly know one that is saved from all sin?

A. We cannot infallibly know one that is thus saved (no nor even one that is justified), unless it should please God to endow us with the miraculous discernment of spirits. But we apprehend those would be sufficient proofs to any reasonable man, and such as would leave little room to doubt either the truth or depth of the work: (1) If we had clear evidence of his exemplary behaviour for some time before this supposed change. This would give us reason to believe, he would not 'lie for God', but speak neither more nor less than he felt; (2) If he gave a distinct account of the time and manner wherein the change was wrought, with sound speech which could not be reproved; and, (3) If it appeared that all his subsequent words and actions were holy and unblamable.

The short of the matter is this: (1) I have abundant reason to believe, this person will not lie; (2) He testifies before God, 'I feel no sin, but all love; I pray, rejoice, and give thanks without ceasing; and I have as clear an inward witness, that I am fully renewed, as that I am justified.' Now, if I have nothing to oppose to this plain testimony, I ought in reason to believe it. . . .

Q. When may a person judge himself to have attained this?

A. When, after having been fully convinced of inbred sin, by a far deeper and clearer conviction than that he experienced before justification, and after having experienced a gradual mortification of it, he experiences a total death to sin, and an entire renewal in the love and image of God, so as to rejoice evermore, to pray without ceasing, and in everything to give thanks. Not that 'to feel all love and no sin' is a sufficient proof. Several have experienced this for a time, before their souls were fully renewed. None therefore ought to believe that the work is done, till there is added the testimony of the Spirit, witnessing his entire sanctification, as clearly as his justification.

Q. But whence is it, that some imagine they are thus sanctified, when in reality they are not?

A. It is hence: they do not judge by all the preceding marks, but either by part of them, or by others that are ambiguous. But I know no instance of a person attending to them all, and yet deceived in this matter. I believe, there can be none in the world. If a man be deeply and fully convinced, after justification, of inbred sin; if he then experience a gradual mortification of sin, and afterwards an entire renewal in the image of God; if to this change, immensely greater than that wrought when he was justified, be added a clear, direct witness of the renewal; I judge it as impossible this man should be deceived herein, as that God should lie. And if one whom I know to be a man of veracity testify these things to me, I ought not, without some sufficient reason, to reject his testimony.

Q. Is this death to sin, and renewal in love, gradual or instantaneous?

A. A man may be dying for some time; yet he does not, properly speaking, die, till the instant the soul is separated from the body; and in that instant he lives the life of eternity. In like manner, he may be dying to sin for some time; yet he is not dead to sin, till sin is separated from his soul; and in that instant he lives the full life of love. And as the change undergone, when the body dies, is of a different kind, and infinitely greater than any we had known before, yea, such as till then it is impossible to conceive; so the change wrought, when the soul dies to sin, is of a different kind, and infinitely greater than any before, and than any can conceive till he experiences it. Yet he still grows in grace, in the knowledge of Christ, in the love and image of God; and will do so, not only till death, but to all eternity.

Q. How are we to wait for this change?

A. Not in careless indifference, or indolent inactivity; but in vigorous, universal obedience, in a zealous keeping of all the commandments, in watchfulness and painfulness, in denying ourselves, and taking up our cross daily; as well as in earnest prayer and fasting, and a close attendance on all the ordinances of God. And if any man dream of attaining it any other way (yea, or of keeping it when it is attained, when he has received it even in the largest measure), he deceiveth his own soul. It is true, we receive it by simple faith: But God does not, will not, give that faith, unless we seek it with all diligence, in the way which he hath ordained.

This consideration may satisfy those who inquire, why so few have received the blessing. Inquire, how many are seeking it in this way; and you have a sufficient answer. . . .

Q. But may we not continue in peace and joy till we are perfected in love?

A. Certainly we may; for the kingdom of God is not divided against itself; therefore, let not believers be discouraged from 'rejoicing in the Lord always.' And yet we may be sensibly pained at the sinful nature that still remains in us. It is good for us to have a piercing sense of this, and a vehement desire to be delivered from it. But this should only incite us the more zealously to fly every moment to our strong Helper, the more earnestly to 'press forward to the mark, the prize of our high calling in Christ Jesus.' And when the sense of our sin most abounds, the sense of his love should much more abound.

Q. How should we treat those who think they have attained?

A. Examine them candidly, and exhort them to pray fervently, that God would show them all that is in their hearts. The most earnest exhortations to abound in every grace, and the strongest cautions to avoid all evil, are given throughout the New Testament, to those who are in the highest state of grace. But this should be done with the utmost tenderness; and without any harshness, sternness, or sourness. We should carefully avoid the very appearance of anger, unkindness, or contempt. Leave it to Satan thus to tempt, and to his children to cry out, 'Let us examine him with despitefulness and torture, that we may know his meekness and prove his patience.' If they are faithful to the grace given, they are in no danger of perishing thereby; no, not if they remain in that mistake till their spirit is returning to God . . .

Q. But what does it signify, whether any have attained it or no, seeing so many scriptures witness for it?

A. If I were convinced that none in England had attained what has been so clearly and strongly preached by such a number of Preachers, in so many places, and for so long a time, I should be clearly convinced that we had all mistaken the meaning of those scriptures; and therefore, for the time to come, I too must teach that 'sin will remain till death.'

The Temptation to 'Locate'

Christopher Hopper to Charles Wesley; Newcastle, December 16, 1759

(Ms at Emory University)

Hopper, born in 1722, entered the itinerancy in 1750 and accompanied John Wesley on his first visit to Scotland the following year. At the time of his death in 1802 he was the oldest itinerant preacher.

Wherever I settle, I hope I shall never settle upon my lees or bury my small talent. Whether I may turn Dissenting Parson I cannot tell. But this I'll presume to say: If you'll find me a loving converted B—p who will ordain me upon honourable terms, viz. to preach when, where & as often as unerring Providence shall direct, to believe & subscribe nothing but which is agreeable to the Word of God, and to keep up a close connexion with the happy People called Methodists, I think I'll never turn Dissenting Parson. But, dear Sir, give me leave to ask you, what will the end of Methodism be? If a Methodist preacher live till he be weak and worn out with travelling, I apprehend he must either be ordained or turn Dissenting Teacher, or sit down by his own fire (if he has one) or be cast out & rejected like an old superannuated Hottentot left in his hut to die in mercy to his old age. Now, Sir, if matters should come to this conclusion, I'll ask you in the fear of God, which of these would you have a poor worn-out brother to choose? All this, & more, has been answered with one word, 'You want faith', You've lost your zeal. This may soon be said, but still I'm to believe that true faith, though above, never contradicts sound reason. However, be as it will, I'm a Methodist yet, & if my brethren will do me justice, I think they never saw anything in my whole deportment very bad, but there are some born to find fault, & those are the unhappy men. I've preached since I was m[arrie]d as I did before, but those men say, He is silent; I've kept my Circuit constantly, which I suppose is near three hundred miles in a month, as before, but those men say, Christopher Hopper will travel no more, therefore those men will say what they please or rather whatever an evil spirit dictates. But blessed be God, all this is nothing to me. I've nothing to do but please my dear Lord & Master, & if I stand approved in his sight I shall enjoy peace in my way, victory over death, & then a crown of glory.

We enjoy great peace without Pilgrim's Gate & in all our borders. I can say little for Scotland. The North Britons are full of words but little power. Yet I believe there are a few precious souls in Dunbar & Musselburgh. We revive in Alnwick. We revive & increase in Plassey, no house in the place will contain the hearers. We hold our own at Newcastle. We've no reason to complain. The Master of the Vineyard removes now and then one to his Eternal House. You've heard of Sister Millener's death. I visited her. She had many violent storms in her passage, but calm uninterrupted peace in the end. I think your old friend Henry will bury all his children. He still appears in the Orphan House under the pulpit with his gray hairs. He can read the smallest print without his glass eyes. He's a wonder. We have many old saints in this Church near the borders of eternity. There is a good work in North & South Shields. Lions are become lambs, & God is glorified. We've built a glorious house in Sunderland, & the work of the Lord prospers. Sinners are reclaimed, mourners comforted, saints built up, Sion watered & God glorified. We gain ground in Durham, where Law & Gospel reign. God has been on our side this year & has given us many victories. May we give Him all the glory. Till this be done, all the danger is not past. But the Lord is our Rock, may Israel say, therefore we shall stand & be safe in the evil day.

Christopher Hopper in Scotland

(*EMP*, I, 210–11)

In the year 1760 I again visited Scotland. The work of the Lord prospered in our hands. Sinners were converted, mourners comforted, and saints built up in their most holy faith. We had now a fair prospect of a great harvest in North Britain, till men of corrupt minds stirred up the spirit of vain controversy: we then spent our time and strength about the meaning of words, instead of promoting the fear and love of God. My soul was troubled, and my spirit grieved within me, to see so many precious souls turned out of the way of holiness and happiness, by noisy disputes and foolish jangling. These men will blush in the last day who have done this great evil. Let me live with men of peace, who love God and the brethren, and enjoy the life of religion in their own souls.

Prosperity and Worldliness

The improved social and economic status of the Methodist people increasingly became a matter of concern to Wesley.

John Wesley's *Journal*

(*JWJ*, IV, 417; V, 30–1, 245; VI, 271)

Oct. 16, 1760. On the three following days I spoke severally to the members of the [Bristol] society. As many of them increase in wordly goods, the great danger I apprehend now is their relapsing into the spirit of the world; and then their religion is but a dream.

Sept. 19, 1763. On Monday evening I gave our brethren [at Bristol] a solemn caution not 'to love the world, neither the things of the world'. This will be their grand danger; as they are industrious and frugal, they must needs increase in goods. This appears already. In London, Bristol, and most other trading towns, those who are in business have increased in substance sevenfold, some of them twenty, yea, an hundredfold. What need, then, have these of the strongest warnings, lest they be entangled therein, and perish!

Dec. 13, 1767. I was desired to preach a funeral sermon for William Osgood. He came to London near thirty years ago, and, from nothing, increased more and more, till he was worth several thousand pounds. He was a good man, and died in peace. Nevertheless, I believe his money was a great clog to him, and kept him in a poor, low state all his days, making no such advance as he might have done, either in holiness or happiness.

April 4, 1780. [At Manchester] I . . . strongly applied, 'What could I have done more to my vineyard that I have not done?' At present there are many here that 'bring forth good grapes.' But many swiftly increase in goods; and I fear very few sufficiently watch and pray that they may not set their hearts upon them.

John Wesley to Freeborn Garrettson; London, September 30, 1786

(*JWL*, VII, 343–4)

Most of those in England who have riches love money, even the Methodists – at least, those who are called so. The poor are the Christians. I am quite out of conceit with almost all those who have this world's goods. Let us take care to lay up our treasure in heaven.

Sermon CVIII: 'On Riches' (1788)

(*JWW*, VII, 221; *Sermons* III, 527–8)

10. Touching this important point, of denying ourselves, and taking up our cross daily, let us appeal to matter of fact; let us appeal to every man's conscience in the sight of God. How many rich men are there among the Methodists (observe, there was not one, when they were first joined together) who actually do 'deny themselves and take up their cross daily'? who resolutely abstain from every pleasure, either of sense or imagination, unless they know by experience that it prepares them for taking pleasure in God? Who declines no cross, no labour or pain, which lies in the way of his duty? Who of you that are now rich, deny yourselves just as you did when you were poor? Who as willingly endure labour or pain now, as you did when you were not worth five pounds? Come to particulars. Do you fast now as often as you did then? Do you rise as early in the morning? Do you endure cold or heat, wind or rain, as cheerfully as ever? See one reason among many, why so few increase in goods, without decreasing in grace! Because they no longer deny themselves and take up their daily cross. They no longer, alas! endure hardship, as good soldiers of Jesus Christ!

Sermon CXVI: 'Causes of the Inefficacy of Christianity' (1789)

(*JWW*, VII, 288–90; *Sermons* IV, 93–6)

13. But to return to the main question. Why has Christianity done so little good, even among us? among the Methodists, – among them that hear and receive the whole Christian doctrine, and that have Christian discipline added thereto, in the most essential parts of it? Plainly, because we have forgot, or at least not duly attended to, those solemn words of our Lord, 'If any man will come after me, let him deny himself, and take up his cross daily, and follow me.' It was the remark of a holy

man, several years ago, 'Never was there before a people in the Christian Church, who had so much of the power of God among them, with so little self-denial.' Indeed the work of God does go on, and in a surprising manner, notwithstanding this capital defect; but it cannot go on in the same degree as it otherwise would; neither can the word of God have its full effect, unless the hearers of it 'deny themselves, and take up their cross daily.'

14. It would be easy to show, in how many respects the Methodists, in general, are deplorably wanting in the practice of Christian self-denial; from which, indeed, they have been continually frighted by the silly outcries of the Antinomians. To instance only in one: While we were at Oxford, the rule of every Methodist was (unless in case of sickness) to *fast* every Wednesday and Friday in the year, in imitation of the Primitive Church; for which they had the highest reverence. Now this practice of the Primitive Church is universally allowed. 'Who does not know,' says Epiphanius, an ancient writer, 'that the fasts of the fourth and sixth days of the week' (Wednesday and Friday) 'are observed by the Christians throughout the whole world?' So they were by the Methodists for several years; by them all, without any exception; but afterwards, some in London carried this to excess, and fasted so as to impair their health. It was not long before others made this a pretence for not fasting at all. And I fear there are now thousands of Methodists, so called, both in England and Ireland, who, following the same bad example, have entirely left off fasting; who are so far from fasting twice in the week (as all the stricter Pharisees did) that they do not fast twice in the month. Yea, are there not some of you who do not fast one day from the beginning of the year to the end? But what excuse can there be for this? I do not say for those that call themselves members of the Church of England; but for any who profess to believe the Scripture to be the word of God. Since, according to this, the man that never fasts is no more in the way to heaven, than the man that never prays. . . .

16. But why is self-denial in general so little practised at present among the Methodists? Why is so exceedingly little of it to be found even in the oldest and largest societies? The more I observe and consider things, the more clearly it appears what is the cause of this in London, in Bristol, in Birmingham, in Manchester, in Leeds, in Dublin, in Cork. The Methodists grow more and more self-indulgent, because they *grow rich*. Although many of them are still deplorably poor ('tell it not in Gath; publish it not in the streets of Askelon!'), yet many others, in the space of twenty, thirty, or forty years, are twenty, thirty, yea, a hundred times richer than they were when they first entered the society. And it is an observation which admits of few exceptions, that nine in ten of these decreased in grace, in the same proportion as they increased in

wealth. Indeed, according to the natural tendency of riches, we cannot expect it to be otherwise.

17. But how astonishing a thing is this! How can we understand it? Does it not seem (and yet this cannot be) that Christianity, true scriptural Christianity, has a tendency, in process of time, to undermine and destroy itself? For wherever true Christianity spreads, it must cause diligence and frugality, which, in the natural course of things, must beget riches! and riches naturally beget pride, love of the world, and every temper that is destructive of Christianity. Now, if there be no way to prevent this, Christianity is inconsistent with itself, and, of consequence, cannot stand, cannot continue long among any people; since, wherever it generally prevails, it saps its own foundation.

18. But is there no way to prevent this? – to continue Christianity among a people? Allowing that diligence and frugality must produce riches, is there no means to hinder riches from destroying the religion of those that possess them? I can see only one possible way; find out another who can. Do you gain all you can, and save all you can? Then you must, in the nature of things, grow rich. Then if you have any desire to escape the damnation of hell, *give* all you can; otherwise I can have no more hope of your salvation, than of that of Judas Iscariot.

Thomas Taylor in South Wales, 1761

(*EMP*,V, 18–20)

As a young man of 22, Taylor met Wesley at Birstall, Yorks, and was advised to attend the forthcoming conference in London in order to offer for the itinerancy.

I intimated a desire of spending a year in that place, that I might be fully informed both in the doctrines and discipline of the Methodists. Accordingly, I disposed of some small effects which I had, and set out on foot. When I came thither I expected to undergo a close examination, with regard to my principles, experience, and abilities; and therefore, as I did not in everything agree with Mr. Wesley, it was a doubt with me whether I should not be rejected. But, to my surprise, I was not asked one question relative to any of these things; but was appointed for Wales, and was the only travelling preacher of our Connexion in those parts. This I have sometimes thought was not prudently done, as I was but just come into the Connexion. However, I set out for Bristol, and so into Wales; and truly a rough region it was. A preacher at Bristol said to me, 'You seem pretty well dressed, and will hold out well enough for a year; but you must expect nothing to buy any more clothes with when those are worn out.' However, I did not regard that; for I was determined to spend and be spent in doing all the good I could. I therefore began preaching out of doors in the first town I came to, which was Chepstow, and determined to do so in every town I came to. Thus I went on till after Christmas, and endured a good deal of hardship from hunger and cold; especially in passing those dreadful mountains from Neath to Brecon, which were nearly forty miles over, and have a most dismal aspect in winter. On these I travelled a long way, and saw neither house nor field, hedge nor tree; nor yet any living creature, excepting here and there a poor sheep or two, nor scarcely any visible track to know my way by. This was not pleasing to flesh and blood; but still I determined to go on.

In February there seemed a prospect of much good in a large tract of land called Gower, in Glamorganshire: the inhabitants of it were nearly heathens. I went down into this miserable country in very cold, rainy weather: the people flocked to hear, but we were ill provided with convenient places to preach in. Meantime the rain was excessive, and the cold intense, while we had but little fire; so that I put on my wet clothes several days successively, yet without any inconvenience afterwards. Here God blessed my word: I collected several societies, and many were at this time brought to experience the knowledge of salvation by the remission of sins.

Towards summer, a circumstance seemed to open my way sixty or seventy miles farther down to Pembrokeshire: I went thither, and preached at Carmarthen in my way. Afterwards I preached at Pembroke, and had multitudes to hear, who behaved in a respectful manner, and generously paid all my expenses; for at this time there was no provision made for missionaries. I preached in several places round Milford-Haven, and had many to hear. Indeed, the prospect was so promising, and the people were so loving, that I was almost tempted to embrace their pressing invitations to stay with them. But I thought that would be a betrayal of my trust; so I returned to my own Circuit, promising that I would return again after the Conference was over. When I returned into the old Circuit, I was seized with a slow fever. I believe it was in some measure occasioned by fatigues. But Providence was kind to me: for though I was in a poor place, where little assistance was to be had; yet, by the blessing of God, I did without it. Mr. Mather then came from Staffordshire, to help me to put things into some order, and went with me through the rambling Cricuit; and indeed his advice has been of use to me ever since.

The 'Model Deed'

Wesley's first attempt to settle the Bristol 'New Room' on a body of trustees quickly proved abortive (pp. 000–0 above). His second attempt, in 1746, was an important step towards the final solution in the form of the Model Deed of 1763.

The 'New Room' deed of 1746

(Enrolled copy at the Public Record Office)

The following version omits some of the repetitive legal verbiage in order to highlight the main features of the deed.

This Indenture made the fifth day of March in the Year of our Lord 1745 and the nineteenth year of the Reign of [George II][1] between John Wesley Clerk fellow of Lincoln College in the University of Oxford of the one part and John Hodges Clerk rector of Wenvoe in the county of Glamorgan, South Wales, John Dyer of the City of Bristol, Gentleman, Henry Durbin of Bristol Chemist, Daniel Jenkins of Bristol cork cutter, Thomas Willis of Barton Hundred in the county of Gloucester Gentleman, James Wheatley of Painswick, Gloucester Gentleman and Thomas Whittington of Kingswood, Gloucester Collier WITNESSETH that for the settlement and conveyancing the Messuage Tenements and Hereditaments hereinafter mentioned to be granted upon such Trusts and for such pious and charitable purposes as are hereinafter therof mentioned or expressed and in consideration of the sum of five shillings . . . by the said [Trustees] to the said John Wesley before the sealing and delivery hereof well and truly paid, the receipt whereof he the said John Wesley doth hereby acknowledge, and for diverse other considerations him thereunto moving, he the said John Wesley hath bargained and sold . . . unto the said [Trustees] All that lately erected Messuage House or Tenement . . . situate standing and being in the Horsefair within the city of Bristol . . . commonly called or known by the name of the New room and now in the said John Wesley's own occupation . . . To have and to hold the same to the said [Trustees] their Heirs and assigns for ever, Nevertheless upon the Trusts and for the purposes hereinafter mentioned or expressed, that is to say upon special Trust and confidence and to the intent that they . . . shall permit and suffer the said John Wesley and such other person and persons as he shall for that purpose from time to time nominate or appoint from time to time and at all times during his life at his will and pleasure, to have and enjoy the house and benefit of the said premises as he . . . hath heretofore done, and that he and such other persons as he shall so nominate or appoint shall and may therein preach and expound God's Holy word, and after his decease upon further Trust and Confidence and to the Intent that [they] shall permit and suffer Charles Wesley . . . and such other persons as [he] shall for that purpose . . . nominate . . . to have use and enjoy the said premises . . . and after the decease of the survivor of them . . . then upon further Trust . . . [the Trustees or their survivors] shall from time to time and at all times for ever thereafter monthly or oftener at their discretion nominate and appoint one or more fit person or persons to preach and expound God's holy word in the said house in the same manner as near as may be as God's holy word is now preached and expounded there . . .

[Also] that the school now subsisting and taught in part of the said house and premises shall from henceforth for ever be and continue and be kept up and shall consist of one Master and one Mistress and such forty poor children as the said John Wesley . . . shall . . . appoint, and that such of them the said children being boys shall be committed solely to the care of such Master and be by him taught and instructed in reading writing and arithmetick, and that such of them the said children as shall happen to be girls shall likewise be under the sole care and instruction of such Mistress and by her be taught reading writing and needlework . . . and that the said Master and Mistress and Scholars . . . shall submit to be and be governed by the Rules, Orders and Constitutions already made and ordained and from time to time to be made and ordained by the Trustees or the major part of them . . . for the good order and government of the said school . . .

And upon farther Trust and Confidence and to the Intent that when and as often as the said Trustees or any of them . . . shall happen to die or shall remove their or his place of abode or residence for the space of forty Miles or more from the said House or shall resign . . . that then and so often so soon afterwards as conveniently may be the rest of the Trustees . . . shall and may elect and choose other fit person or persons to be Trustee or Trustees to fill up such Vacancy and keep up the number of seven Trustees.

---

[1] The deed is dated 1745 Old Style, which is 1746 by the new calendar adopted in 1750. Wesley himself further confused the matter by an error in his *Journal* under the date 19 March 1747 (*JWJ*, III, 286): '. . . the Houses at Bristol, Kingswood and Newcastle are safe; the deeds whereby they are conveyed to the Trustees took place on the 5th inst.'

The first Model Deed, 1763

(*Large Minutes*, 1763, pp. 25–7)

Q. What do you advise with regard to public Buildings?
A. Let none be undertaken without the consent of the Assistant.

2, Build, if possible, in the form of Rotherham house. 3. Settle it in the following form:

This Indenture made   between *B. Heap* of *Manchester*, in the county of   on the one Part, and *Tho.
Phillips*, Hatter, &c. on the other Part, WITNESSETH, That in Consideration of five Shillings, lawful Money of *Great Britain*, by the said *T.P.* &c.
to the said *B.H.* truly paid, before the Sealing and Delivery hereof (the
Receit whereof the said *B.H.* doth hereby acknowledge) and for divers
other Considerations him thereunto moving, the said *B.H.* hath
granted, bargained, and sold; and by these presents doth grant, bargain,
and sell unto the said *T.P.* &c. their Heirs and Assigns for ever, All that
lately erected House or Tenement, with the yard thereunto adjoining,
situate near the upper End of *Market-street Lane* in *Manchester* aforesaid,
now in the Tenure or Occupation of *T. Woolfinden*; together with all the
Ways, Drains, Walls and Privileges to the said Premises, or any Part
thereof appertaining, as the same were purchased of *S. Hope*, of Manchester aforesaid, Bricklayer, before the said House or Tenement was
built; and all the Profits thereof, and all the Right, Title and Interest, in
Law and Equity. To HAVE AND TO HOLD the said House or Tenement,
Yard and other Premises, to the said *T.P.* &c. their Heirs, and Assigns
for ever: NEVERTHELESS upon special Trust and Confidence, and to
the Intent, that they and the Survivors of them, and the Trustees for
the Time being, do and shall permit *John Wesley*, late of *Lincoln College,
Oxford*, Clerk, and such other persons as he shall from Time to Time
appoint, and at all Times, during his natural Life, *and no other Persons*, to
have and enjoy the free Use and Benefit of the said Premises; that the
said *J.W.* and such other Persons as he appoints, may therein preach and
expound God's holy Word: and after his Decease, upon farther Trust
and Confidence, and to the Intent that the said Trustees and the Survivors of them, and the Trustees for the Time being, do and shall permit
Charles Wesley, late of *Christ Church College, Oxford*, Clerk, and such other
Persons as he shall from Time to Time appoint, during his Life, and no
others, to have and enjoy the said Premises for the Purposes aforesaid:
and after his decease, upon farther Trust and Confidence, and to the
Intent that the said Trustees and the Survivors of them, and the Trustees
for the Time being, do and shall permit *Wm. Grimshaw*, Clerk, and such
other Persons as he shall from Time to Time appoint, during his Life,
and no others, to have and enjoy the said Premises for the Purposes
aforesaid: and after the decease of the Survivor of the said *J.W.*, *C.W.*
and *W.G.* Then upon farther Trust and Confidence, and to the Intent
that the said *T.P.* &c. or the major Part of them, or the Survivors of
them, and the major Part of the Trustees of the said Premises, for the
Time being, shall from Time to Time, and at all Times, for ever there-

after, permit such Persons as shall be appointed, at the Yearly Conference of the People called *Methodists*, in *London, Bristol* or *Leeds*, and no others, to have and enjoy the said Premises, for the Purpose aforesaid: *Provided always, that the said Persons preach no other Doctrine than is contained in Mr. W.'s Notes upon the New Testament, and four Vols. of Sermons; Provided also that they preach in the said House   Evenings in every Week, and at Five a Clock on each Morning following:* And upon farther Trust and Confidence that as often as any of these Trustees, or of the Trustees for the Time being shall die, *or cease to a Member of the Society, commonly called Methodists*, the rest of the said Trustees, or of the Trustees for the Time being, as soon as conveniently may be, shall and may chuse another Trustee, or Trustees, in order to keep up the Number of Nine Trustees for ever. In Witness whereof the said *B.H.* hath hereunto set his Hand and Seal, the Day and Year first above written.

In this form the first Proprietors of the House are to make it over to Trustees.

One Thing more should be done without delay.

Let the Vacancies every where be filled up with New Trustees. We know not what Danger may ensue from Delay.

Apostate Will

(Thomas Chatterton, *Complete Works*, 1971, Vol. I, pp. 1–2)

Growing up in mid-eighteenth-century Bristol, the young Chatterton had opportunities to observe Methodism at close quarters. The poem has been likened to 'Holy Willie's Prayer' by Robert Burns.

> In days of old, when Wesley's pow'r,
> Gather'd new strength by every hour;
> Apostate Will just sunk in trade,
> Resolv'd his bargain should be made;
> Then strait to Wesley he repairs,
> And puts on grave and solemn airs,
> Then thus the pious man address'd,
> Good Sir, I think your doctrine best,
> Your Servant will a Wesley be,
> Therefore the principles teach me.
> The preacher then instructions gave,
> How he in this world should behave,
> He hears, assents, and gives a nod

Says every word's the word of God.
Then lifting his dissembling eyes,
How blessed is the sect he cries,
Nor Bingham, Young, nor Stillingfleet[1]
Shall make me from this sect retreat.
He then his circumstance declar'd,
How hardly with him matters far'd,
Begg'd him next meeting for to make
A small collection for his sake;
The preacher said, do not repine,
The whole collection shall be thine.
With looks demure and cringing bows,
About his business strait he goes;
His outward acts were grave and prim,
The Methodist appear'd in him;
But, be his outward what it will,
His heart was an Apostate's still;
He'd oft profess an hallow'd flame,
And every where preach'd Wesley's name;
He was a preacher and what not,
As long as money could be got;
He'd oft profess with holy fire,
The labourer's worthy of his hire.

It happen'd once upon a time,
When all his works were in their prime,
A noble place appear'd in view,
Then – to the Methodists, adieu;
A Methodist no more he'll be,
The Protestants[2] serve best for *he*;
Then to the curate strait he ran,
And thus address'd the rev'rend man;
I was a Methodist, 'tis true,
With penitence I turn to you;
O that it were your bounteous will
That I the vacant place might fill!
With justice I'd myself acquit,
Do every thing that's right and fit.
The curate straitway gave consent –
To take the place he quickly went.
Accordingly he took the place,
And keeps it with dissembled grace.

April 14th, 1764.   T. C.

[1] Joseph Bingham (1668–1723), Arthur Young (1693–1759) and Edward Stilling-fleet (1635–99), Bishop of Worcester, were all Anglican divines and religious writers. Stillingfleet's *Irenicon* had an influence on Wesley's views on church order.
[2] I.e., the Anglicans.

A Receipt to make a true Methodist

(Undated ms at Wesley Theological Seminary, Washington DC)

Take of the herbs of hypocrisy & the roots of spiritual pride, of each 2 large handfuls, 2 ounces of ambition, vainglory & impudence, of each a sufficient quantity. Boil them over the fire of sedition, until you can perceive the ingredients to swim on the top. Then add to them 6 ounces of sugar of deceit, one quart of dissembling tears. Put them into the bottle of envy, & stop them up with the cork of malice. When those ingredients are subsided make them into pills. Warm 5 at night & 5 in the morning. Take with them[3] the tongue of slander and go into the society house to hear nonsense and stupidity. By way of gentle exercise fall into pretended fits. Then go home: cant, sing hymns, say your prayers, till you are heard all round the neighbourhood. This will produce such an effect that your chief study will be to cheat all you converse with, play the whore under the cloak of sanctity, revile the Church, rail against the ministers & government, when opportunity suits; & cut the throats of all your oppressors. These ingredients if rightly prepared are an infallible receipt & without which you cannot be a true Methodist.

[3] Possibly a slip for 'Take them with . . .'

Advice to the Bristol Societies

John Wesley's letter of October 1764

(*JWL*, IV, 271–4)

My Dear Brethren, – I was much comforted among you when I was with you last, finding my labour had not been in vain. Many of you I found rejoicing in God your Saviour, walking in the light of His countenance, and studying to have a conscience void of offence towards God and man. In order to assist you therein, suffer me to remind you of a few things, which I think are of no small concern, in order to your retaining the life of faith and the testimony of a good conscience towards God. And, –

1. For God's sake, for the honour of the gospel, for your country's sake, and for the sake of your own souls, beware of bribery. Before you

see me again the trial will come at the General Election for Members of Parliament. On no account take money or money's worth. Keep yourselves pure. Give, not sell, your vote. Touch not the accursed thing, lest it bring a blast upon you and your household.

2. Have nothing to do with stolen goods. Neither sell nor buy anything that has not paid the duty – no, not if you could have it at half price. Defraud not the King any more than your fellow subject. Never think of being religious unless you are honest. What has a thief to do with religion? Herein mind not men but the Word of God; and, whatever others do, keep yourselves pure.

3. Lose no opportunity of receiving the sacrament. All who have neglected this have suffered loss; most of them are as dead as stones: therefore be you constant herein, not only for example, but for the sake of your own souls.

4. To the public, constantly add the private means of grace, particularly prayer and reading. Most of you have been greatly wanting in this; and without this you can never grow in grace. You may as well expect a child to grow without food as a soul without private prayer; and reading is an excellent help to this. I advise you to read in particular, constantly and carefully, the New Testament; *Lessons for Children*, which are all the choicest parts of the Old Testament, with short notes; *Instructions for Children*, which are a body of divinity for plain people; and that golden treatise *The Christian Pattern*[1]; the *Plain Account of the Methodists*. No Methodist ought to be without these, nor the *Primitive Physick*, which (if you have any regard for your bodies or your children) ought to be in every house. To all that can understand it, I recommend one book more, *A Preservative Against Unsettled Notions*; a book which, by the blessing of God, may help you from being tossed about with divers winds of doctrines. Permit me to give you one advice more under this head: do not encourage young raw men to exhort among you. It does little good either to you or them. Rather, in every Society, where you have not an experienced preacher, let one of the leaders read the *Notes*[2] or the *Christian Library*. By this the wisest among you may profit much, a thousand times more than by listening to forward youths who neither speak English nor common sense.

5. Let all of you who have faith meet in band without excuse and without delay. There has been a shameful neglect of this. Remove this scandal. As soon as the Assistant has fixed your band make it a point of conscience never to miss without an absolute necessity; and the preacher's meeting you all together one night out of two will be an additional blessing.

6. If you constantly meet your band, I make no doubt that you will constantly meet your class; indeed, otherwise you are not of our Society. Whoever misses his class thrice together thereby excludes himself, and

the preacher that comes next ought to put out his name. I wish you would consider this. Halt not between two. Meet the brethren, or leave them. It is not honest to profess yourself of a Society and not observe the rules of it. Be therefore consistent with yourself. Never miss your class till you miss it for good and all. And when you meet it, be merciful after your power; give as God enables you. If you are not in pressing want, give something, and you will be no poorer for it. Grudge not, fear not; lend unto the Lord, and He will surely repay . . .

8. I mention but one thing more. Let all who are able constantly attend the morning preaching. Whenever the Methodist preachers or people leave off this, they will soon sink into nothing.

¹ I.e. Thomas à Kempis, *The Imitation of Christ.*
² I.e. the *Explanatory Notes upon the New Testament*, 1754.

John Wesley in Scotland

An extract from the *Journal*

(*JWJ*, V, 75)

1764: Monday 11 [June]. [Preaching in the high kirk at Inverness] . . . I think the church was fuller now than before, and I could not but observe the remarkable behaviour of the whole congregation after service. Neither man, woman, nor child spoke one word all the way down the main street. Indeed, the seriousness of the people is the less surprising when it is considered that for at least a hundred years this town has had a succession of pious ministers as very few in Great Britain have known.
. . . While we were dining at Nairn the inn-keeper said, 'Sir, the gentlemen of the town have read the little book you gave me on Saturday, and would be glad if you would please to give them a sermon.' Upon my consenting, the bell was immediately rung, and the congregation was quickly in the kirk. Oh what a difference is there between South and North Britain! Every one here at least loves to hear the word of God; and none takes it into his head to speak one uncivil word to any for endeavouring to save their souls.

John Wesley to Dr. John Erskine; April 24, 1765

(*JWL*, IV, 295–6)

Erskine was pastor of the Old Greyfriars Church, Edinburgh and had taken James Hervey's side in his controversy with Wesley.

When I was first invited into Scotland (about fourteen years ago), Mr. Whitefield told me: 'You have no business there; for your principles are so well known, that if you spoke like an angel none would hear you. And if they did, you would have nothing to do but to dispute with one and another from morning to night.'

I answered: 'If God sends me, people will hear. And I will give them no provocation to dispute; for I will studiously avoid controverted points, and keep to the fundamental truths of Christianity. And if any still begin to dispute, they may; but I will not dispute with them.'

I came: hundreds and thousands flocked to hear. But I was enabled to keep my word. I avoided whatever might engender strife, and insisted upon the grand points – the religion of the heart and salvation by faith – at all times and in all places. And by this means I have cut off all occasion of dispute from the first day to this very hour. And this you amazingly improve into a fault, construe into a proof of dishonesty. You likewise charge me with holding unsound principles, and with saying, 'Right opinions are (sometimes) no part of religion.'

The last charge I have answered over and over, and very lately to Bishop Warburton.[1] Certainly, had you read that single tract, you would never have repeated that stale objection . . .

As to your main objection, convince me that it is my duty to preach on controverted subjects, Predestination in particular, and I will do it. At present I think it would be a sin. I think it would create still more divisions. And are there not enough already? I have seen a book written by one who styles himself *Ecclesiae direptae et gementis Presbyter.*[2] Shall I tear *ecclesiam direptam et gementem*? God forbid! No: I will so far as I can, heal her breaches. And if you really love her (as I doubt not you do), why should you hinder me from so doing? Has she so many friends and helpers left, that you should strive to lessen their number? Would you wish to turn any of her friends, even though weak and mistaken, into enemies? If you must contend, have you not Arians, Socinians, Seceders, infidels to contend with; to say nothing of whoremongers, adulterers, Sabbath-breakers, drunkards, common swearers? *O ecclesia gemens!* And will you pass by all these, and single out me to fight with? Nay, but I will not. I do and will fight with all these, but not with you. I cannot; I dare not. You are the son of my Father, my fellow labourer in the gospel of His dear Son. I love your person; I love your character; I love the work wherein you are engaged. And if you will still shoot at me (because Mr. Hervey has painted me as a monster), even with arrows drawn from Bishop Warburton's quiver (how unfit for Mr. Erskine's hand!), I can only say, as I always did before, the Lord Jesus bless you in your soul, in your body, in your relations, in your work, in whatever tends to His own glory!

¹ For Wesley's letter to Bishop Warburton, correcting his treatise on *The Office and Operations of the Holy Spirit*, see *JWL*, IV, 338–84.

² 'Presbyter of a divided and groaning Church.'

Further visits

(*JWJ*, VI, 20; VII, 387)

1774: Saturday 21 [May]: I returned to Perth, and preached in the evening to a large congregation. But I could not find the way to their hearts. The generality of the people here are so wise that they need no more knowledge, and so good that they need no more religion! Who can warn them that are brimful of wisdom and goodness to flee from the wrath to come?

1788: Tuesday 13 [May]: . . . In the evening I preached abroad in a convenient street on one side of the town [Dumfries]. Rich and poor attended from every quarter, of whatever denomination; and every one seemed to hear for life. Surely the Scots are the best hearers in Europe!

'The Scotch Seceder's Prayer'

(Ms at Duke University)

As heard by Mr. Bradburn and repeated in Conference (recorded by Henry Moore, who was present). Undated, but presumably at a Conference between 1791 and Bradburn's death in 1816. Bradburn was never stationed in a Scottish circuit.

> O Lord, remember the fallen Kirk of Scotland,
> And, Lord, remember her fallen sister, the Kirk of England;
> And remember that man of error, George Whitefield,
> *But above all*, remember that man of sin, John Wesley, the
> Perfectionist.

Further Thoughts on Christian Perfection

John Fletcher to John Wesley; Madeley, February 17, 1766

(Ms at Drew University)

In response to this letter, Wesley published his *Plain Account of Christian Perfection* later in the year.

I think we must define exactly that we mean by the perfection which is attainable here, and in so doing we may through mercy obviate the scoffs of the carnal and the misapprehension of the spiritual world at least in part. The light that I now see the thing in is this: as the body is not capable of perfection on this side the grave, all those powers of the soul whose exertion depends, in part, on the frame and well-being of the body or the happy flow of the animal spirits, will not, can not be perfected here. Of this sort, I apprehend, are 1. The understanding. 2. The memory and 3. The passionate affections, or the affections as they work by means of the animal spirits on the animal frame. These are no doubt susceptible of admirable impressions and very high improvements, but still *corpus affiget humi divinae particulam aurae*,[1] more or less. The one power that I see can be perfected here, because it is altogether independent from the body, is the will, and of course the affections so far as they work in the will.

[1] An inexact quotation from Horace, *Satires* II, 2.77: 'The body fastens to earth a fragment of the divine spirit.'

Thomas Taylor to Joseph Benson; Manchester, July 7, 1771

(Ms at Emory University)

What you say with regard to Mr. Wesley setting justification as high as sanctification is in some respects true, and sometimes I am apt to think he has set the Christian standard too high, unless his expressions are to be understood in a limited sense; and I am afraid, my dear friend, you are rather leaning to an extreme [sc. in your interpretation of the doctrine of perfection].

John Wesley to Ann Bolton of Witney; Otley, July 1, 1772

(*JWL*, V, 325)

I am exceeding jealous over you lest you should go one step too far to the right hand or to the left. You are my glory and joy (though you are nothing), and I want you to be exactly right in all things. I am not content that anything should be wrong about you either in your temper or words or actions. And I bless God I generally have my desire over you: you are in good measure what I would have you to be. I do not observe anything to reprove in the account which you now give me. Go on! Watch in all things! Be zealous for God! Continue instant in prayer! And the God of peace Himself shall sanctify you wholly and preserve you blameless unto the coming of our Lord Jesus Christ!

I believe you have been in one danger which you was not sensible of. You seemed a little inclined to that new opinion which lately sprung up among you – that we are (properly) *sanctified* when we are justified. You did not observe that this strikes at the root of perfection; it leaves no room for it at all. If we are never sanctified in any other sense than we are sanctified then, Christian perfection has no being. Consider the sermon on the Repentance of Believers, and you will see this clearly. O may God give you to have a right judgement in all things, and evermore to rejoice in His holy comfort!

John Wesley to Adam Clarke; London, November 26, 1790

(*JWL*, VIII, 249)

To retain the grace of God is much more than to gain it: hardly one in three does this. And this should be strongly and explicitly urged on all who have tasted of perfect love. If we can prove that any of our Local Preachers or Leaders, either directly or indirectly, speak against it, let him be a Local Preacher or Leader no longer. I doubt whether he shall continue in the Society. Because he that can speak thus in our congregations cannot be an honest man.

Letters of Horace Walpole

(*Letters*, edited by Paget Toynbee, 1903–5, VII, 49–50, 152; X, 280–1; XV, 6)

To John Chute, Bath, October 10, 1766

My health advances faster than my amusement. However, I have been at one opera, Mr. Wesley's. They have boys and girls with charming voices, that sing hymns, in parts, to Scotch ballad tunes; but indeed so long, that one would think they were already in eternity, and knew how much time they had before them. The chapel is very neat, with true Gothic windows (yet I am not converted); but I was glad to see that luxury is creeping in upon them before persecution: they have very neat mahogany stands for branches, and brackets of the same in taste. At the upper end is a broad *haut-pas* of four steps, advancing in the middle: at each end of the broadest part are two of *my* eagles,[1] with red cushions for the parson and clerk. Behind them rise three more steps, in the midst of which is a third eagle for pulpit. Scarlet armed-chairs to all three. On either hand, a balcony for elect ladies. The rest of the congregation sit on forms. Behind the pit, in a dark niche, is a plain table within rails; so you see the throne is for the apostle. Wesley is a lean elderly man, fresh-coloured, his hair smoothly combed, but with a *soupçon* of curl at the ends. Wondrous clean, but as evidently an actor as Garrick. He spoke his sermon, but so fast, and with so little accent, that I am sure he has often uttered it, for it was like a lesson. There were parts and eloquence in it; but towards the end he exalted his voice, and acted very ugly enthusiasm; decried learning, and told stories, like Latimer, of the fool of his college, who said, 'I *thanks* God for everything.' Except a few from curiosity, and *some honourable women*, the congregation was very mean.

¹ The reference is to marble eagles which Walpole had at Strawberry Hill and indicates that Walpole is referring to the Countess of Huntingdon's chapel in Bath.

To the Rev. William Cole, Strawberry Hill, December 19, 1767

For the Catholic religion, I think it very consumptive – with a little patience, if Whit[e]field, Wesley, my Lady Huntingdon, and that rogue Madan live, I do not doubt but we shall have something very like it here. And yet I had rather live at the end of a tawdry religion, than at the beginning, which is always more stern and hypocritic.

To the Rev. William Cole, July 12, 1778

Exalted notions of Church matters are contradictions in terms to the low-liness and humility of the Gospel. There is nothing sublime but the Divinity. Nothing is sacred but as His work. A tree or a brute stone is more respectable as such, than a mortal called an Archbishop, or an edifice called a Church, which are the puny and perishable productions of men. Calvin and Wesley had just the same views as the Popes; power and wealth their objects. I abhor both . . .

To Miss Mary Berry. Strawberry Hill, June 23, 1791

The patriarchess of the Methodists, Lady Huntingdon, is dead. Now she and Whit[e]field and Wesley are gone, the sect will probably decline: a second crop of apostles seldom acquire the influence of the founders.

Thomas Taylor in Scotland

(*EMP*, V, 28–37)

One great obstacle in my way was, a new edition of the 'Eleven Letters', ascribed to Mr. Hervey, had just come out, prefaced by a minister in Edinburgh, a man much esteemed in Scotland.¹ These Letters fully answered their design. They carried gall and wormwood wherever they came. So that it was a sufficient reason for everyone to keep his distance, because I was connected with Mr. Wesley. I laboured to keep as clear as possible of controversy, dwelling chiefly upon repentance, faith, and the new birth. Indeed, as I then leaned much both to the doctrine of the imputed righteousness of Christ, and final perseverance, I had no temptation to bring in controversy.

I soon found that persons may easily learn to con over several Gospel topics, – such as original sin, the offices of Christ, His being the only Saviour, and the like, – and yet be haughty, self-sufficient, unbroken-hearted sinners. This I saw, and levelled all my powers against it. I soon found their pharisaic hearts could not brook it. Hence I drew their resentment upon me, and plenty of lies and calumnies were soon spread abroad.

I continued preaching night and morning, when opportunity offered; and tried much to procure a place to preach in, as the winter was now come on. I believe I was disappointed in ten or twelve different places. I sold my horse; and a preacher who passed through Glasgow, to Ireland, having his horse lamed, and little money left, I spared about three guineas to help him on his way. This brought my stock into a small compass; and having everything to pay for, I was reduced to a short allowance. I paid three shillings per week for my room, fire, and attendance; but I really kept a very poor house. I confess that I never kept so many fast-days, either before or since. But how to keep up my credit was a difficulty; for I was afraid my landlady would think me either poor or covetous. I frequently desired her not to provide anything for dinner; and a little before noon, I dressed myself, and walked out, till after dinner, and then came home to my hungry room, with a hungry belly. However, she thought I had dined out somewhere; so I saved my credit . . .

After the society was increased to forty or fifty, some of them began to inquire how I was maintained. They asked me if I had an estate, or some supplies from England. I told them I had neither; but having sold my horse, I had made what little I had go as far as I could. I then explained our custom to them. I told them of the little matter we usually received from our people. The poor souls were much affected, and they very liberally supplied my wants, as also those that came after me. I stayed with them till the middle of April [1766], and then bade them an affectionate farewell; leaving about seventy persons joined together. Though I had many trials in Glasgow, yet I had much opportunity to pursue my study; and the privilege of the college library was of singular advantage to me. But I own I did not live so near to God, the latter part of my time, as I did in the beginning. I seldom enlarge my acquaintance, but I find it enlarges my temptations: so I found cause to cry out, 'Lord, pardon my trifling and want of deep seriousness!'

In order to establish societies betwixt Edinburgh and Glasgow, I preached in several towns which lie between, such as Burrowstounness, Linlithgow, Falkirk, and Killsyth; but I fear with little fruit. The Scots are naturally shy, and suspicious of strangers; and anything in religion that appears new, or not agreeing with their established forms, they are exceeding jealous of. Hence class-meeting has the appearance of novelty, and has often been suspected to border upon the Popish auricular confession of sins, though a different thing: hence many in Scotland have been startled at it, and very loth to engage in it.

Before I dismiss Scotland, I would just take notice, that I have reason to bless God, some good was done by my poor endeavours: some sinners were brought to God; my labours, in the general, were acceptable; and the people gave me many proofs of their friendship, although my entrance among them was unpromising. On the other hand, I see much cause for humility and deep self-abasement. I see that I might have managed my mission abundantly better; I really was neither so holy nor steady as I might have been. I have reason to cry to the Lord, and also to apply to the blood of sprinkling, or I should be an outcast from God, and an heir of eternal misery.

¹ Dr John Erskine: see p. 155 above.

The Future of the Methodist Connexion

(*Minutes*, I, 87–9; cf. *JWL*, V, 143–5)

In May 1769 John Wesley sent a copy of the following letter to his brother, asking for his comments. He then read it to the Itinerants during the Conference of that year. For his letter of April 19, 1764 to other evangelical clergymen, see *JWL*, IV, 235–9; *JWJ*, V, 60–6.

Friday, August 4th, Mr. W. read the following paper:—

My dear Brethren,

1. It has long been my desire, that all those Ministers of our Church who believe and preach salvation by faith might cordially agree between themselves, and not hinder but help one another. After occasionally pressing this in private conversation, wherever I had opportunity, I wrote down my thoughts upon the head, and sent them to each in a letter. Out of fifty or sixty to whom I wrote, only three vouchsafed me an answer. So I give this up. I can do no more. They are a rope of sand; and such they will continue.

2. But it is otherwise with the Travelling Preachers in our Connexion:

you are at present one body. You act in concert with each other, and by united counsels. And now is the time to consider what can be done in order to continue this union. Indeed, as long as I live, there will be no great difficulty: I am, under God, a centre of union to all our Travelling as well as Local Preachers.

They all know me and my communication. They all love me for my work's sake: and, therefore, were it only out of regard to me, they will continue connected with each other. But by what means may this connexion be preserved when God removes me from you?

3. I take it for granted, it cannot be preserved by any means between those who have not a single eye. Those who aim at anything but the glory of God, and the salvation of men; who desire to seek any earthly thing, whether honour, profit, or ease, will not, cannot continue in the Connexion; it will not answer their design. Some of them, perhaps a fourth of the whole number, will procure preferment in the Church. Others will turn Independents, and get separate congregations, like John Edwards and Charles Skelton. Lay your accounts with this, and be not surprised if some you do not suspect be of this number.

4. But what method can be taken to preserve a firm union between those who choose to remain together?

Perhaps you might take some such steps as these:—

On notice of my death, let all the Preachers in England and Ireland repair to London within six weeks:

Let them seek God by solemn fasting and prayer:

Let them draw up articles of agreement, to be signed by those who choose to act in concert:

Let those be dismissed who do not choose it, in the most friendly manner possible:

Let them choose, by votes, a Committee of three, five, or seven, each of whom is to be Moderator in his turn:

Let the Committee do what I do now; propose Preachers to be tried, admitted, or excluded; fix the place of each Preacher for the ensuing year, and the time of the next Conference.

5. Can anything be done now, in order to lay a foundation for this future union? Would it not be well, for any that are willing, to sign some articles of agreement before God calls me hence? Suppose something like these:—

'We, whose names are underwritten, being thoroughly convinced of the necessity of a close union between those whom God is pleased to use as instruments in this glorious work, in order to preserve this union between ourselves, are resolved, God being our helper,

'I. To devote ourselves entirely to God; denying ourselves, taking up our cross daily; steadily aiming at one thing, to save our own souls, and them that hear us.

'II. To preach the old Methodist doctrines, and no other, contained in the Minutes of the Conferences.

'III. To observe and enforce the whole Methodist discipline, laid down in the said Minutes.'

The Preachers then desired Mr. W. to extract the most material part of the Minutes, and send a copy to each Assistant, which he might communicate to all the Preachers in his Circuit, to be seriously considered. Our Meeting was then concluded with solemn prayer.

The Controversy over Calvinism, 1770

(*Minutes*, 1770)

The old rift between the Arminian and Calvinistic branches of the Methodist movement was widened in the 1770s, largely as a result of the following declaration in the Conference Minutes of 1770. A rejoinder by the Rev. Walter Shirley led to the publication of Fletcher's *Checks to Antinomianism*.

Q. 28. What can be done to revive the work of God where it is decayed?
    A. 1. We must needs visit from house to house, were it only to avoid idleness. I am afraid we are idle still. Do we not loiter away many hours in every week? Try yourselves. Keep a diary of your employment but for a week, and then read it over. No idleness can consist with growth in grace. Nay, without exactness in redeeming time, it is impossible to retain even the life you received in justification. Can we find a better method of visiting than that set down in the Minutes of 1766, pp. 63–68. When will you begin? . . .

    6. Take heed to your doctrine.

We said, in 1744,[1] 'We have leaned too much toward Calvinism.' Wherein?

1. With regard to *man's faithfulness*. Our Lord Himself taught to use the expression. And we ought never to be ashamed of it. We ought steadily to assert, on His authority, that if a man is not 'faithful in the unrighteous mammon,' God will not give him the true riches.

2. With regard to *working for life*. This also our Lord has expressly commanded us. 'Labour' – ἐργάζεσθε, literally, 'work' – 'for the meat that endureth to everlasting life.' And, in fact, every believer, till he comes to glory, works *for* as well as *from* life.

3. We have received it as a maxim, that 'a man is to do nothing in order to justification.' Nothing can be more false. Whoever desires to

find favour with God should 'cease from evil, and learn to do well.'
Whoever repents should do 'works meet for repentance'. And if this is
not in order to find favour, what does he do them for?

Review the whole affair.

1. Who of us is *now* accepted of God?

He that now believes in Christ, with a loving, obedient heart.

2. But who among those that never heard of Christ?

He that feareth God, and worketh righteousness, according to the
light he has.

3. Is this the same with 'he that is sincere'?

Nearly, if not quite.

4. Is not this 'salvation by works'?

Not by the *merit* of works, but by works as a *condition*.

5. What have we then been disputing about for these thirty years?

I am afraid, about words.

6. As to *merit* itself, of which we have been so dreadfully afraid: we
are rewarded '*according to our works*', yea, '*because of our works*'. How does
this differ from *for the sake of our works?* And how differs this from *secundum
merita operum*, – as our works *deserve?* Can you split this hair? I doubt I
cannot.

7. The grand objection to one of the preceding propositions is drawn
from matter of fact. God does in fact justify those who, by their own
confession, neither feared God nor wrought righteousness. Is this an
exception to the general rule?

It is a doubt, God makes any exception at all. But how are we sure that
the person in question never did fear God and work righeousness? His
own saying so is not proof: for we know how all that are convinced of
sin undervalue themselves in every respect.

8. Does not talking of a justified or a sanctified state tend to mislead
men? almost naturally leading them to trust in what was done in one
moment? Whereas, we are every hour and every moment pleasing or
displeasing to God, according to our works; according to the whole of
our inward tempers, and our outward behaviour.

[1] See Minutes of the 1744 Conference, p. 68 above.

Checks to Antinomianism, 1771

(John Fletcher, *First Check to Antinomianism*, 1771)

As a consequence of the doctrine of general redemption, Mr. Wesley lays down two axioms, of which he never loses sight in his preaching. *The first* is, that ALL OUR SALVATION IS OF GOD IN CHRIST, and therefore OF GRACE; – all opportunities, invitations, inclination, and power to believe being bestowed upon us of mere grace; – grace most absolutely free: and so far, I hope, that all who are called Gospel ministers agree with him. But he proceeds farther; for, *secondly*, he asserts with equal confidence, that according to the Gospel dispensation, ALL OUR DAMNATION IS OF OURSELVES, by our obstinate unbelief and avoidable unfaithfulness; as we may 'neglect so great salvation', desire to 'be excused' from coming to the feast of the Lamb, 'make light of' God's gracious offers, refuse to 'occupy', bury our talent, and act the part of the 'slothful servant'; or, in other words, 'resist, grieve, do despite to' and 'quench the Spirit of grace', *by our moral agency* . . .

As to the *moral agency* of man, Mr. Wesley thinks it cannot be denied upon the principles of common sense and civil government; much less upon those of natural and revealed religion; as nothing would be more absurd than to bind us by laws of a civil or spiritual nature; nothing more foolish than to propose to us punishments and rewards; and nothing more capricious than to inflict the one or bestow the other upon us; if we were not *moral agents*.

He is therefore persuaded, the most complete system of divinity is that in which neither of those two axioms is superseded: He thinks it is bold and unscriptural to set up the one at the expense of the other, convinced that the prophets, the apostles, and Jesus Christ left us no such precedent; and that, to avoid what is termed *legality*, we must not run into refinements which they knew nothing of, and make them perpetually contradict themselves: nor can we, he believes, without an open violation of the laws of candour and criticism, lay a greater stress upon a few obscure and controverted passages, than upon a hundred plain and irrefragable Scripture proofs. He therefore supposes that those persons are under a capital mistake who maintain only the first Gospel axiom, and under pretence of securing to God *all* the glory of the salvation of *one* elect, give to perhaps *twenty* reprobates full room to lay *all* the blame of their damnation either upon their first parents, or their Creator. This way of making twenty *real* holes, in order to stop a *supposed* one, he cannot see consistent either with wisdom or Scripture.

Thinking it therefore safest not to 'put asunder' the truths which 'God has joined together', he makes all extremes meet in one blessed

Scriptural medium. With the Antinomian he preaches, 'God worketh in you both to will and to do of his good pleasure;' and with the Legalist he cries, 'Work out, therefore, your own salvation with fear and trembling;' and thus he has all St. Paul's doctrine. With the Ranter he says, 'God has chosen you, you are elect;' but, as it is 'through sancti-fication of the Spirit and belief of the truth', with the disciples of Moses he infers, 'make your calling and election sure, for if ye do these things ye shall never fall.' Thus he presents his hearers with all St. Peter's system of truth, which the others had rent to pieces.

Again, according to the *first* axiom, he says with the perfect Preacher, 'All things are now ready;' but with him he adds also, according to the *second*, 'Come, lest you never taste the Gospel feast.' Thinking it ex-tremely dangerous not to divide the word of God aright, he endeavours to give to every one the portion of it that suits him, cutting, according to times, persons, and circumstances, either with the smooth or the rough edge of his two-edged sword. Therefore, when he addresses those that are steady, and 'partakers of the *Gospel* grace from the first day until now', as the Philippians, he makes use of the *first* principle, and testifies his confidence, 'that he who hath begun a good work in them, will perform it until the day of Christ.' But when he expostulates with per-sons, 'that ran well, and do not now obey the truth,' according to his *second* axiom, he says to them, as St. Paul did to the Galatians, 'I stand in doubt of you; ye are fallen from grace.'

In short, he would think that he mangled the Gospel, and forgot part of his awful commission, if, when he has declared that 'he who believeth shall be saved,' he did not also add, that he 'who believeth not shall be damned;' or, which is the same, that none perish merely for Adam's sin, but for their own unbelief, and wilful rejection of the Saviour's grace. Thus he advances God's glory every way, entirely ascribing to his mercy and grace all the salvation of the elect, and completely freeing him from the blame of directly or indirectly hanging the millstone of damnation about the neck of the reprobate. And this he effectually does, by showing that the former owe all they are, and all they have, to creating, preserv-ing, and redeeming love, whose innumerable bounties they freely and continually receive; and that the rejection of the latter has absolutely no cause but their obstinate rejecting of that astonishing mercy which wept over Jerusalem; and prayed, and bled even for those that shed the atoning blood – the blood that expiated all sin but that of final unbelief.

Women Preachers

Mary Bosanquet to John Wesley, 1771

(Copy in Mary Bosanquet's letter book, Duke University)

Very dear & Honoured Sir,

Various have been my hindrances in writing, but none sufficient to have kept me so long silent to you, had I not been at a loss on one particular subject. I wanted your advice and direction in an important point, viz to know if you approved my light in it. Yet I have been toss'd between the temptations of Satan and the arguments of men, that I really could not tell what I thought myself nor how to state the case fairly at all; but at present I think, both outward and inward circumstances tend to bring me to a crisis, and my light been [being?] clearer, I will now open all my mind: and I feel a faith God will make you my Director in this thing, so as to remove my scruples one way or the other.

My soul desires peace & would follow after it with all, especially with God's children, and more particularly with those that act as heads among us. I would hold up their hands in every point that lays within the short limits of my power, and perhaps can say more strongly than many, I honour them for their works' sake. Yet that word of the prophets has oft come to my mind, 'Woe is me that my mother has borne me a man of contention;' how painful is it to be forced to contend with those with whom one desires above all things to live in peace, is well known to you, Sir, by experience. My present situation is very peculiar –

When we first settled at Leytonstone, Sr. Ryan & I began with little kind of prayer meetings, and they were productive of a blessing. Afterwards, on coming into Yorkshire, Sr. Crosby, Br. S. & I did the same now and then, till the people desiring us to come to such and such of their houses the number of these meetings increased so as to return sometimes three or four times a week; the numbers of persons that came to them increased also, hundreds of carnal persons coming to them, who would not go near a preaching-house; and it is enough to say God was with us and made it known by the effects in many places.

However, about a month ago, one of our preachers began to express great dislike to it many ways. We conversed on it in a friendly manner and I asked him, if my abstaining from any more meetings in a particular place would satisfy him (tho' Mr. O. had desired me to come there). He said no. He thought it quite unscriptural for women to speak in the Church & his conscience constrained him to prevent it. We had a good deal more conversation but got no nearer, tho' were very friendly. Afterwards some others conversed with me on the same point, alledging the same objections and Satan strongly persuaded me to swallow them down altogether, and I found it very comfortable and easy to nature. However, on weighing the thing before the Lord, I think it appears to me thus: I believe I am called to do all I can for God, and in order thereto, when I am asked to go with Br. T. to a prayer meeting, I may both sing, pray and converse with them, either particularly, or in general, according to the numbers. Likewise when Br. T. goes to preach in little country places, after he has done, I believe I may speak a few words to the people and pray with them. Twice it has happened, thro' the zeal of the people, that they gave out a meeting in a preaching house, because they had no private house that would hold the people, nor one quarter of them. When we came I was sorry, but could not tell what to do; hundreds of unawakened persons were there, & my heart yearned over them. I feared my Master should say, 'Their blood will I require of you.' So after Br. T. had preached I spoke to them. I believe I may go as far as I have mentioned above. But several object to this in our own round, & out of it, saying, 'A woman ought not to teach, nor take authority over the man.' I understand that text to mean no more than that a woman shall not take authority over her husband, but be in subjection, neither shall she teach at all by usurping authority, she shall not meddle in Church discipline, neither order nor regulate anything in which men are concerned in the matters of the Church; but I do not apprehend it means she shall not entreat sinners to come to Jesus, nor say, Come, and I will tell you what God hath done for my soul.

Ob:— But the Apostle says, I suffer not a woman to speak in the Church – but learn at home. I answer – was not that spoke in reference to a time of dispute and contention, when many were striving to be heads and leaders, so that his saying, She is not to speak, here seems to me to imply no more than the other, she is not to meddle with Church Government.

Ob:— Nay, but it meant literally, not to speak by way of Edification, while in the Church, or company of promiscuous worshippers.

An:— Then why is it said, Let the woman prophesy with her head covered, or can she prophesy without speaking? or ought she to speak but not to edification?

Ob:— She may now and then, if under a peculiar impulse, but never else.

An:— But how often is she to feel this impulse? Perhaps you will say, two or three times in her life; perhaps *God* will say, two or three times in a week, or day – and where shall we find the Rule for this? But the consequences (here I acknowledge is my own objection, that all I do is *lawful*, I have no doubt, but is it expedient? that, my dear Sir, I want your light in) but what are the consequences feared?

Ob:— Why, for forty that comes to hear the preaching, one hundred & fifty will come to your meetings. Will not this cause their hands to hang down?

An:— That only forty comes to preaching, I am sorry for, but that perhaps a hundred careless carnal sinners comes to our meetings (who would not otherwise hear at all) I am not sorry for, neither should I think this would make the hands of any sensible, gracious man hang down. He must know tis no excellence in us that draws them, but the novelty of the thing; and does it not bring many to preaching, let any impartial person judge.

Ob:— But a worse consequence than this is to be feared: will not some improper woman follow your example?

An:— This I acknowledge I have feared; but the same might be said of preachers that come out, will not some improper man follow them?

Ob:— But if an improper man comes out, the Church has power to stop his mouth, but you will not let yours be stopped.

An:— Yes, on the same condition I will. You would not say to him, no *man* must speak, therefore be silent; but only, *You* are not the proper man. Now allowing women may speak, prove to me, it is not my personal call, and I will both lovingly and cheerfully obey.

Ob:— But is it safe to trust women to teach? Does not the Apostle say, She was first in the transgression, therefore let her take no authority, and does not Mr. Wesley observe, She is more easily deceived, and more easily deceives?

An:— He does, and there is much truth in it. On this supposition, the man's understanding is stronger, and his passions harder, consequently not so easily wrought on; and on the other hand, supposing the woman's understanding weaker, & her passions more tender, she is certainly more liable to be deceived; and probably speaking more to the affections than to the understanding, she is more likely to deceive; so far I allow. But may not all this objection be removed by this single caution: Let no woman be allowed to speak among the people any longer than she speaks and acts according to the Oracles of God; and while she speaks according to the truth she cannot lead the people into an error.

Ob:— Well, but is it consistent with that modesty the Christian religion requires in a woman professing godliness?

An:— It may be, and is, painful to it, but I do not see it inconsistent with it, and that for this reason: does not Christian modesty stand in these two particulars, Purity and Humility? 1st I apprehend it consists in cutting off every act, word and thought that in the least infringes on the purity God delights in. 2dly in cutting off every act, word, and thought, which in the least infringes on *humility*, knowing throughly our own place, and rendering to every one their due. Endeavouring to be little, and unknown, as far as the order of God will permit, and simply following that order, leaving the event to God. Now I do not apprehend Mary sinned against either of these heads, or could in the least be accused of immodesty, when she carried the joyful news of her Lord's

Resurrection and in that sense taught the Teachers of Mankind. Neither was the woman of Samaria to be accused of immodesty when she invited the whole city to come to Christ. Neither do I think the woman mentioned in the 20th chapter of the 2nd Samuel could be said to sin against modesty, tho' she called the General of the opposite army to converse with her, and then (verse the 22nd) went to all the people, both Heads and others, to give them her advice and by it the City was saved. Neither do I suppose Deborah did wrong in publicly declaring the message of the Lord, and afterwards accompanying Barak to war, because his hands hung down at going without her.

Ob:— But all these were extraordinary calls; sure you will not say yours is an extraordinary call?

An:— If I did not believe so, I would not act in an extraordinary manner. I do not believe every woman is called to speak publicly, no more than every man to be a Methodist preacher, yet some have an extraordinary call to it, and woe be to them if they obey it not.

Ob:— But do you believe you have this public call?

An:— Not as absolute as some others, nevertheless, I feel a part of it, and what little I see to be my call, I dare not leave undone.

Ob:—But if the people are continually coming to your Meetings, they will not have time to attend the stated ones.

An:— That I have often thought of, and therefore, I know no place except home where I meet more than once a month, and sometimes not that, as there is so many places to go to, and that caution, not to multiply meetings, I see very necessary.

Now, my dear Sir, I have told you all my mind on this head, and taken the freedom to incroach a deal on your time and I find a liberty to say, I believe your exact direction I shall be enabled to follow, and shall be greatly obliged to you for the same.

Mr. Oliver is very desirous of our doing all the good we can; and indeed I am pained for the trouble he has had on our account. But it is not only on ours, for various difficulties have, I believe, interrupted some of his comfort this year; if he stays another year with us, I hope he will see more fruit of his labours: the Lord gives him a patient, loving spirit, and his preaching is very animating and profitable.

I praise my God I feel Him very near, and I prove His faithfulness every day, but I want to live as I do not, and to feel every moment that word, My God and my all. I am &c. M.B.

Wesley's reply; Londonderry, June 13, 1771

(*JWL*, V, 257; cf. Frank Baker, *John Wesley and the Church of England*, 1969, p. 204)

Londonderry, June 13, 1771.

My dear sister,

I think the strength of the cause rests there, in your having an *Extra-ordinary* Call. So, I am persuaded, has every one of our Lay-preachers: otherwise I could not countenance his preaching at all. It is plain to me that the whole Work of God termed Methodism is an extraordinary dispensation of His Providence. Therefore I do not wonder if several things occur therein which do not fall under ordinary rules of discipline. St. Paul's ordinary rule was, 'I permit not a woman to speak in the congregation'. Yet in extraordinary cases he made a few exceptions; at Corinth, in particular.

I am, my dear sister,

Your affectionate brother,
J. WESLEY.

The Madeley Saint

John Fletcher was vicar of Madeley, Shropshire, from 1760 until his death in 1785, firmly withstanding pressure from Wesley to abandon his parish for an itinerant ministry (see pp. 176–8). Here we have glimpses of both his spiritual life and his parish work.

Fletcher to Charles Wesley; Madeley, May 26, 1771

(Ms at Duke University)

My very dear friend,

Tho' I am as a dead man out of mind I do not forget you; while I wander in one part of the wilderness, methinks, I see you turning in another. You hope better days, my hopes of seeing them at times fails me. Were it not for a *Whither should we go*[1] &c. I know not at times where I would betake myself. I have seen I think but *one awakening* in my parish these six years. Offences of the most public sort arise daily among the few professors, and those who call Jesus Lord do not seem to me to have the seal of heaven, the power of the living God with them and in them. This reflection is levelled at myself first, I am at times tempted to believe we live in the hardest gospel-days as to power and internal life; tho' we hear so much about the evangelical letter, which keeps (as I fear) poor stinking Lazaruses quiet in their graves.

I was not more satisfied about Trevecka than about my parish. A deep sense of my incapacity, love of peace, a sight of the absolute necessity of openly standing it out against some concerned in the Work [at Trevecka: deleted] or wounding my conscience: Difficulties every day arising with respect to doctrinal points, a conviction that an Arminian is not a proper person to preside over a college that takes a pretty strong Calvinist turn, and a persuasion that a Calvinist itinerant ministry will go out from thence to feed the professors of that sentimental denomination, and that a moderate Calvinist must superintend (to say nothing of some particular steps relative to Mr. Benson's dismission & your brother's minutes) are the reasons that have engaged *me to resign* my charge in Wales. I have only left it as Under Director, we parted in love, and I am still the servant of the College and the admirer of its extraordinary Foundress.[2]

I want a heart filled with the Spirit and power of Jesus. I am *not yet established* in the contemplation of his glorious love: nor am I yet light in the Lord, and free from the carnal mind. In short, where the Spirit of the Lord [is] there is liberty, but I am still in bondage to [many?] things, nor does it avail me to make a profession which my heart, my life, my want of power and the Holy Ghost shew to be more apparent than substantial. I always fail in persevering in prayer and self-denial; and therefore am always a backslider in heart, filled with my own ways. I open my case to you that you may know how to advise and pray for your unworthy friend

J. FLETCHER

Fletcher to Joseph Benson; Madeley c. 1776

(Ms at Duke University)

The few professors I see in these parts are so far from being what I could wish them and myself to be, that I cannot but cry out, 'Lord, how long wilt thou give thine heritage up to desolation or barrenness? How long shall the heathen say, Where is now their indwelling God?' I hope it is better with you in the North.[3]

---

[1] Perhaps an allusion to the words of Peter in John vi.68.

[2] From 1768 until just before writing this letter, Fletcher had also served as visiting principal of Lady Huntingdon's college at Trevecka, near Brecon, despite his differences from the Countess on doctrinal matters.

[3] Benson was stationed in the Newcastle Circuit in 1775 and 1776.

The Itinerants

(Ms at Drew University)

A letter endorsed by Wesley 'March 3, 1772'. Described in the catalogue as written by 'E. Marriott': possibly Elizabeth Marriott, wife of the City businessman, William Marriott, who was one of Wesley's executors.

Revd. Sir,

I think I can truly say in the presence of God that I desire to do good and to glorify Him. For this only I desire to live, and from this motive alone I offer the following things to your consideration, which I hope you will receive with *candour*, and pardon what you observe *weak* or *wrong* in them. I look upon you as a person whom God has peculiarly chosen and raised up to be the chief instrument of the *present* revival of his work among us. He has exalted you to an higher station in his Church and Kingdom, than any man living upon the face of the earth. He has made you instrumental of more good, has committed more to your care, and consequently more is required from you. It is peculiarly your province to inspect the affairs of the Church, and to determine the expediency and fitness of every thing that is proposed as a means of the increase and prosperity of the work of God. Considering things in this light, I was the more encouraged to trouble you with these lines.

We all know of how vast importance it is in this work, that the Preachers should be truly alive unto God, that they enjoy a sense of his favour and the witness of his Spirit within them that they are his children and heirs of his glory; and that their hearts be earnestly engaged in this great work. Yet I think it is too plain to be denied that there are some Preachers in the Connection, whose tempers and private character strongly indicate that they are neither alive to God nor heartily engaged in his work. Of this I believe you are sufficiently sensible, and doubtless mourn on account of it. Whatever therefore tends to remedy this must be of universal advantage and tend to the benefit of the whole body of the Methodists.

The most probable means to remove the evil and to promote this universal good, I think is for *you* to meet all the preachers once in 12 months, and spend an hour with three, never more than four at once, in the closest conversation possible, by way of band meeting. This you may with great care do, without breaking in upon your settled plan in any respect (excepting a few Preachers who remain in Ireland) partly as you go on your long journey, and partly at the Conference. For as you lay the plan of your journey before you set out, you might give every Assistant timely notice when you will be on his Circuit, and what places you intend to visit, with orders that he shall appoint the most convenient place for all the Preachers on his Circuit to meet you. The few that you could not see this way you might see at the Conference.

The usefulness of this plan would be unspeakably great. It would surprisingly awaken the minds of the Preachers; it would endear you to them, and them to you; it would engage them more seriously and earnestly in the work of the Gospel, and I am persuaded would not be without its comfortable effects on your own mind. But in order to do this effectually (pardon, dear Sir, my great freedom, which proceeds from a fulness of love and desire of good) you will need to call in to your assistance all your *wisdom,* your *zeal* and your *firmness* and *resolution* of mind. A few general questions will be of no service. To meet them in a loose or general way will be nearly as bad as not meeting them at all. Their consciences must be well searched and their private conduct strictly examined. And this will exercise all the wisdom and penetration of one as well versed in Divinity as yourself; so that I know of no other man living that is capable of the work. Here you will have an opportunity of speaking to everyone without any apparent design, what you either know or fear concerning him. And this will prevent that disagreeable and *pernicious* method of appointing one person to reprove another. They will receive *your* reproof and advice as from the mouth of God: it will break their hearts in pieces; it will humble them in the dust and make them more deeply concerned for the salvation of their own soul and of those that hear them. O who can conceive the blessed fruit that would attend this labour of love. In speaking to the Preachers you speak, as it were, to all the people at once, and effectually profit them. In being a means of quickening and stirring up a Preacher, you are perhaps instrumental of the conversion of hundreds. Surely no time could be spent with equal advantage to this. I am confident that you would do [more] good by speaking to the Preachers in this manner for one hour than by [speaking], writing and preaching for a whole week. In the station [in which God has] placed you it is certainly a duty which He requires at your [hand?].

O how will you give up your account with joy to the great Shepherd and Bishop of souls, if you should omit so principal a part of your charge? You are indeed the Father of the people; but the Preachers are in a peculiar sense your Sons in the Gospel. They therefore claim your first attention. For according to their spirit and temper, their zeal and diligence, all your other labours will be rendered more or less extensively useful. It seems therefore a piece of necessary prudence to pay a particular regard to their state in the first place, that every other thing may be done with success. These, Sir, are the thoughts that have occurred to me on this subject, which I do not dictate as a certain rule for your conduct, but only offer to your consideration, that your superior wisdom may determine of them as shall appear most for the general good.

I am, dear Sir, with great sincerity,

Your Friend and Admirer.

'Wesley's Designated Successor'

John Wesley to John Fletcher; Shoreham, January 15, 1773

(*JWL*, VI, 10–12)

Dear Sir,

What an amazing work has God wrought in these kingdoms in less than forty years! And it not only continues but increases throughout England, Scotland, and Ireland; nay, it has lately spread into New York, Pennsylvania, Virginia, Maryland, and Carolina. But the wise men of the world say, 'When Mr. Wesley drops, then all this is at an end!' And so it surely will unless, before God calls him hence, one is found to stand in his place. For οὐκ ἀγαθὸν πολυκοιρανίη·εἷς κοίρανος ἔστω.[1] I see more and more, unless there be one προεστώς,[2] the work can never be carried on. The body of the preachers are not united; nor will any part of them submit to the rest: so that either there must be *one* to preside over *all* or the work will indeed come to an end.

But who is sufficient for these things? qualified to preside both over the preachers and people? He must be a man of faith and love and one that has a single eye to the advancement of the kingdom of God. He must have a clear understanding; a knowledge of men and things, particularly of the Methodist doctrine and discipline; a ready utterance; diligence and activity, with a tolerable share of health. There must be added to these, favour with the people, with the Methodists in general. For unless God turn their eyes and their hearts towards him, he will be quite incapable of the work. He must likewise have some degree of learning; because there are many adversaries, learned as well as unlearned, whose mouths must be stopped. But this cannot be done unless he be able to meet them on their own ground.

But has God provided one so qualified? Who is he? *Thou art the man!* God has given you a measure of loving faith and a single eye to His glory. He has given you some knowledge of men and things, particularly of the whole plan of Methodism. You are blessed with some health, activity, and diligence, together with a degree of learning. And to all these He has lately added, by a way none could have foreseen, favour both with the preachers and the whole people.

Come out in the name of God! Come to the help of the Lord against the mighty! Come while I am alive and capable of labour!

> Dum superest Lachesi quod torqueat, et pedibus me
> Porto meis, nullo dextram subeunte bacillo.[3]

Come while I am able, God assisting, to build you up in faith, to ripen your gifts, and to introduce you to the people. *Nil tanti.* What possible employment can you have which is of *so great importance*?

But you will naturally say, 'I am not equal to the task; I have neither grace nor gifts for such an employment.' You say true; it is certain you have not. And who has? But do you not know *Him* who is able to give them? perhaps not at once, but rather day by day: as each is, so shall your strength be.

'But this implies,' you may say, 'a thousand crosses, such as I feel I am not able to bear.' You are not able to bear them now; and they are not now come. Whenever they do come, will He not send them in due number, weight, and measure? And will they not all be for your profit, that you may be a partaker of His holiness?

Without conferring, therefore, with flesh and blood, come and strengthen the hands, comfort the heart, and share the labour of

Your affectionate friend and brother.

---

[1] Homer, *Iliad*, II, 204: 'The rule of many is not good; let there be one ruler.'
[2] 'leader'.
[3] Juvenal, *Satires*, III, 27–8: 'While Lachesis has something left to spin, and I still walk without the help of a staff.'

John Fletcher to John Wesley; Madeley, February 6, 1773

(Henry Moore, *Life of Wesley*, 1824–5, II, 259–60)

I hope the Lord, who has so wonderfully stood by you hitherto, will preserve you to see many of your sheep, and *me* among the rest, enter into rest. Should Providence call you *first*, I shall do my best, by the Lord's assistance, to help *your brother* to gather the wreck, and keep together those who are not absolutely bent upon throwing away the Methodist doctrine or discipline, as soon as he that now letteth shall be removed out of their way. Every little help will then be necessary; and I hope, I shall not be backward to throw in my mite.

In the mean time, you stand sometimes in need of an assistant to serve tables, and occasionally to fill up a gap. Providence visibly appointed me to that office many years ago: And though it no less evidently called me here, yet I have not been without doubt, especially for some years past, whether it would not be expedient that I should resume my place, as your Deacon; not with any view of presiding over the Methodists after you (God knows!), but to save you a little in your old age, and be in the way of receiving, and perhaps of doing, more good. I have sometimes considered, how shameful it was that no Clergyman should join you, to keep in the church the work which the Lord had enabled you to carry on therein; and, as the little estate I have in my native country is sufficient for my maintenance, I have thought I would, one day or other, offer you and the Methodists my *free* services.

While my love of retirement, and my dread of appearing upon a higher stage than that I stand upon here, made me linger, I was providentially called to do something in Lady Huntingdon's plan; but being shut out there, it appears to me, I am again called to my first work.

Nevertheless, I would not leave this place, without a *fuller* persuasion that the time is quite come. Not that God uses me much *now* among my parishioners, but because I have not sufficiently cleared my conscience from the blood of all men, especially with regard to ferreting out the poor, and expostulating with the rich, who make it their business to fly from me. In the mean time, it shall be my employment to beg the Lord to give me light, to guide me by his counsel, and make me willing to go any where or no where, to be any thing or nothing.

Entire Sanctification

Sarah Crosby to John Wesley; Cross Hall, Jan. 26, 1773

(Ms at Duke University)

I own I have been long silent to your important questions, tho' not for want of regard; but travelling and many engagements prevented my having the quiet, undisturbed time for reading over the plain account of perfection &c., which I thought was quite needful in order to answer you justly & particularly.

But now I can assure you with a pleasing satisfaction, that I was blest in reading it, finding it solid food for my soul. But when that tract was first published, I did not altogether see with my own eyes; so did not fully approve.

Though there is one word which I have heard many express their dislike of, nor can I say that I like it. You say, 'The most perfect have continual need of the merits of Christ, even for their *actual transgressions.*' Would it not have been less exceptionable in some other words? As, *for their transgressions through ignorance*, which I humbly presume, dear Sir, is your meaning? Pardon the liberty I have taken in thus [writing?] to my truly honoured father.

I think I can likewise assure you, my judgment is the same *now* that it was *10* years ago, or more; unless for that space of time wherin I preferred S——R's judgment to my own; & to speak simply, I preferred it to everybody's. But I believe there is some difference in my judgment now from what it was 20 years past.

It is now 23 years since I felt a want of something more than I had; having been justified near 6 months. But the *Predestinarians* made perfection to appear such a bugbear, I was affrighted at the thought of it: yet continued to be very uneasy at times. When reading your sermon on Perfection I said, provided this is what Mr. Wesley means by perfection, this is what I want: & I believe God *can*, & that He *will*, make me thus perfect: and I can never rest till I attain it. After this time, I often thought of the only words I remembered in your sermon, the first time I heard you, which were, 'If it is possible for God to give us a little love, is it not possible for Him to fill us with love?' I then answered in my heart, 'Yes; it is possible, but *He won't do it.*' But now my language was changed, and I often said, Lord it is *possible*; O! that Thou wouldst fill my soul with love.

Soon after this I told you my case. You gave me a ticket: O blessed time, never to be forgotten by me. I now expected *soon* to be filled with pure love. And I felt great need of it, for my evil nature raged more than ever; & I was very unexperienced in the knowledge of God or myself. I had constant need of saying,

> Force my violence to be still.
> Captivate my every thought,
> *Charm*, & *melt*, & *change* my *will*,
> And bring me down to *naught*.

As I was now very simple, I freely & frequently expressed my desire & expectation and was willing to part with whatever could hinder my being closely united to Jesus. For my one desire was to love Him *perfectly*. But I was often told, I must have more knowledge of myself *first*, till I believed so *too*; and have sometimes thought myself better for knowing more of my evil nature than those that were happy in Jesus, whom I thought did not know themselves.

And now my judgment was changed for near five years to come; wherein I laboured and prayed for a deeper & deeper knowledge of myself, & a perfection that would save me from every natural infirmity & every deviation (though through ignorance) from the perfect Law of God: till at length the keen sense of want of constant union and communion with Him, who was indeed the beloved of my soul, constrained me to cry mightily to Him for help; for though I was favoured with much nearness to & *communion* with Him at times, I knew not how any longer to bear the feeling of anything that I knew displeased him, though in a less degree than ever. And my prayers and tears were not in vain: for Jesus shewed me that as He had answered for my actual transgressions in His own body on the Tree, so He had answered for my original sin, & for every deviation from the perfect Law. He then gave my heart a power to believe Him thus my whole Saviour, which I never could do before: & now I felt a peace come into my soul, superior to *all* I had ever known, & which I could not tell how to explain, till it came as though some one had spoken: It is the peace that ruled the heart of Christ in the days of His flesh. There was many more particulars, which I han't room for, and have acquainted you with many years ago. O may my every breath be praise.

And now my Lord instructed me as a little child, daily shewing me how wrong my former judgment had been; from feeling myself still surrounded with various infirmities, & yet a sweet, constant union with Him, which these did not interrupt nor would they have interrupted before but through want of faith. So that I now saw every failure in *obedience* was for want of more *faith*. And as I received freely, so I freely gave; labouring to shew all with whom I conversed the way of faith more perfectly.

And thus I *now* believe and endeavour to practise, and have so believed from the time above mentioned. (Only when I observed the wrong use some made of what *they* called faith, and how likely many more was thus to err, I spoke more of the *necessity* & *blessing* of self-knowledge: & doubtless a blessing it is to know much of our own helplessness & natural tendencies to depart from the living God, which faith *only*, as the instrument, saves us from.)

But in answer to your question, dear Sir, whether I *now* experience what I did *then*? I freely acknowledge I have not uninterruptedly enjoyed so great a degree of the glorious liberty wherewith Christ made me free 16 years past, as I did then: for although I have been kept in many a close & sore trial & temptation, yet in others I think I have sunk below my privilege: and I have sometimes been drawn in some degree from my centre, by preferring others' lights to my own. But gratefully do I praise my Heavenly Father that I could never find my rest below this blessed mark. Viz. Loving God with *all* my redeemed powers, & aiming to serve Him the best I could.

And glory be to His ever adorable name, I now find Him as precious and present with me as ever: He is the centre of all my hopes, the end of my enlarged desires. I have no pursuits nor wishes but to please Him, & no fears but to offend Him. I would live to do His *will*, or I would die to see *Him*. He knows I love Him with a measure of the same love wherewith He *has* & *does* love me: & I know He will be my friend in life & death the same.

All my good comes from Him; He is the life & strength of my soul,

& without Him I can do nothing: yea I am nothing. A poor, weak worm, helpless as infancy, and surrounded with numerous infirmities; Lord, help & humble me.

As one intirely unworthy your notice, dear Sir, I commend myself to your prayers, wishing you all the blessings of the new Covenant, with long life & life everlasting.

I remain with all due respect, in divine bonds,
Yr. Affly, obedient child & servant,
S. Crosby

The State of Methodism, 1773

Charles Wesley to Joseph Benson, January 19, 1773

(Ms at Duke University)

The grand want of our preachers is personal improvement, personal holiness. A man is never safe but in one of these two *frames*. Either happy in the presence of Christ, or miserable in the absence . . .

You seem a little too severe when you say, We are a fallen *people*. The love of many is surely waxt cold: not of *all*. Considering we have no persecution, & so many witnesses of their *own* perfection, I wonder there is so much life left among us. Be thankful for *that*. Don't fear the worst, but hope the best. You have more of Melanchthon's spirit than of Luther's.

The 'Benson/Fletcher Plan'

John Fletcher to John Wesley; August 1st, 1775

(*JWJ*, VIII, 331–4; taken from ms life of Benson by his son at MA)

Fletcher's proposals for the future of Methodism were based on suggestions made to him by Joseph Benson (ibid., pp. 328–30).

This is the day your conference with the Methodist preachers begins. As I pray'd early in the morning that God would give you all the spirit of wisdom and love to consult about the spread of the power of godliness the motion made by Mr. Benson in the letter I sent you came into my mind: And I saw it in a much more favourable light than I had done before: The wish of my soul was that you might be directed to see, and weigh things in a proper manner. About the middle of the day, as I met with you in spirit, the matter occurred to me again in so strong a manner that I think it my duty to put my thoughts upon paper, and send them to you.

You love the Church of England, and yet you are not blind to her freckles, nor insensible of her shackles. Your life is precarious; you have lately been shaken over the grave; you are spared it may be to take yet some important step, which may influence generations yet unborn. What, Sir, if you used your liberty as an Englishman, a Christian, a divine, and an extraordinary messenger of God? What, if with bold modesty you took a farther step towards the reformation of the Church of England? The admirers of the Confessional, and the gentlemen who have petitioned the Parliament from the Feathers' tavern,[1] cry aloud that our Church stands in need of being reform'd; but do not they want to corrupt her in some things, while they talk of reforming her in others? Now, Sir, God has given you that light, that influence, and that intrepidity which many of those gentlemen have not. You can reform, so far as your influence goes, without perverting; and, indeed, you have done it already. But have you done it professedly enough? Have you ever explicitly borne your testimony against all the defects of our Church? Might you not do this without departing from your professed attachment to her? Nay, might you not, by this means, do her the greatest of services? If the mother who gave you suck were yet alive, could you not reverence her, without reverencing her little whims and sinful peculiarities (if she had any)? If Alexander's good sense had not been clouded by his pride, would he have thought that his courtiers honoured him when they awkwardly carried their head upon one shoulder as he did, that they might look like him? I love the Church of England, I hope, as much as you do. But I do not love her so as to take her blemishes for ornaments. You know, Sir, that she is almost totally deficient in discipline, and she publicly owns it herself every Ash-Wednesday. What are her spiritual courts in general, but a catchpenny? As for her doctrine, although it is pure upon the whole, you know that some specks of Pelagian, Calvinian, and Popish dirt cleave to her articles, homilies, liturgy, and rubricks. These specks could with care be taken off, and doing it in the circle of your influence might, sooner or later, provoke our superiors to godly jealousy and a complete reformation. In order to this it is proposed:—

(1) That the growing body of the Methodists in Great Britain, Ireland, and America be formed into a general society – a daughter church of our holy mother.

(2) That this society shall recede from the Church of England in nothing but in some palpable defects, about doctrine, discipline, and unevangelical hierarchy.

(3) That this society shall be the *methodist*-church of England, ready to defend the as yet *unmethodized* church against all the unjust attacks of the dissenters – willing to submit to her in all things that are not unscriptural – approving of her ordination – partaking of her sacraments, and attending her service at every convenient opportunity.

(4) That a pamphlet be published containing the 39 articles of the Church of England rectified according to the purity of the gospel, together with some needful alterations in the liturgy and homilies – such as the expunging the damnatory clauses of the Athanasian creed, etc.

(5) That Messrs. Wesley, the preachers, and the most substantial methodists in London, in the name of the societies scattered thro' the kingdom, would draw up a petition and present it to the Archbishop of Canterbury informing his Grace, and by him the bench of the Bishops, of this design; proposing the reformed articles of religion, asking the protection of the Church of England, begging that this step might not be considered as a *schism*, but only as an attempt to avail ourselves of the liberty of English men, and Protestants, to serve God according to the purity of the gospel, the strictness of primitive discipline, and the original design of the Church of England, which was to reform, so far as time and circumstances would allow, *what ever* needed reformation.

(6) That this petition contain a request to the Bishops to ordain the methodist preachers which can pass their examination according to what is *indispensably* required in the canons of the Church. That instead of the ordinary testimonials the Bishops would allow of testimonials signed by Messrs. Wesley and some more clergymen, who would make it their business to enquire into the morals and principles of the candidates for orders. And that instead of a title, their Lordships would accept of a bond signed by twelve stewards of the Methodist societies, certifying that the candidate for holy orders shall have a proper maintenance. That if his Grace, etc., does not condescend to grant this request, Messrs. Wesley will be obliged to take an irregular (not unevangelical) step, and to ordain upon a church of England-independent plan such lay preachers as appear to them qualified for holy orders.

(7) That the preachers so ordained be the assistants in their respective circuits. That the helpers who are thought worthy be ordained Deacons, and that doubtful candidates be kept upon trial as they now are.

(8) That the Methodist preachers assembled in conference shall have the liberty to suspend and degrade any methodist preacher ordained or unordained, who shall act the part of a Balaam or a Demas.

(9) That when Messrs. W. are dead, the power of Methodist ordination be lodged, in three or five of the most steady methodist ministers under the title of *Moderators*, who shall overlook the flocks, and the other preachers as Mr. Wesley does now.

(10) That the most spiritual part of the common prayer shall be

extracted and published with the 39 rectified articles, and the minutes of the conferences (or the methodist canons) which (together with such regulations as may be made at the time of this establishment) shall be, next to the Bible, the vade mecum of the methodist preachers.

(12) That the important office of confirmation shall be performed with the utmost solemnity by Mr. Wesley or by the Moderators, and that none shall be admitted to the Sacrament of the Lord's Supper but such as have been confirmed or who are ready to be confirmed.

(13) That the grand plan upon which the Methodist preachers shall go, shall be to preach the doctrine of *grace* against the Socinians – the doctrine of *justice* against the Calvinists – and the doctrine of *holiness* against all the world: And that of consequence 3 such questions as these be put to the candidates for orders at the time of ordination—

I. Wilt thou maintain with all thy might the scripture doctrines of *grace*, especially the doctrine of a SINNER's *free* justification merely by a living faith in the blood and merits of Christ?

II. Wilt thou maintain with all thy might the scripture doctrines of *justice*, especially the doctrine of a BELIEVER's *remunerative* justification by the good works which ought to spring from justifying faith?

III. Wilt thou preach up Christian perfection, or the fulfilling of the law of Christ, against all the antinomians of the age; and wilt thou ardently press after it thyself, never resting till thou art perfected in humble love?

Perhaps to keep the work in the Church it might be proper to add:—

IV. Wilt thou consider thyself as a son of the Church of England, receding from her as little as possible: never railing against her clergy, and being ready to submit to her ordination, if any of the bishops will confer it upon thee?

(14) And lastly, that Kingswood school be entirely appropriated: (1) To the reception and improvement of the candidates for methodist orders: (2) To the education of the children of the preachers: and (3) to the keeping of the worn out methodist preachers, whose employment shall be to preserve the spirit of faith and primitive Christianity in the place; by which means alone the curse of a little *unsanctified* learning may be kept out.

---

[1] This was a petition for the abolition of subscription to the Thirty-nine Articles presented in 1772. It was defeated in Parliament, largely through the opposition of Edmund Burke.

John Wesley 'On Predestination'

(Sermon LVIII; originally published as *A Sermon on Romans VIII. 29, 30* in 1776. *JWW*, II, 226, 230; *Sermons* II, 416, 420–21)

Whom he did foreknow, he also did predestinate to be conformed to the image of his Son:—Whom he did predestinate, them he also called: And whom he called, them he also justified: And whom he justified, them he also glorified. Romans viii. 29, 30.

4. The more frequently and carefully I have considered it, the more I have been inclined to think that the Apostle is not here (as many have supposed) describing a chain of causes and effects; (this does not seem to have entered into his heart;) but simply showing *the method in which God works; the order* in which the several branches of salvation constantly follow each other. And this, I apprehend, will be clear to any serious and impartial inquirer, surveying the work of God either forward or backward; either from the beginning to the end, or from the end to the beginning. . . .

15. The sum of all is this: The almighty, all-wise God sees and knows, from everlasting to everlasting, all that is, that was, and that is to come, through one eternal *now*. With him nothing is either past or future, but all things equally present. He has, therefore, if we speak according to the truth of things, no foreknowledge, no afterknowledge. This would be ill consistent with the Apostle's words, 'With him is no variableness or shadow of turning;' and with the account he gives of himself by the Prophet, 'I the Lord change not.' Yet when he speaks to us, knowing whereof we are made, knowing the scantiness of our understanding, he lets himself down to our capacity, and speaks of himself after the manner of men. Thus, in condescension to our weakness, he speaks of his own purpose, counsel, plan, foreknowledge. Not that God has any need of counsel, of purpose, or of planning his work beforehand. Far be it from us to impute these to the Most High; to measure him by ourselves! It is merely in compassion to us that he speaks thus of himself, as foreknowing the things in heaven or earth, and as predestinating or fore-ordaining them. But can we possibly imagine that these expressions are to be taken literally? To one who was so gross in his conceptions might he not say, 'Thinkest thou I am such an one as thyself?' Not so: As the heavens are higher than the earth, so are my ways higher than thy ways. I know, decree, work, in such a manner as it is not possible for thee to conceive: But to give thee some faint, glimmering knowledge of my ways, I use the language of men, and suit myself to thy apprehensions in this thy infant state of existence.

16. What is it, then, that we learn from this whole account? It is this, and no more:—(1) God knows all believers; (2) wills that they should be saved from sin; (3) to that end, justifies them, (4) sanctifies, and (5) takes them to glory.

O that men would praise the Lord for this his goodness; and that they would be content with this plain account of it, and not endeavour to wade into those mysteries which are too deep for angels to fathom!

Toplady on Arminianism

Augustus Montague Toplady to John Fletcher, *c.* 1777

(Ms at Garrett-Evangelical Seminary)

An undated draft in Toplady's own hand, showing the levels to which even religious controversy could descend in the eighteenth century.

Sir,

It is always with concern that I find myself under a *necessity* of hanging any man in chains; by gibbetting him, on paper, in the view of posterity. I feel, on these occasions, something of that *reluctance* and mental *pain*, with which you & your system suppose the Deity to be afflicted, when, having done all he *can* to convert omnipotent sinners from the errors of their ways, he finds THEIR obstinacy *invincible* & his compassionate efforts unsuccessful; COMPELLED by the independent creatures whom he hath unfortunately made too strong for himself, he pronounces on them the sentence which he *wishes* might have been reversed into 'Come, ye blessed!' & lays on them that punishment which, sorely against his will, they oblige him to inflict.

This Arminian representation of GOD is blasphemous in itself & atheistical in its consequences. But it exhibits a very just portraiture of *Man* (& of myself among others), under such circumstances as those in which, through your own rashness & self-sufficiency, I now stand[?] in relation to you.

You have very lately favoured me with two pamphlets, one of which is mistakenly Christened 'An ANSWER to' my Vindication of the Decrees.[1] The other with much greater regard for modesty & truth, is humbly entitled 'Remarks on' my scheme of Christian and philosophical Necessity.[2]

The Switz mountain is, at length, delivered of its mice; which were begotten upon it, by the pressing necessity of Mr. John Wesley. And, to give the little squeakers their due, they resemble their progenitors to an hair.

Mr. Wesley has several highly prudential reasons for deputing you to enter the lists in his defence. The very bad use he has made of his free will, & his consciousness of *perfect love*, have rendered him additionally cautious, instead of casting out his fear.

¹ *An Answer to the Rev. Mr. Toplady's Vindication of the Decrees,* 1776.
² *A Reply to the Principal Arguments . . . being remarks on the Rev. Mr.Toplady's 'Scheme of Christian and Philosophical Necessity'*, 1777.

'The Catholic Spirit'

John Wesley, preface to *Hymns and Spiritual Songs, intended for the Use of Christians of all Denominations*, 1777

(*JWW*, XIV, 351–2)

For other expressions of Wesley's proto-ecumenism, see his sermons *A Caution against Bigotry* and *Catholic Spirit*.

1. The innumerable mischiefs which have arisen from bigotry, an immoderate attachment to particular opinions or modes of worship, have been observed and lamented, in all ages, by men of a calm and loving spirit. O when will it be banished from the face of the earth! When will all who sincerely love God employ their zeal, not upon ceremonies and notions, but upon justice, mercy, and the love of God!

2. The ease and happiness that attend, the unspeakable advantages that flow from, a truly catholic spirit, a spirit of universal love, (which is the very reverse of bigotry,) one would imagine, might recommend this amiable temper to every person of cool reflection. And who that has tasted of this happiness can refrain from wishing it to all mankind? Who that has experienced the real comfort, the solid satisfaction, of a heart enlarged in love toward all men, and, in a peculiar manner, to all that love God and the Lord Jesus Christ in sincerity, can avoid earnestly desiring that all men may be partakers of the same comfort?

3. It is with unspeakable joy, that these observe the spirit of bigotry greatly declining (at least, in every Protestant nation of Europe), end the spirit of love proportionably increasing. Men of every opinion and denomination now begin to bear with each other. They seem weary of tearing each other to pieces on account of small and unessential differences; and rather desire to build up each other in the great point wherein they all agree, – the faith which worketh by love, and produces in them the mind which was in Christ Jesus.

4. It is hoped, the ensuing collection of Hymns may in some measure contribute, through the blessing of God, to advance this glorious end, to promote this spirit of love, not confined to any opinion or party. There is not an hymn, not one verse, inserted here, but what relates to the common salvation; and what every serious and unprejudiced Christian, of whatever denomination, may join in. It is true, none but those who either already experience the kingdom of God within them, or, at least, earnestly desire so to do, will either relish or understand them. But all these may find either such prayers as speak the language of their souls when they are in heaviness; or such thanksgivings as express, in a low degree, what they feel, when rejoicing with joy unspeakable. Come, then, all ye children of the Most High, and let us magnify his name together; and let us with one mind and one mouth glorify God, even the Father of our Lord Jesus Christ!

Anglican Worship and Doctrine

John Wesley to Mary Bishop; London, October 10, 1778

(*JWL*, VI, 326–7)

The original Methodists were all of the Church of England; and the more awakened they were, the more zealously they adhered to it in every point, both of doctrine and discipline. Hence we inserted in the first Rules of our Society, 'They that leave the Church leave *us*.' And this we did, not as a point of prudence, but a point of conscience. We believe it utterly unlawful to separate from the Church unless sinful terms of communion were imposed; just as did Mr. Philip Henry, and most of those holy men that were contemporary with them.

'But the ministers of it do not preach the gospel.' Neither do the Independent or Anabaptist ministers. Calvinism is not the gospel; nay, it is farther from it than most of the sermons I hear at church. These are very frequently unevangelical; but those are anti-evangelical. They are (to say no more) equally wrong; and they are far more dangerously wrong. Few of the Methodists are now in danger from imbibing error from the Church ministers; but they are in great danger of imbibing the grand error – Calvinism – from the Dissenting ministers. Perhaps thousands have done it already, most of whom have drawn back to perdition. I see more instances of this than any one else can do; and on this ground also exhort all who would keep to the Methodists, and *from* Calvinism, 'Go to the church, and not to the meeting.'

But, to speak freely, I myself find more life in the Church prayers than in the formal extemporary prayers of Dissenters. Nay, I find more profit in sermons on either good temper or good works than in what are vulgarly called gospel sermons. That term is now become a mere *cant* word. I wish none of our Society would use it. It has no determinate meaning. Let but a pert, self-sufficient animal, that has neither sense nor grace, bawl out something about Christ and His blood or justification by faith, and his hearers cry out, 'What a fine gospel sermon!' Surely the Methodists have not so learnt Christ. We know no gospel without salvation from sin.

There is a Romish error which many Protestants sanction unawares. It is an avowed doctrine of the Romish Church that 'the pure intention of the minister is essential to the validity of the sacraments'. If so, we ought not to attend the ministrations of an unholy man; but, in flat opposition to this, our Church teaches in the 28th Article that 'the unworthiness of the minister does not hinder the validity of the sacraments.' Although, therefore, there are many disagreeable circumstances, yet I advise all our friends to keep to the Church. God has surely raised us up for the Church chiefly that a little leaven may leaven the whole lump. I wish you would seriously consider that little tract *Reasons against a Separation from the Church of England*.[1] These reasons were never answered yet, and I believe they never will be.

[1] See above, pp. 128–34.

'For Several of the Methodist Preachers'

'Written [by Charles Wesley] Oct. 10, 1779'

(Ms at MA)

In the course of the controversy at Bath over the Rev. Edward Smyth, Alexander McNab, the Assistant in the Bristol Circuit, defied John Wesley's authority, and Charles saw this as evidence of a conspiracy among the preachers. He remained suspicious of many of the itinerants during the rest of his life.

> 1 Lord over all, thy people hear
> For every favour'd messenger
> Whom Thou hast own[e]d for thine,
> For every chosen instrument
> Without our rules or orders sent
> To serve the cause divine.

2 Sent forth they were to prophesy,
  Their lack of service to supply
    Who sit in Moses' chair,
  But love the world, and seek their own,
  Neglect their ministry, and shun
    The gospel to declare.

3 Because the prophets held their peace
  The stones, thy quicken'd witnesses,
    Cried out on every side,
  In streets, and houses, and high-ways
  They spread the news of pard[o]ning grace,
    They preach'd the Crucified.

4 Their doctrine sinsick spirits heal'd,
  The Lord himself their mission seal'd
    By daily signs from heaven,
  Blind souls their inward sight receiv'd,
  The dead were rais'd, the poor believ'd,
    And felt their sins forgiven.

5 By ceaseless toils of humble love
  Thy serv[an]ts sought their faith t'approve,
    They spake, and liv'd the word,
  Simple & poor, despis'd of men,
  They liv'd immortal souls to gain,
    And glorify their Lord.

6 With tears we own, They *did* run well!
  But where is now their fervent zeal,
    Their meek humility,
  Their upright heart, their single eye,
  Their vows the Lord to magnify
    And live, and die for Thee?

7 The love of ease, and earthly things
  The pride from which contention springs,
    The fond desire of praise,
  Have imperceptibly stole in,
  Brought back the old besetting sin,
    And poison'd all their grace.

8 They now preeminence affect
  Eager to form the rising Sect,
    Some better thing to gain:
  Like hireling priests, they serve for hire,
  And thro' ambition blind, aspire
    Without the cross to reign.

9 The flock they w[oul]d in pieces tear,
  That each may seize the largest share,
    May feed himself alone:
  'Come, see my zeal' at first they cried,
  But now they ask 'W[h]o's on my side
    Will make my cause his own?'

10 The men w[h]o have their savour lost
  Themselves ag[ains]t the branches boast,
    And dignities despise:
  Their greedy hopes the flock devour,
  As all were left within their power
    To glut their avarice.

11 But O thou Shepherd great & good,
  The sheep redeem'd by thy own blood
    Into thine arms receive;
  If still with England's Church Thou art
  True pastors after thy own heart
    To thy own people give.

12 Thy flock out of their hands redeem
  Who of their own importance dream
    As God had need of man:
  Send whom Thou wilt, in mercy send,
  Thy cause and gospel to defend,
    Thy glory to maintain.

13 And O their faithful hearts inflame
  With love of our Jerusalem
    Thy Church Establish'd here:
  Still may they cry, & never rest:
  Till Glory, in thy face exprest,
    Throughout our land appear:

14 Till Thee, the Glory of the Lord,
  In truth and righteousness restor'd
    All flesh together see,
  Salute Thee on thy great white throne
  And sink in speechless raptures down
    For ever lost in Thee.

A Collection of Hymns for the use of the People Called Methodists

The '1780 Hymnbook' was designed as a comprehensive but compact collection to replace the many smaller collections issued by the Wesleys during the previous forty years.

From the Preface
'What we want is a collection neither too large, that it may be cheap and portable, nor too small, that it may contain a sufficient variety for all ordinary occasions.' Such a hymn-book you now have before you . . . It is large enough to contain all the important truths of our most holy religion, whether speculative or practical; yea, to illustrate them all, and to prove them both by Scripture and reason. And this is done in a regular order. The hymns are not carelessly jumbled together, but carefully ranged under proper heads, according to the experience of real Christians. So that this book is in effect a little body of experimental and practical divinity.

The Contents

Discipline

John Valton to Matthew Mayer; Daw Green [Dewsbury],
Dec. 13, 1781

(Ms at Drew University)

So you have got the Manchester House settled and I am very thankful
on this account. I feared you would have very disagreeable work before
things could have been brought to a favourable crisis; but is anything
too hard for the Lord? I hope that all will now be peace and harmony,
and that the work of the Lord will prosper in the circuit.

I have had a trying time since I have been in my new circuit.[1] I found
the societies had well nigh lost and forgot all discipline. However, the
Lord has stood by me, and things now wear a more favourable aspect
than they did, and I am in hopes that I shall see good days yet. O my dear
brother, I see without strict discipline the work must come to ruin. A
man may preach like an angel, but without strict attention to economy
we cannot long survive; we shall become a poor, dry, Laodicean Church,
and God will soon spew us out of his mouth. I hope my dear successor
in Manchester will complete what I began and see the blessed fruit of
his labour. I should be thankful to follow some good disciplinarian for it
is really very trying work to divide classes and reduce them almost in

every place. I had here very large classes, even to fifty nine, and near three hours taken up in meeting them; enough to destroy the work. I hope that dear Sister Mayer is able to meet her class. I believe that was one of the best things that I did among you. I have made three women's classes here, and they all wonderfully prosper and increase. I am likely very soon to lose the most pious useful person in England, dear Mrs. Fletcher; she leaves us in about three weeks.[2] Many will surely feel her loss. Come on, my dear brother, let us do our work betimes and we shall not fail of a reward; let us do all we can for our gracious God and we shall abundantly prosper. Preach as much as you can while health and strength remains, and many at last shall welcome you into the everlasting habitations.

[1] According to the 1781 stations, Valton was still in the Manchester Circuit, but this letter makes it clear that he had been moved to Birstall Circuit. The evidence suggests that Thomas Brisco, the Assistant there, was proving unsatisfactory in matters of discipline, and it may be significant that the following year Valton was listed as the Assistant, with Brisco as third preacher in the circuit.

[2] Mary Bosanquet, of Crosby Hall, was married in Batley parish church to John Fletcher on 12 November 1781 and left for Madeley the following January.

The Future of Methodism

(Printed cutting in notebook of Joseph Entwisle; Methodist Archives)

Original anecdote of the late Rev. John Wesley communicated to the Preachers assembled in Conference at Liverpool, August 1820 by Mr. Robert Miller.

The first time I had the pleasure of being in company with the Rev. John Wesley, was in the year 1783. I asked him what must be done to keep Methodism alive when he was dead: to which he immediately answered, 'The Methodists must take heed to their doctrine, their experience, their practice, and their discipline. If they attend to their doctrines *only*, they will make the people *antinomians*; if to the experimental part of religion *only*, they will make them *enthusiasts*; if to the practical part *only*, they will make them *Pharisees*; and if they do not attend to their discipline, they will be like persons who bestow much pains in cultivating their garden, and put no fence round it, to save it from the wild boar of the forest.

The Deed of Declaration, 1784

(Smith, *History*, I, 705–9)

The Deed was enrolled in Chancery as a means of giving legal status to the Conference after Wesley's death. The following is an abbreviated version of the original.

To all to whom these presents shall come, John Wesley, late of Lincoln College, Oxford, but now of the City Road, London, Clerk, sendeth greeting:

Whereas divers buildings commonly called chapels . . . situate in various parts of Great Britain, have been given and conveyed from time to time, by the said John Wesley to certain persons and their heirs . . . upon trust, that the trustees . . . should permit and suffer the said John Wesley, and such other . . . persons as he should for that purpose from time to time nominate and appoint, at all times during his life . . . to have and enjoy the free use and benefit of the said premises:
and whereas divers persons have in like manner given, or conveyed, many chapels . . . for the same uses and purposes as aforesaid . . .
and whereas, for rendering effectual the trusts created by the said several gifts or conveyances, and that no doubt or litigation may arise with respect unto the same, or the interpretation and true meaning thereof, it has been thought expedient, by the said John Wesley, . . . to explain the words *Yearly Conference of the people called Methodists,* contained in all the said trust-deeds, and to declare what persons are members of the said Conference, and how the *succession* and *identity* thereof is to be continued: *Now therefore these presents witness,* that, for accomplishing the aforesaid purposes, the said John Wesley doth hereby declare, that the Conference of the people called Methodists in London, Bristol, or Leeds . . . hath always heretofore consisted of the preachers and expounders of God's holy word, commonly called Methodist preachers, in connexion with, and under the care of, the said John Wesley, whom he hath thought expedient, year after year, to summons to meet him, . . . to advise with them for the promotion of the Gospel of Christ . . .

And these presents further witness, and the said John Wesley doth hereby avouch and further declare, that the several persons herein-after named [here follows a list of those preachers nominated by Wesley to form what became known as the 'Legal Hundred'] . . . do, on the day of the date hereof, constitute *the members of the said Conference* . . . and shall for ever be construed, taken and be *the Conference of the People called Methodists.* Nevertheless upon the terms, and subject to the regulations herein-after prescribed, that is to say,

First, That the members of the said Conference, and their successors for the time being for ever, shall assemble once in every year, at London, Bristol, or Leeds . . .

Second, The act of the majority in number of the Conference assembled as aforesaid shall be had, taken, and be the act of the whole Conference . . .

Third, That after the Conference shall be assembled as aforesaid, they shall first proceed to fill up all the vacancies occasioned by death, or absence . . .

Fourth, No act of the Conference . . . shall . . . be the act of the Conference, until forty of the members thereof are assembled . . . and during the assembly of the Conference, there shall always be forty members present at the doing of any act . . .

Fifth, The duration of the yearly assembly of the Conference shall not be less than five days, nor more than three weeks . . .

Sixth, Immediately after all the vacancies occasioned by death, or absence, are filled up . . ., the Conference shall choose a president, and secretary, of their assembly, out of themselves, who shall continue such until the election of another president, or secretary, in the next or other subsequent Conference; and the said president shall have the privilege and power of two members in all acts of the Conference during his presidency, and such other powers, privileges, and authorities, as the Conference shall from time to time see fit to intrust into his hands.

Seventh, Any member of the Conference absenting himself from the yearly assembly thereof for two years successively, without the consent, or dispensation of the Conference, and being not present on the first day of the third yearly assembly thereof, at the time and place appointed for the holding of the same, shall cease to be a member of the Conference . . .

Eighth, The Conference shall and may expel . . . any person . . . for any cause which to the Conference may seem fit or necessary . . .

Twelfth, That the Conference shall and may appoint the place of holding the yearly assembly thereof at any other city, town or place, than London, Bristol, or Leeds, when it shall seem expedient so to do . . .

Fourteenth, All resolutions and orders touching elections, admissions, expulsions, consents, dispensations, delegations, or appointments, and acts whatsoever of the Conference, shall be entered and written in the Journals or Minutes of the Conference, which shall be kept for the purpose, publicly read, and then subscribed by the president and secretary thereof . . .

Lastly, Whenever the said Conference shall be reduced under the number of forty members, and continue so reduced for three yearly assemblies thereof successively, or whenever the members thereof shall decline or neglect to meet together annually for the purposes aforesaid, during the space of three years, that then . . . the Conference of the people called Methodists shall be extinguished, and all the aforesaid powers, privileges, and advantages shall cease; and the said chapels and premises, and all other chapels and premises . . . shall vest in the trustees for the time being of the said chapels and premises respectively, and their successors for ever; *upon trust* that they . . . may appoint such person and persons to preach and expound God's holy word therein . . .

Provided always, that nothing herein contained shall extend . . . to extinguish, lessen, or abridge the life-estate of the said John Wesley, and Charles Wesley, or either of them, of and in any of the said chapels and premises . . .

The Right to Ordain

Wesley's letter to Coke, Asbury and 'our Brethren in North-America' ascribed his conviction that Bishops and Presbyters in the early church had been the same order to a reading of Lord Peter King's *Enquiry*. But only the changed circumstances following the American War of Independence persuaded him that the time had come to act on this conviction.

John Wesley, Bristol, Sept. 10, 1784

(*JWL* VII, 238)

2. Lord King's account of the primitive church convinced me many years ago, that Bishops and Presbyters are the same order, and consequently have the same right to ordain. For many years I have been importuned from time to time, to exercise this right, by ordaining part of our travelling preachers. But I have still refused, not only for peace' sake: but because I was determined, as little as possible to violate the established order of the national church to which I belonged.

3. But the case is widely different between England and North-America. Here there are Bishops who have a legal jurisdiction. In America there are none, neither any parish ministers. So that for some four hundred miles together there is none either to baptize or to administer the Lord's supper. Here therefore my scruples are at an end: and I conceive myself at full liberty, as I violate no order and invade no man's right, by appointing and sending labourers into the harvest.

[Lord Peter King], *An Enquiry into the Constitution, Discipline, Unity & Worship of the Primitive Church* by an Impartial Hand (1691)

Ch. IV [On Presbyters]

Now the Definition of a Presbyter may be this: *A Person in Holy Orders, having thereby an inherent Right to perform the whole Office of a Bishop; but being possessed of no Place or Parish, not actually discharging it, without the Permission and Consent of the Bishop of a Place or Parish. . . .*

Now this is what I understand by a Presbyter, for the Confirmation of which, these two things are to be proved.

1. That the Presbyters were the Bishops' Curates and Assistants, and so inferior to them in the actual Exercise of their Ecclesiastical Commission.

II. That yet notwithstanding, they had the same inherent Right with the Bishops, and so were not of a distinct specific Order from them.

But though the Presbyters were thus different from the Bishops in degree, yet they were of the very same specific Order with them, having the same inherent Right to perform those Ecclesiastical Offices, which the Bishop did, as will appear from these three Arguments.

1. That by the Bishop's permission they discharged all those Offices, which a Bishop did. 2. That they were called by the same Titles and Appellations as the Bishops were: And, 3. That they are expressly said to be of the same Order with the Bishops . . .

As for Ordination, I find but little said of this in Antiquity, yet as little as there is, there are clearer Proofs of the Presbyters Ordaining, than there are of their administering the Lord's Supper . . .

Now then if the Presbyters could supply the place of an Absent Bishop, and in general discharge all those Offices, to which a Bishop had been obliged, if he had been present, it naturally follows that the Presbyter could discharge every particular Act and part thereof . . . For what is affirmed of an Universal is affirmed of every one of its Particulars. So when the Fathers say, that the Presbyters performed the whole Office of the Bishop, it naturally ensues, that they Confirmed, Ordained, Baptized, &c. because those are Particulars of that Universal.

The Ordinations of 1784

Thomas Coke to John Wesley, August 9, 1784

(Moore, *Life of Wesley*, II, 530)

Honoured and dear Sir,

The more maturely I consider the subject, the more expedient it seems to me that the power of ordaining others should be received by me from you, by the imposition of your hands; and that you should lay hands on Brother Whatcoat and Brother Vasey, for the following reasons:—
1. It seems to me the most scriptural way, and most agreeable to the

practice of the primitive churches. 2. I may want all the influence in America which you can throw into my scale. Mr. Brackenbury informed me at Leeds that he saw a letter in London from Mr. Asbury, in which he observed 'that he should not receive any person deputed by you to take any part of the superintendency of the work invested in him,' – or words that implied so much. I do not find the least degree of prejudice in my mind against Mr. Asbury; on the contrary, a very great love and esteem; and I am determined not to stir a finger without his consent, unless sheer necessity obliges me; but rather to lie at his feet in all things. But as the journey is long, and you cannot spare me often, and it is well to provide against all events, and an authority *formally* received from you will be fully admitted by the people, and my exercising the office of ordination without that formal authority may be disputed, if there be any opposition on any other account; I could therefore earnestly wish you would exercise that power in this instance, which I have not the shadow of a doubt but God hath invested you with for the good of the Connexion. I think you have tried me too often to doubt whether I will in any degree use the power you are pleased to invest me with further than I believe absolutely necessary for the prosperity of the work . . . In short, it appears to me that everything should be prepared, and everything proper to be done, that can possibly be done, this side of the water . . .

Thomas Coke's 'Certificate of Ordination'

(MCOD Archives)

To all to whom these Presents shall come, John Wesley, late Fellow of Lincoln College in Oxford, Presbyter of the Church of England, sendeth greeting.

Whereas many of the People in the Southern Provinces of North America who desire to continue under my care, and still adhere to the Doctrines and Discipline of the Church of England, are greatly distressed for want of Ministers to administer the Sacraments of Baptism and the Lord's Supper according to the usage of the same Church: And whereas there does not appear to be any other way of Supplying them with Ministers:

Know all men, that I John Wesley think myself to be providentially called at this time to set apart some persons for the work of the ministry in America. And therefore under the Protection of Almighty God, and with a single eye to his Glory, I have this day set apart as a Superintendent, by the imposition of my hands and prayer, (being assisted by other ordained Ministers,) Thomas Coke, Doctor of Civil Law, a Presbyter of the Church of England, and a man whom I judge to be well qualified for that great work. And I do hereby recommend him to all whom it may concern as a fit person to preside over the Flock of Christ. In testimony whereof I have hereunto set my hand and seal this second day of September, in the year of our Lord one thousand seven hundred and eighty four.

JOHN WESLEY

Charles Wesley on the ordinations

(Frank Baker, Representative Verse, 1962, 367–8)

Wesley himself and friends betrays,
    By his good sense foresook,
When suddenly his hands he lays
    On the hot head of C——.

But we alas should spare the weak,
    His weak coevals we,
Nor blame a hoary schismatic
    A saint of eighty-three.

So easily are Bishops made
    By man's or woman's whim?
W—— his hands on C—— hath laid,
    But who laid hands on him?

Hands on himself he laid, and *took*
    An Apostolic Chair:
And then ordain'd his creature C——
    His heir and successor.

Episcopalians, now no more
    With Presbyterians fight,
But give your needless contest o're,
    'Whose ordination's right?'

It matters not, if both are one,
    Or different in degree,
For lo! ye see contained in John
    The whole Presbytery!

'The Sunday Service of the Methodists'

In his letter to Coke, Asbury and 'our Brethren in North-America', September 10, 1784, Wesley wrote: 'I have prepared a liturgy little differing from that of the Church of England (I think, the best constituted national church in the world) which I advise all the travelling-preachers to use, on the Lord's day, in all their congregations, reading the litany only on Wednesdays and

Fridays, also praying extempore on all other days. I also advise the elders to administer the supper of the Lord on every Lord's day.' This liturgy was contained in *The Sunday Service of the Methodists in North America*, to which he wrote the following preface.

I believe there is no LITURGY in the World, either in ancient or modern language, which breathes more of a solid, scriptural, rational Piety, than the COMMON PRAYER of the CHURCH OF ENGLAND. And though the main of it was compiled considerably more than two hundred years ago, yet is the language of it, not only pure, but strong and elegant in the highest degree.

Little alteration is made in the following edition of it, (which I recommend to our SOCIETIES IN AMERICA) except in the following instances:

1. Most of the holy-days (so called) are omitted, as at present answering no valuable end.

2. The service of the LORD's DAY, the length of which has been often complained of, is considerably shortened.

3. Some sentences in the offices of Baptism, and for the Burial of the Dead, are omitted. And,

4. Many Psalms left out, and many parts of the others, as being highly improper for the mouths of a Christian Congregation.

Bristol, September 9, 1784   JOHN WESLEY

The PRAYER OF CONSECRATION from *The Sunday Service of the Methodists*, showing the two versions (a) with and (b) without the manual acts (see following pages).

136 *The Communion.*

redemption; who made there (by his oblation of himſelf once offered) a full, perfect, and ſufficient ſacrifice, oblation, and ſatisfaction for the ſins of the whole world; and did inſtitute, and in his holy Goſpel command us to continue, a perpetual memory of that his precious death until his coming again; hear us, O merciful Father, we moſt humbly beſeech thee, and grant that we, receiving theſe thy creatures of bread and wine, according to thy Son our Saviour Jeſus Chriſt's holy inſtitution, in remembrance of his death and paſſion, may be partakers of his moſt bleſſed Body and Blood: who,

in the ſame night that he was betrayed * took bread; and when he had given thanks, he brake it †; and gave it to his diſciples, ſaying, Take, eat; ‡ this is my Body which is given for you; do this in remembrance of me. Likewiſe after Supper § he took the Cup; and when he had given thanks, he gave it to them, ſaying, Drink ye all of this; for this ‖ is my Blood of the New Teſtament, which is ſhed for you, and for many, for the remiſſion of ſins: Do this as oft as ye ſhall drink it, in remembrance of me. *Amen.*

> * *Here the Elder is to take the Patten into his Hands:*
> † *And here to break the Bread:*
> ‡ *And here to lay his Hand upon all the Bread.*
> § *Here he is to take the Cup into his Hand:*
>
> ‖ *And here to lay his Hand upon every Veſſel (be it Chalice or Flaggon) in which there is any Wine to be conſecrated.*

Then ſhall the Miniſter firſt receive the Communion in both kinds himſelf, and then proceed to deliver the ſame to the other Miniſters in like manner, (if any be preſent) and after that to the People alſo, in order, into their Hands. And when he delivereth the Bread to any one, he ſhall ſay,

THE Body of our Lord Jeſus Chriſt, which was given for thee, preſerve thy body and ſoul unto everlaſting life. Take and eat this in remembrance

136   *The Communion.*

Then the Elder shall say the Prayer of Consecration, as followeth:

ALmighty God, our heavenly Father, who, of thy tender mercy, didst give thine only Son Jesus Christ to suffer death upon the cross for our redemption; who made there (by his oblation of himself once offered) a full, perfect, and sufficient sacrifice, oblation, and satisfaction for the sins of the whole world; and did institute, and in his holy Gospel command us to continue, a perpetual memory of that his precious death until his coming again; hear us, O merciful Father, we most humbly beseech thee, and grant that we, receiving these thy creatures of bread and wine, according to thy Son our Saviour Jesus Christ's holy institution, in remembrance of his death and passion, may be partakers of his most blessed Body and Blood: who, in the same night that he was betrayed, took bread; and when he had given thanks, he brake it, and gave it to his disciples, saying, Take, eat; this is my Body which is given for you : Do this in remembrance of me. Likewise, after supper, he took the cup; and when he had given thanks, he gave it to them, saying, Drink ye all of this; for this is my blood of the New Testament, which is shed for you, and for many, for the remission of sins : Do this, as oft as ye shall drink it, in remembrance of me. *Amen.*

Then shall the Minister first receive the Communion in both kinds himself, and then proceed to deliver the same to the other Ministers in like manner, (if any be present) and after that to the People also, in order, into their Hands. And when he delivereth the Bread to any one, he shall say,

THE Body of our Lord Jesus Christ, which was given for thee, preserve thy body and soul unto everlasting life. Take and eat this in remem-

I   brance

Charles Wesley: A Retrospect

Charles Wesley to Dr. Thomas Bradbury Chandler; London, April 28, 1785

(Maryland Diocesan Archives; copy at Duke University endorsed 'A genuine copy from the New York Gazette' and containing the postscript).

As you are setting out for America, & I for a more distant Country, I think it needful to leave with you some account of myself & my companion through life. At eight years old in 1715, I was sent by my father, Rector of Epworth, to Westminster School, & placed under the care of my eldest brother Samuel, a strict churchman who brought me up in his own principles. In 1727 I was elected student of Christ Church. My brother John was then Fellow of Lincoln.

The first year at College I lost in diversions; the next I betook myself to study. Diligence led me into serious thinking. I went to the weekly sacrament & persuaded two or three young scholars to accompany me & likewise to observe the Method of Study prescribed by the trustees of the University. This gained me the harmless name of a Methodist.

In half a year my brother left his curacy of Epworth & came to our assistance. We then proceeded regularly in our Studies, & in doing what good we could to the bodies & souls of men.

I took my degree, & only thought of spending all my days at Oxford; but my brother, who always had the ascendant over me, persuaded me to accompany him & Mr. Oglethorpe to Georgia.

I exceedingly dreaded entering into Holy Orders, but he over-ruled me here also; & I was ordained Deacon by the Bishop of Oxford one Sunday, & the next Priest by the Bishop of London.

Our only design was to do all the good we could as ministers of the Church of England, to which we were firmly attached both by education and principle. My brother still acknowledges her the best national Church in the world.

In 1736 we arrived as missionaries in Georgia. My brother took charge of Savannah & I of Frederica, waiting for an opportunity of preaching to the Indians. I was, in the meantime, secretary to Mr. Oglethorpe, & also Secretary of Indian Affairs.

The hardships of lying upon the ground, &c soon threw me into a fever & dysentry, which forced me in half-a-year to return to England. My brother returned the next year. Still we had no plan but to serve God & the Church of England. The lost sheep of this fold were our principal care, not excluding any Christians, of whatever denomination, who were willing to add the power of godliness to their own particular form.

Our eldest brother Samuel was alarmed at our going on, & strongly expressed his fears in its ending in a separation from the Church. All our enemies prophesied the same. This confirmed us the more in our resolution to continue in our calling, which we constantly avowed both in public & private, by word & preaching & writing, exhorting all our hearers to follow our example.

My brother drew up Rules for our Society, one of which was, constantly to attend the Church Prayers & Sacrament. When we were no longer permitted to preach in churches, we preached (but never in Church Hours) in houses or fields, & sent from thence, or rather carried, multitudes to Church who had never been there before.

Our Society, in most places, made the bulk of the congregation, both at Prayers and at Sacrament.

I never lost my dread of separation, or ceased to guard our Society against it. I frequently told them, 'I am your servant, as long as you remain members of the Church of England, but no longer. Should you ever forsake her, you renounce me.' Some of our lay-preachers very early discovered an inclination to separate, which induced my brother to publish *Reasons against a Separation*. As often as it appeared, we beat down the schismatical spirit. If any one did leave the Church, at the same time he left our Society. For 50 years we kept the sheep in the fold, & having fulfilled the number of our days, only wanted to depart in peace.

After our having continued friends for above 70 years & fellow-labourers for above 50, can anything but death part us?

I can scarcely yet believe that in his 82nd year, my brother, my old intimate friend & companion, should have assumed the episcopal character, ordained elders, consecrated a bishop, & sent him to ordain the lay preachers in America. I was then in Bristol at his elbow, yet he never gave me the least hint of his intention. How was he surprised into so rash an action? He certainly persuaded himself that it was right.

Lord Mansfield told me last year that ordination was *separation*. This my brother does not, & will not see; or that he has renounced the principles & practice of his whole life, that he has acted contrary to his declarations, protestations & writings; robbed his friends of their boasting; realized the Nag's Head ordination, & left an indelible blot on his name, as long as it shall be remembered.

Thus our partnership dissolved, but not our friendship. I have taken him for better for worse till death us do part – or rather re-unite us in love inseparable. I have lived on earth a little too long, who have lived to see this evil day; but I shall very soon be taken from it, in steadfast faith that the Lord will maintain his own cause & carry on his work, & fulfil his promise to his Church – 'Lo, I am with you always, even unto the End of the World.'

P.S. What will become of those poor sheep in the wilderness, the American Methodists? How have they been betrayed into a separation from the Church of England which their preachers & they no more intended than the Methodists here. Had they had patience a little longer they would have seen a real primitive bishop in America duly consecrated by those bishops who had their consecration from the English bishops & are acknowledged by them as the same with themselves. There is therefore not the least difference between Bishop Seabury's Church and the Church of England. You know I had the happiness to converse with that truly apostolic man who is esteemed by all who know him as well as by you & me. He told me he looked upon the Methodists in America as sound members of the Church & was ready to ordain any of their preachers whom he should find duly qualified. His ordination would be indeed genuine, valid & episcopal: but what are your poor, ignorant Methodists now? Only a new set of Presbyterians and after my Brother's death, which is now so very near, what will be their destiny? They will forfeit the consideration of all who are wise enough not to join them. They will lose their usefulness and importance. They will settle again upon their lees & like other dissenters come to nothing.

John Pawson in Scotland

John Pawson to Charles Atmore; Edinburgh, October 8, 1785

(*WHS*, XI, 50–1)

The Scots in general are unaccountably prejudiced against us, and, to the last degree, bigotted to their own way. And really it is very melancholy to think that their best and most pious ministers are our very worst enemies, and think it their duty to warn the people against us. O cursed Calvinism! What havoc hast thou made with the souls of men in this once highly favoured nation! No heart can conceive what a bar this wretched doctrine is to our usefulness, and how far and wide it spreads among people of all sorts. Those among them who are pious cannot conceive how we can be right at all except we believe in Election and the rest of those absurd notions connected with it. However, I bless the Lord I think there is a prospect of doing good. Our congregations on Sunday nights increase very much, and the people are exceedingly attentive, and I have hitherto found very great liberty among them, so that I do hope good will be done. We expect Dr. Coke here next week, when I shall give him your letter. He also intends to be with us on Sunday the 23rd, when we are to have the Sacrament again, if all is well. I think I told you in my last that we have had it once, and that it was a time of refreshing from the presence of the Lord. But I do not know what we shall do, as Mr. Wesley is against us having it in the Scotch form, and if he is determined then I am well satisfied that our new plan will answer no end at all in Scotland, but will prove a hindrance to the work of God. The people in general take the very name of the Prayer Book, and everything belonging to it (as they have always been taught to believe it) a limb of Antichrist, and very little better than the Romish Mass book. Popery, prelacy, and all such like things are held by them in the greatest detestation, and you may depend upon it they will not submit to bow the knee to Baal, as they would call it. One and another would soon tell us, 'I dinna ken what you mean by these wicked new inventions; we belong to the gude old Kirk of Scotland, and will not join with the whore of Babylon at all.'

John Pawson to James Oddie; Glasgow, December 14, 1785

(Ms at Drew University)

As far as I am able to judge there is a prospect of doing much good both here and in Edinburgh. The congregations are large, serious and attentive, especially on Sundays; and we have had a good many joined Society, which I hear has also been the case in Dundee and Aberdeen. We have introduced no form of prayer. That would answer no good end in Scotland, but quite the contrary. We are obliged to comply with the Kirk in every part of our public worship, and also in administering the Lord's Supper. We have had that ordinance three times in Edinburgh and were very much favoured with the presence of the Lord, so that the people were well satisfied with our proceedings, and I trust that it will answer the end proposed. Mr. Wesley would have been glad to have had everything done according to the Church of England, but it could not be, so he has given us leave to go on in the Scotch way for the present, and [so?] I hope it will continue, as I am well persuaded that it is the [best?] for this country at least . . .

John Pawson to Charles Atmore; Glasgow, December 15, 1785

(*WHS*, XI, 52)

You cannot conceive how bigotted and how bitterly prejudiced the Scots in the general are to their own opinions and ways of all sorts, and yet divided among themselves amazingly. I think that if John Hurst, with all his high flown notions, was in Scotland a month, it would be enough to give even him a surfeit of his own bad opinions, as he would find

thousands as hot Calvinists as himself, who would nevertheless reprobate him, as he could not come up to their standard in everything. What
think you of the following pious prayer offered up to the God of Love
in public by a Seceder Minister: 'Lord, sweep away the Methodists from
the face of the earth with the besom of destruction! Lord, bless some of
us this day, it would be an unkah thing if Thou shouldst bless us all.'
They call Mr. Whitefield the Great White Devil, and Mr. Wesley the
Man of Sin,[1] and pray that the Lord would save them from him and his
perfection and his billets – that is, his hymns. Was there ever anything
like this, think you? And yet these, and such as these, are the Saints of
Scotland. O! my Brother, let us praise the Lord who has taught us
better, who has given us another Spirit, even the Spirit of holiness and
meekness and love.

[1] Cf. p. 157 above.

John Pawson to Charles Atmore; Glasgow, February 13, 1786

(*WHS*, XI, 53)

I have not seen any Magazines for the present year, but am unkah well
pleased at the hint you gave respecting our leaving the old Kirk. It
appears to me high time to come out from among *Heathenish Priests* and
Mitered Infidels. What may we call that Church where such blessed
wretches preside but an old withered harlot who has lost all that is truly
excellent in the religion of Jesus Christ? I hope that Mr. Wesley is now
paving the way for our complete deliverance from all that yoke of bondage by which we have been held down too long. I hear that the Dr. and
Mr. Chas. Wesley are publishing to the world their thoughts on this
subject. I hope that the Dr. will come off more than conqueror. I never
thought so much of the loss you sustain in England for want of the
service at the proper hours on Sundays, as I have since I tasted the sweetness of those happy seasons. Our Sunday forenoons are precious times
indeed. The minds of the people at that time are best prepared to receive
divine impressions, and is it not a pity that this hour should be lost, no
one knows how. You have very few high-flown church folks in your
country, I think.

The 'World Parish' Surveyed

(Thomas Coke, *An Address to the Pious and Benevolent, proposing an annual subscription for the support of the missionaries in the Highlands and adjacent islands of Scotland, the Isles of Jersey, Guernsey and Newfoundland, the West Indies, and the Provinces of Nova Scotia and Quebec,* 1786)

Coke's first *Plan . . . for the Establishment of Missions* had foundered partly because he failed to enlist Wesley's support in advance. He did not make this mistake a second time. Wesley's letter commending the proposals of 1786 prefaces Coke's *Address.*

Bristol, March 12, 1786

Dear Sir,

I greatly approve of your proposal for raising a subscription in order to send missionaries to the Highlands of Scotland, the Islands of Guernsey and Jersey, the Leeward Islands, Quebec, Nova Scotia, and Newfoundland.

It is not easy to conceive the extreme want there is, in all those places, of men that will not count their lives dear unto themselves, so they may testify the Gospel of the Grace of God.

I am, Dear Sir,
Your affectionate Brother,
John Wesley

Dearly beloved in the Lord,

Some time past I took the liberty of addressing you in behalf of a mission intended to be established in the British dominions in Asia; and many of you very generously entered into that important plan. We have not indeed lost sight of it at present; on the contrary, we have lately received a letter of encouragement from a principal gentleman in the province of Bengal.[1] But the providence of God has lately opened to us so many doors nearer home, that Mr. Wesley thinks it imprudent to hazard at present the lives of any of our preachers, by sending them to so great a distance, and amidst so many uncertainties and difficulties; when so large a field of action is afforded us in countries to which we have so much easier admittance, and where the success, through the blessing of God, is more or less certain.

We cannot but be sensible of the fallen state of Christendom, and the extensive room for labour which faithful ministers may find in every country therein. But some of the nations which are called Christian, are deeper sunk in ignorance and impiety than others; and even of the most enlightened, various parts are still buried in the grossest darkness.

No kingdom under heaven, I believe, has been more blessed with the light of the gospel than *North Britain.* Numerous have been the men of most eminent piety and abilities, whom God in his providence and grace has been pleased to raise among that people. And yet, in the *Highlands* and adjacent *Islands*, many scores, perhaps I may say hundreds of thousands, are little better than the rudest barbarians . . . The Lord seems to be pointing out our way in the present instance, for he has lately raised up a zealous young man, well versed in the *Erse* (the language spoken by the people of whom we are now treating), to whom Mr. Wesley has given an unlimited commission to visit the Highlands and adjacent Islands of *Scotland*.[2] We have also one or two more in our view, who are masters of the *Erse* language, who, we have reason to believe, would accept of a similar commission. But the charges would be considerable, and our present regular expenses in *Scotland*, beyond what the poverty of our Scotch societies can afford, are full as great as our contingent fund will bear . . .

The Isles of Jersey and Guernsey make the second object of our institution. The Lord has been pleased, by our much respected brother Mr. *Brackenbury*, to begin a very promising work in those islands. Several societies have been formed: and the Lord has also raised up a very sensible and zealous young man, whose native language is the *French*, and who is likely to be highly useful to the cause of God.[3] He is now stationed in *Guernsey*, where some assistance has been already given him to supply his necessary wants, and probably more will be yet required. In *Jersey* Mr. Brackenbury bears the whole burden of the expense at present, but we cannot expect this to be always the case. No doubt but the larger societies will soon be enabled to support their own expenses: but still, as the work increases, the infant societies will stand in need of assistance . . .

The third object we have in view, is our *West India* islands, where a field is opened to us among the negroes beyond anything that could have been expected. *Eleven hundred* blacks have been already united in society in the island of *Antigua* through the successful labours of Mr. *Baxter*;[4] and the greatest part of them, we have reason to believe, are converted to God. But we have only that single minister in those islands, Mr. *Lambert*, whom we sent from the States, being obliged to return on account of his ill state of health. Nor can our brethren in the States afford us any assistance in the *West India* islands, the call for preachers being so great on the continent. In the islands of *St. Christopher's* we have received considerable encouragement. And the planters in general are constrained to acknowledge, that the negroes who are united to *us* and the *Moravians*, are the most laborious and faithful servants they have: which favourable sentiment, through the blessing of God, has laid open the whole country to our labours among the blacks; and we seem to want nothing but preachers, under the divine influence, to gather in many thousands of them. And these islands seem to have a

peculiar claim on the inhabitants of *Britain*. Our country is enriched by
the labours of the poor slaves who cultivate the soil, and surely the least
compensation we can make them, is to endeavour to enrich them in
return with the riches of grace. But the grand consideration to the
children of God, is the value of the souls of these negroes, a set of people
utterly despised by all the world, except the Methodists and Moravians.
And yet I have no doubt but a most glorious gospel-harvest would soon
be displayed to our view among that miserable people, if they were
sufficiently supplied with gospel-ministers . . .

The provinces of Nova Scotia and Quebec and the island of Newfoundland, make the fourth and last object of the present plan. We have
lately sent a Missionary to *Harbour Grace* in *Newfoundland*, and his labours
have been blessed; but his single endeavours are not likely to carry the
work of God to that extent which every pious soul must wish for. In
Nova Scotia we have about *three hundred* whites and *two hundred* blacks in
society according to the last accounts, but have only three travelling
preachers for the whole province; so that most of our congregations
have preaching but once in a month. In the province of *Quebec* a few
pious soldiers have formed societies at Quebec and Montreal on the
Methodist plan, among whom we have reason to believe that our
preachers would be gladly received.

Such an open door has not been known perhaps for many ages, as is
now presented to us on the continent of America . . . How attentive
should we be to the times of refreshing from the presence of the Lord,
to improve to the utmost all those blessed occasions. Nor should any
lover of Zion object to the distance of those countries from us. Oceans
are nothing to God, and they should be no obstruction to his people in
respect to the love they should bear one towards another . . .

A particular account of the missions, with any letters or extracts of
letters from the missionaries or others, that are worthy of publication,
shall be printed as soon as possible after every one of our annual conferences, and a copy presented to every subscriber: in which also the
receipts and disbursements of the preceding year, with an alphabetical
list of the names of the subscribers (except where it is otherwise desired),
shall be laid before the Public. The assistants of our circuits respectively
will be so kind as to bring the money subscribed to the ensuing conference, and so from year to year.

The preaching of the gospel is an object of the greatest importance;
and the present state of mankind must cause very frequent and painful
sensations to the truly pious – that the kingdom of Jesus Christ should
be circumscribed by such narrow bounds, and Satan rule so great a part
of the world . . .

The *Roman Catholics* have manifested astonishing zeal in the missions
they have established in *China* and other parts of the East. Their

contributions for the purpose have been almost boundless: And shall *Protestants* be less zealous for the glory of God, when their religion is so much more pure? Alas! this is really the case. Nor let us object that the *Romanists* are richer than we – that even crowned heads have used their utmost influence in the former case. But let us rather remember that God works by the smallest means, yea he delights to do so. He rejoices to 'perfect strength in weakness, and to ordain praise out of the mouths of babes and sucklings.' Hitherto the Lord has blessed us in this very way, raising very large and lively societies from very small beginnings. And if we engage in the present undertaking in the spirit of faith, our endeavours shall be successful . . .

Blessed be God! our spiritual resources are amazing. Numerous, I am fully persuaded, are the preachers among us, who, in the true spirit of apostles, count all things but dung, that they may win Christ, and win souls to him; who carry their lives in their hands, and long to spend and be spent in their Master's glorious cause. Let us therefore endeavour to draw forth these resources and spread them out to the uttermost. Then shall the little leaven imperceptibly win its widening way, till it has leavened the whole lump of mankind. And while we are unitedly watering the whole world around us, our own souls shall be watered again: the Methodist Connection shall become a seminary to fill the vineyard of Christ with devoted labourers, and be made the most valuable, the most extensive blessing, not only to the present age, but to the generations that are yet to come.

London, March 13, 1786

[1] Charles Grant, a merchant serving with the East India Company near Calcutta.
[2] Duncan M'Allum became an itinerant in 1775 and served forty years in Scottish circuits.
[3] Jean de Quetteville, a native of Jersey.
[4] John Baxter; see pp. 218–19 below.

Separation from the Church

John Pawson to Charles Atmore; Glasgow, March 30, 1786

(*WHS*, XI, 112–13)

I think that I can see far greater difficulties which would attend a separation from the Church than any mentioned in the Pamphlet.[1] To pass by every other how will these be got over? Every Circuit would want more

Preachers than they have at present in order that we might have the church service at the proper time in all the large places. But where shall we find, or how shall we provide for them? I do notice we have not a sufficient number of Preachers who are proper to be ordained; very far from it. I am well assured that there are not a few in our Connexion who pass tolerably well upon our present plan, who if they were set to read the prayers and the scriptures in a public congregation, would make but poor work. I ever found it exceedingly difficult to read the scriptures well, and altho' I may perhaps be able to read as well as some who travel, yet I never could please myself, setting aside other people. What miserable readers are nine in ten (not to say ninety nine in a hundred) of the Clergy with all their learning! Indeed, altho' I do really believe that to separate from the Church would be much the better for our people, and therefore I wish it from the ground of my heart, yet at the same time I do not see how it can be done all at once, but by degrees. I could wish that Mr. Wesley would ordain preachers this next Conference for those places where the bulk of the people greatly desire it, and so go on from time to time as providence may open the way, and let those places remain upon the old plan, who wish to be as they are.

John Pawson to Charles Atmore; Edinburgh, June 2, 1786

(*WHS*, XII, 107–8)

I have heard from various quarters of Mr. Wesley expressing himself in very strong terms in favour of the Church. I was not at all surprised at this; but nevertheless I do not see it to be any more difficult for him to leave the Church than it was before. For if he was to see it his duty to have the Church Service in any of our places he would not call it separation from the Church, but just the contrary. He has already shewed you that the word Schism does not signify a separation from any Church whatsoever; & he has also proved beyond all contradiction that the Methodists are the very Church of England itself, & that from one of the Articles of that Church. So that all he has said lately would just stand for nothing. But the truth is the good old man has been so pestered with his brother & the High Church bigots on all sides that I really believe he does not know what to do. And you may add to this that Dr. Coke, with his well meant zeal drives quite too fast, & by that means defeats his own designs. When Mr. W. was here he told the whole Sunday night's Congregation that it never came into his head to separate from the Church of Scotland, but that Dr. Coke had entirely mistaken his meaning throughout the whole business, and that there never should be public worship in that Chapel with his consent. So that it is quite evident that he has forgotten what he himself said on that subject last Conference. Poor dear

Soul, his memory fails him, therefore he speaks in a very unguarded manner sometimes.

[1] Probably a reference to Wesley's thoughts 'Of separation from the Church', written at Camelford on August 30, 1785 (*JWW*, XIII, 222–3).

Advice to Preachers

(*Minutes*, 1786)

I advise the assistants,
   1. To re-establish morning-preaching, in all large towns at least.
   2. To exert themselves in restoring the bands.
   3. And the select societies.
   4. Change both a general and a particular steward in each Circuit.

I advise all preachers
   1. Always to conclude the service in about an hour.
   2. Never scream.
   3. Never lean upon, or beat the bible.
   4. Wherever you preach, meet the society.
   5. Do not, without the utmost necessity, go home at night.
   6. Never take part against the assistant.
   7. Never preach a funeral sermon, but for an eminently holy person: Nor then, without consulting the assistant. Preach none for hire. Beware of panegyric, particularly in London.
   8. Have love-feasts in more places.
   9. Introduce no new tunes. See that none sing too slow, and the women sing their parts. Exhort all to sing, and all to stand at singing, as well as to kneel at prayers.
   10. Let none repeat the last line, unless the preacher does.
   11. Inform the Leaders, that every assistant is to change both the stewards and leaders when he sees good. And that no leader has power to put any person either into or out of the society.

John Wesley to Joseph Taylor; Hinckley, February 14, 1787

(*JWL*, VII, 368–9)

On Sunday morning the whole service may continue an hour and an half. At any other time morning and evening our service should not exceed an hour. I cannot at all approve of that dull way of spinning out many sermons from the same text, unless your text be the 13th of the First Epistle to the Corinthians or the Sermon on the Mount. It is this chiefly which occasions so many sermons in Scotland without any application. A sermon should be rather all application. This is the better extreme.

It seemed to be the design and endeavour of Mr. Henry[1] to say all that could be said on every subject; but he will never be imitated herein by any who take either our Lord or His apostles for their pattern.

[1] Matthew Henry, the biblical commentator.

Services in Church Hours

(*Minutes*, 1786)

In what cases do we allow of service in church hours? I answer,

1. When the Minister is a notoriously wicked man.
2. When he preaches Arian, or any equally pernicious, doctrine.
3. When there are not churches in the town sufficient to contain half the people; and,
4. When there is no church at all within two or three miles. And we advise every one who preaches in the church hours to read the Psalms and Lessons with part of the Church Prayers; because we apprehend this will endear the Church service to our brethren, who probably would be prejudiced against it, if they heard none but extemporary prayer.

Wesley's application of these principles

(*JWJ*, VII, 217, 232, 340)

Oct. 24, 1786. I met the classes at Deptford, and was vehemently importuned to order the Sunday service in our room at the same time with that of the church. It is easy to see that this would be a formal separation from the Church. We fixed both our morning and evening service, all over England, at such hours as not to interfere with the Church; with this very design – that those of the Church, if they chose it, might attend both the one and the other. But to fix it at the same hour is obliging them to separate either from the Church or us; and this I judge to be not only inexpedient, but totally unlawful for me to do.

Jan. 2, 1787. I went over to Deptford; but it seemed, I was got into a den of lions. Most of the leading men of the society were mad for separating from the Church. I endeavoured to reason with them, but in vain; they had neither sense nor even good manners left. At length, after meeting the whole society, I told them: 'If you are resolved, you may have your service in church hours; but, remember, from that time you will see my face no more.' This struck deep; and from that hour I have heard no more of separating from the Church.

Nov. 5, 1787. The congregation [at Dorking] was, as usual, large and serious. But there is no increase in the society. So that we have profited nothing by having our service in the church-hours, which some imagined would have done wonders. I do not know that it has done more good anywhere in England; in Scotland I believe it has.

John Wesley, Sermon 'On Attending the Church Service', 1787

(*JWW*, VII, 175, 184–5; *Sermons* III, 466, 477–8)

From the text, 'The sin of the young men was very great' (1 Sam. ii.17), Wesley argued against the view that Methodists should leave the Church because its clergy were 'unholy men'.

4. For more than twenty years this never entered into the thoughts of those that were called Methodists. But as more and more who had been brought up Dissenters joined with them, they brought in more and more prejudice against the Church. In process of time, various circumstances concurred to increase and to confirm it. Many had forgotten that we were all at our first setting out determined members of the Established Church. Yea, it was one of our original rules, that every member of our society should attend the church and sacrament, unless he had been bred among Christians of any other denomination.

5. In order, therefore, to prevent others from being puzzled and perplexed, as so many have been already, it is necessary, in the highest degree, to consider this matter thoroughly; calmly to inquire, whether God ever did bless the ministry of ungodly men, and whether he does so at this hour. Here is a plain matter of fact: If God never did bless it, we ought to separate from the Church; at least where we have reason to believe that the Minister is an unholy man: If he ever did bless it, and does so still, then we ought to continue therein. . . .

31. Another consequence would follow from the supposition that no grace is conveyed by wicked Ministers; namely, that a conscientious person cannot be a member of any national Church in the world. For wherever he is, it is great odds whether a holy Minister be stationed there; and if there be not, it is mere lost labour to worship in that congregation. But, blessed be God, this is not the case; we know by our

own happy experience, and by the experience of thousands, that the word of the Lord is not bound, though uttered by an unholy Minister; and the sacraments are not dry breasts, whether he that administers be holy or unholy.

32. Consider one more consequence of this supposition, should it ever be generally received. Were all men to separate from those Churches where the Minister was an unholy man (as they ought to do, if the grace of God never did nor could attend his ministry), what confusion, what tumults, what commotions would this occasion throughout Christendom! What evil-surmisings, heart-burning, jealousies, envyings must everywhere arise! What censuring, tale-bearing, strife, contention! Neither would it stop here; but from evil words the contending parties would soon proceed to evil deeds; and rivers of blood would soon be shed, to the utter scandal of Mahometans and Heathens.

Coke's First Visit to the West Indies

(Coke's *Journals*, 1816, pp. 76, 81–3)

Antigua, Jan. 2, 1787

By the powerful hand of God we have been brought to this island, as you will see by the following journal:
On Sunday the 24th of September, we sailed from *Gravesend*, and the next day were opposite the *Isle of Wight*. . . .

Thursday, November 30. A dreadful gale blew from the north-west. At ten at night, I heard the captain's wife crying out in the most dreadful fright, and presently Mr. *Hilditch*, (one of the passengers) came running and crying, 'Pray for us, Doctor, pray for us, for we are just gone!' I came out of my state-room, and found that a dreadful hurricane (I assuredly may call it) had just arisen. The ship was on her beam-ends. They had not time to take down the foresail, and were just going to cut away the main-mast as the last remedy, expecting every moment that the ship would be filled with water and sink. My brethren and myself at this awful moment retired into a corner to pray, and I think I may say we all felt a perfect resignation to the will of God. Through grace, I think I may assert, that I was entirely delivered from the fear of death. But brother *Hammet* was superior to us all in faith for the occasion. His first prayer (if it could be called by that name) was little else than a declaration of the full assurance he possessed that God would deliver us: and his second address to God was a thanksgiving for our deliverance. It was not till after this, and after we had sung a hymn together, that the fore-sail was shivered in pieces, and by that means the masts were saved, and probably the ship itself . . . After the immediate danger was over, we drove with the wind, which carried us with nothing but the bare poles, at the rate of six miles an hour for eight hours and a half.

Monday, Dec. 4 [After a night of violent storm, during which 'the whole ship began to ooze at every joint'] The next morning we held a little council. The captain being convinced of the impossibility of reaching the port of *Halifax* this winter, it was the unanimous opinion of all [sic] that no other refuge was left us, under God, but to sail with all possible expedition for the *West-Indies*. At present our sails appear like wafers. Our ropes are quite white, all the tar being washed off; in short, the ship may already be said to be half a wreck. . . . It is very remarkable, that since we came near the Banks of *Newfoundland*, I have had a strong persuasion, and I believe, a divine one, that we shall be driven to the *West-Indies*. . . .

Dec. 25. This day we landed in *Antigua*, and in going up the town of St. *John's* we met brother *Baxter* in his band,[1] going to perform divine service. After a little refreshment I went to our Chapel, and read prayers, preached, and administered the sacrament. I had one of the cleanest audiences I ever saw. All the negro women were dressed in white linen gowns, petticoats, handkerchiefs and caps: and I did not see the least spot on any of them. The men were also dressed as neatly. In the afternoon and evening I had very large congregations.

Jan. 5, 1787 . . . Our Society in this island is near two thousand: but the ladies and gentlemen of the town have so filled the house, that the poor, dear negroes who built it, have been almost entirely shut out, except in the mornings: and yet they bear this, not only with patience, but with joy. Two or three times I have preached in the country. Our friends who invite us to their houses, entertain us rather like princes than subjects: herein, perhaps, lies part of our danger in this country. . . .

We have held an Infant-Conference. A pressing invitation has been sent us to visit St. *Vincent's*; and this evening we are to sail for that island. Brother *Warrener* is to remain here. We have about twenty recommendatory letters. There is, as far as we can at present judge, a fair opening in St. *Eustatius*. A little while ago brother *Baxter* received two warm letters of recommendation for that island: and brother *Hammet* has just received one for St. *Kitt's*. We are all in remarkable good health. All is of God. I have no doubt but it would be an open resistance to the clear providences of the Almighty, to remove any one of the Missionaries at present from this country.[2]

¹ I.e. in clerical attire: John Baxter had been ordained by Coke in Baltimore in May, 1785. He had gone out to Antigua in 1778 to work in the naval dockyard, and as a Methodist local preacher had taken over leadership of the society there.

² Of the preachers accompanying Coke on this voyage, only William Warrener had been intended for Antigua. William Hammet and John Clarke were appointed by the Conference to work in Newfoundland, but never arrived there.

Ordination and the Sacrament

Thomas Hanby was ordained by Wesley in 1785 for the work in Scotland, after thirty years as an itinerant. When he was brought back to an English circuit in 1787, Wesley ordered him to cease administering the sacrament. His case vividly illustrates the moral dilemma in which this generation of the people called Methodists found themselves.

Hanby to James Oddie; Rotherham, October 22, 1787

(Ms at Drew University)

Rotherham, Oct. 22, 1787

As for the honours of the gown and ordination, *weel o' wot*, there is no great cause for glory: for W—y has stripped us of the former, and the other is of no use, as we are forbidden to act in a ministerial character. I assure you I am ashamed of my dignities, and poor Pawson and I look upon ourselves as two poor degraded parsons, which makes us sink lower in our own eyes than we were before this great honour was conferred upon us. For had we never stood, we never should have fallen. How mortifying! However, we do not fail to remonstrate, and to plead the unreasonableness of his earnest desire for us to take this upon us, and now to forbid us the use of our office. And for no offence that we have given, whilst we are solicited on every hand to administer the ordinances. Is not this a strange conduct and a new thing in earth? Can you advise? . . . I feel a great desire to be useful. I sometimes think we have too much preaching, there is a danger of the people loathing the manna. I fear our rounds are too much crowded with preachers which in time will make a burden to our people, too much like the Tithing Parsons, as we are obliged to strain every nerve to get money to support our numerous wants. Lord help us!

Hanby to Oddie; Grantham, May 21, 1789

(*WHS*, IV, 171–2)

Grantham, May 21, 1789

Since I wrote last I have been in deep waters on account of my administering the Lord's Supper, which I think it is my duty to do and especially to those who for conscience cannot go to the Church. Mr. Wesley has written and ordered me to lay it aside. I wrote and told him if I did I should sin, because I was persuaded it was my duty and therefore I could not oblige him. Then he ordered the clergy and preachers in London to undertake me. I have received their letters and [have] written answers, that I must do as I have done, and provided Mr. W. has given me up in their hands, they must act according to their judgments for what I did was from a divine conviction. I have for some time expected another preacher to take my place, but as he is not come, perhaps they will refer the matter till the Conference. Mr. W. has ordered Joseph Taylor, who opposes me all he can, to remove the leaders who have been the promoters of the Sacraments and provided he does it, there will be a division I expect. See, my brother, my situation! I wish first for an interest in your prayers, and secondly your advice. I am much afraid of myself, least I should turn coward, and defile my conscience by yielding to the preachers' importunity. I am of all others the most improper person to make a stand in defence of Christ's precious and much neglected ordinance. However, hitherto, through infinite mercy, I have been quite firm and unmovable and our solemnities are much owned of God, and I have much employment in the sacred office. I meet with great opposition from the High Church bigots, but yet there are many who will stand by me let the consequence be what it will, who see and feel the privilege very great.

Charles Wesley

'Facts from memory' written by his daughter Sarah

(Ms at Emory University; undated, but clearly written after his death in 1788)

My father gave up all Church preferment from a sort of knight-errantry in virtue. In the younger part of his life he went to Georgia to convert the Indians. On his return to England, the peculiar sanctity he felt it his duty to enforce offended the more indolent clergy, and he was either to disguise his principles or be denied their pulpits. The consequence of this was, meeting houses were built, and before they were finished, preaching in the fields introduced.

From hymn-books & other devotional tracts, of which the profits were very great, he received only £160 annually, devoting the rest to the general support of the Methodist cause. Whenever he visited the different chapels over England, he resided at them, or lived amongst a people for whom he had sacrificed all worldly emoluments and honours.

When he married, and had an increasing family, it did not alter his mode of life. He travelled, generally without my mother, whose love of a domestic sphere confined her more than any other cause, to an humble home, distinguished however by hospitality & peace.

They lived at Bristol, where Mrs. Stafford's family acted the part of relations, attending her in her lyings-in, were always present if illness or solitude rendered their kind sympathy needful.

Pecuniary assistance they could not be said to need, everyone knowing that their circumstances & their minds were well suited and that the luxuries of life were excluded not merely from their power, but their idea of enjoyment.

When we grew up my father removed to London, and bought a house there, and I believe no family ever regretted this removal more than Mrs. Stafford's did. But the education of his children & the line which their particular genius pointed out, rendered such a situation necessary.

His visits to Bristol, however, were annual. I think twice, by particular invitation, he took a bed at Mrs. Stafford's during his continuance, which has usually been one month. My mother once was with him; all his family, never. . . .

I have been endeavouring to recollect the events which have fallen within my knowledge concerning my respected father's life, and am surprised to find them so few and inconsiderable.

Much as I was with him & many as are the precious *words* which I have treasured up, he spoke so little of himself & so reluctantly, that I often had recourse of those who knew him in his early years for the most common information. Nor did he keep any Journal for his latter days; some remarkable circumstances he has committed to writing, but they are not, I apprehend, of a nature admissible in such a work as yours. One of the longest is, concerning a Mr. Davis, who wronged him of a horse, and only important as it evinces my father's meekness & forbearance under ill treatment & injustice: with others of this kind, which I can procure on my return to London.

His conduct indeed, under various trials, was most exemplary. Whenever he lost a friend by death (and no one regarded a friend more tenderly), whenever he met with any of those dispensations of providence

which the world calls evils, whether contempt of his ministry, ingratitude towards himself, bodily pain or disappointment, it seemed to add
to his faith *patience*, & he received all at the hands & in the name of the
Lord resignedly.

Even his constitutional warmth of temper was the means of producing
such acts of humility as I never yet saw equalled. He would apologise
even to his children for a hasty word, & indeed on every occasion in
domestic life displayed sweet condescension & kindness.

His self-denial was remarkable. He always preferred the coarsest fare,
the meanest things, in little & great, & in such a manner, that it might
appear a matter of indifference or choice rather than a virtue.

He was in everything unostentatious. He once owned to me that the
reason he did not give money to beggars was lest anyone should see him.[1]

He strove to be little & unknown; to *conceal* his graces; acting under
the divine eye he shunned all others & whenever he spoke of himself, it
was in such humble terms as I am sure he would not have applied to any
other servant of God.

But when he was called to bear his testimony, publickly or privately,
in the line of duty, he had no respect of persons; all the zeal of his soul
would be poured out, earnestly and valiantly he would contend for the
truth.

> With holy indignation fired [filled?]
> When by the Prince of Hell withstood,
> Firm to resist & grasp the shield,
> And quench his fiery darts with blood.

It was the man he wished to hide from view, not the minister from
shame, nor soften the message for favour, & he who in one capacity
took for his motto

> Nec vixit male qui natus moriensque fefellit.[2]

in the other would speak rebuke, exhort, with all long suffering and with
all authority witnessing a good confession before men & angels.

---

[1] Cf. a letter from Sally Wesley to her uncle John, December 29, 1786, but
endorsed: 'Never sent' (ms at Emory University). She asks his advice on visiting the
poor and sick and giving them money, because she has been warned by 'a person
whom I know meant well' of the dangers, including the temptation to 'ostentation'.

[2] Horace, *Epistles*, I.17.10: 'He who is born and dies in obscurity has not lived
badly.'

Wesley in Old Age

(William Jay, *Autobiography*, 1854, pp. 412–13)

This encounter probably occurred on Saturday, September 26, 1789 (see Wesley's diary for that date).

During my stay at Hope Chapel, I had the honour and pleasure of dining at Lady Maxwell's house, with the venerable Mr. Wesley. He kindly noticed me, and inquired after Mr. Winter, adding, 'Cornelius is an excellent man.' This was the more candid, as Mr. Winter, in a letter, a copy of which I have, had testified freely against some of Mr. Wesley's opinions. At the first interview, there were in the company the Rev. Mr. Moore, one of Mr. Wesley's biographers, and several other preachers in his connexion; and among these was a Captain Webb, deprived of one eye at the battle of Bunker's Hill, who held forth commonly without-doors in regimentals. As I wished to hear Mr. Wesley talk, nothing could be more mortifying than the incessant garrulity of this fanatical rodo-montader; and I much wondered Mr. Wesley, who had such influence over his adherents, did not repress, or at least rebuke, some of his spiritual vagaries and supernatural exploits. Did this master in Israel think it harmless to tolerate a kind of visionary agency, and suppose that it was better for the common people to believe too much rather than too little?

[Jay then gives details of a recent case of exorcism in Bristol.]

I should not have related this, but it unfortunately engrossed the con-versation for nearly the whole of the afternoon; and because, to my great surprise, Mr. Wesley seemed to admit the reality of the possession and dispossession, and to consider it as nothing less than a wonderful work of God. After tea I went with him in his carriage into Bristol, and heard him preach from Ephes. v. 8 – 'Ye were sometimes darkness, but now are ye light in the Lord: walk as children of light.' It was the only oppor-tunity I ever had of hearing this truly apostolical man. The whole scene was very picturesque and striking. Several preachers stood in the large pulpit around him: the sermon was short, the language terse and good, but entirely devoid of expansion and imagery, while the delivery was low and unanimated. This surprised me. Was it the influence and effect of age? If it was originally the same, how came he to be so popular, among the rude multitudes which always attended him, and so hung upon his lips? Whit[e]field's voice and vehemence, and strong emotions, will in some measure account for the impressions he produced, even regardless of the grace of God which accompanied them. How popular and useful was Berridge! yet he had nothing of the vulgar orator in his manner; it was plain and unimpassioned. This was the case also with many of the original corps of evangelists.

Recalled by Henry Crabbe Robinson

(From his *Reminiscences*, 1870, I, 12)

It was, I believe, in October, 1790, and not long before his death, that I heard John Wesley in the great round meeting-house at Colchester. He stood in a wide pulpit, and on each side of him stood a minister, and the two held him up, having their hands under his armpits. His feeble voice was barely audible. But his reverend countenance, especially his long white locks, formed a picture never to be forgotten. There was a vast crowd of lovers and admirers. It was for the most part pantomime, but the pantomime went to the heart. Of the kind I never saw anything comparable to it in after life.

The following letter enters a little more into particulars respecting this interesting occasion:—

October 18, 1790

Dear Brother:—

. . . I felt a great Satisfaction last Week, on Monday, in hearing (excuse me now) that veteran in the Service of God, the Rev. John Wesley. I was informed in the Afternoon that he was in Town and would preach that Evening . . . At another time, and not knowing the Man, I should almost have ridiculed his figure. Far from it now. I lookt upon him with a respect bordering upon Enthusiasm. After the people had sung one Verse of a hymn he arose, and said: 'It gives me a great pleasure to find that you have not lost your Singing. Neither Men nor Women – you have not forgot a single Note. And I hope that by the assistance of the same God which enables you to sing well, you may do all other things well.' A Universal Amen followed. At the End of every Head or Division of his Discourse, he finished by a kind of Prayer, a Momentary Wish as it were, not consisting of more than three or four words, which was always followed by a Universal Buzz. His discourse was short – the Text I could not hear. After the last Prayer, he rose up and addressed the People on Liberality of Sentiment, and spoke much against refusing to join with any Congregation on account of difference of Opinion. He said, 'If they do but fear God, work righteousness, and keep his commandments, we have nothing to object to.'

'On the Ministerial Office'

(Sermon CXV, on the text Hebrews v.4; *JWW*, VII, 277–80; *Sermons* IV, 79–80, 82–3)

11. In 1744, all the Methodist Preachers had their first Conference. But none of them dreamed, that the being called to preach gave them any right to administer sacraments. And when that question was proposed, 'In what light are we to consider ourselves?' it was answered, 'As *extraordinary messengers*, raised up to provoke the *ordinary* ones to jealousy.' In order hereto, one of our first rules was, given to each Preacher, 'You are to do *that part* of the work which we appoint.' But *what work* was this? Did we ever appoint you to administer sacraments; to exercise the priestly office? Such a design never entered into our mind; it was the farthest from our thoughts: And if any Preacher had taken such a step, we should have looked upon it as a palpable breach of this rule, and consequently as a recantation of our connexion.

12. For, supposing (what I utterly deny) that the receiving you as a Preacher, at the same time gave an authority to administer the sacraments; yet it gave you no other authority than to do it, or anything else, *where I appoint*. But where did I appoint you to do this? Nowhere at all. Therefore, by this very rule you are excluded from doing it. And in doing it, you renounce the first principle of Methodism, which was wholly and solely to preach the gospel . . .

18. I wish all of you who are vulgarly termed Methodists would seriously consider what has been said. And particularly you whom God hath commissioned to call sinners to repentance. It does by no means follow from hence, that ye are commissioned to baptize, or to administer the Lord's Supper. Ye never dreamed of this, for ten or twenty years after ye began to preach. Ye did not then, like Korah, Dathan and Abiram, 'seek the priesthood also'. Ye knew, 'no man taketh this honour unto himself, but he that is called of God, as was Aaron.' O contain yourselves within your own bounds; be content with preaching the gospel; 'do the work of Evangelists; proclaim to all the world the loving-kindness of God our Saviour; declare to all, 'The kingdom of heaven is at hand: Repent ye, and believe the gospel!' I earnestly advise you, abide in your place; keep your own station. Ye were, fifty years ago, those of you that were then Methodist Preachers, *extraordinary messengers* of God, not going in your own will, but *thrust out*, not to supersede, but to 'provoke to jealousy' the ordinary messengers. In God's name, stop there! Both by your preaching and example provoke them to love and to good works. Ye are a new phenomenon in the earth, – a body of people who, being of no sect or party, are friends to all parties, and endeavour to

forward all in heart-religion, in the knowledge and love of God and man. Ye yourselves were at first called in the Church of England; and though ye have and will have a thousand temptations to leave it, and set up for yourselves, regard them not; be Church-of-England men still; do not cast away the peculiar glory which God hath put upon you, and frustrate the design of Providence, the very end for which God raised you up.

Methodism in the Channel Islands

Adam Clarke to John Wesley, July 1789

(R. D. Moore, *Methodism in the Channel Islands*, 1952, pp. 55–6)

My reverend father in Christ,

In my last letter I gave you a short account of the prosperity of the work of God in our midst and of the perspective we have of an increase. Since then, the Lord has done wonderful things in our midst. You may perhaps recollect that I spoke to you of the special prayer-meeting I had established for those who had obtained or who yearned after entire sanctification. I thought that, being met with one accord, in one place, we were justified in expecting a glorious descent of the purifying flame. It has even been so. Presently five or six persons could attest that God had purified their souls from all sin. This could not remain hid and was known outside, it could not be otherwise, the change was so palpable in these Christians. Moreover, many others were urged to seek the same blessing and were provoked to jealousy, amongst whom one of the chief was Mr. de Quetteville. He questioned me at length with regard to our little meeting and of the good that was done by it. I satisfied him in all points; then, filled with emotion he said to me: 'It is a lamentable thing that those who began seeking God after me have left me so far behind. By the grace of Christ I want to commence seeking with greater eagerness the same blessing, and give myself no rest until I have joined and gone beyond them if possible.' During two or three days he wrestled with God almost without ceasing. The 30th June he came in my room greatly depressed in spirit, and asked me this question: 'How shall I receive the blessing, and how shall I recognize it?' I gave him all the directions I could, I exhorted him to expect it at the present moment and I assured him that he was not far from the Kingdom of God. He returned to his room, and after a few minutes engaged in the fight of faith, his soul was completely and gloriously delivered. He left then for the country, and went off, as a flame of fire, throughout all the Societies in the Island, carrying the glorious news wherever he went. God accompanied him with the mighty demonstration of His Spirit, and a great number of souls were urged to seek, and many found the promised rest.

I announced then a love-feast for the 5th instant. Never before has my soul felt heaven open in like manner on earth. Many were filled with the pure love; and some, then and since, have, with a pure heart, obtained deliverance of inveterate physical disorders from which they had long suffered. This is an absolutely true fact of which I have such full proofs as reason may demand. There has been one remarkable thing, there has been no false flame, no, not a spark that I would not have wished to have in my own soul all eternity. God was working in the bodies and in the souls, but everything was under the direction of His Spirit and proclaimed loudly His action alone. To summarize, there are not less than fifty or sixty souls who, in less than a fortnight, have entered into the good land, and many of them are established therein, strengthened and fixed. And the hallowed work continues.

A Provincial Look at London Methodism

(*Diary of Julius Hardy*, privately printed, 1973)

Julius Hardy (1763–1816) was a button-manufacturer in Birmingham, whose business took him from time to time to London.

24th [October, 1789]. Being informed that the Revd. Mr. Wesley came to town today, I called upon him in the afternoon. The old gentleman looked very hearty; his sight, to be sure, evidently fails him: for on my saying I cd. wish to speak *to him*, and on our leaving his front parlour, where was his own sister and some others going to tea, and going to a back room, he could hardly see his way.

By my putting a few questions to him relating to the subject, I presently found he was irritated at Dr. Coke's making a collection in Birmingham for the cause he is engaged in, in the West Indies. How far this conduct in Mr. W. is right or not I will not, because I cannot, by any means determine. 'Tis true I was not convinced of the Doctor's committing any crime therein by anything that dropped at this time . . .

25th. In the forenoon some revd. Divine read the prayers and Mr. Wesley preached at West Street Meeting House, where attended a tolerably full congregation, the men on one side, the women opposite. Afterwards the ordinance of the Lord's Supper was administered by the two ministers before noted, and one other whom I did not know, in their surplices, the people kneeling at receiving. They sung two or more hymns out of Mr. Wesley's Collection during the ceremony. One asked me, and repeated his request, that I would join the communicants, but I did not chuse to do it, and so continued a spectator in the men's gallery till the whole concluded. Only in the business of singing the hymns, otherwise I suppose the whole form of the administration was gone thro', as in use with the Establishment . . .

At five o'clock Service begun at the New Meeting House in the City Road. Mr. Jno. Broadbent officiated, beginning with extemporate prayer, then an hymn, and the sermon, etc., the same as at most other Methodist Meeting Houses is commonly the practice.

The public Service being ended, Mr. Wesley spoke for some time to the Society, and many others as well as myself who were not in connection. He reprimanded him for preaching so loud, saying that was by no means acceptable – to offer God Murder for Sacrifice. Then he scolded the leaders (so termed) for not attending their weekly appointed meeting, as I suppose for mutual consultation. He ended his oration by saying he was about to publish more at large, again, his thoughts on the impropriety as well as the inexpedience of the Methodists forsaking the Established Church and becoming a distinct body separated from and unconnected with it. Whether this can be proved or not, will be best known when the publication comes out.

Pastor and People

John Wesley to John Mason; near London, January 13, 1790

(*JWL*, VIII, 196–7, from *WM Magazine*, 1830, p. 251)

Mason was the Assistant in the St. Austell circuit, Cornwall.

As long as I live the people shall have no share in choosing either stewards or leaders among the Methodists. We have not, and never had, any such custom. We are no republicans, and never intend to be. It would be better for those that are so minded to go quietly away. I have been uniform both in doctrine and discipline for above these fifty years; and it is a little too late for me to turn into a new path now I am grey-headed.[1] Neither good old Brother Pascoe[2] (God bless him!) expects it from me, nor Brother Wood,[3] nor Brother Flamank.[4] If you and I should[5] be called hence this year, we may bless God that we have not lived in vain. Come, let us have a few more strokes at Satan's kingdom, and then we shall depart in peace!

¹ A copy of this letter at Duke University reads: 'old and grey-headed'.

² Identified by Telford as the grocer at St John, near Torpoint, but the Duke ms gives the name as 'Porner'.

³ Richard Wood of Port Isaac.

⁴ George Flamank, excise officer, of Plymouth.

⁵ Duke ms: 'shall'.

Extempore Preaching

Adam Clarke to R. C. Brackenbury; Bristol, June 15, 1790

(Ms at Drew University)

As to the remarks you make concerning the *mode* of preaching which is obtaining among us, suffice it to say, I am wholly of your mind. To reduce preaching into the *Rules of Science* & to *learn* the *Art* of it, is a something of which my soul cannot form too horrid an Idea. I bless J. Christ I have never *learnt to preach*, but thro' his eternal mercy I am *taught* from time to time by him as I need instruction. *I* cannot *make* a sermon before I go into the pulpit, therefore I am obliged to hang nakedly on the arm & wisdom of the Lord. Yet I *read* a good deal, & *write* a very little & strive to *study*: but these things I know will be of no avail either to myself or the people if they are unsealed by the Holy Ghost. A preacher who depends on his *collections, divisions* & *articulations* is highly despicable in the sight of God: & the lazy Potto¹ who neglects to improve himself under the gracious influence of the Holy Spirit, & then fathers his ignorance and absurdities on its teachings, is a blasphemer against the Trinity. O how few escape one or the other of these perils! The adage is in general verified here: 'Incidit in Scylam qui vult vitare Charybdim'.²

¹ Potto: a West African sloth.

² 'He who wishes to avoid Charybdis falls into Scylla' – a loose quotation from the twelfth-century poet Philippe Gaultier, *Alexandreis* V. 301.

Dublin Methodism

Adam Clarke to John Wesley; Dublin, September 5th [17]90

(Ms at Wesley College, Bristol)

Endorsed: 'To be forwarded with speed'.

Thro' the tender mercy of God we have got to this City in Safety. Our journey by Land was long & fatiguing, particularly to my dr. Wife & Children who were unwell during the whole: blessed be God, they are now in a measure recover'd.

I came in good time, as Mr. Rutherford had been laid up for some time in a severe Rheumatic Fever, & the People being destitute of their Spiritual Director, were rather in Confusion, especially in their meetings for Prayer &c.

The Work which was so remarkable about the time of Conference was hardly discernible when I came – owing as I am inform'd to some Extravagance & Irregularity in the Conduct of those who took on them the chief management during Mr. Rutherford's indisposition.

However, all the times of Prayer-meeting were & are continued, but to an unwarrantable length; hardly ever breaking up before Ten or Eleven o'clock, & frequently continued to Twelve & One: and in those meetings some have taken on them to give Exhortations of half an hour & sometimes 45 minutes in length. This had a tendency to wear out the People.

I have advis'd them to shorten their Prayer-meeting at Whitefriars on Sabbath Evening after Preaching; as I find the families of many are shockingly neglected: for how can there be family Religion especially on the Lord's Day which you know is here fill'd up with Ordinances, if Prayer meetings are continued as they are here to 10 or 11 o'clock at Night? But in these things I would take no decisive Step but as you, my dr. Sir, should be pleased to direct me. Indeed I am led to be the more cautious in this Respect as I find that those who were made particularly useful in the beginning of this work are possess'd of a very jealous Spirit, which, when anything is attempted to be done in order to regulate or help them, leads them to think & say, 'This is in opposition to us, & is intended to destroy the Work.' Thoughts of this kin[d?] are uncharitable, & corresponding Speeches are horrid: but this I hope will not spread as it is now confined to a few. I am fully convinc'd that we can hardly expect a Revival of the Work of God without Irregularities & Stumbling Blocks: but my Heart joins fully with one of the last Prayers I heard my Revd. Father pray in Bristol. 'Lord! if possible give us this work without the Stumbling Blocks, but if this cannot be, give us Stumbling Blocks &

all, rather than not have thy work!' My whole soul says Amen!

We are now visiting the Classes: when this is finished I hope to transmit an i[mpartia?]l account of the good which has been done as far as I can discern it. I trust this has been considerable.

I wait, Revd. Sir, for any Directions you may be pleased to give me: I humbly trust I shall strive to be faithful to God, & the trust you repose in me.

John Wesley to Adam Clarke; Bristol, September 9, 1790

(*JWL*, VIII, 237)

You will have need of all the courage and prudence which God has given you. Indeed, you will want constant supplies of both. Very gently and very steadily you should proceed between the rocks on either hand. In the great revival at London my first difficulty was to bring in temper those who opposed the work, and my next to check and regulate the extravagancies of those that promoted it. And this was far the hardest part of the work, for many of them would bear no check at all. But I followed one rule, though with all calmness: 'You must either bend or break.' Meantime, while you act exactly right, expect to be blamed by both sides. I will give you a few directions: (1) See that no prayer-meeting continue later than nine at night, particularly on Sunday. Let the house be emptied before the clock strikes nine. (2) Let there be no exhortation at any prayer-meeting. (3) Beware of jealousy or judging another. (4) Never think a man is an enemy to the work because he reproves irregularities. Peace be with you and yours!

John Wesley's Last Conference

(Joseph Sutcliffe's ms 'History of Methodism', at MA)

The forty-seventh Conference opened in Bristol on Tuesday July 27, 1790. About one hundred and thirty preachers were present; and assuredly it was a friendly meeting of the brethren. Mr. Wesley, amidst his sons, looked fresh and lively, & likely to run out his course for years to come. But he himself, having other views, had prepared a book of minutes in 12mo, from the year 1744 to 1789[1] and a copy was put into the hands of about a dozen of us, who came for admission into full connexion, with this inscription: 'J.S. As long as you continue to walk by these Rules, we shall rejoice to acknowledge you as a fellow-labourer: John Wesley.'

Bristol, August 4, 1790:

A long table being placed across the chapel, which had no pews, Mr. Wesley sat in a chair at the head on the table, and about twenty venerable men on the benches, ten on each side, distinguished by bushy or cauli-flower wigs, aged men that had borne the heat and burden of the day. Mr. Mather, as a sort of Archdeacon, a man of clear head and command-ing voice, conducted the whole business of the Conference. Mr. Valton was the secretary, with his small quarto ledger. The rest of the preachers were distributed on the benches, the more aged sitting nearer to the long table.

The first business of the Conference was the cares of the ministry, the examination of probationers, & the strictest [enquiry?] about the can-didates coming out on trial. These are the first cares of heaven; the aged prophet Elijah was not allowed to die till he had thrown his mantle on Elisha.

The second general business was the call of names and characters, present and absent. Mr. Mather asked, Are there any objections to Alex Mather?; any against our venerable father in the chair? The voices were prayers that God would prolong his life. While thus proceeding, he asked, Are there any objections to Andrew Inglis? A pause; he was superintendent of the Sheffield circuit, and a popular man in the pulpit. On his way to Bristol, he had in some visit preached abroad, and the clerical magistrate had fined him £20 as the Act directs.[2] It was in vain that he pleaded being a native of Scotland, a presbyterian, and a licensed preacher: the magistrate knowing what was doing in Lincolnshire, felt disposed, how contrary soever it might be to law, to play the same game. His case before the Conference was worse, because he had paid the fine out of the public collections! The preachers regarded his timidity with great displeasure, as having dishonoured himself & all our former suf-ferers. Dr. Coke, in particular, was much moved, and said, 'I envy the situation in which you then stood;' being ready to go to prison for the Lord's work.

The next, and in some views the main business of the Conference was to ask, How are the preachers stationed this year? Mr. Wesley then put his hand into his pocket and pulled out the manuscript order of the Stations, which it is believed no one had seen since he transcribed it in Newcastle on his way to the Conference. While proceeding, very many changes were made for mutual accommodation in regard to the prayers of the people, & for personal and family reasons, Mr. Wesley rarely interfering, except now & then saying, that he had made such a circuit a promise that brother —— should go to them the next year. It had been reported by some, that Mr. Wesley was tyrannical on those points. Certainly no such idea struck me; all was paternal and fair.

One rub indeed I did hear; it was said that a certain point of discipline had been altogether neglected in one circuit. On hearing that, Mr. Wesley coloured up a little & stamped with his foot, declaring that he would expel the preacher, be he who he might, that should dare to do it. Hearing that, Mr. Robert Roberts rose and looking round on the preachers, said, 'Brethren, I think it very hard that we should be threatened in language so strong. We have left our homes and all behind to travel with Mr. Wesley as sons in the gospel, and to be expelled for a local error in discipline is very severe.' Mr. Wesley patted him on the head with a smile, and all was right again. I have since thought of a couplet in Walter Churchey's poems in his eulogy on Wesley:

> He carried anger as a flint bears fire,
> Which when struck, emits a sudden spark,
> And straight is cold again.

The remaining business of the Conference was to provide for widows, the worn out preachers, the children, & all the incidental cases of chapels, circuits & the missions abroad, for which during Dr. Coke's absence a committee of six preachers was appointed. A building committee was also nominated, but of feeble power; for when men have money, and land, & credit, they disregard committees, till beset with poverty and obliged to utter their humble petitions for aid.

On the Sunday during the Conference Mr. Wesley preached as usual in Carolina-court, King's Square, where fame gave him always two thousand hearers; he might have fourteen hundred.[3] What struck me was his animation and vocal powers. He preached as though he had been a young man for the space it would seem of nearly forty minutes. He seemed on taking the field against the world to resemble the aged Nestor in camps and wars, with all the [gaieties?] of youth sporting on his temples. But alas! on the Monday evening, he desired Mr. Hanby to take the pulpit, having gone beyond his strength in the Court. The order of preaching, then, was for the old men to take the mornings at five and the clergy to preach in the evening. The people were eager to hear their aged fathers, & would rise to hear them once more. The chapels were full at five. . . .

The close of the Conference was very impressive. The twelve young men, or perhaps but eleven, stood on one of the benches, spoke briefly of their experience, their call to preach, & confessed their faith. After this Dr. Coke came on the fore bench with the large Minutes on his left arm. and delivered a copy to each, putting his right hand on each of our heads. This was ordination in every view; what else could it designate, having sworn thus to the faith and devotion to the work of the Lord?

I do not recollect that this was continued in future Conferences; but am told it followed the Scottish ordinations, & though it was not called ordination, what else could it be?

Mr. Wesley took no part in these proceedings; he kept his seat, but saw the Doctor deliver the Minutes to the twelve, laying his right hand in silence on the head of each. His presence sanctioned the whole; for though bound [to] him by countless [ties?], he saw and felt that half a million people could not be kept together with[out] the bread hallowed by the Lord. The words of Peter apply here: 'What was I that I could withstand God?'

After this, the Sacrament followed; and the crowd being great, Dr. Coke and the Rev. Mr. Baddiley,[4] a retired clergyman, stepped in among the people in the best manner they could & delivered the sacred elements. We parted as brothers in joyful hopes to meet again; we parted as the sons of Wesley from whose hand through the Dr. we had received the blessing . . .

Mr. Wesley, and all his laborious sons, had not laboured in vain. The very exact Mr. William Myles[5] gave the following schedule of the work at the close of this Conference:

	Circuits	Preachers	Members
In England	65	195	52,832
In Ireland	29	67	14,106
In Wales	3	7	566
In Scotland	8	18	1,086
In the Isle of Man	1	3	2,580
In the Norman Isles	2	4	498
In the West Indies	7	13	4,500
British America	4	6	800
United States	97	198	43,265
Total	216	511	120,233

The increase being sixteen thousand the next year, the real number of members at his death could not have been less than one hundred and thirty thousand. 'What hath God wrought?'

[1] This was the sixth edition of the so called 'Large Minutes', a compendium of Methodist doctrine and discipline first issued in 1753.

[2] This was the Conventicle Act of 1664, under which Lincolnshire magistrates had recently fined a man for allowing a prayer meeting to be held in his home.

[3] King Square, adjoining Dighton Street, was a favourite site for Wesley's open-air preaching in Bristol.

[4] The Rev. William Baddiley, rector of Nailsea.

[5] The table is taken from William Myles, *Chronological History*, 1799, p. 142.

British Methodism in 1790

(Minutes, 1790)

However problematical, the membership figures reported in 1790 reflect the uneven distribution of Methodism at the end of Wesley's life.

Q.10. What numbers are in the societies?
A.   As follows:

London	2740	Liverpool	1020
Sussex	249	Blackburn	930
Kent	570	Coln[e]	976
Colchester	300	Leicester	775
Norwich	900	Nottingham	910
Lynn	385	Derby	736
Bedford	376	Sheffield	1690
Northampton	406	Grimsby	584
Oxfordshire	636	Horncastle	643
Gloucestershire	354	Gainsborough	585
Worcestershire	339	Epworth	697
Sarum	556	Leeds	2157
Isle of Wight	150	Wakefield	706
Isles of Jersey,		Huddersfield	846
Guernsey and		Birstal	1266
Alderney	498	Bradford	1085
Bradford	730	Halifax	1111
Shepton-Mallet	880	Keighley	1480
Bristol	1841	Whitehaven	302
Taunton	226	Isle of Man	2580
Tiverton	380	York	880
Bideford	140	Pocklington	830
Plymouth	804	Hull	665
St. Austel	762	Scarborough	652
Redruth	1840	Whitby	582
St. Ives	1391	Thirsk	674
Pembroke	159	Yarm	525
Glamorganshire	240	The Dales	980
Brecon	167	Sunderland	1300
Birmingham	1400	Newcastle	700
Wolverhampton	559	Alnwick	290
Burslem	1400	Edinburgh	204
Macclesfield	1090	Glasgow	300
Stockport	830	Dundee	132
Manchester	2060	Aberdeen	260
Bolton	1152	Inverness	190
Chester	604		

Wicklow	117	Brookborough	800
Wexford	260	Iniskillin	530
Waterford	186	Ballyshannon	838
Cork	660	Lisleen	520
Bandon	250	Omagh	290
Limerick	330	Charlemount	1023
Birr	240	Londonderry	300
Castlebar	155	Coleraine	440
Athlone	560	Belfast	560
Longford	450	Lisburn	380
Sligo	371	Downpatrick	340
Ballyconnell	875	Tandaragee	856
Cavan	580	Newry	355
Clones	800	Dublin	1040

The Orphaned Connexion

From the diary of Richard Reece

(Ms at MA)

Reece entered the itinerancy in 1787 and at this time was junior preacher in the Wakefield circuit.

Saturday March 5 [1791]. Wakefield. This day tidings, distressing tidings, are arrived at W—: 'Mr. Wesley is no more.' O thou Head of the Church, we look to thee in this hour of her distress; make bare thine arm, let wisdom & power divine interpose & dissipate our fears. There is no Pilot proper for the Helm at this critical period. Take the conduct of the Ship into thine own hand. O let one principle govern us, let our common interest engage our views; that while we lament the loss of thy Servant we may love one another, & each endeavour by the most fervent zeal to supply his lack. How is earth impoverished! What a deduction from this world! He died *well*, after an illness of five days. A life of 88 years well spent. What a Prodigy! O may I be a follower of him in the practice of those virtues for which he was eminent. My mind has been very solemn since I heard of his D[eath] & has been led out to agonize for the welfare of the Church. *Let Zion be thy chief care.*

    Sunday 6. Wakefield. This morning after preaching I went with one of the friends to Church & stay'd to receive the Sacrament. I found it a precious season. The Lord was there of a truth, notwithstanding the common objection which many of our people urge, 'The Clergymen are wicked.' I am well persuaded if our h[ear]ts are sincere, the Clergy be what they may, we shall not be altogether disappointed of our hopes.

I felt my heart pray in an agony for more of the meekness & gentleness of Jesus Xt, which I perceive such an essential part of the minister's character that I cannot be content without a plenitude of it.

Wednesday [April] 13. Wakefield. . . . A few days ago Mr. M[ather][1] & Mr. Pawson had an interview for the purpose of settling the Policy of Methodism, when their notions of Government by no means agreeing Mr. M. came home much chagrin'd. Mr. M. is for the absolute Monarchial, & Mr. P. for the Republican mode of G[overnment]. Mr. M. argues his right to the reins upon this principle: 'His long service to the Connection'. But this plea has no weight, since there are those who are his seniors & who have served the Connection as effectually as he. The lust of Power which is the characteristic virtue of Mr. M. will but appear from the most arduous enterprises, & like another Proteus transform himself into a thousand different shapes to serve his own purposes: so that were we not to see a gleam of real character breaking through the clouds occasionally in the exercise of dominion, we should mistake it for solid virtue. I see the deceitfulness of all those pleasures which the exercise of power promises. O may I always feel disposed to become the Servant of all.

[1] Alexander Mather was superintendent of the Wakefield Circuit from 1788. Reece was his junior colleague in 1790 and 1791. (George Highfield was appointed to the Circuit in 1790, but for some reason Mather stayed on. The diary confirms this in an entry under Monday March 7: 'I am firmly persuaded his staying this year has been the greatest curse to the Society here.')

2. From 1791 to 1851

Tensions in the Connexion

Wesley's death brought into immediate focus unresolved issues that were crucial to the future of the Methodist movement.

The 'Halifax Circular'

(Smith, *History*, II, 688–9)

To the METHODIST-PREACHERS in general, and to the *Conference* and *Assistants,* in particular.

Dear Brethren,

We whose names are underwritten, having seriously weighed the present State of our Affairs, beg leave to lay before you the results of our deliberations.

Ought not the Preachers in each Circuit to consult with their neighbouring Brethren, and appoint who shall attend the ensuing Conference? For, would it be prudent for *all* to go? as the Circuits would then be left for a considerable time without Preachers: and it would be impossible to find accommodation for *all* among our own friends in Manchester. Yet, ought not as many of the Members of the Conference as possible, with the Assistants, and Preachers who are to be admitted, to attend? Likewise to take into consideration our form or mode of government for the future; that you may not have *all* to do, when you meet in Manchester.

There appear to us but two ways: either to appoint another King in Israel; or to be governed by the Conference Plan, by forming ourselves into Committees. If you adopt the first, who is the Man? What power is he to be invested with? and what revenue is he to be allowed? – But this is incompatible with the *Conference Deed*. If the latter, we take the liberty to offer our thoughts upon that subject.

1. Fill up the vacant places in the Conference Deed with Preachers, according to their *seniority in the Work.*

2. Chuse a President for *one year only*, according to the enrolled Deed.

3. Appoint a Secretary and Stewards for one year only, except for the Preachers' Fund.

4. Appoint a person from year to year to hold a Conference in Ireland.

5. Appoint different Committees, which will take in all the Circuits in the three Kingdoms, to manage the affairs of their respective Districts from one Conference to another.

6. Let these Committees, during the time of Conference, appoint their own Presidents for the *ensuing year*. And let their names be inserted in the Minutes, that they may convene the Committee in case of the bad behaviour or death of a Preacher, or any other emergency.

7. Let each of the Presidents bring an account of their proceedings to the Conference, and *there* let them be *finally determined*.

8. Let every Preacher that is recommended at the Conference, and approved of, but not *then* wanted, have his name inserted at the end of the Minutes, that the aforesaid Presidents, or Committees, may know where to apply for a Preacher, when one is wanted in any of their respective Districts.

9. In case the number of these Preachers be not sufficient to supply the vacancies that happen between Conference and Conference, let the Committee agree with a Local Preacher to supply till the *next Conference only*.

10. If the number of Clergymen who do not travel, Superannuated and Supernumerary Preachers, be not limited, may not our government, in process of time, fall into the hands of men who cannot, properly, be called Travelling Preachers! ! !

11. Should it be necessary to *settle any more Clergymen*, or to make more Supernumerary Preachers than a *given number*, will it not be wise to put out of the Deed the *first Clergymen*, or *Supernumerary Preacher*, and put a Travelling Preacher in his place? George Whitfield, or the Book Steward, for the time being excepted.

N.B. Read the Conference Deed, and you will be convinced that *no Person has a right, by that Deed*, to go to *Ireland*, or *elsewhere*, to *hold a Conference*: and, had not our last Conference appointed our ensuing meeting at *Manchester*, by *that Deed*, we must have gone to *London, Bristol*, or *Leeds*.

We submit these thoughts to your consideration, and earnestly pray to God that you may have wisdom to improve, amend, or reject them, as shall be most for His glory, and the CONTINUATION of ITINERACY AMONG the METHODISTS !

We are, Dear Brethren,
Your affectionate Brethren,

William Thompson
John Pawson
Robert Roberts
John Allen
Richard Rodda
Samuel Bradburn
Thomas Tennant
Thomas Hanby
Christopher Hopper

Halifax, March 30th, 1791

Redruth 'Proposals'
(Smith, *History*, II, 690)

At a meeting of the DELEGATES, and others, from the METHODIST SOCIETIES, in the County of CORNWALL, held at REDRUTH, June 14th, 1791, it was agreed, that an AMENDMENT of our Discipline is necessary. We therefore resolve,

1. That in the forming of Classes, the Members constituting every Class (or a majority of them) shall chuse their Leader.

2. That the people in every Society (or a majority of them) shall choose the Society Stewards.

3. That no Preacher shall admit into, or expel from, the Society any Member, without the consent of a majority of such Society.

4. That the Stewards assembled at Quarter Meeting shall choose the Circuit Stewards.

5. That there shall be no division of Circuits, without the consent of a majority of the Stewards at Quarter Meeting.

6. That no person be recommended to Conference (or sent out) as a Travelling Preacher without a certificate from the Stewards assembled at Quarter Meeting.

7. That if any Preacher be charged with not walking worthy of his vocation, or with being deficient in abilities, the Circuit Stewards (on complaint to them made) shall convene the Stewards of the several Societies in their Circuit, who, from among themselves, shall choose an equal number with the Preachers present, to judge of the charge or charges that shall be produced; and, according to the decision of the majority, such Preacher shall be continued in, or expelled the Circuit.

8. That WE will on all occasions support the Itinerant Plan, and chearfully contribute our proportion of the expence.

We propose

That every Preacher coming from a distant Circuit, shall bring a certificate of his good conduct (while in that Circuit) from a majority of the Stewards assembled at Quarter Meeting.

That, for the advantage of the Connection in general, the Preachers (who are not included in the Conference Deed) be admitted to an equal share of the government, and have a vote in all cases; the affairs of Preaching Houses only excepted.

We highly disapprove of the proposal for dividing the Kingdom into Districts, conceiving it would be injurious to Methodism.

Resolved,

That a copy of these Resolutions, Proposals, &c., be transmitted to every Traveling Preacher in the Kingdom. Wishing you peace, amity, and harmony at the ensuing Conference: Our prayer is that prosperity may attend the cause in which you are embarked. We subscribe ourselves your affectionate Brethren,

[Signed by 51 'Delegates']

The Conference of 1791

At the first Conference after Wesley's death, unity in the face of various threats to the future of the Connexion seemed more important to the itinerants than the immediate resolution of the issues they had inherited.

Joseph Bradford to his wife; Manchester, July 30, [17]91

(Ms at Duke University)

It is with the greatest pleasure I inform my truly precious Eliz. that all things are conducted in love, and with the greatest concord, everyone seeming determined to guard against division ... We have about 170 preachers present, such a company I never saw together before, and probably never shall again, until we meet our late venerable head and honoured Father in the Kingdom of Christ and of God.

Henry Moore's account

(Henry Moore, 'A Plain Account of the Conduct of Dr. Whitehead ...'; ms at SMU)

On the 26th day of July ... the Conference assembled at Manchester according to the appointment of the former year. There were present upwards of 200 Travelling Preachers from various parts of the three kingdoms. Every person present seemed deeply sensible of the importance of the occasion. For more than fifty years Mr. Wesley had been under God the Father and Head of the whole Connexion; and though far the greater part of the Societies had been formed by the labours of the Preachers and many of them Mr. Wesley had never visited, yet having begun the work and formed the Rules by which the whole was governed, having by unwearied labour in travelling, preaching and writing for upwards of half a century, given to the whole work a consistency and order which under God ensured its stability, he was justly considered a centre of union both to preachers and people, and as having an apostolic and fatherly authority over the whole Body. He still continued to visit the principal places every two years, and to preside at the Conference.

The death of such a man was no common loss. It was deeply felt by every person present. The Preachers conversed together previously to the regular opening of the Conference, and were greatly strengthened and comforted by knowing each other's mind, that they were determined to abide in the good way in which they had been called, and to be followers of their deceased Father as he was of Christ.

The business being ended, the Conference broke up. Great was the comfort of the Preachers that such a foundation was laid for the peace and prosperity of the Societies. The Lord they saw was better to them than their boding fears. His servants were of one heart and of one mind! The voice of thanksgiving ascended up on high, and they departed to their several circuits blessing and praising God.

'Our future economy'

(*Minutes*, 1791)

Q.8.   What regulations are necessary for the preservation of our whole Economy, as the Rev. Mr. Wesley left it?
A.   Let the three kingdoms be divided into Districts; England into nineteen . . .; Scotland into two . . .; and Ireland into six . . .

Q.24.   Is it necessary to enter into any arrangements in respect of our future economy?
A.   We engage to follow strictly the plan which Mr. Wesley left us at his death.

Correspondence of 'a Man of Peace'

William Thompson was chosen as the first President of the Conference after Wesley's death because of his reputation as a moderate. His correspondence before and after the Conference of 1791 reveals some of the tensions beneath the issues which had to be faced.

Thompson to Richard Rodda; May 1791

(Ms at Drew University)

I am inclined to think that every member of Conference, and every preacher who is to be admitted, which will not be many above the usual number, ought to meet at Manchester next July. Can you settle our future government without such a meeting? If it be necessary that so many members according to the Deed meet next Conference, what need

is there for a Conference either in Scotland or Ireland? Read the Enrolled
Deed, and you will see that no person has any authority to go either to
Ireland or Scotland to hold any Conference, and had not our last Conference appointed our next meeting at Manchester, we must have gone
to London, Bristol, or Leeds according to the Deed. Mr. Mather set out
for London, as soon as he heard that Mr. Wesley was dead, and is not
yet returned to his new and young wife. I have heard that the preachers
in London have appointed Mr. Mather to go to Ireland to hold a Conference; but in so doing they have gone beyond the power which the
Deed gives them. But perhaps they have been so much accustomed to
this rule, that they have forgotten that the king is dead. It is my judgment,
that a number of the oldest preachers ought to meet at Manchester or
Leeds, to consult what is best to be done in our present circumstances:
but how to do this, is what I am at a loss to know. The preachers in
London, you see, in Mr. Wesley's name, have ordered us all to keep our
places till we go to Manchester next July.[1] What is to be done? shall we
obey or not? I hope none of the brethren will find any fault with any of
us for speaking all the good we can of Mr. Wesley: and I cannot see why
your writing good of him should displease any of them. I should be glad
to go to Manchester next Monday; but fear it will not be in my power,
as we have not got all our classes met yet, and our Quarter day will be
that day week. I hope you and all the members of Conference will take
care what you do and what you say at this time. You have now an opportunity of setting your future government so as to be a blessing to yourselves and many; but if you let it slip you may never have such another.
If I live to see you I shall tell you my mind fully; but I am a man of
peace, and hope we shall all pray much to God for grace and wisdom to
assist us at this time. I find a second Thomas Atherton[2] has sent out a
printed letter among the young preachers, but hope it will not do much
hurt.

[1] The preachers stationed in London sent a letter to each itinerant, dated March
2nd, 1791, in which they reported the news of Wesley's death and his dying injunc-
tion that they should all continue in their 'respective stations' until the Conference
met, as appointed, in Manchester (Smith, *History*, II, 199–200).
[2] A reference to Alexander Kilham.

Thompson to Joseph Benson; Halifax, June 28, 1791

(Ms at Emory University)

I was sorry to see your printed letter & the letters from Hull, not because
I think the design of the authors wrong, but that they have a tendency to
accomplish the very end they wish to prevent: 1. To set the people who
are for, & those who are against a separation to contend with each other
& thereby to make a division among the people who are now quiet & at

peace. 2. To bring the people who are for a separation to the knowledge of the preachers, if there are any among us, who are inclined that way, & thereby accomplish that which they intended to prevent. The people in these parts are very peaceable among themselves at present, & have much confidence in the wisdom & goodness of the preachers in general; & therefore Mr. E[ntwisle][3] and I shall not disturb them with your letter. You read prayers & preach in church hours; we pray without book, in some places, & preach at the same time, baptise children & bury the dead, but still we all keep close to the Church & are very strong church-men!

You wish to know my mind & what I think of a separation, the Lord's Supper, & baptising children; & I shall tell you, without the least reserve. I would have the preachers to follow the Methodist Plan just as Mr. Wesley left it, without attempting the smallest alteration in it, one way or other. That is, where they then read prayers continue to do so, where they prayed without book, do so still; where they preached in Church hours, & where they did not, still continue to preach at the same time, & where they baptised & buried the dead, do so still, & where they did not these things, let them not begin till the people force them to do otherwise. But at the same time, make no public or private declarations of what they will do in future; but follow the footsteps of Providence, as he shall see proper to open their way. If you will settle the Preachers Fund upon a proper foundation, & keep, in all your appointments, from unjust & unchristian influence, I have no doubt but we shall go on well. But I must tell you, that I fear the latter abundantly more than preaching in church hours, baptising children & burying the dead; yea, than even a separation from the Church of England.

No preacher has said one word to me of any change in our Plan; all with whom I correspond, seem resolved to follow the good old way without turning to the right or left: but just as they did from last Conference to Mr. Wesley's death . . .

[3] Joseph Entwisle was the junior preacher in Thompson's circuit.

Thompson to Richard Rodda; Wakefield, Feb. 8, 1792

(Ms at Drew University)

I have heard that Dr. Whitehead has published against us all, but hope it is not quite so severe, as what James the first said of the Puritans; viz That they should all be burnt. But by the by, I suspect little mercy from him; for the wrath of a disappointed proud man is such. I am sorry to say, that some of our preachers have been so foolish, as to give me a good deal of trouble 'on his account' to keep them quiet, but hope, they are now pretty well satisfied. I believe many of them were disturbed by the Holy Women in different places, who were attached to the Dr., and therefore, said and reported many unjust things of the preachers in general. But his raising the price of his book, and keeping Mr. Wesley's papers unjustly, have, if not convinced, stopped their mouths at present. Poor souls, I pity them, for they have been accustomed to rule among us, but now find the hope of their government is at an end, and not having that measure of grace which they profess, are not willing to be what God and their brethren would have them be; that is peaceable members of Society. It is more than probable, they expected that the executors and trustees would have been our masters; and Dr. Whitehead King among them: in such a government they hoped to be their eyes in different parts of the land, and therefore still to keep their places. To be disappointed here also is very provoking. Hope deferred maketh the heart sick and the wise woman mad.

I am sorry to inform you, that some of the priests among us, I fear, without consent of Conference or consulting the district have been administering the Sacrament in different places. Nay, even some that are no priests, and not even admitted, have ventured to put forth their hand to that Holy Thing. This I impute to two causes, first the not appointing chairmen in the districts; and secondly, to the example of their Reverend brethren, who have not kept their agreement in the last Conference. I fear if there be not some method adopted next Conference, that this will grow till we shall have local preachers, likewise, climbing into the priest's office; and thereby, many of our people offended and the work of God destroyed. To me there appears no better way, than the receiving that part of our plan which Mr. Benson, Mather, and Dr. Coke objected to last Conference; for had it been received it would have prevented Taylor, Hanby, Pawson, Cownley, Elliott[4] from doing what they have done, as none of them durst have made any alteration in our plan, without the consent of their district. It is shameful to have such a boy as Elliott administering the Sacrament in Huddersfield circuit, is not this a violation of order in the church of Christ and opposed to common sense, and will actually ruin our course if not prevented. I think the committee in London ought to write to Elliott, to inform them wherefore or why he did so. Dr. Whitehead has not got one subscriber in my circuit. I hope you will let me know in your next how you are getting on in London, and what you hear from other quarters, as you see I have kept nothing back from you . . .

---

[4] The preachers named had all taken upon themselves to administer the sacrament despite the position adopted at the Conference of 1791. Richard Elliott, then stationed in Huddersfield Circuit, had become an itinerant only one year earlier.

Thompson to Richard Rodda; Wakefield, May 14, 1792

(Ms at Drew University)

Your letters are so far from being a trouble to me, that they are a pleasure, but to tell you the truth I do not know whether I am a letter in your debt, or you in mine. I am nearly of the same mind with respect to the District meeting at Manchester; only think their ordination was not Episcopal, Presbyterian or Methodistical, and know not how to baptize it unless I call it a creature proceeding from the pride of their own hearts, which I am convinced will die with them.[4] But have no doubt that it tends to sap the foundation of our usefulness, by destroying the union of preachers and people. I am a Methodist preacher, and will do nothing contrary to the mind of my brethren at large; nor can I see an order which is likely to be produced by our Manchester brethren, and their proceedings, equal to, much less superior, to the order among us antecedent to their meeting. I think that all who are called to the ministry, and admitted by their brethren at our Conference, are as scripturally ordained as any men in the world: but think we ought to decline the lesser parts of the ministry, that we may perform the greater with advantage. Our chief call was to preach the gospel, and I shall not submit to have authority given me by the laying on of the hands of my junior brethren; till they can show me 'Thus sayeth the Lord' for it, which I think will not be easily done. I fear the Liverpool affair is a melancholy one, and I doubt will stand upon our records as a full proof of the folly if not the sinful proceedings of our brethren in that district. I am sorry that anything they have done in Manchester should strengthen the hand of the opposition in London; but hope as the Lord reigneth, he will take care of his own cause. I think if Mr. Rogers follows your advice in giving the tickets for the pews into the hands of the leaders, it may preserve the body of the society on our side; but I cannot say that the dividing the London circuit at present meets my approbation. I am inclined to think the fewer alterations we make at present, and the more we comply with the judgment of the body of our people, the better; as our usefulness in a great measure depends upon the confidence the people have in us. The world in general and our people in particular give credit to the declaration which we made last Conference, and I, as well as you, did it from my heart; and am determined with you to consent to no change without the judgment of my brethren. If my brethren shall think proper to appoint me for London next year, I at present have no objection; but do not wish any division of the circuit, and hope you and I shall by the blessing of God be enabled to take care of it, especially if we get such fellow labourers as we shall desire.

Our district met the 2nd of this instant, and thank God we were of one mind in supporting the declaration of last Conference, and following the Methodist plan as Mr. Wesley left it; and hope our brethren at the next Conference will approve of our resolution. Whether a layman as you call him, or a gownsman shall sit in the chair next Conference is a matter of indifference to me, but hope it will be better filled than last year, and I thank God I shall be free of it. The Districts, so far as I can hear, over the three kingdoms, except Manchester and Newcastle, are in a state of peace and prosperity; and trust, we shall by the blessing of God be able by next Conference to settle there also. You see by this that I am not easily shaken in mind, as a company of self-ordained priests cannot affright me; as I can trust in God, and in my lay brethren, to support the good old cause of Methodism.

4 Both Manchester and Liverpool were Circuits where there was dissatisfaction with the Conference decision to follow 'Mr. Wesley's plan' at least for the time being, to give time for deliberation on the 'future economy' of the Connexion. Three of the Manchester preachers were ordained at a District Meeting.

Kilham in Scotland

Alexander Kilham to John Gaulter; Aberdeen, November 10th, 1792

(Ms at MA)

Kilham, at the age of thirty, had been an itinerant for six years and was Superintendent of the Aberdeen circuit, with James Anderson as the junior minister. Wesley had reluctantly agreed to the use of the Presbyterian form of Communion in Scotland.

The people are exceeding kind and obliging. The Elders of this Society appear of one heart & mind. They are men fearing God & hating covetousness. They are willing to do everything in their power to make us comfortable & happy. We have good Congregations on the Sundays. Our weeknight Congregations are equal to Newcastle's now. But we are new. By what I learn the people of this Kingdom do not make it their duty to hear any days but Sundays. If they do it, they consider it rather of choice than necessity.

Yesterday we had the Sacrament. The preaching began at half past ten. About 160 communicated or near 200. Near 90, who were not of the society, were with us. It was a most solemn season. It was half past 2 before we had done. About 500 persons were spectators. All was still as death. I had the plan given me by Mr. Anderson & kept it in every point. The Lord manifested himself gloriously in the midst. The hearts of many were glad in his salvation. Mr. Anderson was obliged to be in the country. The whole burthen rested on me. I had to speak most of the time. At night our congregation was uncommonly large. The Lord gave me the strength according to my day. The people here are perfectly reconciled to the Methodists being separate from all others. Our friends declare they have been uncommonly happy & blessed since they had the ordinances among themselves. We have several joined already. I hope God will give us to see the travail of our Redeemer's soul . . .

Most of our friends, as well as the people in general, are revolutionists. Scotland appears ripening fast for a reform. The sentiments of the most enlightened in these parts are much of the same nature with yours & mine.

[He goes on speak of the friendly support of the local minister, deplores the situation over the Newcastle chapel and advocates building a new one for the friends of liberty. He is about to leave for Inverness, where he will spend the next four Sundays, giving the Sacrament and preaching, while Mr. Doncaster (the second of the four ministers in the Inverness Circuit) takes his place in Aberdeen.]

Benson's Defence of Methodism

(Joseph Benson, *A Defence of Methodism in five letters addressed to the Rev. Dr. Tatham*, 1793)

Edward Tatham's *Sermon suitable to the times: Preached before the University of Oxford* was an attack not only on Methodists, but on Enthusiasts, Anabaptists and Dissenters, and provoked a number of replies. The author was Rector of Lincoln College. Benson's letters are dated from Manchester in February, 1793.

Are the Methodists found by experience to be such *nuisances* on the one hand, or of *so little use* on the other, in the nation; such enemies to *good order*, or so *remiss* and *slothful* in *good works*, that people in general desire their extinction? Sure I am, Sir, in places where the Methodists are numerous, as in this neighbourhood [Manchester], throughout the West of Yorkshire, in the populous parts of Staffordshire, Worcestershire, and Cornwall, at Birmingham, Bristol and London, Liverpool, Hull, Newcastle-upon-Tyne, Sunderland, and many other of the manufacturing and trading Towns, the *Parish Officers*, *Overseers*, and *inhabitants* in *general*, would have no cause to praise you, were you to effectuate, what, blessed be God, will never be in your power, the extermination of the Methodists. The effect of their preaching in rendering *drunkards* sober, *thieves* honest, the *idle* and *slothful* diligent and industrious, the provision they make for their own poor, many of whom they keep from being troublesome to the parish, the *benevolent* Societies which they have instituted in almost all the large Towns, as at London, Bristol, Birmingham, Manchester, Liverpool &c. for the relief of the *poor*, *afflicted*, and *destitute* of every denomination; their liberal contributions to charitable institutions of *every kind*, as to *Infirmaries*, *Hospitals* and *Sunday Schools*, which in very many places they have introduced and which, in very many places they alone keep on foot, these things demonstrate that they are public blessings, in the Towns and Countries where divine Providence has favoured with increase. – In this Town alone, Sir, the last year, the collections in the Methodist Chapels for the Infirmary and Lunatic Hospital amounted to 102£, for the Sunday School 114£, for the poor of their own Society to about 200£, while the subscriptions for the *Strangers Friend* or benevolent *Society*, instituted for visiting and relieving the *poor*, the *fatherless*, the *widows*, the *afflicted*, and such as have *no helper*, of *any* and *every* denomination, amounted from Nov. 7, 1791 to Nov. 1, 1792, to no less sum than 427£. It is true this last mentioned charity meets with very liberal support from many gentlemen and ladies in this Town and neighbourhood, who are not members of the Methodist Society; but the Methodists had the happiness of first instituting, as they still have of conducting this admirable beneficence; the *Visitors* and *Committee* being *all* of their Community.

Pressure for Change

(*Diary of Julius Hardy*; see p. 227 above)

Samuel Bradburn was a leading advocate of the 'new plan'. Soon after taking up his appointment in the Bristol circuit in 1792, he aroused fierce controversy by donning vestments and reading the Liturgy at the opening of Portland Chapel. Of his travels the following May, he himself wrote: 'This month has been well filled. I have travelled about six hundred miles, preached forty-two sermons, expounded frequently, and prayed in public about one hundred times ...' A year later he was a participant in the meeting at Lichfield.

May 26th [1793]. Late in the evening of yesterday, Mr. Sam. Bradburn reached this place [Birmingham] ... This morning it was given out at Cherry Street Meeting House that he would preach in the forenoon at Coleshill Street Meeting House, which he did to a tolerably large and very attentive congregation; as also in the afternoon at three. In the evening, at six, he preached again at Cherry Street. I think I never saw people more earnest in my life to catch every expression from the speaker. He too was very animated, all alive, appearing in that pulpit quite in his element. The conclusion I thought admirable indeed; taking occasion to speak of the war, and how closely it affected the poorer part of the congregation, he said he considered it as a scourge sent to chastise a guilty land, and the likeliest means of shortening its duration was by national and personal repentance and reformation – tho', he observed, its termination did not appear speedy.

It seems he has been from his circuit some time, on a journey through South and North Wales, Cheshire, Lancashire, and is now on his return to Bristol. Suspicion, I doubt not, has attended him; several with us ask, what has he been about? How can he presume to leave Bristol so long? Surely he must have some fresh scheme in contemplation, in order to which he has been sounding the disposition of the people and preachers too. These and other conjectures I find already occupy the minds of high-flyers, zealous churchmen.

May 27th. Early in the morning I accompanied Mr. Bradburn on horseback to Bromsgrove . . . I understand it is the determination of the liberal part of the Methodist ministers to be shackled no longer than till their ensuing yearly Conference. After that, it is their intention to drop that slavish adherence to the Established Church, and by celebrating the Lord's Supper in their own congregations, and baptising the children of such people as desire it, to assume the appearance of an independent body of themselves. This, it appears, Mr. Benson and that party are not disposed to acquiesce; at least, he tells Mr. Bradburn it is not yet the proper time, and is desirous of putting it off another year. Which of the two will prevail, time must discover. Thus much I am persuaded of, the Methodists in Birmingham taking them in general are much more inclined to moderation than at the period of last Conference. Nay, several who some time ago were quite averse to the celebration of that divine ordinance out of the Established Church, I learn are now quite otherwiseminded and not only have no objection to it, but are desirous of it. Others I believe have become neutral who, but a little while ago, opposed its introduction with all their might. Thus far, it was best perhaps to defer the public celebration thereof one more year, as was resolved upon last Conference. Since then, the body of Methodists have had an opportunity of considering still further the propriety of the measure; the consequence of which is, I believe, an acquisition of numbers, both ministers and people, to the liberal side.

An Address to the Methodist Societies

The first of two Addresses 'to the members of the Methodist Societies' from the Conference of 1793. The second, dated August 8th, was a reply to charges made by the London and Bristol trustees that they had 'departed from the original plan of Methodism'.

(*Minutes*, 1793)

An ADDRESS *to the Members of the Methodist Societies throughout England, from the Conference assembled at Leeds, August 6, 1793.*

Dear Brethren,

We feel it our duty to send you this Address, lest the insinuations of any who are enemies to our prosperity and unity should grieve your minds, and injure the work of God.

Our venerable father, who is gone to his great reward, lived and died a member and friend of the Church of England. His attachment to it was so strong and so unshaken, that nothing but irresistible necessity induced him to deviate from it in any degree. In many instances God Himself obliged him to do this; He powerfully called him forth into the streets and open fields, and afterwards raised to his assistance hundreds of men who never passed through the usual forms of ordination. To all these evident providences of God Mr. Wesley submitted, though at first with great reluctance. In consequence, he found himself obliged to erect chapels, which were neither consecrated according to the usual method of the Church of England, nor in the least subject to the direction of the National Episcopacy. In all these things he deviated from the Establishment merely on the ground of unavoidable necessity; or, which is the same to a truly pious soul, from the clear manifested providence and will of God.

A dilemma, or difficulty, of a similar kind has been experienced by us since the death of Mr. Wesley. A few of our Societies have repeatedly importuned us to grant them the liberty of receiving the Lord's Supper from their own Preachers. But, desirous of adhering most strictly to the plan which Mr. Wesley laid down, we again and again denied their request. The subject, however, is now come to its crisis. We find that we have no alternative, but to comply with their requisition, or entirely to lose them. O, brethren, we 'hate putting away!' – especially those who are members of the mystical body of Christ, and our dearly beloved brethren; and whose only error, where they do err, is that of the judgment, and not of the heart. And can we suffer these to forsake their faithful Pastors, and possibly to run into the jaws of some ravening wolf, when the point in contest must be allowed by all to be *unessential* to salvation?

But we are not insensible that our brethren on the other side may justly urge, 'Are not our interests as dear to you as theirs? Why then will you grieve us in so tender a point? Why will you oppose us in those particulars which we think of very great importance to the prosperity of Zion? Why will you force upon us a term of communion to which we never consented, or expect us to remain united to those who will be ever grieving us by pressing the necessity of compliance with *that* which we judge to be highly injurious to the cause of God?'

Such is the dilemma, dear brethren, to which we have been reduced. We allow the full force of the arguments which the brethren who disapprove of the administration of the Lord's Supper urge as above: nor can we, on any consideration, lay on them a new term of communion, or suffer *a single person* among them to be grieved by the reasonings of those who wish for an innovation in our plan. We therefore weighed this delicate subject with the greatest seriousness and deliberation, feeling the tenderest pity for those of our brethren who thought themselves aggrieved; and came finally to the following resolution: 'That the sacrament of the Lord's Supper shall not be administered by the Preachers in any part of our Connexion, except where the whole Society is unanimous for it, and *will not be contented without it*; and, even in those few exempt Societies, it shall be administered, as far as practicable, in the evening only, and according to the form of the Church of England.' For we could not bear that the Sacrament, which was instituted by our Lord as a bond of peace and union, should become a bone of contention; and are determined never to sanction the administration of that holy ordinance for the purpose of strife and division.

You may clearly see from hence, dear brethren, that it is *the people*, in the instances referred to, who have forced us into this further deviation from our union to the Church of England. Still, we wish to be united to it as a body at large. The few Societies which answer the description mentioned in the above resolution, need but have a small influence on the whole Connexion. We cannot, however, we will not, part with any of our dear flock, who love God and man, on account of unessential points. For we love you *all*, and are the servants of you all for Jesus' sake. But we entreat our Societies at large (the few exempt cases excepted) to continue, as usual, in connexion with the Church of England; and we shall, with great cheerfulness and contentment, labour among them according to that simple original plan of Methodism established and left to us by our venerable friend.

We must observe to you, in conclusion, that we feel the most unfeigned loyalty to the King, and a sincere attachment to the Constitution. We reverence the Government; are conscious of the many blessings we enjoy under our gracious Sovereign, and are thankful to God for them; and do earnestly and sincerely recommend the same principles and spirit to you.

We remain, dear Brethren,

You most affectionate Servants and faithful Pastors.

A Comment from John Pawson

John Pawson to Charles Atmore; December 13th, 1793

(Ms at MA)

... It will by no means answer our end to dispute one with another which is the most Scriptural form of Church government, but we should consider our present circumstances, and try to agree upon some method by which our people may have the Ordinances of God, and we may at the same time be preserved from divisions. I care not a rush whether it be Episcopal or Presbyterian. I believe neither of them Scriptural. But our Preachers and people in general are prejudiced against the latter, and therefore if the former will answer our end, we ought in our present circumstances to embrace it. Indeed, I believe it will suit our present plan far better than the other. My reason for thinking so is, we have a great many very little men among us, who cannot get forward except they are under proper governors.

The design of Mr. Wesley will weigh very much with many, both Preachers and people, which now evidently appears to have been this. He foresaw that the Methodists would soon after his death become a distinct body of people. He was deeply prejudiced against Presbyterian, and as much prejudiced in favour of Episcopal government. In order therefore to preserve all that is valuable in the Church of England among the Methodists, he ordained Mr. Mather and Dr. Coke Bishops. These he undoubtedly designed should ordain others. Mr. Mather told us so at the Manchester Conference, but we did not at all understand him. We could not see how a Scotch Presbyterian Bishop could support the Church of England. The mystery was here. By the Church of England was meant the body of Methodists, who were to have the Doctrine and Discipline of the Church of England among them. I can see no way to come to any good settlement but that which I mentioned before. The District meetings do not answer the end at all. My very soul is weary of them. And in reality we have no government. I do therefore most sincerely wish that Dr. Coke and Dr. Mather may be allowed to be what they are, Bishops. That they should ordain two more chosen by the

Conference. That these four should have the government put into their hands, for one year, each one in his own District. They being stationed, one suppose in London, one in Bristol, one in Leeds and one in Newcastle. We can give them what degree of power we please, but I would not cramp them. If any of them should abuse their powers, woe be to them, for they would never be intrusted with it any more. And even supposing these four had authority to station the Preachers, who would have any cause to fear? Not a man in the Connection who is good for anything. It is only a parcel of poor worthless creatures that we do not know where to find a place for, that will have any occasion to shrink back from this plan. I am so weary of Districts and of the shadow of being a Chairman that I would give my vote that either Mr. Mather or Dr. Coke should be King in our Israel rather than that we should be as we are.

We must have Ordination among us at any rate. We have so many little, very little, men in the Connection. Men who would quite disgrace that sacred Ordinance were they to have anything to do with it.

When you write to the Dr., for goodness sake do not raise difficulties, but whatever you do endeavour to make every thing as easy as you can. Tell him you have not the least objection in the world to his being a Bishop. I am sure I have not, no, nor hath my most blessed, my faithful and affectionate friend Adam Clarke. A man of God if ever there was one. The Lord bless him, his very name is precious to me.

The Lichfield Meeting

Minutes of a Meeting held at Lichfield, April 2nd, 1794

(Ms at Wesley College, Bristol. Printed, with some variations, in Smith, *History*, II, 691)

1. A Promise of Secrecy
2. All the company except Mr. H[?] promise to abide by the decisions of the Majority except where he believes the Bible is against it or his conscience cannot approve of it.
3. We will make no avowed separation from the Church of England.
4. The sacrament of the Lord's Supper shall be administered wherever there is a majority of the Society who desire it; but the preachers must not canvass for votes, or do anything to obtain a majority which may lead to division or strife; nor should the Lord's Supper be administered in any chapel when a majority of the trustees are against it, except a fair

and full indemnification be afforded them for all the debts which they were responsible for, supposing they require such indemnity.

5. That there be an order of superintendents appointed by the Conference.

6. That all the preachers who shall be approved by the Conference shall from time to time be ordained as elders.

7. That all the preachers, when admitted into full Connexion, shall receive their admission by being ordained deacons by the superintendents, appointed by the Conference: provided, 1. That no preacher at present on probation, or in full Connexion, shall be under any obligation to submit to ordination. 2. That no preacher shall receive letters of orders till he has been ordained an elder.

8. That the superintendents appointed among us, by the Conference, shall be annually changed, if it be good [Smith: if necessary].

9. That the Connexion be formed into seven or eight general divisions.

10. That each superintendent shall visit the principal Societies in his division, at least once a year; that he shall have authority to execute, or see executed, all the branches of Methodist discipline, and to determine, after having consulted the preachers who are with him, in all cases of difficulty, till the Conference.

11. That the superintendent of any division, where he judge himself inadequate to determine in any given case, shall have authority to call in the president to his assistance; in which case the president shall, if possible, attend, and shall have the ultimate determination of the case till the next Conference.

12. The divisions for the present:—

1. London, Sussex, Rochester, Canterbury, Godalming, Norwich, Yarmouth, Diss, St. Ives, Bury, Colchester, Lynn, Walsingham, Bedford, Higham Ferrers.

2. Bristol, Bath, Portsmouth, Sarum, Isles[1], Bradford, Wilts, Gloucester, Shepton Mallett, Taunton, Collumpton, Plymouth, St. Austle, Redruth, Penzance.

2. Birmingham, Oxford, Worcester, Pembroke, Glamorgan, Brecon, Wolverhampton, Shrewsbury, Burslem, Hinckley.

4. Manchester, Macclesfield, Leek, Stockport, Oldham, Bolton, Wigan, Chester, Liverpool, Northwich, Blackburn, Colne.

5. Sheffield, Nottingham, Northampton, Banbury, Castle Donnington, Newark, Derby, Ashby-de-la-Zouch, Grimsby, Horncastle, Gainsborough, Epworth, Rotherham.

6. Leeds, Wakefield, Huddersfield, Birstal, Dewsbury, Bradford, Halifax, Keighley, Otley, York, Thirsk, Pocklington, Hull, Bridlington.

7. Newcastle, Sunderland, Alnwick, Hexham, Barnard Castle, Whitehaven, Whitby, Stockton, Scarbro', Isle of Man.

8. Scotland and Ireland and the Norman Isles.[1]
Proposed superintendents,
Dr. Coke, Dr. Mather, Dr. Pawson, Dr. Taylor, Dr. Moore, Mr. Hanby, Mr. Bradburn.
Present: T. Coke, A. Mather, T. Taylor, J. Pawson, S. Bradburn, J. Rogers, H. Moore, A. Clarke.
The whole of the above plan to be laid before the ensuing Conference, to be adopted or rejected, as they may think proper [Smith: fit]; but those present agree to recommend and support it as a thing greatly wanted, and likely to be of much advantage to the work of God.

[1] Smith lists the Norman Isles in division 2, where the manuscript has simply 'Isles', referring presumably to Portland and the Isle of Wight.

William Thompson to Richard Rodda; London, May 19, 1794

(Ms at Drew University)

The Minutes of our district which met on Tuesday the 6th, as far as they relate to the Lichfield convention, are as follows: 1. We think it entirely contrary to the existing constitution of Methodism and prejudicial to the work of God in which we are engaged. 2. That it was contrary to the declaration of last Conference. 3. That the contents thereof ought not to be introduced into our Conference, till the person or persons who appointed it be known. 4. It is our judgment that every preacher in the Methodist connexion ought to be appointed by Conference to some circuit and to continue in that circuit unless in case of necessity.

I have asked the following questions of Dr. Coke and some of the Lichfield conventioners, but have received no answer: 1. Which ordination do you wish to introduce among us? Episcopal or Presbyterian? 2. What preachers would you have ordained? 3. What are they to be ordained for? or what are they to do by virtue of their ordination? 4. What change do you wish to make thereby in our mode of government?

You may see by the above that the members of our district will not support your motion to give £60 to Mr. B. for his labour in going through the kingdom. It appears to me that the love of power moved the persons who met at Lichfield, but I trust in God they will be disappointed. I am inclined to think all the power necessary to govern the church of Christ is rightly divided among the districts and annually centres in the Conference, where it ought. If we keep at these, we shall do well, but should we create London Bishops to wander about under pretence of administering the Sacrament or anything else, I fear the consequences will prove fatal. If we continue the same simple, plain and holy men we were when we set out, the Lord will be with us. But if we seek after titles, lawn sleeves, gowns and bands, I fear the present revival will come to nothing. You see by this that there are more preachers who are opposed to the Lichfield meeting than you; and I hope you will find 19 out of every 20 at Conference of the same mind . . .

The Bristol Dispute, 1794–5

The power-struggle between Conference and trustees erupted at Bristol in August 1794. Henry Moore, who had been ordained by Wesley in 1787 for the English work, assisted Coke in administering the sacrament at Portland Chapel and was accordingly debarred from the New Room pulpit by the trustees. Joseph Benson, appointed as Superintendent of the Bristol circuit that year, was the leading advocate of the 'old plan' among the itinerants and the unity of the 'Conference party' was thereby threatened. The issues were connexional rather than local.

John Pawson to Joseph Benson; Liverpool, August 16, 1794
(Ms at Emory University)

Mr. Wesley himself could not govern [the Bristol trustees]. They gave him infinite trouble, and he was obliged to give them up. I know that Mr. Pine & Mr. Roberts are by far the best men among them. But take them all together and the richer part of the people who are their principal friends, and you cannot think that they are the most deeply pious among the people, that they ought to govern the preachers.

John Pawson to Joseph Benson; Liverpool, September 5, 1794
(Ms at Drew University)

It pains my mind very much to differ from persons in judgment I so highly and so justly esteem as I certainly do you and Mr. Mather. The Bristol trustees also are my old and very good friends, and I should be sorry to give either them or you a moment's pain. Nevertheless I cannot help thinking that they [have done?] wrong in the highest degree. It appears to me not a little thing to shut the door of the church against a faithful, long & justly approved servant of God. As we all know Henry Moore to be. I never had the happiness of being intimate with him. But I most sincerely and highly esteem him as greatly my superior in many respects.

The following considerations weigh very much with me. Ever since the death of Mr. Wesley we all know that the trustees have been trying to lessen our influence with the people, and as far as they can prevail here they at the same time lessen our usefulness also. We all know that of late their avowed design has been to divide us and they have done all they could in order to it. Those trustees at Bristol have got possession of a most extravagant degree of power, committed to them by the owner of those premises when he did not understand what he was doing, which they would never part with, no not to the owner of the premises himself, although oft entreated so to do. They have now without any good or lawful reason exercised this unjust power in excluding a man of God, a faithful minister of Christ, a man of long approved integrity, none more so, that I know of in the whole Connection, from preaching in their Chapels, although appointed by the Conference. And will Mr. Benson sanction this? Can any Methodist preacher countenance this! Here I stand and wonder. Why so! What will be the consequence if you suffer these trustees to exercise their power? Why, they will no doubt exercise the same power in all time coming. And then please them with preachers if you can. How many then will you find in the whole Connection that you will be suffered to station in Bristol? Will J. Brittle or Frank Wrigley[1] stand the first chance? I fear not. But bad as this is, it is not the worst. It will no sooner be known that the trustees in Bristol exercise this power in the choice of preachers, but all the large towns in the kingdom will claim the same power, and whether their Deeds give it to them or not, they will use it. Witness the trustees of Stockport in the case of poor Billy Simpson last year. You know how this is so.

What then will become of the Itinerant plan? It is dashed all to pieces at once, and we must have done with it for ever. On the present occasion I should have thought that the preachers would have been united as one man, and would at once have convinced those trustees that they would never, no never on any consideration whatsoever, put their necks under the yoke of those men. We certainly have a fair opportunity to convince them that we will not be brought into bondage, by obliging them to give up that unreasonable power, as the trustees of Newcastle have done, or else by building a good and sufficient new chapel, and let them make the best of the old ones . . .

I must live and die, I hope, with my brethren. I should have been glad if you could have gone upon the healing plan that you proposed. But it seems by our brethren's letter to you that this would have been impracticable. As to their having no authority to act and write thus: Alas! that is true enough, nor have you [or] any one else authority to ask us to come to Bristol, nor have we any authority to come there, be the case ever so extraordinary. We have no government at all, and what is more we are resolved we never will have any.

---

[1] John Brettell and Francis Wrigley had been itinerants since 1771 and 1769 respectively.

Joseph Benson to George Merryweather[1]; Bristol, December 12, 1794

(Ms at Drew University)

Our disputes here are very unhappy indeed, and I fear not likely to be soon ended, as it seems nothing will satisfy a part of the preachers but the introduction of the Ordinances every [week?], which would first divide and scatter the societies, and secondly in time make us a complete body of Dissenters: which I confess I do not wish to become. I was much obliged by the [letter?] from the preachers, trustees &c, of the principal places of your circuit. It, with some scores of a similar nature from other places, gave me much encouragement. It is evident that the body [of] our people yet want nothing but to go on in the old way. But, let me observe, nothing is wanting to throw any Society [into?] as much confusion as this Society is, but for some of the [Sacra]mentarian preachers to come among them. They would [effectively?] divide and scatter any Society in a few weeks. Something, if possible, must be done to prevent this, or we are ruined.

[1] George Merryweather was a leading Yorkshire layman and trustee at Yarm, and represented the conservative wing of the membership.

Samuel Bradburn to ? ; Bath, May 12, 1795

(Ms at Drew University)

I have taken a great deal of pains to bring matters to some good conclusion; but hitherto it has been lost labour. Mr. Benson seems very desirous of peace. I have met him several times, and spent many hours with him, in contriving a plan of reconciliation. But some on his side have objected to my terms; and some on my side have objected to his. So that all we have yet done is the being, in a great measure, reconciled to each other. I have appointed our District-Meeting for the 27th inst. and have agreed with Mr. Benson for him to invite Mr. Mather and Mr. Pawson to meet with us, in hopes of healing the breach in Bristol. Should we succeed there, I hope we shall be enabled to strike out a plan for general peace. I absolutely would rather we should all die before August than live to divide. I cannot think of a division but with horror! Yet even that is better than to give up liberty of conscience. You need not fear my granting too much to those trustees. I see them in proper light, and will beware of them. Indeed, I shall act in concert with the Brethren. Dr. Coke has acted nobly through the whole. I intend to do all in my power to get him chosen President at the Conference. He deserves it of us, for his steady support of *our cause*. And he will be very proper for the President.

Josiah Dornford[2] to Joseph Benson; Deptford Road, Dec. 7th, 1794
(Ms at the New Room, Bristol)

Dear Sir,

Tho' I am almost wholly unknown to you, yet I have long conceived a sincere esteem and regard for you, and as one who has been connected with the Methodists more than thirty years, I must honor you for the part you have taken in asserting the cause of *old Methodism*. I have with great satisfaction read the letter you have lately published, I have also read some of the others and I have read the publication by Mr. Knox, and I have read Mr. Moor[e]'s. Every sincere Christian, especially among the Methodists, must lament the bitterness of spirit which has attended the disagreements which have happened in London, since the death of Mr. Wesley, between Mr. Wesley's Executors, the Trustees, and the Preachers. All this, I hesitate not to say, has been promoted and widen'd by James Rogers, Henry Moor[e] & Dr. Coke, whose heart [head?] has been wrought upon by the art of others. Indeed, Rogers had the honor of driving me out of the Society, first in altering the Preaching into the Church-hours at Deptford, contrary to Mr. Wesley's will, so that as a Magistrate I could not consistently attend *there* after that, nor did I think I ought to do it because it was wholly inconsistent when Mr. Wesley in his 'twelve reasons against a separation from the Church of England' had declared against it, as I with those same reasons in my hand, observed to Mr. Wesley and James Rogers at the same time. Mr. Wesley then ordered the preaching to be altered back again to seven in the Morning and five in the afternoon, but Rogers said it could not be done then, but promised it should, which *promise* was never fulfilled. I saw at that time, Mr. Wesley had lost the reins in 1789, and that (as he told me himself) he could not do as he would.

On the reading of Mr. Moor[e]'s pamphlet which I confess is well wrote, though not in a good spirit, his sheet anchor seems the copy of the Ordination which Mr. Wesley gave him. This is what the friends of Old Methodism hardly know how to get over, because it casts up Mr. Wesley's writings, and the general tenor of his conduct for fifty years before. This, I say, is difficult to manage, and I am persuaded that calm and dispassionate men must see and feel the same difficulty in that as I do. There might a good deal be said by way of vindication for the Ordinations for America, and even for the Highlands and Scotland in general, where the Methodists were deny'd the Ordinances, but that Mr. Wesley should ordain others but a few months before his death, and let that Ordinance lay dormant, and no use be made thereof, is what I confess I know not how to account for. Therefore wish I could hear what some, whom I could believe what they say, that which Mr. Wesley

[sic] uttered in vindication of his own conduct, since it seems so contradictory to me. . . .

As to my own part, I contend not against the Ordination, either of the Methodists or any others; all [?] and moderate men must acknowledge that Episcopal and Presbyterian Ordination were both practiced by the primitive Church, but I believe the Methodists will do much more good, to abide in their original calling, which was to christianize men of all Denominations, and leave them in the Form to which they are attached, either by principle or by education[3]; but should it so happen that even among those so brought to God, that they cannot be content unless they are joined to a Meeting and have the Sacrament as regular Dissenters, let them in the name of the God of Peace have them, and depart, but let not the Methodists at large become such as it spoils and perverts their original plan & design of becoming an universal blessing to the Nation at large.

[2] Josiah Dornford, a London merchant, was another of the 'old school'. He and his wife were active and prominent members of the Deptford society and had been long-standing friends of Wesley. He had sided with Wesley in resisting strong agitation at Deptford in 1786 for services in Church hours (*JWJ*, VII, 217, 232, 241, see pp. 215f.). As he was a member of the Court of Common Council of the City of London and a Justice of the Peace for Kent, Methodist loyalty to the Church of England was of particular importance to him.

[3] Cf. a further letter of May 29, 1795 in which Dornford says: 'If I rightly conceive the call of the body of Methodist preachers, it was, it is, to Christianize the different sects of Professors and the various denominations thereof into which the Reformed are split and divided. This being the case, they should leave these in their various forms and various communities, to which they have formerly been attached by the prejudice of their educations.'

'Peace in Our Time'

The Plan of Pacification, 1795

(Smith, *History* II, 688, 693–4, taken from *Minutes*, 1795)

Part 1: Concerning the Lord's Supper, Baptism etc.

1. The Sacrament of the Lord's Supper shall not be administered in any chapel, except the majority of the trustees of that chapel on the one hand, and the majority of the stewards and leaders belonging to that chapel (as the best qualified to give the sense of the people) on the other hand, allow of it. Nevertheless, in all cases, the consent of the Conference shall be obtained, before the Lord's Supper be administered.

2. Wherever there is a Society, but no chapel, if the majority of the stewards and leaders of that Society testify, that it is the wish of the people that the Lord's Supper should be administered to them, their desire shall be gratified: provided that the consent of the Conference be previously obtained.

3. Provided nevertheless, that in Mount Pleasant chapel in Liverpool, and in all other chapels where the Lord's Supper has been already peaceably administered, the administration of it shall continue in future.

4. The administration of baptism, the burial of the dead, and service in Church-hours, shall be determined according to the regulations above-mentioned.

5. Wherever the Lord's Supper shall be administered according to the before-mentioned regulations, it shall always be continued, except the Conference order the contrary.

6. The Lord's Supper shall be administered by those *only* who are authorized by the Conference; and at such times, and in such manner *only*, as the Conference shall appoint.

7. The administration of baptism, and the Lord's Supper, according to the above regulations, is intended only for members of our own Society.

8. We agree that the Lord's Supper be administered among us on Sunday evenings only; except where the majority of the stewards and leaders desire it in Church-hours; or where it has already been administered in those hours. Nevertheless, it shall never be administered on those Sundays on which it is administered in the parochial church.

9. The Lord's Supper shall be always administered in England according to the form of the Established Church; but the person who administers shall have full liberty to give out hymns, and to use exhortation and extemporary prayer.

10. Wherever Divine service is performed in England on the Lord's Day in Church-hours, the officiating preacher shall read either the service of the Established Church, our venerable father's abridgement, or, at least, the lessons appointed by the Calendar. But we recommend either the full service, or the abridgement.

Part 2: Concerning Discipline.

1. The appointment of preachers shall remain solely with the Conference; and no trustee, or number of trustees, shall expel or exclude from their chapel or chapels, any preacher so appointed.

2. Nevertheless, if the majority of the trustees, or the majority of the stewards and leaders of any Society, believe that any preacher appointed for their Circuit is immoral, erroneous in doctrines, deficient in abilities, or that he has broken any of the rules above-mentioned, they shall have

authority to summon the preachers of the District, and all the trustees, stewards, and leaders of the Circuit, to meet in their chapel on a day and hour appointed, (sufficient time being given). The chairman of the District shall be president of the assembly; and every preacher, trustee, steward, and leader shall have a single vote, the chairman also possessing the casting vote. And if the majority of the meeting judge that the accused preacher is immoral, erroneous in doctrines, deficient in abilities, or has broken any of the rules above-mentioned, he shall be considered as removed from that Circuit . . .

3. If any preacher refuse to submit to the above mode of trial, in any of the cases mentioned above, he shall be considered as suspended till the Conference. And if any trustees expel from any chapel a preacher by their own *separate* authority, the preachers appointed for that Circuit shall not preach in that chapel till the ensuing Conference, or till a trial take place, according to the mode mentioned above.

4. If any trustees expel or exclude a preacher, by their own *separate* authority, from any chapel in any Circuit, the chairman of the District shall summon the members of the District Committee, the trustees of that Circuit who have not offended, and the stewards and leaders of the Circuit. And the members of such assembly shall examine into the evidence on both sides; and if the majority of them determine, that the state of the Society in which the exclusion took place, requires that a new chapel should be built previous to the meeting of the Conference, every proper step shall be immediately taken for erecting such a chapel. And no step shall on any account be taken to erect a chapel for *such purpose* before the meeting of the Conference, till such meeting be summoned, and such determination be made . . .

6. The hundred preachers mentioned in the enrolled deed, and their successors, are the only *legal* persons who constitute the Conference; and we think the junior brethren have no reason to object to this proposition, as they are regularly elected according to seniority.

7. Inasmuch as in drawing up the preceding regulations, we have laboured to restore and preserve the peace and unity of the Society, and, in order thereto, have endeavoured to keep the preachers out of all disputes on the subjects therein specified:— be it understood, that any preacher who shall disturb the peace of the Society by speaking for or against the introduction of the Lord's Supper in our Societies, or concerning the old or new plan, so called, shall be subject to the trial and penalties before mentioned.

8. And in order that the utmost impartiality may be manifest in these regulations, for the peace of the whole body, we also resolve, that if any local preacher, trustee, steward, or leader, shall disturb the peace of the Society by speaking for or against the introduction of the Lord's Supper,

or concerning the old or new plan, so called, the superintendent of the Circuit, or the majority of the trustees, stewards, and leaders of the Society so disturbed, shall have authority to summon a meeting of the travelling preachers of the Circuit, and the trustees, stewards, and leaders of that Society. Evidence shall be examined on both sides; and, if the charge be proved, the superintendent preacher shall expel from the Society the person so offending.

Letters of Joseph Benson to the Rev. Peard Dickinson

(Mss at Duke University)

Dickinson was one of the clergymen who served at Wesley's Chapel, London, having been Vincent Perronet's curate at Shoreham.

Bristol,[1] Oct. 8, 1795

It gave me great pleasure, indeed, to be informed of the termination of the dispute in London, & of the prospect which, it seems, there is of returning peace. I trust nothing will occur to prevent the very desirable blessing. I find by a letter from Mr. Pawson, received yesterday, that the Trustees, in general, have returned to the Chapels, & are very friendly. I hope individuals of both sides will endeavour to the uttermost of their power, to manifest & confirm their love to each other. This will be the way to bring about an entire union and perfect harmony.

I thank God things are in a better situation here than I once thought they ever would be. The parties are so far united that the bulk of the people on both sides hear, promiscuously, at all the chapels: but there are individuals, not a few, who will not yet be prevailed upon to go to the New Chapel, & some have left the Society on account of the Old Room being shut up on a Sunday evening. However, I hope, by degrees all remaining prejudice will be done away & a spirit of love will generally prevail . . .

I am perfectly of your mind, that the restoration of peace, here, at London, & throughout the whole connexion, as far as it is restored, is entirely the Lord's doing, & in answer to the many prayers put up by thousands for that blessing. I trust we shall ever acknowledge his goodness & more than ever live to his praise.

[1] Benson had been appointed to the Leeds circuit, but was delayed in moving from Bristol by his wife's pregnancy.

Weatherby, near Leeds, March 17, 1796

The difference of opinion that has taken place among sundry members of our community, both Preachers and people, certainly tends to make us more united and attracted to those whose views of things are similar to our own, especially when we find them possessed of piety & virtue equal or superior to that of those who differ from us. It is true the grand bond of union among the people is not any *opinion* or mode of worship, but piety alone, or as our Lord expresses it Matt. 12.50, *doing the will of our Father who is in heaven*, & we should be careful that we do not put anything on a level with that. Yet still in this imperfect state in which we know so little of one another & have so many reasons to call one another's sincerity in question, a known difference of sentiment on any point, judged to be of importance, will always be a great drawback from our love, at least our love of *esteem, approbation & delight*, & a bar to our union. A consideration of this makes me fear that we shall never again see the Methodists closely united as a body of people, & that in defiance of all that can be done a division among them will in the end take place. However, if the evil can be prevented during our days, it may be so far well. And I agree with you that, like the first Christians, it will be our duty & wisdom to maintain the *unity of the Spirit in the bond of peace* & in *righteousness of life*, even when we differ about lesser matters. May the Lord enable us to do so more & more!

Your determination to avoid disputes in matters of religion, that you may give yourself the more up to the *word of God & prayer*, is mine also. Only my situation is so different from yours that it will not be possible to do it so much as you. I assure you I am exceeding critically situated at present & unavoidably engaged in more debates then I could wish, unless I chused to give up entirely the reins of government & let every man do what is right in his own eyes.

Leeds, Dec. 17, 1796

It is true, as you observe, the times are trying, but not more so than they have been in former ages. The Church of Christ, like the ship with the disciples in it upon the lake, is frequently tossed with tempests. It never enjoys a long calm. It is well that Jesus has his eye upon it. He will take care that it does not sink. He will, in the end, bring it safe to land . . .

I thank God we have gone on very well here since Conference. Kilham & a few of his abettors here have endeavoured to excite commotions & divisions, but have not been able. We have peace in all our borders, & see the work of God much deepened & enlarged among the people. Our connexion, however, is still in a very critical situation. Our Preachers & people are far from being united in sentiment, & a difference of judgment in matters apprehended to be of importance fails not to produce an alienation of affection from one another. Our Oeconomy & Plan, also, is far from being established, & our Laws & Rules from being observed as they ought to be. What will be the end God knows. I cannot foresee: only I hope for the sake of the work of God in this nation & the multitude of pious & upright souls that are concerned, the head of the Church will interpose & not suffer us to go to pieces. [I find] no way but to endeavour to live near to God & to take care of my own soul & do what little I can to promote true & spiritual religion.

Alexander Kilham

On the Bristol controversy: letter to James Bogie; Newburgh [Fife], Jan. 12, 1795

(Ms at MA)

Kilham's comments on the Bristol fracas were published in November 1794 under the pseudonym 'Aquila and Priscilla'.

You were perfectly right in your conjecture respecting Aquilla & Priscilla. I thought none of the letters gave a fair statement of the business, and, therefore, determined to give my opinion amongst the lave. I have received many flattering incomiums upon it: some of them by persons that did not know it was mine: & all of them by men whose judgment I respect . . . I hope it will have its use among those that have gone out to the help of the Lord against the mighty . . .

I had a long letter from London a few days ago and am informed by it, that the old Gentlemen are resolved on a bishops plan, if they can only bring it about. Messrs Mather and Thompson, as far as I can learn, are both in this sentiment. How far their scheme may answer the purposes they intend, I am not able to determine. But I trust in the Lord they will not have the power to bring it into existence. Something is brewing about Bristol as a plan far more excellent, if my friend does not mistake the signs of the times. I am told that Jonathan Crowther is forging off something on the subject. If he, with the help of Bradburn and Moore, undertake this work, it will be worthy of all acceptation. My friend presses me to give them a letter or a pamphlet on this subject and offers to bear part of the expence. If my ghost should make a second appearance I am hoping it will be more to the advantage of our camp than its late apparition in England. I have nearly completed the outlines of what I could wish to publish, and should I determine to send it abroad, it will be addressed to the preachers in full connection everywhere.

I undertook the last from a conviction of its being a duty I owed to God and the connection; and I think the same spirit influences me in my present undertaking. If I go forward with my plan, it will be several weeks before it can make its appearance; only I will promise that far, that you shall have one as soon as possible . . . I would have gladly signed by name [sic] to the last, but knew that every churchified fool would have been plaguing me with letters. And many of them would have been sent back. Besides, my youth, and my republican principles would have hindered many from reading my sentiments impartially. When the Editor of the Patriot published four long letters of mine under the signature of Independent, many persons were delighted with them who would have spurned them if they had known they were mine. This taught me a good lesson which I shall not very soon forget. The war being continued will hasten the business of reform, beyond anything that could have happened. Nothing can be more calculated to serve the interest of the great.

On the Plan of Pacification

(Preface to *The Progress of Liberty among the People called Methodists*, 1795, pp. vii–viii)

In the time of the Conference, many of us refused to vote for different articles of pacification. We entered our protest against them at the time they were read. When we saw an appearance of some of our rules[1] being capable of two meanings, I drew up the following address to the conference, which was signed by 57[2] of the preachers. Many more would have signed it, if they had had an opportunity. Most of those that did sign, were *very respectable* men, as their names would testify, were I to publish them.[3]

Honoured Fathers and Brethren,

We are *extremely sorry*, that anything should cause us to differ in sentiment, from a majority of the conference. We are *constrained* to do it, from a principle of truth and honesty. It appears to us, that no rule made in this house should be capable of bearing a double meaning. We are sorry to find an *appearance* of duplicity in some of our rules. We exceedingly object to the addition which is made to the first proposition of reconciliation, unless you add to it Messrs Thompson, Benson and Bradburn's explanation of the word *separation*. If this be not granted, we jointly enter our protest against that, and every other rule of the same nature. And intreat the preachers met in conference, to respect their character, by making their rules so explicit, that no person may misunderstand them. We are your affectionate brethren in the Gospel, &c.

Is there anything in this address, but what *reason* and the *Bible* require? A clamour, however, was made against us, before it was read, and the president *actually suppressed it*, without its being publicly read to the preachers. Several cried out it was designed to divide us: and it was some time before they would cease complaining on this head. Does not this address breathe the spirit of the gospel, in advising the conference to make its rules and laws so explicit, that they may be known by all? And in recommending truth and honesty in all our measures? If this divide us, *what is it that keeps us together?* If our opposing brethren had suffered it to have been read, it is very probable, they would have been of a different mind.

¹ The original reads 'rulers', corrected to 'rules' in John Blackwell's *Life* of Kilham, 1838, p. 229.

² Blackwell has '58', probably by the inclusion of Kilham himself.

³ Blackwell, pp. 229–30 lists the signatories from a note in Kilham's own hand. They include such familiar names as Thomas Hanby, Richard Reece, Robert Lomas, Alexander Suter, John Hickling, James Rogers, Charles Atmore, Joseph Sutcliffe, Joseph Entwisle, Jonathan Crowther and Theophilus Lessey.

'A few reflections'

(The Progress of Liberty, pp. 18–20)

1. Liberty of conscience is one of the most valuable blessings which a people can enjoy. It leaves every person perfectly free to examine all the doctrines and discipline of the different national churches, and dissenting congregations, that are established. Creeds, articles and confessions of faith, homilies, &c, &c, are all brought to the law and the testimony; and everything is rejected that does not agree with the word of God: which is the only and sufficient rule, both of our faith and practice . . . If bigotry, superstition, attachment to modes of worship, which have not been examined, and to creeds and articles of faith which never have been seriously thought upon, should compose our religion in such a state, will it not be to our present condemnation and to our eternal reproach?

2. In these nations we have a very great portion of liberty of conscience. Our excellent laws allow us to prove all things in religion, and to hold fast that which is good. If we are *forced* to support the church by tithes and offerings, we are not constrained to be members of her body. We may renounce her doctrines and discipline with impunity, and worship God according to the desire of our heart. Our fathers looked with *earnest desire* to these days, and rejoiced at the prospect of the followers of Jesus ever being blessed with them.

3. Is it not amazingly strange, that any sect or party should refuse to give to their brethren what the laws of our country so cheerfully allow? Is it not cruelty and persecution to restrict one another in those things which are not essential to the salvation of the soul? Does not every man that would force his brother to submit to any modes of worship against his own mind act the part of a spiritual tyrant, and lord it over God's

heritage? We detest the conduct of persecuting Neros, and all the bloody actions of the great Whore of Babylon, and yet in our measure we tread in their steps. If a man of any sect or party should force his creed of faith upon us, and constrain us to worship in his way contrary to our will, or prevent us from worshipping according to the convictions of our own mind, he is a Nero to us – a true son of the great Whore of Babylon.

4. Nothing can be easier than tolerating one another in matters that are indifferent. Can anything be more *easy* or more *equitable* than the following simple rule, for us as a people to walk by? Those of our friends who desire to worship with the national church in those hours she devotes to the service of God, and to receive the sacrament with her members, let them do it in the name of the Lord Jesus. If you can fairly convince them that their conduct is wrong, do it in simplicity and godly sincerity. But if you cannot, as you *value your salvation*, do not hinder them from going forward in their worship. Let those of our friends that cannot join the church in her worship, nor receive the sacrament with her members, be allowed to worship where they please, and to have the Lord's Supper either among themselves, or where they can receive it to the glory of God and their own satisfaction. Is not this *simple plan* exactly according to the rules which our Lord and his apostles have given us? And does not reason speak in favour of it in each of our breasts? We should lose sight of what we call *old* or *new* plans, and follow the unerring rules of the scriptures; and those principles of reason which are found in the most pious followers of the Lord Jesus, as well as in the rest of the world.

Letter to George Smith; Alnwick, 22 Dec., 1795

(Photocopy at MA)

. . . I wrote with the purest motives, & with a design to promote the glory of God. In these parts, as well as in Sunderland and Newcastle, many of our most pious and sensible friends highly approve of the steps I have taken. And are hoping it will end in good to our cause at large. But I find several of the preachers are highly offended, and are determined, if possible, to have me expelled the connexion before the next conference. Dr. Coke, Sam[ue]l Wrigley &c &c have been holding a convention upon it, and have written a most violent letter to the chairman of our district, requesting, and even claiming a meeting immediately.[4] They have gone so far as to pre-judge me, and seem only to want a district-meeting to sanction what they have proposed. Mr. Hunter has passed me a copy of their letter to him, and is taking the advice of the preachers in the District to know whether a meeting should be called or not. I have answered their *popish bull* (designed to apprehend poor Martin) and sent it to London. I have told them, should a district meeting be called, I shall be obliged to justify my character before all, and make the pamphlet more public than I have yet done: and that I shall publish their letter to Mr. Hunter, and my answer to it[5] . . . I cannot yet tell whether Mr. Hunter will call a meeting or not. I am confident they cannot prove anything in the pamphlet which is either false or which is mis-represented. And instead of being terrified by their opposition, I consider it a badge of honour. I have told them my mind fully, and given them to understand if they go so far as to expel me from the connexion this will not in the least prevent my happiness and prosperity.

[4] For the letter from the London preachers to Hunter, Chairman of the Newcastle District, see Blackwell, op. cit., pp. 243–4.
[5] *A Candid Examination of the London Methodistical Bull*; see next extract.

A Candid Examination of the London Methodistical Bull

(Op. cit., 1796, pp. iii–v, vii–viii)

While Mr. Wesley lived, he had the chief management of our affairs. Since his death, they have been managed principally by the preachers. There are no ministers, in any national churches, or among any denomination of dissenters, that have such power over their people as we have, according to the present rules of our connexion. Can it be supposed that in such a large body of ministers nothing should be instituted contrary to the nature and design of true religion? When the whole management of the church is left to the preachers, and the societies are not allowed to have a voice by their representatives, is it possible for us to stand in that relation to our people in all things which the scriptures direct? Would it not be the greatest miracle that ever was known, for us to have laws and rules in everything according to the interests of our people, when they have no hand in making them? Is it not more than probable, that in half a century several things have insensibly crept in amongst us which militate against the interests of our societies? If it were not so, we might be considered more than human. And if evils do exist among us as a people, is it our wisdom to shut our eyes and refuse to see them; or to stand open to conviction and renounce them immediately?

For a number of years, many of our most sensible and pious friends have complained of many evils which are found amongst us. They thought, after Mr. Wesley's death, we should immediately remove them. But to their unspeakable sorrow they saw many of them continued, and others added to their number. This occasioned murmurings and complaints in many places . . . For two years the petitions and requests of the people, which were sent to the Manchester and London conferences, were only seen by the presidents and a few individuals. On a motion being made, they were all destroyed, without examination. This was a very easy and ready way to answer the complaints of our people. Perhaps history would not furnish an instance of such a large body of ministers treating their followers with such contempt in any age or nation. If their petitions &c. had been read, this would have given them a degree of satisfaction. But to have them destroyed without examination was, what many of them considered, an insult offered to our people everywhere. Wherever this was known, our leading men were grieved beyond expression. And since that time, a spirit of jealousy has spread its influence through many places.

In the course of last year, several things were hinted in many of the letters and pamphlets that were circulated, to have our affairs better managed. The Nottingham and Ashby letters⁶ were particular on this subject. Several of the rules of pacification are proofs of the influence of those remonstrances. There never was greater liberty granted in some cases among the Methodists than by the last conference. But every thinking person must be convinced that our people have not the privileges which belong to them as Christians. And until they come forward to help in managing our affairs, it will be impossible to give them satisfaction.

At our last conference, many of us were conscious that a more equitable plan must be adopted, or we shall soon see the wheels of Methodism stand still . . . After pondering these matters over in my mind, with prayer for direction from God, I wrote the pamphlet called 'The Progress of Liberty &c.' The God that searches all hearts knows that I entered upon this work from the purest motives. It was to promote the interests of the Redeemer's kingdom amongst us as a people. Every line of the pamphlet was written with this intention. Many things I suppressed, determining to introduce none but what appeared necessary to answer the end I aimed at. If I could not write gravely upon subjects that appear to sensible persons both childish and ridiculous, this was my infirmity and will be pardoned by the candid. It would require the gravity of an angel to write seriously upon the subjects I have treated with a little humour. The *thing* called Bishop, to be introduced among us, appeared so contemptible to me, that I could not write seriously about it. 'To make merry with our friends' over this, in my judgment, is as innocent as Elijah's making merry over the poor priests of Baal, when they made wry faces, cut themselves, and cried out to a dumb idol, 'O Baal, hear us.' . . .

This plan was first invented at the Lichfield meeting. But when it was revealed to the preachers, a vast majority of them determined to oppose it. In the letters published last year several things were said on the subject. It was supposed, no person would have attempted to have brought it forward in our last conference. It was however introduced and sup- ported in the manner I have mentioned: and was rejected three times by a great majority of the preachers. When I wrote my pamphlet, I thought, to prevent it from being brought forward again, and to cause every preacher and sensible friend to abhor it, was to place it in as ridiculous a light as the subject would admit of. It appeared both childish and un- scriptural to have bishops on the plan proposed; which led me to place the three attempts in a sarcastical light, that our people might *innocently* laugh them out of countenance. I had not the least design to injure the character of any man, or to raise indignation in the breasts of our people against any who supported those plans. It was the system I attacked; and I only wished to meddle with those that countenanced it so far as appeared necessary to make it sink into contempt for ever.

⁶ Two of many circular letters through which groups of trustees and other lay- men canvassed their views at this time.

A recollection of Kilham by a member of the congregation at Mossley, Lancs., in 1796

(*MNC Magazine*)

From many things I had heard of him I was very eager to see him, but both his appearance and his preaching greatly disappointed my expecta- tions. His bodily presence was weak, and his speech contemptible. As I remember, his stature low, his countenance common almost to coarse- ness, he had a clumsy hobbling sort of walk, as though his toes might stumble against his heels at every step. In preaching, his delivery was slow, his voice weak and faltering and unharmonious; but there was a solemnity in his look, an earnestness in his manner, a richness in his matter, and an unction accompanied his word, which more than com- pensated for every natural defect: he commanded attention still as night.

Kilham's Expulsion

Henry Moore to his wife; London, July 26, 1796

(Ms at Drew University)

Soon after the Conference met Mr. Kilham delivered a written paper, which was a recapitulation of several things in his pamphlets, but no answer to the queries. A motion was then made, that we confirm the engagement entered into in Manchester 1791, namely, That we will abide by the Plan Mr. Wesley has left us; and that we will abide by the Rules in the Large Minutes both with respect to doctrine and discipline; this was unanimously carried. Mr. Kilham, when asked, replied, 'I agree to them so far as they are agreeable to Scripture.' It was replied, 'We all agree to the Koran of Mahomet, *so far as it is agreeable to Scripture*. We agree to the Rules, because we believe they are agreeable to Scripture.' To this he would give no further answer.

The Secretary then read the articles taken from Mr. Kilham's books as charges against the preachers, and he was called for proof.

1. That the preachers want ability for the work. To this he would only answer, 'I ask *you* if it is not so?'

2. That they tyrannize over and oppress the people. To this he replied, 'I have written these things; if that does not satisfy you, I have nothing more to say.'

3. That the preachers are immoral in various instances. To this he replied, 'I am not willing to mention names.' He was answered, 'The cruelty stands in your not naming them. We desire you to name them. He would then only say, 'What I have written are *suppositions*: things which *may* happen according to our Rules.'

4. That the trial of preachers is a farce. He replied, 'I think it was so.' It was asked, 'Can you produce any instance, or name any person so tried?' To this he would only say, 'I think it *all* wrong, unless the people were present.'

5. Wasting the public money. To this he replied, 'I only meant want of *economy*.' He was asked to produce instances, on which he mentioned three or four long removed. These were considered, and found to be necessary either for the family or the circuit. Mr. Kilham's own removal from Aberdeen to Alnwick was mentioned, and found to be at his own desire on account of his wife's illness. He said, 'There were other inst-ances,' but he did not mention them.

6. Swindling in getting money by false pretences. To this he replied by mentioning two instances of *expelled* men, and yet when even these cases were examined, they were found to be *misrepresentations*. He then mentioned the case of a person who bought a horse from Mr. Kilham, but upon trial the person was found perfectly innocent. He would then produce no other instances.

7. He then produced a letter, which a person in Manchester *stole* from Mr. Mather, and sent to him. The assertions in that letter were then examined, and Mr. Kilham himself, as well as the Conference, declared he was perfectly satisfied.

8. That he had represented Mr. Wesley as unscriptural and oppressive in his conduct. To this he would only answer, 'I do not think I have injured Mr. Wesley's character at all.'

9. That he used slanderous and indecent expressions. To this he answered, 'I acknowledge I have used improper expression, and am sorry for them.' There was also an examination of every other fact alleged in Mr. Kilham's writings, not one of which he could *prove*.

Wednesday morning, 27. After a few preliminary observations, it was ordered that the Secretary should read over the Articles again with the answers, which was accordingly done, and Mr. Kilham was called upon to add to these answers anything which he should think proper. He made a few additions, but nothing material. He was then ordered to withdraw, and the Conference, having considered the case, ordered, That any letters which were in Mr. Kilham's *favour* should be read, but that no letters *against* him with respect to his plans &c. should be read, which was done accordingly. The charges were then read over again one by one, and the question put on each. They were all unanimously pronounced *Unproved* and *Slanderous*. The following Motion was then made. 'Whereas Mr. Kilham has brought several charges against Mr. Wesley and the body of preachers, of a scandalous and criminal nature which charges he declared he could prove, and yet on examination he could not prove one of them; and also considering the disunion, strife &c. which he has occasioned, we adjudge him unworthy of being a member of the Methodist connexion. This was carried unanimously, not one person against it. He was then called and the judgment read to him. Thus this business is ended, unless he repent, which would rejoice my heart; but there is no appearance of it at present. Thus, my dearest, I have given you a hasty account of this painful matter. The preachers are as the heart of one man.

The Aftermath of the Disruption: a dispassionate verdict

William Smith to Joseph Benson; Newcastle, Oct. 6, 1796

(Ms at the New Room, Bristol)

Smith was Wesley's stepson-in-law. His long friendship with Benson is attested by another letter, also at the New Room, following Benson's departure from the Newcastle circuit in 1777.

I sincerely thank you for your kind remembrance of me and the affectionate manner in which you make it known in your letter to Mr. Embleton. I assure my dear friend my friendship and affection for you is still the same and tho' we differ in opinion respecting matters lately agitated in the Methodist connection, I find no alteration in my love and regard for you. I readily give you full credit for the purity of your intentions in what you have done, at the same time I would assure you I am no party man. I have no private interests to serve, I sincerely wish the prosperity of the Christian religion in general and the cause of Methodism in particular, and as far as it is in my power I wou'd gladly contribute to its success. The notice I took of the Newcastle address[1] I judged to be one of the best proofs I cou'd then give of my love to the connection. I entertain'd fears (as I had done for many years before) that something had crept into the system of Methodism that wou'd shortly be found very injurious to it, some of those things were pointed out in a very friendly yet plain and earnest manner. The sudden alarm several of the Preachers took at this has confirmed and considerably increased my fears, but if any future time discover I am mistaken and my fears are groundless I will rejoice, for my chief wish is the unanimity and prosperity of the whole body. Yet I cannot suppress my apprehensions that even some of the late rules of Conference will be found very grievous to many of the people. What was the design and what is likely to be the tendency of the 24th and 31st rules[2] of last Conference? Is this a proof the Methodist Preachers consult the people in their government? How many of the local Preachers and of the more considerate of the People will submit to them? As to you, I can say anything with freedom and without reserve. I declare I think these rules are an insult on both Preachers and people, and shou'd they ever be applied to me and the observance of them made a condition of membership, well as I love the connection, I shou'd certainly leave it. What the sentiments of others may be concerning these rules I know not as I have conversed with very few upon the subject, but I expect they will be pretty generally reprobated.

I rejoice to hear the Lord's work prospers with you and that the Society is in a flourishing state; sorry shall I be if Mr. Kilham in any degree counteracts your pious labours or hinders the prosperity of the Redeemer's Kingdom among you. Were I in your place I would endeavour to turn the point of his keen sword, not against me, but against the kingdom of darkness. This, I think might be done by treating him more as a friend than an enemy, for, if I know the man, an enemy he is not to either Preachers or People, but only to what he thinks will be hurtful to both. His little publications have undoubtedly occasioned much altercation in the connection, but this I believe was owing more to the violent opposition he met with from Conference than anything contained in his pamphlets. His expulsion I cannot but think was impolitick, unchristian and un[just?]. Conference may act more wisely for the time to come. [   ] members here have lately left our Society, perhaps about 6, most of them have withdrawn on account of the illiberal treatment Kilham met with at the District meeting and at Conference. The appointment of the same two preachers another year[3] has grieved the minds of many. What their success will be time will discover. Amidst all this agitation I keep my place and go on my way as usual, desirous of doing what good I can, for my day of usefulness is drawing towards an end. I feel I am older than when you were last at N.Castle . . .

[1] Probably the approval given by the Newcastle trustees to the circular in which the Manchester and Stockport trustees supported the trustees at Bristol in their dispute with the Conference.

[2] *Minutes*, 1796: Q.24: What can be done to bring certain Local Preachers more fully to observe our discipline? A. 1. Let no one be permitted to preach, who will not meet in Class, and who is not regularly planned by the Superintendent of the Circuit where he resides. 2. Let no Local Preacher be allowed to preach in any other Circuit without producing a recommendation from the Superintendent of the Circuit where he lives . . . 3. Let no Local Preacher keep Love-feasts without the appointment of the Superintendent, nor any way interfere with his business, as mentioned in the Large Minutes. We must carefully attend to our Rules, that all things may be done decently, and in order.

Q.31: What can be done to prevent unruly or unthinking men from disturbing our people? A. Let no man, nor number of men, in our Connection, on any account or occasion circulate letters, call meetings, do, or attempt to do, any thing *new*, till it has been first appointed by the Conference.

[3] Robert Johnson and Richard Condy were both reappointed to the circuit in 1796 for a second year.

Samuel Taylor Coleridge on Methodism

The Watchman, No. 1, March 1, 1796: Introductory Essay

(*Collected Works*, ed. Lewis Patton, II, 12–13)

The very act of dissenting from established opinions must generate habits precursive to the love of freedom. Man begins to be free when he begins to examine. To this we may add, that men can hardly apply themselves with such perseverant zeal to the instruction and comforting of the Poor, without feeling affection for them; and these feelings of love must necessarily lead to a blameless indignation against the authors of their complicated miseries. Nor should we forget, that however absurd their enthusiasm may be, yet if Methodism produce sobriety and domestic habits among the lower classes, it makes them susceptible of liberty; and this very enthusiasm does perhaps supersede the use of spiritous liquors, and bring on the same pleasing tumult of the brain without injuring the health or exhausting the wages.

A Preacher's Reading

John Pawson to George Marsden; London, Feb. 7, 1797

(Ms at Emory University)

I make no doubt but you are still giving up yourself to God, in prayer, in reading and in meditation, so that he may fit you for greater usefulness in his Church. A great deal depends on your spending your time profitably, especially upon what books you read. The longer I live in the world, the more fully I am convinced that the men among us who have given up themselves to what I will call universal reading, or reading every curious book that they can meet with, greatly hurt themselves. The knowledge they acquire is not of that kind which renders them more useful in the hand of the Lord, and their minds are somehow diverted from their proper centre, so that they do not increase in spiritual-mindedness at all.

To mention names on a disagreeable subject is not pleasing, else I could easily point out the men who would have been burning and shining lights indeed, had they retained their simplicity. But that sort of reading in my opinion has a natural tendency to destroy it. I do not know one single instance, no not one among all whom I have been acquainted with who have got into that line of reading, who have escaped. I am more shocked than ever I was in my life in hearing a preacher so zealously recommend to the people what I know he does not practise himself. Let us, my dear brother, study uniformity in religion. Let us try if we cannot so live in the presence of God as that we may be universally conscientious. Surely, if this is needful for the people, it is tenfold more so, for us. I mean, you have lived with those whom you might turn round about and view on every side, and you have been with those who would not bear looking at in any wise. But let Jesus be your pattern and you will never go wrong.

Dr. Coke in Scotland

(Thomas Coke's *Journals*, 1816, pp. 251–2)

On Monday the 27th [March, 1797] I set out for *Ayr*, where I preached in the evening, and the next day reached *Port Patrick*. Frequently in this journey I was led into serious meditations on the miserable state of religion in *Scotland*, and of the cause thereof: and to Antinomianism, that bane of inward holiness, I was obliged to refer the whole. There was a time, when *Scotland* was the glory of all the Churches; but that time is passed. Speculative knowledge is the all in all among the generality of the Professors; whilst the Infidels who compose a very considerable part of the nation, beholding nothing in religion but a bare profession – nothing of that image of God, which is the only desirable thing in the universe – fly naturally to Deism for a refuge from hypocrisy. And who can be surprised? For what sensible man in the world can believe, that God would give his only-begotten Son to die upon a Cross, in order to make us *orthodox*? Never will *Scotland* rise again out of its ashes, till the Antinomians and Hypocrites become in general Infidels, and the little City on the Hill begins to shine through the nation. Nor have we, I am persuaded, any object in view, worthy of our present toil and expenses in that Kingdom, but the preservation of a seed of grace to wait for that blessed day! I by no means confine my ideas of a seed of grace to the faithful who hold the doctrine of General Redemption. But when the Lord is pleased again to visit *Scotland* with times of refreshing, we shall certainly be glad to give a helping hand, to make that country flame again with the glory of God! There is nothing, which can more clearly evidence the height to which Antinomianism has arisen in *Scotland*, than that single circumstance – that the most zealous Professors in the land should consider one of the most eminent Divines, who have lived since the times of the Apostles, Mr. *George Whitefield*, as an Imp of the Devil! The effusions of the Holy Ghost, the pressing of mourners through the pangs of the New Birth into the liberty of God's Children, the witness of the Spirit, and all those deep experimental truths of Christianity, which, when realised to the soul, form it into the image of God, seem to be entirely forgotten among them.

Formation of the Methodist New Connexion

(*Minutes of Conversations between Travelling Preachers and delegates from the People Late in Connexion with the Rev Mr Wesley, held in Ebenezer Chapel, Leeds, in August 1797,* pp. 4–8)

Dear Fathers and Brethren,

We came to Leeds with no other design than to seek the glory of God, in the future prosperity of Methodism. When the major part of the trustee-meeting did not think proper to admit several of our friends to meet with them, who were delegated from the people, we thought it necessary to meet together, to converse upon such objects as the present state of our affairs suggested.

When the trustees were not assembled in their room, those of our friends who met with them, attended with us. But we refused to form ourselves, when together, into a regular meeting, because of their union with the other meeting. However, that no time might be lost, we resolved to enter into business, without any provision for future unity, we mutually agreed to draw up, and preface what we should attend to, by the following declaration:—

'At a meeting of the People's Delegates, held at Leeds, the third of August, 1797, in the Ebenezer Chapel, it was unanimously agreed, That the meeting should proceed to organize their plan of future conduct, according to the utmost of their ability and information; and that all their decisions should remain in full force until the issue of the committee of preachers and delegates should be known; but if the issue of that meeting should be favourable to our views, all proceedings of this evening, in regard to making provisions for a new itinerancy, should be null and void.'

When the preachers rejected the proposal from the trustees, and refused to admit delegates from the districts into the conference, our hopes of reconciliation languished; but when we heard the result of the meeting, held between a committee of delegates and some of the preachers, we were conscious that nothing could restore peace and unity, without the singular interposition of Divine Providence. But as all things are possible with God, we have agreed to send in to the conference the particulars we have drawn up and agreed to, for our future conduct. If the preachers can unite with us upon this, or a similar plan, we shall exceedingly rejoice, but if they are resolved not to do it – we must divide. Because all that we propose appears to be founded on the Scriptures, and in every respect both reasonable and just.

Signed in behalf of the Friends

JOHN SHORE

1. Let one or more delegates, chosen by the quarterly meeting, composed of trustees, stewards, local preachers and leaders, attend, with an equal number of travelling preachers, at the district meetings, possessed of equal powers to transact all business relative to the respective circuits which they represent.

2. Let trustees in legal matters of necessity only, as it respects their powers of trust for the people, have a delegate in district meetings, and in conference, during the time of their particular business.

3. Let these delegates when assembled together at a district meeting, elect one or more from their body to attend an equal number of travelling preachers at the conference. These delegates shall possess equal powers with the travelling preachers, in every respect. They shall carry in all the public collections, and assist in disbursing them. No new laws

or rules shall be made, without their concurrence; and all the laws and rules respecting discipline, that already exist, shall only be binding by being revised, with their special sanction: particularly those laws and rules made since the death of Mr Wesley: and the power of the delegates shall cease when the conference is ended.

4. Let members be received into society in the following manner:— 1. No leader shall bring a person to a travelling preacher for a note of admission, until he has met four times. No person received on trial only, shall have his name in the class-paper. 2. Every person shall be considered on trial until he has met in class two months. 3. Every leader shall bring a list of those persons who have met two months, to the leaders' meeting. The preacher shall read the list in the meeting, and if the majority approve, he shall receive them into connexion, in the society meeting, the Sunday evening following, by exhortation and prayer. 4. The leaders shall give those persons who are to be received, timely notice in their respective classes. 5. The leaders, with the preachers, shall judge of exempt cases, whether arising from modesty, natural relations, &c.

5. Let members be excluded from the society in the following manner:—1. Those who do not renew their tickets quarterly, or omit their class without a sufficient reason being given, exclude themselves. No member shall be privately put out of society. 2. Every fourth leaders' meeting, the travelling preacher shall enquire whether there be any in their different classes, that do not meet regularly, or walk disorderly and will not be reproved; and whether sufficient means have been used to reclaim them. The preacher shall, if the majority judge them unworthy of a place in the society, exclude them by crossing their names out of the class papers. No person shall be expelled until such measures have been adopted. But if any person think himself aggrieved, he shall have a fair trial by a jury chosen from among the society, he choosing five, and the leaders' meeting choosing an equal number, and the travelling preacher attending, shall have the casting voice.

6. The method of choosing leaders. 1. In new places, leaders shall be appointed by the mutual concurrence of the travelling preachers, and the people. 2. But in other places, when a new leader is wanted, the leaders' meeting shall nominate a person to supply the class for one month, and if the class approve of the nomination, the person shall be appointed; but if a class be dissatisfied with the leader, they shall state their complaints to the leaders' meeting, and shall have them properly attended to. Other leaders shall be appointed till the majority of the class are satisfied. If any in the minority cannot submit, they shall be admitted to meet in what classes they please, provided their objections are deemed valid by the major part of the leaders' meeting.

7. Let stewards be appointed to, or removed from their office, by the

concurrence of the major part of a full leaders' meeting; notice thereof being previously given in the society meeting.

8. Let no circuit stewards be appointed to, or removed from their office, without the concurrence of a majority of a quarterly meeting; and let no town, or circuit, stewards abide longer in that office than two years, unless in particular cases, mutually agreed upon by the brethren that are present in such a quarterly meeting. But in large towns, and in circuits, let not all the stewards be changed at once, unless other persons can be brought forward, deemed sufficiently acquainted with the business.

9. Method of appointing local preachers. 1. If any person think it his duty to preach amongst us, let him first consult his leader on the subject, and then let the leader mention it to a leaders' meeting; and they shall give their opinion for or against his admission. 2. Let no person act as a local preacher, until proposed at, and approved by the majority of a quarterly meeting: and a local preachers' meeting, if there be one in the circuit.*

10. Let no person go out to travel under any pretence whatever, untill he be mentioned and approved of by a majority of a leaders', local preachers', quarterly, and district meeting. But if there can be no local preachers' meeting held in a circuit, the decisions of the other three meetings shall be sufficient.

11. 1. Let no person be admitted into full connexion untill he has travelled four years. 2. Let no person received on trial be admitted into full connexion, without being recommended by the two last circuits where he has travelled, expressed in writing from their quarterly meetings, to the district meeting and the conference.

12. Let every private member of society, censured or expelled, who thinks himself aggrieved, and cannot have redress in the place where he resides, have a power of appealing from a leaders' meeting, and have a fair examination of his case before the brethren in the quarterly meeting, and their decision shall be final, unless in very particular cases. And every trustee, steward, local preacher, and leader, shall have an appeal from the quarterly to the district meeting; where every thing shall be fully examined, and finally settled: unless the case be so particularly important, that an appeal to the conference be deemed necessary by a majority of that district meeting.

* If it be reported to the leaders' meeting, that any person takes upon himself to pray, exhort, and expound the scriptures in public, without their consent, they shall immediately take the matter into consideration, and act as the majority of that meeting deem the most proper.

Principles of the New Connexion.

These were enunciated in the Nottingham Jubilee Volume of 1876, the year in which laymen were first admitted to the Wesleyan Conference.

The Methodist New Connexion came into being for the establishment of the following principles:

1. The right of the people to hold their public religious worship at such hours as were most convenient, without being restricted to the mere intervals of the hours appointed for service at the Established Church.

2. The right of the people to receive the ordinances of Baptism and the Lord's Supper from the hands of their own ministers and in their own places of worship.

3. The right of the people to a representation in the District Meetings and in the Annual Conference, and thereby to participate in the government of the community and in the appropriation of its funds.

4. The right of the church to have a voice, through its local business meetings, in the reception and expulsion of members, and the choice of local officers and in the calling out of candidates for the ministry.

Letter to the Methodist Societies

(*Minutes*, 1797)

Dear Brethren,   August 7, 1797.
                                                          Leeds,

We think it our duty to inform you by the earliest opportunity, of the measures we have taken, in order to satisfy those of our Brethren, who have been made more or less uneasy by sundry publications circulated through the Societies: and we trust, that on a serious consideration of the regulations we have agreed to at this Conference, you will see, that the sacrifices in respect to authority which we have made on the part of of the whole Body of Travelling Preachers, evidence our willingness to meet our Brethren in every thing which is consistent with the existence of the Methodist Discipline, and our readiness to be their servants for Jesu's sake.

1st, In respect to finances, or money-matters:

1. We have determined to publish annually a very minute account of the disbursements or applications of the yearly collection: And,

2. A full account of the affairs of Kingswood-school.

2dly, In respect to all other temporal matters:

1. It has been determined that no circuits shall be divided, till such division has been approved of by their respective quarter-meetings, and signed by the circuit stewards.

2. That no other temporal matter shall be transacted by the district-committees, till the approbation of the respective quarterly-meetings be first given, signed by the circuit stewards.

3dly, In respect to the receiving and excluding private members of society:

1. The leaders'-meeting shall have a right to declare any person on trial, improper to be received into the society: and after such declaration the superintendent shall not admit such person into the society.

2. No person shall be expelled from the society for immorality, till such immorality be proved at a leader's-meeting.

4thly, In respect to the appointment and removal of leaders, stewards, and local preachers, and concerning meetings:

1. No person shall be appointed a leader or steward, or be removed from his office, but in conjunction with the leaders'-meeting . . .

2. The former rule concerning local-preachers is confirmed: viz. That no person shall receive a plan as a local-preacher without the approbation of a local-preachers' meeting.

3. In compliance with a request made by the committee of persons from various parts, namely, 'That the Conference be requested to re-consider and revise those rules, which relate to the calling of meetings, and appointing local-preachers, made last year,' we say, 'No local-preacher shall be permitted to preach in any other circuit than his own, without producing a recommendation from the superintendent of the circuit in which he lives; nor suffer any invitation to be admitted as a plea, but from men in office, who act in conjunction with the super-intendent of that circuit which he visits.' The design of this rule is to prevent any, under the character of local-preachers, from burthening the people, either by collecting money, or by living upon them; and to prevent improper persons, who bear no part of the expence, from invit-ing local preachers thus to visit them. But it never was intended to reflect the least disrespect on any of our worthy brethren, the local-preachers, who, considered as a body, we greatly respect. And it should not be lost sight of, that several of the most respectable local-preachers in the king-dom, who were in the committee which met the committee of preachers appointed by the conference, declared their high approbation of the rule, and desired that it might be strengthened as much as possible, as none could justly complain of it . . .

7thly. In respect to all new rules, which shall be made by the conference, It is determined, that if at any time the conference see it necessary to make any new rule for the societies at large, and such rule should be objected to at the first quarterly meeting in any given circuit; and if the major part of that meeting, in conjunction with the preachers, be of opinion, that the enforcing of such rule in that circuit will be injurious to the prosperity of that circuit; it shall not be enforced in opposition to the judgment of such quarterly meeting before the second conference. But if the rule be confirmed by the second conference, it shall be binding to the whole connexion. Nevertheless, the quarterly meetings rejecting a new rule, shall not by publications, public meetings, or otherwise, make that rule a cause of contention; but shall strive by every means to preserve the peace of the connexion.

Thus, brethren, we have given up the greatest part of our executive government into your hands, as represented in your different public meetings . . .

Administration of the Sacrament in the New Connexion

T. Hannam to Jas. Harrop; Leeds, Sept. 15, 1797.

(Ms at MA)

We have no fixed plan; consequently cannot say that we *do* not nor *may* ever vary. Our present mode as you will recollect if present is to place the Bread & Wine upon the Table, then gather round the Travelling & local Preachers with any other leader or praying Friend. The Travelling or local Preacher begins with singing, then Prayer – then Exhortation suited to the Occasion – whilst 2 or more Friends called Deacons hand round the Bread to the people kneeling, sitting or standing as they shall please individually – this done sung to a verse – another exhortation whilst the wine is carried about, from any person who may be asked or find an impulse – or between the Bread and the Wine, the Friends sometimes may pray – or give out a short verse and exhort a moment, or Pray – anything suitable for the occasion . . . This continuing for quarter [to] half an hour or more, then singing again, during which time a collection is made by the Deacons & the money given afterwards to the poor.

(Outlines of a Constitution, 1797, pp. 19–20)

Sect. VIII. *Directions respecting the Lord's Supper.*
. . . To make this ordinance a singular blessing, 1. Let it be administered with primitive simplicity. All the incumbrances which the wisdom

of man has added to it, should be thrown off immediately. It is the duty of Christians to imitate their Lord and his apostles, in their manner of communicating, as well as in the duty itself. It appears that sitting is the posture they made use of at this ordinance. If any, however, among us had rather kneel in their pews, or at the rails of the communion table, they ought to be indulged, without any reflections being made on their conduct. 2. Let none be admitted, but those who sincerely desire to save their souls. Great care should be taken, to prevent any from eating and drinking unworthily. Notes should be given to all, who do not belong to the society. The leaders should let no motives induce them to give notes to any, whom they are conscious would dishonour the Lord Jesus, or eat and drink judgments to themselves, not discerning his body. 3. When the people assemble together, the nature and design of the institution should be briefly stated, and suitable exhortation given, that they may come with a lively faith, expecting to meet the Prince of Peace, in his own appointed ways. 4. Singing and prayer should open the meeting – and exhortation, singing and prayer, at certain intervals should accompany it. 5. The persons appointed to carry the elements to the people, should do it with that decency and seriousness, which becomes the solemnity of the occasion. 6. After the collection is made for the poor, the communicants should be informed, that they have professed themselves the disciples of Christ in this ordinance, and that they ought all to determine to ornament their profession. If they do this, God will be glorified – and the people will be constrained to acknowledge that they have been with Jesus. But if they live contrary to the gospel afterwards, the religion of Jesus will be reproached, and their own souls be in danger of being lost for ever. 7. The meeting should be concluded with earnest prayer to God, for his blessing to attend what has been delivered. If several persons were to pray for a few moments, perhaps the Lord might be entreated, and our souls be abundantly blessed.

Methodism Past and Present

(Joseph Entwisle, 'Thoughts on Methodism'; ms at Duke University; printed in *Memoir of Entwisle* by his son, Ch. VI)

[November 26th, 1797]
Reflecting last night on the agitated state of the Methodist Connexion, I was led into a chain of thoughts on the subject which greatly affected my mind & induced me to mourn over existing differences. My thoughts fixed chiefly upon two things, the state & circumstances of the Metho-

dists & their opportunities of getting & doing good 50 years ago & at
the present time.

In the infancy of Methodism its professors were few in number. But
they were, in general, deeply pious, & were as the 'salt of the earth'.
The members were scattered abroad, & the Preachers few, so that they
could seldom visit the country Societies. Hence, of necessity, the people
enjoyed few opportunities of hearing the preaching of the word, & not
unfrequently had to travel several miles to hear a Gospel Sermon. The
public opinion was against them. They were generally accounted weak-
headed enthusiasts & fanatics, they were represented as enemies to the
state & were even scandalized with the charge of obscenity, lewdness
&c. which their enemies affirmed they practised in their private, noc-
turnal meetings. In short, they were accounted, & by many *treated* as the
'refuse and offscouring' of the people . . .

Under all these disadvantages, we, with heartfelt pleasure, mark their
progress. It was the work of God, & therefore, could not be over-
thrown, could not be hindered by men or devils. Most who bore the
name of Methodist were persons who had experienced a thorough
change of heart, & breathed the pure spirit of Christianity. The line
between them and the world was drawn on the one hand by themselves;
for they were not conformed to the world, but were transformed by the
renewing of their minds: and on the other, by the violent opposition
of their enemies. They appeared, therefore, as the true successors of the
primitive followers of Jesus. They were united to God by one spirit, &
to each other by the bonds of Christian charity. And, though there were
among them partial contentions (which are unavoidable in the present
state of human nature) yet, *in the general,* the members of the respective
Societies were blended into one by divine love, & the whole body was
animated by one soul, nor did they count their lives dear unto themselves, so they might finish their course with joy & the M[inistr]y they
had received of the Lord Jesus, to testify the gospel of the grace of God.

Living in this spirit, though pressed sometimes beyond measure, they
flourished like the palm-tree. Those who had been planted in the courts
of the Lord, grew in grace, & their good fruit abounded to the glory of
God. The Preachers, aided by the prayers of the people, rushed into
every open door. The hand of the Lord was with them, & many believed
& turned unto God, almost daily. Thus, in opposition to the 'wisdom
of the wise', the understandings of the prudent, the threatenings of the
great & the fury of outrageous mobs, Methodism extended its influence
more & more . . . A few persons are still alive who saw the foundation
when newly laid, & with various emotions of hope & fear, joy &
sorrow, have observed the progress of the spiritual building. And now
their fears are alarmed at the probable consequences of the violent disputes which exist about the ornaments and management of it. Let every

member of our community pray that God may be the glory in the midst of us & a wall of fire around us.

The present state of Methodism is very different from what it was 50 years ago. The Methodists are become a numerous and respectable body. In the 3 Kingdoms upwards of 90,000 persons have united in Christian fellowship, and, perhaps, more than four times that number constantly attend preaching & approve of the doctrines they hear. Many of these are persons of fortune, respectable tradesmen and men of good repute among their neighbours. Persecution has in a great measure ceased, and the Methodists, as a body, have great influence on the nation at large. God hath spoken the word, and great is the multitude of them that preach it. In consequence of this, the word of God is preached in almost every corner of the land, & the means of Grace abound. The Methodists, at present, enjoy great advantages for their own improvement in knowledge & holiness & opportunities of extensive usefulness to mankind . . .

How great the danger [of their losing their ancient glory]! Outward peace & rest, though in itself an unspeakable blessing, may be the *accidental* cause of an undue attachment to the world, & an *unprofitable* & *unlawful* friendship with worldly men. The whole body of Methodists are in danger from this quarter, & their temptations are continually increasing. The Preachers, also, from their situations & circumstances, may, *unawares*, lose the spirit of primitive Christian ministers. They are generally well provided for, much respected by the people, frequently invited to the tables of the most opulent of their flocks, by whom they are treated as gentlemen, their labour is moderate, & their circuits contracted. Methodist Preachers, especially in respectable circuits, fill up more honourable stations, & are placed in more comfortable circumstances, than vast numbers of the inferior Clergy. Without much watchfulness & prayer, self-denial & deadness to the world & a resolute and strict observance of their excellent rules, the above advantages, which might be improved to good purpose, will become occasions of great evil. And in a few years, we may see the Methodist Preachers soft, effeminate and inactive in the Vineyard of the Lord.

But that which is most alarming is, the present agitated state of the community about Church Government &c. This occasions a great loss of time, & foments unchristian tempers, &, unless it subside, may be followed with the most dreadful consequences. May God bring good out of this evil!

The Spectre of Republicanism

Elizabeth Hurrell[1] to Joseph Benson; London, Dec. 23, 1797

(Ms at the New Room, Bristol)

Your time is always precious to the Church, but especially so when innovations & innovators are gaining ground on all sides; the fury of our restless enemy is great; surely he has but a short time? . . .

The worst trait of this critical time appears to me to be the Proud Republican Spirit which stalks round our Land, among professors & prophane. I cannot but think, had our Preachers endeavour'd to crush the Viper's head, when it first peep'd, neither Church nor King would have been in the danger they are now in, nor would Kilham or any of his friends have found such multitudes to join them. I look on him as a scourge for the wrong steps we have, as a body, taken, & where these sad disasters will end, who can see? Would to God, Men at the helm of our Society, would drop the fatal Idea of becoming great, & in a true scriptural poverty of Spirit, with simplicity and godly sincerity, seek God's glory, in the conversion of precious souls. This a few of you, blessed be God, do; but O! Sir, is it not *evident*, too, too many that are allowed to travel as Preachers, are of a contrary Spirit: Achans in the Camp. Golden wedges, and babylonish garments &c, coveted will cause us to flee before our enemies, as in the days of old. Ye faithful ones, come out to the help of the Lord, against the mighty. You say, dear Sir, how strange it is that pious people & persons united to the mystical body of Christians in bands of brotherly love, should suffer themselves to be separated from their brethren, about such matters! Has not experience both in civil & religious Connections, for ages, *shown*, that when the mind is diverted from the *Grand principle* both become like a rope of sand? And are not very many pious people very *ignorant*, & thro' that ignorance are exposed to the sophistry of designing men, who by specious arguments beguile them & lead them into bypaths? I believe the Friends of God, both in the Church and State, are verily guilty in this day. The Enemies of God, against both Church & State, strain every nerve, leave no stone unturn'd, to bring about its overthrow; while the others seem to stand neuter, as if our civil & religious rights where [sic] not worth a struggle . . .

I hear Mr. Kilham has got friends in this Metropolis & some local preachers have assembled among them; but I cannot say whether they prosper: but, I fear, party spirit is so much in fashion, and religion so low, that if anything is presented in the Republican order, many will join them; Mr. A.C.'s party,[2] I fear, gains ground; he is much follow'd since Conference; fine folk love something fine; plain truths suit plain unvisiated palates. I hope, if we live to another Conference, London will be favoured by having *you*, our Superintendent: for if you do not give us suitable & acceptable Preachers, we shall go astray to other places.

Mrs. Keysall & I were at Bristol near 3 months; but I suppose Mrs. K. has given you an account of the Bristol people. I cannot say I think either party in a flourishing state, how can they? 'A House divided against a a house cannot stand!' Our fatal divisions stab religion, & strengthen Infidelity; 'tis amazing to me, to hear that there is any good at all, where there is Divisions.

---

¹ Elizabeth Hurrell travelled widely and preached for many years with Wesley's approval. See Z. Taft, *Holy Women*, pp. 175–81. This letter is endorsed, apparently by Benson: 'Dead, I hope in the Lord.'

² Probably Adam Clarke, who was stationed at this time in the London circuit.

Advice to Young Preachers

(Adam Clarke, *Letter to a Methodist Preacher on his entrance into the work of the Ministry*, 1800)

Adam Clarke's advice to young preachers went through several British and American editions and in 1821 was incorporated in his *Preacher's Manual*. It provides a glimpse of the strengths and weaknesses of Methodist preaching at the turn of the century.

III. *Concerning your Behaviour in the Pulpit.*

1. Go from your knees to the chapel. Get a renewal of your commission every time you go to preach, in a renewed sense of the favour of God. Carry your authority to declare the gospel of Christ, not in your hand, but in your heart. When in the pulpit, be always solemn: say nothing to make your congregation laugh. Remember you are speaking for eternity; and trifling is inconsistent with such awful subjects as the great God, the agony and the death of Christ, the torments of hell, and the happiness of heaven.

2. Never assume an air of importance while in the pulpit; you stand in an awful place, and God hates the proud man.

3. Avoid all quaint and fantastic attitudes. I once knew a pious and sensible young man who, through a bad habit which he had unfortunately acquired, made so many *antics*, as the people termed them, in the pulpit, as to prejudice and grieve many ... As there are a thousand reasons why a young man should not wish the people to form such an opinion of him, so there is all the reason in the world why he should

avoid *queer nodding, ridiculous stoopings,* and *erections* of his body, skipping from side to side of the desk, knitting his brows, and every other theatrical or foppish air, which tends to disgrace the pulpit, and to render himself contemptible.

4. Never shake or flourish your handkerchief: this is abominable. Do not gaze about on your congregation, before you begin your work: if you take a view of them at all, let it be as transient as possible.

5. Endeavour to gain the attention of your congregation. Remind them of the presence of God. Get their spirits deeply impressed with this truth, *Thou, God, seest me!* . . . I have ever found that a few words of this kind, spoken before the sermon, have done very great good.

6. The pulpit appears to me analogous to the *box* in which the witnesses are sworn in a court of justice, 'To say the truth, the whole truth, and nothing but the truth.' You are a *witness* for God; and are bound by more, if possible, than an oath, to speak the truth in righteousness; and to declare faithfully and solemnly, according to the best of your knowledge, the whole counsel of God.

7. Give out the *page*, and *measure* of the hymn, and the hymn itself distinctly and with a full voice; and do not hold the book before your face while giving out the hymn, for this hinders the progress of the sound.

8. While praying, keep you eyes closed; at such a time you have nothing to do with outward objects; the most important matters are at issue between God and you; and he is to be contemplated with the eye of the mind. I cannot conceive how it is possible to have the spirit of devotion in prayer, while he is engaged in gazing about on his congregation. Such a one may *say* his prayers, but he certainly cannot *pray* them . . . In your prayers avoid long prefaces and circumlocutions. You find none of these in the Bible. Some have got a method of complimenting the Most High on the dignity of his nature, and the glory of his heavens: this you should studiously avoid. . . .

9. Say the Lord's Prayer in the same tone and elevation of voice in which you said your own. I have observed many, when they came to this solemn form, suddenly dropping their voice, and repeating it as if it made no part of their devotion. Is this treating the institution of Christ with becoming reverence? . . .

12. Be sure to have the *matter* of your text well arranged in your own mind before you come into the pulpit, that you may not be confused while speaking. But beware of too much *dividing* and *subdividing*: by these means the word of God has been made to speak something, anything, or nothing, according to the creed or prejudices of the preacher. How little of this *division* work do you meet with in the discourses of the apostles. Besides, this mode of preaching is hackneyed to death; and can

never succeed but in judicious hands. Unless the matter of the text be abundant, it rather fetters than enlarges the mind; and that which is ominously called the *skeleton*, i.e. a system of *mere bones*, is in general but ill clothed with muscles, worse strung with nerves, and often without the breath either of a spiritual or intellectual life. On this subject, a man of deep sense and piety once observed: 'The major part of what we hear at present in sermons is, *Three heads and a conclusion.*'

13. In whatever way you handle your text, take care, when you have exhausted the matter of it, not to go over it again. Apply everything of importance as you go along; and when you have *done*, learn to make an *end*. It is not essential to a sermon that it be half an hour or an hour long. Some preach more in ten minutes than others do in sixty. At any rate, the length of time spent in preaching can never compensate for the want of matter; and the evil is doubled when a man brings forth *little* and is *long* about it. There are some who sing long hymns, and pray long prayers, merely *to fill up the time*; this is a shocking profanation of these sacred ordinances, and has the most direct tendency to bring them into contempt. If they are of no more importance to the preacher or his work than merely *to fill up the time*, the people act wisely who stay at home and mind their business till the time in which the sermon commences. Have you never heard the following observation? 'You need not be in such haste to go to the chapel; you will be time enough to hear the sermon, for Mr. X.Y. always sings a *long* hymn, and makes a *long* prayer.'

14. As to the *matter* of your preaching, I will only say, Preach Jesus, preach his atonement, preach his dying love; and through him proclaim a *free*, *full*, and *present* salvation;[1] and God will bless your labours wherever you go.

Therefore never sing long hymns, pray long prayers, nor preach long sermons – these last are intolerable, unless there be a great variety of interesting matter in them, accompanied with great animation. I have often preached only *ten* or *fifteen* minutes at a time. Why? Because I had no more to say on that subject, and I did not think that what I had already uttered was of consequence enough to entitle it, then and there, to a *second* hearing.

IV. *Concerning your Behaviour in your Circuit*.

1. Never disappoint a place: this would be contrary to your covenant with God, your agreement with your brethren, and your engagements to the people. Keep your own *watch* always to true time, and begin precisely at the time appointed. Never be a minute later than true time, except in the country, where there is no public clock; then *five* minutes may be allowed for the difference between clocks and watches. Do not many preachers, of all denominations, sin against God and their own souls by not attending to this? ... I never knew a preacher who acted in this

way who did not lose the confidence of the people to such a degree as essentially to injure his public usefulness. Add to this, that the congregations are ever ruined by such conduct.

2. Be punctual in getting in proper time to the place where you are to dine and lodge. Do not make a whole family wait upon *you*. This is both injustice and insolence. While I readily grant, with our blessed Lord, that *the labourer is worthy of his meat*, yet he should certainly come to receive it in due time: and he who *habitually* neglects this, disappointing and confusing the families wherever he comes, is not worthy of a morsel of bread. I have known some, of more than common ministerial abilities, lose their importance, and ruin themselves in the opinion of the people, by their want of punctuality in this respect.

3. Never leave any place you visit without praying with the family; and seize the most convenient time for family prayer in the houses where you lodge. Just before they sit down to meat is, in my opinion. the best time; *then* the several members of the family are generally present. But I have often observed, that one, and another, after having *hurried* down their victuals, have either gone, or have been called away to business; so that before the whole family had finished their meal, one third of the members of it were not to be found . . . Should you be invited to any place where you are not permitted to pray with the family, never go thither again; and give them your reason . . .

4. If you wish to keep a good conscience, you must walk as in the presence of God. Extremes beget extremes. Take heed, then, that while you avoid *levity* on the one hand, you fall not into *sour godliness* on the other. There are some who have the unhappy art of making a *jest* out of everything; and even apply Scripture in this way. Such conduct is execrable. There are others, who, being of an *unhappy* cast of mind, through a kind of natural or factitious melancholy, strip a man of salvation for a smile, and condemn him to the pit for being cheerful. Avoid both these extremes; and remember that *levity* will ape *religious cheerfulness*, and *sourness of temper* will endeavour to pass itself off for *Christian gravity*. But do not judge from such appearances . . .

5. Tell your secret trials and temptations to very few. Your weakness, &c., should be known only to God and yourself . . .

6. Wherever you go, discountenance that disgraceful custom (properly enough termed) bibliomancy; i.e. divination by the Bible. I need scarcely observe that this consists in what is called dipping into the Bible, taking passages of Scripture at hazard, and drawing indications thence concerning the present and future state of the soul. This is a scandal to Christianity. So also are those religious trifles, impiously and ominously called *Scripture cards*. Thank God! these have never been very common among us; and are certainly not of Methodist growth. In an evil hour they were first introduced; and have since been criminally

tolerated. I have found them the constant companions of religious *gossips*; and have seen them *drawn* for the purpose of showing the success of journeys, enterprises, &c. Very great mischief they have done, to my knowledge; and sensible persons have, through them, been led to despise the whole of that system from which they never sprang, on which they have never been ingrafted, and in which they have never been more than barely *tolerated*. Giving the authors of them all the credit we can for the goodness of their intention, we cannot help saying of their productions (and this is giving them the very best character they deserve) that they are the drivellings of a religious *nonage*, or of piety in *superannuation*. I do not find that Mr. Wesley ever made, used, or approved of these things; but as they were tolerated in his time, they have been attributed to himself . . . I am glad to find that they are daily *dying* among the few that did use them: I hope soon to hear that they are all finally *buried*; and earnestly pray that they may never have a RESURRECTION, except to shame and everlasting contempt.

7. Never go in debt for food, clothes, or anything else: it is no sin to die in a ditch through hunger or cold; but it is a crime to go in debt, when there is not the fullest prospect of being able to pay. It is the most certain and honourable way never to sit down to the food, nor put on the clothes, till the bills for both are discharged. By these means you will keep clear of the world, and make most of the little you have. Every word of the old adage is true: 'Live not on *trust*, for that is the way to pay *double*.'

8. Never go out on parties of pleasure, however innocent they may be; what, in this case, would be considered as no evil in another, might be reputed a crime in you.

9. Never choose a circuit for yourself. If you do, and succeed in getting the object of your choice, make up your mind to bear all the crosses *alone* which you may meet with in it: for how can you look to God for strength to support you under trials which you may reasonably conclude are of your own procuring? You are God's messenger; pray him, therefore, to send you where you may *do* and *get* most good. In such a place the crosses you meet with are God's crosses; and he is bound not only to support you under them, but to sanctify them to the good of your soul . . .

V. *Concerning your Behaviour in the house where you lodge.*

1. On your arrival, get as speedily as possible to private prayer; and earnestly beg God to bless your coming . . .

2. Show yourself satisfied with every thing you receive. Be not nice in your food. Do not keep a lordly distance from the family: be so familiar with them as to gain their confidence . . . At the same time keep a due distance, that, while you are esteemed as a *brother* in Christ, you may be

acknowledged as his *minister*. There is much truth in that proverb, 'Too much familiarity breeds contempt.'

3. Speak closely and lovingly to every person in the family; but let it be as much apart as possible: for members of the same household seldom speak freely before each other.

He who despises *little things*, shall fall by *little* and *little*. Do not, therefore, disregard the following small advices.

4. Give the family where you lodge as little trouble as possible: never desire any of them, not even the servants, to do anything for you that you can conveniently do for yourself . . . A man of a truly Christian and noble mind finds it his highest interest to have few wants; and esteems it a luxury to minister to his own necessities.

5. Never pull off your boots in a parlour or sitting room. Leave your hat, whip, great coat, &c., in the hall, lobby, or some such place. Do not leave your foul linen, dirty clothes, shoes, &c., about in the room where you lodge. After having left your bed uncovered for some time to cool and air, lay on the clothes neatly when you quit your room; and always throw up your window when you go out. Empty the basin in which you have washed your hands, &c., and leave it always *clean*. Don't splash the walls nor the floor. Wipe every drop of water off the washstand, and spread your towel always to dry; and when dry, fold it loosely up, and place it on the head of the water bottle. Never comb out hair in a sitting room, or before company; this is an unpardonable vulgarity: nor brush your clothes in a bedroom; this spoils the furniture. See that you spill no ink on the floors, tables, &c. . . .

6. Observe rule and order in every thing . . . Remember, that cannot be considered as a *small* thing to you, which either prejudices a family against you, or is instrumental in acquiring you their good graces.

7. Shun tea-drinking visits: these, in general, murder time, and can answer no good purpose either to your body or soul . . .

8. Go out as little as possible to eat and drink . . . Stay in your own lodgings as much as possible, that you may have time for prayer and study . . . Seldom frequent the tables of the rich or great . . . Visit the people, and speak to them about their souls, as often and as much as you can; but be not at the mercy of every invitation to go out for a morsel of bread . . . When you do go out, let your visit be short. The only time that a man of *study* and *business* can spare is the *evening*, after all his work is done. But take care, if you sup out, never to do it to the prejudice either of early rising or morning preaching.

---

[1] This is the earliest known use of what became a standard summary of 'Methodist doctrine'.

The earliest known Circuit Plan for Manchester, 1799

The deployment of both itinerant and local preachers throughout widely scattered circuits necessitated detailed plans of preaching appointments from an early date. The first known examples are hand-written plans from the Leeds circuit in 1777. Before long they were being printed. In this example Jabez Bunting is listed as one of the junior local preachers.

Manchester Circuit. 1799.

PREACHERS' PLAN.	JULY 7	14	21	28	AUGUST 4	11	18	25	SEPTEMBER 1	8	15	22	29	OCTOB. 6	13	PREACHERS' NAMES.	No.
Oldham-ftreet 7, Salford 2½ & 6	1	11/3	2	1	11/3	2	1	11/3	2	1	6/3	2	1	13/3	2	John Barber	1
Salford 10, Oldham-ftreet 5½	2	1	3	2	1	3	2	1	3	2	1	3	2	1	3	John Farrar	2
Altringham 10, 2 & 5½	12	2	11	3	19	1	26	2	6	3	18	1	10	2	23	Thomas Prefton	3
Barton 9, Davyhulme 1 & 5	3	8	1	12	2	26	3	17	1	15	2	16	3	19	1	John Holt	4
Barton 1 & 5	5	22	25	20	4	14	15	12	9	27	23	28	26	17	7	Robert Brierley	5
Carrifhed 9, Irlam 1		15		17		19		5		16		23		9		~~Robert Oughton~~	6
Sodom 10, North-ftr. 6, & Monday 8	*13	26	*27	5	*21	9	*20	6	*16	18	*15	12	*4	7	*11	John Smith	7
Stanney-ftreet 10, Worfley 3	9	17	21	8	5	11	16	26	18	20	12	14	23	6	28	Thomas Painter	8
Partington 10 & 2	23	11	28	6	17	5	27	8	13	24	19	18	17	16	14	John Gadd	9
Blackley 4	4	7	20	26	22	21	13	25	31	9	11	15	12	4	5	Stephen Ruffell	10
Longfight 5½	20	4	13	22	18	25	9	7	19	8	24	21	15	23	12	John Birkinhead	11
Pendleton 6	8	6	7	27	31	28	12	4	15	25	13	22	16	11	18	William James	12
Crofs-lane 6	22	25	9	13	14	27	6	19	28	7	16	4	8	5	20	Thomas Owen	13
North-ftreet 10, Miles-platting 6	15	5	19	11	8	4	19	13	12	14	9	20	18	15	16	Hugh Emett	14
St. Mary's-gate 5½	16	10	14	7	9	6	31	20	5	13	8	11	24	21	15	Holland Hoole	15
* Baguley-fold 5, Bradford 5	11	*9	16	*14	6	*20	25	*21	22	*19	26	*13	31	*8	24	James Dewhurft	16
* Hoole Hill 6, Rufholme 5½	*6	12	*5	4	*24	16	*7	11	*8	21	*22	31	*13	25	*19	William Walton	17
Sale 10 & 2		18		24		7		9		5		10		14		Thomas Patrick	18
Rhodes 6	18	21	10	25	7	12	4	22	14	6	5	26	20	31	27	George Burton	19
Droylefden 5½	14	20	31	15	16	13	5	18	7	11	21	24	22	10	25	John Hughes	20
Oldham 2 & 6						8						6				Robert Shepley	21
Delph 10 & 1, Mofley 4½		19		9						12				13		John Bamber	22
Middleton 1 & 5½			6				8				14				21	James Wood	23
Ardwick 5½	7	14	22	21	25	24	11	16	20	26	4	5	6	18	9	Solomon Afhton	24
Newtown.....Monday after date 8	20	5	26	9	19	14	25	13	21	11	12	15	16	5	20	George Leigh	25
Hulme......... Ditto......7½	19	10	11	26	13	15	5	14	25	9	16	23	10	20	7	Jonathan Hern	26
Clowes's-ftreet, Salford ....Ditto 8	5	9	12	14	16	24	19	11	26	13	23	7	15	10	21	Richard Hulme	27
Strand-ftreet, Fleet-ftreet .. Ditto 8	11	19	16	26	21	25	9	12	5	14	15	13	11	19	26	Lee Speakman	28
Long Mill-gate, No. 44.....Ditto 8	16	15	5	20	26	13	12	7	11	19	21	14	25	26	5	John Heywood	29
Bank-top..... Tuefday after date 7	21	3	13	1	12	2	16	3	26	1	23	2	5	3	11	Jabez Bunting	30
Jackfon's-row..Thurfday Ditto 8	1	5	2	12	3	26	1	16	2	11	3	10	1	13	2	Robert Crofs	31
Bloom-ftreet, Salford, Ditto Ditto 8	12		14		15		26		25		9		21		23		
Brierley-ftreet, Bank-top ...Ditto 8	5	12	15	16	20	7	13	26	9	25	11	5	10	26	14		

The Brearer hereof, Stephen Russell *is an approved Local Preacher here, and may be employed as such wherever he comes.*

Sowier & Russell, Printers.

The earliest known Circuit Plan for Manchester, 1799.
(original: 10″ × 13″)

Home Missions in North Wales

During Wesley's lifetime, Wales had been left largely to the Calvinistic Methodists. The work in the north of the country, in particular, made a late start.

'A Short Account of the Welsh Missions'

From Thomas Coke, *An Account of the Rise, Progress and Present State of the Methodist Missions*, 1804, pp. 35–6

In travelling annually, for many years, thro' North-Wales, in his way to Ireland, and on his return, Dr. Coke felt exceedingly for his country-men the Welch, and wished that the everlasting Gospel of Jesus Christ might be preached universally among them. It is true, there are many pious Clergymen in the Churches of Wales, and many pious Dissenting Ministers in that Principality. But he was, notwithstanding, fully satis-fied, that myriads of the Welch were still in spiritual darkness, and lived in the practice of vice, to whom Ministers, on the Itinerant Plan, might find access thro' the blessing of God, when the settled Ministers were not able to reach them, from their reluctance to receive the Gospel in the first instance, unless it were brought to them, as it were, in the highways and hedges. He was at the same time convinced, that no extensive good could be accomplished, unless Itinerant Preachers were found, who were Masters of the Welch Language. Soon after, the Doctor was incited to enter upon this undertaking by the arguments of a pious person in Anglesea. He then requested his worthy and highly esteemed friend, Mr. Owen Davies, to go and travel thro' North Wales, if the Conference should consent, and a proper colleague were found out to travel with him. Mr. Davies complied, and the Doctor then proposed his plan to the Conference. – The Conference most readily gave him their utmost support: And Mr. Hughes, a very suitable colleague for Mr. Davies, having offered himself, the Missionaries immediately commenced their labours.

Some Account of the Success of the Missions in North-Wales, from the Conference 1800, to the Conference 1803, by Mr. Owen Davies.

(*Methodist Magazine*, 1803, pp. 537–40)

Previous to the Conference in the year 1800, my mind was impressed with a strong desire, that a Missionary should be sent into North-Wales, believing it would be attended with good, especially if he were one that could preach in the Welch language. Being at that time in Cornwall, and

Dr. Coke visiting those parts, I acquainted him with my thoughts. He said, his mind had been influenced by a similar desire for some time, and that he intended making a proposal to this effect, at the next Conference. At the same time he requested me to offer myself to this work. But being at that time in an agreeable Circuit, and our friends in it requesting me to stay with them, which I had engaged to do, I was induced to decline accepting the proposal. When Conference came, the business was brought forward, and Mr. Hughes and I were requested, by the general voice of the Brethren, to enter on the Mission. When I found it to be the request of so many men of God, I considered it as a divine call, and therefore could not but comply therewith, altho' there was every reason to believe it would be putting myself and my wife into a very uncomfortable situation . . .

When the Conference was ended, my colleague and I set out for Wales, where we found two societies raised, thro' the instrumentality of the preachers employed in the Chester Circuit, one consisting of thirty, the other of fifteen members. We immediately entered on our office, and, as Missionaries, we visited the principal towns in Denbighshire, Flintshire, Carnarvonshire, Anglesea, and some parts of Merionethshire. And after some time, we thought it prudent to confine our labours chiefly to Denbighshire and Flintshire, and to form a Circuit so as to visit each place, at least, once a fortnight, just as if we had societies to receive us, and friends to encourage us in the way. We preached sometimes in the market-places, sometimes in the corners of streets, and often in the inns where we put up. And thro' the good pleasure of our God, we had not long pursued this plan, before we found favour in the sight of the people, insomuch, that one and another began to receive us into their houses. At that time we thought it a mercy when we found *one* friend in a place; for it was not always the case, altho' we seldom met with any persecution. And, I must say this in behalf of my country people, that, in general, there is not so much ungodliness among them, as I have seen in many parts of England. In general, they will attend the preaching of the Word somewhere, and that with seriousness. I have sometimes been surprised, when preaching out of doors, to see the people fall on their knees, when I began to pray, with as much apparent devotion as if they were surrounding the altar. In the course of this year our two societies increased to fourteen, whereby our expenses were lessened, and our way was made more comfortable. Our numbers also increased from forty-five, to two hundred and eighty-two.

At the Conference 1801, Mr. Bryan was appointed to labour with Mr. Hughes and me. We had now two that could preach as well in Welch as in English. We immediately adopted the same plan we had done the preceding year, taking in as many places as were needful to employ three preachers. By this time, the cross became much lighter than it had been the preceding year, when we were obliged to have a cryer to publish our preaching, or do it ourselves by going from door to door. For now, when we had to go to a new place, we could often get a few friends to accompany us, which tended to make our preaching public, and wonderfully strengthened our hands in God. The Lord continued to succeed this plan. By going regularly, at least, once a fortnight to a place, we knew how to publish for each other, and the people knew when to expect us. In this way we raised societies almost in every place we visited. We were much comforted also in another respect. A few young men, lately brought to the knowledge of God, began to exhort a little, and to assist us as Local Preachers, and their labours were owned of God, and rendered acceptable and useful among the people. The invitations we had to new places were now more than we could accept of: So that we saw it necessary to call two more preachers to our help, brother Edward Jones, and brother Morris. By this means, we had an opportunity of visiting Carnarvonshire and Anglesea, and found the people ripe for the reception of the gospel. Pressing, indeed, were the invitations we had to visit them as often as possible . . . We have now eight Travelling Preachers in the Circuit, which takes in eight different Counties, and is upward of one hundred miles in length, and five hundred in circumference. Nevertheless, it is as regular a Circuit as any we have in the Kingdom. The fruit of our labours this year has far exceeded our expectations. Our twenty-three societies are increased to fifty-seven, and our five hundred and forty-four members, to one thousand three hundred and forty-two . . .

At our Love-feasts, which sometimes last five or six hours, we have no need to exhort the people to speak, for the whole time is taken up in testifying the grace of God. Having the Spirit of God, they find liberty to speak of and for him. But, I calculate concerning the good work that is done, by the fruit that is produced. For, altho' we have met with some exceptions, yet, in general, their lives correspond with their professions. Many wives bless the day that we came into Wales; for, thro' our ministry, the worst of husbands have become the best. We have made the hearts of many parents to rejoice; for, by the Word of Grace, their profligate children have become truly pious. Indeed, our enemies allow, that a great reformation has taken place since we came into the country. It is true, the work is yet in its infancy, and who will endure to the end, is not for me to say. However, of the many who have joined us, very few have left us as yet; and I can only hope and pray, that all who have begun in the Spirit, may be found faithful unto death.

The Edinburgh Circuit

Letters of Thomas Preston to Jabez Bunting

(Hayes and Gowland, pp. 25–6)

Preston was a probationer in the Edinburgh circuit from 1799 to 1801.

Dunbar, March 11, 1800

I am very fond of Scotland, also for the many opportunitys I have for making improvement in usefull knowledge. Our Circuit is different from most in England. We have but three place[s] where we preach on a Sunday, Edinburgh, Dalkeith and Dunbar. The preachers in Edinburgh and Dalkeith change every fortnight. At Dunbar (which is 27 miles east of Edinburgh) we stay for three months, except the Superintendent who stays only about one month.

Dunbar is my province at present, and will be till about the 15th of May. Here I have to preach five times a week, (and once a fortnight to walk eleven miles to preach at Haddington) and meet two small classes and attend three prayer meetings. I take a walk out by the sea-side before breakfast and then sit down to read till three or four o'clock in the afternoon . . .

The people of Scotland for the most part are a knowing sencible [sic] people; but there is not that depth of piety, which knowledge require[s] to keep it in its proper place. Nevertheless, there are a few pious persons, as any I have ever known. This is the only thing I have against Scotland, or else according to my present views, I would live and die among them. But there [is] no necessity that a preacher should drink into their spirit, and the more he is spiritual in his conviction, the more he is respected by them.

Our success in the work of the Lord is small, but we have good reason to believe that we do not labour altogether in vain.

Edinburgh, March 6, 1801

You ask what is the state of Methodism & Religion in Scotland? Both are very low. Very little of the power of Godliness is known amongst them. The Scotch are for the most part a well informed people; they are very partial to a learn[ed] discourse from the Pulpit, & think it little better than blasphemy for a person to preach who has not had an Academical Education. I have more than once been asked at what College I study'd. We never hear any Amens. This is altogether unfashionable. We have a few very pious persons amongst us, & thro' mercy we are increasing a little. We have added a few to the Society since Conference, & have reason to hope several have got good.

The great bar which prevents Methodism from prospering in this Country is the Doctrines of Calvin [being] nearly universally received; so that as soon as a general salvation is offer'd we are looked upon as deceiver[s] of the People and many to this day believe the Methodists to be the false prophets mentioned in Scripture. At present Salvation is seldom heard in the churches, the Gospel being preach'd rather as a system of Doctrines than as truths which are to be experienced.

Cause for Concern (1)

(*Minutes*, 1802)

Q. 21. Are there any evils existing among us?

A. There are: 1. Many of the wives of the Preachers dress like the vain women of the world: 2. Some of the Preachers set them the example. 3. A great many of our people stand or sit at prayer, instead of kneeling. 4. It is become too common a custom to sit while singing the praises of God. 5. Too many of our people sit, whilst a blessing is asked, and thanks returned, at meals. 6. Some of the wives and children of Preachers, we fear, are remiss in their attendance on the preaching of God's holy word; yea, it appears that some Preachers' wives will continue in their houses, while divine service is performed, even when their houses join the chapels, and will keep their grown-up children from hearing the word preached.

Q. 22. What can be done to remove these evils?

A. 1. We exhort our sisters to dress as becometh those who profess to walk with God; and we direct their husbands to use all the influences of love and piety in this behalf.

2. We insist upon it, that the Preachers set the best example in dress and every thing. If the Preachers be not moderate in every thing, a torrent of luxury will irresistibly break in upon us, and destroy the work of God.

3. We strongly recommend it to all our people to kneel at prayer: and we desire that all our pews may, as far as possible, be so formed as to admit of this in the easiest manner; and we request that the pews and pulpits be supplied with hassocks.

4. We beg that our people will keep close to the excellent rules drawn up by our venerable father in the gospel Mr. Wesley, in respect to singing. The celebrating of the praises of the most high God is an important part of divine worship, and a part in which the whole congregation should endeavour vocally to join. It is therefore very indecorous not to stand up on so solemn an occasion.

5. Though it is our privilege and duty to set God always before us, we should manifest our sense of his divine presence on all occasions, when we join in solemnly addressing him in public company, by our actions as well as words.

6. The last-mentioned evil is so great, that we trust there are but very few whom it concerns. But such as it does concern, we must exhort to flee from the wrath to come. If they have no savour for the word of God they can have no savour of God himself.

Conformity to the World

John Pawson to Francis Asbury and Richard Whatcoat; Bristol, October 14, 1803

(Ms at Garrett-Evangelical Seminary)

Whatcoat was one of those ordained by Wesley in 1784 for America. In 1800 he was elected bishop and so shared with Asbury in the leadership of the American Methodists, despite his failing health. Both he and Asbury had known the Wednesbury society in its early days.

If I have not formed a wrong judgment of you and the brethren united with you, you still retain a good degree of the ancient simplicity and plainness of the old primitive Methodists, and that you preach a full, free and present salvation[1] through faith in the Lord Jesus Christ. All this I very highly approve of. Christian simplicity appears to me exceedingly amiable and I have long thought that our gracious Lord gives a good degree of it, as well as of tenderness of conscience, to everyone that he received into his favour. This simplicity prepares and disposes the person possessed of it to receive instruction, and every good thing, from every quarter, and such persons will surely prosper in the life and power of religion. But I have seen in my life's short day, too many instances where this simplicity has been lost, and instead of it a nice, critical reasoning spirit hath been imbibed. This I greatly fear is too much the case with some of our young men here. There seems a very strong inclination in them to refine and philosophize upon divine truth, so as to reason the witness of the Spirit, and the life and power of religion quite away. Nay, some have begun to deny the necessity of a divine influence to attend our ministry in order to its having a saving effect upon the minds of the people. But, blessed be the name of the Lord, the whole body of the preachers have set their faces against this pernicious and destructive opinion, so that those that hold it have left us.

I am now grown old in the service of a good Master, being very near 66 years old, and am the oldest man now travelling. I have attended 42 Conferences and never missed one, which is more than anyone living besides me has done, yet good brother Thomas Taylor has travelled one year more than I have done, but although he is one year younger than I am, yet he has more of the infirmities of age than me. Such is the goodness and mercy of God to an unworthy creature, and such abundant cause have I to praise him for his unmerited mercy and never-failing love.

I am inclined to think that our Societies in general, as well as the preachers, are in as good a state as I have ever known them. For this we have infinite cause to praise the Lord. But notwithstanding this, there are some things which I have long seen and lamented, but cannot cure. We have not had since the death of Mr. Wesley any proper government. We are a very large body without a head, and what is still worse, the preachers in general are strongly opposed to everything of the kind. They will not bear to hear anything of that sort mentioned. Conformity to this world, following the various fashions of this world in dress &c. has strongly [?strangely] broken in upon us everywhere. And very few of the preachers see any harm therein, nay very many of them follow every fashion which makes its appearance. A Methodist is no longer known (as formerly) by the plainness and gravity of his dress and behaviour, these days are over and gone. Yet there are some still in every large Society who continue in the old primitive simplicity and plainness.

I am inclined to think that all the old preachers, and very many of the younger, are fully determined to abide by the original doctrines of Methodism, and see as great a necessity to preach all the grand leading truths of the gospel in the plainest, clearest and most pointed manner possible, as they ever did at any time. As to myself, I am sure this is highly necessary, and although it may be said by some, that these truths are become so familiar to many of the people that except the preachers study variety their word will have little effect, I am well persuaded that where these truths are lost sight of, very little good will be done . . .

I doubt we are in danger of forgetting too much the necessity of constantly pressing believers to look for full salvation. The truth of the doctrine itself is not denied. But I fear not many of our preachers see that it is the design of God wholly to sanctify the soul instantaneously . . .

O what changes have taken place since I met you first at the house of good brother King of Stroud, and since I sent honest Br. Whatcoat out to travel from Wednesbury[2] . . .

---

[1] For this expression, which occurs twice in this letter, see above, p. 295.

[2] Pawson was appointed to the Staffordshire circuit in 1768, and Whatcoat entered the ministry from that circuit the following year.

Sarah Crosby to John Pawson; Leeds, Dec. 14, 1803

(Ms at MA; Lamplough Collection)

Sarah Crosby, born in 1729, was within a year of her death. She could look back over many years of experience as a Methodist.

We will praise God that there are *some* in different places who still dare to be *singularly good*! But we, as you observe in your good letter, cannot help lamenting that the greater part of the *Methodists* are in full conformity with the *World*, with regard to *dress* & many other things. & to me it seems a pity to grieve a beginner or one that has not been long in the way about their dress, seeing so many of the preachers' *wives* set the example, unless they were led to lay aside any part thereof from conviction. Indeed, if all our preachers kept strictly to the Rule of not admitting any into Society or *Bands*, unless they would conform to the proper Rules, and told them so in Society Meetings! But then we should not have so many members. Should we have more of the presence and power, and love of God! Does Mr. Pawson think? Or should we have 10 or 20 thousand more members, would that do us good? Without more of the power & love of God? You don't think it would. I believe I know your thoughts on this subject. The silent language of your soul to God is, 'Nothing in heaven or earth I want, but only to be filled with love.'

Pawson's 'last words' to his fellow preachers

(*Methodist Magazine*, 1806, pp. 595–6)

The letter is dated from Wakefield, February 26, 1806. He died on March 19th.

May I be permitted, as a dying man, to give you a little advice, which I hope, when I am no more, you will seriously think of:—

1. Take great care that you all constantly maintain the primitive Methodist spirit. Be serious, spiritual, and heavenly-minded. Be lively, zealous and active in the service of God. Be crucified to this vain world, and filled with that Holy Spirit, which raises the soul from earth to heaven. You are in great danger of conforming to the world in your dress, in your manners, and in your spirit and temper of mind. O! watch and pray against this deadly evil; and let not your wives and children fall into this snare of the devil.

2. Take care that you constantly, clearly, fully, and pointedly, preach the good old Methodist doctrines. They are the very truth, as revealed in God's own Book. Never lose sight of the knowledge of salvation by the forgiveness of sins: And the full renewal of the soul in righteousness and true holiness. Constantly preach Christ, in all the riches of his grace,

and offer, in his Name, a present, free, and full salvation: a salvation from the guilt, the power, and the very being of sin.

3. Abide by every branch of our discipline. You have known the blessing which has attended it: But never try to make the door of the church narrower than God hath made the door of heaven. Never, no, never while you live, give the least countenance to any thing like a persecuting spirit.

4. Take all possible care to maintain a lively, spiritual, heart-searching Ministry. To this end I intreat you, by the mercies of God in Christ Jesus, never, no never try to make Ministers, by substituting learning, or any thing else, in the room of the call of God, and those spiritual gifts and graces, which he always did, and always will bestow upon those whom he sends to labour in his vineyard. The Great Head of the Church will always take care to provide a sufficient number of faithful men, to publish the glad tidings of salvation in his name. It is your duty to pray that the Lord of the harvest may send forth labourers; but never try to make them: he will do that himself. Religion has been utterly ruined, in almost every particular body of Christians, by this deadly evil; the establishing a learned, instead of a lively, spiritual Ministry.

5. Be exceeding careful in receiving Candidates for the Ministry. On no account whatsoever admit any, but what you have sufficient reason to believe are soundly converted to God, are zealous for his glory, and who only wish to spend, and be spent in his work. If ever the life and power of godliness begin to decay among the Methodists, look well to your selves, for the first cause will be with the Preachers. As long as you are truly devoted to God, and faithfully preach his word, a blessing must attend it, and the work of the Lord will prosper in your hands. But if you do not live in the Spirit, and copy the example of your Lord, you have no right to expect that he will cause his blessing to attend your labours; and your spirit will but too soon be observed by the people, and they will lose the life and power of godliness, as well as yourselves.

Persecution Renewed

Joseph Butterworth, on behalf of the Committee of Privileges, to the Right Honourable Lord Hobart, one of His Majesty's Principal Secretaries of State &c., 9 November 1803

(Lambeth Palace Library, Fulham Papers, XVIII, 125)

My Lord,

It is with real concern that in the present peculiar state of public affairs, and amidst the very important avocations of His Majesty's Ministers, the

Committee of the People called Methodists (*of the late Rev. Mr. Wesley's Connexion*) should be under the painful necessity of entreating any attention from those occupations which are of such vast importance at this awful crisis . . . [However,] we presume to address your Lordship upon this occasion and to state some grievances which have lately occurred to the detriment of Religion and to the serious injury of His Majesty's faithful subjects . . . But before we relate the particulars in question, we would just observe that it has been the common fate of religious characters to be greatly misrepresented by the generality of the World; and the Methodists have had their full share of public odium, both from persons wilfully and wickedly averse to all virtue, as well as from those who have either been strongly prejudiced against them, or ignorant of their principles and practice.

We have not, my Lord, so much vanity as to say, or even to imagine, that the Methodists are an immaculate people, and free from all human failings; but this we can truly affirm, that our aim and intention is to have always a conscience void of offence, towards God and towards men.

That we may not be further tedious to your Lordship, we proceed to state, that considerable coercion has been exercised by Officers of the Army over the tender rights of conscience. We conceive, my Lord, that if soldiers are exact in every part of duty and discipline, they should, under the British Constitution, be allowed to worship the Almighty as their own judgment directs, but nevertheless in conformity to the Laws. At Gibraltar in particular, this privilege has been refused, and two men of the Methodist Society have been cruelly flogged (as an example to the rest) for attending a religious meeting; and others threatened with the like punishment, if they should ever spend their leisure hours in the same manner; but the details of this affair are transmitted to the Right Honourable The Secretary at War, and it may not be necessary to repeat them in this place.

The circumstances to which we would more immediately entreat your Lordship's attention relate to Jamaica. We have the honour to enclose a brief account of our Missions to the West India Islands, published by the Rev. Dr. Coke in the year 1798. The efforts of our people have been crowned with great success in several of these islands; but at Jamaica they have experienced very considerable opposition, and in December last, an Act was passed the Legislature there entitled 'an Act to prevent preaching by Persons not duly qualified by Law', which has occasioned very considerable anxiety for the interests of Religion, both at home and abroad; as it gives authority to misrepresentation, and commits uncontrolled power into the hands of prejudice.

This act has been put in force in a very extraordinary manner, to the great grief of numbers of His Majesty's loyal and faithful Subjects.

In the town of Kingston, Jamaica, we have many persons in our

Society; & at Morant Bay there were nearly one hundred persons seriously inclined; and our preachers considered it necessary that they should have a proper teacher appointed over them. For this purpose, Mr. John Williams (a man of good character and genuine piety) was chosen, and he applied to the Court of Quarter Sessions there, on the 4th January 1803 for a Qualification to preach according to the Law of Toleration, but he was refused this Qualification by the Magistrates without any reason whatever being assigned for such a refusal.

On account of the Act above-mentioned, Mr. Williams did not venture to preach or teach without being qualified, but he was shortly after apprehended and closely imprisoned in the House of Correction as a 'rogue and a vagabond' under this new Law, for having prayed to Almighty God and having sung hymns in company with some religious people.

On the 7th February following, Mr. Daniel Campbell, one of our regular Missionaries (who has been some time in Jamaica) visited Montego Bay & preached as usual, for which he was instantly apprehended, and altho' he produced his British Qualification, he was also committed to the same prison, without even a formal sentence, but was told that his British licence would not do there. Thus, my Lord, if the Act above-mentioned remain in force, the Magistrates may effectually destroy the blessing of Religion in Jamaica. Those at Morant Bay seem determined neither to give licences to preach, nor permit those Preachers to exercise the sacred functions of their office, who are already duly qualified by Law.

Our Friends in Jamaica obtained Mr. Campbell's removal by Writ of Habeas Corpus from the House of Correction at Morant Bay to the Supreme Court at Spanish Town, where the Chief Justice of the Island, *Lawyer*, gave it as his opinion, that Mr. Campbell's Qualification was valid: but when the Counsel for the Magistrates hinted that their clients would be rendered liable to a prosecution for false imprisonment if the Court determined the Qualification to be sufficient, the other two Judges on the Bench, *who are not of the Profession of the Law*, supported the Magistrates, and determined the Cause in their favour.

We are perfectly aware, my Lord, of the importance of supporting the authority of Magistrates, particularly in the West Indies, but this should not be done at the expense of Justice. Our sole object in maintaining these Missions is the benefit of Mankind; and we are well persuaded that our Missionaries can have no other end in view whatsoever; we also trust that a wise and temperate Government will patronize our laudable designs.

The Act in question imposes fine, imprisonment, & flogging, for the various *offences* of religious worship therein described; and also enacts that whenever the 'offence' of preaching &c. 'appear of *extraordinary heinousness'*, the offender, on conviction, '*to suffer such punishment as the court shall see fit to inflict*, not extending to Life'!

For the honour of the British Name, we hope that such a Law will not long disgrace the Annals of Christianity! . . .

The preamble to the Act insinuates that 'an evil threatens much danger to the peace and safety of the Island by reason of the preaching of *ill-disposed, illiterate* or ignorant *enthusiasts* whereby the minds of the hearers are perverted with fanatical notions &c.' We shall only observe upon these uncharitable assertions, that our two Missionaries in Jamaica (Messrs Campbell & Fish) do not to our own certain knowledge come under the character described, with any sort of truth or justice: they are men of good sense, and sound, exemplary piety; and our correspondence with Mr. John Williams proves him to be a *well-disposed, intelligent, sober-minded Christian*, and does great honour to the encomiums we have received of his character.

If, my Lord, we might be allowed to venture a political opinion respecting the West Indies, we should not hesitate to say, that their best defence and security would be in a general diffusion of religious knowledge among the Negroes; we are confident that this would be the surest means of preserving internal safety, and in case of foreign attack, we are certain that dependence could not be better placed than in persons whom religion inspires with valour and integrity. This is not our hasty opinion, taken up at random, but founded upon observation and experience. The Methodists have upon various occasions manifested those qualities, which are of the utmost consequence in the hour of trial. During the Rebellion in Ireland, our people in the Volunteer Corps rendered many most important services to their King & country; and at this moment the members of our Society who are inhabitants of the Island of Guernsey & who bear arms for the defence of the State are well known for their steady good conduct & discipline, and have received public thanks for the same . . .

The Conversion of William Clowes

(*The Journals of William Clowes*, 1844, pp. 18–21)

This turning point in Clowes's life occurred on January 20, 1805, when he was twenty-four years old.

The deliverance of my soul from the heavy sorrows that oppressed it, was preceded by a circumstance in which may be traced the finger of God: it occurred about a fortnight prior to my conversion. In taking up

the prayer-book to read, that passage in it powerfully struck my attention – 'They that eat and drink the Lord's Supper unworthily eat and
drink their own damnation.' This made a deep impression on me at the
time, and I resolved that, wicked as I was, I should never do this thing;
for I conceived this to be the sin against the Holy Ghost which was unpardonable. The Sunday following, a neighbour of mine called upon me,
and asked me if I would accompany him to Burslem, to a preaching.
Well, thought I, it is dark, I shall not be seen; accordingly, I assented to
the proposition of my neighbour, and went with him. After preaching
was concluded, and the congregation was dismissed, it was announced
that there would be a love-feast immediately, and that the members of
the Society would be admitted to the meeting by presenting their Society
tickets to the door-keepers. The individual who was my companion on
this occasion, asked me if I should like to go into the love-feast. I inquired
of him what the meeting was for, and what the people did; for I was
totally ignorant of such matters. The man, however, replied, that if I
wished to go in, he would go home, and I should have the ticket which
he had borrowed of his mother-in-law, for the purpose of getting in.

So, feeling inclined to see this meeting, and my curiosity being thus
excited, I took the ticket, and with it directions how to act, in order to
gain admission. The person told me, in showing the ticket to the door-
keeper, I was to cover the name written upon it with my thumb, and just
let him see the alphabetical letter, and thus I should be allowed to pass
on into the chapel. Accordingly, we both went up to the chapel door,
and my companion, observing that the door-keeper, instead of giving a
rapid glance at the presented tickets, took them out of the hands of the
individuals, and examined them minutely, said to me, 'Come, we must
go home; I see neither of us can get in.' But, at the moment, I neither felt
any disposition to return, nor to give my friend his ticket back; and,
just as I stood in this undecided state, a puff of wind came, and blew the
door-keeper's candle out. In a moment, I presented him my ticket; but
on taking it into his hand, he called for another light, and just as he was
going to read the ticket, another puff came, and away went the light a
second time. The man being fluttered and disappointed, hastily pushed
back the ticket into my hand, saying, 'Here, here, move on.' So I passed
into the gallery of the chapel. I was no sooner seated than I felt disturbed
with a variety of thoughts. I thought, 'What shall I do here? How must
I act amongst this people?' I, however, concluded in my mind that I
would sit still when the people did, kneel when they knelt, and regulate
matters as well as I could in this way, taking care to be always on the
watch. The service had only proceeded a short way, when I observed, to
my uncommon surprise, certain individuals going round, and handing
bread and water among the congregation. Immediately the thought
struck me like lightning – 'This is the sacrament!' – and what I had read

in the prayer-book respecting eating and drinking it unworthily rushed in upon my mind, and shook me from head to foot. I glanced rapidly round on the people to see if there were any that did not receive; that if there were, I should do as they did, and thus I would escape the damnation threatened; but to my anguish and distress I observed every individual partook. At last, I thought, 'Well, if I take it as these people do, and never commit sin afterwards, but serve the Lord, it will not be eating and drinking unworthily.' So I prayed to God in my heart, that if this was a good thought, he would give me peace of mind. I therefore received the bread and water in the love-feast, under the idea of the sacrament, persuaded that, if I sinned after this, I must be damned to all eternity. So ignorant was I, at this period of my life, of religious things. From this time, however, I became conscious of a stronger power working in my soul, and I resolved, with my besetting sins, to give up my wicked companions, and to attend religious meetings. Now it was that I began to see the folly of trying to serve God in my own strength, and clinging to the society of dissipated and ungodly associates. The pall of spiritual darkness with which my soul had been so long enveloped, was about to be withdrawn. Some rays from the eternal Sun of Righteousness had already fallen upon me; for, on my return from the love-feast, I told my wife where I had been, and what I purposed to do in future. She said nothing in opposition to the determination thus expressed; for she saw by this time that if I held to my purpose it would be to her own advantage. Indeed, I am persuaded, had she zealously supported me in my wishes to change my practices, and had any pious individual taken me by the hand at the period of my marriage, my conversion to God would then have taken place; but in a certain sense I might adopt the language of inspiration, and say, 'No man careth for my soul!'

On the morning subsequent to the love-feast (to which reference has been made) I went to a prayer-meeting which commenced at seven o'clock. The meeting was what some would term a noisy one, but I was not affected on that account; I felt I had enough to do for myself. The power of Heaven came down upon me, and I cried for help to Him who is mighty to save. It was towards the close of the meeting, when I felt my bands breaking; and when this change was taking place, I thought within myself, What is this? This, I said, is what the Methodists mean by being converted: yes, this is it – God is converting my soul. In an agony of prayer, I believed God would save me, – then I believed he was saving me, – then I believed he had saved me, and it was so. I did not praise God aloud, at the moment of my deliverance; but I was fully persuaded that God had wrought the glorious work – that I was justified by faith, and had peace with God through Jesus Christ. Accordingly, when the meeting was concluded, some one asked me how I was going on. I instantly replied, 'God has pardoned all my sins.' All the people then fell upon their knees and returned thanks to God for my deliverance. Thus, sorrow, which had continued for a night, passed away, and joy came in the morning.

Music in Worship

(*Minutes*, 1805)

Q. 20. Are any regulations necessary with regard to singing?

A. 1. Let no instruments of music be introduced into the singers' seats, except a bass viol, should the principal singer require it.

2. Let no books of hymns be henceforth used in our chapels except the hymn-books printed for our Book-Room.

[3.] Let no *Pieces*, as they are called, in which *Recitatives*, by single men, *Solos*, by single women, *Fuguing* (or different words sung by different voices at the same time) are introduced, be sung in our chapels.

4. Let the original, simple, grave, and devotional style be carefully preserved, which, instead of drawing the attention to singing and the singers, is so admirably calculated to draw off the attention from both, and to raise the soul to God only.

5. Let no musical *Festivals*, or, as they are sometimes termed, *Selections of Sacred Music*, be either encouraged or permitted in any of our chapels: in which performances, the genuine dignity of spiritual worship is grossly abused, under the pretence of getting money for charitable purposes, which we have sufficient proof, has been procured as amply, where nothing of the kind has been introduced, but the charity recommended to the people in the name of God.

6. Let no Preacher suffer any thing to be done in the chapel where he officiates but what is according to the established usages of Methodism; knowing that he is accountable to God for whatever he does, or permits to be done, during the times he is in possession of the pulpit.

7. Let no Preacher, therefore, suffer his right to conduct every part of the worship of Almighty God, to be infringed on, either by singers or others, but let him sacredly preserve, and calmly maintain his authority, as he who sacrifices this, sacrifices not only Methodism, but the spirit and design of Christianity.

(*Minutes*, 1808)

3. The Conference judge it expedient to refuse, after this present year, their sanction or consent to the erection of any organ in our chapels.

4. Where organs have been already introduced, the Conference requires that they shall be so used as not to *overpower* or *supersede*, but only to assist our *congregational singing*: and that they shall be considered as under the control of the Superintendant, or of the officiating Preacher for the time being, whose right and duty it is to conduct every part of the public worship of God. Let no voluntaries be played during the time of divine service; and let all the rules respecting singing and instrumental music, which were made at the Sheffield Conference in 1805, and published in the Minutes of that year, be uniformly enforced.

Cause for Concern (2)

Joseph Benson to George Marsden; London, January 6, 1807

(Ms at the New Room, Bristol)

Marsden was stationed at Stockport and had sent news of affairs in the circuit. Hillgate Chapel, built in 1784, had become too small by 1800, but plans for a larger building were delayed by the competing demands of the Sunday School. The latter had grown rapidly in the closing years of the eighteenth century, until it was easily the largest in the town. The 'larger and more commodious chapel' at Tiviot Dale was not built until 1826.

I rejoice to find that peace is in a great measure restored to the Society & congregation at Stockport, & am of opinion that every effort should be used to get a larger & more commodious Chapel erected. I think it a shame that, while they are laying out such an immense sum of money on a Sunday School, in which, I believe, *writing* & *accounts* are taught on the Lord's Day (a mere secular business, certainly, like teaching to *knit*, *weave* or anything else whereby a man or woman may get bread) – that the rich and, I hope, pious congregation in Stockport are still content to be couped up in that old & paltry chapel. They should have one as large as the New Chapel in Sheffield.

For some time the Sunday School at Stockport went on well, and the Managers of it acted in unison with Preachers, [Trustees?], Stewards & Leaders of the Society. But it appears of late that a very different Plan has been adopted which I am, indeed, very sorry for. I am apprehensive, that in a little time, instead of serving the cause of genuine religion in Stockport, the Sunday School there will militate against it. Whatever lessens the reverence of young persons for divine worship, & for the Lord's Day opposes the interests of true Piety.

George Morley to Jabez Bunting; Bury, March 23, 1807

(Ms at Emory University)

We live in strange times. Everything foreign & domestic, political & religious, appears to be unsettled. I was going to say human nature itself has lately undergone a great alteration. But perhaps that would be saying too much. There always were discontented men: and discontented men have always wished to be reformers. I see I have written a preface to my letter without intending any such thing.

I am informed that there is a fund in Manchester for the relief of Local Preachers when they are sick. I want to know whether you have such a fund, and if you have, how it is supported, whether you and the other travelling preachers approve of it, or whether you fear that it may be productive of evil consequences. My reason for requesting this information from you is what has lately taken place in this and the Rochdale circuits.

Many of the Local Preachers in these circuits have formed themselves into a kind of independent association. Their professed design is to make provision for themselves in time of sickness, for horse-hire, and for their widows and children after their death. The means they proposed are a subsciption of 10/6 from each local preacher annually, public annual collections in all our congregations in both circuits, and private subscriptions from friends to the institution. They have determined not to preach in any places where a public collection shall not be allowed. They intend to print their rules and circulate them, I believe with a design to promote similar plans in other parts of the connexion.

They themselves are to have the whole management and disposal of the above mentioned funds, without being subject to any control, either from the society or circuit stewards, or Quarterly Meetings, or any other whatever. This would be to establish a new authority in our Connexion, which would obstruct, and perhaps soon destroy our discipline. It would also establish two temporal interests in the connexion, between which there would be everlasting jealousies. It originated in ill-nature, is unnecessary, and on many accounts unreasonable. I have spoken my mind freely to those Local Preachers whom I have seen since I heard of their scheme. Our principal friends in Bury are decidedly against the plan, and say they would rather subscribe towards the support of a third preacher in the circuit than submit to it.

Would you be so kind as to advise with the Manchester preachers on the business and let me know as soon as you can how you think I ought to act. Should I endeavour to crush it at once or try to prevail on them to refer it to the Conference? Perhaps the latter plan would only give them time to strengthen themselves by corresponding with the disaffected in other circuits. If they should join Broadhurst's party, they would do us uncalculable mischief in these little circuits. The business will come forward at our Quarterly Meeting next Monday at Accrington. I shall leave this town on Saturday. Can you favour me with a letter before then?

The First English Camp Meetings

Observations on Camp Meetings, with an Account of a Camp Meeting held on Sunday, May 31st, 1807, at Mow, near Harriseahead.

By Hugh Bourne. Price One Penny.

(Reprinted in John Walford, *Life of Hugh Bourne*, 1855, I, 119–25)

The first institution of camp meetings, for the solemn worship of Almighty God, appears to have been very ancient. In Leviticus xxiii. 39, to the end of the chapter, we find that the God of Israel commanded his people to build them booths of the boughs of trees, of different kinds, and dwell in them seven days. And that this was to be done annually, immediately after gathering in the fruits of the land . . .

Matt. xiv. 13–21. Here we find, that a great multitude of men, women, and children collected together out of the cities, &c., into the desert place where Jesus was, and that they continued with him until the evening, and were fed by his interposition. Our Lord, then, was not displeased with such large and promiscuous collections of people . . . It would seem, therefore, that our Lord himself, on finding the multitude willing to receive instruction in the ways of salvation, had no objection to continue with them in the mountain, or desert, even three days together. See a defence of camp meetings, by the Rev. S. K. Jennings, A.M.

America has had the honour and happiness of again reviving the long neglected institution of sacred camp meetings, and they are there become very frequent and respectable. – High and low, rich and poor, chief magistrates, judges, &c., attend, and hundreds get converted. They were begun in Kentucky, by an opening of Providence about the year 1797, and from thence they were introduced into North Carolina, and afterward into all the United States.

These meetings are held (by preachings, exhortations, prayer, and other godly exercises) day and night, for three, four, or five days. Families will go above fifty miles to a camp meeting, in covered waggons, carriages, &c. Taking with them several days' provision, with equipage of blankets, sheets, coverlets, &c., for tents to sleep in, &c. Immediately the camp resembles a very populous town, enclosing a large square of ground. And the thousands of people, attentive and solemn, preparing to seek the most high God, strike the mind with a most pious awe; and the vast number of fires, during the night, together with lamps, lanterns, &c., suspended, and burning, in every direction, and illuminating all round, to a great distance, have a grand and pleasing effect.

Letters concerning these extraordinary things being published in the methodist magazines, paved the way for camp meetings in England. And Lorenzo Dow, the celebrated American preacher (who lately visited this country), published a defence of camp meetings, by the Rev. S. K. Jennings, A.M., with other remarks on the subject; which, together with the lively and wonderful descriptions of the work which he gave, both in the pulpit, and in conversation, appear to have been the chief means of fully introducing them.

Mow camp meeting was appointed to be held on Sunday, May 31st, 1807. The morning proved rainy and unfavourable, which rather put it back; but about six o'clock, the Lord sent the clouds off, and gave us a very pleasant day.

The meeting was opened by two holy men from Knutsford – Captain Anderson having previously erected a flag on the mountain to direct strangers, and these three, with some pious people from Macclesfield, carried on and sustained the meeting a considerable time, in a most vigorous and lively manner. They conducted it by preaching, prayer, exhortations, relating experiences, &c. The Lord owned their labours, grace descended, and the people of God were greatly quickened. The congregation rapidly increased, and others began to join in holy exercises.

One of the men from Knutsford, a lawyer, and an Irishman (who had been converted under the Ministry of Lorenzo Dow), related the troubles he had passed through in Ireland. In the late rebellion in that unhappy land, he had been deprived of thousands; from a state of wealth and affluence, in which he had been brought up, and in which he had lived, he with his family had been reduced. But for this he thanked God, the taking away his substance had been the cause of his gaining the true riches; and he had since given up his profession of an attorney, because he found it too difficult to keep his religion in that profession. This man exhorted all to pray for our gracious king, who was worthy, because he granted liberty of conscience; but he himself had seen a time in Ireland when a protestant knew not at night but his house and family might be burned before morning.

Another man had been in many parts of the world, had been preferred in the army, and had left his leg in Africa. He was a great scholar and philosopher, had renounced christianity and turned to deism, afterwards to atheism; but being drawn by curiosity to hear Lorenzo preach, heard him relate the following circumstance: —At a camp meeting in America, a black was converted, and in the fulness of joy, praised God with a loud voice. A deist standing by, who with his fellow deists had endeavoured to believe that blacks have no souls, said; 'You black rascal, why do you go on in this manner? You have no soul to save.' The poor black replied: 'Massa, if black man no soul, religion make body happy.' – Hearing this made such an impression on him, that he began to pray, and the Lord made him feel the weight of his sins; he cried for mercy, and the Lord pardoned him. Jesus Christ was manifested to him, and he was born of God: he soon after obtained full sanctification; and now lived by faith in the Son of God. He was so overpowered by the love of God, that he was obliged to be supported while he spoke.

Meanwhile, the people were flocking in from every quarter. The wind was cold, but a large grove of fir-trees kept the wind off, and made it very comfortable. So many hundreds now covered the ground that another preaching-stand was erected in a distant part of the field, under the cover of a stone wall. Returning over the field, I met a company at a distance from the first stand, praying for a man in distress. I could not get near: but I there found such a measure of the power of God, such a weighty burning of joy and love, that it was beyond description. I should gladly have stopped there, but other matters called me away. I perceived that the Lord was beginning to work mightily. Nearer the first stand was another company praying with mourners. Immediately the man in the other company was praising God, and I found that he had obtained the pardon of his sins, and was born again. I believe this man to have been the first that was born of God at this meeting. Many were afterwards born again or converted in the other company; the number I could not ascertain: but from what information I was able to collect, I suppose, about six.

Meantime, preaching went on without intermission at both stands, and, about noon, the congregation was so much increased, that we were obliged to erect a third preaching-stand; we fixed it a distance below the first, by the side of the fir-tree grove. I got upon this stand, after the first preaching, and was extremely surprised at the amazing sight that appeared before me. The people were nearly all under my eye; and I had not before conceived that such a vast multitude were present; but the thousands hearing with attention as solemn as death, presented a scene of the most sublime and awfully-pleasing grandeur that my eyes ever beheld.

The preachers seemed to be fired with an uncommon zeal, and an extraordinary unction attended their word, while tears were seen flowing, and sinners trembling on every side. Numbers were convinced, and saints were uncommonly quickened. And the extraordinary steadiness and decorum that were maintained during the whole day (notwithstanding the vast concourse of people who attended) seemed to make a great impression upon every mind.

Many preachers were now upon the ground, from Knutsford, Congleton, Wheelock, Burslem, Macclesfield, and other places: and a most extraordinary variety appeared. The man who was turned from deism had been in the field of war, when the grandees of the earth drew the sword and bid the battle bleed. He had seen death flying in every direction, and men falling slain on every side. He had walked in blood, over fields covered with mountains of dying and dead. He shewed the happiness of our land, and the gratitude we owed to God for being exempted from being the seat of war. Another, who had seen the horrors of rebellion lately in Ireland, persuaded us to turn to righteousness, because we were exempt from these calamities. E. Anderson related the devotion he had beheld in many parts of the world, which we suppose to be in darkness and superstition, and exhorted us to turn to God, lest they should rise up in judgment against us. All the preachers seemed to be strenthened in the work. Persuasion dwelt upon their tongues while the multitudes, were trembling or rejoicing around.

The congregation increased so rapidly that a fourth preaching-stand was called for. The work now became general, and the scene was most awful and interesting. In this glass, any one might have viewed the worth of souls. To see the thousands of people, all (except a few stragglers) in solemn attention; a company near the first stand wrestling in prayer for mourners; and four preachers dealing out their lives at every stroke. These things made an impression on my mind, not soon to be forgotten; this extraordinary scene continued till about four o'clock, when the people began to retire; and before six, they were confined to one stand.

About seven o'clock in the evening, a work began among children: six of whom were converted, or born again, before the meeting broke up; and the power of God seemed to have a great effect upon the people present. At about half-past eight o'clock at night, the meeting was finally closed. A meeting, such as our eyes had never beheld! a meeting, for which many will praise God in time and eternity! such a day as this we never before enjoyed! a day spent in the active service of the living God! a Sabbath in which Jesus Christ made glad the hearts of his saints, and sent his arrows to the hearts of sinners. The propriety and great utility of camp meetings appeared to every one; so great was the work, that the people were ready to say, 'We have seen strange things to-day.' O may the Lord carry on his work, till righteousness cover the earth, for Jesus' sake. Amen.

Second Mow camp meeting

I have now to inform our friends, that (God willing) there will be a camp meeting held in the same place, to begin on Saturday, July 18, 1807, at four o'clock in the afternoon, to be held day and night, for two or three days, or more; and also, that a camp meeting is appointed (Providence permitting) to be held at Norton-in-the-Moors, in the county of Stafford, near the chapel, to begin on Saturday, August 22nd, 1807, at four o'clock in the afternoon, to be held day and night as above.

The provision made for strangers at the camp meeting that is past was small, the cause of which was, that such a meeting being a new thing in England, the managers were unacquainted with the proper method of making preparations for it. In those that are now appointed, they intend to follow the advice of their friends, that is:

1. To get the ground regularly licensed under the toleration act, that all interruption, or misbehaviour, in the time of meeting, may be prevented, or else punished as the law directs.

2. To provide a sufficient quantity of stands and seats.

3. To provide tents, &c., sufficient to defend the people from the inclemency of the weather.

4. To provide a large supply of coals, lanterns, candles, &c., to light the camp during the night.

5. To get provision sufficient to supply all distant comers during the Sabbath.

6. To defray these expenses by public collections during the meeting.

An attentive observer will soon perceive some difference between America and England, with regard to camp meetings. There the people are more employed in farming, which enables them with more convenience to bring provisions, and equipage for tents. With regard to tents, the difficulties will be removed, by the managers erecting them; and trades-people, who are accustomed to buy their provisions, may, when the Sabbath is past, buy them with as much convenience at Harriseahead and Norton, as at other places.

The Wesleyan reaction

(*Minutes*, 1807)

Q. 20. What is the judgment of the Conference concerning what are called Camp-Meetings?

A. It is our judgment, that even supposing such meetings to be allowable in America, they are highly improper in England, and likely to be productive of considerable mischief. And we disclaim all connexion with them.

Q. 21. Have our people been sufficiently cautious respecting the permission of strangers to preach to our congregations?

A. We fear not: and we, therefore, again direct, that no stranger, from America or elsewhere, be suffered to preach in any of our places, unless he come fully accredited; if an Itinerant Preacher, by having his name entered on the Minutes of the Conference of which he is a member; and if a Local Preacher, by a recommendatory note from his Superintendent.

Early Home Missions

(Thomas Coke, *The Annual Report of the State of the Missions . . . addressed in particular to those generous subscribers who have contributed to their support, and to the benevolent public at large,* 1808, pp. 26–8).

XVII. THE IRISH MISSIONS

The numerous accounts of these Missions, which have been given in our Magazines since our last Report, will render it less necessary to enlarge on the important and successful attempts which have been made of late years, to introduce the gospel among the Roman Catholics of Ireland. The benefits which have already resulted from the institution of these Missions, are almost incalculable. Great numbers, through grace, have had fortitude sufficient to break off the shackles of Popery, in which both they and their ancestors had been held from time immemorial. Multitudes of others, who cannot be induced to believe that salvation is attainable out of the pale of that tyrannical and corrupt communion, have been so far enlightened as to perceive many of the impositions which have been practised on them by their priests. Even great numbers of the Protestants in Ireland, both nominal and real, have, through these means, been stirred up to seek that salvation which they had habitually neglected; and many of them have been awakened by that alarm which the Missionaries have sounded.

As the English and Irish languages are spoken in most places where they preach, it has been found highly expedient that they should travel in pairs, one of them preaching in the former, and the other in the latter tongue. The happy effects which have succeeded to this regulation, have already become visible. At present we have ten Missionaries employed on this important errand; but the extent of the country and population demands the labours of twice that number. These could be found without much difficulty, if the pecuniary aid which is wanting did not lay an embargo on our designs. Those of our opulent friends who have money to spare for beneficent purposes, may here find ample room to exercise their benevolence, and, under the blessings and promises of God, procure unto themselves perpetual gratification, and greatly promote the glory of God.

XVIII. The Welsh Missions

Perhaps in no part of the globe in which we have established Missions, have the benefits resulting from them been more conspicuous, more extensive, or more genuine, than in the Principality of Wales. Ten years have not yet elapsed since their first institution; and so greatly has God blessed the endeavours of his servants, that no less than sixty chapels have been erected, which are filled with large and attentive congregations. A Society has been raised, which consists of 5,218 members, besides our Welsh Societies in London, Manchester, Liverpool, and the Swansea, Cardiff, Merthyr-Tydville, Brecon, Kington, Caermarthen, and Wrexham circuits, which probably amount to at least 1,000 more. This very extraordinary work was begun about nine years and a half since, by two pious men who understood the Welsh language. From this small beginning no less than thirty-six Travelling Preachers have sprung up; and these have been accompanied by a still greater number of men who act in a local capacity.

Nor is this work apparently more rapid than real. The Preachers do, indeed, breathe the genuine Missionary spirit. The people seem actuated by the same disposition. Their words and actions manifest a spirit of love; and the life and power of true religion evidently dwell and rule in their hearts. The little cloud which first appeared so remarkably in North Wales, and shed that sacred shower of which we have just spoken, is now grown larger, and gloriously moves over, and covers a more extensive tract. From North Wales it is speading over South Wales. Cardiganshire, Caermarthenshire, Glamorganshire, and Breconshire, are refreshed with the dews of heaven: and Pembrokeshire, Radnorshire, and Monmouthshire, begin to feel the influences of this great revival: all seem to be preparing for a largish shower which, we trust, will shortly fall upon them. For this glorious outpouring of the Spirit the people seem to be devoutly waiting; and we believe the day is not very remote, when the mountains shall break forth into singing on the right-hand and on the left . . .

XIX. The Home Missions in England

When our friends and brethren reflect on the vast extent to which the gospel has been published through this kingdom within the last twenty years, many of them may be led to wonder why these Missions should be thought necessary. But their astonishment will cease when they are informed that out of the 11,000 parishes which England and Wales contain, perhaps one half of them seldom or never hear the gospel. In numerous small towns villages, and hamlets, a very considerable part of the inhabitants attend no place of worship whatever, nor once think of entering a religious edifice, except when marriages, baptisms, or funerals occur. It is among people of this description that our Missions have been chiefly established.

Within the three last years God has so blessed these means, that great numbers who had been living without hope and without God in the world, have, through Divine grace, been brought to know in whom they have believed. In addition to these, vast numbers have been induced to entertain a relish for the gospel, of which they had scarcely ever before had any conception. Among these, several new circuits have been formed, and considerable congregations collected; so that we have reason to believe that God will soon 'call them a people who were not a people', and 'her beloved who was not beloved'. Thirty-five Missionaries were appointed by our last Conference for this home department; and we are happy to find from their labours and those of their predecessors, that the predominant vices are considerably on the decline in many parts, and that multitudes flock to the standard of Christ as doves to the windows. In short, though they were but lately perishing for lack of knowledge, they appear ripe for the gospel, and many of them already embrace the overtures of salvation through Jesus Christ.

Sydney Smith on Methodism

(*Edinburgh Review*, January 1808)

In his letter to Marsden on January 6, 1807 (see p. 314 above), Benson wrote: 'You'll observe that anecdotes attesting or illustrating the Divine Providence are the most acceptable materials that can be sent to me for the Magazines, because I have fewer of that kind of article sent. On most other subjects I abound, especially in accounts of Deaths &c.' The Methodist understanding of the workings of Providence was one of the targets for Sydney Smith's attack, in a lengthy review of R. A. Ingram's *The Cause of the Increase of Methodism and Dissension* (1807). Despite the criticism, we find James Macdonald, Assistant Connexional Editor from 1811, writing to Joshua Fielden in 1815: 'Extraordinary and well authenticated providential occurrences, especially when well written, are very desirable and Mr. Benson and I will be obliged to you for any communications of that kind.' (Ms at SMU)

The article gives examples of 'providential' events from evangelical and Methodist sources, before proceeding to the general comments below.

Upon the foregoing facts, and upon the spirit evinced by these extracts, we shall make a few comments.

1. It is obvious that this description of Christians entertain very erroneous and dangerous notions of the present judgments of God. A belief that Providence interferes in all the little actions of our lives refers all merit and demerit to bad and good fortune, and causes the successful

man to be always considered as a good man, and the unhappy man as the object of divine vengeance. It furnishes ignorant and designing men with a power which is sure to be abused: the cry of, *a judgment, a judgment*, it is always easy to make, but not easy to resist. It encourages the grossest superstititions; for if the Deity rewards and punishes on every slight occasion, it is quite impossible but that such a helpless being as man will set himself at work to discover the will of Heaven in the appearances of outward nature, . . . as the poor Methodist, when he rode into Piccadilly in a thunder-storm, and imagined that all the uproar of the elements was a mere hint to him not to preach at Mr Romaine's chapel. Hence a great deal of error and a great deal of secret misery. This doctrine of a theocracy must necessarily place an excessive power in the hands of the clergy: it applies so instantly and so tremendously to men's hopes and fears, that it must make the priest omnipotent over the people, as it always has done where it has been established. It has a great tendency to check human exertions and to prevent the employment of those secondary means of effecting an object which Providence has placed in our power. The doctrine of the immediate and perpetual interference of Divine Providence is not true . . . Have not the soundest divines of both churches always urged this unequal distribution of good and evil, in the present state of retribution? Have not they contended, and well and admirably contended, that the supposition of such a state is absolutely necessary to our notion of the justice of God, absolutely necessary to restore order to that moral confusion which we all observe and deplore in the present world? The man who places religion upon a false basis is the greatest enemy to religion. . . .

2. The second doctrine which it is necessary to notice among the Methodists, is the doctrine of inward impulse and emotions, which, it is quite plain, must lead, if universally insisted upon and preached among the common people, to every species of folly and enormity. When a human being believes that his internal feelings are the monitions of God, and that these monitions must govern his conduct, and when a great stress is purposely laid upon these inward feelings in all the discourses from the pulpit, it is of course impossible to say to what a pitch of extravagance mankind may not be carried, under the influence of such dangerous doctrines.

3. The Methodists hate pleasure and amusements; no theatre, no cards, no dancing, no punchinello, no dancing dogs, no blind fiddlers; – all the amusements of the rich and of the poor must disappear, wherever these gloomy people get a footing. It is not the abuse of pleasure which they attack, but the interspersion of pleasure, however much it is guided by good sense and moderation. It is not only wicked to hear the licentious plays of Congreve, but wicked to hear Henry the Fifth, or the School for

Scandal. It is not only dissipated to run about to all the parties in London and Edinburgh, but dancing is not *fit for a being who is preparing himself for Eternity*. Ennui, wretchedness, melancholy, groans and sighs, are the offerings which these unhappy men make to a Deity who has covered the earth with gay colours and scented it with rich perfumes, and shown us, by the plan and order of his works, that he has given to man something better than a bare existence and scattered over his creation a thousand superfluous joys which are totally unnecessary to the mere support of life.

4. The Methodists lay very little stress upon practical righteousness. They do not say to their people: Do not be deceitful, do not be idle, get rid of your bad passions. Or at least (if they do say these things) they say them very seldom. Not that they preach faith without works; for if they told the people that they might rob and murder with impunity, the civil magistrate must be compelled to interfere with such doctrine; but they say a great deal about faith and very little about works. What are commonly called the mysterious parts of our religion are brought into the foreground, much more than the doctrines which lead to practice; – and this among the lowest of the community.

The Methodists have hitherto been accused of dissenting from the Church of England. This, as far as relates to mere subscription to articles, is not true; but they differ in their choice of the articles upon which they dilate and expand, and to which they appear to give a preference, from the stress which they place upon them. There is nothing heretical in saying that God *sometimes* intervenes with his special providence; but these people differ from the Established Church in the degree in which they insist upon this doctrine. In the hands of a man of sense and education it is a safe doctrine; in the management of the Methodists, we have seen how ridiculous and degrading it becomes. In the same manner, a clergyman of the Church of England would not do his duty if he did not insist upon the necessity of faith as well as of good works; but, as he believes that it is much more easy to give credit to doctrines than to live well, he labours most in those points where human nature is the *most* liable to prove defective. Because he does so, he is accused of giving up the articles of his faith, by men who have their partialities also in doctrine, but partialities not founded upon the same sound discretion and knowledge of human nature.

5. The Methodists are always desirous of making men more religious than it is possible, from the constitution of human nature, to make them. If they could succeed as much as they wish to succeed, there would be at once an end of delving and spinning, and of every exertion of human industry. Men must eat, and drink, and work; and if you wish to fix upon them high and elevated notions, as the *ordinary* furniture of their minds, you do these two things: you drive men of warm temperaments mad, and you introduce, in the rest of the world, a low and shocking

familiarity with words and images which every real friend to religion would wish to keep sacred. *The friends of the dear Redeemer who are in the habit of visiting the Isle of Thanet* – (as in the extract we have quoted) – Is it possible that this mixture of the most awful with the most familiar images, so common among Methodists now and with the enthusiasts in the time of Cromwell, must not, in the end, divest religion of all the deep and solemn impressions which it is calculated to produce? In a man of common imagination (as we have before observed) the terror and the feeling which it first excited must necessarily be soon separated, but where the fervour of impression is long preserved piety ends in Bedlam. Accordingly there is not a mad-house in England where a considerable part of the patients have not been driven to insanity by the extravagance of these people. We cannot enter such places without seeing a number of honest artisans, covered with blankets, and calling themselves angels and apostles, who, if they had remained contented with the instruction of men of learning and education, would still have been sound masters of their own trade, sober Christians, and useful members of society.

6. It is impossible not to observe how directly all the doctrine of the Methodists is calculated to gain power among the poor and ignorant. To say that the Deity governs this world by general rules and that we must wait for another and a final scene of existence before vice meets with its merited punishment and virtue with its merited reward, to preach this up daily, would not add a single votary to the Tabernacle nor sell a Number of the Methodistical Magazine; but to publish an account of a man who was cured of scrofula by a single sermon, of Providence destroying the innkeeper at Garstang for appointing a cock-fight near the Tabernacle, this promptness of judgment and immediate execution is so much like human justice, and so much better adapted to vulgar capacities, that the system is at once admitted as soon as any one can be found who is impudent or ignorant enough to teach it; and, being once admitted, it produces too strong an effect upon the passions to be easily relinquished. The case is the same with the doctrine of inward impulse, or, as they term it, experience. If you preach up to ploughmen and artisans that every singular feeling which comes across them is a visitation of the Divine Spirit, can there be any difficulty, *under* the influence of this nonsense, in converting these simple creatures into active and mysterious fools, and making them your slaves for life? It is not possible to raise up any dangerous enthusiasm by telling men to be just, and good, and charitable; but keep this part of Christianity out of sight, and talk long and enthusiastically, before ignorant people, of the mysteries of our religion, and you will not fail to attract a crowd of followers: verily the Tabernacle loveth not that which is simple, intelligible, and leadeth to good sound practice.

Toleration under Threat

Joseph Butterworth to Joseph Benson; Bristol, 4th August 1809

(Ms at Emory University)

I was much obliged to your note respecting the Bishop of Exeter's charge[1] to his clergy in Cornwall, as it is very desirable to collect all the information we can of the wishes & intentions of the higher powers relative to toleration. Mr. Griffiths I expect informed you that I sent a copy of our resolutions respecting Local Preachers[2] (as printed in Conference Minutes of 1803) to Lord Sidmouth, which by his Lordship's calling & writing to me I am sure has done good.

It is indeed our wisest way to prevent mischief to remove as much as possible all cause of complaint. In our zeal for lay preaching I fear we have not always been sufficiently on our guard against admitting improper persons as Local Preachers; & although we have been always ready to rejoice at any good done by any man, we have not I think paid suitable attention to the prejudices which have been created or strengthened against us by encouraging some persons to preach who have been altogether unsuitable. In consequence of the advantage taken by licensed teachers by claiming exemption from offices, though not I think among the Methodists, & of the obviously unfit persons who are continually applying for licenses, it certainly is intended to abridge this privilege, & we cannot wonder at it; but it will be a serious evil for magistrates to have discretional powers, or for testimonials to be required from ministers already licensed. This would be placing many in very unpleasant situations & eventually injure the cause of God, and although we know that the Lord will guard his Church, yet we also know that we must be co-workers with Him, and it is a question whether we have any more right to expect He will guard our privileges if we wantonly trifle with them, than we have a right to expect unconditional election without repentance or faith.

Our resolutions of 1803 have stood us in good stead, & I really think if the Conference were to adopt some prudent regulations respecting Local Preachers it would do much good, both politically & in our Societies. The Travelling Preachers are called out by the voice of the Church, expressed by the Quarterly Meetings, & I see no good reason why Local Preachers should not be called out in the same way – and some declaration of caution in admitting Preachers printed in the Minutes might meet & obviate objections that we might expect to be made against us in the next Session of Parliament. What think you of something like the following for Conference to adopt:

Q. What further regulations can be adopted to prevent improper persons from becoming preachers in the Connexion?

A. In addition to the rules already established by the Large Minutes of 1797* for admitting travelling Preachers on Trial, let no *local* Preacher in future be admitted into the regular Preachers plan till he has been proposed at one Quarterly Meeting & approved at the subsequent Quarterly Meeting of the Circuit in which he resides, nor be fully admitted as a local Preacher in general till approved at the District Meeting after one year's trial. His approval or testimonial to be signed by the Chairman of the District.

I think something of this kind would be good & wholesome in itself for the Connexion & such a measure would certainly gain us credit with Government, as I believe that Lord Sidmouth & many well meaning people think we bring religion into contempt by setting up as teachers very unsuitable persons. Such a resolution as the above would not prevent occasional exhortations from young men to try their gifts, but merely guard the regular local Preachers from improper colleagues.

In addition to the above a letter might be written in the Magazine giving a more decided opinion about legal restraints on preaching, which it would not be prudent for Conference to express lest it should be considered as hostility against Government; but an opinion is necessary, to give tone to the Dissenters, who are divided in sentiment on the subject in question.

I think it will be highly proper for the Conference to do as the Dissenters have done, return thanks to the Privy Council for their late liberal measures respecting toleration in the Colonies. I intend to sketch an address & send for your amendment in a post or two.

I am very glad to hear that the Conference have done so much honour to Mr. Taylor & to themselves by making him President. I hear he has travelled 50 years. If he intends now to sit down & the Conference cannot make suitable provision for an old servant according to the length and usefulness of his labours & it should be thought advisable to raise our venerable friend a little annuity, I dare say the Trustees of Hinde Street Chapel would give £10 for any money that might be advanced during the life of Mr. & Mrs. Taylor & perhaps 7/– for the life of his son Thomas. You can mention this privately to a few of the Preachers & if a Subscription be opened I would gladly give 10 guineas.

I consider the Methodist Body of growing importance to Great Britain & to the world at large. I hope the Conference will have wisdom & divine influence in all their measures & with all gravity, devotion & sobermindedness regulate their affairs.

---

* I have not the Minutes of 1797 by me and therefore only *suppose* the plan of admitting travelling Preachers is therein regulated.

¹ The Bishop of Exeter in 1809 was George Pelham (1766–1827), described in DNB as 'notorious for his greed of lucrative office'. The Charge referred to in this letter does not seem to have been published.

² Resolutions of 1803: Initiated by the London Circuit Quarterly Meeting and endorsed by the Conference, these were concerned with local preachers who claimed exemption from civil and military obligations under the Toleration Act. See Smith, *History* ii. 387–9.

Bible Christian Origins

William O'Bryan's separation from the Wesleyans, 1810

('Some Account of the Rise and Progress of the Missions belonging to the Arminian Bible Christians', 1818, prefaced to *The Rules of Society*, 1818 and reprinted in the *BC Magazine*, 1905, pp. 300–7)

I believe I am where God would have me to be, separate from my old friends. It seems there must be something severe to separate me from a people to whom I was strongly attached, and in whose doctrinal senti-ments I was fixed and riveted; having found the truth of them in my own experience. My creed was formed. I had found truth the fountain of living waters, and was constrained to cry to others, 'Come taste and see that the Lord is gracious.' And was further convinced that it was my duty to follow those who could not hear while I remained in one place. The Cross appearing formidable, for awhile I lingered. But it was like fire in my bones; I was weary of forbearing and could not stay, being convinced I must go at the command of God, or go to Hell. I yielded obedience, and went into the highways and hedges, seeking those of whom it might be said,

"No man cared their souls to save."

It was suggested to me, by one of the Travelling Preachers, that this was likely to lead to a separation from the Methodists, and persuaded me to offer myself to travel with them. I had not the least intention to form a separate Church, but had one only end in view – to do good. Neverthe-less, I attended to the arguments used and consented, being willing to do whatever was for the best, and offered myself accordingly, but was rejected at the Cornish District Meeting in June, 1810, on account of having a family, although I had offered to give security for the entire support of my children.

In about half-a-year before this, God had blessed my labours; so that in that short period I had established preaching in eight different parishes on the north coast of Cornwall, in most of which promising Societies were formed (if, through being compelled, I may become a fool in boasting), and God had greatly revived His work in some of the neighbouring Societies, which, I doubt not, is yet fresh in the minds of some who will read these lines.

This was known, and the Chairman of the District acknowledged that he believed that I was called to preach, yet persuaded me to return to business, which I could not do consistent with a good conscience, and resolved to proceed as I had done before.

The following autumn the Preachers in Bodmin Circuit changed. The Superintendent who now came into the Circuit wished me to confine myself to a Local Preachers' Plan; I informed him of my design, which I was convinced was my duty to do; namely, to go into the highways and hedges, as I had done before. But to my surprise when I came to the Quarterly Meeting following at Bodmin, where the new Plan for the Local Preachers was read over, my name was continued, to which I again objected in the presence of the people assembled, observing that if they were disappointed they should not blame me, not having consented to take the Plan, as I might on the Saturday be twenty miles from the Sunday's appointment, and very probably should have my own Missionary engagements to fulfil, that being the most eligible day for getting a congregation in new places. Finding me determined, the Superintendent threatened to shut their Chapel doors against me. To which I replied, 'I was not careful about that.' For before this I had made up my mind to obey God rather than man and take all consequences. Upon cool reflection, I am led to think, not all the men, nor all the fire and faggots on earth, could have moved me from my purpose.

At the same time, I had to plead on behalf of one of the Societies God had enabled me to gather, which was the first I had planted after I set off as a missionary, namely, Newquay, a little fishing town on the north coast of Cornwall. They were a very poor people, their living depending chiefly on the fishery, and this summer, no pilchards appearing on their coast, they were much distressed. This was increased by having built a house for preaching, and having incurred a debt, which they could not devise how to pay; the tradesmen's bills, &c., were due before the fishing season came on. To this season they had looked forward with joyful hope, but now that hope was cut off.

Under all these trying and struggling circumstances the Superintendent insisted on their paying quarterage, that is, so much each member quarterly. This appeared to me unreasonable and unjust for several reasons; and, as they were my charge, I pleaded in their behalf that it was more reasonable to send them a few pounds as a present to help them in their trying circumstances than to take money from them, especially as the circuit had a great increase of money through the additions, as before alluded to. I had not objected to any of the other Societies paying quarterage to the travelling preachers, although I had been the means of forming them at my own expense, and never received one farthing towards it. In this peculiar case I considered I had a right to plead for the people of Newquay an exemption; for if any person had a right to take quarterage from them it was me; but so far from doing which, I freely gave them my labours, and had actually gone begging for them among my friends and others, to get them some aid in discharging the debt incurred in building the house. Another reason against the tax was that it had not been taken into the travelling preachers' plan, and, of course, on that account they had not been at any expense in forming the Society; and it appeared unreasonable, as well as unjust, that I should be opposed in thus forming Societies, and even be threatened with having their chapel doors shut against me (which implies, being excluded from them as a preacher) for no other reason than for travelling into the highways and hedges to bring souls to God . . .

[In November 1810, O'Bryan found himself publicly excluded from membership.]

Public exclusion is the highest censure among the Methodists. They went their utmost length, and which is but seldom done, except for something more than an ordinary offence. But what had I done? There was no offence stated. I answered to the congregation immediately in the preacher's presence, alleging it was for nothing more than for taking the Bible for my rule, and Christ for my example, and gave him an opportunity before the congregation to accuse me of anything worse, which he did not attempt to do, but left the house to the people and me. This was done without calling me to a leaders' meeting, according to the Methodist rule, or so much as calling me to any other meeting to answer any charge.

I had been a member of the Methodist Society about twenty years, had spoken in public about nine years, and was excluded without having a charge of immorality brought against me. When I consented to take a plan, I made it a point of conscience to follow it or get it supplied, although some have taken the liberty to say to the contrary. What! had a professor of twenty years' standing no trial before he was excluded? A preacher of nine years' standing no trial before he was excluded? I know of none. If there was, I was not present. But what was I excluded for? For doing any harm? No, only for doing good. Trying to save poor souls out of the fire, to snatch them from the verge of hell, and vindicating the rights of the poor. None of the preachers ever attempted to assign any other reason (if you may call this a reason). If they ever assigned any other reason to me than this, let them declare what it was, when and where . . .

But let none think all the Preachers are alike, or all that are called Methodists are alike; no, they are not. I believe there are some of the wisest and some of the best people in the nation among the Methodists. Was there ever yet a pure Church on earth? Even when Christ was in person in the Church, there was a Judas; and can we expect it better now? It appears to have been my lot to meet with some of the worse just at this time. Someone may say, why did you not appeal to those who might have undertaken to do you justice? I answer, a friend of mine had stated something of my case to one, and I had written to another of the principal persons of the Conference, to which I received no answer. I resigned it in the hands of Him who judgeth righteously, and who is a Friend sticking closer than a brother; the Lord of Hosts is His Name.

WILLIAM O'BRYAN.

Launceston, August 12th, 1818.

The society at Lake Farm, Shebbear, 1815

('The Rise and Progress of the Connexion of People, called Arminian Bible Christians' by William O'Bryan, in *The Arminian Magazine*,[1] Vol. II No. 8, August, 1823, pp. 257–9)

At Cookbury [in North Devon] on the 5th [October], Brother James Thorne being there, gave me another invitation to come to Shebbear to preach. A young man of Shebbear had some months before heard me at Milton Damarel, and given me an invitation; but as they had a pious clergyman, I thought the people of Shebbear did not stand in need of preaching, so much as some other parishes that had unconverted and wicked parsons; and further, I told him it might displease their Minister, who might not understand my motive; and as I understood that he was one that feared God, I was not willing to give him any offence, &c. The young man, whose name was William Western, assured me that their Minister was a good man, and would not be displeased at my coming into the parish to preach. Other engagements occupying my time, I did not go. In August, Brothers John and James Thorne, came to Cookbury, and gave me an invitation also; and then I was engaged for some weeks forward and could not conveniently go. I appointed with Brother James Thorne to preach at his father's house at Lake, in Shebbear, on Monday the 9th [October] . . .

That evening [Sunday, October 8th], Brother John Thorne came to Langtree, and took me to Lake with him that night. When I came there, I found a well disposed hospitable family, with whom I felt much union of spirit. Notice had been given for preaching there at six o'clock the Monday evening. Such a spirit of hearing was excited, that some came about five, and by six o'clock, both kitchen and parlour were well filled with attentive hearers, who seemed to hear for eternity. After preaching I desired those who were seriously inclined, to stay a little longer. I intended to form a class, having been desired so to do by the family; but finding nearly all the congregation like people pinned to the floor, I began again, and gave an exhortation, and again concluded. The people still appeared unwilling to go, and I was afraid they were not all convinced of sin, consequently not fit to join in class, so I went down in the kitchen. They followed me, and I was again pressed by the family to join a class that night. Finding the people were nearly all gone, I returned to the parlour: about thirty followed me. I sung a verse and stated to them the nature of class-meetings, and proposed forming a class. I then met those who gave me their names, which, were *twenty-two* in number. Two more gave me their names the next morning.

So here at Lake, a class of twenty-four was formed the first time of my going there. I have since thought, that if I had proceeded, nearly all the congregation would have given in their names to join society at that time. How well to steer between the two extremes, of over-cautious prudence, and incautious zeal. One thing must not pass unnoticed. A clergyman had a few years before come to take charge of the parish, from the neighbourhood of Padstow, in Cornwall, whose name was [Daniel] Evans. For some years he had been enlightened; and his word had been attended with a blessing to many, in turning them from their former errors, though but few of them had experienced the forgiveness of their sins. By this means the people were prepared for the reception of a *present*, *free*, and *full* salvation, which many of them discovering to be their privilege, soon realised in their own experience. What a blessing a spiritual clergyman may be to his parish!

[1] This was the earliest title under which the *Bible Christian Magazine* was published; not to be confused with its Wesleyan predecessor.

Religious Liberties

The 'Sidmouth Bill' of 1811

(George Pellew, *Life of Sidmouth*, 1847, III, 40–7)

Lord Sidmouth's attempt to tighten the licensing controls on nonconformist preachers was an establishment response to the spread of itinerant preaching both in Methodism and on the fringes of the older dissent. Resistance to it as an attack on religious liberty showed how far the Wesleyans, even when making common cause with the dissenting camp, still stood aloof from it.

Coke at first pinned his hopes on co-operation with the government, but later came to suspect the motives of both Sidmouth and Wilberforce.

Shute Barrington, Bishop of Durham, to Lord Sidmouth, 11 July 1809:

The framers [of the Toleration Act of 1689] conceived that the religious duties of the respective congregations would never be performed but in

places exclusively appropriated to divine service, and by ministers qualified by education, by attested respectability in point of morals, and of a
proper age to add weight to their prayers and impression to their instructions. So long as the Toleration Act was thus understood, dissenting
teachers were respected by their own people, and esteemed by the
Establishment; but with modern sectaries the case is very different. They
assemble in barns, in rooms of private houses, or in other buildings of
the most improper kind, to hear the wild effusions of a mechanic or a
ploughboy, perhaps not more than 15 years of age, destitute of the first
rudiments of learning, sacred or profane.

Thomas Coke to Lord Sidmouth, 23 April 1811:

I recommend to your Lordship John Wilson Esq, Islington, as the most
proper person to give your Lordship information in respect to the
society and congregations in London late in connexion with Mr. George
Whit[e]field . . .

    I have been maturely considering the nature of the probationary
licenses which your Lordship spoke of when I had the honour of an
interview with you. The plan of a year's probation would be quite sufficient for the Dissenters, as they have academies for the previous instruction of those who are to be called to the ministry. But we have no such
academies . . . As we believe that the Unitarian sentiments and doctrines
were introduced among the Dissenters by their means, and as we have
no regular confession of faith (the thirty-nine Articles of the Established
Church excepted), we should be in greater danger of fatal errors than the
Dissenters if we had academies like them. Our local preachers, therefore,
begin to exercise their talents at a low state of improvement, so that it is
highly expedient that their probationary license should be for *two* years.
This would do perfectly well, and a less time than this would do considerable injury to Mr. Wesley's connexion; whilst, on the other hand,
it would be of little consequence to the Dissenters whether it were one
year or two: and I am confident, my Lord, from the love of religion and
morality which you discovered when I was indulged with an interview,
that you will lengthen out the probation to two years, if you view the
subject as I do.

Thomas Allan, solicitor to the Wesleyan Committee of Privileges, to the
Rt. Hon. Spencer Perceval, 15 February 1812

(British Library, Manuscript Department: Add Mss 38,248 ff. 27–8)

Although Sidmouth's bill had been dropped, the interpretation of the 1689
Toleration Act by local magistrates was giving cause for concern. The

following letter initiated a dialogue between the Wesleyans and the Prime Minister which continued until the eve of Perceval's assassination and was successfully taken up with his successor, the Earl of Liverpool.

Sir,

I am directed by the General Committee of the Societies founded by the late Rev. John Wesley commonly called Methodists, to address you respecting the situation in which those Societies are now placed as a religious Body, by the construction which the Act of Toleration has lately received, and by an appearance of the revival of the obsolete Penal Laws on the subject of Religion.

The Methodist Societies have now existed for nearly 80 years, during which time they have enjoyed the happiness of a free toleration in matters of Religion; & they have worshipped God agreeably to the dictates of their consciences.

They imagined that this sacred right was secured to them by the liberal laws and enlightened policy of this free country; at least this right has not, 'till now, been disputed from the rise of their societies; nor at periods when their character was not known, & when they had to combat the prejudices of Mankind. Under a general interpretation of the Law which secured those inestimable privileges, the Societies have flourished; & their beneficial operation has been felt through the various classes of the community. Places of Worship were necessary, and under the most implicit confidence that the Laws as well as the disposition of the Government would give security to their religious rights, the Societies have expended an immense sum of money in the erection of Chapels in different parts of the United Kingdom. But the Societies are suddenly placed in a state of complete insecurity, and are exceedingly alarmed not only by the new interpretation of the Law at the different Quarter Sessions held after last Christmas and the late determinations of the Court of King's Bench; but from strong indications of a revival of the old penal Statutes. Indeed, if the Law were to remain as it is now construed to be, the Enforcing of the Penalties of the Conventicle & other antiquated acts of a similar nature, would deprive thousands of His Majesty's loyal Subjects of their property and their personal liberty.

[The letter concludes with a request that Perceval receive a Wesleyan deputation.]

Village Methodism: An Anglican View

(John Skinner's Journal, mss. in British Library; published as *Journal of a Somerset Rector, 1803–1834* (1971), pp. 66–7, 92–4)

Skinner was rector of Camerton, near Radstock.

Memoranda respecting a conversation with a Methodist, called Green, living in one of the cottages at Bridge Place,

July 18 [*1811*]

Whilst walking my usual round in the village Sunday evening in order to see things were going on quietly I saw this Green, who is a very staunch Methodist, standing at his door reading a book out loud as I passed by. I stopped for a moment to hear the subject on which he was haranguing in this public manner. When he saw I stopped he said he was looking over a book of instruction for young people to see whether it had a catechism in it, as he wished to find it there. I said I was very glad to hear him say so, as I thought it was proper that all young people of the school lately instituted at the Meeting House should be instructed in the Catechism, as it was the ground work of religion, and that John Wesley himself, the founder of Methodism, always recommended it to his followers. He replied, to be sure John Wesley had recommended many good things, but there were other things of much importance to be attended to besides what he had mentioned. I said, from what dropped from him, I must then suppose alterations had taken place in the doctrines of the Methodists since John Wesley's time. Certainly, he said, there were some alterations. I said I also had observed them myself. John Wesley recommended his followers to go to Church, and receive the Sacrament at stated periods; both these injunctions were rarely complied with at present, and I did not know how any number of persons professing to be the disciples of Christ could neglect so important a command and abstain from the Communion. He said he did not himself abstain from it, and had received it in my Church. The conversation then took quite a spiritual turn, when he strongly insisted on the efficacy of the Spirit in working immediate conviction and enabling men to preach the gospel although they had originally no idea of being called to the ministry. Knowing that this man himself had set up for a *pray-er*, though he had not arrived at the honour of a *preacher*, I told him that many who set up for teachers, even in this country, could not speak their own language, much less that of another country. Then he said, 'I suppose you will deny there is such a thing as the gift of repentance,' indeed, he continued, in a sarcastic manner, 'I can easily suppose you know but little about this gift.' Not heeding his insolence (for he began to be nettled when he became entangled in the argument,) I continued, 'religion is not that easy thing you think it to be. When you have committed a fault you must be sorry for it. God will give his assistance that the grace of repentance may grow and increase if it be your wish and you fervently pray for it, but the labour and efforts must be your own.' He concluded by telling me I was myself quite blind as to repentance, and was sure I knew not what it was. Finding he began to be insolent, I thought I had better leave him before he said anything to irritate my feelings. Accordingly I quitted him, after an hour's conversation.

Memorandum of a conversation with Hill and Bush, two colliers, now chief instructors of the Methodists at Camerton.

February 16 [1816]

On going down to the village to visit Mrs. Hillman who was lying ill, Joseph Goold's wife spoke to me and asked whether I had heard of the extraordinary meeting of the Methodists which took place last night at Lewis's house. She said that she understood that it was one of the most extraordinary that had occurred, since they were all crying and bewailing their sins, and continued in that state until 11 o'clock at night. I replied that I was sorry to hear that they had suffered their feelings to be worked upon in such a manner by the ignorant and designing; that it would be much better for them to come to Church to convince their reason and understanding, instead of suffering themselves to be misled by the heats of a disordered imagination. On leaving her, as I returned towards the Parsonage, I saw Bush and Hill going into the cottage of Hall, who lives about 100 yards from my house. Supposing what might be the object of their visit I also went and asked Mrs. Hall who with her two daughters was listening to them (the latter of whom I had taken some pains to instruct at the Sunday School), whether they were about to be converted to Methodism. Hill replied that they wished not only to convert them but everyone in the parish of Camerton, which they trusted in Christ they should do ere long. Bush then declared with great vehemence that Christ had begun the work, and could not leave it unfinished. I told them that it would be much better for such ignorant and uninformed persons as they were to attend to their own business as colliers and leave me to direct the souls of my parishioners which were committed to my charge; that it was my business and office to do so, and that they had no place or pretence to take that office from my hands. They both at once declared that Christ had sent them to perform His work, and that they would do it in spite of all opposition, and that their object in coming to Mrs. Hall was to pray; that with regard to the conversion I alluded to that it was their duty to save the souls of as many poor wretches as they could, for unless they were born again it was impossible they could enter into the Kingdom of Heaven, that our Saviour Himself had said so, and if I contradicted that I contradicted Scripture. I replied that that text, like so many others, had been wrested from its true meaning and import, which shewed the necessity there was for a well-educated instructor to explain the proper meaning of the Scriptures; that those who took on themselves to instruct others, without being instructed themselves, incurred a great share of responsibility, since they not only continued in ignorance themselves but prevented many of their companions from learning their duty; that our Saviour had declared that it were better for a millstone to be tied around their necks and that they should be thrown into the sea than to offend or otherwise mislead the weak. They then broke out in the most violent way, saying that I with all my learning had never converted one since I had been in the parish, and that instead of being able to assist others by my doctrines I was in the greatest need of divine assistance myself; that if I had only been with them yesterday I might have shed tears too and been pricked to the heart and perhaps converted also, so powerfully did Christ work amongst them. I said that if I shed tears it would have been to have seen so many deluded by presumptuous imposters; that as there were two meeting houses licensed in my parish they had no right to assemble in this manner in private houses, that it was my duty to prevent it, and they might depend on my making a proper representation to the magistrates on the subject. They replied that they knew I had no power to prevent them meeting at each other's houses, and Hill said as he paid rent for his house he had a right to call in as many neighbours as he chose to pray with, and would do it in spite of *any* magistrate; that the magistrates, if they were only reasonable men, would approve of what they did for the conversion of souls; but even if they should oppose it, as I did oppose it, they did not care, they must attend to God rather than man and would continue to do so. Bush continued, if they did not pray in their houses they might in the fields, and that there would be plenty to follow them there; that the work of God was now begun, and would not be hindered by any opposition; that lately at Bristol 500 were added to their Church, and that ere long Methodism would be universal. I asked him what he meant by *their Church*. He said any congregation of the faithful, that it was not a building of stones like that out there (pointing to Camerton Church, for he was then standing in Hall's garden,) but any place wherein the word of God was properly taught and expounded. This was the substance of the conversation which passed between us but a great deal more was said in direct terms relative to the success of their cause and the depression of the Church. Having again in a serious and solemn manner warned them not to persevere in their meetings at private houses, as being contrary to the law, and having again heard their defiance as to my inability to prevent them, I returned home ...

Memorandum. Hill, when I was remonstrating with him on his presumption, made quotation from Acts viii, 23 where St. Paul reproves Simon

Magus. The very same quotation was employed on a similar occasion some time ago by another Methodist of the name of Green when I was endeavouring to convince him of his errors. Quare, do they suppose that they are in the light of the Apostles, gifted with the Spirit, and we, the clergy, like Simon Magus, wish to purchase it for money?

A Dissenting View of Wesleyanism

(David Bogue and James Bennett, *A History of the Dissenters*, Vol. IV, 1812, pp. 337–8, 391–2)

The authors represent the new evangelical spirit among the Dissenters.

Against the Wesleyan methodists a charge of want of zeal for the increase of their body will not readily be adduced, or if adduced, be credited. Next to the regular dissenters, they constitute the most considerable portion of those who have separated from the established church. Their separation some of them have stoutly denied. But can those who have different places of worship, different ministers dispensing all the ordinances of religion, and different rules of discipline; who acknowledge no jurisdiction of the ecclesiastical rulers; who allow no interference of the state with their proceedings; who would scorn the thought of the clergyman of the parish exercising any authority over them, – with the slightest shadow either of propriety or truth call themselves members of the established church? This sect was happy in a leader who possessed the skill of governing a religious body, beyond any protestant in modern times; and his long life enabled him to nurture it to maturity and strength. Whatever effects his death produced, it did not lessen the ardour of their zeal, nor prevent their increase; for they have continued to multiply with accelerating rapidity to the present time . . .

The Wesleyan methodists have not suffered by the death of their founder, but have perhaps increased in religious excellence as well as in numbers and in influence during the latter part of this period. They have among them able men who aim at the noblest objects, and see their recompence in a number of pious people who are the salt of the communion. Though much deduction be allowed for the sectarian zeal which prevails among them, great praise is still due to their persevering efforts to call sinners to repentance. But the want of competent knowledge in the great body of their preachers, has nourished error and enthusiasm among the people, and too fully justified the heavy censure which has been passed upon this communion, as containing a greater sum of ignorance of the Scriptures than was ever found in any body of protestants since the reformation.

Financial Constraints

The connexion's extended resources were put under further pressure by the post-war recession. For Jonathan Crowther's assessment of a worsening situation, see pp. 352–5 below.

Joseph Entwisle to George Marsden; Bristol, June 19, 1813

(Ms at Drew University)

I understand one District recommends to the Conference to take out no more Preachers, but to fill up the vacancies by reducing the numbers in some of the Circuits. There seems to exist a *general alarm as though the ship were sinking.* And indeed, if we don't work hard at the pumps, she will sink. The building of Chapels injudiciously has hurt us. I find, *even in London,* they are embarrassed by the debts & rents of chapels recently built or rented, though some of them answer well.

William Myles to Robert Blunt; Southwark, November 1, 1813

(Ms at MA)

Myles was answering a letter appealing for financial support for the newly formed Frome circuit, where he himself had been stationed before coming to London.

Our congregations on the Lord's Day are very great in all our Chapels since the late Conference. We have just collected £200 for the Kingswood and Woodhouse Grove Schools in our Circuit, this is £30 more than last year.

We have five travelling Preachers on our Circuit this year, but we were between two and three hundred pounds in debt when we were last year but four. You naturally enquire why did we get another additional family? The answer is, we increased the number of our Chapels. And the Congregations will not hear Local Preachers. We have in our Circuit ten Chapels in the City and two little ones in the country. The people of London for many years had too few Chapels, but now they have too many, more than they can comfortably support.

When I was here ten years ago, we had but three principal Chapels and five Preachers, where we now have fifteen Preachers and upwards of twenty Chapels that have travelling Preachers very nearly every Sunday.

Every principal member is satisfied we have gone too far, and we are greatly burthen'd with debt.

[He then reports various pieces of missionary news, especially Coke's preparations for his mission to Asia, and concludes:]

My own opinion is, we must lessen our sails: we cannot support the work we are engag'd in. The Trustees of several Chapels are greatly distress'd. Even in Chelsea, the Chapel does not bring in as much as pays the Interest without anything for the support of the Preachers.

William Myles to Joseph Dutton; Southwark, June 3, 1814

(Ms at MA)

Dutton was a Liverpool merchant.

I received your circular letter in January last. I am much obliged to you for it. I am sure you love the Methodists, and rejoice in their prosperity ... This being premised, I must beg leave to tell you my opinion of your plan. 1. If it was practicable which I very much doubt, it would not answer the end proposed: For if we were out of debt tomorrow, we should be involved in debt again, before twelve months: while the present rage for building Chapels, and purchasing meeting-houses continue. The getting chapels necessarily calls for Travelling Preachers, this as necessarily leads to marriage, and marriages multiply families and expences, so that if the Methodists subscribed sixpence per week and Chapels multiplied as they have been for these last ten years, we should be as much involved as ever.

I had the happiness of an acquaintance with Mr. Wesley. He told me he considered himself as 'bound for every Chapel in the connection that he consented should be built, also for the support of every family of the travelling Preachers; this, said he, makes me cautious; and should make me cautious what Chapels I consent should be built and to what Preachers I give leave to marry.' These being his views, you may see, there never were more than one third of the Preachers married while he lived. And he would not let a Chapel be built unless two thirds of the money was subscribed before a stone was laid, and it stated whether it would call for an additional Preacher. Now, near three fourths of the Preachers are married, and Chapels are built, or purchased without, in some cases, one fifth of the money subscribed, and immediately a travelling Preacher called out, as it is said, 'We shall never let the seats if we only have Local Preachers to supply them.' This is the real cause of our embarrassment and of the uneasiness in our Societies.

The influence and interest which travelling and local Preachers, and poor people, find in the erection of new Chapels, or purchase of Chapels, always cause a majority to vote at the Quarterly Meetings for such things whenever they are proposed. Then the Trustees and Lessees are left to struggle with their burdens; and the majority that voted for these things are as free as air . . .

I think that no poor person should vote for the erection of a Chapel . . .

Jabez Bunting to Isaac Clayton; Leeds, July 14, 1815

(Ms at Garrett Evangelical Seminary)

Clayton was junior minister in the Skipton circuit.

I am sorry to find that six months have elapsed, without my having answered your friendly letter. The truth is, I have been so variously occupied this year by urgent engagements, as to be under the necessity of almost entirely relinquishing the attempt to maintain any epistolatory intercourse with distant friends.

To your plan for relieving our finances by paying off or materially reducing our Chapel Debts, I feel some objections:

1. I do not think it desirable, that any *large* or *considerable* portion of the Supplies necessary for the maintenance of our Ministry should come from the Chapels. This I know is the Dissenting Plan. But the longer I live, the less I am disposed to assimilate our system to theirs. Our plan is to support our Ministry by the voluntary subscriptions of our *Societies*. This I think is almost infinitely preferable; and if the Chapels have a surplus, let it be employed in assisting other Chapels, in building new ones, in providing & furnishing *houses* for Preachers, and in defraying the *occasional* & *extraordinary* expences which will sometimes occur in all Circuits.

2. If the object were good & eligible, I must question the efficacy of your means. Very few Chapels can spare much of their income for deposits in a Sinking Fund. The deposits would usually be so small as to prevent our hoping for any speedy relief from them. And in many cases we can have no security that the Chapels, if got out of debt, will apply their surplus in aid of the general work.

Perhaps, however, I do not fully understand your Plan. In that case, if I have the pleasure of seeing you at the Conference, you can correct my mis-apprehensions of it . . .

The First District Missionary Society

(Report of the Principal Speeches delivered at the Formation of the Methodist Missionary Society for the Leeds District, October 6th 1813, pp. 8–10, 18–20, 25–6)

Growing demands on the Mission Fund, coupled with Coke's impending departure for the East, led to this initiative in the Leeds District, which was quickly followed elsewhere. A series of formal resolutions were the occasion for extensive speech-making.

The Rev. James Wood [moving the 1st Resolution giving 'hearty approval' to the missions already established]:

Such has lately been the embarrassed state of our Mission-Fund, that we could not comply with the wishes of many friends. It was truly distressing at our last Conference to find that a large number of accredited young men – well recommended for their piety and abilities, who were willing to sacrifice all their prospects of acquiring wealth, to leave their friends and connexions, to encounter the perils of the ocean, and the danger of disease from climate – could not be employed, because we could not find means for their maintenance. We have men, but we have not money to send them into Missionary ground. This want must have resulted from a want of its publicity. Our members of society, and others, our numerous valuable friends and well-wishers, are able and willing to help, when they are fully informed of our necessities.

For several years past, the exertions of the Methodists have far exceeded their pecuniary ability. Our annual expenditure has been about £6,000: but our income from Collections, inclusive of the fruit of Dr. Coke's diligence and zeal, has seldom been much more than £4,000. Hence we were deficient, at our last Conference but one, about £6,000: but, by an extra Collection, and the very great application of our highly-esteemed friend, Dr. Coke, this debt is nearly liquidated.

As the Doctor is about to leave England, his aid, in begging for the Methodist Missions, will be lost to us: while an additional burden will be brought upon us by the expences of equipment and support for six or seven Missionaries, who are going out with him, to preach the word of life in the East Indies. We are therefore brought to this alternative, – either to withdraw our Missionaries, and give up the souls whom they have been instrumental in saving, or to augment our income.

With a view to the latter, this Meeting has been called, that our dear friends might know our wants, and feel an interest in the cause in which we are embarked. A plan of this kind was devised, about six months ago; an 'Address' was written, and the outlines of some Rules were drawn up. But things did not then appear ripe for its adoption. However, I am now happy to see such a prospect of a Society being formed in this District; and hope the example will be followed in every District throughout the kingdom.

The Rev. George Morley [moving the 3rd Resolution, that 'the Society be denominated "The Methodist Missionary Society for the Leeds District" ']:

Never, perhaps, Sir, in this land, if in any other, were exertions made, in support of Missions, equal to those at present making. The sacred flame warms the hearts of religious professors among all denominations. All are striving to advance the interests of the Messiah's kingdom, not in the bitter jealousy of party-spirit as formerly, much less in opposition to each other; but, in the spirit of Christian benevolence, each, praying for the success of others, and rejoicing in it, endeavours to excel in love and good works. But while we are favoured with a goodly portion of this Christian liberality, we feel a peculiar degree of interest in the Methodist Missions. And such feelings are natural to us; for these Missions are our own. The doctrines propagated by them, and the discipline which they have established in foreign lands, exactly coincide with our own views and practices. We know the men who are employed as Missionaries. They are children of our venerable father in the Gospel; and, we may say, they were born in our house, nourished at our table, educated in our school; and, though now separated from us by the wide Atlantic, or other intervening seas, they are still our brethren. We know their motives. Many of us have heard them declare their conversion to God, their call to the ministry, and their reasons for devoting themselves to Missionary labours. We have no cause to doubt that the love of Christ has constrained them to expose themselves to the piercing colds of Newfoundland, or to the burning sun of the torrid zone, in seeking the salvation of their fellow-creatures.

We, Sir, are not now assembled to institute a new Mission, to select suitable men for the work, to inquire where they shall make their first attacks on the dominion of sin and error, or to present our first prayers to heaven for their success. No: the Mission is established, the men are appointed, Providence has marked out their way, and grace has already crowned their labours with great success . . .

Having thus ventured on the experiment, seen it succeed, and appreciated its advantages, we have the strongest reasons for giving these Missions our zealous support, and for providing the means of extending them, if possible, to other countries.

When, at the last Conference, the subject of Missions was brought forward, and proposals were made for extending them to the East; though all joined in the common wish for sending Christianity to those countries, many were discouraged, and some absolutely terrified, from making the attempt at this time, on account of the exhausted state of the funds. But it was at last agreed to diminish the number of Preachers at home, in order that we might be enabled, by our frugal savings, to maintain a greater number of Missionaries in foreign countries. That was an anxious, painful, and important hour. It was then that I resolved, on returning to my Circuit, to propose some extraordinary efforts for the continuance, on their present scale, of our important Missions, and for their yet further extension. On mentioning the subject to the brethren, my colleagues in the ministry, though they felt the difficulties in our way, they were hearty in the cause, and willing to give it all their aid. I spoke of it also to some respectable individuals in Leeds, and in the Circuit around; and not an objection was raised, but all were willing to assist. We took measures for forming the Society for this Circuit. Our views soon extended to Bramley; but further than Bramley we never thought of going, till we invited the Wakefield Preachers to assist in the services of this day; when they kindly offered, not only to attend and assist, but to join us in our good design. This morning, on the earnest recommendation of many respectable Preachers and friends from other Circuits, it has been agreed to form the Society for as many Circuits in this District, as shall choose to enrol themselves with us in this Association.

Mr. John Wood, of Wakefield [moving the 6th Resolution, appointing a General Committee]:

We are met together this day under peculiar circumstances; for, on the one hand, we have to regret the loss of the labours (in this country) of our venerable friend, Dr. Coke, in behalf of the Missions; while, on the other, we have to congratulate the cause on the transfer of his services to a part of the world which has excited a more than ordinary interest in our minds. I have waited, with some degree of impatience, in the hope of hearing some one, more competent than myself, do justice to the merit and services of that valuable Minister of Christ. Few men, indeed, deserve more of the respect of Christians than he; because there are few who have endured greater hardships, or made greater sacrifices, in the cause of Christianity. We consider him, in conjunction with Mr. Wesley, as the founder of our very important Missions; and to his activity, in a great measure, attended by the Divine blessing, may be attributed their present flourishing state and success. Regardless of his own ease, he has cheerfully relinquished the congenial comforts of his country and climate, that he might preach the Gospel to the Heathen, on the continent of America and in the West-India Islands. There he has been the honoured instrument of forming many churches for God; and has cultivated that barren wilderness, which is now fertilized and fruitful as the garden of the Lord. At a period of life, when most men are anxious to retire from the busy scenes of the world, to enjoy in private the fruit of their labours, he has devised for himself new plans of usefulness, which will inevitably require more painful sacrifices, and oblige him to sustain yet severer toils . . .

Deprived as we are, Sir, of the benefits of his services, some permanent plan must be adopted to supply the defect. For, notwithstanding all that has been done towards the great work of evangelizing the world, much still remains to engage the benevolent attention of Christians. Whichever quarter of the globe we survey, we see in it the necessity of continuing, and even increasing, our exertions.

Glimpses of Circuit Life

Joseph Taylor to Richard Rodda; Derby, October 28, 1814

(Ms at Drew University)

Taylor was President of the Conference in 1802.

I was only one year in Dudley, for they keep no horse, the walks are considerable, and the dirt in winter can hardly be described. I am now removed to my old friends at Derby;[1] only about 4 miles from the place where I first drew my breath . . . We are only two Preachers, and one horse, and are 2 weeks in and 2 weeks out.[2] In the time we are in we walk to 5 places in the country, the most distant of which is about 4 miles. I have great cause to thank the Lord, that although I am not without infirmities, I am able to do my work. I am in the 62nd year of my age, and in the 38th year of my itinerant labours! And perhaps the Lord may prop me up 2 years more to make it 40. My times are in his hand, let him do what he will with his own.

[1] Taylor had been stationed in the Derby circuit once before, from 1790 to 1792.

[2] I.e., each preacher spent half his time in the circuit town and the other half travelling round the circuit.

John Barber to Adam Clarke; Bristol, December 21, 1814

(Ms at Drew University)

I find our people in the city in general very friendly, and some of them much devoted to God; but here as in some other places we suffer from want of good Leaders.

We have lately been obliged to put one out of his office and out of the Society also for extreme bad conduct.

Our congregations in the towns are very large, particularly at King Street and Guinea Street, where I understand many go away on the Sabbath evening for want of room. Two additional chapels would do well if we could get them, but we want men of public spirit; and our chapels that have been erected of late have cost so much that the people are frightened at the idea of building.

Jonathan Crowther to Timothy Crowther; Wednesbury, December 14, 1815

(Ms at Garrett-Evangelical Seminary)

Our house is the best, and the best furnished, we have ever gone to. We have five good beds, all feathers, and the worst is better than the best at Stockport. If you were near, we would invite you and Sister to come and spend a while with us; for we have a bed & room to spare, and two parlours, with carpets on the floors. We have also a good and genteel garden . . .

We have ten chapels in the circuit. But four or five of them have the heaviest debts upon them of any I ever knew & with such small incomes. To relieve them, we have a public collection in each chapel once every month: and as most of these are on my days, I beg almost every Sunday for the relief of Trustees. But habit makes almost anything easy. We keep no horse; have a good deal of [walking?]; and preach about seven times a week, upon the average thrice every Sunday and four nights in the week. But I make no complaints; and I am so far from being worn down, that my health and flesh improve. Probably one reason is that ever since I came hither, I have enjoyed undisturbed peace and quietness. To be sure, this was not the most likely circuit in which to find tranquillity; but as I have sometimes said before, every circuit is to us just what God pleases to make it. I found the circuit in a shattered, divided and disheartening state, having been going worse and worse for several years. Our first Quarterly Meeting was expected to be a very boisterous one, from the party spirit which was expected to be displayed. But God helping me, I was enabled so to manage them, that all the difficulties were got well over, and they departed declaring that it was the best Quarterly Meeting they had had for some years. Since then it has appeared as if the Demon of Discord had fled out of the circuit. Peace and harmony seem to be returning, and several of our principal congregations are improved. This is the more remarkable, as both my colleagues were here last year and I am the only substitute for two who removed at the Conference[3] . . .

I have lately feared that Methodism has seen its zenith, and is displaying symptoms indicative of a decline. I write in confidence. I think that the affairs of the connexion are gotten chiefly into hands incapable of managing them to the good and improvement of the body. I think our being on the verge of bankruptcy, without any prospect of relief, the whole feeling of the last Conference, and other circumstances furnish reasons for fearing this.[4]

[3] Crowther had replaced John Ogilvie and John Hodson. His junior colleagues were William Rennison and John Thompson.

[4] See further pp. 352–5 below.

The Mission to Ceylon

Sir Alexander Johnstone to his mother, the Hon. H. M. Johnstone

(Notebook of Joseph Entwisle in MA; endorsed: 'A true Copy. J. Entwisle')

The death of Dr. Coke at sea in May 1814 left his party of young missionaries leaderless. But both in Bombay and in Ceylon, where Johnstone was Chief Justice, they met with encouragement and support.

Jaffna, 20th June 1815
Received by the Brigg Sphynx, Nov. 11, 1815

I request that you will have the goodness to mention to Mr. Wilberforce, Mr. Butterworth &c. that the Wesleyan Missionaries whom Mr. Stephens & they recommended to me, and who came out under the late Dr. Coke, are getting on wonderfully well: they have, besides making a great many Converts, among whom are some Budha priests, established Sunday Schools, and command the highest respect possible from the great decorum of their conduct. Will you tell Mr. B—— also that I have just given 500 Rix Dollars to help them build a church at Colombo and erecting their Press, & establishing a permanent building for the Mission. Many have followed my example, & they will soon accomplish their object.

I see Dr. Clarke is the President of their Society this year. Will you mention to him, through Mr. Butterworth, in case he does not receive a letter which I have written to him, that he must determine upon some plan of sending out at least 40 or 50 Wesleyan Missionaries to this Island. Government will be able to save the Society much of the expence of paying for their outfit, & giving them their passages free in the King's Transports.

Tell Mr. Butterworth, that their discipline & zeal point them out as the *only* class of Missionaries which can succeed here. Now that their character is established in this Island, advantage ought to be taken of the respect which the people entertain for them – and *numbers* ought to be sent out to carry their object into immediate effect.

Revival in Cornwall

George Russell to Isaac Clayton; Helston, July 7, 1815

(Ms at MA; printed in *Journal* of CMHA, 1963, pp. 163–4, 175–6)

You wish me to give some account of the revival in these parts. This I will endeavour to do. The revival began last year in the chapel at Redruth where the doors were scarcely closed for eight successive days. It spread with amazing rapidity through the Redruth circuit and their number soon increased from 1,980 to 4,000. About the same time the revival began at Laddock and spread rapidly through their circuit also. The increase was from 2,000 to 3,200 and nearly 1,000 of the increase was made within the last quarter before I came hither.

When I entered on this circuit it was never the expectation that I should soon have to labour on backsliding ground, an expectation which I have sufficiently realised. A large proportion of the new converts consisted of young people. Very many of the leaders were men of but little experience. The dwellings of the people are widely scattered and but very few of the members could be seen by their leaders unless they continued to come to their meetings. These and other considerations connected with the suddenness, and in many cases shallowness of the work accounts for the loss we have suffered which amounts to about 200.

Notwithstanding some disorder and extravagance which appeared during the height of the work, there was none of that *Ranterism* and *false fire* which have followed the revivals in Yorkshire, Nottinghamshire, Lancashire, Derbyshire &c. This is a characteristic of the Cornish revival which in my opinion speaks loudly in its favour. I know not of one individual who is disposed to speak of a Preacher as a 'Dead Stick', 'a dead soul' &c.

From this account you may be ready to infer that I am attached to these parts, but I cannot say so. I cannot avoid the idea that the Cornish Methodists, though generally as pious as others elsewhere, are less social, friendly and affectionate, than any I have met before. I am told

this circuit is the worst in the district in respect of religion and attachment to Preachers. I have not one to whom I am warmly united but there
is one or two whom I would soon send to heaven if I could.

Finally, though our labour is so great as to justify me in calling it
drudgery; though not a few of the Cornish Methodists are filling their
heads with foolish notions about Conference corruptions – the great
danger of settling chapels on the Methodist Plan &c, and though with
all their religion they cannot think of paying so much for heaven as
Methodists do generally; yet our having to preach to full congregations,
our having large and numerous societies, our covering the county from
sea to sea are circumstances which operate powerfully against the dis-
agreeables I have noticed.

I and my colleagues have gone on well together. Mr. Sibly is an excellent disciplinarian, a good preacher, and agreeable companion, and well
read. Our greatest Thunderer in the District is Charles Haime at Redruth,
our most popular and warm William Martin . . .

The State of the Connexion: A More Optimistic View

Joshua Marsden to Francis Hall, Commercial Advertiser, 41 John Street,
New York City

(Mss at Garrett Evangelical Seminary)

Plymouth Dock, October 3, 1815
[After giving the latest membership figures for British Methodism] Thus
you see, my dear brother, that Providence still smiles upon our Connection. You would be astonished at the number and beauty of our Chapels,
they exceed in simplicity and elegance anything I ever saw. But while I
am detailing the beauty of the outward court, I must not omit to mention
that we have a great deal of piety, vital piety among our people. In this
place we have a prayer meeting in the Chapel every morning at 5 o'clock
and the men go from the Chapel into the dockyard to work.

May 3, 1816
Things are dull in England, I mean trade, as 25 years warfare has made
the transit to a state of peace a difficult and trying affair . . . In England,
trade is dull and thousands who are out of work would be glad to get to
America if they could. Such vast numbers being discharged from the
Army and Navy have caused labour to sink to a low ebb, so that the

farmers around this place only give from seven to nine shillings per week, without meat or anything else . . .

With regard to the state of our own affairs, I send you the Minutes of our last Conference. Things are much in the same state, only we have had several great revivals in Cornwall, Leeds, Bristol, Salisbury, Plymouth &c &c &c. We are still sending missionaries to foreign lands. Thus you see the work of God is deepening and widening through all the earth.

William Hazlitt, 'On the Causes of Methodism'

(*The Examiner*, October 22, 1815, pp. 684–5)

Hazlitt describes David as 'the first Methodist on record' because 'he made a regular compromise between religion and morality, between faith and goods works'.

The principle of Methodism is nearly allied to hypocrisy, and almost unavoidably slides into it: yet it is not the same thing; for we can hardly call anyone a hypocrite, however much at variance his professions and his actions, who really wishes to be what he would be thought . . .

The same reason makes a man a religious enthusiast that makes a man an enthusiast in any other way, an uncomfortable mind in an uncomfortable body . . . If you live near a chapel or tabernacle in London, you may almost always tell, from physiognomical signs, which of the passengers will turn the corner to go there. We were once staying in a remote place in the country, where a chapel of this sort had been erected by the force of missionary zeal; and one morning, we perceived a long procession of people coming from the next town to the consecration of this same chapel. Never was there such a set of scarecrows. Melancholy tailors, consumptive hair-dressers, squinting cobblers, women with child or in the ague, made up the forlorn hope of the pious cavalcade . . .

Again, Methodism, by its leading doctrines, has a peculiar charm for all those, who have an equal facility in sinning and repenting, – in whom the spirit is willing but the flesh is weak, – who have neither fortitude to withstand temptation, nor to silence the admonitions of conscience, – who like the theory of religion better than the practice, and are willing to indulge in all the raptures of speculative devotion, without being tied down to the dull, literal performance of its duties . . . This scheme happily turns morality into a sinecure, takes all the practical drudgery and trouble off your hands, 'and sweet religion makes a rhapsody of words.' Its proselytes besiege the gates of heaven, like sturdy beggars about the doors of the great, lie and bask in the sunshine of divine grace, sigh and groan and bawl out for mercy, expose their sores and blotches to excite commiseration, and cover the deformities of their nature with a garb of borrowed righteousness!

The jargon and nonsense which are so studiously inculcated in the system, are another powerful recommendation of it to the vulgar. It does not impose any tax upon the understanding. Its essence is to be unintelligible ... 'Vital Christianity' is no other than an attempt to lower all religion to the level of the capacities of the lowest of the people.

'Temporal Affairs'

(Jonathan Crowther, *Thoughts upon the finances or temporal affairs of the Methodist Connexion ... written just before the Conference of 1817*, pp. 5–6, 16, 17–18, 27–9)

Crowther had been in the itinerancy since 1784 and was elected President at the 1819 Conference.

It is one of the greatest afflictions in Methodism, that our temporal affairs are so frequently in a state of embarrassment. This is productive of anxiety of mind, and especially in those who take the most lively interest in our concerns: and at no period did our pecuniary matters exhibit such alarming symptoms, as at the present; and particularly what stands connected with the Contingent Fund, or Yearly Subscription.

There is such a looking and leaning to this collection, in many Circuits, that some have doubted, whether the advantages or disadvantages arising from it be the greater. If many Circuits were entirely excused from raising any Yearly Collection, upon condition that they paid their own expenses, it would be a great saving to the connection. But so long as they continue to subscribe to it, they view it somewhat in the light of a sick-club-box, or a parish fund; to which all sick and needy subscribers may make application.

The original institution of the Yearly Subscription, was for purposes very little different from those of the present Mission Fund, except in the nearness or remoteness of the object. The Yearly Subscription had for its object chiefly Home Missions, while the Mission Fund is employed chiefly in Foreign ones. At that time, many of the Circuits might properly enough be considered as Missions, and so may sundry Circuits now, in Scotland, Wales, and even in England itself. But, besides these, a number of Circuits have long been in the habit of bringing demands for deficiencies, ordinary and extraordinary, upon the Yearly Subscription. And to a certain extent, this might have been borne. But the claims for some years, have been so many and so great, as totally to overpower us. So that they which should have been for our relief and support, has been to us an occasion of falling into extreme difficulty. Our embarrassments are exceedingly great and alarming.

It is a point of the highest importance, to trace all our chief deficiencies to their true sources. A principal source will be found to be, the sending so many additional labourers, to cultivate the same extent of ground, occasioned chiefly by the demand of more preaching on the sabbath-days, from the Travelling Preachers, which has arisen chiefly from the building so many new chapels. This has led to an increase of Travelling Preachers; that to an increase of wives; and that to an increase of children, house-rent, and other expenses. The result has frequently been, that additional demands have been brought upon the Contingent Fund. Whereas no additional Preacher ought to be sent to any Circuit, nor any division of Circuits made, that will require an additional Preacher, except an additional and adequate support be provided for the maintenance of such additional Preacher; either from an increase of class-money, ticket-money, some part of the produce of the seat-rents of the chapels, or extra subscriptions.

Every chapel-building concern ought to be so managed, as to pay its own way, besides doing something towards the support of the Preachers, when need requires. And, if persons who propose to build new chapels, had such statements laid before them, it might deter some from injudicious and extravagant proceedings: it might prevent the erection of some chapels which have no visible sanction from God; which become dead weights upon the Connection; and rather hurt than help the cause of religion in the places where they are built . . .

I would observe, that a considerable share of demands upon the Contingent Fund has arisen from those Circuits, which were formerly considered as Home Missions. A few years ago, Dr. Coke boasted, that by these Missions, he had given us forty Circuits. But alas! in a temporal point of view, most of them have proved so many Mill stones hung about the neck of the Connexion, through which it has been sinking every year. And even in a spiritual sense, few of them have been very prosperous. But this was not owing to any want of integrity or zeal in the Doctor. In many instances, however, there has been a flagrant want of judgment, economy and prudence . . .

While writing the preceding observations, I have anticipated the unfair advantage which some will probably take of them, by representing me as an enemy to the poor and feeble, and as proposing measures inimical to brotherly love and christian union. But, whoever shall propagate such an idea will bear false witness against his neighbour. I believe myself to be advocating, not only the cause of justice, but to a considerable extent, the cause of the poor of this world. In the Manchester,

Halifax, and Leeds Districts, which with the addition of the Liverpool District, contain nearly one fourth of all the Methodists in England, there are, perhaps almost as many really poor people, as in all the Connexion besides; together with many thousands more in very limited circumstances, and who therefore have little to spare for any purpose however good. Manufacturing Dictricts abound with poor people, and people but one degree removed from poverty. And probably there are as many labouring manufacturers in the Leeds, Halifax, and Manchester Districts, as in all the other parts of the Methodist Connexion. Yet each of these Districts, not only pay their own expenses, but spare part of their Yearly Collection, and give up the whole of the profits of the Book-trade, to aid and assist the other Districts. And this they do willingly; and they would do still more if possible; only they would not give, *as the payment of a debt*, what would be an act of pure brotherly kindness . . .

The first business must be to reduce the number of Preachers in those Circuits where they bring large demands for the payment of deficiencies; and especially where the numbers in the Societies, and the Congregations, are but small, and not on the increase, and more especially, where they are on the decline. We should direct our chief attention to the parts where God seems most disposed to work. Wherever he opens a door, and especially a great and effectual one, we should rush in, and be workers together with him. Meantime, according to our means and opportunities, we should visit, and cultivate the more barren parts of the vineyard. One thing, however, we should always bear in mind, namely, that God never calls us to do what he has not furnished us with the ways and means of doing.

In reducing the number of the Preachers, our attention should be first drawn to those parts where we have long laboured to little purpose, and at a vast expense of men and money. And the moment we think of this, Wales and Scotland, start into view. Edinburgh, Glasgow, Aberdeen, Dundee, and one or two other places, should have continued to them a moderate supply; but with regard to sundry other stations, it is high time to give over whipping a dead horse. After an immense expenditure of men and money, for forty years, in a stretch of more than seventy miles, from Banff to Inverness, what fruit is there of our labours to this day? There was more thirty years ago than now. In a few weeks, it will be thirty years, since I was appointed for that barren and dreary region. After being tossed in a storm at sea, and enduring much fatiguing travel by land, I arrived at Keith, the first place in the Circuit, where I found one of my predecessors, Mr. Edward Burbeck, dying of a fever, in a lousy bed. The next day I travelled eighteen miles to Elgin, chiefly on foot, and there found, in our lodging-room, the clothes of Mr. Joshua Keighley, who was just buried. I stayed two years in Scotland, and was an attentive observer of every thing around me. I left Scotland with a

higher opinion of the Scotch than I had when I went thither. I found
them as a nation, considerably superior to the English in morality,
knowledge of the scriptures, and general and serious attention to the
worship of God. But this did not convince me the more of our call to
that country. After attentively weighing the subject, I informed Mr.
Wesley, that I seriously doubted, whether God ever intended the
Methodists for Scotland: 1. Because there was so little need for them,
when compared with England and Ireland. 2. Because we are not suited
to the genius and taste of the people of that country. 3. Because the
number of our adherents was very small; and many of those were rather
proselytes to our Doctrines and Discipline than converts from sin to
holiness. 4. Because numbers of them would have gone to heaven,
though they had never seen us: and 5. Because some of them would go
to hell after all we could do for them.

To this day, I have not seen any reason, that I think sufficient, to
induce me to change my views upon this subject. I am not influenced
by hatred or prejudice, but by conviction founded upon observation and
reflection.

The Wesleyan Methodist Missionary Society

(*Minutes*, 1818)

The Conference of 1817 gave approval to a 'Plan of a General Wesleyan
Missionary Society', to co-ordinate and regulate the activities of the District
Missionary Societies which had sprung up since 1813. The plan was imple-
mented the following year, in answer to the question: 'What improvement
can be made in the General Management of our Foreign Missions?'

LAWS AND REGULATIONS OF THE GENERAL WESLEYAN METHODIST MISSIONARY SOCIETY.

1. This Institution shall be designated *The General Wesleyan Methodist
Missionary Society*.
2. The object of this Society is to excite and combine, on a plan more
systematic and efficient than has heretofore been accomplished, the
exertions of the Societies and Congregations of the Wesleyan-Methodists
(and of others, who are friends to the conversion of the Heathen World,
and to the preaching of the Gospel, generally, in Foreign Lands) in
support and enlargement of the Foreign Missions, which were first
established by the Rev. John Wesley, A.M., the Rev. Thomas Coke,
LL.D., and others, and which are now, or shall be from year to year,

carried on under the sanction and direction of the Conference of the People called Methodists.

3. Every Person subscribing annually the sum of One Guinea and upwards, and every Benefactor presenting a Donation of Ten Pounds and upwards, shall be deemed a Member of this Society, and entitled as such to a copy of the General Annual Report.

4. All Methodist Missionary Societies which have already been formed, and those which it is intended to form as soon as it shall be found practicable, for the several *Districts* of this Kingdom into which the Methodist Connexion is divided, shall be entitled 'Methodist Missionary Auxiliary Societies' for the *Districts* in which they have been or may be formed. All Methodist Missionary Societies already formed or hereafter to be formed, in the particular *Circuits* of any District, shall be entitled 'Methodist Missionary Branch Societies' for the *Circuit*, (or where there are or shall be more than one such Society in the same Circuit) for the *City*, *Town*, or *Village*, in which they are or shall be established. – And, the formation of *Ladies' Branch Associations*, and *Juvenile Branch Societies*, in connection with the Auxiliary Societies of the several Districts, is also earnestly recommended, wherever separate Institutions of that nature are likely to be advantageous. . . .

6. The Secretaries of every Branch Society, or other Local Association, shall forward annually to the Secretaries of the Auxiliary Society for their District, an Alphabetical List of all the Benefactors and Subscribers during the preceding twelve Months, with an account of their respective Contributions; stating at the same time what portion of the sums so received has been detained for local expenses, and what portion has been paid in to the Treasurer for the District. – And the Secretaries of every District Auxiliary Society shall also forward annually to the Secretaries of the General Society in London a similar List of the Benefactors and Subscribers in all the Circuits of their District, an abstract of the accounts of the Auxiliary Society, shewing its gross receipts, its local payments, and its remittances to the General Treasurers.

7. All Benefactors of Ten Pounds and upwards, and all subscribers of One Guinea and upwards annually, to any of the Auxiliary or Branch Societies, or other Local Associations, in connection with this Institution, shall be deemed, in right of such Benefaction or Subscription, Members of the General Society.

8. All Persons who collect to the amount of One Shilling and upwards weekly, or Five Shillings and upwards monthly, for this Institution, or for any of its Auxiliaries, Branches, or Associations, shall also be Members of the General Society, and entitled to receive a Copy of each Annual Report, and of each Number of the Methodist Missionary Notices.

9. An Annual Public Meeting of the Members and Friends of the Society, connected with such Religious Services as may be deemed expedient, shall be held in London, on the first Monday in May, unless that day shall happen to fall on the 6th or 7th of May, in which case the Meeting shall be held for that year on the 29th or 30th of April.

10. A General Committee shall be appointed by the Conference, to whom shall be entrusted, in the intervals of the Annual Assemblies of that Body, the superintendance of the Collection and Disbursement of all Monies raised for Foreign Missions which are now, or may hereafter be carried on under its sanction, and by the Preachers in connection with it, and also the *General Management* of those Missions, according to the Rules hereinafter provided. . . .

13. Three of the Methodist Ministers, stationed in or near London, shall be appointed to conduct the Official Correspondence of the Missions, and to perform the other duties of *Secretaries*. One of the Secretaries shall always reside, during the period of his remaining in that office, at the Wesleyan-Mission-House, and be expected to devote himself on the Week-Days, in general, to the service of the Missions exclusively: being subject, however, to all the General Rules of the Connexion, respecting a regular change of station. . . .

18. It is earnestly recommended to the Members of this Society, and of the Auxiliary Societies, and other Local Associations, in connection with it, to consider it as an indispensable part of their daily Christian duty, to pray to Almighty God, for a blessing upon its designs, and upon those of all similar Societies of other Denominations, engaged in the Propagation of the Gospel of Jesus Christ; under the full conviction, that unless He 'prevent us in all our doings with his most gracious favour, and further us with his continual help' we cannot reasonably hope for a succession of Persons of proper spirit and qualifications for the Office of Missionaries, nor expect their labours to be crowned with the desired success. And it is further hoped that with the same view, all the Members and Friends of this Society will sanction, in their several neighbourhoods, by their presence and influence, the Monthly Missionary Prayer Meetings, which should be held in every Chapel in the Methodist Connexion, according to the Recommendation of the Conference, published in their Minutes for 1815: at which Meetings, Extracts from the Missionary Notices, containing recent intelligence from Foreign Stations, may be read, and united supplications offered up for the salvation of the world.

Connexional Affairs

William Myles to Jabez Bunting; Hull, June 5th, 1819

(Ms at MA)

I feel a desire to communicate my thoughts to you on the present state of our connection, because I know it is a subject that occupies your thoughts. I do not particularly desire an answer, because I know your time is fully occupy'd: but if you should answer me, I shall be greatly oblig'd to you. . . .

I think it would be well if the Conference would send an affectionate address to the people, telling them they must get Houses for married Preachers or else be without their complement of Preachers, for we have not single Preachers to send to them. At present we have only two single men in our District, but some of the Circuits intend to remonstrate against second and third Families this ensuing Conference. The language of the Trustees and Stewards is, 'Send the deficiencies to the Conference'; and our brethren feel it easier to make their wants known to their brethren, than to speak out manfully at a Quarterly Meeting, or a Meeting of Trustees.

I know not whether I am singular in the following opinion, but I will mention it. I think the great Circuits should be contracted. The present plan of the Preachers living in great Towns, such as Hull, York, Sheffield & Leeds, and only just preaching in the Country is the real cause of the increase of the Ranters. The pastoral duty is neglected; and you cannot get some of the brethren to think they are accountable to God or his people, as they are not Superintendents. If it could be, there should not be more than two Preachers, or three, on a Circuit.

The objection the people have against divisions is the fear of not getting good Preachers; and yet Facts prove we do no good in a Town where we have not a married preacher or two settled.

With respect to Scotland. We must send fewer Preachers there. It is considered here, by many persons, downright folly to be sending such large sums to a people so well instructed as the Scotch are.

The Rule of the last Conference respecting collections for Chapels[1] will I believe give every coming year greater satisfaction than what it will do this year. At first it was objected to, now the friends begin to see its utility. A list of all the Chapels should be ordered by the Conference, and publish'd, distinguishing those that are private property. Those persons who own their Chapels are very stiff, they threaten the Preachers with calling in the Ranters or New Connection, if their will is opposed.

I have no doubt but the Lord is with us, in all things. If spared, I intend with God's blessing to be in my place at the stationing committee. I hope and trust the Lord will direct me to a Circuit where I shall be useful, and where the labour will not be above my strength. I hope, indeed I expect you will be my friend. My prayer is that the Lord may direct me. There is no Circuit in these parts that would suit me. This year we are suffering here, on account of so many Miss[ionar]y Meetings appointed in these parts during the Ticket Months. If we do not attend them we hurt the Miss[ionar]y Fund: if we do, we injure our Ticket-money. We have been forc'd to employ Local Preachers to give Tickets. This subject I hope will be taken up at Conference, and brought under proper regulations.

¹ The Conference of 1818 agreed 'that a *General Chapel Fund*, to be supported by Private Subscriptions, by Public Collections, by Legacies and by Annual Subscriptions from the Trust Funds of Chapels . . . shall be immediately instituted,' and confirmed a decision of the previous year that no chapel should be built or enlarged without the previous consent of the Chapel-Building Committees.

Impressions of Ireland

Jonathan Edmondson to his wife; Drogheda, June 9, 1819

(Ms at Duke University)

Edmondson had been elected President at the 1818 Conference and was in Ireland to preside over the Conference there.

On Sunday last I preached twice in Dublin. In the morning at Wesley Chapel, from 1 John iii.2; and in the evening at Whitefriar Street Chapel, from Tit. ii.11–14. Wesley Chapel is large and elegant; but they are about to sell it, as they cannot raise the interest of the money upon it. White Friar Street Chapel is about the size of Cherry Street Chapel [Birmingham], a dull, heavy old place where a man cannot be heard unless he has a voice like that of a bull. The galleries, which are almost as flat as a house floor, are supported by hugh pillars sufficiently strong to prop up St. Paul's or Westminster Abbey. Above all, there are a number of classrooms, which I did not see. To say the truth, I had no inclination to ascend to the top of the building.

The family where I slept are truly affectionate . . .

Some of our friends in Dublin are famous for what they call perfection. You know I am a strong advocate for the doctrine as it was taught by Wesley & Fletcher, but, in my opinion, they are in great error. Mr. Cooke, brother to Mrs. Butterworth and Mrs. Clarke, told me he had not had a temptation the last twelve years; & he believes the devil cannot tempt a perfect man.

Yesterday morning at 6 o'clock I left Dublin, and came to this town by the stage coach. The distance is about 23 Irish miles, or 30 English. The roads are remarkably good, and the country beautiful . . . I preached last night to about 150 people in a neat chapel, about the size of that at Deritend [Birmingham] . . . Nine inhabitants out of ten are Roman Catholics. They are all very still at present; but one has no dependence on them. Indeed, the whole country is remarkably tranquil, and a man may travel with as much safety as in England . . . But I keep your rules: 1. never to go on the outside of the coach, unless I cannot get an inside place; and 2. never to travel in the night on any account.

I am not in love with Irish meal times. They breakfast at 9, dine at 4, drink tea at 6 or 7, and sup, very sparingly, about 10. I have seen no fire since I came except once; and yet it is very cold and wet. Their beds are clean and good, and, what is best of all, perfectly dry.

The Irish who have left our Connexion here[1] think we are a fallen people in England, especially since we have been guilty of receiving the holy sacrament at the hands of our own pastors; but, I assure you, my dear love, there appears to be very little either of the form or power of religion here.

[1] I.e., the Primitive Wesleyan Methodists.

Joseph Entwisle, 'Notes and Observations on my Tour thro' part of Wales and Ireland, from June 19 to July 16th, 1821'

(Ms at MA)

Case of the Bishop of Waterford

The Clonites[2] applied to the Bishop of Waterford, requesting him to give something towards their new chapel, alleging that they were the proper, original Methodists, and that *we* had left the Church &c. The Bishop subscribed £10. Sometime after when called upon for his subscription he refused to pay, saying 'That the Methodists in any form are inimical to the Church. That if they are Methodists there is room enough for them in the old Chapel &c. – Chapel on the Quay; and if they are Church people, there is room enough for them in the Cathedral. And that if the Clonites had left the Body of Methodists, it is not unlikely but they might leave the Church also.'

[2] This name also refers to the Primitive Wesleyan Methodists.

Female Itinerants in the Bible Christian Connexion

Minutes of the Bible Christian Conference, 1819

Q.4. What are our thoughts on female preaching?
A. First; we believe God can enable a Woman, as well as a Man, to *'Speak to edification, and exhortation, and comfort'*.
   2. God has promised, or declared, that females shall prophesy in His Name; Joel ii.28, 29 . . .
   3. It hath been practised in different ages.
   4. In our days as well as heretofore, the Lord hath owned their labours, in *turning many to righteousness* through their word; and what but this is the end of all preaching? Namely; that sinners may be converted to God, and eternally saved. We believe, we ought to praise God, that the kingdom of darkness is shaken, and the kingdom of the Redeemer is enlarged, *whoever* be the instruments God is pleased to use; and that we dare not be so insolent, as to dictate to HIM, who He shall employ, to accomplish His gracious purposes . . .

Practical advice

(*Minutes,* 1820)

[Q.15] . . . Our sisters who travel as helpers, should keep their own place, be watchful, always neat, plain, and clean, discreet, humble, grave as mothers in Israel; diligent according to their sex, as well as our brethren, being as much as they can, their own servants, and helps to the families where they go: and when they leave their room in the morning, leave everything in its proper place.

An extract from *A Digest of the Rules, Regulations and Usages of the People Denominated Bible Christians*

(Op. cit. 5th edition, 1882, p. 21)

The last female itinerant died in 1896, having been retired since 1870; but the possibility of female itinerants long outlived the actuality.

Itinerant Female Preachers

We believe that God, in certain instances, calls women as well as men to publish salvation to their fellow-sinners; and that the following scriptures sanction it – Joel ii.28, 29; Acts ii. 17, 18; xxi.9; and 1 Cor. xi. 5, 6; and seeing that in numerous instances the Almighty seals their ministrations by the conversion of souls, we dare not prevent them from engaging in this work when they possess unquèstionable piety and acceptable talents, and believe themselves to be called of God to engage therein. They do not, however, take part among us in Church Government; they are entitled to attend meetings for business, but not to vote.

Before they are taken out to travel, their Pastor converses with them respecting their Christian experience, call to the work, and state of health, and submits their case to the Quarterly Meeting, when, if approved, a certificate of recommendation, signed by the Circuit Stewards, is sent to the District Meeting and the Conference. They remain three years on trial, but do not undergo any examination at the Conference. When they become disabled in their labours, after they are admitted into full connexion, they receive such support as their necessities require, so long as they maintain a becoming character, and are unmarried.

Records of the Hull Primitive Methodist Circuit, 1819–20

(Ms at MA)

Quarterly Meeting Minutes

13 Sept. 1819. A man to be called out immediately as a Hired Local Preacher who shall travel on a Single Man's Allowance. John Dent proposed by R. Woolhouse to go out as a Hired Local Preacher – to be sent out immediately.

14 Sept. Wm. Clowes will reprove and give J. Dent such instructions and information as he thinks proper and also take a tour with him &c. Hannah Johnson acting as a Missionary for one Quarter shall receive £1.

12 Dec. 1819 . . .
5. The Travelling Preachers to be allowed to attend the Circuit Committee Meetings, but only two to have a voice in this meeting & those two to be the Senior Preachers.
11. Thos. Johnson of Newbold to receive 15/– for supplying J. Harrison's Plan 10 days.
12. E. Taylor to take care of the Singers Pew and to let none in only those that appear in a plain dress. Men plain coats & no pantaloons. Women no frills, no bunches of ribbons, no curls & no superfluities whatever. All the Preachers & Leaders are requested to get a plain dress as soon as possible in order that they may insist upon plainness in all the Society.

March 13, 1820 . . .

A letter to be sent to Ann Carr to know whether she be at liberty to labour amongst us & if she be to request her to do so.

A letter to be sent to Geo. Lazenby to inform him that we have no need of him . . . John Dent to be paid immediately for the time he laboured amongst us & that he shall not continue any longer amongst us either as a Local Preacher or Member of our Society until he shews true repentance for his faults &c.

June 13, 1820.

Every member of the Quarter Board shall in future be fined for non-attendance at the time appointed sixpence and 3d for every quarter of an hour after. The fines to be given to the poor.

The [Circuit] Committee to meet once a fortnight on the Tuesday nights at 7 o'clock & any brother not being present at the time whose business it shall have been to have brought on the business of the meeting shall forfeit 1/– to be paid to the poor. . . .

No preacher shall be allowed to take with him any child or other person who shall be encumbersome to the people.

Circuit Committee Minutes:

March 30, 1820.

A letter to be sent to Bro. Coats of Newbold to inform him we are not in particular want of a Preacher at present, but we have a call into Holderness & if the Lord should open our way there we will then take his case into consideration . . .

May 3, 1820.

In consequence of Bro. Clowes not being regularly chose at the Quarter Board as a Delegate for the Annual Meeting, he is now chose by Circuit Committee . . .

No Preacher to be taken out by this Committee until they hear him preach and examine him respecting his doctrines &c.

May 5.

In consequence of a Preacher being wanted to go out immediately, Nathaniel West is requested to come down to Hull & preach & be examined on various points (to bear his own expenses) if he think proper or to send us an answer.

May 8.

No expenses are to be paid by this Committee for any person or persons going to any Camp Meeting or other place without the sanction of this meeting.

John Abey having preached before & been examined by the Circuit Committee, he shall go out as a Travelling Preacher as soon as he can (say a fortnight).

Local Preachers' Meeting Minutes:

September 13, 1819.
John Oxtoby to be reproved by R. Woolhouse for neglecting his appointments. And to have only one or two appointments in the next Plan . . .
W. Rickateson to be spoken to by W. Clowes for long preaching & praying & for talking about philosophy & Astronomy &c . . .
Josh. Taylor to be censured from this meeting for indiscretion &c by Jno. Harrison . . .

December 12, 1819.
J. Taylor to be reproved for the doctrines he preaches by W. Clowes and J. Harrison & also to be instructed further into the doctrines he ought to preach . . .

March 13, 1820.
Josh. Taylor to be put on the Plan as an Exhorter in consequence of his not being generally received as a Local Preacher.

The Liverpool Conference of 1820

This was the first Conference over which Jabez Bunting presided and the first attended by a representative of the Methodist Episcopal Church. Difficulties had arisen over the division of the work in Canada between the American and British Churches; the issue was discussed with 'much mutual good will' and a *modus vivendi* worked out. The state of the British connexion gave rise to lengthy discussions and much heart-searching, and the result was the 'Liverpool Minutes'. Revised in 1885, these remained for many years a blueprint for the pastoral ministry.

Diary of the Rev. John Emory of the Methodist Episcopal Church

(Ms at SMU)

The version published in *The Life of the Rev. John Emory, D.D.* by his eldest son, 1841, pp. 84–131 is toned down by the omission of several interesting details from the manuscript reproduced below.

Wednesday 26th [July]. Went to Mr. Peter Sowerby's, where I am appointed to lodge. My reception was of the most friendly kind, and I am honoured with the chamber which was formerly occupied by Dr. Coke, and with the bed in which he was accustomed to sleep. The family are truly hospitable. The Conference sent Mr. Joseph Taylor as a messenger to invite me to sit with them. In the afternoon I went accordingly and was introduced first to the President (Mr. Bunting) and by him to the Conference, all in a very handsome manner. I was requested to occupy a seat on the right of the President between him and the Ex-President (Mr. J. Crowther). The members of the Conference take their seats by seniority. They sit in the Brunswick Chapel, which is large, in the form of an amphitheatre, no gallery, but circular pews raised one above another. Behind the pulpit is a large organ.

Dr. Clarke proposed a loyal address to the King, a sketch of which he read. After hearing it the Ex-President turned to me and said, 'It is singular that on your first visit to us you should hear such a piece (or parcel) of balderdash.' I replied that it was not a subject proper for me to express any opinion about. 'I know not', said he, 'what you may think of it, but it is too strong for my stomach.'

The Conference hours are from 6 to 8 in the morning, from 9 to near one, and from ½ past two till five.

The President speaks with much authority and is very particular in keeping the members in their places and to their business . . .

The preachers to be admitted into full Connexion were examined before the Conference long and closely, having been previously examined by their District Meetings and also by the President and Secretary. On the several points of doctrine and the answers of the young men, the elderly preachers expressed their sentiments as they proceeded. The whole was very profitable.

Preachers who had once travelled and been expelled cannot be admitted even as members into any society again without leave of the Annual Conference. . . .

Monday 31st . . . The Conference proceeded to read the Stations. They were first read through and the Preachers allowed to make any note concerning them. They were then taken up and read again with liberty for any Preacher to make any objection. After hearing and considering, the Conference determined. Frequent objections were made which produced considerable discussion. I understand the appointments were formerly kept secret till read in Conference, but now the Stationing Committee meet some time before, and as soon as a plan is made give information to their constituents. The Circuits also generally know. If objections are made the Committee meet again and consider them; after which they submit the improved plan to the final decision of the Conference . . .

This and tomorrow evening are appointed for the public reception of the young Preachers into full connexion . . . The President examines them severally, after which they severally address the Congregation respecting their experience, exercises etc., with anything particular in their travels and labours . . .

[Tuesday 1st August] Stationing continued in Conference with considerable trouble. At six o'clock I witnessed the form of receiving the Preachers into full Connexion. The President and Conference were assembled in Conference order, a large congregation around, and the candidates standing on a bench before the President. Having spoken their experience last night this was not continued tonight. The President went through a general examination of them nearly in the same manner as in Conference, but shorter, (singing and prayer having been first). He then read the address in our form of ordination. It was then moved and seconded that they be admitted into full Connexion, the mover, seconder and others speaking on the occasion; after this the vote was taken and the President then declared to the candidates in a body (without imposition of hands or giving the hand) in the name of the Father, Son and Holy Ghost, that they were admitted into full connexion with the Methodist Conference. There was then singing and prayer again. The Ex-President then addressed those admitted at some length on the ministerial office &c. after which the service was concluded with singing and prayer.

[Wednesday 2nd. Agreement to exchange representatives every 4 years, and to adjustments to the line of demarcation in the Canadas. 'An open Conference was held from breakfast till one o'clock with much order and edification.']

Thursday 3rd. Morning session before and after breakfast spent in conversation on the best means of reviving religion etc; excellent speeches by many of the elder brethren, summed up and concluded by the President.

Friday and Saturday occupied in going over the Stations again. The appointments having been communicated throughout the country afforded an opportunity to Preachers and people to petition or remonstrate. This is often done in strong terms and gives much trouble. A Preacher of any standing is very seldom sent where he is not willing to go. [A subsequent memo says: 'The printed Stations confirmed, yet changes afterwards made when agreed to by the parties.']

[Memo] Prayers[1] read in one Chapel in most large towns, but omitted in far the greater part of the Connexion.

Tuesday Aug. 8th. The Conference met at 6 o'clock. Some miscellaneous matters were attended to . . . The Minutes were read in a general way, legalised by a formal vote, and signed in open Conference by the President and Secretary . . . The Conference then partook of the Lord's Supper together and closed in the greatest harmony, love and order. I heard several of the Preachers say it was the best Conference they had ever had. It lasted nearly a fortnight and closed a little before 10 o'clock A.M.

Monday 14th. Dined with Samuel Drew. Local preachers in England – about 10 for one of travelling (others say 5 for one) – All the variety of talents as among the travelling – generally preach on the Sabbath twice – expenses *allowed* out of a fund for this purpose, made up of the surplus of the sales of the Stations and collections for the purpose etc. Their names on the local plan is their authority. – This plan made out by the Superintendent. The local preachers, Mr. D. thinks, are looked down on by the travelling and held in too much degradation, which is sorely felt and will in time cause an explosion. There have been no movements, however, for a change.

'Are you American?' 'Yes.' 'Why, you speak English very well! Is English much spoken in America?' Such are queries which have been frequently put to me . . .

Memo: 2 or 3 Preachers on one circuit keep one horse, owned and kept by the Circuit. One [preacher] out and one in. Many circuits no horse.

¹ I.e., the Methodist version of Morning Prayer.

The 'Liverpool Minutes'

(*Minutes*, 1820)

Q. XXVI. What measures can we adopt for the increase of Spiritual Religion among our Societies and Congregations, and for the extension of the work of God in our native country?

A. After long and deeply serious deliberation on this important Question, we have unanimously agreed to the following results:

1. We, on this solemn occasion, devote ourselves afresh to God; and resolve, in humble dependance on his grace, to be more than ever attentive to Personal Religion, and to the Christian Instruction and Government of our own Families.

2. Let us endeavour, in our public Ministry, to preach constantly all those leading and vital Doctrines of the Gospel, which peculiarly distinguished the original Methodist Preachers, whose labours were so signally blessed by the Lord, and to preach them in our primitive method, – evangelically, experimentally, zealously, and with great plainness and simplicity; giving to them a decided prominence in *every* Sermon, and labouring to *apply* them closely, affectionately, and energetically to the consciences of the different classes of our hearers.

3. Let us consecrate ourselves fully and entirely to our proper work, as servants of Christ and his Church, giving ourselves 'wholly' to it, both in public and in private, and guarding against all occupations of our

time and thoughts, which have no direct connexion with our great calling, and which would injuriously divert our attention from the momentous task of saving souls, and taking care of the flock of Christ.

4. Let us 'covet earnestly the best gifts', to qualify us for an acceptable and useful ministry; let us seek them in prayer from Him who is the Father of Lights and Fountain of Wisdom; let us 'stir up', and improve by study and diligent cultivation, 'the gift that is in us'; and strive in every way to be 'workmen who need not to be ashamed, rightly dividing the Word of Truth'; – taking care, however, that, whatever other qualifications we may acquire and use, our Ministry shall, at least, by the divine blessing, be always characterized by sound, evangelical doctrine, by plainness of speech, and by a spirit of tender affection and burning zeal.

5. Let us frequently read, and carefully study, Mr. Wesley's 'Rules of a Helper', and other parts of the large Minutes which relate to the duties of a Preacher and Pastor.

6. In order to promote an increase of the congregations, and a revival of the work of God, let us have recourse, even in our old-established Circuits, to the practice of *preaching out of doors; seeking,* in order to *save,* that which is lost.

7. In every Circuit, let us try to open new Places; let us try *again* places which have not been *recently* visited; let us be increasingly attentive to the supply and superintendence of the *country-places* already on the Plan; let us not be satisfied till every town, village, and hamlet in our respective neighbourhoods shall be blessed, as far as we can possibly accomplish it, with the means of grace and salvation; – in a word, let *every* Methodist Preacher consider himself as called to be, in point of enterprise, zeal, and diligence, a *Home-Missionary,* and to *enlarge* and extend, as well as *keep,* the Circuit to which he is appointed.

8. Let us, wherever it shall appear to be practicable, especially in the old and large Societies, employ some active, zealous men, whose piety and general character shall be approved by the Leaders' Meetings, to attempt the formation of new *Classes* in suitable neighbourhoods, where we may hope by that method to gather into the fold of Christ some persons who are 'not far from the kingdom of God', but who need special invitation, and are not likely to 'give themselves' fully 'to the Lord and to us by the will of God', without more than ordinary labour and spiritual attention.

9. Let us speak plainly and pointedly in every place, both in those occasional meetings of the Society at which strangers are allowed to be present, and in our sermons, on the duty and advantage of Christian Communion; and exhort all who are seeking salvation, to avail themselves, without delay, of the help of our more private means of grace.

10. Let us encourage public Prayer-Meetings, especially those which

are held at times which do not interfere with our general worship, in the houses of our friends, in different parts of a town or neighbourhood; such meetings having been long proved to be, when prudently conducted by persons of established piety and competent gifts, and duly super-intended by the Preachers, and by the Leaders' Meetings, valuable nurseries for our Congregations and Societies, and means of salvation to many who could not have been reached at first in any other method.

11. In country places, where a full supply of preaching cannot be obtained, either by Travelling or Local Preachers, let suitable persons, belonging to the nearest Societies, be encouraged to attend, under the direction of the Superintendent, for the purpose of Public Prayer and Exhortation, and occasionally to read to the Congregations a short and plain Sermon on the First Principles of the Doctrine of Christ, until such places can be favoured with other and more regular opportunities of instruction in righteousness.

12. Let us ourselves remember, and endeavour to impress on our people, that we, as a Body, do not exist for the purposes of party; and that we are especially bound by the example of our Founder, by the original principle on which our Societies are formed, and by our constant professions before the world, to avoid a narrow, bigoted, and sectarian spirit, to abstain from needless and unprofitable disputes on minor subjects of theological controversy, and as far as we innocently can, to 'please all men for their good unto edification'. Let us, therefore, main-tain towards all denominations of Christians, who 'hold the Head', the kind and catholic spirit of primitive Methodism; and, according to the noble maxim of our Fathers in the Gospel, 'be the friends of all, the enemies of none'.

13. Let us, at least in every large town, establish weekly meetings for the Children of our friends, according to our ancient custom; and let us pay particular spiritual attention, in public and in private, to the young people of our Societies and Congregations.

14. Let us meet the Societies regularly on the Lord's Day; and fre-quently on the week-day evenings, in *country* places, where we do not preach on the Lord's Day: – Let the Members be accustomed, on such occasions, to show their Society Tickets; – and let us endeavour to make these Meetings interesting and appropriate to our Members, as such, – by giving to our Addresses an immediate reference to the state of the people, to the circumstances of each Society, and to their peculiar duties, both personal and domestic, as professors of religion, and as Methodists, and by frequently explaining and enforcing our own Rules.

15. Let us revive, where it has been neglected, and promote in every place, the observance of those parts of our discipline, which refer to Watch-Nights, Private and Public Bands, and Quarterly Days for solemn Fasting and Prayer.

16. Let us, wherever we have access and opportunity, be diligent in *pastoral* visits to our people, at their own houses, especially to the sick, the careless, and the lukewarm.

17. But as such private visits must, in many cases, from our plan of continual itinerancy and village-preaching, and from the number of Members in the larger Societies, be greatly limited, let us endeavour so to arrange in our several Circuits the Plans for the Quarterly Public Visitation of the Classes, as to allow full time for a more minute examination into the christian knowledge, experience, and practice of the Members, and for pastoral inquiries, instructions, and counsels, respecting personal and family religion.

18. Let us regularly meet the Class-Leaders, and examine their Class-Papers, in town and country; and do all we can to engage both them, and our respected Brethren, the Local Preachers, to co-operate with us, in their respective departments, in promoting vital godliness among our people, and extending the work of the Lord.

19. As much depends, under the blessing of God, on the piety, knowledge, zeal, activity, and christian temper, of our Leaders, as well as on their firm attachment to the doctrines, discipline, and cause of Methodism, let us never nominate a new Leader, until we have conscientiously satisfied ourselves by previous inquiry, and personal examination, as to the character and qualifications of the person proposed; and let us act uniformly on the Rule respecting the Public Examination of Leaders, which is found in our Minutes of 1811.

20. Let us, whenever a new Leader, nominated by us, and accepted by the Leaders' Meeting, shall be first introduced into the Meeting, take that opportunity of stating the duties which belong to the office, and of enforcing them on all present.

21. Let us affectionately, but firmly, enforce on the Leaders, as an essential article of our pastoral discipline, and one, which, in consequence of our own constant itinerancy, cannot be dispensed with, the Rule of the Society in which it is stated to be the duty of a Leader 'to see every Member in his Class *once in every week*'.

22. Let us pay particular attention to Backsliders, and endeavour, in the spirit of meekness, to restore them that have been overtaken in a fault, and by private efforts, as well as by our public ministrations, to recover the fallen out of the snare of the Devil.

23. Let us afresh enforce on all our people a conscientious attendance on the Lord's Supper.

24. Let us earnestly exhort our Societies to make the best and most religious use of the rest and leisure of the Lord's Day; – let us admonish any individuals who shall be found to neglect our public worship, under pretence of visiting the sick, or other similar engagements; – let us show our People the evil of *wasting* those portions of the Sabbath, which are not

spent in public worship, in visits, or in receiving company, to the neglect of private prayer, of the perusal of the Scriptures, and of family duties, and, often, to the serious spiritual injury of servants, who are thus improperly employed, and deprived of the public means of grace; – let us set an example in this matter, by refusing for ourselves and for our families, to spend in visits, when there is no call of duty or necessity, the sacred hours of the Holy Sabbath; – and let us never allow the Lord's Day to be *secularized* by meetings of mere *business*, when such business refers only to the *temporal affairs* of the Church of God.

25. With a view to promote, in the families and schools of our Connexion, the uniform and regular practice of *Catechetical* instruction, which, especially in the present state of our Body, and of our Country at large, we deem to be of the highest importance, – we agree that a series of Catechisms shall be prepared, and recommended for general use among us: and we earnestly request MR. BENSON and MR. WATSON, to draw up such Catechisms, and to submit them to the examination of the next Conference.

26. In conducting our Leaders' and Quarterly Meetings, and all other official Meetings among us, let us affectionately and steadily discountenance the spirit of strife and debate, and promote, in the management of all our affairs, both by our advice and example, the temper and manner of men who are acting for God in the service of his Church. – Let the introduction of all topics of useless or irritating discussion, not legitimately connected with the proper business of such Meetings, be prudently repressed. – Let us remember that in a large Body, the only way to *live in peace* and comfort, is to *walk by rule*, and (to use the language of MR. WESLEY) 'not to mend our Rules, but to keep them for conscience' sake'. – And while we readily and cheerfully protect all our Members, in Meetings in which we preside, in the exercise of such functions as belong to them, according to our laws and general usages, let us not forget that we are under solemn obligations to conduct ourselves on such occasions, not as the mere *Chairmen* of public Meetings, but as the *Pastors* of Christian Societies, put in trust by the ordinance of God, and by their own voluntary association with us, with the scriptural superintendence of their spiritual affairs, and responsible to the great Head of the Church for the faithful discharge of the duties of that trust.

27. We affectionately exhort those of our own people, who are laudably active in various benevolent Institutions, while they persevere in every good word and work, to guard against the danger of expending all their leisure and influence on mere local and subordinate Charities, so as to neglect God's own direct and immediate Institutions, such as the public preaching of the Gospel, or to deprive themselves of the opportunity of regularly attending their Classes, and of private prayer and reading of the Holy Scriptures. It should not be forgotten that the *great*

spiritual work of God depends, under the divine blessing, on the general and conscientious use of his Institutions; and that, in the success of *that* work, all other good undertakings among us had their origin, and must ever have their principal support. 'These things ought ye to have done, and not to have left the other undone.'

28. In order that the state of the Work may be constantly under the eye of the Preachers, we agree to revive uniformly the good old custom of keeping Quarterly Schedules in every Circuit, each of which shall contain a correct Statement, for the Quarter to which it belongs, of Persons admitted on Trial, – New Members, fully admitted into Society after due probation, – Removals into other Circuits, – Deaths, – Backsliders, – Conversions, – Number in the Bands, – and Total Number of Members then in the Society. – The Book-Steward shall prepare, and furnish to every Circuit, a sufficient number of Printed Forms of such a Schedule, to be filled up by the Preachers, in reference to every distinct Class, during their Quarterly Visitations: – And from these, each Superintendent shall draw up every Quarter one General Schedule, containing an Account of all the Societies in his Circuit, in relation to the several particulars above-mentioned. These General Circuit-Schedules each Superintendent is expected to produce, whenever required so to do, at the Annual District-Meeting, or at the Conference.

29. Every Superintendent is required to leave for his Successor in the Circuit-Book, not only a List of the Town and Circuit-Stewards, and of the Annual Subscribers to our several Funds, &c., but especially an exact List of the Names of all the Members in his Circuit, arranged in their several Classes and Societies, as found at the preceding Midsummer-Visitation.

30. But as we are deeply sensible that the great thing to be desired, in order to a Revival and Extension of the Work of God, without which no resolutions, or labours, or regulations will avail, is A NEW AND MORE ABUNDANT EFFUSION OF THE Holy Spirit on ourselves, on our Societies, and on our Congregations, – we solemnly agree to seek that blessing in humble and earnest prayer. And we hereby appoint that the day of the next Quarterly Fast, *namely, the Friday after Michaelmas-Day, October 6th,* shall be observed in all our Circuits, as a day of *special* Fasting and Prayer to Almighty God. – Let Meetings for Public Supplication be held, in as many places as possible, in every Circuit; and let the Preachers speak largely and particularly on the subject in their Sermons on the preceding Lord's Day.

31. The various articles included in this Minute, shall be read by every Chairman at the next regular annual Meeting of his District; and shall then be made the subject of serious conversation among the Brethren, with a view to their particular bearing on the spiritual state and circumstances of each District respectively.

'Fears Respecting the Local Preachers'

William Myles to Jabez Bunting; Halifax, Aug. 18th, 1820

(Ms at MA)

Without any flattery I can truly say, I greatly approved of your public conduct as President in Liverpool. The Office now means something besides the mere name . . .

    I have some fears respecting the Local Preachers. They well know we cannot do without them. Some of them appear to be jealous and envious of us . . . I fear it would not be good policy to get at present an exact number of our Chapels with the debts on each. It would give us to see how dependent we are on the Local Preachers, and the whole of the debts would frighten us. Some of our Local Preachers are still urging the people to build Chapels in country places where we cannot visit them on the Lord's day. The people of Mixenden in this Circuit are building a Chapel without consulting the Building Committee. I did what I could to prevent it, or to get them to consult the Committee. But I could not prevent them . . . I hope it will be stated in the Report of the Chapel Fund, that one good effect will follow from it, Namely, The preventing people from making Collections for Chapels. None but the Preachers should do this accompanied by a Trustee or two for the Chapel Fund.

Sunday School Rules

Rules and Regulations of the Wesleyan Methodist Sunday School, Grimsby, 1820

(Skelton Collection, Grimsby Borough Library; printed in Rex. C. Russell, *Sunday Schools in Lindsey*, 1965, pp. 61–2)

At a Meeting of the Committee of the Methodist Sunday School, Grimsby, held on the 24th of November, 1820, the following Resolutions were adopted, viz.

1st.   That the Two Schools shall be united.

2nd.   That no writing shall be taught on the Lord's Day.[1]

3rd.   That the Children, or at least the senior part of them, shall be taken to the Chapel every Lord's Day afternoon, attended by their respective Teachers: and that the Preachers be respectfully re-requested to conclude the service by the end of the hour, or within one hour and five minutes.

4th. That the Committee shall meet regularly once a quarter, according to notice, which shall be previously given, in writing, in the months of November, February, May, and August: and each Member being absent at such Meeting, without giving a reason, which may be deemed by the Committee satisfactory, shall pay Sixpence as a fine.

5th. That certain Rewards, in Books, shall be given to the Scholars for regular attendance; and such Books shall be given as the Committee may think proper.

6th. That all the Members of this Committee shall exert their influence to promote the interest and prosperity of the School, and procure accession to the number of Scholars.

7th. That an Anniversary Sermon, for the benefit of the School, shall be preached in the Month of April or May, by some Minister, selected by the Committee, and invited by the Superintendent of this Circuit, at their request.

TEACHERS

At a Meeting of the Committee and Teachers of the Sunday School, held in the Methodist Chapel, Grimsby, on Monday the 27th of November, 1820, the following Resolutions were adopted, viz.

1st. That if any Teacher be too late five minutes, such Teacher shall be fined one penny; if half an hour, two pence; if absent the whole morning or afternoon, three-pence; if absent the whole day, without providing a proper Substitute, six-pence.

2nd. That these fines shall be applied to the sole use and benefit of the School.

3rd. That the Superintendent and Secretary shall revise and correct the Old Rules, belonging to the School; and the Rules so revised and corrected, together with these Resolutions, shall be printed.

4th. That each Teacher wishing to resign, shall send in his or her resignation in writing: those who neglect to do so, shall in case of absence, be subject to the fines, as the first Rule directs.

5th. That each Teacher, leaving the School, without leave, or not returning from the Chapel, with the Scholars, shall be subject to a fine of three-pence.

SCHOLARS

1st. The School shall commence precisely at Half-past Nine o'clock in the Morning, and at Half-past One o'clock in the Afternoon; at which time all the Scholars are expected to be there.

2nd. The names of the Scholars will be called over immediately, and those who are not present will be marked for late attendance, and dealt with accordingly.

3rd. All the Scholars must come clean washed and combed.

4th. Not one word must be spoken in School hours, to any person, but
      the Teachers: the Scholars are not allowed to look off their Books,
      or get their Lessons aloud.

5th. If any Scholar neglect coming to the School, or sending a reason-
      able excuse, for Three Sundays together, such Scholar shall be
      excluded.

6th. Those Scholars, who are frequently absent from School, without
      giving sufficient reason will be excluded.

7th. If a Scholar be guilty of either cursing, swearing, quarreling, wil-
      ful lying, calling names, or despising another on account of his
      dress, or any thing else, he shall be admonished for the first
      offence, punished for the second, and excluded for the third.

8th. When the Scholars are dismissed, they must go straight home,
      without loitering in the streets; and if any be seen playing at any
      game, or in any other respects misbehaving upon the Lord's Day,
      they shall be treated as the seventh Rule directs.

9th. When the Scholars go to Chapel, they must walk regularly, two
      and two, along the street, neither thronging, nor pushing against
      each other, nor speaking one word, from the time they leave the
      School, to the time they come out of the Chapel. They must
      reverently enter the Chapel, and follow their Teachers to their
      seats, without any disorder or confusion. They must sit, stand, or
      kneel, always with the congregation. They must not go out of the
      Chapel, during the service; and if either by word or action, they
      disturb those who are near them, their names will be taken down,
      that they may be reported, when they return to the School.

[1] In a later set of rules for the same school (1842) this is spelled out more fully,
reflecting the 'Principles and Rules' adopted connexionally in 1827 (pp. 399–404
below): 'That the sale of books, teaching the art of writing, or any other merely
secular branch of knowledge shall not be practised on the Lord's Day.'

The First Primitive Methodist Annual Conference

(PM *Minutes*, 1820, printed in the *PM Magazine*, 1820, pp. 206–21)

The Minutes of the first 'Annual Meeting' incorporated the recommendations of the 'preparatory meeting' held at Nottingham in August 1819.

The first Annual Meeting commenced at Hull, on Tuesday, May 2nd,
1820, and closed the Wednesday but one following. Evening preachings
were carried on in one street or other on most nights: to these were

added, morning preachings in chapels at 5 o'clock, and evening preachings at seven, as long as the Annual Meeting continued; excepting only
on the love-feast night. At the close of the evening preachings in the
chapel, the service with the mourners usually commenced, and the pious
people frequently prayed and laboured with them till a late hour, and
with considerable success; many obtained true conversion, many were
born of God.

Q. Of whom shall the Annual Meetings be composed?

A. Of three delegates from each circuit, one only of whom shall be a
travelling preacher. But the travelling preachers shall not vote on any
subject relative to preachers' salaries.

2. Q. How shall the delegates be chosen?

A. By the Quarter day boards of the respective circuits; and it is
recommended that they be chosen immediately after dinner the first day.

3. Q. How shall the Quarter day boards proceed in electing lay
delegates?

A. Every person nominated to serve the office of lay delegate, shall,
before his election, be asked the following questions:—

1. Have you been a travelling preacher within the last six months?

2. Have you, in any case, during the last six months laboured in the
capacity of a travelling preacher, and have received, or expect to receive,
any pay or compensation for such service or labour, either from an
individual or individuals, or from a quarter day board?

3. Have you any intention or desire to be employed as a travelling
preacher receiving pay, within the next twelve months?

Any person who does not answer these questions decidedly in the
negative, shall not be appointed to the office of lay delegate . . .

N. B. The circuits are requested to choose delegates, who can be present
at the opening of the meeting, and can stay till the close of it . . .

8. Q. How are the travelling preachers distinguished?

A. By the terms travelling preachers, and hired local preachers.

9. Q. What is the difference between them?

A. Those termed travelling preachers are removable from circuit to
circuit by the Annual Meeting. Those termed hired local preachers are
not so removable. This is the whole difference: in all other respects they
are equal and alike.

N. B. Those termed hired local preachers, may remove by agreement of
one circuit with another. . . .

14. Q. What particulars shall be sent from the quarter day board, to
the Annual Meeting, relative to a candidate for the ministry?

A. An account of his age, and station in life; whether he has made any
engagements relative to marriage, and whether his circumstances are

embarrassed, and if a married man what family; a description of his talents; the time he has been a local preacher, with an account of his usefulness, christian experience, and conduct in the society; and a statement of the doctrines he holds.

16. Q. Wherein may the legislative power of the Annual Meetings restrain the circuits [?]

A. In all cases where one circuit might injure another . . .

34. Q. By what means shall the circuit committee be informed of the spread of the work of God amongst us, and of the general state of our societies?

A. Every travelling preacher shall be required to keep a regular journal or journals, and shall transmit the same to the circuit committee, either monthly or otherwise, as the circuit committee or quarter day shall direct.

Any travelling preacher who does not comply with this rule, shall have no voice nor vote, neither at a circuit quarter day, nor at a branch quarter day. . . .

37. Q. In what dress shall our members in office appear in public?

A. In a plain one: the men to wear single breasted coats, single breasted waistcoats, and their hair in its natural form; and not to be allowed to wear pantaloons, fashionable trowsers, nor white hats. . . .

40. Q. Under what circumstances shall a circuit be divided?

A. When the business of a circuit is become too extensive for the quarter day board, and there are found in a branch or part of it, a sufficient number of experienced persons to conduct the affairs of a circuit, and all parties are agreeable. . . .

43. Q. How shall the circuits be managed?

A. I. Each circuit shall have a general quarterly meeting, which shall form its local government.

II. The quarter board shall be composed of Travelling and Local Preachers, Leaders, Stewards, and Delegates, and such other persons as the several general quarterly meetings shall think proper.

III. The general quarterly meetings shall have power to make such regulations as they may think proper; providing that such regulations do not interfere with the general rules.

44. Q. On whom shall the management of the circuit devolve between the quarterly meetings?

A. On a committee chosen by the quarter day board, and consisting of not less that four persons besides travelling preachers, and circuit stewards.

N. B. Two travelling preachers only shall be allowed to vote, by virtue of office, at any one sitting of the committee. . . .

53. Q. Of whom shall the Leaders' meeting be composed?

A. This meeting shall be composed of Preachers, Stewards, and Leaders, none of whom shall leave the meeting till it be concluded, without permission of the President: it shall be held every week, or every fortnight, as is found most convenient. And should any Leader, Steward, or preacher, absent himself three times together, without assigning a satisfactory reason, he shall be removed from his office.

54. Q. What are the duties of the Leaders' meeting?

A. 1. The Leaders' meeting shall remove all improper Leaders from their office, shall inquire into the state of the society, and see that proper measures are adopted for its regulation and prosperity.

2. The Leaders shall bring their class papers to be examined by the President; they shall collect the class money weekly, and pay it to the Treasurer the following meeting: they shall likewise collect the quarter-age when the tickets are given, and pay it in at the next meeting.

55. Q. By whom shall the Leaders be appointed?

A. The appointment of Leaders shall be with the Leaders' meeting. The class may recommend a person; but he must be approved of by the Leaders' meeting. But should the person appointed not be agreeable to the class, another shall be chosen.

56. Q. What other regulations will be necessary to adopt, relative to our society?

A. 1. Any person who earnestly desires to flee from the wrath to come, may be admitted to meet in class, *on trial*. But the earnest desire must be manifested, at least, three months before such person is received into full membership . . .

9. No person shall be continued a member of our society, who visits public or worldly amusements; nor those who waste their time at public-houses, follow the fashions of the world, buy unaccustomed goods, who are not honest in all their dealings, or who are guilty of other acts of immorality. . . .

11. If any member transgress the rules, he shall be required to appear before a leaders' meeting, to answer such charge, or charges as may be brought against him. And if the offender wish it, he or she, may have a copy of all such charges together with the names of the principal evidences who are to appear against them. And the Leaders' meeting shall in no case whatever, give judgment against any person who has not had such privileges or who has not had an opportunity of answering for him, or herself. And in case any are aggrieved, they may appeal to the quarterly meeting, the decisions of which shall be final.

A Primitive Methodist Broadsheet

ON
Primitive Methodism.

I.

PRIMITIVE METHODISM duly enforces the doctrine of a full, free, and present salvation, through and by faith. This is essential to it, and constitutes its grand and chief distinguishing mark. Mr. Wesley explicitly laid down, and duly enforced the doctrine of a present salvation. On this the Wesleyan Connexion first originated. And this, under God, was the chief cause of the many revivals of religion, that rose under Mr. Wesley's auspices.

II.

WORSHIP in the open air. This was practised by Adam in Paradise; and also in the first ages of the world, and under the law, and by Christ and his apostles; and it was revived, and practised extensively, and with great success, by Mr. Wesley. This then is another mark of Primitive Methodism.

III.

Short preaching was revived and established by Mr. Wesley. And this is a third mark.

IV.

Mr. Wesley also revived and established ministerial family visiting, and teaching from house to house. This then is a fourth mark of Primitive Methodism. So the

CONCLUSION OF THE MATTER
Is as follows.

1.

When a present Salvation is not duly enforced, there Primitive Methodism is not. And no sermon can with propriety be called a Primitive Methodist sermon, if this doctrine be omitted, or not duly enforced.

2.

Where worship in the open air is not duly attended to, there Primitive Methodism is dying.

3.

No one can, with propriety, be called a Primitive Methodist Preacher, either travelling or local, unless, in addition to these things, he also duly attends to Mr. Wesley's system of short preaching.

4.

Also, no one can, with propriety, be called a Primitive Methodist travelling preacher, unless, in addition to all these things, he duly attends to ministerial family visiting, and teaching from house to house.

By these marks it may be easily known, who are, and who are not duly entitled to the appellation of PRIMITIVE METHODISTS.

Reasons why the Primitive Methodist Connexion appears to be entitled to that appellation.

1.

It originated like Mr. Wesley's. in the enforcing of the doctrine of a present salvation; and not in any split or division from any other Connexion.

2.

It duly established worship in the open air, and that with great success.

3.

Its first preachers attended to Mr. Wesley's system.

4.

It duly, and with great success, established ministerial family visiting, and teaching from house to house.

Price One Penny,   *Bemersley: Printed by J. Bourne.*

Bible Christian Preaching Services

Advice to the preachers

(BC *Minutes*, 1820)

. . . 7. Begin preaching at the time appointed, and do not be long and tedious, either in singing, praying, or preaching. 'It is better to let the people go away *longing*, than *loathing*.'

8. Suppress (in the tenderest manner) *false fire or wild unwarrantable conduct*** among the people; especially in the meetings; but beware, not to check the *true fire*; and recommend going solemnly, and silently, from the place of worship; unless in returning, they discourse on the sermon, or experience heard.

9. Never suffer talking in the meeting house after meeting is over; because it is apt to erase from the memory, the truths that have been heard. . . .

15. Suffer no Choirs of singers in our preaching-houses; encourage singing by all the congregation. If singing be a part of worship, why not all the people join in it? But Choir-singing, not only cuts off a great part of the congregation, from this part of the worship: but it has also a tendency to beget formality. Let none take the lead in singing, who do not fear God. Caution all, against singing what they do not experience, or understand. Stop sometimes and ask: Do you know what you said last? Do you feel the importance of what you sang? If it can be done, let one of the society set the tune, and take the lead in singing; promote this as much as possible. By this means, singing will be improved and be more melodious, and edifying. Of all parts of our worship, singing comes nearest to the heavenly worship; as it raises the affections to heaven when the soul is happy in God; and makes us almost forget that we are in the body.

---

* By *false fire*, or *wild unwarrantable conduct*, we mean the expressions of sorrow, or joy, by outward gestures, &c. when the *heart* is not *affected*. As the conviction for sin, and a knowledge of pardoning mercy, are often attended with gestures of the body; we consider, that Satan excites some to mimic this. It being somewhat difficult to know the *pretended*, from the *real* work; therefore we need act with caution, lest while we gather up the tares, we root up also the wheat with them! We believe many revivals of religion, have been hindered, and sometimes stopped, through running into one or other extreme! It is true some tell us that it is all *enthusiasm*, and *delusion*, to talk about *feeling in religion*; as though all life, and power accompanying religious experience were false; and as though there were no true life, animation, or fire (as it is sometimes called) . . . The *true fire* is that which is produced by the operation of the Spirit of God on the heart, subduing its stubbornness, softening its hardness, humbling its pride, and bringing everything in subjection to the will of God . . .

Instructions to the Wesleyan Missionaries

At a meeting of the Missionary Committee on December 18, 1817, it was decided to codify the 'various Advices and Directions' given over the years to the missionaries and to have them printed. They were revised from time to time to take account of such changes of circumstance as the emancipation of slaves in the British West Indies. The following version dates from 1825.

I. We recommend to you, *in the first place and above all things*, to pay due attention to your personal piety; which, by prayer, self-denial, holy diligence, and active faith in Him who loved you and gave himself for you, must be kept in a lively, vigorous, and growing state . . . Amidst all your reading, studies, journeyings, preaching, and other labours, let the prosperity of your own souls in the Divine life be carefully cultivated . . .

II. We wish to impress on your minds the absolute necessity of using every means of mental improvement with an express view to your great work as Christian Ministers. You are furnished with useful books, the work of men of distinguished learning and piety. We recommend you to acquire an increase of that general knowledge which, if the handmaid of Piety, will increase your qualifications for extensive usefulness. But more especially, we press upon you the absolute necessity of studying Christian divinity, the doctrines of salvation by the cross of Christ . . . You are to teach Religion: you must, therefore, understand Religion well. You are to disseminate the knowledge of Christianity, in order to the salvation of men; let the Bible then be your book; and let all other books be read only in order to obtain a better acquaintance with the Holy Scriptures, and a greater facility in explaining, illustrating, and applying their important contents. We particularly recommend to you to read and digest the writings of Wesley and Fletcher, and the useful commentaries with which you are furnished, which are designed and calculated to increase your knowledge of the Sacred Volume . . .

III. We exhort you, Brethren, to unity of affection, which will not fail to produce unity of action. Let your love be without dissimulation. In honour prefer one another . . .

IV. Remember always, dear Brethren, that you are by choice and on conviction Wesleyan-Methodist Preachers; and, therefore, it is expected and required of you, to act in all things in a way consistent with that character. In your manner of preaching, and of administering the various ordinances of God's house, keep closely to the model exhibited by your Brethren at home. Indeed, you have solemnly pledged yourselves so to do. *You have promised to preach, in the most explicit terms, the doctrines held* as scriptural, and therefore sacred, in the Connexion to which you belong. We advise, however, in so doing, that you avoid all appearance of controversy, in your mode of stating and enforcing divine truths. While you firmly maintain that ground which we, as a body, have seen it right to take, cultivate a catholic spirit towards all your fellow-labourers in the work of evangelizing the heathen; and aid them to the utmost of your power in their benevolent exertions. You have engaged also to pay a conscientious regard to our discipline. We need not tell you, that *all the parts* of that discipline are of importance; and that, taken together, they form a body of rules and usages, which appear to meet all the wants of individuals who are seeking the salvation of their souls; and, under the divine influence and blessing, to promote the prosperity of every society. We also particularly press upon your constant attention and observation Mr. Wesley's Twelve Rules of a Helper.

V. We cannot omit, without neglecting our duty, to warn you against meddling with political parties, or secular disputes. You are teachers of Religion; and that alone should be kept in view. It is, however, a part of your duty as Ministers to enforce, by precept and example, a cheerful obedience to lawful authority. You know that the venerable Wesley was always distinguished by his love to his country, by his conscientious loyalty, and by his attachment to that illustrious family which has so long filled the throne of Great Britain. You know that your Brethren at home are actuated by the same principles and walk by the same rule; and we have confidence in you that you will preserve the same character of religious regard to good order and submission 'to the powers that be' – in which we glory . . .

VI. You will, on a foreign station, find yourselves in circumstances very different from those in which you are at home, with regard to those who are in authority under our gracious Sovereign. It is probable you will frequently come under their immediate notice and observation. We are, however, persuaded that while you demean yourselves as you ought, you will be generally favoured with their protection. On your arrival at your stations, you will be instructed what steps to take in order to obtain the protection of the local Governments: and we trust that your subsequent good behaviour towards Governors, and *all* who are in authority, will be such as shall secure you the enjoyment of liberty to instruct and promote the salvation of those to whom you are sent.

VII. Those of you who are appointed to the West-India Colonies, being placed in stations of considerable delicacy, and which require, from the state of society there, a particular circumspection and prudence on the one hand, and of zeal, diligence, and patient perseverance on the other; you are required to attend to the following directions, as specially applicable to your Mission there:

1. Your particular designation is to endeavour the religious instruction and conversion of the ignorant, pagan and neglected black and coloured population of the island, or station, to which you may be appointed, and of all others who may be willing to hear you.

2. Where Societies are already formed, you are required to watch over them with the fidelity of those who must give up their accounts to Him who hath purchased them with his blood, and in whose Providence they are placed under your care. Your labours must be constantly directed to improve them in the knowledge of Christianity, and to enforce upon them the experience and practice of its doctrines and duties ... And in order to this, we recommend that your sermons should consist chiefly of clear expositions of the most important truths of Holy Writ, enforced with affection and fervour on the consciences and conduct of them that hear you; that you frequently and familiarly explain portions of the Scriptures; and that, as extensively as you possibly can, you introduce the method of teaching children, and the less instructed of the adult slaves and others, by the excellent Catechisms with which you are furnished.

3. It is enforced upon you, that you continue no person as a member of your Societies, whose 'conversation is not as becometh the Gospel of Christ'. That any member of Society who may relapse into his former habits, and become a polygamist, or an adulterer; who shall be idle and disorderly; disobedient to his owner (if a slave)[1]; who shall steal, or be in any other way immoral or irreligious, shall be put away, after due admonition and proper attempts to reclaim him from the 'error of his way'.

4. Before you receive any person into Society, you shall be satisfied of his desire to become acquainted with the Religion of Christ, and to obey it; and if he has not previously been under Christian instruction, nor baptized, you are, before his admission as a member, diligently to teach him the Christian faith, and the obligations which he takes upon himself by baptism; so as to be assured of his having obtained such knowledge of the principles of religion, and such belief of them as to warrant you to administer to him that ordinance. Beside this, no person is to be admitted into Society, without being placed first on trial, for such time as shall be sufficient to prove whether his conduct has been reformed, and that he has wholly renounced all those vices to which he may have been before addicted.

5. You are to consider the children of the negroes and coloured people of your Societies and Congregations as a part of your charge; and it is recommended to you, wherever it is practicable and prudent, to establish Sunday or other Schools for their instruction. It is to be considered by you as a very important part of your duty as a Missionary to catechise them as often as you conveniently can, at stated periods; and to give your utmost aid to their being brought up in Christian knowledge, and in industrious and moral habits.

6. As in the Colonies in which you are called to labour, a great proportion of the inhabitants are in a state of slavery[2], the Committee most

strongly call to your recollection, what was so fully stated to you when you were accepted as a Missionary to the West Indies, that your only business is to promote the moral and religious improvement of the slaves to whom you may have access, without, in the least degree, in public or private, interfering with their civil condition. On all persons, in the state of slaves, you are diligently and implicitly to enforce the same exhortations which the Apostles of our Lord administered to the slaves of ancient nations, when by their ministry they embraced Christianity. Eph. vi.5–8, 'Servants, be obedient to them that are your masters according to the flesh, with fear and trembling, in singleness of your heart, as unto Christ; not with eye-service, as men-pleasers; but as the servants of Christ, doing the will of God from the heart; with good will doing service, as to the Lord, and not to men: knowing that whatsoever good thing any man doeth, the same shall he receive of the Lord, whether he be bond or free.' . . .[3]

7. You are directed to avail yourselves of every opportunity to extend your labours among the slaves of the islands where you may be stationed; but you are in no case to visit the slaves of any plantation without the permission of the owner or manager; nor are the times which you may appoint for their religious services, to interfere with their owner's employ; nor are you to suffer any protracted meetings in the evening, not even at negro burials, on any account whatever. In all these cases, you are to meet even unreasonable prejudices, and attempt to disarm suspicions, however groundless, so far as you can do it consistently with your duties as faithful and laborious Ministers of the Gospel.

8. As many of the negroes live in a state of polygamy, or in a promiscuous intercourse of the sexes, your particular exertions are to be directed to the discountenancing and correcting of these vices, by pointing out their evil, both in public and in private, and by maintaining the strictest discipline in the Societies. No man, living in a state of polygamy, is to be admitted a member, or even on trial, who will not consent to live with one woman as his wife, to whom you shall join him in matrimony, or ascertain that this rite has been performed by some other Minister; and the same rule is to be applied, in the same manner, to a woman proposing to become a member of Society. No female, living in a state of concubinage with any person, is to be admitted into Society so long as she continues in that sin.

9. The Committee caution you against engaging in any of the civil disputes or local politics of the Colony to which you may be appointed, either verbally or by correspondence with any persons at home, or in the Colonies. The whole period of your temporary residence in the West Indies is to be filled up with the proper work of your Mission. You are not to become parties in any civil quarrel; but are to 'please all men for

their good to edification'; intent upon the solemn work of your office, and upon that eternal state, in the views of which the Committee trust you will ever think and act.

10. In cases of opposition to your ministry, which may arise on the part of individuals, or of any of the colonial legislatures, a meek and patient spirit and conduct are recommended to you. You will in particular guard against all angry and resentful speeches, and in no case attempt to inflame your Societies and hearers with resentment against your persecutors or opposers. Your business, in such cases, after every prudent means of obtaining relief has failed in your own hands, is with the Committee at home; who will immediately take such steps as may secure to you that protection, from a mild and tolerant Government, which they hope your peaceable and pious conduct, your labours and successes, will ever merit for you.

N.B. The Directions to the West India Missionaries are also to be considered as strictly obligatory on all others, as far as they are applicable to the circumstances of their respective stations.

VIII. It is *peremptorily required* of every Missionary in our Connexion to keep a Journal, and to send home frequently such copious abstracts of it as may give a full and particular account of his labours, success, and prospects. He is also required to give such details of a religious kind as may be generally interesting to the friends of Missions at home; particularly, accounts of conversions. Only, we recommend to you, not to allow yourselves, under the influence of religious joy, to give any *high colouring* of facts; but always write such accounts as you [would] not object to see return in print to the place where the facts reported may have occurred.

IX. It is a positive rule amongst the Wesleyan Methodists, that no Travelling Preacher shall 'follow trade'. You are to consider this rule as binding upon you, and all Foreign Missionaries in our Connexion. We wish you to be at the remotest distance from all temptation to a secular or mercenary temper . . . Independently of the moral and religious considerations which enforce this principle, we here take occasion to remind you, that all your time and energies should be the more sacredly devoted to the duties of your Mission, because the Committee feel themselves fully pledged to pay an affectionate attention to all your wants, and to afford them every reasonable and necessary supply . . .

And now, Brethren, we commend you to God and the word of his grace. We unite with tens of thousands in fervent prayer to God for you. May he open to you a great door and effectual; and make you, immediately or remotely, the instruments of the salvation of myriads. We shall incessantly pray, that 'you may go out with joy, and be led forth with peace; that instead of the thorn may come up the fir-tree, and instead of the briar the myrtle-tree; and it shall be to the Lord for a name, for an everlasting sign that shall not be cut off.' 'Blessed be the Lord God, the God of Israel, who only doeth wondrous things; and blessed be his glorious name for ever, and let the whole earth be filled with his glory: Amen and Amen.'

[1] This clause is omitted in the 1834 edition.

[2] Following the emancipation of the West Indian slaves, the 1834 version reads: 'As in most of the Colonies in which you are called to labour a great proportion of the inhabitants, though happily emancipated from their former state of slavery, are yet placed by law in certain peculiar relations, as apprenticed labourers . . .'

[3] Col. iii.22–25 is also quoted at this point.

Instructions of the Wesleyan Methodist Missionary Society

to Mr. [Samuel] Leigh and to Mr. [John] Morgan, the former going out to establish Missions in New Zealand and the Friendly Islands; the other to the River Gambia in West Africa, read to them at a Public Ordination Service in the New Chapel, City Road, January 17th, 1821

You are both appointed to the important work of undertaking new Missions. You are going among the heathen, and to those stations in the heathen world where Christ is not named. You are appointed not to enter upon other men's labours, but to lay the foundations: not to reap the fruits of others' toils, but for the first time to clear away the encumbrances of the ground, and to put the plough into an unbroken soil. Such an undertaking, we need scarcely remind you, demands your most solemn consideration. It is one which from its difficulties and hazards, requires you, in an especial manner, to gird up the loins of your mind, to summon all your courage and to put your trust in God.

You are both going not only beyond the bounds of the church of Christ, the ordinances and privileges of which you must for a time be deprived of, but also beyond the bounds of the British Empire; and will not, like most of your fellow Missionaries, enjoy the protection of its power and its laws. You, Brother Leigh, will fix your residence among the rude savages of New Zealand, and you, Brother Morgan, are appointed to penetrate the dense negro population of the Gambia, where power only is law, and where there are few restraints on the violence of men. In this respect you are placed in circumstances similar to many of the first preachers of the gospel. You carry in an emphatic sense your lives in your hand . . . It was to the primitive Missionaries that Jesus, their Master, said, 'The very hairs of your head are all numbered.'

Among some of the tribes of New Zealand, and of Africa, you will be the first Christian residents. Of Christians by profession they have heard, some of them have been their visitants; and unhappily from the conduct of many they must have imbibed notions of our religion not in the least tending to recommend it. But they have also heard of Christian Missionaries, and have learned to distinguish between them and others. Let this circumstance impress you. You have a high character to sustain; and closely as every word and action will be scrutinised by the people to whom you will each be sent, remember that it is from your daily spirit and walk that they will form their estimate both of your motives and the religion you would enjoin upon them. He who would recommend a new religion to others as the only true religion, coming from the only living and true God, is especially called upon to show that it is of God by the effects produced upon himself. In the habitual kindness of your tempers therefore, in your holy and even scrupulous demeanour; in the openness and rectitude of all your intercourse with others; in the impressive love you shall manifest to your fellow-labourers, who may go out with you, or may follow after you; and in the orderly and religious management of your families, earnestly pray and strive, that you may be the living example of the superior purity and excellence of the religion of our Lord Jesus.

It is an important circumstance that in New Zealand, and the Committee have reason to believe also among the negroes up the Gambia, the heathen are ready to place their children under the care of Christian Missionaries. In the humble but important task of superintending, teaching and catechising in schools, your earliest efforts will therefore be demanded; and even when assistants are raised up, a careful and affectionate oversight of them will be necessary. To this part of your work you are therefore required to pay great attention. It is the first instrument for undermining the prejudice and superstititions of the heathen put into your hand. A number of immortal souls will thus be brought under your influence and early imbued with right principles . . . Let all your plans of education, however, be strictly Christian, and let the conversion of youth confided to you be the object of your most solicitous regard.

You are nevertheless preachers of the gospel, and are to watch every opportunity to gain access to the minds of the adults. For this purpose your study of the native languages must be assiduous and conscientious. You are to consider this as a sacred and religious duty, rather than as a matter of literature and in this study you are to seek for Divine help in all your endeavours. . . .

In giving instruction to the natives, it is of importance that you rather propose and enforce with meekness the glorious truths of the gospel, than dispute with their superstitions and absurd opinions. No true Christians have anywhere been made by mere disputations, however well conducted. You are to propose the gospel in its simplest and most explicit truths, as an undoubted revelation from God, to dwell upon the wretched and guilty state of man, and upon the love and grace of our Lord Jesus Christ; and invite and persuade them to be reconciled to God. Do all this, not with the air and spirit of a dogmatist, but with the sympathy and kind solicitude of him who came 'to seek and save that which was lost'. Nor let it be ever absent from your minds, that all your hopes of success depend upon the Divine influence and power accompanying truths thus spoken in the benevolent spirit and according to the true doctrine of the gospel. Let every word of advice, and every public discourse, be given and delivered in the spirit of prayer, and steadfastly fix your hopes in God.

As you will be appointed to assist the natives in acquiring the knowledge of agriculture, and some of the useful arts of life, habits of labour and industry must be cultivated by you, at least in the early stages of your Mission. To all things by which you can promote the real good of the natives you must apply yourselves, even as the great Apostle of the Gentiles, working with your own hands. In all this beware of the secular spirit. These are works to be done in the name of the Lord Jesus, and for Him. Whatsoever you are called to in this respect, 'do it heartily, and do it unto the Lord'. . . .

Should you acquire influence and consideration with the natives of the place of your destination, as we trust by the blessing of God you will, you may be placed in circumstances of some difficulty arising from the quarrels and different views of the various chiefs. Your plain line of duty is to take no part in their civil affairs and to make it understood that interference in these matters is no part of your object, and that you are sent to do good to all men. This, however, will not prevent you giving them such advice as may be beneficial to all parties when it is desired, and more especially you ought earnestly to endeavour to induce them to abandon those cruel practices which are so frequent in their wars. Kind and prudent remonstrances against cruelty of every description may be the means of softening the barbarism of their manners, even before they are efficiently brought under the influence of the gospel.

The rules in the General Instruction, as to the administration of Baptism, and discipline in general, are specially recommended for your guidance. Our aim is not merely to civilise but to convert, and in every instance careful instruction in the Christian Faith and evidence of a true turning of the heart unto the Lord is to be required before that sacred ordinance is administered.

As in New Zealand especially, and ultimately on the banks of the Gambia, the brethren with their families must live together in the Mission-house, the careful cultivation of the kindest brotherly affection is solemnly enjoined. To promote and establish this, let the rules for your conduct towards each other in the General Instructions be sacredly adhered to. Let the heathen around you behold and say, 'See how these Christians love.' In honour prefer one another. Remember your great work, your brief and uncertain life; your solemn account. Live in peace, and the God of love and peace will be with you.

Objects of the West Indian Missions

Richard Watson[1] to Charles Janion[2]; London, November 27, 1821

(Ms at Drew University)

Your letters and Extracts from your Journal[3], giving the account of the progress of the Mission in which you labour, have given us satisfaction. These are the details with which all our missionaries ought to furnish us, and we are happy that you set an example to the negligent, rather than fall under the influence of theirs.

I need not impress it upon you that the Mission in which you are engaged is an important one. Wherever souls are to be saved, and a corrupt state of society purified, the most important work is to be done, and it is to be done in the spirit and temper of those who know that they are nothing of themselves, nothing but what they are made by God and can do nothing but what God does by them.

The great objects to be aimed at in a West India Mission appear to be the following:

1. A holy, zealous, provident and meek conduct on the part of the missionary, that he may obtain the confidence of at least reasonable men, who are without;

2. A ministry, expository of the leading doctrines and most important parts of the Sacred Scriptures, plain, affectionate, evangelical and practical;

3. The appointment of as suitable leaders as can be found without partiality, and the making leaders' meetings rather the means of instruction and edification to the leaders than for *discussions* or discipline or anything else;

4. The effectual catechising of the children of *all* our friends, and as many of the adults in Society as need it, that they may not be ignorant of the first principles of religion;

5. The extension of this benefit to as many others as possible, that so the work may spread among the heathen.

But who is sufficient for all this? For what labour, patience, self-denial and holy zeal does this require? Well, my dear Brother, you are aiming, I doubt not, at all these objects and by this time you know the dangers, the discouragements, and the hopes & joys of a West India Mission. Continue to go to that source which has never failed you, and you will be girded with strength. In a more glorious sphere of labour you could not be placed; for the result of the labours of you and your brethren will finally be, if persevered in, to banish darkness from the West Indies and fill every negro mind with the knowledge of the glory of God. So be it, and quickly!

¹ Watson was one of the secretaries of the Missionary Society from 1821 to 1825.

² Janion was appointed to the West Indian mission in 1819. This letter was addressed to him at the Methodist Chapel, Montserrat, thuogh according to the *Minutes* for 1821 he was appointed to Tortola that year.

³ For Janion's letter to the Missionary Committee, see *WM Magazine*, 1822, pp. 191–2.

The Lord's Supper among the Bible Christians

(BC *Minutes*, 1821)

Q.15. What are our thoughts on what is called the Sacrament of the Lord's Supper?

A. We believe it is an institution of Christ, to keep his *meritorious death in remembrance*.

Q.16. What are the essential parts of the Sacrament of the Lord's Supper?

A. *Bread* and *wine* used as a *memorial* of the *death of Christ*.

Q.17. In what manner should this be done?

A. As we cannot approach too near to the original institution, in which our Lord used *unleavened* bread, and *brake* (not cut) it, and gave it to the disciples as they were sitting (not kneeling); we think it safest to follow *his* example; especially as *kneeling* was introduced with the *monstrous* doctrine of *transubstantiation*; a doctrine replete with *absurdity*, *superstition*, and *idolatry*.¹

¹ A more flexible attitude later developed: 'The elements are usually received in a sitting posture, . . . but persons are at liberty to kneel if it be more suitable to their views and feelings to do so.' (*Digest of the Rules*, 1882, p. 46).

William Cobbett on Methodist Preaching

(*Rural Rides* (Penguin edition, 1967), pp. 181–2, 187–8)

Sunday, August 31, 1823

Coming through the village of Benenden, I heard a man, at my right, talking very loud about *houses! houses! houses!* It was a Methodist parson, in a house, close by the road side. I pulled up, and stood still, in the middle of the road, but looking, in silent soberness, into the window (which was open) of the room in which the preacher was at work. I believe my stopping rather disconcerted him; for he got into shocking *repetition.* 'Do you KNOW,' said he, laying great stress on the word KNOW: 'do you KNOW, that you have ready for you houses, houses I say; I say do you KNOW; do you KNOW that you have houses in the heavens not made with hands? Do you KNOW this from *experience?* Has the blessed Jesus *told you so?*' And, on he went to say, that, if Jesus had told them so, they would be saved, and that if he had not, and did not, they would be damned. Some girls whom I saw in the room, plump and rosy as could be, did not seem at all daunted by these menaces; and indeed, they appeared to me to be thinking much more about getting houses for themselves *in this world first*: just to *see a little* before they entered, or endeavoured to enter, or even thought much about, those '*houses*' of which the parson was speaking: *houses* with pig-styes and little snug gardens attached to them, together with all the other domestic and conjugal circumstances, these girls seemed to me to be preparing themselves for. The truth is, these fellows have no power on the minds of any but the miserable . . .

This evening I have been to the Methodist Meeting-house [at Tenterden]. I was attracted, fairly drawn all down the street, by the *singing.* When I came to the place the parson was got into prayer. His hands were clenched together and held up, his face turned up and back so as to be nearly parallel with the ceiling, and he was bawling away, with his '*do thou,*' and '*mayest thou,*' and '*may we,*' enough to stun one. Noisy, however, as he was, he was unable to fix the attention of a parcel of girls in the gallery, whose eyes were *all over the place*, while his eyes were so devoutly shut up. After a deal of this rigmarole called prayer, came the *preachy*, as the negroes call it; and a *preachy* it really was. Such a mixture of whining cant and of foppish affectation I scarcely ever heard in my life. The text was (I speak from memory) one of Saint Peter's Epistles (if he have more than one) the 18th Chapter and 4th Verse. The words were to this amount: that, *as the righteous would be saved with difficulty, what must become of the ungodly and the sinner!* After as neat a dish of nonsense and of impertinences as one could wish to have served up, came the distinction between the *ungodly* and the *sinner*. The sinner was one who *did moral wrong*; the ungodly one, who did *no moral wrong*, but who was not *regenerated. Both*, he positively told us, were to be DAMNED. One was just as bad as the other. Moral rectitude was to do nothing in saving the man. He was to be damned, unless born again, unless he came to the regeneration shop, and gave the fellows money? He distinctly told us, that a man *perfectly moral*, might be *damned*; and that 'the *vilest of the vile*, and the *basest of the base*' (I quote his very words) 'would be saved if they became *regenerate*; and that *Colliers*, whose souls had been as *black* as their *coals*, had, by regeneration, become bright as the saints that sing before

God and the Lamb.' And will the *Edinburgh Reviewers* again find fault
with me for cutting at this bawling, canting crew? Monstrous it is to
think that the Clergy of the Church really encourage these roving
fanatics. The Church seems aware of its loss of credit and of power. It
seems willing to lean even upon these men; who, be it observed, seem,
on their part, to have taken the Church *under their protection*. They always
pray for the *Ministry*; I mean the ministry at *Whitehall*. They are most
'*loyal*' souls. The THING *protects them*; and they lend their aid *in upholding
the* THING. What silly, nay, what base creatures those must be, who really
give their *money*, give their pennies, which ought to buy bread for their
own children; who thus give their money to these lazy and impudent
fellows, who call themselves *ministers of God*, who prowl about the
country, living easy and jovial lives upon the fruit of the labour of other
people. However, it is, in some measure, these people's fault. If they did
not *give*, the others could not *receive*.

Primitive Methodist Discipline

('A Private Communication', reprinted in John Walford, *Life of Hugh Bourne*, II,
132–5)

Disciplinary weaknesses in the Connexion provoked the following statement from Bourne in 1824 and inaugurated a 'period of crisis' in Primitive
Methodism.

It is evident the Lord has, in an extraordinary manner, prospered the
labours of the Primitive Methodist Connexion, which proves that the
preachers have in their hands a great power in the ministry. But a few
things have been complained of, and they will come before the next
annual meeting.[1] It was therefore thought best, by this private communication, to make them known to the travelling preachers in general,
and to the official people in the respective circuits, in order that the
annual meeting delegates may be prepared beforehand with proper
instructions. And as the cases are but few, the travelling preachers are
requested to weigh them over, and, if possible, to devise the best means
to correct them. If they be not corrected, the reproach of them will be
attached to the whole of the travelling preachers.

1. In the year 1822, a preacher on the annual list was appointed to
labour for three months in a flourishing circuit; and during that time,
chiefly by neglect of duty, he so ran the circuit out as to render it unable
to pay him his salary. It is true the people borrowed money to pay him;
but it appears the money so borrowed has not been paid to this day.
Now the question to be decided by the annual meeting is this, – From

what source shall a preacher's salary be paid, in future, in all such cases? 2. If such preacher was stationed in a circuit for twelve months, and such running out of the circuit should happen in the first or second quarter, is the circuit obliged to keep him the whole twelve months? And if it be obliged to keep him, then from what sources shall his salary be paid? 3. In 1822 a preacher on the annual list often neglected his appointments, going among other professors of religion. By this neglect he caused much embarrassment to the circuit, yet at the quarter-day he required a full salary. 4. Also a preacher occasionally neglected his appointments, without any apparent cause but mere indolence. 5. In 1823 a complaint was made of a preacher neglecting appointments, – spending the time in smoking and tattling. 6. In 1823 a circuit-steward complained, saying, that one travelling preacher's wife had been setting up in a line of business, and he had frequently neglected his appointments to assist her. By these neglects he greatly injured the circuit; yet at the quarter-day he required a full salary. Some thought it wrong to pay a man for work he had not done. 7. In 1823 it was stated that two travelling preachers refused to take any appointments but what were given to them in print, yet they required a full salary. 8. In the former part of 1823 a circuit complained that the travelling preachers were almost constantly too late at their appointments. The circuit tried a variety of means to correct the evil, but was not able to correct it. 9. In 1823 two travelling preachers in one circuit, and one in another, did much injury by trailing about with women. 10. In 1823 two single travelling preachers, one of whom is on the annual list, took an advantage of the regulation about board and lodging, and by improper conduct brought embarrassment upon the circuit. On that account that circuit thinks the regulation ought to stand as it did in 1822. It will be difficult for the annual meeting to correct the evil without causing the whole of the single preachers to suffer for the improper conduct of two individuals. 11. One annual meeting admonished the societies to beware of impostors. But since then a travelling preacher has done much injury by introducing an impostor among the people. And in September, 1823, two travelling preachers, by their own authority, took up a woman, an entire stranger, and of doubtful report, and put her up to preach, without the consent of the leaders' meeting. 12. There have been other complaints of travelling preachers, by their own authority, introducing improper persons among the people as preachers, and thereby doing injury. All these cases will come before the annual meeting, when the names of all the preachers referred to will be given in, if required; and the annual meeting will be called upon to lay down a line of proceedings for the circuits in future, in all similar cases.

CIRCUIT EMBARRASSMENTS

These are becoming serious, and will require the united wisdom of the Connexion. And the annual meeting must, as far as possible, point out to the embarrassed circuits such means and plans as shall be the most likely to enable them to rise out of their embarrassments. Also, the annual meeting must make such regulations as will, if possible, prevent embarrassments in future. On one occasion the annual meeting acted with effect. Some of the travelling preachers had got into a habit of embarrassing circuits by hand-over-head proceedings about places of worship. The annual meeting took it up, and made a regulation which appears to have cut it off. And in some of the before-mentioned cases, the annual meeting may cut off embarrassments. Also, they may do something in the following:—

1. On one occasion, on the forming a new circuit, a preacher neglected his station where he was appointed, and stationed himself in the new circuit; and his so doing was the means of bringing a great embarrassment on that new circuit. The annual meeting must absolutely do something decisive on this point, as it is a growing evil. 2. Two or three travelling preachers, by their own authority, and in breach of discipline, fetched an improper man into a circuit, from another circuit, but no member thereof; and they actually put him upon the people as a travelling preacher. This, as might have been foreseen, brought on a most dreadful embarrassment. 3. Three women were suffered to go loose from circuit to circuit; and one of the larger circuits not only connived at them, but actually encouraged them. At first they appeared to be useful; but after a time the evil over-balanced the good; and finally, they acted in the most treacherous manner, and made great ravage of religion on one of the circuits. 4. One circuit has been embarrassed through illness among the travelling preachers. This of course is and has been providential; and the circuit might have been greatly assisted out of the contingent fund, – there being in it thirty-two pounds of unapplied money, in May, 1823. But, unhappily, the travelling preachers had neglected to make the contingent fund collection, and by such neglect the circuit was deprived of the benefit. The annual meeting, it is thought, may do something serviceable in all such cases as these, and in a variety of other cases.

Further to assist the annual meeting, it is requested that every circuit that has been embarrassed, and has risen out of its embarrassment, will send to the annual meeting a statement in writing of how the embarrassment occurred, and by what means the circuit was enabled to rise out of its embarrassment. Also, the preachers, and others, who occupy official stations, are requested to weigh over this important matter, and try to devise the most likely means to preserve the circuits. It will be well to put the remarks in writing. Every embarrassed circuit is distinctly requested to send to the annual meeting a statement in writing, giving a full account of its embarrassment, shewing how it first arose, and by what means it has been lowered or increased. Also stating distinctly what travelling preachers laboured in such circuit when the embarrassment was first brought on; and what travelling preachers succeeded them from that time. Also when, and how, the embarrassment has been lowered or increased.

N.B. – It is requested that one of these be sent to each travelling preacher as speedily as it well can.

¹ I.e., of the Primitive Methodist Conference.

Irish Methodist Missionary Report, 1826

(William Smith, *Consecutive History*, 1830, pp. 171–2; HMGB, Vol. 3, 246)

The 21 missionaries stationed in different parts of Ireland, have continued to exert themselves throughout the year, in spreading the knowledge of evangelical truth, and in leading the peasantry, in many of the most neglected districts, from their superstitition and vices, to the knowledge and practice of the religion of the Holy Scripture. In this work, their journeys have been long and arduous, their privations many, and their dangers sometimes great.

They have preached the Gospel in the fields and streets, the fairs and markets, and in the cabins of the peasantry, and have had many instances of direct success, besides diffusing some knowledge of Scriptural Christianity, through a considerable part of the population. Small religious societies have been raised up, in various places, which are as lights of example and doctrine, in the surrounding darkness.

The schools connected with the missions, which are under the care of pious and qualified schoolmasters, have been conducted with great regularity, throughout the year, and the effects produced by them, upon the morals of the children, and the neighbourhoods in which they are situated, have been, in many instances, great.

Missionary schools in 1826:

Masters	Schools	Children	Bible Readers	Catechumens	Sunday Scholars
20	20	1,412	626	559	880

The 'Leeds Organ Case'

Petition to the Leaders' Meeting, signed by sixty of the Circuit's loca preachers, October 13, 1826.

(John Barr, *A Statement of Facts*, 1827, pp. 2–4)

We, the undersigned local preachers, beg respectfully to state to the Leaders of the Leeds East circuit (in meeting assembled) our sentiments on the subject of an organ in Brunswick Chapel.

United with our brethren, the leaders, in one common object, namely, the glory of God in the salvation of sinners, and in the building up of his church, we naturally feel interested in every thing relating to Methodism, and are anxious to see such measures adopted throughout our system and economy, as will best produce so great and important a design.

But, brethren, we cannot but feel alarmed, at the attempts which we understand are now making, to change the mode of conducting the devotional part of our religious services, by erecting an organ in Bruns-wick Chapel: a measure, which, whilst it destroys at once the excellent form of our venerable founder, is one which almost universal experience goes to prove to be at variance with, and subversive of, that spirituality in our congregational worship, which has so long characterized the Methodists of Leeds, and which we believe to be so acceptable in the sight of God.

The Leeds society has hitherto set a noble example to the whole con-nexion, for its steady and uniform adherence to the original and simple forms of religious worship; and we fear, brethren, that the wish for such innovation as that now contemplated, proceeds not so much from a desire to increase holy and hallowing influence upon the hearts and lives of the congregation, as to please the ear and captivate the passions, and ought in our humble opinion to be regarded, not only as an approxi-mation to the spirit of the world, but also as the first step towards other, and still more important changes. If the friends of such a measure seek only to increase spirituality of worship, which surely ought to be the end and design of every change, it appears to us, that such an object would be best promoted by their habitual search after greater personal enjoyment of its power and influence, and then from their hearts would they be enabled to 'make melody unto God'.

We would seriously recommend to the solemn and attentive con-sideration of the friends of organs, what account can be given at the final day of retribution, for the expenditure of so large a sum of money as would be necessary for a purpose which we have every reason to believe would prove an actual evil; especially at a period like the present, when many members of our society are wanting the common necessaries of life.

In conclusion, brethren, we believe and trust, that a matter so fraught with such serious consequences to vital religion among us, as that upon which we now address you, will not receive that sanction from you, which by the laws of Methodism is indispensable to its adoption . . .

George Cubitt to George Birley; Bristol, October 10, 1827

(Ms at SMU)

I have no Methodistical news. Everything, I think, seems to be very quiet among us . . .

The public papers will have told you, as they have told me, of the disturbances at Leeds. I had forgotten this when I said 'things seem to be very quiet among us'. There is a very black cloud there – but I will hope it will disperse. It will never do for the Local Preachers to intermeddle, *as such*, with Society matters. At the same time, I hope Mr. Grindrod[1] has not been guilty of claiming and exercising absolute power, as the papers I have seen state. I wait anxiously to hear news. At present I hear none.

[1] Edmund Grindrod was Superintendent of the Leeds circuit at the time.

Adam Clarke to George Marsden; Stockport, October 31, 1828

(Ms copies at Duke and Emory Universities)

They have earnestly requested me to visit Liverpool, where their schools are in a ruinous state. We can get plenty of money for *organs* and other *matters*, by which the Church of God is rent, but we feel less, at least less than we did, for the poor, especially for the poor of God's people . . .

The Leeds business is a fearful matter. After all that I have heard at Conference, I am satisfied in my *conscience* that *we alone* were the aggressors, and that we have done wrong, if not wickedly, from the first to the last. I saw what the decisions of the last Conference would do, nothing could be worse in the case as it then stood, than our decisions relative to it. We have sacrificed 1,000 members, if not souls, to our *organism* and attempts at *despotic power*. This is my opinion, my creed in the present business.

Rules of the Societies of the Wesleyan Protestant Methodists

(Op. cit., 1829, pp. 10–11)

WORSHIP

The worship of the Almighty should be conducted in a humble, spiritual manner:— all Pomp and Parade should be most scrupulously avoided. – No Instruments of Music shall be introduced into our Chapels; nor shall any person be employed to conduct the Singing therein, unless known to be a pious man. In every case Simplicity must be joined with Piety, Prudence with Zeal, and solemn Reverence be the Guide of the most ardent Devotion. In all these points, we think, we have an excellent example in the practice of Original Methodism. We also read of both our Lord and his Disciples singing Hymns, and this was evidently the practice of all the Primitive Churches: but we hear of no Instruments of Music being ever sanctioned by either Christ or his Apostles. In this respect, the Simplicity and heart-felt Devotion of the Christian Religion is evidently distinguished from the Splendour, Costliness, and Pomp attached to the ceremonial Institutions of the Mosaic economy. The Collection of Hymns by Mr. Wesley 'for the use of the people called Methodists', shall be used in all our Places of Worship.

With respect to the Reading of the Church Liturgy in our Chapels, it is agreed, 1. That our brethren in London be allowed the use of Mr. Wesley's Abridgement of the Liturgy in their Chapels, where a majority of the Preachers, Leaders, Stewards, and Trustees desire it, inasmuch as they have been accustomed to it from the early periods of Methodism. But, as a general principle, this Meeting entertains a very strong objection to the Liturgy being read in our Chapels. 2. That the permission, in reference to the Reading of the Liturgy in the Chapels in London, shall not be extended to any other place.

Management of Sunday Schools

(*Minutes*, 1827)

As a means of exercising control of the growing number of Wesleyan Sunday Schools, the following recommendations were adopted.

General Principles and Rules to be observed in the management of Methodist Sunday-Schools

(I) General Principles

First principle. – Sunday-schools should be *strictly and entirely religious* institutions; and ought therefore to be schools for the *Christian* instruction and education of the children of the poor; as it is only on this ground that the occupation of the Lord's day in tuition can be held to consist with the due observation of the Christian Sabbath.

Second principle. – Schools designed for the religious education of poor children ought to be conducted in distinct and avowed *connexion* with some particular branch of the visible *church of Christ*.

1. Because the Pastors, and other official members of a Christian church or society, are not left at liberty to commit the religious education of *the children of their own poorer members* to any persons, except those, for whose character and principles they possess some adequate security, and over whose modes of instruction and discipline they have the means of exercising an efficient influence and control. The children of members, and those even of constant hearers in the congregation, are, in an important sense, *the children of the church*, and of that portion of it, especially, with which their parents stand connected. Many of them have been by holy baptism solemnly recognised as among the objects of pastoral charge, and as entitled to the care and spiritual assistance of Christian people. In all such cases, a responsibility attaches to the church and its Ministers, which they cannot, without blame, transfer into other hands, except under such circumstances as will allow them still to *observe* and to *direct*, in all points of vital importance, the manner in which the trust is executed by those to whom they confide it.

2. Because every Christian church or society is not only obliged in duty to exert a proper control over the religious education of its own youth, but has also a deep and permanent *interest* in the results of that education; and is therefore required, in justice to itself, to retain those Sunday-schools which are supported, wholly or principally, by its contributions, its labours, or its influence, under the superintendence and scriptural jurisdiction of its Pastors, and of its other regular authorities.

3. Because, in reference to *children of every class* admitted into Sunday-schools (whether their parents be directly connected with any Christian

church or not), those who piously and liberally support such institutions have a clear right to receive a decisive pledge, in the *known Christian character and principles* of their leading managers, and in their connexion with some religious body whose creed is avowed before the world, and whose right of superintendence is expressly recognised, that the influence exerted by them upon the opinions and habits of the rising generation shall be, as far as human prudence can secure it, a sound and salutary one.

4. Because *general experience* seems now to have decided in favour of the superior advantages of placing every Sunday-school under the care of some particular religious community, which shall be held responsible to the parents of the children educated in it, and to the public who may choose to support it, for its sound principles and good management. Instructed by that experience, almost every branch of the Christian church in this country has now *its own Sunday-schools*; open indeed to all poor children who apply; but conducted chiefly by its own members; superintended by its own Ministers, and other ecclesiastical officers; governed according to its own peculiar views of the *fundamental* doctrines and duties of Christianity; and connected *generally* with its own places of worship. Thus the labour of religiously educating the poor is amicably divided, and, for that reason, better performed: and sufficient scope is left for the exercise of a truly Christian liberality, in the interchange of mutual good offices, and in the occasional aids afforded by the affluent of one body to the funds of others; while no temptation is in any case held out to a compromise of principle, and the danger of practical collision or controversy, among persons of different sentiments, is in a great measure precluded.

Third principle. – Sunday-schools should be most conscientiously and anxiously so conducted, that they may not interfere, farther than an invincible necessity may compel, with the *primary and universal* duties of the holy Sabbath, and, in particular, with the constant attendance of teachers and children on the public worship of God's house, at the hours most generally devoted to that purpose, and best adapted to secure their edification:—

1. Because one essential part of a truly *Christian* education must ever consist in the formation of an early and fixed *habit* of reverence for the Christian Sabbath, and of regard for the ordinances of the Christian sanctuary.

2. Because those who act as teachers in these schools, in common with all other persons, are under an immutable obligation to attend with regularity the public means of grace, and to pay their vows to God in the presence of all his people. They actually need, for themselves, all the help and instruction provided for them in the house of God; from which, as experience has often proved, they cannot be *frequently* and *needlessly*

detained, even by the well-meant endeavour to serve the souls of others, without great danger of weakening in their own minds the proper tone of Christian feeling, and of suffering (especially if they be young in years and in religious profession) a spiritual loss, most prejudicial in the issue to their piety, and to their general usefulness in the church of Christ.

Fourth principle. – On the same ground of vigilant concern for the best interests both of children and of their teachers, the *bustle* and the *secularity* of mere *school-business* should be as much as possible avoided in the management of Sunday-schools; and the spiritual objects and character of the institutions should be so carefully kept in mind, as to regulate and control the whole plan and process of Sabbath-education.

In conformity to these PRINCIPLES the following *outline* of

(II) GENERAL RULES

has been drawn up, with a direct reference to the circumstances of *Methodist* Sunday-schools: viz., –

1. Sunday-schools supported, wholly or principally, by the contributions, labours, and influence of our body, and sanctioned by our Preachers, shall be denominated *Wesleyan-Methodist* Sunday-schools; – in order that the Connexion and the public may possess, in the very name and title of the institutions, the means of ascertaining the principles on which they profess to be conducted, and a pledge and security for the maintenance of those principles, under every change of local management; and in order, also, that parents, not connected with our societies and congregations, who shall choose to send their children to our schools, may be fully apprized of the nature and tendency of the instruction and discipline there administered.

2. The general management of such schools shall be entrusted to a Committee, consisting,

(1) Of all the *Travelling Preachers* of the Circuit.

(2) Of all the *officers* of the school or schools; appointed as hereinafter mentioned.

(3) Of twelve, sixteen, twenty, twenty-four, or thirty-six *other persons* (the number being determined according to local circumstances), to be appointed by the annual meeting of the subscribers; but of this number, –

One-fourth shall always be selected from those *teachers* in the schools, who are also *members* of the Methodist Society:

One half shall be chosen from the general body of *subscribers*, being also *members* of the Methodist Society:— and

The remaining *one-fourth* shall be selected from those respectable members of our *congregations*, or *other subscribers*, who, though not of our Society, are believed to agree with us in their general views of the great and leading doctrines of Christianity.

3. The Superintendent Preacher of the Circuit, as the chief Pastor of our Societies, and the official representative of Methodism in the Circuit

where he is stationed, shall *preside* in all meetings of the Subscribers and of the Committee at which he may be present. In his absence, his place shall be supplied by one of the other Preachers; or, if no Preacher be present, by some other officer of the institution appointed for that purpose by the persons assembled . . .

5. All the officers, with the exception of the Treasurer and Auditors, shall be selected *exclusively* from the members of the Methodist Society; and, before their final appointment, shall be proposed and approved in the Leaders' Meeting of the Society to which each school shall be attached, as persons deemed eligible, in point of *general religious character*, to be put in nomination at the Meeting by which the election is to be made.

6. The *teachers* shall be appointed by the Conductors or Local Superintendents of each school; subject, however, to the subsequent approbation of the Committee, if, in any instance, they deem it necessary to interpose their authority. And no person shall be continued in office as a teacher, who shall at any time be declared by the Committee, or by the Leaders' Meeting, ineligible in point of general character, or of religious opinions, to take a part in the Christian education of the children placed under our care. In the selection of teachers for the *elder* classes, peculiar attention should be paid to their *Christian experience*; and those only should be so employed, who are able to teach their pupils, clearly and fully, 'what they must do to be saved'.

7. As it is the great and primary object of Sunday-schools to teach the children of the poor to read and understand the holy Scriptures, with a view to their being made 'wise unto salvation', the elementary books employed in the tuition even of the younger scholars shall be such as contain the largest portion of *scriptural instruction*; and the Bible or New Testament shall be regularly used every Sabbath-day by those classes which are farther advanced.

8. *Catechetical exercises* shall form a regular part of the system of our schools. And, in order to prevent the evils which might result from an unlimited private discretion in the selection of Catechisms, it is earnestly recommended that the Catechisms employed shall be those compiled and published under the sanction of the Conference, in which are embodied the most important portions of Mr. Wesley's Instructions, of the Church of England's Catechism, of the Assembly's, and of Dr. Watts's. For the same reason, we recommend to our schools the uniform adoption, as soon as it can be made convenient, either of the Large Hymn-Book generally used in our chapels, or of the Methodist Sunday-school Hymn-Book recently published.

9. Neither the *art of writing*, nor any other merely secular branch of knowledge, shall be taught on the Lord's day. But we strongly recommend that writing, and the elements of arithmetic, shall be taught to the

leder scholars, both male and female, on one or more week-day evenings, as a reward for their regular attendance and good conduct on the Sabbath.

10. Where Sunday-school *libraries* are instituted, no book shall on any account be admitted without the previous approbation of the Committee. The distribution of books shall take place, wherever it is practicable, on some week-day evening, so as not to occasion, either to the librarian or the readers, an unnecessary and injurious diversion of any portion of the Sabbath from employments directly spiritual. And we recommend, where there are more schools than one in the same town, the plan of *one central library*, accessible at suitable hours to those persons connected with each school, who shall be duly furnished with tickets by their respective Conductors or local Superintendents, as likely in most cases to be most judiciously managed, and to afford a greater variety of suitable books, and therefore much to be preferred to the plan of separate libraries for every such school.

11. No *sales of books*, or of other articles used in the schools, shall on any account be suffered to take place on the Lord's day; but suitable facilities for the supply of the scholars shall be afforded on week-day evenings. 'The profaning the day of the Lord by buying or selling' is a sin explicitly prohibited by the standing 'Rules of the Methodist Society'; and ought not to be tolerated in any Methodist institution.

12. The *Meetings of the Committee*, for purposes of ordinary *business*, shall not be held on the Lord's day. And the *Teachers' Meetings*, if *unavoidably* held on that day, shall be fixed for such *hours* as will not prevent those who belong to our body from regularly attending on our public worship, on our Society-meetings, or at the administration of the Lord's Supper.

13. All the children of our schools shall be trained up in the habit of a regular and invariable attendance on *public worship, at least once on every Lord's day*. Wherever they can be accommodated with room, we strongly, and for many reasons, recommend their attendance at the house of God, with their teachers, in the *forenoon* especially of every Sabbath; and the elder classes should be advised and encouraged to hear the word of God in the evening also, where we have an evening service. We earnestly entreat our friends, who may be concerned in the future erection or enlargement of chapels, to have this object in view, as one of unspeakable importance to the interests of religion and of our country; and to include in their plans the provision of large and convenient accommodation, not only for the *adult* poor, but for their *children* also.

14. Where separate buildings shall be erected for Sunday-schools, by the contributions or influence of our members and friends, they shall be *legally secured* for the purposes which they are intended to serve. And we recommend, as the best general method of accomplishing this object,

that the Trustees of the *nearest chapel*, in the Circuit to which the school may belong, shall also be constituted the Trustees for the school, under suitable provisions and regulations. This plan, without at all interfering with the internal management of the school on the principles and rules above-mentioned, would sufficiently connect our schools with our chapels; and would afford to the Trustees of chapels that safeguard against possible injury to their trust-concerns, which their pecuniary liabilities give them a just right to expect from their Christian brethren of the same community.

15. To all Methodist Sunday-schools established in their respective Circuits, on the principles maintained in this Plan, and governed, *substantially and generally*, according to the preceding Rules and Regulations, our Preachers are directed to afford all possible countenance and assistance; by occasionally visiting the schools; by giving counsel and advice to the teachers, parents, and children; by earnestly recommending such institutions to the prayers, and to the pecuniary support, of our societies and congregations; and by so arranging their Circuit-Plans, as to afford themselves the opportunity of attending at all the principal meetings of the Committees and of the Subscribers.

The Bible Christian Disruption of 1829

Edward Hocken to William Bailey, March 5, 1828

(*WHS*, XXXIII (1961), 33–5)

I shall proceed to answer your kind letter without any apology only the contents are to be kept Secret, and first as to the Connexion. I am fully perswaded there are many good people with us and the Lord has wrought A great work and if more care had been taken in takeing out Preachers more might have been done. As to the temporal state it is bad; the people are in general poor, that I admitt, but I fear they have not been taught their Duty; for instance, the Quarterage in this Circuit at Michaelmas did not amount to *Sixpence* A member, at Christmas not full *Seven pence* (but then they can indulge in the fashions of Life). This is low work and unless we can increase our income it will be bad. I want time and oppertunity to see how much a member through the whole Connexn., Secondly as to the Traveling Preachers my knowledge does not reach far beyond Cornwall, but I believe as far as my knowledge reaches they are *Closely* united, never more so since I knew them. They begin to

see and *feel too* and are determined to stand together, and in the Lord too,
I am fully aware that there are many Holy men that are as pillars in those
parts, men who are truly Devoted to God. . . .

Thirdly the Conference, and first from some Conversation with
W.O'B[ryan] (before I last wrote you) I was led to conclude that you
were dissatisfied with the proceedings of the Conference and were
opposed to the steps the preachers had taken and indeed it was that that
induced me to write you. But he never intimated his intention of goeing
to America. It is impossible for me to state the trials we had to pass
through at the Conference. The General Acct was £156. 3s and the
Missionary Fund £164. 12s in Debt and W.O'B. would not strive to get
money to pay it. He said they might wait or the Conference might pay it,
but then he claimed the right of stationing all the preachers and of takeing out whom he pleased or of sending home whom he thought fit, so if
money were wanting then the Conference [must find it?]; but no Conference to Controul him, in fact we were to pay all and he be master with
the wip in one hand and the reins in the other, and go on at the beck of
A POPE! To this the preachers *one* and *all* objected, and then came on
the storm which I can not enter into. At last the Committee was chosen
and the Money borrowed and the Debts paid. Then the Book Room
Concern came on. W.O'B. found fault with the management tho he himself had allways been consulted; he wished to have the concern in his
own hand and not for the Conference to have the Liberty to controul
(acct. of which you may see in the last *Circular*), but I suppose you have
seen it already; we would not consent to it so he was *paid off*; since that
he has done all he can to get the whole into his *Clutches*; So far we have
resisted for the general good.
    Fourthly the Chapels, which with the view that I have is the worst of
all. It is generally thought by the Preachers and people that they are made
to him only for his Life and then back to the Connexion; but I am fully
aware it's A mistake; they are gone for *Ever* unless some alterations takes
place and that can only be done in Enrolling the Conference (tho I never
yet hinted my mind to anyone). At present the Chapels are made to him
and then to fall to the Connexion after him; *but what Connexion?* Why,
those that are Enrolled with him, and as he refuses to Enroll the present
Conference he may separate and Enroll whom he pleases, possibly his own
family, and it's theirs. This is my decided opinion on the features of the
old Deed and if he can get the Book Room, if he pleases he may play the
same *trick*. We shall prepare the form of A deed to submit to the preachers for their Consideration, but I do not see how we can Enroll without
him unless we do seperate from him for the above reasons, and unless he
alters his maner of proceeding a seperation must take place, but if we
could be enrolled with him then he might be managed and if he would

not submit he might be proceeded against as another preacher, and the Chapels after him would fall to the Connexn. I shall give you but an imperfect view in this paper but must pass on.

Fifthly to W.O'B, and I must plainly tell you he is not A fit person to fill *any* Important office, if he be fit to be a preacher at all. He cares not how much he loads us with Expences, I will instance a few *Trifels*. In the year 1824 his Coals and Candles cost £16. 5s. 4d; the same year he charged for people comeing at his house £45. 17s. 0d. In 1825 I have but three Quarter which amounts for Coals and Candels £15. 15s. 7d, Comers and Goers at the house £24. 5s. 0d (mind, this does not include the Preacher in the Circuit). Last year he went to take Missionary Collections at the Portsmouth District and Collected about £9. 0s. 0d and Charged about £6 0s. 0d for Expences. Last Qr Meeting he had to come from Torpoint to St Neot, he hired A post horse, gave 4/- a day, came to Liskeard the first day about 17 or 18 miles, slept at A publick house, 3/8 Expences, and St Neot the next day about 5 miles which was 4/- more makeing 11/8 to travel 23 miles. I objected to it and *Insisted* it should not be entered on the Circuit Book. He did not say much, I suppose ashamed of it, as James Thorne did not Expend but 6/8 in goeing all round the District the whole of last year. I only observe this to show you that his Expences must be curbed or we are ruined, and this makes him uneasy; but this is not all. His word cannot be taken in Conversation; he so speaks that when called on for an Explanation he so turns and twists his Words that no one knows what they are at and I observe he allways leaves A hole to creep out at. This is not upright work, and in particular amongst the Preachers I have reason to think he represents things in a wrong light. This he did to me in reference to the letter you wrote him and I have reason to believe he has to others: and as long as those things continue to Exist the Lord cannot be pleased. On last Monday week he came to see me and *seemed* to wish things were setteled. I urged the necessity of an Enrollment but he seemed to wave that and I told him candidly my thoughts on his proceedings. What Effect it will have on him I do not know. I wish him well. We parted friendly, but as to his words they are wind. I love honesty. One thing I may add, that is if we do seperate I do not think that many will go with him as it's getting amongst the members and they seem to stand by the preachers in general and declare against his proceedings. Let us pray the Lord to take the matter into his hands and all will be well.

James Thorne's account

(Jubilee *Memorial Volume*, 1866, pp. 103–4, 106, 109–12)

As O'Bryan's successor, Thorne gives the official view of the disruption.

At the 1827 Conference

There was dissatisfaction again manifested in reference to the authority claimed by Mr. O'Bryan, and after some discussion he requested those who were dissatisfied to draw up a paper setting forth how they wished to have Connexional affairs managed in future. The paper was hastily prepared, proposing—

1. That the Conference be the organ of Government.

2. That the Conference be annually composed of the Superintendents and Representatives of Districts, and as many Itinerant preachers in Full Connexion as may be sent by their District Meetings.

3. The Conference yearly to appoint where the next should be held – that Mr. O'Bryan be the President, if in attendance, and no moral obstacle prevent.

4. That Mr. O'Bryan take a Circuit, if requested; but that he be allowed to choose on what Circuit he wishes to be stationed.

5. That a Deed to identify the Conference be enrolled in Chancery.

6. That either Mr. O'Bryan take off the Book Concern on the conditions specified, or else the Committee take it on those terms.

The above was signed by all present – twenty Itinerant Brethren, and three Representatives.

It was proposed to drop the term 'Arminian,' in the Connexional name; but as Mr. O'Bryan seemed unwilling to acquiesce in the proposal, it was not put to the vote . . .

At the 1828 Conference

The agitation respecting the authority claimed by Mr. O'Bryan was greater than it had hitherto been, and matters occurred which induced him to relinquish the Presidential chair for this Conference. William Mason was therefore chosen President, and James Thorne was re-elected Secretary. It would serve no good purpose to detail particulars of the unpleasantness experienced at the Conference, and through the year. It all grew out of Mr. O'Bryan's supposing it to be his duty to claim and exercise supreme authority, and the resistance offered thereto by the preachers and people. It was now clearly seen that, unless a great alteration took place in the views of the Founder of the Denomination, a crisis was imminent. The brethren had been refreshed while together; but they had also been greatly pained, and they separated with gloomy forebodings as regarded the future . . .

At the 1829 Conference

The eleventh Annual Conference was appointed to be held in Ebenezer chapel, Lake, Shebbear, Devon. The agitation respecting the authority claimed by Mr. O'Bryan having now extended throughout the Societies, a number of influential friends attended on Thursday, July 23rd, 1829, the day the Conference was appointed to assemble. Some had been invited by Mr. O'Bryan, and others came from the love they bore to the Connexion. In the interval between the last Conference and this, Mr. O'Bryan had issued a pamphlet complaining of the treatment he had received from the Financial Committee (first appointed in 1826, for managing the General Account and enrolling the Connexion), and a reply to it was issued by that Committee; and thus the whole question was brought before the people. There were many things stated on both sides which there is no necessity for repeating here; but, as may well be conceived, this induced many, who loved and respected Mr. O'Bryan and the rest of the preachers, to be present on the occasion. A preliminary meeting was held, and a venerable, judicious Christian of many years standing, Mr. JOHN BLEWETT, of Truro, the Representative of the Luxillian[1] District, was called to preside. One question had been decided contrary to Mr. O'Bryan's views, and another was brought forward. In the midst of the discussion, he said, 'I will do no more business with you – I adjourn this Conference to Liskeard next Monday.' Mr. O'Bryan having left the Conference, the question was discussed, whether the persons present were satisfied with the proceedings of the Financial Committee with respect to their conduct towards Mr. O'Bryan; and nearly all present – 26 Itinerant preachers, the three Representatives, and 22 local preachers and friends – 51 in all, signified their satisfaction by signing their names to a paper which was copied into the Journals of the Conference and published in the Minutes . . .

Lessons of the separation

This sad separation has its lessons, which it will be well for christians to learn. It was indeed sad; for although the Conference was satisfied that it was better to endure this painful disruption, than to submit to un-scriptural authority, yet to sever the ties of affectionate regard they had many of them so long cherished towards their Founder, made some weep, and all to feel acute grief; and but for the painful agitation by which it had been preceded, and which had prepared them in some measure for the stroke, would have been still more distressing.

It also occasioned the loss of Mr. O'Bryan's labours, which would otherwise, to this day, have been prized and highly beneficial.

Perhaps the worst evil it produced was the strife and contention which followed, in the older stations where Mr. O'Bryan was best known, and had been rendered most useful. Before this severance, when the brethren and friends met, the tenor of their converse was respecting their christian experience and the prosperity of the work of God; but afterward it was more frequently respecting the opposition, unkind remarks, and perhaps highly coloured reports of doings and sayings calculated to widen the breach. This, to some extent, checked that large measure of spiritual enjoyment which many had attained, blunted the keen longing for the salvation of souls, cooled the intense ardour of pure, 'brotherly love,' and was calculated to make a root of bitterness again to grow. It may be doubtful whether the almost seraphic enjoyments for which many of the earlier converts were so remarkable, have yet been fully regained; and whether that 'mighty faith' which expected conversions as the result of the application of Divine truth to men's consciences by the Holy Spirit, so generally prevails.

¹ I.e. Luxulyan.

Catholic Emancipation

Adam Clarke to William Reed of Manchester; Pinner, April 14, 1829

(Ms at Wesley Theological Seminary, Washington DC)

Our great men have lately done what I believe will endanger the Crown of these realms & what every genuine Christian man must deplore; and true religion has, I fear, been wounded, even by its professors. If *we* have been faithful to the trust God has delivered to us, it is more than we can prove, & much more than I can believe. And, if *we* have got nothing of that tincture of *Religious Indifference*, which is the vice of the times, it will be the better for us, when God comes to examine who they are who have confessed him before men. I do not like to think of these things, but they press themselves upon me, & I have had too much to do with the Ark of the Lord for more than half a century, not to tremble for its safety when I see it has fallen into the hands of the Philistines.

Anecdotes of Irish Missionaries

From an account of his Irish tour in the diary of Elijah Hoole, August–September, 1830.

(Ms at Drew University)

John Hamilton,[1] Irish missionary, often ate only once in two days, the country and the people where he laboured not affording him more frequent refreshment. One day when quite exhausted he entered a hut. In the first room was no person. In the inner chamber he found a large family seated round a basket of potatoes boiled for their dinner. 'You're welcome, honest man,' said John aloud, addressing himself, at which all gazed at him with astonishment and one laid down his fork or spoon to laugh. John seized the unoccupied instrument and began to eat heartily. No one interrupted him, but when he had satisfied his hunger he told who he was and his errand through the country. A congregation was collected in the evening, the people of the house were converted and true religion established in the neighbourhood.

On one occasion, having preached the previous evening in a cottage where he lodged, he prepared to proceed to another part of the circuit. The good woman prepared an oaten cake and put it before the fire to bake for his breakfast. He wished to have prayer before breakfast, to save time; three neighbouring women came in to prayer, each having an infant in her arms. During prayer one of the women became so distressed in her soul, she could not take care of her child; John, still on his knees & praying, took it from her and laid it on a shakedown of straw, when it was quiet. Another of the women became affected in like manner, and John took her child in the same way. The third became equally troubled in soul, and John still praying took charge of her infant also. He then perceived by the smell that the cake was burning; knowing there would be no other provision for his breakfast, he turned it. He continued praying till the three women successively found peace, keeping the children quiet meantime, and had the cake nicely baked also.

A young woman was about to be married to an ungodly man. 'Well,' said John, 'I hear you are going to be married; I am sorry you should form such a connection as to have the Devil for your Father-in-law.' The proposed union did not take place.

When recovering from in [sic] a severe fever, he one day could fancy nothing to eat but a peculiar kind of fish, which his poor host had not the manner to procure. The fish was provided for him; an unknown dog brought in a fish of the kind and laid it at his feet. It is thought the dog must have carried it two miles at least.

John Howe,[2] when preaching in some part of Ireland near a market was disturbed by a ruffian who opposed the Gospel. The preacher, being a powerful man, seized his antagonist by the collar and the breech and taking him to the market hung him on one of the hooks of the market by his waistband of his leathern small clothes, and then concluded his sermon.

He subsequently lost his piety. While in this state, in a fit of sickness, a Romish priest came to visit him. When he was announced, 'Show him in,' said John. The priest entered & after a friendly conversation was about to depart. 'Stay,' said he, 'you will not go without praying with me.' 'Why,' said the priest, 'I had no expectation of being called to perform that service and I have not brought my book.' 'Oh well, then,' replied John, 'kneel down and *I* will pray for *you*.' The priest did as he was desired, & John raising himself in bed uttered a prayer in his own energetic style. When he had concluded the priest rose and assured him that it was the best *sermon* he had ever heard in his life. 'Well, but,' said John, 'I now want you to anoint me. You profess to be successors of the Apostles and to have the same power, and you anoint sick people in imitation of them. Now they anointed the sick to cure them & I want you to cure me. My pain is here,' pointing to his side, 'and if you cure me I will become a Catholic – and if not,' pointing to the pistols that hung in his room, 'I will shoot you as an impostor.' The priest was terrified. John disarmed his fears, talked to him seriously on his character & professions. The man was affected by what he said; he drooped and three months afterwards died. It was thought his death was occasioned by the pain & fears of his mind.

---

[1] Hamilton, an itinerant from 1794 to 1825, has been described by R. H. Gallagher as 'a man of humble talents and undistinguished as a preacher. But his whole spirit, soul and body were completely surrendered to God.'

[2] Howe (1780–1839) entered the Irish itinerancy in 1802.

Worship and Preaching

'On Profiting from Hearing Sermons' by E.T.

(*WM Magazine*, 1831, p. 25)

Here I must advert to an important difference between the circumstances of earlier and modern Methodism. Originally, the religious services of the Methodists were rather *appendages and auxiliaries to worship*, than worship itself. It was supposed that the duties of worship had been elsewhere observed. Mr. Wesley himself considered the preaching of himself and coadjutors to be as the sermons before the University, in the University church; at which times the accustomed prayers are not read; as it is presumed that these have been both read and attended in the respective chapels of the different colleges. The people were gathered together *to hear preaching*. All the service had reference to this. The hymns were ordinarily selected so that their subject might be connected with that of the discourse: and the prayer was a *brief address*, in which a blessing on the ministry in the present exercise of it was earnestly solicited. Mr. Wesley, therefore, always recommended (and set an example of his own recommendation) *short prayers*. Not that he thought public prayers ought to be so when they were considered as constituting public worship, but because he acted on the principle, that the Methodists *heard preaching* in his *preaching-houses and rooms*, and *worshipped elsewhere*. Hence, a significant reason which he gave on one occasion against leaving the Church amounted to this, – *the Methodists have no regular worship*. A very different state of things now exists; we believe, in the order of divine Providence, and according to the will of God. The Methodists are now become, by the growth and operation of Wesleyan principles and plans, a distinct body, enjoying all the privileges of a Christian Church. Of course, all the obligations and duties of a Church are devolved upon them; and, among the rest, public worship in all its parts. Unhappily, I had almost said, a mode of speaking derived from the former practice still prevails, and sometimes, I fear, influences us. The Minister is *the Preacher*. Are we asked where we are going? The reply is, *To preaching*. Is there no danger in this mode of speaking, I will not say, that *too much should be attributed to preaching*, but *too little to worship*? It is both dangerous and wrong to compare duties among themselves, and to ask which is the most important. In the case before us, Christian obligation binds us to both; and I will therefore say to all whom it may concern, Still think highly of preaching, ... but think highly of divine worship too. The mind is never more prepared to derive good from the ministry of the word, than when a proper portion of time has been spent in humble, fervent, and joint communing with God.

The 'Minor Wesleyans' (Y Wesle Bach) of North Wales

(Translation in A. H. Williams, *Welsh Wesleyan Methodism 1800–1858* (1935), pp. 222–3)

At a meeting of local preachers in Llanrwst on September 6, 1831, a number of grievances were aired. Certain resolutions were passed and a minor secession resulted. The following summary appeared in the reformers' magazine, *Blaguryny Diwygiad*, i, 66.

1. First and foremost, the state of the denomination was considered. It was found to be unsatisfactory. The obstacles to progress must therefore be removed.

2. It was agreed that the local preachers of one circuit should interchange as often as possible with those of another, and that they should be recompensed for their labours.

3. It was decided that 'foreign' local preachers should visit each circuit, so that congregations should hear a greater variety of talents; and that at least two should visit each congregation every quarter.

4. A quarterly collection should be made in each chapel towards defraying the expenses of such visiting preachers. A secretary and treasurer were to be appointed to deal with this.

5. It was agreed that a married preacher with a family should receive 14s. per week, and a single man 9s. per week, while travelling in a circuit other than his own.

6. It was resolved that a meeting should be held in North Wales to station preachers for the coming year, to which every circuit should send a local preacher and a leader. Circuit ministers could attend if they so wished.

7. It was 'earnestly requested' that ministers should interchange once a quarter, again in order to secure a variety of preaching.

West Indian Slavery

(*Minutes*, 1832)

Q. XXV. Shall any farther means be adopted by the Conference to promote the EARLY AND ENTIRE ABOLITION OF SLAVERY IN THE BRITISH DOMINIONS?

A. 1. The Conference feels that it is rendered imperative upon it, by every disclosure of the real character of colonial slavery, to repeat its solemn conviction of the great moral guilt which the maintenance of that system entails upon our country; and year by year, until some effectual step shall be taken by Government to terminate it, to call upon the members of the Wesleyan Societies throughout Great Britain and Ireland, to promote that important event, by their prayers; by their influence; by diffusing all such publications as convey correct information on this subject; by supporting those institutions which are actively engaged in obtaining for our enslaved fellow-men and fellow-subjects the rights and privileges of civil freedom; and by considerately and most conscientiously giving their votes, at the election of Members of Parliament, only to those candidates for their suffrages, in whose just views and honest conduct on this important question they have entire confidence.

2. The Conference also feels itself called upon to express its deep sense of the injustice done to its Missionaries in the island of Jamaica, and of the outrages committed upon the property of the Mission there, in the destruction of five chapels by lawless mobs of white persons, notwithstanding the peaceable conduct of the slaves connected with the Wesleyan Societies, during the late insurrection, and the acknowledged prudent conduct of their Missionaries. These circumstances serve to impress the Conference more deeply with the painful truth, that the system of slavery is frequently even more corrupting to the heart, and more destructive of religious influence, in the agents of the slave-proprietors in the colonies, than in the slaves themselves; and afford additional and most powerful reasons for the renewed efforts of the friends of religious liberty, of negro-instruction, and of the extension of the kingdom of our Saviour in the world by the instrumentality of Christian Missions, to obtain for the slaves, and for those who labour in the charitable work of their instruction, a security for the exercise of the rights of conscience, which nothing can effect but the entire and speedy abolition of the system of slavery itself. The Conference farther expresses its affectionate sympathy with the Missionaries in the island of Jamaica, in the sufferings and injuries to which they have been so unrighteously subjected through the intolerance and violence of 'wicked and unreasonable men'. And, whilst it gratefully records its testimony to their excellent conduct, in neither betraying the principles of eternal justice and morality as to the civil wrongs of the slaves, nor mixing themselves up, whilst employed in their Mission, with such discussions on the case as might be dangerous, it exhorts them still to cultivate the same spirit, to exert the same zeal for the instruction and salvation of the population of the West India colonies, and to walk steadfastly by those excellent rules which are embodied in their printed Instructions. The Conference more especially expresses its approbation of the conduct of the Missionaries who have been now for several years employed in Jamaica, because, at a former period, through the unfaithfulness of one, and the timid apprehensions of two others, some Resolutions were published in the year 1824, bearing a construction far too favourable as to the condition of the slaves, and the general state of society there; which Resolutions were condemned by the Missionary Committee for the time being, and by the ensuing Conference. And since these Resolutions have been lately made use of as evidence in favour of the system of slavery, the Conference repeats its strong disapprobation of them, as conveying sentiments

opposed to those which the Conference has at all times held on the subject of negro-slavery; and not less so to the views and convictions of the great majority of its Missionaries, who have been and now are employed in the West India colonies.

The Liverpool Circuit, 1832

Samuel Jackson to his parents; Liverpool, September 22, 1832

(Ms at Drew University)

As I know you are interested in our welfare you will perhaps like to know a little about our prospects here.

First of all, Jabez[1] is a very great man, but is very kind and affable so far. Indeed, I know not how he can well be otherwise. It was my wish to have gone to London. My coming to Liverpool is entirely his own act and deed. So that he is bound in honour to use me well . . .

In our principal chapel[2] we have an organ, the Church prayers, and the congregation on the whole is the most splendid affair with which I have been connected for some time. In the Society there seem to be many holy and excellent people, but upon the whole it is not in a sound or pleasant state. There is a discontented and radical party. A kind of magazine is published here which is open to all the complainers in the connexion; and whenever these gents cannot have their own way, off they go trotting to the Editor of this same periodical. And forthwith comes out an article on the tyranny of the Methodist preachers.

I am, however, determined by God's help to try to do them nothing but good. Here is a large mass of ignorant weaker people in the town. God grant I may be of some use to some of them.

[1] Jabez Bunting was Jackson's superintendent minister in the Liverpool (North) circuit.

[2] Bunting had been instrumental in obtaining Conference permission for an organ to be installed in the new Brunswick Chapel in 1811, despite its ruling in 1808 that no further organs should be authorised.

Regulation of Camp Meetings

(Primitive Methodist *General Minutes*, 1832)

2. Q. How may the Camp Meetings be rendered more efficient, and useful? there having heretofore frequently been over much preaching.

A. Let the praying services be as fully supported as possible. And as reading services have been rendered very useful, let, at least, one reading service, if possible, take the place of a preaching, in the forenoon, and another in the afternoon. Let one sermon, at least, be preached to the children. Also, if need be, let any preacher have two minutes' notice to conclude. Also when the work so breaks out that there is praying with mourners to be attended to, then one or more of the preachings must be given up, unless a permanent praying company can be formed, expressly for praying with mourners. N. B. At the Conference Camp Meeting, at Bradford, missionary speeches were delivered with good effect. This perhaps might be useful in general.

3. Q. How may religion be further promoted?

A. When the weather permits, let open-air meetings be held on the Camp Meeting system, for one hour, or longer, if circumstances warrant it; as was done with so much success in the infancy of Burland circuit. This means prayer-meetings accompanied with a short preaching service, or something of the kind.

4. Q. What may be further done in towns?

A. Let similar open-air meetings be held on Sunday mornings: say from seven o'clock to eight; sometimes in one place, and sometimes in another. If the society be strong, several such meetings may be held each morning.

Also when it can be done, let such open-air meetings be held: to begin about one hour before preaching time; to be held about three quarters of an hour; sing to the chapel, and be sure to arrive full five minutes before preaching time.

The Theological Institution

Letters of Richard Treffry Jr.

(*Memoirs*, 1838, pp. 142–3, 157–8)

To Mrs. Blaine of Hull, May 1833

So well am I pleased with it [the scheme for a theological college] that it shall have my pittance, though, like Dr. Primrose, I go upon short commons for a fortnight afterwards. Yet, let me not be understood to look at the measure without apprehension. My first object, I mean after the cultivation of an active, stirring piety, should be theology. Day and night, without intermission, bending all things to this object, waiving every other consideration, I would try to make a man a good theologian, so fully that he should have an ample and well-arranged store of *materiel* for all occasions. Then, as much Hebrew, and Greek, and general literature, as possible. A man, it is true, cannot be a finished divine till he has read his Bible in these tongues; but he may, without them, be a well-furnished and ready divine; and as literature is only a secondary, subsidiary thing, I would rather defer the study of that till he had, by his own exertions, well stored his mind with theological truth, and imbued his heart with its spirit. Then, when his habits are formed, when he is so much absorbed by his great work as to make every thing subservient to it; then, and not till then, would I turn him loose upon the classics. But create a passion for literature; give to a mind not yet determined in its bent a strong desire for superiority in scholarship; fill it with Cicero, and Xenophon, instead of Barrow and Jeremy Taylor; let Demosthenes be a model for oratory, and Homer the spirit of inspiration, and the Lord have mercy upon the poor wretch; he is as fit for a Methodist preacher as ——. But we will hope better things of our Institution; and pray that from all the great and serious hazards to which it is liable, it may be mercifully preserved.

To George Osborn, November 1833.

I hope you are getting on in public matters with increasing delight and profit. I am more than ever impressed with the need which ministers have to devote their undivided attention to the word of God. The present state of the church, its appetite for feverish excitement, its general fastidiousness, and the superficiality of its scriptural knowledge, lead me to the conclusion that the study of exegetical, rather than systematic, divinity, – of the meaning of God's word, rather than human arrangements of its doctrines, – belongs to the present duties of the minister.

A man ought now especially to imbue his sermons with the very spirit of the Bible. Happily, Epictetus and Seneca are not popular as pulpit-models; but I am satisfied that Paul and John are not so fully the objects of study as they ought to be, especially taken in connexion with Moses and the prophets. I have no wish to complain of the present attainments of ministers. To a certain extent, they are highly encouraging; yet still, with a full allowance of their merits, I am disposed to think that we too often pander to a vitiated taste, rather than aim at creating, or at least renovating, the intellectual appetities of our auditors. It requires much strength of mind, much nerve of resolution, and much grace, to act rightly under such circumstances; especially among our people, where we have not time to see the correctness of our plans approved by their results: and where their results are not obvious, we need much patience to endure the listlessness of some, and the frowns of others. That, however, does not affect the question of duty; and I do not at all doubt that biblical study is the peculiar duty of the ministers of the age. It is really marvellous how deficient we are in this matter.

The Conference debate: Elijah Hoole's account[1]

(Ms diary at Drew University)

[Wednesday, August 6th, 1834] *Institution* introduced by Mr. Bunting. Moved by Mr. Leach and seconded by Mr. B. Slater in an admirable speech.

Dr. Warren rose to move an amendment. Rob[ert] Wood rose to order: a member of a committee could not move an amendment on propositions to which his name was attached. Lessey & others joined the conversation, which was closed to examine the young men.

Thursday, 7: After report of committee for sale of chapels, Dr. Warren resumed. The time is not yet come for the Institution: 1. The projected Institution would be found something different from Methodism from the beginning. 2. That the improved and improving state of society will offer candidates improving. 3. Tendency to increase power in certain hands and destroy the liberty of the Connexion. Amendment. To the order of the day . . .

Bromley seconded Dr. Warren's amendment. 1. Because the projected Institution would add two years to the constrained celibacy of the junior preachers. 2. It would effect a great revolution of our District Meetings: by instituting a tribunal between the District Meeting and the Conference. 3. The scheme involved a practical disregard to the advantage of the present system, especially as respects the local preachers. 4. Danger of loss of piety. 5. Impossibility of being carried into effect.

Ven. James Wood: because of the character of the work hitherto, rather prefers the plan mentioned at the close of the pamphlet – lists of books for each year. Opposes the Institution.

Burdsall: Thinks it impossible to support it. The people are unfavourable to it. It would be the loss of love & therefore the loss of power. Supports the amendment.

John Gaulter: asserts it is not a novel project. Learning & piety not irreconcilable. Mr. Wesley always had the plan in his head. Supports the Institution.

Val[entine] Ward: supports the Institution.

Shipman: Charged with res[olution] from Colchester Quarterly Meeting in favour of Institution.

Abraham Farrar gives way. Sutcliffe supports. Scott also; defended Mr. B[untin]g, argued well. Reece: admirably supported the object. Thos. Rowland: spoke at large & loosely, asking time. John Anderson: came to Conference in favour of the Institution. Still so. Thos. Waugh: Admirably supported, insisting on immediate decision to prevent agitation. Wm. Lord: spoke in favour. The Brethren will learn the discipline. There is not so extensive prejudices against the Institution as is feared. Mr. Waddy: opposes but will support & subscribe if carried. Haswell: opposed. Blackett, Everett, Smith &c. gave up.

The question was put. 31 voted for Dr. Warren's amendment, i.e. the order of the day. All the rest for the resolution, *That the principle of the Institution as recommended by the Committee be adopted by this Conference*.

[1] Cf. Joseph Fowler's account in *Sidelights*, pp. 169–78.

Warren's speech against the proposal

(Samuel Warren, *Remarks on the Wesleyan Theological Institution*, 1834, pp. 11–32)

The special reasons which have led me to this general conclusion [that 'the time is not yet come for adopting the Recommendations of the Committee'], I would, with the utmost respect, but, at the same time, with all plainness of speech, and without reserve, lay before my honoured Fathers and Brethren.

In the first place, That the projected Institution, however plausible it may appear in theory, would be found in fact and in working, to be a very considerable departure from the original and uniform practice of Methodism hitherto. God himself has impressed on Methodism an extraordinary character, as if purposely to teach *us* especially, and also to shew the nations of the earth, that its success is not to be attributed to human 'might or power', or political patronage, or worldly embellishments, 'but to my Spirit, saith the Lord of Hosts.' I need only instance the character and qualifications of the instruments chosen by divine Providence, in the commencement of its history, and the contempt in which they were held by 'the wise and prudent' of their day. . . .

In the second place, That the improved and improving state of Society generally, will not fail to furnish suitable men for the work to which they may be called, conformably to our ordinary manner of training. Could we suppose, that those men only who are candidates for our ministry, partook not of the the improving state of society, – that they alone remained stationary, whilst all about them were advancing; this would be a powerful argument for having recourse to extraordinary measures to meet the exigency. But is this the case? Certainly not: far otherwise! Such is the peculiar character of Methodism, that whatever may be the elements of existing society, at any given period, it possesses the special faculty of availing itself of those resources which are best suited to promote its interests. The men thus raised up are indigenous to the soil and climate in which they are reared. Instead of being improved by the insalubrious fumes of a hot-house Institution, they would degenerate and become worthless, if not even noxious. . . .

In the third place, That the signal success with which it has pleased Almighty God to own the course hitherto pursued, indicates rather the wisdom of 'walking by the same rule, and minding the same things', than of commencing a new course, however small the divergency may seem at the outset . . . Are we not correct in attributing this unprecedented success to the special blessing of Almighty God, on our working the machinery of Methodism *as it is at present constituted*? . . . Besides, in a measure of such vast importance, is it not proper to take into mature consideration, not only, nor even *chiefly*, what is the opinion of a few more wealthy individuals among us; but also what thousands of the most pious, the most judicious, and the longest tried members of our Societies, think of the projected Institution? for I hesitate not to express my opinion, that thousands of our most valuable members, deprecate this new scheme as fraught with incalculable mischief to our Connexion.

Nor ought we to lose sight of one special aspect of the affair. With whom did this question of an Institution orginate? Did it originate with the *People* – the party of all others the most deeply concerned? Had any official, or general expression, complaining of the insufficiency and inefficacy of our Ministry, emanated from *them*? – Nothing of the kind! . . .

These, Sir, are some of the reasons why I demur to the measures proposed by the Committee. But the weightiest reason of all the rest, because all the rest appear to me to be contained in it, and naturally to flow from it, is *this*, – That the Institution now proposed, has an obvious tendency to increase such power in the hands of *a few individuals*, as is likely to be detrimental to the liberty of the Preachers, and perilous to the unity of the Body itself . . . I therefore crave a few more minutes, whilst, in the most unreserved manner, I state my reasons for entertaining fears on this subject.

And *first*, that the Committee entered at all upon the question of the Officers to be appointed over the Institution, was a very suspicious circumstance, – thus attempting *themselves* to create the Faculty . . . Although this may appear somewhat strange, . . . it must appear still more remarkable, that of all the Officers proposed to superintend the Institution, not one was nominated but from among *themselves!* . . .

Secondly, That one and the same individual was proposed to occupy the following Offices; – First, to be President of the Institution: Secondly, to be a Theological Tutor: and, Thirdly, still to retain the senior Secretaryship of our Foreign Missions. Now, I ask, in the first place, are the duties of these respective offices of such a nature, as to allow of any individual man discharging them all, in such a manner as they ought to be discharged? I ask, in the next place, whether such is indeed the dearth of intellect and learning amongst us, – of religious, of moral, of literary qualifications, that throughout the whole length and breadth of the Connexion, not one preacher, beyond the limits of their own Committee, can be found, to rescue this individual from being overwhelmed and smothered under this accumulation of Offices! . . .

Thirdly, That a proposal was actually made in the Committee, – That, having nominated the President of the Institution, the choice of all the other Officers might be left to himself! Now if such a proposal as this could be made in the very outset of the scheme, for what are we not to prepare ourselves next? . . .

What . . . will become of our original . . . characteristic simplicity and piety? . . . And where will be the liberty of the great body of the Preachers?

Fourthly, That the methods had recourse to, in order to represent to the Connexion, the *unanimity* of the Committee in their Conclusions, were not sufficiently characterized by simplicity and godly sincerity.

A Tractarian Viewpoint

('Advertisement' in *Tracts for the Times*, 1834)

Methodism and Popery are in different ways the refuge of those whom the Church stints of the gifts of grace; they are the foster-mothers of abandoned children. The neglect of the daily service, the desecration of festivals, the Eucharist scantily administered, insubordination permitted in all ranks of the Church, orders and offices imperfectly developed, the want of Societies for particular religious objects, and the like deficiencies, lead the feverish mind, desirous of a vent to its feelings, and a stricter way of life, to the smaller religious Communities, to prayer and bible meetings, and ill-advised institutions and societies on the one hand, – on the other, to the solemn and captivating services by which Popery gains its proselytes.

J. H. Newman to Mrs. John Mozley; January 19, 1837

(*Letters and Correspondence*, ed. A. Mozley, 1891, Vol. II, p. 224)

I have nearly finished Southey's 'Wesley', which is a very superficial concern indeed: interesting, of course. He does not treat it historically in its connexion with the age, and he cannot treat it theologically, if he would ... I do not like Wesley – putting aside his exceeding self-confidence, he seems to me to have a black self-will, a bitterness of religious passion, which is very unamiable. Whit[e]field seems far better.

J. H. Newman, Extracts from an essay on the Countess of Huntingdon

(*Essays Critical and Historical*, Vol. 1, 1871, pp. 387–8, 404–5, reprinted from the *Dublin Review of 1846*)

The history of Methodism is, we do not scruple to say, the history of a heresy; but never surely was a heresy so mixed up with what was good and true, with high feeling and honest exertion, – never a heresy which admitted of more specious colouring or more plausible excuse, – never a heresy in which partizan must be more carefully discriminated from partizan, persons from their tenets, their intentions from their conduct, their words from their meaning, what they held of truth from what they held of error, their beginnings from their endings. Being nothing short of a formal heresy, ultimately good could not come of it, nor will good come of it. We have not yet seen its termination, and therefore as yet can but partially argue *ab eventu*, which in theological matters is an evidence so solemn, so conclusive. 'Ye shall know them by their fruits' is our Lord's canon concerning all schemes of doctrine, however attractive or fair of promise, which come not of the Catholic Church. Already has one of the two branches of Methodism, and that the principal one, borne, in the person of its most learned divine, the bitter fruit of error in the most sacred doctrine of theology. We hope nothing, then, we fear everything, from a religious movement, which nevertheless in its rise excites our sympathy, and of which we do not deny, as of any event in the world, the incidental benefits. Yet interest, pity and admiration we do feel for many of the principal agents in it; and if the choice lay between them and the reformers of the sixteenth century (as we thankfully acknowledge it does not,) a serious inquirer would have greater reason for saying, 'Sit anima mea cum Westleio,' than 'cum Luthero,' or 'cum Calvino,' and 'cum multis aliis,' as the grammar has it, 'quos nunc perscribere longum est.'[1] . . .

But at the period in question [the Church] was under eclipse, or at least behind a thick fog, in these our northern parts. She indeed herself was ever what she has been, for she is one; but the English Establishment, which is the aspect in which she looks and has looked upon us from her native heavens, sent out at that time a wan and feeble ray, and exerted a languid influence, and was as little able to warn and guide her children, as the moon is to cheer the shivering wayfarer, and to light him amid the perils of wilderness or morass. Wesley and Whit[e]field doubtless had their places in her economy, as truly as St. Francis, or St. Philip Neri, had there been minds able and free to solve the problem. Repentance and conversion have their place in the gospel and the Church; field preaching has its place; the poor have their place; and, if that place cannot be found in an existing system, which claims to be the Church, that system is, so far, but the figure of the narrow Jewish polity, not of that which overshadows the whole earth and penetrates into the recesses of the heart.

But such seems to have been, more or less, the English Church at that day. It saw that there was excellence in the Methodistic system, it saw there was evil; – it saw there was strength, it saw there was weakness; – – it praised the good, it censured the faulty; – it feared its strength, it ridiculed its weakness: and that was all. It had no one clear consistent *view* of Methodism as a phenomenon: it did not take it as a whole – it did not meet it, – it gave out no authoritative judgment on it – it formed no definition of it – it had no line of policy towards it – it could but speak of it negatively, as going *too* far, or vaguely, as wanting in *discretion* and *temper*; whereas it on the contrary, defective as it was, was a living, acting thing, which spoke and did, and made progress, amid the scattered, unconnected, and inconsistent notions of religion which feebly resisted it.

---

[1] 'May my soul be with Wesley [rather] than with Luther or with Calvin, and with many others whom it would be tedious to list now.'

Emblems of the Polity of Methodism

Reform Agitation

Richard Treffry Sr. to an unidentified correspondent; Bristol, July 4, 1835

(Ms at Drew University)

The state of our connexion is certainly peculiarly perilous; and though I have no fears as to the final issue of the present agitations, yet it does appear to me that nothing can save us from a great rent; the agitations at Manchester & Liverpool & other places have it appears to me gone so far, resorted to such measures, & committed such outrages on all rules of order, that to receive them again would be sanctioning their proceedings & furnishing others with a license to do the same deeds. I love moderation as much as any man, & would make every concession to moderate men, but to men who love violence & who seek the subversion of the very first principles of Methodism, I think we can make no compromise.

Thomas Thompson & the delegates who met in Leeds in the year 1795 were men of moderation; they demanded & they deserved the attention of the Conference, & the sequel proved that the Conference was right in listening to their suggestions. But have we such men to deal with now? No. Far from it. The object at which the disturbers of our peace now aim is to deprive us of all pastoral authority, & to take the discipline of the connexion into their own hands; & to make peace with such men would be to do a deed which would reduce us to most abject circumstances & make us the slaves & tools of demagogues.

Joseph Entwisle to John Hanwell; London, February 13, 1836

(Ms at SMU)

I congratulate you on the peace you enjoy; it is no small mercy in these times. S[amuel] W[arren], the grand agitator, is in London, I suppose, as it is given out for him to open a small chapel near Chelsea tomorrow, and to hold a 'Methodist reform meeting' on Monday in Freemason's Hall.

What effects will follow I do not know. But am not apprehensive of any serious injury to our cause. But I am afraid many poor souls will be ruined by their contentions. Our opponents act as if they thought it 'meet, right, and their bounden duty' to say all manner of evil of us. I am sure if they really think we are what they represent us to be, they ought not to wish to have any communication with us.

Ah, me! I was in the storm at Dewsbury 48 years ago, and in that raised by Kilham etc., in 1795 etc. Still Methodism prospers and will prosper. Mr. Wesley often said (as he did one day in Oldham Street Chapel above 50 years ago), 'Many people say when my head is laid, all this work will come to nothing. If it were the work of man, it might. But it is the work of God, & it will increase more and more, till the knowledge of the glory of the Lord shall cover the earth as the waters cover the sea.' I could fancy that I hear now the voice of that venerable man!!!

Reply to the 'Wesleyan Delegates'

(*Minutes*, 1835)

To Mr George Cookman

Sir,

The 'Address to the Methodist Conference assembled in Sheffield', dated August 1st, 1835, professing to proceed 'from a numerous Meeting of Wesleyan Delegates', and signed, 'George Cookman, Chairman, Ralph Grindrod, Secretary,' has been read to the Conference; who have directed me, as their President, to return the following answer:—

I. It is with the greatest surprise that the Conference have listened to a statement in the Address, that the persons described are 'Wesleyan Delegates', and are 'commissioned by a vast number, comprising tens of thousands of members of the Societies'. This surprise is founded on the *fact*, that no information has yet reached the Conference from any quarter, to justify the belief that any considerable number of our Societies have either wished for, or concurred in, the appointment of Delegates to any such meeting. Indeed, not a single Circuit, or Society, nor even any one *collective body* of Trustees, in the whole kingdom, has announced to the Conference its mission of any individual or individuals for purposes so irregular and unconstitutional: so that the Delegation or Commission, if it have really taken place to any thing like the extent asserted in the Address (which is a matter quite unproved), must, at all events, be allowed to have been accomplished by means the reverse of those which are fair, open, and manly, and to come before the Conference and the Connexion in a character singularly unauthenticated and equivocal.

II. But even if this weighty objection to the statement of the 'Address' as to 'Wesleyan *Delegates*' could be removed, there is another, which the Conference considers to be altogether insurmountable. It is founded on the broad and obvious principle of Methodism, and indeed of society in general, whether civil or religious, that such a plan of *confederated* delegations as that to which this Address appears to refer, designed to interrupt, or supersede, or intimidate the regular jurisdictions of our community, is calculated to subserve the purposes of agitation and faction, but can never consist with the maintenance of Christian order, edification, and peace.

III. The Conference are constrained, on a calm review of various circumstances, to entertain the conviction, that the meeting from which the Address has emanated, instead of being, as it is delusively termed, a Meeting of Wesleyan Delegates, is in reality an adjourned Meeting of the body of persons calling themselves 'The Grand Central Associations', of which a 'Provisional Meeting' was held in Manchester in the month of April last. This conviction is confirmed by the notorious facts, that the Manchester Meeting in April formally resolved and agreed that an Adjourned Meeting of Delegates, connected with it, should be procured and assembled in Sheffield at this very period; and that of the placards and other advertisements, published on this occasion, some expressly speak of an 'Adjourned Meeting' of the said Association, and others, though professing to call an 'Adjourned Meeting of Wesleyan Delegates', are as expressly stated to have been issued by 'The Central Committee of the Association'. The last-mentioned advertisements were signed by 'William Smith', and 'William Wood', the Chairman and Secretary of the Association's Committee; and the very Address now under consideration bears the signatures of the Chairman and Secretary of the Provisional Meeting of the Association, held in Manchester. It is, therefore, clear to the Conference, that this Address is in truth a communication, however disguised, from the 'Grand Central Association' itself, or from persons who by attending its meetings, and other unequivocal tokens of sympathy and encouragement, are virtually identified with, and responsible for, the projects and proceedings of that Association.

IV. Taking this view of the origin and character of the present Address, the Conference deems it due, in Christian simplicity and candour, to announce at once its deliberate and unalterable resolution, not to hold any intercourse with the said 'Grand Central Association', or with any other meeting, however denominated, into which persons who continue to be leading and active members of that confederacy shall be notoriously admitted, and receive approbation and sanction.

That Association was avowedly formed on principles which we deem to be subversive of the essential constitution of Wesleyan Methodism. It has, in the Meeting at Manchester, and elsewhere, openly fraternized with various persons belonging to parties who have for a number of years ceased to have any connexion with our Body, and are distinguished by the violence and injustice of their attacks on its members and its system. It has adopted a regular scheme and course of 'agitation', in disgraceful imitation of certain political proceedings; tending, by public

Meetings and other means of disturbance, to the ultimate division of our Societies, and to the great annoyance and discomfort of those of our flocks who are desirous to live in peace and godly quietness. It has most wickedly, though happily with little effect, endeavoured to injure the Public Funds of the Connexion; and thus, by persuading those who hearkened to its counsels to 'stop the supplies', has placed itself in practical hostility to those great Institutions of Piety and Mercy, both at home and abroad, to the promotion of which the Funds in question are devoted. It has, by various publications, attacked, in the most unmeasured and bitter language, that system which alone can with any truth or honesty be designated as *Wesleyan* Methodism, and advocated the substitution for it of other and widely different plans of ecclesiastical government and discipline, – plans which are subversive of the Scriptural rights of the Christian ministry, and inconsistent with the pure and faithful discharge of the functions of the Pastoral Office; – plans which, therefore *are not* Wesleyan Methodism, and which it can only serve the purposes of delusion or self-deception to miscall by that honoured name. It has, both in mixed meetings, and by means of the press, carried on and encouraged a regular course of slander and calumny, directed against the Conference and its members, in reckless violation of the requirements of truth, of piety, of brotherly kindness, and even of common decency itself; and is identified with a system of periodical vituperation and abuse, such as never before assailed a body of Christian Minister and Pastors, on the part of persons still strangely professing, for the most part, to desire religious communion with the very men whom they habitually revile, and hold up to public reprobation and scorn.

With such an Association, or with any Meeting of persons who are directly or indirectly in fellowship with it, or who shall persevere, after due admonition and expostulation, in aiding or abetting its revolutionary and unhallowed projects, the Conference could not hold communication, without violating their duty to God, their fidelity to the great trust and deposit of genuine Methodism committed specially to their care, their pastoral obligations to the immense and overwhelming majority of their beloved Societies, both at home and in foreign lands, by whom the divisive and disorderly principles of the Association are held in just abhorrence, and the proper regard which they owe to their own Ministerial honour and character, so foully aspersed by the leading actors in the present scheme of organized disturbance and agitation.

V. While the Conference, in the fear of God, announce their firm resolution on this subject, and are persuaded that it will have the cordial approbation of the great mass of our Societies, – and especially of those whose standing, piety, intelligence, and active support of Methodism, best entitle their opinions on such topics to respectful consideration, –

they feel it also due to their beloved flocks in general, to those among the dissatisfied portions of their Societies, whom they willingly consider rather as the deluded and misled, than as the deluders and misleaders of the party, and to their own sincere and long-cherished sentiments of what is right and fitting, to make the following Declaration; – viz., That it is their intention to take into their most affectionate and careful consideration, partly at this Conference, as far as time can be found for such a task, when the *indispensable* business of their Session shall have been transacted, and partly at the earliest subsequent opportunity, some of the most material of those subjects of discipline which have of late excited the attention of the Connexion. They will engage in this work, not with the purpose of making any one of those revolutionary changes which the Association has demanded, or of abandoning any one of those vital and important principles of pastoral administration which are embodied in Wesleyan Methodism, as now generally understood and exercised among us; but in order to carry out the principles already recognised into yet more extensive and satisfactory operation, especially in relation to the financial affairs of the Connexion, and to provide, if possible, additional *guards* and *securities* for our people, in reference to the calm and temperate exercise of those scriptural powers which belong of right to the Pastoral Office, and are essential to the faithful discharge of its salutary and divinely-appointed functions.

VI. The Conference also are most happy to take this opportunity of declaring, that, while decidedly opposed to the recognition of any divisive and agitating Association or Confederacy whatsoever, they are at all times ready to receive, with the most respectful attention, the friendly communications and suggestions of any member of their Societies (if unconnected with the 'Grand Central Association,' or any such mischievous combination), on topics tending not to the subversion, but to the conservation, of our doctrines and discipline, and of the great and vital interests of the Connexion. They are willing to appoint proper persons, members of their Body, to converse freely and kindly with any such persons who may request it, in order to afford such friendly explanations and pastoral counsel as they may need in the present crisis. And if any parties, supposing themselves aggrieved or injured by certain acts of local discipline which have occurred during the last year, be disposed to forward their complaints to the Conference, in a peaceful and Christian spirit, and will promise to refrain, in the mean time, from all hostile proceedings, provision shall be made, as far as possible, to meet such cases by Special Deputations from the Conference to the Circuits concerned, which Deputations, in conjunction with the District Committee, shall be charged to enter upon a fair and impartial revision of those transactions, and to do justice to all parties, on the basis of those long-tried and scriptural principles which the laws and usages of

Methodism have ever recognised, and from which the Conference, by
the blessing of God, ARE RESOLVED NEVER TO DEPART.

Signed, on behalf and by order of the Conference,

RICHARD REECE, *President.*

Carver-Street Chapel, Sheffield, August 6th, 1835.

Ordination

The Conference of 1836, presided over by Jabez Bunting, decided to re-
introduce the traditional form of ordination alongside 'reception into full
connexion'.

(*The Watchman*, Vol. II No. 84, August 10, 1836, pp. 251–2)

The PRESIDENT said, he introduced the question of the imposition of
hands, in the ordination of the Young Men, about to be admitted into
full connexion, because he wished to remove from himself to the Conference the responsibility of omitting that circumstance. He believed
that it was a practice of divine authority, – of great antiquity, and was
observed by the universal Church; – and that it tended also to raise the
character of the Christian Ministry . . .

The SECRETARY (Mr. Newton) then moved a resolution – 'The Conference are of opinion, that the Young Men who are this year to be
admitted into full connexion should be received by imposition of
hands, . . .'

The PRESIDENT then put the question, which was carried with only
two dissentients.

The official ruling

(*Minutes*, 1836, p. 85)

Q. XXIV. What is the decision of the Conference on the ORDINATION
OF OUR MINISTERS BY IMPOSITION OF HANDS?

A. The Conference, after mature deliberation, resolves that the
Preachers who are this year to be publicly admitted into full connexion,
shall be ordained by imposition of hands; – that this shall be our standing
rule and usage in future years; – and that any rule of a contrary nature,
which may be in existence, shall be, and is hereby, rescinded.

N.B. The Conference agrees that Returned Missionaries, who have
travelled with acceptance four years and upwards, having been already,
on their appointment to the foreign work, solemnly set apart to the
office of the ministry by the imposition of hands, shall not be re-ordained

with the approved Candidates for the home work, who may be received into full connexion; – but that there shall be a formal *recognition* of them, by the President and Secretary for the time being, acting on behalf of the Conference, in a *separate* public service appointed for that purpose; when they shall be examined with respect to their continued attachment to the doctrines and discipline to which they are already solemnly pledged, and shall also be expected to give an account, if time will permit, of their present Christian experience, and of their labours in the foreign department of our work.

An example of its application

(*Sidelights*, p. 220)

Samuel Dunn, who had not been received into full Connexion on the ground of his disbelief in the *Divine Sonship* of Christ, avowed his having arrived at a firm conviction of that Verity, through reading Wesley's *Works*. He was asked whether he would be ordained with the candidates *publicly*, or in the old form, henceforth to be disused, by simple vote of Conference. He preferred the public ordination by *imposition* of hands. His renunciation of his error caused 'great joy among the brethren'. Ordination by 'laying on of hands of the presbytery', which Mr. Fowler had so earnestly advocated *at the foregoing Conference*, was, notwithstanding the strongly expressed misgivings of Mr. Grindrod, now cordially adopted, with but two dissentients, R. Melson and John Moulton.

Wesleyan Views on Revivalism

(*Sidelights*, pp. 246–7)

Joseph Fowler recorded a conversation during the 1837 Conference, arising out of the reported decrease in membership.

Mr. S. D. Waddy said: 'I think we should be guarded in speaking against revivalism, saying the cause of declension is the having had a revival. We are naturally given to lassitude, and need stirring up.' Mr. Reece: 'If after the revival there comes a decline, I ask, Were the converts nursed? I have found early morning services and band meetings most useful in conserving converts.' Dr. Bunting: 'We may excel in getting revivals, but we have yet to learn how to manage them.' Mr. Lessey: 'Many are called revivalists who are not so; there is too much artificiality in our revivals. A revival of the work of God must begin in the minister's own heart, and we should look for converts in all our services. We should then have a continuous operation of the convincing Spirit. I regret the distinction between a revival-preacher and others.' Dr. Bunting: 'I agree with Mr. Lessey in the main, but as in nature there are thunderstorms, so in grace God sometimes goes out of His ordinary way.' Mr. Lessey: 'If God pours a mighty flood from heaven, we thank Him for it.' Mr. Marsden: 'I was awakened under Mr. Benson.' He then enlarged on the qualities of Benson's preaching, which made him a revivalist from the beginning to the end of every service. He dwelt upon the usefulness of the society meeting in attaching young converts. Mr. McLean dwelt first upon the sovereignty of God in the choice of instruments and seasons, Mr. Fowler thought, unduly and unpractically, to the overlooking of the fixed conditions of ministerial success. Yet he admitted that our unfaithfulness might break the continuity of the Spirit's work. Mr. Burdsall: 'I hope that God will make us all revivalists in the best sense. But I think we may mistake a spirit of excitement for religion. What should be done is this: Do not let revivals get into the hands of persons who are a discredit to us.' The President: 'We are dishonoured by such jigs as "Come to Jesus." ' Mr. Newton: 'I have heard "Come to Jesus" sung by the people with profit, and I am Methodistical.' Dr. Beaumont: 'I would have the ministers themselves take part in revival services. I wish we went more frequently into those meetings, and more willingly. I think this conversation is the most important part of our Conference. This decrease deeply affects me. We need both "the early and the latter rain," the gentle showers and the thunderstorm.' Dr. Bunting: 'Instead of "Come to Jesus" and ranting tunes, we should have "God of all grace and majesty".'

The Cry of the Afflicted

(George Loveless, *The Victims of Whiggery. A Statement of the Persecutions experienced by the Dorchester Labourers* . . . dedicated (without permission) to Lords Melbourne, Grey, Russell, Brougham, and Judge Williams, (1837), pp. 23, 28)

Five of the six 'Tolpuddle Martyrs' were Wesleyans and their leader, George Loveless, was a local preacher. Here is the radical undertow of Wesleyan politics.

But I have been told it is done 'for the good of society, and to uphold our most holy religion!' Good God, what hypocrisy and deceit is here manifested! The most cruel, the most injust, the most atrocious deeds are committed and carried on under the cloak of religion! If I had not learnt what religion meant, such practices would make me detest and abhor the very name. And yet, strange as it may appear, those hypocrites who pretend to be so scrupulous, that rather than submit to have their most holy religion endangered, they would starve hard-working, honest husbands and fathers, and [those] who have solemnly pronounced, 'What God hath joined together, let no man put asunder,' are some of the first to separate man and wife, to send some to banishment, and others to the Poor-law prisons[1]; to oppress the fatherless and widow. From all such religion as this, 'Good Lord, deliver us!' But, again, we are told it is intended to lead to a reformation of their characters, and to make them useful members of society. I much question whether the present system is calculated to have such an effect on the moral conduct of men in general; as far as I have had an opportunity of observing, it has the contrary effect. Nothing can be more absurd than to suppose that you can keep down the conquered for any length of time, by pouring out upon them judgment without mercy. Although I was sent out of the country, and have been subjected to privations, to distress, and wretchedness, transportation has not had that intended effect on me, but, after all, I am returned from my bondage with my views and principles strengthened. It is indelibly fixed in my mind, that labour is ill-rewarded in consequence of a few tyrannizing over the millions; and that through their oppression thousands are now working in chains on the roads, abused by overseers, sentenced by the comitants[2], and punished by the flagellator; young, and once strong able men, now emaciated and worn almost to skeletons. Is this the plan to reform men? I say, no; if they were bad before, they are tenfold more the children of hell now. It has a tendency to harden the heart, stultify the feelings, make them careless and regardless of consequences; and they rush forward, plunging headlong into an abyss from which they are not able to extricate themselves: the groans and cries of the labourers ere long will bring down vengeance on the heads of those who have been, and are still, the authors of so much misery. I believe that nothing will ever be done to relieve the distress of the working-classes, unless they take it into their own hands . . . Nothing but union will or can ever accomplish the great and important object, namely the salvation of the world . . .

England has for many years been lifting her voice against the abominable practice of negro slavery; numbers of her great men have talked, have laboured, have struggled, until at length emancipation has been granted to her black slaves in the West Indies. When will they dream of advocating the cause of England's white slaves? How long will it be, ere they will cease to grind to the dust, trample underfoot, and tread down as the mire of the streets, the hard-working and industrious labourer? How long will it be ere they will cease to 'join house to house, and field to field, until there is no place'; to oppress the hireling in his wages, and to keep back by fraud that to which he is so justly entitled? When will they attempt to raise the working man to that scale in society to which he can lay claim from his utility? Never – no never, will (with a few honourable exceptions) the rich and great devise means to alleviate distress, and remove the misery felt by the working men of England. What then is to be done? Why, the labouring classes must do it themselves, or it will be for ever left undone; the laws of reason and justice demand their doing it. Labour is the poor man's property, from which all protection is withheld. Has not the working man as much right to preserve and protect his labour as the rich man has his capital?

But I am told that the working man ought to remain still and let their [sic] cause work its way – 'that God in his good time will bring it about for him.' However, this is not my creed; I believe that God works by means and men, and that he expects every man who feels an interest in the subject to take an active part in bringing about and hastening on so important a period . . . Arise, men of Britain, and take your stand! rally round the standard of Liberty, or for ever lay [sic] prostrate under the iron hand of your land and money-mongering taskmasters!

Tolpuddle, August 1837

    [1] I.e. the workhouses.
    [2] Literally, 'accompanying circumstances', but Loveless's meaning is unclear at this point.

Educational Policy

First Report of the Wesleyan Educational Committee, presented to the Conference of 1837

(Printed in the annual report of the Wesleyan Education Committee, 1889–90, pp. 114–15)

Mr. Wesley gave it as his opinion, That the great design of God in raising up the Methodists was, by their instrumentality, to spread Scriptural holiness throughout the land; which means, we suppose, that they were to put forth an influence, partly direct and partly indirect, the effect of which should be to make the people of this country generally and truly religious. If this be indeed our calling, we cannot begin to deal with that portion of the public mind to which we have access at too early a period of life. There can be no wisdom in leaving children and youth to themselves, until they are confirmed in habits of irreligion and vice, and then seeking by the use of extraordinary means to instruct and convert them. If it is our duty to evangelise the masses of our countrymen, the sooner we begin with each individual the better. Methodism, by God's blessing, has done a good thing, and a great thing; but it has not yet done every-thing. Many hundreds and even thousands of profligates have been re-claimed, and formed into Christian churches; but the land is not yet leavened with religion. Perhaps this will never be done until the various denominations of Christians zealously unite in giving to the rising generation a thoroughly religious education. Very great, and praise-worthy, and successful efforts, in this particular department of duty, have been made both by the Established Church, and by Dissenters from her Communion; and without wishing in any way to interfere with them, but, on the contrary, rejoicing in their success, we think that Methodism *can* and *ought* to do the following things:—

1. To bestow an increased attention upon the Sunday-schools already established among ourselves.

There are 3,339 Schools, including 341,442 Scholars; – there are, on an average, in actual attendance every Sabbath Day, 264,445 children; – the number of Teachers employed is 59,277; and the Annual Expense about £17,800 . . .

2. Some inquiry should also be made into the cases of those Chapels and Societies with which no Schools are connected.[1]

There are 1,766 preaching-places, connected with 30,017 Members of Society, 99,438 stated hearers, and a population of 736,994, unconnected with a single Methodist School of any sort. In these places there are 915 Chapels, – 20,202 Members, – and 67,789 Stated Hearers, – and a Population of 465,929; and yet no Wesleyan School.* Surely, there can be no impropriety in asking, 'Why are these things so?'

3. There are about Nine Daily Infant Schools, under the immediate direction of the Members of our Society; and there is reason to think that if the attempt were made, it would prove by no means a difficult task, to multiply these very useful institutions to an indefinite extent.

4. There are, immediately connected with our Societies, about 22 Week-day Schools for elder children; and there are already about as many favourable openings for the introduction of others; but, assuredly, these valuable institutions ought to be greatly extended; they should also be placed under our pastoral oversight, and closely connected with the Church of God.

5. As there are many places in which our friends are unable to main-tain Week-day Schools of their own, and are therefore led to act with other denominations of Christians, it is desirable that some principles were laid down for their guidance in this matter, in order that the children of our own people, at least, may be duly instructed in religion, and brought to a place of worship on the Lord's Day.

6. It is also very desirable that some plan should be devised for the purpose of retaining some hold of a large class of young persons who are, by birth, education, and habit, attached to Methodism, and who, if

unwilling to join the Society, should not, if possible, be left wholly to themselves.

7. For the accomplishment of these and similar objects, we request the appointment of a Committee, or a Provisional Committee, which, under the official sanction of the Conference, may proceed to work this very year, and push their plans in every direction, wherever the providence of God may open a door, and supply the ways and means of success.

What we wish for is, not merely Schools, but *Church* Schools, which, being systematically visited by the Preachers, may prove doors of entrance into the Church of God:—not merely education, but an education which may begin in an Infant School, and end in heaven; and which will thus subserve the high ends of Methodism, which are to fill the world with saints, and paradise with glorified spirits.

If the matter appear difficult and impracticable, let us remember that Methodism is the heroism of Christianity; and that it began, even in its cradle, to do good on a large scale.

The only thing which has been advanced in the shape of an objection is the probability that, at no distant period, the Government will take up the subject of national education; and that the effect of a legislative measure would be to empty our schools, and involve our friends in difficulties. This may be a reason why we should not, just at present, venture upon any considerable outlay of money; but it is no reason why we should not immediately attempt such Schools as can be closed at any time, without hazard or material inconvenience. Mr. Wesley said he would not neglect the performance of a present duty through a fear of distant and uncertain consequences. But, supposing that the necessity for our labours should, a few years hence, be superseded by a better system of education, why should not we do what we can in the meantime? Should Popery and infidelity ever attempt, under any pretence, to take the direction of the youthful mind of this country, it is to be hoped that Methodism will resist the attempt, even to the death; and, in order that we may then be in a condition to resist with success, let us now hasten to the field, and, as far as possible, pre-occupy the ground.

---

[1] In the following paragraph two sets of figures are given: the first is for *all* preaching-places, the second for those places only where a chapel had been built.

* The 'population' is that of the townships or parishes in which the chapels are situated. In many of these places there are schools conducted by other denominations; but where the Methodists have a chapel, and a society, and a congregation, in the centre of a considerable population, there must be work for *them* to do among the children.

Charles Prest to George Osborn; Bristol, February 22, 1839

(Ms at Drew University)

The Conference of 1837 appointed an enlarged committee to carry the Report's suggestions into effect. This was reappointed in 1838 with the task of 'collecting information; of exciting in our Connexion ... an increased attention to the utility and necessity of Wesleyan Infant and Day Schools; ... of watching over the rights and interests of our Societies, as they may be involved in any legislative or other proceedings on the question of National Education; and of preparing ... some general plan for the promotion of Religious Education in connection with the Wesleyan body'.

Now then a word on Education. Pray, what are the Committee re-appointed last Conference doing? The position of the question of Education in Parliament should arouse us. We cannot submit either to the mode likely to emanate from thence or to that so offensively & foolishly talked about by the Clergy. There seems a strange fatality about the recent movements of the latter. What with the Apostolical Succession and their claim to instruct the children of right, it appears as though that judicial blindness which in the order of God precedes destruction or calamity had come upon them. We as Methodists must educate our own children; and I do wish we were more fully aroused to it. Will anything be matured by Conference or are all things *in statu quo*?

NATIONAL EDUCATION

(*Minutes*, 1839)

Q. XXIII. What is the judgment of the Conference with respect to the measures which were adopted by the London United Committees, to promote PETITIONS in the various Societies and Congregations of the Connexion against the grant of public money in support of the plans of Education proposed by the recently appointed Committee of Privy Council?

A. 1. The Conference, in its deliberate judgment, resolves, that the OCCASION, which especially called for vigilant and active exertions, constituted a full and perfect justification of the proceedings in question. The attempt to allow the introduction of the Roman Catholic version of the Scriptures into the Normal School, which it was proposed to establish and support by a grant of public money, could not but appear eminently calculated to afford facilities and means for the countenance and propagation of the corrupt and tyrannical system of Popery, highly detrimental to the best interests of this country, the security of the Protestant faith, and the spiritual welfare of the community at large, particularly of its children and youth. Besides, as several parts of the proposed measure had a directly religious bearing and tendency, deeply affecting our body, in common with all other Protestant Churches, it was imperative on our regularly constituted authorities to pursue such a course as might most promptly and effectually call forth the united efforts of the Wesleyan Connexion, to defeat a project so fraught with danger. The Conference takes this opportunity of recording its sorrow and alarm at the methods employed by different parties to revive and extend the influence of Popery in the United Kingdom, as well as in our Colonies; and considers itself called upon, by fidelity to God and his truth, as also to its own well-known principles, to pledge itself to the employment of all the Christian and legitimate means in its power to arrest the progress of this evil, and to support the general Protestantism of the country, as well as our own faith and institutions in particular.

2. The thanks of the Conference are due, and are hereby respectfully and cordially tendered, to the Preachers and Gentlemen who formed the London United Committees, for their watchful attention, exemplary zeal, and wise and Christian exertions, on this important occasion. And, farther, as the Committee of Privy Council is still in existence, and retains the POWER of promoting a scheme of National Education which would, if carried into effect, put to hazard the scriptural Christianity of the country, – trench on the right and duty of Christian Churches to educate in their own principles the children of their charge, – endanger the foundations and progress of evangelical truth, by introducing a merely secular or essentially pernicious system of education in its place, – taint society at its very springs, by bringing the children and youth of the age under a defective, irreligious, and worldly system, – and thus, in several ways, prepare the public mind for the reception of the dangerous errors of Popery, – these United Committees are affectionately directed by the Conference to watch the progress of this great national and religious question, with a view to afford a Connexional assistance to the defeat of all movements tending to establish a corrupt and anti-scriptural scheme of Education at the public expense.

3. As these Committees are especially appointed by the Conference to be the official and executive organs of its business and discipline during the intervals of its sittings, and, moreover, as their proceedings must necessarily pass in review before that body, it is obviously improper for any Wesleyan Minister to assail those proceedings, previously to the deliberation and judgment of the Conference, by appeals to the world through the medium of the public press, or otherwise: and such a practice is hereby prohibited.

The Wesleyan Centenary Fund

(*WM Magazine*, 1838, pp. 938–40)

The *Magazine* reported in detail a meeting of the Centenary Committee in Oldham Street Chapel, Manchester on November 7, 1838, at which the purposes for which the proposed Funds should be used were agreed.

In the first place, – To the erection and preparation of suitable premises for the accommodation of those Students who, after satisfactory evidence . . . of their sound conversion to God, their solid piety, and their divine call to the Christian ministry, shall be received into the *Wesleyan Theological Institution,* whether such Students be designed for Home or for Missionary Service;

In the second place, – To the provision of commodious premises in London for the use of the *Wesleyan Missionary Society,* adequate to the greatly augmented and augmenting extent of its multifarious and important business . . .

. . . This Meeting, after much inquiry and careful deliberation as to the other *Connexional* objects to which further sums may be best appropriated, unanimously adopts the following conclusions:

1. That the sum of *eighty thousand pounds* is considered as the very lowest which must be raised, by the universal effort now contemplated, for the Centenary Fund.

2. That after a liberal reserve for the purposes of the Theological Institution and for the new Mission-House, &c., . . . the remainder of the said sum of £80,000 should be employed as follows:

(1) In providing a Wesleyan Missionary Ship, for the purpose of forwarding Missionaries and Missionary stores, as may from time to time be found necessary and expedient, from New South Wales and Van Dieman's Land to our Mission Stations in New Zealand, in the Friendly Islands, in the Feejee Islands, and in other Polynesian groups; such a ship being exceedingly wanted, both for the comfort of the Missionaries labouring in those islands, and for the general advantage and security of the Missions themselves.

(2) In finally liquidating a Building-Debt of about five thousand pounds, yet remaining on the premises of our two Connexional Schools at Kingswood and Woodhouse Grove . . .

(3) In placing at the disposal of the *Chapel-Loan Fund* Committee a considerable sum, sufficient to enable it to continue, without material interruption, its most beneficial and important operations . . . and thus to relieve many cases of distressed Trustees and over-burdened chapels from the pressure of debt and difficulty.

Tabular View of Methodism in England, 1838

The table on page 441 appeared in *Dearden's Miscellany*, Vol. 1, January 1839 and is reproduced in *WHS*, Vol. XXVI, 1947, facing p. 1. It was the work of Simeon Woodhouse, Methodist New Connexion minister from 1808 to 1854. No figures are given for the Bible Christians, whose connexional membership in England in 1838 was recorded as 9,532. The final column, giving Wesleyan figures for 1823, is based on a table said by the editor to have been drawn up by a Wesleyan minister, Arthur Jewitt.

The Wesleyan Association in Sunderland

(*Principles of Doctrine and Church Discipline held by the Methodists of the Wesleyan Association in the Sunderland Circuit*, 1838; reprinted in *The Diary of John Young*, ed. G. E. Milburn, 1983)

PREFACE

In April, 1836, several persons – being local preachers, leaders, or members of the Wesleyan Methodist societies in Sunderland and its vicinity – seceded from that body. Their fundamental objection to the constitution of Wesleyan Methodism, consisted in the irresponsible and irresistible power of the conference in its legislative and executive character. The conference, as is well known, consists of preachers only, to the entire exclusion of lay-members, however high in character, talent, or office in the church. From the supreme and irresponsible power of the conference, and the entire exclusion of laymen from its deliberations, many evils and grievances had originated, of which a numerous body of the members complained. Efforts to remedy those evils, and to obtain a redress of the grievances complained of, had for some time been made, in various parts of the kingdom, by those who participated in these views, but without success; whilst the ruling party in Methodism seemed determined to confirm and strengthen the authority from which these evils arose. Under these circumstances, many of the local preachers, leaders, and members of the Sunderland circuit, to the number of about 600, withdrew from the communion of the Wesleyan Methodists, and formed themselves into separate societies, under the denomination of *Wesleyan Seceders*. These societies, whilst they held the same doctrines, and adopted the same religious usages, as the Wesleyans, in their class meetings, love feasts, &c. were founded on principles of church government which they conceived to be more in accordance with the spirit and precepts of our Lord and Saviour Jesus Christ.

Tabular View of Methodism in England, 1838

Methodism in England in 1838.
Number of Members

Counties	Area in Square Miles	Population in 1831	Crime in 1835, Committals as one in	Wesleyan Connexion	Methodist New Connexion	Primitive Methodists	Wesleyan Association 1837	Total	Proportion to Population, as one in	Proportion of Wesleyans in 1823, *Vide* Jewitt's Tables
Bedford	463	95383	552	3473	..	..	..	3473	27	46
Berks	752	145289	769	2261	..	2079	..	4340	33	91
Buckingham	202	146529	660	1208	..	260	..	1468	99	139
Cambridge	857	143955	682	1572	..	535	..	2107	68	114
Chester	1052	334410	627	6836	1491	2827	1284	12438	27	43
Cornwall	1330	302440	1461	18980	313	1466	1155	21914	14	17
Cumberland	1523	169681	1697	2752	..	967	300	4019	42	60
Derby	1028	237170	1088	7160	360	2446	900	10866	22	33
Devon	2585	494168	955	7523	..	..	500	8023	61	75
Dorset	1006	159252	861	3024	..	..	700	3724	43	61
Durham	1097	253827	1567	8619	1006	3446	1488	14559	17	27
Essex	1533	317233	546	2248	..	..	..	2248	136	178
Gloucester	1258	386904	512	6501	..	200	..	6701	58	69
Hampshire	1625	314313	714	2434	..	620	..	3054	102	161
Hereford	863	110976	800	1174	..	1432	..	2603	43	121
Hertford	630	143341	602	517	..	..	..	517	277	888
Huntingdon	372	53149	794	832	..	..	..	832	64	67
Kent	1557	477155	536	7305	..	..	..	7305	65	66
Lancaster	1766	1336854	503	24588	3643	6374	8295	42900	31	48
Leicester	806	197003	716	4887	..	1643	438	6958	28	42
Lincoln	2611	317244	1629	16960	75	3665	..	20703	15	26
Middlesex	282	1358541	395	9537	..	..	660	10197	133	113
Monmouth	496	98136	818	1637	..	..	..	1637	60	276
Norfolk	2024	390054	582	7619	189	6013	..	13821	28	56
Northampton	1016	179276	1188	4471	..	206	..	4677	38	56
Northumberland	1871	222912	1755	4176	914	1629	79	6446	33	63
Nottingham	837	225320	656	6744	1386	1257	400	9787	23	35
Oxford	756	151726	561	2685	..	330	..	3015	50	75
Rutland	149	19385	1292	286	..	..	..	286	75	74
Shropshire	1343	222503	1082	3558	517	2162	..	6237	36	76
Somerset	1645	403908	591	8167	..	763	..	8930	45	57
Stafford	1184	410485	574	9680	2417	3681	..	15778	26	40
Suffolk	1515	296304	658	2355	..	2053	..	4408	67	155
Surrey	759	486326	483	3110	188	..	..	3298	147	*
Sussex	1466	272328	754	1462	..	..	..	1462	186	204
Warwick	897	336988	445	3267	266	800	..	4333	78	125
Westmoreland	762	55041	2201	978	..	..	191	1169	47	69
Wilts	1367	239181	717	2202	..	960	..	3162	79	104
Worcester	723	211356	760	3567	1897	965	257	6686	31	92
York	5836	1371296	956	65456	5905	15445	3086	89892	15	48
Totals[1]	50380	13091005	740	270801	20567	66244	19733	377315	35	55

* In 1824, the number of members for Surrey was included in the Middlesex Raturn, which gives the appearance of there being a smaller number now in Middlesex than there was at that time.

[1] The totals as shown in the original have not been corrected.

They continued to stand alone, and to act independently, until August, 1837, when, having had the previous concurrence of each separate society in the circuit, they formed a union with the Wesleyan Association, at their annual assembly, held at Liverpool . . .

PRINCIPLES OF CHURCH ORDER AND DISCIPLINE

1. We hold it to be the will of Christ, that true believers should voluntarily assemble together to observe religious ordinances, to promote mutual edification and holiness, to perpetuate and propagate the gospel in the world, and to advance the glory and worship of God through Jesus Christ; and that each society of believers, having these objects in view in its formation, is properly a Christian church.

2. That the New Testament contains, either in the form of express precepts, or in the example and practice of the apostles and apostolic churches, all the principles of order and discipline requisite for the constituting and governing of Christian societies; and that human traditions, canons, and creeds, possess no authority over the faith and practice of Christians.

3. That Christ is the only head of the church; that the officers of each church under him are appointed to administer his laws impartially to all; and that the only appeal, in all questions touching religious faith and practice, is to the sacred scriptures.

4. That the New Testament authorises every Christian church to elect its own officers, to manage its own affairs, and to stand responsible only to the supreme and divine head of the church, the Lord Jesus Christ.

5. That the only officers placed by the apostles over individual churches are pastors and deacons;* the number of these being dependent on the numbers of the church; and that to these, as the officers of the church, was committed respectively the administration of its spiritual and temporal concerns, subject, however, to the approbation of the church.

6. That none should be received as members of Christian churches but converted or awakened persons, who walk according to the gospel; and that none should be excluded from the fellowship of the church, but such as deny the faith of Christ, violate his laws, or refuse to submit themselves to the discipline which the word of God enjoins.

7. That the power of admission into any Christian church and rejection from it, we believe to be vested in the church itself, and to be exercised through the medium of its own officers.

8. That the power of a Christian church is purely spiritual and that the authority of ministers and officers is simply executive, not legislative; their office is to interpret and enforce the laws of Christ, not to make laws of their own; agreeably to the commission given to the apostles by

Jesus Christ, 'teaching them,' says he, 'to observe all things whatsoever I have commanded you.'

9. That it is the duty of Christian churches to hold communion with each other, to entertain an enlarged affection for each other as members of the same body, and to co-operate for the promotion of the Christian cause.

10. That the fellowship of every Christian church should be so liberal as to admit to communion in the Lord's supper all whose faith and piety are approved, though conscientiously differing in points of minor importance; and that this outward sign of brotherhood in Christ should be co-extensive with the brotherhood itself.

* The terms pastors, bishops, elders, and presbyters, we are of opinion all mean the same class of officers, variously endowed, some for leading or guiding the flock, others for preaching the word, and some gifted for both; and that the office of deacon is to visit the sick and poor, and to distribute the contributions of the church.

The View from Nottingham

George Marsden to Jabez Bunting; Nottingham, December 3rd, 1839

(Ms at SMU)

This part of the kingdom is almost new to me, and it is pleasing to see the hold which Methodism has upon the population, both in the town and in the surrounding country. The villages within six miles of the town are many of them manufacturing places, and some of them very large, and the Chapels a good size, and in most of them Methodism seems to be the prevailing religion. I suppose the low politics have been very prevalent in Nottingham, but I hear very little upon the subject among our people . . .

It appears to me that Methodism never was in a better state than at the present time. We have general peace in our Connexion, the purity and fulness of our doctrines are preserved, our Discipline is not now disputed, and the good work is spreading rapidly abroad, and gaining some ground at home. Some time ago it was thought we were in danger from the increasing wealth of our people; but we have had full proof that if they lose their piety, Class meeting becomes irksome, and they generally withdraw. In that way the general purity of our body may be preserved, and while time shall continue Methodism prove a blessing to the World.

Primitive Methodist Urban Mission

(Diary of Thomas Proctor; Canterbury Circuit records)

Canterbury, July 20th, 1839. During this week I have been engaged in various parts of this city pointed out for my visitation, in order to ascertain as far as possible the true condition of the people; & after calling upon most of the families in these districts of the city, I find they comprise some 600 families comprehending more than 2,000 souls. Of these families more than 100 are destitute of the Word of God, and some 400 families are not in the habit of frequenting a place of worship on the Lord's Day. Theoretical infidelity does not appear to have obtained among the people, yet practical infidelity abounds to a tremendous extent under the colours of formalism, hypocrisy & carelessness. Here & there an isolated individual is found who wishes in his heart there were no God. Of Roman Catholics there are but very few.

July 21st (Sabbath). On the afternoon of this day preached to 9 souls assembled in a house in Milit[ary] Road. I observed one was impressed under the word even to tears, whilst others whose spirits seemed unwilling and whose flesh was weak were closing their eyes in sleep.

July 22nd . . . Was well received by all the families visited today with one exception of a woman who when she thought she knew the object of my visit ran out of the room, telling me that she went to her Church.

In Jewry Lane I found three adults in a state of great ignorance who when asked if they knew who Jesus Christ is & what he has done? could answer neither of these important questions.

[July] 24th. In Fortune's Passage are several houses of ill fame. Visited several of them in conjunction with a friend & warned them of their danger. No *signs* of penitence were manifested.

[July] 25th. Fortune's Passage. Mrs. Stone says that the thunderstorm which came on several weeks ago made her think that the day of judgment was come & feeling unprepared was much alarmed; but since she has abandoned many of her evil ways, in consequence of which reformation she professes to be much happier than she was formerly. But fearing the poor woman was looking for justification by the 'deeds of the law' I directed her to the work of the Messiah as that on account of which we alone can be justified before God.

[July] 30th. Visiting in Chantry Lane and finding the people in this place in a most ignorant condition. One man named Hall who professes to go to a place of worship & to hear his wife read the Bible could not tell me who the Lord Jesus Christ is. Another named Roberts says she can read but could not tell who Christ is. A person named Hay told me not to come to her house any more as she could go to her church or chapel & did not approve of people going about praying with old wives, & that she had as good book in her house as the Bible is & did not think it right to go about in the manner I was doing. Others express themselves grateful for my visits.

[July] 31st. Visiting today in Ivy Lane. Although many of the people in this place profess to go some time upon the Sabbath to some place of worship, yet they substitute this for Christ & many of them stand in as much need of our Christian visits as the inhabitants of central Africa!!! During this month (besides calls made upon many hundred families), visits made: 145, of which

5 were made to the sick
Tracts distributed   155
Meetings holden   6
Attendance at these   60
Families who have given me their names as subscribers for the work
    of God   7

By a visit is meant not merely a call and delivery of a tract, but a religious conversation or the reading of a portion of scripture accompanied with exhortation or reading scripture, exhortation & prayer. From 15 to 20 visits are made per day.

Changing Fortunes of Scottish Methodism

(Hayes and Gowland, pp. 87–8, 111–12)

Jonathan J. Bates to Jabez Bunting; Edinburgh, July 31, 1839

We have three preachers appointed to this circuit; but one resides at Leith, the other at Dalkeith 6 miles from Edin[burg]h so that I am virtually left alone in the midst of this large place & immense population. I can assure you that I am often ready to weep because I cannot find time to attend to things as I am expected, and as they require. No one can conceive of the labours and interruptions to which a Superintendent is subject in this city unless he is actually in the place; and unless the Preacher is first and last in everything Methodism cannot (humanly speaking) be maintained. I hope, by a vigilant attention to the interests of the people, they are really improving in piety altho[ugh] our numbers are greatly diminished. I do not see how I can pay any efficient attention beyond the present circuit. And then as to help from local preachers I have very little to employ. We have seven places and eight local preachers, three or four of whom are advanced in years and incapable of hard work and long journeys; besides the appointments for their own circuit keep them fully employed. . . .

I am quite sure that the religion and morality of the Scotch people are amazingly over-rated, while their wide spread Calvanism [sic] and their good opinion of themselves, do very much to prevent the spread of vital godliness. There is a good deal of practical preaching but not anything of a corresponding share of experimental and practical religion. Our good friend Dr Coldstream often says instead of their religion leading them to God, they make a god of their religion. It is surprising also to observe what ignorance and what prejudice exist against the very name of Methodism; and yet a mighty friend of the Kirk said to me some time since he believed we were living it down. I do sincerely wish some thing could be done to bring Methodism more forcibly to bear upon the place & to make it a praise & a glory in this part of the earth. Our missionary meetings have done something to bring it before the public, & several respectable & popular ministers of the Episcopal and Presbyterian Churches have kindly assisted, and thus lent their influence to help us forward. Many pious persons believe it would be an awful thing for Scotland if Methodism were to be withdrawn . . .

John M'Lean to Jabez Bunting; Edinburgh, March 24, 1845

We have had several very remarkable awakenings lately – our people are becoming more devout; and getting better principles put into them. They are a worthy people; but just think of the succession of Super-intendents they have had since good Mr Grindrod left & you will not be surprised that they have much to learn, and some little to unlearn. The Warrenite Association is breaking up. Their preacher has come over to us & twenty or thirty of the best of them; old friends of my own who never would have left; had Methodism not been betrayed by the man who was sent here to be its guardian.[1] I pray you, dear and honoured Sir, let us have sound men sent here and Scottish Methodism will do you good and not evil. We must have no equivocal character – no man who comes for his own popularity more than the credit of the Conference. I would rather have the worst radical that could be picked up out of the small residuum of the Warrenite clique, than one of the modern few who affect to run with the hare and hunt with the hounds. You can do with them in England, for they are a supple bending race; and will not break violently out of the traces, but here they would play the very mischief with us. I am much favoured with my colleagues. They are men of the right stamp; genuine Methodists. Mr Duncan[2] has been very poorly & sometimes low during the winter; but I trust is now better – he is a noble little fellow; has some capital principles in him as deep as Metternich, but he has not had the advantage of sufficient intercourse with our lead-ing men. His plans are a little too popular for my taste; and a little too Scottish. We are working harmoniously together however, and I am not

without strong hope that a little of my toryism, sweetening and sanctifying his Whiggism will make him just what the Chairman of Scotland
ought to be.

¹ The reference is to Samuel Warren, who was Superintendent of the Edinburgh
circuit from 1827 to 1830.
² Peter Duncan, M'Lean's predecessor in the circuit, had moved to Glasgow.

The Ashanti Mission

(*Missionary Notices*, January 1840, pp. 204–25)

Thomas Birch Freeman, son of an African father and an English mother,
was the first Wesleyan missionary to survive the notorious climate of West
Africa (known as 'the white man's grave'). Scarcely a year after arriving at
Cape Coast in January 1838, he set out on a hazardous visit to the inland
kingdom of Ashanti. His diary of this journey was sent back to the Missionary Committee and its publication created immense interest.

On his way to Kumasi he was detained for several weeks at Fomunnah,
awaiting permission to proceed.

Saturday, [February] 9th [1839]. This morning, the Chief informed me
that Corintchie, the Chief of Fomunnah, had sent over for him, in order
to converse with him respecting me; and shortly afterwards a messenger
arrived from Corintchie, requesting me to go over and visit him, which
I immediately prepared to do. When I entered the town, Corintchie was
sitting before the front of his house, under his large umbrella, waiting to
receive me; his Captains and people occupying the ground on his right
and left. After the usual compliments on meeting, he asked me what
object I had in view in wishing to pass up to Coomassie. I told him I had
nothing to do with trade or palavers, but was come into the country to
promote the best interests of the King of Ashantee and his people, by
directing them in the way of peace and happiness through the preaching
of the Gospel. He then said he should like to hear the Gospel in his town,
before I proceeded any farther into the country. I hereupon proceeded
to speak to him and all present on the Being of a God. I commenced by
taking into my hand a leaf which had fallen from a banyan-tree, under
which I was standing, and asking them if they could make one like it;
and they answered, *Debida*, 'No.' I then asked them if they thought it
possible for all the wisdom, power and genius in the world, united, to
make such a leaf; they answered again, *Debida*. I directed their attention
to the almighty power, mercy, and truth of 'God, who made the world
and all things therein'; and spoke to them on the nature of the Christian

religion. They readily gave their assent to all I said; and Cornitchie requested me to pay them a visit on the morrow, that they might hear more from me concerning the Christian religion. On my remarking, that as I was a Minister of the Gospel, I could not prudently make them presents according to the usual custom, it being beneath the dignity of Christianity, which is so truly excellent in itself, that it requires no recommendation except a conviction of its value; he answered, 'We do not desire any of the customary presents from you, but wish rather to become acquainted with Christianity.' I then asked him when I could proceed to Coomassie, to which he answered that I should know more about it on the morrow ...

Knowing their jealous disposition, I thought it prudent to make them as sensible as I possibly could of the disinterested character of my Mission; I therefore told them, that it was my love to God, and the souls of my fellow creatures, which caused me to leave my happy native land behind me, and come among them, and that this love was the fruit of my having embraced Christianity, as I was once as ignorant of practical religion as they were, and did not feel the desire to benefit my fellow-men until I had repented of my own sins, and turned to God. On hearing this, they were struck with astonishment, and said that the religion which I thus recommended to them from practical experience, was good. There were about five hundred persons present ...

Thursday, 14th. At eight a.m. Corinthie sent to my lodgings, requesting me to pay him a visit. I immediately repaired to his house, where I found him seated with his Captains, ready to receive me. He informed me that they were waiting to hear me explain some of the truths of Christianity. Knowing the injurious effects of talking much in this climate with an empty stomach, I asked Corintchie to excuse me for a few minutes while I stepped home to take my breakfast, which I was about to do at the moment he sent for me. After hastily taking breakfast, I again repaired to Corintchie's house, and conversed with him and his Captains on the doctrine of the General Resurrection; on which subject their minds seemed very much confused. By divine assistance I succeeded in convincing them of the possibility of such an event; after which I directed their attention to the doctrine of future rewards and punishments ...

Tuesday, 19th. Last night a sister of Corintchie died, after a long sickness. Her death was announced by the firing of muskets and the 'mourners going about the streets'. When an Ashantee of any distinction dies, several of the deceased's slaves are sacrificed. This horrible custom originates in some shadowy ideas of a future state of existence; in which they imagine that those who have departed hence stand in need of material food, clothing, &c., the same as in the present world; and that, as a vast number of concubines, slaves, &c., are the chief marks of superiority among them here, so it must also be in a future state. Accordingly, as I walked out early in the morning, I saw the mangled corpse of a poor female slave, who had been beheaded during the night, lying in the public street. It was partially covered with a common mat, (made from the stem of the plantain tree), and, as this covering is unusual, I concluded that it was thrown over it merely in order to hide it from my view. In the course of the day I saw groups of the natives dancing round this victim of superstitious cruelty, with all manner of frantic gestures, appearing to be in the very zenith of their happiness. In the evening I was informed, that as Corintchie and his Captains did not wish me to see more headless trunks lying in the streets, they had not sacrificed any other persons during the day, but would most probably do so during the night. I am happy to say, however, that I could not ascertain that any more sacrifices were made. That only one person was sacrificed, I believe, resulted entirely from my presence in the town . . .

[Freeman was eventually allowed to continue towards Kumasi on March 28th, and reached the capital on Monday April 1st.]

At two p.m. a messenger arrived from the King, requesting me to proceed as early as possible. I immediately dressed myself; and while so doing, three other messengers arrived, each bearing a gold sword, requesting me to hasten forward. I then proceeded towards the town, preceded by the messengers and some soldiers bearing arms. Having reached the outside of the town, we halted under a large tree, and there waited for another royal invitation. In a short time, His Majesty's chief linguist, Apoko, came in a palanquin, shaded by an immense umbrella, and accompanied by messengers bearing canes nearly covered with gold, to take charge of my luggage, and see it safe lodged in the residence intended for me. All these things being properly arranged, another messenger arrived, accompanied by troops, and men bearing large umbrellas, requesting me to proceed to the market-place. 'The King's commandment' being 'urgent', we pushed along with speed, preceded by a band of music. As soon as we arrived at the market-place, I got out of my little travelling chair, and walked through the midst of an immense concourse of persons, a narrow path being kept clear for me, paying my respects to the King and his numerous Chiefs and Captains, who were seated on wooden chairs, richly decorated with brass and gold, under the shade of their splendid umbrellas, some of them large enough to screen twelve or fourteen persons from the burning rays of the sun, and crowned with images of beasts covered with gold, surrounded by their troops and numerous attendants. I was occupied for half an hour in walking slowly through the midst of this immense assembly, touching my hat and waving my hand, except before the King, in whose presence I of course stood for a moment uncovered. I then took my seat at a distance, accompanied by my people and several respectable Fantee traders who are staying in the town, to receive the compliments of the King &c., according to their usual custom . . .

In this ostentatious display, I also saw what was calculated to harrow up the strongest and most painful feelings, – the royal executioners, bearing the blood-stained stools on which hundreds, and perhaps thousands, of human victims have been sacrificed by decapitation, and also the large *death-drum*, which is beaten at the moment when the fatal knife severs the head from the body, the very sound of which carries with it a thrill of horror. This rude instrument, connected with which are the most dreadful associations, was literally covered with dried cloths of blood, and decorated (awful sight!) with the jaw-bones and skulls of human victims. Then followed the King, Quacoe Dooah, under the shade of three splendid umbrellas, the cloth of which was silk-velvet of different colours, supported by some of his numerous attendants . . .

The arduous duties of the day being over, I immediately repaired to my quarters; and, spreading a cloth upon the floor, sunk, tired and weary, into the arms of sleep . . .

Friday, 5th [April] . . . This morning I received information that the King had lost one of his relations by death, and that, in consequence thereof, four human victims were already sacrificed, and their mangled bodies lying in the streets. I therefore concluded that I should not have an opportunity of seeing the King for a day or two. Shortly afterwards I saw Apoko, the chief linguist, and told him that I was aware that there was bloody work going on today, as I saw a number of large hawks and turkey-buzzards hovering over a certain spot, where I judged these poor victims were lying . . . He said it was even so, and, in consequence thereof, I should not have an opportunity of seeing the King today, and perhaps not tomorrow. I told him that I did not like being confined at one small place, in a low, unhealthy part of the town, and that I must walk out and take exercise, otherwise my health would suffer. I also told him that I was anxious to commence my journey home to the coast on Monday next . . .

Throughout the day I heard the horrid sound of the death-drum, and was informed in the evening, that about twenty-five human victims had been sacrificed; some in the town, and some in the surrounding villages, the heads of those killed in the villages being brought into the town in baskets. I fear there will be more of this awful work tomorrow.

Saturday, 6th. This morning I again talked of walking out into the town, when Apoko informed me that more sacrifices would be made during the day, and that I must not go out until tomorrow. I therefore remained in my quarters until the afternoon, when, on finding myself in rather a dangerous state for want of exercise, I insisted upon walking out at one end of the town for half an hour. In the evening I learned that several more human victims had been sacrificed during the day, but could not ascertain the exact number. The most accurate account I could obtain was, that fifteen more had suffered, making a total of FORTY IN TWO DAYS!!

While speaking to Apoko, I did not fail to remind him that the law of God forbids this awful practice, and that they were under a great error in supposing that the persons sacrificed would attend on the deceased relative of the King in some other state of existence.

These poor victims were allowed to lie naked and exposed in the street, until they began to swell like dead dogs; and such is the callous state of mind in which the people live, that many were walking about among the putrefying bodies, smoking their pipes, with astonishing indifference . . .

Tuesday, 9th . . . About half-past nine this morning, I went to the King's residence to thank him for the handsome present which he made me yesterday. He appears to be about thirty-six years of age. He is of middle stature; his complexion is not so dark as that of many of his subjects; his manners are pleasing and agreeable. He has an aversion to drinking and smoking, a quality this quite unusual among the Ashantees . . .

Thursday, 11th . . . In the course of the day, I reminded Apoko of my anxiety to obtain an answer from His Majesty, respecting the establishment of Schools, &c., in Ashantee; who answered, 'The King will speedily give you an answer; and we hope you will come to Coomassie again and pay us another visit, as we shall be always glad to see you. The King believes that you wish to do him and the people good.'

[Returning to the Coast, Freeman reported to the President, George Maclean, and then sent the following letter to the Missionary Committee in London.]

I trust, my dear Sirs, that these copious extracts from my Journal will convince you, that God, in his infinite mercy, is gently opening before us our way into the interior of this vast continent. Future difficulties will doubtless arise; but I am fully confident that they will not be of such a nature as to hinder the Christian Missionary from pressing on in the glorious conflict. It is true, that this spiritual Jericho at present stands strong, and that Satan, its monster king, still has the triumph of seeing thousands of helpless men, for whom Christ died, dashed into the dust in dishonour: but Israel shall surely triumph; the mystical rams' horns shall not be blown in vain; the enemy shall be taken in his strong-hold, and the Redeemer shall have these 'Heathen' for his 'inheritance', and these 'uttermost parts of the earth' for his 'possession'.

I believe that my long detention at Fomunnah, on my way to Coomassie, was all the Lord's doing. The great length of time which I remained there, gave me an excellent opportunity of becoming acquainted with the people, and, of gaining their affections. I also became accustomed, by gentle degrees, to those horrid and awful scenes, which are everyday occurrences in Coomassie.

Fomunnah is a much more desirable place for the establishment of a Mission, at the present time, than Coomassie. The people are more prepared for the reception of the Gospel; and their Chief, Corintchie, is exceedingly well disposed towards us. Nevertheless, I should have no hesitation in attempting the establishment of a Mission even in Coomassie itself.

To carry on this glorious work in Ashantee, and other parts of the interior, it will require men of great nerve, patience, forbearance, and perseverance. I also here deem it necessary to remind you of the importance of sending persons who are rather light than heavy in weight, as the hammock-men will not carry them if they are very heavy. Yet, on the other hand, they must not be too small and weak; if so, they will never (humanly speaking) bear the very heavy toils of travelling in this climate. If I were a little larger than I am, I should meet with almost insuperable difficulties in travelling. If I were not very strong, through divine goodness, I could not have borne half the toils through which I have passed.

I have no doubt as to getting up to Ashantee for the future with much less expense than has been incurred in my first visit. The King would not make so much ado the second time, as I am no longer a stranger. I also think, that even with a stranger he would not adopt the same course as he did with me, inasmuch as the novelty is over . . .

It was manifest that a mighty change had taken place respecting me in the mind of the King, after I had been a few days in Coomassie; for he seemed very anxious to detain me, if possible; and I believe he would have kept me several weeks longer, thereby placing my life in the greatest danger from the rains, &c., but for the kindness of President Maclean, who, knowing the probable consequences of my being detained in that manner, wrote to the King, some time after I left Cape Coast, requesting him to let me leave Coomassie whenever I thought proper.

I certainly deeply regretted the necessity of leaving so early; but had I stayed longer, I must, in all probability, have stayed until the rainy season was over, which I was not prepared to do.

Doubtless, there has been a great advantage gained by this enterprise; and I trust, my dear Sirs, you will, by the liberality of British Christians, and especially those of our own body, be enabled to follow up that advantage, by sending out, as early as possible, three or four Missionaries, at the least, that more attention may be paid to Ashantee.

I intend sending up a messenger to the King, to keep the communication open, as soon as the rains are over; and shall wait with great anxiety for an answer from you, as to what steps are to be taken. If it were practicable, a handsome present, of the description I mentioned in my last [namely, a poney-phaeton, and harness, suitable to the country], would be well received by the King, and be of much importance in influencing his mind in our favour . . .

Thus, my dear Sirs, I have endeavoured to discharge what I feel to be a very important duty. And casting myself, as usual, on your kind indulgence, for having used so many words in support of a cause which I know would strongly recommend itself to your hearts and affections without my saying anything,

I subscribe myself, &c.,
T. B. Freeman

Mission-House
Cape-Coast Castle,
July 10th, 1839

The Mission to Fiji

James Calvert to Joseph Entwisle; Lakemba, Feejee, June 25, 1839

(Ms at MA)

Calvert spent one year, 1837–8, at the Hoxton Theological Institution before being designated for the new mission in the South Pacific. He had known Entwisle there.

I think I promised you & Mrs. Entwisle that I would write, & therefore I must do it. I also love you both very much, and therefore should like to [do] it; perhaps it is a lawful gratification. But really, Sir, I must be excused from doing more than just plainly stating a few things to you as they rise in my mind, without any adornment; for time, which is everywhere precious, appears to be at least doubly needed, & therefore doubly valuable here. We have here many sorts of work, and very much of each sort.

You know of our voyage. It was speedy, and on the whole very comfortable. I have resided in a small house in order to save expense, & that I might not have anything to interfere with my acquiring knowledge of the language of the people among whom I am placed. I have conversed with them & preached a few times – married two couples, & baptized 16. And Mrs. Calvert has attended the school, to teach the natives the art of reading.

We were very anxious to get our press in operation as soon as possible, as there had only been 12 chapters of the Gospel of Matthew printed in the Feejeean language on our arrival. We therefore exerted ourselves, &

got the first part of the Conference Catechism printed by the 13th of March, & have since printed part of the Gospel of Mark.[1]

We have had 2 very severe storms of rain & wind, which downed several of our houses. My small house was secure, in which the two other Mission families[2] took refuge. These kept us back very much in the language . . .

Oh! Mr. Entwisle, how I am rejoiced when I think about the Institution. Brother Hunt[3] and I in coming often talked about you, & all the good things connected with that best of all places that I know in this world. So we did at Rewa; frequently indeed, contrary to the good Institution Rules, until 12 o'clock or later. And now that I am alone my soul is often filled with gladness & encouragement by a recollection of the spiritual blessedness with which I was there favoured: as well as the clear System of Christian Theology, expositions &c. &c. that I there received. If I had remained my full term it would have been a much greater blessing to me. I should have got the rudiments of various branches of knowledge, that I fear I shall ever be totally ignorant of, or know but little about them. Amidst the variety of work that a Missionary has here, it seems almost impossible to begin to learn anything new: perhaps I may do something in those things on which I have had elementary instruction, outlines, & good plans for study. However, I am very happy in my work. Here is plenty of it, & good work too. They are a very superior people. Good looking, strong, very quick and ingenious. They are also very bad – having been steeped in crimes the most polluting for a long time. There is an alteration among them. Cannibalism is not nearly so prevalent as it formerly was. We seldom hear of it. Indeed, we believe it is not practised at all in this island. We heard that 7 human beings were sacrificed at the opening of Tanoa's new house at Mbau, and that the inhabitants of a whole city or island are appointed to death at the dedication of a new and splendid temple which Tanoa is building. However, I hope that will be prevented through Mr. Cross's residence there; or that we may have some influence over it through the king at Rewa, who is a most powerful chieftain.

Their prejudices in favour of their priests are great, though they are somewhat shaken. The king here refused to present an offering to the god of Lakemba during our great storms, but said he should just sit, thinking that the god had no love for him or he would not have sent such storms. A Tonga chief, who has been waiting a long time to go to Tonga, came 50 miles to offer a piece of firewood through the priest to the god at Lakemba that he might be propitious, & grant him a favourable wind. But Mr. Hunt and such like are wanted here. A very noted priest at Rewa has dreamed a dream (his dreams the great chiefs say are always true). It is this. 'The god of Rewa was not at all afraid when Mr. Cross alone lived at Rewa; but now that Mr. Hunt has come, who is

'Ubalambalavu sara', that is, very great or tall, the god of Rewa, judging that the God of such a great man must be very great indeed, was alarmed, has fled to a considerable distance, & would shortly leave Feejee altogether.' They have no images, I believe, but worship imaginary deities, to whom they give names. In some instances they worship birds & reptiles . . .

While we were detained at Ovalau by contrary winds we went into the heathen temple & begged a bowl that was sacred to the priest to drink out [of]. He gave it to us rather unwillingly. Being detained some time he, the chief & people said the god was angry at us for taking away the priest's sacred bowl, & therefore sent a contrary wind. They wished us to present an offering to the god through the priest. We told them that there was but one God, that Jehovah was his name, & him only we worshipped & served.

[A postscript dated July 8th, reports that one of his colleagues, John Spinney, is very ill and therefore on his way to New South Wales.]

On account of our present prospects it seemed necessary to leave one alone. I am the person fixed upon. I remain at Lakemba & shall be at least 120 miles from any other station. Our correspondence will be seldom and uncertain. However, I am perfectly willing to do anything that is calculated to benefit the cause. Will you & Mrs. Entwisle be so good as to favour me with a letter. Oh! it would be an excellent thing to receive a letter from you. We have not had one yet since we left dear England.

We have pigs, fowls, yams (an excellent vegetable), coconuts, fish, wild ducks, & many other good things produced here; and as many from England and other countries as we please to buy. We buy the produce of the island with articles supplied by the Mission, and have £30 a year allowed for goods from the Colony,[4] and our flour is also paid for by the Mission. I got a good supply at Sydney, and am well off – yet I am out of debt this quarter, & have therefore said in a letter to Dr. Bunting that he may pay £5 for us to the Institution – or the Mission Fund.

[1] Calvert had been trained as a printer before entering the ministry.

[2] His colleagues in the Lakemba circuit were David Cargill (Chairman of the Fiji District), John Spinney and Thomas James Jagger.

[3] John Hunt had travelled out with Calvert and was stationed at Rewa on the much larger island of Viti Levu to the west. Calvert and Cargill had recently visited Rewa to arrange for the transfer of the printing press there, as it was a more central, populous and important place.

[4] I.e. New South Wales.

The Mission Funds

Jabez Bunting to Thomas Chalmers; Wesleyan Mission House, London, January 23, 1841

(Hayes and Gowland, pp. 92–3, from ms at New College, Edinburgh)

Chalmers was a prominent Presbyterian divine who, in 1843, became the leading member of the Scottish Free Church.

When I last had the honour & pleasure of seeing you in London, I mentioned to you the very strong wish, which the Committee of the Wesleyan Society had for many past years entertained, to be favoured with your invaluable assistance in preaching one of the Annual Sermons on behalf of their Funds. Their Anniversary being necessarily held in the last week of April, or first week in May, & your official engagement in Scotland being such as to prevent your visiting London at that time of year, you had more than once expressed your inability to meet our wishes, but had stated in the kindest terms your disposition to befriend us . . .

You were . . . pleased to say that I might write to you on the subject, when the time of exigency should arrive, and that you would be good enough to direct your attention on the matter. That exigency *now* exists in greater force & pressure than ever before. Our funds are quite exhausted; we are greatly in debt already; our expenditure annually much exceeds our income: our Missionary progress is arrested, though our calls & openings for usefulness are multiplied; and some new & powerful impulse is wanted, to extricate us from present embarrassments, and to enable us to re-commence a career, which God had condescended greatly to honour & to bless. Our usual practice has been to secure the services of One Minister, *not* of our own Denomination at our London Anniversary. This year we are in peculiar difficulties on that point; as not a few of our Dissenting Brethren in England stand aloof from us at present, being offended by our support of the Establishment principle in the recent struggles. We therefore venture to look for help in our emergency to some eminent and zealous & catholic-spirited Minister of the Church of Scotland; and anxiously hope that guided and aided by your counsel & influence, we shall not look in vain. Will you Rev. and dear Sir, do us this friendly & important service, by naming to us one or more individuals, whom you would deem *able*, & likely to be willing & at liberty, thus to aid the Cause of Missions as carried on by our section of the Universal Church of our common Saviour. What we should request of such an individual would be, to preach once in Great Queen St. Chapel, on Friday Forenoon, April 30th, & once in City Road Chapel on Sunday, May 2, and to take some part in our Meetings at Exeter Hall, on Monday, May 3rd.

Pusey on Methodism

(Thomas Jackson, *A Letter to the Rev. E. B. Pusey, . . . being a vindication of the Tenets and Character of the Wesleyan Methodists against his misrepresentations and censures*, 1842, pp. 4–7, 15, 32–3, 51–3)

Pusey, the Regius Professor of Hebrew at Oxford, succeeded Newman as leader of the Oxford Movement in 1841. His *Letter to the Archbishop of Canterbury* had enough truth in its condemnation of 'Wesleyan heresy' to provoke a detailed response from the autodidact Thomas Jackson, connexional editor from 1824 until he became theological tutor at Richmond College in 1842.

The following is that part of your publication upon which I feel it my duty to offer some animadversions:—
> *Meaning of the title heresy as applied to Wesleyanism.*

Having been informed, that some have been offended by my having said 'that Wesleyanism is degenera*ting* into developed heresy', and been requested to explain my meaning, it seems right to do it, although the statement was made too incidentally to justify in the first instance an explanation, which would have been only a prolonged censure. I may say, then, at once, that the conviction on my mind was, that the result of the present movement in the Wesleyan body would be, that the better part would, sooner or later, return to the Church, the remainder were *in the course* of 'degenerating into developed heresy'. The root of that heresy consists in the way in which the doctrine of Justification is held, being in fact, and *practically*, a 'Justification by feelings'. 'Believe (not "in Christ" but) that you will be saved, and you will be saved,' was early a Wesleyan doctrine; but its character was long held in check, partly by the Church-system, in which those who adopted it had been educated, partly by the continued use of the Sacraments of the Church. In the section of the Wesleyan body, which is becoming more alienated from the Church, and ceases to communicate with it, the original error has been more fatally developing itself. They who go over to it, are taught to look for 'present salvation', *i.e.* a sensible assurance of salvation, such as is vouchsafed often to God's servants on their dying beds, probably but rarely until the close of life, and still less at the first conversion of a sinner. What (if true) would be a direct revelation from Almighty God, persons are taught indiscriminately to expect, as the infallible accompaniment and test of a sincere conversion; so that they may not hope that they are really converted, or will be saved, unless they obtain it; what God, when He is pleased to vouchsafe it, ordinarily bestows as the reward at the end, the Wesleyan is taught to look for at the outset, as the very condition of his ultimate salvation, and as securing it. Practically he is taught to hold his salvation to be assured, as soon as he has obtained this first persuasion.

The persuasion that a person will be saved is made the condition, and, virtually, the *only* condition, of his salvation. As long as he believes he is saved, so long, according to them, he is so. The workings of repentance and penitence are thus suddenly checked in the convert, as being thought to be attained. It is with them made an object to check the strong emotions of compunction which God has raised in the sinner. To feel 'the burden of our sins to be intolerable' is accounted want of faith.* The mind is worked up until it lose its fear, and gain what it thinks an assurance of salvation. In other words, permanent repentance and anxiety and grief for sin are accounted contrary to the Gospel. . . . The state of their feelings, not God's commandments, are the standard whereby they try themselves . . .

Persons, of no very strict lives, have been able to profess that they have been without a sinful thought for weeks together, others, for even twenty years. Again: persons esteemed sober-minded among them, have held, 'that by one act of faith, a person may become perfectly sanctified; and that it is the privilege of believers, whenever they choose to claim it.' These things are not said as any reflection on the body, but as pointing out the germ whence an heretical system is springing, which threatens to be more desolating, because more delusive, than open Antinomianism. For, all these things follow from the first principle, that the feelings, or the persuasion that a man is saved, are the test of his faith. He has no need then to examine himself, except as to this one point; he may take it for granted that he is obedient, humble, meek, has all 'the fruits of the Spirit.' Since, then, life is a daily struggle against the powers of evil, since watchfulness is enjoined as essential, since habitual self-denial and bearing the cross is a test of our Lord's true disciples, how must such a system, in the end, be a delusion?

Wesleyanism, then, was said to be 'degenerating into a developed heresy', in that it substitutes for the Catholic teaching, a doctrine of justification for which there is 'no warrant in the Word of God', involv-

---

* The following, which has been furnished me out of a very popular Wesleyan book, 'The Life of Carvosso,' a Class-Leader, may serve as an illustration of what is taking place daily. The writer knows of similar cases, where the ultimate effect (as was to be expected) was very injurious. 'I found a poor heavy-laden penitent. I laboured to encourage her; but such were her strong crying and tears, that I thought best to pray with her. Her mind apparently becoming a little more composed, I asked her how she felt? She said, *I see I must go home and pray more.* Aware that this was a snare of Satan's, [!] I replied, *There is no necessity for that: the Lord is here, and is now waiting to bless you. There is nothing wanting, but for you to believe in Jesus as your Saviour. And if He died for you, ought you not at once to believe in Him, and to love Him?* The light of faith soon appeared, and her soul found liberty through the blood of the Lamb. Full of the assurance of faith, she cried out, *Now I know my sins are forgiven.*' Belief in Christ, and belief in the individual's assured personal salvation, are represented as equivalent.

ing the principle of Antinomianism, and, in many cases, practically leading into it, effacing the doctrine of Repentance, and the real character of good works, and virtually superseding the Sacraments. Painful as it is to say it, on account of the many good men, doubtless, still entangled in it, it 'preaches another Gospel from that which has been delivered unto us', substituting practically the feelings and experiences for repentance, good works, and the Sacraments. – *Letter to the Archbishop of Canterbury* [1842], pp. 159–163. Third Edition [1843].

Let us analyse the several allegations which you have here made, and thus endeavour to ascertain whether the tenets and character of the Wesleyan societies generally are what you describe, or whether you have been led by your prejudices to publish statements which are not true, to the injury of an unoffending people. To an impartial reader your whole account must appear very suspicious, in this view, – that while you express the strongest condemnation of what you are pleased to call 'Wesleyanism', you make no reference to the acknowledged writings of its Founder. It is well known that he has written largely on all the subjects which you have here mooted, and his works are accessible to all who choose to read them; yet have you carefully abstained from quoting a single word that he ever uttered. . . .

[Jackson then deals in detail with the Wesleyan teaching on justification and assurance and with the charge of Antinomianism.]

The subject is now before the reader, and every one may judge of the question at issue. Mr. Wesley declares, in language the most direct and explicit, that Christ crucified, or God in Christ, is the object of justifying faith. On this point the people who bear his name have not departed a hair's breadth from his views. They declare, with one heart and voice, that there is no way of justification before God, for fallen and guilty men, but that of faith in Christ, as the divinely-appointed sacrifice for sin, or in God through Christ. In opposition to this, you aver, that, in order to justification, they teach their hearers to 'believe (*not in Christ*, but) that they will be saved', and then assure them that salvation will infallibly follow. The belief that the parties 'will be saved', you describe as a mere 'feeling', and not as either a principle or an act. A more palpable mis-representation was never palmed upon the world. You declare the thing that is not. Without adducing the slightest proof, and in defiance of the most decisive evidence to the contrary, you describe a body of Christian people, not only as heretics, but as consummate fools, who teach mankind to exercise faith without an object. According to 'Wesleyanism', it seems, men are neither justified by faith in God, nor by faith in the one Mediator between God and man, but by faith in a contingency! . . . 'Wesleyanism' teaches that an 'assurance' – a satisfying evidence – of acceptance with God, arising from the joint testimony of the Holy Spirit, and the believer's own conscience, is directly consequent upon the exercise of faith in Christ, on the part of a truly penitent sinner. This you boldly declare to be 'heresy', and assert, that such an 'assurance' is rarely (if ever) given, except on the bed of death, and as a 'reward'. Let the reader judge on which side the truth lies. For myself, I know not a single text of the New Testament, when fairly interpreted, that gives even the semblance of countenance to your theory, confident though the language be in which you express yourself. . . .

Antinomianism, or opposition to the law of God, whether in theory or in practice, is justly considered one of the foulest heresies that ever afflicted the Church, and dishonoured the sacred cause of religion. This heresy you charge upon the Wesleyan body, and profess to state its origin, as well as to trace its developement and effects, among them. Its principle, you say, is to be found in their doctrine of salvation by faith; and to substantiate this allegation, as we have already seen, you invent and place to their account a doctrine on this subject which they never believed, and which they hold in righteous abhorrence . . .

But you have not confined yourself to doctrine. The practice of the Wesleyans you also declare to be in many respects lax, reprehensible, and, in fact, Antinomian. Your allegations on this score shall be fully met, and the question then submitted to those who take an interest in its decision.

You charge the Wesleyans with setting up a false test of acceptance with God, so that they judge of their spiritual state with little or no regard for religious and moral duties. . . . They do indeed believe that there is a witness of the Holy Spirit, consequent upon faith in Christ, as St. Paul teaches, both in his Epistle to the Romans, and in that to the Galatians, and that this witness is direct and immediate; but it is never alone. It is always preceded by unfeigned repentance, in the exercise of which sin in every form is confessed, lamented, and renounced; and is immediately followed by purity of heart, and by obedience to all the will of God, so far as it is known and understood. Whatever you may assert, the Wesleyans acknowledge as a test of faith no 'feelings' that are unconnected with holy tempers and an obedient life. In declaring the contrary, you misrepresent their creed, and unjustly reproach their character. A man's state of trial does not cease when he obtains the forgiveness of his past sins, and is 'accepted in the Beloved'. To the end of life, says Mr. Wesley, 'we are every moment either pleasing or displeasing to God, according to our works; according to our inward tempers and outward behaviour.' There is no subject on which he has expressed himself more distinctly and copiously than on this, as every candid reader of his works will confess.

Revival at Hinde Street Chapel, London

(Extract of a letter from the Rev. Robert Young, June 8, 1843, printed as a leaflet)

On my coming to this Circuit, after the last Conference, I found the people dwelling together in unity, and very generally expecting that the Lord was about more abundantly to bless his heritage. At the Michaelmas visitation of the classes, it was found, on close inquiry, that, although there was much in the society over which we could rejoice, many of its members were resting without a scriptural evidence of their adoption into the family of God, and but few of them enjoyed the blessing of entire sanctification. Special attention was therefore called to these important privileges, which were explained and enforced, not only in the assemblies of the saints, but frequently on occasions for pastoral visitation. Happy effects followed: a delightful influence was felt in all the means of grace; and the Lord added to the church daily such as were saved. Nothing, however, very extraordinary occurred until December 25th. On the evening of that day, a love-feast was held in Hinde Street Chapel, at which about nine hundred people were present. Thirty-four persons spoke with much propriety and power; twenty-five of whom gave a clear and delightful account of the grace of entire sanctification, which they professed to have recently received. When the hour arrived for bringing this interesting meeting to a close, the officiating Minister made some remarks on the blessing so frequently alluded to; gave a few plain directions for its attainment; presented to the mind several clear promises; exhorted the people at once to seek for it; and then called upon two persons to engage in prayer. During the prayer of the first (Mr. Thompson) an indescribable awe rested upon the assembly; the place was indeed 'dreadful', and every soul appeared bowed down, under a sense of Jehovah's presence.

When the second – 'Father' Jones – pleaded with God, an intelligent and sober-minded young man (Mr. James Richardson) who felt, as he afterwards declared, great objection to excitement and noise in the house of God, cried with a loud voice, 'I have got it! I have got it!' – In a moment, the whole assembly appeared as if convulsed. Such a scene as now presented itself cannot be adequately described. No man moved from his place; but each one seemed to lose sight of all around him, and to draw near the mercy-seat with as much earnestness as if the last hour of his life had approached. 'The kingdom of heaven suffereth violence,' and, on that memorable night, 'the violent took it by by force.' Every few seconds, the affecting cries of penitence were lost amid the bursting joy of triumphant faith, until, like the scene witnessed when the foundation of God's House was laid, it was impossible to discern the noise of the shout of joy from the noise of the weeping of the people. For ten minutes this glory filled the temple, during which period many obtained the spirit of adoption, and not fewer than one hundred persons, according to their subsequent profession, received the blessing of entire sanctification. The effect of this remarkable visitation was soon felt, more or less, in all our religious services; and a great number believed, and turned unto the Lord. The work has continued to advance; and local preachers, leaders, stewards, and many private members, as well as my excellent colleagues, have successfully co-operated in its promotion. Under the ministry of the Word, at the table of the Lord, in class meetings, in the closet, and at the family altar, has the power of God been present to heal; but in no means of grace have conversions been so numerous as in the public prayer meetings, held immediately after the preaching of the Word. Those meetings, conducted with Christian order, have been invariably attended with encouraging results; and in some of them more than twenty broken-hearted penitents have professed to receive 'beauty for ashes, the oil of joy for mourning, and the garments of praise for the spirit of heaviness.' This time of refreshing has extended to 'young men and maidens, old men, and children,' it has visited the mansions of the wealthy, and the cottages of the poor, and whilst it has called forth the derision of a few, it has led many others seriously to enquire, 'What meaneth this?'

Our net increase of members, taken in March, as the result of this gracious visitation, is two hundred and forty-seven, besides one hundred and sixty-seven on trial, and upwards of fifty children that give evidence of having received, in various degrees, the grace of God. But as a large number in church-fellowship, resting without a clear evidence of their acceptance in the Beloved, have happily received that blessing, and many others, living in a comparatively low state of grace, have been 'sanctified wholly'; a much larger amount of good has obviously been accomplished than these statistics show. The finances of the Circuit have been greatly benefited by this revival; and notwithstanding the depression of trade, an augmented sum has been contributed to each of our connexional funds. Needing as we do, 'church extension', we are preparing to build another chapel, for which the friends are subscribing very liberally; and the prospect of seeing yet greater things than these is cheering. It is true, we have seen Popery in several of the churches around us, and under its dire influence numerous and vigorous efforts are being made to arrest the progress of Methodism 'at the West End'; but we no more fear the Priests of Babylon than did Israel's Prophet the Priests of Baal, while the Lord thus graciously answers by fire.

Early Methodism in Retrospect

Jacob Stanley to Henry Moore; Bristol, Dec. 20, 1843

(Ms at Drew University)

When you receive this you will have completed your 92nd year; a long life and in a period of the world's history which has been full of incident both in the Church and the world. Many ancient landmarks have been removed, many revolutions have taken place and many important changes have been effected, some of a doubtful, some of an injurious and some of a useful character. Among the latter may we not rank an increase of missionary zeal which has led to the spread of the gospel in many parts of the heathen world where it has proved to be the power of God to the salvation of many thousands? Under this head too may we not place the increased interest manifested in the religious education of the rising generation? And under this head may we not also place the secession from the Church of Scotland? This appears to me to be one of the noblest instances of Christian principle that has ever been given. A body of Christian ministers, rather than offend their Lord by rejecting his absolute and supreme authority, have nobly sacrificed their homes and dwelling houses amounting in value to three millions annually. Will this, think you, have any effect upon our own Establishment? Does our Church contain 500 men who would make such a sacrifice? I fear not – I fear that most of them would be like the Vicar of Bray.

In our own body I know of nothing remarkable going on. In these parts we have peace, and in South Bristol some prosperity. But not so much as might be expected from the agency employed. I sometimes fear that our numerous applications for money has an injurious operation. We beg for missions, for Sunday Schools, for Tract & Benevolent Societies, for Kingswood School, the Chapel Fund, the Auxiliary, the Contingent Fund & the Theological Institution, besides our Quarterly Collections. There is, however, this consolation in the midst of all – our people are in no danger of dying of apoplexy . . .

Bible Christian Nurture

(BC *Minutes*, 1843)

Q. 13: What can be done to afford increased means of Religious Instruction for the children of the friends composing our congregations?

    A. Being convinced that all the children whom we baptize should be regarded as part of our flock; that it is our duty to endeavour to provide them with means of religious instruction and to assist their parents to bring them up 'in the nurture and admonition of the Lord'; we resolve,

1. To form Sunday schools in connection with all our places of worship, where practicable; and that the children of these Schools be regarded as a part of the flock over whose spiritual state the Pastors and Elders should watch, as 'those who must give account'.

2. That in order to bring our Sunday Scholars under the influence of saving grace, let all the children who are willing to attend, be met weekly by such of their teachers or other persons as the Elders' meeting shall appoint; the boys and girls to meet separately; . . . but the children who attend these meetings shall not be numbered among the members of society, until they have given such evidence that they are the subjects of a work of grace, as shall induce the members of the church to receive them into church-fellowship . . .

3. That no illegitimate child shall be baptized in any of our places of worship.

4. That, ordinarily, no child be baptized by us, except one of its parents, at least, be a member of society, a seat-holder, or a regular attendant on our ministry. The parents shall be expected to attend when the ordinance is administered.[1]

5. That our friends be earnestly entreated to endeavour to establish day schools, to promote the education of the rising generation, in connexion with our places of worship, where it may be practicable.

---

[1] The provisos in paras. 3 and 4 remained in operation for many years, being repeated for example, in the 1882 edition of the *Digest of the Rules . . . of the Bible Christians.*

Work among the Young People

(Mss at Duke University)

Francis A. West to George Osborn; Leeds, Feb. 3, 1844

West was stationed in the Leeds (Brunswick) circuit, with William Kelk as his Superintendent and Frederick J. Jobson as the junior minister. Kelk left after only one year in the circuit.

I am sadly overworked, like you. When I am Superintendent I will make a leisure night for the young men, – a matter of far greater moment than preaching to 15 saints and sinners who are crammed with sermons. At present, I am obliged to meet them in the morning, which neither suits me nor them. I had about 50 young men when I met them a few times in the evening, but they do not meet so numerously in the morning. The young ladies, for they are such, except a few matrons, number from 40 to 50 at a meeting, on Monday afternoon. Kelk will do nothing but talk about pastoral visitations 'on a grand scale' and 'special services'. Jobson I hope to link with in a little time, for the young men.

F. A. West to George Osborn; undated, but probably from the same period

As to my teaching the Young People. I have hitherto confined myself to Scripture Antiquities, with collateral illustration of Scripture, and inculcation of religion . . . The Lecture usually occupies me from 70 minutes to 1½ hours. Of course the interest varies not only with the *subject*, but my *mood*; for sometimes I *cannot* throw off illustrations as at others. I used to meet the young men at 6 a.m., but when they fell off to 6, I gave it up; and I generally meet the ladies at 6 p.m., & the young men at 8. Perhaps I have 35 of the former, & about 20 or 25 of the latter. They give me great satisfaction, & I believe count it a great privilege. I know I should have done at their age.

'In Labours More Abundant': A Primitive Methodist Retrospect

(Petty, *History*, pp. 441–3)

In January 1844, William Garner looked back on twenty-one years in the itinerancy which he claimed to be 'a pretty fair specimen of the labours of his brethren in general'.

I was called out to travel by the Quarterly Meeting of Hull circuit, in December, 1822, and I entered on my new and important vocation on January 8th, 1823. From the day that I left my paternal roof for the work of the holy ministry, to the present date, I have kept a diurnal record of my journeys and my regular pulpit labours. By the grace of God, I have now completed three times seven years' service in the vineyard of Jesus Christ. In three months hence I shall be forty-two years of age. And, after having reviewed 'my manner of life', from the period of my accountability to God to the present day, I feel thankful to Heaven, that I can rationally come to the conclusion, that the time which I have spent in the Gospel field, has been far the happiest, and, notwithstanding my imperfections, I doubt not, far the most useful portion of my existence. I *feel* that this is not a mean stimulus to be 'faithful unto death'. In the space of twenty-one years, I have travelled on *foot*, with comparatively trifling exceptions, 44,936 miles, and have preached 6278 sermons. The journeys do not include my daily perambulations in the cities, towns, villages, &c., where my lot has been cast; nor do the sermons include exhortations, addresses, missionary speeches, &c., which amount to a great number. Some of my fellow-labourers, of equally long standing in the ministry with myself, have probably not travelled and preached so extensively as I have; but by others, in these respects, I have undoubtedly been exceeded. So that the extent of my preachings and travels may be regarded as a fair specimen of that of the first race of Primitive Methodist Preachers in general. Frequently, after having walked twenty and (occasionally) thirty miles a day, I have been enabled to stand up and preach, or assist at a missionary meeting. Some of my old and esteemed companions in toil, are able to confirm this statement. And to their honour be it recorded, I know that they have endured similar fatigues.

On many days, of course, I have not travelled at all. And I gratefully acknowledge that very many of my journeys have been agreeable, and recreative to both body and mind; but not a few of them have been extremely exhausting, especially in the early years of my ministry.

It appears, from my diary, that forty-eight of my principal journeys, which were performed on foot, between January 8th, 1823, to July 27, 1830, amount to 1,068 miles, which average rather more than twenty-two miles a-day. And the reader must bear in mind that some of these journeys were performed beneath a scorching sun – some through depths of snow – some, through windy storms and tempests – and some, through drenching rains in the cold winter, while I was encumbered with an umbrella over my head, and a library and wardrobe on my back; though others were performed beneath a serene sky, and while I was surrounded with all the charms of a delightful spring. Nor should it be forgotten, that preaching and travelling do not form the *whole* of the work of a Primitive Methodist preacher: in addition to these he has to 'give attention to reading', to 'study to show himself a workman that needeth not to be ashamed', especially to '*search* the Scriptures' – to use the pen extensively – and to 'visit from house to house'; besides attending to those things which come upon him daily – the cares of the church.

Under the arduous toils of the Primitive Methodist ministry, many of our fellow-labourers have fainted, and have either returned to their secular employments, or withdrawn from the Connexion, and entered the ministry of other churches. Some of these, we hope, left us for conscience' sake; others, we fear, 'went out from us because they were not of us'. They sought an *easier life* and a *larger income* than the Primitive

Methodist ministry could afford: verily these are enjoying their reward
NOW. Others, regardless of invitations and lucrative proffers, have

> Nobly for their Master stood,
> Valiant champions for their God.

These look for their reward HEREAFTER.

If the preceding remarks be a means of cheering my young brethren
in the ministry, in the prosecution of their arduous, but blessed toil
(which they may, at times, be tempted to regard as insupportable), and
if they be, in any measure, instrumental in confirming the love of our lay
brethren to a class of ministers who are not seeking *theirs* but *them*, they
are not written in vain.

Primitive Methodism in the Villages

(*PM Magazine*, 1845, pp. 278–80)

The first of three letters written by the Rev. William Thorn, the Independent
minister at Winchester, to Sir Thomas Baring, protesting at his treatment of
the Primitive Methodist society in Micheldever, Hants. Baring was an
Anglican professing liberal sentiments. When he failed to respond in any
way to Thorn's protests, the letters were sent to the press. For Cobbett's
verdict on Baring, see *Rural Rides* (Penguin edition, 1967), pp. 44–5, 74–5.

September 2, 1844

Sir Thomas,

I fear you will deem me improperly officious in sending you the subsequent remarks; but as they solely concern the cause of Christ and the
salvation of souls, in which you avowedly take a lively interest, I think
you will pardon the intrusion . . .

The facts I wish to bring under your serious consideration are soon
narrated. The Primitive Methodists had agreed to purchase, of Mr.
Winkworth, a cottage and garden at Northbrook, in the parish of
Micheldever, for £100, on which to erect a chapel for the worship of
God. The time was fixed, and had all but arrived for signing the agreement and settling the bargain; in fact they had virtually and morally
bought the premises.

The evening previous to the legal accomplishment of this object, the
Rev. Mr. Clark having, by some means, heard of the transaction, applied
either to you personally or to your steward, and persuaded you, or him

in your name, to offer the seller £20 more for the property than its real value, or than the Primitives were to have paid for it. This was immediately done; and the cottage and garden were wrested from their hands, and added to the ample estate of Sir Thomas Baring.

The manifest motive of Mr. Clark was to prevent the Primitives from having a suitable place in which to worship God according to the dictates of their own consciences, and, if possible, ultimately to drive them out of the parish and neighbourhood altogether. This, I hear, he has openly avowed, and exults in his superior generalship in the transaction. The Lord pardon his iniquity!

The injury done to these good people is aggravated by the circumstance that they are now obliged to worship in a small inconvenient cottage, the pious occupants of which have a large family, and in which they are not sure how long they shall be enabled to carry on the service of God; and as Mr. Winkworth's house and garden were the only premises obtainable for their purposes in the parish, your securing these has well-nigh blasted all their hopes of future usefulness in that neighbourhood.

I would charitably presume that you were not cognisant of the above facts when you purchased the property in question. I cannot conceive that you, a professed disciple of Christ, an avowed advocate of liberty of conscience, and the generous supporter of many noble institutions formed to extend the saving knowledge of Christ, would have tempted a poor man to violate his positive agreement to sell his premises to others by the offer of a larger sum for them, in order that they might not be converted into a humble sanctuary for the honour of God and the conversion of immortal souls.

You well know, and you have candidly stated, that the Primitive Methodists have been greatly blessed of God among the formerly profane and ignorant peasantry of Micheldever and neighbouring places. And as a Christian, I think you cannot question that they have done ten times more good to the people, both in soul and conduct, than the clergyman under whose sectarian and persecuting influence you have now and on former occasions been induced to oppose them. Hence, for these useful and self-denying Methodists to find in *you* an opponent is strange indeed! But whether you have acted ignorantly or knowingly, your *might* has overcome their *right*; and, instead of encouraging and helping them as a wealthy disciple of our common Lord ought to have done, you have hindered them by the power of a heavier purse, too much like an exclusive and intolerant member of the church of England . . .

You will bear in mind that all the souls which may be lost through your driving away or opposing the Methodists, will, in a great measure, be laid to your account; and that many will probably be so lost is unhappily too manifest. The labourers in general greatly dislike the state clergyman of the parish; will not hear him; and, of course, can derive no benefit from his ministration.

May the gracious Spirit of God incline you to do justly towards his people, even if you do not exercise mercy and benevolence. Your obedient humble servant,

W. Thorn

Overseas Missions: Primitive Methodist Regulations

(Petty, *History*, pp. 378–80)

The Primitive Methodist Conference of 1843 set up a new General Missionary Committee charged with the oversight of the work of both home and overseas missionaries. But the initiative at this period in its history still lay not with the Connexion so much as with the circuits; and it was the North Shields Circuit which later that year took the lead in sending missionaries to New Zealand and Australia. In April 1844 the following regulations were agreed upon, just before the first missionaries sailed.

1. All the Committee's resolutions shall be understood to be subject to the allowance or disallowance of the Conference, to be held in the year 1844; though the Committee does not anticipate the Conference's disallowance of any of them, unless it be to promote the interests of Christ and the missionaries; and the Committee will exert itself to secure the Conference's allowance, unless it shall appear that these important ends will thereby be endangered.

2. The costs of the missionaries' passages, their victuals and outfittings for their voyages, the salaries of the single men while on their passages, as well as their salaries, board, and lodgings for nine months after their arrival, (and the salaries and allowances of married men for the same length of time after theirs), shall be either paid into a bank, so as to be drawn by them when they arrive, or be placed in their possession when they set sail, as shall be found most safe and convenient; and the Conference of 1844 shall be desired to fix what shall be allowed to married men, in addition to the victuals and outfittings for their passages.

3. If the missionaries employed shall conduct themselves uprightly and efficiently, they shall not be expected to remain on foreign stations longer than ten years, except by the mutual concurrence of themselves, and the officiating organs of the Connexion; and when they shall remove under official sanction, they and their families, if they have any, shall be placed in home stations.

4. They shall, at the discretion of any Conference of the Primitive Methodist Connexion, or General Missionary Committee appointed

thereby, be liable to be removed before the end of ten years hence to either home stations or to other foreign ones, than those which they shall be occupying at the time being.

5. If the health of any missionary shall, within ten years hence, fail so much as to disqualify him from prosecuting his ministerial labours, and if there shall not at the time be any default in his missionary character, then his removal shall take place as speedily as it can be prudently effected.

6. When the removal of a missionary shall take place, and that of his family, if he shall have one (if his conduct shall have been upright and Primitive Methodistic, and if his removal be effected under proper official direction), the expenses occasioned thereby shall be borne by the Connexion; but if his conduct or his removal shall be found otherwise than is herein expressed – then it shall be at the Connexion's option whether these expenses shall be borne wholly or in part by himself or not.

7. If a married missionary shall die on a foreign station, and if his widow shall, within three months after his death, write to the officiating organs of the Connexion, to solicit the removal of herself and her children, if she shall have any, – then the Connexion shall bear the expenses of the removal, provided it be effected, as to time and manner, under proper official direction.

8. The missionaries shall receive salaries, rents, book-profits, travelling expenses, and other immunities, to such extent as will be equal to the average allowances made to their brethren in home stations; and in order hereto they shall furnish, in detail to the Missionary Committee, a list of rents, and of the prices of provisions, and wearing apparel in their respective stations, that an equality may be fixed.

9. In purchasing furniture for married missionaries, obtaining board and lodgings for single ones, and otherwise expending the missionary money, there shall be observed the same economy as that which has been generally practised in the Connexion, and as will befit the means by which such money is raised.

10. The duties and interests of every foreign missionary, respecting the Primitive Methodist Itinerant Preachers' Friendly Society (including those of his family, if he have one), shall be deemed the same as if he occupied a home station. Hence, if the duties be fulfilled, the interests will be secured; as the Committee is confident that the next yearly meeting will sanction this resolution.

11. As the work of our missionaries is spiritual, they shall not directly or indirectly embark in business or trade to secure personal profit, but shall devote their energies to the spreading of His interests, who says, 'My kingdom is not of this world.'

12. As our missionaries are emphatically teachers of religion, they shall not be members of political associations, nor take any part in public

political disputes, but shall enforce, by precept and example, a cheerful obedience to the lawful authorities and institutions recognized in the countries to which their respective stations shall belong. And, in order that they may observe this regulation, they are desired to acquaint themselves with the governors and the laws of those stations, and to demean themselves towards the former, and observe the latter, in such a manner as to secure every possible facility to the spreading of the work of God among the unsaved of mankind; which must be the *alpha* and *omega* of all their conduct.

13. Before receiving any person as a member of society they shall be satisfied of his desire to become a decided Christian, and if he be un-baptized, shall perform the rite of baptism by sprinkling in the name of the Father, Son, and Holy Ghost; and they shall not allow members to repeat faults with impunity, but shall meekly, and yet firmly enforce the wholesome discipline observed by the Connexion at home, except where difference of circumstances shall render any of its unessential details inexpedient; and the exceptions must always be subject to the allowance or disallowance of the home authorities.

14. Wherever it is practicable they shall establish Sunday, week-day, and infant-schools; and shall at stated times catechise the pupils thereof on subjects calculated to render them intelligent, industrious and reputable Christians.

15. If they shall have to endure persecution in the discharge of their duties, or witness the endurance of it by any of our members or friends, they are hereby exhorted to cherish and enforce meekness and prayerfulness, and to elude suffering by such means only as are in accordance with the Gospel and the laws of the country in which the persecution shall take place.

16. They shall keep journals of their labours, regular accounts of the receipts and disbursements of their missions, memorandums of suggestions likely to improve the spiritual and financial interests of those missions, and to improve our legislation respecting them; and these journals, &c., with plans of the missionaries' appointments, shall be transmitted to the General Missionary Committee in London once in three months at the least, and oftener if the Committee shall desire them.

17. If a missionary shall, within six years after his arrival at his first foreign station, wish to dissever himself from the Primitive Methodist Connexion he shall refund to the General Treasurer of the Missionary Fund the money expended in conveying him from England to the station.

Fly Sheets from the 'Private Correspondent'

The series of anonymous 'Fly Sheets' issued between 1844 and 1849 mounted a virulent attack on the 'London hierarchy' and on its leader, Jabez Bunting, in particular. The first was sub-titled 'On Location, Centralization, and Secularization' and prefaced by quotation from 'Wesley's Advice to his Preachers' and the 'General Report of the Wesleyan Centenary Fund'.

We have selected these two mottos, with a view, first, to show, that Dr. Bunting's whole system of government has been opposed to the advice and practice of Mr. Wesley; his system being of EXCLUSIVENESS, FAVOUR-ITISM, and SELFISHNESS, as exemplified in the formation and packings of his Committees, his opposition to open, free discussion, in the general assembly, on the more politic and public affairs of the Connexion, and his invariable attempt to confine the knowledge, the power, the privileges of the body to his own chosen few: and, secondly, to show the slender influence the rules, which he has imposed upon others, have had upon his own principles, habits and ministerial character; adopting, by his conduct, the language of those of the clergy of the Established Church, who, in consequence of having run themselves out of health, wealth, and credit, insist on their parishioners 'doing as they say, not as they do' . . .

One of the earliest subjects to which we direct attention, and to which we turn the more readily because of its lying at the base of several other evils, is:—

I. LOCATION. This is opposed to:—

1. The Apostolic plan of spreading Christianity through the nations of the earth . . .

2. Location is opposed to the spirit and practice of Methodism, as introduced and established by its Founder . . . And shall any calling themselves his sons in the gospel, and affecting to be zealous in the main-tenance and promotion of the cause which he had at heart, fritter down his system of Itinerancy? Shall Messrs. Bunting, Alder, Beecham, Jack-son, Hoole, &c., &c., whose presence is falsely assumed to be so neces-sary, not to say vitally important, to the right management of our mis-sionary and other interests in London and elsewhere; – shall these be the privileged few, who, at the very time they are lauding Mr. Wesley's plan and procedure, and affecting to be so anxious for its conservation, destroy it, by locating themselves in London, and by bartering the spirit of the ministers of Jesus for one of fleshly ease and sloth? Spirit of consistency and honesty! whither art thou fled!

3. There is an incongruity between the location of ministerial secre-taries and the christian ministers sent forth on foreign missions; implying separate calls to the same apostolic office; sending forth others, while

luxuriating at home themselves; hesitating about taking excellent young men out, who offer themselves for the home work only; and manifesting an anxiety to keep the men out in the missionary field during the period of life!

4. It is inimical to a fair distribution of ministerial talent; depriving an important part of the Connexion of the diversity of gifts which God has conferred upon different men, and which are necessary for the perfecting of the saints . . .

5. An argument may be drawn from its prejudicial effects upon health. While some are worn down by incessant application to study in one department, others present – not through hard labour – an unnatural degree of obesity: the well-clothed skeletons of the latter of whom, we leave to speak for themselves . . .

6. Another view of it is, its flagrant injustice towards others, who are compelled to be out in all weathers, and to experience all the inconveniences entailed on itinerancy, without the slightest prospect of enjoying the repose of location for a given period. And what, it may be demanded, renders the presence of Dr. Bunting and his coadjutors so necessary to the best management of our connexional interests in London? What talents have these men that are peculiar to themselves, or that may not be found in one, two, or more hundreds of their brethren? We know of none, unless it be unseemly vanity, in arrogating, either directly or indirectly, this superiority over their brother ministers . . .

8. Dissatisfaction with itinerancy is one of the natural consequences, owing to its various inconveniences; and it thus becomes the forerunner of a settled ministry. Let the experiment be tried on the four Secretaries at home, which they are trying on others abroad; send the easy Dr. Bunting to Alstone, the dainty Dr. Alder to Shetland, the stately Mr. Beecham to Whitehaven, and the 'illustrious' Mr. Hoole among the Welsh mountains! How would they work, and feel, and walk, and eat, after the sweets of metropolitan localization? . . . We contend that the preacher on the poorest circuit is serving the connexion, by his example and by his labours, much more effectually than our locators; for such an one preserves the spirit of itinerancy, is the immediate instrument of bringing sinners to God, and exhibits to the more luxurious the self-denying example of our Lord. Imitate the example of Dr. Bunting, and itinerancy is at an end; imbibe the spirit of localizers, and self-indulgence will be the order of the day.

The Human Face of 'Buntingism'

(James H. Rigg, *Wesleyan Methodist Reminiscences, Sixty Years Ago*, 1904, pp. 26–9)

While attending the July Examination Committee as a candidate for the ministry in 1845, Rigg was surprised to be invited to breakfast by the great Dr. Bunting.

Of course I gratefully accepted the invitation, given with such courtesy as well as kindness, and in good time the following morning I found myself at Dr. Bunting's house, the only guest. Mrs. Bunting, and I think also Miss Bunting, was there, and it was evident that breakfast would not keep us waiting. The house was a plain, family house, by no means large, in a dull square in Pentonville – a house of moderate rent in an unfashionable quarter. A quieter, a more perfectly home-like meal it would not be possible to imagine. The charm was the greater because the courteous host, dignified without effort or pretence, was so distinguished and influential a man – one whose eminence and importance as a Christian teacher and leader were universally recognised. There was not a trace of self-importance or of aloofness from first to last. I was at once put at my ease – made perfectly at home. He knew something of Biggleswade, . . . and more than a little of Bedfordshire Methodism, and he quietly elicited what I might have properly to say on the subjects touched on. Of course, he had known my father long and well. He spoke about the state of 'the Connexion', and did not disdain to intimate quietly – I might almost say modestly – his own views as to some difficult points then pending, and to encourage me to speak also. In short, nothing about this great man, as I then met him, and learnt afterwards to know him, was more remarkable than his modesty and candour, his moderation even when he felt bound to censure, his large tolerance and generous breadth of view, though on some all-important questions his views were, on critical occasions, emphatically expressed. At that time there were well-meaning men and women, some of them strangers to England, whose peculiar views and masterful irregularities were making trouble in the Methodist Church. I was especially struck by his tenderness of judgment when referring to such cases. Nothing that I saw or learned afterwards altered the judgment which I then formed as to the charity and wise discrimination which habitually ruled Dr. Bunting's views of men and things, though I was never called to work with him or under him in the service of the Church, but was always a more or less distinterested junior.

Some years later, when I was still a very junior minister, I felt it my duty more than once respectfully to differ from Dr. Bunting as to certain points that were in question, and to express my views in Conference discussion, as I ventured also to do more than once in Committee. But from Dr. Bunting I never experienced anything, in the way of opposition or correction, but courteous dissent. On one occasion, at the Birmingham Conference of 1854, I well remember meeting Dr. Bunting in the vestry after he had replied to some view I had expressed, and his saying to me words to this effect:—

'Mr. James Rigg, you must not suppose when I disagree with you, as I have done to-day, that I fail to respect your character or your motives, though I may sometimes differ from your views.' . . .

Dr. Bunting was a man of surpassing wisdom, and of an unpretending greatness, recognised by the most distinguished ministers of all Evangelical Churches in his day, but he was not, of course, infallible. Nor did he count those his best or wisest friends who held it necessary never to allow any to differ from his judgment. How the leading laymen of Methodism honoured this great and modest man was shown in an enthusiastic public meeting held in Leeds in 1850, and in another not less enthusiastic held in London in 1851.

Morning Prayer at Wesley's Chapel, 1846: An American Impression

(Tobias Spicer, *Autobiography*, 1851, pp. 180–1)

Spicer was an American Methodist minister.

I spent six Sabbaths in London, and attended public worship in several different places. The first Sabbath I attended at the City Road chapel. Here the morning service of the Established Church was read, as is the case in most of the Wesleyan chapels in London. The service is used by our people, without much alteration; however, for a few years past, they omit to pray for Bishops as a distinct order in the ministry; they pray for all the ministers of the Gospel, instead of 'Bishops and other clergy'. I suppose our Wesleyan brethren in England think as we do here, namely, that 'Bishop' is an *office* in the church, and not a distinct *order*. This is the light in which Mr. Wesley viewed it, and accordingly, in 'The Sunday Service of the Methodists in the United States', which he prepared, he omitted the term 'Bishops', and substituted 'Ministers'.

The reading of the service occupied about three quarters of an hour, and was attended with the responses of a regular clerk. In this chapel the service is seldom read by the man who delivers the sermon, but by a man who is employed to read the service, administer baptism, and bury the dead.

Only a few besides the Sabbath school and their teachers were present,

The New Chapel, City Road, London, a pencil sketch made c. 1850

Opened in 1778, the 'New Foundery' was a social and cultural landmark in the development of London Methodism, as well as a symbol of Wesley's ambivalent relationship with the Church of England. Following the pattern of eighteenth-century auditory parish churches, the sanctuary was hidden behind a central three-decker pulpit which provided for preacher, reader and precentor. Men and women sat apart. Until well into the new century, worship was conducted only by Anglican clergy. Bunting was the first itinerant to read prayers there, in 1820; and the veteran Henry Moore was the first to administer the Sacrament, on May 27, 1826.

when the reading of the service commenced, but the congregation were all in and quietly seated by the time the reader was through. Just before the service closed, the preacher came in from the vestry, and went into the pulpit and kneeled down, and remained on his knees until the benediction was pronounced. After a few moments, he gave out a hymn; this was followed by prayer and singing again. Then followed the sermon, as is usual among us. I could not learn the minister's name who preached that morning, but he gave us an excellent sermon. It certainly was among the best that I heard in London.

The Wesleyan Conference of 1846 through American Eyes

(Tobias Spicer, *Autobiography*, 1851, pp. 165–9, 178–80)

As the Wesleyan Conference was to be held in Bristol, I resolved to visit this place. Bristol lies one hundred and eighteen miles west of London. I took the cars at London, and reached Bristol in about nine hours . . .

On my arrival, I found the Conference was held in Ebenezer Chapel, in Old King street. Next morning I went to the place, and found the preachers assembling. The chapel is about fifty-five feet by eighty-five; the pulpit stands about ten feet from the rear, having the communion table and altar behind it, leaving a narrow passage between the altar and rear of the pulpit. Around the pulpit was erected a temporary platform, about four feet high; this would accommodate about twenty persons, and was designed for seating the most distinguished members. Directly in the front of the pulpit was an armed chair for the president. At his left sat the two secretaries at a table, and at his right sat the ex-presidents.

The doors of the chapel being open I went in, and sat down near the door. Soon one of the preachers came to me and inquired who I was. Upon informing him, and expressing a wish to be permitted to sit with them a day or two, he said he would introduce me to Mr. Atherton, the president, who would pass in very shortly. Soon Mr. Atherton came in; he introduced me, and Mr. Atherton took my hand and just inquired whether I was from the Northern or the Southern States. I told him, and he passed on, giving me no opportunity to hand him my letter of introduction from Bishop Janes . . .

The president had taken his seat on the platform, and soon Mr. Newton was in his place, and the Conference was opened by singing, reading the Scriptures, and prayer. During these religious exercises the preachers were coming in, and there was much noise. When they were through, the president spoke a few words, but to me they were inaudible. Then Mr. Newton commenced speaking, and, after a while, I heard him mention my name, and he beckoned to me to come forward. So I started, scarcely knowing whether I was right or wrong, crowding my way along the aisle, till I got alongside the platform, when a brother conducted me around in the rear of the pulpit, and up the steps to the platform.

I supposed the secretary would have introduced me to the Conference, as is usual in our country; but he only turned round, and, pointing to a seat in the rear, desired me to be seated. On observing Dr. Peck, from New York, and Dr. Emory, sitting there, I took a seat beside them, and said to one of them quite softly, 'I suppose this must pass for an introduction to the British Conference.' He replied, 'It is as good an introduction as I have had.' I doubt whether one in twenty heard my name announced, or knew who I was, whence I came, or whither I was going. I suppose it was just as well, for I doubt whether one in fifty cared one pin about me.

Thus far, great noise and confusion seemed to prevail; but the president took it into his head to still the noisy elements. He cried at the top of his voice, and in a manner that showed he was really in earnest, 'Order!' and comparative order ensued. The whirlwind was hushed to a gentle breeze.

The manner of doing business was a little singular; it was certainly different from anything I had ever seen before.

1st. There was not that order observed, and that attention to business, that I have generally seen. Men were talking in every direction, so that the speaker could sometimes scarcely be heard.

2d. The president sometimes took part in the discussion, and he would occasionally interrupt the speaker, if he did not like the argument.

3d. It several times happened that some one would interrupt a speaker in the midst of his argument, by inquiring, 'How do you know that?' which question the speaker would stop to answer, and then proceed with his argument.

4th. The frequent cry of, 'Hear, hear', which was sometimes uttered by perhaps fifty voices, to me was a great annoyance, for they often so drowned the voice of the speaker that I could not hear him at all.

5th. They frequently would respond to the speaker, if he expressed himself in the form of an interrogation; it may be sometimes fifty voices would cry out, 'Yes, yes,' or, 'No, no,' as they happened to view the question.

6th. The president did not always put the question, and call for the ayes and noes; but often made up the decision from the ayes and noes that were uttered during the discussion. When these ayes and noes became so frequent and uproarious that the speaker could no longer be heard, the president sometimes would say, 'I think the ayes have it,' or,

'I think the noes have it'; and that arrested all further discussion, and decided the case.

7th. Not unfrequently, the Conference broke out into an uproarious laughter, at some remark of the speaker, and once or twice they clapped and stamped as sinners do at their political meetings in our own country.

I know that much allowance must be made for the customs and usages of the country; but to me it does seem strange that a body of grave divines should fall into such disagreeable and inconvenient habits. I should think that those who had visited our country, and had seen a more excellent way, would, ere this, have labored to bring about a reform.

There were present, at this Conference, *four hundred* ministers, and they were as fine, healthy, and intelligent looking set of men as I ever looked upon in my life. I shall never see the like again.

I am sure, from what I saw and heard while in England, that too many of our members and ministers, as well as others, are far behind the times in their views and feelings on the subject of temperance. As a further proof of this, I will mention what took place at the Conference in my presence, at Bristol. Mr. Atherton, the president of the Conference, arose in his place, and said that he was sorry to say he had never known so many insolent things sent up to any Conference as had been sent up to that by the tee-totallers. 'They make us,' said he, 'a great deal of trouble. Not content with having their own way, they undertake to direct us, and tell us what is our duty. They plainly show that they are not of us. I wish they would take themselves away from us. They are at liberty to leave us, and go where they can be better pleased. I think,' said he, 'there is no body of ministers who are so much troubled by them as we are.' Upon this, not waiting for the president to finish his speech, or, if he had finished, he had not taken his seat, Dr. Beaumont sprang up and said, 'Perhaps there is no body of ministers that has assailed and provoked them as much as we have.' Here the president interrupted the doctor, and replied, 'We do not design to provoke them, but we act in self-defence.' I afterwards inquired what the president meant by the assault of the tee-totallers, to which he alluded, and was told that many brethren from Preston and elsewhere, who had become tee-totallers, had sent up petitions and remonstrances on the subject of temperance, asking the co-operation of all the preachers in the great temperance movement, and requesting, especially, that they would abstain from wine and beer as a beverage.

Another instance occurred. I was sitting beside Rev. Dr. Peck on the rear seat of the platform, when he whispered to me to look down behind me; so I turned round, and saw a man passing between the platform and the communion table, bearing a waiter in his hands; he appeared to have come out of the vestry, and was going across to the opposite door which leads into the sexton's house, or the parsonage. I supposed it was the sexton. On the waiter which he bore, there were, I should think, not less than twenty-five wine-glasses, all of which were empty, except one. Just as I first saw him, he stopped, and a minister, who sat within the altar by the communion-table, took the glass which had wine and drank it, and set back the glass, and the sexton passed on to the opposite door. I learned, upon inquiry, that the committee who made out the preachers' appointments for the ensuing year were at that time occupying the vestry, engaged in their appropriate work, and I suppose the wine had been carried in as refreshment for these venerable fathers, to strengthen them in the performance of their arduous labors. But of this I know nothing.

An Important Meeting on State Education

(J. H. Rigg, *Wesleyan Methodist Reminiscences*, 1904, pp. 104–14)

Mr. Arthur happened at this time [early 1847] to be over from Paris, to lecture at Exeter Hall, and he and I had naturally come together, and together had learnt from Mr. Scott about the Committee that was to be held at Centenary Hall, at which, through his kind influence, on the condition that we kept absolute silence, and treated all we heard and learned as confidential, we were allowed to be present within the Committee Room, hanging on the skirts of the Committee. It was not a large Committee, but it was an influential selection from the Conference Committee on Education. No one had any idea, not even Mr. Scott, that Lord Ashley was to call at the House.[1] Of course, he was not admitted to the Committee. But I am anticipating.

So far as I remember, the principal ministers present, in addition to Mr. Scott and Dr. Bunting, included Samuel Jackson, W. M. Bunting, George (not yet Dr.) Osborn, T. Vasey, John C. Pengelly. John Lomas, I seem to remember, was there, and also R. Newstead. I think also that S. R. Hall was present. Mr. Prest, no doubt, was there, though he did not take a leading part. There were others of whom I have no distinct recollection. The two speakers, who were never to be forgotten, and who made the chief impression on Mr. Arthur and myself, were Samuel Jackson and W. M. Bunting. Abler argumentative speeches I have rarely heard, and both were entirely opposed to allowing Government to have any share whatever in the matter of organised National Education. Both held the strong Dissenting position on this subject. Mr. Samuel Jackson opposed the idea of State co-operation by searching arguments which might have been, in part – though probably they were not – borrowed from Adam Smith. He pleaded for individual liberty in the interest of teachers, and on the principles of Free Trade, and for parental right of choice as to the education of their children. He pleaded also for the rights and liberties of Christian Churches in respect of their members and adherents, and their Mission Day Schools. Mr. William Bunting power-fully supported him at length and with many parentheses, but with characteristic force and felicity of phrase. My impression is that Mr. Bunting insisted strongly on the danger – on the certainty – that if the Evangelical Churches consented to share the task of National Education with the State, the Roman Catholics could not be excluded from State countenance and pecuniary help in their Day School work. The effect of these addresses on the Committee was evident, and seemed to be all but decisive . . .

Mr. Arthur and myself agreed that if abstract reasoning had prevailed, the result must have been the refusal of all negotiations with the Govern-ment . . . If, however, their logic and the loftiness of their Christian ideal seemed to take strong hold of the Committee generally, none the less there was left a feeling of helplessness. Practical men, the men most widely and completely acquainted in detail with all the facts involved in the question, and especially with the actual conditions of the people and the Churches – while feeling the force of the arguments which had been advanced, were painfully, if not hopelessly, conscious of the irresponsive immobility of the upper and middle classes, and even of the Churches generally, of the utterly discouraging contrast between the ideal view which warned the State to hold its hands from the work of organising National Education, in the faith that the Churches both could and would do the work, and the hard reality which had to be faced in the unprepared-ness and indisposition of the Churches generally to accept that ideal as defining their practical duty.

I scarcely remember to have seen at any time a Committee more helpless-seeming than was that Committee after the two speeches had been delivered. Dr. Bunting had no word to offer; Dr. Osborn, who was acting as Secretary, was visibly perplexed and was silent. The Com-mittee was waiting for Mr. Scott, and it was evident that he was not in haste to intervene.

Whilst the Committee was thus at fault, a messenger came up to the room to say that a gentleman – whose name was not at first made known – had called to see Mr. Scott. Mr. Scott, after a few words to one or two members of the Committee, made haste to go down to the visitor. By-and-by, the word went round that Lord Ashley had called.

Lord Ashley was not a member of the Government, nor was he in any sense a party man; he . . . came as a voluntary, unofficial philanthrop-ist, to find out what might best and most fittingly be done in the way of securing the co-operation of the Wesleyan Methodists in the painfully necessary work of National Education, and in interpreting to the Government the ideas and requirements of the Wesleyan leaders. The sensation that went through the Committee may be imagined, when such a Christian nobleman, the most influential philanthropist in the kingdom, felt constrained, as a mere Christian and entirely apart from any thought of politics, to call on Mr. Scott, whose character and influence as a Christian educationist were already known, on both sides of politics, to see if he could render help in the great work which the Queen, in her own personality, and all statesmen alike, felt to be the vital question of the hour for the country and all classes, although the multitude were so utterly indifferent to the question of national education, both moral and material, and yet more to the question of moral than of material education. Mr. Scott was absent some time with his visitor, half an hour, or more. When he returned he was guarded and more than usually deliberate in his statement to the Committee of the general purport of Lord Ashley's communication, and the special object of his visit. He did not enter directly into controversy, but insisted on the established facts as to the nation's educational needs, which had so profoundly impressed alike philanthropists and statesmen of every colour; he gave evidence that all leading statesmen were deeply convinced that moral and Christian instruction was yet more necessary than any outward advance or reform, and if he did not refute the arguments of Mr. Jackson and Mr. Bunting, he showed that they could hardly be carried out in practice, or contribute to the practical solution of the very grave and pressing question then before the country.

The question which Methodism had to determine in 1846–7, was whether, or upon what terms, the Wesleyan Methodist Church would be prepared also to accept the pecuniary help and general guidance of the State in the establishment and organisation of its Training Colleges and Church Schools.

The Committee in Centenary Hall, which met early in 1847, was the first company assembled on behalf of Wesleyan Methodism to take this momentous question into consideration.

After Mr. Scott had spoken, the business of framing a resolution was taken up, and Dr. Bunting at length said a few words, regretting that at his time of life he should be obliged to take any leading part in the framing of a resolution on the subject. He had a right now to look to younger men to do such work, at least, in first draft. Dr. Osborn then at length made an essay in this direction. The Committee could not forget the speeches of Mr. Jackson and Mr. William Bunting. There was also the question whether the Roman Catholics would also be taken into partnership, as to which Mr. Scott informed the meeting that he had mentioned that difficulty to Lord Ashley, who assured him that no grant would be made to any school where the Holy Scriptures were not regularly read, which would be likely to exclude the Romanists. This was the most serious difficulty of all in the view of Dr Osborn, who, I have reason to believe, mainly on that ground, felt repugnance to association with a State National System.

The practical result of that Committee was that Mr. Scott and a few other ministers were entrusted with the difficult work of drawing up a resolution which should give a guarded and conditional consent to co-operate with the Government, a resolution to be suggested by Mr. Scott for acceptance by a large representative Committee, which was to meet at the next Conference (1847). That Resolution is to be found in the 'Minutes of Conference' for 1847, and shows traces of the perplexity which had puzzled the select Committee six months before. The Resolution speaks of the circumstances of great practical difficulty in which the question of General Education was placed, and approves of the very negative recommendation to the Wesleyan Societies and Congregations 'not to offer any further Connexional opposition to the scheme embodied in the Minutes [of Council] after the authorised explanations which had been given by the Committee of Conference on several important points deeply affecting the interests of Scriptural and Protestant Religion throughout the country.' Thus carefully, after jealous study and scrutiny of the whole matter, did the Conference give permission to Mr. Scott and the Education Committee to consent to work with the Government, and to go forward with their already agreed upon proposals to erect seven hundred Day Schools and a Connexional Training College, by means of which permission a status and recognised influence has been secured for our Church as a national force in Christian Education, and hundreds of Christian teachers with tens of thousands of Evangelically-trained scholars have become a power and glory in this country. Other Methodist Churches have followed in our steps. But it is no wonder that there have always been difficulties and perplexities felt in dealing with this profound and far-reaching national problem.

[1] The Mission House in Bishopsgate. Lord Ashley: Anthony Ashley Cooper, who became the seventh Earl of Shaftesbury in 1851.

Everett v. Wesleyan Authorities

(Mss at Garrett-Evangelical Seminary)

Robert Newton to James Everett; Edinburgh, Nov. 9, 1848

Dear Bro^r,

I am directed by Tho. P. Bunting Esq.[1] to summon you to attend a Minor District Meeting as a witness, regarding a charge preferred by Mr. Bunting against the Rev. D. Walton[2] on the subject of the Fly Sheets. The meeting will be in the Stewards Room, Oldham Street, Manchester on the 13th inst at 10 o'clock in the morning.

I am
Yours truly
R^t Newton

[1] Thomas Percival Bunting, a son of Jabez Bunting. His older brother, the Rev. William Maclardie Bunting, deplored the charges and the way in which they were brought. (*Sidelights*, p. 449).

[2] Daniel Walton had been in the ministry since 1814. He remained silent in the face of questioning at the 1849 Conference about his complicity in the *Fly Sheets* and received an official rebuke.

James Everett to Robert Newton; York, Nov. 10, 1848

To the Rev. Robert Newton D.D., President of the Wesleyan Conference:

Rev. and Honoured Sir,

As a Wesleyan Minister, I consider myself bound by the laws of the Wesleyan Body, and am disposed to obey them. You profess, in your 'summons', to be 'directed by Thos. P. Bunting Esqr', but as I am not bound to be guided in my decisions and movements by the said Mr. Bunting, or any other, you will oblige me, honoured sir, by stating the *law* of the case; by what law a man like Mr. Bunting is authorized to subpoena a brother, and oblige him to bear witness against a late colleague, both against his will and against his most cherished sentiments of high honour and generosity? I offer no factious opposition; I am afraid of the precedent, and wish to be informed. I am ignorant of any law of the kind; and my ignorance must be my apology. It is not the *will* of Mr. T. P. Bunting, but the *Law* of Methodism that must guide me.

In the next place, honoured sir, as your notice is based upon the request of Mr. T. P. Bunting, and he, in his letter to me of the 7th instant, states it to be 'in consequence of a communication received from York the same morning', I wish to know, through you, sir, as the only official organ in the case,

1. What the nature of the 'communication' is, said to be 'received from York'; and whether sufficient to warrant in this special case such a 'summons' from Mr. T. P. Bunting?

2. Who the party is that makes the 'communication'; and whether of sufficient integrity and respectability to be attended to? I may know the party better than Mr. Bunting.

3. Whether the party or parties in York, at whose instigation I am to be sent across the country between one and two hundred miles, will be in Manchester themselves?

Pardon, honoured sir, another trespass on your valuable time. I am summoned as a 'witness'. If I am called to '*witness*' to the *character* of Mr. Walton, all I have to say, and all I shall say, is – I know nothing of him but what is good and praiseworthy. Further I shall not proceed. If I am called to 'witness' to the *authorship* of the 'Fly-Sheets', I have no answer to give, pro or con. My reasons for this are the following:

1. I object to answer any question as to authorship till a searching enquiry is made into the truth or falsehood of the allegations made in the 'Fly-Sheets', this appearing to me, and for the peace and interests of the body, of greater importance than the enquiry now set on foot, which can only affect the individual. I commit myself neither to their truth nor falsehood.

2. I object to the manner in which the present enquiry was begun; being in my humble view unbrotherly, uncourteous, and unscriptural, Matt. xviii. 15–17; and will not, therefore, so far as law will lend me aid, assist and abet it in its progress.

3. I objected, in companionship with 256 other christian ministers, to sign the 'Declaration', of which the present enquiry, in my judgment, is part and parcel; both that and the commencement of this present enquiry being placed in the un-English form of leading a man to criminate himself.

With all respect, honoured sir, both for yourself and your high office, I am

Your's
Most truly
James Everett

The 1849 Expulsions

Thomas Jackson's account

(*Recollections of my own Life and Times*, 1873, pp. 335–8, 342)

Jackson was President in 1849 and therefore played a prominent part in the Conference which expelled those suspected of publishing the Fly Sheets.

The Conference resolved at length to deal with this enormous evil, which, being left unchecked, gathered strength from year to year; and one of its members, the Rev. Dr. Hannah, in the presence of about five hundred Ministers, in a spirit of deep seriousness, and in the fear of God, asked the man whom every one suspected, whether or not he was concerned in the publication of the pamphlets which were known by the name of the 'Fly Sheets'. 'Why is that question proposed to me,' said he, 'rather than to other brethren?' 'Because universal suspicion falls upon you,' was the answer given; which was assented to by nearly five hundred Ministers then present, whose eyes were fixed upon him, and who as with one voice responded, 'Hear, hear.' He at once shrunk from the sound of those voices, and the earnest looks by which they were accompanied, and said, 'That question I will not answer. I will submit to expulsion rather than answer it.' He was expostulated with, and time was given him for reflection; but he was inflexible. It was then felt that the man who would not purge himself from the attempt to destroy the reputation and ministerial usefulness of his brethren, by the pertinacious and deliberate propagation of anonymous slander, ought no longer to receive the sanction of the Methodist Conference as a co-Pastor and a Minister of Christ. If other parties chose to receive him in these characters, be it so; to their own Master they must stand or fall; but the body of Methodist Preachers refused to partake of the sin by conniving at it.

Two other men, against whom direct and formal charges were preferred for commencing a periodical publication, which was declared to promote actual strife and contention in the Societies, and which they positively refused to discontinue, were severed from the Body at the same time . . .

These acts of discipline it was my painful duty to perform, as the organ of the Conference; but acts of *duty* I then felt them to be, and as such I still regard them. They were not acts of personal hostility to the offenders, whom I was sincerely grieved to see in such a position; and some of whom I had formerly regarded as my friends; but such was their spirit at the time, that their further connexion with the Conference was impossible. . . .

The three men who were at this time severed from their connexion with the Conference entered immediately upon a course of public agitation, which they carried on from one end of the kingdom to the other, through a series of years, using every means in their power to injure the funds of the Connexion, especially that of the Missions to the Heathen; to bring the Conference and the Wesleyan Ministers in general into disrepute; and to divide and scatter the Societies.

Some of the most popular topics upon which the itinerant agitators dwelt in the public meetings which they convened were these: That they had been expelled without a trial; that the discipline of Methodism is an interference with the liberty of free-born Englishmen; and that no man is bound to criminate himself. These announcements, of course, were eagerly received by mixed assemblies, convened by public advertisement, containing frequenters of public-houses, and many others, who hate all restraint, and are glad to hear that, as 'freeborn Englishmen', they may live as they list, in defiance of all ecclesiastical regulations. The editors of 'liberal' newspapers endorsed these statements as exactly adapted to the popular taste, and condemned the Methodist Conference as an arbitrary and intolerant Body. The *Times* led the way on this occasion, and pronounced me a 'fanatic', for speaking of spiritual religion as the work of God.

From *The Times*, September 3, 1849

It is very rarely that we are called on to remark on the ecclesiastical proceedings of the numerous dissenting communities which divide with the Church the vagrant affections of this isle. Their foundation and government is on the voluntary principle; and they are generally administered with sufficient regard to those notions of liberty and fair play which guide the public opinion of this country. *Volenti non fit injuria*,[1] and it would be a very idle piece of knight-errantry to protect an injured Wesleyan or Independent who has of course in his own hands the most effectual remedy. If we are led to depart from the rule of non-interference, it is because we find a very large and respectable body of Englishmen committing an apparent violation of English usage and principle. Speaking only from our first impressions, after a perusal of the statements published by the aggrieved parties on the one hand, and the Wesleyan Conference on the other, we must say that the latter has just taken a step which smacks more of the Inquisition than of a British tribunal. So far, of course, the character of England is concerned; and, as guardians of that character, we are justified in expressing at least our surprise, and asking for further explanation.

The Wesleyan Connexion, as everybody knows, is governed by a 'Conference' of Ministers, and in that Conference certain divines of remarkable talents, high character, of long standing, enjoy the prominence they deserve . . . But this spiritual senate and its leaders have not escaped the invariable consequences of power. They have been charged with the vices of Prime Ministers, Bishops, and Kings. For three or four years certain anonymous papers have appeared under the name of *Fly Sheets*, reflecting on their proceedings. As we have not seen these papers, and have indeed no wish to see them, we will take the word of the Conference itself for the tone of their contents: 'These papers,' it says in a published manifesto, 'were characterized by intense bitterness of feeling in reference to certain excellent Ministers, whom they described as 'indolent', 'selfish', 'artful', 'ambitious', and 'tyrannical'; and also by other personalities, so grossly offensive and libellous, that the parties issuing them did not dare to affix the name of either printer or publisher. Not content with endeavouring to damage the character of individuals who had hitherto been regarded with the highest esteem, the writers attacked the administration of the affairs of the Connexion in general. They declared that its resources were perverted to uphold a system of favouritism, oppression, and extravagance; that many public acts of the Conference proceeded from corrupt motives or were of a mischievous tendency; and, while suggesting extensive changes in its system of proceeding, and representing the members of the Conference as enslaved, and longing for emancipation, they exhorted them to vigorous and united efforts to shake off the unhallowed yoke. The certain and obvious tendency – not to say the avowed design – of these publications was to destroy the mutual confidence upon which our connexion is based, and to subvert, or at least greatly impede, the operation of our several institutions.' All this of course is very shocking, and we can easily imagine that it would sound rank blasphemy in the ears of the excellent gentlemen assailed by these coarse insinuations and vulgar invectives. To us, however, who are no such tender exotics and do not live in a hothouse, strictures of this sort are matters of course. We are accustomed to see everybody treated in this manner, from the Premier to a station-clerk, from a Bishop to a curate, from an Archdeacon to a sexton. The conduct and motives here referred to are continually ascribed to public men by antagonist journals. Periodicals professing a religious character are daily, weekly, monthly or quarterly charging bishops and clergy with rapacity, dishonesty, Jesuitism, and a systematic design to revolutionize the Church in one direction or another. The *Fly Sheets*, therefore, have not that unusual and prodigious character in our eyes which they evidently have in the eyes of the Conference, and we cannot see why they should not have been treated as such attacks usually are.

But how were they treated? In the first place with a gravity at which we must beg to express our amusement and surprise. It is confessed, with singular imprudence, that they could not be left alone to work their own cure. One of the authors being discovered, and having made his submission, was sentenced to a solemn admonition from the chair, and disqualified from the superintendence of a circuit. As the nuisance went on, the President made a solemn appeal to the sympathy, not to say the fanaticism, of the Conference. 'He must advert to one painful particular. He had mourned over the attempts which had been made to innovate upon their system. A *secret irresponsible power* had risen up which interfered with the just rights of the Conference – *which reflected on its acts and appointments* – and which endeavoured, in various instances, to render these acts and appointments nul and void.' 'He mourned over this state of things, because it interfered with the blessed work of God.' – 'The Conference, the highest authority in this community, was bearded by this secret and irresponsible power. He had a full conviction that the time was come when this evil should be dealt with and effectually corrected, and, by the grace of God, done away with, he trusted, for ever. He believed they were all inclined to unite in the prayer suggested by a line in one of their hymns, –

End, Jesus, end this war within.

This war among themselves must be terminated. It was a stumbling block to their people, and the occasion of scandal to other Christian communities.'

The tone of this appeal sufficiently prepares one for the subsequent proceedings of the Conference. The Rev. J. Everett and the Rev. J. Burdsall were suspected of a hand in these obnoxious *Fly Sheets*. So on the strength of various declaratory resolutions, and particularly of a vague expression in an early minute of Conference enjoining the personal examination of candidates suspected of having forfeited their calling, the Conference deemed it to be its solemn duty to God and to itself, to put a *brotherly question* to these two gentlemen touching their concern in the *Fly Sheets*, which question they both declined to answer. On their obstinate silence Mr. Everett was expelled and put out from being a member of the Conference, or being in connexion therewith. Mr. Burdsall, being an old man, was affectionately admonished. Mr. John C. George, having also declined to criminate himself, was reproved and 'disqualified'. The Rev. Messrs. Samuel Dunn and William Griffith, Jun., being openly compromised in the *Wesleyan Times* and the *Wesley Banner*, and being also suspected of a hand in the *Fly Sheets*, but refusing to answer thereupon, shared Mr. Everett's fate, and were expelled the Connexion; and so with an affectionate and grateful recognition of the exemplary Christian temper uniformly displayed by the President, the Rev. Thomas Jackson, amidst the labours and trying circumstances of the sitting, and with a special prayer for his health and peace, the Conference terminated its proceedings.

Whether such a course be right or wrong, it is at best perfectly unique in this country. No other British tribunal possesses or claims the authority to put 'a brotherly question' to a suspected person, and require 'a frank and brotherly answer'. The rule of all our Courts, both ecclesiastical and civil, is charity, which 'hopeth all things', and which assumes everybody to be innocent till he is proved to be guilty. These gentlemen are punished on mere suspicion, and for refusing to criminate themselves. We never heard the like in this country, at least in modern and peaceable times. Talk of the Star Chamber! A man might hold his tongue before that Court, stand his trial, and escape if the evidence failed to support the charge. Of the parties themselves, of the *Fly Sheets*, or the usual practice of the Conference, we know next to nothing. We take these proceedings on the statement of the Conference, and we pronounce them at once a gross outrage on our old English principles of fair play.

[1] 'The man who has chosen for himself cannot complain of injury.'

The response of a reader

(*The Times*, September 14, 1849)

To the Editor of *The Times*.

Sir, The Wesleyan Conference, in certain recent decisions, declared its determination not to tolerate among its members the practice of anonymous slander. On this principle, one of its ministers (lying under strong suspicions, on his peremptory and repeated refusal to answer a query respecting the authorship of a series of gross libels attacking the personal and official character of some of his brethren) was declared unworthy of ministerial recognition.

The Times, in an article published on the 3rd of September, describes these proceedings as surpassing in tyranny the doings of Star-chambers or Inquisitions. Without imputing to the writer of this article any wilful perversion of facts, it may be easily proved – first, that the case is misstated as to its chief feature, an aggravated instance of defamation being represented as nothing more than a party struggle, in which the weapons customary in such contests had been, perhaps, somewhat too licentiously employed; and, secondly, that one at least of the principles which should have guided the verdict has been overlooked.

The primary considerations by which the disciplinary acts of Christian churches must be tested are religious; and for this discussion newspapers may not be the most appropriate vehicle.

Analogous cases, however, falling legitimately within the province of public journalists, may exist. To one somewhat analogous to that on which we presume to think an over-hasty and not very impartial judgment has been pronounced, we respectfully call the notice of the editors, and follow it by one question. It is, we believe, usual among military officers, as well as in other associations bound by the ties of honour, when a secret libel affecting the general character is propagated, to require each individual to disown participation in the offence. Our question is – how would he be treated who should refuse submission to this usage of honourable society, and would *The Times* characterize its enforcement in the terms applied to the acts of the Wesleyan Conference?

Hackney, Sept. 13, 1849.

*** If the Wesleyan Conference professes to govern the many hundred thousand members of Connexion with no other securities of justice than are necessary among a dozen officers meeting daily at one dinner table, it will expedite the present controversy if the Conference will say so at once. We have ascribed to it pretensions of a more public character. As a fact, however, there are numerous cases in which the officers of a mess have unanimously refused to answer just such a question as that put to the expelled Wesleyan ministers.

Chapel Architecture

(F. J. Jobson, *Chapel & School Architecture as appropriate to the buildings of nonconformists, particularly to those of the Wesleyan Methodists*, 1850, pp. 40–45, 49, 55–6, 58–61)

Jobson had served an apprenticeship in architecture. His book had a widespread influence on the style of chapel building in the second half of the century.

Some pious and well meaning Christians are fearful of the application of Art, in any form, to the service of the Almighty. I honour the feeling; and should regret deeply to see carelessness arise as to the outward representations of Christianity. In these times of Tractarian heresy, caution is especially needed. But safety is in Truth, and not in extremes. I hope and pray that the day will never come when painted scenes and sculptured figures shall be introduced into Methodist chapels; and I am of opinion that, already, there is too much 'music', as it is called, in some places of worship. But shall not Art be eventually employed in the service of Christ; or shall it always be an instrument for the unbelieving and sinful world? . . .

And, already, the organ-loft has re-appeared, even in Nonconforming chapels. That grand and solemn instrument has banished therefrom the reedy, squeaking pipes and string-breaking fiddles, which too often broke the harmony of religious worship; and it begins to be admitted that Christians ought to have their hymning melody as harmoniously attuned in the House of God, as when they gather in choral groups for social enjoyment, in their own homes . . .

And so with Gothic Architecture: it shall, with all its surpassing flexibility and unbounded power of adaptation, be again used in the service of God. It is now reviving; and is, more or less, employed by every Christian denomination. The general feeling is already in its favour, as the outward representation of Christian worship in this country . . .

Let us not dishonour the religion we profess, by imitating Pagan temples in the erection of buildings where 'the blood of bulls and goats' is not to be shed, – but where is to be worshipped, in faith and love, the Divine Saviour of Mankind.

The propriety of employing Gothic Architecture on houses for Christian worship might be argued on other grounds – such as the confusion of apprehension or knowledge occasioned by our use of Pagan Architecture. Who has not felt the uncertainty of apprehension, and the incongruity of ideas, arising from the sight of a Chapel in Roman or Grecian Architecture when he entered a city or town for the first time? On looking upon the building (unless an inscription-board was on it) he could not tell whether it was a Concert-room, a Theatre, a Town-hall, or a Chapel. But who, on seeing a Gothic chapel, has had any difficulty in determining its appointed purpose? Its ecclesiastical form made known its use, at first sight, and without any possibility of mistake. What can more fully manifest the fitness and propriety of erecting buildings for Christian worship in the Gothic style of architecture? . . .

I could refer to large Chapels in commercial and manufacturing towns which are more like warehouses or factories than Houses of God; and where, if in any case, a tall chimney were added on one side, the building would immediately appear ready for use as a cotton-mill or a wool-factory. And others might be named that look much more like concert-rooms or theatres, than erections for Christian worship; – others, with made-up shop-like fronts, having sham windows, readily seen to be such, – by their situation, – being placed higher than the roof; and the whole, perhaps, propped up behind by an iron bar; while the sides are as plain and barn-like as could well be conceived, and disfigured by a clumsy heap of chimneys . . .

The Scriptures do not condemn 'the *form* of godliness'. They sanction and enjoin it by plain and positive commands. It is the form *without the power* they condemn; and Methodism is not likely to be less spiritual in its inward life, nor less influential on the world, by having, in its outward representations, *appropriate* and *economical* forms. Will it be said that Methodism will be less alive and powerful in its services within the Gothic Chapels than it was in the old, irregular, and suffocating buildings they have superseded? – or, than it would be, if, in architectural style, it was more nearly associated with Concert-halls and Theatres? There is Truth in all things that are good; and force it down for a time as men may, and hold it under water by prejudice, as long as they can, yet, eventually, it will rise and be uppermost. Things will have their right place in the world, however disordered for a time; and so will Gothic Architecture . . .

Wesleyan Methodism has particular wants to be provided for in the arrangements of its public buildings. It is not the ordinary oblong Chapel, however correct in its proportions, and consistent in its architecture, that will supply all it requires. It has its social means of grace; its religious education of the young; and its benevolent institutions for the relief of the sick and the poor, which must be considered, as well as the exercises of public worship, if the Chapel premises shall provide what is requisite to the efficient working of the Wesleyan system of Christian means and agencies. This has been increasingly felt in late years; and it being evident that some general principles of Chapel-Building were required by the Connexion, the subject was introduced to the Bristol Conference of 1846, by James Heald, Esq.; and, on his proposal, a Committee was appointed to consider the requirements of Methodism, in its Chapel-Building department . . . The members of it met frequently, and carefully considered, in the first place, what were *the wants of Methodism in the arrangements of their buildings, for social and public worship*; and, as their Secretary, I may here avail myself of the advantage I possess, in this respect, and give the results of their deliberations, while, at the same time, I hold myself alone responsible for the reasons and terms by which I shall in these pages endeavour to support those results.

1. It appeared to the Committee that, in preparing to erect Wesleyan chapels, sufficient consideration had not generally, been given to the want of *Class-Rooms* and *Vestries*. These are indispensable to the working of Methodism, in the present day. Formerly, they were less needed than they are now. In the past time, classes were scattered, as to their places of weekly meeting, throughout a city or town; but, of late years, there has been a growing feeling towards meeting for weekly fellowship on the chapel premises. Though this feeling should not be hastily encouraged, (for there are very great advantages resulting to Methodism in the meeting of members in different localities) yet, the wants and desires of a religious people must be reasonably met; and class-rooms on chapel premises must, in the present day, to a much greater extent than formerly, be provided. In addition to these, it is also requisite that, in connection with a chapel of considerable dimensions, at least one larger room for *prayer-meetings* and *social gatherings* should be supplied. The increased agencies of Methodism require this. Of course, additional buildings will require additional expense; and it is important that ministers and trustees, in their first meetings for the erection of a new

chapel, should consider that, as Methodists, they have not only to build a chapel, but also vestries, class-rooms, and a larger room for prayer-meetings, annual or other tea-meetings, &c.

2. Another consideration which engaged the attention of the Committee, was *the arrangement of the buildings in such a manner as most easily to admit of enlargement when required*. The enlargement of our Chapels has, of late years, been so frequent, that, to prepare for it in the original plan of a chapel, so that, when necessary, it may be executed in the readiest and least expensive mode, becomes a measure of common prudence. And the Committee found, by applications to practical men, that it would be easy, generally, to provide for enlargement, by including the class-rooms, and the larger room over or below them, under the roof at the farther end of the chapel . . .

3. Another and a very important object to be secured in Methodist chapels, and which was carefully and anxiously considered by the Committee, was *the furnishing of seat-room for the children of Sabbath and Week-day Schools*. This was not required in the earlier days of Methodism, but it must be amply supplied now, if Wesleyans are to maintain their consistency, and keep their position among the Christian churches of the land. The Methodist education of the young is avowedly *religious*; therefore, all the children under training in Methodist schools ought to be habituated to regular attendance on Public worship. In former years, Sabbath-school instruction was chiefly secular; but the time has happily come, when children may easily learn to read and write on the week-days. The Sabbath-school is now made, more consistently than it used to be when otherwise employed, the means of dealing with the consciences and hearts of children, rather than with their intellects: it is now, confessedly, the training-place for eternity, rather than for time. This fact renders it imperatively necessary that increased attention should be paid to the children of our Sabbath-schools, with regard to providing places for their attendance in the House of God.

The time has also come when Sabbath and Week-day schools must be more closely allied with the churches, and more manifestly under the care of Ministers. They must be regarded, more than they have been, as an important part of our church system.

3. From 1851 to 1932

The Census of Religious Worship, 1851

Summary Tables of estimated accommodation and attendance by denomination

(*Report*, pp. clxxxi and clxxxii)

For these tables see pp. 498–9, 500–01

Extracts from the Census Returns on Religious Worship, 1851

(Appendix to Charles Prest, *Fourteen Letters on the Home-Work of Wesleyan Methodism, its sustentation and extension . . . addressed to the editors of the 'Watchman' newspaper*, 1856)

I. The following Table shows the rate of advancement, since 1770, in Great Britain:—

Dates	Number of Ministers	Number of members or communicants*	Dates	Number of Ministers	Number of members or communicants*
1770	119	26,283	1820	718	191,217
1780	170	37,721	1830	824	248,592
1790	278	58,673	1840	1,167	323,178
1800	442	90,619	1850	1,034	358,277
1810	672	137,997			

* It is estimated that the number of persons attending upon the ministrations of the Wesleyan Societies is about three times the number of communicants. (P. lxxviii.)

II. The Census accounts show 6,579 chapels in England and Wales, belonging to this Connexion in March, 1851; containing (allowance being made for defective returns) accommodation for 1,447,580 persons. The number of attendants on the Census Sunday was – morning, 492,714; afternoon, 383,964; evening, 667,850; including an estimate for 133 chapels for which the number of attendants was not stated. (P. lxxviii.)

III. The following Table [on p. 502] shows the principal Societies and Institutions for religious objects supported by the original Wesleyan Connexion:—

Supplement I. to Table A

Showing the total Accommodation provided by each Religious Body;
including Estimates for defective Returns

Religious Denomination	Number of Places of Worship		
	Returns complete as to Sittings	Returns defective as to Sittings	Total
TOTAL	31.943	2524	34,467
PROTESTANT CHURCHES			
BRITISH:			
Church of England	13,051	1026	14,077
Scottish Presbyterians:			
Church of Scotland	17	1	18
United Presbyterian Church	64	2	66
Presbyterian Church in England	74	2	76
Reformed Irish Presbyterians	1	..	1
Indepedents, or Congregationalists	3,058	186	3,244
Baptists:			
General	82	9	93
Particular	1,847	100	1,947
Seventh-Day	2	..	2
Scotch	12	3	15
New Connexion, General	177	5	182
Undefined	486	64	550
Society of Friends	362	9	371
Unitarians	212	17	229
Moravians	30	2	32
Wesleyan Methodists:			
Original Connexion	6,193	386	6,579
New Connexion	281	16	297
Primitive Methodists	2,562	309	2,871
Bible Christians	440	42	482
Wesleyan Methodist Association	385	34	419
Independent Methodists	18	2	20
Wesleyan Reformers	288	51	339
Calvinistic Methodists:			
Welsh Calvinistic Methodists	775	53	828
Lady Huntingdon's Connexion	104	5	109
Sandemanians	4	2	6
New Church	49	1	50
Brethren	112	20	132
Isolated Congregations	468	71	539
FOREIGN:			
Lutherans	5	1	6
French Protestants	3	..	3
Reformed Church of the Netherlands	1	..	1
German Protestant Reformers	1	..	1
OTHER CHRISTIAN CHURCHES:			
Roman Catholics	522	48	570
Greek Church	3	..	3
German Catholics	1	..	1
Italian Reformers	1	..	1
Catholic and Apostolic Church	31	1	32
Latter Day Saints	169	53	222
Jews	50	3	53

| Number of Sittings | | | Average number of Sittings to one Place of Worship |
In the complete Returns	Estimate for the defective Returns	Total	
9,467,738	744,825	10,212,563	296
4,922,412	395,503	5,317,915	377
12,914	875	13,789	760
30,401	950	31,351	475
40,458	1,094	41,552	547
120	..	120	120
1,002,507	65,253	1,067,760	328
18,532	2,007	20,539	223
550,775	32,178	582,953	299
390	..	390	195
2,037	510	2,547	170
51,159	1,445	52,604	289
82,770	10,540	93,310	170
89,551	2,048	91,599	247
63,770	4,784	68,554	299
8,723	582	9,305	291
1,361,443	86,137	1,447,580	220
91,716	5,248	96,964	328
369,216	44,814	414,030	144
60,341	6,493	66,834	137
90,789	8,024	98,813	236
2,144	119	2,263	119
57,126	10,688	67,814	199
198,242	13,709	211,951	256
35,210	3,517	38,727	339
638	318	956	159
11,865	242	12,107	242
15,869	2,660	18,529	140
90,048	14,433	104,481	192
2,172	434	2,606	434
560	..	560	187
350	..	350	350
200	..	200	200
164,664	21,447	186,111	314
291	..	291	97
300	..	300	300
150	..	150	150
6,973	464	7,437	232
22,951	7,832	30,783	135
7,961	477	8,438	159

Supplement II. to Table A

Showing the total number of Attendants at Public Worship;
in connection with each Religious Body; including
Estimates for defective Returns

Religious Denomination	Number of Places of Worship		
	Returns complete as to Attendance	Returns defective as to Attendance	Total
TOTAL	33,073	1,394	34,467
PROTESTANT CHURCHES			
BRITISH			
Church of England	13,138	939	14,077
Scottish Presbyterians:			
Church of Scotland	18	..	18
United Presbyterian Church	64	2	66
Presbyterian Church in England	75	1	76
Reformed Irish Presbyterians	..	1	1
Independents	3,185	59	3,244
Baptists			
General	90	3	93
Particular	1,909	38	1,947
Seventh Day	2	..	2
Scotch	15	..	15
New Connexion, General	180	2	182
Undefined	526	24	550
Society of Friends	362	9	371
Unitarians	222	7	229
Moravians	30	2	32
Wesleyan Methodists:			
Original Connexion	6,446	133	6,579
New Connexion	294	3	297
Primitive Methodists	2,810	61	2,871
Bible Christians	474	8	482
W.M. Association	414	5	419
Independent Methodists	19	1	20
Wesleyan Reformers	334	5	339
Calvinistic Methodists:			
Welsh Calvinistic Methodists	828	..	828
Lady Huntingdon's Connexion	102	7	109
Sandemanians	6	..	6
New Church	48	2	50
Brethren	130	2	132
Isolated Congregations	506	33	539
FOREIGN:			
Lutherans	5	1	6
French Protestants	2	1	3
Reformed Church of the Netherlands	1	..	1
German Protestant Reformers	1	..	1
OTHER CHRISTIAN CHURCHES			
Roman Catholics	543	27	570
Greek Church	3	..	3
German Catholics	1	..	1
Italian Reformers	1	..	1
Catholic and Apostolic Church	30	2	32
Latter Day Saints	213	9	222
Jews	46	7	53

Number of Attendants						Total Number of Attend-ances
In the Places of Worship sending complete Returns			In the total Number of Places of Worship (including an Estimate for the Places which sent defective Returns)			
Morning	Afternoon	Evening	Morning	Afternoon	Evening	
4,428,338	3,030,280	2,960,772	4,647,482	3,184,135	3,064,449	10,896,066
2,371,732	1,764,641	803,141	2,541,244	1,890,764	860,543	5,292,551
6,949	960	3,849	6,949	960	3,849	11,758
17,188	4,931	8,551	17,725	5,085	8,818	31,628
22,607	3,345	10,684	22,908	3,390	10,826	37,124
..	..	..	..	..	..	..
515,071	228,060	448,847	524,612	232,285	457,162	1,214,059
5,228	7,865	8,283	5,404	8,130	8,562	22,096
286,944	172,145	267,205	292,656	175,572	272,524	740,752
27	43	16	27	40	16	83
649	986	312	649	986	312	1,947
23,688	15,545	24,381	23,951	15,718	24,652	64,321
36,525	22,826	37,417	38,119	23,822	39,050	100,991
14,016	6,458	1,459	14,364	6,619	1,495	22,478
27,612	8,610	12,406	28,483	8,881	12,697	50,061
4,681	2,312	3,202	4,993	2,466	3,415	10,874
482,753	376,202	654,349	492,714	383,964	667,850	1,544,528
36,428	22,391	39,222	36,801	22,620	39,624	99,045
98,001	172,684	229,646	100,125	176,435	234,635	511,195
14,655	24,002	34,038	14,902	24,345	34,612	73,859
31,922	20,888	40,170	32,308	21,140	40,655	94,103
571	1,245	1,148	601	1,311	1,208	3,120
30,018	1,5841	44,286	30,470	16,080	44,953	91,503
79,728	59,140	125,244	79,728	59,140	125,244	264,112
19,966	4,099	17,929	21,103	4,380	19,159	44,642
439	256	61	439	256	61	756
4,652	2,308	2,978	4,846	2,404	3,102	10,352
5,613	4,441	7,272	5,699	4,509	7,384	17,592
34,706	22,726	40,835	36,969	24,208	43,498	104,675
960	220	..	1,152	264	..	1,416
150	21	100	225	32	150	407
70	..	..	70	..	..	70
120	..	60	120	..	60	180
240,792	51,406	73,232	252,783	53,967	76,880	383,630
240	..	..	240	..	..	240
500	..	200	500	..	200	700
..	20	..	..	20	..	20
3,077	1,607	2,622	3,176	1,659	2,707	7,542
7,212	11,016	15,954	7,517	11,481	16,628	35,626
2,848	1,043	1,673	2,910	1,202	1,918	6,030

Name of Society or Institution	Date of formation A.D.	Annual Income £
Contingent Fund	1756	10,065
Auxiliary Fund	1813	7,163
The Children's Fund	1818	3,280
Wesleyan Theological Institution	1834	4,688
General Chapel Fund	1818	3,984
Wesleyan Seamen's Mission	1843	100
Wesleyan Missionary Society	1817	105,370
Kingswood and Woodhouse-Grove Schools	{ 1748 1811 }	8,048
Education Fund	1837	2,800

(P. lxxviii.)

IV. The Wesleyan Methodists in 6,579 places of worship provide 1,447,580 sittings, being in the proportion of 8.1 per cent. to the whole population, and of 14.1 per cent. to total number of sittings provided by all Bodies. (P. cxxxvii.)

V. The number of places mentioned in the returns as 'not separate buildings' used by the Wesleyan Methodists (all the different bodies of Arminian Methodists are included) is 2,155. For the number belonging to the Original Connexion, see No. XI [below].

VI. The Wesleyan Methodists are found in greatest force in Cornwall, Yorkshire, Lincolnshire, Derbyshire, Durham, and Nottinghamshire; their fewest numbers are in Middlesex, Surrey, Sussex, Essex, Warwickshire, and Hertfordshire. (P. cxliv.)

VII. Rate of increase of the Wesleyan Methodists, in decennial periods, in the whole of England and Wales. (All branches.)

Date	Places of worship	Sittings	Rate of increase per cent. at each period
1801	825	165,000	
1811	1,485	296,000	80.0
1821	2,748	549,600	85.0
1831	4,622	924,400	68.2
1841	7,819	1,563,800	69.2
1851	11,007	2,194,298	40.3

It appears that neither the Wesleyans, the Independents, nor the Baptists are advancing at a rate so rapid as formerly. But then it must be remembered that neither is there *room* for such a rapid increase, since the aggregate rate of increase during the half century has been so much more rapid than the increase of the population, that whereas, in 1801, the number of sittings provided for every 1,000 persons was – by Wesleyans, 18, by Independents 34, and by Baptists 20; in 1851 the provision was – by Wesleyans 123, by Independents 59, and by Baptists 42. (P. cxliv.)

VIII. Out of a total number of 11,007 places of worship belonging to the various sections of Wesleyan Methodists, 4,990 were open for morning worship, 6,796 in the afternoon, and 8,930 in the evening. (P.cxlv.)

IX. The number of free-sittings provided by Wesleyan Methodists (all branches) is 1,066,312, out of a total of 2,194,298, or 48.6 per cent. The Independents provide 41.0, and the Baptists 50.2, per cent. (P. cxlvi.)

X. Estimated total number of attendants at places of worship belonging to the Wesleyan Methodists, original Connexion, 907,313, being 51 per 1,000 of the population, and 125 per 1,000 of the number of attendants of all Denominations.

The proportion per cent. of attendants to sittings in Wesleyan Chapels on the Census Sunday was 35; Independents, 38; Particular Baptists, 42; Church of England, 33; Society of Friends, 8. (P. clvi.: see also table M.)

XI. The original Connexion, March, 1851, had places of worship, –

Separate buildings	5,625	No. of sittings.	
Not separate buildings	954	Free	626,434
		Appropriated	729,928
Total	6,579	Not distinguished	5,081
			1,361,443*

Number of attendants on public worship in these places on Sunday, March 30, 1851, –

Morning	482,753
Afternoon	376,202
Evening	654,349

Number of these places of worship open for worship at each period of the day, on Sunday, March 30th, 1851, and number of sittings thus available, –

Places open		Number of sittings
Morning	3,124	923,615
Afternoon	3,881	758,315
Evening	5,288	1,211,884

Dates at which the buildings were erected or appropriated to religious purposes, –

Before 1801	644	1831 to 1841	1,411
1801 to 1811	523	1841 to 1851	1,247
1811 to 1821	927	Not stated	752
1821 to 1831	1,075		
		Total	6,579

The average number of sittings to each place of worship is said to be 220. (Pp. clxxviii., clxxxi.)

* Another table, p. clxxxii, including estimates for defective returns, gives the number 1,544,528.

XII. Number of Ministers, Places of Worship, Sittings, and Attendants (Wesleyan Methodists, original Connexion) in Counties:—

| Names of Counties | Population | Ministers | Number of Places of Worship, and Sittings | | Number of Attendants at Public Worship on Sunday, March 30th, 1851 | | | Number of Places open for Worship at each period of the Day, on Sunday, March 30th, 1851; and Number of Sittings then available | | | | | |
| | | | | | | | | Places of Worship open | | | Sittings | | |
			Places of Worship	Sittings	Morning	Afternoon	Evening	Morning	Afternoon	Evening	Morning	Afternoon	Evening
Bedford	124,478	12	78	16,736	6,807	11,017	12,839	29	66	76	9,514	14,951	16,566
Berks	170,065	13	72	10,084	3,523	2,113	4,902	28	34	58	5,814	4,050	
Buckingham	163,723	6	81	13,023	3,827	7,293	7,964	35	70	75	6,287	11,467	12,070
Cambridge	185,405	10	57	11,764	5,498	7,908	7,782	38	53	50	9,235	11,458	10,976
Chester	455,725	24	188	37,877	13,791	11,695	17,133	76	128	136	23,511	22,949	30,485
Cornwall	355,558	46	412	95,061	30,795	14,969	54,209	194	180	300	64,776	29,034	81,646
Cumberland	195,492	14	96	14,774	3,579	2,487	5,131	42	46	62	10,514	5,321	13,567
Derby	296,084	20	222	39,734	8,466	12,994	14,769	57	145	173	17,329	22,422	32,564
Devon	567,098	32	219	39,839	16,829	11,527	22,884	122	141	184	30,087	27,782	36,464
Dorset	184,207	15	101	14,148	5,748	4,200	9,192	49	53	85	9,714	7,222	13,062
Durham	390,997	28	192	43,079	9,922	8,435	18,187	66	99	169	24,404	18,221	39,366
Essex	369,318	9	63	11,375	5,973	6,069	5,396	47	47	49	9,844	8,333	9,476
Gloucester	458,805	22	144	30,930	8,248	5,525	11,645	73	70	114	21,370	15,465	28,468
Hereford	115,489	6	44	4,502	1,536	765	1,844	23	20	31	3,094	1,953	3,787
Hertford	167,298	4	46	8,530	3,213	4,094	5,497	25	31	44	6,318	6,301	8,353
Huntingdon	64,183	6	34	6,272	3,592	3,843	4,105	21	27	31	4,894	5,655	5,997
Kent	615,766	31	184	33,759	14,128	9,581	17,992	83	135	156	22,573	23,211	31,441
Lancaster	2,031,236	75	300	107,983	53,797	23,771	43,542	202	155	247	91,511	47,274	98,420
Leicester	230,308	14	129	21,739	4,704	6,044	10,761	38	70	107	9,874	10,641	19,301
Lincoln	407,222	44	462	78,862	20,532	23,554	38,760	155	274	360	39,221	49,899	66,796
Middlesex	1,886,576	22	81	33,887	19,016	2,608	18,005	76	15	70	32,161	13,322	32,164
Monmouth	157,418	10	59	15,506	7,394	1,877	9,066	41	21	44	13,654	3,770	13,113
Norfolk	442,714	17	213	34,285	8,129	13,324	13,052	95	173	164	19,399	29,724	28,457
Northampton	212,380	15	97	18,620	5,628	9,915	21,146	52	88	91	11,078	16,701	16,996
Northumberl'd	303,568	12	110	20,114	4,889	3,555	7,663	42	62	76	11,533	8,052	17,473
Nottingham	270,427	17	160	32,006	8,534	9,079	16,374	45	91	141	15,522	16,879	29,757
Oxford	170,439	10	74	10,988	4,127	4,245	7,442	32	43	66	6,461	6,610	10,049
Rutland	22,983	1	17	1,901	470	614	1,139	5	8	14	752	855	1,643
Salop	229,341	13	80	14,022	5,853	3,093	6,355	39	41	61	10,477	5,084	12,442
Somerset	443,916	22	202	39,553	11,359	6,128	19,006	101	87	176	26,983	12,313	36,087
Southampton	405,370	13	80	15,384	7,252	3,936	9,518	45	53	75	11,918	10,515	15,249
Stafford	608,716	31	191	50,443	23,991	13,998	15,284	92	125	150	37,593	28,843	48,094
Suffolk	337,215	10	84	13,779	4,779	6,473	5,581	48	65	58	9,683	11,350	10,421
Surrey	683,082	13	55	14,435	6,885	639	7,336	44	9	50	13,715	870	14,116
Sussex	336,844	8	63	11,018	4,293	3,639	5,587	32	42	50	7,439	7,246	9,625
Warwick	475,013	14	91	19,379	7,403	4,412	9,126	45	61	74	14,647	14,072	17,972
Westmoreland	58,287	4	29	4,368	1,284	1,189	1,474	12	18	24	2,935	2,842	3,783
Wilts	254,221	9	97	15,531	7,140	5,738	10,360	52	59	82	10,823	9,982	14,183
Worcester	276,926	14	67	15,155	6,259	3,081	7,495	30	44	53	11,022	9,163	13,808
City of York	36,303	4	4	3,719	1,759	120	1,833	4	1	4	3,719	1,000	3,719
York, E. Rid.	220,983	22	223	39,360	11,425	9,507	18,745	91	110	178	21,971	19,185	34,811
York N. Rid.	215,214	25	304	46,898	10,592	15,062	19,713	123	176	234	23,552	29,794	41,885
York, W.Rid.	1,325,495	101	646	173,962	67,199	58,695	63,515	338	428	478	134,736	125,747	147,311
North Wales	412,114	32	260	45,782	12,612	13,087	26,918	144	154	230	28,600	23,338	42,629
South Wales	593,607	37	168	31,313	9,973	4,304	17,082	93	63	138	23,478	7,449	28,467

(Table C.)

XIII. The Wesleyan Methodists held on Sunday, March 30th, 1851, the following services at different periods of the day:—

IN TOWNS		IN RURAL DISTRICTS	
In the Morning only	25	In the morning only	231
— Afternoon only	43	— Afternoon only	526
— Evening only	49	— Evening only	838
— Morning and Afternoon	24	— Morning and Afternoon	442
— Morning and Evening	482	— Morning and Evening	1,073
— Afternoon and Evening	193	— Afternoon and Evening	1,806
— Morning, Afternoon, and Evening	266	— Morning, Afternoon, and Evening	581
	1,082		5,497

(Table L.)

A Camp Meeting on Mousehold Heath, Norwich

(George Borrow, *Lavengro*, 1851, Ch. XXV)

One day, whilst I bent my way to the heath of which I have spoken on a former occasion, at the foot of the hills which formed it, I came to a place where a wagon was standing, but without horses, the shafts resting on the ground; there was a crowd about it, which extended half-way up the side of the neighbouring hill. The wagon was occupied by some half a dozen men – some sitting, others standing; they were dressed in sober-coloured habiliments of black or brown, cut in a plain and rather uncouth fashion, and partially white with dust; their hair was short, and seemed to have been smoothed down by the application of the hand: all were bareheaded – sitting or standing, all were bareheaded. One of them, a tall man, was speaking as I arrived; ere, however, I could distinguish what he was saying, he left off, and then there was a cry for a hymn 'to the glory of God' – that was the word. It was a strange-sounding hymn, as well it might be, for everybody joined in it: there were voices of all kinds, of men, of women, and of children – of those who could sing and of those who could not – a thousand voices all joined, and all joined heartily; no voice of all the multitude was silent save mine. The crowd consisted entirely of the lower classes, labourers and mechanics, and their wives and children – dusty people, unwashed people, people of no account whatever, and yet they did not look a mob. And when that hymn was over – another man in the wagon proceeded to address the people. He was a much younger man than the last speaker, somewhat square built and about the middle height; his face was rather broad, but expressive of much intelligence, and with a peculiar calm and serious look. The accent in which he spoke indicated that he was not of these parts, but from some distant district. The subject of his address was faith, and how it could remove mountains. It was a plain address, without any attempt at ornament, and delivered in a tone which was neither loud nor vehement. The speaker was evidently not a practised one – once or twice he hesitated as if for words to express his meaning, but still he held on, talking of faith, and how it could remove mountains: 'It is the only thing we want, brethren, in this world; if we have that, we are indeed rich, as it will enable us to do our duty under all circumstances, and to bear our lot, however hard it may be – and the lot of all mankind is hard. The lot of the poor is hard, brethren; and who knows more of the poor than I – a poor man myself, and the son of a poor man? But are the rich better off? Not so, brethren, for God is just. The rich have their trials too; I am not rich myself, but I have seen the rich with careworn countenances; I have also seen them in mad-houses. From which you may learn, brethren, that the lot of mankind is hard – that is, till we lay hold of faith, which makes us comfortable under all circumstances; whether we ride in gilded chariots or walk barefooted in quest of bread; whether we be ignorant, whether we be wise – for riches and poverty, ignorance and wisdom, brethren, each brings with it its peculiar temptations. Well, under all these troubles, the same which I would recommend you to seek is one and the same – faith; faith in our Lord Jesus Christ, who made us and allotted to each his station. Each has something to do, brethren. Do it, therefore, but always in faith. Without faith we shall find ourselves sometimes at fault; but with faith never, for faith can remove the difficulty. It will teach us to love life, brethren, when life is becoming bitter, and to prize the blessings around us; for as every man has his cares, brethren, so has each man his blessings. It will likewise teach us not to love life overmuch, seeing that we must one day part with it. It will teach us to face death with resignation, and will preserve us from sinking amidst the swelling of the river Jordan.'

And when he had concluded his address he said, 'Let us sing a hymn, one composed by Master Charles Wesley – he was my countryman, brethren.

> "Jesus, I cast my soul on Thee,
> Mighty and merciful to save;
> Thou shalt to death go down with me,
> And lay me gently in the grave.

> "This body then shall rest in hope,
> This body which the worms destroy;
> For Thou shalt surely raise me up,
> To glorious life and endless joy." '

Farewell, preacher with the plain coat, and the calm, serious look! I saw thee once again, and that was lately – only the other day. It was near a fishing hamlet, by the seaside, that I saw the preacher again. He stood on the top of a steep monticle, used by pilots as a look-out for vessels approaching that coast, a dangerous one, abounding in rocks and quicksands. There he stood on the monticle, preaching to weather-worn fishermen and mariners, gathered below upon the sand. 'Who is he?' said I to an old fisherman who stood beside me with a book of hymns in his hand; but the old man put his hand to his lips, and that was the only answer I received. Not a sound was heard but the voice of the preacher and the roaring of the waves; but the voice was heard loud above the roaring of the sea, for the preacher now spoke with power, and his voice was not that of one who hesitates. There he stood – no longer a young man, for his black locks were become grey, even like my own; but there was the intelligent face, and the calm, serious look which had struck me of yore. There stood the preacher, one of those men – and, thank God, their number is not few – who, animated by the spirit of Christ, amidst much poverty, and alas! much contempt, persist in carrying the light of the Gospel amidst the dark parishes of what, but for their instrumentality, would scarcely be Christian England.

The 'Rules' of a Wesleyan Reform Circuit

(Salisbury Circuit, Quarterly Meeting minutes, July 16, 1851)

1. That this meeting recognises the Church in its collective capacity as the highest court for all its affairs, whether financial, executive or disciplinary . . .

2. Leaders to be elected by ballot, with notice given from the pulpit.

3. Leaders' meeting to consist of Leaders, Stewards and Preachers.

4. The Leaders have power to admit on trial any person making application for Church Membership, and after three months' trial the final reception or rejection of such individuals shall be decided by the votes of the Church Meeting.

5. That no accusation be received against any member before the accuser or accusers have fulfilled the directions of the Scriptures, Matt. xviii.15–17, after which the exercise of discipline shall rest with the Leaders' Meeting, the accused having the right of appeal first to those members of the Church who worship in the same place with the accused and subsequently to the Quarterly Meeting, whose decision shall be final.

6. Society and Poor Stewards to be elected annually by ballot in each place at a meeting of the members.

7. A meeting of all the members in the Circuit to be held quarterly.

8. Circuit Stewards to be elected annually by ballot at the Lady Day Quarterly Meeting.

9. System of quarterly tickets to continue.

10. No person to be admitted as a Preacher without the joint consent of the Preachers and Quarterly Meeting.

11. The ordinance of the Lord's Supper to be duly celebrated in all places where there are separate services.[1]

12. Any member may propose the repeal or alteration of any existing rule or the introduction of any new rule at a Quarterly Meeting.

[1] Several laymen had earlier been appointed to officiate at the Sacrament, and it had been decided 'that we celebrate the Lord's Supper in a sitting posture' – a move away from the Anglican background of Wesleyanism towards the nonconformist camp. Cf. p. 288 above.

From Mission to Church

George Osborn to William Moister; London, October 2, 1852

(Ms at MA)

The move towards autonomy began in Australasia, where an independent Conference held its first meetings in Sydney in 1855. Both political and economic factors played a part in this. The situation in Canada was complicated by the existence of both Wesleyan and Methodist Episcopal work there. Osborn was writing as one of the Missionary Secretaries. Moister was serving as a missionary at Cape Town.

Of the object of [Robert Young's] Mission to Australia you will have been already apprized, and I hope it commends itself to your judgment & will have the help of your earnest prayers. It is a great comfort to us to reflect that we had come to our resolutions in reference to Australia before anything was heard of Gold being found there; and that the project has, generally speaking, received the warm concurrence of our brethren and the friends of Missions at home. We have a further encouragement in the circumstances that the new organisation of a French Conference has been so successfully prosecuted. We have lately heard from Dr. Cook[1] of the holding of the first French Conference, & the unanimous accord to our brethren there with the plan which had been proposed for their acceptance on our part.

We hope that things will soon be ripe for a similar proceeding in reference to British North America & then we shall have more time & more funds for the service of places & parts of the world which stand more in need of our help. God grant it soon! For we cannot but feel that viewed in reference to the masses of paganism all around us, the movements of Missionary Societies are fearfully slow & comparatively feeble.

¹ Charles Cook, pioneer of French Methodism, became President of the autonomous French Conference at its formation in 1852.

Methodism Triumphant

The peroration to John B. Dyson's *Wesleyan Methodism in the Leek Circuit* (1853) encapsulates the buoyant but parochial confidence of Wesleyans in the wake of the Religious Census.

We cannot bring to an end this narrative without a remark or two. Time has amply proved that Methodism is a modification of Christianity admirably adapted to meet the moral necessities of man anywhere and everywhere, under all the varied circumstances in which he is found, whether civilized or barbarian, learned or illiterate, bond or free. The present results of the Wesleyan system have fully justified the character which was given it by the great Northern Divine, when he styled it 'Christianity in earnest'. While, however, we rejoice, not only in the success of Methodism, but also of Protestantism in general, let us not forget that there are other systems in earnest. What is Secularism, but Infidel Naturalism in earnest? What is Puseyism, but Formalism in earnest? What is Popery, but – I will not say corrupted Christianity – but the Devil's substitute, in earnest? Never was there a time when we, as a body, were more imperatively called upon to be true to our principles and character, than now. Methodism finds an appropriate place and work for every man individually, and for all its members collectively. Let each one with Paul say, 'Lord, what wouldest thou have *me* to do?' And as a body, let us in the same earnest and submissive spirit enquire, What can *we* do? We shall then joyfully prove that Methodism does not so much need mending as working – well working – working in a prayerful and unaffected dependence on the promised presence and aid of the Holy Spirit. Then shall our Zion be as the 'sun when he goeth forth in his might'. She shall enlighten and bless thousands upon thousands now sitting in the 'region and shadow of death'.

We are happy to state that the friends in Leek are taking a step in the right direction. It is in contemplation to commence a Day School. £60 per annum has been already promised towards this most desirable and important object.

A Report on the Wesleyan Training College, Westminster, 1853

(Matthew Arnold, *Reports on Elementary Schools 1852–1882*, 1889, pp. 261–5)

There can be no question as to the advantage which the students enjoy in the lectures of their head-master, or as to the zeal and ability with which the other officers of the institution discharge their duties. Neither can there be any question as to the acquaintance with all subjects of ordinary secular instruction shown by most of the students, both when examined themselves, and when giving lessons in the practising schools. The secular instruction here is no doubt well and adequately given; those who conduct the institution are anxious to perfect their students in it, and are of opinion that the attention which is paid to religious teaching will not affect their success in doing so. And the institution has been so recently established, that it cannot, perhaps, yet be determined what that success will be. But the whole spirit of the proceedings in this institution, the language held by its promoters, the subjects constantly preferred by the students on which to give their lessons, the tenor of these lessons themselves, the very arrangement and organization of the practising schools, remind the observer that this is not the sole, nor even the chief thing aimed at. The Wesleyan Education Committee, and the connexion on behalf of which they act, put it forth as their first principle, 'that the week-day schools should secure the means of *religious* as well as secular instruction, in such a manner as to make the latter *strictly subordinate* to the former.' And again, '*religious teaching* is the leading and paramount object in the system of week-day schools, which it is the business of the committee to promote.' And, therefore, as '*religious character* is the primary consideration in the selection of the students, it is also the main end regarded in their discipline and training.' The daily attendance at morning and evening worship required of every student, their weekly conversations with the principal on religious subjects, their meetings for prayer among themselves, the supplementary examination paper on Scripture doctrines and Scripture history, set by the Wesleyan committee to all candidates examined at their institution for Government certificates, are all of them so many endeavours towards securing this end. For this end too, the committee placed the institution where it is, rather than in a less miserable and necessitous neighbourhood, because, to use the principal's own words, 'they did not wish their students to be spoiled in training; and by a lengthened residence away from the dwellings of the poor, and amongst the attractions of superior life, disinclined and rendered unfit to undertake the arduous and self-denying duties of school teachers. They hoped that, surrounded as their students are at Westminster by the families of the poor, their want of education, with its attendant degradation and misery, would excite their best feeling.' A *moral* end, then, a *moral* effect to be produced upon the student, was in view, even in planting the institution where it now stands.

It is right to remember these things when one notices, perhaps, points in the proceedings of the training college or of the practising schools which seem unfavourable to the perfection of secular instruction; when a spectator, attending exclusively to this, remarks that the galleries are too large, the number of children collected in them too great, the lessons on religious subjects or which are made to take a religious turn too frequent, the method of the teacher too often one of exhortation and lectures, rather than one of searching question and answer; it is right to remember that much of this is done with special aims, in the view to produce a special result both in the teachers and in the children; that it was because they had these special aims that the Wesleyan connexion, like the Church of England, for the most part withheld their assent from the principle of British schools, to establish schools of a strictly connexional character.

And, perhaps, considering how far more important to the young is the personal influence of the teacher than the things taught; considering, too, how narrow is the range of subjects in which it can be expected that the children of the poor shall really acquire instruction in school, it is no matter of regret that a training college should be established with these aims, even though the pursuit of them should cause it to send forth somewhat less finished scholars, if the same pursuit enables it to send forth more formed and serious men.

But, however this may be, by no member of the Methodist body will it be esteemed a reproach to have sacrificed something of intellectual smartness and showy acquirement in the paramount endeavour to train a band of serious and religious men to send among the poor; of that body, which already in other ways has laboured so long and so well in this cause; of that body, which from the first has devoted itself above all to matters of religious concernment, just as, even in its separation from the established Church, it was actuated by spiritual, and not by political, grounds.

Methodist Preaching and Dissent

(William Jay, *Autobiography*, 1854, pp. 144–5)

I have always thought the regular Dissenters were to blame at the origin of Methodism. They did not indeed oppose, as the Church generally did, on the ground of doctrine; for in this they essentially acquiesced, but as to the mode of preaching. The Dissenters were educated ministers themselves (for at that time there was scarcely a lay-preacher among them), and their sermons were not only orthodox but studied, grammatically correct, and methodical; but, with a very few exceptions, pointless, cold, and drawled off from notes. On the other hand, many of the new preachers had not been trained for the ministry; and delivered themselves in a way very unacceptable, in many respects, to cultivated minds. They were often boisterous, rude, coarse, incoherent. Yet they were powerful and efficient; and noise and novelty will not account for all the effect they produced. Reflecting men might have perceived this. Our ministers saw that the Meeting was thinly attended, and that crowds were drawn to the Tabernacle. Instead of listening to reports, which always magnified the mistakes of these men, and dwelling so much upon their deficiencies, they should have owned that God honoured them and did much good by them; they should have heard and judged for themselves; they should have examined whether there were not some things in which these labourers, (for such *indeed* they were) deserved not only to be tolerated, but even imitated. And there were a few who nobly differed from the many of the general body. They were candid and judicious enough to own these men, without approving everything in them. They perceived, that, with all their supposed or real faults, they had an earnestness in their manner, with strokes of fancy, touches of passion, striking metaphors, plain anecdotes, bold addresses and characteristic applications to the conscience, which might be detached from their accompanying improprieties, and adopted in an improved state, in combination with elements of their own. Accordingly, these ministers soon displayed, in addition to their own superior learning, accuracy, and order, an ease and a liveliness which they knew not before.

And it is this union, so to speak, of the Dissenter and Methodist, that has produced the better style of preaching than either of them had separately attained. They have corrected and improved each other; and introduced freedom without irregularity, arrangement without stiffness, animation without violence, soberness without dulness, solemnity without sanctimoniousness, readiness without rapidity, and plainness without vulgarity.

Democracy in the Church

John M'Lean to Jabez Bunting; Edinburgh, August 18, 1855

(Hayes and Gowland, pp. 131–2)

You will not I am sure suppose from my letter yesterday, that I have turned Democrat since I came to Scotland, which it must be admitted is a region, perhaps, somewhat unusually charged with that spirit. I quite believe in the sentiment which your enemies charged you with, when I had the honour of living under your roof, and of which I think you have no reason to be ashamed, that Methodism is as opposed to democracy as it is to sin. By which I understood you to mean, that Methodism was unmistakeably and irreconcilably opposed to democracy as a system of government. But I also believe that you recognise the existence of a Christian people or flock as distinct from the Pastors; and that next to the glory of God all church arrangements should be made with a view to their benefit. Neither do I doubt that any powers which might with safety be put into the hands of the flock would by you be most freely and gladly consented to. In England, however, you are accustomed to regard the flock or people or congregation, as embodied or condensed (certainly *you* never thought that they were *represented*) in the Leaders' and Quarterly Meetings &c. For the south of the Tweed this perhaps is the best; because in truth I fear you have given such powers to those meetings, that I greatly doubt, whether without the hazard of some fearful tumult you could apportion any of them, to the congregation. In Scotland it is different, because our entire ecclesiastical system may be considered to be yet in a state of solution; and also because in this country, the existence and rights, or as it would be more Wesleyan & scriptural to call them, the duties of the congregation are universally acknowledged. In the Free Church as well as in the Established Church this is undoubtedly the case. So also in the United, and other Presbyterian sections. You have no parallel to this state of things in England. Now I recommend the Veto Act in yesterday's letter with a view to this peculiar constitution of religious opinion and society on this side of the Tweed. I do not deny that I should without scruple place it myself upon much higher ground than that of *mere* expediency, though of course I am too established a Wesleyan to suppose that the scriptures make this or any similar detail of church arrangement, imperative, except where the prosperity of the work of God demands it. The reality of a *visible* Church, should I think be carefully kept up, along with the reality (not of an *invisible* Church, as our Calvinistic friends are too apt at once to run the thing to) – but of a *spiritual* and *converted* church such as I believe we have; visibly embodied in own own beloved and precious Methodist Societies.

Now such a regulated power of vetoing a minister, as I described in my last, might I think be safely and very advantageously committed to our congregations in Scotland. They are all supposed to be baptised. We admit their children to baptism. They are thus with their families, members of the visible community of Christ's people, even if they do not feel themselves worthy to be communicants. I am not sure whether the Free Church extends the veto law so far; but I am satisfied that it might be done with our system of Government with perfect safety and advantage. As for having lay Elders in this country, that I believe is absurd and unscriptural, and I am yet to be convinced that Mr Wesley ever gave the slightest sanction to it. That our Presbyterian friends emerging from Roman Catholic errors three hundred years since, should have fallen into this Protestant error, is no reason, why any section of the followers of John Wesley should adopt it. But a proper recognition of the Congregation, would have the effect I believe of making one class of our lay officers more decidedly scriptural, while it would render another class more exclusively secular and financial, agreeably as I cannot but believe with the state of things in the *primitive Church* and *certainly* in our primitive Methodism. Have you not noticed how the godly men of business of Mr Wesley's days, got superseded by the spiritual men, and how the secular spirit, accumulated upon our poor but pious leaders thereby, has been exploding in our Leaders' and Quarterly Meetings whenever the external atmosphere has become favourable from that day to this?

Scottish Methodism in 1856

(Peter Prescott, *The Case of Scottish Methodism Impartially Considered*, 1856, pp. 4–6, 35, 37, 86–7)

When the writer was appointed at the Conference of 1851, to the Airdrie Circuit – a circuit comprising almost the entire extent of country between Edinburgh and Glasgow, and uniting, in fact, the difficulties of an English, with those of a Scottish circuit – he felt deeply and painfully the condition of that and all circuits north of the Tweed. Their condition was a burden upon his mind; a burden which impelled him to the continual study of the subject, and to the endeavour to trace the operation of the causes at work which have produced so deplorable a state of things. To this study he devoted the greater portion of his available time during the years of his residence there.

. . . The time seems to be fully come, when all who know anything of the subject and think upon it, have reached, or are fast reaching, the conclusion, that the present state of things ought either to be mended or ended; that its condition, hovering between life and death, is such as must be terminated, and will, at on distant day, terminate itself, unless vigorous and effectual measures be resorted to for its renovation.

Now, let us view the actual working of Itinerancy in Scotland. The outer Itinerancy which originated in evangelistic effort, may be taken to represent that principle. Well, then, have we any evangelistic effort in Scotland – any effort to act upon the masses who are sinking into virtual heathenism? We have none, none whatever. The inner Itinerancy which is the interchange between ministers – have we that? In the great majority of the few churches we possess, we have it not. In another letter written by *Mr. Wesley* to Mr. Benson, we find the following statement; 'You will be buried in Scotland, if you sit still.' We *do* sit still, and *are* buried; and conversely – being buried, we therefore, of necessity, sit still. In other words, the sitting-still system, has caused the extinction of so many churches that those which remain are so 'few and far between' that it is with the utmost difficulty that an interchange is effected.

Thus, in whatever light we look upon Itinerancy in the form in which it now exists, we find that it is in a state of utter decay; its strength and substance are eaten out of it; it is rotten to the core.

Itinerancy then, which is the blending of the evangelistic and pastoral offices in the same minister, has utterly failed to answer the purposes for which it was instituted in Scotland. What then is the remedy? We reply, the question answers itself. If the attempt to blend these offices has not succeeded, the only plan which remains, is to EFFECT A SEPARATION BETWEEN THEM, *devolving the former upon Evangelists, and the latter upon Pastors.* . . .

The question here arises – if it is a question – Does Scotland *need* Methodism? There are some in this country who hint to us, in terms not obscure, that we scarcely are needed; that, though it may be very benevolent on our part to put ourselves to so much trouble, our efforts and our presence might well be dispensed with. But those who feel the most inclined to speak thus, are not persons, the condition of whose churches would lead us to a similar conclusion. There are none who feel aright with regard to the large 'outfield' population, but would gladly hail as co-adjutors those, whose system has produced elsewhere, as is confessed on all hands, results so beneficial, causing the moral 'wilderness to rejoice and blossom as the rose'. Nor can it be said that the churches of this country are contending successfully with the ungodliness of the multitudes who are never found within the walls of the sanctuary. Their action is denominational and antipopish rather than directly spiritual. And precisely such a population as that in which Methodism won the most glorious of its early triumphs in England, is on the increase in Scotland. And who that looks upon the torpor which to so great an extent pervades the Scottish churches, can doubt that a church exhibiting a higher standard of spirituality, and a nearer approach to the warm, free life of primitive Christianity, is needed? And if Methodism is not that church, if we are not prepared to 'come to the help of the LORD against the mighty', God will assign the work which must be accomplished, and *will* be accomplished by ourselves or by others, to a people 'raised up' as 'from the stones', who will fulfil all His pleasure.

The Baptism of Fire

(William Arthur, *The Tongue of Fire: or the True Power of Christianity*, 1856, Ch. VI)

Religion has never, in any period, sustained itself except by the instrumentality of the tongue of fire. Only where some men, more or less imbued with this primitive power, have spoken the words of the Lord, not with 'the words which man's wisdom teacheth, but which the Holy Ghost teacheth,' have sinners been converted, and saints prompted to a saintlier life. In many periods of the history of the Church, as this gift has waned, every natural advantage has come to replace it:—more learning, more system, more calmness, more profoundness of reflection, everything, in fact, which, according to the ordinary rules of human thought, would insure to the Christian Church a greater command over the intellect of mankind, and give to her arguments in favour of a holy life a more potent efficacy. Yet it has ever proved that the gain of all this, when accompanied with an abatement of the 'fire', has left the Church less efficient; and her elaborate and weighty lessons have transformed few into saints, though her simple tongue of fire had continually reared up its monuments of wonder. This has been not less the case in modern times than in ancient.

If the amazing revival which characterised the last century, be viewed merely as a natural progress of mental influences, no analysis can find elements of power greater than have often existed in a corrupting and falling Church, or than are found at many periods when no blessed effects are produced. Men equally learned, eloquent, orthodox, instructive, may be found in many ages of Christianity. It is utterly impossible to assign a natural reason why Whitefield should have been the means of converting so many more sinners than other men. Without one trace of logic, philosophy, or anything worthy to be called systematic theology, his sermons, viewed intellectually, take a humble place among humble efforts. Turning again to his friend, Wesley, we find calmness, clearness, logic, theology, discussion, definition, point, appeal, but none of that prodigious and unaccountable power which the human intellect would naturally connect with movements so amazing as those which took place under his word. Neither the logic of the one, nor the declamation of the other, furnishes us with the secret of his success. There is enough to account for men being affected, excited, or convinced; but that does not account for their living holy lives ever after. Thousands of pulpit orators have swayed their audience, as a wind sways standing corn; but, in the result, those who were most affected differed nothing from their former selves. An effect of eloquence is sufficient to account for a vast amount of feeling at the moment; but to trace to this a moral power, by which a man, for his life long, overcomes his besetting sins, and adorns his name with Christian virtues, is to make sport of human nature.

Why should these men have done what many equally learned and able, as divines and orators, never did? There must have been an element of power in them which criticism cannot discover. What was that power? It must be judged of by its sphere and its effects. Where did it act? and what did it produce? Every power has its own sphere. The strongest arm will never convince the understanding, the most forcible reasoning will never lift a weight, the brightest sunbeam will never pierce a plate of iron, nor the most powerful magnet move a pane of glass. The soul of man has separate regions, and that which merely convinces the intellect may leave the emotions untouched, that which merely operates on the emotions may leave the understanding unsatisfied, and that which affects both may yet leave the moral powers uninspired. The crowning power of the messenger of God is power over the moral man; power which, whether it approaches the soul through the avenue of the intellect or of the affection, *does* reach into the soul. The sphere of true Christian power is the heart – the moral man; and the result of its action is not to be surely distinguished from that of mere eloquence by instantaneous emotion, but by subsequent moral fruit. Power which cleanses the heart, and produces holy living, is the power of the Holy Ghost. It may be through the logic of Wesley, the declamation of Whitefield, or the simple common-sense of a plain servant woman or labouring man; but whenever this power is in action, it strikes deeper into human nature than any mere reasoning or pathos. Possibly it does not so soon bring a tear to the eye, or throw the judgment into a posture of acquiescence; but it raises in the breast thoughts of God, eternity, sin, death, heaven, and hell; raises them, not as mere ideas, opinions, or articles of faith, but as the images and echoes of real things.

We may find in many parts of the country, where much has been done to dispel darkness and diffuse true religion, that some of the first triumphs of grace were entirely due to the wonderful effects produced by the private and fire-side talking of some humble Christians, who had themselves gone to the throne of grace, and waited there until they received the baptism of fire. In proportion as the power of this one instrument is overlooked, and other means are trusted in to supply its place, does the true force of Christian agency decline; and it may without hesitation be said, that when men holding the Christian ministry, habitually and constantly manifest their distrust in the power of the Holy Ghost to give them utterance, they publicly abjure the true theory of Christian preaching.

A 'Protracted Meeting' in Norfolk

(*PM Magazine*, 1857, pp. 170–1)

CASTLE ACRE, SWAFFHAM CIRCUIT ... Previous to the December quarter-day, 1855, there appeared a growing desire for a revival of the work of God; and many earnest prayers for the purpose were offered up both in private and public.

Castle Acre was speedily visited with showers of blessings, many were converted to God, and added to the church; but, alas! some at the Whitsuntide, and others during the harvest, unhappily fell from grace, and returned to the world. Many, however, kept on their way, and can still rejoice in the God of their salvation.

January 25th, 1857, being the day appointed for the commencement of a fresh and protracted attack on the strongholds of sin and Satan, the friends wisely devoted the previous week to special prayer for a mighty outpouring of God's Spirit upon the appointed means.

'It is not by might, nor by power, but by my Spirit, saith the Lord of Hosts.'

The congregation at each service was good, and on two nights it was so large, that the friends were obliged to light up the gallery, which was soon thronged with attentive hearers. The preaching was plain and pointed. The aim of each speaker seemed to be to impress the mind of the people with the shortness of time, the certainty of death, the necessity of preparation for it, and the happiness of being found ready. The shouts of praise from the assemblies, as well as the many tears that were shed, bespoke the deep interest that was felt in the various addresses.

The singing was lively and powerful, especially in the procession; the voice of which was 'as the sound of many waters', and the noise was heard afar off. The ancient castle hills echoed with the well-known hymn,

The gospel news is sounding
To nations far and near, etc.
And as the inhabitants opened their doors to view the crowd, the
invitation rung in their ears,
Come, listen to the echo,
Now, while 'tis sounding here.
And many did listen, and followed us to the chapel, and some did
Taste the virtue of the blood
Of him who died for all.

The afternoon prayer-meetings were well sustained; at each a gracious
influence was felt, and three broken-hearted penitents professed to
obtain 'peace with God'. The result of these services will not be fully
known in time, but as far as we can ascertain at present, they are very
encouraging.

The week was one of physical and mental toil, but our labour was not
in vain; the church was quickened, backsliders were reclaimed, and a
few sinners converted to God.

'Women's Work'

'The Ladies' Committee for the Amelioration of the Condition of Women in
Heathen Countries, and for Education etc.' was formed in 1858 and marked
the beginning of what was to become known as 'Women's Work' within the
Missionary Society's structure.

Minutes of the first committee meeting of the Ladies' Auxiliary

(MCOD Archives)

On Dec. 20th, 1858, a meeting of Ladies was assembled at the Wesleyan
Mission House, Bishopsgate Street Within, for the purpose of directing
attention to the subject of Female Education in Heathen Countries . . .
The Rev. William Arthur opened the meeting with prayer, after which
he & Dr. Hoole made a general statement of the plan proposed, & then
retired. The following extract from the Minutes of the General Committee was then brought forward:
'General Committee, Oct. 13, 1858. Read a letter from Miss Farmer,[1]
accompanying one from Mrs. Batchelor of Negapatam, recommending the formation of a Ladies' Society for Female Education in India.
Resolved, that the subject of Female Education in India is regarded
by this Committee with lively interest. They rejoice in the help which

has been afforded by many Ladies' Societies in London & elsewhere, & look favourably on the project for organising those Societies more extensively for the promotion of Female Education in India & other parts of the Mission field.'

It further appeared from statements made by Mrs. Farmer & Mrs. Hoole,[2] that the good resulting from the efforts of various Ladies' Societies was marred by the want of general direction & arrangement in disposing of the work. Some Missionary stations received supplied from many quarters, while others, more needy, were neglected. In some cases the operation of zeal was delayed, if not checked, by the want of a definite object. Mrs. Hoole read a letter from a lady in Manchester, stating that in one of the Manchester circuits the ladies were anxious to work, & only waited to have an object put before them. Miss Farmer remarked that the same thing occurred in two or three places in the North. After a free discussion of the subject, it was resolved,

I. That in accordance with the minute of the General Committee now read, the Ladies present at this meeting form themselves into a Committee, to be called the Ladies' Committee for the Amelioration of the Condition of Women in Heathen Countries, Female Education, &c.

II. That the Committee consists of twenty-four Ladies, who shall be invited to meet on the second Tuesday in each month, from November to June, at 11 o'clock.

III. That any vacancies which may occur in the Committee shall be filled up at the November or December meeting each year.

IV. That three Secretaries shall be appointed to conduct the business of the Committee, one for Foreign correspondence, one for Home correspondence, & one for Minutes & Finance . . .

V. That the object of the Committee shall be to promote & extend the education of Females in Heathen Countries, in accordance with the teaching of the Wesleyan Missionary Society,

1. By corresponding with the wives of Missionaries & others who are engaged in Female Education in Heathen Countries, inviting full information on the state of their schools & the best methods of aiding & extending them.

2. By communicating with Ladies & Ladies' Committees throughout this country, furnishing information & requesting co-operation & increased effort in behalf of this great work.

3. By selecting & training suitable persons for Female school teachers, to be sent out at the expense of the Funds of this Committee.

VI. That the Secretaries of the General Committee be requested to draw up a Circular to all the Home Circuits, stating the plan now formed, & asking all workers in connection with Miss[ionar]y Baskets &c. to communicate with the Ladies' Committee, so that all agencies may combine in one centre – the decision as to distribution of funds & work to rest with the Committee, but always to be guided by the wishes of the senders.

VII. That a Quarterly Paper be published to report results and give extracts from correspondence &c.; to be printed in large type.

VIII. That notice of the monthly meetings be sent by the Minute Secretary to each Lady of the Committee.

[1] Mary Farmer, daughter of Thomas Farmer, lay treasurer of the Missionary Society. She and her mother were both actively involved in the launching of the Ladies' Auxiliary.

[2] Elizabeth Hoole (née Chubb), wife of one of the secretaries of the Missionary Society, Elijah Hoole, who had served as a missionary in India from 1819 to 1828.

The first woman missionary

(Minutes of Ladies' Committee; *Occasional Papers*, Vol. 1, pp. 131, 67–9, 93–5)

Susannah Goulding Beal was sent out to British Honduras in the autumn of 1859, after six months' training at the Westminster Normal College. Within a year she had died of yellow fever.

March 22, 1859: Dr. Hoole mentioned the urgent need of a female teacher at the station of Belize, Central America, where a school of 168 girls was left entirely to the care of the Missionary & his wife, Mr. & Mrs. Webb. The question was raised & left open, how far would Miss Lister be suited to fill this post?

May 17, 1859: Mrs. Farmer mentioned the case of Miss Beal, who, in regard to religious character, Methodistical bias, age & health, was considered very suitable. Being at the Mission House at the time, Miss Beal was called in, & answered readily to the questions put to her by the Ladies, expressing her willingness to go to any part of the Mission field. It was suggested that Miss Beal might go to the school at Belize, Central America.

From Miss Beal's diary

September, 1859. – Early in the year my mind was very much exercised in reference to Mission work. I was then meeting in Mr. John Corderoy's class. One evening I was led to mention the feelings that had been influencing my mind through the day. After the class Mr. Corderoy had some conversation with me, which resulted in an application to the Ladies' Committee. On the 4th of May, I received a letter from one of the Secretaries, requesting an interview; on the 17th, I met the Committee; on the 26th, I came to the Westminster College. It is decided that I shall leave England for Belize, Honduras Bay, on the 17th of October.

I shall have charge of a girls' school, where there are one hundred and thirty in attendance. The more I mark all the way by which God has led me, the more my heart bounds with gratitude to Him who doeth all things well. Every circumstance has been a link in one great chain of Providence, leading to the same issue. God is claiming the fulfilment of reiterated vows. I do trust that I shall be enabled to live for Him alone. I feel deeply parting with all whom I love on earth: but I am so persuaded that I am only obeying the command of my Father in heaven, that, were the deadly shores of Western Africa my destination, I would go with willing feet.

Miss Beal to Mrs. Hoole; Mission House, Belize, November 16, 1859

We left Jamaica at six o'clock A.M., on Monday, and had a most uncomfortable journey to Belize. It scarcely ceased raining, not as we generally have it in England, but pouring in torrents; but through mercy we reached here in safety and peace . . .

I visited both of the Schools yesterday; but I do not think I shall commence duty before Christmas. Next week will be their annual examination by the Board of Education; and, during the following week, there will be circumstances to interfere with ordinary School duties; after that, we expect the Schools will have their usual holiday . . .

You will be quite surprised to hear that I have felt it cold since I have been here. On Monday morning I was quite glad to put on a thoroughly warm dress. I like Belize, or, at least, what I have seen of it, much better than I do Kingston, and am glad that my residence is fixed here rather than there. I keep hearing of the degraded state of the people, and the necessity there will be to use a cane in School. This is quite new to me, and I do trust the occasion for such extremes will be very rare. I do feel that I shall need great wisdom to enable me to discharge my duty aright; but I do believe that all needful grace will be given, and I expect to have success.

I am very much pleased with what I have seen of my Assistant Teacher. She is quiet, unassuming, willing to be led, and has hitherto given great satisfaction. She took tea with me last evening; also her sister and Mrs. Lewis, who has kindly taken charge of the School for the last two months. After tea, some of the girls came to work. We spent two or three hours very pleasantly; it reminded me of the Pupil Teachers' working class at Westminster. I can scarcely realize that I am now more than five thousand miles from England, and that, while I am writing this, it is midnight at home. I am enjoying a good degree of health, only suffering from the stings of mosquitoes and sand-flies; these are comparatively little evils.

Miss Beal to Miss Farmer; Belize, January 14, 1860

Our Schools re-opened on the 9th of the present month, so that I am now in full work, and find great delight in it; but at the same time I feel that my position is indeed a responsible one; a large number of children, some in their earliest childhood, others ripening into youth, and others verging into womanhood, looking to me for guidance and instruction, who will become, to a very great extent, just what those instructions tend to make them. O! what need there is that I should be guided from on high, living every moment under the teaching of the good Spirit of God! I am very much pleased with the spirit in which the duties of School have been resumed by the children: they seem determined to try and do their best. The attendance has been very good. We commenced this year by having a uniform charge of three-halfpence per week. This has been responded to by a large number of the parents; but we hope it will become more general in the course of a few weeks. Mr. Fletcher will be writing upon this subject, so that it scarcely needs many remarks from me. I have enclosed you a routine of school duties. I have found it necessary, in consequence of there being such a large number requiring to be taught how to read, to re-model the first class; but I trust the present arrangement will be attended with advantage. In addition to the duties stated upon that programme, I meet the monitors for an hour from two until three o'clock. On Sunday I have a tract district and a juvenile class. On Monday, from five to six, I have a Bible class, and on Thursday, at the same time, I meet the assistant teacher and her sister for the study of History and Geography, &c. These engagements, the week-night services, and the attention which it is necessary for me to give to the needle-work after school-hours, keep my time well occupied, and furnish me with good reasons for declining to pay frequent visits.

Mr. Fletcher has declined retaining Miss J. V. Cowel for the Day School (which is entirely an infant one), on account of the increase of expense. I have not a monitor in the school capable of taking charge of these little ones, of whom there are frequently upwards of forty in daily attendance; so I have decided to retain her at my own expense. This will render extra carefulness in my own personal expenditure necessary; but I am persuaded it will increase the efficiency of the School . . .

Should you ever have contributions of sheeting, towelling, or muslin for mosquito nets, they would be very acceptable in this part of the world, where they are either not to be had, or of such indifferent quality as to wear out very quickly. I have had some difficulty in this matter. I should already have saved two or three pounds by bringing such things from home.

The great difficulty in securing regular attendance with some of the children is want of clothes. Their parents will not let them come unless they are clean and tidy; and sometimes it is so wet on Saturday that they are unable to get the clothes in which they have appeared at school washed and dried ready for the following week. Then, when these wear out, which they do in an amazingly short time, they have to wait until they can get new ones; so that, should there be any pieces of print or calico, &c., among your boxes, you would find it better to send such here, rather than ready-made articles. We could thus employ a large number of children who can work very nicely. Thimbles, needles, cottons, will also be very acceptable. You will think I am commencing early with a list of wants; but what Mrs. Hoole said upon the subject rather directed my attention to it.

A Probationer in the Wigan Circuit

Thomas Major to Henry Oldfield; Wigan, October 15, [18]60

(Ms at Duke University)

This was Major's first year in the ministry. He died only seven years later.

I have just returned from Hindley where I have been visiting for about a couple of hours. Generally speaking the people receive me kindly, some even press me to call again, while on the other hand others are very cool in their manner and some treat me rudely. At times I feel an extraordinary love for the work, and at other times I am cast down, & dispirited. I have had numbers of people promising me to come to our chapels, but such is the deep-rooted indifference to things spiritual and divine, that these promises are but seldom kept. Hindley, Ince[-in-Makerfield] and Lamberhead Green I am expected to pay attention to in the way of visiting. The former of these places has been in low water, & is yet even depressed. The Society only numbers about 18 members, many being lost through a Sunday School squabble. I was preaching there last night, and there were nearly sixty persons present.

Lamberhead Green through Topping's expulsion has decreased from about 60 members to 29 – so that instead of their being 480 members in this circuit as on the Minutes, there were only 450 at the last quarter day. But for all this the people made an effort, and at the quarter board presented eight pounds more than last quarter. Peace reigns in our borders, and through the blessing of God we shall yet see better days . . .

We are just now commencing with our Missionary Meetings. Two of these I am required to attend, as next week. A Dorcas tea-meeting is held on Wednesday next, and I see that I am down as a speaker. I suppose I must not [?   ] at this, but as I have begun to lead the life of a Methodist Preacher, I must take with it all the duties which belong to that office.

Education of the Poor

An Address to the Students of the Wesleyan Training Institution, Westminster, on commencing the Session of 1862, by the Principal, the Rev. John Scott

(*Annual Report* of the Wesleyan Education Committee, 1861, pp. 51–5, 58, 66)

The Wesleyan Education Committee strongly opposed Robert Lowe's 'Revised Code', which introduced a system of 'payment by results' likely to lower educational standards, especially for the children of the poor.

The education which you will be called to give in Wesleyan schools, while it carefully instructs every junior scholar in what is primary, will never, we hope, be solely initiatory: for then it might be again left in the hands of 'dames,' and such other persons as were the educators of the people thirty years ago. This brings me to the *second* point which I wish you to settle in your minds; namely, that the education provided and offered in Wesleyan schools *must be good*, and that it cannot be *too good* for those who are to receive it.

The children of your schools, though of the labouring classes, are not machines, made to work in the fields, in the mines, at the forge, in the mill, – which, being nevertheless human, may work all the better if able to read a newspaper, write a fair hand, and do a rule of three or practice sum. They may, and probably will, have to work; but they are the children of *men*. We wish you to have just conception of man, *as man*, – a thorough sympathy with human feelings and human interests, irrespective of worldly condition. Is a child less rational, less capable of intellectual and moral improvement, – of living an orderly, creditable, and useful life in society, – of serving God, and ensuring a blissful immortality, – because his parents are poor? obliged to work hard six days of the week, and perhaps for small wages? What reason can be assigned, of which the persons assigning it ought not to be ashamed, why a poor man's child ought to have only a poor education? The 'humble classes' are represented as having 'contracted minds', into which it is the business of education to 'throw some glimmering of light and knowledge'! Are the minds of *children* of the poorer classes, as matter of fact, more contracted than those of the more affluent classes? Take a

poor child, born in a hovel, of the poorest parents; and when you educate him, place him in equally favourable circumstances, you will find
his mind open and expand as kindly, receive instruction as readily, and
retain it as tenaciously, as a child of higher birth. Afford him the same
right tuition, and his heart will unfold as noble and generous affections,
his taste and manners will form to as correct a model, in the one case as
in the other. We do not propose, because we are not able, to place him
in equally favourable circumstances: our argument is, that *in his education*
we ought to do the best for him that we can. No person, however
jealous he may be lest poor children rise too high and advance too far,
need be alarmed on hearing it said that too good an education cannot
be given to them. Give our schools the best teachers, and let them do
their best, still only a few, comparatively, of the great mass will remain
long enough at school to make a proficiency which can render them
objects of jealousy to the higher classes . . .

Our views of that education may be shortly stated. Six years ago
(1856), in an address entitled 'The best Teachers and the best Schools',
we said, that while in elementary schools now, as in former days, certain
work – to teach the children to read, write, and cipher – is indispensable,
instruction in grammar, geography, and history, must in these days be
added. But it was further remarked, that true education forms the mind
to *think*, to *reason*, to *deduce*; that a child should not only be trained to
remember, but taught to understand; that what, by the teacher's skill in
leading his thought from one thing to another, he is enabled to make
out for himself, he will most certainly remember, and most readily
reproduce and make serviceable in after life; that thus he will be shown
how one thing involves another, how antecedent is followed by consequent, premises by conclusions . . .

Is this carrying the education of the labouring people of the country
too far? Must that largest class of children, to whom 'the Lord, the
Maker of them all,' has given capabilities equal in every respect to the
children of the classes above them, be restricted to something much
humbler? We answer, No! Our opinion remains unchanged; and every
year's observation, every day's reflection, more fully satisfies us that
such an education should be given to every child whose parents will
allow him to remain long enough in the school to receive it. Will a
labouring man's home be less happy, and less loved, when, after a day
of toil, he can read at night a few pages, more or less as his fatigue may
permit, of a good book, to an intelligent wife, who has, like himself,
received a good education; their children, as they grow up and are
educated, as much interested in what he reads as themselves? and will he
work the next day the less cheerfully, because he can ruminate on what
he read last night? The New Code does not, at present, declare that
schools receiving Government aid shall *not* give such an education: but

it offers no inducement to do so; it places no such standard before us. And among the many objections which our Committee have publicly alleged against this crude and mischievous attempt at educational legislation, *this* we have felt most strongly, and placed most prominently before the Lord President of the Council . . .

I wish to express to you my belief that, so long as the Wesleyans pretend to give education to the poor, they will give them an education which it will be worth their while to receive, and to pay for as far as they are able. Should Parliament, in disappointment of our hope, make this New Code law, it may be difficult to keep the education *up* in Wesleyan schools, with the whole scheme of public encouragement arranged to bring it *down*. But with this difficulty you must prepare yourselves to contend . . .

In your school-life, if you are Wesleyan school-teachers, you will have extensively to do with people of the middle class. The promoters of our schools, the members of managing committees, those who contribute the large funds raised among us for education, are mostly of that class. You will find in them no paltry jealousy lest their poorer neighbours should rise to a level with themselves. The great body of Wesleyan people knew well what they did, when, in the course of years, they built their Sunday-schools, capable of accommodating half a million of children; and when they set up this Training Institution at an expense *to themselves* of between thirty and forty thousand pounds, – which they did not agree to do without ample discussion. They know what they now do when they build their schools in different localities at a great outlay of their own money, and, on opening them, in every case urge us to send them the best teacher we have. By this course of action, they can have left no room for doubts as to their feeling on the present question. You may, perhaps, hear them complain that they have not schools equally accessible with yours, and of equal merit, for the education of their own children; and, where there is room to admit them, they may send their children to your schools. I do not wonder at them: I would do so myself, were I in their case. But I will venture to say, that, within the whole range of Wesleyan school-promoters, and within a much wider range, you would not find one in a hundred that would rob his poorer brethren of the advantage which our primary schools afford for the education of their children, to serve himself. It has never been the manner of our community to call, *Excelsior!* to the upper or '*lower* middle classes,' – content to leave the crowd grovelling below. Through the century or more of their existence, their great aim has been to promote the upward and onward progress of society, by directing an enlightened attention to the masses. Once they were nearly alone in this aim; they rejoice that now they are joined in it, and in active exertion to attain it, by a multitude of others, not of their own denomination . . .

In concluding, let me remind you that the Christian's hope at all times is in God; and we may, with every assurance of His interest in it, confide our cause to Him, the great Moral Ruler, and almighty Disposer of all things. Our cause in this contention is the cause of our poorer brethren: He is the common Father, and 'we *all* are His offspring'. We cannot read the Bible without perceiving that the cause of the poor in all ages has been His cause. When our Saviour came down from heaven, He exercised His ministry chiefly among the poor; and to congregations of them He enunciated much of that Divine truth which 'abideth for ever', and which men, having means of knowing it, must receive in the love thereof in order to be saved. HE cannot be pleased that masses of His creatures should remain in so sunken a condition as at present. He would see them rise; and He cannot but approve of those who, by the use of His own instituted means, seek to raise them. Our Christian school-system, with its Bible, its godly teachers, and its religion, is well adapted to this end. Let us trust that He will not suffer it to be stripped of all that adapts it to its purpose, but that it will be preserved to us in unimpaired efficiency. Then, vigorously working it, we may hope in time to see the most gratifying and striking moral transformations extensively produced by the almighty power of Him 'who raiseth up the poor out of the dust, and lifteth the needy out of the dunghill; that He may set them with the princes of His people.'

A Charge to the Ordinands, 1862

(Charles Prest, *A Charge delivered to fifty-seven newly ordained Ministers, in Brunswick Chapel, Sheffield*, 1862, pp. 32–5)

Prest was President of the Conference in 1862.

There is yet the need of our ministry in this country; and our mission, notwithstanding the fears of some, and the hopes of others, is not yet accomplished. In the presence of popish activities and tendencies, amidst the developments of varied pestilent errors, and the alarming aboundings of iniquity, it is still needed in that distinctive character which has been impressed upon it by the Providence of God. The comprehension of Methodism into or its coalition with the Church of England, or its absorption into any other ecclesiastical organization, is impossible! The idea is ill timed, and the change could not be accomplished, even were extraneous difficulties removed, without the sacrifice of opportunities of usefulness, without the renunciation of responsibilities which are incumbent upon us, nor without a fatal schism in the body.

We are not called upon to retire and to make way for others, but rather to prosecute, with increased zeal and assiduity, the work which has been given *us* to do. Thankful for past and for present success, we are admonished by the moral and religious condition of the kingdom of the need of our ministry to spread scriptural holiness yet more widely through the land. The evangelical agency of Methodism is now as necessary as at any former time; and, if vigorously developed, will reap a richer harvest than that which at present rewards its former toils. The increase of the population fearfully outstrips all efforts made to provide for the due ministration of religion; and we are imperatively summoned to renew and enlarge our exertions in stemming the tide of iniquity, in meeting the claims of neglected spiritual destitution, and in preaching Christ to the vicious, the careless, and the dangerous classes, that, from these lost ones, multitudes may be brought to God. We cannot but see, in the irreligion of so large a portion of the inhabitants of this country, a terrific, though a latent power, most dangerous to the social and political well-being of the nation; equal, if roused into action, to the wrecking of all that is dear to Christian and patriotic men. The quickened zeal and activities of other denominations do not, in any degree, render our best exertions unnecessary. Were our evangelical work to cease, a blank would be created with could not be easily supplied by other Churches, and our glory would have departed.

While our zeal for Foreign Missions has not abated, and must not be allowed to subside, it is satisfactory, that the need of Missions at home is now again fully and officially recognized among us. We have heathens here, as much requiring our solicitude and labour as any of those abroad to whom we direct our Foreign Missions; who, as our countrymen, have the first claim on our sympathy, and who must be dealt with on Missionary principles and plans. . . .

Our ministry must be more and more animated by its primitive spirit and be conducted upon its primitive principles. So far as the claims of existing congregations allow, it must be aggressive everywhere. We are 'not to be satisfied till every town, village, and hamlet, in our respective neighbourhoods,' and we may add, every destitute locality in our large towns, 'shall be blessed, so far as we can possibly accomplish it, with the means of grace and salvation.' Every minister among us 'should consider himself as called to be in enterprise, zeal, and diligence, a *Home Missionary*, and to *enlarge* and extend, as well as *keep*, the Circuit to which he may be appointed.' – (*Minutes of Conference*, 1820.)

Far more extensive arrangements to pervade the masses with our preaching and teaching must be made before we shall have done our share in the great work of evangelizing the nation. It will be in vain that we have contributed to send the Gospel to heathens abroad – in vain that we have assisted to send the Bible to distant nations – if we have neglected our perishing brethren in this land, for whom Christ died, who are within our reach, to whom we can at once bring the Gospel, and to whom we are bound, as God may enable us, to make the offer of everlasting life.

The Class Meeting in Decline

Editorial from the *Methodist Recorder*, November 10, 1865

The communication of the Rev. James Bayley refers to a subject which must always be regarded as important by Methodists of every name and persuasion ... Our remark that 'the English method of reckoning members is much more strict and searching than the American' was not intended to convey the insinuation that the Methodist Episcopal Church neglects to inquire with sufficient strictness into the spiritual state of persons admitted to membership. We believe the reverse of this to be the case ... What we endeavoured to point out in the article in question was simply this, that the relative numerical strength of British and American Methodism cannot be fairly estimated merely from a comparison of the number of members in Society as published by the two Churches. In England, as a general rule, continued attendance at Class is necessary to continual membership; in America it is not necessary. In our English congregations, there are no doubt tens of thousands of serious and excellent persons, who would be delighted to have their names enrolled as Church members according to the plan described by Mr. Bayley. Where is there a congregation of any magnitude in which numbers of persons may not be found, who, if they were called together, addressed by the Minister, and forthwith enrolled as members, with the understanding that their continued and regular attendance at Class would be optional, would at once and gladly give in their names to be added to the Church-roll? We see no reason to doubt that the membership of the Wesleyan Body in England might soon be increased by scores of thousands, if its discipline were conformed on this point to the American model. Whether this would be an improvement is altogether another question. Mr. Bayley has pointed out that what is suitable for one place is not always suitable for another; and while we unfeignedly admire the wonderful skill with which American Methodism has adapted adapted itself to the varied conditions and requirements of the inhabitants of the United States, he will agree with us in maintaining that similar plans might not necessarily be productive of similar results in England ...

Letter to the Editor, *Methodist Recorder*, November 24, 1865

Dear Sir,

Your last week's issue raised the subject of the Methodist Class Meeting in a way which induces me to trouble you with a few remarks . . . My object is not to enter into the question which seems to have prompted both letter and article, viz., the relative value of the numerical statistics furnished on either side of the Atlantic, but to call more particular attention to the fact, not now for the first time made apparent, that a wide difference exists between the places assigned in British and American Methodism to the Class Meeting as a part of Church organisation. This difference will be found not to arise from any dispute as to its value as a means of spiritual edification to the Church. On that point there are probably no two opinions. But the difference is, nevertheless, highly important, being one of constitutional principle, which may be simply stated thus:— British Methodism insists upon meeting in Class as the condition of Church membership; American Methodism does not. In the one case, the Class Meeting is the corner-stone, the basis upon which the entire superstructure is raised; in the other, it is adopted as an accessory of strength and security to the building reared to some extent independently of it. Or, to vary the figure, the British Methodist must go through the Class Meeting as the only door to the sheep-fold; while the American has access by a gate which, with all deference to your opinion of it, does not appear to my mind to be any less strait, though in an easier level. Now this question of principle as affecting Church Membership is, in the present position of British Methodism, one that demands with increasing urgency the most serious consideration of all who have the best interests of Methodism at heart. It is no less than the question whether the fault of non-membership with the Church rests upon many thousands who, Christian and Methodist too in every respect except that of being registered in a Class-book, are yet outside the pale, or whether the Church itself, by interposing a supra-Scriptural bar, is not chargeable with the solemn responsibility of hindering many men's salvation. It is because no arguments I have yet met with have been sufficient to justify to my mind our practice in this country – old-established as it is – on grounds either of expediency or of Scripture, and because I believe that Methodism would gain both in spirituality and in power, were meeting in Class allowed to become voluntary instead of compulsory, that I am inclined to think our American brethren are ahead of us in this matter, and that we might take a leaf out of their book with advantage to ourselves. Methodism should surely be as capable of adapting herself to circumstances in this country as in the United States. In its embryo state, as a Society of individuals within the Church, Methodism might with propriety insist upon its own terms.

Exclusion from the 'Society' was not then exclusion from the Church. But seeing that the 'Society' has expanded into a 'Church', it becomes a fair question whether the 'Society' foundation is broad enough to meet all the requirements of the more comprehensive 'Church' edifice. In the light of the New Testament, your present correspondent is humbly inclined to think not, and remains,

Your obedient servant,

Liverpool, Nov. 15 LIBERAL

Rev. Luke H. Wiseman[1] to the Rev. J. H. Norton, November 30, 1865

(Ms at Emory University)

I am exceedingly obliged by your kind & friendly letter. The question of class meeting is one of the most difficult with which we have to deal: but I am not aware that the *Recorder*, in its articles, has ever taken the wrong side. The *British Standard* quoted one of its articles on class meeting lately as a proof how vigorously it could be defended. Your local paper, if it quoted from the letter of 'Liberal' last week, ought not to have treated it as an expression of the opinion of the *Recorder* itself; and a reply to that letter will be forthcoming this week.

Personally, I would be very slow to drop a name, rich or poor, for non-attendance merely, if their conduct continues right, and if they keep up their contributions. I fear we are too hasty, both in receiving & in dropping members, so that membership loses some of its significance & value. The discussion of the question, sooner or later, is inevitable, chiefly perhaps owing to the opinions held and pretty freely expressed by not a few of our own brethren on the subject. In the *Recorder* we have acted on the plan of allowing the matter to be ventilated (which cannot be done without both sides having a voice), taking care that the preponderance is on the right side. Your suggestion however should not be lost sight of, that it is better *not* to discuss the question at all, but only to enforce our old practice, but I fear that if this were done, the controversy would reappear in another & perhaps a less pleasant form.

[1] Wiseman was the author of *Thoughts on Class Meetings and their Improvement*, 1854.

Dr Pusey's appeal to the Wesleyan Conference rejected

REJECTED ADDRESSES.

Doctor Pusey. " AND, MY DEAR YOUNG LADY, IF I COULD INDUCE YOU AND YOUR FRIENDS TO LOOK KINDLY UPON MY PROPOSAL——"

Miss Methodist. " BUT YOU CAN'T, SIR. I DON'T WANT TO GO TO CHURCH AT ALL; AND IF I DID, I 'M SURE I WOULDN'T GO WITH YOU."

[" Dr. Pusey appeals for sympathy to the Wesleyan Conference. His sincerity and earnestness encountered a harsh rebuff."—*Times.*

Pusey's bid to enlist Wesleyan and Nonconformist support in opposing a Parliamentary move to end the Anglican monopoly in the universities was scathingly dismissed by *The Times* (August 15 and 17, 1868) as a discreditable *Volte-face*. It revealed clearly enough the extent to which the Establishment had been driven onto the defensive since the middle of the century. The response of the Wesleyan Conference to Pusey's overtures was entirely predictable.

Matthew Arnold on Methodism and its Founder

(*St. Paul and Protestantism*, 1870, pp. 15–19, 123–4)

The other great division of English Puritanism is formed by the Methodists. Wesleyan Methodism is, as is well known, not Calvinist, but Arminian. The *Methodist Magazine* was called by Wesley the *Arminian Magazine*, and kept that title all through its life. Arminianism is an attempt made with the best intentions, and with much truth of practical sense, but not in a very profound philosophical spirit, to escape from what perplexes and shocks in Calvinism . . .

In truth, Calvinism is both theologically more coherent, and also shows a deeper sense of reality than Arminianism, which, in the practical man's fashion, is apt to scrape the surface of things only . . .

Arminian Methodism, however, puts aside the Calvinistic doctrine of predestination. The foremost place, which in the Calvinist scheme belongs to the doctrine of predestination, belongs in the Methodist scheme to the doctrine of justification by faith. More and more prominently does modern Methodism elevate this as its essential doctrine; and the era in their founder's life which Methodists select to celebrate is the era of his conversion to it. It is the doctrine of Anselm, adopted and developed by Luther, set forth in the Confession of Augsburg, and current all through the popular theology of our day.

It is true that from the same reason which prevents, as we have said, those who know their Bible and nothing else from really knowing even their Bible, Methodists, who for the most part know nothing but Wesley, do not really know even Wesley. It is true that what really characterises this most interesting and most attractive man, is not his doctrine of justification by faith, or any other of his set doctrines, but is entirely what we may call his *genius for godliness*. Mr. Alexander Knox, in his remarks on his friend's life and character, insists much on an entry in Wesley's Journal in 1767, where he seems impatient at the endless harping on the tenet of justification, and where he asks 'if it is not high time to return to the plain word: "He that feareth God and worketh righteousness is accepted with him." ' Mr. Knox is right in thinking that the feeling which made Wesley ask this is what gave him his vital worth and character as a man; but it is not what gives him his character as the teacher of Methodism. Methodism rejects Mr. Knox's version of its founder, and insists on making the article of justification the very corner-stone of the Wesleyan edifice.

And the truth undoubtedly is, that not by his assertion of what man brings, but by his assertion of what God gives, by his doctrines of conversion, instantaneous justification and sanctification, assurance and sinless perfection, does Wesley live and operate in Methodism.

This is the teaching of Wesley which has made the great Methodist half of English Puritanism what it is, and not his hesitations and recoils at the dangers of his own teaching.

No doubt, as the seriousness of Calvinism, its perpetual conversance with deep matters and with the Bible, have given force and fervency to Calvinist Puritans, so the loveliness of Wesley's piety, and what I have called his genius for godliness, have sweetened and made amiable numberless lives of Methodist Puritans. But as a religious teacher, Wesley is to be judged by his doctrine; and his doctrine, like the Calvinistic scheme, rests with all its weight on the assertion of certain minutely described proceedings on God's part, independent of us, our experience, and our will; and leads its recipients to look, in religion, not so much for an arduous progress on their own part, and the exercise of their activity, as for strokes of magic, and what may be called a sensational character . . .

Both Calvinism and Methodism appeal, therefore, to the Bible, and, above all, to St. Paul, for the history they propound of the relations between God and man; but Calvinism relies most, in enforcing it, on man's fears, Methodism on man's hopes. Calvinism insists on man's being under a curse; it then works the sense of sin, misery, and terror in him, and appeals pre-eminently to the desire to flee from the wrath to come. Methodism, too, insists on his being under a curse; but it works most the sense of hope in him, the craving for happiness, and appeals pre-eminently to the desire for eternal bliss . . .

The Wesleyans, who used always to refuse to call themselves Dissenters, whose best men still shrink from the name, the Wesleyans, a wing of the Church, founded for Godliness, the Wesleyans more and more, with their very growth as a separate denomination, feel the secular ambition of being great as a denomination, of being effaced by nobody, of giving contentment to this self-importance, of indulging this ordinary self; and I should not wonder if within twenty years they were keen political Dissenters.

('A Word about America', 1882)

I have a sincere admiration for Wesley, and a sincere esteem for the Wesleyan Methodist body in this country; I have seen much of it, and for many of its members my esteem is not only sincere but also affectionate. I know how one's religious connections and religious attachments are determined by the circumstances of one's birth and bringing up; and probably, if I had been born and brought up among the Wesleyans, I should never have left their body. But certainly I should have wished my children to leave it; because to live with one's mind, in regard to a matter of absorbing importance as Wesleyans believe religion to be, to live with one's mind, as to a matter of this sort, fixed constantly upon a mind of the third order, such as was Mr. Wesley's, seems to me extremely trying and injurious for the minds of men in general.

Higher Education, 1871

By the 1870s nonconformist access to Oxford and Cambridge was opening up new cultural and academic vistas and prompting misgivings about the consequences.

'Methodism and the University of Oxford' by Benjamin Alfred Gregory, Scholar of Brasenose College

(*City Road Magazine*, November 1871, pp. 496–9)

The condition and prospects of Methodism in the place of its birth may well demand the attention of all the spiritual children of the Wesleys. Apart from the present loss we suffer from neglect, and the future gain we may make with care, the associations of Oxford should alone secure a watchful interest. Yet is it not true that the bulk of our people look upon Oxford with distrust? It is only of late that the Methodist public has shown any lively consciousness of the claims of the Universities. Still with little aid and little sympathy, there have grown up Methodist undergraduates in Oxford, and there is a reasonable hope of Methodist Fellows. A Society-class of members of the University assembles regularly in term-time within a few hundred yards of the meeting-place of the Godly Club. A beginning has been made. There is a nucleus to work upon.

We only ask help and countenance in our endeavours to hold to the religion of our fathers against so great odds. When the present writer entered Oxford there was one attendant at the Circuit Chapel from the University, and not one member of Society. Now there are nine or ten names on the Class-book, and about fifteen present with tolerable regularity at the public worship. Besides, there are a few Methodists by descent who, there is reason to think, would under more favourable circumstances have identified themselves with us. There are, of course, others who no longer call themselves by our name. Most of these, however, are to be reckoned as lost to us through influences that acted upon them before they entered Oxford. Roughly estimated there are some thirty undergraduates who are, or might be, more or less within the spiritual charge of Methodism. And, if we may judge by the last few years, the number is rapidly growing, while the removal of legal obstacles to the ordinary academic career cannot but increase it. We are indeed few compared to the large fields of labour offered in crowded populations. But when it is recollected that these few are mostly men who have proved their strength in arduous competition, and may hope to render future service in some proportion to their educational advantages, it may, perhaps, appear worthwhile to accord them special attention.

In Cambridge the number of Methodists is somewhat larger. But of that it is not for us to speak. The fact that so many young men do, amid all the discouragements and distractions of Oxford, retain their attachment to Methodism and their personal religion is, surely, of itself a sufficient answer to those who look upon such faithfulness as impossible. We have not yet, it is true, given the Connexion any ministers or influential laymen trained in Oxford. We have not had time. None of us has passed through the University since there has been special provision made for Methodist students. Meanwhile let the objectors remember they have no right to blame Oxford for losses they took no trouble to prevent. Young Methodists have been left to stand alone where church influences are the strongest. Were they alone to blame if they yielded to such formidable odds? . . .

It is obvious that such a study [reading for Greats] cannot be pursued without exciting thought on most of the permanent problems of human life and history. Familiarity with the many-changing course of opinion is likely to lead to a somewhat searching examination of the grounds of one's own beliefs. It need not, however, bring about habitual scepticism in all matters of religion and morals. Its natural product is not the 'sceptical' but the 'historical' spirit. It generates a habit of mind extremely careful not to interpret a past thinker or system apart from the circumstances of the time. It makes a man – perhaps sometimes morbidly – afraid of mixing his own subjectivity with his views of truth. It should lead not to the abandonment of all belief but to a firm resolve to be able to give a good reason for what one professes to hold. Oxford teaches no system. It provides that those it trains shall not hastily adopt a side in ignorance of rival claims. With scarcely an exception those who have experienced this training pronounce it invaluable.

The position of a young man during the two years of this study is naturally somewhat critical. The dangers are different from, perhaps greater than, those of other society and pursuits. They are very much increased when, as at present, counteracting influences are weak. There is a want, if we can but supply it, of a clear, manly theology like that of Methodism, free from the strength-less Calvinism, the unthinking High Churchmanship, and the indefinite Liberalism which now represent Christianity in Oxford. . . .

The universities need also a proper representation of cultivated and thoughtful Methodism. There are fatal objections to any scheme, such as have been proposed, for gathering Methodists in Oxford into a separate College or boarding-house. The expense would be enormous; the staff almost impossible to provide; the permission of the authorities unobtainable; the success of the scheme in itself dubious and not to be desired. The Oxford Circuit is very poor and the Society small. We consider that we have a claim upon the Connexion for such assistance as may be necessary for strengthening Methodism in its historic home, especially as the benefit will accrue much more to the Connexion than to local interests.

Opportunities to be taken

The Conference of 1871 authorised the setting up of a committee to consider the Church's response to the new opportunities for nonconformist undergraduates. Among the proposals put forward were secondary schools and student hostels at both Oxford and Cambridge, scholarship funds and opportunies for theological students to study at the universities.

(Ms of Joseph Ryder, printed in Derek Baker, *Partnership in Excellence* (1975), pp. 69–73)

Recommendations

1. As to the Schools:

(1) The University towns present advantages in respect of teachers such as no other places can offer. Men who have taken high places in the Triposes and hope in the course of a year or two to obtain fellowships, wish to obtain employment in the interval as tutors, especially men of limited means. The great Public Schools, such as Rugby, Harrow, Eton, Marlborough, Westminster etc., secure such men, and by this means maintain their high position; and the youths from those schools having been trained by men fresh from the Universities secure an advantage in the Examinations for Scholarships etc. The number of such men is considerable, and they would much prefer to remain in the University, and could be obtained as Masters or Lecturers in the proposed schools at less than in Schools at a distance from the Universities.

(2) It is common for youths intending to enter the Universities to go to Oxford and Cambridge after leaving school to read with private tutors so that they may successfully compete for scholarships etc. The scholars at the proposed schools would have the advantage of doing so at an earlier age than those at a distance, by which means they might matriculate and graduate at an earlier period.

(3) It will also be an advantage to the boys at the proposed schools that they will have continually before them in the Universities the highest

standards of Education and the great honours and emoluments which may be obtained by learning, which will naturally supply incentives to diligence and effort.

2. As to the Hostels:

(1) Financial. One half of the undergraduates in Cambridge University lodge in private houses licensed by the Authorities of the University. The average cost of lodgings without board is £30 for the University year. It is believed that board and lodgings could be provided in the proposed Hostels at less cost, the expenses being reduced by the Students taking their meals together with the Governors.

(2) Moral and Religious. Parents frequently hesitate to send their sons to the Universities fearing that their moral and religious principles should suffer harm; and not without cause.

The danger arises chiefly from the undergraduates being associated on the same staircases and in the same courts in the Colleges, or in the same lodging houses with men of idle and dissolute habits; and being left without any direct moral and religious supervision. At the University of Cambridge in 1858, statutes were confirmed providing for the establishment and regulation of Hostels for the reception of Students who should be matriculated and admitted to all the privileges of the University without being of necessity entered as members of any College. In 1868 and 1869 both the Universities passed statutes in accordance with which students may be admitted members of the University without being members of any College or Hostel, such students residing with their parents or in lodgings duly licensed. The proposed Hostel would afford a home to which parents might with confidence send their sons; assured that they would be placed under proper moral and religious supervision.

In the case of youths going to Oxford and Cambridge to read with private tutors preparatory to entering the Universities it is extremely difficult to find lodgings of such a character as parents would allow their sons at about 17 years of age to occupy; inasmuch as all the more respectable lodgings are occupied by the members of the University under the necessary licence which provides that no other lodgers shall be received without a special permission from the Authorities of the University. The proposed Hostel would offer accommodation for youths of this class as have been educated at home and wish to prepare for the Universities.

It has long been a complaint that the sons of Methodists in passing through the Universities become alienated from the Church of their fathers. This it must be confessed has been the rule, to which however there are a few honourable exceptions. In the altered circumstances of the Universities it is the duty of the Methodist Connexion to take steps to remedy this evil.

To this end it is important that the sons of Methodists should be under Methodist influence and oversight.

The establishment of such a Hostel as is proposed would supply these. The youths would have all the privileges of a Methodist home, would be required to attend the Methodist Chapels; and would be under the Pastoral oversight of the Governors of the Institutions.

The proposed Institutions would enable a youth to continue in the same establishment from his admission to the schools, say at the age of ten, until he graduated in the University.

An Anglican Verdict

(G. H. Curteis, *Dissent in relation to the Church of England* (Bampton Lectures, 1871), pp. 344–6, 385–6)

Had John Wesley been appointed a bishop in the middle of the eighteenth century (a thing quite impossible to conceive then, – though, thank God, quite possible now), who can say how different might have been the fortunes of the English Church, and of her American and colonial daughters, through all succeeding times! . . .

It is indeed with the greatest possible reluctance, that any Churchman can bring himself to speak of the Wesleyan body as if its secession were complete. Even yet, it is believed, there are many thousands (and those among the best of 'the people called Methodists') who refuse to lift up their hand against the Church of England, or to be borne away by that rushing stream of Puritan hostility which is bent on doing her a mischief. Even yet, secession can hardly be said to be accomplished, – when so many Wesleyans habitually avail themselves of the ministrations of the Church; when so many cordially welcome the visits of her clergy; and when, amid all confusions and party-cries, there are still so many indications abroad that the Methodist societies have never forgotten, and will never be able to forget, their venerable founder's almost dying words: 'I live and die a member of the Church of England; and none who regard my judgment or advice will ever separate from it.'. . .

And surely we, who remain loyal members of the Church of England, ought – in two ways especially – to derive instruction from the deeply interesting spectacle afforded us by the past history, and the present condition, of Wesleyanism.

(1) We should learn the *negative* lesson: viz. *to guard against the danger of 'drifting' into disunion*, and against the sin of pushing our ecclesiastical dissensions to the sad extremity of mutual alienation and of actual Dissent. . . .

(2) But still more earnestly, if possible, should we Churchmen arouse ourselves to learn the all-important *positive* and practical lesson, that Wesleyanism – by its wonderful successes – ought to teach us. And that lesson is, above all things (in the words of my text), to ' *condescend to men of low estate.*' In Dr. Johnson's judgment – who lived in the midst of the great Methodist movement, – the whole secret of its success was, that the preachers 'expressed themselves in a plain and familiar manner, which is the only way to do good to the common people; and which clergymen of genius and learning ought to do from a principle of duty.' We know it was something more than that. But still, one clear lesson of Methodism is here pointed out to us. *The lower classes cannot be drawn to religion, by dry and cold addresses to their reason,* which in them is only half cultivated. We must not, therefore, be afraid of appealing to their emotions. We must not shrink from touching their enthusiasm. We must not allow *refinement* to stand between us and our Master's work. But we must venture to incur some risks, and even approach – while we diligently guard against – the evils of fanaticism. Nor again, can persons of this class – nor perhaps of any class – be *kept* in the ways of religion, without some sort of Methodism: i.e. without some skilfully devised plans for religious association and mutual help.

A Primitive Methodist Farm-Hand

(George Edwards, *From Crow-scaring to Westminster: an Autobiography* (1922), pp. 29–36)

Born in 1850 at Marsham, Norfolk, the son of a farm-worker, Edwards grew up in desperate poverty. Resentful of the exploitation of his class, he played an active role in the early days of the agricultural workers' union and in 1920 became a Labour M.P.

... I attended a little Primitive Methodist chapel one Sunday evening, when a very earnest lay-preacher, by name Samuel Harrison, was preaching ... I became what we used to call in those days 'saved', but which I term now the spiritual forces coming into contact with the forces of evil, which up till then were completely controlling my life, and which, had I not been brought under the influence of the Eternal Spirit at this particular time, might have altered the whole course of my life.

I at once embraced the simple faith of Christ as the Great Saviour of man, although in a rather different light then to what I do now. I still love my Church, and remain a loyal supporter of that great section of the Methodist Church, namely the Primitive Methodists, which has during the last hundred years done so much for the uplifting of the toiling masses of England, and brought light and comfort into thousands of homes. . . .

The September Quarterly Meeting of 1872, of the Aylsham Primitive Methodist Circuit decided that my name should appear on the preachers' plan as an 'Exhorter', and I was planned to take my first service on the third Sunday in October of that year.

Up to this time I could not read. I merely knew my letters, but I set myself to work. My dear wife came to my rescue and undertook to teach me to read. For the purposes of this first service she helped me to commit three hymns to memory and also the first chapter of the Gospel according to St. John. . . .

My first three were good old Primitive Methodist hymns. The opening verse of the first hymn I learned was:

> Hark, the Gospel news is sounding,
>   Christ has suffered on the tree,
> Streams of mercy are abounding,
>   Grace for all is rich and free,
>   Now, poor sinner,
> Look to Him who died for thee.

The second hymn was:

> There is a fountain filled with blood
>   Drawn from Immanuel's veins,
> And sinners, plunged beneath that flood,
>   Lose all their guilty stains.

The third hymn was:

> Stop, poor sinner, stop and think
>   Before you further go.
> Will you sport upon the brink
>   Of everlasting woe?
> On the verge of ruin stop,
>   Now the friendly warning take,
> Stay your footsteps or you'll drop
>   Into the burning lake.

The last hymn does not appear in the present-day Primitive Methodist hymnal.[1] Needless to say, I have long ceased to use the hymn. It was too horrible for my humanitarian spirit. I might say that at my first service I was not quite sure that I held the book the right way up, as I was not quite certain of the figures. I had, however, committed the hymns to memory correctly, and also the lesson, and I made no mistakes. In those days we used to give out the hymns two lines at a time, as very few people could read, and they could possibly remember the two lines. There was no musical instrument in many of the small village chapels at that time . . .

By the time the next plan came out I could just manage to read my lessons and hymns, but not until I had gone through them many times with my wife and had mistakes rectified . . .

The different Primitive Methodist services of my early days would be out of date now, and the quaint sayings of those days, though effective then, would cause some amount of amusement to our young educated folk of today. One form of service was called a 'love-feast', at which small pieces of bread were taken round with water. The meeting was thrown open for anyone to speak, and then the simple, faithful, uneducated, saintly people, in relating what to them was Christian experience, would express themselves in peculiar phrases. I call to mind the statement made by a brother at one meeting who said he felt 'like a fool at a fair'. At the same meeting another said he thanked God that although that was the first time he had attempted to speak, he was getting used to it. Others would relate what dreadful characters they had been and what religion had done for them.

Although my preaching efforts did not give me entire satisfaction, still I can look back with pleasure at some of the results of my labours . . . I can recall instances of ten or twelve of my hearers at my Sunday services making a stand for righteousness. Many of them in after years became stalwarts for truth.

They also soon began to be dissatisfied with the conditions under which they worked and lived. Seeing no hope of any improvement they migrated to the North of England, and found work in the coalfields, and never returned to their native county. When in Newcastle last December I met several of my old converts and friends.

With my study of theology, I soon began to realise that the social conditions of the people were not as God intended they should be. The gross injustices meted out to my parents and the terrible sufferings I had undergone in my boyhood burned themselves into my soul like a hot iron. Many a time did I vow I would do something to better the condition of my class.

[1] The hymnal known to Edwards in his early years would be the one edited by John Flesher in 1854. This was replaced by a new book in 1886, to which a supplement was added in 1912. The first of the quoted hymns survived as no. 262 in the 1886 book. William Cowper's 'There is a fountain filled with blood' was, of course, by no means confined to Primitive Methodism.

Village Methodism

(Frederick J. Jobson, *A Plea for the Support and Spread of Methodism in the Villages*, 1873, pp. 4–8)

It must . . . be evident to those who are observant of the altered and advancing state of the population in the rural parts of the kingdom, that what served, and, to a certain extent satisfied Methodists, during past years, is wholly insufficient for doing so at the present time. Not only is education, both by Day and Sunday-schools, raising the minds and habits of the people in the country, as well as in the towns, so as to produce increased desire for more immediate ministerial instruction and pastoral oversight; but the proselyting activities of other religious communities, whose influence for Christ and for Protestantism is more than doubtful, demand that for continuance of what God has given to Methodism, closer and more watchful ministerial attention should be secured for its work in the villages. It is not now, as it was in former times, that villages are largely supplied in public services of the Establishment by clergymen resident in towns and cities, who, after ministering in Churches or Cathedrals in the morning, would ride forth to adjacent villages to 'do duty' there in the afternoon, and then return home, leaving them without any provision for further services in the evening. Clergymen of the Church of England have, in later years, been properly deprived of pluralities of livings to a considerable extent, and, for the most part, they now reside among their own parishioners, and are with them continuously, to instruct and to watch over them.

This just and praiseworthy change would be satisfactory and encouraging, if the shepherd among his sheep could, in all cases, be trusted; and, if it were so, none would rejoice in it more than Wesleyan-Methodists. If the country people were adequately and safely provided with religious teaching and oversight by any other church, Wesleyan-Methodists would be content to leave them to such, and would direct its aggressive efforts where more needed. But, while rejoicing in the presence and services of good and faithful evangelical clergymen among their parishioners, wherever they are found, yet it is a lamentable fact, openly acknowledged by Episcopal dignitaries of the Anglican Church, that many of its clergy are unfaithful to their vows, betraying their trust for Protestantism, corrupting the people under their influence by superstitious and idolatrous performances, and are preparing them for rank Popery. Witness, the increasing number of such clergymen who pass yearly over as perverts to the Church of Rome; – the four hundred and eighty-three signatures to the petition recently presented from clergymen of the Church of England to the Archbishops and Bishops for formal restoration of auricular confession; – the pleas made for licence to use freely the 'Catholic element', as it is termed, of what remains from Popish times in the 'Book of Common Prayer'; – the actual doings of many of the clergy in the villages, in dressing up churches on feast and fast days after the Romish fashion, – the setting up of crosses, embroidering them on priestly garments, on covers of book-boards, and of the communion-table; – the lighted candles in day-time; – the elevation of the host, and bowing before it; – the mumbling over words not distinctly audible; – the 'Holy Communion' apart from the people, as well as professed priestly absolution after secret confession to man!

These errors, superstitions, and idolatrous practices, more or less found in different parts of the country, and which, through imposing shows and captivating music, are made acceptable where fifty or even twenty years ago they would not have been tolerated, cannot do otherwise than convince true Protestants that Great Britain must not be left for religious teaching and training to the Church of England. More especially is this conviction confirmed by the consideration of the pitiable helplessness of the Episcopacy to restrain and correct such erring, rebellious, and defiant under-shepherds of the people. Wesleyan-Methodism, which, whatever it may be besides, is soundly Protestant at the core, and, throughout its whole system, cannot listlessly resign the country to such destructive frauds and falsehoods practised under the guise of religion; but must rise in its united strength to provide better and safer instruction for the people.

And, it is also to be observed, that more than a few members of the Church of England in the country, as well as in towns and cities, despairing of deliverance from Romish teaching and performances in their parish churches, are looking round for more congenial places of worship. Methodism is nearest akin, both in doctrine and discipline, to the Church in which they have been brought up, and like themselves, has no antipathy to the Establishment, if faithful to its professed principles and trusts. But, for such, more regular and efficient ministry and pastorate must be provided, if they and their families are to attach themselves to it. And, while scorning mere proselytism, or coaxing of members from other churches, yet, with the want of sounder and safer instruction than the Church of England supplies, – which want is widening more and more as time progresses, – it is not only patriotic, but a solemn Christian duty to provide for it as far as practicable, and that before the habit of absence from public worship shall be formed by repelled and scattered members of that Church.

For this, there must be, not only increased care bestowed upon the preparation of Local-preachers and Exhorters for their important services, but there must also be considerable increase in the number of Circuit-Ministers. With such increase of Ministers, much might be done, by judicious arrangements, for more Ministers of town-circuits to reside in and among the villages belonging to them. In many instances, doubtless, Ministers now resident in towns and cities, might live in country places; and while taking their turn for Sabbath services in the towns and cities wherein their colleagues reside, yet should have special charge for Week-night Services, and for more immediate pastoral oversight of the people in the villages; being mostly freed from ministerial responsibility towards Societies and Schools in the towns . . .

But, what is most needed in the present day, both for the villages themselves, and for the relief of towns not unfrequently hampered by the claims of numerous country places attached to them, is the organization of VILLAGE-CIRCUITS, specifically such. Circuits to be formed by the grouping of villages and hamlets together in their respective localities, to which Ministers should be appointed, whose position and maintenance should be such as to give them equal status with their brethren in towns. A Clergyman of the Established Church is not lowered in rank by appointment to a country parish, if the 'living' is a good one; and if Methodist Ministers were duly provided for in country stations, the old tradition in Methodism of a Minister 'going down' when removed to a country Circuit, would soon pass away. Indeed, to many a Minister of superior ability and attainments, overtaxed by heavy drains upon his mental resources from successive appointments to large exciting towns, such a residence in the country, where he could pursue his studies for a season, uninterrupted by public turmoil, and where he could compass the ground allotted to him, could not fail to be attractive, – provided that he had there secured to himself and his family adequate support.

The advantages of this to the country-places would be great. They would have Ministers immediately and confessedly in charge of them, who would not only preach and administer the Sacraments in them more frequently, but who would live personally among Methodist families and households for pastoral instruction and oversight. As many Circuits are now constituted, it is unreasonable to expect that the Ministers of such should pay attention to the villages equal to their necessities. A Minister resident in a town, finds, in most instances, that he cannot meet the requirements of the large and increasing population around him. Labour as he will, and that by system and plan, he cannot do all that is needful to be done; and the neglect of the many in the towns seems more to be deprecated than the neglect of the smaller number in the country. So he lingers with his overwhelming charge in the town, and hastens off at the last hour into the country; and then, after public service there, hastens back as soon as possible.

Lay Representation at Conference

(*Report of the Proceedings of a Special Committee on Lay Representation . . . June 6th, 7th and 8th, 1876, at the Centenary Hall, London,* 1876, pp. 13–18, 52–3, 58–60, 106–8)

The admission of laymen to the Wesleyan Conference in 1878 was a significant landmark and laid to rest a contentious issue. Early in the meeting of the special committee the tone was set by the veteran Irish figure, William Arthur, who quoted the dying Jabez Bunting as saying, 'My policy has been misunderstood. My real policy was to secure the just rights of the people, or the proper representation of the people, and many of the old preachers thought I went too far.'

Rev. William Arthur:

From the day that I read Mr. Bunting's pamphlet[1] my great anxiety has been that the question should not be treated as one either of orders or of interests, but as one of scriptural principles and godly regulations. With preachers, my effort has been to get it settled speedily if possible, and quietly as might be; always saying, what I firmly believed, that the more generously the better for them, and for the work of God. With laymen, my effort has been to stave off urgency and prevent excitement, and to assure them of the kind and generous feeling that seemed to animate every one in any reference I ever heard to the question. I am bound now to say – and I do it in my present circumstances with solemnity, as a witness – that I have not heard anything from preachers behind the backs of laymen that all the laymen in the world might not fitly hear; and that I have not heard anything from laymen behind the backs of preachers that was not worthy to be said before the face of us all . . .

Within the last twelvemonth, however, judging from what I have read in my retirement, I have feared that some preachers were putting forward the interests of our order, and some laymen were provoked to reply by asserting the claims of theirs. Yet both preachers and laymen feel that, far beyond any interests of any class, our one common interest is 'the Church of God, which He hath purchased with His own blood,' and both preachers and laymen are so just at heart, so reasonable, so full of love one to another – ay, love much greater than we sometimes think – that I doubt not that our blessed Master will lead us to common accord.

Discussion I have never feared; but ever since 1849 my deep dread – my soul's horror – has been agitation, and that alienation of large portions of the people from the Conference and the preachers which first gave the agitation its foothold, and then its deadly power. And very strange it is how alienation and attachment may meet in the same person and struggle together. Ever since that time it has proved that discussion has been the best means of dissipating the ignorance and misunderstanding out of which alienation arises. But, in those times, preachers came to sore trials. My own health, already frail, was then so broken as never to recover. What the experience of others was I cannot say. I will record one point in my own – that more alienation was produced by unguarded assertions of Conference prerogative, and what the people called priestly power, than by the attacks of disaffected laymen or disaffected preachers. In those dark days it seemed to me that the holiest connexional service which could be done by layman or preacher was to draw Conference and people so close together that similar misunderstanding should be impossible, and similar estrangement difficult. Many of both laymen and preachers evidently learned the same lesson, and have remembered it ever since; and, surely, with blessed results. The waste places have been built up. The people have a sense of strength, and capability of expansion. The ministers are respected and provided for very differently from what they were. The public ear – which had to a great extent been closed against us by the belief that we were priestly, exclusive, despotic, and fifty things of that sort – has to no small extent been re-opened, so that our access to those whom we seek to convince and convert is growing. Best of all, God is with us . . .

The last Conference resolved in favour of some plan for 'some direct and adequate representation of the laity in the business of the Conference.' I take it that any attempt made by ministers to go back from that resolution would be one of the gravest mistakes ever made since we were a Connexion. It seems to me that it might lead to results not only blighting to the Church we all love, but, if human interests are to be named at all, seriously hurtful to the interests – not merely to the occasional gratification, but to the solid interests – of the preachers, whether viewed as ministers of God or as men with human ties and cares. The Committee appointed to devise a plan for giving effect to the above resolution has recommended the formation of a mixed body. That is what every District-meeting, during part of its sittings, and what every administrative Conference Committee but one, is. This mixed body is simply a growth of the constitution, and will like branches of constitutions which do grow, prove strong . . .

The more I reflect, the more does it seem to me as if we were pointed to the experience and to the model of the District-meeting – pointed to them by the old plan of letting the constitution advance step by step upon lines already proved. If we put our imagination under the guidance of hope, we may fancy that they would bring in some wonderful improvements. If we put it under the guidance of fear, we may picture them as doing terrible things. If we put it under the guidance of experience, we shall fancy them as doing much as they do in the District-meetings, the Missionary Committee, and other places in which they and we know, and help, and love one another . . .

Mr. Ensor[2]:

I come from the rural parts of Methodism; and I may say that in the Bath District there exists at this time a feeling that the laity should have more power in our Connexion. Those who hold this opinion are not men who are likely to be moved by mere vulgar clamour, but men who are wholly devoted to Methodism, and who take the deepest interest in spiritual work. I am not aware that as yet there is any demand of this kind coming from the masses of our people; but as we all know, the masses do not move quickly. A preceding speaker, whom I very much respect, asked us to state our reasons for desiring this change. With all due deference to that venerable gentleman, I would say that, to my mind, the case is patent. I cannot see any sound argument which can be derived either from Scripture or reason, or from the practice of other Churches, why the laity of Methodism should be excluded from the government of the Church in matters not strictly appertaining to the pastoral office. In matters of business there is room for the presence of business men, and the presence of such men would be of great assistance to the Conference in the management of the various Connexional funds. I believe, further, that the presence of laymen in the Conference would give our people more confidence in the governing body of the Church. I remember the dark days of agitation in 1849. My opinion is, that if laymen had been admitted into Conference the parties who took the lead in that agitation would have had no power . . .

This question is now being argued in a calm, deliberate, friendly, brotherly, and prayerful spirit, and at a time when the whole Connexion is united in the bonds of love. Surely this is the time, therefore, for this question to be settled. Settled it will be, sooner or later. That is certain. The time is coming when laymen will be admitted into Conference, either in response to the modest request put forward at the present time, or as the result of passionate agitation. There may be – and certainly there are – difficulties in this matter; but, if the principle be conceded, these difficulties may be overcome. Let it not be forgotten that what the laity ask is – not the appearance of power, but a share in the real power, and on a basis similar to that of the District-meeting. I am not very wishful to see laymen in the Conference in large numbers. If we could secure the presence of one hundred, or one hundred and twenty representative men, that would meet my own idea of 'adequate representation'. There are not two distinct interests to be represented. We are all united in a common love to the Church of our choice, and I can't see what difficulty there is in the way of our working harmoniously together. Laymen co-operate with ministers in all the other work of the Church – why should we stop short at the Conference? I firmly believe that if laymen be admitted into the Conference according to the plan already indicated, there will be in the future more glorious times of prosperity in Methodism than there have been in the past . . .

[1] One or other of the two pamphlets written by Thomas Percival Bunting: *Laymen in Conference ?* (1871) or his more recent *Lay-representation; the present state of the question* (1876).
[2] Charles Ensor of Milborne Port, Somerset.

Rev. Edward J. Robinson:

As in the District Committees, so in the Conference, it may be declared what matters there are within the province of laymen conjointly with ministers. We just extend the lines. We do not destroy any of the lines of our constitution. I hope that nothing will be said to-day about any attempts being made by some of us to New-Connexionalise the old body. The Kilhamites say that the Deed of Declaration was not the work of John Wesley, except that when he was a very old man he yielded to the counsels of others. We believe, Sir, that it was the deliberate work of John Wesley, when he was a very wise man and most dutiful to Providence; and, so long as we have that Deed Poll as our safeguard, it is utterly impossible for us to degenerate into New-Connexionalism. I once asked a New-Connexion minister how the ministers of his denomination, when cases of ministerial character were under consideration, liked being examined and tried by laymen in conjunction with ministers. He answered, 'Oh! the laymen are our most considerate and tender friends!' intimating that they were more willing to pass over a transgression. Now, Sir, I for one want nothing of that kind. I wish that we should adhere faithfully to the severity which has always characterised the examination of ministerial character . . .

Let us, therefore, think of the young laity in Methodism. What is asked for in this resolution is, the admission into Conference of direct and adequate representation of the laymen. We do not want any representatives of another separate assembly to come climbing up to the window outside the Conference Chapel, and to be informing us of their decisions through some broken pane of glass. We wish to have them alongside of us, and as nearly as possible on equal terms. If the laymen were in Conference we should get rid of an anomaly which in the present arrangements of Methodism exists. There are gentlemen here who belong to the House of Commons, gentlemen who belong to Town Councils, gentlemen who belong to School Boards, and so on, and the Committees that they form are constituted from among themselves; but it has been the custom of the Methodist Conference, consisting only of ministers, to appoint committees including laymen. When we get laymen into Conference the mode of appointing committees will then correspond with that adopted in other bodies. I spoke of the forbearance of the Hundred. Let me now speak of the forbearance of the laity. I wonder at them. The agitating spirit certainly is not in them, or they would have taken a course different from the one they have pursued; but now, when there is the new light that these legal opinions throw upon the minds of the laity, can we think that they will be so extremely forbearing in the future? Surely they must now insist upon their rights.

Rev. Alexander M'Aulay[3]:

I have looked at the word of God, at the history of Methodism, and at the Minutes of Conference, and I see that history repeats itself. There was a time in the history of the Methodist Conference when its financial business was very small indeed. As that financial business increased, the ministers very wisely, and in an ever-increasing degree, introduced the men of business whom God had given to them as children in the Gospel, and they incorporated them with themselves in certain offices and courts, for the more efficient working of that system which God, in His great mercy, had sent them to extend. I see the same thing in the New Testament, and I am always thrown upon that when any accusation is brought against me . . .

I am told that my chief business is to save souls. Now, Sir, what is the real point and pith of the change which it is now proposed to make? Is it not this – that we will put laymen more and more over this secular business, whilst we, as ministers, give ourselves more and more to the Word of God and prayer? If I understand my ordination vow, it is not so much to look after finances as to win souls; and it is because I feel the pressure of that vow that I am anxious for Mr. Robinson's resolution to pass. How much of my time and strength during the last fifteen years of my life has been given to the work of collecting subscriptions, &c. – work which would have been much better performed by Christian laymen? When I look at my ordination vows, I feel that I can stand before the great Head of the Church and say that my compact with men and my obedience to Him are both better performed by handing over these affairs to the laity of the Church. I may say, further, that I think the whole ministry and the whole Connexion will be benefited by the proposed change. The ministry want relief from these financial burdens. . . .

I hope that as little will be done as possible to diminish the number of ministers attending Conference. Every man who goes to Conference is a better Methodist preacher when he leaves it. One reason why I want to see the incorporation of laymen with the Conference is, that they may catch its loving and united spirit. Don't look upon us in any other light than as men, who are prepared to sacrifice everything for the furtherance of the Gospel. I don't wish, and I never expect, to be engaged in anything like making constitutions. From the beginning I have tried, as God has helped me, to win souls. I have preached in the streets, and given my best hours to mission work. My heart is in that. My impression is, that that work will be extended by the carrying out of the resolution which is now before us.

[3] Pioneer missioner in the East End of London; elected President of the Conference in 1876.

Thomas Jackson of Whitechapel

(H. B. Kendall, *History of the Primitive Methodist Church* [1905], II, 507–8)

Jackson's name is inseparably linked with the founding of the Whitechapel Mission. Here he describes his first days in the East End of London, following his acceptance for the Primitive Methodist ministry in 1876.

My instructions were to open a new mission at Walthamstow and superintend, *pro tem.*, the Bethnal Green Mission, which at that time was without a minister. The enterprise of Rev. R. S. Blair had secured at a nominal rent for three years a disused Independent Chapel (with sitting accommodation for 600 persons) in Marsh Street (now High Street), Walthamstow, and services had been held in it for nine months by the Poplar Circuit and good work done in the open air. But the conditions were unfavourable to progress, and Mr. Blair, with the circuit's approval, offered the chapel to the General Missionary Committee. The two small mission-rooms that comprised the Bethnal Green station – West Street and Squirries Street – were in squalid neighbourhoods. One was a rented room, and in an unfit condition for services; the other was Connexional property and seated sixty persons. It had cost £250, and had that amount of debt upon it. The former was given up at once, and the other subsequently sold to the London City Mission.

I entered upon my new duties on October 13th. The first Sunday I preached in London I preached at West Street in the morning and had three persons as congregation. In the evening I preached at Squirries Street when, during the earlier portion of the service, I had only the chapel-keeper as my congregation. In the afternoon I visited the notorious Mile End Waste, and was shocked by the profanity and Sabbath desecration that I witnessed. I took my stand amidst the hubbub and alone commenced to sing a hymn, and then exhorted the unsaved to turn from their sins and serve God. The experience of that first Sunday greatly distressed me; but it so profoundly stirred my soul that I resolved with the help of God, I would devote myself unreservedly to the work of serving and saving the poor in the East End. A mission in notorious, defiled and squalid Whitechapel from that day was the goal of my missionary ambition; but for twenty years the way did not open. It did come at last with the acquisition of the Working Lads' Institute.

The second Sunday in London was spent at Walthamstow, where my congregation numbered three persons in the morning and five in the evening. For a time my wife and I had to act as chapel-keepers. I resolved to devote my attention to the poorest districts, and systematically visited from room to room and house to house. The sights of suffering and privation I met with powerfully affected me. My rule was to pray with every person or family I visited whenever possible. But to pray with starving persons and not do something to relieve their suffering I felt to be impossible. As we had no funds, and my salary was only one pound per week, my wife and I resolved to consecrate to our mission-work the few hundred pounds we had saved and the proceeds of the sale of our Sheffield house and furniture. On Lord Mayor's Day, November 9th, 1876, we held our first gathering of destitute men and women from the slums. A meat-tea was provided, followed by an evangelistic service. During the subsequent winter months when distress was acute, fifty families were provided with a breakfast each Sunday morning in our schoolroom, the proceedings being closed with a short gospel address and prayer. The late Marquis Townshend, hearing of my efforts for the destitute poor of Bethnal Green and Walthamstow, sent me several liberal donations. The idea of appealing to the public for funds to carry on this benevolent ministry did not occur to me until all our private means had been expended and we had experienced considerable domestic impoverishment. The effect of this personal contact with the poor in their homes and of the manifestation of interest in their struggles, was to induce many to attend the services, and scores were converted. Being pitchforked into the superintendency, the arduous duties of a new station, the demands of probationary studies, the erection of two new school chapels during probation, and details associated with the social ministries to the needy, rendered the demands upon health and strength at times very exacting.

Independent Methodism

(A. Mounfield, *A Short History of Independent Methodism* (1905), p. 60)

The following outline of the principles of Independent Methodism was adopted by the Annual Meeting of the denomination in 1880.

I.   Doctrines, those commonly expressed by the term Evangelical.

II.   Worship and services, those usual among Methodist Societies.

III. Every Church self-governed, managing its own financial and other internal affairs.
IV. Equality of Christian brotherhood, all members sharing in the government of the Church.
V. Ministry open and free, in contradistinction to an exclusive Ministry in which public teaching is confined to a Clerical or Ministerial Order. Every Christian is called by God to actively labour in His cause, and none can discharge his responsibility by proxy.
VI. We recognise no Clerical Titles or Designations.
VII. Our Ministry is purely voluntary and unpaid.
VIII. We have an Evangelistic Agency, brethren being appointed to go from place to place, preaching the Gospel, visiting weak and planting new Churches; and whilst so engaged they may be maintained, Evangelists having 'liberty to live of the Gospel'.
IX. Groups of Churches in adjacent neighbourhoods are associated in Districts, for ministerial and other mutual advantages.

Worldly Pastimes

(*Minutes*, 1881, pp. 318–19)

We wholly fail to understand 'the liberty wherewith Christ hath made us free', if we suffer ourselves to become 'entangled again with the yoke of bondage', in endless discussion as to the more or less harmlessness of this or that thing. It is not thus that we are to show forth 'the victory that overcometh the world'. The only way, alike of safety and freedom, lies far above the distraction of these petty disputings. A life made strong and satisfied with the fulness of the love of God, and consecrated, with joyous devotion, to His service, passes on its way unhindered by the world's fashion and pleasure, and will not stop to argue about that which it neither needs nor desires.

On this ground only can we deal successfully with the young people of our families, our schools, and our congregations. We both commit a grievous blunder and put our Lord to shame, when we try to attract these to His religion by making concessions to their worldly tastes. Such an attempt must defeat itself: for those, whom we would thus seek to lure, are keen to discover the meaning of the bait held out to them, and the practical insincerity of the faith which thus acknowledges that it hopes to succeed by false pretences. How often is the question anxiously discussed: How shall we attach our young people to us? The answer is one, and plain, and sure: Get them converted. You can never conciliate the carnal mind. It is as great a folly as a fault to try. Your own observation will bear out our assertion, that when our youth are saved through faith in Christ they very rarely leave us.

We are the more disposed to lay affectionate stress upon this point, inasmuch as we have heard with great sorrow, that, in some places, our chapel and school-premises, set apart as they are for the worship and service of God, have been unlawfully abused by the holding therein of entertainments, which were not only utterly devoid of religious tendency, but seemed to enter into undisguised competition with the music-hall and the theatre. Brethren, we call upon you everywhere to stand by us in an uncompromising opposition to this mistaken and dangerous policy. Even if any success were to be gained thereby, it is too dearly bought to be worth having. And, in truth, such gain is unreal, and must, in the end, bring damage and loss to the Church which seeks it. Here, again, the cure is to be found in the spread of fervent piety, and active devotion to the work of the Lord. Where these are, the evil will not only be escaped, but made impossible.

Chess and draughts at Croft Street School [Preston]

(*Information for the Wesleyan Conference*, 1882, pp. 2–4)

Allow me to put before your readers as briefly as possible the history of the reading-room and recreation-room at Croft Street.

The members of the young men's class, not satisfied with the bleak and bare room in which they were accustomed to meet from Sunday to Sunday, determined on improving the same at their own cost; they also considered that, if the trustees would grant them the use of the room on week-nights for reading and innocent games, such a course would tend to unite the elder scholars more firmly to the school and would give greater facilities for becoming more intimately associated with each other than could possibly be the case in a class consisting of 160 scholars meeting only on the Sabbath.

Consequently application was made to the trustees, and permission was generously conceded by them. The room has been beautifully painted and decorated, the floor covered with kamptulicon, the seats upholstered, the walls tastefully hung with pictures, the reading-room supplied with daily papers, periodicals, chess, and draughts, at a cost of over £100, for which sum the scholars of the first male class are responsible, and which, with the spirit that now animates them, they will shortly repay . . .

Preston, Oct. 25th, 1881

Mr. F——, in your last issue, contends that Wesleyan trust property can be legally used for playing chess and draughts during six days of every week. In the case to which he refers the youths who attend the Bible-class on Sunday have the privilege of using the same premises during the week as a kind of club-room for chess and draughts, perusing the leading daily and other papers, periodicals, lectures etc. Are the girls in Preston to have the same privileges as the boys? If not, why not?

I know a Congregational church where the young men were allowed to play games during the week on the school premises; and they quietly laid bets; and I saw the public-house to which they retired to drink them afterwards. Of course, when this was discovered the use of the school was forbidden. But did they stop their games? Bets are as likely to be made as raffles are to take place in bazaars opened with prayer.

Mr. F—— argues – if I understand him – that the prosperity of the school proves the utility of *using the premises regularly* for playing chess and draughts. If so, surely all branches of Methodists, and all Episcopalians, Presbyterians, Baptists, and Congregationalists should also open their school-rooms everywhere, without delay, for chess and draughts, etc., *throughout the week*. Why should any colliery village or foreign mission station not have the same privileges as the Bible-class of the largest Wesleyan Sunday-school at Preston? Should that have a monopoly?

When the gaming becomes *universally* associated with Bible classes and Sunday-schools, will the world call the organisations 'Christianity in earnest', or 'Christianity in fun'? If the Bible and chess and draughts are to be joined in spreading Scriptural holiness among our young men, I cannot see why the Bible and billiards and bagatelle should not be leagued together in Sunday-school organisations for the same purpose.

. . . Games and politics, if introduced on Wesleyan trust property – the newspapers are already introduced – would transform the school-room into something very like a Liberal club. In Methodism, Whig, Tory, and Radical have hitherto been happily united; but 'New Methodism' is to be a political and amusement Church. Rather let Methodism perish at once, and its past glorious history alone remain.

Chess and draughts are unnecessary, unfitting, untimely, and will be injurious, if tolerated during six days of the week on Wesleyan trust property. The whole religious arrangements there are designed to 'warn men to flee from the wrath to come': but let these games be placed in the midst of them and wounded consciences may fly to them to forget strong strivings of the Spirit and to divert attention during 'seasons of refreshing' and thus they may destroy many souls at the great crisis of being. The craving for games and amusements is at present inordinate, and needs rather to be repressed than encouraged in the sanctuary. I see many proofs that the proverb is true, spiritually and temporarily, 'He that loveth pleasure shall be a poor man.'

Dr. Morley Punshon, Orator Extraordinary

(Thomas Hayes, *Recollections of Sixty-three Years of Methodist Life*, 1902, pp. 210–13)

Punshon was an outstanding performer in the heyday of the Victorian public lecture; but there were less patent aspects to his career.

The scene was Exeter Hall, filled with a congregation to the full, on the tiptoe of expectation, for Mr. Punshon was about to lecture before the Young Men's Christian Association on 'John Bunyan'. I was there with a fellow-clerk. Perfect silence reigned when the orator commenced, so that not a word might be lost. His lectures were always more largely attended than any others. As the oratory rolled forth, what varied emotions followed! We sat with bated breath, and now and then looked at each other with wonderment. But when the peroration came, such a bursting forth of cheers I never witnessed. That utterance, in my judgment, was one of the great orations of the world. I want the Rev. T. M Cullagh's descriptive powers to show forth the splendour of his intimate friend's lecture. If I had paid a guinea for admission it would have been money well spent, for the memory of that lecture and its associations abide with me still. It was not the only lecture I heard Dr. Punshon give, but that in my judgment was his grandest.

In course of time Dr. Punshon came to the Mission House as Missionary Secretary, and afterwards was appointed Deputy Treasurer. It was my privilege to act under him in receiving and banking the Society's receipts. Now and then he took me home to tea and to spend an evening among his autographs, of which he had a choice collection, the taste for which he occasionally indulged in amidst such a busy life as rarely falls to the lot of man.

[Following Punshon's early death in 1881]

I sent the following to the *Methodist Recorder*, and I am sure I shall be excused for its insertion here:—

To the Editor of the *Methodist Recorder*

Dear Sir,

I cannot forbear, while the memory of our beloved senior Secretary is still fresh upon us, and when the tears shed by us for him are still undried, to add this expression of the love and esteem which myself and fellow-clerks at this House cherish for the memory of the late Dr.

Punshon. Not only did we respect him for his brilliant powers as a public speaker, of which some of us were witnesses in his early days, but we also respected him for his stern integrity, deep insight, and devotion to the cause of our Missions – a cause which was ingrained in his very being. His duties were not mere perfunctory ones, for he made himself thoroughly informed of every detail of his treasurership. Not a cheque would he sign without well knowing the reason for its being drawn. His acquaintance with his work was *thorough*. All this won respect from us. The inadequacy of the Society's income to meet its expenditure was a source of deep anxiety to him. If the morning's post brought but a small sum to the Society's funds his concern was visible, but a good day's remittance was a source of real joy to him, and, when occasionally a handsome donation came to hand, the formal acknowledgment was invariably accompanied by words from his pen of special thankfulness. It was a painful task to him to have to borrow so often from our bankers large sums of money, to meet the incessant demands made upon us as bills became due. He made the Mission cause his own, and how deeply he was devoted to his work is well known. His was a large diocese, embracing correspondence with the officials of the Australian and Canadian Conferences, together with France, Germany, Italy, and Spain. Some of the European stations he occasionally visited.

A Cornish Revival in 1882

(Ms account of his ministry by the Rev. W. H. Lockley of the Methodist New Connexion; original in the hands of Mr. E. A. Rose)

Known in his own district of Barrow-in-Furness as 'the Boy Preacher', Lockley was accepted for the ministry later in 1882. This account was written in 1916.

... None of the people were well-to-do & the bulk of them poor. Revivals were less common in Cornwall than formerly, still they were prayed for & looked for, but only periodically, as the Cornish folk look at certain seasons for large catches of fish. The fire burned & blazed [up] & then went down into white dust. Not that the results were lost, but the work stopped, was expected to stop. I had experience of a revival in the sparsely populated district of Lady Downs, a very lonely & difficult-to-find hamlet, midway between St. Ives & Penzance. Though few people lived there, yet there was a Bible Christian as well as a M.N.C. chapel. Special services were held in Jan. & Feb. 1882 of which I conducted several. Here we had an old-fashioned revival in all its primitive character. The services went on quietly for several nights & then suddenly the people were roused as though a bomb had fallen. Moans & groans, lamentations & strong crying & tears burst on every side. The scene might almost be described as one of 'weeping & gnashing of teeth'. A young man at my left (Richard Rowe's son) fell to his knees & began to hammer the pew with his hands in a violent way; in such a violent way indeed that his hands began to bleed, & by & by his face was smeared with the blood. Then swift as a gunshot he rose & darted out of the chapel. In a few minutes he came back, fell on his knees on the sanded floor in front of the little pulpit, shrieked for mercy in a way to alarm sensitive souls. He was soon on his feet again: he had got the blessing; with haste & energy he embraced & kissed his sister (who forthwith burst into tears) & a few other females who were not his sisters. I meekly kept out of his way, not fearing the kisses of his mouth so much as the length of his arm, & the weight of his feet. I had never seen anything like this before, & nothing so realistic has appeared since.

Joyful News

(First issue of *Joyful News*, Thursday, February 22, 1883)

The publication of Thomas Champness's evangelical paper led eventually to the founding of Cliff College.

FIRST WORDS
We begin our task in the spirit of thankfulness. This enterprise comes to the front in a time of peace and increase, and it is our work, as it will be our joy, to tell of the kindling and spreading of the holy flame of Revival. Why should there not be a spiritual awakening all over the country? and why should not the Methodist people be the widest awake of all? The years that are past can tell enough of hours wasted in sleep or idleness, while the plough has been left in the unfinished furrow, and the precious grain, which might have been 'seed for the sower and bread for the eater', has been devoured by the fowls of the air. Thank God, there are already the signs of a glorious season. The fields, if not in every place 'white unto harvest', are green with promise for the reaper, whose sickle, it may be, has well nigh rusted on the nail for want of the brave and industrious hand to wield it. 'He that soweth and he that reapeth' shall 'rejoice together'. It is so, even now, in part, and we confidently look for an abundant harvest of souls to be ingathered to the Lord's garner. It is with the hope of encouraging all kinds of 'labourers for the

harvest', and of fostering revival ideas, that we have taken our place among the religious agencies of the day. Will not our readers pray that we may have the desire of our hearts, in spreading the intelligence of a general outpouring of the Holy Spirit? It will be our delight to chronicle both works and results, at home and abroad, and in every way that lies in our power to push the frontier line of our King's territory further and still further, till He comes Himself to take possession of the kingdom promised to Him by the Father.

As we wish to set out contributors an example of brevity it only remains for us to say, in the words of Boaz, 'The Lord be with you'; and we shall be glad if the toilers in the Lord's field reply, 'The Lord bless thee.'

HINTS FOR THOSE WHO WRITE FOR THIS PAPER
1. Be Interesting.
2. Never use two words when one will do.
3. Do not exaggerate.
4. Write on one side of the paper only.
5. If you are not an educated person, do not worry about grammar, or spelling; we will make it all right.
6. Sign your name, and send it to
   Rev. Thomas Champness, 80 Bradford Street, Bolton.

WHAT WE WANT
News of recent revival
Stories of remarkable conversions
Answers to prayer
Illustrations of providence

WHAT WE DO NOT WANT
Politics
Controversy
Connexional Finance.

HOW TO BE CHARITABLE, AND AT THE SAME TIME HELP THE CIRCULATION OF 'JOYFUL NEWS'.
Buy sixpence worth of this number[1], and give them to a hungry boy to sell. He will earn his bread, and put good reading into the hands of some who would not have seen our paper.

---

[1] The paper sold at a halfpenny.

Methodist Catholicity

Hannah E. Pipe to Miss Huggins; July 4, 1883

(Anna M. Stoddart, *Life and Letters of Hannah E. Pipe*, 1908, pp. 308–11)

Born in Manchester of Methodist stock and educated at a Quaker school, Hannah Pipe established a fashionable girls' school in Clapham. She represents a new cultural and ecclesiastical mutation in Wesleyanism.

I am a Wesleyan not on conviction, but by birth, and I feel pretty sure that if I had been born *anywhere* within the precincts of the Christian Church, there I should have remained, – in Congregationalism, Quakerism, Anglicanism, Plymouth Brotherism, Romanism, Greek Orthodoxy, – as contentedly as in Methodism. They all seem to me noble in their way. I am proud of my Methodism, but then I think I should have been proud of any other *ism*, though of course for different reasons. What is best in each I hope I should have found, and on it cast anchor. The thing I dislike is *d*issent (not *D*issent). I dislike the dissenting temper. I don't mean that I dislike Dissent from the Anglican or any other Established Church, though no man made on my pattern would ever do the work of a Luther or a Wesley, – but I dislike the disposition which cannot find rest in its appointed surroundings and go in heartily for what lies nearest. I love Methodism, because one has room to breathe in it: it is the largest of all the Protestant Churches. I love it because better than any other religious organisation it has known how to deal with the poor. I love and honour it because it is believed by many to have saved us from a French Revolution. I love it, because if you hear of any one particularly good and energetic in the Church of England, or anywhere else, you usually find that his mother or his grandmother held the unfeigned faith of a good Methodist. I love it and believe and rejoice in it, because it has recovered many brutes into the human form divine, and is going on with such recovery. I love it for the good work done and doing in the world by the sons of Methodist preachers. The Senior and Second Wranglers this summer are both Methodist preachers' sons. Plain living and high thinking are still to be found in such houses. I love it for its hymns and liturgy, and its good and great men, – its Dr Pope, and Mr Piggott, and Mr Davison, and Richard Green, and Watson, – for Dr Osborn, who taught me the true doctrine of the Incarnation when I was a little girl, and made me (much against his intention) the happy heretic that I am now. I tell him so sometimes. I think I love it also a little because it is unfashionable and accidentally, poor thing! though by no means necessarily, a little vulgar. But this is a feeling which I cannot quite explain, though a person of more subtlety could. The fashions of this world are somehow so infinitely remote from the awful, majestic, and radiant Simplicities of the Faith, that one is almost jealous of fashion when it allies itself to the Faith. But this is foolish, for the Holy Catholic Faith has no more to do really with the vulgarity of the poor than with the puerilities of the imperfectly cultivated. To look for a perfect Church in the present condition of society seems to me an amazing sort of hopefulness. I for my part am ready to kneel down beside any human creature that repents of his sins, and feels his need of heaven-sent bread and wine to sustain and cheer him on the journey to our Father's final Home. The things in which we who believe in Christ are one, dwarf into immeasurable insignificance the trifles in which, if we think of them at all, we differ, or might differ. I seldom dream. But a few nights ago I had one dream, short, simple, and vivid – darkness and nothingness before it and after. We were standing in a dimly lighted church to recite the shortest of the creeds. I could not see the whole congregation; but at one point, not content with bowing at the name of Christ, my whole school of girls without an exception went down on their knees, leaving me alone standing, and delighted at their decision, unanimity, and fervour. It was not at the name of Jesus in the usual place that this happened, but nearer the end. It might be at 'Jesus Christ risen from the dead,' or at 'I believe in the Holy Ghost.' It was on the eve of Whitsunday that I saw this vision. Ah! to have it realised! This is what I thirst and long for. Methodist? Quaker? let them be what they please. Or rather let them be what their parents were, or their husbands shall be. The only Church that I *in the full and high sense of the word believe in,* is the Holy Catholic Church, which follows from belief in the Holy Ghost, and leads on to belief in the Communion of Saints. The company of the faithful who are led by the Spirit, they are the Church – and they understand one another, are in communion and fellowship with one another, as one in Spirit.

The Social Gospel

Hugh Price Hughes to William Unsworth; Oxford, March 7, 1884

(Ms at MA)

I have read your tracts[1] with great pleasure & satisfaction ... The Gospel you preach is the true Gospel, & the whole Gospel. The body, the mind & the social environment must receive more attention. I pray that you may inspire more & more of our people with your ideas and methods. Have you read Lavelaye's 'Le socialisme contemporaire'? It gives a wonderfully complete & exact account of all the phases of modern socialism. That is the coming question, & our great need is to ally all that is true & good in Socialism with Christianity. Many of the skilled artizans are to be reached first, not by individualistic, but by socialistic Christianity. What a use Bradlaugh makes of his sympathy with the social needs of the toiling masses. How difficult it is to shake off the influences of conventional, aristocratic Christianity & to become as democratic as Christ was. Moody's success shows how ready the masses still are to respond to divine truth and human sympathy. Trustees & pew rents are a great hindrance to the evangelization of the poor. Mrs Grundy must be put down.

¹ E.g. *The Brotherhood of Man: its Laws and Lessons*, 1872; *The Aggressive Character of Christianity*, 1878.

Hugh Price Hughes on *Social Christianity*

(Op. cit., 1889; 4th edition, 1890, pp. viii, xll–xiii, 21–2)

In our reaction from mediaeval ecclesiasticism we have gone too far. We have practically neglected the fact that Christ came to save the Nation as well as the Individual, and that it is an essential feature of His mission to reconstruct human society on a basis of Justice and Love. It has been well said that 'the power of love as the basis of a State has not yet been tried.' But Christ rose from the dead to try it, and to do it . . .

The following sermons are a brief and fragmentary attempt to show that the social failure of Christianity is not the fault of Christianity or of Christ, but of us Christians who have been selfishly individualistic. Bushnell's felicitous epigram is indeed true: 'The soul of all improvement is the improvement of the soul.' But that is the beginning, not the end of our work. We must not be 'so busy saving souls that we have no time to save men and women'. We must not forget that 'all authority' is given to our Lord Jesus Christ 'on earth' as well as 'in heaven'; and that our work will never be completed until the prayer which He Himself taught us is fulfilled, and the will of God is done *on earth* as angels do it in heaven.

Already there are many hopeful signs. Canon Westcott is not alone in realizing that 'we are suffering on all sides from a tyrannical individualism.' Many have already come round to Charles Kingsley's 'belief that not self-interest but self-sacrifice is the only law upon which human society can be grounded with any hope of prosperity and permanence.' One of the best and most useful events of this new year is the proposal just made by Lord Nelson, first in *Church Bells* and then in the *Contemporary Review*, that all Christians, however widely they may differ on theological and ecclesiastical topics, should co-operate in the promotion of Social Christianity. It is impossible to exaggerate the importance and blessedness of this proposal. We Christians, when we unite our forces, are simply irresistible. Let us, then, in the name of God and humanity, combine heartily to abolish Slavery, Drunkenness, Lust, Gambling, Ignorance, Pauperism, Mammonism, and War. After that is done, we shall not have much difficulty in settling all our theological and ecclesiastical differences; and the glory of God, which is the happiness of men, will fill the whole earth.

I have long been persuaded that the reason why the masses of the people have to so great an extent failed to realize that their best friend is Jesus Christ, is the fact that we ministers of religion have taken the very course which my excellent correspondent urged upon me last Monday. We have dealt too exclusively with the individual aspect of the Christian faith. We have constantly acted as if Christianity had nothing to do with business, with pleasure, and with politics; as if it were simply a question of private life and of prayer-meetings. It is because the spirit of Christ has not been introduced into public life that Europe is in a perilous condition to-day. I have often thought how distressing it was that so great and illustrious a man, and so devout a believer in God, as Mazzini should have deliberately rejected the Christian religion on this ground: That he believed Christianity taught men to be selfish; that it taught them to be so absorbed in their own individual salvation, and to be so wrapped up in thoughts of the future that they neglected their duty on earth. Now, I absolutely deny that this is the case. I protest that it is contradicted by history. I contend that everything that is best in Mazzini himself is due to Christ. We have been so accustomed to breathe a Christian atmosphere that very few of us have any conception of the intolerable condition of the human race when Jesus Christ came. But so gifted a man as Mazzini would never have made such a terrible mistake unless we Christians had neglected to declare that the teaching of Christ was applicable to every phase of life.

The London Mission

(*Minutes*, 1885)

The Conference approves the following Scheme:—

I. The Movement shall be called 'The London Wesleyan-Methodist Mission.'

II. Object of the Mission:—

To carry the Gospel to such regions of London, and especially of Central London, as are most spiritually destitute and degraded . . .

IV. Scope of the Mission:—

(A) Missions not worked by Circuits.

1. In order to facilitate the work of the Mission, and prevent friction, certain districts, the spiritual needs of which cannot be provided for by the Circuits to which they belong, shall be detached from such Circuits, and constituted special ground for Home-Mission work, the boundaries of such Mission districts being carefully defined. In cases where all parties are agreed, the Committee shall have power to complete the necessary negotiations. In cases where all parties are not agreed, the course of procedure shall be in accordance with our established Rules.

2. Prosperous Suburban Circuits shall be invited to take under their care any such detached district or portion of a district as may be agreed upon with the Committee.

3. The Committee shall have power, with the consent of all parties interested, and on terms to be agreed upon, to take over Chapels or Mission Halls not efficiently worked by existing agencies. The boundaries of the districts assigned to such Chapels or Mission Halls shall be carefully defined, and due regard had to any legal questions that might arise. In all cases, the Committee shall decide, subject to the proviso contained in (A) 3, whether such transfers come within the sphere of their special work.

4. The Committee shall have power to rent, purchase or build Mission-premises in the detached Mission districts, care being taken to secure properly drawn agreements, and in the case of purchase or building, the due settlement of the estate. In building Mission-premises, the Committee hope to receive assistance from the Metropolitan Chapel Building Fund, under its amended rules.

5. Wherever the Committee may think it desirable, they shall have power to provide, in connection with any Chapels or Mission Halls, additional premises to be used for the social and philanthropic work of the Mission.

6. The Committee shall have power to maintain, in whole or in part, suitable Ministerial and Lay agents for Mission work in these districts.

7. The Committee shall have power to negotiate for the restoration to Circuits, or incorporation with adjacent Circuits, of any detached Mission districts in which Societies have been formed, and which can be efficiently worked by such Circuits.

(B) Missions in 'the most spiritually destitute parts of London', worked by the Circuits in which they are situate.

1. The Committee may assist by means of annual grants, or otherwise, any Missions (in such parts of London) which with such help may be

efficiently worked by the Circuits to which they belong. In each case a Quarterly Report shall be presented to the Committee.

2. The Committee may also assist in the hire or erection of Mission-premises in such Circuits.

3. It is not proposed, at present at least, to lay down any specific regulations under which such assistance shall be granted, as, in almost all the cases contemplated, the degree of poverty in the neighbourhood will be the main fact to be considered.

(c) Existing Chapels.

Inasmuch as several existing Chapels, situate in the midst of 'the most spiritually destitute parts of London,' have small and diminishing congregations, and fail under the ordinary methods to attract the multitudes living around them, the Committee may assist the Trustees of any such Chapels as shall be thrown open for Mission Services, by undertaking some portion of the expense incident to such Services.

(D) Missions outside 'the most spiritually destitute parts of London.'

1. The Committee shall have power, from such portions of the annual income of the Fund as are not otherwise specifically appropriated, to make Grants towards the support of Lay Agents employed in Mission work within the City and Metropolitan Police Area.

2. The Committee may also aid in the extension of Mission work by voluntary agencies under Circuit control.

Salvationist Greetings

William and Catherine Booth to 'the Wesleyan Methodist Ministers assembled in the Metropolitan Monthly Meeting'

(Undated ms, c . 1885, in MA)

Mrs. Booth was stricken with cancer in 1884. Writing on his wife's behalf to their 'dear comrades and friends', William Booth thanks them for their expression of sympathy.

During these weary months her thoughts have frequently reverted to the days of her youth when she listened to Wesleyan ministers, was a member of a Wesleyan Class, and loved and served the interests of the Wesleyan Church with all the ardour of her nature.

She has never forgotten how much blessing she received in those early days from the lives and writings of some of the holy men and women connected with your Denomination.

She wishes now to express her gratitude for it all, and it is no little comfort to her to be told that in the opinion of so large an assembly of Ministers she has accomplished a work for God in which the Church of her early days is able to rejoice . . .

She earnestly implores you to beware, both of the 'Antinomian fiend' so powerful amongst the Evangelical forces of today which deludes men into a false peace without either real repentance, living faith, or practical godliness, and of the 'Latitudinarian fiend' now so popular, which would encourage and help the world to seek good anywhere and everywhere rather than in the 'Sinner's only Friend', and which would attempt to make up for the loss of a simple faith in the Bleeding Sacrifice of Calvary by profuse attention to the external needs of the miserable and oppressed.

The West London Mission

The launching of the new mission represented a shift in the direction of 'secularisation' about which George Osborn, as one of the older generation of Wesleyanism, had misgivings.

Hugh Price Hughes to George Osborn

(Mss at MA)

October 14, 1887

I have hesitated to ask you to take part in the opening services of the West Central Mission on Friday next, the 21st inst, because you said in the London Conference that you did not trust me as the principal agent of such an enterprise. I feared therefore that you would not feel free to identify yourself in any way with the movement.

Still, there is nothing that would give me more gratification than to secure your presence. Satan's seal is on the West End, & it will be supremely blessed, if we can present a united front, when we attack his strongholds. The President will be with us, & every prominent minister in London, except yourself, will either be with us, or send a letter of sympathy and regret for unavoidable absence.

Under these circumstances your absence would be very conspicuous, and your presence correspondingly helpful to the work of God.

It has occurred to me today that perhaps you might see your way to come to the *afternoon devotional* meeting in Wardour Hall, & give us a short address on *entire sanctification*, such as you gave at the City Road conventions. Wardour Hall is a small building, & you could be heard without exerting your voice unduly. We want to give the utmost prominence to Wesley's doctrine of scriptural holiness, & who could strike the keynote so appropriate as you?

[Osborn's reply has not survived, but is clearly reflected in Hughes's next letter.]

October 21, 1887

I have not had time to answer your letter until now, & now I am just starting to hear Mr. Spurgeon strike the keynote of our Mission. I very much regret your absence, especially as it is founded upon entire misconception.

It never entered my head to encourage a 'holiness party'. If the same men speak often about entire sanctification, it is simply because we cannot get other men to follow Wesley's example in that matter. We lose no opportunity of doing our utmost to induce everybody to preach & experience this truth.

Secondly, there will be no disparagement whatever of the sermon. We simply use music as an auxiliary, as Wesley himself did. Moreover we have no faith in anything except the blessing of God. But to win that blessing we must do all in our power in every way – but when all is done without Christ we are nothing! Methods must change in a changing age, but our motives & principles change not.

At any rate *pray* for us.

A recollection of the first service

(Katherine Price Hughes, *The Story of my Life*, 1945, pp. 72–4)

The first service[1] held at the old St. James's Hall of Victorian fame was a great event, and we looked forward to it with mingled hopes and fears. I shall always remember the suppressed excitement with which I walked down the hall with my husband on the night of October 27th, 1887, and my first anxious glance at the assembled congregation. To my joy and also to my surprise, the hall was absolutely full. I had imagined that it would take time to build up a congregation there, but no building-up was needed. From that night until November 17th, 1902, St. James's Hall was crowded, so much so that later on Prince's Hall, on the other side of Piccadilly, had to be taken for the people who could not get into St. James's. I have a vision before my eyes of that old St. James's Hall on Sunday evenings – one that will never fade away.

On the platform the band, conducted by Mr. Heath Mills, was playing music suitable for a religious service, and the balcony on the left of the hall was filled with soldiers from the Wellington Barracks close by. Their scarlet uniforms made a striking blaze of colour, and special seats were also reserved for nurses in uniform and for policemen in plain dress. H.P.H. once said that if he had not been a Methodist minister he was to have been a barrister, and his duty would then have been to win a decision for his client. Now he said his foremost duty was to win a decision for Christ. That first service proved the force of that conviction and decisions were won from many present who became firm workers in and supporters of the Mission. From that time onwards those Sunday evening services became a spiritual force in West London, attracting crowds of people, from members of the Government and aristocracy down to the unhappy outcast women who paraded Piccadilly outside.

I have received testimonies from people all over the world who were present at one or other of those services, telling me of the deep impression made upon their hearts which nothing could ever efface and of changed lives devoted to the service of Christ.

Oh, the tragedies and confessions that I heard in those days in that little room behind the orchestra where we had opportunity to talk quietly with those who sought our advice! They alone would have filled a book of poignant interest . . .

Before long our house at 8 Taviton Street became the workshop of the Mission. Our door-bell rang so constantly that I had to employ some one to answer it, for no ordinary maid could undertake the task. I never knew how many people we should have to provide for at our midday meal. At the last minute my husband would run down from his study: 'Katie, Mr. —— is here; we were in the midst of an important conversation, and I must bring him down to have a little lunch with us.' I look back now and wonder at the extraordinary variety of people who sat round our dining table; ministers of many different Churches and creeds, politicians, artists, authors, and friends of all sorts and conditions.

[1] Mrs. Hughes' recollections seem to be of the first Sunday evening service, not the inaugural service on the morning of Friday October 21st, when Spurgeon had been the guest preacher. The date she gives is, in any case, clearly in error.

Wesleyan Day Schools

Principles on which Wesleyan [Day] Schools are to be conducted

(*Annual Report* of Wesleyan Education Committee, 1887–8, pp. 10–12)

(I) RELIGIOUS INSTRUCTION AND WORSHIP
Such Schools shall be of a distinctively religious character; and, as practical means to realize this important purpose, the following elementary arrangements are deemed indispensable; viz., –

1. The BIBLE, in the Authorized Version only, shall be the basis of all the religious instruction; and a certain portion of every day, at least half-an-hour, shall be set apart for the devotional reading of the Holy Scriptures, with explanations by the Teacher, Minister, or duly appointed Visitor, or for Catechetical instruction.

2. The Authorized WESLEYAN CATECHISMS shall be used in all our Schools, subject to such provisions of the Elementary Education Act of 1870, as are commonly known collectively as 'The Conscience Clause'.

3. CHRISTIAN PSALMODY – in which the Wesleyan Hymn-Book, or other Hymn-Book, published or approved by the Wesleyan Education Committee, shall be used – shall form a part of the daily exercises.

4. The School duties of each day shall begin and end with PRAYER.

(II) GOVERNMENT

Each Day-School shall be under the immediate care and direction of a Local Committee, annually appointed, which shall include the Wesleyan Ministers of the Circuit, for the time being; the Officers of the School, such as the Treasurer, Secretaries, and Visitors; and a suitable number of the friends of education connected with our Body, either as members of our Society, or at least as worshippers in our chapels.

(III) SUPPORT

The pecuniary support of each School shall be provided for by the Local Committee, from the weekly payments of the Scholars, from Local Subscriptions and Collections, and from any other available sources.

(IV) TEACHERS

1. Every Teacher employed in the Schools, or trained for them, shall be of a decidedly religious character, and in connection with the Wesleyan-Methodist Society.

2. Every such Teacher shall be recommended by the Superintendent Minister of the Circuit in which he or she resides; and, previously to his or her actual nomination to a School by the General Committee of Education, shall have been examined and approved by them, or by persons deputed to examine on their behalf . . .

IV. – GENERAL CONNEXIONAL AID AND CO-OPERATION

THE RULES OF THE CONFERENCE ARE AS FOLLOWS:—

1. The following questions shall be considered in each May District Meeting, during that portion of the business of the District Committee when both Ministers and Laymen are present; and the answers obtained shall be recorded in the Minutes of each District, viz., –

(1) What is the number and state of the Wesleyan Sunday and Week-Day Schools in this District?

(2) Are all possible care and effort used to promote the formation and

success of Week-Day Schools in connection with our Societies in this District?

(3) Has any Wesleyan Day-School been discontinued, or transferred to other management, since the last May District Meeting; and if so, have the directions of the Conference relating thereto been observed? (*Min. Conf.*, 1874, p. 195.) . . .

4. Arrangements shall be made upon each Circuit Plan for the regular Visitation of each Day-School in the Circuit, by one or more of the Ministers of the Circuit, for religious instruction and catechizing during the time shown to be allotted for such purposes by the time-table of each school.

5. It is earnestly urged upon all the Societies to promote the formation of Week-Day Schools in connection with every principal Chapel in each Circuit, and to encourage the formation of School Libraries and Bible-classes, for the explanation, illustration, and religious application of the Scriptures, whenever practicable.

6. The Conference expresses its opinion that, in view of the working of existing arrangements for Public Elementary Education, it is highly desirable that the number of Wesleyan Day-Schools should at least be maintained. The Conference therefore strongly recommends that before any steps are taken towards the closing or transfer of any Wesleyan Day-School, the proposal to close or transfer it be communicated to the Educational Committee, in order that they may have an opportunity of suggesting alternative proposals for the consideration of Local Managers.

Church Membership and the Class Meeting

The report of a special Conference committee.

(*Minutes*, 1889, Appendix XI)

It is necessary to introduce at the outset a caution against hasty and discouraging statements concerning the present condition of Methodism as indicated by the numerical returns of membership in recent years. It is true that for two years a small decrease was reported, namely, 87 in the year 1887, and 779 in the year 1886 – a total of 866. But it is also true that in the four years previous to 1886 an increase of 32,207 was reported, and that during the two years in which the decreases above-mentioned were recorded there was an increase in the membershp in Junior Society Classes of 8,328; whilst during the last two years (1887–8 and 1888–9) the number of members 'in Society' has increased by 8,684 . . .

On the other hand, the Conference does not desire to conceal the fact that the advance indicated in recent years by our returns of membership is far from satisfactory, when viewed in relation either to the Agents and appliances now employed by Methodism, to the increase of our Chapels, Mission Halls, and Congregations, or to the growth of the population. The Conference also feels that the proportion between the number of members in our Church, and of persons who regularly attend our Ministry, demands serious consideration.

It appears, first of all, to be our duty, as ministers of the Church, humbly to recognise that we ourselves need a deeper and more religious sense of our solemn responsibility to God, whether in official work and service or in private conduct and relations. . . .

Holding this conviction, it becomes our duty to inquire whether there is anything connected with our ordinances of fellowship, and especially our Class-meeting, or with our administration of them, which at the present time calls for reform or improvement. No answer can safely or wisely be given to any inquiry on this subject without remembering the peculiar position of the Class-meeting in Methodism, and its relation to all parts of the Methodist economy.

It is not merely a gateway of entrance into membership; it is not merely a gauge by which fitness for continuing in membership with a living and spiritual Church may be tested. It is all this, but it is more. It is an opportunity systematically provided for the giving of testimony to the power and willingness of Christ to save the soul. It is an organized form of Christian Fellowship, and is at least one of the modes of that Christian Fellowship which is enjoined by the New Testament upon all believers. It is a form of fellowship also which the history of our Church has proved to be, when duly administered, of the highest efficiency and of manifold and far-reaching influence. It is pre-eminently a method for sheltering, encouraging and developing the spiritual life. It brings every member under godly oversight, and subjects him to a thorough but congenial discipline. Such a system, moulded for us by the hand of Providence, hallowed and sanctioned during a century and a half by the manifest and abundant blessing of God upon its continual use, – a system after which, or some equivalent for it, other Evangelical Churches are anxiously feeling, – we surely ought not in any way to weaken or discredit, but rather bend every energy to make it more widely and spiritually influential.

The relation of the Class-meeting to all the agencies of Methodism must not be overlooked. It is to be feared that in many cases the Class-meeting is not now what it once was, and what it might again be made. The Class-meeting, when rightly conducted, is a fountain of incalculable blessing. It is in the Class-meeting that the young convert first tests his power to speak of the things of God. In the prayers and testimonies of the Class-meeting are to be found the first training of Prayer Leaders, Mission Workers, Sunday-school Teachers, Local-Preachers, and Ministers. But for the practice of simple and fervent utterance in the Class-meeting, it is very doubtful whether such a harvest of Christian Workers as has been reaped, year by year, could ever have been grown or gathered amongst us. In the Class-meeting the finest evangelical instruments have been shaped and tempered.

Nor must the relation of the Class-meeting to every part of our Church organization be overlooked. The Leaders' Meeting, our first court of discipline, is, as its name indicates, mainly a meeting of 'Leaders of Classes,' and its jurisdiction extends as far as the Classes themselves extend. But the Leaders' Meeting represents and embodies in a peculiar way Pastoral care, because the Leaders may be described as Sub-Pastors, and are links between the members and the ministers. In a Leaders' Meeting, if it be rightly and regularly conducted, the minister is made aware of the condition of the Church; the needs of the poor, the sick, the spiritually feeble and tempted, are brought under his attention, and Pastoral oversight is thereby made in all cases easier, and in some cases possible, where it would otherwise have been impossible. . . .

The Class-meeting then is not a mere appendage to the Methodist system – not a limb which can be removed without endangering the vital organs, but is the very heart of the system, having relations most intimate and essential to all the discipline and fellowship of Methodism. The Class-meeting fellowship has been, in fact, the very tissue and substance of living Methodism, from its beginning hitherto. It has indeed been said by some that this vital and essential element of Methodism has lost its former hold upon the attachment of our people. In some parts of the country this is lamentably true. Too many persons attend the Class-meeting very irregularly. In other cases, membership is very lightly estimated, so that absence for any reason during a few weeks leads to a quiet abandonment of it. Often through carelessness, sometimes of set purpose, removal to another place becomes the occasion of ceasing to meet. Complaints of this character are by no means new in Methodism. They are indeed as old as the days of Wesley. But the evil has been aggravated by the circumstances of our modern life. Removals from place to place are much more frequent than formerly. The claims of secular business are both more numerous and more urgent than ever. Social life is more restless, and makes greater demands upon the time of our people, especially in the evening. Religious meetings are multiplied; so that the Class and the Week-night Services are no longer the only calls on the religious interest and attention of our people when the business of the day is over. Perhaps, too, an increase of self-consciousness, and the growth of a fastidious spirit arising from the influences of modern culture, may, in some cases, have fostered a distaste to speaking freely of the deepest thoughts and feelings. On the other hand, we have gratifying evidence that many of our educated people value not less than others the privilege of Class-meeting fellowship; and that even in many parts of restless and busy London, the Classes are exceedingly well attended.

It is of the greatest importance that the Leaders' Meeting should be restored to its former place of spiritual influence and power. It should be remembered that the Leaders' Meeting is not a mere instrument for collecting the contributions of the Classes, for administering poor relief, and for making certain administrative arrangements. Its purpose is to enable the ministers, with the help of the leaders, to guard and promote the spiritual well-being of the Societies. The meeting should therefore be held frequently and regularly; if possible, weekly, according to rule. The Class-books should be examined by the minister, and note taken of any members who because of affliction or poverty or spiritual declension need special attention. The Leaders themselves should be conversed with as to how they are prospering in their own souls, and how their Classes are prospering. In accordance with a regulation passed many years ago, and productive of great blessing, an entire meeting should at least once a quarter be given up to prayer and testimony, and heart-searching conversation in reference to the leaders' special work. Further, the introduction of a new leader should be made with all solemnity; our rules as to his examination being carefully observed. In a word, the Leaders' Meeting should be made the spiritual centre of the Society. If this were done, not only would the existing leaders be more efficient and useful, but the succession of competent and spiritually powerful leaders would more easily be maintained . . .

An earnest and united effort should be made to restore our ancient discipline as to the showing of tickets at those meetings which, according to our constitution, are intended for the special benefit of the members of our Church. Wherever possible, we should return to our former plan of holding Lovefeasts in the afternoon of the Lord's day, allowing no admission except by Class or Communicant's ticket, or by note from the minister. Where it is necessary to hold them after the evening service, distinct intimation should be given previously that only those persons are entitled to remain who are members of our Church, or who shall have received from the Minister a special note of admission. Then the stewards should pass from pew to pew to see the tickets, or in some other way ascertain that only qualified persons are present. This rule should also be strictly observed in reference to the Covenant service, and, so far as practicable, in reference to Society Meetings.

Further, it is most important that a united and earnest attempt should be made to secure the presence of all our members, and the showing of tickets at the Lord's Supper. As regards strangers occasionally attending our services, who desire to participate with us, they may reasonably be expected to assure the minister of their fitness by explaining to him that they are members of another Church, or for what reason, not being members of any Church, they desire to be Communicants; and such occasional cases can be met by the issue of a special note of admission by the minister. That the Table of the Lord should be open to all comers is surely a great discredit and a serious peril to any Church. . . .

It appears to be of the greatest possible importance, for the lessening of the present great loss of members, that a roll of membership shall be kept in every Society. Such a roll should be, in fact, the aggregate of the Class-books, and it should be corrected, if possible, quarter by quarter, or at least once a year. While the Superintendent must be responsible for seeing that this roll is duly kept, the actual work of correction, from quarter to quarter, might be done by one of his junior colleagues.

'The Missionary Controversy'

(*The Missionary Controversy, 1890*, pp. 82–91, 314–19)

On the basis of a brief period of service as a missionary in India, Henry Lunn wrote four articles for the *Methodist Times* in 1889, criticising the Indian missions for the failure of their educational work and the social gulf between missionaries and the native population. In this he was backed by Hugh Price Hughes, his Superintendent in the West London Mission and editor of the *Methodist Times*. The following quotations are from the official *Report* on the controversy.

The charges
Our Comparative failure in India

There is no part of the mission field where our comparative failure is more marked than in India, where we might reasonably expect our greatest triumphs. Rev. H. Little, chairman and general superintendent of the Negapatam and Trichinopoly district, forwarded to us last year the following tabular statement of the relative position of the principal Indian missionary societies in 1881, when the last census was taken:—

NAME OF SOCIETY	Foreign Mission- aries 1881	Native Mission- aries 1881	NATIVE CHRISTIANS		
			1851	1871	1881
Church Missionary Society	95	110	35,162	69,114	98,983
Gospel Propagation Society	41	57	22,621	45,083	80,812
American Baptist Mission	13	59	122	6,810	57,070
London Missionary Society	46	37	20,077	39,879	55,138
Gossner's Missionary Society	14	2	123	14,804	32,800
American Board	24	30	2,852	8,161	13,816
Leipsic Lutheran Mission	17	8	2,957	9,265	12,272
American Methodist Mission	32	17		1,835	7,054
Wesleyan Methodist Mission	38	9	440	1,011	3,591

This statement, with our society at the bottom of the list, speaks only too plainly for itself.

In the *Harvest Field* for last November, Rev. W. H. Findlay calls attention to the fact that in 1885 the Wesleyan Missionary Society, while occupying, amongst English societies that work in India the *sixth* position in age, and the *seventh* in the number of missionaries employed, was only *fifteenth* in the number of its communicants, and *sixteenth* in the number of its adherents. Rev. H. Little, in a letter to the *Methodist Recorder*, threw a very vivid light upon the state of affairs in India. He showed that out of 316 teachers employed in our mission schools in the Madras and Negatapam districts 128 *were heathen.* It was yet more impressive to read that out of 410 members of society in his own district, only 111 were gaining an *independent livelihood.* He added

> In my District we have to day six native ministers; two of them may be regarded as the fruit of our own work. We have 21 catechists, of whom one was won by us from Romanism, and the rest were all baptised outside our mission. *With one exception they have joined us for the work and pay we give them. It is 26 years since I landed in India, and every year has deepened the impression that we are on the wrong tack.*

Mr. Little and Mr. Findlay believe that the failure which they so emphatically record, is due to the fact that our work there has been fatally devoid of concentration, continuity, and thoroughness. We heartily agree with these distinguished missionaries in tracing failure to our policy and not to our agents. WE NEVER FOR A SINGLE MOMENT IMPUTED PERSONAL BLAME TO OUR MISSIONARY BRETHREN. We were well aware that Indian missionaries are always picked men; and we sincerely believed that the average Indian missionary was superior both in ability and in devotion to the average minister at home. It never occurred to us that anyone could misconstrue our criticism of policy into a personal attack, and we are still of opinion that our proved love of the missionary cause ought to have protected us from such an imputation. We have the highest confidence in the integrity and devotion of our Indian brethren; and we are, therefore, quite sure that our comparative failure in India is due not to personal shortcomings, but to mistaken policy, for which our missionaries are not responsible.

The Secret of our Failure

What is the mistake? We entirely agree with Mr. Little and Mr. Findlay that we ought to establish powerful and well-manned mission centres in India. But we think their reform does not go far enough. In addition to that, we hold that we ought to completely transform our educational policy. We believe (1) that educational agencies should be quite subordinate to the direct work of preaching the gospel; (2) that educational agents should be, as far as possible, laymen; and (3) that the advantages of education should be given mainly to our own native converts, and especially to those of them who may become catechists or ministers. No one can seriously believe that we disparage education. But we do hold that in India it has been allowed to absorb far too much of our limited resources of men and of money. Success there has been in direct proportion to the prominence which the various missionary societies have given to the evangelization of the masses. We may quote for example the following extract from a letter written to Mr. Champness by one of the most energetic of our Indian missionaries, Rev. G. Mackenzie Cobban:—

If you need any arguments for sending out men for evangelistic work, here are one or two:— Evangelistic Missions have won *thousands* of converts where we have only won *hundreds*, sometimes *tens*. We gained *six hundred* converts in *sixty years*; the Arcot Mission (Presbyterian) gained *six thousand* in *thirty* years. Among all the *five thousand* villages in our district there are not *six* efficient itinerating Evangelists belonging to all the Missionary Societies professing to work there. In the city of Madras there is *less preaching to the heathen than there was forty-five years ago. Eleven* Englishmen are at work in the Madras Christian College among 1,400 students. In my circuit are 1,400 villages, among them only one Scotchman.

In South India, the chief scene of our educational work, we spend £13,582 a year, and report 2,038 members. The Church Missionary Society spends in the same region £3,000 a year more than we, and reports 67,533 members. The Propagation Society spends £600 a year less than we, and reports 46,466 members and 12,617 catechumens. Whatever allowance we may make for the greater severity of our church membership test, it will not bridge over the immense chasm between 2,038 and 46,466 . . .

The Missionary Style of Living

The special prominence which we desire to give to the direct evangelization of the masses of the Indian peoples, raises the question of the style of living which Committees at home should encourage missionary evangelists to adopt. If we could have foreseen the way in which this subordinate issue would excite personal feeling and divert attention from the main point, we would have said nothing about it until the main point was settled. But we were influenced partly by a desire to present a complete programme, and yet more by a desire to protect Indian missionaries from an extreme policy which was being vehemently advocated in influential quarters at the beginning of last year. Distinguished men both in Church and State were loudly contending for the ascetic method which members of the Salvation Army and some High Anglican celibates had adopted. We believe that the maintenance of a Christian Home is essential to the healthy evangelization of India. Therefore we strongly opposed the ascetic extreme, whilst paying our tribute to the saintly disinterestedness which prompted it. Seeing how apt the public, when disaffected, are to run to extremes, we feared they might be led to favour the ascetic method. We therefore proposed a 'Via Media,' believing that it was our duty to bring our missionary evangelists as near those to whom they preach, as is consistent with health, civilization, and reasonable comfort. We felt deeply the force of the social circumstances described by the Rev. Robert Stephenson, B.A., in the following letter to Rev. Thomas Champness:

> Even at home it is often painful to the minister of a congregation in a poor part of a great town to *live away in a pleasant suburb*. He feels the danger that more than the mere distance in space should separate him from the people. *The poorer people are under restraint* in coming to a house that seems to them a mansion, and in himself he dreads the *subtle temptation* to imagine that his more pleasant surroundings are his rights, and indicate personal superiority. It was this feeling in an *intensified degree* I realized on going to India and finding myself located, like other Englishmen, IN A LARGE HOUSE SURROUNDED BY BROAD GROUNDS. I felt there was quite enough to make intercourse with the people to whom I was sent as a messenger of Christ difficult, almost impossible, in their language, their manners and customs, and modes of thought, and it seemed to me a *great aggravation* of the evil that we should live SO APART FROM THEM, as the character and position of our homes implied and almost necessitated. I should have liked to live in the midst of the people, and when after a while, I had to find my own

house I longed to go into the native town and take a house in a street of respectable Hindoos. But I soon found it could not be.

We believe it is not so impossible as Mr. Stephenson imagines. Christian missionaries during the last two thousand years have overcome much more serious difficulties. Be that as it may, Mr. Stephenson expresses exactly the social difficulty we wish to overcome. We never stated that English missionaries generally yielded to the temptation of their circumstances, but only that such temptation exists, and that it is the duty of the Committees at home to reduce such temptation to a minimum.

Inferior Status of Native Ministers

It is exceedingly difficult for any Englishman in India to maintain always towards the natives that attitude of absolute brotherly equality which Jesus Christ maintained towards all men. We cannot but think that even our brethren have unwittingly and unintentionally fallen short.

In the first place, it is the custom in South India, and, we believe, in the North also, to hold two District Meetings. The first is styled the European, and the second the Native District Meeting. During the first meeting the ORDAINED native ministers who are in full connexion with the Wesleyan Conference, and whose names are printed in the minutes of the Conference in the alphabetical list of the ministers of our church, are excluded. It may be said that this meeting discusses only the policy and work of the society and its finances in so far as they affect the European brethren. This is true with regard to the finances, but it is impossible, or ought to be, to draw any hard and fast line between the work of the European missionary and that of his native helper, and the policy which should guide the efforts of both. It is useless to assert that native ministers are regarded as in any real sense the equal colleagues of the European missionary when they are excluded from half the deliberations of the annual District Meeting.

This gulf between the European and the native minister is further accentuated by the fact that, at any rate in the Negapatam and Trichinopoly District, the native ministers only dine on one day of the whole District Meeting week with their European brethren, and that is regarded by all concerned as a praiseworthy endeavour to bridge the gulf. During the whole of Dr. Lunn's twelve-months' residence in India he never, so far as his memory serves him, excepting on that one occasion, was invited to take a meal at the same table as a native Wesleyan minister.

But the Bangalore Conference itself affords the strongest proof of the fact that this gulf does exist. At this Triennial Conference of the Wesleyan Methodist Church in India, the fifth gathering of its kind, how was the spirit of brotherhood with the native ministry manifested? This

Conference was not summoned for the mere purpose of replying to criticism. It was, the great triennial gathering of our church. It considered the gravest questions of church polity in which the native ministers as representatives of the Indian Methodist Church were, if possible, more interested than the English missionaries. It considered the propriety of giving a 'definite constitution to the triennial meetings which have been held during the past twelve years', a subject of the gravest import to all native Christians. It debated at considerable length the question of Educational versus Evangelistic work. It considered carefully the question of handing over a part of our Indian work to the Australian Conferences, and numerous other issues momentous in their bearing on the future of Indian Methodism. Under these circumstances it might have been anticipated that English missionaries, careful to assert their full recognition of the brotherly equality of their Indian colleagues, would have secured their full representation in the *personnel* of the Conference. The facts however are far otherwise . . .

Twenty-four English missionaries represented their countrymen at the Bangalore Conference. *Not a single Native minister had a place in that assembly.* What would be thought in this country if the British Conference were specially summoned to discuss Welsh affairs, and from first to last not a single Welshman was present? Would that either represent or conciliate Wales? It may doubtless be said that the native ministers were not deliberately excluded at Bangalore; and we are glad to see that some provision has now been made for their representation at future Conferences. But the fact that they were totally unrepresented on such an occasion as the present indicates an unconscious attitude of mind in relation to the natives which no Englishman in India can overcome without ceaseless vigilance and effort . . .

The official response

From these passages when taken together it will be observed that the contentions of our critics are –

(*a*) That the style of life adopted by missionaries is such as (1) to interpose a serious obstacle to the growth of sympathy and confidence between them and the native population; (2) to expose the missionaries to the temptation of lordly indifference and isolation; (3) to lead the natives frequently to misunderstand the motives which bring missionaries to India and prompt them in their work, and consequently to beget suspicion and mistrust of them.

(*b*) That this whole evil might be remedied by a change in the outward circumstances of the missionary's life which (1) would not make it necessary for him to discard that mode and fashion of life which his English birth and training have made natural and necessary to him; or

(2) endanger his health, or deprive him of these reasonable comforts upon which the efficiency of his work in part depends; or (3) hinder him exhibiting to the Hindu the beauty and sweetness of a Christian home. . . .

The issue, it will be observed, is not 'Is there a wide social gulf between the European and the native in India?' nor yet 'Is this gulf of such a nature as to oppose very serious hindrances to the growth of perfect mutual understanding and confidence?' To both of these questions every one who has even a slight knowledge of India would give an affirmative answer. All Europeans in India feel this gulf, and many even outside missionary circles are seeking in various ways to bridge it. The missionary sees it and feels it every day. It is one of his constant hindrances and trials. He longs to come nearer to the natives, to be more thoroughly in touch with them; and how to bring himself nearer to them and to obtain his intimacy of touch is one of the many problems which his whole life is an effort to solve. The question before us however is this:— *'Is the gulf between the European missionary and the native of India one that is caused – or mainly caused – by the difference in their style of life, and which the missionary can bridge by adopting a style of life different from that which he does now adopt?'* To this question our answer must be a clear and emphatic negative.

Before we proceed to indicate the grounds on which this answer is based, we may be permitted to point out some extraordinary conclusions which would seem necessarily to follow from the assertions which we traverse. If it be true that the 'social gulf' which impedes mission work is created by differences in the merely outward conditions of life, and that it may be abolished by a change in these conditions so trifling as not to involve the surrender on the part of missionaries of that mode of life which to every Englishman is at once a heritage and a necessity; and if it be further true that these facts lie so plainly on the surface that a young man whose acquaintance with missionary life is of the most superficial character and whose knowledge of native life is *nil* can detect them, then how extraordinary it is that a long succession of Indian missionaries of all societies should have remained through whole lifetimes of service either blind to them, or if not blind, culpably silent! Was there no serious study of Indian problems till the 'Friend of Missions' appeared? Or have Indian missionaries of all societies and times preferred their own comfort to the interests of their work? Then indeed has the Church fallen upon evil days! And yet serious as these conclusions are – dishonouring either to the intellect or the heart of missionaries past and present – it seems to us that the acceptance of one or other of them is tacitly involved in any serious discussion of Mr. Hughes' proposals. If it be really so patent that a reduction of £80 in the stipends of missionaries will suffice to remove one of the great hindrances to the spread of the Gospel in India, and to open a great and effectual door for the evangelization of 'the masses,' and your missionaries have never suggested and now oppose this change, then plainly they must be either selfish knaves or short-sighted fools, and in neither case is it worth the Church's while to retain them in its service. It is true that Mr. Hughes refuses to go on to either of these conclusions, and we give him the fullest credit for sincerity in his professions of confidence and love. But Mr. Hughes has to deal with a public more logical than himself – a public that is not able to accept premises and reject the conclusion that is wrapped up in them. The 'Friend of Missions' seems to have felt this logical difficulty when he wrote his second article. 'And to-day,' said he, 'there are many men at work in India, as the writer can testify from personal knowledge, who would welcome gladly and heartily a general and sweeping reduction in missionary stipends which would compel a change in the style of living all round.' Where are these men, and why do they not come forward? They do not, and never did, exist. In this, as in so many other points, the 'Friend of Missions' has drawn on his imagination for his 'facts'.

Let us now proceed to ask – What is the gulf that separates the English missionary from the Hindu? Is it such a one as Mr. Hughes supposes? Can it be bridged in the simple fashion that he suggests?

To this last question every missionary – indeed every European of any calling who has lived half a dozen years in India – will answer in the negative. The gulf that separates him from the Hindu is not a *material* but a *moral* one. It does not consist in food and dress and habitation at all, nor in anything else that can be touched and modified by any change in financial policy or style of life. It consists in an incompatibility of sentiments and feelings and modes or habits of thought, and is the net result of three thousand years of diverse development. For a hundred generations the European and the Hindu have been growing apart, and while the faith and philosophy of the West have been quickening the conscience and fostering the growth of individuality, liberty and responsibility, these have been almost destroyed in India by a subtle pantheism and a crushing ceremonial system. The result of this is that the Hindu and the Englishman view everything from different standpoints – often opposite standpoints, – and it is years before they can enter with intelligent comprehension into each other's thoughts. This is a gulf which separates more or less all alien peoples, but which is wider between the Englishman and the Hindu than between any other two races under heaven. It is so wide and so apparently impassable that it often fills the young missionary – who has known nothing of such gulfs before – with a feeling akin to despair. He may be in the midst of Hindus, associating with them on terms of equality all day long, but he feels that he only touches the outer shell of their life. He may orientalize himself outwardly, but he is still occidental in thought and feeling, and the gulf remains as wide and as impassable as ever. It may be passed, it is passed, but not in one year or in five, and not by any change in the form and fashion of outward life. It is passed by patient study and long-continued intercourses, by ever widening sympathy and ever increasing acquaintance with Eastern conceptions, by opening the mind to every orientalizing influence, and seeking to view everything as far as may be through an oriental glass. It is thus and thus only that the European missionary can bring himself into close and intimate contact with the people he seeks to win for Christ, and the process is one that demands years. There is no potent spell in a turban, no insurmountable obstacle in knives and forks, no open sesame in any '*Via Media*'. The outward form and fashion of life is a thing wholly apart, and to one whose knowledge of India is based upon the experience of years, a suggestion that a 'simpler life' would bring the missionary 'nearer to the natives', in anything but space, is the *ne plus ultra* of childishness.

But it may be said that the 'Friend of Missions' did not refer to the great moral chasm, but only to the comparative absence of social intercourse and fellowship between the European missionary and the natives of India, and that his contention was that this was brought about by the exclusive style of life adopted by the former. But what, we must ask, does the 'Friend of Missions' mean by social intercourse? Eating and drinking together? Then we acknowledge that there is an entire absence of it. But we do not regard this as an evil, and are not anxious to remedy it. The Kingdom of God is not meat and drink. It would, however, be an insult to the intelligence of the 'Friend of Missions' to suppose that this is his meaning, for the veriest tyro in Indian affairs knows very well that the hindrance to this form of social intercourse is not on our side. *But beyond this there is no social gulf, no separation.* If Dr. Lunn means – and this is undoubtedly the primary and natural sense of his words – that there are circumstances in the style of the missionary's life which keep the natives at a distance from him, whether it be that his house is so far from theirs that they cannot come to see him, or that it is so grand that it frightens them away, or that the missionary himself does not encourage their visits or bid them welcome, or that his haughty spirit and bearing repels them: if these, or any of these, are the meaning which his words are intended to convey, then we assert that his words are simply untrue, and that Dr. Lunn has had sufficient experience of the life of missionaries to know that they are untrue. During his brief stay in India he lived for considerable periods in the houses of at least five of his brethren, and if he took any notice at all of what was going on he must often have been aware of an almost continuous stream of native visitors of all ranks who came to see the missionary or his wife on all conceivable errands, some to seek his sympathy in their troubles, others to share with him some new joy, but more to ask his advice and help in difficulties of every kind. He must have observed that all were welcome, that all came with fearless confidence, knowing that they never had been and never would be repelled. He must have known that the problem which the overwrought missionary had to solve was not how to attract the natives to his house, but how to find time for all who came.

Methodism and the Miner

At Staveley, north Derbyshire

(David Barr, *Climbing the Ladder*, 1910, pp. 40–1)

Leaving home as a young man, the author found himself living in a mining community.

There were several earnest Methodists living in the same terrace, and it was their custom to hold frequent prayer-meetings, getting access to each cottage and taking them in turn for these gatherings. These men, most of whom were colliers, knew the secret of prevailing prayer. In their flannels, with bare chests, they called upon God in stentorian tones which could be heard for a considerable distance. 'The kingdom of heaven suffereth violence,' and the cottages were often crowded, while their simple but powerful wrestling brought Heaven's blessing down. There were glad and fervent responses from those who were of the Household of Faith, and now and again the cry of the penitent almost drowned the voice of the suppliant. At the first opportunity I repaired to the chapel in the village and made the acquaintance of the people, especially of two young men with whom I chummed and worked in God's cause.

In the Durham coalfield

(Jack Lawson, *A Man's Life*, 1932, pp. 111–13)

Lawson began his working life as a miner and later became an M.P. and held office in the first Labour Government of 1924.

Their hymns and sermons may have been of another world, but the first fighters and speakers for unions, Co-op. Societies, political freedom, and improved conditions, were Methodist preachers. That is beyond argument. And the Gospel expressed in social terms has been more of a driving-power in northern mining circles than all the economic teaching put together. Room for criticism there may be, but that the eighteenth-century Revival has been a motive power in the personal, domestic, and social life in the Kingdom of Collieries is beyond doubt. And here and now I wish to pay my tribute to that movement, and to the humble people who composed the Society of Methodists which I joined in my youth, and of which I remain a loyal member to this day. It was composed of men and women who in many cases had received no education worth speaking of, but who had become really cultured, though their reading was limited to certain schools of thought.

One there was who would sing you a 'spiritual' or equally a comic song in fine style, or he would preach a sermon. Others would lead a choir, play the organ or piano, or preach a sermon. One, who had only been taught by his wife to read when he was in his thirties, used to wait for me when I was putting and he was hewing at the same flat. As we went 'out bye,' my pony trotting before, we would talk books while we walked, bent double in the dark roadway. I remember well when this elderly man first struck Nietzsche. That was a 'find' – and I also remember how the man turned me upside down mentally. Which was all to my good.

This man read the New Testament in Greek, and oratorios were as easy to him as the latest song is to the man in the street. Many of the members of course were illiterate, but they were fine types of men and women, and had individuality – and that is not a common thing. All, even the most ordinary – or, if you like, ignorant as far as education goes – all of them were 'something'. Methodism took the 'nobodies', and made the most humble and hopeless 'somebody'. They set aside the things that are not good for a man; they had some little pride in their dress; they made their homes to be things of beauty, and aspired and worked to give their children a better life and opportunity than themselves. They are as a whole among the best men and women I have ever known ...

The Wesley Deaconess Order

(T. B. Stephenson, letter to the religious press, 1890, reprinted in William Bradfield, *Life of the Rev. Thomas Bowman Stephenson* (1913), pp. 290–5)

In his *Concerning Sisterhoods* Stephenson set out three basic principles: '1. There must be vocation, though no vow. 2. There must be discipline without servility. 3. There must be association, not excluding freedom.'

For some years past the subject of women's work in the Church has been creating much interest. The attention excited by the accounts of the work of the 'Sisters of the People' has quickened and deepened that interest. It is known to some of my friends that for many years I have felt a deep concern in this subject; and it has been one of the hopes of my life that I might be permitted to aid in the establishment upon a secure basis of an association of Christian Sisters in connexion with our own Church. Indeed, there has long been such an organization in connexion with the Children's Home. For fifteen years we have been steadily and quietly developing one great branch of the Female Diaconate, namely, that which deals mainly, though not exclusively, with the ministry of women to the spiritual wants of children and young people. The 'Sisters of the Children' pass through a stated period of probation, and their work is systematized and regulated. But in connexion with our recent evangelistic enterprises another phase of women's work has attracted attention and curiosity, and the time has become rapidly ripe for some definite organization by which women of suitable character might be trained for the service of Christ and the nation. . . .

Any such scheme must, of course, be of a private character, and must depend for its public acceptance upon whatever amount of faith is put in its promoters. Before any large and general scheme could be established and developed, the Conference would have to give its judgement, because any such scheme must touch our Church organization at a great many points. The relation of the 'Sisters' who might go out to work in the various circuits to the Circuit authorities, and to the Church at large, must be carefully defined; and the Church must make up its mind upon the preliminary question of whether the employment of such agents on so large a scale is desirable, and, if so, whether it be possible, considering all that it must involve. The true way to prepare for the employment of such an agency is that the experiment should be tried upon a small scale. A little experience in such a matter is worth a vast amount of theory . . .

The scheme, so far as I am able to state it within the limits of this letter, is, in rough outline, as follows: A house will be taken within convenient reach of this spot, capable of accommodating ten or twelve Probationary Sisters. They must be women of good education as well as of fervent spirit. It is not intended, however, to exclude persons of exceptional force and spiritual gifts, even if they have not had the advantage of a complete early education. Applicants must be members of a Methodist Church, unless in exceptional cases. It is hoped that some will be able to pay their own expenses, but board and lodging will be provided. Three months' preliminary trial will be required; then a further period of nine months' training. The second year of probation will be spent in actual work. Instruction in Bible subjects will be given, also in such medical subjects as would be likely to be useful in the after work of the Sisters; and a portion of each day will be spent in practical work.

I need hardly say that no vow will be required or received of any Sister; but it is expected that candidates will be moved by a deep conviction that God has called them to their work, and that they will intend to spend at least a considerable number of years in it; otherwise the labour and expense of training would be thrown away.

Three great fields of usefulness lie before the Sisters.

1. Moral and spiritual education, in connexion with orphanages and industrial schools, both at home and in the missionary field.

2. The ministry to the sick, especially the sick poor. The noble vocation of the nurse is not open, as it should be, to Nonconformist girls. It is hoped that, if not immediately, yet after a time, arrangements may be made for an Hospital Training Branch of the Institute.

3. Evangelistic visitation, in connexion with circuits, with congregations, perhaps with groups of village congregations, and certainly in connexion with mission centres. This is such work as is being done by the 'Sisters of the People',[1] and by Mr. Thompson's[2] and Mr. Clegg's workers, and to some extent by our 'Sisters of the Children'.

---

[1] The 'Sisters of the People', organised by Hugh Price Hughes as part of the West London Mission, anticipated some features of the Deaconess Order.

[2] Peter Thompson (1847–1909), pioneer missioner in the East End of London.

A Response to the Lambeth Conference

(*Minutes*, 1890)

A Conference of Bishops of the Anglican Communion met at Lambeth Palace in July 1888. That Conference appointed a Committee to consider the question of Home Re-Union. The Report of that Committee laid down as a basis for Home Re-Union four Articles, referring to the Holy Scriptures, the Creeds, the Sacraments, and 'the Historic Episcopate'.

The Conference of Bishops adopted these Articles, and requested the constituted authorities of the various Branches of the Anglican Communion to 'make it known that they hold themselves in readiness to enter into brotherly conference with the representatives of other chief Christian Communions in the English-speaking races'.

In accordance with the wish so expressed, letters from the Archbishop of Canterbury on this subject were considered by the Conference, which ordered the following reply to be forwarded:—

My Lord Archbishop,—

Your letters on the subject of 'Home Re-Union' addressed to the Rev. Joseph Bush, who was President of the Wesleyan-Methodist Conference of 1888, have been laid before the Conference. I regret that, owing to some doubt as to your Grace's wish respecting the first letter, this answer has been delayed.

The Conference has received your letters with the respect due to your Grace, and to the venerable body of Bishops at whose instance this communication, with others similar to it, was sent forth. The Conference cordially joins with you in prayer for the unity of the Church of Christ, that thus may be fulfilled the prayer of the Blessed Saviour Himself: 'That they all may be one; as Thou, Father, art in Me, and I in Thee, that they also may be one in Us.'

It appears to the Conference that very much might be done by all the Christian Communions to promote that unity of spirit, without which corporal unity is impossible, and if possible, would be of little worth. By frankly acknowledging the Christian character of the members of the several Churches, by recognising cordially and practically the status and work of their Ministers, and by abstaining from everything in public teaching and in our more private ministries which would injure the influence or destroy the fruit of godly labour beyond our own Communions, we might approach much nearer to that state of heart and mind on which the Divine Head of the Holy Church universal would doubtless look with approval. In your Grace's efforts, and those of your Right Reverend Brethren to produce this happier state of feeling, the Conference would desire very heartily to co-operate; for it is the traditional policy of Methodism to be in its relation to other Christian Churches 'the friend of all, the enemy of none'.

The Conference, whilst deploring needless divisions, and still more a schismatical spirit, is of opinion that the true unity of the Church of Christ does not necessarily require the corporate union of the several Churches, or their acceptance of any form of polity and government.

And whilst fully recognising the spirit which animated the Committee on 'Home Re-Union' appointed by the Bishops, the Conference is of opinion that the Articles presented as a basis for possible Re-Union (especially the fourth, which relates to 'the Historic Episcopate') do not, in the absence of fuller information and more exact definition, provide a practical ground for the discussion of the subject.

I have the honour to be,

My Lord Archbishop,

Your Grace's faithful servant and brother in Christ,

WILLIAM F. MOULTON,

President of the Wesleyan-Methodist Conference.

Bristol, 7th August, 1890.

Methodism in the Yorkshire Dales

(J. C. Atkinson, *Forty Years in a Moorland Parish: Reminiscences and Researches in Danby in Cleveland*, 1891, pp. 14–16)

Speaking of the state of the parish as he found it on arrival, after years under an elderly and infirm incumbent, the author comments: 'I could well understand how the only religious life in the district should be among and due to the exertions of the Wesleyans and Primitive Methodists' (p. 48).

Shortly after my acceptance of the incumbency the patron wrote to me, 'You will find the Wesleyans worthy of much consideration. Indeed I think that if it had not been for them and their influence, religion would practically have died altogether out in these Dales.' And I am very much inclined to think there was more truth in the remark than a stickler for the influence of the Church would find it pleasant to have to admit. The days were but lately passed away when one 'minister' (or 'church priest', as he was quite as often called) found himself charged with the burden of three, in one or two cases I knew of, even four parishes; and where parishes are such as this moorland district necessitates in point of area, that is equivalent to saying that even one service in the week and a proportionate amount of visiting was a thing to be desired rather than statedly enjoyed. My immediate predecessor had Danby (of 13,600 acres) and Westerdale (of about 9000) on his hands, and was neither strong nor good at reading, let alone preaching. One of his predecessors had Danby, Rosedale, and Farndale. Another parson in the same district, and not a century ago, had Glaisdale, Egton, and Goathland. And I have reason to think that even thus the pittance earned by such men was barely up to the proverbial wealthiness of 'forty pounds a year'. Thus, the Wesleyans with their admirable organisation were an important factor in the condition of religious life in the Dale, and had more than merely a claim to consideration. And they are still a strong and influential body. And I think they will continue to be so yet awhile, although they are but barely holding their own at present. The religious fervour and earnestness of the old days seems to have lost warmth and energy, and to have been in part replaced by more secular feelings and objects. And the change will be fatal in the end. Nor do I think that the Primitive Methodists, who constitute another strong element in the religious life of the parish, quite reach the point of making up what is missing. There is one defect in the organisation of both bodies, the weakness of which is already becoming more than apparent, and which will be but the more evident as time rolls on and the advancing tide of information, knowledge, and especially inquiry, more than keeps pace with the times. They can multiply chapels, but the local-preacher system will not supply the teachers that are, and will increasingly be, wanted. 'Mean of light and leading' do not grow up like mushrooms in remote places like these, and will be slow of growth even where the culture can be and is attended to.

Public Elementary Education

(*Minutes*, 1891)

I. The Conference receives and adopts the Report of the Representative Committee, appointed by the Conference of 1890, in view of Prospective Parliamentary Legislation affecting Public Elementary Education, held on January 27th and 28th, 1891; and directs that the following Resolutions be printed in the *Minutes*, viz.:—

1. That the primary object of Methodist policy in the matter of Elementary Education should be the establishment of School Boards everywhere, acting in districts of sufficient area, and the placing of a Christian unsectarian school within reasonable distance of every family, especially in the rural districts.

2. That no National system of Education will meet the necessity of the country, which shall exclude from the Day Schools the Bible and religious instruction therefrom by the Teachers, suited to the capacities of children.

3. That all modifications of the National policy in respect to Elementary Education should be made in view of the ultimate establishment of a complete National system of Schools under adequate and representative public management.

4. That so long as Denominational Schools form part of the National system of Education, our Connexional Day Schools and Training Colleges should be maintained in full vigour and efficiency.

5. That the Committee is prepared to accept any reasonable proposals for Free Education; but insists that all Schools freed by the aid of public grants must be so far placed under public management, as – (1) To secure the efficiency of the Schools, and (*p*) To prevent their misuse for sectarian purposes.

6. That no scheme of Free or Assisted Education can be acceptable to Wesleyan-Methodists which will place the Schools of Protestant Nonconformists at a disadvantage in comparison with those of the Church of England or of the Roman Catholics.

7. That no measure will be satisfactory to Wesleyan-Methodists which provides for the payment from the Consolidated Fund of a sum in lieu of school fees, while it makes no provision for the due representation of the public on the Committees of Management.

8. That a measure merely for giving further assistance to different sorts of inspected Schools, provided and managed as at present and organized on existing lines, must be deficient alike in symmetry and elasticity, and altogether inadequate to meet the requirements of the nation in respect of public education of various grades and kinds in town and country.

9. That the experience of twenty years has shown that the Conscience Clause has, to a considerable extent, proved to be ineffectual and unreal as a protection for parents and children against religious intolerance and oppression; that, moreover, in not a few Day Schools of the Church of England, religious intolerance and bigotry of an exceedingly offensive character are systematically taught the scholars during the hours set apart for religious instruction by means of a special Catechism, such as it ought not to be possible to teach in connection with any public school of the Nation; and that the way of appeal to the Education Department against such grievances is difficult, tedious, and often altogether unavailable. This Committee, therefore, would strongly urge upon the Government that the Local Education Authority, which is responsible for enforcing educational compulsion on children and their parents, should have authority to take cognizance of any complaints which may be made by parents or guardians of offences against conscience or religious liberty in the conduct of any inspected School, and may make representations on the subject either to the Managers of the School or to the Education Department, or to both these authorities, as the case may require.

And further, that it shall be within the competency of the same local authority to take cognizance of the sanitary conditions of the Schools within their Districts which it may be their duty to require children to attend, and to make representations on this subject to the Managers of any School or to the Education Department, or to both these authorities.

Aims of the Bermondsey Settlement

(J. Scott Lidgett, *Reminiscences*, 1928, pp. 29–31)

I shall never forget the experiences of the next two years. The powerful influence of Dr. Moulton had procured official and formal approval of the undertaking, yet there was very little real conviction behind it. Some years later, when the Report of the Settlement was brought before the Conference Dr. Rigg expressed his satisfaction with the success of an enterprise, which, he said, he had felt bound to support at the beginning owing to the advocacy of Dr. Moulton, but which he had believed was foredoomed to failured. This, I think, was the general attitude; and as I travelled over the country raising the all too small Building Fund I often felt like a mendicant, hawking his patent in the hope of its being eventually taken up. Moreover, there were many who supposed that I desired in large measure to substitute social activities pursued in a somewhat secular spirit for the gospel and spirituality. I think this impression was largely dissipated by the publication of my book on the Atonement some years later.

Nor were things better on my first appearance in Bermondsey itself. My reception by the large firms was chilly in the extreme. Nor did the clergy and ministers welcome me much more warmly. They assured me that there was no demand in Bermondsey for such a scheme, and that I should meet with little response. They also seemed nervous lest I should bring financial support from outside to inaugurate a work which would damage their own struggling churches. The difficulty was increased by reason of the fact that the enterprise had to be plunged complete on the neighbourhood instead of springing from small beginnings. The one exception was the late Colonel S. B. Bevington, a man of the highest position in the commercial and public life of Bermondsey, who stood by me from the first and right on to the end of his life. However, I set my teeth and toiled on, with the result that the Committee felt justified in taking a building contract early in 1891, that the foundaton stone was laid by the Lord Mayor, Sir Joseph Savory, on July 14, and that the main Settlement building was opened for educational work on January 6, 1892. Owing to lack of funds the building could not be completed until 1898, and the plans of the architect, Mr. Elijah Hoole, were to some extent damaged by the rigid economy that had to be imposed.

Before this time, however, I had come to the conclusion that a Settlement for women must be established side by side with that for men. I had therefore sought the help of the late Miss Alice Barlow of Edgeworth, who at once joined me in taking the responsibility for this additional enterprise, a partnership which lasted, on terms of the most intimate friendship and generous support, till her death in 1919. To her and to Miss Mary Simmons, who was head of the Women's House from January 1893 till 1916, and continued in the work for some years longer, I owe the most grateful thanks for their unfailing comradeship and cooperation. The work of the Women's House began in October 1891 by our undertaking, under the Queen Victoria Jubilee Institute, the District Nursing of Rotherhithe, for which I have been responsible ever since.

AIMS OF THE SETTLEMENT

The main object of the Settlement was to bring a force of educated workers to give help to all the higher interests of the neighbourhood, religious, educational, social, and administrative. Its aims were defined at the outset in the following terms:

1. To bring additional force and attractiveness to Christian work.
2. To become a centre of social life, where all classes may meet together on equal terms for healthful intercourse and recreation.
3. To give facilities for the study of Literature, History, Science, and Art.
4. To bring men together to discuss general and special social evils and to seek their remedy.
5. To take such part in local administration and philanthropy as may be possible.
6. And so to do all this that it shall be perfectly clear that no mere sectarian advantage is sought, but that it shall be possible for all good men to associate themselves with our work.

It is clear from all that has been said that the Settlement differs considerably in aim and therefore in development from a Mission. A Settlement is or should be a community of social workers who come to a poor neighbourhood to assist by the methods of friendship and co-operation those who are concerned in upholding all that is essential to the well-being of the neighbourhood. Hence freedom and initiative are of its essence. Men and women who come to it must be encouraged to see with their own eyes and to respond with a large measure of independence to the calls that are made upon them. A cut-and-dried programme would be fatal both to the conception and to the development of a Settlement. Its head should not stereotype, but guide and co-ordinate all its activities, encouraging adventure, though tempering it with prudence. Much, therefore, will depend upon the temperament and outlook of the settlers who rally to his banner. Moreover, the mental, moral, and material conditions of the particular neighbourhood that is served by any Settlement may encourage and necessitate certain forms of activity, and equally may hinder or thwart certain other endeavours that may be intrinsically desirable. Hence for more than the ordinary reasons there must needs be a considerable interval between the ideal and the practicable. All this has been true of the Bermondsey Settlement.

The 'New Look' of Methodism

Saturday Night at the Central Hall, Manchester.

From *Manchester Old and New* by W. A. Shaw, c. 1894, Vol. 2, facing p. 145

The Manchester Mission

Extracts from the Mission's magazine, *Greeting*.

Sunday in Manchester (by a London Minister)

(*Greeting*, November 1893, p. 125)

Nothing is more surprising about the Manchester Mission than its many-sidedness. The great Central Hall is like a beehive. There is a ceaseless, restless activity, which offers a strange and striking contrast to the sedate orderliness of the ordinary place of worship. In the street, at the doors, along the corridors, and in the numerous committee and class rooms it was the same. There was life everywhere.

The Mission has set hundreds of men and women to work, and this is at once the secret of its power and the proof of its success.

The Saturday gathering is almost unique. More than two thousand people were packed in the large Hall. All sorts and conditions were represented, and for about nearly half-an-hour they were treated to a racy and musical entertainment of a broad but perfectly healthy kind, and while straightlacedness was conspicuously absent, one could not spend an evening here without feeling the wholesome influence of the great spiritual organisation.

But it is of course in the great Sabbath gatherings that the influence of the Mission is felt. In the Mission is an aggregate of congregations numbering at least nine or ten thousand, and this is not on special days or with big preachers, it is the normal condition of the Halls and Chapels of this Mission.

On Sunday afternoons again an audience, mostly men, fills the Central Hall! Here an hour's service is held. Perhaps this is the most remarkable congregation of all, never have I seen so many 'men of the street' in a religious service.

In the evening the great Free Trade Hall is crowded to the doors. Here assembles a congregation equal in numbers to the two other largest gatherings in all Methodism. It is a glorious sight to see the thousands of working men and women crowding this large building. The services at the Free Trade Hall has [sic] not lessened in the slightest degree the attendance at the Central Hall, for on each Sunday night on which I have visited Manchester the one Hall is as densely packed as the other.

Now it is when these two services are going on that one gets some adequate idea of the forces of this Mission. There are hundreds of helpers and all their activity tends in one direction, namely towards the Enquiry room. This is the furnace into which all the metal, often largely mixed with dross, is drawn. Genteel sinners kneel side by side with sinners who are tramps. Ladies and factory girls seek Christ together and scores who enter these rooms depressed and heartsick come out radiant with a strange joy born of a new life.

From the *Manchester Guardian*, November 18th, 1895

(*Greeting*, December 1895, p. 147)

The Manchester Mission in its present form has been in existence ten years. Its operations cover a good deal of hitherto untouched ground, and produce results of which one only hears on such occasions as the Anniversary meetings of this week. The Central Hall in Oldham Street is the headquarters of the Mission, the centre of Administration, and the common rallying ground of the workers in the different agencies in the slum districts round about Deansgate, Hulme, Red Bank, and Ancoats. The statistics relating to the growth of the Mission are impressive enough. This year the membership numbers 1,804, exclusive of 415 on trial for membership and 306 junior members; the congregation regularly in attendance at the various mission centres averages more than 10,000 every Sunday evening; there are 2,500 children in the Sunday Schools; 1,200 men and women in Bible Classes; an average weekly attendance of over 2,000 people at the Temperance Meetings; and large crowds at the twenty-five Open-air Services which are held weekly. These figures tell a story of their own, but they give no idea of what is known as the 'social' side of the Mission's work. They leave out of account the operations of the homes and shelters for men and women in Ancoats, the preventative and training home for girls at Reddish, the medical mission and district nursing organisation, the employment bureau, the food depot, and other branches of charitable enterprise.

The Preventive Home at Reddish is a good example of the methods adopted by the Mission. It is not a rescue home, but, as the name implies, is intended to shelter and protect and train girls whose domestic surroundings are of a perilous or unhappy nature. About thirty girls are constantly housed in the institution, their ages varying from nine to twenty-two years. Sooner or later they are taught laundry work, housework, plain sewing and dressmaking. The intention of the home, it is said, has been most successfully realised.

Another aspect of the Mission's social work may be studied in Ancoats, where some of the workers are sanguine enough to believe that they have fallen on the solution of a problem upon which poor-law guardians and their forerunners have been breaking their brains ever since the first tramp turned his face northwards from Land's End or towards the south from John-o'-Groat's. If the system does not quite settle the tramp question, it forms at least an interesting complement to the efforts in that direction of the Local Government Board on the one hand and the Salvation Army on the other. A mere outline of the Ancoats scheme will indicate the points of difference between this and older methods. To begin with, the tramp is expected to make his application for food and lodging at a comparatively early hour, so that he may earn both before going to bed. Provided with a ticket for the men's night shelter in Hood-street, he goes to the labour yard in Pott-street, and works at wood-chopping until he has earned the price of bed, supper, and breakfast. The rate of remuneration, it is important to note, is calculated on the trade union basis. At eight o'clock, after supper, he and his fellow casuals meet, if they please, in Hood-street for family worship, and in the morning each man is called at half-past five and sent out to look for work. An hour or two later he returns for breakfast which he earned on the previous day, and then again sallies forth, conscious that he has paid in labour for what he has received . . . On the Mission system, if the man does not succeed in finding work during the first day he can return to the labour yard at two o'clock, make up his fifty bundles of wood, and earn another night's lodging. He may repeat this for two or three days. But there is no hard and fast rule; each case is treated on its merits. Many of the casuals obtain work the day after their admission. If they fail to find work, but stand the labour test and show that they are honest and anxious to do well, they may pass into the labour home, which is described as a kind of upper house. Here the men pay for bed and board . . . The advantage of residence in such an institution is that the lodgers are cared for and helped in a variety of ways, and the great feature of the whole system is that at no stage is a man pauperised.

Women Representatives to the Wesleyan Conference

Minutes, 1894, p. 320

1. The attention of the Conference having been called to the presence of a woman Representative, elected by the Third London District Synod, the Conference resolves, in view of all the special circumstances of the case, and without deciding the question of the validity of the election, to proceed to the order of the day.

2. The Conference directs that in future no Chairman of any Synod shall receive the nomination of a woman Representative until the Conference shall have determined, by legislative action, to admit women as Representatives, and until such new legislation has been submitted for approval to the District Synods . . .

Wesleyan Methodist Church Record, March 1895, p. 54 ('Notes of the Month')

At the last Conference, when the Representative Session met, a lady, who had been elected as one of the Second London Lay Representatives, took her place in the pew allotted to that district. It is a mistake to suppose that this was absolutely the first occasion on which a woman attended a Methodist Conference. Long ago, when John Wesley himself ruled the Conference, an illustrious lady once was present and took part. Lady Huntingdon was at the Conference which met in Leeds in 1762 . . . But those were days when Methodism was still a mere society within the Church. The presence of Miss Dawson raised the question whether a woman might in harmony with constitutional law and usage sit as a representative in the Conference. After a long discussion the Conference came to the conclusion that so serious an innovation could not be tolerated except as the result of careful consideration. A Committee was appointed. It has met and discussed the matter in admirable temper. Our readers will be interested to see the resolution which was carried by a majority of five on the first vote and six on the second.

> The Committee having considered in all its bearings and question of the election of Women Representatives to the Conference, reports that in its judgment it is not probable many women will be elected, but in view of the great services which women render to Methodism, of the increasing activity of women in all spheres of life, and of the fact that women are already eligible for every lay office of our Church, this Committee recommends that after due legislation the Conference should permit the election of a Woman Representative to the Conference when, in the judgment of any District Synod, such an election would secure the best interests of the work of God.

. . . Of course this resolution only goes as a recommendation to the Conference, and it is impossible to say at present what view the Conference may take. The matter does not seem to excite very much interest. And this is not difficult to account for. No one has yet seen very clearly what women can do in the Conference that cannot be done quite as well by men; whilst, undoubtedly, in many places those who have to make the ever increasingly difficult arrangements for the Conference would find their labours complicated, if not increased, if any large number of women representatives had to be provided for. On all sides, however, it is seen that very few women are likely to be elected, except perhaps whilst the novelty lasts.

Minutes, 1895, p. 319

The Conference receives the Report of the Committee, but does not adopt its recommendation.

Minutes, 1909, p. 119

The Conference *provisionally* resolves that the time has come when duly qualified and elected women shall be eligible as Lay Representatives to the Conference.

'Pleasant Sunday Afternoons'

The Annual Address to the Methodist Societies

(*Minutes*, 1895)

We have had occasion during the Conference to consider a special report on the Sunday afternoon meetings which are a conspicuous feature in Church life to-day. When conducted as Bible-classes, they afford a fruitful field for service, in which much may be done for the spiritual benefit of the people, especially for thoughtful and intelligent young men; but, as popular services, they are not without dangers, against which we bid you be on your guard. It is possible to attempt to brighten the hours of the day of rest at the expense of its sacredness. Let your zeal in these things be tempered with discretion. Suffer nothing to interfere with the sanctity of the Lord's day; and remember there can be no real substitute for the great message of reconciliation with God through Christ. We rejoice to know there is a strong desire to hear the word of God, and that large numbers of young people attend the services of our sanctuaries; but we exhort you not to be content with the mere desire to hear preaching. Come to the house of the Lord with hearts prepared for the incorruptible seed of the kingdom. Resolve to receive the word 'with all readiness of mind', and to allow it to exert its mighty influence on life and conduct.

Constitution of the Wesley Guild

(*Minutes*, 1896)

2. Definition.
A Wesley Guild is a Young People's Society, closely linked to the Church, holding weekly or periodical meetings for devotional, literary, and social purposes, and centring around itself various branches of Young People's work.

4. Aim.

The main principle is comradeship in the highest aims of life; and its objects, briefly stated are—

(1) To awaken and deepen the Christian Life in the Young People of the Congregation and Sunday School.

(2) To form and strengthen such associations and agencies as will be helpful to the Church.

(3) To link together the various departments of Christian work in which Young People are engaged.

(4) To provide for the oversight of Young People by Young People, especially in welcoming those newly settled in a neighbourhood, and in following with letters of recommendation those who remove.

(5) To provide facilities for social and friendly intercourse and literary improvement in harmony with the above objects.

5. Membership.

The Guild shall comprise Active, Companion, and Associate Members.

Active Members of the Guild are Young People who are *Members of the Church*, and wishful to help others.

Companion Members of the Guild are Young People of the Congregation or Sunday School, who wish to join any section of the Guild and who are in sympathy with its spirit of friendship and service.

Associate Members of the Guild. Older workers and friends who are in sympathy with the movement.

6. Pledges.

Active Member's Pledge:

I will earnestly endeavour, in the strength of Christ, to live a truly Christian life, to daily read the Holy Scriptures, and to attend to the duty of private prayer. I will attend my Class with regularity, and fulfil to the best of my ability my duties as a member of the Christian Church. Whenever possible, I will be present at the Devotional Meeting of the Guild, and take an active part in the proceedings, if desired.

Companion Member's Pledge:

I will try to avoid in my daily life anything that would bring discredit upon myself or upon the Church of Christ, and will do my best to maintain the friendly spirit of the Guild.

10. Guild Meetings

(1) Devotional Meetings of the Guild.

(i) Monthly Devotional Meeting.

This shall be a meeting for praise, prayer, and testimony at which, if possible, one of the Ministers shall preside.

The roll of Guild Members shall be read, and each Active Member shall be expected, not only to answer to his name, but to be willing to take part, by either prayer or brief testimony, or at least by reciting a verse of Scripture or of a hymn.

The names of new members proposed shall be read by the Look-out Secretary, and they shall be received and welcomed by the members rising or holding up a hand.

Any Active Member unable to be present shall, if practicable, send a message by some other member.

Companion Members of the Guild shall be heartily encouraged to be present. . . .

(2) Plans for Weekly Meetings.
  (i) Rotation of Meetings.
     (*a*) Monthly Devotional Meeting.
     (*b*) Literary Meeting.
     (*c*) Social and Musical Evening.
     (*d*) Bible Reading, Literary Meeting or Lecture. . . .

(3) Notes.
  (i) The objects of the Social and Musical Evening shall be:—
     (*a*) To give the Minister and others an opportunity for conversation and friendly intercourse with the members of the Guild.
     (*b*) To enable the Secretaries of the different sections to canvass for new workers.
     (*c*) To afford the Look-out Committee a chance of introducing new members to suitable friends.

The Twentieth Century Fund

(*Minutes*, 1898)

1. In the judgment of the Conference it is desirable to raise a special Connexional Fund for the maintenance and extension of the work of God at home and abroad, and the commencement of the Twentieth Century will afford a suitable occasion for the Wesleyan Methodist Church and its adherents to gratefully acknowledge the way in which God has led them, and also to prepare for further evangelistic, educational, and philanthropic service.

2. The Conference therefore resolves:

(1) A Special Connexional Fund, to be called the Wesleyan Methodist

Twentieth Century Fund, shall be raised and applied to the Evangelistic, Educational, and Philanthropic purposes of our Church at home and abroad.

(2) The amount which the Wesleyan Methodist Church and its adherents shall endeavour to raise shall be not less than One Million Guineas.

(3) With a view to secure the co-operation of as large a number as possible of Wesleyan Methodists, whether members of the Church or adherents at home or abroad, the proposed Century Fund shall be raised by at least one million Methodists, who shall between January 1, 1899, and January 1, 1901, give or collect a sum of at least One Million Guineas.

Each person should aim at giving or collecting one guinea, thus preserving the fundamental principle of 'one person one guinea', but it is believed that many will desire to subscribe sums greatly in excess of that amount. The General Committee is therefore instructed to make some provision whereby the wishes of such subscribers may be met.

(4) The first day of the Twentieth Century, *viz.* January 1, 1901, shall be observed as a day of prayer and thanksgiving, when suitable devotional services shall be held in all our places of worship.

(5) A Roll shall be opened on January 1, 1899, upon which there shall be entered the names of all subscribers and collectors, whether members of our Church, teachers or scholars in our Sunday and Day Schools, communicants, seatholders, or other worshippers and adherents or friends of Methodism at home and abroad.

The proposed Roll shall be closed on January 1, 1901, and the list of the donors in every Society or Circuit shall be read at the services on that day. The original Roll, upon which subscribers or collectors should, if possible, themselves inscribe their names, shall be preserved among the historical documents of the Wesleyan Methodist Church.

(8) The following shall be the objects of the Fund and the general scheme of allocation; but the General Committee shall have power to more exactly determine the amounts to be devoted to the several purposes named:

(i) To assist in the purchase of sites and the erection of Wesleyan Methodist places of worship, whether Chapels, Sunday Schools, or Mission Halls in any part of the United Kingdom, and Soldiers' and Sailors' Homes, and to help the completion of extension schemes already begun, £300,000.

(ii) For educational work in connexion with the Higher, Secondary, Elementary, or other Educational Institutions associated with the Wesleyan Methodist Church, and for furthering the mental improvement and training of Local Preachers, £200,000.

N.B. – Special provision shall be mad efor the erection of Day Schools in rural and other districts where at present Nonconformists are compelled to attend either Anglican or Roman Catholic schools, and also to provide for the reasonable requirements of pupil teachers who desire to be trained for their profession in a congenial religious atmosphere.

(iii) For Foreign Missionary work, £100,000.

(iv) For Home Missionary work, including Temperance work, £100,000.

(v) For the purchase of a suitable site in London in a convenient and prominent situation, and the erection thereon of a monumental Connexional Building, £250,000.

(vi) For the development of the work of the Children's Home, with a view to save all children of Methodist and other Nonconformist parentage from workhouse schools, and to provide also for the orphan children of Methodist Soldiers and Sailors, £50,000.

A view from the wings

(Charles Booth, *Life and Labour of the People in London*, 1902, Series III, Vol. 2, pp. 220–2)

A special week-day service and meeting was held at Wesley's Chapel, City Road, to inaugurate the collection of this fund. The originator of the idea occupied the chair, and was supported by a number of leading men of the denomination. The chapel, which is a building of some size with large galleries, was already full at 6.20, and I with difficulty found a place in the gallery, but from it could hear and see very well. The audience of men and women, in nearly equal proportions, looked extremely respectable; working class partly, but all well dressed and very earnest and orderly. The platform filled, and the service began at once, before the advertised time. There had been some other functions previously, including a 'love-feast', and the remains of the tea could be seen in a sort of corridor building at one side of the chapel as one entered the church. The pleasant friendliness of such functions is, I imagine, one of the secrets of the strength of Methodism.

The singing of an eight-verse hymn, in which the last line of each verse was repeated in chorus, occupied some time, and the audience was then led in prayer by one of the ministers present. It was more a short address than a prayer, consisting of direct appeals to us as well as to the Almighty, by the minister individually, and also as speaking for us. After this the chairman explained the scheme and others spoke on the subject. A long first list of subscriptions already promised by London circuits was read, and continually added to during the evening, representatives standing up one after another to make promises, till a total of sixty-five thousand guineas was reached.

The plan is to associate guineas with names. Ostensibly all are to be equally subscribers of one guinea, neither more nor less. It was explained that those who could afford more could make up the money for those who could not afford so much, but all the names would stand equal on the 'roll'. The total sum would be paid by each circuit, the number of guineas matching that of the names given, or, stretching this principle a little further, a rich circuit would perhaps help a poorer one 'out of its abundance'. In one way or another each guinea must mean a name, and almost any plan might be adopted to swell the number of names, especially, for instance, the paying for children, those of a man's own family or, in more wholesale fashion, those from Sunday-school classes, whose connection with Wesleyanism might be very slight indeed. Nor did some speakers shrink from suggesting (perhaps partly in joke) that it would be admissible to add the names of the dead as well as the living to this immortal roll.

The main purposes to which the million guineas shall be devoted have been laid down beforehand, and the allotment is evidently the result of carefully balanced claims. I gathered that 300,000 guineas were to go to the aid and support of village Methodism all over the country, and 250,000 to the building of central London quarters: a kind of cathedral for the body. Then 200,000 were set aside for education, and other objects filled up the total. It is a very large sum to raise, and some anxiety may have been felt, but the confidence expressed in the success of the attempt has since been justified.

What surprised me was the low level spiritually and intellectually of all that was said. No high note was ever struck, or only once (and I stayed to the end). This was when an old man 'trusted that the effort to obtain money might not choke spirituality', or something to that effect. At this meeting there was no spark of spirituality to choke: nothing appeared but the pursuit of success. The audience seemed thoroughly to enjoy the electioneering style in which the meeting was conducted, with the 'state of the poll' read out every few minutes amid a shower of feeble jokes. I looked for some deeper note of feeling. If a deeper note be not sounded, what good can come?

A Fin de Siecle View from the Presidential Chair

(F. W. Macdonald, *As a Tale that is Told*, 1919, pp. 236–42)

Macdonald followed Hugh Price Hughes as President in 1899. These extracts are from his Presidential Address, reprinted in his autobiography.

The Domestic Annals of Methodism. – The general course of our church's history is well known, but the domestic annals which that history in-

cludes are, from the nature of the case, private memories and possessions.
It has been said that the political history of this country might almost be
written from the letters and journals of its great political families. Something like it is true of Methodism. Much of its history is interpreted when
we read the correspondence of our fathers, and are enabled to see the
humble round of life and duty of which the Methodist preacher's home
was the centre. I have had this privilege in an exceptional degree in
traditions of more than a century. The simple records that I possess,
letters written to near relations and diaries intended for no eye but the
writer's, afford 'side-lights of Methodism' more edifying than the controversies whose echoes reach us still; plain living and high thinking,
family life just above the level of actual poverty, but bright with affection
and intelligence, sweet and gracious in its simple piety, serious in its aims
but touched with imagination and humour. It has been given to some of
my grandfather's descendants to achieve distinction that is widely recognised; but the moral picturesque of that brave old Methodist preacher's
life, his courage and cheerfulness, his manly piety, his love of his children
and of his books, and of the people among whom he laboured – the
memory of these will still remain a principal part of the inheritance of
those who claim descent from him. In thinking of these things I have
often felt that but a small part of the church's life is represented by our
conferences and congresses, by organisations and demonstrations visible
to every observer . . .

Relations with Other Churches. – Our church system seems to me to hold
in happy balance different elements of polity on whose equilibrium
stability depends. The theory and position of the ministry among us are
as far removed from sacerdotalism as from anarchy, and we have no
intention of going further in the direction of Rome on the one hand, or
of Plymouth on the other. Our laity are neither the slaves nor the taskmasters of their ministers, but their brethren and fellow-labourers. As
to our relations with other churches, they were never more cordial or
fruitful than they now are. So far as the Nonconformist churches are
concerned, there are no grudges or grievances between us, no differences
that hinder co-operation of the happiest kind. With regard to the Church
of England, the relation is not so clear or so easily summed up, but I by
no means take a despondent view of it. It is true we regret many of the
developments that have marked recent years, both in a sacerdotal and
in a rationalistic direction. We shall meet them, not by controversy,
which embitters and seldom persuades, but by working out our own
convictions as witnesses for an Evangelical theology and church life.
Meanwhile, we see much to admire in the zeal and industry of her clergy,
and much to imitate in the piety of many of her children. We honour her
scholars, love her missionaries, and count many of her people amongst
our dearest friends. And when, tired of looking for recognition on the

part of Rome, she thinks of possible union with the non-episcopal churches, I trust we shall frankly respond.

A Pastoral Ministry. – The subject of preaching is too large a one for me to touch under the limits of this occasion, but if anything I can say may have weight with my younger brethren, I would urge them to consider the question of their efficiency as pastors. I sometimes fear it has not its due place among our ideals. There is a laudable ambition in the minds of most of us when we are young to attain to pulpit excellence. There is intellectual and moral gratification in preaching, especially to those who appreciate it as our people generally do. To be popular is delightful, and ministers win popularity and take rank in the church more directly by their pulpit powers than by anything else. Now my point is not that too much pains are given to preaching, but that the duties of the pastoral office are liable to be underestimated in comparison with it. Perhaps it is because I am growing older, and have larger experience of what is involved in the life of a family, but it is my strong conviction that no minister does a better or more abiding work than he who interests himself in the daily life of his people, who wins the confidence and esteem of the young, whose sympathy is quick in times of sorrow, who visits the sick, and brings his personal influence to bear upon the homes to which he has access. I know well the difficulty of our itinerant ministry, how easily it may produce an itinerant cast of mind unfavourable to local concentration, and a sustained interest in individuals; but it remains true that we must be pastors as well as preachers if we are to win the hearts of those under our charge . . .

Ministerial Training. – I think that we must make up our minds steadily to raise the standard of ministerial education. The Methodist ministry has always been a practically efficient ministry, but a training that would be sufficient in one period and under one set of circumstances is not necessarily adequate in another period and under other conditions, and it is my strong conviction that in the England of the twentieth century that will not be an efficient ministry that is not highly trained. We have entered upon what is in many respects an age of transition, and not least so in the sphere of religious thought and church polity. I do not say that old truths are crumbling – truths do not crumble – but old modes of expressing and applying truth may need to be revised. Ministers must know what currents are running, what tendencies are making themselves felt. Our universities and high schools are giving us in every congregation young men and women who, though they do not ask us to give them university extension lectures slightly tinged with Christian thought, have a right to expect the preacher to speak as one who shares the knowledge and culture of our time. Now does any one of us regard the present training of our ministry in this respect as ideal, or even adequate? Is the three years' term – too often cut short by the demands of our system –

sufficient? And that three years' training, be it remembered, is not a course of theological instruction given to men who have already had a training in arts, but one that for the majority of students includes general education.

I do not know whether Methodism, that was born at Oxford, will go back to Oxford, whether that or any other university will in the future give a part at least of the training our ministers receive; but in any case we must seek to draw into our ministry the choicest products of all classes in our church, and aim at giving them the best training both in arts and in theology that is to be had, and so equip them for the great and varied duties the twentieth century will bring.

Methodism and Politics. – One of the possible dangers to which I have referred is that of seeking to use our compact and organised strength in the sphere of politics. There is some juncture of public affairs on which, say, some of us feel strongly, a phase of policy, some action, real or imagined, on the part of a government or an opposition which we desire or dislike. Well, we have a compact organisation. There are eight hundred circuits, and the address of every superintendent can be found in the minutes of conference, and a circular letter would reach every one of them in the course of two posts. There are thirty-four district synods, and surely a brother would be found in each of them to move an identical resolution if he were furnished with it. And there is the Conference itself, with its enormous weight and influence. What a machinery to use! What a power to wield! And here is an occasion when it could be used to such good effect! I do not wonder that the possibility of capturing this Conference should haunt the minds of public men looking round for allies and reinforcements. But I trust we shall continue to maintain as a church our independence and neutrality, and preserve our individual civic freedom on public questions. There are indeed few political issues of such a nature that all good men must necessarily be on the same side; and when such an issue does arise there will be little need of denominational action as such – the motives that govern good men generally will then suffice. . . . I believe that concerted action in the political sphere is about the last use we should make of our influence as a church, and that in the meantime the best political service we can render to our country is to bring the power of a living Christianity to bear upon the people at large, and so to assist in the formation of a public opinion hostile to wrong-doing of every kind, and favourable to truth and justice, to religion and virtue.

Temperance and Total Abstinence

A debate in the Wesleyan Conference

(*Methodist Recorder*, 1 August 1901)

The Rev. Thomas Champness moved the following motion, of which he had given notice:

> That, in view of the sorrow and sin caused by the drinking habits of the people, the Conference thinks it in the highest degree undesirable that any persons directly engaged in the liquor traffic should be nominated for office in the Wesleyan Methodist Church . . .

The Rev. Enoch Salt presented the report of the Memorials Committee upon this question. Memorials had been received from twenty-two circuits, all of them almost identically in the terms of Mr. Champness's motion, and, after a prolonged consideration of those memorials, the Committee came unanimously to the decision to advise the Conference to reply in the following terms:

> The Conference, having in 1898, 1899 and 1900, expressed its judgment upon this subject, this Conference thinks it unnecessary to do more than order the resolutions of 1899 to be printed in the forthcoming 'Minutes of Conference.' . . .

Mr. Champness having moved his resolution, the Rev. William Bradfield, B.A. seconded . . . He did not approach that subject from the same point of view as Mr. Champness, and a great many more of the more vigorous teetotal party with whom he was not able to join. He believed they were wrong in their theology and wrong in their science. He was one of those who, in spite of all that had been spoken on the subject over these many years, would not hesitate to call alcoholic liquors 'good creatures of God'. It must be perfectly obvious, then, that he, at any rate, could not take up the position that there was anything wrong *per se* in selling a liquor of which he, for one, was sure there was nothing wrong in drinking it. But they must look at the actual facts of the case. The sale of alcoholic liquors in this country, as carried on, depended for its profit upon their excessive and wasteful consumption . . . One half of the liquors sold were used to wasteful consumption, and the great harm of the moral and physical condition of the community . . . As a part of the Church of the Lord Jesus Christ they ought to use the power they had of denouncing the traffic, so that the world should understand what their denunciation meant. It was the great sin of covetousness which, after all, was responsible. They ought to speak. They could stand on solid New Testament lines in that matter, and they certainly could say that the man whom they would not put into office was the man who took dirty profits . . .

The Ex-President [Dr. Thomas Allen] moved, as an amendment, the recommendation of the Memorials Committee . . . It might be said . . . that there was not very much difference between Mr. Champness's proposal and the resolutions of the Conference, which they proposed that day to re-affirm. The Ex-President here read the resolutions of Conference of 1899, as follow:

The Conference having received suggestions and memorials on the subject of 'Persons interested in the traffic in intoxicating liquors, occupying official positions in the Methodist Church', resolves as follows:

1. The Conference reaffirms its resolutions of last year, namely: (1) The Conference was never more alive than at the present time to the dire results of the liquor traffic, and rejoices in the progress of Temperance sentiment and practice in the Wesleyan Methodist Church, but feels that to interfere with the constitutional method of appointing our Church officers is undesirable, in the interests of Temperance work itself, as well as on other grounds. (2) At the same time the Conference recommends our people to keep free from complicity with a traffic, the results of which are so injurious to the interests of religion, morality, and social life.

2. The Conference, while deeply deploring the manifold evils – spiritual, moral and physical – arising from the existing liquor traffic, confidently relies on the continued growth of moral conviction in the community, by the blessing of God, to remove the present national disgrace and danger. It once more earnestly exhorts our people to keep themselves free from complicity with the traffic, and to give their active support to well-considered efforts on behalf of Temperance reform.

3. The Conference cannot, however, impose disabilities upon those who sell drink which would not apply to those who buy and use it; neither is it prepared to interfere with the rights and responsibilities of circuit authorities in the election of Church officers.

4. Furthermore, the Conference believes that the great ends of the Temperance movement can be secured without resort to methods of coercion, which raise the gravest issues respecting the constitution of the Christian Church and the rights of the individual Christian conscience . . .

The fact that these resolutions were strong showed very clearly that the Conference had been anxious to go as far as possible in order to meet Mr. Champness – (hear, hear) – and it seemed to some of them that that fact demanded, on the part of Mr. Champness and those who thought with him, some definite practical response. But, unfortunately, that notice of motion could not be separated from Mr. Champness himself, or from methods of action and policy which he had felt it to be right to take. He referred to certain articles which had appeared in the 'Joyful News', also to letters which had been written to people in the trade. Mr.

Champness, by the action which he had taken – conscientiously and deliberately – had already driven families out of the Methodist Church. ('No, no.') All that was known in many quarters, and it was greatly regretted. He (the Ex-President) had travelled about the country a great deal, as they knew, during the year, and he had met with people who had said this: 'We respect Mr. Champness; we admire the great work which he has done in the Methodist Church – (hear, hear) – but Mr. Champness is an individual – he must have freedom of speech, like all other individual members of the Conference and of the Methodist Church. But if the supreme assembly of the Church takes up this question, and puts its stamp on this resolution, and on the methods employed by what one of them called 'this new Connexional Censor' – if the supreme deliberative assembly of the Church does that, that is a very different matter; let that be done, and we retire from Methodism at once.' . . .

The Rev. Thomas Champness, speaking from the platform, then proceeded to reply. He said he had been asked by a distinguished member of that platform to pause. He had paused for years. Those who knew him knew that he was not given to running counter to his brethren. He liked to agree with them. He had paused year after year, until the cries and sobs and tears of strong men weeping over their sons carried to their graves before their time – the sorrows of humanity, especially of those who spoke his native tongue – their sorrows had compelled him to pause, and speak, and write. He signed his name when he wrote. (Hear, hear.) He wished everybody else did. (Hear, hear.) He wrote in the fear of God. He knew his brethren there, the Ex-President and others, had spoken in the fear of God. He respected them, and believed these brethren to be sincere. God forbid that he should say a word against any of them. But he was sincere also – (hear, hear) – and he said he had no ulterior motive. . . . He did not want to hurt anybody, except this wicked traffic. He had sworn before God that as long as he was outside his coffin he would fight that till he died. (Hear, hear.) The Ex-President had said the drink traffic was a great source of misery and crime. Was that true? And was the source of misery and crime to be dignified by office in that Church? That was an important question. He paused for a reply. What was their reply? The vote would be the reply. ('No, no.') The Ex-President had said that no one would nominate any person for office who was directly connected with the drink traffic. There was a man directly connected with the drink traffic in the Conference, sent there by his Synod, sent to the highest court of their Church. As long as any Synod could send a man to that Conference who was connected directly with that which was a source of misery and crime, it was time for them to say strong things, and he said he was a traitor in the camp. ('No, no,' and 'Withdraw.') He had only to say he had been asked when this was to cease. Every time he came to that Conference he should act legally. No one could refuse to him the right to give notice of motion. He should do so respectfully. But he wanted to say now that he feared lest that vote would strengthen the hands that were dirtied with this drink. There were men in that Connexion who got their living by that which ruined the people. He knew a nice little town, where there were Methodist brewers, who kept very respectable public-houses, that were closed on the Lord's Day, but they had thirty-two houses in a big city in this country. They did not act the same there, and there was not the same care for the family name in that big city. And because these men would be strengthened if they refused to entertain his motion he begged of them to vote with him. (Hear, hear.)

The President then put the amendment moved by the Ex-President to the vote, and it was carried by a large majority.

Bible Christian Temperance Report, 1905

(BC *Minutes*, 1905)

The annual returns indicate continued interest and activity in Temperance work. We are thankful to record an increase of 7 Bands of Hope, the total number now being 324. We have been urging for years past that every Sunday School should recognize the Band of Hope as an integral part of its work, and this recognition is being given in increasing measure, though the increase is not as rapid as we could wish to see it.

Will Elders' Meetings and Sunday School Teachers' Meetings please note, as a great present day necessity, that there must be
A BAND OF HOPE IN EVERY CHURCH
Its purpose is to safeguard the children from the perils of the drink-habit and the drink-traffic. Who does not realize the necessity of this? Strong drink is England's curse and shame. For its sake the dearest ties are every day severed, the costliest sacrifices every day made; and the greatest sacrifice placed on the blood-stained altar of Bacchus is the life of England's children.

If the nation has not the moral sense to see the evil and to take measures for its removal, then the duty is laid all the more clearly and urgently on the Church of Christ to raise her voice in indignant protest and to use every means in her power for the protection of its child-life, which is a nation's most precious possession.

Save the children!! That is the Church's watchword for the twentieth century. Our Bible Christian Church has an honourable record. Our fathers were among the first and foremost of Temperance Reformers. Our Chapels were open for the advocacy of teetotal principles when other places of worship were closed against them.

We are bound by the traditions of the past, as well as by the imperative needs of the present, to the principle and the practice of total abstinence.

The number of members in the Bands of Hope is 26,530. This is a decrease of 250, but the decrease is more than counter-balanced by the return of Sunday School scholars who are teetotalers. These number 34,953, or an increase of 2,403 on last year, while for the previous year the increase was 6,910.

It is a fact over which we greatly rejoice that the vast majority of children in our schools are teetotalers. If we can send them out into the battle of life as decided followers of Christ and pledged abstainers, we have done the greatest work possible for our day and generation.

The number of Temperance Societies is the same as last year, viz., 78. The membership is 5,508, an increase of 773. A large number of our churches have no separate temperance society for the reason that the church is a temperance society in itself, and also because many of our people are identified with one or other of the great temperance organisations of the country.

We have striven to obtain an approximate number of the members of churches who are total abstainers, but without success. The column for such a return is absolutely disregarded by some districts, in others only partially filled, so that no accurate statement can be made.

On the general and public aspects of the question every legitimate weapon has been used to fight the drink foe. The present Government, in alliance with the liquor traffic, has placed a new Licensing Act upon the Statute Book, which makes our work as Temperance Reformers more difficult than ever. It has lessened the power of magistrates in local areas in the control of licences, and has recognised the vicious principle of compensation as part of the law of the land. It is deeply felt by all the Free Churches, and by all who have the cause of temperance reformation at heart, that this Act must be vitally amended. Such legislation is worse than barren. It is pernicious and corrupting.

We eagerly long for the day when the nation shall have the opportunity to shake itself free from the incubus of a Government dominated by the priest and the publican. In that day let every man amongst us exercise his franchise as in the sight of God and the Throne of Judgment.

Justice! Freedom! Equality! Righteousness! These are lost ideals that wait for a time of restoration.

The Central Sunday Closing Association is taking steps to unite all the Temperance forces in the country to secure an English Sunday Closing Act during the next Parliament.

Most heartily do we support the proposal. In itself it is of the first necessity, and it would help, rather than hinder, other temperance reforms.

Sunday Closing would be an instalment of the legislation sought by all the temperance organisations. It is one of the few temperance reforms of which the people of Great Britain and Ireland have had actual experience; its undoubted success in promoting sobriety and good order in Scotland, Ireland and Wales gives the claim for its extension to England a pre-eminence over every other.

It is re-assuring in all our work and warfare to remember that 'the battle is the Lord's. The Lord of Hosts is with us, the God of Jacob is our refuge.' 'They that be with us are more than they that with with them.'

If defeat awaited us our duty would be the same; but we may hearten ourselves for the conflict by the confidence that victory is sure.

London Methodism

(Charles Booth, *Life and Labour of the People in London*, 1902, Series III, Vol. 1, pp. 233–4; Vol. 2, pp. 217–18)

On Sunday morning Mr. Peter Thompson was preaching at the Wesleyan East-End Mission. His subject was the calling of Matthew, and the feast he made to attract those for whose conversion he hoped, the preacher describing very forcibly the presence of Christ among these people. It was all said in support of missionary work, and was very curious as a commentary on the Mission's own methods: the tables spread to attract those to whom should be preached the Word of God and hope of salvation. Mr. Thompson in the pulpit is exactly the same as out of it; a big burly man, with a great voice and strong practical way of saying what he has to say. I was struck (as I had been in the case of the young Catholic priest mentioned above) that he preached as to fellow-workers, and not as to those themselves in the present need of salvation. In the congregation there were many children (the galleries were filled by them both morning and evening), and those in the body of the hall, about one hundred, were mostly young persons. As regards the children the sermon was hardly applicable at all, and as to the young persons, seemed apt to encourage spiritual conceit.

The chapel of the Methodist New Connexion is a truly hideous building, formed into an exact oval by its galleries, which are carried round so as to meet. At the further end there is an organ, and in front of the gallery a high pulpit, from which the minister expounded the Scriptures in an extraordinarily simple, realistic fashion, as to the relations between God and Christ and the angels. He pointed out that God could never grow old; had never been young; if He had ever been young at all He must once have been very young, must once have had a beginning, &c. Then as to the etiquette of heaven: the angels *stood* in the presence of God; Christ *sat*, the work of mediation being finished, but *got up* from His seat to welcome Stephen the proto-martyr, &c., &c. In the morning there was a congregation of about one hundred strictly lower middle class, and in the evening about one hundred and fifty, when there was more exposition, dealing this time, in an exhaustively definite way, with David's poetical language, 'As far as the East is from the West, so far has Thou removed my transgression from me.'

Sunday Evening at Cleveland Hall (*West London Mission*)

At 7 o'clock the hall, which may hold four hundred to five hundred, was already almost full, and eventually there was scarcely a vacant seat. There were about five women to one man, and a considerable sprinkling of children. Those seated near me were young women of the servant or shop class, and the congregation, as a whole, were of the highest working class, with a small number of the poor and a larger number of those obviously on or over the border of the middle class. The order of the service was as usual, and the sermon a strong emotional appeal on the love of the Cross. There was an after-meeting, which lasted thirty-five minutes, for which a large number stayed; I should think quite one hundred and fifty. This meeting was directed at the unconverted. Hymns and prayers (by men specially called on by the leader) followed alternately, interspersed by strongly-worded appeals to those who were touched to come out and indicate it in some way, by lifting a hand or by standing up in their place. There was no visible response. The leader would not, he said, address any individual personally, because 'people were so touchy', but one of the Sisters sat down beside a woman evidently trying to move her, and a man passed from one to another, but apparently without success. He came to me with 'Are you trusting in the Saviour?' 'Are you sure?' I bent my head, and he went on to another man with whom he appeared to plead and wrestle for the remainder of the time – a stubborn, but perhaps a hopeful case.

On another Sunday evening, at the same hall, there may have been one hundred and fifty present, of whom about one hundred were adults. Many were quite distinctly middle class, and with the rarest exception none looked poor. The numbers probably depend on the preacher. On this occasion it was an elderly man, who preached a hopelessly dull sermon lasting half an hour.

Prospects of Methodist Union

(T. Bowman Stephenson, *Proceedings of the Third Oecumenical Methodist Conference*, 1901, Introduction, pp. xi–xii)

The winning of souls to Christ, and building them up in their most holy faith, is the prime work of the Church, without which all else is vain, and by reference to which everything else should be judged. To alter the constitution of a Church, to draw the Churches nearer to each other, or to unite those who have been disparted, is not in itself of any importance, except as it improves the capacity of the Church for its great work of saving mankind. Whatever promotes this, directly or indirectly, is worthy of all care and effort; nothing that will not help this is worth the time spent upon it. For the Church's business is salvation; and it is a matter for rejoicing that Methodism is still a fruitful bough, even 'a fruitful bough whose branches run over the wall'.

Nevertheless, the needless existence of separate Churches is to be regretted, and separation is needless, except when sufficiently grave variations of creed, method, or polity compel it. It can scarcely be denied that in some of the now divided Churches of Methodism there are no sufficient causes for their separation. In such cases economy of men and means might well be promoted, and a larger result of the highest kind expected from labours which would be no longer in any degree expended upon rivalry or self-protection. True everywhere, this is especially true in new and sparsely-populated countries. Hence it was a cause of deep thankfulness that, whilst the second Œcumenical Conference was heralded by Methodist Union in Canada, the third could rejoice over a like Union in Australasia, all but completed.

It would have added to the joy of the Conference if any decisive step could have been reported towards Union between some at least of the several Methodist Churches in Great Britain and in the United States. But it was tacitly recognised that in the countries where Methodism has been longest planted, is most widely and strongly entrenched, and has the memory of past struggles still surviving, the difficulties in the way of Union are the greatest. The Conference, however, greatly rejoiced in the fact that controversy between Methodist Churches is a thing of the past, and the relations between those Churches are cordially harmonious, and show promise of an increasing intimacy of relation and feeling as the years pass on.

State Education

(*Minutes*, 1902, 1906)

Education Bill, 1902.

The Conference once more declares that the primary object of Methodist policy in the matter of Elementary Education is the establishment of School Boards everywhere, acting in districts of sufficient area, and the placing of a Christian unsectarian school within reasonable distance of every family. The Conference, therefore, deeply regrets that the present Education Bill is intended to destroy the School Board system, and to make no adequate provision for the just claims of those parents who do not desire their children to be driven into denominational schools. The Conference has no wish to abolish the denominational schools, or to prevent them from being used, with equitable restrictions, for the purpose of giving denominational education to those children whose parents desire it. But the Conference expresses once more its deep conviction that no increased grant from public funds should be made to denominational schools, unless that increased grant is accompanied by adequate and representative public management. If, however, denominational schools are to be almost wholly maintained from imperial taxes and local rates, the irreducible minimum of the rights of conscience and of public justice demands that at least a majority of the local education authority and of the governing Committee of every school shall consist of publicly elected persons.

Education Bill, 1906
Joint Meeting of the Ordinary Committee of Privileges of the Wesleyan Methodist Church, the Education Committee, and the Secondary Education Committee.

The Conference receives and adopts the Report of the Committee. The following are the resolutions:—
(1) That the proposed national system of education should be complete, and should grant no preferential treatment to any particular denomination, as such.
(2) That the abolition of ecclesiastical tests imposed upon teachers should be complete. That no inducements to teachers should be permitted which constitute an indirect ecclesiastical test, and that suitable provision should be made that no teacher should be called upon to give religious instruction in which he does not believe.
(3) That the simple Biblical instruction to be provided in the schools should be given by the teachers within school hours, by means of a syllabus to be prepared by the local education authority, under the

conditions of the Cowper-Temple clause, and should be subject to a conscience clause.

(4) That the facilities for giving special religious instruction should only be provided in any particular school when a sufficient number of parents of children attending the school demand it. Such instruction should be given outside the regular school hours, should be at the expense of the denomination providing it, and should not be given by means of the staff of the school . . .

An Executive Committee was appointed to lay these Resolutions before the Right Hon. Augustine Birrell, K.C., M.P., President of the Board of Education, and to take such action as might be necessary to secure the objects of the Conference while the Education Bill is before Parliament. The Committee was received by the President of the Board of Education at a private interview on March 13.

The Executive Committee met on Thursday, April 26, to consider the Education Bill, and unanimously passed the following Resolutions:

1. The Committee expresses its warm approval of the Education Bill introduced by his Majesty's Government in that it adopts the principle of a national system of elementary education, abolishes ecclesiastical tests for teachers, and provides for the continuance of simple Biblical instruction in the schools.

2. While reserving its rights to submit amendments to the Bill, especially in reference to the special facilities to be afforded for sectarian teaching, the Committee recommends the Wesleyan Methodist Church to give its strong support to a measure which in its main features entirely accords with the declared educational policy of our Church . . .

A further meeting of the Joint Committee met by instruction of the President of the Conference on Monday, May 28, when the following Resolutions were passed unanimously:

(1) The Committee expresses its warm approval of the Education Bill introduced by his Majesty's Government in so far as it adopts the principle of a national system of elementary education, abolishes ecclesiastical tests for teachers, and provides for the continuance of simple Biblical instruction in the schools.

(2) The Committee strongly objects to Clause IV in its present form, on the ground that it is an indirect violation of the main principles of the Bill, namely, the abolition of tests and the adoption of full popular control. The Committee therefore recommends his Majesty's Government to withdraw this Clause, unless it can be amended in accordance with the above-named principles.

(3) That the religious instruction under the Cowper-Temple Clause should be given by the teachers within school hours.

(4) That this Committee urges upon his Majesty's Government the

importance of building new schools in all cases where that course is possible, rather than allow the public elementary education to be carried on in schools which are either private property or are subject to private rights, and of making financial provision for carrying out this policy throughout the country.

These Resolutions were forwarded to the President of the Board of Education, and a copy was sent to all members of the House of Commons.

The Coming of the Miao: Bible Christian Missions in South West China

(*Eyes of the Earth: the Diary of Samuel Pollard*, edited by R. Elliott Kendall, 1954, pp. 73–8, 86–8)

July 12th [1904]. Several Miao, four of them in fact, came in from the country and stayed here until Saturday morning. Their strange story was this. They had walked for nine days to An-shuen, in the neighbouring province, to see a Mr. Adam who was a missionary with whom a Miao hunting party had once stayed the night. He had told them that as they had come so far they would find it better to go to Chaotung, which could be only two days' journey from their home. Accordingly they had returned to Chaotung.

The first thing was, they were very much in earnest in wanting to read. They brought with them small bags of food, oatmeal chiefly. I let them sleep in the old schoolroom. I sincerely hope this will turn out to be the opening of a new field. God save them all. Our people here are very stirred up by this event.

July 22nd. Five more Miao came, and we tried to teach them.

July 23rd. Thirteen more Miao came. They say that there are thousands more waiting to come. On Friday night I spoke to them for some time, as simply as I could, and tried to tell them the Gospel story. As I spoke to them of God as the Father and Mother of all races their faces brightened up and they nodded assent. Presently I was called away. When I returned I questioned them on what I had just told them and they answered, 'We cannot remember'. It is so difficult to know how to teach these primitive folk.

I asked them if they were afraid of us and one answered, 'We heard the Chinese and No-su talking about "Foreigner! Foreigner!" We were afraid at first, but by and by we went to see, and then found that they were not foreign, but like our own people. We are one family, only you come from a distance.' This is said as a great compliment . . .

Aug. 7th. Sunday. More Miao have been coming every few days. Altogether about eighty have been here. Today a party of twelve arrived who had been out all night on the road in torrential rain. These fellows were on the hillsides all through the wet night, on their way here to hear the Gospel. In some places the Chinese have tried to stop the Miao coming in to visit me, and that is why they were travelling through the night. So far they have come from ten different villages.

In the evening, after the Chinese service, I held a Miao service with them, by speaking through two of them as interpreters. It was so interesting to watch them. I would say a few words and then turn to my interpreters and tell them to repeat what I said in Miao. In this way I got hold of some words as well as they. . . .

[In September] an invitation came to me to visit an aboriginal chief. He lived at Heh-tu-ho, about thirty miles east of Chaotung in the hills. Men arrived in the city with a horse all ready for our departure. We left about noon and reached there after dark. I found there were three brothers living together, the oldest was only thirty-four, and he managed all the affairs of a large estate. His house, a primitive chateau, was bigger and more impressive than the Yamen of Chaotung.

There were some indications of their manner of life which impressed me. Outside the main gate was a canque, a wooden affair which is fastened round a prisoner's neck like a yoke. It was not there as a relic but was obviously in use. Men were armed with spears and guns, and prepared for the defence of the buildings was a handy supply of tridents. However, they treated us very kindly.

They were clearly the landlords and a power to be reckoned with in this area. They asked us a lot of questions about the Church and at my request gathered all the local people together for me to preach to. . . .

Sept. 4th. While in the country I heard a lot more details of the rumours that are sweeping through the countryside with the coming of the Miao to Chaotung. The whole country is alive with rumours. The most common story is that the oppressed Miao get poison from the foreigner and with it they are going to kill off all the Nosu landlords and the Chinese. Three Miao that I know of have been tied up and told that, if they do not deliver up the person who gave them the poison, they would be killed. In many places the Miao are now prohibited from attending the weekly markets. Their visits to Chaotung are bringing them into serious trouble.

One of the rumours is that when the Miao come into the city I put a drop of water into their mouths and then they can read splendidly. At other times I stroke their hair once or twice, and then their memory becomes marvellous.

Sept. 5th. The Miao in the country are being annoyed and ostracised. Most of them appear to live in Weining County, so today Wong-lao-tai, Chong-ming-tsai, two of the Chinese preachers, and I set off for the Yamen at Weining, 75 miles away, to see if we can settle the affair at headquarters. . . .

Sept. 8th. [At Weining] I saw the authorities and brought up the question of the Miao in the country because of their attempt to hear the Christian religion. In the evening the officer sent over a copy of the proclamation to see if it would do. The first line began, 'Whereas we have repeatedly received edicts commanding us to protect the Western men . . .' I cut out the last two words and altered them to 'Christian'. This was later accepted, and the whole proclamation will be made known throughout the area. . . . I discovered that the inns that refused us were not full, but would just not have a foreigner. We should not have had an inn at all had it not been for the fact that we brought with us an escort of men from the Chaotung Yamen. After two places had refused us, the escort saw that the next did not.

Sept. 10th. After a meal we left Weining and made for Yang-kai, the supposed centre of the Miao oppression. On arrival we settled ourselves in a little inn and visited the local officer. He said that there had been no trouble here, but all local markets the Miao had been prohibited from attending. We visited the local market, held on the hillside; a display of all manner of wares and a crowd of people from all around. The Miao at first were afraid to come near; they had evidently been scared. Later some of them came to see us at the inn.

Sept. 11th. Today was Sunday and my companions strongly urged us to travel to Ta-kai, and so be able to maintain the 'run of the market days' as we journeyed on. We felt tempted to go but I decided to stay and keep the day properly. We went outside a temple and preached to the local soldiers.
    Later on in the day about forty or fifty Miao came to see me, followed by lots more, until there were over a hundred here; some of them had been to Chaotung to learn. Had we not stayed for the Sunday we should have missed seeing them.
    A Miao woman and her husband came in great trouble. It was a strange case of demon possession. The woman was nursing a baby girl. She had been a medium and now wished to give it up, but her neighbours refused to let her. When any trouble befell any of them they said it was her spirit that had done it, and she had to exorcise the spirit. Crying bitterly, she begged us to deliver her from the possession by this spirit. We stood up together and prayed, and I told the woman to call upon Him whenever she was troubled by this demon and she would be freed.

She seemed greatly comforted when it was all over. May God drive the demon away from her and save them all!

I have discovered who are the ring-leaders of the Miao trouble and have written to them warning them to watch their step. The local people are very nervous of a rebellion. In this tense atmosphere an outbreak could occur at any moment. . . .

Dec. 6th. For a while today we were travelling on the road to Ko-kuei. It was on this road that Thorne was travelling when he was struggling back to Chaotung to die. (He fell from his horse a number of times from sheer exhaustion.) We went down and down and down. It was an awful road, bad enough for us, but it must have been torture for a sick man. What brave fellows Thorne and Vanstone were! No two better men have ever been sent out by the Bible Christians.[1]

At night about two hundred people came and a lot of boys and girls. The women stood by listening. They say there are a thousand families hereabouts. In the 8th Moon they were threatened with chains, etc., in the usual way, if they became Christians, but it is quieter now.

The greatness of the work frightens one at times. What are we to do with it? What does the Lord mean?. . . .

Dec. 26th. During the day a Miao wizard came to me in great distress. He was blind in one eye and he had a horn of hair sloping at about 50 degrees up from his forehead. He told me he wished to get rid of the demon which possessed him and to give up all his devil tricks. Could I help him?

At the evening service John Li took charge, and then some Miao spoke; then I called on the wizard and he came to the front. I told the people what we were going to do. Just then I thought that there might be more in the same situation, so I called for any other wizards. Another stood up – excitement began to increase – then another and another, until at last we had five. We cleared the preachers off the platform, so as to have room for action, but the proceedings were interrupted by a voice shouting out 'Another! Another!' Finally we had nine devil-workers in all. Some of the wizards were very repulsive.

Then to our surprise we noticed that one of the men was a Miao who had begun to preach. He told me that since he had come and learned to sing and pray, the devil had left him and never returned again.

Up there at the front I felt as if I could treat a myriad of devils with supreme contempt. 'If God be for us, who can be against us?' I told the people that we were more powerful than all devils, that before Jesus 'devils fear and fly'. Then I questioned each. Each said he wanted to give up his devil practices and to trust Jesus. First of all singly, and then unitedly, they promised to quit it for ever. (Great excitement.) Then I told them all to get on their knees, and all the nine repeated prayers after me. There they were on their faces before God asking for deliverance. We prayed and prayed: 'Lord, help us,' 'Drive the devils away,' then 'Thank you, Jesus,' and last of all, in mounting excitement, the congregation clapped their hands, shouting, 'Thank you, Jesus, for saving us and driving the devils away.' It was all very exciting and wonderful, different from anything I have ever seen before.

Drunkenness and immorality are the twin sins these people suffer from most of all. The former confined chiefly to the men, the latter shared in an almost unthinkable manner by all. Every village of twenty or more houses boasted of a club where the young people, married and unmarried, spent their evenings, and these brothels or clubs were the curse of the people. On the physical side the children have endured terrible suffering from the sins of their parents. When one mentions the 'Miao disease', everyone knows what one means, as it is so typical.

[1] Samuel T. Thorne (a great-grandson of William O'Bryan) and Thomas G. Vanstone were the pioneers of the Bible Christian mission to South-west China, in 1885. Thorne died of fever in 1891; Vanstone returned home in 1893.

The United Methodist Church

UMC *Minutes*, 1907

Requested by the General Connexional Committee of the recent Conference, in London, to write a brief foreword to its published 'Minutes', I yield with goodwill and look for Divine assistance.

For about 110 years the Methodist New Connexion issued 'Minutes of Conference' annually; for 85 years the Bible Christians; and for 50 years the United Methodist Free Churches, under that designation. But with the Conferences and Assembly of 1907 such publication has ceased.

What a tale is told by those 'Minutes' of toil and trouble, persecution and affliction, and, in the midst of general progress, of occasional failure and retrogression! Some of the pages heave with the sob of sorrow on account of disappointments and losses, which for the most part would never have been experienced but for foolish, selfish, and sinful action, and unwise, ungenerous and needless use of the tongue. Nevertheless, there is in the records as a whole a buoyant and grateful tone, and the inward ear of the spiritual can catch the echoes of the jubilant songs of victory which our fathers sang.

A new page now opens in our history. We take a new name. We are now constituted 'The United Methodist Church', and our 'Minutes', of which this is the first volume, will be issued year by year until there shall be a larger Union (which God grant may come soon), when all Methodists, and possibly other Churches too, shall become one in name and inheritance.

There are doubtless hindrances to consolidating our Union, of which we must beware, and which by loyal devotion to Christ and fervent love of the brethren we can remove. We have hitherto been three rivers, running nearly parallel to the same ocean of Heavenly power and Christian achievement. And we have all had our peculiarities, which may yet quicken our pulses and call forth feelings of admiration. But we have come to a confluence and are now flowing on as one river. The stain of the soil through which each river made its way may continue awhile. This may be picturesque, but it is not profitable. These marks of diversity, if let alone, will soon disappear; as a residuum they will sink to the bottom; and the river will flow on, no one guessing from its appearance, that it has not been a pellucid, crystal stream, issuing from one spring flowing in one channel from the beginning. But if we do not carefully sink our slight differences, and especially if we talk about them and magnify their bulk and value by our prejudices and imagination, from one part of the river will come in harsh, unbrotherly tones, 'We are of Paul'; from another, 'We are of Apollos,' which will almost drown the rich music of the sweet and clear water as it goes by softly and winningly resounding, 'We are of Christ.'

Beloved friends, whatever our training and methods may have been, let us avoid polluting the stream by tramplings and shibboleths. Let us accept without a murmur the provisions and modes of administration set forth in these pages. Let them work, and let us try to aid them in working with all sincerity and love of peace, and never do or say anything which, if they fail, will make your conscience whisper upbraidingly, 'You were the guilty cause of the failure.' Make the organization framed with so much care, thought and prayerfulness, go; and if (to change the figure) any joint or pivot in the machinery should prove to be a misfit, the wise men of the future will devise and apply a remedy under the powers set forth in the Constitution.

Thank God, we are one in Christ already. Daily let us grow up into Him more and more. He is our living Head. In Him we have quietness, gentleness, unity, power, and peace.

I am, yours in the one Mediator and Example,

EDWARD BOADEN, *President.*

Circular to Ministers and Church and Circuit Stewards:

Dear Brethren,

The Union which has been so happily consummated, and from which we expect so much blessing, has necessitated the revision of our various

Church courts, and the adoption of a new Constitution which comes into operation forthwith.

Each of the Uniting Churches will find its usual methods of procedure somewhat modified, and it is important that as soon as possible we should all conduct our business on the same general lines.

The Constitution is not rigid, and in certain important respects there is room for variation where desired, but all the Churches will find it to their advantage to accept and to act upon the form of government, which, after careful inquiry and discussion, has been adopted. Any Circuit, however, will be free to make by-laws for itself provided these do not contravene the general Rules.

Statistical Returns of the Uniting Churches, 1907

United Methodist Free Churches
Home Districts

Names of Districts	Itinerant Preachers	Local Preachers	Church Members	Probationers	Jnr. Church Members	Chapels	Other Preaching Places	Schools	Teachers	Scholars
1. Birmingham	19	117	2889	162	62	49	3	48	799	764
2. Bristol	34	219	6585	238	358	97	3	97	1576	1600
3. Cornwall	26	339	5528	414	210	132	3	120	2411	1064
4. Leeds and Bradford	54	290	11990	912	348	136	2	134	3853	2532
5. Lincoln	22	260	4076	269	182	114	9	97	1145	733
6. Liverpool & N. Wales	23	207	4186	208	203	74	3	77	1300	1111
7. London	52	161	7051	130	214	84	1	84	1540	1531
8. Manchester	57	229	8659	459	270	106	2	106	2634	2116
9. Newcastle-on-Tyne	47	400	8987	499	479	146	17	149	2523	1930
10. Norwich	18	197	2929	312	65	91	3	83	946	700
11. Nottingham	30	310	6032	312	332	113	4	110	1956	1618
12. Rochdale	34	114	6641	358	172	67	2	68	2529	1925
13. Sheffield	22	140	4395	243	206	60	3	64	1612	1286
Totals	438	2983	79948	4516	3101	1269	55	1237	24824	18916

Foreign Districts

Names of Districts	Itinerant Preachers	Local Preachers	Church Members	Probationers	Jnr. Church Members	Chapels	Other Preaching Places	Schools	Teachers	Scholars
1. China: Ningpo	3	38	1815	722	32	19	28	11	14	24
2. China: Wenchow	3	177	2303	6082	..	10	152	36	64	125
3. East Africa	5	17	404	..	34	13	3	13	29	38
4. West Africa	9	114	2510	554	1137	21	3	19	104	151
5. Jamaica and Bocas	10	114	3890	459	249	41	11	42	274	258
Totals	30	460	10922	7817	1452	104	197	121	485	598

Methodist New Connexion
Home Districts

Names of Districts	Itinerant Preachers	Local Preachers	Church Members	Probationers	Junior Church Members	Chapels	Other Preaching Places	Schools	Teachers	Scholars
1. Dudley	19	142	4011	534	..	51	..	52	1299	13392
2. Halifax	20	91	4444	391	..	41	..	41	1270	8905
3. Hanley	14	124	3858	620	..	50	..	49	1271	10673
4. Leeds	20	72	3645	476	..	32	..	31	1010	7739
5. Liverpool	14	43	1110	123	..	17	..	17	224	2043
6. London	6	41	871	73	..	16	..	15	173	1556
7. Manchester	28	111	5836	778	..	51	..	55	1885	15433
8. Newcastle	28	221	4514	763	..	80	..	84	1401	10149
9. Nottingham	18	82	3467	335	..	33	..	32	816	6053
10. Sheffield	21	147	3691	507	..	58	..	58	1234	9074
11. Truro	2	9	264	36	..	5	..	5	81	438
12. Home Missions	14	40	1298	230	..	23	..	18	295	2286
Totals	204	1123	37009	4866	..	457	..	457	10959	87741

Foreign Districts

	Itinerant Preachers	Local Preachers	Church Members	Probationers	Junior Church Members	Chapels	Other Preaching Places	Schools	Teachers	Scholars
1. China	11	165	2979	1487	..	215	..	53	53	659

Bible Christian (Methodist) Connexion
Home Districts

Names of Districts	Itinerant Preachers	Local Preachers	Church Members	Probationers	Jnr. Church Members	Chapels	Other Preaching Places	Schools	Teachers	Scholars
1. Falmouth	13	132	2994	10	56	60	..	55	1153	447▪
2. Bodmin	14	223	3597	49	236	89	1	76	1313	551▪
3. Devonport & Plymouth	19	228	4825	97	301	82	1	81	1243	706▪
4. Shebbear	20	241	4696	47	162	92	4	91	793	393▪
5. Exeter	15	168	2598	42	114	63	5	58	418	263▪
6. Bristol	16	100	1676	20	82	46	1	36	266	219▪
7. London	15	43	1791	53	128	17	3	16	281	273▪
8. Portsmouth	22	155	3345	52	230	59	1	52	546	452▪
9. South Wales	18	106	3062	69	308	53	..	48	525	526▪
10. Chatham	10	60	1340	36	54	31	..	29	362	295▪
11. Bradford	9	31	988	41	111	15	..	12	252	226▪
12. Unconnected Stations	10	28	1290	19	112	15	2	16	264	229▪
(Supernumeraries)	25	..	..	..	..	..	..	..	..	..
Totals	206	1515	32202	535	1894	622	18	570	7416	4584▪

Foreign Districts

	Itinerant Preachers	Local Preachers	Church Members	Probationers	Jnr. Church Members	Chapels	Other Preaching Places	Schools	Teachers	Scholars
1. Chao Tong	4	..	33	50	15	2	..	..	10	17▪
2. Tong Chuan	5	..	16	2	10	1	1	..	..	..
3. Miao	5	5	2393	2500	400	3	..	..	20	200▪
Totals	14	5	2442	2552	425	6	1	..	30	217▪

Statistics of the United Methodist Church

		Itinerant Preachers	Local Preachers	Church Members	Probationers	Junior Church Members	Chapels	Other Preaching Places	Schools	Teachers	Scholars
U.M.F.C.	Home	438	2983	79948	4516	3101	1269	55	1237	24824	1891▪
„	Foreign	30	460	10922	7817	1452	104	197	121	485	59▪
M.N.C.	Home	204	1123	37009	4866	..	457	..	457	10959	877▪
„	Foreign	11	165	2979	1487	..	215	..	53	53	6▪
B.C.	Home	206	1515	32202	535	1894	622	18	570	7416	458▪
„	Foreign	14	5	2442	2552	425	6	1	..	30	21▪
	Totals	903	6251	165502	21773	*6872	2673	*271	2438	43767	3315▪

* The M.N.C. do not report the number of Junior Church Members, and 'other Preaching Place

A Christian Socialism

(S. E. Keeble, *The Ideal of the Material Life and other Social Addresses* (1908), pp. 12–17, 124–5, 139–40)

The stance of S. E. Keeble marked a significant advance on the 'Nonconformist conscience' of Hugh Price Hughes in the direction of a radical Christian critique of industrial society.

We modern Christians occupy a wholly different position [from that of the early church]. We dwell in the midst of a civilisation which is largely the creation of Christianity itself, and have, therefore, a potent if not an authoritative voice in matters ethical, social, and even political. So far from being uninfluential, insignificant, and unconscious of the social problem, as the first Christians were, modern Christians are powerful factors in society, and aware of social wrongs. Their duty is therefore to do exactly what the first Christians did not and could not do – namely, help to deal with these matters directly and collectively through the State – not for one moment, however, neglecting the important work of spiritually and ethically saving the individual man. Its attitude towards such evils as Chinese labour, indentured Kaffir labour, the coolie labour of the Assam tea-gardens and elsewhere, as well as the economic 'slavery' at home, must be much less passive than that of the early Christians towards the slavery of their time . . .

It is obvious that [the Epistle to Philemon] has a direct bearing upon the position of our modern employing class. It forbids the treatment of human beings in any factory or business establishment as mere machines, mere 'hands', mere 'machine-minders'. It is unnecessary to say that this is exactly how many employers today, who do not shrink from calling themselves Christians, do regard their workpeople. The lesson of this epistle is that it is the business of the Christian Church fearlessly to teach such men their duty, and if they will not yield to the pleadings of love, to refuse to company with them as Christians. This would leave many churches crippled indeed, but also free from participation in disregard for human relationships, and in the oppression of the helpless . . .

The modern growth of huge limited companies, trusts and syndicates, with their multitude of shareholders and large directorates, intent only on dividends, tends to render the labour problem more acute by removing the actual workers still further from those who employ them. If these brute corporations, industrial Calibans, who 'fear not God nor regard man', are not some day to be swept away by the people with a rough hand or taken over by them, they must be infused with Christian concepts of humanity, and adopt a treatment of their employees in harmony therewith. . . .

Yet another substitute for Justice is *Charity*. This is, with many middle-class and narrow-visioned Christian workers and well-to-do people, by far the most popular refuge from 'considering whatsoever things are *just*' . . . Humane and philanthropic persons busy themselves benevolently, by the thousand, in behalf of the poor, the distressed, and the unemployed. The social side of our Central Missions grows in its ameliorative, palliative, socially redemptive work – and no one would wish to diminish it. But it is no *remedy*, and it may divert men's minds from the real remedy for most of the social misery of the time, *the practice of social justice*. The Christian Church should be the first to listen to those who cry: 'We want not charity but justice.' It should be startled into new life by that banner in the London unemployed procession – 'Curse your Charity, give us work!'

Christian men must not think that because they are kind to the poor, generous to social and ameliorative institutions, that therefore they have discharged their duty. Their first duty is to give heed to the cry for justice, though no doubt, it is much easier to fly to charity and give alms, support unemployed funds, breakfast and holiday funds, hospitals, universities, and free libraries. Nor must we be blinded by those who would obscure the injustice of their methods of amassing wealth by acts of lavish charity and generous donations. Just as the old barons sought to compound with God for their robbery and bloodshed by endowing the Church, so many modern capitalists and financiers seek to cover their sins against society by benefactions of all kinds. The peril is that both the community and individuals should lose their sense of the social injustice of many of the means of acquiring wealth when a fraction of it is bestowed, with apparently gorgeous liberality, upon good causes. It is indeed 'tribute money', but it is tainted money. . . .

Since [Christ's] coming social justice has been attempted upon a scale unknown in history hitherto. But even in Christendom it has been perpetually checked and often defeated by the strength of the persistent primitive passion of selfishness. The only hope for justice lies in Christianity. Christianity is a religion of love. Where it exercises its characteristic and pure influence it creates an element in which justice is easily practised and attained. Only when individuals and communities are raised to a lofty ethical temper in which the virtues of love, unselfishness, and self-sacrifice are gladly pursued and enjoyed, is it likely to achieve justice. Where justice alone is the quest, less than justice will be attained. In order to gain the less, the aim and desire must be to gain more.

Fifty Years in Retrospect

(Charles H. Kelly, *Memories* (1910), pp. 170–5)

Kelly, as secretary of the Wesleyan Sunday School Union, helped to found the Wesley Guild, was President of the Conference in 1889 and Book Steward from 1889 to 1907.

On a review of the past half-century, I have no doubt that the changes in Methodism have for the most part been improvements.

The liberty and freedom of speech in Conference and Synods is very different to-day from what it was when I first attended: that was at the Liverpool Conference of 1857. It was like the explosion of a bomb when the Rev. Alexander M'Aulay, who had only 'travelled' seventeen years, dared to reply to the speech of a prominent man, and to castigate him severely. Going out after the session, I heard the Rev. J. P. Haswell say to the solemn Rev. Peter M'Owan – they were both 'rulers in Israel' – 'A bold young man, that brother M'Aulay!' Mr. M'Owan gravely shook his head, and replied, 'A most indiscreet young man!' At that time ministers were considered young men until they had been at least forty years in the ranks.

At that same Conference the Rev. J. Gilchrist Wilson, M.A., Assistant Editor, made a strong attack on the Book-Room and its officials, and protested against the idea that he should abstain from doing so in full Conference, and against the notion that a man must keep silence until he had been in the ministry for forty years. He had then been a minister in Methodism fifteen years; before that he was a Presbyterian, and he had been trained as a Scotch lawyer. He later submitted to reordination, and went, when an elderly man, into the Church of England. He was a pawky, amiable, and able man, who had given counsel to his superintendent at St. George's, East End, a few years before, to cut off the reformers in the circuit. But he forced a hearing at the Liverpool Conference.

From that time things changed. During that Conference several younger men spoke. Veterans like Osborn, Rattenbury, Scott, Prest, and other gods of the mountain, realized that they would no longer be able to hush voices, and that their word would not be taken for law . . .

The greatest change in modern Methodism was that which authorized Lay Representation in the Conference. It was a revolution, but a revolution accomplished without hard strife or loss. The debates on the subject were long, keen, able, thorough, and conducted almost entirely in good temper. The majorities in favour of the change were large; but when final votes had been taken the considerable minorities in Committees, Synods, and Conference were freed from bitterness, and set themselves to work the new constitution loyally and vigorously. Very few, if any, members were lost through the change. Men of both sides knew that Methodism had nothing to fear when trusting her laymen . . .

The scheme for Lay Representation was brought into operation at the Bradford Conference of 1878, and has worked admirably ever since. Laymen have been made to feel intense interest in the work of their Church. Conference experience has broadened their views, made them understand better the principles and polity of their Church, and enabled them to take a more intelligent interest in all that concerns it. The families of Methodists have felt its blessedness; the representatives themselves, their wives, their sons, and daughters have rejoiced in the glow of the Christian social intercourse of the Conference towns, and gone home far more intense in their attachment to their Church. And, better than all this, there have been some wonderful seasons of grace during the sessions, when great baptisms of the Holy Spirit have been bestowed, – memorable times, never to be forgotten.

Now that more than thirty years have passed since the change in constitution was made, it gives joy when we mark its good results; when we see how conservative of what was of first importance in Methodism the great liberal and democratic action has been.

But it makes me sad to think that it came so late; for if it, and kindred changes, could have been effected years before, probably tens of thousands of members might have been retained, and a power might have been exercised in the Conference that would have curbed the action of extremists of different sets of opinions – for there were faults on both sides.

The Impact of War

Conference Address to the Methodist Societies, 1915

(Wesleyan *Minutes*, 1915, pp. 453–6)

Dear Brethren,
Gathered in our Annual Conference we give thanks to God for His goodness to us as a Church during a year of national anxiety and personal stress. By common consent the crisis through which we are passing is fraught with mighty issues for Christianity and the world. We are thankful that as a united people our Methodist Church from the first recognised the gravity of the issue, and responded to the national call. We believe that the part that Britain is playing in this stupendous conflict has been dictated by national honour, and not by selfish expediency.

We are fully convinced that it was morally impossible for a nation with our obligations and traditions to remain neutral while Belgium was being ravaged, France and Russia imperilled, and the gains of Christianity and civilisation jeopardised by a despotic ambition. Deeply as we deplore the appalling spectacle of bloodshed and widespread misery, we are driven to confess that 'a righteous war is better than an immoral peace'. We rejoice that the crisis through which the Empire has been passing has revealed the strength of the bonds which unite all sections of the King's subjects throughout the world. We give thanks to God for the magnificent loyalty and devotion of our people both to the Church and the State during a year of unexampled difficulty. Nearly one hundred thousand of our young men have responded to the call of the King and the need of the country. Many have laid down their lives in this great war against materialism and inhumanity. Although we keenly mourn their loss, we believe that by the shedding of their blood they have done much to maintain the cause of truth and justice, progress and brotherhood. In the Memorial Service held during the Representative Session, we endeavoured to honour the memory of the dead, to give thanks for their self-sacrifice, and to remember the bereaved in our prayers. The women of Methodism, in common with the women of the Empire, have given of their best in assiduous and sacrificial service for the well-being of our soldiers and sailors and the strangers within our gates. Let us continue to pray and labour for the victory of right over wrong; of spiritual ideals over a soul-degrading materialism; and for the ultimate advent of a world-wide and lasting peace, founded upon law and righteousness, which shall unite all nations in the service of humanity . . .

The world's need of the Gospel of Jesus Christ was never more supremely urgent than to-day. Thank God, Christianity has a message for broken lives and desolated homes. The nation's sorrow and grief call for compassionate ministries. In the throes of a great agony we believe a new world will have its birth. Social problems will have to be solved in the light of Christ's teaching, and the religion of our Lord applied to every department of thought and activity. The faith of our fathers must be lifted out of abstraction and be made incarnate in character and service; and a basis of brotherhood must be found on which all nationalities may unite in freedom and peace.

Conference Address, 1918

(Wesleyan *Minutes*, 1918, pp. 272–5)

We are deeply conscious that the war is creating a new situation which makes fresh demands upon the Church of Jesus Christ and which presents a challenge which we dare not evade. While we sorrow that the

Christian Church has not so far influenced the world as to make war impossible, our conviction is unwavering that in this conflict Britain is wielding the sword of righteousness. The certainty of this belief increases the perplexity of those who are yearning for the peace which is so long delayed.

As we turn our thoughts to the future we cannot ignore the fact that war and its aftermath bring their own perils to the moral and spiritual life of the nations. We would therefore urge you to do all that in you lies to fortify our countrymen against the decline of ideals, the lack of restraint, and the contraction of spiritual vision that so often follow in the wake of war. But while recognising these dangers we rejoice in the manifest signs that God is seeking by His Spirit to over-rule this great evil for good. The old world is passing away, and, for good or for evil, a new world is being born. Ancient institutions are in the melting-pot, and time-honoured customs and beliefs are being questioned. Our sons and daughters are prophesying; young men are seeing visions and old men dreaming dreams. We thank God for the growing recognition of the need of social and industrial reconstruction, for the widespread realisation that the avenues to a full and abundant life must be opened to all classes of the people, and for the deepening determination to end industrial and international strife. In the new spirit that is stirring in the hearts of the peoples we see the energising of the Holy Spirit of God. But neither the dreams of individuals nor those of nations can be realised without careful thought, persistent effort, and the charity that suffereth long and is kind. The need for intelligent, sympathetic, and resolute spiritual leadership will be greater than ever in the day when millions of men, released from the colours, will have to be reabsorbed into civil life, and the nations will have to face once more the task of living together in peace and unity. The removal of patriotic restraints that operate in time of war and the necessity for Capital and Labour to readjust themselves to peace conditions will place a great strain upon the sentiment of social enthusiasm and unity engendered in the stress of the conflict. Unsettlement of opinions, the exchange of military discipline for the freedom and independence of civil life, and a general reaction from the strain of war will inevitably create a tendency towards licence and a casting off of moral restraints. It is for the Church of Jesus Christ, called to be 'the firstfruits of His creatures', to prepare herself to guide the nation both by precept and example.

We recognise with sorrow that at the present time the Church is exercising a diminished influence and authority. We do not believe that the whole blame is to be laid at her door, but none the less, without extenuation, we desire to acknowledge our failures, to discover the sources of our weakness, and to surrender ourselves without reserve to the will of God, that we may be His obedient and efficient instruments.

We are confident that the hearts of the people need as much as ever the inspiration of religion, and that in many secret places the Divine fires still burn . . .

Our Church was called into being to bear witness to the potency of the saving and sanctifying truths of the Gospel. The need for that witness is greater than ever. Methodism has not exhausted its mandate. The sorrowful history of the last four years has brought home to us with a new force that there is no hope for the world apart from the regeneration of the human heart. Diplomacy, legislation, even triumphant armies can do little to heal the world of the ills that oppress it, if the old order of sin and selfishness is to continue, and there is not change of mind and heart in individual and nation. A League of Nations can only endure if founded on the basis of transformed peoples. There is no hope of universal peace and brotherhood save as Jesus Christ makes of the severed nations of mankind 'one new man, so making peace'. The dream of industrial peace and of a commonwealth in which each shall seek not his own but his neighbour's good can only be realised as selfishness makes way for self-sacrifice and self-seeking for love. . . .

Our Methodist fathers emphasised the necessity of proclaiming the *sanctifying* as well as the saving power of the Gospel. They declared that God will carry on and perfect the work which He begins in individuals and communities. We are constrained to acknowledge that this truth has not always been kept prominently before us. In our zeal to win men for the Kingdom, we have sometimes forgotten that both we and they need to be continually learning what are the truths of the Kingdom and how they are to be applied to the common life. We would remind you that the evangelism for which we stand is social as well as individual, ethical as well as spiritual, and aims at the transformation of the mortal life as well as at bringing immortality to light. The process of salvation from sin must be *worked out* both in the individual and in society. We must love the Lord our God with all our *minds* as well as with all our hearts. All the resources of our intelligence and self-sacrifice must be placed at the disposal of the indwelling Spirit of God, if we are to bring the truths of the Gospel effectively to bear upon this world of sin and selfishness. The social ethics of the Gospel, that is, the practical implications of sanctification, constitute a territory that has been very inadequately explored. There is no greater service that Christian men, both individually and corporately, can render to the world to-day, than to think out and to work out the meaning of the Christian ideal as applied to social and national relationships. How is Christianity to be more fully embodied in the life of the State? How is the Golden Rule to be applied to industry? How are competition and co-operation to find a way of reconciliation? These are questions to which the Christian conscience must find an answer. An adequate reply will only be forthcoming as men attain to clarity of vision and steadiness of will through the experience of the grace of Him who redeems from sin and selfishness and gives strength for righteousness. The answer to these complex questions may not be found in a day or a year, but gradually as men surrender themselves to the guidance of the Spirit, think out the practical bearings of the truths they have embraced, and are not afraid of making experiments, even at the cost of sacrifice. Both our origin and our history constitute a call to us to play a worthy part in this sanctification of life.

Methodist Union: The Scheme

The Scheme as presented in 1920 went through three successive revisions. The main points at issue were not constitutional, but doctrinal, especially concerning the nature of the ministry and the sacraments. For the full Scheme, see the Wesleyan *Minutes*, 1920, pp. 71–83; 1922, pp. 68–81; 1924, pp. 69–90; 1926, pp. 70–85.

A statement of principles laid down in the 1919 report on Methodist Union

This was printed at the head of the 1920 Scheme and reiterated in the subsequent revisions.

It is agreed by all that if Union is to be accomplished it must be upon such comprehensive lines that all the various types of thought and temperament represented in the existing denominations could find a home in the United Church. The Committee believes that the way of approaching the problem is not by a consideration of the concessions which one Church should make in favour of another, but by resolutely keeping in view as the main object of the Union, the more effective service of the age and evangelisation of the world, so that the modifications and adjustments made in the constitution or customs of the several Churches should be directed to those ends. As the result of the conversations it is evident that the difference in practice between our Churches is much less than might be suggested by a comparison of the existing Constitutions, and many misunderstandings have been removed.

1920:

(1) The evangelical doctrines for which Methodism has stood from the beginning as held by the three Conferences, and generally contained in Wesley's *Notes on the New Testament* and the first four volumes of his

Sermons, subject to the authority of Divine Revelation recorded in the Holy Scriptures, shall be the doctrinal standard of the Methodist Church.

(2) In any necessary Act of Parliament provision shall be made to give the Conference final authority with regard to all questions concerning the interpretation of the doctrines of the United Church.

(3) In order to ensure the continuous fidelity of Ministers to the doctrines of Methodism, the following question shall be asked in the Ministerial Session of the May Synod: Is there any charge against any Minister in the District? The Chairman of the District shall inquire whether due notice in writing of any such charge has been given to the Minister before he allows the charge to be heard.

In order to ensure the continuous fidelity of the Local Preachers to the doctrines of Methodism, the following question shall be asked annually in the Local Preachers' Meeting: Is there any charge against any Local Preacher in the Circuit? The Superintendent of the Circuit shall inquire as to whether due notice in writing of any such charge has been given to the Local Preacher before allowing the charge to be heard.

(4) It is the universal conviction of the Methodist people that the office of the Christian Ministry depends upon the call of God, Who bestows the gifts of the Spirit, the grace, and the fruit which indicate those whom He has chosen.

(5) Those whom the Church recognises as called of God, and therefore receives into its Ministry, shall be ordained by the imposition of hands, as expressive of the Church's recognition of the Minister's personal call.

(6) The general usage of the three uniting Churches whereby the Sacrament of the Lord's Supper is administered by Ministers shall continue to be observed. In any area where special provision for the regular administration is required, the Conference shall be responsible for the authorisation of duly qualified persons set apart for the purpose.

1922:

(1) The evangelical doctrines which Methodism has held from the beginning and still holds are generally contained in Wesley's Notes on the New Testament and the first four volumes of his Sermons. These doctrines are based upon the Divine Revelation recorded in the Holy Scriptures. The Methodist Church acknowledges this revelation as the supreme rule of faith and practice.

(2) The Conference shall be the final authority within the Church with regard to all questions concerning the interpretation of its doctrines. In any necessary Act of Parliament provisions shall be made to secure the recognition of this power.

(3) [As 1920].

(4) [As 1920].

(5) The general usage of the three uniting Churches whereby the Sacrament of the Lord's Supper is administered by Ministers shall continue to be observed. In any area where special provision for the regular administration is required, the Conference shall be responsible for the authorisation of duly qualified persons set apart for the purpose. The Circuit shall, if it so desire, submit the names of suitable persons to the Synod and Conference for authorisation. The persons selected shall be set apart in a special Service of Dedication arranged by the Synod.

1924:

(1) The Doctrines of the Evangelical Faith which Methodism has held from the beginning, and still holds, are based upon the Divine revelation recorded in the Holy Scriptures. The Methodist Church acknowledges this revelation as the supreme rule of faith and practice. These doctrines are contained in Wesley's *Notes on the New Testament* and the first four volumes of his *Sermons*.

(2) [As 1922].

(3) 'Christ's ministers in the Church are stewards in the household of God, and shepherds of His flock. Some are called and ordained to this sole occupation, and have a principal and directing part in these great duties; but they hold no priesthood differing in kind from that which is common to the Lord's people, and they have no exclusive title to the preaching of the gospel or the care of souls. These ministries are shared with them by others, to whom also the Spirit divides His gifts severally as He wills.'*

(4) [As 1920].

(5) [As 1920].

(6) The general usage of the three uniting Churches, whereby the Sacrament of the Lord's Supper is administered by Ministers, shall continued to be observed. Exceptions to the general usage may be continued until the Conference, with fuller knowledge of the needs and resources of the United Church, is able to determine how to provide for all the Methodist people to partake of the Sacrament with regularity and frequency.

* Statement concerning Church Membership adopted by the Wesleyan Methodist Conference, 1908, to accompany the 'Rules of the Society of People called Methodists '

1926:

(1) The Methodist Church claims and cherishes its place in the holy Catholic Church, which is the Body of Christ. It rejoices in the inheritance of the Apostolic faith, and loyally accepts the fundamental principles of the historic creeds and of the Protestant Reformation. It ever

remembers that in the Providence of God Methodism was raised up to spread Scriptural Holiness through the land by the proclamation of the Evangelical Faith, and declares its unfaltering resolve to be true to its Divinely appointed mission.

The Doctrines of the Evangelical Faith, which Methodism has held from the beginning, and still holds, are based upon the Divine revelation recorded in the Holy Scriptures. The Methodist Church acknowledges this revelation as the supreme rule of faith and practice. These Evangelical Doctrines to which the preachers of the Methodist Church, Ministerial and Lay, are pledged are contained in Wesley's Notes on the New Testament and the first four volumes of his Sermons.

The Notes on the New Testament and the forty-four Sermons are not intended to impose a system of formal or speculative theology on Methodist Preachers, but to set up standards of preaching and belief which should secure loyalty to the fundamental truths of the Gospel of Redemption and ensure the continued witness of the Church to the realities of the Christian experience of salvation.

(2) The Conference shall be the final authority within the Church with regard to all questions concerning the interpretation of its doctrines. In any necessary Act of Parliament provision shall be made to secure the recognition of this power.

(3) Christ's ministers in the Church are stewards in the household of God, and shepherds of His flock. Some are called and ordained to this sole occupation, and have a principal and directing part in these great duties; but they hold no priesthood differing in kind from that which is common to the Lord's people, and they have no exclusive title to the preaching of the gospel or the care of souls. These ministries are shared with them by others, to whom also the Spirit divides His gifts severally as He wills.

(4) It is the universal conviction of the Methodist people that the office of the Christian Ministry depends upon the call of God, Who bestows the gifts of the Spirit, the grace, and the fruit which indicate those whom He has chosen.

(5) Those whom the Church recognises as called of God, and therefore receives into its Ministry, shall be ordained by the imposition of hands, as expressive of the Church's recognition of the Minister's personal call.

(6) The Methodist Church holds the doctrine of the priesthood of all believers and consequently believes that no priesthood exists which belongs exclusively to a particular order or class of men.

But in the exercise of its corporate life and worship special qualifications for the discharge of special duties are required and thus the principle of representative selection is recognised.

The preachers, itinerant and lay, are examined, tested, and approved before they are authorised to minister in holy things. For the sake of Church order, and not because of any priestly virtue inherent in the office, the Ministers of the Church are set apart by ordination to the Ministry of the Word and Sacraments.

The general usage of the three uniting Churches whereby the Sacrament of the Lord's Supper is administered by Ministers shall continue to be observed.

There will necessarily be a transitional period during which the Circuits are being gradually amalgamated. During this period in areas in which local unions have not been consummated, it will be natural on account of variations from the general usage for each Circuit to continue the practice of the Church to which it originally belonged.

When local unions take place, the general usage of administration by Ministers, as stated above, will continue. Where, however, it can be shown that any Church is deprived of a reasonably frequent and regular administration through lack of Ministers, the Circuit concerned may apply to Conference for the authorisation of persons other than Ministers to administer the Sacrament. All nominations of such persons shall be made annually by the June Quarterly Meeting. The authorisation shall be made from year to year by Conference in its Representative Session, and shall be duly certified by the President and the Secretary on behalf of the Conference.

Methodist Union: 'The Other Side'

This Manifesto, signed by 76 Wesleyan ministers, was sent to all 'ministers in the English Work' with an invitation to them to indicate their approval. At the time it was printed in the *Methodist Recorder*, on April 27, 1922, 538 had done so.

At the request of a large number of brethren who are alarmed at the precipitancy with which it is sought to rush our Wesleyan Methodist Church into Organic Union with the other Methodist Churches, at the sacrifice of our valuable historic individuality, the following Manifesto has been prepared.

We are of opinion that the scheme for Methodist Union is not the expression of any general demand on the part of our people, and that the absence of such a demand is fatal to permanent unity. We are convinced that the true way to Union is through a natural and irresistible unity, rather than that unity should be sought by an artificial union. Many of us, moreover, regard a variety of organisation as a sign of healthy life, provided the spirit of unity be not grieved; and we believe that the obliteration of the Wesleyan type would inflict a real loss upon the Universal Church, while causing deep pain to a large section of strongly attached people.

We hold that the view-point of Wesleyan Methodism is essentially different from that of the other Methodist Churches in regard to doctrinal standards, the Sacraments, forms of worship, the ministry, party politics, and other matters of the first importance. The proposed scheme of Union involves a large accession of those whose sentiment and training will inevitably lead farther and farther away from the Wesleyan tradition and usages. We are convinced that the Church Universal will lose rather than gain by the absorption of the Wesleyan and other Churches concerned in an artificial organisation which has not grown out of the activities of life but is the creation of an official Committee.

We appeal as on a former occasion to all the brethren who are in general agreement with the views here set forth, and do not desire to see Wesleyan Methodism sacrificed to this Scheme, to signify their assent on the form enclosed, that we may confer with them upon the action to be taken at Conference.

Reply of the Rev. J. Ernest Rattenbury to Dr. A. S. Peake

(*Methodist Recorder*, June 8, 1922)

Rattenbury was one of the signatories of the Manifesto.

. . . Dr. Peake takes objection to one sentence of the Manifesto because he says it doesn't state facts. I do not think Dr. Peake has read this sentence fairly. But I have to admit that some of our own ministers have refused to sign the Manifesto because they hold Dr. Peake's views as to its meaning. This apparently ambiguous sentence has lost us many signatures, so Dr. Peake should be pleased! . . .

Here are the words he criticises so severely:— 'We hold that the view-point of Wesleyan Methodism is essentially different from that of the other Methodist Churches in regard to doctrinal standards, the Sacraments, forms of worship, the ministry, party politics, and other matters of the first importance.'

The vital word in this sentence is the word 'view-point'. Our statement is not that there is an essential difference in doctrine, but in view-point. 'View-point' obviously means the point from which things are viewed. This view-point is different by reason of our history, and separate corporate experience, and, we think, so distinctive that Union will be impossible until there is a much better understanding. Therefore we think the time is not ripe for Union, and that attempts to press it now are unduly precipitant.

To illustrate our meaning is simple. We are not asserting that all Primitives are Radicals, and all Wesleyans Tories – or that Primitives generally are higher critics like Dr. Peake – or that all Wesleyans are conservative theologians like Mr. Dinsdale Young – no such sort of thing is claimed. All that we say is that our *view-points* are essentially different. I will not write at undue length by dealing with each point; it will be sufficient to illustrate from three – Politics, Forms of Worship, and Doctrine.

Take Politics. Each Church contains people of different political parties, although the variations have been more marked in the Wesleyan than the other Churches. But can there be any question that Wesleyans and Primitives have regarded, and do regard, politics from a different corporate point-of-view? The Wesleyan Conference has always been reluctant to speak as a Conference on political questions, because it corporately supported no party. It has insisted strongly that its Chapels should not be used for political meetings, and has even disapproved the use of Public Halls like the Central and Kingsway Halls for such purposes. Nothing has characterised Wesleyan Methodism more than its determination not to support, as a Church, a particular party, or commit itself to a political policy, even where the majority of Wesleyans have approved of it, if such a committal lays it open to a charge of supporting a party. Can this really be claimed of Primitive Methodism? I hardly think Dr. Peake would make the claim. I am arguing neither for the Wesleyan nor against the Primitive position in respect to the duty of the Church in the political sphere. But I shall need very forceful evidence to convince me that there is no difference in point-of-view.

Take Forms of Worship. Of course, it is true that the normal Nonconformist type of worship is commonest in Wesleyan Chapels, and it is practically universal in Primitive Methodist Chapels. But we have used the Anglican Liturgy in many of our Chapels from the beginning on Sunday mornings. And we use Liturgical forms in the Sacraments. Our only authorised form of service for Holy Communion in England is a very slightly altered version of the Anglican rite. In these matters thousands of Wesleyans would greatly resent any change – particularly in Holy Communion. How can a Church like Primitive Methodism view these things from our standpoint? Of course, there are Wesleyans who would prefer the Primitive Methodist methods, and what we fear is, not that Liturgies would be immediately abolished, but that the left-wing Methodists would be so enormously re-inforced, that the old-fashioned Wesleyan would lose the distinctive Wesleyan history he prizes . . .

(3) *Doctrine.* This, I am informed, is the point on which Dr. Peake is most chagrined by the Manifesto. To my mind it is the point in which our attitude is most defensible. When I saw the first draft of the Manifesto, I admit I questioned the meaning of the phrase. The reply which

convinced me of its fairness, and still convinces me, was, 'The United Methodist Church has taken power to change its doctrine once every ten years.' This, to my mind, expresses a view-point which is not ours.

A study of the amendments in the 1921 Synods of the United Methodist Church particularly, but also of some Primitive Methodist Synods, will illustrate a point-of-view on this matter very different from that of the Wesleyan Synods.

I venture to assert that the view-point of Dr. Peake himself is not that of Wesleyan Methodists on this subject. He has always insisted in Committee on the Representative Session of the Conference – and so far he has got his way – being the final authority in doctrine, because doctrine is a matter for the whole Church. I say emphatically that, right or wrong, this has never been the view-point of Wesleyan Methodism! Wesleyan Methodism has never considered the people as judges on doctrine, not because it despised the people, but because it never has imposed doctrinal tests upon them, always safeguarding religion from intellectual assents, and insisting that constitutional Christianity only implied doing all the good you can, abstaining from all harm, and attending the means of grace.

Social Concerns in Primitive Methodism

(PM *Minutes*, 1924, pp. 229–32)

LEAGUE OF NATIONS. INTERNATIONAL QUESTIONS

The Conference rejoices that, in spite of some disquieting signs, world conditions are more settled, and the prospects of abiding peace brighter. We desire to see friendly relations established between Germany and France, and though the difficulties are grave and embarrassing, European nations seem to be approaching that mutual understanding and goodwill which is the necessary basis of social reconstruction.

We welcome the recognition of Russia by our Government; for while there may be many things in Russian policy with which we disagree, we believe that the resuming of diplomatic and commercial relations with the government of that great nation is right and will result in good.

We reaffirm our passionate faith in the League of Nations. Already it has justified its creation by its pacific influence in cases of international dispute, and its humanitarian efforts in many directions. We recognise many weaknesses in it, especially the fact that, with the U.S.A., Germany and Russia still outside, it is not universal, and we are glad that our

Government is making patient efforts to secure their inclusion. We commend the League of Nations Union to all our people and Churches, and urge them to join it individually and corporately, and so increase the moral force behind this international institution.

Resolution on Housing

That we heartily congratulate the Government on its determination to deal with the housing problem. We view with extreme concern the great shortage of workmen's dwellings in many parts of the country, resulting in over-crowding, with its host of attendant evils, physical, moral and spiritual. While we recognise the difficulties that lie in the way of an adequate and thorough solution of this problem, we affirm our earnest belief that the Christian ideal of the family demands the opportunity for an adequate home life. At present this is impossible for large numbers of the community, and believing as we do that the homes of the nation are of vital concern to its well-being, we welcome the increasing attention which the State and some municipalities are giving to this most important matter, and the earnest efforts they are making to realise housing conditions that are more worthy of a Christian civilisation.

Unemployment

That we deplore the continuance of widespread unemployment.

We accept the principle on which recent Governments have acted, that sustenance must be given to the workless. This, however, is a mere palliative and does not touch some of the worst consequences. For example, the unemployed are deprived of the rightful pride and satisfaction of providing for their needs by their own energies. This often produces bitterness of soul and deterioration of character.

We therefore urge that every effort should be made by the Government and all others concerned to lessen and prevent recurring cycles of unemployment.

One of the gravest evils is that so many young people are idle during the formative years of life. When employment cannot be found, opportunities for continuing their education should be provided and financial assistance should be dependent on their availing themselves of such opportunities.

Our hearts go out in sympathy to all who are suffering from this great evil.

Education

That we record that no further steps have been taken towards the solution of the difficult problem of dual control in the educational system of this country. We would heartily welcome any equitable arrangement by which this anomaly could be removed. We deeply regret the breakdown of the Welsh Concordat after two years of strenuous negotiations, which only shows how difficult is the problem, but we cannot conceive that it is an insoluble problem. We re-affirm our strong desire that some settlement of this question should be reached, but we cannot relax our opposition to the right of entry into our Public Schools or the imposition of any religious test for the teachers in our Elementary Schools. With these reservations we are prepared to welcome any proposals that may be made.

ROYALTY AND THE TURF

This Conference affirms its loyal adherence to the Royal House, but views with grave concern and pain the increasingly close association of Royalty with the Turf. We regard horse-racing as most largely responsible for the widespread practice of gambling, which all of us must admit, has become terribly menacing in its effects upon the young life of our nation. And in their interests and also of morality generally some steps be taken to ascertain and focus the opinion of all Free Churchmen in order that our emphatic protest shall be made to reach the ears of our Ruling House in this matter.

RODEO EXHIBITIONS

That this Conference strongly deprecates the cruelty to animals inevitably involved in Rodeo Exhibitions; it recognises that rude methods of rounding up cattle are inevitable in frontier and backwoods life, but it wholeheartedly opposes a form of entertainment which is only possible through the suffering of dumb creatures. It urges the Government to take immediate steps to prevent all such exhibitions at Wembley or elsewhere.

GAMBLING

1. That we express to the Home Secretary and His Majesty's Government our pleasure at the steps which have recently been taken to prevent the holding of certain sweeps, and assure them of our strong conviction that in view of the terrible menace of the gambling evil, no steps can be too drastic in the way of prevention.

2. That we urge upon His Majesty's Government the urgent necessity of dealing seriously with one of the root causes of gambling; namely, the publication of betting news in the Press. We would strongly and earnestly urge that in the best interests of the community this should be absolutely prohibited. We trust that the removal of so flagrant a temptation may have early attention, and legislative and administrative means be taken to give effect to a sorely-needed reform.

COPEC RESOLUTION

That this Conference cordially welcomes the movement known as COPEC[1] and very warmly commends its finding to the earnest and prayerful consideration of all our people. The Commissions, whose findings are now before us, aimed at discovering the social implications of Christianity both in relation to national and international affairs, believing that only the ideals of Christ are adequate for the manifold and complex needs of human Society.

We rejoice especially that the Birmingham Conference, while reflecting wide differences of political outlook, revealed the consciousness of a deeper fundamental unity, born of the common impulse to discover the mind of Christ and to realise His Lordship in all human affairs; and it is in this spirit of absolute loyalty to Christ that we desire our people to face the complete social situation of the moment.

We would commend the published reports of the Commissions and Recommendations of the Conference to the careful study of our Ministers, Local Preachers, Christian Endeavourers, Sunday School Teachers and our people in general, and would urge them to support wherever possible the work of the COPEC Continuation Committee and the Regional Conferences which will be held from time to time.

We would assure the Continuation Committee of our prayerful co-operation and our unwavering desire to secure the triumph of Christian ideals in every domain of industrial, social and international life.

[1] The Conference on Christian Politics, Economics and Citizenship, held at Birmingham in April 1924.

John Scott Lidgett on Ministerial Training, 1927

(W. Bardsley Brash, *The Story of our Colleges 1835–1935*, 1935, pp. 114–16)

The preparation and training of the ministry is the greatest concern of Methodism at the present time. The Church has, in recent years, carried through great schemes of material expansion, in buildings. Educational standards have risen throughout the country, and increased educational facilities of all kinds have been multiplied. The educational requirements of every profession, business and industry have become more and more exacting. Yet the Wesleyan Methodist Church has done little or nothing for more than forty years either to raise the standard expected of Candidates for the ministry or to improve their training when received. The establishment of Wesley House, Cambridge, has been the work of a handful of enlightened and generous men, rather than of the Connexion as a whole. Yet the supreme question is not that of church buildings, but of the character, capacity, and equipment of the men who minister in them.

The highest concern of the Connexion, and the all-embracing aim of the Colleges is spiritual and evangelical. We need, above all, men of spiritual power to proclaim the Gospel, and so to present it as, by the blessing of God, to arouse, sustain and instruct the living faith that accepts it. Yet such faith is the act of a man's whole personality. The mind must co-operate with the heart and the will in its exercise. Hence, at the very least, the preacher must command the intellectual respect of his hearers, must be on a level with his congregation, and be in touch with their thought and difficulties, and particularly with those of the young. This requirement is made of the minister by all sections of society, not least of all by the most intelligent of the industrial classes.

Furthermore, both the young minister and his hearers are confronted with problems of thought and life which go to the very heart of the Christian revelation and religion. When the minister as pastor comes into close and sympathetic contact with the young, he will be called upon not only to enter into their perplexities, but to give them such guidance as can only be furnished by one who has reached the level of intelligence, knowledge and outlook at which these perplexities chiefly arise. And this not as a merely intellectual end, but in order to win and maintain their allegiance to our Lord Jesus Christ. Hence the minister urgently needs, not indeed exact and expert scholarship, but reserves of thought and knowledge which can be mobilized and brought to bear upon his duties as both preacher and pastor.

Yet even this vital necessity is secondary. What is even more important is the morale and virility of the minister. He must have grit, energy, and self-discipline if he is to discharge his task, and maintain his spiritual influence. The demand for these qualities must be made upon men at the outset . . .

If the minimum standard for Candidates be raised, and if such steps be taken to enable those who fall short of it to reach it, not only will the general level of the ministry be raised and the work of the Colleges be made more effective, but a preliminary 'discipline' will be applied, which will improve the morale of the Candidate and thus be of inestimable advantage to his character throughout the whole of his future ministry.

The Deed of Union of the Methodist Church, 1932

(*Minutes of the Uniting Conference*, 1932, pp. 286–306)

This deed formally constituted the Methodist Church on the basis of the Methodist Church Union Act of 1929. It incorporates the statement on doctrinal standards and the regulations as to the Lord's Supper from the 1926 Scheme. (See pp. 637–8 above.)

36. *Basis of Membership.* – (*a*) All persons are welcomed into membership of The Methodist Church who sincerely desire to be saved from their sins through faith in the Lord Jesus Christ and evidence the same in life and conduct and who seek to have fellowship with Christ Himself and His people by taking up the duties and privileges of The Methodist Church.

(*b*) It is the privilege and duty of Members of The Methodist Church to avail themselves of the two sacraments namely Baptism and the Lord's Supper. As membership of The Methodist Church also involves fellowship it is the duty of all Members of The Methodist Church to seek to cultivate this in every possible way. The Weekly Class Meeting has from the beginning proved to be the most effective means of maintaining among Methodists true fellowship in Christian experience. All Members of The Methodist Church shall have their names entered on a Class Book shall be placed under the pastoral care of a Class Leader and shall receive a quarterly ticket of membership.

(*c*) According to Methodist usage the Sacrament of Baptism is administered to infants and regular oversight should be given by the local Church and its Minister to all who have been dedicated to God by this sign. If any have not received Christian Baptism that Sacrament should be administered either before or in connection with the Recognition Service.

(*d*) After a probation of not less than three months those approved shall be admitted to full membership by the Leaders' Meeting and be publicly recognised at a service conducted by the Minister in the presence of the Church at the earliest opportunity which shall be followed by the administration of the Lord's Supper.

(*e*) Any Member of The Methodist Church who without sufficient reason persistently absents himself from the Lord's Supper and from the meetings for Christian Fellowship shall be visited by both his Leader and his Minister. The name of any such person who by such prolonged absence severs himself from Christian Fellowship shall be removed by the Leaders' Meeting from the Class Book and he shall thereupon cease to be a Member of The Methodist Church.

(*f*) In connection with the Societies of The Methodist Church Classes shall be generally established which shall directly provide for the religious instruction of young people. The object of these classes shall be to secure the decision of children for Christ their instruction and training in Christian Doctrine and ethics and the development in Christian experience and character. The Holy Scripture shall be the basis of instruction and these classes shall be met wherever possible weekly. . . .

39. *Power to Unite with other Churches.* – The Methodist Church may by a resolution of the Conference passed and confirmed as in this clause provided unite or amalgamate with any other Church or religious body or association upon such terms and conditions as The Methodist Church by a resolution of the Conference passed and confirmed as in this clause provided may determine Provided that the power conferred by this clause shall not be exercised except subject to and in conformity with such provisions relating to such union or amalgamation as aforesaid as shall be contained in this Deed or in any alteration or amendment thereof made or new provisions adopted under any power in that behalf herein contained Provided also that notwithstanding any provision to the contrary herein contained or in any such alteration amendment or new provision as aforesaid every resolution to which this clause refers shall be passed in one year by the votes of not less than three-fourths of the members of the Conference of that year present and voting upon such resolution and confirmed in the next subsequent year by a resolution of the Conference of that year similarly passed.

World Methodism, 1932

(*Minutes*, 1932)

On the eve of the union between the main branches of British Methodism, nearly two centuries after the conversion of the Wesley brothers, the movement had become a world communion.

XI. GENERAL STATISTICS OF METHODISM, 1932

N.B.—These statistics are the latest procurable.

Denomination	Ministers	Lay Preachers
Wesleyan Methodists:		
Great Britain	2,510	18,785
Ireland	250	578
Foreign Missions	683	8,768
French Conference	24	65
South African Conference	455	8,792
Primitive Methodists	1,131	12,896
United Methodist Church	729	5,232
Wesleyan Reform Union	30	497
Independent Methodist Churches	400	—
Australasian Methodist Church	1,306	10,065
New Zealand Methodist Church**	191	752
United States:		
Methodist Episcopal†	20,040	13,585
Methodist Episcopal, South	8,127	4,329
Methodist Protestant	2,175	—
African Methodist Episcopal (coloured)	7,315	—
African Methodist Episcopal Zion (coloured)	3,460	—
Coloured Methodist Episcopal	3,208	2,162
Free Methodist	1,399	—
Wesleyan Methodist	700	474
Primitive Methodist	90	73
Congregational Methodist	487	—
New Congregational Methodist	25	—
Union American Methodist Episcopal (coloured)	324	—
African Union Methodist Protestant (coloured)	675	—
Reformed Zion Union Apostolic (coloured)	43	—
Reformed Methodist Union Episcopal (coloured)	51	—
Coloured Methodist Protestant	33	—
Reformed Methodist Church	14	—
Independent African Methodist Episcopal	—	—
Union Church of Canada	3,767	—
Japan Methodist Church	227	111
Totals	59,869	87,164

* Seating accommodation, 2,339,771. ** These figures include the Solomon Islands with native ministers 3, lay preachers 198, members 5,510, Sunday schools 3, scholars 253, churches 98. † Methodism is also represented in several European countries by Conferences and Missions affiliated to the Methodist Episcopal Church of America, and their membership is included in the figures given above. The latest returns available are: Austria, 717 members; Baltic and Slavic, 1,882; Bulgaria, 619; Denmark, 3,475; Finland, 1,663; France, 904; Germany, 31,237; Hungary, 575; Italy, 2,947; Jugo-Slavia, 809; Norway, 7,002; Russia, 1,814; Sweden, 14,644; Switzerland, 11,226.

The members in Junior Classes are not reckoned

Church Members and Probationers	Sunday Schools	Officers and Teachers	Sunday Scholars	Churches, etc.
517,551	6,952	115,624	770,716	*8,152
30,057	323	2,213	20,396	406
289,221	2,970	10,401	158,375	4,298
1,411	21	95	641	48
303,148	293	2,548	21,958	732
222,021	4,006	52,457	377,792	4,356
179,527	2,152	36,474	223,395	2,900
13,919	235	2,535	26,255	231
10,786	164	3,136	22,574	163
189,437	3,709	33,133	221,377	3,993
24,813	429	3,347	30,231	901
4,658,862	31,527	394,865	4,375,598	26,722
2,621,900	15,339	175,740	1,930,552	17,272
195,460	1,850	17,351	181,373	2,218
781,692	7,200	—	320,000	7,390
500,000	2,429	45,087	267,141	3,882
467,520	2,964	23,020	310,210	3,101
40,827	—	—	—	1,279
23,000	584	6,110	43,632	650
13,000	87	383	14,600	85
21,050	80	—	4,807	357
1,229	3	—	126	26
22,259	—	—	—	307
27,000	42	273	2,581	650
4,086	36	212	1,500	58
1,904	15	—	400	27
533	24	125	1,016	3
401	—	—	—	14
1,003	—	—	—	29
671,349	5,962	—	653,007	7,622
37,451	625	2,507	50,707	350
11,872,417	90,021	927,636	10,030,960	98,222

PART TWO

Bibliography

Introductory Notes

Method of Compilation

Research for the project was undertaken in three main phases. Between August 1984 and March 1985 an alphabetical author file of approximately seven thousand references was constructed from

the compiler's 'Bibliography of Methodist historical literature' which has appeared annually in the *Proceedings of the Wesley Historical Society* since June 1976 (and which, incidentally, will provide the necessary updating service to the present guide);[1]

a thorough search of fifteen indexing serials, four periodical runs, twenty-four non-recurrent bibliographies and of the footnotes and reading lists in a substantial number of individual monographs;

suggestions made by some of the contributors to *A History of the Methodist Church in Great Britain.*

During the course of April 1985 this file was reduced to about four and a half thousand items by the elimination of duplicates and an initial application of the selection criteria as detailed in the ensuing paragraph. Final editing and revision took place from May 1985 to October 1986 and involved direct handling of hundreds of original volumes in Manchester and Oxford as well as consultation of book reviews, abstracts, library catalogues and the like with a view to controlling entries for quality and relevance, verifying bibliographical data and ensuring an exact classification of subject matter.

Scope

In order to contain this bibliography within manageable limits it has proved necessary to restrict its scope in a number of directions. Readers are especially asked to note that

---

[1] The 'Bibliography of Methodist historical literature, 1986', which will feature in the February 1988 issue of the Society's *Proceedings*, is the first such update. It lists 138 items in all, of which 60 would have qualified for inclusion in the present Bibliography, either as additional or replacement references, had they been available at the time of its compilation. Amongst them are some quite seminal works, not the least of which is *Religion in England, 1688–1791* (Oxford: Clarendon Press, 1986, xiii + 584p.) by the late Ernest Gordon Rupp, one of the general editors of this *History*.

the principal aim has been to provide an introduction to the secondary literature of Methodism and not to duplicate listings of primary sources which are readily available in Kenneth Rowe's *Methodist union catalog* and other reference tools;

the geographical framework is Great Britain and Ireland with no more than a token representation of studies of the expansion of Methodism in the overseas mission field;

emphasis has been placed on developments at the connexional level to the neglect of all but the most important regional, county, community and circuit histories;

there is an overall bias in favour of more recent (1945–85) material although some attempt has also been made to chart the evolving historiography of Methodism by recording significant examples of 'classical' scholarship;

preference has been given to works written in or translated into English but not to the exclusion of key titles in Welsh, French, German and other languages;

unpublished items have not been cited except in the case of postgraduate research theses presented to institutions of higher education, generally in the United Kingdom or in the United States of America, which may be obtained without undue difficulty through the national and international inter-library loan network;

length as well as quality has been invoked as a criterion in pruning the more densely populated sections of the bibliography – in particular, contributions of fewer than five pages, even when published in the *Proceedings of the Wesley Historical Society*, have been omitted in the main;

with regard to books only one imprint of one edition (usually the last revised issue to appear within the British Isles) has been included;

no references are given for the chapters by Herbert Butterfield (1.I), William Reginald Ward (2.I) and Thomas Edmund Jessop (2.V) which concern the general background to the rise and development of Methodism.

Structure

It has not proved possible to classify the entries according to the strict sequence of chapters in Volumes 1–3 of *A History of the Methodist Church in Great Britain* since certain topics are tackled there by more than one contributor whilst others are not examined in detail at all (as the general editors explained in their original preface of 1965, the intention was never 'to encompass all the facts or to narrate all the happenings' but merely to select 'such salient features as enable the story of Methodism to be considered within an ecumenical perspective'); Appendix I, however, does attempt to cater for the needs of those readers who would have preferred such an approach. The alternative framework which has been devised for use in this bibliography, after much careful research and pilot testing, is of a modular design which permits the constituent elements to be linked horizontally or vertically in any number of logical ways.

Although considerations of space dictate that each item be represented by a single bibliographical description only, advantage has been taken of the digitalized hierarchical system to supply up to four cross-references per entry. The main exceptions to this rule occur

in Section 2 where works about John and, to a lesser extent, Charles Wesley have been assumed to be coterminous with those on eighteenth-century Methodism;

in the case of all other biographies where an individual has been located in the period of primary activity (thus, references and cross-references to Thomas Coke have been assembled in Sub-Section 2.3 rather than in 4.2 despite the fact that he did not die until 1814, whilst lives of James Everett are noted in 6.3.5 and not in 4.2);

in relation to items on the doctrine of the ministry which have been placed, as appropriate, with ordained or lay ministry in preference to theology.

Table of Contents

1. LONG-TERM PERSPECTIVES

1.1 Study Aids

1.1.1 Bibliography and historiography

1.1.1.1   BAKER, Frank: *Methodism, our history and heritage: A reading list,* London: Dudley Press, [1948], [8]p.

1.1.1.2   BOWMER, John Coates: 'Seventy-five years with Methodist history: The story of the Wesley Historical Society', *Methodist History,* Vol. VIII, No. 1, October 1969, pp. 20–4.

1.1.1.3   BOWMER, John Coates: 'Twenty-five years (1943–68): II. Methodist studies', *Proceedings of the Wesley Historical Society,* Vol. XXXVII, 1969–70, pp. 61–6.

1.1.1.4   BRETHERTON, Francis Fletcher: 'The W[esley] H[istorical] S[ociety]: Its origin and progress', *Proceedings of the Wesley Historical Society,* Vol. XXIV, 1943–44, pp. 26–35, 41–4.

1.1.1.5   FIELD, Clive Douglas: 'Bibliography of Methodist historical literature, 1974[–83]', *Proceedings of the Wesley Historical Society,* Vol. XL, 1975–76, pp. 145–9, Vol. XLI, 1977–78, pp. 53–60, 143–51, Vol. XLII, 1979–80, pp. 55–63, 134–8, Vol. XLIII, 1981–82, pp. 21–4, 88–91, Vol. XLIV, 1983–84, pp. 16–21, 103–8, Vol. XLV, 1985–86, pp. 8–14.

1.1.1.6   FORTNEY, Edward L.: 'The literature of the history of Methodism', *Religion in Life,* Vol. XXIV, 1954–55, pp. 443–51.

1.1.1.7   GAGE, Laurie E.: *English Methodism: A bibliographical view,* Westcliff-on-Sea: Gage Postal Books, 1985, [3]+16+[10]p.

1.1.1.8   HARDMAN, Keith Jordan: 'A checklist of doctoral dissertations on Methodist, Evangelical United Brethren and related subjects, 1912–1968', *Methodist History,* Vol. VIII, No. 3, April 1970, pp. 38–42.

1.1.1.9   HARRISON, Archibald Harold Walter: 'Fifty years of studies in Methodist history', *Proceedings of the Wesley Historical Society,* Vol. XXIV, 1943–44, pp. 17–26.

1.1.1.10   LENHART, Thomas Emerson & NORWOOD, Frederick Abbott: *A checklist of Wesleyan and Methodist studies, 1970–1975,* Evanston: Institute for Methodist Studies and Related Movements, Garrett-Evangelical Theological Seminary, 1976, 19p.

1.1.1.11   *Methodist union catalog of history, biography, disciplines and hymnals,* preliminary edition, edited by Brooks Bivens Little, Lake Junaluska: Association of Methodist Historical Societies, 1967, vii+478p.

1.1.1.12 *Methodist union catalog, pre-1976 imprints*, edited by Kenneth Elmer Rowe, Metuchen: Scarecrow Press, 1975– , 6 vol., A–I, to date.

1.1.1.13 NORWOOD, Frederick Abbott: 'Methodist historical studies, 1930–1959', *Church History*, Vol. XXVIII, 1959, pp. 391–417.

1.1.1.14 NORWOOD, Frederick Abbott: 'Wesleyan and Methodist historical studies, 1960–70: A bibliographical article', *Church History*, Vol. 40, 1971, pp. 182–99 and *Methodist History*, Vol. X, No. 2, January 1972, pp. 23–44.

1.1.1.15 RACK, Henry Derman: 'Recent books on Methodism', *Epworth Review*, Vol. 7, No. 1, January 1980, pp. 82–8.

1.1.1.16 ROSE, Edward Alan: *A checklist of British Methodist periodicals*, Bognor Regis: W.M.H.S. Publications, 1981, [29]p.

1.1.1.17 [SHARP, John Alfred]: *A catalogue of manuscripts and relics, engravings and photographs, medals, books and pamphlets, pottery, medallions, etc. belonging to the Wesleyan Methodist Conference, and preserved at the office of the Conference, 25–35 City Road, London, E.C.1, together with some of the principal books, mss. etc. in the possession of the United Methodist Church*, London: Methodist Publishing House, 1921, vii+217p.

1.1.1.18 STAMPE, George: 'List of local histories, compiled chiefly by Mr. George Stampe from his collection', *Proceedings of the Wesley Historical Society*, Vol. I, 1897–98, pp. 3–14.

1.1.1.19 STAMPE, George: 'A supplemental list of local Methodist histories in George Stampe's collection', *Proceedings of the Wesley Historical Society*, Vol. VI, 1907–08, pp. 70–4.

1.1.1.20 THORNE, Roger Frank Sidney: *Methodism in the South-West: An historical bibliography*, [Topsham: the author, 1983], 56p.

1.1.1.21 VICKERS, John Ashley: *Wesley Historical Society: General index to the 'Proceedings', Vols. I–XXX and Publications I–IV (1897–1956)*, Leicester: printed for the Wesley Historical Society by Alfred A. Taberer, 1960, vi+61p.

1.1.1.22 WORKMAN, Herbert Brook: 'General list of authorities' [for the history of Methodism], *A new history of Methodism*, edited by William John Townsend, Herbert Brook Workman & George Eayrs, London: Hodder and Stoughton, 1909, Vol. II, pp. 533–50.

1.1.2 Sources and archives

1.1.2.1 BAKER, Frank: *The Methodist pilgrim in England*, third edition, revised, Rutland, Vt.: Academy Books, 1976, 110p.

1.1.2.2 CUMBERS, Frank Henry: *The Book Room: The story of the Methodist Publishing House and Epworth Press*, Wesley Historical Society Lecture No. 22, London: Epworth Press, 1956, xii+153p.

1.1.2.3 CUMMINGS, Arthur Dagg: *A portrait in pottery* [of John Wesley], Wesley Historical Society Lecture No. 28, London: Epworth Press, 1962, 48p.

1.1.2.4 HIMSWORTH, Sheila J.: *Survey of Methodist records*, [London]: Methodist Church Archives and History Committee, 1978, 30p.

1.1.2.5　LEARY, William: *Local Methodist records: A brief explanation of local Methodist archival material deposited in county record offices*, Bognor Regis: W.M.H.S. Publications, 1981, 11p.

1.1.2.6　LEARY, William: 'The Methodist Archives', *Archives*, Vol. XVI, 1983–84, pp. 16–27.

1.1.2.7　LEARY, William: *Methodist artefacts*, [Manchester: Methodist Church Connexional Archivist, 1979], iii+34p.

1.1.2.8　LEARY, William: *Methodist preaching plans: A guide to their usefulness to the historian*, Sudbrooke: the author, 1977, [3]+25p.

1.1.2.9　LEARY, William: *My ancestor was a Methodist: How can I find out more about him?*, London: Society of Genealogists, 1982, [3]+12p.

1.1.2.10　ROSE, Edward Alan: 'The evolution of the circuit plan', *Proceedings of the Wesley Historical Society*, Vol. XXXVII, 1969–70, pp. 50–4.

1.1.2.11　ROSE, Edward Alan: *A register of Methodist circuit plans, 1777–1860* [with supplements to 1907], [Manchester]: Society of Cirplanologists, 1961–80, 6 vol.

1.1.2.12　STEEL, Donald John: *Sources for Nonconformist genealogy and family history*, National Index of Parish Registers Vol. 2, London: Society of Genealogists, 1973, vi+501–798p.

1.1.2.13　STRAWSON, William: ' "The London Quarterly and Holborn Review", 1853–1968', *Church Quarterly*, Vol. 1, 1968–69, pp. 41–52.

1.1.2.14　SWIFT, Wesley Frank: *How to write a local history of Methodism*, third revision with additions by Thomas Shaw & Edward Alan Rose, Bunbury: Alfred A. Taberer, 1981, 24p.

1.1.2.15　WRIGHT, Joseph G.: 'Class and band tickets: A guide to collectors', *Proceedings of the Wesley Historical Society*, Vol. V, 1905–06, pp. 33–44.

See also 1.4.1.2, 2.1.1.32.

1.2 General Histories

1.2.1 Connexional histories

1.2.1.1　ANDREWS, Stuart: *Methodism and society*, London: Longman, 1970, x+140p.

1.2.1.2　BAKER, Frank: *A charge to keep: An introduction to the people called Methodists*, London: Epworth Press, 1947, viii+232p.

1.2.1.3　BERTRAND, Claude-Jean: *Le Méthodisme*, Paris: Armand Colin, 1971, 416p.

1.2.1.4　BRASH, William Bardsley: *Methodism*, London: Methuen & Co., 1928, xi+207p.

1.2.1.5　CHAMBERLAYNE, John Henry: 'From sect to Church in British Methodism', *British Journal of Sociology*, Vol. XV, 1964, pp. 139–49.

1.2.1.6　CURRIE, Robert: 'A micro-theory of Methodist growth', *Proceedings of the Wesley Historical Society*, Vol. XXXVI, 1967–68, pp. 65–73.

1.2.1.7 CURRIE, Robert, GILBERT, Alan David & HORSLEY, Lee: *Churches and churchgoers: Patterns of church growth in the British Isles since 1700*, Oxford: Clarendon Press, 1977, xi+244p.

1.2.1.8 DAVEY, Cyril James: *The Methodist story*, London: Epworth Press, 1955, 190p.

1.2.1.9 DAVIES, Rupert Eric: *Methodism*, second revised edition, London: Epworth Press, 1985, 196p.

1.2.1.10 EDWARDS, Maldwyn Lloyd: *This Methodism: Eight studies*, London: Epworth Press, 1939, 152p.

1.2.1.11 *The encyclopedia of world Methodism*, Nolan Bailey Harmon, general editor, Nashville: United Methodist Publishing House, 1974, 2 vol.

1.2.1.12 FIELD, Clive Douglas: 'The social structure of English Methodism: Eighteenth–twentieth centuries', *British Journal of Sociology*, Vol. XXVIII, 1977, pp. 199–225.

1.2.1.13 GAY, John Dennis: *The geography of religion in England*, London: Duckworth, 1971, xviii+334p.

1.2.1.14 GILBERT, Alan David: *Religion and society in industrial England: Church, chapel and social change, 1740–1914*, London: Longman, 1976, x+251p.

1.2.1.15 GREGORY, John Robinson: *A history of Methodism, chiefly for the use of students*, London: Charles H. Kelly, 1911, 2 vol.

1.2.1.16 HARRISON, Archibald Harold Walter, BARBER, Benjamin Aquila, HORNBY, George Goodall & DAVIES, Edward Tegla: *The Methodist Church: Its origin, divisions and reunion*, London: Methodist Publishing House, 1932, 229p.

1.2.1.17 HARRISON, Grace Elizabeth Simon: *Methodist good companions*, London: Epworth Press, 1935, 154p.

1.2.1.18 HURST, John Fletcher: *The history of Methodism*, London: Charles H. Kelly, 1901–04, 7 vol.

1.2.1.19 HYDE, Ammi Bradford: *The story of Methodism throughout the world, from the beginning to the present time, tracing the rise and progress of that wonderful religious movement which, like the Gulf Stream, has given warmth to wide waters and verdure to many lands; and giving an account of its various influences and institutions of to-day*, revised and enlarged [edition], Chicago: Johns Publishing House, [1888], 827+xivp.

1.2.1.20 KELLOGG, Amherst W.: *A concise history of Methodism in England and America, of its origin, founders, development and institutions*, Milwaukee: H. O. Brown & Company, 1893, 409p.

1.2.1.21 PARKINSON, George Anthony: *The people called Methodists: A short survey of the history of the Methodist Church*, Croydon: Martell's Methodist Publications, [1937], 128p.

1.2.1.22 RACK, Henry Derman: *The future of John Wesley's Methodism*, London: Lutterworth Press, 1965, 80p.

1.2.1.23 WORKMAN, Herbert Brook: *Methodism*, Cambridge: at the University Press, 1912, vii+133p.

See also 1.6.1.1, 7.2.1.1.

1.2.2 Local histories: England

1.2.2.1 BURGESS, John: 'The growth and development of Methodism in Cumbria', University of Durham M.Litt. thesis, 1979, xiv+714p.

1.2.2.2 BURGESS, John: *A history of Cumbrian Methodism*, Kendal: Titus Wilson, 1980, viii+168p.

1.2.2.3 CLARKE, David Frederick: *This other Eden* [being a history of Methodism in the Upper Eden Valley, Westmorland], Milburn: Thomas K. Clarke, 1985, 139p.

1.2.2.4 HALL, Michael: ' "Who knows but it may continue?" (A history of Methodism in Quinton from 1781 to 1981)', University of Birmingham M.A. thesis, 1983, [13]+286p.

1.2.2.5 MOORE, Richard Douglas: *Methodism in the Channel Islands*, London: Epworth Press, 1952, viii+175p.

1.2.2.6 PROBERT, John Charles Cripps: *The sociology of Cornish Methodism to the present day*, Cornish Methodist Historical Association Occasional Publications No. 17, Redruth: Cornish Methodist Historical Association, 1971, [2]+80+[4]p.

1.2.2.7 RICHARDSON, W. F.: *Preston Methodism's 200 fascinating years and their background, local and national*, Preston: Henry L. Kirby, 1975, xii+220p.

1.2.2.8 SHAW, Thomas: *A history of Cornish Methodism*, Truro: D. Bradford Barton, 1967, 145p.

1.2.2.9 SWIFT, Rowland Cook: *Lively people: Methodism in Nottingham, 1740–1979*, Nottingham: Department of Adult Education, University of Nottingham, 1982, x+189p.

1.2.2.10 TICE, Frank: *The history of Methodism in Cambridge*, London: Epworth Press, 1966, vi+143p.

See also 1.1.1.18, 1.1.1.19, 1.1.1.20, 1.1.2.5, 1.1.2.11, 1.1.2.14, 1.3.4.6, 1.4.3.3, 1.5.3.2, 1.5.3.4.

1.2.3 Local histories: Wales

1.2.3.1 EDWARDS, Eric: *Yr Eglwys Fethodistaidd: Hanes ystadegol am aelodau, gweinidogion, capelau &c. yn y taleithiau Cymraeg*, Llandysul: Gwasg Gomer, 1980, 132p.

1.2.3.2 ROBERTS, Griffith Thomas: 'Methodism in Wales', *A history of the Methodist Church in Great Britain*, Vol. 3, general editors: Rupert Eric Davies, Alfred Raymond George & Ernest Gordon Rupp, London: Epworth Press, 1983, pp. 253–64.

1.2.4 Local histories: Scotland

1.2.4.1 HAYES, Alan J.: *Edinburgh Methodism, 1761–1975: The mother churches*, Edinburgh: printed for the author, 1976, x+260p.

1.2.4.2 MACFARLANE, David Laing: 'The introduction and development of Wesleyanism in Scotland', University of Edinburgh Ph.D. thesis, 1931, [13]+xxii+341+[1]+58+13+[1]+17+32+12p.

1.2.4.3   Wood, Arthur Skevington: 'Methodism in Scotland', *A history of the Methodist Church in Great Britain*, Vol. 3, general editors: Rupert Eric Davies, Alfred Raymond George & Ernest Gordon Rupp, London: Epworth Press, 1983, pp. 265–78.

1.2.5 Local histories: Ireland

1.2.5.1   Cole, Richard Lee: *A history of Methodism in Dublin*, Dublin: printed for the author by R. T. White, 1932, 145p.

1.2.5.2   Cole, Richard Lee: *History of Methodism in Ireland, Volume IV: One Methodist Church* [1860–1960], Belfast: Irish Methodist Publishing Co., 1960, xiv+203p.

1.2.5.3   Cooke, Joseph Henry: 'The development and distribution of Methodism in Ireland: A demographic study', Queen's University of Belfast M.A. thesis, 1964, 167p.

1.2.5.4   Crookshank, Charles Henry: *History of Methodism in Ireland*, Belfast: R. S. Allen, Son & Allen, 1885–88, 3 vol.

1.2.5.5   Crookshank, Charles Henry: '[Methodism] in Ireland', *A new history of Methodism*, edited by William John Townsend, Herbert Brook Workman & George Eayrs, London: Hodder and Stoughton, 1909, Vol. II, pp. 1–38.

1.2.5.6   Gallagher, Robert David Eric: 'Methodism in Ireland', *A history of the Methodist Church in Great Britain*, Vol. 3, general editors: Rupert Eric Davies, Alfred Raymond George & Ernest Gordon Rupp, London: Epworth Press, 1983, pp. 232–52.

1.2.5.7   Jeffery, Frederick: 'The Irish contribution to Methodism', *World Methodist Historical Society quinquennial meeting, August 24 1976, Dun Laoghaire Methodist Church, Ireland: Lectures*, [Lake Junaluska]: World Methodist Historical Society, 1977, pp. 1–18.

1.2.5.8   Jeffery, Frederick: *Irish Methodism: An historical account of its traditions, theology and influence*, Belfast: Epworth House, 1964, 104p.

1.2.5.9   Jeffery, Frederick: *Methodism and the Irish problem*, Wesley Historical Society Lecture 1973, Belfast: Christian Journals Ltd., 1973, vi+40p.

See also 1.4.4.4.

1.3 Spirituality

1.3.1 Theology

1.3.1.1   Langford, Thomas Anderson: *Practical divinity: Theology in the Wesleyan tradition*, Nashville: Abingdon Press, 1983, 303p.

See also 1.3.5.2.

1.3.2 Doctrine of the Church

1.3.2.1   Kissack, Reginald: *Church or no Church? A study of the development*

of the concept of Church in British Methodism, London: Epworth Press, 1964, 164p.
See also 1.2.1.5.

1.3.3 Sacraments

1.3.3.1 RUPP, Ernest Gordon: 'The Holy Communion in the Methodist Church', *The Holy Communion: A symposium*, edited by Hugh Martin, London: SCM Press, 1947, pp. 113–26.

1.3.4 Worship and devotion

1.3.4.1 BAKER, Frank: *Methodism and the love-feast*, London: Epworth Press, 1957, 83p.
1.3.4.2 BISHOP, John: *Methodist worship in relation to Free Church worship*, New York: Scholars Studies Press, 1975, xvii+173p.
1.3.4.3 GEORGE, Alfred Raymond: 'Private devotion in the Methodist tradition', *Studia Liturgica*, Vol. II, 1963, pp. 223–36.
1.3.4.4 LOCKETT, George Herbert: 'The Methodist tradition of worship', *In church: An introduction to worship and preaching*, edited by John Stacey, London: Local Preachers' Department of the Methodist Church, 1971, pp. 51–66.
1.3.4.5 PEASTON, Alexander Elliott: *The Prayer book tradition in the Free Churches*, London: James Clarke & Co., 1964, xiii+201p.
1.3.4.6 PROBERT, John Charles Cripps: *The worship and devotion of Cornish Methodism*, [Redruth: the author], 1978, [2]+120p.
1.3.4.7 TRIPP, David Howard: *The renewal of the covenant in the Methodist tradition*, London: Epworth Press, 1969, vii+220p.
1.3.4.8 WALLWORK, Charles Norman Robert: 'Origins and development of the Methodist preaching service', University of Birmingham M.A. thesis, 1984, [5]+178p.
See also 1.3.5.2, 1.3.5.3, 1.4.3.1.

1.3.5 Hymnology and music

1.3.5.1 BUCKROYD, Elizabeth Ann: 'Hymns for children', *Methodist Church Music Society Bulletin*, Vol. 3, 1977–82, pp. 82–5.
1.3.5.2 DIXON, Neil: 'English hymnody: Its relation to theology and worship in the eighteenth and nineteenth centuries', University of London M.Phil. thesis, 1970, 319p.
1.3.5.3 ELLIS, Miriam [née Tuckwell] & ELLIS, Martin: 'The origins and growth of choirs in Methodism', *Methodist Church Music Society Bulletin*, Vol. 3, 1977–82, pp. 55–9, 109–13.
1.3.5.4 GREGORY, Arthur Stephen: *Praises with understanding, illustrated from the words and music of the Methodist Hymn-Book*, London: Epworth Press, 1936, 348p.
1.3.5.5 KER, Robert Ernest: 'The sources of Methodist hymnody', *Hymn*

Society of Great Britain and Ireland Bulletin, Vol. 3, 1951–55, pp. 107–16, 134–6.

1.3.5.6   MANKIN, Kenneth: '*Our hymns*': *A commentary on Methodist hymnology, 1737–1984*, [London: the author], 1984, 27+4p.

1.3.5.7   WESTBROOK, Francis Brotherton: 'A short history of Methodist music', *Hinrichsen's Musical Year Book*, Vol. IV–V, 1947–48, pp. 180–6.

1.4 Polity and Mission

1.4.1 Ordained ministry

1.4.1.1   CANNON, William Ragsdale: 'The meaning of the ministry in Methodism', *Methodist History*, Vol. VIII, No. 1, October 1969, pp. 3–19.

1.4.1.2   GARLICK, Kenneth Benjamin: 'Ministers and probationers of the Methodist Church: "Hill's arrangement"', *Proceedings of the Wesley Historical Society*, Vol. XL, 1975–76, pp. 2–5, 45–7.

1.4.2 Lay ministry

1.4.2.1   BATTY, Margaret: 'The contribution of local preachers to the life of the Wesleyan Methodist Church until 1932, and to the Methodist Church after 1932, in England', University of Leeds M.A. thesis, 1969, [3]+372p.

See also 1.4.1.1.

1.4.3 Buildings and finance

1.4.3.1   BUTLER, John Francis: 'Methodist architecture in relation to Methodist liturgy', *University of Birmingham Institute for the Study of Worship and Religious Architecture Research Bulletin*, 1977, pp. 20–45.

1.4.3.2   PERKINS, Ernest Benson: *Methodist preaching houses and the law: The story of the model deed*, Wesley Historical Society Lecture No. 18, London: Epworth Press, 1952, 94p.

1.4.3.3   PROBERT, John Charles Cripps: *The architecture of Cornish Methodism*, Cornish Methodist Historical Association Occasional Publication No. 10, Redruth: Cornish Methodist Historical Association, 1966, 34p.

1.4.4 Overseas missions

1.4.4.1   BIRTWHISTLE, Norman Allen: 'Methodist missions', *A history of the Methodist Church in Great Britain*, Vol. 3, general editors: Rupert Eric Davies, Alfred Raymond George & Ernest Gordon Rupp, London: Epworth Press, 1983, pp. 1–116.

1.4.4.2   DAVEY, Cyril James: *The march of Methodism: The story of Methodist missionary work overseas*, London: Epworth Press, 1951, xi+209p.

1.4.4.3   DAVEY, Cyril James & THOMAS, Hugh: *Together travel on: A history of Women's Work*, London: Cargate Press (Methodist Church Overseas Division), 1984, 23p.

1.4.4.4   TAGGART, Norman Wilson: *The Irish in world Methodism, 1760–1900*, London: Epworth Press, 1986, xvii+222p.

1.5 Social Aspects

1.5.1 Political impact

1.5.1.1   TURNER, Bryan Stanley & HILL, Michael: 'Methodism and the pietist definition of politics: Historical development and contemporary evidence', *A sociological yearbook of religion in Britain, 8*, edited by Michael Hill, London: SCM Press, 1975, pp. 159–80.

1.5.2 Social witness

1.5.2.1   BRAKE, George Thompson: *Drink: Ups and downs of Methodist attitudes to temperance*, London: Oliphants, 1974, xvi+151p.

1.5.2.2   URWIN, Evelyn Clifford: *Methodism and sobriety: The story of a great transformation*, London: Epworth Press, 1943, 68p.

1.5.3 Educational work

1.5.3.1   CLOKE, Henry: 'Wesleyan Methodism's contribution to national education (1739–1902)', University of London M.A. thesis, 1936, 225p.

1.5.3.2   HASTLING, Arthur Henry Law, WILLIS, Walter Addington & WORKMAN, Walter Percy: *The history of Kingswood School; together with registers of Kingswood School and Woodhouse Grove School, and a list of masters*, London: Charles H. Kelly, 1898, 371+204p.

1.5.3.3   HUBERY, Douglas Stanley: *The Methodist contribution to education in England (1738–1977)*, London: Methodist Church Division of Education and Youth, 1977, 61p.

1.5.3.4   IVES, Arthur Glendinning Loveless: *Kingswood School in Wesley's day and since*, London: Epworth Press, 1970, xv+264p.

1.5.3.5   PRITCHARD, Frank Cyril: 'Education', *A history of the Methodist Church in Great Britain*, Vol. 3, general editors: Rupert Eric Davies, Alfred Raymond George & Ernest Gordon Rupp, London: Epworth Press, 1983, pp. 279–308.

1.5.3.6   PRITCHARD, Frank Cyril: *Methodist secondary education: A history of the contribution of Methodism to secondary education in the United Kingdom*, London: Epworth Press, 1949, 351p.

1.5.4 Literary and cultural influence

See 1.1.2.2.

1.6 Reactions to Methodism

1.6.1 Relations with other Churches

1.6.1.1   Turner, John Munsey: *Conflict and reconciliation: Studies in Methodism and ecumenism in England, 1740–1982*, London: Epworth Press, 1985, xiv +306p.

2. JOHN WESLEY AND EIGHTEENTH-CENTURY METHODISM

2.1 General Histories

2.1.1 Connexional histories

2.1.1.1 ARMSTRONG, Anthony: *The Church of England, the Methodists and society, 1700–1850*, London: University of London Press, 1973, 224p.

2.1.1.2 BETT, Henry: *The Spirit of Methodism*, London: Epworth Press, 1937, 254p.

2.1.1.3 BROOK, David: 'The Oxford Methodists', *A new history of Methodism*, edited by William John Townsend, Herbert Brook Workman & George Eayrs, London: Hodder and Stoughton, 1909, Vol. I, pp. 135–58.

2.1.1.4 BURKHARD, Johann Gottlieb: *Vollständige Geschichte der Methodisten in England, aus glaubwürdigen Quellen; nebst den Lebensbeschreibungen ihrer beyden Stifter, des Herrn Johann Wesley und George Whitefield*, Nürnberg: Verlag der Rauschen Buchhandlung, 1795, viii+186p.

2.1.1.5 CAMERON, Richard Morgan: *The rise of Methodism: A source book*, New York: Philosophical Library, 1954, xv+397p.

2.1.1.6 CARTER, Henry: *The Methodist heritage*, London: Epworth Press, 1951, xiv+246p.

2.1.1.7 CHUBB, James Stoskopf: 'Some contributing factors in the rise of Methodism', Northwestern University Ph.D. thesis, 1930.

2.1.1.8 CHURCH, Leslie Frederic: *The early Methodist people*, London: Epworth Press, 1948, ix+286p.

2.1.1.9 CHURCH, Leslie Frederic: *More about the early Methodist people*, London: Epworth Press, 1949, xix+324p.

2.1.1.10 CROWTHER, Jonathan: *A portraiture of Methodism; or, The history of the Wesleyan Methodists, shewing their rise, progress and present state; biographical sketches of some of their most eminent ministers; the doctrines the Methodists believe and teach, fully and explicitly stated; with the whole plan of their discipline, including their original rules and subsequent regulations; also a defence of Methodism, containing remarks on toleration, etc.*, second edition, enlarged and considerably improved, London: Richard Edwards, 1815, xii+512p.

2.1.1.11 DIMOND, Sydney George: *The psychology of the Methodist revival: An empirical & descriptive study*, London: Oxford University Press, 1926, xv+296p.

2.1.1.12 EAYRS, George: 'Developments, institutions, helpers, opposition' [in eighteenth-century Methodism], *A new history of Methodism*, edited by William John Townsend, Herbert Brook Workman & George Eayrs, London: Hodder and Stoughton, 1909, Vol. I, pp. 277–331.

2.1.1.13 HALÉVY, Elie: *The birth of Methodism in England*, translated and edited by Bernard Semmel, Chicago: University of Chicago Press, 1971, ix+81p.

2.1.1.14 HARWOOD, George H.: *The history of Wesleyan Methodism*, London: Whittaker and Co., 1854, 244p.

2.1.1.15 JACKSON, Thomas: *The centenary of Wesleyan Methodism: A brief sketch of the rise, progress and present state of the Wesleyan-Methodist societies throughout the world*, London: John Mason, 1839, viii+384p.

2.1.1.16 JONES, Wilfred Lawson: 'The social and psychological conditions of the rise and development of Methodism', University of Liverpool Ph.D. thesis, 1939, 492p.

2.1.1.17 JONES, Wilfred Lawson: 'Some psychological conditions of the development of Methodism up to 1850', *British Journal of Psychology*, Vol. XLII, 1951, pp. 345–54.

2.1.1.18 LEE, John David: *The evangelical revival: A re-appraisal*, Evanston: Seabury-Western Theological Seminary, 1951, 32p.

2.1.1.19 McTYEIRE, Holland Nimmons: *A history of Methodism; comprising a view of the rise of this revival of spiritual religion in the first half of the eighteenth century and of the principal agents by whom it was promoted in Europe and America, with some account of the doctrine and polity of Episcopal Methodism in the United States and the means and manner of its extension down to A.D. 1884*, London: Richard D. Dickinson, 1885, 692p.

2.1.1.20 MYLES, William: *A chronological history of the people called Methodists, of the connexion of the late Rev. John Wesley, from their rise in the year 1729 to their last conference in 1812*, fourth edition, considerably enlarged, London: printed at the Conference Office by Thomas Cordeux, 1813, xi+486p.

2.1.1.21 NIGHTINGALE, Joseph: *A portraiture of Methodism; being an impartial view of the rise, progress, doctrines, discipline and manners of the Wesleyan Methodists, in a series of letters addressed to a lady*, London: Longman, Hurst, Rees and Orme, 1807, xvi+496p.

2.1.1.22 ONG, Walter Jackson: 'Peter Ramus and the naming of Methodism: Medieval science through Ramist homiletic', *Journal of the History of Ideas*, Vol. XIV, 1953, pp. 235–48.

2.1.1.23 RATTENBURY, John Ernest: *Wesley's legacy to the world: Six studies in the permanent values of the evangelical revival*, London: Epworth Press, 1928, 309p.

2.1.1.24 SEMMEL, Bernard: *The Methodist revolution*, London: Heinemann, 1974, ix+273p.

2.1.1.25 SIMON, John Smith: *The revival of religion in England in the eighteenth century*, London: Charles H. Kelly, [1907], 331p.

2.1.1.26 STEVENS, Abel: *The history of the religious movement of the eighteenth century called Methodism, considered in its different denominational forms and its relations to British and American Protestantism*, New York: Carlton & Porter, [1858–61], 3 vol.

2.1.1.27 WALSH, John Dixon: 'The Cambridge Methodists', *Christian spirituality: Essays in honour of Gordon Rupp*, edited by Peter Brooks, London: SCM Press, 1975, pp. 249–83.

2.1.1.28 WALSH, John Dixon: 'Elie Halévy and the birth of Methodism', *Transactions of the Royal Historical Society*, Fifth Series, Vol. 25, 1975, pp. 1–20.

2.1.1.29 WALSH, John Dixon: 'Origins of the evangelical revival', *Essays in modern English church history in memory of Norman Sykes*, edited by Gareth Vaughan Bennett & John Dixon Walsh, London: Adam & Charles Black, 1966, pp. 132–62.

2.1.1.30 WEARMOUTH, Robert Featherstone: *Methodism and the common people of the eighteenth century*, London: Epworth Press, 1945, 276p.

2.1.1.31 WEDGWOOD, Julia: *John Wesley and the evangelical reaction of the eighteenth century*, London: Macmillan and Co., 1870, xi+412p.

2.1.1.32 WELCH, Charles Edwin: 'The early Methodists and their records', *Journal of the Society of Archivists*, Vol. 4, 1970–73, pp. 200–11.

2.1.1.33 WOOD, Arthur Skevington: 'The eighteenth-century Methodist revival reconsidered', *Evangelical Quarterly*, Vol. LIII, 1981, pp. 130–48.

2.1.1.34 WOOD, Arthur Skevington: *The inextinguishable blaze: Spiritual renewal and advance in the eighteenth century*, London: Paternoster Press, 1960, 256p.

See also 2.2.6.9, 2.2.6.17, 2.2.6.31, 2.2.6.34, 2.2.6.41, 2.2.6.50, 2.2.7.7, 2.2.7.8, 2.2.20.5, 2.7.2.1, 4.1.2.20.

2.1.2 Local histories: England

2.1.2.1 BIGGS, Barry John: 'Methodism in a rural society: North Nottinghamshire, 1740–1851', University of Nottingham Ph.D. thesis, 1975, xiv+557p.

2.1.2.2 BRETHERTON, Francis Fletcher: *Early Methodism in and around Chester, 1749–1812*, Chester: Phillipson & Golder, 1903, xv+300p.

2.1.2.3 BRIGG, Gordon Teasdale: 'The contribution of John Wesley to the social and educational life of Bristol and its neighbourhood', University of Bristol M.A. thesis, 1959, x+[158]p.

2.1.2.4 BROWN, Howard Miles: 'Early days of Cornish Methodism', *Proceedings of the Wesley Historical Society*, Vol. XXVI, 1947–48, pp. 49–54, 69–76, 89–96, 137–40.

2.1.2.5 BROWN, Howard Miles: 'Methodism and the Church of England in Cornwall, 1738–1838: A historical survey of Cornish Methodism, its rise, growth and relation to the Church of England', University of London Ph.D. thesis, 1947, 617p.

2.1.2.6 DYSON, John B.: *Methodism in the Isle of Wight: Its origin and progress*

down to the present times, Ventnor: George M. Burt, 1865, viii+
344p.

2.1.2.7 EVERETT, James: *Historical sketches of Wesleyan Methodism in Sheffield and its vicinity*, Vol. 1, Sheffield: printed by James Montgomery, 1823, xviii+268p [no more published].

2.1.2.8 EVERETT, James: *Wesleyan Methodism in Manchester and its vicinity*, Vol. 1, Manchester: printed by the executors of S. Russell, 1827, xvi+190p [no more published].

2.1.2.9 Goss, Walter Arthur: 'Early Methodism in Bristol, with special reference to John Wesley's visits to the city, 1739–90 and their impression on the people', *Proceedings of the Wesley Historical Society*, Vol. XIX, 1933–34, pp. 30–7, 57–65, 81–9, 101–6, 133–42, 161–8, 183–8, Vol. XX, 1935–36, pp. 1–9, 25–8.

2.1.2.10 GREAVES, Brian: 'Methodism in Yorkshire, 1740–1851', University of Liverpool Ph.D. thesis, 1968, 354p.

2.1.2.11 LAYCOCK, John William: *Methodist heroes in the Great Haworth Round, 1734–1784*, Keighley: Rydal Press, 1909, vii+380+vp.

2.1.2.12 LYTH, John: *Glimpses of early Methodism in York and the surrounding district*, York: William Sessions, 1885, [3]+320p.

2.1.2.13 Moss, Reginald: 'The origins and influence of Methodism in the north Staffordshire Potteries before 1820', University of London M.A. thesis, 1949, 160p.

2.1.2.14 RAIMO, John William: 'Spiritual harvest: The Anglo-American revival in Boston, Massachusetts and Bristol, England, 1739–1742', University of Wisconsin Ph.D. thesis, 1974, vii+279p.

2.1.2.15 ROGAL, Samuel J.: 'John Wesley's London', *Asbury Seminarian*, Vol. XXXIV, 1979, pp. 23–33.

2.1.2.16 ROSE, Edward Alan: 'Methodism in Cheshire to 1800', *Transactions of the Lancashire and Cheshire Antiquarian Society*, Vol. 78, 1975, pp. 22–37.

2.1.2.17 ROSE, Edward Alan: 'Methodism in south Lancashire to 1800', *Transactions of the Lancashire and Cheshire Antiquarian Society*, Vol. 81, 1982, pp. 67–91.

2.1.2.18 SMITH, Benjamin: *Methodism in Macclesfield*, London: Wesleyan Conference Office, 1875, xv+382p.

2.1.2.19 STAMP, William Wood: *The Orphan-House of Wesley; with notices of early Methodism in Newcastle-upon-Tyne and its vicinity*, London: John Mason, 1863, xii+299p.

2.1.2.20 STEELE, Anthony: *History of Methodism in Barnard Castle and the principal places in the Dales Circuit*, London: George Vickers, 1857, x+239p.

2.1.2.21 WALKER, John Uriah: *A history of Wesleyan Methodism in Halifax and its vicinity from its commencement to the present period*, Halifax: Hartley and Walker, 1836, viii+279p.

2.1.2.22 WALLACE, Charles Isaac: 'Religion and society in eighteenth-century England: Geographic, demographic and occupational patterns of Dissent in the West Riding of Yorkshire, 1715–1801', Duke University Ph.D. thesis, 1975, xv+542p.

2.1.2.23 WATMOUGH, Abraham: *A history of Methodism in the town and neighbourhood of Great Yarmouth, including biographical sketches of some of the leading characters who have been among the Methodists at that place,* London: printed for John Kershaw, 1826, 233p.

2.1.2.24 WILKINSON, John F.: 'Aspects in the rise of the Methodist movement in the industrial area of west Yorkshire, 1740–1830', University of Birmingham M.A. thesis, 1964, 139+[23]p.

See also 2.8.3.9, 2.9.1.3, 2.9.4.9, 2.9.5.8, 3.1.3.12, 4.1.3.9.

2.1.3 Local histories: Wales

2.1.3.1 EVANS, Richard William: 'The eighteenth-century Welsh awakening with its relationships to the contemporary English evangelical revival', University of Edinburgh Ph.D. thesis, 1956, 254p.

2.1.3.2 JENKINS, Robert Thomas: 'John Wesley in north Wales', *Bathafarn*, Vol. 2, 1947, pp. 35–54.

2.1.3.3 ROBERTS, Griffith Thomas: 'Seiadau cynnar John Wesley yng Nghymru', *Bathafarn*, Vol. 1, 1946, pp. 25–39.

2.1.3.4 WESLEY, John: *John Wesley in Wales, 1739–1790: Entries from his journal and diary relating to Wales,* edited, with an introduction, by Albert Hughes Williams, Cardiff: University of Wales Press, 1971, xxxix+141p.

2.1.3.5 WILLIAMS, Albert Hughes: 'John Wesley and the Archdeaconry of Brecon', *Links with the past: Swansea & Brecon historical essays,* edited by Owain William Jones & David Walker, Llandybie: Christopher Davies, 1974, pp. 143–64.

See also 2.3.5 *passim*, 4.1.4.12.

2.1.4 Local histories: Scotland

2.1.4.1 BUTLER, Dugald: *John Wesley and George Whitefield in Scotland; or, The influence of the Oxford Methodists on Scottish religion,* Edinburgh: W. Blackwood and Sons, 1898, vii+318p.

2.1.4.2 DAW, A. R.: 'John Wesley in Scotland: The bicentenary of Methodism', *Scots Magazine*, Vol. XXIX, April–September 1938, pp. 127–32.

2.1.4.3 GRAHAM, Ena Dorothy: 'The contribution of Lady Glenorchy and her circle to the evangelical revival', University of Leeds B.D. thesis, 1964, [2]+217p.

2.1.4.4 GRAY, William Forbes: 'John Wesley and Scotland', *Records of the Scottish Church History Society*, Vol. VIII, 1942–44, pp. 209–24.

2.1.4.5 JEFFERIES, Alfred: 'John Wesley in Scotland', *Scottish Geographical Magazine*, Vol. 83, 1967, pp. 105–12.

2.1.4.6 ROGAL, Samuel J.: 'John Wesley at Edinburgh, 1751–1790', *Trinity Journal*, New Series, Vol. 4, 1983, pp. 18–34.

2.1.4.7 SWIFT, Wesley Frank: *Methodism in Scotland: The first hundred years,* Wesley Historical Society Lecture No. 13, London: Epworth Press, 1947, 96p.

2.1.5 Local histories: Ireland

2.1.5.1   BOWMER, John Coates: 'John Wesley and Ireland', *London Quarterly and Holborn Review*, Vol. CLXXVIII, 1953, pp. 252–62, Vol. CLXXIX, 1954, pp. 38–45.

2.1.5.2   COLE, Francis Joseph: 'John Wesley and his Ulster contacts', *Proceedings and Reports of the Belfast Natural History and Philosophical Society*, Second Series, Vol. II, 1940–45, pp. 199–215.

2.1.5.3   COLE, Richard Lee: *The Wesleys came to Dublin*, London: Epworth Press, 1947, 32p.

2.1.5.4   CROOKSHANK, Charles Henry: *Memorable women of Irish Methodism in the last century*, London: Wesleyan Methodist Book Room, 1882, 203p.

2.1.5.5   FREEMAN, Thomas Walter: 'John Wesley in Ireland', *Irish Geography*, Vol. VIII, 1975, pp. 86–96.

2.1.5.6   GALLAGHER, Robert Henry: *Pioneer preachers of Irish Methodism who were called to their eternal reward during the first century of Methodism*, Belfast: Nelson & Knox, 1965, [14]+173p.

2.1.5.7   HAIRE, Robert: *Wesley's one-and-twenty visits to Ireland: A short survey*, London: Epworth Press, 1947, vi+186p.

2.1.5.8   PHILLIPS, Randall Canning: *Irish Methodism*, London: Charles H. Kelly, 1897, 107p.

2.1.5.9   PLUNKETT, Hedley Washington: *The adventure and faith of the Irish pioneers*, Belfast: Dorman & Sons, 1964, 63p.

2.1.5.10   WARNER, Thomas Edward: 'The impact of Wesley on Ireland', University of London Ph.D. thesis, 1954, iv+337p.

See also 2.2.1.3, 4.1.6.8.

2.2 Biographies: The Wesleys

2.2.1 Wesley family

2.2.1.1   BEAL, William: *The fathers of the Wesley family, clergymen in Dorsetshire, 1650–1662, (the present, the bi-centenary of their ejection), and references to events and changes of their times*, second edition, with many additions, London: William Freeman, [1862], 80p.

2.2.1.2   CLARKE, Adam: *Memoirs of the Wesley family; collected principally from original documents*, second edition, revised, corrected and considerably enlarged, London: printed for T. Tegg & Son, 1836, 2 vol.

2.2.1.3   CROOK, William: *The ancestry of the Wesleys, with special reference to their connexion with Ireland*, London: Epworth Press, 1938, 84p.

2.2.1.4   DOVE, John: *Biographical history of the Wesley family, more particularly its earlier branches*, London: Simpkin and Marshall, 1833, 300p.

2.2.1.5   EVANS, Charles: 'The ancestry of the Wesleys', *Notes and Queries*, Vol. CXCIII, 1948, pp. 255–9.

2.2.1.6   PINHORN, Malcolm: 'Wesley family', *Blackmansbury*, Vol. 1, No. 5–6, December 1964/February 1965, pp. 36–51.

2.2.1.7   ROUTLEY, Erik Reginald: *The musical Wesleys*, London: Herbert Jenkins, 1968, xv+272p.

2.2.1.8   STEVENSON, George John: *Memorials of the Wesley family; including biographical and historical sketches of all the members of the family for two hundred and fifty years, together with a genealogical table of the Wesleys, with historical notes, for more than nine hundred years*, London: S. W. Partridge and Co., [1876], xxiii+562p.

2.2.1.9   WINTERS, William: *An account of the remarkable musical talents of several members of the Wesley family, collected from original manuscripts &c.; with memorial introduction and notes*, London: F. Davis, 1874, iv+92p.

See also 2.2.4.3, 2.2.6.5, 2.2.6.6, 2.2.6.31, 2.2.6.50, 2.4.7.1, 2.4.7.3.

2.2.2 Samuel Wesley

2.2.2.1   BEECHAM, Helen Audrey: 'Samuel Wesley senior: New biographical evidence', *Renaissance and Modern Studies*, Vol. VII, 1963, pp. 78–109.

2.2.2.2   TYERMAN, Luke: *The life and times of the Rev. Samuel Wesley, M.A., Rector of Epworth and father of the Revs. John and Charles Wesley, the founders of the Methodists*, London: Simpkin, Marshall & Co., 1866, xvi+472p.

2.2.2.3   WILDER, Franklin: *Father of the Wesleys: A biography*, New York: Exposition Press, 1971, 220p.

See also 2.2.4.4.

2.2.3 Susanna Wesley

2.2.3.1   BAKER, Frank: 'Salute to Susanna', *Methodist History*, Vol. VII, No. 3, April 1969, pp. 3–12.

2.2.3.2   BAKER, Frank: 'Susanna Wesley: Puritan, parent, pastor, protagonist, pattern', *Dig or die: Papers given at the World Methodist Historical Society Wesley Heritage Conference at Wesley College within the University of Sydney, 10–15 August 1980*, edited by James Stuart Udy & Eric Gerald Clancy, Sydney: World Methodist Historical Society Australasian Section, 1981, pp. 77–88, *Women in new worlds*, Vol. II, edited by Rosemary Skinner Keller, Louise L. Queen & Hilah Frances Thomas, Nashville: Abingdon, 1982, pp. 112–31 and *Epworth Review*, Vol. 9, No. 2, May 1982, pp. 39–46.

2.2.3.3   BRAILSFORD, Mabel Richmond: *Susanna Wesley, the mother of Methodism*, London: Charles H. Kelly, 1910, 128p.

2.2.3.4   CLARKE, Eliza: *Susanna Wesley*, London: W. H. Allen & Co., 1886, vi+239p.

2.2.3.5   HARMON, Rebecca Lamar: *Susanna, mother of the Wesleys*, London: Hodder and Stoughton, 1968, 175p.

2.2.3.6   KIRK, John: *The mother of the Wesleys: A biography*, London: Henry James Tresidder, 1864, xx+351p.

2.2.3.7   NEWTON, John Anthony: *Susanna Wesley and the puritan tradition in Methodism*, London: Epworth Press, 1968, 216p.

2.2.3.8   NEWTON, John Anthony: 'Susanna Wesley (1669–1742): A bibliographical survey', *Proceedings of the Wesley Historical Society*, Vol. XXXVII, 1969–70, pp. 37–40.

2.2.3.9   ROGAL, Samuel J.: 'The Epworth women: Susanna Wesley and her daughters', *Wesleyan Theological Journal*, Vol. 18, No. 2, Fall 1983, pp. 80–9.

2.2.3.10 WALLACE, Charles Isaac: 'Susanna Wesley's spirituality: The freedom of a Christian woman', *Methodist History*, Vol. XXII, 1983–84, pp. 158–73.

2.2.3.11 WILDER, Franklin: *Immortal mother*, New York: Vantage Press, 1966, 230p.

2.2.3.12 YOUNG, Betty Irene: 'Sources for the Annesley family', *Proceedings of the Wesley Historical Society*, Vol. XLV, 1985–86, pp. 47–57.

See also 2.4.7.8.

2.2.4 John and Charles Wesley

2.2.4.1   BAKER, Frank: *A union catalogue of the publications of John and Charles Wesley*, Durham, North Carolina: Divinity School, Duke University, 1966, 230p.

2.2.4.2   BRAILSFORD, Mabel Richmond: *A tale of two brothers: John and Charles Wesley*, London: Rupert Hart-Davis, 1954, 301p.

2.2.4.3   EDWARDS, Maldwyn Lloyd: *Family circle: A study of the Epworth household in relation to John and Charles Wesley*, London: Epworth Press, 1949, ix+192p.

2.2.4.4   EDWARDS, Maldwyn Lloyd: *Sons to Samuel*, London: Epworth Press, 1961, xii+134p.

2.2.4.5   GREEN, Richard: *The works of John and Charles Wesley: A bibliography, containing an exact account of all the publications issued by the brothers Wesley, arranged in chronological order, with a list of the early editions, and descriptive and illustrative notes*, second edition, revised and with many additional notes, London: Methodist Publishing House, 1906, 291p.

2.2.4.6   LOFTHOUSE, William Frederick: 'John Wesley's letters to his brother', *London Quarterly and Holborn Review*, Vol. CLXXXV, 1960, pp. 60–5, 133–9.

2.2.4.7   OSBORN, George: *Outlines of Wesleyan bibliography; or, A record of Methodist literature from the beginning, in two parts: the first containing the publications of John and Charles Wesley, arranged in order of time, the second those of Methodist preachers, alphabetically arranged*, London: Wesleyan Conference Office, 1869, xi+220p.

2.2.4.8   ROGAL, Samuel J.: 'The contributions of John and Charles Wesley to the spread of popular religion', *Grace Theological Journal*, Vol. 4, 1983, pp. 233–44.

2.2.4.9   ROGAL, Samuel J.: 'The Wesleys: A checklist of critical commentary', *Bulletin of Bibliography & Magazine Notes*, Vol. 28, 1971, pp. 22–35.

2.2.4.10 SWIFT, Wesley Frank: 'Brothers Charles and John', *London Quarterly and Holborn Review*, Vol. CLXXXII, 1957, pp. 275–80.

2.2.4.11 WESLEY, John & WESLEY, Charles: *John and Charles Wesley: Selected prayers, hymns, journal notes, sermons, letters and treatises*, edited, with an introduction, by Frank Whaling, London: SPCK, 1981, xx+412p.

See also 2.2.1.7, 2.2.7.3, 2.2.9.7, 2.2.9.11, 2.2.12.12, 2.2.20.3, 2.6.4.22.

2.2.5 John Wesley: bibliography and historiography

2.2.5.1 BAKER, Frank: 'Unfolding John Wesley: A survey of twenty years' studies in Wesley's thought', *Quarterly Review: A Scholarly Journal for Reflection on Ministry*, Vol. 1, No. 1, Fall 1980, pp. 44–58.

2.2.5.2 GREEN, Richard: 'A list (chiefly) of published biographies and biographical notices of John Wesley, arranged in alphabetical order for the use of students of Wesley's life', *Proceedings of the Wesley Historical Society*, Vol. III, 1901–02, pp. 217–36.

2.2.5.3 HEITZENRATER, Richard Paul: 'The present state of Wesley studies', *Methodist History*, Vol. XXII, 1983–84, pp. 221–33.

2.2.5.4 JUDSON, Sandra: 'Biographical and descriptive works on the Rev. John Wesley', bibliography submitted in part requirement for University of London Diploma in Librarianship, 1963, vi+259p.

2.2.5.5 LORING, Herbert Richard: 'A comparison of biographies of John Wesley since 1850 in the light of biographical and critical materials', Boston University Ph.D. thesis, 1951.

2.2.5.6 McCONNELL, Francis John: 'New interest in John Wesley', *Journal of Religion*, Vol. XX, 1940, pp. 340–58.

2.2.5.7 M'CULLAGH, Thomas: 'The biographers of Wesley', *London Quarterly Review*, Vol. XCVII, January–April 1902, pp. 129–52.

2.2.5.8 McINTOSH, Lawrence Dennis: 'The place of John Wesley in the Christian tradition: A selected bibliography', *The place of Wesley in the Christian tradition: Essays delivered at Drew University in celebration of the commencement of the publication of the Oxford edition of the works of John Wesley*, edited by Kenneth Elmer Rowe, Metuchen: Scarecrow Press, 1976, pp. 134–59.

2.2.5.9 MASER, Frederick Ernest: 'The early biographers of John Wesley', *Methodist History*, Vol. I, No. 2, January 1963, pp. 29–42.

2.2.5.10 MELTON, John Gordon: 'An annotated bibliography of publications about the life and work of John Wesley, 1791–1966', *Methodist History*, Vol. VII, No. 4, July 1969, pp. 29–46.

2.2.5.11 OUTLER, Albert Cook: 'A new future for Wesley studies: An agenda for "Phase III"', *The future of the Methodist theological traditions*, edited by Merrill Douglas Meeks, Nashville: Abingdon Press, 1985, pp. 34–52.

2.2.5.12 ROGAL, Samuel J.: 'Methodism on the hustings: Woodrow Wilson and "John Wesley's place in history" ', *Perkins School of Theology Journal*, Vol. 38, No. 3, Spring 1985, pp. 9–18.

2.2.5.13　SOMMER, E. F.: 'John Wesley: eine bibliographische Skizze', *Mitteilungen der Studiengemeinschaft für Geschichte des Methodismus*, Bd. IV, 1966–67, pp. 4–47.

See also 2.2.4.1, 2.2.4.5, 2.2.4.7, 2.2.4.9, 2.2.6.19, 2.2.12.3, 2.2.12.13, 2.4.4.5.

2.2.6 John Wesley: lives in general

2.2.6.1　ABELOVE, Henry Diamond: 'John Wesley's influence during his lifetime on the Methodists', Yale University Ph.D. thesis, 1978, vi+244p.

2.2.6.2　ARMSTRONG, Clinton Cornelius: 'The religious leadership of John Wesley', Boston University Ph.D. thesis, 1950, iv+246+ixp.

2.2.6.3　AYLING, Stanley Edward: *John Wesley*, London: Collins, 1979, 350p.

2.2.6.4　BEVAN, Emma Frances: *John Wesley*, London: Alfred Holness, [?1877], vi+348p.

2.2.6.5　BOURNE, George: *The life of the Rev. John Wesley, A.M., with memoirs of the Wesley family; to which are subjoined, Dr. Whitehead's funeral sermon and a comprehensive history of American Methodism*, Baltimore: printed by George Dobbin and Murphy for themselves, John Hagerty and Abner Neal, 1807, 351p.

2.2.6.6　BOWEN, Marjorie *pseud.* [i.e. Gabrielle Margaret Vere Campbell]: *Wrestling Jacob: A study of the life of John Wesley and some members of the family*, London: William Heinemann, 1937, x+395p.

2.2.6.7　BRIGDEN, Thomas Edwin: 'John Wesley, 1703–1791', *A new history of Methodism*, edited by William John Townsend, Herbert Brook Workman & George Eayrs, London: Hodder and Stoughton, 1909, Vol. I, pp. 159–233.

2.2.6.8　[BRIGDEN, Thomas Edwin]: *John Wesley the Methodist: A plain account of his life and work*, New York: Eaton and Mains, 1903, 319p.

2.2.6.9　COKE, Thomas & MOORE, Henry: *The life of the Rev. John Wesley, A.M., including an account of the great revival of religion, in Europe and America, of which he was the first and chief instrument*, London: printed by G. Paramore, 1792, x+542p.

2.2.6.10　EAYRS, George: *John Wesley, Christian philosopher and Church founder*, London: Epworth Press, 1926, 288p.

2.2.6.11　EDWARDS, Maldwyn Lloyd: *The astonishing youth: A study of John Wesley as men saw him*, London: Epworth Press, 1959, 128p.

2.2.6.12　EDWARDS, Maldwyn Lloyd: 'John Wesley', *A history of the Methodist Church in Great Britain*, Vol. 1, general editors: Rupert Eric Davies & Ernest Gordon Rupp, London: Epworth Press, 1965, pp. 35–79.

2.2.6.13　EVANS, John: *John Wesley: Ei fywyd a'i lafur*, Treffynnon: P. M. Evans & Son, 1880, xxi+552p.

2.2.6.14 FITCHETT, William Henry: *Wesley and his century: A study in spiritual forces*, London: Smith, Elder & Co., 1906, vii+537p.

2.2.6.15 GREEN, Richard: *John Wesley, evangelist*, London: Religious Tract Society, 1905, 542p.

2.2.6.16 GREEN, Vivian Hubert Howard: *John Wesley*, London: Thomas Nelson, 1964, 168p.

2.2.6.17 HAMPSON, John: *Memoirs of the late Rev. John Wesley, A.M.; with a review of his life and writings, and a history of Methodism from its commencement in 1729 to the present time*, Sunderland: printed for the author by James Graham, 1791, 3 vol.

2.2.6.18 HARRISON, Grace Elizabeth Simon: *Son to Susanna: The private life of John Wesley*, London: Ivor Nicholson and Watson Ltd., 1937, 353p.

2.2.6.19 HEITZENRATER, Richard Paul: *The elusive Mr. Wesley*, Nashville: Abingdon Press, 1984, 2 vol.

2.2.6.20 HOLMES, David: *The Wesley offering; or, Wesley and his times*, Auburn: Derby and Miller, 1852, 308p.

2.2.6.21 JEFFERY, Thomas Reed: *John Wesley's religious quest*, New York: Vantage Press, [1960], 439p.

2.2.6.22 KENYON, Edith C.: *The centenary life of Wesley*, London: Walter Scott, [1891], vi+404p.

2.2.6.23 LA GORCE, Agnès de: *Wesley: Maître d'un peuple, 1703–1791*, Paris: Albin Michel, 1940, 366p.

2.2.6.24 LEE, Umphrey: *The Lord's horseman*, New York: Century Company, 1928, xi+358p.

2.2.6.25 LELIEVRE, Matthieu: *John Wesley: His life and his work*, new edition, revised and enlarged, London: Charles H. Kelly, 1900, xvi+473p.

2.2.6.26 LIPSKY, Abram: *John Wesley: A portrait*, New York: Simon and Schuster, 1928, ix+305p.

2.2.6.27 LUNN, Arnold Henry Moore: *John Wesley*, London: Cassell, 1929, 381p.

2.2.6.28 McCONNELL, Francis John: *John Wesley*, London: Epworth Press, 1939, 355p.

2.2.6.29 MASER, Frederick Ernest: 'Second thoughts on John Wesley', *Drew Gateway*, Vol. 49, No. 2, Winter 1978, pp. 1–56.

2.2.6.30 MEREDITH, William Henry: *The real John Wesley*, Cincinnati: Jennings and Pye, 1903, 425p.

2.2.6.31 MOORE, Henry: *The life of the Rev. John Wesley, A.M., Fellow of Lincoln College, Oxford; in which are included the life of his brother, the Rev. Charles Wesley, A.M., Student of Christ Church, and memoirs of their family, comprehending an account of the great revival of religion in which they were the first and chief instruments*, London: John Kershaw, 1824–25, 2 vol.

2.2.6.32 MOORE, Robert Louis: *John Wesley and authority: A psychological perspective*, American Academy of Religion Dissertation Series No. 29, Missoula: Scholars Press, 1979, ix+245p.

2.2.6.33 NORO, Yoshio: *Wesurei no shogai to shingaku*, Tokyo: Shinkyo Shuppan Sha, 1975, 668p.

2.2.6.34 PIETTE, Maximin: *John Wesley in the evolution of Protestantism*, London: Sheed & Ward, 1937, xlviii+569p.

2.2.6.35 SCHMIDT, Martin: *John Wesley: A theological biography*, London: Epworth Press, 1962–73, 2 vol. [in 3].

2.2.6.36 SIMON, John Smith: *John Wesley and the advance of Methodism*, London: Epworth Press, 1925, 352p.

2.2.6.37 SIMON, John Smith: *John Wesley and the Methodist societies*, London: Epworth Press, 1923, 381p.

2.2.6.38 SIMON, John Smith: *John Wesley and the religious societies*, London: Epworth Press, 1921, 363p.

2.2.6.39 SIMON, John Smith: *John Wesley: The last phase*, London: Epworth Press, 1934, 355p.

2.2.6.40 SIMON, John Smith: *John Wesley: The master-builder*, London: Epworth Press, 1927, 344p.

2.2.6.41 SOUTHEY, Robert: *The life of Wesley, and the rise and progress of Methodism*, London: Longman, Hurst, Rees, Orme and Brown, 1820, 2 vol.

2.2.6.42 TELFORD, John: *The life of John Wesley*, revised and enlarged edition, London: Wesleyan Methodist Book Room, 1899, xviii+406p.

2.2.6.43 TUTTLE, Robert Gregory: *John Wesley: His life and theology*, Exeter: Paternoster Press, 1979, 368p.

2.2.6.44 TYERMAN, Luke: *The life and times of the Rev. John Wesley, M.A., founder of the Methodists*, London: Hodder and Stoughton, 1870–71, 3 vol.

2.2.6.45 URLIN, Richard Denny: *The Churchman's life of Wesley*, new edition, revised and corrected, London: Society for Promoting Christian Knowledge, 1886, vi+352p.

2.2.6.46 VULLIAMY, Colwyn Edward: *John Wesley*, London: Geoffrey Bles, 1931, x+370p.

2.2.6.47 WADE, John Donald: *John Wesley*, New York: Coward-McCann, 1930, xvii+301p.

2.2.6.48 WATSON, Richard: *The life of the Rev. John Wesley, A.M., sometime Fellow of Lincoln College, Oxford and founder of the Methodist societies*, London: John Mason, 1831, viii+379p.

2.2.6.49 WESLEY, John: *Sayings and portraits of John Wesley*, compiled and edited by John Telford, London: Epworth Press, 1924, 267p.

2.2.6.50 WHITEHEAD, John: *The life of the Rev. John Wesley, M.A., sometime Fellow of Lincoln College, Oxford, collected from his private papers and printed works, and written at the request of his executors, to which is prefixed some account of his ancestors and relations; with the life of the Rev. Charles Wesley, M.A., collected from his private journal and never before published, the whole forming a history of Methodism in which the principles and economy of the Methodists are unfolded*, London: printed by Stephen Couchman, 1793–96, 2 vol.

2.2.6.51 WINCHESTER, Caleb Thomas: *The life of John Wesley*, New York: Macmillan, 1906, xiii+301p.

2.2.6.52 WOOD, Arthur Skevington: *The burning heart: John Wesley, evangelist*, Exeter: Paternoster Press, 1967, 302p.

See also 2.2.5.5, 2.2.20.12.

2.2.7 John Wesley: life to 1735

2.2.7.1   BATES, Edmund Ralph: 'John Wesley's first preaching Sunday', *Proceedings of the Wesley Historical Society*, Vol. XL, 1975–76, pp. 7–16.

2.2.7.2   BATES, Edmund Ralph: 'The Methodist legend of South Leigh: An article in celebration of the 250th. anniversary of the ordination of John Wesley, Sunday, September 19, 1725', *Methodist History*, Vol. XIII, No. 4, July 1975, pp. 18–24.

2.2.7.3   DOUGLASS, Paul Franklin: *Wesleys at Oxford: The religion of university men*, Bryn Mawr: Bryn Mawr Press, 1953, 107p.

2.2.7.4   FOWLER, James Wiley: 'John Wesley's development in faith', *The future of the Methodist theological traditions*, edited by Merrill Douglas Meeks, Nashville: Abingdon Press, 1985, pp. 172–92.

2.2.7.5   GREEN, Vivian Hubert Howard: *The young Mr. Wesley: A study of John Wesley and Oxford*, London: Edward Arnold, 1961, viii+342p.

2.2.7.6   HARPER, J. Steven: 'The devotional life of John Wesley, 1703–38', Duke University Ph.D. thesis, 1981, xiii+711p.

2.2.7.7   HEITZENRATER, Richard Paul: 'John Wesley and the Oxford Methodists, 1725–1735', Duke University Ph.D. thesis, 1972, xvi+548p.

2.2.7.8   HEITZENRATER, Richard Paul: 'The Oxford diaries and the first rise of Methodism', *Methodist History*, Vol. XII, No. 4, July 1974, pp. 110–35.

2.2.7.9   KÄLLSTAD, Thorvald: 'John Wesleys religiösa Utveckling, 1703–1738', Licentiatavhandling, Lunds Universitet, 1959.

2.2.7.10   LEGER, J. Augustin: *L'Angleterre religieuse et les origines du méthodisme au XVIIIᵉ siècle: La jeunesse de Wesley*, Paris: Librarie Hachette, 1910, xxxi+446+137p.

2.2.7.11   MOORE, Robert Louis: 'Justification without joy: Psychohistorical reflections on John Wesley's childhood and conversion', *History of Childhood Quarterly*, Vol. 2, 1974–75, pp. 31–52.

2.2.7.12   NOTTINGHAM, Elizabeth Kristine: *The making of an evangelist: A study of John Wesley's early years*, Upper Darby: C. S. McIver, 1938, v+178p.

2.2.7.13   THOMPSON, Edgar Wesley: *Wesley at Charterhouse*, London: Epworth Press, 1938, vii+17p.

See also 2.2.15.3, 2.2.15.10.

2.2.8 John Wesley: Georgia ministry

2.2.8.1   BAKER, Frank: 'John Wesley's last visit to Charleston', *South Carolina Historical Magazine*, Vol. 78, 1977, pp. 265–71.

2.2.8.2   CANNON, William Ragsdale: 'John Wesley's years in Georgia', *Methodist History*, Vol. I, No. 4, July 1963, pp. 1–7.

2.2.8.3   COULTER, Ellis Merton: 'When John Wesley preached in Georgia', *Georgia Historical Quarterly*, Vol. IX, 1925, pp. 317–51.

2.2.8.4   MASER, Frederick Ernest: 'Preface to victory: An analysis of John Wesley's mission to Georgia', *Religion in Life*, Vol. XXV, 1955–56, pp. 280–93.

2.2.8.5   MORGAN, David Taft: 'John Wesley's sojourn in Georgia revisited', *Georgia Historical Quarterly*, Vol. 64, 1980, pp. 253–62.

2.2.8.6   PENNINGTON, Edgar Legare: 'John Wesley's Georgia ministry', *Church History*, Vol. VIII, 1939, pp. 231–54.

2.2.8.7   RANDOLPH, Jerry Ralph: 'John Wesley and the American Indian: A study in disillusionment', *Methodist History*, Vol. X, No. 3, April 1972, pp. 3–11.

2.2.8.8   ROBBINS, Peggy: 'God, man, woman and the Wesleys', *American Heritage*, Vol. 35, No. 3, April/May 1984, pp. 96–103.

2.2.8.9   SCHMIDT, Martin: *Der junge Wesley als Heidenmissionar und Missionstheologe: Ein Beitrag zur Entstehungsgeschichte des Methodismus*, 2., völlig neu bearbeitete Auflage, Gütersloh: Gütersloher Verlagshaus Mohn, 1973, 66p.

2.2.8.10 SMITH, Warren Thomas: 'The Wesleys in Georgia: An evaluation', *Journal of the Interdenominational Theological Center*, Vol. VI, 1978–79, pp. 157–67.

See also 2.2.7.11, 2.2.7.12, 2.2.14.4, 2.2.16.1, 2.2.16.5, 2.2.16.11, 2.2.16.13, 2.2.18.9, 2.2.18.10.

2.2.9 John Wesley: Aldersgate experience

2.2.9.1   BAKER, Frank: ' "Aldersgate" and Wesley's editors', *London Quarterly and Holborn Review*, Vol. CXCI, 1966, pp. 310–19.

2.2.9.2   BAKER, Frank: 'Aldersgate, 1738–1963: The challenge of Aldersgate', *Duke Divinity School Bulletin*, Vol. 28, 1963, pp. 67–80.

2.2.9.3   CAMERON, Richard Morgan: 'John Wesley's Aldersgate Street experience', *Drew Gateway*, Vol. 25, 1954–55, pp. 210–19.

2.2.9.4   CLARK, Elmer Talmage: *The warm heart of Wesley*, New York: Association of Methodist Historical Societies, 1950, 78p.

2.2.9.5   ELTZHOLTZ, Carl Frederik: *John Wesley's conversion and sanctification*, Cincinnati: Jennings and Graham, 1908, 41p.

2.2.9.6   GREEN, Richard: *The conversion of John Wesley*, edited, with an introduction, by Thomas Frederick Lockyer, London: Francis Griffiths, 1909, 46p.

2.2.9.7   HOLLAND, Bernard George: 'The conversions of John and Charles Wesley and their place in Methodist tradition', *Proceedings of the Wesley Historical Society*, Vol. XXXVIII, 1971–72, pp. 46–53, 65–71.

2.2.9.8   LEE, John David: 'The conversion experience of May 24, 1738 in the life of John Wesley', Boston University Ph.D. thesis, 1937.

2.2.9.9   MCINTOSH, Lawrence Dennis: 'John Wesley: Conversion as a continuum', *Mid-Stream*, Vol. 8, No. 3, Spring 1969, pp. 50–65.

2.2.9.10 MCNEILL, John Thomas: 'Luther at Aldersgate', *London Quarterly and Holborn Review*, Vol. CLXIV, 1939, pp. 200–17.

2.2.9.11 RATTENBURY, John Ernest: *The conversion of the Wesleys: A critical study*, London: Epworth Press, 1938, 243p.

2.2.9.12 SCHMIDT, Martin: 'Die Bedeutung Luthers für John Wesleys Bekehrung', *Luther-Jahrbuch*, Bd. XX, 1938, pp. 125–59.

2.2.9.13 SCHMIDT, Martin: *John Wesleys Bekehrung*, Bremen: Buchdruckerei des Traktathauses, 1937, 108p.

2.2.9.14 *What happened at Aldersgate*, edited by Elmer Talmage Clark, Nashville: Methodist Publishing House, 1938, 239p.

See also 2.2.7.11.

2.2.10   John Wesley: preacher

2.2.10.1 BISHOP, John: 'John Wesley as a preacher', *Religion in Life*, Vol. XXVI, 1956–57, pp. 264–73.

2.2.10.2 BORAINE, Alexander Lionel: 'The nature of evangelism in the theology and practice of John Wesley', Drew University Ph.D. thesis, 1969, ix+276p.

2.2.10.3 DOUGHTY, William Lamplough: *John Wesley, preacher*, London: Epworth Press, 1955, x+213p.

2.2.10.4 DYGOSKI, Louise Annie: 'The journals and letters of John Wesley on preaching', University of Wisconsin Ph.D. thesis, 1961, viii+363p.

2.2.10.5 GRANT, Frank R.: 'The revolution in religious rhetoric: John Wesley and the evangelical impact on England', *Historian*, Vol. XXXIX, 1976–77, pp. 439–54.

2.2.10.6 HOLLAND, Bernard George: ' "A species of madness": The effect of John Wesley's early preaching', *Proceedings of the Wesley Historical Society*, Vol. XXXIX, 1973–74, pp. 77–85.

2.2.10.7 MASER, Frederick Ernest: 'Problem in preaching: An analysis of the preaching power of John Wesley', *London Quarterly and Holborn Review*, Vol. CLXXXII, 1957, pp. 110–17.

2.2.10.8 RAMAGE, Ian: *Battle for the free mind* [with special reference to John Wesley], London: George Allen & Unwin, 1967, 269p.

2.2.10.9 SIMON, John Smith: 'John Wesley and field preaching', *Proceedings of the Wesley Historical Society*, Vol. XI, 1917–18, pp. 54–63.

See also 2.2.6.15, 2.2.6.52, 2.2.7.1, 2.2.15 *passim*.

2.2.11   John Wesley: his reading

2.2.11.1 BAKER, Frank: 'A study of John Wesley's readings', *London Quarterly and Holborn Review*, Vol. CLXVIII, 1943, pp. 140–5, 234–42.

2.2.11.2 BOSHEARS, Onva K.: 'The books in John Wesley's life', *Wesleyan Theological Journal*, Vol. 3, Spring 1968, pp. 48–56.

2.2.11.3 BOSHEARS, Onva K.: 'John Wesley, the bookman: A study of his reading interests in the eighteenth century', University of Michigan Ph.D. thesis, 1972, vii+425p.

2.2.11.4 JACKSON, George: 'John Wesley as a bookman', *London Quarterly and Holborn Review*, Vol. CLX, 1935, pp. 294–305 and *Religion in Life*, Vol. IV, 1935, pp. 599–608.

2.2.11.5 Joy, James Richard: 'Wesley: Man of a thousand books and a book', *Religion in Life*, Vol. VIII, 1939, pp. 71–84.

2.2.11.6 Rogal, Samuel J.: 'A Journal and diary checklist of John Wesley's reading, 14 October 1735–23 February 1791', *Serif*, Vol. 11, 1974, pp. 11–33.

2.2.11.7 Rogal, Samuel J.: 'Pope and the Wesleys', *University of Dayton Review*, Vol. 9, 1972, pp. 47–57.

2.2.11.8 Rogal, Samuel J.: 'The role of "Paradise lost" in works by John and Charles Wesley', *Milton Quarterly*, Vol. 13, 1979, pp. 114–19.

2.2.11.9 Smith, Neil Gregor: 'The literary taste of John Wesley', *Queen's Quarterly*, Vol. XLV, 1938, pp. 353–8.

2.2.11.10 Wright, Louis Booker: 'John Wesley, scholar and critic', *South Atlantic Quarterly*, Vol. XXIX, 1930, pp. 262–81.

2.2.12   John Wesley: writings in general

2.2.12.1 Baker, Frank: 'John Wesley, literary arbiter: An introduction to his use of the asterisk', *Proceedings of the Wesley Historical Society*, Vol. XL, 1975–76, pp. 25–33.

2.2.12.2 Baker, Frank: *John Wesley, London publisher, 1733–1791: A lecture to the Friends of Wesley's Chapel, given on Thursday, May 24th. 1984 at Wesley's Chapel*, Friends of Wesley's Chapel Annual Lecture No. 3, [London: Friends of Wesley's Chapel, 1984, 15p].

2.2.12.3 Baker, Frank: 'The Oxford edition of Wesley's works and its text', *The place of Wesley in the Christian tradition: Essays delivered at Drew University in celebration of the commencement of the publication of the Oxford edition of the works of John Wesley*, edited by Kenneth Elmer Rowe, Metuchen: Scarecrow Press, 1976, pp. 117–33.

2.2.12.4 Baker, Frank: 'Publishing to the glory of God: John Wesley as seen in his writings', *Historical Bulletin, World Methodist Historical Society*, Vol. 11, First Quarter 1982, pp. 2–5.

2.2.12.5 Baker, Frank: 'The re-printing of Wesley's publications', *Proceedings of the Wesley Historical Society*, Vol. XXII, 1939–40, pp. 57–61.

2.2.12.6 Baker, Frank: 'Wesley's printers and booksellers', *Proceedings of the Wesley Historical Society*, Vol. XXII, 1939–40, pp. 61–5, 97–101, 131–40, 164–8.

2.2.12.7 Golden, James L.: 'John Wesley on rhetoric and belles lettres', *Speech Monographs*, Vol. 28, 1961, pp. 250–64.

2.2.12.8 Herbert, Thomas Walter: *John Wesley as editor and author*, Princeton: Princeton University Press, 1940, vii+146p.

2.2.12.9 Lawton, George: 'John Wesley and proverbs: A concluding essay with special reference to proverb lexicography', *Proceedings of the Wesley Historical Society*, Vol. XXX, 1955–56, pp. 73–81, 108–13.

2.2.12.10 Lawton, George: *John Wesley's English: A study of his literary style*, London: George Allen & Unwin, 1962, 320p.

2.2.12.11 RIVERS, Isabel: 'Dissenting and Methodist books of practical divinity', *Books and their readers in eighteenth-century England*, edited by Isabel Rivers, Leicester: Leicester University Press, 1982, pp. 127–64.

2.2.12.12 ROGAL, Samuel J.: *John and Charles Wesley* [as authors], Boston: Twayne Publishers, 1983, [18]+178p.

2.2.12.13 SWIFT, Wesley Frank: 'The works of John Wesley', *Proceedings of the Wesley Historical Society*, Vol. XXXI, 1957–58, pp. 173–7.

2.2.12.14 VALLINS, George Henry: *The Wesleys and the English language: Four essays*, London: Epworth Press, 1957, 88p.

2.2.12.15 WESLEY, John: *The works of the Rev. John Wesley, A.M.*, third edition, edited by Thomas Jackson, London: John Mason, 1829–31, 14 vol.

See also 2.2.4.1, 2.2.4.5, 2.2.4.7, 2.5.1.24, 2.8.5.4, 2.8.5.12.

2.2.13 John Wesley: letters

2.2.13.1 BAKER, Frank: 'John Wesley, postal pastor', *Dig or die: Papers given at the World Methodist Historical Society Wesley Heritage Conference at Wesley College within the University of Sydney, 10–15 August 1980*, edited by James Stuart Udy & Eric Gerald Clancy, Sydney: World Methodist Historical Society Australasian Section, 1981, pp. 37–47.

2.2.13.2 GRAHAM, William Creighton: *John Wesley as a letter writer*, Toronto: Methodist Book and Publishing House, 1923, 35p.

2.2.13.3 HOWARD, Wilbert Francis: 'John Wesley in his letters', *Proceedings of the Wesley Historical Society*, Vol. XXIX, 1953–54, pp. 3–11.

2.2.13.4 LAWTON, George: 'Proverbs and proverbial echoes in John Wesley's letters', *Proceedings of the Wesley Historical Society*, Vol. XXVI, 1947–48, pp. 111–14, 129–34.

2.2.13.5 LAWTON, George: 'The slang and colloquial expressions in Wesley's letters', *Proceedings of the Wesley Historical Society*, Vol. XXXII, 1959–60, pp. 5–11, 25–33.

2.2.13.6 ROGAL, Samuel J.: ' "The elder unto the well-beloved": The letters of John Wesley', *Journal of Religious Studies*, Vol. 7, Fall 1979, pp. 73–87.

2.2.13.7 TELFORD, John: 'On editing Wesley's letters', *London Quarterly Review*, Vol. CLVI, 1931, pp. 145–58.

2.2.13.8 WESLEY, John: *The letters of the Rev. John Wesley, A.M., sometime Fellow of Lincoln College, Oxford*, edited by John Telford, standard edition, London: Epworth Press, 1931, 8 vol.

2.2.13.9 WESLEY, John: *The works of John Wesley, Volume 25: Letters I, 1721–1739*, edited by Frank Baker, Oxford: Clarendon Press, 1980, xxii+763p.

2.2.13.10 WESLEY, John: *The works of John Wesley, Volume 26: Letters II, 1740–1755*, edited by Frank Baker, Oxford: Clarendon Press, 1982, xx+684p.

See also 2.2.4.6, 2.2.10.4.

2.2.14 John Wesley: diaries and journal

2.2.14.1 BAKER, Frank: 'The birth of John Wesley's journal', *Methodist History*, Vol. VIII, No. 2, January 1970, pp. 25–32.

2.2.14.2 COLE, Richard Lee: *John Wesley's 'Journal': An appreciation*, Wesley Historical Society Lecture No. 4, London: Epworth Press, 1938, 47p.

2.2.14.3 HEITZENRATER, Richard Paul: 'Rediscovering John Wesley through his diaries', *Historical Bulletin, World Methodist Historical Society*, Vol. 11, Third Quarter 1982, pp. 2–5.

2.2.14.4 HENDRIX, Eugene Russell: 'Wesley's original American journal', *Methodist Review*, Vol. LXXXIII, 1901, pp. 513–23.

2.2.14.5 JENSON, Evelyn Gene van Til: 'John Wesley's use of three types of classical oratory – forensic, epideictic and deliberative – in his "Journal"', Ball State University Ed.D. thesis, 1980, 195p.

2.2.14.6 LAWTON, George: 'The colloquial element in the English of Wesley's "Journal"', *Proceedings of the Wesley Historical Society*, Vol. XXXII, 1959–60, pp. 159–65, 178–85.

2.2.14.7 LAWTON, George: 'The proverbial element in Wesley's "Journal"' *Proceedings of the Wesley Historical Society*, Vol. XXIX, 1953–54, pp. 58–65.

2.2.14.8 TENNEY, Mary Alice: 'Early Methodist autobiography, 1739–1791: A study in the literature of the inner life', University of Wisconsin Ph.D. thesis, 1939, iv+360+6p.

2.2.14.9 WESLEY, John: *The journal of the Rev. John Wesley, A.M., sometime Fellow of Lincoln College, Oxford; enlarged from original mss., with notes from unpublished diaries, annotations, maps and illustrations*, edited by Nehemiah Curnock, London: Robert Culley, [1909–16], 8 vol.

See also 2.1.3.4, 2.2.7.8, 2.2.10.4, 2.2.11.6.

2.2.15 John Wesley: sermons

2.2.15.1 COLLINS, Edward McDaniel: 'A critical edition of the thirteen sermons by John Wesley on the Sermon on the Mount', Ohio University Ph.D. thesis, 1965, [5]+214p.

2.2.15.2 DOWNEY, James: *The eighteenth-century pulpit: A study of the sermons of Butler, Berkeley, Secker, Sterne, Whitefield and Wesley*, Oxford: Clarendon Press, 1969, xiv+254p.

2.2.15.3 HEITZENRATER, Richard Paul: 'John Wesley's early sermons', *Proceedings of the Wesley Historical Society*, Vol. XXXVII, 1969–70, pp. 110–28.

2.2.15.4 LAWTON, George: 'The "illustrious vulgar" in John Wesley's sermons', *Proceedings of the Wesley Historical Society*, Vol. XXXIII, 1961–62, pp. 53–62, 112–17.

2.2.15.5 LAWTON, George: 'Wesley's homiletic use of proverbial lore', *Proceedings of the Wesley Historical Society*, Vol. XXVIII, 1951–52, pp. 2–7, 25–7.

2.2.15.6 SIMON, John Smith: 'The first four volumes of Wesley's sermons',

Proceedings of the Wesley Historical Society, Vol. IX, 1913–14, pp. 36–45.

2.2.15.7 SMITH, Timothy Lawrence: 'Chronological list of John Wesley's sermons and doctrinal essays', *Wesleyan Theological Journal*, Vol. 17, No. 2, Fall 1982, pp. 88–110.

2.2.15.8 WESLEY, John: *Wesley's standard sermons; consisting of forty-four discourses, published in four volumes in 1746, 1748, 1750 and 1760 (fourth edition, 1787) to which are added nine additional sermons published in Vols. I to IV of Wesley's collected works, 1771*, edited and annotated by Edward Holdsworth Sugden, London: Epworth Press, 1921, 2 vol.

2.2.15.9 WESLEY, John: *The works of John Wesley, Volume 1: Sermons I, 1–33*, edited by Albert Cook Outler, Nashville: Abingdon Press, 1984, xxi+722p.

2.2.15.10 WHITED, Harold Vaughn: 'A rhetorical analysis of the published sermons preached by John Wesley at Oxford University', University of Michigan Ph.D. thesis, 1959, xiv+359p.

See also 2.4.2.7, 2.5.3.17.

2.2.16 John Wesley: hymns

2.2.16.1 BAKER, Frank: 'The sources of John Wesley's "Collection of psalms and hymns", Charleston, 1737', *Proceedings of the Wesley Historical Society*, Vol. XXXI, 1957–58, pp. 186–93.

2.2.16.2 BETT, Henry: 'John Wesley's translations of German hymns', *Proceedings of the Wesley Historical Society*, Vol. VIII, 1911–12, pp. 141–6.

2.2.16.3 BETT, Henry: 'John Wesley's translations of German hymns in reference to metre and rhyme', *London Quarterly and Holborn Review*, Vol. CLXV, 1940, pp. 288–94.

2.2.16.4 DRURY, Brian C.: 'John Wesley, hymnologist', *Proceedings of the Wesley Historical Society*, Vol. XXXII, 1959–60, pp. 102–8, 132–5.

2.2.16.5 ENGLAND, Martha Winburn: 'The first Wesley hymn book', *Bulletin of the New York Public Library*, Vol. 68, 1964, pp. 225–38.

2.2.16.6 GOLDHAWK, Norman Panter: 'Hymns for the use of the people called Methodists, 1780', *Hymn Society of Great Britain and Ireland Bulletin*, Vol. 9, 1978–81, pp. 170–5.

2.2.16.7 HATFIELD, James Taft: 'John Wesley's translations of German hymns', *Publications of the Modern Language Association*, Vol. XI, 1896, pp. 171–99.

2.2.16.8 HODGSON, Elsie Marjorie: 'John – or Charles – Wesley?', *Proceedings of the Wesley Historical Society*, Vol. XLI, 1977–78, pp. 73–6.

2.2.16.9 HOUGHTON, Edward: 'John Wesley or Charles Wesley?', *Hymn Society of Great Britain and Ireland Bulletin*, Vol. 9, 1978–81, pp. 93–9, Vol. 10, 1982–85, pp. 70–6.

2.2.16.10 NUELSEN, John Louis: *John Wesley and the German hymn: A detailed study of John Wesley's translations of thirty-three German hymns*, Calverley: Arthur S. Holbrook, [1972], 171p.

2.2.16.11 STEVENSON, Robert: 'John Wesley's first hymnbook', *Review of Religion*, Vol. XIV, 1949–50, pp. 140–60.

2.2.16.12 WALTERS, Stanley David: 'Strange fires: A biblical allusion in John Wesley's hymns', *Methodist History*, Vol. XVII, 1978–79, pp. 44–58.

2.2.16.13 WESLEY, John: *John Wesley's first hymn-book, A collection of psalms and hymns: A facsimile, with additional material*, edited by Frank Baker & George Walton Williams, Dalcho Historical Society of the Protestant Episcopal Church in South Carolina Publication No. 16, Charleston: Dalcho Historical Society, 1964, xxxvii+74p.

2.2.16.14 WESLEY, John: *The works of John Wesley, Volume 7: A collection of hymns for the use of the people called Methodists*, edited by Franz Hildebrandt & Oliver Aveyard Beckerlegge, with the assistance of James Dale, Oxford: Clarendon Press, 1983, xv+848p.

See also 2.4.6.11, 2.6.2.8, 2.6.2.18, 2.6.4.7, 2.6.4.22, 2.6.6.14, 2.6.6.15, 2.6.7.1, 2.6.7.3, 2.6.7.6.

2.2.17 John Wesley: other writings

2.2.17.1 BARBER, Frank Louis: 'John Wesley edits a novel' [Henry Brooke's "The fool of quality"], *London Quarterly and Holborn Review*, Vol. CLXXI, 1946, pp. 50–4.

2.2.17.2 CLAPPER, Gregory Scott: ' "True religion" and the affections: A study of John Wesley's abridgement of Jonathan Edwards' "Treatise on religious affections" ', *Wesleyan Theological Journal*, Vol. 19, No. 2, Fall 1984, pp. 77–89 and *Wesleyan theology today: A bicentennial theological consultation*, edited by Theodore Runyon, Nashville: Kingswood Books, 1985, pp. 416–23.

2.2.17.3 DOIDGE, Reginald James: *John Wesley's Christian Library*, London: Epworth Press, 1938, 15p.

2.2.17.4 DUNCAN, Ivar Lou: 'John Wesley edits "Paradise lost" ', *Essays in memory of Christine Burleson in language and literature*, edited by Thomas Glen Burton, Johnson City: Research Advisory Council, East Tennessee State University, 1969, pp. 73–85.

2.2.17.5 HANSEN, William Albert: 'John Wesley and the rhetoric of reform', University of Oregon Ph.D. thesis, 1972, v+341p.

2.2.17.6 LAWTON, George: 'Slang and colloquialism in John Wesley's tracts and treatises', *Proceedings of the Wesley Historical Society*, Vol. XXXV, 1965–66, pp. 154–8, 165–7, 185–8.

2.2.17.7 LAWTON, George: 'Wesley's use of proverbs in his treatises and kindred works', *Proceedings of the Wesley Historical Society*, Vol. XXIX, 1953–54, pp. 169–77.

2.2.17.8 MOLIN, Sven Eric: 'John Wesley's techniques in revising literary masterpieces for his Methodist audience with special reference to "Paradise lost" ', University of Pennsylvania Ph.D. thesis, 1956, xvii+317p.

2.2.17.9 PARTRIDGE, Eric: 'John Wesley's dictionary', *London Quarterly and Holborn Review*, Vol. CLVII, 1932, pp. 544–7 and *Proceedings of the Wesley Historical Society*, Vol. XXVII, 1949–50, pp. 170–3.

2.2.17.10 ROGAL, Samuel J.: 'John Wesley's "Arminian Magazine"', *Andrews University Seminary Studies*, Vol. 22, 1984, pp. 231–47.

2.2.17.11 ROGAL, Samuel J.: 'Thoughts on Prior: John Wesley's distortion of Johnson', *Essays in Literature*, Vol. 11, 1984, pp. 137–43.

2.2.17.12 ROGERS, Charles Allen: 'John Wesley and Jonathan Edwards', *Duke Divinity School Review*, Vol. 31, 1966, pp. 20–38.

2.2.17.13 SEABORN, Joseph William: 'John Wesley's use of history as a ministerial and educational tool', Boston University Th.D. thesis, 1985, 265p.

2.2.17.14 SHERWIN, Oscar: 'Milton for the masses: John Wesley's edition of "Paradise lost"', *Modern Language Quarterly*, Vol. XII, 1951, pp. 267–85.

See also 2.4.2.3, 2.4.2.4, 2.4.2.10, 2.4.2.11, 2.4.2.13, 2.4.2.19, 2.4.2.21, 2.4.2.23, 2.4.4.1, 2.4.6.4, 2.4.8.6, 2.5.7.14, 2.6.3.2, 2.6.3.6, 2.6.3.7, 2.6.3.9, 2.6.3.11, 2.6.3.12, 2.6.3.13, 2.8.1.10, 2.8.1.27, 2.8.1.30, 2.8.2.1, 2.8.2.12, 2.8.4.3, 2.8.4.5, 2.8.4.7, 2.8.4.14, 2.8.4.15, 2.8.4.16, 2.8.4.22, 2.9.2.2, 2.9.6.1.

2.2.18 John Wesley: relationships with women

2.2.18.1 BAKER, Frank: 'John Wesley and Sarah Crosby', *Proceedings of the Wesley Historical Society*, Vol. XXVII, 1949–50, pp. 76–82.

2.2.18.2 BAKER, Frank: 'John Wesley's first marriage', *Duke Divinity School Review*, Vol. 31, 1966, pp. 175–88 and *London Quarterly and Holborn Review*, Vol. CXCII, 1967, pp. 305–15.

2.2.18.3 BAKER, Frank: 'Some observations on John Wesley's relationship with Grace Murray', *Methodist History*, Vol. XVI, 1977–78, pp. 42–5.

2.2.18.4 BANKS, John: *'Nancy, Nancy': The life story of Ann Bolton who was the friend, and confidante, of John Wesley, based on her unpublished journal and on letters*, Wilmslow: Penwork (Leeds) Ltd., 1984, [7]+151p.

2.2.18.5 BERESFORD, John Baldwin: 'Wesley and Judith Beresford, 1734–1756', *London Quarterly Review*, Vol. CXLVII, 1927, pp. 35–50.

2.2.18.6 CHILCOTE, Paul Wesley: 'John Wesley as revealed by the journal of Hester Ann Rogers', *Duke Divinity School Review*, Vol. 44, 1979, pp. 33–43 and *Methodist History*, Vol. XX, 1981–82, pp. 111–23.

2.2.18.7 EDWARDS, Maldwyn Lloyd: *My dear sister: The story of John Wesley and the women in his life*, Manchester: Penwork (Leeds) Ltd., [1980], 124p.

2.2.18.8 EDWARDS, Maldwyn Lloyd: 'The reluctant lover: John Wesley as suitor', *Methodist History*, Vol. XII, No. 2, January 1974, pp. 46–62.

2.2.18.9 ETHRIDGE, Willie Snow: *Strange fires: The true story of John Wesley's love affair in Georgia*, New York: Vanguard Press, 1971, 254p.

2.2.18.10 HAYES, Alan Lauffer: 'John Wesley and Sophy Hopkey: A case study in Wesley's attitude toward women', *Women in new worlds*, Vol. II, edited by Rosemary Skinner Keller, Louise L. Queen & Hilah Frances Thomas, Nashville: Abingdon, 1982, pp. 29–44.

2.2.18.11 LEE, Umphrey: 'John Wesley's love affairs', *Methodist Quarterly Review*, Vol. LXXIV, 1925, pp. 476–93.

2.2.18.12 LEGER, J. Augustin: *John Wesley's last love*, London: J. M. Dent & Sons, 1910, xv + 300p.

2.2.18.13 LOFTHOUSE, William Frederick: 'Wesley and his women correspondents', *Wesley's Chapel Magazine*, January 1959, pp. [2–8], April 1959, pp. [6–12].

2.2.18.14 MASER, Frederick Ernest: 'John Wesley's only marriage: An examination of Dr. Frank Baker's article "John Wesley's first marriage" ', *Methodist History*, Vol. XVI, 1977–78, pp. 33–41.

See also 2.7.3.4, 2.8.3.6.

2.2.19 John Wesley: character and life-style

2.2.19.1 BAKER, Frank: 'The real John Wesley', *Methodist History*, Vol. XII, No. 4, July 1974, pp. 183–97.

2.2.19.2 BRASH, William Bardsley: 'Wesley's wit and humour', *London Quarterly Review*, Vol. CXXXV, 1921, pp. 53–67.

2.2.19.3 MASER, Frederick Ernest: 'The human side of John Wesley', *Religion in Life*, Vol. XXVII, 1957–58, pp. 544–56.

2.2.19.4 MASER, Frederick Ernest: 'John Wesley as revealed in his humor', *Historical Bulletin, World Methodist Historical Society*, Vol. 11, Second Quarter 1982, pp. 5–10.

2.2.19.5 ROGAL, Samuel J.: 'John Wesley's daily routine', *Methodist History*, Vol. XIII, No. 1, October 1974, pp. 41–50.

2.2.19.6 WALLACE, Charles Isaac: 'Simple and recollected: John Wesley's life-style', *Religion in Life*, Vol. XLVI, 1977, pp. 198–212.

See also 2.2.6.18.

2.2.20 Charles Wesley

2.2.20.1 BAKER, Frank: *Charles Wesley as revealed by his letters*, Wesley Historical Society Lectures No. 14, London: Epworth Press, 1948, vi + 152p.

2.2.20.2 BAKER, Frank: 'The prose writings of Charles Wesley', *London Quarterly and Holborn Review*, Vol. CLXXXII, 1957, pp. 268–74.

2.2.20.3 FLINT, Charles Wesley: *Charles Wesley and his colleagues*, Washington: Public Affairs Press, 1957, viii + 221p.

2.2.20.4 GILL, Frederick Cyril: *Charles Wesley, the first Methodist*, London: Lutterworth Press, 1964, 238p.

2.2.20.5 JACKSON, Thomas: *The life of the Rev. Charles Wesley, M.A., sometime Student of Christ Church, Oxford; comprising a review of his poetry, sketches of the rise and progress of Methodism, with notices of contemporary events and characters*, London: John Mason, 1841, 2 vol.

2.2.20.6 JONES, D. M.: *Charles Wesley: A study*, London: Skeffington & Son, [1919], 284p.

2.2.20.7 LOFTHOUSE, William Frederick: 'Charles Wesley', *A history of the Methodist Church in Great Britain*, Vol. 1, general editors: Rupert

Eric Davies & Ernest Gordon Rupp, London: Epworth Press, 1965, pp. 113–44.

2.2.20.8   SWIFT, Wesley Frank: 'Portraits and biographies of Charles Wesley', *Proceedings of the Wesley Historical Society*, Vol. XXXI, 1957–58, pp. 86–92.

2.2.20.9   TELFORD, John: *The life of the Rev. Charles Wesley, M.A., sometime Student of Christ Church, Oxford*, revised and enlarged edition, London: Wesleyan Methodist Book Room, 1900, xiv+324p.

2.2.20.10 TYSON, John Rodger & LISTER, Douglas: 'Charles Wesley, pastor: A glimpse inside his shorthand journal', *Quarterly Review: A Scholarly Journal for Reflection on Ministry*, Vol. 4, No. 1, Spring 1984, pp. 9–21.

2.2.20.11 WESLEY, Charles: *The journal of the Rev. Charles Wesley, M.A.; to which are appended selections from his correspondence and poetry*, with an introduction and occasional notes by Thomas Jackson, London: John Mason, 1849, 2 vol.

2.2.20.12 WESLEY, Charles: *Sayings and portraits of Charles Wesley; with family portraits, historic scenes and additional portraits of John Wesley*, compiled and edited by John Telford, London: Epworth Press, 1927, 267p.

2.2.20.13 WILDER, Franklin: *The Methodist riots: The testing of Charles Wesley*, Great Neck: Todd & Honeywell, 1981, 160p.

2.2.20.14 WISEMAN, Frederick Luke: *Charles Wesley, evangelist and poet*, London: Epworth Press, 1933, 232p.

See also 2.2.4.1, 2.2.4.5, 2.2.4.7, 2.2.6.31, 2.2.6.50, 2.6.4.3, 2.6.4.23.

2.3 Biographies: John Wesley's Contemporaries and his Relations with Them

2.3.1 John Cennick

2.3.1.1   BAKER, Frank: *John Cennick (1718–55): A handlist of his writings*, Publication No. 5 of the Wesley Historical Society, Leicester: printed for the Society by Alfred A. Taberer, 1958, 32p.

2.3.1.2   COUILLARD, Vernon Williams: *The theology of John Cennick*, Moravian Historical Society Transactions Vol. 16, Pt. 3, Nazareth, Pa.: Moravian Historical Society, 1957, 216p.

2.3.1.3   HUTTON, Joseph Edmund: *John Cennick: A sketch*, London: Moravian Publication Office, [1906], 78p.

2.3.1.4   KELYNACK, William Sydney: 'John Cennick, 12th. December 1718–4th. July 1755', *London Quarterly and Holborn Review*, Vol. CLXXX, 1955, pp. 209–14.

2.3.1.5   LEARY, William: 'John Cennick, 1718–55: A bi-centenary appreciation', *Proceedings of the Wesley Historical Society*, Vol. XXX, 1955–56, pp. 30–7.

2.3.2 Thomas Coke

2.3.2.1　CANDLER, Warren Akin: *Life of Thomas Coke*, Nashville: Publishing House, M. E. Church South, 1923, vi+408p.

2.3.2.2　CROWTHER, Jonathan: *The life of the Rev. Thomas Coke, LL. D., a clergyman of the Church of England but who laboured among the Wesleyan Methodists for the last thirty-eight years of his life, and who died suddenly on shipboard, after being four months at sea, on his passage to the East Indies whither he was conducting a company of Christian missionaries of whom he was the superintendent*, Leeds: Alexander Cumming, 1815, 544p.

2.3.2.3　DAVEY, Cyril James: *Mad about mission: The story of Dr. Thomas Coke*, Basingstoke: Marshalls, 1985, 127p.

2.3.2.4　DREW, Samuel: *The life of the Rev. Thomas Coke, LL. D., including in detail his various travels and extraordinary missionary exertions in England, Ireland, America and the West-Indies; with an account of his death, on the 3d. of May 1814, while on a missionary voyage to the island of Ceylon in the East-Indies, interspersed with numerous reflections, and concluding with an abstract of his writings and character*, London: printed at the Conference-Office by Thomas Cordeux, 1817, xix+391p.

2.3.2.5　ETHERIDGE, John Wesley: *The life of the Rev. Thomas Coke, D.C.L.*, London: John Mason, 1860, viii+450p.

2.3.2.6　VICKERS, John Ashley: 'The churchmanship of Thomas Coke', *Methodist History*, Vol. VII, No. 4, July 1969, pp. 15–28.

2.3.2.7　VICKERS, John Ashley: *Thomas Coke, apostle of Methodism*, Wesley Historical Society Lecture No. 30, London: Epworth Press, 1969, xiv+394p.

See also 2.7.2.11, 2.7.2.25, 2.7.2.28, 4.1.4.10.

2.3.3 John Fletcher

2.3.3.1　BAKER, Frank: 'John Fletcher, Methodist clergyman', *London Quarterly and Holborn Review*, Vol. CLXXXV, 1960, pp. 291–8.

2.3.3.2　BENSON, Joseph: *The life of the Rev. John W. de la Flechère; compiled from the narratives of the Reverend Mr. Wesley, the biographical notes of the Reverend Mr. Gilpin, from his own letters and other authentic documents, many of which were never before published*, second edition, enlarged, London: printed by Richard Edwards for R. Lomas, 1805, xiv+442p.

2.3.3.3　COX, Robert: *The life of the Rev. John William Fletcher, late Vicar of Madeley, Shropshire*, second edition, carefully revised and enlarged by the insertion of several original documents, London: J. Butterworth & Son, 1825, iv+148p.

2.3.3.4　DAVIES, William Rhys: 'John William Fletcher of Madeley as theologian', University of Manchester Ph.D. thesis, 1965, vi+740p.

2.3.3.5　FIELD, Clive Douglas: 'John William Fletcher (1729–85): A guide to further reading', *John Fletcher, 1729–1785, Vicar of Madeley – a Methodist bicentenary: Catalogue of an exhibition held in the John Rylands University Library of Manchester*, Manchester: John Rylands University Library of Manchester, 1985, pp. 39–46.

2.3.3.6 FORSAITH, Peter S.: *The eagle and the dove: John Fletcher, Vicar of Madeley – towards a new assessment*, [Bristol: the author, 1979], [4]+63p.

2.3.3.7 FORSAITH, Peter S.: 'Wesley's designated successor', *Proceedings of the Wesley Historical Society*, Vol. XLII, 1979–80, pp. 69–74.

2.3.3.8 KINGHORN, Kenneth Cain: 'Faith and works: A study in the theology of John Fletcher', Emory University Ph.D. thesis, 1965, viii+178p.

2.3.3.9 KNIGHT, John Allan: 'John William Fletcher and the early Methodist tradition', Vanderbilt University Ph.D. thesis, 1966, iv+413p.

2.3.3.10 LAWTON, George: *Shropshire saint: A study in the ministry and spirituality of Fletcher of Madeley*, Wesley Historical [Society] Lecture No. 26, London: Epworth Press, 1960, xvii+136p.

2.3.3.11 LOCKHART, Wilfred Cornett: 'The evangelical revival as reflected in the life and works of John William de la Fléchère, 1729–1785', University of Edinburgh Ph.D. thesis, 1936, iv+264p.

2.3.3.12 MACDONALD, Frederic William: *Fletcher of Madeley*, London: Hodder and Stoughton, 1885, viii+196p.

2.3.3.13 MATTKE, Robert A.: 'John Fletcher's methodology in the antinomian controversy of 1770–76', *Wesleyan Theological Journal*, Vol. 3, Spring 1968, pp. 38–47.

2.3.3.14 MAYCOCK, Joseph: 'The Fletcher-Toplady controversy', *London Quarterly and Holborn Review*, Vol. CXCI, 1966, pp. 227–35.

2.3.3.15 NUELSEN, John Louis: *Jean Guillaume de la Fléchère, John William Fletcher, der erste schweizerische Methodist: Ein Gedenkblatt zu seinem zweihundertsten Geburtstag, 12. September 1729*, Zürich: Christliche Vereinsbuchhandlung, 1929, 127p.

2.3.3.16 SHIPLEY, David Clark: 'Methodist Arminianism in the theology of John Fletcher', Yale University Ph.D. thesis, 1942, xx+450p.

2.3.3.17 SLAATTE, Howard Alexander: *The Arminian arm of theology: The theologies of John Fletcher, first Methodist theologian, and his precursor, James Arminius*, Washington: University Press of America, 1977, ii+137p.

2.3.3.18 SOMMER, Carl Ernst: *'Der designierte Nachfolger' John Wesleys*, Stuttgart: Christliches Verlagshaus, 1977.

2.3.3.19 SOMMER, Carl Ernst: 'John William Fletcher (1729–85), Mann der Mitte: Prolegomena zu seinem Verständnis', *Basileia: Walter Freytag zum 60. Geburtstag*, herausgegeben von Jan Hermelink und Hans Jochen Margull, Stuttgart: Evang. Missionsverlag, 1959, pp. 437–53.

2.3.3.20 STREIFF, Patrick Philipp: *Jean Guillaume de la Fléchère, John William Fletcher, 1729–1785: Ein Beitrag zur Geschichte des Methodismus*, Frankfurt am Main: Peter Lang, 1984, 540p.

2.3.3.21   THOMPSON, Claude H.: 'John Fletcher, first theologian of Method-ism', *Emory University Quarterly*, Vol. XVI, 1960, pp. 239–50.

2.3.3.22   TYERMAN, Luke: *Wesley's designated successor: The life, letters and literary labours of the Rev. John William Fletcher, Vicar of Madeley, Shropshire*, London: Hodder and Stoughton, 1882, xvi+581p.

2.3.3.23   WESLEY, John: *A short account of the life and death of the Rev. John Fletcher*, London: printed by J. Paramore, 1786, 227p.

2.3.3.24   WIGGINS, James Bryan: *The embattled saint: Aspects of the life and work of John Fletcher*, Macon: Wesleyan College, 1966, 71p.

2.3.3.25   WIGGINS, James Bryan: 'The pattern of John Fletcher's theology as developed in his poetic, pastoral and polemical writings', Drew University Ph.D. thesis, 1963, viii+322p.

See also 2.4.1.5, 2.4.1.6, 2.5.5.8, 2.5.7.8, 2.5.7.13, 2.5.7.24, 2.5.7.36.

2.3.4 William Grimshaw

2.3.4.1   BAKER, Frank: *William Grimshaw, 1708–1763*, London: Epworth Press, 1963, 288p.

2.3.4.2   CRAGG, George Golden: *Grimshaw of Haworth: A study in eighteenth-century evangelicalism*, London: Canterbury Press, 1947, 128p.

2.3.4.3   HARDY, Robert Spence: *William Grimshaw, incumbent of Haworth, 1742–63*, London: John Mason, 1860, vii+286p.

2.3.4.4   MYLES, William: *The life and writings of the late Reverend Wm. Grimshaw, minister of Haworth in the West Riding of the County of York*, Newcastle-upon-Tyne: printed for the author by Edw. Walker, [1806], v+199p.

2.3.4.5   NEWTON, John: *Memoirs of the life of the late Rev. William Grimshaw, A.B., minister of Haworth in the West Riding of the County of York, with occasional reflections, in six letters to the Rev. Henry Foster*, London: T. Bensley, 1799, 187p.

See also 2.9.4.9.

2.3.5 Howell Harris

2.3.5.1   EVANS, Eifion: *Howel Harris, evangelist, 1714–1773*, Cardiff: University of Wales Press, 1974, x+75p.

2.3.5.2   HUGHES, Hugh Joshua: *Life of Howell Harris, the Welsh reformer*, London: J. Nisbet & Co., 1892, 439p.

2.3.5.3   KNOX, Robert Buick: 'The Wesleys and Howell Harris', *Studies in Church History, Volume III: Papers read at the third winter and summer meetings of the Ecclesiastical History Society*, edited by Geoffrey John Cuming, Leiden: E. J. Brill, 1966, pp. 267–76.

2.3.5.4   MORGAN, Edward: *The life and times of Howel Harris, Esq., the first itinerant preacher in Wales, whose labours were very extraordinary and successful*, Holywell: W. Morris, 1852, xii+298p.

2.3.5.5   NUTTALL, Geoffrey Fillingham: *Howel Harris, 1714–1773: The last enthusiast*, Cardiff: University of Wales Press, 1965, x+87p.

2.3.5.6   ROBERTS, Gomer Morgan: 'Llythyrau Trefeca a Wesley', *Bathafarn*, Vol. 15, 1960, pp. 45–54.

2.3.5.7   ROBERTS, Griffith Thomas: *Howell Harris*, Wesley Historical Society Lectures No. 17, London: Epworth Press, 1951, 87p.

2.3.5.8   ROBERTS, Griffith Thomas: 'Wesley a Harris', *Cylchgrawn Cymdeithas Hanes Eglwys Methodistiaid Calfinaidd Cymru*, Cyfrol XXX, 1945, pp. 65–72, 93–9.

2.3.5.9   WILLIAMS, Albert Hughes: 'The leaders of English and Welsh Methodism, 1738–91', *Bathafarn*, Vol. 16, 1961, pp. 23–40, Vol. 17, 1962, pp. 5–26, Vol. 21, 1966, pp. 23–31, Vol. 22, 1967, pp. 24–36, Vol. 23, 1968, pp. 7–13, Vol. 24, 1969, pp. 20–5.

2.3.5.10 WILLIAMS, Albert Hughes: 'Wesley a Harris', *Er clod: Saith bennod ar hanes Methodistiaeth yng Nghymru*, dan olygiaeth Thomas Richards, Wrecsam: Hughes a'i Fab, 1934, pp. 9–33.

2.3.5.11 WILLIAMS, Robert Richard: *Flames from the altar: Howell Harris and his contemporaries*, Caernarvon: Calvinistic Methodist Book Agency, 1962, viii+99p.

See also 2.1.3.1.

2.3.6 Selina Hastings, Countess of Huntingdon

2.3.6.1   BARKER, Esther T.: *Lady Huntingdon, Whitefield and the Wesleys*, Maryville: E. T. Barker, 1984, 144p.

2.3.6.2   BRETHERTON, Francis Fletcher: *The Countess of Huntingdon*, Wesley Historical Society Lectures No. 6, London: Epworth Press, 1940, 48p.

2.3.6.3   DAVIS, Mollie Camp: 'The Countess of Huntingdon', *Women in new worlds*, Vol. II, editors: Rosemary Skinner Keller, Louise L. Queen & Hilah Frances Thomas, Nashville: Abingdon, 1982, pp. 162–75.

2.3.6.4   FRANCIS, Matthew: 'Selina, Countess of Huntingdon (1707–1791)', University of Oxford B.Litt. thesis, 1957, 4+[6]+iv+229+268+[94]+16p.

2.3.6.5   HULL, James Ernest: 'The controversy between John Wesley and the Countess of Huntingdon: Its origin, development and consequences', University of Edinburgh Ph.D. thesis, 1959, v+353p.

2.3.6.6   KIRBY, Gilbert Walter: *The elect lady*, East Grinstead: Trustees of the Countess of Huntingdon's Connexion, 1972, 79p.

2.3.6.7   KNIGHT, Helen Cross: *Lady Huntington and her friends; or, The revival of the work of God in the days of Wesley, Whitefield, Romaine, Venn and others in the last century*, New York: American Tract Society, 1853, 292p.

2.3.6.8   LANE, Margaret: 'The Queen of the Methodists', *Brycheiniog*, Vol. XV, 1971, pp. 85–99.

2.3.6.9   MITCHELL, David: 'Queen of the Methodists: Selina, Countess of Huntingdon', *History Today*, Vol. XV, 1965, pp. 846–54.

2.3.6.10 MYERS, Lucia: *Lady Huntingdon, friend of the Wesleys*, Montgomery, Ala.: Huntingdon College Alumnae Association, 1956, 60p.

2.3.6.11 NEW, Alfred Henry: *The coronet and the cross; or, Memorials of the Right Hon. Selina, Countess of Huntingdon, compiled from authentic documents*, London: Partridge and Co., 1857, viii+429p.

2.3.6.12 [SEYMOUR, Aaron Crossley Hobart]: *The life and times of Selina, Countess of Huntingdon*, London: William Edward Painter, 1839–40, 2 vol.

2.3.6.13 TYTLER, Sarah *pseud.* [i.e. Henrietta Keddie]: *The Countess of Huntingdon and her circle*, London: Sir Isaac Pitman and Sons, 1907, xi+292p.

2.3.7 James Hervey

2.3.7.1 BAKER, Frank: 'James Hervey, Methodist prose poet', *London Quarterly and Holborn Review*, Vol. CLXXXII, 1957, pp. 62–8.

2.3.7.2 BROWN, John: *Memoirs of the life and character of the late Rev. James Hervey, A.M.*, second edition, with large additions, Edinburgh: Oliphant & Brown, 1809, 407p.

2.3.7.3 COLE, John: *Herveiana; or, Graphic and literary sketches illustrative of the life and writings of the Rev. James Hervey, A.M.*, Scarborough: John Cole, 1822–23, 2 vol.

2.3.7.4 HARSHA, David Addison: *Life of the Rev. James Hervey*, Albany: J. Munsell, 1865, 58p.

2.3.7.5 PORTER, Laurence E.: 'James Hervey (1714–1758): A bicentenary appreciation', *Evangelical Quarterly*, Vol. XXXI, 1959, pp. 4–20.

2.3.7.6 TYERMAN, Luke: *The Oxford Methodists: Memoirs of the Rev. Messrs. Clayton, Ingham, Gambold, Hervey and Broughton, with biographical notices of others*, London: Hodder and Stoughton, 1873, viii+416p.

2.3.8 Benjamin Ingham

2.3.8.1 CLARKE, David Frederick: 'Benjamin Ingham (1712–1772), with special reference to his relations with the Churches (Anglican, Methodist, Moravian and Glassite) of his time', University of Leeds M.Phil. thesis, 1971, [4]+144p.

2.3.8.2 INGHAM, Benjamin: *Diary of an Oxford Methodist: Benjamin Ingham, 1733–1734*, edited by Richard Paul Heitzenrater, Durham, N.C.: Duke University Press, 1985, xvi+304p.

2.3.8.3 THOMPSON, Richard Walker: *Benjamin Ingham and the Inghamites*, Kendal: the author, 1958, 116p.

See also 2.3.7.6, 2.9.2.10.

2.3.9 William Law

2.3.9.1 BAKER, Eric Wilfred: *A herald of the evangelical revival: A critical inquiry into the relation of William Law to John Wesley and the beginnings of Methodism*, London: Epworth Press, 1948, ix+203p.

2.3.9.2 BAKER, Frank: 'John Wesley and William Law: A reconsideration', *Proceedings of the Wesley Historical Society*, Vol. XXXVII, 1969–70, pp. 173–7.

2.3.9.3 BAKER, Frank: 'John Wesley's introduction to William Law', *Proceedings of the Wesley Historical Society*, Vol. XXXVII, 1969–70, pp. 78–82.

2.3.9.4 CASCIO, Robert Jude: 'Mystic and Augustan: A study of the impact of William Law on John Wesley, Edward Gibbon and John Byrom', Fordham University Ph.D. thesis, 1974, vi+194p.

2.3.9.5 CLARKSON, George Edward: 'John Wesley and William Law's mysticism', *Religion in Life*, Vol. XLII, 1973, pp. 537–44.

2.3.9.6 GREEN, John Brazier: *John Wesley and William Law*, London: Epworth Press, 1945, 224p.

2.3.9.7 HARPER, Kenneth: 'Law and Wesley', *Church Quarterly Review*, Vol. CLXIII, 1962, pp. 61–71.

2.3.9.8 HUNTER, Frederick: 'John Wesley's introduction to William Law: A comment', *Proceedings of the Wesley Historical Society*, Vol. XXXVII, 1969–70, pp. 143–50.

2.3.9.9 JONES, John Ellis: 'John Wesley a William Law', *Y Traethodydd*, Cyfrol CII, 1947, pp. 97–105.

2.3.9.10 MALEKIN, Peter: 'William Law and John Wesley', *Studia Neophilologica*, Vol. XXXVII, 1965, pp. 190–8.

2.3.9.11 TYSON, John Rodger: 'John Wesley and William Law: A reappraisal', *Wesleyan Theological Journal*, Vol. 17, No. 2, Fall 1982, pp. 58–78.

2.3.9.12 WALKER, Arthur Keith: *William Law: His life and thought*, London: SPCK, 1973, xiii+274p.

2.3.10 Augustus Montague Toplady

2.3.10.1 LAWTON, George: *Within the rock of ages: The life and work of Augustus Montague Toplady*, Cambridge: James Clarke & Co., 1983, 249p.

2.3.10.2 MAYCOCK, Joseph: 'Augustus Montague Toplady, hymn-writer and theologian, with special reference to his controversy with John Wesley', University of Edinburgh Ph.D. thesis, 1946, vi+572p.

See also 2.3.3.14.

2.3.11 George Whitefield

2.3.11.1 ANDREWS, John Richard: *George Whitefield: A light rising in obscurity*, second edition, revised and enlarged, London: Morgan and Chase, [1871], xviii+445p.

2.3.11.2 AUSTIN, Roland: 'Bibliography of the works of George Whitefield', *Proceedings of the Wesley Historical Society*, Vol. X, 1915–16, pp. 169–84, 211–23.

2.3.11.3 BAKER, Frank: 'Whitefield's break with the Wesleys', *Church Quarterly*, Vol. 3, 1970–71, pp. 103–13.

2.3.11.4 BELDEN, Albert David: *George Whitefield, the awakener: A modern study of the evangelical revival*, second edition, revised, London: Rockliff Publishing Corporation, 1953, xiv+302p.

2.3.11.5 DALLIMORE, Arnold Arthur: *George Whitefield: The life and times of the great evangelist of the eighteenth-century revival*, London: Banner of Truth Trust, 1970–80, 2 vol.

2.3.11.6 DOUGLAS, Walter Benjamin Theophilus: 'George Whitefield: The man and his mission', *Methodist History*, Vol. XVI, 1977–78, pp. 46–53.

2.3.11.7 GILLIES, John: *Memoirs of the late Reverend George Whitefield of Pembroke College, Oxford, chaplain to the late Right Hon. Selina, Countess Dowager of Huntingdon, faithfully selected from his original papers; with an appendix containing extracts from the funeral sermons preached on the occasion of his death*, revised and corrected, with observations illustrative and justificatory, by John Jones, London: T. Williams and L. B. Seeley, 1811, 279+lxivp.

2.3.11.8 GLEDSTONE, James Paterson: *George Whitefield, M.A., field-preacher*, London: Hodder and Stoughton, 1900, xii+359p.

2.3.11.9 HARDY, Edwin Noah: *George Whitefield, the matchless soul winner*, New York: American Tract Society, 1938, 298p.

2.3.11.10 HARRINGTON, Susan F.: 'Friendship under fire: George Whitefield and John Wesley, 1739–1741', *Andover Newton Quarterly*, Vol. 15, 1974–75, pp. 167–81.

2.3.11.11 HENRY, Stuart Clark: *George Whitefield, wayfaring witness*, New York: Abingdon Press, 1957, 224p.

2.3.11.12 KING, Charles Harold: 'George Whitefield, revivalist', Cornell University Ph.D. thesis, 1935, x+364p.

2.3.11.13 PHILIP, Robert: *The life and times of the Reverend George Whitefield, M.A.*, London: George Virtue, 1837, xi+588p.

2.3.11.14 POLLOCK, John Charles: *George Whitefield and the great awakening*, London: Hodder and Stoughton, 1973, xi+272p.

2.3.11.15 SHERRIFF, Collin Bedford: 'The theology of George Whitefield, 1714–1770', University of Edinburgh Ph.D. thesis, 1950, iii+217p.

2.3.11.16 TYERMAN, Luke: *The life of the Rev. George Whitefield, B.A. of Pembroke College, Oxford*, London: Hodder and Stoughton, 1876–77, 2 vol.

2.3.11.17 WHITEFIELD, George: *The works of the Reverend George Whitefield, M.A., late of Pembroke College, Oxford and chaplain to the Rt. Hon. the Countess of Huntingdon, containing all his sermons and tracts which have been already published with a select collection of letters written to his most intimate friends and persons of distinction in England, Scotland, Ireland and America from the year 1734 to 1770, including the whole period of his ministry, also, some other pieces on important subjects never before printed, prepared by himself for the press; to which is prefixed an account of his life compiled from his original papers and letters*, London: printed for Edward and Charles Dilly, 1771–72, 6 vol.

See also 2.1.4.1, 2.2.15.2, 2.2.20.3, 2.3.6.1, 2.5.3.19, 2.5.7.35.

2.4 Spirituality: Theology – Sources of Authority

2.4.1 General works

2.4.1.1 BENNETT, Erman Fay: 'The call of God in the ministry of John Wesley: A study of spiritual authority in Methodist history', Southwestern Baptist Theological Seminary Th.D. thesis, 1963.

2.4.1.2 CHANDLER, Douglas Robson: 'John Wesley and the uses of the past', *Foundations of theological education: The 1972 Willson Lectures, Wesley Theological Seminary, Washington, D.C.*, Washington: Wesley Theological Seminary, [1972], pp. 27–37.

2.4.1.3 COPPEDGE, Allan: 'John Wesley and the issue of authority in theological pluralism', *A spectrum of thought: Essays in honor of Dennis F. Kinlaw*, edited by Michael L. Peterson, Wilmore: Francis Asbury Publishing Company, 1982, pp. 78–94 and *Wesleyan Theological Journal*, Vol. 19, No. 2, Fall 1984, pp. 62–76.

2.4.1.4 FROST, Stanley Brice: *Die Autoritätslehre in den Werken John Wesleys*, München: Ernst Reinhardt, 1938, [8]+110p.

2.4.1.5 KNICKERBOCKER, Waldo Emerson: 'Doctrinal sources and guidelines in early Methodism: Fletcher of Madeley as a case study', *Methodist History*, Vol. XIV, 1975–76, pp. 186–202.

2.4.1.6 KNICKERBOCKER, Waldo Emerson: 'The doctrine of authority in the theology of John Fletcher', Emory University Ph.D. thesis, 1972, 269p.

2.4.1.7 LEE, Umphrey: *The historical backgrounds of early Methodist enthusiasm*, Columbia University Studies in History, Economics and Public Law No. 339, New York: Columbia University Press, 1931, 176p.

2.4.1.8 MCDONALD, Hugh Dermot: *Ideas of revelation: An historical study, A.D. 1700 to A.D. 1860*, London: Macmillan & Co., 1959, xi+300p.

2.4.1.9 McELDOWNEY, James Edward: 'John Wesley's theology in its historical setting', University of Chicago Ph.D. thesis, 1943, 355p.

2.4.1.10 McINTOSH, Lawrence Dennis: 'The nature and design of Christianity in John Wesley's early theology: A study in the relationship of love and faith', Drew University Ph.D. thesis, 1966, ix+255p.

2.4.1.11 RYDER, Mary R.: 'Avoiding the "many-headed monster": Wesley and Johnson on enthusiasm', *Methodist History*, Vol. XXIII, 1984–85, pp. 214–22.

2.4.1.12 WILBERFORCE, David L.: 'A study of the formative influences governing the development of John Wesley's social, political and ecclesiastical methods and practices', University of Newcastle-upon-Tyne M.Litt. thesis, 1976, [8]+405p.

2.4.1.13 WILSON, Kenneth Alexander: 'The devotional relationships and interaction between the spirituality of John Wesley, the Methodist societies and the Book of Common Prayer', Queen's University of Belfast Ph.D. thesis, 1984, xviii+513p.

2.4.1.14 Wood, Laurence Willard: 'Wesley's epistemology', *Wesleyan Theological Journal*, Vol. 10, Spring 1975, pp. 48–59.

2.4.1.15 Workman, Herbert Brook: *The place of Methodism in the Catholic Church*, new edition, revised and enlarged, London: Epworth Press, 1921, 104p.

See also 2.2.6.21, 2.5.1.14, 2.5.6.1, 2.5.7.22, 2.6.3.9, 2.7.2.12, 2.7.3.3, 2.8.1.17.

2.4.2 Scripture

2.4.2.1 Arnett, William Melvin: 'John Wesley and the Bible', *Wesleyan Theological Journal*, Vol. 3, Spring 1968, pp. 3–9.

2.4.2.2 Arnett, William Melvin: 'John Wesley, man of one book: An investigation of the centrality of the Bible in the life and works of John Wesley with special emphasis on his labours as an interpreter of the New Testament', Drew University Ph.D. thesis, 1954, v+262p.

2.4.2.3 Arnett, William Melvin: 'A study in John Wesley's "Explanatory notes upon the Old Testament"', *Wesleyan Theological Journal*, Vol. 8, Spring 1973, pp. 14–32.

2.4.2.4 Casto, Robert Michael: 'Exegetical method in John Wesley's "Explanatory notes upon the Old Testament": A description of his approach, use of sources and practice', Duke University Ph.D. thesis, 1977, ix+551p.

2.4.2.5 Clemons, James Thomas: 'John Wesley: Biblical literalist?', *Religion in Life*, Vol. XLVI, 1977, pp. 332–42.

2.4.2.6 Clemons, James Thomas: 'Was John Wesley a biblical literalist?', *Epworth Review*, Vol. 6, No. 3, September 1979, pp. 61–9.

2.4.2.7 Dillman, Charles N.: 'Wesley's approach to the law in Discourse XXV, on the Sermon on the Mount', *Wesleyan Theological Journal*, Vol. 12, Spring 1977, pp. 60–5.

2.4.2.8 Ferguson, Duncan S.: 'John Wesley on scripture: The hermeneutics of pietism', *Methodist History*, Vol. XXII, 1983–84, pp. 234–45.

2.4.2.9 Garrison, Richard Benjamin: 'Vital interaction – scripture and experience: John Wesley's doctrine of authority', *Religion in Life*, Vol. XXV, 1955–56, pp. 563–73.

2.4.2.10 Glasson, Thomas Francis: 'Wesley's New Testament reconsidered', *Epworth Review*, Vol. 10, No. 2, May 1983, pp. 28–34.

2.4.2.11 Harrison, Archibald Harold Walter: 'The Greek text of Wesley's translation of the New Testament', *Proceedings of the Wesley Historical Society*, Vol. IX, 1913–14, pp. 105–13.

2.4.2.12 Källstad, Thorvald: *John Wesley and the Bible: A psychological study*, Stockholm: Nya Bokförlags Aktiebolaget, 1974, 356p.

2.4.2.13 Lockyer, Thomas Frederick: 'John Wesley's revised version of the New Testament', *London Quarterly Review*, Vol. CXLIII, 1925, pp. 55–62.

2.4.2.14 McCarthy, Daryl: 'Early Wesleyan views of scripture'. *Wesleyan Theological Journal*, Vol. 16, No. 2, Fall 1981, pp. 95–105.

2.4.2.15 Michalson, Carl: 'The hermeneutics of holiness in Wesley', *The heritage of Christian thought: Essays in honor of Robert Lowry Calhoun,* edited by Robert Earl Cushman & Egil Grislis, New York: Harper and Row, 1965, pp. 127–41 and *Interpreting God's word for today: An inquiry into hermeneutics from a biblical theological perspective,* edited by Wayne McCown & James Earl Massey, Anderson: Warner Press, 1982, pp. 31–52.

2.4.2.16   MULLEN, Wilbur H.: 'John Wesley's method of biblical interpretation', *Religion in Life*, Vol. XLVII, 1978, pp. 99–108.

2.4.2.17   OSWALT, John Newell: 'Wesley's use of the Old Testament in his doctrinal teachings', *Wesleyan Theological Journal*, Vol. 12, Spring 1977, pp. 39–53.

2.4.2.18   PELLOWE, William Charles Smithson: 'John Wesley's use of the Bible', *Methodist Review*, Vol. CVI, 1923, pp. 353–74.

2.4.2.19   ROGAL, Samuel J.: 'Scriptural quotation in Wesley's "Earnest appeal"', *Research Studies*, Vol. 47, 1979, pp. 181–90.

2.4.2.20   RUPP, Ernest Gordon: 'Paul and Wesley', *De dertiende apostel en het elfde gebod: Paulus in de loop der eeuwen*, onder redactie van Gerrit Cornelis Berkouwer en Heiko Augustinus Oberman, Kampen: J. H. Kok, 1971, pp. 102–10.

2.4.2.21   SCROGGS, Robin: 'John Wesley as biblical scholar', *Journal of Bible and Religion*, Vol. XXVIII, 1960, pp. 415–22.

2.4.2.22   SHELTON, Raymond Larry: 'John Wesley's approach to scripture in historical perspective', *Wesleyan Theological Journal*, Vol. 16, No. 1, Spring 1981, pp. 23–50.

2.4.2.23   SIMON, John Smith: 'Mr. Wesley's "Notes upon the New Testament"', *Proceedings of the Wesley Historical Society*, Vol. IX, 1913–14, pp. 97–105.

2.4.2.24   SMITH, Timothy Lawrence: 'John Wesley and the wholeness of scripture', *Interpretation*, Vol. XXXIX, 1985, pp. 246–62.

2.4.2.25   TURNER, George Allen: 'John Wesley as an interpreter of scripture', *Inspiration and interpretation*, edited by John F. Walvoord, Grand Rapids: Wm. B. Eerdmans Publishing Co., 1957, pp. 156–88.

2.4.2.26   WATSON, Philip Saville: *Die Autorität der Bibel bei Luther und Wesley*, Stuttgart: Christliches Verlagshaus, 1983, 27p.

See also 2.5.6.8, 2.5.7.39, 2.6.2.20, 2.6.5.7.

2.4.3 Tradition: Christian antiquity

2.4.3.1   ALLCHIN, Arthur Macdonald: 'Our life in Christ: In John Wesley and the Eastern Fathers', *We belong to one another: Methodist, Anglican and Orthodox essays*, edited by Arthur Macdonald Allchin, London: Epworth Press, 1965, pp. 62–78.

2.4.3.2   BRIGHTMAN, Robert Sheffield: 'Gregory of Nyssa and John Wesley in theological dialogue on the Christian life', Boston University Ph.D. thesis, 1969, xi+381p.

2.4.3.3   CAMPBELL, Ted Allen: 'John Wesley's conceptions and uses of

Christian antiquity', Southern Methodist University Ph.D. thesis, 1984, 368p.

2.4.3.4 KEEFER, Luke L.: 'John Wesley, disciple of early Christianity', Temple University Ph.D. thesis, 1982, 2 vol.

2.4.3.5 KEEFER, Luke L.: 'John Wesley, disciple of early Christianity', *Wesleyan Theological Journal*, Vol. 19, No. 1, Spring 1984, pp. 23–32.

2.4.3.6 McCORMICK, Kelley Steve: 'John Wesley's use of John Chrysostom on the Christian life: Faith filled with the energy of love', Drew University Ph.D. thesis, 1983, 45p.

2.4.3.7 OUTLER, Albert Cook: 'John Wesley's interests in the early fathers of the Church', *The Bulletin* [of the Committee on Archives and History of the United Church of Canada,] No. 29, 1980–82, pp. 5–18.

2.4.3.8 WAKEFIELD, Gordon Stevens: 'La littérature du désert chez John Wesley', *Irénikon*, Tome LI, 1978, pp. 155–70.

2.4.3.9 YOUNG, Frances: 'Grace and demand – the heart of preaching' [a comparative study of John Chrysostom and John Wesley], *Epworth Review*, Vol. 12, No. 2, May 1985, pp. 46–55.

2.4.4 Tradition: European Catholicism

2.4.4.1 BAKER, Frank: 'John Wesley and the "Imitatio Christi" ', *London Quarterly and Holborn Review*, Vol. CLXVI, 1941, pp. 74–87.

2.4.4.2 CAMERON, Richard Morgan: 'The little flowers of John Wesley', *Religion in Life*, Vol. XXIII, 1953–54, pp. 267–78.

2.4.4.3 FAULKNER, John Alfred: 'Wesley the mystic', *London Quarterly Review*, Vol. CLIII, 1930, pp. 145–60.

2.4.4.4 HARTMAN, Lewis Oliver: 'Mystical elements in John Wesley's doctrines', Boston University Ph.D. thesis, 1909, 116p.

2.4.4.5 MASSA, Mark S.: 'The Catholic Wesley: A revisionist prolegomenon', *Methodist History*, Vol. XXII, 1983–84, pp. 38–53.

2.4.4.6 ORCIBAL, Jean: 'Les spirituels français et espagnols chez John Wesley et ses contemporains', *Révue de l' Histoire des Religions*, Tome CXXXIX, Janvier–Juin 1951, pp. 50–109.

2.4.4.7 ORCIBAL, Jean: 'The theological originality of John Wesley and continental spirituality', *A history of the Methodist Church in Great Britain*, Vol. 1, general editors: Rupert Eric Davies & Ernest Gordon Rupp, London: Epworth Press, 1965, pp. 81–111.

2.4.4.8 SCHMIDT, Martin: 'John Wesley und die Biographie des französischen Grafen Gaston Jean-Baptiste de Renty (1611–1649): Ein Kapitel aus dem ökumenischen Austausch zwischen romanischer Mystik, reformiertem Pietismus, Anglikanismus und Methodismus im 18. Jahrhundert', *Theologia Viatorum*, Band V, 1953–54, pp. 194–252.

2.4.4.9 SOMMER, Carl Ernst: 'John Wesley und die Mystik', *Mitteilungen der Studiengemeinschaft für Geschichte des Methodismus*, Band III, 1965, pp. 6–22.

2.4.4.10 TAYLOR, Alfred Edward: 'St. John of the Cross and John Wesley', *Journal of Theological Studies*, Vol. XLVI, 1945, pp. 30–8.

2.4.4.11 TODD, John Murray: *John Wesley and the Catholic Church*, London: Hodder and Stoughton, 1958, 195p.

2.4.4.12 TUTTLE, Robert Gregory: 'The influence of Roman Catholic mystics on John Wesley', University of Bristol Ph.D. thesis, 1969, vii+476p.

2.4.4.13 WILSON, David Dunn: 'The influence of mysticism on John Wesley', University of Leeds Ph.D. thesis, 1968, [5]+422p.

2.4.4.14 WILSON, David Dunn: 'John Wesley and "mystical prayer"', *London Quarterly and Holborn Review*, Vol. CXCIII, 1968, pp. 61–9.

2.4.5 Tradition: European Protestantism

2.4.5.1 ASHMAN, Ronald George: 'An examination of the views of John Wesley in relation to the Protestant Reformation', University of Wales (Cardiff) Ph.D. thesis, 1949.

2.4.5.2 BERG, Johannes van den: 'John Wesleys contacten met Nederland', *Nederlands Archief voor Kerkgeschiedenis*, Nieuwe Serie, Deel LII, 1971, pp. 36–96.

2.4.5.3 DAMM, Ulrich F.: *Die Deutschlandreise John Wesleys: Grund, Orte, Begegnungen, Auswirkungen*, herausgegeben von den Studienge-meinschaft für Geschichte der Evangelisch-Methodistischen Kirche, Stuttgart: Christliches Verlagshaus, 1984, 35p.

2.4.5.4 DAVIES, Daniel Horton Marlais: 'Epworth's debt to Geneva: A field for research', *The Livingstonian*, Vol. XXVII, 1951, pp. 105–18.

2.4.5.5 GOUNELLE, Edmond: *Wesley et ses rapports avec les français: Thèse historique*, Nyons: Imprimerie Brevetée F. Bonnardel, 1898, 112p.

2.4.5.6 HALL, Thor: 'The Christian's life: Wesley's alternative to Luther and Calvin', *Duke Divinity School Bulletin*, Vol. 28, 1963, pp. 111–26.

2.4.5.7 HILDEBRANDT, Franz: *From Luther to Wesley*, London: Lutter-worth Press, 1951, 224p.

2.4.5.8 HYNSON, Leon Orville: 'John Wesley and the "Unitas Fratrum": A theological analysis', *Methodist History*, Vol. XVIII, 1979–80, pp. 26–60.

2.4.5.9 IRESON, Roger William: 'The doctrine of faith in John Wesley and the Protestant tradition: A comparative study', University of Manchester Ph.D. thesis, 1973, xvi+445p.

2.4.5.10 MARSHALL, Ronald Philip: 'Wesley and the Reformation', *Religion in Life*, Vol. XXXIX, 1970, pp. 426–33.

2.4.5.11 NAGLER, Arthur Wilford: *Pietism and Methodism; or, The significance of German pietism in the origin and early development of Methodism*, Nashville: Publishing House M.E. Church South, 1918, 200p.

2.4.5.12 PASK, Alfred Henry Speedie: 'The influence of Arminius on John Wesley', *London Quarterly and Holborn Review*, Vol. CLXXXV, 1960, pp. 258–63.

2.4.5.13 PASK, Alfred Henry Speedie: 'The influence of Arminius upon the theology of John Wesley', University of Edinburgh Ph.D. thesis, 1940, [2]+v+170p.

2.4.5.14 PINOMAA, Lennart: 'Tro, lag, helgelse hos Luther, Calvin och John Wesley', *Norsk Teologisk Tidsskrift*, Vol. 69, 1968, pp. 107–18.

2.4.5.15 RUPP, Ernest Gordon: *John Wesley und Martin Luther: Ein Beitrag zum lutherischen-methodistischen Dialog*, Stuttgart: Christliches Verlagshaus, 1983, 24p.

2.4.5.16 SCHMIDT, Martin: 'Wesley's place in church history', *The place of Wesley in the Christian tradition: Essays delivered at Drew University in celebration of the commencement of the publication of the Oxford edition of the works of John Wesley*, edited by Kenneth Elmer Rowe, Metuchen: Scarecrow Press, 1976, pp. 67–93.

2.4.5.17 STOEFFLER, Fred Ernest: 'Pietism, the Wesleys and Methodist beginnings in America', *Continental pietism and early American Christianity*, edited by Fred Ernest Stoeffler, Grand Rapids: William B. Eerdmans Publishing Company, 1976, pp. 184–221.

2.4.5.18 TOWLSON, Clifford William: *Moravian and Methodist: Relationships and influences in the eighteenth century*, London: Epworth Press, 1957, viii+265p.

2.4.5.19 WALLS, Jerry L.: 'John Wesley's critique of Martin Luther', *Methodist History*, Vol. XX, 1981–82, pp. 29–41.

2.4.5.20 WRIGHT, Charles James: 'Comenius and Methodism: A significant tercentenary', *London Quarterly and Holborn Review*, Vol. CLXVI, 1941, pp. 436–50.

2.4.5.21 ZEHRER, Karl: 'The relationship between pietism in Halle and early Methodism', *Methodist History*, Vol. XVII, 1978–79, pp. 211–24.

See also 2.2.9.10, 2.2.9.12, 2.2.16.2, 2.2.16.3, 2.2.16.7, 2.2.16.10, 2.3.3.16, 2.3.3.17, 2.4.2.26, 2.5.1.16, 2.5.3.13, 2.5.3.14, 2.5.5.5, 2.5.7.5, 2.5.7.19, 2.5.7.34, 2.5.7.43, 2.6.4.8, 2.6.4.19.

2.4.6 Tradition: Anglicanism

2.4.6.1 BAKER, Frank: 'Jonathan Swift and the Wesleys', *London Quarterly and Holborn Review*, Vol. CLXXIX, 1954, pp. 290–300.

2.4.6.2 BLANKENSHIP, Paul Freeman: 'The significance of John Wesley's abridgment of the Thirty-Nine Articles as seen from his deletions', *Methodist History*, Vol. II, No. 3, April 1964, pp. 35–47.

2.4.6.3 CLAYPOOL, James Vernon: 'Berkeley and Wesley: A comparison of their lives, influence and writings', Temple University S.T.D. thesis, 1932, 247p.

2.4.6.4 ENGLISH, John Cammel: 'The Cambridge Platonists in Wesley's "Christian library"', *Proceedings of the Wesley Historical Society*, Vol. XXXVI, 1967–68, pp. 161–8.

2.4.6.5 ENGLISH, John Cammel: 'John Wesley and the Anglican moderates of the seventeenth century', *Anglican Theological Review*, Vol. 51, 1969, pp. 203–20.

2.4.6.6   HARMON, Nolan Bailey & BARDSLEY, John W.: 'John Wesley and the articles of religion', *Religion in Life*, Vol. XXII, 1952–53, pp. 280–91.

2.4.6.7   HINDLEY, John Clifford: 'The philosophy of enthusiasm: A study in the origins of "experimental theology" ', *London Quarterly and Holborn Review*, Vol. CLXXXII, 1957, pp. 99–109, 199–210.

2.4.6.8   HUGHES, Henry Trevor: 'Jeremy Taylor and John Wesley', *London Quarterly and Holborn Review*, Vol. CLXXIV, 1949, pp. 296–304.

2.4.6.9   HUNTER, Frederick: 'The influence of the Church of England and Dissent upon Methodism in the eighteenth century', University of Manchester M.A. thesis, 1939, $4+10+68+20+5+10+23+15+7+11+6+6+3+6+5$p.

2.4.6.10   HUNTER, Frederick: 'The Manchester non-jurors and Wesley's high churchism', *London Quarterly and Holborn Review*, Vol. CLXXII, 1947, pp. 56–61.

2.4.6.11   HUTCHINSON, Francis Ernest: 'John Wesley and George Herbert', *London Quarterly and Holborn Review*, Vol. CLXI, 1936, pp. 439–55.

2.4.6.12   LEACH, Elsie A.: 'John Wesley's use of George Herbert', *Huntington Library Quarterly*, Vol. XVI, 1952–53, pp. 183–202.

2.4.6.13   PIKE, David: 'The religious societies in the Church of England, 1678 to 1743, and their influence on John Wesley and the Methodist movement', University of Leeds M.A. thesis, 1960, [2]+231p.

2.4.6.14   ROGERS, Charles Allen: 'John Wesley and William Tilly', *Proceedings of the Wesley Historical Society*, Vol. XXXV, 1965–66, pp. 137–41.

2.4.6.15   RUPP, Ernest Gordon: 'Son of Samuel: John Wesley, Church of England man', *The place of Wesley in the Christian tradition: Essays delivered at Drew University in celebration of the commencement of the publication of the Oxford edition of the works of John Wesley*, edited by Kenneth Elmer Rowe, Metuchen: Scarecrow Press, 1976, pp. 39–66.

2.4.6.16   SELLECK, Jerald Brian: 'The Book of Common Prayer in the theology of John Wesley', Drew University Ph.D. thesis, 1983, 357p.

2.4.6.17   SELLECK, Jerald Brian: 'An historical consideration of worship and the cure of souls' [with reference to John Wesley's theology and the Book of Common Prayer], *Drew Gateway*, Vol. 54, No. 2–3, Winter–Spring 1984, pp. 25–51.

2.4.7 Tradition: Puritanism and Dissent

2.4.7.1   BAKER, Frank: 'Wesley's Puritan ancestry', *London Quarterly and Holborn Review*, Vol. CLXXXVII, 1962, pp. 180–6.

2.4.7.2   BUTLER, Dugald: *Henry Scougal and the Oxford Methodists; or, The influence of a religious teacher of the Scottish Church*, Edinburgh: William Blackwood and Sons, 1899, xi+151p.

2.4.7.3   EAYRS, George: 'Links between the ejected clergy of 1662, the Wesleys and Methodism', *The ejectment of 1662 and the Free Churches*,

London: National Council of Evangelical Free Churches, 1912, pp. 97–119.

2.4.7.4 ENGLISH, John Cammel: 'John Wesley and Francis Rous', *Methodist History*, Vol. VI, No. 4, July 1968, pp. 28–35.

2.4.7.5 LLOYD, Albert Kingsley: 'Charles Wesley's debt to Matthew Henry', *London Quarterly and Holborn Review*, Vol. CLXXI, 1946, pp. 330–7.

2.4.7.6 MONK, Robert Clarence: *John Wesley, his Puritan heritage: A study of the Christian life*, London: Epworth Press, 1966, 286p.

2.4.7.7 NEWTON, John Anthony: *Methodism and the Puritans*, Friends of Dr. Williams's Library Eighteenth Lecture, London: Dr. Williams's Trust, 1964, [6]+19p.

2.4.7.8 NEWTON, John Anthony: 'Samuel Annesley (1620–1696)', *Proceedings of the Wesley Historical Society*, Vol. XLV, 1985–86, pp. 29–45.

2.4.7.9 ROUTLEY, Erik Reginald: 'Charles Wesley and Matthew Henry', *Congregational Quarterly*, Vol. XXXIII, 1955, pp. 345–51.

2.4.7.10 SANDERS, Paul Samuel: 'The Puritans and John Wesley', *Work-Worship*, Vol. 17, No. 2, Whitsuntide 1967, pp. 13–9.

See also 2.2.3.7, 2.4.6.9

2.4.8 Reason and experience

2.4.8.1 BRANTLEY, Richard Estes: *Locke, Wesley and the method of English romanticism*, Gainesville: University of Florida Press, 1984, xi+300p.

2.4.8.2 CLAPPER, Gregory Scott: 'John Wesley on religious affections: His views on experience and emotion and their role in the Christian life and theology', Emory University Ph.D. thesis, 1985, 237p.

2.4.8.3 ENGLISH, John Cammel: 'John Wesley and the Age of Reason', *Freedom under grace: Papers presented to the Methodist History Symposium, Baker University, October 30, 31, November 1 1984*, edited by John Cammel English, Baldwin: Baker University, 1985, pp. 3–36.

2.4.8.4 GRAY, Wallace Gale: 'The place of reason in the theology of John Wesley', Vanderbilt University Ph.D. thesis, 1953, xix+253p.

2.4.8.5 MATTHEWS, Rex Dale: ' "With the eyes of faith": Spiritual experience and the knowledge of God in the theology of John Wesley', *Wesleyan theology today: A bicentennial theological consultation*, edited by Theodore Runyon, Nashville: Kingswood Books, 1985, pp. 406–15.

2.4.8.6 NEWMAN, Leslie Arthur: 'The philosophical thought of John Wesley', University of Durham (Newcastle-upon-Tyne) Ph.D. thesis, 1949, [3]+664p.

2.4.8.7 SHIMIZU, Mitsuo: 'Epistemology in the thought of John Wesley', Drew University Ph.D. thesis, 1980, 245p.

See also 2.2.17.2, 2.4.2.9.

2.5 Spirituality: Theology – the Plan of Salvation

2.5.1 General works

2.5.1.1 ALBIN, Thomas R.: 'An empirical study of early Methodist spirituality', *Wesleyan theology today: A bicentennial theological consultation*, edited by Theodore Runyon, Nashville: Kingswood Books, 1985, pp. 275–90.

2.5.1.2 BENCE, Clarence Luther: 'John Wesley's teleological hermeneutic', Emory University Ph.D. thesis, 1981, 304p.

2.5.1.3 CANNON, William Ragsdale: 'Methodism in a philosophy of history' [with reference to the theology of John Wesley], *Methodist History*, Vol. XII, No. 4, July 1974, pp. 27–43.

2.5.1.4 CANNON, William Ragsdale: 'Salvation in the theology of John Wesley', *Methodist History*, Vol. IX, No. 1, October 1970, pp. 3–12 and *The Bulletin* [of the Committee on Archives of the United Church of Canada], No. 27, 1978, pp. 43–54.

2.5.1.5 CELL, George Croft: *The rediscovery of John Wesley*, New York: Henry Holt and Company, 1935, xviii+420p.

2.5.1.6 COLLINS, Kenneth Joseph: 'A hermeneutical model for the Wesleyan "ordo salutis"', *Wesleyan Theological Journal*, Vol. 19, No. 2, Fall 1984, pp. 23–37.

2.5.1.7 COLLINS, Kenneth Joseph: 'John Wesley's theology of law', Drew University Ph.D. thesis, 1984, 292p.

2.5.1.8 CUSHMAN, Robert Earl: 'Theological landmarks in the revival under Wesley', *Religion in Life*, Vol. XXVII, 1957–58, pp. 105–18.

2.5.1.9 DAVIES, Rupert Eric: 'The people called Methodists: 1. "Our doctrines"', *A history of the Methodist Church in Great Britain*, Vol. 1, general editors: Rupert Eric Davies & Ernest Gordon Rupp, London: Epworth Press, 1965, pp. 145–79.

2.5.1.10 DORR, Donal J.: 'The Wesleyan doctrine of sin and salvation', St. Patrick's College, Maynooth D.D. thesis, 1964, [3]+200+xiiip.

2.5.1.11 DREYER, Frederick: 'Faith and experience in the thought of John Wesley', *American Historical Review*, Vol. 88, 1983, pp. 12–30.

2.5.1.12 EBERLY, Paul F.: 'John Wesley's philosophy of religion', Syracuse University Ph.D. thesis, 1934.

2.5.1.13 ENGLISH, John Cammel: *The heart renewed: John Wesley's doctrine of Christian initiation*, Macon: Wesleyan College, 1967, 82p.

2.5.1.14 ENGLISH, John Cammel: 'The historical antecedents and development of John Wesley's doctrine of Christian initiation', Vanderbilt University Ph.D. thesis, 1965, vi+388p.

2.5.1.15 FUHRMAN, Eldon Ralph: 'Speaking the truth in love: Dual emphases in Wesleyan thought', *Wesleyan Theological Journal*, Vol. 11, Spring 1976, pp. 5–21.

2.5.1.16 GREVE, Lionel: 'Freedom and discipline in the theology of John Calvin, William Perkins and John Wesley: An examination of the origin and nature of pietism', Hartford Seminary Foundation Ph.D. thesis, 1976, 299p.

2.5.1.17   HILDEBRANDT, Franz: *Christianity according to the Wesleys: The Harris Franklin Rall Lectures 1954, delivered at Garrett Biblical Institute, Evanston, Illinois,* London: Epworth Press, 1956, 80p.

2.5.1.18   HOON, Paul Waitman: 'The soteriology of John Wesley', University of Edinburgh Ph.D. thesis, 1936, [6]+x+354p.

2.5.1.19   JORDEN, Eric Evans: 'The ideal of sanctity in Methodism and tractarianism, with special reference to John Wesley and John Henry Newman: A comparative study', University of London Ph.D. thesis, 1958, viii+426p.

2.5.1.20   JOY, Donald Marvin: 'Toward Christian holiness: John Wesley's faith pilgrimage', *Moral development foundations: Judeo-Christian alternatives to Piaget-Kohlberg,* edited by Donald Marvin Joy, Nashville: Abingdon Press, 1983, pp. 207–32.

2.5.1.21   KNIGHT, John Allan: 'Aspects of Wesley's theology after 1770', *Methodist History,* Vol. VI, No. 3, April 1968, pp. 33–42.

2.5.1.22   KNOX, Ronald Arbuthnott: *Enthusiasm: A chapter in the history of religion, with special reference to the XVII and XVIII centuries,* Oxford: Clarendon Press, 1950, viii+622p.

2.5.1.23   LEE, Umphrey: *John Wesley and modern religion,* Nashville: Cokesbury Press, 1936, xiii+354p.

2.5.1.24   LEUPP, Roderick Thomas: 'The art of God: Light and darkness in the thought of John Wesley', Drew University Ph.D. thesis, 1985, 245p.

2.5.1.25   LINDSTRÖM, Harald Gustav Åke: 'The message of John Wesley and the modern man', *Drew Gateway,* Vol. 25, 1954–55, pp. 186–95.

2.5.1.26   MEREDITH, Lawrence: 'Essential doctrine in the theology of John Wesley, with special attention to the Methodist standards of doctrine', Harvard University Ph.D. thesis, 1962, 325p.

2.5.1.27   MULLEN, Wilbur H.: 'John Wesley and liberal religion', *Religion in Life,* Vol. XXXV, 1965–66, pp. 561–74.

2.5.1.28   NEWTON, John Anthony: 'The theology of the Wesleys', *The Methodist heritage: The Principal's Lectures, Southlands College, Spring Term 1984,* [London]: Southlands College, [1984], pp. 1–10.

2.5.1.29   OUTLER, Albert Cook: 'John Wesley as theologian: Then and now', *Methodist History,* Vol. XII, No. 4, July 1974, pp. 63–82.

2.5.1.30   OUTLER, Albert Cook: 'John Wesley, folk-theologian', *Theology Today,* Vol. XXXIV, 1977–78, pp. 150–60.

2.5.1.31   OUTLER, Albert Cook: 'The place of Wesley in the Christian tradition', *The place of Wesley in the Christian tradition: Essays delivered at Drew University in celebration of the commencement of the publication of the Oxford edition of the works of John Wesley,* edited by Kenneth Elmer Rowe, Metuchen: Scarecrow Press, 1976, pp. 11–38.

2.5.1.32   OUTLER, Albert Cook: 'The rediscovery of John Wesley through his faith and doctrine', *Historical Bulletin, World Methodist Historical Society,* Vol. 12, First Quarter 1983, pp. 4–10.

2.5.1.33 OUTLER, Albert Cook: 'Towards a re-appraisal of John Wesley as a theologian', *Perkins School of Theology Journal*, Vol. 14, No. 2, Winter 1961, pp. 5–14.

2.5.1.34 SCANLON, Michael Joseph: 'The Christian anthropology of John Wesley', Catholic University of America S.T.D. thesis, 1969, 154p.

2.5.1.35 SCHEMPP, Johannes: *Seelsorge und Seelenführung bei John Wesley*, Stuttgart: Christliches Verlagshaus, 1949, 248p.

2.5.1.36 SCHNEEBERGER, Vilém D.: 'Der Begriff der christlichen Freiheit bei John Wesley', *Communio Viatorum*, Vol. XX, 1977, pp. 47–61.

2.5.1.37 SCHNEEBERGER, Vilém D.: 'Schlichte Wahrheit: Eine Aufgabe der Theologie?', *Communio Viatorum*, Vol. XVII, 1974, pp. 47–61.

2.5.1.38 SLAATTE, Howard Alexander: *Fire in the brand: An introduction to the creative work and theology of John Wesley*, New York: Exposition Press, 1963, 157p.

2.5.1.39 SWEETLAND, William Ernest: 'A critical study of John Wesley as practical thinker and reformer', Michigan State University Ph.D. thesis, 1955, ii+195p.

2.5.1.40 TURNER, John Munsey: 'John Wesley, people's theologian', *One in Christ*, Vol. XIV, 1978, pp. 328–39.

2.5.1.41 VERHALEN, Philip A.: 'The proclamation of the Word in the writings of John Wesley', Pontificia Universitas Gregoriana S.T.D. thesis, 1969.

2.5.1.42 WEISSBACH, Jürgen: *Der neue Mensch im theologischen Denken John Wesleys*, Stuttgart: Christliches Verlagshaus, 1970, 218+56+ixp.

2.5.1.43 WILLIAMS, Colin Wilbur: *John Wesley's theology today*, London: Epworth Press, 1960, 252p.

See also 2.2.4.11, 2.2.6.33, 2.2.6.35, 2.2.6.43, 2.2.10.2, 2.2.17.5, 2.3.1.2, 2.3.3.4, 2.3.3.8, 2.3.3.9, 2.3.3.14, 2.3.3.16, 2.3.3.17, 2.3.3.25, 2.3.11.15, 2.4.5.7, 2.4.5.9, 2.6.1.13, 2.8.2.7, 2.8.2.16, 2.9.1.6, 2.9.4.6.

2.5.2 Man's fallen state

2.5.2.1 BLAISING, Craig Alan: 'John Wesley's doctrine of original sin', Dallas Theological Seminary Th.D. thesis, 1979.

2.5.2.2 CALAGUI, Jeremias Datu: 'The doctrine of man in John Wesley's theology', Northwestern University M.A. thesis, 1961.

2.5.2.3 CHO, John Chongnahm: 'John Wesley's view of fallen man', *A spectrum of thought: Essays in honor of Dennis F. Kinlaw*, edited by Michael L. Peterson, Wilmore: Francis Asbury Publishing Company, 1982, pp. 67–77.

2.5.2.4 COX, Leo George: 'John Wesley's concept of sin', State University of Iowa M.A. thesis, 1957, 193p.

2.5.2.5 DORR, Donal J.: 'Total corruption and the Wesleyan tradition', *Irish Theological Quarterly*, Vol. XXXI, 1964, pp. 303–21.

2.5.2.6 HODGEN, Margaret Trabue: 'The negro in the anthropology of John Wesley', *Journal of Negro History*, Vol. XIX, 1934, pp. 308–23.

See also 2.5.1.10, 2.5.1.34.

2.5.3 God's sovereign grace

2.5.3.1   ALLBECK, Willard Dow: 'Plenteous grace with thee is found', *Religion in Life*, Vol. XXIX, 1959–60, pp. 501–6.

2.5.3.2   CHILES, Robert Eugene: 'From free grace to free will', *Religion in Life*, Vol. XXVII, 1957–58, pp. 438–49.

2.5.3.3   COPPEDGE, Allan: 'John Wesley and the doctrine of predestination', University of Cambridge Ph.D. thesis, 1976, xxii+357p.

2.5.3.4   CROW, Earl Pickett: 'John Wesley's conflict with antinomianism in relation to the Moravians and Calvinists', University of Manchester Ph.D. thesis, 1964, xi+360p.

2.5.3.5   CROW, Earl Pickett: 'Wesley and antinomianism', *Duke Divinity School Review*, Vol. 31, 1966, pp. 10–19.

2.5.3.6   CUSHMAN, Robert Earl: 'Salvation for all: Wesley and Calvinism'. *Methodism*, edited by William Ketcham Anderson, Cincinnati: Methodist Publishing House, 1947, pp. 103–15.

2.5.3.7   DORR, Donal J.: 'Wesley's teaching on the nature of holiness', *London Quarterly and Holborn Review*, Vol. CXC, 1965, pp. 234–9.

2.5.3.8   FUHRMAN, Eldon Ralph: 'The concept of grace in the theology of John Wesley', University of Iowa Ph.D. thesis, 1963, vii+497p.

2.5.3.9   GERDES, Egon Walter: 'John Wesleys Lehre von der Gottesebenbildlichkeit des Menschen', Dissertation, Christian-Albrechts-Universität Kiel, 1958, x+306p.

2.5.3.10   GREEVES, Frederic: 'John Wesley and divine guidance', *London Quarterly and Holborn Review*, Vol. CLXII, 1937, pp. 379–85.

2.5.3.11   HENDRICKS, Melvin Elton: 'John Wesley and natural theology', *Wesleyan Theological Journal*, Vol. 18, No. 2, Fall 1983, pp. 7–17.

2.5.3.12   HENRY, Granville C.: 'John Wesley's doctrine of free will', *London Quarterly and Holborn Review*, Vol. CLXXXV, 1960, pp. 200–4.

2.5.3.13   HILLMAN, Robert John: 'Grace in the preaching of Calvin and Wesley', *Dig or die: Papers given at the World Methodist Historical Society Wesley Heritage Conference at Wesley College within the University of Sydney, 10–15 August 1980*, edited by James Stuart Udy & Eric Gerald Clancy, Sydney: World Methodist Historical Society Australasian Section, 1981, pp. 279–89.

2.5.3.14   HILLMAN, Robert John: 'Grace in the preaching of Calvin and Wesley: A comparative study', Fuller Theological Seminary Ph.D. thesis, 1978, 2 vol.

2.5.3.15   HYNSON, Leon Orville: 'Creation and grace in Wesley's ethics', *Drew Gateway*, Vol. 46, 1975–76, pp. 41–55.

2.5.3.16   MADDOX, Randy Lynn: 'Responsible grace: The systematic perspective of Wesleyan theology', *Wesleyan Theological Journal*, Vol. 19, No. 2, Fall 1984, pp. 7–22.

2.5.3.17   MERCER, Jerry Lee: 'A study of the concept of man in the sermons of John Wesley', Southern California School of Theology at Claremont Th.D. thesis, 1970, iv+225p.

2.5.3.18   RAKESTRAW, Robert Vincent: 'The concept of grace in the ethics of John Wesley', Drew University Ph.D. thesis, 1985, 435p.

2.5.3.19 REIST, Irwin W.: 'John Wesley and George Whitefield: A study in the integrity of two theologies of grace', *Evangelical Quarterly*, Vol. XLVII, 1975, pp. 26–40.

2.5.3.20 REIST, Irwin W.: 'John Wesley's view of man: A study in free grace versus free will', *Wesleyan Theological Journal*, Vol. 7, Spring 1972, pp. 25–35.

2.5.3.21 ROGERS, Charles Allen: 'The concept of prevenient grace in the theology of John Wesley', Duke University Ph.D. thesis, 1967, xvi + 320p.

2.5.3.22 SANDERS, Paul Samuel: 'What God hath joined together', *Religion in Life*, Vol. XXIX, 1959–60, pp. 491–500.

2.5.3.23 SHERMER, Robert Charles: 'John Wesley's speaking and writing on predestination and free will', Southern Illinois University Ph.D. thesis, 1969, 371p.

2.5.3.24 SHIPLEY, David Clark: 'Wesley and some Calvinistic controversies', *Drew Gateway*, Vol. 25, 1954–55, pp. 195–210.

2.5.3.25 SMITH, James Weldon: 'Some notes on Wesley's doctrine of prevenient grace', *Religion in Life*, Vol. XXXIV, 1964–65, pp. 68–80.

2.5.3.26 WALLS, Jerry L.: 'The free will defense, Calvinism, Wesley and the goodness of God', *Christian Scholar's Review*, Vol. 13, 1984, pp. 19–33.

2.5.3.27 WILSON, Charles Randall: 'The correlation of love and law in the theology of John Wesley', Vanderbilt University Ph.D. thesis, 1959, iii + 208p.

2.5.3.28 WILSON, Charles Randall: 'The relevance of John Wesley's distinctive correlation of love and law', *Wesleyan Theological Journal*, Vol. 12, Spring 1977, pp. 54–9.

2.5.3.29 WOOD, Arthur Skevington: 'The contribution of John Wesley to the theology of grace', *Grace unlimited*, Clark H. Pinnock, editor, Minneapolis: Bethany Fellowship, 1975, pp. 209–22.

See also 2.2.17.12, 2.3.11.3, 2.3.11.10, 2.5.1.34, 2.6.5.4.

2.5.4 Christ's atonement for sin

2.5.4.1 CUSTER, Watson Stanley: 'The doctrine of atonement in the writings of John Wesley', Northwestern University M.A. thesis, 1955.

2.5.4.2 DESCHNER, John William: *Wesley's Christology: An interpretation*, Dallas: Southern Methodist University Press, 1960, ix + 220p.

2.5.4.3 NORMAN, David Douglas Robert: 'The development of the evangelical doctrine of the Atonement in England from the conversion of John Wesley to the present day', University of Nottingham M.A. thesis, 1958, v + 276p.

2.5.4.4 RENSHAW, John Rutherford: 'The Atonement in the theology of John and Charles Wesley', Boston University Th.D. thesis, 1965, vi + 299p.

2.5.4.5 TYSON, John Rodger: 'Charles Wesley's theology of the Cross: An examination of the theology and method of Charles Wesley as seen in his doctrine of the Atonement', Drew University Ph.D. thesis, 1983, 1,003p.

2.5.4.6   WATSON, David Lowes: 'Christ our righteousness: The center of Wesley's evangelistic message', *Perkins School of Theology Journal*, Vol. 37, No. 3, Spring 1984, pp. 34–47.

2.5.4.7   [WEST, Nathaniel]: *John Wesley and premillennialism*, New York: printed for the author by Hunt & Eaton, 1894, 48p.

2.5.5 Justification

2.5.5.1   BOLSTER, George Reed: 'Wesley's doctrine' [of justification], *Evangelical Quarterly*, Vol. XXIV, 1952, pp. 144–55.

2.5.5.2   BROCKWELL, Charles Wilbur: 'John Wesley's doctrine of justification', *Wesleyan Theological Journal*, Vol. 18, No. 2, Fall 1983, pp. 18–32.

2.5.5.3   CANNON, William Ragsdale: *The theology of John Wesley, with special reference to the doctrine of justification*, New York: Abingdon-Cokesbury Press, [1946], 284p.

2.5.5.4   DICKER, Gordon Stanley: 'The concept "simul iustus et peccator" in relation to the thought of Luther, Wesley and Bonhoeffer, and its significance for a doctrine of the Christian life', Union Theological Seminary in the City of New York Th.D. thesis, 1971, 215 + [8]p.

2.5.5.5   EICKEN, Erich von: 'Rechtfertigung und Heiligung bei Wesley, dargestellt unter Vergleichung mit den Anschauungen Luthers und des Luthertums', Dissertation, Universität Heidelberg, 1934, 69p.

2.5.5.6   HODGES, Herbert Arthur: 'A neglected page in Anglican theology' [John Wesley on justification and perfection], *Theology*, Vol. XLVIII, 1945, pp. 104–10.

2.5.5.7   MARQUARDT, Manfred: 'John Wesley's "Synergismus"', *Die Einheit der Kirche: Dimensionen ihrer Heiligkeit, Katholizität und Apostolizität – Festgabe Peter Meinhold zum 70. Geburtstag*, herausgegeben von Lorenz Hein, Veröffentlichungen des Instituts für Europäische Geschichte, Mainz, Band 85, Wiesbaden: Franz Steiner Verlag, 1977, pp. 96–102.

2.5.5.8   MATLOCK, Paul Russell: *The four justifications in John Fletcher's theology*, Salem: Schmul Publishers, 1980, 93p.

2.5.5.9   SMITH, Harmon Lee: 'Wesley's doctrine of justification: Beginning and process', *Duke Divinity School Bulletin*, Vol. 28, 1963, pp. 88–98 and *London Quarterly and Holborn Review*, Vol. CLXXXIX, 1964, pp. 120–8.

See also 2.2.9.7, 2.3.3.13, 2.5.3.4, 2.5.3.5, 2.5.3.22, 2.6.1.6.

2.5.6 New birth and assurance through the Spirit

2.5.6.1   BENNER, Forest T.: 'The immediate antecedents of the Wesleyan doctrine of the witness of the Spirit', Temple University Ph.D. thesis, 1966, 253p.

2.5.6.2 CANNON, William Ragsdale: 'The Holy Spirit in Vatican II and in the writings of Wesley', *Religion in Life*, Vol. XXXVII, 1968, pp. 440–53.

2.5.6.3 KELLETT, Norman Lawrence: 'John Wesley and the restoration of the doctrine of the Holy Spirit to the Church of England in the 18th. century', Brandeis University Ph.D. thesis, 1975, 218p.

2.5.6.4 KIM, Seung Lak: 'John Wesley's doctrine of the witness of the Spirit or the assurance of salvation', Southern Baptist Theological Seminary Ph.D. thesis, 1932.

2.5.6.5 KOERBER, Charles J.: *The theology of conversion according to John Wesley*, Neo-Eboraci: auctore Carolo Koerber, 1967, a–n +82p.

2.5.6.6 McGONIGLE, Herbert: 'Pneumatological nomenclature in early Methodism', *Wesleyan Theological Journal*, Vol. 8, Spring 1973, pp. 61–72.

2.5.6.7 NOLL, Mark Allan: 'John Wesley and the doctrine of assurance', *Bibliotheca Sacra*, Vol. 132, 1975, pp. 161–77.

2.5.6.8 OSWALT, John Newell: 'John Wesley and the Old Testament concept of the Holy Spirit', *Religion in Life*, Vol. XLVIII, 1979, pp. 283–92.

2.5.6.9 RUTTER, Robert Sherman: 'The new birth: Evangelicalism in the transatlantic community during the Great Awakening, 1739–1745', Rutgers University, the State University of New Jersey (New Brunswick) Ph.D. thesis, 1982, 449p.

2.5.6.10 SMITH, Timothy Lawrence: 'The Holy Spirit in the hymns of the Wesleys', *Wesleyan Theological Journal*, Vol. 16, No. 2, Fall 1981, pp. 20–47.

2.5.6.11 STARKEY, Lycurgus Monroe: 'The Holy Spirit and the Wesleyan witness', *Religion in Life*, Vol. XLIX, 1980, pp. 72–80.

2.5.6.12 STARKEY, Lycurgus Monroe: *The work of the Holy Spirit: A study in Wesleyan theology*, New York: Abingdon Press, 1962, 176p.

2.5.6.13 TOWNSEND, James A.: 'Feelings related to assurance in Charles Wesley's hymns', Fuller Theological Seminary Ph.D. thesis, 1979.

2.5.6.14 WINDEMILLER, Duane Arlo: 'The psychodynamics of change in religious conversion and communist brainwashing, with particular reference to the 18th. century evangelical revival and the Chinese thought control movement', Boston University Ph.D. thesis, 1960, viii +178p.

2.5.6.15 WOOD, Arthur Skevington: 'John Wesley, theologian of the Spirit', *Theological Renewal*, No. 6, June/July 1977, pp. 26–34.

2.5.6.16 YATES, Arthur Stanley: *The doctrine of assurance, with special reference to John Wesley*, London: Epworth Press, 1952, xviii +242p.

See also 2.2.10.8, 2.4.1.13, 2.4.6.7, 2.5.7.1.

2.5.7 Sanctification and perfection

2.5.7.1 ARNETT, William Melvin: 'The role of the Holy Spirit in entire sanctification in the writings of John Wesley', *Wesleyan Theological Journal*, Vol. 14, No. 2, Fall 1979, pp. 15–30.

2.5.7.2 BIBLE, Ken: 'The Wesleys' hymns on full redemption and Pentecost: A brief comparison', *Wesleyan Theological Journal*, Vol. 17, No. 2, Fall 1982, pp. 79–87.

2.5.7.3 CANNON, William Ragsdale: 'John Wesley's doctrine of sanctification and perfection', *Mennonite Quarterly Review*, Vol. XXXV, 1961, pp. 91–5.

2.5.7.4 COGGIN, James Earl: 'John Wesley's doctrine of perfection and its influence on subsequent theology', Southwestern Baptist Theological Seminary Th.D. thesis, 1949, vi+236p.

2.5.7.5 COLLIER, John: 'Wesley's Christian perfection in light of Luther and Niebuhr', *Church Divinity, 1981*, edited by John H. Morgan, Notre Dame: Church Divinity Monograph Series, 1981, pp. 12–22.

2.5.7.6 Cox, Leo George: *John Wesley's concept of perfection*, Kansas City: Beacon Hill Press, 1964, vi+227p.

2.5.7.7 CUBIE, David Livingstone: 'John Wesley's concept of perfect love: A motif analysis', Boston University Ph.D. thesis, 1965, xiii+328p.

2.5.7.8 CUBIE, David Livingstone: 'Perfection in Wesley and Fletcher: Inaugural or teleological?', *Wesleyan Theological Journal*, Vol. 11, Spring 1976, pp. 22–37.

2.5.7.9 DARBY, James Carter: 'A study of the historical development of John Wesley's doctrine of Christian perfection as proclaimed in his preaching and tested in the life of the Christian community', Northwestern University M.A. thesis, 1956.

2.5.7.10 FINDLATER, John: *Perfect love: A study of Wesley's view of the ideal Christian life*, Leith: Leith Printing & Publishing Co., 1914, xvi+182p.

2.5.7.11 FLEW, Robert Newton: *The idea of perfection in Christian theology: An historical study of the Christian ideal for the present life*, London: Oxford University Press, 1934, xv+422p.

2.5.7.12 GARRISON, Richard Benjamin: 'Love as the radical element in John Wesley's doctrine of perfection', Drew University M.A. thesis, 1955, iv+304p.

2.5.7.13 IMPETA, Christoffel Nicolaas: *De leer der heiliging en volmaking bij Wesley en Fletcher*, Leiden: P. J. Mulder, [1913], ii+440+iiip.

2.5.7.14 LERCH, David: *Heil und Heiligung bei John Wesley, dargestellt unter besonderer Berücksichtigung seiner Anmerkungen zum Neuen Testament*, Zürich: gedrückt bei der Christlichen Vereinsbuchhandlung, 1941, ix+180p.

2.5.7.15 LEZIUS, Friedrich E.: 'Wesleys Perfektionismus und die Otley-Bewegung', *Reinhold-Seeberg Festschrift*, herausgegeben von Wilhelm Koepp, Leipzig: A. Deichertsche Verlagsbuchhandlung, 1929, Band II, pp. 213–29.

2.5.7.16 LINDSTRÖM, Harald Gustaf Åke: *Wesley and sanctification: A study in the doctrine of salvation*, London: Epworth Press, [1950], xvi+228p.

2.5.7.17 LOFTHOUSE, William Frederick: 'Wesley's doctrine of Christian perfection', *London Quarterly and Holborn Review*, Vol. CLIX, 1934, pp. 178–88.

2.5.7.18 MANIFOLD, Orrin Avery: 'The development of John Wesley's doctrine of Christian perfection', Boston University Ph.D. thesis, 1946, 203p.

2.5.7.19 MARSHALL, Ian Howard: 'Sanctification in the teaching of John Wesley and John Calvin', *Evangelical Quarterly*, Vol. XXXIV, 1962, pp. 75–82.

2.5.7.20 MÍGUEZ BONINO, José: 'Wesley's doctrine of sanctification from a liberationist perspective', *Sanctification & liberation: Liberation theologies in light of the Wesleyan tradition*, edited by Theodore Runyon, Nashville: Abingdon, 1981, pp. 49–63.

2.5.7.21 MOULTON, Wilfrid Johnson: 'John Wesley's doctrine of perfect love', *London Quarterly Review*, Vol. CXLIV, 1925, pp. 14–27.

2.5.7.22 MUSSMAN, Robert Byron: 'A study and evaluation of the primary nonscriptural influences on John Wesley's doctrine of Christian perfection', Southern Baptist Theological Seminary Ph.D. thesis, 1959, vii + 168p.

2.5.7.23 NAUSNER, Helmut: 'John Wesley, ein Reformator: Christliche Vollkommenheit als Lebensthema', *Was bedeutet uns heute die Reformation?*, Linz: Oberösterreichischer Landesverlag, 1973, pp. 99–127.

2.5.7.24 NEFF, Blake J.: 'John Wesley and John Fletcher on entire sanctification: A metaphoric cluster analysis', Bowling Green State University Ph.D. thesis, 1982, 110p.

2.5.7.25 NEWTON, John Anthony: 'Perfection and spirituality in the Methodist tradition', *Church Quarterly*, Vol. 3, 1970–71, pp. 95–103.

2.5.7.26 NICHOLSON, Roy Stephen: 'The holiness emphasis in the Wesleys' hymns', *Wesleyan Theological Journal*, Vol. 5, Spring 1970, pp. 49–61.

2.5.7.27 NICHOLSON, Roy Stephen: 'John Wesley's personal experience of Christian perfection', *Asbury Seminarian*, Vol. VI, 1952, pp. 64–89.

2.5.7.28 NORO, Yoshio: 'Wesley's understanding of Christian perfection', *Japanese contributions to the study of John Wesley*, edited by Clifford Walter Edwards, Macon: Wesleyan College, 1967.

2.5.7.29 PANOSIAN, Edward Miran: 'John Wesley's doctrine of Christian perfection', *Biblical Viewpoint*, Vol. 6, 1972, pp. 120–9.

2.5.7.30 PETERS, John Leland: *Christian perfection and American Methodism*, New York: Abingdon Press, 1956, 252p.

2.5.7.31 RUNYON, Theodore: 'Introduction: Wesley and the theologies of liberation', *Sanctification & liberation: Liberation theologies in light of the Wesleyan tradition*, edited by Theodore Runyon, Nashville: Abingdon, 1981, pp. 9–48.

2.5.7.32 SANGSTER, William Edwin Robert: *The path to perfection: An examination and restatement of John Wesley's doctrine of Christian perfection*, London: Hodder and Stoughton, 1943, 211p.

2.5.7.33 SANGSTER, William Edwin Robert: 'Wesley and sanctification', *London Quarterly and Holborn Review*, Vol. CLXXI, 1946, pp. 214–21.

2.5.7.34 SCOTT. Percy: *John Wesleys Lehre von der Heiligung verglichen mit einem lutherisch-pietistischen Beispiel*, Berlin: Alfred Töpelmann, 1939, xii+97p.

2.5.7.35   SMITH, Timothy Lawrence: 'George Whitefield and Wesleyan perfectionism', *Wesleyan Theological Journal*, Vol. 19, No. 1, Spring 1984, pp. 63–85.

2.5.7.36   SMITH, Timothy Lawrence: 'How John Fletcher became the theologian of Wesleyan perfectionism, 1770–1776', *Wesleyan Theological Journal*, Vol. 15, No. 1, Spring 1980, pp. 68–87.

2.5.7.37   STANGER, Frank Bateman: 'The Wesleyan doctrine of scriptural holiness', *Asbury Seminarian*, Vol. XXXVIV, No. 3, Summer 1984, pp. 8–29.

2.5.7.38   STAPLES, Rob Lyndal: 'John Wesley's doctrine of Christian perfection: A reinterpretation', Pacific School of Religion Th.D. thesis, 1963, ix+357p.

2.5.7.39   THOMAS, Wilhelm: *Heiligung im Neuen Testament und bei John Wesley*, Zürich: Christliche Vereinsbuchhandlung, 1965, 54p.

2.5.7.40   VICK, Edward William Harry: 'John Wesley's teaching concerning perfection', *Andrews University Seminary Studies*, Vol. IV, 1966, pp. 201–17.

2.5.7.41   WALTERS, Orville S.: 'The concept of attainment in John Wesley's Christian perfection', *Methodist History*, Vol. X, No. 3, April 1972, pp. 12–29.

2.5.7.42   WALTERS, Orville S.: 'John Wesley's footnotes to Christian perfection', *Methodist History*, Vol. XII, No. 1, October 1973, pp. 19–36.

2.5.7.43   WATSON, Philip Saville: 'Wesley and Luther on Christian perfection', *Ecumenical Review*, Vol. XV, 1962–63, pp. 291–302.

2.5.7.44   WILSON, Robert Henry: 'John Wesley's doctrine of sanctification', Fuller Theological Seminary D.Min. thesis, 1972, 169p.

2.5.7.45   WOOD, Alfred Harold: 'Charles Wesley's hymns on holiness', *Dig or die: Papers given at the World Methodist Historical Society Wesley Heritage Conference at Wesley College within the University of Sydney, 10–15 August 1980*, edited by James Stuart Udy & Eric Gerald Clancy, Sydney: World Methodist Historical Society Australasian Section, 1981, pp. 67–76.

See also 2.2.9.5, 2.4.1.13, 2.5.3.22, 2.5.5.5. 2.5.5.6, 2.6.1.6, 2.8.2.14.

2.5.8 Eschatology

2.5.8.1   BENCE, Clarence Luther: 'Processive eschatology: A Wesleyan alternative', *Wesleyan Theological Journal*, Vol. 14, No. 1, Spring 1979, pp. 45–59.

2.5.8.2   DOWNES, James Cyril Thomas: 'Eschatological doctrines in the writings of John and Charles Wesley', University of Edinburgh Ph.D. thesis, 1960, iv+271p.

2.5.8.3   MERCER, Jerry Lee: 'The destiny of man in John Wesley's eschatology', *Wesleyan Theological Journal*, Vol. 2, Spring 1967, pp. 56–65.

2.5.8.4   STRAWSON, William: 'Wesley's doctrine of the last things', *London*

Quarterly and Holborn Review, Vol. CLXXXIV, 1959, pp. 240–9.

2.5.8.5   WILSON, David Dunn: 'The importance of hell for John Wesley',
          Proceedings of the Wesley Historical Society, Vol. XXXIV, 1963–64,
          pp. 12–16.

See also 2.2.10.8.

2.6 Spirituality: the Church and the Means of Grace

2.6.1 Doctrine of the Church

2.6.1.1   BAKER, Frank: 'John Wesley's churchmanship', *London Quarterly
          and Holborn Review*, Vol. CLXXXV, 1960, pp. 210–15, 269–74.

2.6.1.2   BAKER, Frank: 'The people called Methodists: 3. Polity', *A history
          of the Methodist Church in Great Britain*, Vol. 1, general editors:
          Rupert Eric Davies & Ernest Gordon Rupp, London: Epworth
          Press, 1965, pp. 211–55.

2.6.1.3   BEALS, James Duane: 'John Wesley's concept of the Church',
          Wesleyan Theological Journal, Vol. 9, Spring 1974, pp. 28–37.

2.6.1.4   CARRUTH, Samuel Enoch: 'John Wesley's concept of the Church',
          Iliff School of Theology, Denver Th.D. thesis, 1952, vi+218p.

2.6.1.5   HILDEBRANDT, Franz: 'The Wesleys' churchmanship', *Drew Gate-
          way*, Vol. 31, 1960–61, pp. 147–62.

2.6.1.6   LANGFORD, Thomas Anderson: 'Wesley's doctrine of the Church,
          ministry and the sacraments; John Wesley's doctrine of justifica-
          tion by faith; John Wesley's doctrine of sanctification', *The Bulletin*
          [of the Committee on Archives and History of the United Church
          of Canada], No. 29, 1980–82, pp. 35–74.

2.6.1.7   LAWSON, John: 'The people called Methodists: 2. " Our disci-
          pline" ', *A history of the Methodist Church in Great Britain*, Vol. 1,
          general editors: Rupert Eric Davies & Ernest Gordon Rupp,
          London: Epworth Press, 1965, pp. 181–209.

2.6.1.8   LOCKYER, Thomas Frederick: 'The churchmanship of John
          Wesley', *London Quarterly Review*, Vol. CXLI, 1924, pp. 57–69.

2.6.1.9   LUCKOCK, Herbert Mortimer & CARRIER, E. Theodore: *John
          Wesley's churchmanship*, London: Longmans, Green and Co., 1891,
          iv+55p.

2.6.1.10 MILLER, James Campbell MacBeath: 'The roots and development
          of John Wesley's organisation', University of Edinburgh Ph.D.
          thesis, 1951, vi+349p.

2.6.1.11 MUMFORD, Norman William: 'The organization of the Methodist
          Church in the time of John Wesley', *London Quarterly and Holborn
          Review*, Vol. CLXXI, 1946, pp. 35–40, 128–35.

2.6.1.12 RIGG, James Harrison: *The churchmanship of John Wesley, and the
          relations of Wesleyan Methodism to the Church of England,* new and
          revised edition, London: Wesleyan-Methodist Book-Room,
          [1887], vi+126p.

2.6.1.13 RUSSELL, Bernard C.: 'The theory and practice of Christian discipline according to John Wesley: Its theological bases and its modern relevance', Drew University Ph.D. thesis, 1951, xi+269p.

2.6.1.14 SCHMIDT, Martin: 'John Wesley als Organisator der methodistischen Bewegung', *Für Kirche und Recht: Festschrift für Johannes Heckel zum 70. Geburtstag*, herausgegeben von Siegfried Grundmann, Köln: Böhlau Verlag, 1959, pp. 313–50.

2.6.1.15 SNYDER, Howard Albert: 'Pietism, Moravianism and Methodism as renewal movements: A comparative and thematic study', University of Notre Dame Ph.D. thesis, 1983, 329p.

2.6.1.16 SNYDER, Howard Albert: *The radical Wesley & patterns for church renewal*, Downers Grove: Inter-Varsity Press, 1980, [14]+189p.

2.6.1.17 STOEFFLER, Fred Ernest: 'Tradition and renewal in the ecclesiology of John Wesley', *Traditio, Krisis, Renovatio aus theologischer Sicht: Festschrift Winfried Zeller zum 65. Geburtstag*, herausgegeben von Bernd Jaspert und Rudolf Mohr, Marburg: N. G. Elwert, 1976, pp. 298–316.

2.6.1.18 WILLIAMS, Ronald Gordon: 'John Wesley's doctrine of the Church', Boston University Th.D. thesis, 1964, x+350p.

See also 2.3.2.6, 2.4.1.13, 2.5.1.35, 2.9.3.2, 2.9.4.2, 2.9.4.6, 2.9.4.7.

2.6.2 Sacraments

2.6.2.1 BARRATT, Thomas H.: 'The place of the Lord's Supper in early Methodism', *London Quarterly Review*, Vol. CXL, 1923, pp. 56–73.

2.6.2.2 BORGEN, Ole Edvard: 'John Wesley and the sacraments', *The Bulletin* [of the Committee on Archives and History of the United Church of Canada], No. 30, 1983–84, pp. 5–30.

2.6.2.3 BORGEN, Ole Edvard: *John Wesley on the sacraments: A theological study*, Nashville: Abingdon Press, 1972, 307p.

2.6.2.4 BOWMER, John Coates: *The sacrament of the Lord's Supper in early Methodism*, London: Dacre Press, 1951, xii+244p.

2.6.2.5 CHO, John Chongnahm: 'John Wesley's view on baptism', *Wesleyan Theological Journal*, Vol. 7, Spring 1972, pp. 60–73 and *Northeast Asia Journal of Theology*, No. 9, September 1972, pp. 29–41.

2.6.2.6 CHO, John Chongnahm: 'A study in John Wesley's doctrine of baptism in the light of current interpretations', Emory University Ph.D. thesis, 1966, viii+219p.

2.6.2.7 ENGLISH, John Cammel: 'The sacrament of baptism according to "The Sunday service" of 1784', *Methodist History*, Vol. V, No. 2, January 1967, pp. 10–16.

2.6.2.8 FLEMING, Richard Lee: 'The concept of sacrifice in the eucharistic hymns of John and Charles Wesley', Southern Methodist University D.Min. thesis, 1980.

2.6.2.9 GALLIERS, Brian James Newby: 'Baptism in the writings of John Wesley', *Proceedings of the Wesley Historical Society*, Vol. XXXII, 1959–60, pp. 121–4, 153–7.

2.6.2.10 GALLIERS, Brian James Newby: 'The theology of baptism in the writings of John Wesley', University of Leeds M.A. thesis, 1957, [3]+iv+279p.

2.6.2.11 GRISLIS, Egil: 'The Wesleyan doctrine of the Lord's Supper', *Duke Divinity School Bulletin*, Vol. 28, 1963, pp. 99–110.

2.6.2.12 HAAS, Alfred Burton: 'John Wesley and the sacrament of Holy Communion', Drew University M.A. thesis, 1946, 61p.

2.6.2.13 HADDAL, Ingvar: 'Nattverden i Charles Wesleys salmer', *Kirke og Kultur*, Vol. LXIII, 1958, pp. 147–55.

2.6.2.14 HOLLAND, Bernard George: *Baptism in early Methodism*, London: Epworth Press, 1970, x+200p.

2.6.2.15 NAGLEE, David Ingersoll: 'The significance of the relationship of infant baptism and Christian nurture in the thought of John Wesley', Temple University Ph.D. thesis, 1966, [4]+349p.

2.6.2.16 PARRIS, John Roland: *John Wesley's doctrine of the sacraments*, London: Epworth Press, 1963, viii+119p.

2.6.2.17 PLUNKETT, Hedley Washington: 'Doctrine and practice of the Lord's Supper in Methodism', *Church and eucharist*, edited by Michael Hurley, Dublin: Gill and Son, 1966, pp. 115–37.

2.6.2.18 RATTENBURY, John Ernest: *The eucharistic hymns of John and Charles Wesley; to which is appended Wesley's preface extracted from Brevint's "Christian sacrament and sacrifice", together with "Hymns on the Lord's Supper"*, London: Epworth Press, 1948, viii+253p.

2.6.2.19 REIST, Irwin W.: 'John Wesley's view of the sacraments: A study in the historical development of a doctrine', *Wesleyan Theological Journal*, Vol. 6, Spring 1971, pp. 41–54.

2.6.2.20 ROGERS, Donald Guy: 'The New Testament basis of the eucharistic hymns of the Wesleys', *Methodist Sacramental Fellowship Bulletin*, No. 88, Lent 1973, pp. 11–14, No. 89, Pentecost 1973, pp. 8–11, No. 90, Feast of All Saints 1973, pp. 7–11, No. 91, Lent 1974, pp. 12–16, No. 92, Pentecost 1974, pp. 6–10, No. 93, Feast of All Saints 1974, pp. 12–15.

2.6.2.21 SANDERS, Paul Samuel: 'An appraisal of John Wesley's sacramentalism in the evolution of early American Methodism', Union Theological Seminary in the City of New York Th.D. thesis, 1954, xxxvii+575p.

2.6.2.22 SANDERS, Paul Samuel: 'John Wesley and baptismal regeneration', *Religion in Life*, Vol. XXIII, 1953–54, pp. 591–603.

2.6.2.23 SANDERS, Paul Samuel: 'Wesley's eucharistic faith and practice', *Anglican Theological Review*, Vol. XLVIII, 1966, pp. 157–74.

2.6.2.24 VAN PELT, John Robert: 'The eucharistic hymns of the Wesleys', *Religion in Life*, Vol. XXII, 1952–53, pp. 449–54.

See also 2.6.1.6, 2.6.3.5, 4.3.2.2.

2.6.3 Worship and devotion

2.6.3.1 BAKER, Frank: 'The beginnings of the Methodist covenant service', *London Quarterly and Holborn Review*, Vol. CLXXX, 1955, pp. 215–20.

2.6.3.2 BARTON, Jesse Hamby: 'The two versions of the first edition of John Wesley's "The Sunday service of the Methodists in North America"', *Methodist History*, Vol. XXIII, 1984–85, pp. 153–62.

2.6.3.3 DAVIES, Daniel Horton Marlais: *Worship and theology in England: From Watts and Wesley to Maurice, 1690–1850*, Princeton: Princeton University Press, 1961, xiv+355p.

2.6.3.4 DEARING, Trevor: *Wesleyan and tractarian worship: An ecumenical study*, London: Epworth Press, 1966, xii+166p.

2.6.3.5 GEORGE, Alfred Raymond: 'The people called Methodists: 4. The means of grace', *A history of the Methodist Church in Great Britain*, Vol. 1, general editors: Rupert Eric Davies & Ernest Gordon Rupp, London: Epworth Press, 1965, pp. 257–73.

2.6.3.6 GEORGE, Alfred Raymond: 'The Sunday service of the Methodists', *Communio sanctorum: Mélanges offerts à Jean-Jacques von Allmen*, Genève: Labor et Fides, 1982, pp. 194–203.

2.6.3.7 GEORGE, Alfred Raymond: *'The Sunday service', 1784: A lecture to the Friends of Wesley's Chapel given on Wednesday, 18th. May 1983 at Wesley's Chapel*, Friends of Wesley's Chapel Annual Lecture No. 2, [London: the Friends of Wesley's Chapel, 1983, 10p].

2.6.3.8 HUNTER, Frederick: 'The origins of Wesley's covenant service', *London Quarterly and Holborn Review*, Vol. CLXIV, 1939, pp. 78–87 and *Proceedings of the Wesley Historical Society*, Vol. XXII, 1939–40, pp. 126–31.

2.6.3.9 HUNTER, Frederick: 'Sources of Wesley's revision of the Prayer Book in 1784–8', *Proceedings of the Wesley Historical Society*, Vol. XXIII, 1941–42, pp. 123–33.

2.6.3.10 STOCKTON, Carl Rex: 'The origin and development of extra-liturgical worship in eighteenth-century Methodism', University of Oxford D.Phil. thesis, 1969, xii+iv+382+[42]p.

2.6.3.11 SWIFT, Wesley Frank: 'John Wesley's lectionary, with notes on some later Methodist lectionaries', *London Quarterly and Holborn Review*, Vol. CLXXXIII, 1958, pp. 298–304.

2.6.3.12 SWIFT, Wesley Frank: 'The Sunday service of the Methodists', *Proceedings of the Wesley Historical Society*, Vol. XXIX, 1953–54, pp. 12–20.

2.6.3.13 WESLEY, John: *John Wesley's Sunday service of the Methodists in North America*, with an introduction by James Floyd White, [Nashville]: Quarterly Review, 1984, 37+[109]p.

See also 2.4.1.13, 2.4.6.16, 2.4.6.17, 2.6.2.7, 4.3.3.1.

2.6.4 Hymnology and music: general works

2.6.4.1 ARNOLD, Richard Alexander: 'The English hymn in the eighteenth century: An historical and critical study', University of Edinburgh Ph.D. thesis, 1983, [5]+326p.

2.6.4.2 BENSON, Louis Fitzgerald: 'The hymnody of the Methodist revival', *Princeton Theological Review*, Vol. XI, 1913, pp. 420–60.

2.6.4.3   BIRD, Frederic Mayer: 'Charles Wesley and Methodist hymns', *Bibliotheca Sacra*, Vol. XXI, 1864, pp. 127–62, 284–318.

2.6.4.4   BUCKROYD, Elizabeth Ann: 'Hymns for children', *Proceedings of the Wesley Historical Society*, Vol. XLI, 1977–78, pp. 117–22.

2.6.4.5   CHRISTOPHERS, Samuel Woolcock: *The poets of Methodism*, London: Haughton & Co., 1875, viii+520p.

2.6.4.6   EDDY, Addie Cornwall: 'The evolution of the eighteenth-century hymn as established by Watts and the Wesleys', University of Washington Ph.D. thesis, 1919.

2.6.4.7   FINDLAY, George Hindson: *Christ's standard bearer: A study in the hymns of Charles Wesley as they are contained in the last edition (1876) of 'A collection of hymns for the use of the people called Methodists' by the Rev. John Wesley*, London: Epworth Press, 1956, 74p.

2.6.4.8   GREGORY, Arthur Stephen: 'Moravian associations of Charles Wesley's hymns', *Hymn Society of Great Britain and Ireland Bulletin*, Vol. 4, 1955–60, pp. 135–41.

2.6.4.9   GREGORY, Theophilus Stephen: 'Charles Wesley's hymns and poems', *London Quarterly and Holborn Review*, Vol. CLXXXII, 1957, pp. 253–62.

2.6.4.10   HAAS, Alfred Burton: *Charles Wesley*, Papers of the Hymn Society 22, New York: Hymn Society of America, 1957, 22p.

2.6.4.11   HOUGHTON, Edward: 'Poetry and piety in Charles Wesley's hymns', *The Hymn*, Vol. VI, 1955, pp. 77–85.

2.6.4.12   MANNING, Bernard Lord: *The hymns of Wesley and Watts: Five informal papers*, London: Epworth Press, 1942, 143p.

2.6.4.13   MARSHALL, Madeleine Forell & TODD, Janet: *English congregational hymns in the eighteenth century*, Lexington: University Press of Kentucky, 1982, 181p.

2.6.4.14   MAYER, Erika: 'Charles Wesleys Hymnen: Eine Untersuchung und literarische Würdigung', Dissertation, Eberhard-Karls-Universität Tübingen, 1957, iv+137p.

2.6.4.15   ROGAL, Samuel J.: 'John Wesley and the organ: The superfluous pipes', *Church Music* [St. Louis], No. 2, 1974, pp. 27–31.

2.6.4.16   ROGAL, Samuel J.: 'The occasional hymns of Charles Wesley', *Cresset*, Vol. 42, January 1979, pp. 8–13.

2.6.4.17   SHEPHERD, Thomas Boswell: 'The children's verse of Dr. Watts and Charles Wesley', *London Quarterly and Holborn Review*, Vol. CLXIV, 1939, pp. 173–84.

2.6.4.18   TOWNSEND, Michael Jonathan: 'The hymns of Charles Wesley: Devotional verse or congregational hymnody?', *The Methodist heritage: The Principal's Lectures, Southlands College, Spring Term 1984*, [London]: Southlands College, [1984], pp. 11–26.

2.6.4.19   TYSON, John Rodger: 'Charles Wesley and the German hymns', *The Hymn*, Vol. 35, 1984, pp. 153–8.

2.6.4.20   WELCH, Barbara Ann: 'Charles Wesley and the celebrations of evangelical experience', University of Michigan Ph.D. thesis, 1971, iii+147p.

2.6.4.21   WESLEY, Charles: *Representative verse of Charles Wesley*, selected and edited with an introduction by Frank Baker, London: Epworth Press, 1962, lxi+413p.

2.6.4.22 WESLEY, John & WESLEY, Charles: *The poetical works of John and Charles Wesley, reprinted from the originals, with the last corrections of the authors; together with the poems of Charles Wesley not before published*, collected and arranged by George Osborn, London: Wesleyan-Methodist Conference Office, 1868–72, 13 vol.

2.6.4.23 WISEMAN, Frederick Luke: 'Charles Wesley and the hymn-writers of Methodism', *A new history of Methodism*, edited by William John Townsend, Herbert Brook Workman & George Eayrs, London: Hodder and Stoughton, 1909, Vol. I, pp. 235–54.

2.6.4.24 WOOD, Alfred Harold: 'Our heritage in Charles Wesley's hymns', *Dig or die: Papers given at the World Methodist Historical Society Wesley Heritage Conference at Wesley College within the University of Sydney, 10–15 August 1980*, edited by James Stuart Udy & Eric Gerald Clancy, Sydney: World Methodist Historical Society Australasian Section, 1981, pp. 48–66.

See also 2.2.1.7, 2.2.1.9, 2.2.4.11, 2.2.16.1, 2.2.16.2, 2.2.16.4, 2.2.16.5, 2.2.16,6, 2.2.16.7, 2.2.16.9, 2.2.16.10, 2.2.16.11, 2.2.16.13, 2.2.16.14, 2.8.1.8, 2.8.5.5, 3.2.4.1.

2.6.5 Hymnology and music: doctrine

2.6.5.1 DALE, James: 'Some echoes of Charles Wesley's hymns in his journal', *London Quarterly and Holborn Review*, Vol. CLXXXIV, 1959, pp. 336–44.

2.6.5.2 DALE, James: 'The theological and literary qualities of the poetry of Charles Wesley in relation to the standards of his age', University of Cambridge Ph.D. thesis, 1960, vii+271p.

2.6.5.3 DENYER, Allen Stewart: 'The Catholic element in the hymns of Charles Wesley', University of Leeds B.D. thesis, 1943, 178p.

2.6.5.4 FROST, Brian: 'The idea of fullness in the hymns of Charles Wesley', *We belong to one another: Methodist, Anglican and Orthodox essays*, edited by Arthur Macdonald Allchin, London: Epworth Press, 1965, pp. 48–61.

2.6.5.5 FROST, Francis: 'Biblical imagery and religious experience in the hymns of the Wesleys', *Proceedings of the Wesley Historical Society*, Vol. XLII, 1979–80, pp. 158–66.

2.6.5.6 RATTENBURY, John Ernest: *The evangelical doctrines of Charles Wesley's hymns*, London: Epworth Press, 1941, 365p.

2.6.5.7 ROGAL, Samuel J.: 'Old Testament prophecy in Charles Wesley's paraphrase of scripture', *Christian Scholar's Review*, Vol. 13, 1984, pp. 205–16.

2.6.5.8 ROTH, Herbert John: 'A literary study of the Calvinistic and deistic implications in the hymns of Isaac Watts, Charles Wesley and William Cowper', Texas Christian University Ph.D. thesis, 1978, 186p.

2.6.5.9 SMITH, Timothy Lawrence, NICHOLSON, Roy Stephen &

MITCHELL, T. Crichton: 'The theology of the Wesleys' hymns', *A contemporary Wesleyan theology: Biblical, systematic and practical*, Charles Webb Carter, editor, Grand Rapids: Zondervan Publishing House, 1983, Vol. 2, pp. 1,011–42.

2.6.5.10 WRIGHT, David & WRIGHT, Jill: *Thirty hymns of the Wesleys*, Exeter: Paternoster Press, 1985, 64p.

See also 2.2.16.12, 2.4.7.5, 2.4.7.9, 2.5.6.10, 2.5.6.13, 2.5.7.2, 2.5.7.26, 2.5.7.45, 2.6.2.8, 2.6.2.13, 2.6.2.18, 2.6.2.20, 2.6.2.24.

2.6.6 Hymnology and music: structure and language

2.6.6.1 BAKER, Frank: *Charles Wesley's verse: An introduction*, London: Epworth Press, 1964, [9]+110p.

2.6.6.2 BECKERLEGGE, Oliver Aveyard: 'An attempt at a classification of Charles Wesley's metres: A contribution to the study of English prosody', *London Quarterly and Holborn Review*, Vol. CLXIX, 1944, pp. 219–27.

2.6.6.3 BECKERLEGGE, Oliver Aveyard: 'Charles Wesley's vocabulary', *London Quarterly and Holborn Review*, Vol. CXCIII, 1968, pp. 152–61.

2.6.6.4 BECKERLEGGE, Oliver Aveyard: 'The metres of Charles Wesley's hymns', *Methodist Church Music Society Bulletin*, Vol. 2, 1974–77, pp. 36–44.

2.6.6.5 BETT, Henry: *The hymns of Methodism*, third edition, revised, recast and greatly enlarged, London: Epworth Press, 1945, 172p.

2.6.6.6 BETT, Henry: 'Some latinisms in the Wesleys' hymns', *London Quarterly and Holborn Review*, Vol. CLXIII, 1938, pp. 308–19.

2.6.6.7 CAPEY, A. C.: 'Charles Wesley and his literary relations', *The Gadfly* [Retford], Vol. 6, 1983, pp. 17–26.

2.6.6.8 CROMPTON, David Jones: 'The development of the language of eighteenth-century hymnody in the work of Isaac Watts and the Wesley brothers', University of Liverpool M.A. thesis, 1967, iv+366+xviiip.

2.6.6.9 DAVIE, Donald: 'The classicism of Charles Wesley', *Purity of diction in English verse*, London: Chatto & Windus, 1952, pp. 70–81.

2.6.6.10 ELLINGWORTH, Paul: ' "I" and "we" in Charles Wesley's hymns', *London Quarterly and Holborn Review*, Vol. CLXXXVIII, 1963, pp. 153–64.

2.6.6.11 FINDLAY, George Hindson: 'First and last words: A study of some Wesley metres', *London Quarterly and Holborn Review*, Vol. CLXXVII, 1952, pp. 123–8.

2.6.6.12 FINDLAY, George Hindson: 'A study in Wesley six-eights', *London Quarterly and Holborn Review*, Vol. CLXXX, 1955, pp. 138–42.

2.6.6.13 FLEW, Robert Newton: *The hymns of Charles Wesley: A study of their structure*, Wesley Historical Society Lectures No. 19, London: Epworth Press, 1953, 79p.

2.6.6.14 HODGSON, Elsie Marjorie: 'Poetry in the hymns of John and

Charles Wesley', *Proceedings of the Wesley Historical Society*, Vol. XXXVIII, 1971–72, pp. 131–5, 161–5.

2.6.6.15 HODGSON, Elsie Marjorie: 'The poetry of John and Charles Wesley, with special reference to their hymns', University of London Ph.D. thesis, 1970, a–e + viii + 478p.

2.6.6.16 MORRIS, Gilbert Leslie: 'Imagery in the hymns of Charles Wesley', University of Arkansas Ph.D. thesis, 1969, 433p.

2.6.6.17 NOLL, Mark Allan: 'Romanticism and the hymns of Charles Wesley', *Evangelical Quarterly*, Vol. XLVI, 1974, pp. 195–223.

2.6.6.18 WILLIAMSON, Karina: 'The English hymn in the eighteenth century: A study of its poetic quality', University of Oxford B.Litt. thesis, 1955, v + 154p.

See also 2.2.11.8, 2.2.12.14, 2.2.16.3, 2.2.16.8, 2.6.5.2, 2.6.5.5, 2.8.5.4.

2.6.7 Hymnology and music: tunes

2.6.7.1 ADAMS, Nelson Falls: 'The musical sources for John Wesley's tune-books: The genealogy of 148 tunes', Union Theological Seminary in the City of New York S.M.D. thesis, 1973, 614p.

2.6.7.2 FROST, Maurice: 'The tunes associated with hymn singing in the lifetime of the Wesleys', *Hymn Society of Great Britain and Ireland Bulletin*, Vol. 4, 1955–60, pp. 118–26.

2.6.7.3 JOHNSON, Ronald Ernest Charles: *The tunes of John Wesley's hymns from the German*, Edinburgh: [the author], 1976, 23p.

2.6.7.4 LIGHTWOOD, James Thomas: *Methodist music in the eighteenth century*, London: Epworth Press, 1927, 56p.

2.6.7.5 STEVENSON, Robert: 'The eighteenth-century hymn tune', *English hymnology in the eighteenth century: Papers read at a Clark Library Seminar, 5 March 1977*, Los Angeles: William Andrews Clark Memorial Library, University of California, Los Angeles, 1980, pp. 21–66.

2.6.7.6 WESTBROOK, Francis Brotherton: *Some early Methodist tune books*, Wesley Historical Society Lecture 1974, Penzance: printed by Headland Printing Company, [1975], 24p.

2.6.8 Class meetings and membership

2.6.8.1 DEAN, William Walter: 'Disciplined fellowship: The rise and decline of cell groups in British Methodism', University of Iowa Ph.D. thesis, 1985, vi + 567p.

2.6.8.2 MACKENZIE, Peter Donald: 'The Methodist class meeting: A historical study', University of St. Andrews M.Th. thesis, 1969, [5] + 126 + vip.

2.6.8.3 VERNEY, John Henry: 'Early Wesleyan class tickets: Comments and catalogue', *Proceedings of the Wesley Historical Society*, Vol. XXXI, 1957–58, pp. 2–9, 34–8, 70–3.

2.6.8.4 WATSON, David Lowes: *The early Methodist class meeting: Its origin and significance*, Nashville: Discipleship Resources, 1985, xiii + 273p.

See also 3.1.2.12, 3.4.1.11.

2.7 Polity and Mission

2.7.1 Conference

2.7.1.1 DOUGHTY, William Lamplough: *John Wesley: His conferences and his preachers*, Wesley Historical Society Lecture No. 10, London: Epworth Press, 1944, 79p.

2.7.1.2 SIMON, John Smith: 'John Wesley's "Deed of declaration" ', *Proceedings of the Wesley Historical Society*, Vol. XII, 1919–20, pp. 81–93.

2.7.1.3 SWIFT, Wesley Frank: 'The "Minutes of conference" ', *Proceedings of the Wesley Historical Society*, Vol. XXXI, 1957–58, pp. 155–60.

2.7.1.4 WEARMOUTH, Robert Featherstone: 'The first Methodist conference, June 25–30, 1744', *London Quarterly and Holborn Review*, Vol. CLXIX, 1944, pp. 205–10.

2.7.2 Itinerant and ordained ministry

2.7.2.1 ATMORE, Charles: *The Methodist memorial; being an impartial sketch of the lives and characters of the preachers who have departed this life since the commencement of the work of God among the people called Methodists late in connection with the Rev. John Wesley deceased, drawn from the most authentic sources and disposed in alphabetical order, introduced with a brief account of the state of religion from the earliest ages and a concise history of Methodism, to which is added a chronological list of the preachers who are now engaged in the same work*, Bristol: printed by Richard Edwards, 1801, 582p.

2.7.2.2 BETT, Henry: 'The alleged illiteracy of the early Methodist preachers', *Proceedings of the Wesley Historical Society*, Vol. XV, 1925–26, pp. 85–92.

2.7.2.3 BETT, Henry: *The early Methodist preachers*, Wesley Historical Society Lectures No. 1, London: Epworth Press, 1935, 48p.

2.7.2.4 CHANDLER, Douglas Robson: 'John Wesley and his preachers', *Religion in Life*, Vol. XXIV, 1954–55, pp. 241–8.

2.7.2.5 CHURCH, Leslie Frederic: 'The call to preach in early Methodism', *London Quarterly and Holborn Review*, Vol. CLXXIX, 1954, pp. 185–91.

2.7.2.6 DURBIN, Linda M.: 'The nature of ordination in Wesley's view of the ministry', *Methodist History*, Vol. IX, No. 3, April 1971, pp. 3–20.

2.7.2.7 ENGLISH, John Cammel: 'John Wesley and the principle of ministerial succession', *Methodist History*, Vol. II, No. 2, January 1964, pp. 31–6.

2.7.2.8 GARLICK, Kenneth Benjamin: *Mr. Wesley's preachers: An alphabetical arrangement of Wesleyan Methodist preachers and missionaries and the stations to which they were appointed, 1739–1818*, London: Pinhorns for the World Methodist Historical Society (British Section), 1977, [2]+54p.

2.7.2.9 GEORGE, Alfred Raymond: 'Ordination', *A history of the Methodist Church in Great Britain*, Vol. 2, general editors: Rupert Eric Davies, Alfred Raymond George & Ernest Gordon Rupp, London: Epworth Press, 1978, pp. 143–60.

2.7.2.10 GEORGE, Alfred Raymond: 'Ordination in Methodism', *London Quarterly and Holborn Review*, Vol. CLXXVI, 1951, pp. 156–69.

2.7.2.11 GEORGE, Alfred Raymond: 'Wesley and Coke', *Proceedings of the Wesley Historical Society*, Vol. XXXI, 1957–58, pp. 27–31.

2.7.2.12 LAWSON, Albert Brown: *John Wesley and the Christian ministry: The sources and development of his opinions and practice*, London: SPCK, 1963, x+210p.

2.7.2.13 *The lives of early Methodist preachers, chiefly written by themselves*, edited, with an introductory essay, by Thomas Jackson, third edition, with additional lives, London: Wesleyan Conference Office, 1865–66, 6 vol.

2.7.2.14 NUELSEN, John Louis: *Die Ordination im Methodismus: Ein Beitrag zur Entstehungsgeschichte der kirchlichen Selbständigkeit der Methodistenkirche*, Bremen: Verlagshaus der Methodistenkirche, 1935, 191p.

2.7.2.15 NYGREN, Ellis Herbert: 'John Wesley's changing concept of the ministry', *Religion in Life*, Vol. XXXI, 1961–62, pp. 264–74.

2.7.2.16 NYGREN, Ellis Herbert: 'John Wesley's interpretation of Christian ordination', New York University Ph.D. thesis, 1960, 265p.

2.7.2.17 PLATT, Frederic: 'Wesley's "ordinations": A retrospect', *London Quarterly and Holborn Review*, Vol. CLX, 1935, pp. 63–73.

2.7.2.18 RIVERS, Isabel: ' "Strangers and pilgrims": Sources and patterns of Methodist narrative', *Augustan worlds: Essays in honour of A. R. Humphreys*, edited by J. C. Hilson, M. Monica B. Jones & John Richard Watson, Leicester: Leicester University Press, 1978, pp. 189–203.

2.7.2.19 SACKETT, Alfred Barrett: 'John Wesley and the Greek Orthodox bishop', *Proceedings of the Wesley Historical Society*, Vol. XXXVIII, 1971–72, pp. 81–7, 97–102.

2.7.2.20 SCORE, John Nelson Russell: 'A study of the concept of the ministry in the thought of John Wesley', Duke University Ph.D. thesis, 1963, xi+375p.

2.7.2.21 SHIPLEY, David Clark: 'The ministry in Methodism in the eighteenth century', *The ministry in the Methodist heritage*, edited by Gerald O. McCulloh, Nashville: Department of Ministerial Education, Division of Educational Institutions, Board of Education, The Methodist Church, 1960, pp. 11–31.

2.7.2.22 SIMON, John Smith: 'Wesley's ordinations', *Proceedings of the Wesley Historical Society*, Vol. IX, 1913–14, pp. 145–54.

2.7.2.23 THOMPSON, Edgar Wesley: 'Episcopacy: John Wesley's view', *London Quarterly and Holborn Review*, Vol. CLXXXI, 1956, pp. 113–17.

2.7.2.24 THOMPSON, Edgar Wesley: 'John Wesley, superintendent', *London Quarterly and Holborn Review*, Vol. CLXXXIV, 1959, pp. 325–30.

2.7.2.25 THOMPSON, Edgar Wesley: *Wesley, apostolic man: Some reflections on Wesley's consecration of Dr. Thomas Coke*, London: Epworth Press, 1957, 84p.

2.7.2.26 TSOUMAS, George J.: 'A critical evaluation of John Wesley's ordinations from a Greek Orthodox viewpoint', Boston University Ph.D. thesis, 1953.

2.7.2.27 TSOUMAS, George J.: 'Methodism and Bishop Erasmus', *Greek Orthodox Theological Review*, Vol. II, No. 2, Christmas 1956, pp. 62–73.

2.7.2.28 VINE, Victor Edward: 'Wesley, King and Coke', *Proceedings of the Wesley Historical Society*, Vol. XXXI, 1957–58, pp. 65–70.

See also 2.6.1.6, 2.7.1.1, 4.4.2.5.

2.7.3 Lay ministry

2.7.3.1 BAKER, Frank: 'Thomas Maxfield's first sermon', *Proceedings of the Wesley Historical Society*, Vol. XXVII, 1949–50, pp. 7–15.

2.7.3.2 BOWMER, John Coates: 'The local preacher in early Methodism', *The preacher's handbook*, No. 8, edited by David Noel Francis, London: Epworth Press, 1963, pp. 1–14.

2.7.3.3 BROWN, Earl Kent: 'Feminist theology and the women of Mr. Wesley's Methodism', *Wesleyan theology today: A bicentennial theological consultation*, edited by Theodore Runyon, Nashville: Kingswood Books, 1985, pp. 143–50.

2.7.3.4 BROWN, Earl Kent: *Women of Mr. Wesley's Methodism*, New York: Edwin Mellen Press, 1983, xvii+261p.

2.7.3.5 BROWN, Earl Kent: 'Women of the word: Selected leadership roles of women in Mr. Wesley's Methodism', *Women in new worlds*, edited by Hilah Frances Thomas & Rosemary Skinner Keller, Nashville: Abingdon, 1981, pp. 69–87.

2.7.3.6 CHILCOTE, Paul Wesley: 'John Wesley and the women preachers of early Methodism', Duke University Ph.D. thesis, 1984, x+454p.

2.7.3.7 CHILCOTE, Paul Wesley: 'The women pioneers of early Methodism', *Wesleyan theology today: A bicentennial theological consultation*, edited by Theodore Runyon, Nashville: Kingswood Books, 1985, pp. 180–4.

2.7.3.8 COOMER, Duncan: 'The local preachers in early Methodism', *Proceedings of the Wesley Historical Society*, Vol. XXV, 1945–46, pp. 33–42.

2.7.3.9 FUNK, Theophil: *Die Anfänge der Laienmitarbeit im Methodismus*, Bremen: Anker-Verlag, 1941, viii+255p.

2.7.3.10 GARLOW, James Lester: 'John Wesley's understanding of the laity as demonstrated by his use of the lay preachers', Drew University Ph.D. thesis, 1979, iv+355p.

2.7.3.11 WILDER, James Simpson: 'The early Methodist lay preachers and their contribution to the eighteenth-century revival in England', University of Edinburgh Ph.D. thesis, 1948, xv+409p.

See also 2.1.5.4.

2.7.4 Buildings and finance

2.7.4.1 CUMBERLAND, Albert George: 'The Toleration Act of 1689 and freedom for Protestant Nonconformists, 1660–1830', University of London Ph.D. thesis, 1957, 352p.

2.7.4.2 DOLBEY, George William: *The architectural expression of Methodism: The first hundred years*, London: Epworth Press, 1964, x+195p.

2.7.4.3 SHAW, Thomas: 'The Methodist chapel interior (1739–1839) in relation to contemporary church arrangement', *Proceedings of the Wesley Historical Society*, Vol. XXXII, 1959–60, pp. 53–8.

See also 4.4.4.1.

2.8 Social Aspects

2.8.1 Political impact

2.8.1.1 ALDERFER, Owen H.: 'British evangelical response to the American Revolution: The Wesleyans', *Fides et Historia*, Vol. 8, No. 2, Fall 1976, pp. 7–34.

2.8.1.2 ANDREWS, Stuart: 'John Wesley and America', *History Today*, Vol. XXVI, 1976, pp. 353–9.

2.8.1.3 BAKER, Donald S.: 'Charles Wesley and the American loyalists', *Proceedings of the Wesley Historical Society*, Vol. XXXV, 1965–66, pp. 5–9.

2.8.1.4 BAKER, Donald S.: 'Charles Wesley and the American War of Independence', *Proceedings of the Wesley Historical Society*, Vol. XXXIV, 1963–64, pp. 159–64.

2.8.1.5 BAKER, Donald S.: 'Charles Wesley and the American War of Independence', *Methodist History*, Vol. V, No. 1, October 1966, pp. 5–37.

2.8.1.6 BAKER, Donald S.: 'Charles Wesley and the American War of Independence', *Proceedings of the Wesley Historical Society*, Vol. XL, 1975–76, pp. 125–34, 165–82.

2.8.1.7 BAKER, Donald S.: 'Patriots and Howe!', *Contemporary Review*, Vol. CCXXX, January–June 1977, pp. 15–23.

2.8.1.8 BAKER, Donald S.: 'Wesley's hymns on patriotism', University of Birmingham M.A. thesis, 1959, 2 vol.

2.8.1.9 BAKER, Frank: 'Methodism and the '45 rebellion', *London Quarterly and Holborn Review*, Vol. CLXXII, 1947, pp. 325–33.

2.8.1.10   BAKER, Frank: 'The shaping of Wesley's "Calm address"', *Methodist History*, Vol. XIV, 1975–76, pp. 3–12.

2.8.1.11   BECKERLEGGE, Oliver Aveyard: 'Charles Wesley's politics', *London Quarterly and Holborn Review*, Vol. CLXXXII, 1957, pp. 280–91.

2.8.1.12   COPPLESTONE, John Tremayne: 'John Wesley and the American Revolution', *Religion in Life*, Vol. XLV, 1976, pp. 89–105.

2.8.1.13   EDWARDS, Maldwyn Lloyd: 'The political views and influence of John Wesley', University of Wales (Bangor) M.A. thesis, 1927, 217p.

2.8.1.14   GERDES, Egon Walter: 'John Wesley's attitude toward war: A study of the historical formation, the theological determination and the practical manifestation of John Wesley's attitude toward war and its place in Methodism', Emory University Ph.D. thesis, 1960, 192p.

2.8.1.15   HARVEY, Marvin Ellis: 'The Wesleyan movement and the American Revolution', University of Washington Ph.D. thesis, 1962, [6]+ iii+401p.

2.8.1.16   HOLLAND, Lynwood Mathis: 'John Wesley and the American Revolution', *Journal of Church and State*, Vol. V, 1963, pp. 199–213.

2.8.1.17   HOLLAND, Lynwood Mathis & HOWELL, Ronald F.: 'John Wesley's concept of religious and political authority', *Journal of Church and State*, Vol. VI, 1964, pp. 296–313.

2.8.1.18   HOSMAN, Glenn Burton: 'The problem of Church and state in the thought of John Wesley as reflecting his understanding of providence and his view of history', Drew University Ph.D. thesis, 1970, v+417p.

2.8.1.19   HYNSON, Leon Orville: 'Church and state in the thought and life of John Wesley', University of Iowa Ph.D. thesis, 1971, iv+334p.

2.8.1.20   HYNSON, Leon Orville: 'Human liberty as divine right: A study in the political maturation of John Wesley', *Journal of Church and State*, Vol. 25, 1983, pp. 57–85.

2.8.1.21   HYNSON, Leon Orville: 'Implications of Wesley's ethical method and political thought', *Wesleyan theology today: A bicentennial theological consultation*, edited by Theodore Runyon, Nashville: Kingswood Books, 1985, pp. 373–88.

2.8.1.22   HYNSON, Leon Orville: 'John Wesley and political reality', *Methodist History*, Vol. XII, No. 1, October 1973, pp. 37–42.

2.8.1.23   HYNSON, Leon Orville: 'John Wesley's concept of liberty of conscience', *Wesleyan Theological Journal*, Vol. 7, Spring 1972, pp. 36–46.

2.8.1.24   HYNSON, Leon Orville: 'War, the state and the Christian citizen in Wesley's thought', *Religion in Life*, Vol. XLV, 1976, pp. 204–19.

2.8.1.25   KAPP, John Ruse: 'John Wesley's idea of authority in the state', Boston University Ph.D. thesis, 1938, vi+262p.

2.8.1.26   KENT, John Henry Somerset: 'Methodism and revolution', *Methodist History*, Vol. XII, No. 4, July 1974, pp. 136–44.

2.8.1.27   KIRKHAM, Donald Henry: 'John Wesley's "Calm address": The response of the critics', *Methodist History*, Vol. XIV, 1975–76, pp. 13–23.

2.8.1.28   LA GORCE, Agnès de: 'Le réformateur Wesley et la monarchie anglaise', *Revue Universelle*, Tome LXXVIII, 1939, pp. 449–60.

2.8.1.29   LEE, Peter A.: 'The political ethics of John Wesley', Yale University Ph.D. thesis, 1940, 211p.

2.8.1.30   LYLES, Albert Marion: 'The hostile reaction to the American views of Johnson and Wesley', *Journal of the Rutgers University Library*, Vol. XXIV, December 1960, pp. 1–13.

2.8.1.31   MADRON, Thomas William: 'The political thought of John Wesley', Tulane University Ph.D. thesis, 1965, xi+253p.

2.8.1.32   MORGAN, David Taft: ' "The dupes of designing men": John Wesley and the American Revolution', *Historical Magazine of the Protestant Episcopal Church*, Vol. XLIV, 1975, pp. 121–31.

2.8.1.33   RAYMOND, Allan: ' "I fear God and honour the King": John Wesley and the American Revolution', *Church History*, Vol. 45, 1976, pp. 316–28.

2.8.1.34   ROGAL, Samuel J.: 'John Wesley on war and peace', *Studies in Eighteenth-Century Culture*, Vol. 7, 1978, pp. 329–44.

2.8.1.35   SIL, Narasingha Prosad: 'Influence of Methodism on the English working class, 1740–1819', *Quarterly Review of Historical Studies*, Vol. XIV, 1974–75, pp. 19–34.

2.8.1.36   SWEET, William Warren: 'John Wesley, Tory', *Methodist Quarterly Review*, Vol. LXXI, 1922, pp. 255–68.

2.8.1.37   WALLACE, Willard Mosher: 'John Wesley and the American Revolution', *Essays in honor of Conyers Read*, edited by Norton Downs, Chicago: University of Chicago Press, 1953, pp. 52–64, 274–6.

2.8.1.38   WESLEY, Charles: *The American war under the conduct of Sir William Howe*, edited, with an introduction & notes, by Donald S. Baker, London: Keepsake Press, 1975, 37p.

See also 2.2.17.5, 2.4.1.12, 2.4.8.6, 2.8.2.4, 2.8.2.7, 2.8.2.8, 2.8.2.17, 2.8.2.23, 2.8.2.28, 2.8.2.30, 2.8.2.34, 2.9.2.2, 2.9.5.8, 4.5.1.9, 4.5.1.18.

2.8.2 Social witness

2.8.2.1   BAKER, Frank: 'The origins, character and influence of John Wesley's "Thoughts upon slavery" ', *Methodist History*, Vol. XXII, 1983–84, pp. 75–86.

2.8.2.2   BLACK, Robert Edwin: 'The social dimensions of John Wesley's ministry as related to his personal piety', Union Theological Seminary in Virginia Ph.D. thesis, 1984, iii+197p.

2.8.2.3   BREADY, John Wesley: *England – before and after Wesley: The evangelical revival and social reform*, London: Hodder and Stoughton, 1938, 463p.

2.8.2.4   BRENDLINGER, Irv A.: 'A study of the views of major eighteenth-century evangelicals on slavery and race, with special reference to

John Wesley', University of Edinburgh Ph.D. thesis, 1982, [9] + xv + 410p.

2.8.2.5 BRIGDEN, Thomas Edwin: 'Wesley on the ethics of dress', *Wesleyan Methodist Magazine*, Vol. CXXVII, 1904, pp. 41–5, 128–34, 190–5.

2.8.2.6 BURNETT, Ivan Blackwell: 'Methodist origins: John Wesley and alcohol', *Methodist History*, Vol. XIII, No. 4, July 1975, pp. 3–17.

2.8.2.7 COOPER, Allen Lamar: 'John Wesley: A study in theology and social ethics', Columbia University Ph.D. thesis, 1962, vi + 251p.

2.8.2.8 EDWARDS, Maldwyn Lloyd: *John Wesley and the eighteenth century: A study of his social and political influence*, revised edition, London: Epworth Press, 1955, 207p.

2.8.2.9 ELLIOTT, Charles Middleton: 'The ideology of economic growth: A case study', *Land, labour and population in the industrial revolution: Essays presented to J. D. Chambers*, edited by Eric Lionel Jones & Gordon Edmund Mingay, London: Edward Arnold, 1967, pp. 75–99.

2.8.2.10 FLACHSMEIER, Horst Reinhold: 'John Wesley als Sozialhygieniker und Arzt', Dissertation zur Erlangung des Grades eines Doktors der Medizin, Hygienisches Institut der Freien- und Hansestadt Hamburg, 1957, [3] + 91p.

2.8.2.11 FORKEL, Frederick William: 'John Wesley's ethics and the rise of capitalism', Lutheran Theological Seminary, Gettysburg S.T.M. thesis, 1950, 121p.

2.8.2.12 HAYWOOD, Clarence Robert: 'Was John Wesley a political economist?', *Church History*, Vol. XXXIII, 1964, pp. 314–21.

2.8.2.13 HOFFMAN, Thomas G.: 'The moral philosophy of John Wesley: The development and nature of his moral dynamic', Temple University Ph.D. thesis, 1968, xv + 262p.

2.8.2.14 HYNSON, Leon Orville: 'Christian love: The key to Wesley's ethics', *Methodist History*, Vol. XIV, 1975–76, pp. 44–55.

2.8.2.15 HYNSON, Leon Orville: 'Evangelism and social ethics in Wesley's theology', *AME Zion Quarterly Review*, Vol. 93, No. 2, July 1981, pp. 2–18.

2.8.2.16 HYNSON, Leon Orville: *To reform the nation: Theological foundations of Wesley's ethics*, Grand Rapids: Francis Asbury Press, 1984, 176p.

2.8.2.17 KINGDON, Robert Maccune: 'Laissez-faire or government control: A problem for John Wesley', *Church History*, Vol. XXVI, 1957, pp. 342–54.

2.8.2.18 KISHIDA, Yuki: 'John Wesley's ethics and Max Weber', *Japanese contributions to the study of John Wesley*, edited by Clifford Walter Edwards, Macon: Wesleyan College, 1967, pp. 39–54 and *Wesleyan Quarterly Review*, Vol. 4, 1967, pp. 43–58.

2.8.2.19 KISHIDA, Yuki: *Jon Uezuri kenkyū*, Kyoto: Minerva, 1977, xvi + 379p.

2.8.2.20 MACARTHUR, Kathleen Walker: *The economic ethics of John Wesley*, New York: Abingdon Press, 1936, 166p.

2.8.2.21 McNULTY, Frank John: 'The moral teaching of John Wesley', Catholic University of America S.T.D. thesis, 1963, vii + 148p.

2.8.2.22 MADRON, Thomas William: 'John Wesley on economics', *Sanctification & liberation: Liberation theologies in light of the Wesleyan tradition*, edited by Theodore Runyon, Nashville: Abingdon, 1981, pp. 102–15.

2.8.2.23 MADRON, Thomas William: 'John Wesley on race: A Christian view of equality', *Methodist History*, Vol. II, No. 4, July 1964, pp. 24–34.

2.8.2.24 MADRON, Thomas William: 'Some economic aspects of John Wesley's thought revisited', *Methodist History*, Vol. IV, No. 1, October 1965, pp. 33–45.

2.8.2.25 MARQUARDT, Manfred: *Praxis und Prinzipien der Sozialethik John Wesleys*, Göttingen: Vandenhoeck & Ruprecht, 1977, 176p.

2.8.2.26 MERCER, Jerry Lee: 'Counterforce: A review of Wesley's ethics', *Christian ethics: An inquiry into Christian ethics from a biblical theological perspective*, edited by Leon Orville Hynson & Lane Austin Scott, Anderson: Warner Press, 1983, pp. 77–95.

2.8.2.27 NORTH, Eric McCoy: *Early Methodist philanthropy*, New York: Methodist Book Concern, 1914, viii+181p.

2.8.2.28 PHIPPS, William E.: 'John Wesley on slavery', *Quarterly Review: A Scholarly Journal for Reflection on Ministry*, Vol. 1, No. 3, Summer 1981, pp. 23–31.

2.8.2.29 ROGAL, Samuel J.: 'John Wesley and the attack on luxury in England', *Eighteenth-Century Life*, Vol. 3, 1976–77, pp. 91–4.

2.8.2.30 ROGAL, Samuel J.: 'John Wesley's role in the abolition of slavery and the slave trade', *Evangelical Journal*, Vol. 3, 1985, pp. 21–36.

2.8.2.31 SCHNEEBERGER, Vilém D.: *Theologische Wurzeln des sozialen Akzents bei John Wesley*, Zürich: Gotthelf Verlag, 1974, 191p.

2.8.2.32 SOMMER, Johann Wilhelm Ernst: *John Wesley und die soziale Frage: Eine Quellenstudie*, Bremen: Verlagshaus der Methodistenkirche, 1930, 55p.

2.8.2.33 THOMPSON, David Decamp: *John Wesley as a social reformer*, New York: Eaton & Mains, 1898, 111p.

2.8.2.34 WARNER, Wellman Joel: *The Wesleyan movement in the industrial revolution*, London: Longmans, Green and Co., 1930, x+299p.

See also 2.2.17.5, 2.4.1.12, 2.4.8.3, 2.4.8.6, 2.5.1.7, 2.5.2.6, 2.5.3.15, 2.5.3.17, 2.5.3.18, 2.8.1.21.

2.8.3 Educational work

2.8.3.1 BODY, Alfred Harris: *John Wesley and education*, London: Epworth Press, 1936, 168p.

2.8.3.2 EDGAR, Frederick Russell: 'A study of John Wesley from the point of view of the educational methodology used by him in fostering the Wesleyan revival in England', Columbia University Ph.D. thesis, 1952, 171p.

2.8.3.3 GROSS, John Owen: *John Wesley, Christian educator*, Nashville: Board of Education, The Methodist Church, [1954], 30p.

2.8.3.4 HENDERSON, David Michael: 'John Wesley's instructional groups', Indiana University Ph.D. thesis, 1980, vii+260p.

2.8.3.5 HUNT, Raymond Fletcher: 'John Wesley as spiritual director', Northwestern University M.A. thesis, 1967.

2.8.3.6 McQUAID, Ina Debord: *Miss Hannah Ball, a lady of High Wycombe*, New York: Vantage Press, 1964, 160p.

2.8.3.7 MORTON, A. W.: 'The contribution of the evangelical revival to the philosophy and practice of education', University of Oxford D.Phil. thesis, 1949, 3 vol.

2.8.3.8 PRINCE, John Wesley: *Wesley on religious education: A study of John Wesley's theories and methods of the education of children in religion*, New York: Methodist Book Concern, 1926, 164p.

2.8.3.9 ROGAL, Samuel J.: 'Kingswood School: John Wesley's educational experiment', *Illinois Quarterly*, Vol. 40, Summer 1978, pp. 5–16.

2.8.3.10 SANGSTER, Paul Edwin: *Pity my simplicity: The evangelical revival and the religious education of children, 1738–1800*, London: Epworth Press, 1963, 200p.

2.8.3.11 TOWNS, Elmer L.: 'John Wesley and religious education', *Religious Education*, Vol. LXV, 1970, pp. 318–28.

See also 2.1.2.3, 2.2.17.13.

2.8.4 Contribution to science and medicine

2.8.4.1 ANDREWS, Stuart: 'John Wesley and the Age of Reason', *History Today*, Vol. XIX, 1969, pp. 25–32.

2.8.4.2 BARAGAR, Charles Arthur: 'John Wesley and medicine', *Annals of Medical History*, Vol. X, 1928, pp. 59–65.

2.8.4.3 BARDELL, Eunice Bonow: ' "Primitive physick": John Wesley's receipts', *Pharmacy in History*, Vol. 21, 1979, pp. 111–21.

2.8.4.4 BOWMER, John Coates: 'John Wesley's philosophy of suffering', *London Quarterly and Holborn Review*, Vol. CLXXXIV, 1959, pp. 60–6.

2.8.4.5 CALLAWAY, Clifford Wayne: 'John Wesley's "Primitive physick": An essay in appreciation', *Mayo Clinic Proceedings*, Vol. 49, 1974, pp. 318–24.

2.8.4.6 COLLIER, Frank Wilbur: *John Wesley among the scientists*, New York: Abingdon Press, 1928, 351p.

2.8.4.7 DOCK, George: 'The "Primitive physic" of Rev. John Wesley: A picture of eighteenth-century medicine', *Journal of the American Medical Association*, Vol. LXIV, January–June 1915, pp. 629–38.

2.8.4.8 HARGITT, Charles Wesley: 'John Wesley and science: A challenge from the eighteenth century', *Methodist Review*, Vol. CX, 1927, pp. 383–93.

2.8.4.9 HILL, Alfred Wesley: *John Wesley among the physicians: A study of eighteenth-century medicine*, Wesley Historical [Society] Lecture No. 24, London: Epworth Press, 1958, viii+135p.

2.8.4.10 HILL, Alfred Wesley: 'Was John Wesley a Methodist?', *Proceedings of the Wesley Historical Society*, Vol. XXX, 1955–56, pp. 82–5.

2.8.4.11 OTT, Philip Wesley: 'John Wesley on health: A word for sensible regimen', *Methodist History*, Vol. XVIII, 1979–80, pp. 193–204.

2.8.4.12 PELLOWE, William Charles Smithson: 'Wesley's use of science', *Methodist Review*, Vol. CX, 1927, pp. 394–403.

2.8.4.13 RACK, Henry Derman: 'Doctors, demons and early Methodist healing', *The Church and healing: Papers read at the twentieth summer meeting and the twenty-first winter meeting of the Ecclesiastical History Society*, edited by William J. Sheils, Studies in Church History 19, Oxford: Basil Blackwell, 1982, pp. 137–52.

2.8.4.14 ROGAL, Samuel J.: 'Pills for the poor: John Wesley's "Primitive physick"', *Yale Journal of Biology and Medicine*, Vol. 51, 1978, pp. 81–90.

2.8.4.15 ROUSSEAU, George Sebastian: 'John Wesley's "Primitive physic" (1747)', *Harvard Library Bulletin*, Vol. XVI, 1968, pp. 242–56.

2.8.4.16 SCHILLER, Francis: 'Reverend Wesley, Doctor Marat and their electric fire', *Clio Medica*, Vol. 15, 1980–81, pp. 159–76.

2.8.4.17 SCHOFIELD, Robert Edwin: 'John Wesley and science in 18th-century England', *Isis*, Vol. 44, 1953, pp. 331–40.

2.8.4.18 STEWART, David: 'John Wesley, the physician', *Wesleyan Theological Journal*, Vol. 4, Spring 1969, pp. 27–38.

2.8.4.19 SYDENHAM, Frederick Reginald: 'The healing miracles of Wesley', *Quarterly Review of the Churches' Fellowship for Psychical and Spiritual Studies*, No. 100, Summer 1979, pp. 6–10, No. 101, Autumn 1979, pp. 8–12.

2.8.4.20 TURRELL, Walter John: *John Wesley, physician & electrotherapist*, Oxford: Basil Blackwell, 1938, 24p.

2.8.4.21 WEINSTEIN, Alfred Abraham: 'John Wesley, physician and apothecary', *Georgia Review*, Vol. X, 1956, pp. 48–54.

2.8.4.22 WESLEY, John: *Primitive physic*, with an introduction by Alfred Wesley Hill, London: Epworth Press, 1960, 127p.

2.8.4.23 WILCOXON, C. D.: 'The whole man: A study of John Wesley's healing ministry', *Religion in Life*, Vol. XXVIII, 1958–59, pp. 580–6.

2.8.4.24 WILDER, Franklin: *The remarkable world of John Wesley, pioneer in mental health*, Hicksville: Exposition Press, 1978, 192p.

See also 2.4.8.3, 2.8.2.10.

2.8.5 Literary and cultural influence

2.8.5.1 BELSHAW, Harry: 'The influence of John Wesley on Dr. Johnson's religion', *London Quarterly and Holborn Review*, Vol. CLXVIII, 1943, pp. 226–34.

2.8.5.2 BOWMER, John Coates: 'Dr. Johnson and John Wesley', *New Rambler*, Vol. C.VIII, January 1970, pp. 12–25.

2.8.5.3 BRANTLEY, Richard Estes: 'Johnson's Wesleyan connection', *Eighteenth-Century Studies*, Vol. 10, 1976–77, pp. 143–68.

2.8.5.4 BURROWS, Richard Frederick: 'Divided men: A study of puritan and early evangelical literary attitudes in the work of Milton,

Bunyan, Watts and the Wesleys', University of Exeter M.Phil. thesis, 1983, 262p.

2.8.5.5 ENGLAND, Martha Winburn: 'Blake and the hymns of Charles Wesley', *Bulletin of the New York Public Library*, Vol. 70, 1966, pp. 7–26, 93–112, 153–68, 251–64.

2.8.5.6 FRANZ, Rolaine Marie: 'All the ship's company: A Wesleyan paradigm for the poetry of Christopher Smart, William Cowper and William Blake', Brown University Ph.D. thesis, 1978, v + 262p.

2.8.5.7 GILL, Frederick Cyril: *The romantic movement and Methodism: A study of English romanticism and the evangelical revival*, London: Epworth Press, 1937, 189p.

2.8.5.8 HORN, Wilhelm: 'Der Methodismus und die romantische Dichtung', *Anglia*, Beiblatt Band XXIX, 1918, pp. 202–12.

2.8.5.9 KAMM, Otto Friedrich: *John Wesley und die englische Romantik*, Marburg-Lahn: Hermann Bauer, 1939, iv + 55p.

2.8.5.10 McELLHENNEY, John Galen: 'John Wesley and Samuel Johnson: A tale of three coincidences', *Methodist History*, Vol. XXI, 1982–83, pp. 143–55.

2.8.5.11 McGOVERN, Terrence Xavier: 'The Methodist revival and the British stage', University of Georgia Ph.D. thesis, 1978, 408p.

2.8.5.12 SHEPHERD, Thomas Boswell: *Methodism and the literature of the eighteenth century*, London: Epworth Press, 1940, 286p.

2.8.5.13 SHEPHERD, Thomas Boswell: 'Methodists and the theatre in the eighteenth century', *Proceedings of the Wesley Historical Society*, Vol. XX, 1935–36, pp. 166–8, 181–5, Vol. XXI, 1937–38, pp. 3–7, 36–8.

2.8.5.14 WORDEN, Barbara Standley: 'The emotional evangelical: Blake and Wesley', *Wesleyan Theological Journal*, Vol. 18, No. 2, Fall 1983, pp. 67–79.

See also 2.4.1.11, 2.4.8.1, 2.6.6.17, 3.4.4.2, 3.5.1.3.

2.9 Reactions to Methodism

2.9.1 Physical opposition

2.9.1.1 BARR, Josiah Henry: *Early Methodists under persecution*, New York: Methodist Book Concern, 1916, 256p.

2.9.1.2 EDWARDS, Maldwyn Lloyd: 'Two early Methodists [John Nelson and Joseph Capper] in prison', *Methodist History*, Vol. VIII, No. 3, April 1970, pp. 21–7.

2.9.1.3 WADDY, John Leonard: *The bitter sacred cup: The Wednesbury riots, 1743–44*, Wesley Historical Society Lecture No. 36, London: Pinhorns for the World Methodist Historical Society (British Section), 1976, viii + 46p.

2.9.1.4 WALSH, John Dixon: 'Methodism and the mob in the eighteenth century', *Popular belief and practice: Papers read at the ninth summer*

> *meeting and the tenth winter meeting of the Ecclesiastical History Society,* edited by Geoffrey John Cuming & Derek Baker, Studies in Church History 8, Cambridge: at the University Press, 1972, pp. 213–27.

2.9.1.5   WHITNEY, Arthur Percy: *The basis of opposition to Methodism in England in the eighteenth century,* New York: New York University Press, 1951, ix+77p.

2.9.1.6   WILSON, David Dunn: *Many waters cannot quench: A study of the sufferings of eighteenth-century Methodism and their significance for John Wesley and the first Methodists,* London: Epworth Press, 1969, x+213p.

See also 2.2.20.13.

2.9.2 Literary opposition and portrayals

2.9.2.1   BELSHAW, Harry: 'An eighteenth-century wit [Horace Walpole]and Methodism', *London Quarterly Review,* Vol. CLVI, 1931, pp. 50–60.

2.9.2.2   DECANVER, H. C. *pseud.* [i.e. Curtis H. Cavender]: *Catalogue of works in refutation of Methodism from its origin in 1729 to the present time, of those by Methodist authors on lay-representation, Methodist episcopacy, etc., etc., and of the political pamphlets relating to Wesley's 'Calm address to our American colonies',* second edition, revised, New York, 1868, 55p.

2.9.2.3   GREAVES, Brian: 'Eighteenth-century opposition to Methodism', *Proceedings of the Wesley Historical Society,* Vol. XXXI, 1957–58, pp. 93–8, 105–11.

2.9.2.4   GREEN, Richard: *Anti-Methodist publications issued during the eighteenth century: A chronologically arranged and annotated bibliography of all known books and pamphlets written in opposition to the Methodist revival during the life of Wesley, together with an account of replies to them and of some other publications – A contribution to Methodist history,* London: C. H. Kelly, 1902, vii+175p.

2.9.2.5   HOOLE, Elijah: *Byrom and the Wesleys,* London: printed by William Nichols, 1864, 48p.

2.9.2.6   HUGHES, Leo: 'Trick upon trick; or, Methodism display'd', *Studies in English,* Vol. XXIX, 1950, pp. 151–61.

2.9.2.7   KIRKHAM, Donald Henry: 'Pamphlet opposition to the rise of Methodism: The eighteenth-century English evangelical revival under attack', Duke University Ph.D. thesis, 1973, x+456p.

2.9.2.8   LYLES, Albert Marion: *Methodism mocked: The satiric reaction to Methodism in the eighteenth century,* London: Epworth Press, 1960, 191p.

2.9.2.9   LYONS, Nicholas J. L.: 'Richard Graves and the Methodist background to "The spiritual quixote" ', University of Sheffield M.A. thesis, 1972, 196p.

2.9.2.10   SCOTT, Beatrice: 'The Dewsbury riots and the Revd. Benjamin Ingham', *Publications of the Thoresby Society,* Vol. LVI, 1978–80, pp. 187–95.

2.9.2.11 SNOW, Michael Lawrence: 'Methodist enthusiasm: Warburton letters, 1738–1740', *Methodist History*, Vol. X, No. 3, April 1972, pp. 30–47.

2.9.2.12 SWALLOW, John Albert: *Methodism in the light of the English literature of the last century*, Erlangen: A. Deichert'sche Verlagsbuchh. Nachf., 1895, ix+160p.

2.9.2.13 SWIFT, Sarah Patricia: 'The treatment of Methodism in eighteenth-century novels', University of Oxford B.Litt. thesis, 1978, [7]+208p.

See also 2.8.1.27, 2.8.1.30, 2.8.5.11, 2.8.5.12, 2.8.5.13, 2.9.1.6, 2.9.4.1, 2.9.4.3, 3.5.1.3.

2.9.3 Relations with other Churches: general works

2.9.3.1 HARRISON, Archibald Harold Walter: *The evangelical revival and Christian reunion*, London: Epworth Press, 1942, 207p.

2.9.3.2 HUNTER, Frederick: *John Wesley and the coming comprehensive Church*, Wesley Historical Society Lecture No. 33, London: Epworth Press, 1968, 112p.

2.9.3.3 NEWTON, John Anthony: 'The ecumenical Wesley', *Ecumenical Review*, Vol. XXIV, 1972, pp. 160–75.

2.9.3.4 NICHOLSON, Roy Stephen: 'John Wesley and ecumenicity', *Wesleyan Theological Journal*, Vol. 2, Spring 1967, pp. 66–81.

2.9.4 Relations with other Churches: Church of England

2.9.4.1 BAKER, Frank: 'Bishop Lavington and the Methodists', *Proceedings of the Wesley Historical Society*, Vol. XXXIV, 1963–64, pp. 37–42.

2.9.4.2 BAKER, Frank: *John Wesley and the Church of England*, London: Epworth Press, 1970, ix+422p.

2.9.4.3 BECKERLEGGE, Oliver Aveyard: 'The Lavington correspondence', *Proceedings of the Wesley Historical Society*, Vol. XLII, 1979–80, pp. 101–11, 139–49, 167–80.

2.9.4.4 DAVIES, William Rhys: 'The relation of Methodism and the Church of England between 1738 and 1850', University of Manchester M.A. thesis, 1959, 345p.

2.9.4.5 HARRISON, Archibald Harold Walter: *The separation of Methodism from the Church of England*, Wesley Historical Society Lecture No. 11, London: Epworth Press, 1945, 66p.

2.9.4.6 LAWSON, Albert Brown: 'John Wesley and some Anglican evangelicals of the eighteenth century: A study in co-operation and separation, with special reference to the calvinistic controversies', University of Sheffield Ph.D. thesis, 1973, ix+502p.

2.9.4.7 SIMPSON, William John Sparrow: *John Wesley and the Church of England*, London: Society for Promoting Christian Knowledge, 1934, xi+100p.

2.9.4.8 TUCKER, Robert Leonard: *The separation of the Methodists from the*

Church of England, New York: printed by the Methodist Book Concern, 1918, 184p.

2.9.4.9 WALSH, John Dixon: 'The Yorkshire evangelicals in the eighteenth century, with especial reference to Methodism', University of Cambridge Ph.D. thesis, 1956, x+407+[34]p.

See also 2.1.2.5, 2.3.2.6, 2.4.6.9, 2.6.1.12.

2.9.5 Relations with other Churches: Dissent

2.9.5.1 BAKER, Frank: 'The relations between the Society of Friends and early Methodism', *London Quarterly and Holborn Review*, Vol. CLXXIII, 1948, pp. 312–23, Vol. CLXXIV, 1949, pp. 239–48.

2.9.5.2 BOWMER, John Coates: 'Early Methodism and the Quakers', *Religion in Life*, Vol. XXIII, 1953–54, pp. 418–29.

2.9.5.3 BOWMER, John Coates: 'The relations between the Society of Friends and early Methodism', *London Quarterly and Holborn Review*, Vol. CLXXV, 1950, pp. 148–53, 222–7.

2.9.5.4 CLIFFORD, Alan C.: 'Philip Doddridge and the Oxford Methodists', *Proceedings of the Wesley Historical Society*, Vol. XLII, 1979–80, pp. 75–80.

2.9.5.5 NUTTALL, Geoffrey Fillingham: 'Methodism and the older Dissent: Some perspectives', *Journal of the United Reformed Church History Society*, Vol. 2, 1978–82, pp. 259–74.

2.9.5.6 PAYNE, Ernest Alexander: 'John Wesley and some Baptist encounters', *Epworth Review*, Vol. 7, No. 2, May 1980, pp. 60–8.

2.9.5.7 SMITH, Warren Thomas: 'Attempts at Methodist and Moravian union', *Methodist History*, Vo'. VIII, No. 2, January 1970, pp. 36–48.

2.9.5.8 WEST, William Morris Schumm: 'Methodists and Baptists in eighteenth-century Bristol', *Proceedings of the Wesley Historical Society*, Vol. XLIV, 1983–84, pp. 157–67.

See also 2.4.5.8, 2.4.5.18.

2.9.6 Relations with other Churches: Roman Catholicism

2.9.6.1 WESLEY, John: *John Wesley's letter to a Roman Catholic,* edited by Michael Hurley, London: Geoffrey Chapman, 1968, 64p.

See also 2.4.4.5, 2.4.4.11.

3. FROM THE DEATH OF JOHN WESLEY TO METHODIST UNION: INTERDENOMINATIONAL TREATMENTS

3.1 General Histories

3.1.1 Bibliography and historiography

3.1.1.1　ROGAL, Samuel J.: 'A survey of Methodist periodicals published in England, 1778–1900', *Victorian Periodicals Review*, Vol. 14, 1981, pp. 66–9.

3.1.2 Connexional histories

3.1.2.1　CURRIE, Robert: *Methodism divided: A study in the sociology of ecumenicalism*, London: Faber and Faber, 1968, 348p.

3.1.2.2　EAYRS, George: *British Methodism as it is, as it was, as it will be: A handbook and short history to help the union of Wesleyan, Primitive, United and other Methodists*, London: Henry Hooks, [1920], 122p.

3.1.2.3　FIELD, Clive Douglas: 'A sociological profile of English Methodism, 1900–1932', *Oral History*, Vol. 4, No. 1, Spring 1976, pp. 73–95.

3.1.2.4　KENT, John Henry Somerset: *The age of disunity*, London: Epworth Press, 1966, xii+209p.

3.1.2.5　KENT, John Henry Somerset: 'The clash between radicalism and conservatism in Methodism, 1815–48', University of Cambridge Ph.D. thesis, 1950, [2]+401p.

3.1.2.6　MEWS, Stuart Paul: 'Religion and English society in the First World War', University of Cambridge Ph.D. thesis, 1973, vii+351p.

3.1.2.7　REDFERN, William: *Modern developments in Methodism*, London: National Council of Evangelical Free Churches, 1906, 168p.

3.1.2.8　SELLERS, Ian: *Nineteenth-century Nonconformity*, London: Edward Arnold, 1977, ix+102p.

3.1.2.9　STEVENSON, George John: *Methodist worthies: Characteristic sketches of Methodist preachers of the several denominations, with historical sketch of each connexion*, London: Thomas C. Jack, 1884–86, 6 vol.

3.1.2.10　TURNER, John Munsey: 'Methodism in England, 1900–1932', *A history of the Methodist Church in Great Britain*, Vol. 3, general editors: Rupert Eric Davies, Alfred Raymond George & Ernest Gordon Rupp, London: Epworth Press, 1983, pp. 309–61.

3.1.2.11   TURNER, John Munsey: 'Methodist religion, 1791–1849', *A history of the Methodist Church in Great Britain*, Vol. 2, general editors: Rupert Eric Davies, Alfred Raymond George & Ernest Gordon Rupp, London: Epworth Press, 1978, pp. 97–112.

3.1.2.12   WALKER, John Dennis: 'Methodist discipline, 1750–1900', University of Manchester M.A. thesis, 1972, [3]+iii+245p.

3.1.2.13   WEARMOUTH, Robert Featherstone: 'Methodism from the death of Wesley, 1791 to the Wesleyan centenary, 1839', University of Birmingham M.A. thesis, 1928, [3]+iv+177p.

3.1.2.14   WEARMOUTH, Robert Featherstone: *The social and political influence of Methodism in the twentieth century*, London: Epworth Press, 1957, xiii+265p.

3.1.2.15   WILKINSON, John Thomas: 'The non-Wesleyan traditions from 1849', *A history of the Methodist Church in Great Britain*, Vol. 3, general editors: Rupert Eric Davies, Alfred Raymond George & Ernest Gordon Rupp, London: Epworth Press, 1983, pp. 167–81.

3.1.2.16   WILKINSON, John Thomas: 'The rise of other Methodist traditions', *A history of the Methodist Church in Great Britain*, Vol. 2, general editors: Rupert Eric Davies, Alfred Raymond George & Ernest Gordon Rupp, London: Epworth Press, 1978, pp. 276–329.

3.1.2.17   YOUNG, Kenneth: *Chapel: The joyous days and prayerful nights of the Nonconformists in their heyday, circa 1850–1950*, London: Eyre Methuen, 1972, 238p.

See also 2.1.1.1, 2.1.1.16, 2.1.1.17, 2.1.1.26, 4.4.2.3, 7.1.1.1, 7.1.1.3.

3.1.3 Local histories: England

3.1.3.1   BARTON, David Anthony: 'Aspects of Nonconformity in six Derbyshire towns, 1850–1914: A comparative study of Derby, Chesterfield, Bakewell, Matlock, Glossop and Belper', University of Sheffield M.A. thesis, 1981, 2 vol.

3.1.3.2   BINFIELD, John Clyde Goodfellow: 'Nonconformity in the eastern counties, 1840–1885, with reference to its social background', University of Cambridge Ph.D. thesis, 1965, xi+492p.

3.1.3.3   BURGESS, John: 'Methodism in Loughborough: Some problems of membership and finance in the Wesleyan, Primitive, New Connexion and United Methodist societies in the nineteenth century', University of Leicester M.A. thesis, 1974, 105p.

3.1.3.4   CARTER, David John: 'The social and political influence of the Bristol churches, 1830–1914', University of Bristol M.Litt. thesis, 1971, 284p.

3.1.3.5   EDWARDS, Michael Stone: 'Cornish Methodism: A study in division, 1814–1857', University of Birmingham M.A. thesis, 1962, [8]+280p.

3.1.3.6   EDWARDS, Michael Stone: *The divisions of Cornish Methodism, 1802 to 1857*, Cornish Methodist Historical Association Occasional Publication No. 7, Redruth: Cornish Methodist Historical Association, 1964, [2]+26p.

3.1.3.7   FIELD, Clive Douglas: 'Methodism in metropolitan London, 1850–1920: A social and sociological study', University of Oxford D.Phil. thesis, 1974, ix+401p.

3.1.3.8   GRIFFIN, Colin P.: 'Methodism in the Leicestershire and South Derbyshire coalfield in the nineteenth century'. *Proceedings of the Wesley Historical Society*, Vol. XXXIX, 1973–74, pp. 62–72.

3.1.3.9   HALL, George David: 'Congregationalists, Methodists and Lancashire Nonconformity during the years 1790–1907', University of Liverpool M.A. thesis, 1974, 167p.

3.1.3.10   HORNER, John Pennock: 'The influence of Methodism on the social structure and culture of rural Northumberland from 1820 to 1914', University of Newcastle-upon-Tyne M.A. thesis, 1971, [6]+223p.

3.1.3.11   KLAPAS, Janina Alina: 'Geographical aspects of religious change in Victorian Liverpool, 1837–1901', University of Liverpool M.A. thesis, 1977, [332]p.

3.1.3.12   LEESE, Roger: 'The impact of Methodism on Black Country society, 1743–1860', University of Manchester Ph.D. thesis, 1972, [2]+vii+395p.

3.1.3.13   MILBURN, Geoffrey Eden: 'Piety, profit and paternalism: Methodists in business in the North-East of England, c. 1760–1920', *Proceedings of the Wesley Historical Society*, Vol. XLIV, 1983–84, pp. 45–92.

3.1.3.14   MOORE, Robert Samuel: *Pit-men, preachers & politics: The effects of Methodism in a Durham mining community*, London: Cambridge University Press, 1974, xi+292p.

3.1.3.15   OBELKEVICH, James: *Religion and rural society: South Lindsey, 1825–1875*, Oxford: Clarendon Press, 1976, xiii+353p.

3.1.3.16   OLLERHEAD, Peter Edward: 'Protestant Nonconformity in Crewe, 1840–1940', University of Keele M.A. thesis, 1975, vii+341+xvip.

3.1.3.17   RULE, John: 'Methodism, popular beliefs and village culture in Cornwall, 1800–50', *Popular culture and custom in nineteenth-century England*, edited by Robert D. Storch, London: Croom Helm, 1982, pp. 48–70.

3.1.3.18   SELLERS, Ian: 'Liverpool Nonconformity, 1786–1914', University of Keele Ph.D. thesis, 1969, 360+96p.

3.1.3.19   TEALE, Albert Emerson: 'Methodism in Halifax and district, 1780 to 1850: A study of the development of Methodism and its impact upon a rapidly changing society in the late eighteenth and early nineteenth centuries', University of Bradford M.Sc. thesis, 1976, iii+407p.

3.1.3.20   WELLER, John Christopher: 'The revival of religion in Nottingham, 1780–1850', University of Nottingham B.D. thesis, 1957, 271p.

See also 2.1.2.1, 2.1.2.4, 2.1.2.5, 2.1.2.10, 2.1.2.13, 2.1.2.24, 3.4.1.8, 3.4.1.9, 3.4.1.10, 3.4.1.13, 3.4.1.15, 3.4.1.16, 3.4.1.17, 3.4.1.20, 3.4.3.3, 3.5.2.1, 7.1.3.1.

3.2 Spirituality

3.2.1 Theology

3.2.1.1   BECKERLEGGE, Oliver Aveyard: 'Our doctrines', *Proceedings of the Wesley Historical Society*, Vol. XL, 1975–76, pp. 69–72, 74–9.
See also 7.1.1.2.

3.2.2 Sacraments

3.2.2.1   BOWMER, John Coates: *The Lord's Supper in Methodism, 1791–1960*, Wesley Historical Society Lecture No. 27, London: Epworth Press, 1961, 64p.

3.2.2.2   HOLLAND, Bernard George: *The doctrine of infant baptism in non-Wesleyan Methodism*, Wesley Historical Society Occasional Publication New Series No. 1, [no place]: Wesley Historical Society, 1970, [27]p.

3.2.2.3   MUMFORD, Norman William: 'The administration of the sacrament of baptism in the Methodist Church', *London Quarterly and Holborn Review*, Vol. CLXXII, 1947, pp. 113–19.

3.2.2.4   MUMFORD, Norman William: 'The administration of the sacrament of the Lord's Supper in the Methodist Church after the death of John Wesley', *London Quarterly and Holborn Review*, Vol. CLXXVI, 1951, pp. 61–70.

3.2.2.5   TRIPP, David Howard: 'The eucharistic prayer in Methodism: The non-Wesleyan traditions', *Bulletin of the Methodist Sacramental Fellowship*, No. 102, Christmas 1978, pp. 6–8, No. 103, Pentecost 1979, pp. 6–7, No. 104, Christmas 1979, pp. 9–11.
See also 3.2.3.3.

3.2.3 Worship and devotion

3.2.3.1   BOWMER, John Coates: 'Some non-Wesleyan service books', *Proceedings of the Wesley Historical Society*, Vol. XXXII, 1959–60, pp. 145–52.

3.2.3.2   DAVIES, Daniel Horton Marlais: *Worship and theology in England: From Newman to Martineau, 1850–1900*, Princeton: Princeton University Press, 1962, xiv+390p.

3.2.3.3   GOLDHAWK, Norman Panter: 'The Methodist people in the early Victorian age: Spirituality and worship', *A history of the Methodist Church in Great Britain*, Vol. 2, general editors: Rupert Eric Davies, Alfred Raymond George & Ernest Gordon Rupp, London: Epworth Press, 1978, pp. 113–42.

3.2.3.4   WAKEFIELD, Gordon Stevens: *Methodist devotion: The spiritual life in the Methodist tradition, 1791–1945*, Wesley Historical Society Lecture No. 32, London: Epworth Press, 1966, 120p.
See also 3.2.2.5.

3.2.4 Hymnology and music

3.2.4.1   HIND, Roland: 'Changes in Methodist hymnody during the eighteenth and nineteenth centuries', University of Durham M.A. thesis, 1968, [3]+201p.

See also 2.6.4.5, 3.2.3.3.

3.2.5 Class meetings and membership

See 3.1.2.12, 3.1.3.3.

3.3 Polity and Mission

3.3.1 Ordained ministry

3.3.1.1   BRASH, William Bardsley: *The story of our colleges, 1835–1935: A centenary record of ministerial training in the Methodist Church*, London: Epworth Press, 1935, 165p.

3.3.1.2   BROWN, Kenneth Douglas: 'Nineteenth-century Methodist theological college principals: A survey', *Proceedings of the Wesley Historical Society*, Vol. XLIV, 1983–84, pp. 93–102.

3.3.1.3   SWIFT, Wesley Frank: 'The women itinerant preachers of early Methodism', *Proceedings of the Wesley Historical Society*, Vol. XXVIII, 1951–52, pp. 89–94, Vol. XXIX, 1953–54, pp. 76–83.

See also 3.1.2.4, 3.4.1.18.

3.3.2 Lay ministry

3.3.2.1   BOWMER, John Coates: 'The local preacher in Methodism, 1791 to 1964', *The preacher's handbook*, No. 9, edited by David Noel Francis, London: Epworth Press, 1965, pp. 1–19.

3.3.2.2   BUSS, Frederick Harold & BURNETT, Richard George: *A goodly fellowship: A history of the hundred years of the Methodist Local Preachers Mutual Aid Association, 1849–1949*, London: Epworth Press, 1949, 223p.

3.3.2.3   *Illustrious local preachers*, edited by David Whiteley, Bradford: Thornton & Pearson, 1891, 320p.

3.3.3 Buildings and finance

3.3.3.1   PHILLIPSON, William Oliver: *Performance and promise: A centenary brochure describing the work of the Trustees for Methodist Church Purposes*, Manchester: printed by Jesse Broad & Co., [1966], 30p.

See also 2.7.4.1, 2.7.4.2, 3.1.3.3.

3.3.4 Home missions

3.3.4.1   CARWARDINE, Richard: *Trans-Atlantic revivalism: Popular evangelicalism in Britain and America, 1790–1865*, Westport: Greenwood Press, 1978, xviii+249p.

3.3.4.2   HAINES, Sheila Rose: 'Am I my brother's keeper? Victorian tract societies and their work, 1840–1875', University of Sussex D.Phil. thesis, 1979, iv+240p.

3.3.4.3   KENT, John Henry Somerset: *Holding the fort: Studies in Victorian revivalism*, London: Epworth Press, 1978, 381p.

3.3.4.4   ORR, James Edwin: *The second evangelical awakening in Britain*, London: Marshall, Morgan & Scott, 1949, 302p.

3.3.4.5   RICE, Robert Jay: 'Religious revivalism and British Methodism, 1855–1865', University of Illinois at Urbana-Champaign Ph.D. thesis, 1979, iv+270p.

3.3.4.6   SHEARD, Michael Rowland: 'Methodist tract-visiting societies in the early nineteenth century', *Proceedings of the Wesley Historical Society*, Vol. XXXIX, 1973–74, pp. 34–40.

3.3.4.7   TIDBALL, Derek John: 'English Nonconformist home missions, 1796–1901', University of Keele Ph.D. thesis, 1982, vi+475p.

3.3.4.8   TYRRELL, Charles W.: 'Methodist vans: Gospel heralds to the villages', *Proceedings of the Wesley Historical Society*, Vol. XXXIX, 1973–74, pp. 170–6.

3.3.5 Overseas missions

3.3.5.1   BARBER, William Theodore Aquila: 'The work of British [Methodist foreign missionary] societies', *A new history of Methodism*, edited by William John Townsend, Herbert Brook Workman & George Eayrs, London: Hodder and Stoughton, 1909, Vol. II, pp. 283–360.

3.3.5.2   GREEN, Frederick Pratt: *Methodism and the mountain summit: A survey of Methodist world missions*, London: Cargate Press, [1932], 192p.

3.4 Social Aspects

3.4.1 Political impact

3.4.1.1   BEBBINGTON, David William: *The Nonconformist Conscience: Chapel and politics, 1870–1914*, London: George Allen & Unwin, 1982, x+193p.

3.4.1.2   CHRISTIAN, Cyril Joseph: 'The relation of the Methodist movement to political thought in England, 1800–1850, with special reference to Methodist records', University of Manchester M.A. thesis, [1936], [5]+246+5p.

3.4.1.3   DANIEL, Wilborn Harrison: 'The reaction of British Methodism to the Civil War and reconstruction in America', *Methodist History*, Vol. XVI, 1977–78, pp. 3–20.

3.4.1.4   EDWARDS, Michael Stone: 'Methodism and the Chartist movement', *London Quarterly and Holborn Review*, Vol. CXCI, 1966, pp. 301–10.

3.4.1.5   FAULKNER, Harold Underwood: *Chartism and the Churches: A study in democracy*, Studies in History, Economics and Public Law edited by the Faculty of Political Science of Columbia University Vol. LXXIII No. 3, New York: Columbia University Press, 1916, 152p.

3.4.1.6   GILBERT, Alan David: 'Methodism, Dissent and political stability in early industrial England', *Journal of Religious History*, Vol. 10, 1978–79, pp. 381–99.

3.4.1.7   GLASER, John Frederic: 'Nonconformity and Liberalism, 1868–1885: A study in English party history', Harvard University Ph.D. thesis, 1949, 2 vol.

3.4.1.8   GRIFFIN, Alan Ramsay: 'Methodism and trade unionism in the Nottinghamshire–Derbyshire coalfield, 1844–90', *Proceedings of the Wesley Historical Society*, Vol. XXXVII, 1969–70, pp. 2–9.

3.4.1.9   HARGREAVES, John Andrew: 'Political attitudes and activities of Methodists in the Parish of Halifax in the age of reform, 1830–48', Council for National Academic Awards (Huddersfield Polytechnic) M.A. thesis, 1985, [2]+iii+141p.

3.4.1.10   HAYDEN, Peter: 'Culture, creed and conflict: Methodism and politics in Cornwall, c. 1832–1979', University of Liverpool Ph.D. thesis, 1982, xiv+465p.

3.4.1.11   HENDERSON, David Michael: 'The class meeting in Methodism and Chartism', Indiana University M.A. thesis, 1976.

3.4.1.12   HOBSBAWM, Eric John: 'Methodism and the threat of revolution in Britain', *History Today*, Vol. VII, 1957, pp. 115–24 and *Labouring men: Studies in the history of labour*, London: Weidenfeld and Nicolson, 1968, pp. 23–33.

3.4.1.13   HORN, Pamela R.: 'Methodism and agricultural trade unionism in Oxfordshire: The 1870s', *Proceedings of the Wesley Historical Society*, Vol. XXXVII, 1969–70, pp. 67–71.

3.4.1.14   KOSS, Stephen Edward: *Nonconformity in modern British politics*, London: B. T. Batsford, 1975, 272p.

3.4.1.15   McLELLAN, Nathaniel Johnston: 'Chartism and the Churches, with special reference to Lancashire: An account of the Churches and social reform in the Chartist period', University of Edinburgh Ph.D. thesis, 1947, xv+439p.

3.4.1.16   MARQUIS, James Wilson: 'Tyne and Wearside coalminers in the early nineteenth century: A study of Methodism, trade unionism and radical politics', University of California, Berkeley Ph.D. thesis, 1974, iv+678p.

3.4.1.17   MOORE, Robert Samuel: 'The political effects of village Methodism', *A sociological yearbook of religion in Britain, 6,* edited by Michael Hill, London: SCM Press, 1973, pp. 156–82.

3.4.1.18 MUNSON, James Edward Bradbury: 'A study of Nonconformity in Edwardian England as revealed by the passive resistance movement against the 1902 Education Act', University of Oxford D.Phil. thesis, 1973, vii+448+8p.

3.4.1.19 SAINT, Julia Guy: 'The influence of the Non-conformist religions on the character of the British labour movement, 1875–1895', McGill University M.A. thesis, 1962.

3.4.1.20 SCOTLAND, Nigel Adrian D.: *Methodism and the Revolt of the Field: A study of the Methodist contribution to agricultural trade unionism in East Anglia, 1872–96*, Gloucester: Alan Sutton, 1981, 296p.

3.4.1.21 TAYLOR, Ernest Richard: *Methodism & politics, 1791–1851*, Cambridge: at the University Press, 1935, xi+227p.

3.4.1.22 THOMPSON, Edward Palmer: *The making of the English working class*, [revised edition], Harmondsworth: Penguin Books, 1968, 958p.

3.4.1.23 TURNER, John Munsey: 'Methodism, revolution and social change', *Wesley Historical Society West Midlands Branch Bulletin*, Vol. 2, 1970–76, pp. 61–6, 71–8.

3.4.1.24 WEARMOUTH, Robert Featherstone: *Methodism and the struggle of the working classes, 1850–1900*, Leicester: Edgar Backus, 1954, xiii+269p.

3.4.1.25 WEARMOUTH, Robert Featherstone: *Methodism and the trade unions*, Wesley Historical [Society] Lecture No. 25, London: Epworth Press, 1959, 78p.

3.4.1.26 WEARMOUTH, Robert Featherstone: *Methodism and the working-class movements of England, 1800–1850*, London: Epworth Press, 1937, 289p.

See also 3.1.2.6, 3.1.2.14, 3.1.3.4, 3.1.3.8, 3.1.3.14, 3.4.3.1.

3.4.2 Social witness

3.4.2.1 HUTSON, Harry Marshall: 'Methodist concern with social problems in England, 1848–1873', University of Iowa Ph.D. thesis, 1952, iv+330p.

3.4.2.2 HUTSON, Harry Marshall: 'Methodist concern with social problems in England, 1848–1873', *Methodist History*, Vol. VII, No. 3, April 1969, pp. 13–23.

3.4.2.3 WOLFENDEN, James W.: 'English Nonconformity and the social conscience, 1880–1906', Yale University Ph.D. thesis, 1954.

See also 3.1.3.17, 3.4.1.15.

3.4.3 Educational work

3.4.3.1 FOREMAN, Henry: 'Nonconformity and education in England and Wales, 1870–1902', University of London M.A. thesis, 1967, 258p.

3.4.3.2 LAQUEUR, Thomas Walter: *Religion and respectability: Sunday schools and working class culture, 1780–1850*, New Haven: Yale University Press, 1976, xv+293p.

3.4.3.3 OWEN, Raymond Mark: 'The Methodist contribution to education in North-West England from 1850', University of Liverpool M.Ed. thesis, 1965.

3.4.3.4   WILKINSON, Thomas Gordon: 'Methodism and education in the nineteenth century', University of Bristol M.Ed. thesis, 1977, [3]+74p.

See also 3.4.1.18.

3.4.4 Literary and cultural influence

3.4.4.1   BRANTLEY, Richard Estes: *Wordsworth's 'natural Methodism'*, New Haven: Yale University Press, 1975, xvi+205p.

3.4.4.2   FEATHER, Howard Rodney: 'Romanticism and Methodism, 1780–1850: A sociological interpretation', University of Lancaster M.Litt. thesis, 1977, ix+280p.

3.4.4.3   MINOR, Mark: 'John Clare and the Methodists: A reconsideration', *Studies in Romanticism*, Vol. 19, 1980, pp. 31–50.

See also 2.4.8.1, 2.8.5.7, 2.8.5.11.

3.5 Reactions to Methodism

3.5.1 Literary opposition and portrayals

3.5.1.1   CUNNINGHAM, Valentine David: *Everywhere spoken against: Dissent in the Victorian novel*, Oxford: Clarendon Press, 1975, xv+311p.

3.5.1.2   DAKIN, Donald Hubert: 'The Methodist and the influence of Methodism as depicted in Victorian fiction', University of Sheffield M.A. thesis, 1980, ii+258p.

3.5.1.3   MILBANK, Douglas: 'A mirror to Methodism: Methodists in, on and around literature', *The Methodist heritage: The Principal's Lectures, Southlands College, Spring Term 1984*, [London]: Southlands College, [1984], pp. 34–55.

3.5.1.4   PERZL, Anton: 'Der Methodismus im englischen Roman von George Eliot bis Arnold Bennett', Dissertation, Universität Wien, 1928.

3.5.1.5   SHEPHERD, Thomas Boswell: 'George Crabbe and Methodism', *London Quarterly and Holborn Review*, Vol. CLXVI, 1941, pp. 166–74.

3.5.1.6   THORBURN, Donald Burns: 'The effects of the Wesleyan movement on the Bronte sisters as evidenced by an examination of certain of their novels', New York University Ph.D. thesis, 1947, ii+252p.

3.5.1.7   WATSON, Kathleen: 'Dinah Morris and Mrs. Evans: A comparative study of Methodist diction', *Review of English Studies*, New Series, Vol. XXII, 1971, pp. 282–94.

See also 2.8.5.11, 2.9.2.2.

3.5.2 Relations with other Churches

3.5.2.1   FREEMAN, Clifford Ball: *Mary Simpson of Boynton Vicarage, teacher of ploughboys and critic of Methodism*, East Yorkshire Local History

Series No. 28, York: East Yorkshire Local History Society, 1972, 44p.

3.5.2.2   HARRIS, Jeffrey Wallace: 'The development of world Methodism in the nineteenth and twentieth centuries: The growth of ecumenical Methodism up to the 1956 Lake Junaluska World Methodist Conference', University of Manchester M.A. thesis, 1961, [2]+321p.

3.5.2.3   JORDAN, Edward Kenneth Henry: *Free Church unity: History of the Free Church Council movement, 1896–1941*, London: Lutterworth Press, 1956, 254p.

See also 2.1.2.5, 3.1.2.1.

4. FROM THE DEATH OF JOHN WESLEY TO METHODIST UNION: WESLEYAN METHODISM

4.1 General Histories

4.1.1 Bibliography and historiography

4.1.1.1   HEMPTON, David Neil: 'Evangelical revival and society: A historiographical review of Methodism and British society, c. 1750–1850', *Themelios*, New Series, Vol. 8, No. 3, April 1983, pp. 19–25.
See also 2.2.4.7, 4.1.2.11.

4.1.2 Connexional histories

4.1.2.1   CLELAND, Ivan David: 'The development of Wesleyan Methodist principles and ideas, 1791–1914', University of Nottingham M. Phil. thesis, 1970, iii + [1] + 467p.

4.1.2.2   DOWNEY, Herman Jackson: 'The Bristol dispute of 1794–5: A crucial period in English Methodism, with a clarification and an assessment of the role of Joseph Benson', University of Edinburgh Ph.D. thesis, 1957, v + 251p.

4.1.2.3   *The early correspondence of Jabez Bunting, 1820–1829*, edited by William Reginald Ward, Camden Fourth Series Vol. 11, London: Royal Historical Society, 1972, viii + 240p.

4.1.2.4   *Early Victorian Methodism: The correspondence of Jabez Bunting, 1830–1858*, [edited by] William Reginald Ward, Oxford: Oxford University Press, 1976, xxiii + 440p.

4.1.2.5   EDWARDS, Maldwyn Lloyd: *After Wesley: A study of the social and political influence of Methodism in the middle period (1791–1849)*, London: Epworth Press, 1935, 190p.

4.1.2.6   EDWARDS, Maldwyn Lloyd: *Methodism and England: A study of Methodism in its social and political aspects during the period 1850–1932*, London: Epworth Press, 1943, 252p.

4.1.2.7   EDWARDS, Maldwyn Lloyd: 'The years of unrest, 1790–1800', *London Quarterly and Holborn Review*, Vol. CLXVI, 1941, pp. 451–8, Vol. CLXVII, 1942, pp. 84–93.

4.1.2.8   GREGORY, Benjamin: *Side lights on the conflicts of Methodism during the second quarter of the nineteenth century, 1827–1852, taken chiefly from the notes of the late Rev. Joseph Fowler of the debates in the Wesleyan Conference: A centenary contribution to the constitutional history of Methodism with a biographical sketch*, London: Cassell and Company, 1898, viii +584p.

4.1.2.9 GREGORY, John Robinson & GREGORY, Arthur Edwin: 'Wesleyan Methodism: The middle period, 1791–1849', *A new history of Methodism*, edited by William John Townsend, Herbert Brook Workman & George Eayrs, London: Hodder and Stoughton, 1909, Vol. I, pp. 379–433.

4.1.2.10 GWYTHER, Cyril Edward: 'Methodist social and political theory and practice, 1848 to 1914, with particular reference to the Forward Movement', University of Liverpool M.A. thesis, 1961, [7]+347 +[12]p.

4.1.2.11 KENT, John Henry Somerset: 'M. Elie Halévy on Methodism', *Proceedings of the Wesley Historical Society*, Vol. XXIX, 1953–54, pp. 84–91.

4.1.2.12 KENT, John Henry Somerset: 'The Wesleyan Methodists to 1849', *A history of the Methodist Church in Great Britain*, Vol. 2, general editors: Rupert Eric Davies, Alfred Raymond George & Ernest Gordon Rupp, London: Epworth Press, 1978, pp. 213–75.

4.1.2.13 MOSS, Richard Waddy: 'Wesleyan Methodism: The last fifty years, 1849–1908', *A new history of Methodism*, edited by William John Townsend, Herbert Brook Workman & George Eayrs, London: Hodder and Stoughton, 1909, Vol. I, pp. 435–80.

4.1.2.14 MURRAY, Nancy Uhlar: 'The influence of the French Revolution on the Church of England and its rivals, 1789–1802', University of Oxford D.Phil. thesis, 1975, 7+iv+443p.

4.1.2.15 PEARSON, Philip Chisholm: 'Wesleyan Methodism from 1850 to 1900 in relation to the life and thought of the Victorian age', University of Manchester M.A. thesis, 1965, [6]+vii+445p.

4.1.2.16 RACK, Henry Derman: 'Wesleyanism and "the world" in the later nineteenth century', *Proceedings of the Wesley Historical Society*, Vol. XLII, 1979–80, pp. 35–54.

4.1.2.17 RACK, Henry Derman: 'Wesleyan Methodism, 1849–1902', *A history of the Methodist Church in Great Britain*, Vol. 3, general editors: Rupert Eric Davies, Alfred Raymond George & Ernest Gordon Rupp, London: Epworth Press, 1983, pp. 119–66.

4.1.2.18 SEMMENS, Bernard L.: *The conferences after Wesley – an attempt to keep the record straight: A study of the basic documents of early Methodism*, Melbourne: National Press, 1971, 106p.

4.1.2.19 [SIMON, John Smith]: 'The Methodist "Plan of pacification", 1791–1795', *London Quarterly Review*, Vol. LXIII, October 1884–January 1885, pp. 1–24.

4.1.2.20 SMITH, George: *History of Wesleyan Methodism*, London: Longman, Brown, Green, Longmans and Roberts, 1857–61, 3 vol.

4.1.2.21 WALKER, Robin Berwick: 'The growth of Wesleyan Methodism in Victorian England and Wales', *Journal of Ecclesiastical History*, Vol. XXIV, 1973, pp. 267–84.

4.1.2.22 WALSH, John Dixon: 'Methodism at the end of the eighteenth century', *A history of the Methodist Church in Great Britain*, Vol. 1, general editors: Rupert Eric Davies & Ernest Gordon Rupp, London: Epworth Press, 1965, pp. 275–315.

4.1.2.23   WARD, William Reginald: *Religion and society in England, 1790–1850*, London: B. T. Batsford, 1972, x+339p.

4.1.2.24   WARD, William Reginald: 'The religion of the people and the problem of control, 1790–1830', *Popular belief and practice: Papers read at the ninth summer meeting and the tenth winter meeting of the Ecclesiastical History Society*, edited by Geoffrey John Cuming & Derek Baker, Studies in Church History 8, Cambridge: at the University Press, 1972, pp. 237–57.

See also 2.1.1.10, 2.1.1.14, 2.1.1.15, 2.1.1.20, 2.1.1.24, 4.2.5.3, 4.4.2.3, 6.5.8.1.

4.1.3 Local histories: England

4.1.3.1   BRAITHWAITE, Matthew: *History of Methodism in the Bishop Auckland Circuit*, Bishop Auckland: Matthew Braithwaite, 1885, 235p.

4.1.3.2   COCKING, Thomas: *The history of Wesleyan Methodism in Grantham and its vicinity; with preliminary observations on the rise, progress and utility, the discipline and doctrines of the connexion, the life of its founder, etc.*, London: Simpkin, Marshall & Co., 1836, x+418p.

4.1.3.3   ELLIOTT, Charles Middleton: 'The social and economic history of the principal Protestant denominations in Leeds, 1760–1844', University of Oxford D.Phil. thesis, 1962, [16]+570p.

4.1.3.4   FRANCIS, Patricia Rose: 'Wesleyan opposition to Buntingism in Middlesex, 1825–55, with special reference to the importance of the press', Council for National Academic Awards (Polytechnic of North London) M.Phil. thesis, 1980, iv+176p.

4.1.3.5   GILL, Josiah: *The history of Wesleyan Methodism in Melton Mowbray and the vicinity, 1769–1909*, Melton Mowbray: John Wartnaby Warner, 1909, xi+268p.

4.1.3.6   GRAHAM, John Joseph: *A history of Wesleyan Methodism in Sheffield Park, Sheffield*, Sheffield: Sir W. C. Leng & Co., 1914, 300p.

4.1.3.7   GUITON, François: *Histoire du méthodisme wesleyen dans les Iles de la Manche*, Londres: John Mason, [1846], vii+312p.

4.1.3.8   HARWOOD, George H.: *The history of Wesleyan Methodism in Nottingham and its vicinity*, new and enlarged edition, Nottingham: John Ellis, 1872, 242p.

4.1.3.9   JESSOP, William: *An account of Methodism in Rossendale and the neighbourhood; with some notices of the rise and progress of the united societies and of contemporary events*, Manchester: Tubbs, Brook and Chrystal, [1880], [8]+403p.

4.1.3.10   LELIEVRE, Matthieu: *Histoire du méthodisme dans les Iles de la Manche; précédée de l'histoire de la réformation huguenote dans cet archipel*, Paris: Librairie Evangélique, 1885, x+580p.

4.1.3.11   MALLINSON, Joel: *History of Methodism in Huddersfield, Holmfirth and Denby Dale*, London: Charles H. Kelly, 1898, 224p.

4.1.3.12   MILBURN, Geoffrey Eden: 'Wesleyanism in Sunderland in the later

18th. and early 19th. century', *Antiquities of Sunderland,* Vol. XXVI, 1974–76, pp. 85–108, Vol. XXVII, 1977–79, pp. 3–30.

4.1.3.13 MOORE, Benjamin: *History of Wesleyan Methodism in Burnley and east Lancashire: Burnley, Colne, Padiham, Nelson, Barnoldswick,* Burnley: 'Gazette' Printing Works, 1899, viii+268p.

4.1.3.14 PILKINGTON, W.: *The makers of Wesleyan Methodism in Preston and the relation of Methodism to the temperance & teetotal movements,* London: Charles H. Kelly, 1890, viii+275p.

4.1.3.15 RAWLINSON, Arthur: *A centenary history of Wesleyan Methodism in Swinton (Lancashire),* London: printed by William Clowes and Sons, 1910, xii+233p.

See also 2.1.2.2, 2.1.2.6, 2.1.2.12, 2.1.2.18, 2.1.2.19, 2.1.2.20, 2.1.2.21, 2.1.2.23, 4.1.2.2, 4.4.2.6. 4.4.2.7, 4.4.2.11, 4.4.2.13, 4.4.5.1, 4.4.5.2, 4.4.5.3, 4.4.5.7, 4.4.5.8, 4.5.1.7, 4.5.1.19, 4.5.3.1, 4.5.3.2, 4.5.3.4, 4.5.3.6, 4.5.3.15, 4.5.3.16, 4.5.3.19, 4.5.3.20, 4.5.3.21, 4.5.3.22, 4.5.3.23, 4.5.3.24, 4.5.3.26, 4.5.3.27, 4.5.3.28, 4.5.3.29, 4.5.3.30, 4.6.2.1.

4.1.4 Local histories: Wales

4.1.4.1 BOWMER, John Coates: 'Sidelights on Methodism in Wales in the first half of the nineteenth century', *Bathafarn,* Cyfrol 27, 1973, pp. 28–41.

4.1.4.2 EDWARDS, Eric: 'Llyfrfa'r Methodistiaid Wesleaidd Cymraeg, 1809–1909', *Bathafarn,* Vol. 22, 1967, pp. 8–23.

4.1.4.3 EVANS, William Abraham: 'A statistical study of the development of Nonconformity in N. Wales in the 19th century, with special reference to the period 1850–1901', University of Liverpool M.A. thesis, 1928, 216+[23]p.

4.1.4.4 HUMPHREYS, Thomas Jones: *Methodistiaeth Wesleyaidd Cymreig: Sef trem ar ei sefydliad, ei gwaith, a'i llwyddiant yn ystod y ganrif gyntaf o'i hanes,* Treffynnon: W. Williams a'i Fab, 1900, 218p.

4.1.4.5 JONES, David Llewelyn: 'Drych o ddechrau'r ganrif', *Bathafarn,* Vol. 14, 1959, pp. 5–23, Vol. 15, 1960, pp. 5–24.

4.1.4.6 JONES, Hugh: *Hanes Wesleyaeth Cymreig,* Bangor: Y Llyfrfa Wesleyaidd, 1911–14, 4 vol.

4.1.4.7 MORGAN, William Islwyn: ' "Yr Eurgrawn Wesleyaidd": The Welsh Wesleyan Methodist magazine, 1809–1983', *Proceedings of the Wesley Historical Society,* Vol. XLIV, 1983–84, pp. 168–73.

4.1.4.8 MORGAN, William Islwyn: ' "Y Gwyliedydd" ', *Bathafarn,* Vol. 25, 1970, pp. 7–27.

4.1.4.9 MORGAN, William Islwyn: 'Wesleaeth yn Neheudir Cymru, 1872–88', *Bathafarn,* Vol. 13, 1958, pp. 7–39.

4.1.4.10 WILLIAMS, Albert Hughes: 'Thomas Coke and the origins of Welsh Wesleyan Methodism', *Proceedings of the Wesley Historical Society,* Vol. XVIII, 1931–32, pp. 54–8, 78–84, 93–8.

4.1.4.11 WILLIAMS, Albert Hughes: *Welsh Wesleyan Methodism, 1800–1858: Its origins, growth and secessions,* Bangor: cyhoeddwyd gan Lyfrfa'r Methodistiaid, 1935, 378p.

4.1.4.12　Young, David: *The origin and history of Methodism in Wales and the Borders*, London: Charles H. Kelly, 1893, xxvii+731p.
See also 4.2.1.2, 4.3.1.4, 4.5.1.21, 4.5.3.10, 4.5.3.17, 4.5.3.18.

4.1.5 Local histories: Scotland

4.1.5.1　*Scottish Methodism in the early Victorian period: The Scottish correspondence of the Rev. Jabez Bunting, 1800–57*, edited by Alan J. Hayes & David Alexander Gowland, Edinburgh: Edinburgh University Press, 1981, viii+144p.

4.1.5.2　Ward, William Reginald: 'Scottish Methodism in the age of Jabez Bunting', *Records of the Scottish Church History Society*, Vol. XX, 1978–80, pp. 47–63.
See also 2.1.4.7.

4.1.6 Local histories: Ireland

4.1.6.1　Binns, June Rhodes: 'A history of Methodism in Ireland from Wesley's death in 1791 to the re-union of Primitives and Wesleyans in 1878', Queen's University of Belfast M.A. thesis, 1960, 204p.

4.1.6.2　Cooke, Joseph Henry: 'Church Methodists in Ireland: Statistical evidence', *Proceedings of the Wesley Historical Society*, Vol. XXXIV, 1963–64, pp. 135–40.

4.1.6.3　Hempton, David Neil: 'The Methodist crusade in Ireland, 1795–1845', *Irish Historical Studies*, Vol. XXII, 1980–81, pp. 33–48.

4.1.6.4　Huston, Robert: *Sketches from my note book: A record of facts illustrative of Methodism and ministerial life in Ireland*, London: Wesleyan Conference Office, [1869], 191p.

4.1.6.5　Hynes, John Arthur: *Signs infallible: Six generations of Irish Methodism*, London: Epworth Press, 1949, 96p.

4.1.6.6　*Irish Methodism in the twentieth century: A symposium*, [edited by Alexander McCrea], Belfast: Irish Methodist Publishing Co., 1931, 202p.

4.1.6.7　Ker, R. Alan: 'The origins of Primitive Wesleyan Methodism in Ireland', *Proceedings of the Wesley Historical Society*, Vol. XLIII, 1981–82, pp. 77–85.

4.1.6.8　Smith, William: *A consecutive history of the rise, progress and present state of Wesleyan Methodism in Ireland*, Dublin: T. W. Doolittle, 1830, iv+320p.
See also 1.2.5.2, 2.1.5.6, 2.1.5.8, 4.2.19 *passim*, 4.2.27.7, 4.2.27.12, 4.2.27.13, 4.2.27.18, 4.4.5.4, 4.5.3.5, 4.5.3.9, 4.5.3.12, 4.6.2.3.

4.2 Biographies

4.2.1 Collective

4.2.1.1　Hall, Joseph: *Memorials of Wesleyan Methodist ministers; or, The yearly death roll from 1777 to 1840*, London: Haughton & Co., 1876, 312p.

4.2.1.2   JONES, John: *Y bywgraffydd Wesleyaidd: Yn cynwys bras-hanes am un-a-thriugain o weinidogion Wesleyaidd Cymreig yn nghyda 35 o weinidogion a gwyr lleyg saesonig,* Machynlleth: J. Williams, 1866, viii + 296p.

4.2.1.3   *Wesley and his successors: A centenary memorial of the death of John Wesley,* London: Charles H. Kelly, 1891, 257p.

4.2.1.4   WEST, Robert Athow: *Sketches of Wesleyan preachers,* London: Simpkin, Marshall & Co., 1849, [7] + 386p.

See also 2.1.5.6, 3.1.2.9, 4.4.3.1, 4.4.6.6.

4.2.2 Individual: Joseph Beaumont

4.2.2.1   BEAUMONT, Joseph: *The life of the Rev. Joseph Beaumont, M.D.,* London: Hamilton, Adams and Co., 1856, xv + 403p.

4.2.2.2   WRENCH, Richard: *A biographical & critical sketch of Dr. Beaumont, the eloquent orator,* London: Partridge and Co., 1859, 54p.

4.2.3 Individual: Joseph Benson

4.2.3.1   MACDONALD, James: *Memoirs of the Rev. Joseph Benson,* London: T. Blanshard, 1822, viii + 541p.

4.2.3.2   TREFFRY, Richard: *Memoirs of the Rev. Joseph Benson,* London: John Mason, 1840, 363p.

See also 4.1.2.2.

4.2.4 Individual: Samuel Bradburn

4.2.4.1   BLANSHARD, Thomas W.: *The life of Samuel Bradburn, the Methodist Demosthenes,* London: Elliot Stock, 1870, xi + 292p.

4.2.4.2   BRADBURN, Samuel: *Memoirs of the late Rev. Samuel Bradburn, consisting principally of a narrative of his early life, written by himself, and extracts from a journal which he kept upwards of forty years; to which is added a selection from his manuscripts by Eliza Weaver Bradburn,* London: Richard Edwards, 1816, xi + 237p.

4.2.5 Individual: Jabez Bunting

4.2.5.1   BUNTING, Thomas Percival: *The life of Jabez Bunting, D.D., with notices of contemporary persons and events,* [completed by George Stringer Rowe], London: Longman, Brown, Green, Longmans & Roberts, 1859–87, 2 vol.

4.2.5.2   KENT, John Henry Somerset: 'The interpretation of Jabez Bunting', *Proceedings of the Wesley Historical Society,* Vol. XXXI, 1957–58, pp. 125–32, 150–4, Vol. XXXII, 1959–60, pp. 13–17.

4.2.5.3   MAYNARD, William B.: 'The constitutional authority of Dr. Jabez Bunting over Wesleyan Methodism as seen through his correspondence', University of Durham M.A. thesis, 1970, [4] + iii + 192p.

4.2.5.4   RIGG, James Harrison: *Jabez Bunting, a great Methodist leader,* London: Charles H. Kelly, [1905], 126p.

See also 3.1.2.4, 3.1.2.5, 4.1.2.3, 4.1.2.4, 4.1.5.1, 4.1.5.2, 4.4.2.9.

4.2.6 Individual: Samuel Chadwick

4.2.6.1   DUNNING, Norman Grove: *Samuel Chadwick*, London: Hodder and Stoughton, 1933, 250p.

4.2.6.2   HOWARTH, David Heighton: *How great a flame: Samuel Chadwick, 50 years on*, Ilkeston: Moorley's Bible & Bookshop Ltd., 1983, 41p.

4.2.6.3   HOWARTH, David Heighton: 'Samuel Chadwick and some aspects of Wesleyan Methodist evangelism, 1860–1932', University of Lancaster M.Litt. thesis, 1977, viii+341p.

4.2.7 Individual: Thomas Champness

4.2.7.1   CHAMPNESS, Eliza M.: *The life-story of Thomas Champness*, London: Charles H. Kelly, [1907], xiii+370p.

4.2.7.2   MEADLEY, Thomas Donald: *Kindled by a spark: The story of Thomas Champness*, Ilkeston: Moorley's Bible & Bookshop Ltd., 1983, 48p.

4.2.7.3   MEE, Josiah: *Thomas Champness as I knew him*, London: Charles H. Kelly, [1906], 128p.

See also 4.4.5.2.

4.2.8 Individual: Adam Clarke

4.2.8.1   DUNN, Samuel: *The life of Adam Clarke, LL.D., author of a commentary on the Old and New Testaments, etc.*, London: William Tegg, 1863, vii+250p.

4.2.8.2   EDWARDS, Maldwyn Lloyd: *Adam Clarke*, Wesley Historical Society Lectures No. 8, London: Epworth Press, 1942, 48p.

4.2.8.3   ETHERIDGE, John Wesley: *The life of the Rev. Adam Clarke*, London: John Mason, 1858, viii+439p.

4.2.8.4   EVERETT, James: *Adam Clarke portrayed*, second edition, carefully revised and enlarged, London: W. Reed, 1866, 2 vol.

4.2.8.5   GALLAGHER, Robert Henry: *Adam Clarke, saint and scholar: A Memoir*, [Belfast: Wesley Historical Society (Irish Branch), 1963], 106p.

4.2.8.6   [HARE, John Middleton]: *The life and labours of Adam Clarke, LL.D.*, second edition [revised], London: Longman, Brown, Green and Longmans, 1842, xi+416p.

4.2.8.7   JONES, William: *Memoirs of the life, ministry and writings of the Rev. Adam Clarke, LL.D., F.S.A.*, London: printed by J. M'Gowan, 1834, xiii+700p.

4.2.8.8   NEWNES, T. M.: *Memoirs of the life of the Rev. Adam Clarke, LL.D., F.A.S.: A new narrative, with strictures on his creed, commentary and other works, remarks on preaching*, Halifax: printed by Milner and Sowerby, 1858, 384p.

4.2.8.9   [SMITH, Mary Ann]: *An account of the infancy, religious and literary life of Adam Clarke, written by one who was intimately acquainted with him from his boyhood to the sixtieth year of his age*, edited by Joseph Butterworth Bulmer Clarke, London: T. S. Clarke, 1833, 3 vol.

4.2.8.10 WELLS, Raymond James: 'Adam Clarke, LL.D. (1760?–1832) as Church leader in early Methodism', University of Edinburgh Ph.D. thesis, 1957, xiv + 404p.

4.2.8.11 A WESLEYAN PREACHER: *The life of the Rev. Adam Clarke, LL.D., compiled from authentic documents*, London: Joseph Smith, 1837, 299p.

See also 4.3.1.2, 4.3.1.6.

4.2.9 Individual: Thomas Cook

4.2.9.1 COOK, Vallance Cole: *Thomas Cook, evangelist-saint: An appreciation*, London: Hazell, Watson & Viney, 1913, 221p.

4.2.9.2 SMART, Henry Thomas: *The life of Thomas Cook, evangelist and first principal of Cliff College, Calver*, London: Charles H. Kelly, 1913, 316p.

4.2.9.3 SMART, Henry Thomas: *Thomas Cook's early ministry, with incidents and suggestions concerning Christian work*, London: Charles H. Kelly, 1892, ix + 246p.

4.2.9.4 WOOD, Arthur Skevington: *On fire for God: Thomas Cook*, Ilkeston: Moorley's Bible & Bookshop Ltd., 1983, 32p.

See also 4.4.5.2.

4.2.10 Individual: Hugh Price Hughes

4.2.10.1 HUGHES, Dorothea Price: *The life of Hugh Price Hughes*, London: Hodder and Stoughton, 1904, xii + 679p.

4.2.10.2 KENT, John Henry Somerset: 'Hugh Price Hughes and the Nonconformist Conscience', *Essays in modern English church history in memory of Norman Sykes*, edited by Gareth Vaughan Bennett & John Dixon Walsh, London: Adam & Charles Black, 1966, pp. 181–205.

4.2.10.3 KING, William McGuire: 'Hugh Price Hughes and the British "social gospel"', *Journal of Religious History*, Vol. 13, 1984–85, pp. 66–82.

4.2.10.4 MANTLE, John Gregory: *Hugh Price Hughes*, London: S. W. Partridge & Co., 1901, 158p.

4.2.10.5 ROBERTS, John Price: *Hugh Price Hughes, un o Gymry enwocaf yr oes: Ei fywyd a'i lafur*, Bangor: Evan Thomas, 1903, vi + 224p.

4.2.10.6 WALTERS, Arthur: *Hugh Price Hughes, pioneer and reformer*, London: Robert Culley, [1907], 128p.

See also 4.5.1.6, 4.5.2.1, 4.5.2.4.

4.2.11 Individual: Thomas Jackson

4.2.11.1 JACKSON, Thomas: *Recollections of my own life and times*, edited by Benjamin Frankland, London: Wesleyan Conference Office, 1873, xviii + 524p.

4.2.11.2 RUPP, Ernest Gordon: *Thomas Jackson, Methodist patriarch*, Wesley Historical Society Lecture 1954, London: Epworth Press, 1954, 54p.

4.2.12 Individual: Samuel Keeble

4.2.12.1 EDWARDS, Maldwyn Lloyd: *S. E. Keeble, pioneer and prophet*, London: Epworth Press, 1949, xviii+106p.

4.2.12.2 EDWARDS, Michael Stone: 'S. E. Keeble and Nonconformist social thinking, 1880–1939', University of Bristol M.Litt. thesis, 1969, [4]+283p.

4.2.12.3 EDWARDS, Michael Stone: *S. E. Keeble, the rejected prophet*, Broxton: Wesley Historical Society, 1977, [2]+71p.

See also 4.5.2.1.

4.2.13 Individual: John Scott Lidgett

4.2.13.1 *John Scott Lidgett: A symposium*, edited by Rupert Eric Davies, London: Epworth Press, 1957, xi+212p.

4.2.13.2 LIDGETT, John Scott: *My guided life*, London: Methuen & Co., 1936, vii+279p.

4.2.13.3 LIDGETT, John Scott: *Reminiscences*, London: Epworth Press, [1928], 95p.

See also 4.4.2.12, 4.5.3.6, 4.5.3.25.

4.2.14 Individual: Frederic William Macdonald

4.2.14.1 MACDONALD, Frederic William: *As a tale that is told: Recollections of many years*, London: Cassell & Company, 1919, ix+394p.

4.2.14.2 MACDONALD, Frederic William: *Reminiscences of my early ministry*, London: Jarrold & Sons, [1913], 232p.

4.2.15 Individual: Peter Mackenzie

4.2.15.1 DAWSON, Joseph: *Peter Mackenzie: His life and labours*, London: Charles H. Kelly, 1896, xi+348p.

4.2.15.2 YOUNG, Dinsdale Thomas: *Peter Mackenzie as I knew him*, London: Hodder and Stoughton, 1904, 127p.

4.2.16 Individual: James Hope Moulton

4.2.16.1 MOULTON, Harold Keeling: *James Hope Moulton, 11th October 1863–7th April 1917*, London: Epworth Press, 1963, 60p.

4.2.16.2 [MOULTON, William Fiddian]: *James Hope Moulton*, London: Epworth Press, 1919, 200p.

4.2.17 Individual: William F. Moulton

4.2.17.1 FINDLAY, George Gillanders: *William F. Moulton, the Methodist scholar*, London: Robert Culley, 1910, 127p.

4.2.17.2 Moulton, William Fiddian: *William F. Moulton: A memoir*, London: Isbister and Company, 1899, 295p.

4.2.18 Individual: Robert Newton

4.2.18.1 Jackson, Thomas: *The life of the Rev. Robert Newton, D.D.*, London: John Mason, 1855, xiv+427p.

4.2.18.2 A Wesleyan Preacher: *The life, labours and travels of the Rev. Robert Newton*, London: Simpkin, Marshall and Co., 1854, 184p.

4.2.18.3 Young, Dinsdale Thomas: *Robert Newton, the eloquent divine*, London: Charles H. Kelly, [1907], 128p.

4.2.19 Individual: Gideon Ouseley

4.2.19.1 Arthur, William: *The life of Gideon Ouseley*, London: Wesleyan Conference Office, 1876, ix+304p.

4.2.19.2 Reilly, William: *A memorial of the ministerial life of the Rev. Gideon Ouseley, Irish missionary; comprising sketches of the mission in connection with which he laboured, under the direction of the Wesleyan Conference, with notices of some of the most distinguished Irish Methodist missionaries*, London: John Mason, 1847, xiii+318p.

4.2.20 Individual: William Burt Pope

4.2.20.1 Moss, Richard Waddy: *The Rev. W. B. Pope, D.D., theologian and saint*, London: Robert Culley, [1909], 126p.
See also 4.3.1.2, 4.3.1.5.

4.2.21 Individual: William Morley Punshon

4.2.21.1 Dawson, Joseph: *William Morley Punshon, the orator of Methodism*, London: Charles H. Kelly, [1906], 128p.

4.2.21.2 M'Cullagh, Thomas: *The Reverend William Morley Punshon: A memorial sermon preached at George Street Chapel, Grimsby before the Hull District Meeting, with some personal recollections of Dr. Punshon's earlier life and ministry*, London: Wesleyan Conference Office, 1881, 78p.

4.2.21.3 Macdonald, Frederic William: *The life of William Morley Punshon, LL.D.*, London: Hodder and Stoughton, 1887, xi+514p.

4.2.22 Individual: James Harrison Rigg

4.2.22.1 Rigg, James Harrison: *Wesleyan Methodist reminiscences sixty years ago*, London: Robert Culley, 1904, viii+164p.

4.2.22.2 Telford, John: *The life of James Harrison Rigg, D.D., 1821–1909*, London: Robert Culley, [1909], ix+423p.

4.2.23 Individual: Joseph Rayner Stephens

4.2.23.1 EDWARDS, Michael Stone: *Joseph Rayner Stephens, 1805–1879: A lecture delivered at Stamford St. Methodist Church, Ashton-under-Lyne on July 3rd. 1967*, Wesley Historical Society (Lancashire & Cheshire Branch) Occasional Publication No. 3, Hyde: Wesley Historical Society (Lancashire & Cheshire Branch), 1968, 20p.

4.2.23.2 EDWARDS, Michael Stone: 'The resignation of Joseph Rayner Stephens', *Proceedings of the Wesley Historical Society*, Vol. XXXVI, 1967–68, pp. 16–21.

4.2.23.3 HOLYOAKE, George Jacob: *The life of Joseph Rayner Stephens, preacher and political orator*, London: Williams and Norgate, [1881], 244p.

4.2.23.4 JOHNSON, Dale Arthur: 'Between evangelicalism and a social gospel: The case of Joseph Rayner Stephens', *Church History*, Vol. XLII, 1973, pp. 229–42.

4.2.23.5 KEMNITZ, Thomas Milton & JACQUES, Fleurange: 'J. R. Stephens and the Chartist movement', *International Review of Social History*, Vol. XIX, 1974, pp. 211–27.

4.2.23.6 MICKLEWRIGHT, Frederick Henry Amphlett: 'Joseph Rayner Stephens: A reassessment', *London Quarterly and Holborn Review*, Vol. CLXVIII, 1943, pp. 51–8.

4.2.23.7 TAYLOR, Michael: 'Joseph Rayner Stephens, political preacher', University of California, Los Angeles Ph.D. thesis, 1966, xiii + 338p.

4.2.23.8 WARD, John Towers: 'Revolutionary Tory: The life of Joseph Rayner Stephens of Ashton-under-Lyne (1805–1879)', *Transactions of the Lancashire and Cheshire Antiquarian Society*, Vol. LXVIII, 1958, pp. 93–116.

4.2.24 Individual: Thomas Bowman Stephenson

4.2.24.1 BRADFIELD, William: *The life of the Reverend Thomas Bowman Stephenson, B.A., LL.D., D.D., founder of 'The Children's Home' and of the Wesley Deaconess Institute*, London: Charles H. Kelly, 1913, 459p.

4.2.24.2 DAVEY, Cyril James: *A man for all children: The story of Thomas Bowman Stephenson*, London: Epworth Press, 1968, 128p.

4.2.25 Individual: Richard Watson

4.2.25.1 BRAILSFORD, Edward John: *Richard Watson, theologian and missionary advocate*, London: Charles H. Kelly, [1906], 128p.

4.2.25.2 FENNELL, William O.: 'Reflections on the life and work of Richard Watson (1781–1833), with special attention to the question of the role of reason in the life of faith', *The Bulletin* [of the Committee on Archives of the United Church of Canada], No. 27, 1978, pp. 57–68.

4.2.25.3 JACKSON, Thomas: *Memoirs of the life and writings of the Rev. Richard Watson, late Secretary to the Wesleyan Missionary Society*, London: John Mason, 1834, xv + 667p.

4.2.25.4 LITTLETON, William Harvey: 'Rev. Richard Watson, 1781–1833: His work and religious thought', University of Edinburgh Ph.D. thesis, 1956, iii + 438p.

See also 4.3.1.2.

4.2.26 Individual: Dinsdale Young

4.2.26.1 MURRAY, Harold: *Dinsdale Young, the preacher: An intimate sketch of Dr. Dinsdale T. Young*, London: Marshall, Morgan & Scott, [1938], 144p.

4.2.26.2 YOUNG, Dinsdale Thomas: *Stars of retrospect: Frank chapters of autobiography*, London: Hodder and Stoughton, [1920], ix + 242p.

4.2.27 Individual: other ministers

4.2.27.1 ARMSTRONG, Walter Henry: *John Alfred Sharp: A memoir*, London: Epworth Press, 1932, 132p.

4.2.27.2 CHILCOTE, Paul Wesley: 'The legacy of J. Ernest Rattenbury', *Methodist History*, Vol. XXI, 1982–83, pp. 207–24.

4.2.27.3 COLEY, Samuel: *The life of the Rev. Thomas Collins*, London: Hamilton, Adams and Co., 1868, 493p.

4.2.27.4 DICKINSON, Robert: *The life of the Rev. John Braithwaite, Wesleyan Methodist preacher, containing an account of his travels, labours in the ministry and writings, with a short memoir of his wife, Mrs. Mary Braithwaite; compiled from his letters and other authentic documents*, London: printed for John Broadbent, 1825, viii + 603p.

4.2.27.5 DIXON, Richard Watson: *The life of James Dixon, D.D., Wesleyan minister*, London: published for the author at the Wesleyan Conference Office, 1874, xii + 500p.

4.2.27.6 ENTWISLE, Joseph: *Memoir of the Rev. Joseph Entwisle, fifty-four years a Wesleyan minister; with copious extracts from his journals and correspondence and occasional notices of contemporary events in the history of Methodism*, Bristol: N. Lomas, 1848, xvi + 576p.

4.2.27.7 FULLERTON, Alexander: *Fifty years an itinerant preacher, being reminiscences of fifty years in the Irish Methodist ministry*, Belfast: Irish Methodist Publishing Co., [1912], 268p.

4.2.27.8 GREGORY, Benjamin: *Benjamin Gregory, D.D.: Autobiographical recollections*, edited, with memorials of his later life, by [John Robinson Gregory], London: Hodder and Stoughton, 1903, viii + 463p.

4.2.27.9 GREGORY, Benjamin: *The life of Frederick James Jobson; with the funeral memorials of Dr. Osborn and Dr. Pope and ten original sermons printed from Dr. Jobson's own manuscripts*, edited by Elizabeth Jobson, London: T. Woolmer, 1884, vi + 328p.

4.2.27.10 HANNAH, John: *Memorials of the life, ministry and correspondence of the Rev. Theophilus Lessey; to which is added a sermon preached on occasion of his death*, London: Hamilton, Adams & Co., 1842, xii + 352p.

4.2.27.11 HARE, John Middleton: *The ministry and character of Robert Henry Hare, Wesleyan minister*, London: published for the author at the Wesleyan Conference Office, 1874, vi + 480p.

4.2.27.12 HARTE, Frederick Edward: *The road I have travelled: The experiences of an Irish Methodist minister*, Belfast: Wm. Mullan & Son, [1947], 207p.

4.2.27.13 HUSTON, Robert: *Life and labours of the Rev. Fossey Tackaberry; with notices of Methodism in Ireland*, second edition, revised and improved, London: John Mason, 1860, xii + 274p.

4.2.27.14 JACKSON, George: *Collier of Manchester: A friend's tribute*, London: Hodder and Stoughton, [1923], x + 207p.

4.2.27.15 JENKINS, James Heald: *Ebenezer E. Jenkins: A memoir*, London: Charles H. Kelly, [1906], 285p.

4.2.27.16 *Joseph Bush: A memorial*, edited by Jane Bush, with a brief memoir by Arthur Hoyle, London: Robert Culley, [1907], 222p.

4.2.27.17 KELLY, Charles Henry: *Memories*, London: Robert Culley, 1910, 368p.

4.2.27.18 LANKTREE, Matthew: *A biographical narrative of Matthew Lanktree, Wesleyan minister, embracing a period of upwards of forty years; comprising numerous characteristic sketches of contemporaries and historical notices of the rise, progress and influence of Methodism in various parts of Ireland*, Belfast: printed by James Wilson, 1836, xiii + 396p.

4.2.27.19 M'CULLAGH, Henry Hays: *Thomas M'Cullagh: A short story of a long life*, London: Robert Culley, [1909], 144p.

4.2.27.20 MALINS, Joseph: *Wilson Stuart: A memoir*, London: J. Clarke & Co., [1935], 159p.

4.2.27.21 MORTON, Elizabeth & DEWAR, Douglas: *A voice crying in the wilderness: A memoir of Harold Christopherson Morton*, London: Thynne & Co., 1937, 270p.

4.2.27.22 [POPE, Robert Martin]: *The life of Henry J. Pope*, London: Charles H. Kelly, 1913, 284p.

4.2.27.23 *The Rev. Gervase Smith, D.D.: A memorial volume*, edited by Alfred Owen Smith, London: T. Woolmer, 1882, xlvii + 432p.

4.2.27.24 RULE, William Harris: *Recollections of my life and work at home and abroad in connection with the Wesleyan Methodist Conference*, London: T. Woolmer, 1886, viii + 319p.

4.2.27.25 SHARPLEY, Arthur Edward: *The life of David James Waller, D.D., consisting chiefly of selections from his journals*, London: Charles H. Kelly, 1913, 228p.

4.2.27.26 SHREWSBURY, John Vincent Brainerd: *Memorials of the Rev. William J. Shrewsbury*, second edition, London: Hamilton, Adams & Co., [1868], 520p.

4.2.27.27 SMITH, Mary Ann: *The life of the Rev. Mr. Henry Moore, the biographer and executor of the Rev. John Wesley; including the autobiography and the continuation, written from his own papers,* London: Simpkin, Marshall and Co., 1844, viii+408p.

4.2.27.28 STEPHENSON, Thomas Bowman: *William Arthur: A brief biography,* London: Charles H. Kelly, [1907], 126p.

4.2.27.29 THOMPSON, Rosalie Budgett: *Peter Thompson,* London: Charles H. Kelly, 1910, 214p.

4.2.27.30 URWIN, Evelyn Clifford: *Henry Carter, C.B.E.: A memoir,* London: Epworth Press, 1955, 127p.

4.2.27.31 [WADDY, Adeline]: *The life of the Rev. Samuel D. Waddy, D.D.,* London: published for the authoress at the Wesleyan Conference Office, 1878, xiv+464p.

4.2.27.32 WITHINGTON, Thomas: *Reminiscences of the ministerial life of Rev. T. Withington (octogenarian),* Devonport: Josiah Clark and Sons, printers, 1895, xvi+446p.

4.2.27.33 YOUNG, Dinsdale Thomas: *Richard Roberts: A memoir,* London: Charles H. Kelly, [1910], 218p.

See also 4.1.6.4, 4.1.6.5, 4.3.1.1.

4.2.28 Individual: laity

4.2.28.1 BURNETT, Richard George: *Through the mill* [the life of Joseph Rank], London: Epworth Press, 1945, 226p.

4.2.28.2 CRANE, Denis *pseud.* [i.e. Walter Thomas Cranfield]: *The life-story of Sir Robert W. Perks, Baronet, M.P.,* London: Robert Culley, [1909], 240p.

4.2.28.3 [DREW, Jacob Halls]: *The life, character and literary labours of Samuel Drew, A.M.,* London: Longman, Rees, Orme, Brown, Green and Longman, 1834, xii+530p.

4.2.28.4 FOWLER, Edith Henrietta: *The life of Henry Hartley Fowler, first Viscount Wolverhampton, G.C.S.I.,* London: Hutchinson & Co., 1912, x+668p.

4.2.28.5 HAMILTON, Mary Agnes: *Arthur Henderson: A biography,* London: William Heinemann, 1938, viii+461p.

4.2.28.6 HAYES, Thomas: *Recollections of sixty-three years of Methodist life,* London: Charles H. Kelly, 1902, vii+222p.

4.2.28.7 JENNINGS, Elizabeth: 'Sir Isaac Holden, Bart. (1807–97): His place in the Wesleyan connexion', *Proceedings of the Wesley Historical Society,* Vol. XLIII, 1981–82, pp. 117–26, 150–8.

4.2.28.8 JONES, John Harry: *Josiah Stamp, public servant: The life of the first Baron Stamp of Shortlands,* London: Sir Isaac Pitman, 1964, x+365p.

4.2.28.9 LUNN, Henry Simpson: *Chapters from my life, with special reference to reunion,* London: Cassell and Company, 1918, xiii+422p.

4.2.28.10 LUNN, Henry Simpson: *Nearing harbour,* London: Ivor Nicholson & Watson, 1934, vii+328p.

4.2.28.11 M'CULLAGH, Thomas: *Sir William M'Arthur, K.C.M.G.: A biography, religious, parliamentary, municipal, commercial,* London: Hodder and Stoughton, 1891, xvi+398p.

4.2.28.12 WALTERS, Arthur & WALTERS, Charles Ensor: *Sir John Bamford-Slack, preacher and politician*, London: Charles H. Kelly, 1910, 128p.
See also 4.5.1.10, 4.5.3.2.

4.3 Spirituality

4.3.1 Theology

4.3.1.1 BEBBINGTON, David William: 'The persecution of George Jackson: A British fundamentalist controversy', *Persecution and toleration: Papers read at the twenty-second summer meeting and the twenty-third winter meeting of the Ecclesiastical History Society*, edited by William J. Sheils, Studies in Church History 21, [Oxford]: Basil Blackwell, 1984, pp. 421–33.

4.3.1.2 DUNLAP, Elden Dale: 'Methodist theology in Great Britain in the nineteenth century, with special reference to the theology of Adam Clarke, Richard Watson and William Burt Pope', Yale University Ph.D. thesis, 1956, viii+515+[1]p.

4.3.1.3 HOLIFIELD, Elmer Brooks: 'The English Methodist response to Darwin', *Methodist History*, Vol. X, No. 2, January 1972, pp. 14–22.

4.3.1.4 RICHARDS, Glyn: 'A study of the theological developments among Nonconformists in Wales during the nineteenth century', University of Oxford B.Litt. thesis, 1956, [6]+351p.

4.3.1.5 SELL, Alan Philip Frederick: 'An Englishman, an Irishman and a Scotsman . . .' [the theology of William Burt Pope, Robert Watts and Andrew Martin Fairbairn], *Scottish Journal of Theology*, Vol. 38, 1985, pp. 41–83.

4.3.1.6 SELLERS, Ian: *Adam Clarke, controversialist: Wesleyanism and the historic faith in the age of Bunting*, Wesley Historical Society Lecture 1975, [St. Columb Major: Wesley Historical Society, 1976], [9]+21+a–hp.

4.3.1.7 STRAWSON, William: 'Methodist theology, 1850–1950', *A history of the Methodist Church in Great Britain*, Vol. 3, general editors: Rupert Eric Davies, Alfred Raymond George & Ernest Gordon Rupp, London: Epworth Press, 1983, pp. 182–231.

4.3.1.8 *To the uttermost: Commemorating the diamond jubilee of the Southport Methodist Holiness Convention, 1885–1945*, London: Epworth Press, 1945, 79p.

4.3.1.9 WOOD, Arthur Skevington: *Let us go on: One hundred years of the Southport Convention*, Ilkeston: Moorley's Bible & Bookshop Ltd., [1985], 44p.
See also 2.4.2.14, 4.2.8 *passim*, 4.2.16 *passim*, 4.2.17 *passim*, 4.2.20 *passim*, 4.2.25 *passim*, 4.2.27.21, 4.4.2.3.

4.3.2 Sacraments

4.3.2.1 HOLLAND, Bernard George: 'The background to the 1967 Methodist service for infant baptism', *Church Quarterly*, Vol. 2, 1969–70, pp. 43–54.

4.3.2.2   HOLLAND, Bernard George: 'Baptism in Wesleyan Methodism;
          Practice and doctrine to 1882', University of London Ph.D. thesis,
          1966.
See also 4.1.2.2.

4.3.3 Worship and devotion

4.3.3.1   SWIFT, Wesley Frank: 'Methodism and the Book of Common
          Prayer', *Proceedings of the Wesley Historical Society*, Vol. XXVII,
          1949–50, pp. 33–41.
4.3.3.2   SWIFT, Wesley Frank: ' "The Sunday service of the Methodists":
          A study of nineteenth-century liturgy', *Proceedings of the Wesley
          Historical Society*, Vol. XXXI, 1957–58, pp. 112–18, 133–43.
See also 2.6.3.11, 4.4.2.2.

4.3.4 Hymnology and music

4.3.4.1   SPINNEY, Bryan Frank: *Methodist hymn-book revision, 1904 and 1933*,
          [Farnborough: the author], 1980, 15p.
See also 4.5.3.3.

4.3.5 Class meetings and membership

4.3.5.1   DEAN, William Walter: 'The Methodist class meeting: The signi-
          ficance of its decline', *Proceedings of the Wesley Historical Society*,
          Vol. XLIII, 1981–82, pp. 41–8.
4.3.5.2   JONES, Bernard Ewart: 'Society and Church in Wesleyan Method-
          ism, 1878–93', *Proceedings of the Wesley Historical Society*, Vol.
          XXXVI, 1967–68, pp. 134–8.
4.3.5.3   RACK, Henry Derman: 'The decline of the class-meeting and the
          problem of church-membership in nineteenth-century Wesleyan-
          ism', *Proceedings of the Wesley Historical Society*, Vol. XXXIX,
          1973–74, pp. 12–21.
See also 2.6.8.1.

4.4 Polity and Mission

4.4.1 Conference

4.4.1.1   WANSBROUGH, Charles E.: *Handbook and index to the minutes of the
          Conference, showing the growth and development of the Wesleyan Methodist
          constitution from the first Conference, 1744 to 1890*, London: Wesleyan
          Methodist Book-Room, 1890, 311p.
See also 2.7.1.3, 4.1.2.8, 4.1.2.18, 4.2.8.6.

4.4.2 Ordained ministry

4.4.2.1   BOWMER, John Coates: 'Ordination in Wesleyan Methodism,

1791–1850', *Proceedings of the Wesley Historical Society*, Vol. XXXIX, 1973–74, pp. 121–7.

4.4.2.2 BOWMER, John Coates: 'The ordination service in Wesleyan Methodism, 1791–1850', *Proceedings of the Wesley Historical Society*, Vol. XXXIX, 1973–74, pp. 153–7.

4.4.2.3 BOWMER, John Coates: *Pastor and people: A study of Church and ministry in Wesleyan Methodism from the death of John Wesley (1791) to the death of Jabez Bunting (1858)*, London: Epworth Press, 1975, 272p.

4.4.2.4 BOWMER, John Coates: 'The Wesleyan conception of the ministry', *Religion in Life*, Vol. XL, 1971, pp. 85–96.

4.4.2.5 BURGESS, Stuart John: *Seeds of joy* [the development of theological training in Wesleyan Methodism, 1744–1842], Birmingham: Ecumenical Chaplaincy, University of Birmingham, 1985, [9] + 69 + iip.

4.4.2.6 *Didsbury College centenary, 1842–1942*, edited by William Bardsley Brash & Charles James Wright, London: Epworth Press, 1942, 158p.

4.4.2.7 GARLICK, Kenneth Benjamin: 'The Wesleyan Theological Institution: Hoxton and Abney House, 1834–42', *Proceedings of the Wesley Historical Society*, Vol. XXXIX, 1973–74, pp. 104–12.

4.4.2.8 JOHNSON, Dale Arthur: 'The Methodist quest for an educated ministry', *Church History*, Vol. 51, 1982, pp. 304–20.

4.4.2.9 KENT, John Henry Somerset: *Jabez Bunting, the last Wesleyan: A study in the Methodist ministry after the death of John Wesley*, Wesley Historical Society Lecture 1955, London: Epworth Press, 1955, 62p.

4.4.2.10 LIDGETT, John Scott: 'The Theological Institution: Some noted tutors of yesterday', *London Quarterly and Holborn Review*, Vol. CLXI, 1936, pp. 1–13.

4.4.2.11 LOWERY, Ralph: 'The Wesleyan Theological Institution, Hoxton: A further study', *Proceedings of the Wesley Historical Society*, Vol. XXXIX, 1973–74, pp. 128–36.

4.4.2.12 RICHARDS, Edgar: 'The nature of the Free Church ministry, with special reference to (a) the writings of A. M. Fairbairn, J. Oman, P. T. Forsyth and J. Scott Lidgett, and (b) recent reunion proposals', University of London Ph.D. thesis, 1967, 389p.

4.4.2.13 *Richmond College, 1843–1943*, edited by Frank Henry Cumbers, London: Epworth Press, 1944, 190p.

4.4.2.14 VINE, Victor Edward: ' "Episcopé" in Methodism', *Proceedings of the Wesley Historical Society*, Vol. XXX, 1955–56, pp. 162–70.

4.4.2.15 WARD, William Reginald: 'The legacy of John Wesley: The pastoral office in Britain and America', *Statesmen, scholars and merchants: Essays in eighteenth-century history presented to Dame Lucy Sutherland*, edited by Anne Whiteman, John Selwyn Bromley & Peter George Muir Dickson, Oxford: Clarendon Press, 1973, pp. 323–50.

See also 2.7.2.8, 2.7.2.9, 2.7.2.10, 2.7.2.14, 4.1.3.3, 4.2.1.1, 4.4.5.12, 4.5.3.9, 4.5.3.12, 6.3.1.11.

4.4.3 Lay ministry

4.4.3.1   [LAWSON, William D.]: *Wesleyan local preachers: Biographical illustrations of their position in the Connexion, utility in the Church and influence in the world*, Newcastle-upon-Tyne: Wm. D. Lawson, 1874, xv + 334p.
See also 1.4.2.1, 2.7.3.6, 4.2.24.1, 4.4.6.3.

4.4.4 Buildings and finance

4.4.4.1   DOLBEY, George William: 'The architectural expression of Methodism in the eighteenth and nineteenth centuries', University of Manchester M.A. thesis, 1962, [5] + 440 + [3]p.
See also 2.7.4.3, 4.1.3.3, 4.2.28.1.

4.4.5 Home missions

4.4.5.1   BAXTER, John L.: 'The great Yorkshire revival, 1792–6: A study of mass revival among the Methodists', *A sociological yearbook of religion in Britain, 7*, edited by Michael Hill, London: SCM Press, 1974, pp. 46–76.

4.4.5.2   BRICE, Joseph Isaac: *The crowd for Christ* [a study of the evangelistic work of Thomas Champness, Thomas Cook and others, with special reference to Cliff College], London: Hodder and Stoughton, 1934, 160p.

4.4.5.3   CRESSWELL, Amos Samuel: *The story of Cliff* [College], [revised edition], Calver: Joyful News Book Room, 1983, 43p.

4.4.5.4   HAIRE, Robert: *The story of the '59 revival, with some Methodist sidelights*, Belfast: Nelson & Knox Ltd., Printers, [1959], 36p.

4.4.5.5   HOWARTH, David Heighton: ' "Joyful News" (1883–1963): Some reflections', *Proceedings of the Wesley Historical Society*, Vol. XLIV, 1983–84, pp. 2–15.

4.4.5.6   INGLIS, Kenneth Stanley: *Churches and the working classes in Victorian England*, London: Routledge and Kegan Paul, 1963, viii + 350p.

4.4.5.7   LAMBERT, David Willoughby: *What hath God wrought: The story of Cliff College, 1904–1954*, [Calver: Cliff College, 1954], 83p.

4.4.5.8   MOULTON, William Fiddian: *The story of Cliff: A college of the unprivileged, for the training of evangelists*, London: Epworth Press, 1928, 64p.

4.4.5.9   *Quest and crusade – the story of a spiritual adventure: Issued by the editorial board of the Fellowship of the Kingdom to mark the twenty-first anniversary of the movement*, London: Epworth Press, 1939, 52p.

4.4.5.10   RULE, William Harris: *An account of the establishment of Wesleyan Methodism in the British army*, London: T. Woolmer, 1883, 128p.

4.4.5.11   SAILS, George William: *At the centre: The story of Methodism's central missions,* Home Mission Occasional Papers No. 15, London: Methodist Church Home Mission Department, 1970, [6] + 103p.

4.4.5.12   WATKINS, Owen Spencer: *Soldiers and preachers too; being the romantic story of Methodism in the British army, with a complete record of the war service of Wesleyan chaplains to the forces*, London: Charles H. Kelly, [1906], xiv + 267p.

See also 4.1.2.10, 4.2.6 *passim*, 4.2.7 *passim*, 4.2.9 *passim*, 4.2.27.14, 4.2.27.22, 4.2.27.29.

4.4.6 Overseas missions

4.4.6.1   FINDLAY, George Gillanders & FINDLAY, Mary Grace: *Wesley's world parish: A sketch of the hundred years' work of the Wesleyan Methodist Missionary Society*, London: Hodder and Stoughton, 1913, 224p.

4.4.6.2   FINDLAY, George Gillanders & HOLDSWORTH, William West: *The history of the Wesleyan Methodist Missionary Society*, London: Epworth Press, 1921–24, 5 vol.

4.4.6.3   HELLIER, Anna Maria: *Workers together: The story of the Women's Auxiliary of the Wesleyan Methodist Missionary Society*, new and revised edition, London: Cargate Press, [1931], 64p.

4.4.6.4   MARTIN, Roger Harry: 'Missionary competition between evangelical Dissenters and Wesleyan Methodists in the early nineteenth century: A footnote to the founding of the Methodist Missionary Society', *Proceedings of the Wesley Historical Society*, Vol. XLII, 1979–80, pp. 81–6.

4.4.6.5   MOISTER, William: *A history of Wesleyan missions in all parts of the world from their commencement to the present time*, second and revised edition, London: Elliot Stock, 1871, xv + 557p.

4.4.6.6   MOISTER, William: *Missionary worthies; being brief memorial sketches of ministers sent forth by the Wesleyan Missionary Society who have died in the work from the beginning*, London: T. Woolmer, 1885, viii + 438p.

4.4.6.7   PIGGIN, Frederic Stuart: 'Halévy revisited: The origins of the Wesleyan Methodist Missionary Society – an examination of Semmel's thesis', *Journal of Imperial and Commonwealth History*, Vol. IX, 1980–81, pp. 17–37.

4.4.6.8   POTTER, Sarah Caroline: 'The social origins and recruitment of English Protestant missionaries in the nineteenth century', University of London Ph.D. thesis, 1974, 274p.

4.4.6.9   SARGANT, Norman Carr: 'The missionary controversy, 1889–1900', *London Quarterly and Holborn Review*, Vol. CXC, 1965, pp. 304–10.

4.4.6.10   STANLEY, Brian: 'Home support for overseas missions in early Victorian England, c. 1838–1873', University of Cambridge Ph.D. thesis, 1979, 361p.

4.4.6.11   TELFORD, John: *A short history of Wesleyan Methodist foreign missions*, London: Charles H. Kelly, [1906], viii + 281p.

4.4.6.12   WILLIAMS, Cecil Peter: 'The recruitment and training of overseas missionaries in England between 1850 and 1900, with special reference to the records of the Church Missionary Society, the Wesleyan

Methodist Missionary Society, the London Missionary Society and the China Inland Mission', University of Bristol M.Litt. thesis, 1976, xi + 409p.
See also 2.3.2 *passim*, 4.2.25 *passim*, 4.2.27.15, 4.2.27.24, 4.2.28.6, 4.4.2.13.

4.5 Social Aspects

4.5.1 Political impact

4.5.1.1 ANSTEY, Roger Thomas: 'Parliamentary reform, Methodism and anti-slavery politics, 1829–1833', *Slavery and Abolition*, Vol. 2, 1981, pp. 209–26.

4.5.1.2 ANSTEY, Roger Thomas: 'Religion and British slave emancipation', *The abolition of the Atlantic slave trade: Origins and effects in Europe, Africa and the Americas*, edited by David Eltis & James Walvin, Madison: University of Wisconsin Press, 1981, pp. 37–61.

4.5.1.3 BEBBINGTON, David William: 'Nonconformity and electoral sociology, 1867–1918', *Historical Journal*, Vol. 27, 1984, pp. 633–56.

4.5.1.4 BROWN, Brian Dennis: 'Methodism, the labour movement and the General Strike of 1926', University of Birmingham M.A. thesis, 1977, 62p.

4.5.1.5 ENGEMAN, Thomas Sledge: 'Religion and political reform: Wesleyan Methodism in nineteenth-century Britain', *Journal of Church and State*, Vol. 24, 1982, pp. 321–36.

4.5.1.6 GLASER, John Frederic: 'Parnell's fall and the Nonconformist Conscience', *Irish Historical Studies*, Vol. XII, 1960–61, pp. 119–38.

4.5.1.7 GOWLAND, David Alexander: 'Political opinion in Manchester Wesleyanism, 1832–57', *Proceedings of the Wesley Historical Society*, Vol. XXXVI, 1967–68, pp. 93–104.

4.5.1.8 HEMPTON, David Neil: 'Methodism and anti-Catholic politics, 1800–1846', University of St. Andrews Ph.D. thesis, 1977, [4] + 343p.

4.5.1.9 HEMPTON, David Neil: *Methodism and politics in British society, 1750–1850*, London: Hutchinson, 1984, 276p.

4.5.1.10 HEMPTON, David Neil: 'Thomas Allan and Methodist politics, 1800–1840', *History*, Vol. 67, 1982, pp. 13–31.

4.5.1.11 HEMPTON, David Neil: ' "The Watchman" and "religious politics" in the 1830s', *Proceedings of the Wesley Historical Society*, Vol. XLII, 1979–80, pp. 2–13.

4.5.1.12 HEMPTON, David Neil: 'Wesleyan Methodism and educational politics in early nineteenth-century England', *History of Education*, Vol. 8, 1979, pp. 207–21.

4.5.1.13 ITZKIN, Elissa S.: 'The Halévy thesis – a working hypothesis? English revivalism: antidote for revolution and radicalism, 1789–1815', *Church History*, Vol. 44, 1975, pp. 47–56.

4.5.1.14 KOSS, Stephen Edward: 'Wesleyanism and empire', *Historical Journal*, Vol. XVIII, 1975, pp. 105–18.

4.5.1.15   MARLOW, Joyce *pseud.* [i.e. Joyce Mary Connor]: *The Tolpuddle martyrs*, London: André Deutsch, 1971, 320p.

4.5.1.16   PIGGIN, Frederic Stuart: 'A Marxist looks at Methodism: A critique of E. P. Thompson's assessment of the role of Methodism in an age of revolution', *Dig or die: Papers given at the World Methodist Historical Society Wesley Heritage Conference at Wesley College within the University of Sydney, 10–15 August 1980*, edited by James Stuart Udy & Eric Gerald Clancy, Sydney: World Methodist Historical Society Australasian Section, 1981, pp. 290–305.

4.5.1.17   SIMON, John Smith: 'The repeal of the Conventicle Act', *Proceedings of the Wesley Historical Society*, Vol. XI, 1917–18, pp. 103–8, 130–7.

4.5.1.18   STIGANT, Edward Paul: 'Methodism and the working class, 1760–1821: A study in social and political conflict', University of Keele M.A. thesis, 1968, 361p.

4.5.1.19   STIGANT, Edward Paul: 'Wesleyan Methodism and working-class radicalism in the North, 1792–1821', *Northern History*, Vol. VI, 1971, pp. 98–116.

4.5.1.20   WHITNEY, Arthur Percy: 'Wesleyanism and the French Revolution', New York University M.A. thesis, 1942.

4.5.1.21   WILLIAMS, Albert Hughes: 'Wesleaeth Gymreig a pholitics, 1800–1900', *Bathafarn*, Vol. 6, 1951, pp. 5–49.

See also 2.8.1.35, 4.1.2.5, 4.1.2.6, 4.1.2.10, 4.2.10.2, 4.2.23 *passim*, 4.2.28.2, 4.2.28.4, 4.2.28.5, 4.2.28.11, 4.2.28.12, 4.6.2.2.

4.5.2 Social witness

4.5.2.1   CHEATHAM, Carl Wade: 'Social Christianity: A study of English Nonconformist social attitudes, 1880–1914' [with special reference to Hugh Price Hughes, Samuel Edward Keeble, John Clifford and Reginald John Campbell], Vanderbilt University Ph.D. thesis, 1982, 377p.

4.5.2.2   INGLIS, Kenneth Stanley: 'English Nonconformity and social reform, 1880–1900', *Past & Present*, No. 13, April 1958, pp. 73–88.

4.5.2.3   JACKA, Alan Ashby: *The story of the Children's Home*, London: National Children's Home, 1969, 64p.

4.5.2.4   RATLEDGE, Wilbert Harold: 'Evangelicals and social change: The social thought of three British evangelical preachers [Robert William Dale, Hugh Price Hughes and William Connor Magee], 1850–1900', North Texas State University Ph.D. thesis, 1982, 430p.

See also 2.8.2.9, 4.1.3.3, 4.1.3.14, 4.2.10.3, 4.2.12 *passim*, 4.2.24 *passim*, 4.2.27.1, 4.2.27.20, 4.2.27.30, 4.5.1.2, 6.5.6.1.

4.5.3 Educational work

4.5.3.1   BAKER, Derek: *Partnership in excellence: A late-Victorian educational venture, the Leys School, Cambridge, 1875–1975*, Cambridge: Governors of the Leys School, 1975, xvi+272p.

4.5.3.2 BROWN, Anne: 'William Spencer: His influence on Wesleyan education in Beverley, 1848–1887', University of Hull M.Ed. thesis, 1983, [5]+i+152p.

4.5.3.3 BUCKROYD, Elizabeth Ann: *Education or indoctrination? The role of authorized hymnody in the early Sunday schools of the Wesleyan Methodist connexion*, Robert Raikes Historical Society Annual Lecture 1978, [Nutfield: Robert Raikes Historical Society, 1979, 29p.].

4.5.3.4 CHANNON, Henry James: *History of Queen's College, Taunton*, Taunton: Old Queenians' Association, [1957], 215p.

4.5.3.5 COLE, Richard Lee: *Wesley College, Dublin: An historical summary, 1845–1962*, Dublin: A.P.C.K., 1963, xi+152p.

4.5.3.6 CREWES, Frederick Ronald: 'An evaluation of the contribution to education of Rev. Dr. John Scott Lidgett, with special reference to his work at the Bermondsey Settlement', University of London M.A. thesis, 1973, 66p.

4.5.3.7 GOWLAND, David Alexander: 'Methodism and the education of the people', *Journal of the Scottish Branch of the Wesley Historical Society*, Vol. 12, May 1980, pp. 16–24, Vol. 13, August 1981, pp. 2–6.

4.5.3.8 GREENER, Tom: 'Methodism and primary education', *Wesley Historical Society North-East Branch Bulletin*, No. 36, August 1981, pp. 14–18, No. 37, March 1982, pp. 19–26, No. 38, September 1982, pp. 5–14.

4.5.3.9 HENDERSON, John Watson: *Methodist College, Belfast, 1868–1938: A survey and retrospect*, Belfast: Governors of the Methodist College, 1939, 2 vol.

4.5.3.10 HOVEY, Rosa: *Penrhos, 1880–1930*, [Colwyn Bay: Penrhos College, 1930], 83p.

4.5.3.11 INGRAM, Leonard E.: *Fifty years for youth* [the story of the Wesley Guild], London: Methodist Youth Department, 1945, 47p.

4.5.3.12 MARSHALL, Ronald: *Methodist College, Belfast: The first hundred years*, Belfast: Governors of Methodist College, Belfast, [1968], xi+220p.

4.5.3.13 MATHEWS, Horace Frederick: *Methodism and the education of the people, 1791–1851*, London: Epworth Press, 1949, 215p.

4.5.3.14 MATHEWS, Horace Frederick: 'Methodism and the education of the people (since 1851)', University of London Ph.D. thesis, 1954, 521p.

4.5.3.15 PRITCHARD, Frank Cyril: *The story of Westminster College, 1851–1951*, London: Epworth Press, 1951, viii+213p.

4.5.3.16 PRITCHARD, Frank Cyril: *The story of Woodhouse Grove School*, Apperley Bridge: Woodhouse Grove School, 1978, xiv+411p.

4.5.3.17 *Rydal School, 1885–1935*, Colwyn Bay: Rydal Press, [1935], 240p.

4.5.3.18 *Rydal, the first hundred years: A short illustrated history of the School*, Ernest Bradfield, editor, [Colwyn Bay: Rydal School], 1985, 52p.

4.5.3.19 SKINNER, John William: *Culford School, 1881–1951*, Bury St. Edmunds: printed by West Suffolk Newspapers Limited, [1951], 52p.

4.5.3.20 SLATER, A. P. L.: *10,001 facts about Kent College*, [Canterbury: Kent College, 1985], 63p.

4.5.3.21 SLUGG, Josiah Thomas: *Woodhouse Grove School: Memorials and reminiscences*, London: T. Woolmer, 1885, ix+353p.

4.5.3.22 STAFFORD, Helen Muriel: *Queenswood: The first sixty years, 1894–1954*, [Hatfield: Queenswood School], 1954, 64p.

4.5.3.23 [STARKEY, Henry Walton]: *Woodhouse Grove School: A brief sketch of the history of the Grove under the old foundation followed by a short account of the School from the establishment of the new foundation in 1883 to the celebration of the centenary in 1912*, Bradford: W. N. Sharpe, 1912, 112p.

4.5.3.24 THOMAS, Antony Charles: *Methodism and self-improvement in nineteenth-century Cornwall*, Cornish Methodist Historical Association Occasional Publication No. 9, Redruth: Cornish Methodist Historical Association, 1965, 26p.

4.5.3.25 THOMAS, David Hubert: 'John Scott Lidgett, 1854–1953 and the education of the people', University of London Ph.D. thesis, 1960, 486p.

4.5.3.26 *Truro School centenary, 1880–1980*, Nigel Baker, editor, [Truro: Truro School, 1979], 56p.

4.5.3.27 WATSON, F. E.: *Culford School: The first hundred years, 1881–1981*, [Bury St. Edmunds]: Governors of Culford School, 1980, 216p.

4.5.3.28 WILLIAMS, Eva: *The history of Southlands College, 1872–1972*, [London: Southlands College, 1972], 95p.

4.5.3.29 *Woodhouse Grove School, 1812–1962: A hundred and fifty years of memories and recollections*, Clifford William Towlson, editor, [Apperley Bridge]: Old Grovian Association, [1962], viii+155p.

4.5.3.30 WRIGHT, Christopher: *The Kent College centenary book*, London: B. T. Batsford, 1985, 160p.

See also 4.2.27.25, 4.5.1.12, 4.6.2.2.

4.5.4 Contribution to science and medicine

4.5.4.1 ANDREWS, Stuart: ' "The Wesley naturalist" ', *History Today*, Vol. XXI, 1971, pp. 810–17.

4.6 Reactions to Methodism

4.6.1 Literary opposition and portrayals

4.6.1.1 HUGHES, Dorothea Price: 'The novels of Mr. Arnold Bennett and Wesleyan Methodism', *Contemporary Review*, Vol. CX, July–December 1916, pp. 602–10.

4.6.1.2 PILKINGTON, Frederick: 'Methodism in Arnold Bennett's novels', *Contemporary Review*, Vol. CLXXXIX, January–June 1956, pp. 109–15.

4.6.2 Relations with other Churches

4.6.2.1 EDWARDS, Michael Stone: 'The "Tuck net" controversy of 1824', *Proceedings of the Wesley Historical Society*, Vol. XXXVIII, 1971–72, pp. 33–41.

4.6.2.2 HAINES, Meredith C.: 'The Nonconformists and the Nonconformist periodical press in mid-nineteenth-century England' [with special reference to attitudes towards Catholicism, education and disestablishment], Indiana University Ph.D. thesis, 1966, vi+ 300p.

4.6.2.3 JEFFERY, Frederick: 'Anglican-Methodist relations', *Irish Anglicanism, 1869–1969: Essays on the role of Anglicanism in Irish life presented to the Church of Ireland on the occasion of the centenary of its disestablishment*, edited by Michael Hurley, Dublin: Allen Figgis, 1970, pp. 79–92.

4.6.2.4 TURNER, John Munsey: 'Methodism and Anglicanism, 1791–1850', University of Bristol M.A. thesis, 1956, 96+iip.

See also 2.6.1.12, 2.9.4.4, 2.9.4.5, 4.1.2.19, 4.2.28.9, 4.4.6.4, 4.5.1.8.

5. FROM THE DEATH OF JOHN WESLEY TO
METHODIST UNION: PRIMITIVE METHODISM

5.1 General Histories

5.1.1 Bibliography and historiography

5.1.1.1 HATCHER, Stephen George: *A Primitive Methodist bibliography*, [Leigh-on-Sea]: Laurie Gage Books, 1980, [88]p.

5.1.2 Connexional histories

5.1.2.1 BARBER, Benjamin Aquila: *A Methodist pageant: A souvenir of the Primitive Methodist Church*, London: Holborn Publishing House, 1932, xv+317p.

5.1.2.2 BOURNE, Hugh: *History of the Primitive Methodists, giving an account of their rise and progress up to the year 1823*, Bemersley: printed for the author, at the office of the Primitive Methodist Connexion, by J. Bourne, 1823, iv+68p.

5.1.2.3 BROWN, Leonard: 'The origins of Primitive Methodism', *Proceedings of the Wesley Historical Society*, Vol. XXXIV, 1963–64, pp. 79–86, 114–25.

5.1.2.4 CHURCH, Thomas: *A history of the Primitive Methodists,* third edition, revised, enlarged and approved by the London District Publishing Committee, London: Bemrose and Sons, 1869, 80p.

5.1.2.5 FARNDALE, William Edward: *The secret of Mow Cop: A new appraisal of the origins of Primitive Methodism*, Wesley Historical Society Lectures No. 16, London: Epworth Press, 1950, 76p.

5.1.2.6 GARNER, William: *Jubilee of English camp meetings*, London: Thomas King, 1857, 176p.

5.1.2.7 KENDALL, Holliday Bickerstaffe: *History of the Primitive Methodist Church*, revised and enlarged edition, London: Joseph Johnson, 1919, vii+177p.

5.1.2.8 KENDALL, Holliday Bickerstaffe: *The origin and history of the Primitive Methodist Church*, London: Edwin Dalton, [1906], 2 vol.

5.1.2.9 KENDALL, Holliday Bickerstaffe: 'The Primitive Methodist Church and the Independent Methodist Churches, 1796–1908', *A new history of Methodism*, edited by William John Townsend, Herbert Brook Workman & George Eayrs, London: Hodder and Stoughton, 1909, Vol. I, pp. 553–98.

5.1.2.10 McKEON, Francis James: 'Religion, education and leisure in

Primitive Methodism: A study of the social significance of lay predominance within an evangelical sect, 1812–1932', University of Keele M.A. (Ed.) thesis, 1973, v+332p.

5.1.2.11 MORRIS, Geoffrey Malcolm: 'The origin of Primitive Methodism in North Staffordshire, 1800–1812', *North Staffordshire Journal of Field Studies*, Vol. 9, 1969, pp. 62–73.

5.1.2.12 NUTTALL, Geoffrey Fillingham: 'Early Quakerism and early Primitive Methodism', *Friends' Quarterly*, Vol. 7, 1953, pp. 179–87 and *The Puritan spirit: Essays and addresses*, London: Epworth Press, 1967, pp. 204–13.

5.1.2.13 PETTY, John: *The history of the Primitive Methodist Connexion from its origin to the Conference of 1860, the first jubilee year of the Connexion*, new edition, revised and enlarged by James MacPherson, London: John Dickenson, 1880, xv+662p.

5.1.2.14 RITSON, Joseph: *The romance of Primitive Methodism*, London: Edwin Dalton, 1909, vii+312p.

5.1.2.15 RUSSELL, Thomas: *Record of events in Primitive Methodism*, London: William Lister, 1869, 244p.

5.1.2.16 [SIMON, John Smith]: 'The origin of the Primitive Methodist Connexion', *London Quarterly Review*, Vol. LXVII, October 1886–January 1887, pp. 18–40.

5.1.2.17 SMITH, Samuel: *Anecdotes, facts and biographical sketches connected with the great revival of the work of God in raising up and progressing the Primitive Methodist Connexion; to which is added an account of the introduction of Primitive Methodism into Lancashire*, Douglas: Matthew Glover, 1872, 130p.

5.1.2.18 THOMPSON, John Day: *The Church that found herself: The story of our centenary commemoration, 1907–1911*, London: W. A. Hammond, 1912, 96p.

5.1.2.19 TURNER, John Munsey: 'Primitive Methodism from Mow Cop to Peake's "Commentary"', *From Mow Cop to Peake, 1807–1932: Essays to commemorate the one hundred & seventy-fifth anniversary of the beginnings of Primitive Methodism, May 1982*, Wesley Historical Society Yorkshire Branch Occasional Paper No. 4, [Leeds]: Wesley Historical Society Yorkshire Branch, 1982, pp. 1–13.

5.1.2.20 VALENZE, Deborah Mary: *Prophetic sons and daughters: Female preaching and popular religion in industrial England*, Princeton: Princeton University Press, 1985, xvi+308p.

5.1.2.21 WERNER, Julia Stewart: *The Primitive Methodist Connexion: Its background and early history*, Madison: University of Wisconsin Press, 1984, xv+251p.

5.1.2.22 WILKES, Arthur & LOVATT, Joseph: *Mow Cop and the camp meeting movement: Sketches of Primitive Methodism*, Leominster: Orphans' Printing Press, [1942], xx+242p.

5.1.3 Local histories: England

5.1.3.1 BECKWORTH, William Harold: *A book of remembrance; being records* of Leeds Primitive Methodism, compiled during the centenary year 1910, London: W. A. Hammond, [1910], viii+336p.

5.1.3.2   MORRIS, Geoffrey Malcolm: 'The origin and early development of Primitive Methodism in Derbyshire, 1810–1870', University of Nottingham M.A. thesis, 1960, 288p.

5.1.3.3   MORRIS, Geoffrey Malcolm: 'Primitive Methodism in Nottinghamshire, 1815–1932', University of Nottingham Ph.D. thesis, 1967, 424p.

5.1.3.4   MORRIS, Geoffrey Malcolm: 'Primitive Methodism in Nottinghamshire, 1815–1932', *Transactions of the Thoroton Society of Nottinghamshire*, Vol. LXXII, 1968, pp. 81–100.

5.1.3.5   MYERS, James: *Eventide review of Primitive Methodism in the Otley Circuit*, Leeds: printed by Rhodes & Sons, 1920, 195p.

5.1.3.6   PATTERSON, Arthur Henry: *From hayloft to temple: The story of Primitive Methodism in Yarmouth, biographical, reminiscent, chronological, etc.*, London: Robert Bryant, 1903, xvi+175p.

5.1.3.7   PATTERSON, William M.: *Northern Primitive Methodism: A record of the rise and progress of the circuits in the old Sunderland District*, London: Edwin Dalton, 1909, vi+385p.

5.1.3.8   PHILLIPS, Scott Kershaw: 'Popular evangelicalism and society: Primitive Methodism in Tunstall Circuit, 1812–1843', La Trobe University M.A. thesis, 1980, [6]+278p.

5.1.3.9   PROBERT, John Charles Cripps: *Primitive Methodism in Cornwall (a history and sociology)*, Redruth: [the author, 1966], [4]+128p.

5.1.3.10   SHEARD, Michael Rowland: 'The origins and early development of Primitive Methodism in Cheshire and south Lancashire, 1800–1860', University of Manchester Ph.D. thesis, 1980, 3 vol.

5.1.3.11   SHEARD, Michael Rowland: *The origins and early development of Primitive Methodism in the Manchester area, 1820–1830*, Wesley Historical Society Lancashire & Cheshire Branch Occasional Publication No. 4, [no place]: Wesley Historical Society Lancashire & Cheshire Branch, 1976, 29+5p.

5.1.3.12   *Silsden Primitive Methodism: Historical records and reminiscences*, edited by William J. Robson, Silsden: Briggs Bros., 1910, xi+606p.

5.1.3.13   TONKS, William C.: *Victory in the villages: The history of the Brinkworth Circuit*, Aberdare: printed by William Wilcox, 1907, 175p.

5.1.3.14   WOODCOCK, Henry: *Piety among the peasantry; being sketches of Primitive Methodism on the Yorkshire Wolds*, London: Joseph Toulson, [1889], viii+268p.

5.1.3.15   YARROW, William Henry: *The history of Primitive Methodism in London from its commencement in 1822 to the year 1876*, London: John Dickenson, [1876], 181p.

See also 5.1.2.11, 5.1.2.17, 5.2.6.9, 5.4.1.4, 5.5.1.1, 5.5.1.2, 5.5.1.3, 5.5.1.4, 6.3.11.1, 6.5.9.1, 6.5.9.2.

5.1.4 Local histories: Wales

5.1.4.1   HOWELL, David: 'Primitive Methodism in Pembrokeshire: The chapel in a rural society', *Pembrokeshire Historian*, Vol. 7, 1981, pp. 52–60.

5.2 Biographies

5.2.1 Collective

5.2.1.1 BROWNSON, William James, GAIR, John, MITCHELL, Thomas & PROSSER, David Samuel: *Heroic men: The death roll of the Primitive Methodist ministry, being sketches of the ministers who have died between the Conferences of 1888–9, with more extended memoirs of Revs. Thomas Russell, Charles Lace, James Prosser, John Dickenson, John T. Neale and William B. Luddington,* London: Joseph Toulson, [1889], xvi + 367p.

5.2.1.2 HEROD, George: *Biographical sketches of some of those preachers whose labours contributed to the origination and early extension of the Primitive Methodist Connexion,* London: T. King, [1855], 493p.

5.2.1.3 HURD, F. H.: *Earnest men: Sketches of eminent Primitive Methodists, ministers and laymen,* London: F. H. Hurd, 1872, iv + 244p.

5.2.1.4 PEARCE, Joseph: *Burning and shining lights: A souvenir of Primitive Methodist radiant personalities,* Halesowen: H. Parkes Ltd., 1935, 104p.

5.2.1.5 PEARCE, Joseph: *Dinna forget: A souvenir of Primitive Methodist soul-winning personalities,* Leominster: Orphans' Printing Press, 1932, 103p.

5.2.2 Individual: Hugh Bourne

5.2.2.1 ANTLIFF, William: *The life of Hugh Bourne, founder of the Primitive Methodist Connexion,* new edition, revised [by Colin Campbell McKechnie], London: James B. Knapp, 1892, vii + 332p.

5.2.2.2 ASHWORTH, Jesse: *The life of the venerable Hugh Bourne,* London: Joseph Toulson, [1888], 132p.

5.2.2.3 BIRCHENOUGH, Albert Allen: 'The Quaker Methodist friendships of Hugh Bourne', *Primitive Methodist Quarterly Review*, Vol. XLIX, 1907, pp. 245–58.

5.2.2.4 BROWN, Leonard: 'Hugh Bourne, born 3rd. April 1772: A bicentenary reflection', *Proceedings of the Wesley Historical Society*, Vol. XXXVIII, 1971–72, pp. 121–6.

5.2.2.5 FARNDALE, William Edward: 'Hugh Bourne and the "spiritual manifestation"', *Proceedings of the Wesley Historical Society*, Vol. XXVIII, 1951–52, pp. 131–7.

5.2.2.6 SIMPSON, John: *Recollections and characteristic anecdotes of the late Rev. Hugh Bourne,* London: John Day, 1859, 24p.

5.2.2.7 WALFORD, John: *Memoirs of the life and labours of the late venerable Hugh Bourne, founder of the English camp meetings and the originator, and for twenty-two years editor, of the Primitive Methodist magazines,* edited by William Antliff, London: T. King, 1855–56, 2 vol.

5.2.2.8   WILKINSON, John Thomas: *Hugh Bourne, 1772–1852*, London: Epworth Press, 1952, 203p.

5.2.2.9   WILKINSON, John Thomas: 'Hugh Bourne, 1772–1852: A centenary tribute', *Proceedings of the Wesley Historical Society*, Vol. XXVIII, 1951–52, pp. 126–30.

See also 5.1.2.2, 5.1.2.3.

5.2.3 Individual: William Clowes

5.2.3.1   CLOWES, William: *The journals of William Clowes, a Primitive Methodist preacher; containing chronicles of events relative to his unregenerate state, his conversion to God, his call to the ministry, the commencement and progress of the Primitive Methodist Connexion, and to his itinerant labours therein from the year 1810 to that of 1838*, London: Hallam and Holliday, 1844, iv+367p.

5.2.3.2   DAVISON, John: *The life of the venerable William Clowes, one of the founders of the Primitive Methodist Connexion*, London: Thomas King, 1854, viii+295p.

5.2.3.3   GARNER, William: *The life of the Rev. and venerable William Clowes, one of the patriarchs of the Primitive Methodist Connexion*, new edition, London: William Lister, 1868, 418p.

5.2.3.4   GUTTERY, Thomas: *The venerable William Clowes: A sketch*, London: Joseph Toulson, [?1890], 132p.

5.2.3.5   WILKINSON, John Thomas: *William Clowes, 1780–1851*, London: Epworth Press, 1951, xiii+104p.

5.2.3.6   WILKINSON, John Thomas: 'William Clowes, 1780–1851: A centenary tribute', *Proceedings of the Wesley Historical Society*, Vol. XXVIII, 1951–52, pp. 8–12.

5.2.4 Individual: James Flanagan

5.2.4.1   CRANE, Denis *pseud*. [i.e. Walter Thomas Cranfield]: *James Flanagan: The story of a remarkable career*, London: S. W. Partridge & Co., [1906], 240p.

5.2.4.2   FLANAGAN, James: *Scenes from my life, both grave and gay*, London: Hodder and Stoughton, 1907, xvi+335p.

5.2.4.3   RUSSELL, Robert William: *The life of James Flanagan, preacher, evangelist, author*, London: Holborn Publishing House, [1920], viii+251p.

5.2.5 Individual: John Petty

5.2.5.1   MACPHERSON, James: *The life and labours of the Rev. John Petty, late minister of the Primitive Methodist Connexion, first governor of the Jubilee School, York, and first connexional theological tutor of candidates for the ministry*, London: George Lamb, 1870, iv+526p.

5.2.5.2   MILBURN, Geoffrey Eden: 'John Petty, 1807–1868: Insights into Victorian Primitive Methodism from the life and work of a travel-

ling preacher', *From Mow Cop to Peake, 1807–1932: Essays to commemorate the one hundred & seventy-fifth anniversary of the beginnings of
Primitive Methodism, May 1982*, Wesley Historical Society Yorkshire Branch Occasional Paper No. 4, [Leeds]: Wesley Historical
Society Yorkshire Branch, 1982, pp. 59–72.

5.2.6 Individual: other ministers

5.2.6.1   ATKINSON, John: *Life of Rev. Colin C. McKechnie*, London: T.
           Mitchell, 1898, xv+252p.

5.2.6.2   BAKER, Frank: 'James Bourne (1781–1860) and the Bemersley
           Book-Room', *Proceedings of the Wesley Historical Society*, Vol. XXX,
           1955–56, pp. 138–50.

5.2.6.3   BOWRAN, John George: *The life of Arthur Thomas Guttery, D.D.*,
           London: Holborn Publishing House, [1922], viii+336p.

5.2.6.4   DORRICOTT, Isaac: *Memorials of an earnest life; or, Records of the Rev.
           William Peacefull, Primitive Methodist minister*, London: Elliot
           Stock, [1878], [7]+104p.

5.2.6.5   GARNER, William: *The life of Mr. John Garner, Sen., one of the early
           ministers of the Primitive Methodist Connexion and an original deed poll
           member of the Conference*, London: Thomas King, 1856, xii+
           177p.

5.2.6.6   HALL, Ebenezer: *The earnest preacher: Memoirs of the Rev. Joseph
           Spoor*, London: George Lamb, 1870, xxiv+142p.

5.2.6.7   KENDALL, Charles: *Life of the Rev. W. Sanderson*, London: George
           Lamb, 1875, viii+165p.

5.2.6.8   PETTY, John: *Memoir of the life and labours of the Rev. Thomas Batty,
           one of the early Primitive Methodist preachers, chiefly compiled from his
           own papers and other authentic documents*, London: Thomas King,
           1857, 198p.

5.2.6.9   POTTER, William: *Thomas Jackson of Whitechapel: A record of fifty
           years of social and evangelistic enterprise*, Liverpool: C. Tinling & Co.,
           [1929], xix+170p.

5.2.6.10   PRITCHARD, James: *Memoirs of the literary and itinerant labours of the
           Rev. Philip Pugh*, London: George Lamb, 1871, 318p.

5.2.6.11   PRITCHARD, James: *The poet of the million; or, Memorials of the life
           and labours of the late Rev. Richard Jukes of Westbromwich, forty-two
           years a Primitive Methodist and forty-one a preacher*, London: William
           Lister, 1867, iii+193p.

5.2.6.12   RUSSELL, Thomas: *Autobiography of Thomas Russell, one of the
           pioneers of the Primitive Methodist Connexion*, revised [edition], Lon-
           don: James B. Knapp, [1889], 174p.

5.2.6.13   SHAW, George: *Life of Rev. Parkinson Milson (Primitive Methodist
           minister)*, London: Simpkin, Marshall, Hamilton, Kent & Co.,
           1893, xii+443p.

5.2.6.14   TRAVIS, James: *Seventy-five years: The life and work of James Travis
           as seen by himself and as judged by others*, London: W. A. Hammond,
           1914, vii+194p.

5.2.7 Individual: Joseph Arch

5.2.7.1   ARCH, Joseph: *Joseph Arch: The story of his life, told by himself*, edited, with a preface, by the Countess of Warwick [i.e. Frances Evelyn Greville], London: Hutchinson & Co., 1898, xx+412p.

5.2.7.2   HORN, Pamela R.: *Joseph Arch (1826–1919), the farm workers' leader*, Kineton: Roundwood Press, 1971, x+262p.

5.2.8 Individual: Sir William Hartley

5.2.8.1   MILBURN, Geoffrey Eden: 'Big business and denominational developments in Methodism during the late nineteenth and early twentieth centuries' [with reference to the life of Sir William Hartley], *Epworth Review*, Vol. 10, No. 3, September 1983, pp. 33–41.

5.2.8.2   PEAKE, Arthur Samuel: *The life of Sir William Hartley*, London: Hodder and Stoughton, 1926, 224p.

5.2.9 Individual: Arthur Samuel Peake

5.2.9.1   *Arthur Samuel Peake, 1865–1929: Essays in commemoration and selections from his writings*, edited by John Thomas Wilkinson, London: Epworth Press, 1958, 167p.

5.2.9.2   PEAKE, Arthur Samuel: *Recollections and appreciations*, edited by Wilbert Francis Howard, London: Epworth Press, 1938, 231p.

5.2.9.3   PEAKE, Leslie Sillman: *Arthur Samuel Peake: A memoir*, London: Hodder and Stoughton, 1930, 319p.

5.2.9.4   WILKINSON, John Thomas: *Arthur Samuel Peake: A biography*, London: Epworth Press, 1971, xii+212p.

See also 5.4.1.2.

5.2.10 Individual: other laity

5.2.10.1   ANDERSON, Barbara Vogwill: 'The life and work of John Wilson, Primitive Methodist, miners' leader and Member of Parliament', *Wesley Historical Society North-East Branch Bulletin*, No. 26, September 1976, pp. 9–30.

5.2.10.2   BURT, Thomas: *Thomas Burt, M.P., D.C.L., pitman & Privy Councillor: An autobiography*, with supplementary chapters by Aaron Watson, London: T. Fisher Unwin, 1924, 319p.

5.2.10.3   EDWARDS, George: *From crow-scaring to Westminster: An autobiography*, London: Labour Publishing Co., 1922, 240p.

5.2.10.4   LAWSON, John James: *Peter Lee*, London: Hodder and Stoughton, 1936, 316p.

5.2.10.5   WILSON, John: *Memories of a labour leader: The autobiography of John Wilson, J.P., M.P.*, London: T. Fisher Unwin, 1910, 320p.

See also 5.5.1.4.

5.3 Spirituality

5.3.1 Theology

See 5.2.9 *passim*.

5.4 Polity and Mission

5.4.1 Ordained ministry

5.4.1.1   GRAHAM, Ena Dorothy: 'Women itinerants of early Primitive Methodism', *Cirplan*, Vol. 8, 1983–87, pp. 106–15.
5.4.1.2   HOOKER, Morna Dorothy: 'Ministerial training: The contribution of A. S. Peake', *Epworth Review*, Vol. 12, No. 3, September 1985, pp. 64–76.
5.4.1.3   MILBURN, Geoffrey Eden: *A school for the prophets: The origins of ministerial education in the Primitive Methodist Church*, [Sunderland: the author, 1981], 36p.
5.4.1.4   *The story of the Hartley Primitive Methodist College, Manchester, 1881–1931, with illustrations and programme of the jubilee celebrations, July 7th. and 8th. 1931*, editors: Albert Lewis Humphries & William Barker, [Manchester: Hartley Primitive Methodist College, 1931], 32p.
See also 5.2.1.1, 5.2.5.1, 5.2.9 *passim*.

5.4.2 Lay ministry

See 5.1.2.10, 5.1.2.20.

5.4.3 Buildings and finance

See 5.2.8 *passim*.

5.4.4 Home missions

See 5.2.4 *passim*, 5.2.6.9.

5.5 Social Aspects

5.5.1 Political impact

5.5.1.1   GURDEN, Helen: 'Primitive Methodism and agricultural trade unionism in Warwickshire, 1872–5', *Society for the Study of Labour History Bulletin*, No. 33, Autumn 1976, pp. 4–5.
5.5.1.2   GURDEN, Helen: 'Trade unionism, education and religion: Aspects of the social history of Warwickshire agricultural labourers in the 1870s', University of Warwick M.Phil. thesis, 1975, 262p.

5.5.1.3   HOWKINS, Alun: *Poor labouring men: Rural radicalism in Norfolk, 1872–1923*, London: Routledge & Kegan Paul, 1985, xiv+225p.

5.5.1.4   RICHARDSON, Sidney Yearsley: 'John Skevington of Loughborough: Primitive Methodism and Chartism', *From Mow Cop to Peake, 1807–1932: Essays to commemorate the one hundred & seventyfifth anniversary of the beginnings of Primitive Methodism, May 1982*, Wesley Historical Society Yorkshire Branch Occasional Paper No. 4, [Leeds]: Wesley Historical Society Yorkshire Branch, 1982, pp. 47–58.

See also 2.9.1.2, 5.2.7 *passim*, 5.2.10 *passim*.

5.5.2 Social witness

See 5.2.6.9.

5.5.3 Educational work

5.5.3.1   HENSHAW, Samuel Shipley: *The romance of our Sunday schools: A brief centenary narrative of the origin, history and wonderful progress of the Sunday-schools of the Primitive Methodist Church*, London: W. A. Hammond, [1911], 158p.

See also 5.1.2.10, 6.3.11.1.

5.6 Reactions to Methodism

5.6.1 Physical opposition

5.6.1.1   CHURCH, Thomas: *Gospel-victories; or, Missionary anecdotes of imprisonments, labours and persecutions endured by Primitive Methodist preachers between the years 1812 and 1844*, London: Aylott and Jones, 1851, 148p.

See also 2.9.1.2.

5.6.2 Relations with other Churches

See 5.1.2.12.

6. FROM THE DEATH OF JOHN WESLEY TO METHODIST UNION: OTHER TRADITIONS

6.1 Methodist New Connexion

6.1.1 Connexional histories

6.1.1.1   [ALLIN, Thomas, COOKE, William, HULME, Samuel & WRIGHT, Philip James]: *The jubilee of the Methodist New Connexion; being a grateful memorial of the origin, government and history of the denomination,* London: John Bakewell, 1848, 450p.

6.1.1.2   CROTHERS, Thomas Dickson: 'Historical sketch of the Methodist New Connexion', *The centenary of the Methodist New Connexion, 1797–1897,* editor: George Packer, London: Geo. Burroughs, [1897], pp. 71–177.

6.1.1.3   EAYRS, George: 'The United Methodist Church and the Wesleyan Reform Union, 1797–1908', *A new history of Methodism,* edited by William John Townsend, Herbert Brook Workman & George Eayrs, London: Hodder and Stoughton, 1909, Vol. I, pp. 481–551.

6.1.1.4   ROSE, Edward Alan: 'The first Methodist New Connexion chapels', *Proceedings of the Wesley Historical Society,* Vol. XXXVI, 1967–68, pp. 7–15.

6.1.1.5   SALT, William: *A memorial of the Wesleyan Methodist New Connexion; containing a short account of the circuit preachers who have died and a general statement of the leading transactions of the Connexion from its formation in 1797 to the present time,* Nottingham: printed and sold by Sutton and Son, 1822, ix+256p.

6.1.1.6   [SIMON, John Smith]: 'The origin of the first important Methodist secession', *London Quarterly Review,* Vol. LXV, October 1885–January 1886, pp. 136–58.

See also 6.1.5.1, 6.1.6.3, 6.4.1.1, 6.4.1.3.

6.1.2 Local histories: England

6.1.2.1   EAYRS, George: *A history of Zion Church, Batley and the churches of the United Methodist Batley Circuit,* London: Andrew Crombie, 1909, vi+134p.

6.1.2.2   LOCKLEY, Walter Henry: *The story of Stockport Circuit of the United Methodist Church: A series of lectures,* Stockport: T. Hooley & Co., 1909, vii+200p.

6.1.2.3   ROSE, Edward Alan: 'The Methodist New Connexion in London, 1797–1907', *Proceedings of the Wesley Historical Society*, Vol. XXXVIII, 1971–72, pp. 177–87.

6.1.3 Local histories: Ireland

See 6.1.6.6.

6.1.4 Biographies: collective

6.1.4.1   BECKERLEGGE, Oliver Aveyard: *United Methodist ministers and their circuits; being an arrangement in alphabetical order of the stations of ministers of the Methodist New Connexion, Bible Christians, Arminian Methodists, Protestant Methodists, Wesleyan Methodist Association, Wesleyan Reformers, United Methodist Free Churches and the United Methodist Church, 1797–1932*, London: Epworth Press, 1968, [8] + 268p.

6.1.4.2   SMITH, Henry: *Sketches of eminent Methodist New Connexion ministers*, London: Geo. Burroughs, 1893, 144p.

See also 6.1.1.5.

6.1.5 Biographies: individual - Alexander Kilham

6.1.5.1   [BLACKWELL, John]: *Life of the Rev. Alexander Kilham, formerly a preacher under the Rev. J. Wesley, and one of the founders of the Methodist New Connexion in the year 1797; including a full account of the disputes which occasioned the separation*, London: R. Groombridge, 1838, 408p.

6.1.5.2   COOKE, William: *Methodist reform and its originator; or, A true estimate of Alexander Kilham and his principles*, London: Partridge and Oakey, 1850, 95p.

6.1.5.3   KILHAM, Alexander: *The life of Mr. Alexander Kilham, Methodist preacher, who was expelled from the Conference, or society of Methodist preachers, for publicly remonstrating with them for countenancing various corruptions and abuses; to which are added extracts of letters (in favour of reform) written by a number of preachers to Mr. Kilham during the time of his undertaking the cause of religious liberty*, [edited by] John Grundell & Robert Hall, Nottingham: printed and sold by C. Sutton, [1799], xxviii+222p.

6.1.5.4   TOWNSEND, William John: *Alexander Kilham, the first Methodist reformer*, London: J. C. Watts, [1890], 128p.

6.1.6 Biographies: individual - other ministers

6.1.6.1   COOKE, William: *The man of all work: A memoir of the life and labours of the Rev. James Maughan, with selections from his sermons and lectures*, London: Hodder and Stoughton, 1872, vi+312p.

6.1.6.2   EAYRS, George: *William John Townsend, D.D., Methodist preacher,*

Free Church leader; with tributes and reminiscences, London: Henry Hooks, 1916, 229p.

6.1.6.3 HULME, Samuel: *Memoir of the Rev. Thomas Allin, author of discourses on 'The character and folly of modern atheism', etc., etc., with notices of the contemporary history of the Methodist New Connexion*, London: Hamilton, Adams and Co., 1881, xii+265p.

6.1.6.4 HULME, Samuel: *Memoir of the Rev. William Cooke, D.D.*, London: C. D. Ward, 1886, viii+393p.

6.1.6.5 LYNN, Andrew: *Methodist records; or, Selections from the journal of the Rev. Andrew Lynn, designed to promote spiritual Christianity*, edited by John Stokoe, London: J. B. Cooke, 1858, xv+460p.

6.1.6.6 THOMAS, Edward: *Irish Methodist reminiscences; being mainly memorials of the life and labours of the Rev. Samuel Nicholson*, London: J. C. Watts, 1889, xi+247p.

6.1.6.7 TOWNSEND, William John: *James Stacey, D.D.: Reminiscences and memorials*, London: Hodder and Stoughton, 1891, viii+412p.

See also 6.5.7 *passim*.

6.1.7 Biographies: individual - laity

6.1.7.1 STACEY, James: *A prince in Israel; or, Sketches of the life of John Ridgway, Esq.*, London: Hamilton, Adams and Co., 1862, xii+315p.

6.2 Bible Christians

6.2.1 Bibliography and historiography

6.2.1.1 BECKERLEGGE, Oliver Aveyard: 'The bibliography of the Bible Christians', *Proceedings of the Wesley Historical Society*, Vol. XXXV, 1965–66, pp. 45–50, 74–6, 100–4, 128–9, Vol. XXXVII, 1969–70, pp. 48–9.

6.2.2 Connexional histories

6.2.2.1 ANDREWS, J. H. B.: 'The rise of the Bible Christians and the state of the Church in North Devon in the early 19th century', *Devonshire Association Report and Transactions*, Vol. XCVI, 1964, pp. 147–85.

6.2.2.2 BOURNE, Frederick William: *The Bible Christians: Their origin and history, 1815–1900*, [London]: Bible Christian Book Room, 1905, vii+567p.

6.2.2.3 COURT, A. W. Glyn: 'The Bible Christians, 1815–?', *London Quarterly and Holborn Review*, Vol. CXC, 1965, pp. 295–303.

6.2.2.4 [O'BRYAN, William]: 'The rise and progress of the connexion of people called Arminian Bible Christians', *Arminian Magazine*, Vol. II, 1823, pp. 3–15, 37–46, 73–87, 109–20, 145–59, 181–93, 217–24,

253–67, 289–303, 325–34, 361–9, 397–405, Vol. III, 1824, pp. 7–12, 41–53, 77–86, 113–27, 149–58, 185–94, 221–9, 257–66, 293–301, 329–39, 365–71, 401–6, Vol. IV, 1825, pp. 3–9, 37–46, 73–7, 109–15, 145–50, 181–5, 217–26, 253–62, 289–93, 325–9, 361–71, 397–9, Vol. V, 1826, pp. 3–9, 37–41, 73–8, 109–13, 145–9, 181–6, 217–24, 253–9, 289–96, 325–38, 361–7, 397–402, Vol. VI, 1827, pp. 3–8, 37–41, 73–5, 109–14, 145–9, 181–6, 217–29, 243–63, 289–93, 325–30, 361–7, 397–401.

6.2.2.5   PYKE, Richard: *The early Bible Christians*, Wesley Historical Society Lectures No. 7, London: Epworth Press, 1941, 46p.

6.2.2.6   PYKE, Richard: *The golden chain: The story of the Bible Christian Methodists from the formation of the first society in 1815 to the union of the denomination in 1907 with the Methodist New Connexion and the United Methodist Free Churches in forming the United Methodist Church*, London: Henry Hooks, [1915], 215p.

6.2.2.7   SHAW, Thomas: *The Bible Christians, 1815–1907*, Wesley Historical Society Lecture No. 31, London: Epworth Press, 1965, xii + 120p.

6.2.2.8   SHAW, Thomas: 'The Stratton Mission (1811–18) and Bible Christian origins', *Proceedings of the Wesley Historical Society*, Vol. XXX, 1955–56, pp. 120–6.

6.2.2.9   [SIMON, John Smith]: 'The origin of the Bible Christian Connexion', *London Quarterly Review*, Vol. LXVIII, April–July 1887, pp. 322–37.

6.2.2.10   [THORNE, James, KINSMAN, Richard, PRIOR, Jacob Hunt & ROBINS, Matthew]: *A jubilee memorial of incidents in the rise and progress of the Bible Christian Connexion*, Shebbear: published for the Bible Christian Book Committee by James Thorne, 1865, vi + 292p.

See also 6.1.1.3, 6.4.1.1, 6.4.1.3.

6.2.3 Local histories: England

6.2.3.1   BECKERLEGGE, Oliver Aveyard: 'The northern Bible Christians', *Proceedings of the Wesley Historical Society*, Vol. XXXI, 1957–58, pp. 39–43.

6.2.3.2   THORNE, Roger Frank Sidney: 'The last Bible Christians: Their Church in Devon in 1907', *Report and Transactions of the Devonshire Association*, Vol. 107, 1975, pp. 47–75.

6.2.3.3   WOOLCOCK, James: *A history of the Bible Christian churches on the Isle of Wight*, Newport, I.O.W.: Fredk. Lee, 1897, xi + 108p.

See also 6.2.7.1, 6.2.7.2, 6.2.7.3, 6.2.7.4.

6.2.4 Biographies: collective

6.2.4.1   MICHELL, William John: *Brief biographical sketches of Bible Christian ministers and laymen*, Jersey: Beresford Press, 1906, 2 vol.

See also 6.1.4.1.

6.2.5 Biographies: individual - ministers

6.2.5.1 BOURNE, Frederick William: *All for Christ, Christ for all; illustrated by the life and labours of William M. Bailey*, London: Bible Christian Book-Room, 1880, vi+117p.

6.2.5.2 BOURNE, Frederick William: *The centenary life of James Thorne of Shebbear*, London: Bible Christian Book-Room, 1895, viii+179p.

6.2.5.3 LUKE, William Balkwill: *Memorials of Frederick William Bourne*, London: W. H. Gregory, 1906, 220p.

6.2.5.4 PYKE, Richard: *Men and memories*, London: Epworth Press, 1948, 144p.

6.2.5.5 THORNE, James: *Memoir of William Reed, Bible Christian minister*, Shebbear: Bible Christian Book Committee, 1869, 157p.

6.2.5.6 [THORNE, John]: *James Thorne of Shebbear: A memoir compiled from his diary and letters*, London: Bible Christian Bookroom, 1873, vi +312p.

6.2.5.7 THORNE, Samuel Ley: *The maiden preacher, wife and mother: Miss Mary O'Bryan – Mrs. Thorne*, London: Partridge & Co., 1889, 194p.

6.2.5.8 THORNE, Samuel Ley: *Samuel Thorne, printer*, second edition, London: Elliot Stock, 1875, 191p.

6.2.5.9 THORNE, Samuel Ley: *William O'Bryan, founder of the Bible Christians: The man and his work, chiefly from original documents,* second edition, Plymouth: J. C. Holland, 1888, 126p.

6.2.6 Biographies: individual - laity

6.2.6.1 DYMOND, George Pearse: *Thomas Ruddle of Shebbear, a North Devon Arnold: His life and selections from his letters*, London: Henry Hooks, [1913], 219p.

6.2.7 Educational work

6.2.7.1 PYKE, Richard: *Edgehill College, 1884–1934*, London: Epworth Press, 1934, 80p.

6.2.7.2 PYKE, Richard: *Edgehill College, 1884–1957: A triumph of faith*, London: Epworth Press, 1957, 74p.

6.2.7.3 PYKE, Richard: *The story of Shebbear College*, [Shebbear: Shebbear College, ?1953], [12]+100p.

6.2.7.4 SHAW, A. Mary: *When you were there: Reflections on Edgehill College, 1884–1984*, South Molton: printed by G. P. Printers, 1983, [8]+ 173p.

See also 6.2.6.1.

6.3 United Methodist Free Churches

6.3.1 Connexional histories

6.3.1.1 BAXTER, Matthew: *Methodism: Memorials of the United Methodist Free Churches, with recollections of the Rev. Robert Eckett and some of his contemporaries*, London: W. Reed, 1865, ix+514p.

6.3.1.2 BECKERLEGGE, Oliver Aveyard: *The United Methodist Free Churches: A study in freedom*, Wesley Historical Society Lectures No. 23, London: Epworth Press, 1957, 112p.

6.3.1.3 *Free Methodist manual; comprising a statement of the origin, doctrines and constitution of the United Methodist Free Churches, with alphabetical arrangements of ministers and circuits, historical and statistical accounts of connexional institutions, funds, &c. from 1836 to 1898*, Edwin Askew, editor, London: Andrew Crombie, 1899, xvi+415p.

6.3.1.4 HUGHES, John Thomas: 'The story of the Leeds "Non-cons" ', *Proceedings of the Wesley Historical Society*, Vol. XXXV, 1965–66, pp. 81–7, 122–4, Vol. XXXVII, 1969–70, pp. 133–9, Vol. XXXIX, 1973–74, pp. 73–6.

6.3.1.5 KIRSOP, Joseph: *Historic sketches of Free Methodism*, London: Andrew Crombie, 1885, viii+113p.

6.3.1.6 [SIMON, John Smith]: 'The Methodist agitation of 1835', *London Quarterly Review*, Vol. LXXIX, October 1892–January 1893, pp. 129–54, Vol. LXXXI, October 1893–January 1894, pp. 48–65.

6.3.1.7 [SIMON, John Smith]: 'The Methodist controversy of 1835', *London Quarterly Review*, Vol. LXXVII, October 1891–January 1892, pp. 327–51.

6.3.1.8 [SIMON, John Smith]: 'The Protestant Methodist controversy of 1827', *London Quarterly Review*, Vol. LXX, April–July 1888, pp. 271–91.

6.3.1.9 [SIMON, John Smith]: 'The second great schism in Wesleyan Methodism', *London Quarterly Review*, Vol. LXXV, October 1890–January 1891, pp. 49–72.

6.3.1.10 [SIMON, John Smith]: 'Second stage in the Methodist controversy of 1835', *London Quarterly Review*, Vol. LXXVIII, April–July 1892, pp. 100–21.

6.3.1.11 [SIMON, John Smith]: 'The Theological Institution controversy in Methodism', *London Quarterly Review*, Vol. LXXIV, April–July 1890, pp. 61–86.

6.3.1.12 SWALLOW, Thomas: *Disruptions and secessions in Methodism: Their causes, consequences and lessons*, London: Ralph Fenwick, 1880, viii+215p.

6.3.1.13 URWIN, Evelyn Clifford: *The significance of 1849: Methodism's greatest upheaval*, Wesley Historical Society Lecture No. 15, London: Epworth Press, 1949, 27p.

See also 3.1.2.12, 6.1.1.3, 6.4.1.1, 6.4.1.3.

6.3.2 Local histories: England

6.3.2.1   BECKERLEGGE, Oliver Aveyard: *Free Methodism in Cornwall*, Cornish Methodist Historical Association Occasional Publications No. 2, Truro: Cornish Methodist Historical Association, [1961], ii+26p.

6.3.2.2   BECKERLEGGE, Oliver Aveyard: 'Free Methodism in Devon', *Proceedings of the Plymouth and Exeter Branch of the Wesley Historical Society*, Vol. 2, 1968–73, pp. 10–17, 56–66.

6.3.2.3   GOWLAND, David Alexander: *Methodist secessions: The origins of Free Methodism in three Lancashire towns – Manchester, Rochdale, Liverpool*, Chetham Society Third Series, Vol. XXVI, Manchester: Manchester University Press, 1979, ix+191p.

6.3.2.4   SUNMAN, William Robert: *The history of Free Methodism in and about Newcastle-on-Tyne*, Newcastle-on-Tyne: A. Dickson, 1902, xv+302p.

See also 4.1.3.4, 6.3.1.4, 6.3.8.2, 6.3.8.3, 6.3.9.1, 6.3.11.1.

6.3.3 Local histories: Wales

6.3.3.1   WILLIAMS, Albert Hughes: 'The Wesleyan Methodist Association and Wales, 1838–1857', *Bathafarn*, Vol. 4, 1949, pp. 25–53.

6.3.4 Biographies: collective

See 6.1.4.1.

6.3.5 Biographies: individual - James Everett

6.3.5.1   BECKERLEGGE, Oliver Aveyard: 'James Everett: 1784–1984', *Proceedings of the Wesley Historical Society*, Vol. XLIV, 1983–84, pp. 135–44.

6.3.5.2   CHEW, Richard: *James Everett: A biography*, London: Hodder and Stoughton, 1875, xvi+546p.

6.3.6 Biographies: individual - William Griffith

6.3.6.1   BARTON, David Anthony: 'William Griffith (1806–83), the "Hercules of the Reform Movement" ', *Proceedings of the Wesley Historical Society*, Vol. XLIII, 1981–82, pp. 165–70.

6.3.6.2   CHEW, Richard: *William Griffith: Memorials and letters*, London: Andrew Crombie, 1885, viii+247p.

6.3.7 Biographies: individual - other ministers

6.3.7.1   BOADEN, Edward: *Memoir of the Rev. Richard Chew*, London: Andrew Crombie, 1896, xiii+388p.

6.3.7.2   HOCKING, Silas Kitto: *My book of memory: A string of reminiscences and reflections*, London: Cassell and Co., 1923, viii + 305p.
See also 6.3.1.1.

6.3.8 Biographies: individual - laity

6.3.8.1   MALLINSON, William: *A sketch of my life*, London: Epworth Press, 1936, 173p.
6.3.8.2   STOVIN, Cornelius: *Journals of a Methodist farmer, 1871–1875*, edited by Jean Stovin, London: Croom Helm, 1982, [17] + 251p.
6.3.8.3   YOUNG, John: *The diary of John Young, Sunderland chemist and Methodist lay preacher, covering the years 1841–1843*, edited by Geoffrey Eden Milburn, Publications of the Surtees Society Vol. CXCV, Durham: Surtees Society, 1983, xxx + 218p.

6.3.9 Ordained ministry

6.3.9.1   HORNBY, George Goodall: *The Methodist College, Victoria Park, Manchester: A souvenir*, Manchester: Richard Bates Limited, Printers, [1934], 23p.

6.3.10 Lay ministry

6.3.10.1   SMITH, Henry: *Ministering women: The story of the work of the sisters connected with the United Methodist Deaconess Institute together with some account of the origin and history of the Institute*, London: A. Crombie, [1913], 205p.

6.3.11 Educational work

6.3.11.1   BOOTH, William: *Centenary history of Ashville College incorporating New College, Harrogate (1930), Elmfield College, York (1932)*, [Bradford: Ashville College Centenary Celebrations Committee, 1977], 40p.

6.4 United Methodist Church

6.4.1 Connexional histories

6.4.1.1   EAYRS, George: *A short history and handbook of the United Methodist Church*, London: Henry Hooks, [1913], iv + 108p.
6.4.1.2   *The story of the United Methodist Church*, edited by Henry Smith, John Edward Swallow & William Treffry, London: Henry Hooks, [1932], xi + 406p.
6.4.1.3   TOWNSEND, William John: *The story of Methodist union*, London: Milner & Co., [1906], xiii + 254 + viiip.

6.4.2 Biographies: collective

See 6.1.4.1.

6.5 Other Movements

6.5.1 Independent Methodism

6.5.1.1   KELLY, Hugh: *An impartial history of Independent Methodism in the counties of Durham and Northumberland from its commencement in the year 1819 up to 1824*, Newcastle: printed by Edw. Walker, 1824, 64p.

6.5.1.2   MURRAY, James: *Independent Methodist history: The third fifty years, 1905–1955*, Wigan: Independent Methodist Bookroom, 1955, viii +150p.

6.5.1.3   *A short history of Independent Methodism: A souvenir of the hundredth annual meeting of the Independent Methodist Churches, 1905*, Arthur Mounfield, editor, Wigan: Independent Methodist Book Room, [1905], viii+203p.

6.5.1.4   VICKERS, James: *History of Independent Methodism: Sketches of worthies, origins of circuits, expositions of principles and polity*, [Nelson]: Independent Methodist Bookroom, 1920, xii+318p.

See also 5.1.2.9, 5.1.2.20, 5.2.2.3, 6.5.9.1.

6.5.2 Methodist Unitarian Movement

6.5.2.1   McLACHLAN, Herbert John: *The Methodist Unitarian Movement*, Publications of the University of Manchester Historical Series No. XXXIII, Manchester: the University Press, 1919, xi+151p.

6.5.2.2   McLACHLAN, Herbert John: 'Methodist Unitarians and the beginnings of the Co-operative Movement in Rochdale in 1844', *Essays and addresses*, Manchester: Manchester University Press, 1950, pp. 213–29.

6.5.3 Magic Methodists

6.5.3.1   HORNE, John T.: 'James Crawfoot: A character study', *Primitive Methodist Quarterly Review*, Vol. XLIV, 1902, pp. 578–92.

6.5.4 Tent Methodists

6.5.4.1   RUSSELL, Kate Pyer: *Memoirs of the Rev. John Pyer*, London: John Snow, 1865, xv+336p.

6.5.5 Original Methodists

6.5.5.1   GRUNDY, Donald M.: 'A history of the Original Methodists', *Proceedings of the Wesley Historical Society*, Vol. XXXV, 1965–66, pp. 116–21, 149–53, 170–2, 189–95, Vol. XXXVI, 1967–68, pp. 22–7, 49–58, 80–5, 115–18, 143–8, 181–6.

6.5.5.2 PARKES, William: 'The Original Methodists, Primitive Methodist reformers', *Proceedings of the Wesley Historical Society*, Vol. XXXV, 1965–66, pp. 57–64.

6.5.6 Teetotal Wesleyan Methodists

6.5.6.1 EDWARDS, Michael Stone: 'The Teetotal Wesleyan Methodists', *Proceedings of the Wesley Historical Society*, Vol. XXXIII, 1961–62, pp. 63–70.

6.5.7 Barkerite secession

6.5.7.1 BARKER, Joseph: *The life of Joseph Barker, written by himself*, edited by John Thomas Barker, London: Hodder and Stoughton, 1880, xiv + 385p.

6.5.7.2 BROOK, Michael: 'Joseph Barker and "The People", the true emigrant's guide', *Publications of the Thoresby Society*, Vol. XLVI, 1957–61, pp. 331–78.

6.5.7.3 HOWORTH, Franklin: 'Anti-trinitarian churches in connexion with Joseph Barker', *Unitarianism exhibited in its actual condition; consisting of essays by several Unitarian ministers and others illustrative of the rise, progress and principles of Christian anti-trinitarianism in different parts of the world*, edited by John Relly Beard, London: Simpkin, Marshall and Co., 1846, pp. 165–71.

6.5.7.4 MCLACHLAN, Herbert John: 'The Christian Brethren movement', *The story of a Nonconformist library* [and other essays], Publications of the University of Manchester Historical Series No. XLI, Manchester: at the University Press, 1923, pp. 152–83.

6.5.8 Wesleyan Reform Union

6.5.8.1 JONES, William Harold: *History of the Wesleyan Reform Union*, London: Epworth Press, 1952, 62p.

6.5.8.2 *Origin and history of the Wesleyan Reform Union; with a brief summary of Methodist secessions*, Sheffield: Wesleyan Reform Union Book Room, 1896, 116p.

See also 6.1.1.3.

6.5.9 Christian Lay Churches

6.5.9.1 MILBURN, Geoffrey Eden: *The Christian Lay Churches*, Sunderland: published by authority of the Sunderland Independent Methodist Circuit, 1977, 49p.

6.5.9.2 MILBURN, Geoffrey Eden: 'Tensions in Primitive Methodism in the eighteen-seventies and the origins of the Christian Lay Churches in the North-East', *Proceedings of the Wesley Historical Society*, Vol. XL, 1975–76, pp. 93–101, 135–44.

7. METHODISM SINCE 1932

7.1 General Histories

7.1.1 Connexional histories: Methodist union

7.1.1.1   BOWMER, John Coates: 'Methodist union', *Proceedings of the Wesley Historical Society*, Vol. XLIII, 1981–82, pp. 101–10.

7.1.1.2   DREWERY, Benjamin: 'Methodist union: Some theological issues', *Epworth Review*, Vol. 9, No. 2, May 1982, pp. 32–9.

7.1.1.3   KENT, John Henry Somerset: 'The Methodist union in England, 1932', *Institutionalism and Church unity: A symposium prepared by the Study Commission on Institutionalism, Commission on Faith and Order, World Council of Churches*, edited by Nils Ehrenstrom & Walter George Muelder, London: SCM Press, 1963, pp. 195–220.

7.1.1.4   WYCHERLEY, Richard Newman: *The pageantry of Methodist union; being a pictorial record of events leading up to and consummating in the historic uniting Conference of 1932*, London: Epworth Press, 1936, 411p.

See also 3.1.2.1, 3.1.2.4, 3.1.2.10.

7.1.2 Connexional histories: other

7.1.2.1   BRAKE, George Thompson: *Policy and politics in British Methodism, 1932–1982*, London: Edsall, 1984, xii+880p.

7.1.2.2   DAVIES, Rupert Eric: 'Methodism', *The testing of the Churches, 1932–1982: A symposium*, edited by Rupert Eric Davies, London: Epworth Press, 1982, pp. 32–59.

7.1.2.3   DAVIES, Rupert Eric: 'Since 1932', *A history of the Methodist Church in Great Britain*, Vol. 3, general editors: Rupert Eric Davies, Alfred Raymond George & Ernest Gordon Rupp, London: Epworth Press, 1983, pp. 362–90.

7.1.2.4   TURNER, Bryan Stanley: 'Discord in modern Methodism', *Proceedings of the Wesley Historical Society*, Vol. XXXVII, 1969–70, pp. 154–9.

7.1.3 Local histories: England

7.1.3.1   HARRISON, Kevin Kenneth: 'The decline of Methodism in Kingston-upon-Hull in the twentieth century', University of Hull M.A. thesis, 1973, 270p.

See also 3.4.1.10, 3.4.3.3, 4.4.5.3, 4.4.5.7, 4.5.3.1, 4.5.3.4, 4.5.3.16, 4.5.3.19, 4.5.3.20, 4.5.3.22, 4.5.3.26, 4.5.3.27, 4.5.3.28, 4.5.3.29, 4.5.3.30, 6.2.7.2, 6.2.7.3, 6.2.7.4, 6.3.11.1, 7.5.3.1.

7.1.4 Local histories: Wales

See 4.5.3.18, 7.5.3.2, 7.5.3.4.

7.1.5 Local histories: Ireland

See 1.2.5.2, 4.5.3.5, 4.5.3.12, 4.6.2.3.

7.2 Biographies

7.2.1 Collective

7.2.1.1 GARLICK, Kenneth Benjamin: *Garlick's Methodist registry, 1983*, London: Edsall, 1983, 373+xxiii+xvii+vip.

7.2.1.2 *The Methodist local preachers' who's who, 1934: A complete record of the lives and careers of Methodist local preachers*, London: Shaw Publishing Co., 1934, 632p.

7.2.1.3 *Who's who in Methodism, 1933: An encyclopaedia of the personnel and departments, ministerial and lay, in the united Church of Methodism*, London: Methodist Times and Leader, 1933, xvi+433p.

7.2.1.4 *Who's who in the Free Churches (and other denominations)*, editor: Leslie Gilbert Pine, London: Shaw Publishing Co., 1951, xxxvi+500p.

7.2.2 Individual: ministers

7.2.2.1 NEWELL, Roy Norman: *Methodist preacher and statesman: Eric W. Baker (1899–1973)*, Taunton: printed by Quantock Printers, [1984], [4]+39p.

7.2.2.2 NEWTON, John Anthony: *A man for all Churches: Marcus Ward, 1906–1978*, London: Epworth Press, 1984, viii+87p.

7.2.2.3 PERKINS, Ernest Benson: *So appointed: An autobiography*, London: Epworth Press, 1964, xiv+204p.

7.2.2.4 PURCELL, William Ernest: *Odd man out: A biography of Lord Soper of Kingsway*, revised edition, London: Mowbray, 1983, 196p.

7.2.2.5 RADFORD, G. Elizabeth: *My providential way: A biography of Francis Brotherton Westbrook*, [Bristol: Methodist Church Music Society, 1978], [6]+149p.

7.2.2.6 SANGSTER, Paul Edwin: *Doctor Sangster*, London: Epworth Press, 1962, 372p.

7.2.2.7 THOMPSON, Douglas Weddell: *Donald Soper: A biography*, Nutfield: Denholm House Press, 1971, 224p.

7.2.2.8   WAKEFIELD, Gordon Stevens: *Robert Newton Flew, 1886–1962,* London: Epworth Press, 1971, xii+268p.
7.2.2.9   WEATHERHEAD, Andrew Kingsley: *Leslie Weatherhead: A personal portrait,* London: Hodder and Stoughton, 1975, 222p.
See also 4.2.27.30, 7.3.1.1.

7.2.3 Individual: laity

7.2.3.1   MACKINTOSH, Harold Vincent: *By faith and work: The autobiography of the Rt. Hon. the first Viscount Mackintosh of Halifax, D.L., LL.D.,* edited and arranged by Arthur Alexander Thomson, London: Hutchinson, 1966, 296p.
See also 7.5.3.1, 7.5.4.1.

7.3 Spirituality

7.3.1 Theology

7.3.1.1   ODOM, Stephen Allan: ' "Identification" as a key to effectiveness in the preaching of Leslie Dixon Weatherhead', Southern Baptist Theological Seminary Ph.D. thesis, 1985, 274p.
See also 4.3.1.7, 4.3.1.9, 7.2.2.2, 7.2.2.8.

7.3.2 Sacraments

7.3.2.1   JENNINGS, Robert H.: 'Recent eucharistic renewal in the Roman, Anglican and Methodist Churches', University of Durham M.A. thesis, 1978, [3]+106p.
7.3.2.2   TRIPP, David Howard: 'Behind the "Alternative order" ', *Proceedings of the Wesley Historical Society,* Vol. XLIII, 1981–82, pp. 4–8.
See also 3.2.2.1, 4.3.2.1.

7.3.3 Worship and devotion

7.3.3.1   BOWMER, John Coates: 'The Methodist Book of Offices: An essay in liturgical revision', *London Quarterly and Holborn Review,* Vol. CXCI, 1966, pp. 268–76.
7.3.3.2   GEORGE, Alfred Raymond: 'The changing face of Methodism: I. The Methodist Service Book', *Proceedings of the Wesley Historical Society,* Vol. XLI, 1977–78, pp. 65–72.
7.3.3.3   THOMAS, John A.: 'Liturgy and architecture, 1932–60: Methodist influences and ideas', *Proceedings of the Wesley Historical Society,* Vol. XL, 1975–76, pp. 106–13.
See also 2.6.3.11, 7.3.2.2.

7.3.4 Hymnology and music

7.3.4.1   GREGORY, Arthur Stephen: 'M[ethodist] C[hurch] M[usic]

S[ociety]: The first five years', *Methodist Church Music Society Bulletin*, Vol. 3, 1977–82, pp. 42–6, 68–72.
See also 4.3.4.1, 7.2.2.5.

7.4 Polity and Mission

7.4.1 Ordained ministry

See 7.2.1.1, 7.2.2.2.

7.4.2 Lay ministry

See 3.3.2.2, 7.2.1.2.

7.4.3 Buildings and finance

See 3.3.3.1, 7.3.3.3.

7.4.4 Home missions

See 4.4.5.3, 4.4.5.7, 4.4.5.11, 7.2.2.6.

7.5 Social Aspects

7.5.1 Political impact

See 3.4.1.10.

7.5.2 Social witness

7.5.2.1 DAVEY, Cyril James: *Home for good: The Methodist Homes for the Aged, 1943–1983*, London: Methodist Homes for the Aged, 1983, [3]+48p.
7.5.2.2 DAVEY, Cyril James: *Home from home: The story of the Methodist Homes for the Aged*, London: Epworth Press, 1976, 168p.
7.5.2.3 *MIH silver jubilee, 1950–75*, [London: Methodist International House, 1975], 24p.
See also 4.5.2.3.

7.5.3 Educational work

7.5.3.1 *A. B. Sackett: A memoir*, edited by John Dixon Walsh, [London]: Epworth Press in association with the Governors of Kingswood School, 1979, 127p.
7.5.3.2 BEARDSWORTH, Monica: *Penrhos College, 1880–1980: The second fifty years*, Bristol: printed by Bristol Typesetting Co., [1980], 103p.
7.5.3.3 [HINSON, David Francis]: *50 years with the Methodist Study Centre*, London: Methodist Study Centre, [1978], 11p.

7.5.3.4   *Rydal School, 1936–1963*, [edited by Frank William Pilling], Colwyn Bay: Rydal Press, [1964], 232p.

See also 3.4.3.3, 4.5.3.1, 4.5.3.4, 4.5.3.5, 4.5.3.12, 4.5.3.16, 4.5.3.19, 4.5.3.20, 4.5.3.22, 4.5.3.26, 4.5.3.27, 4.5.3.28, 4.5.3.29, 4.5.3.30, 6.2.7.2, 6.2.7.3, 6.2.7.4, 6.3.11.1.

7.5.4 Literary and cultural influence

7.5.4.1   Wood, Alan: *Mr. Rank: A study of J. Arthur Rank and British films*, London: Hodder and Stoughton, 1952, 288p.

7.6 Reactions to Methodism

7.6.1 Relations with other Churches

See 4.6.2.3.

Appendix I
Chapter Conversion Table

The following table lists the chapters of *A History of the Methodist Church in Great Britain* in order of their appearance and identifies the principal subsections of the bibliography which correspond to them. It will be recalled from the introductory notes that no references have been given for the essays by Herbert Butterfield, William Reginald Ward and Thomas Edmund Jessop which concern the general background to the rise and development of Methodism.

VOLUME 1

2.	'John Wesley'	2.1.1, 2.2.4–2.2.19
3.	'The theological originality of John Wesley and continental spirituality'	2.4.4, 2.5.1
4.	'Charles Wesley'	2.2.4, 2.2.20, 2.6.4–2.6.6
5.	'The people called Methodists: 1. "Our doctrines"'	2.5.1–2.5.8
6.	'The people called Methodists: 2. "Our discipline"'	2.5.7, 2.6.1, 2.6.3, 2.8.2
7.	'The people called Methodists: 3. Polity'	2.6.1, 2.6.8, 2.7.1, 2.7.2, 2.7.4
8.	'The people called Methodists: 4. The means of grace'	2.6.2, 2.6.3
9.	'Methodism at the end of the eighteenth century'	2.1.1, 2.9.3–2.9.5, 4.1.2, 4.4.2, 4.5.1

VOLUME 2

II.	'Methodist religion, 1791–1849'	3.1.2, 3.2.3, 3.3.4, 3.4.3, 4.1.2
III.	'The Methodist people in the early Victorian age: Spirituality and worship'	3.2.2, 3.2.3, 4.3.1, 4.3.3
IV.	'Ordination'	2.3.2, 2.7.2, 4.4.2
VI.	'The Wesleyan Methodists to 1849'	3.4.1, 4.1.2, 4.2.5, 4.2.8, 4.2.11, 4.2.18, 4.2.25, 4.3.3, 4.5.1, 4.5.3
VII.	'The rise of other Methodist traditions'	5.1.2, 5.2.2, 5.2.3, 6.1.1, 6.1.5, 6.2.2, 6.3.1, 6.5.1, 6.5.2

VOLUME 3

Appendix II

Index of Authors and Editors

Note: Asterisks are used to distinguish the contributions of editors from those of authors.

ABELOVE, Henry Diamond – 2.2.6.1.
ADAMS, Nelson Falls – 2.6.7.1.
ALBIN, Thomas R. – 2.5.1.1.
ALDERFER, Owen H. – 2.8.1.1.
ALLBECK, Willard Dow – 2.5.3.1.
ALLCHIN, Arthur Macdonald – 2.4.3.1, 2.6.5.4*.
ALLIN, Thomas – 6.1.1.1.
ANDERSON, Barbara Vogwill – 5.2.10.1.
ANDERSON, William Ketcham – 2.5.3.6*.
ANDREWS, J. H. B. – 6.2.2.1.
ANDREWS, John Richard – 2.3.11.1.
ANDREWS, Stuart – 1.2.1.1, 2.8.1.2, 2.8.4.1, 4.5.4.1.
ANSTEY, Roger Thomas – 4.5.1.1, 4.5.1.2.
ANTLIFF, William – 5.2.2.1, 5.2.2.7*.
ARCH, Joseph – 5.2.7.1.
ARMSTRONG, Anthony – 2.1.1.1.
ARMSTRONG, Clinton Cornelius – 2.2.6.2.
ARMSTRONG, Walter Henry – 4.2.27.1.
ARNETT, William Melvin – 2.4.2.1, 2.4.2.2, 2.4.2.3, 2.5.7.1.
ARNOLD, Richard Alexander – 2.6.4.1.
ARTHUR, William – 4.2.19.1.
ASHMAN, Ronald George – 2.4.5.1.
ASHWORTH, Jesse – 5.2.2.2.
ASKEW, Edwin – 6.3.1.3*.
ATKINSON, John – 5.2.6.1.
ATMORE, Charles – 2.7.2.1.
AUSTIN, Roland – 2.3.11.2.
AYLING, Stanley Edward – 2.2.6.3.

BAKER, Derek – 2.9.1.4*, 4.1.2.24*, 4.5.3.1.
BAKER, Donald S. – 2.8.1.3, 2.8.1.4, 2.8.1.5, 2.8.1.6, 2.8.1.7, 2.8.1.8, 2.8.1.38*.
BAKER, Eric Wilfred – 2.3.9.1.
BAKER, Frank – 1.1.1.1, 1.1.2.1, 1.2.1.2, 1.3.4.1, 2.2.3.1, 2.2.3.2, 2.2.4.1, 2.2.5.1, 2.2.8.1, 2.2.9.1, 2.2.9.2, 2.2.11.1, 2.2.12.1, 2.2.12.2, 2.2.12.3, 2.2.12.4, 2.2.12.5, 2.2.12.6, 2.2.13.1, 2.2.13.9*, 2.2.13.10*, 2.2.14.1,

2.2.16.1, 2.2.16.13*, 2.2.18.1, 2.2.18.2, 2.2.18.3, 2.2.19.1, 2.2.20.1, 2.2.20.2, 2.3.1.1, 2.3.3.1, 2.3.4.1, 2.3.7.1, 2.3.9.2, 2.3.9.3, 2.3.11.3, 2.4.4.1, 2.4.6.1, 2.4.7.1, 2.6.1.1, 2.6.1.2, 2.6.3.1, 2.6.4.21*, 2.6.6.1, 2.7.3.1, 2.8.1.9, 2.8.1.10, 2.8.2.1, 2.9.4.1, 2.9.4.2, 2.9.5.1, 5.2.6.2.

BAKER, Nigel – 4.5.3.26*.

BANKS, John – 2.2.18.4.

BARAGAR, Charles Arthur – 2.8.4.2.

BARBER, Benjamin Aquila – 1.2.1.16, 5.1.2.1.

BARBER, Frank Louis – 2.2.17.1.

BARBER, William Theodore Aquila – 3.3.5.1.

BARDELL, Eunice Bonow – 2.8.4.3.

BARDSLEY, John W. – 2.4.6.6.

BARKER, Esther T. – 2.3.6.1.

BARKER, John Thomas – 6.5.7.1*.

BARKER, Joseph – 6.5.7.1.

BARKER, William – 5.4.1.4*.

BARR, Josiah Henry – 2.9.1.1.

BARRATT, Thomas H. – 2.6.2.1.

BARTON, David Anthony – 3.1.3.1, 6.3.6.1.

BARTON, Jessie Hamby – 2.6.3.2.

BATES, Edmund Ralph – 2.2.7.1, 2.2.7.2.

BATTY, Margaret – 1.4.2.1.

BAXTER, John L. – 4.4.5.1.

BAXTER, Matthew – 6.3.1.1.

BEAL, William – 2.2.1.1.

BEALS, James Duane – 2.6.1.3.

BEARD, John Relly – 6.5.7.3*.

BEARDSWORTH, Monica – 7.5.3.2.

BEAUMONT, Joseph – 4.2.2.1.

BEBBINGTON, David William – 3.4.1.1, 4.3.1.1, 4.5.1.3.

BECKERLEGGE, Oliver Aveyard – 2.2.16.14*, 2.6.6.2, 2.6.6.3, 2.6.6.4, 2.8.1.11, 2.9.4.3, 3.2.1.1, 6.1.4.1, 6.2.1.1, 6.2.3.1, 6.3.1.2, 6.3.2.1, 6.3.2.2, 6.3.5.1.

BECKWORTH, William Harold – 5.1.3.1.

BEECHAM, Helen Audrey – 2.2.2.1.

BELDEN, Albert David – 2.3.11.4.

BELSHAW, Harry – 2.8.5.1, 2.9.2.1.

BENCE, Clarence Luther – 2.5.1.2, 2.5.8.1.

BENNER, Forest T. – 2.5.6.1.

BENNETT, Erman Fay – 2.4.1.1.

BENNETT, Gareth Vaughan – 2.1.1.29*, 4.2.10.2*.

BENSON, Joseph – 2.3.3.2.

BENSON, Louis Fitzgerald – 2.6.4.2.

BERESFORD, John Baldwin – 2.2.18.5.

BERG, Johannes van den – 2.4.5.2.

BERKOUWER, Gerrit Cornelis – 2.4.2.20*.

BERTRAND, Claude-Jean – 1.2.1.3.

BETT, Henry – 2.1.1.2, 2.2.16.2, 2.2.16.3, 2.6.6.5, 2.6.6.6, 2.7.2.2, 2.7.2.3.

BEVAN, Emma Frances – 2.2.6.4.

Brook, Michael – 6.5.7.2.
Brooks, Peter – 2.1.1.27*.
Brown, Anne – 4.5.3.2.
Brown, Brian Dennis – 4.5.1.4.
Brown, Earl Kent – 2.7.3.3, 2.7.3.4, 2.7.3.5.
Brown, Howard Miles – 2.1.2.4, 2.1.2.5.
Brown, John – 2.3.7.2.
Brown, Kenneth Douglas – 3.3.1.2.
Brown, Leonard – 5.1.2.3, 5.2.2.4.
Brownson, William James – 5.2.1.1.
Buckroyd, Elizabeth Ann – 1.3.5.1, 2.6.4.4, 4.5.3.3.
Bunting, Thomas Percival – 4.2.5.1.
Burgess, John – 1.2.2.1, 1.2.2.2, 3.1.3.3.
Burgess, Stuart John – 4.4.2.5.
Burkhard, Johann Gottlieb – 2.1.1.4.
Burnett, Ivan Blackwell – 2.8.2.6.
Burnett, Richard George – 3.3.2.2, 4.2.28.1.
Burrows, Richard Frederick – 2.8.5.4.
Burt, Thomas – 5.2.10.2.
Burton, Thomas Glen – 2.2.17.4*.
Bush, Jane – 4.2.27.16*.
Buss, Frederick Harold – 3.3.2.2.
Butler, Dugald – 2.1.4.1, 2.4.7.2.
Butler, John Francis – 1.4.3.1.

Calagui, Jeremias Datu – 2.5.2.2.
Callaway, Clifford Wayne – 2.8.4.5.
Cameron, Richard Morgan – 2.1.1.5, 2.2.9.3, 2.4.4.2.
Campbell, Gabrielle Margaret Vere – see Bowen, Marjorie *pseud.*
Campbell, Ted Allen – 2.4.3.3.
Candler, Warren Akin – 2.3.2.1.
Cannon, William Ragsdale – 1.4.1.1, 2.2.8.2, 2.5.1.3, 2.5.1.4, 2.5.5.3, 2.5.6.2, 2.5.7.3.
Capey, A. C. – 2.6.6.7.
Carrier, E. Theodore – 2.6.1.9.
Carruth, Samuel Enoch – 2.6.1.4.
Carter, Charles Webb – 2.6.5.9*.
Carter, David John – 3.1.3.4.
Carter, Henry – 2.1.1.6.
Carwardine, Richard – 3.3.4.1.
Cascio, Robert Jude – 2.3.9.4.
Casto, Robert Michael – 2.4.2.4.
Cavender, Curtis H. – see Decanver, H. C. *pseud.*
Cell, George Croft – 2.5.1.5.
Chamberlayne, John Henry – 1.2.1.5.
Champness, Eliza M. – 4.2.7.1.
Chandler, Douglas Robson – 2.4.1.2, 2.7.2.4.
Channon, Henry James – 4.5.3.4.

CHEATHAM, Carl Wade – 4.5.2.1.
CHEW, Richard – 6.3.5.2, 6.3.6.2.
CHILCOTE, Paul Wesley – 2.2.18.6, 2.7.3.6, 2.7.3.7, 4.2.27.2.
CHILES, Robert Eugene – 2.5.3.2.
CHO, John Chongnahm – 2.5.2.3, 2.6.2.5, 2.6.2.6.
CHRISTIAN, Cyril Joseph – 3.4.1.2.
CHRISTOPHERS, Samuel Woolcock – 2.6.4.5.
CHUBB, James Stoskopf – 2.1.1.7.
CHURCH, Leslie Frederic – 2.1.1.8, 2.1.1.9, 2.7.2.5.
CHURCH, Thomas – 5.1.2.4, 5.6.1.1.
CLANCY, Eric Gerald – 2.2.3.2*, 2.2.13.1*, 2.5.3.13*, 2.5.7.45*, 2.6.4.24*,
   4.5.1.16*.
CLAPPER, Gregory Scott – 2.2.17.2, 2.4.8.2.
CLARK, Elmer Talmage – 2.2.9.4, 2.2.9.14*.
CLARKE, Adam – 2.2.1.2.
CLARKE, David Frederick – 1.2.2.3, 2.3.8.1.
CLARKE, Eliza – 2.2.3.4.
CLARKE, Joseph Butterworth Bulmer – 4.2.8.9*.
CLARKSON, George Edward – 2.3.9.5.
CLAYPOOL, James Vernon – 2.4.6.3.
CLELAND, Ivan David – 4.1.2.1.
CLEMONS, James Thomas – 2.4.2.5, 2.4.2.6.
CLIFFORD, Alan C. – 2.9.5.4.
CLOKE, Henry – 1.5.3.1.
CLOWES, William – 5.2.3.1.
COCKING, Thomas – 4.1.3.2.
COGGIN, James Earl – 2.5.7.4.
COKE, Thomas – 2.2.6.9.
COLE, Francis Joseph – 2.1.5.2.
COLE, John – 2.3.7.3.
COLE, Richard Lee – 1.2.5.1, 1.2.5.2, 2.1.5.3, 2.2.14.2, 4.5.3.5.
COLEY, Samuel – 4.2.27.3.
COLLIER, Frank Wilbur – 2.8.4.6.
COLLIER, John – 2.5.7.5.
COLLINS, Edward McDaniel – 2.2.15.1.
COLLINS, Kenneth Joseph – 2.5.1.6, 2.5.1.7.
CONNOR, Joyce Mary – see MARLOW, Joyce *pseud*.
COOK, Vallance Cole – 4.2.9.1.
COOKE, Joseph Henry – 1.2.5.3, 4.1.6.2.
COOKE, William – 6.1.1.1, 6.1.5.2, 6.1.6.1.
COOMER, Duncan – 2.7.3.8.
COOPER, Allen Lamar – 2.8.2.7.
COPPEDGE, Allan – 2.4.1.3, 2.5.3.3.
COPPLESTONE, John Tremayne – 2.8.1.12.
COUILLARD, Vernon Williams – 2.3.1.2.
COULTER, Ellis Merton – 2.2.8.3.
COURT, A. W. Glyn – 6.2.2.3.
COX, Leo George – 2.5.2.4, 2.5.7.6.

Cox, Robert – 2.3.3.3.
CRAGG, George Golden – 2.3.4.2.
CRANE, Denis *pseud.* – 4.2.28.2, 5.2.4.1.
CRANFIELD, Walter Thomas – see CRANE, Denis *pseud.*
CRESSWELL, Amos Samuel – 4.4.5.3.
CREWES, Frederick Ronald – 4.5.3.6.
CROMPTON, David Jones – 2.6.6.8.
CROOK, William – 2.2.1.3.
CROOKSHANK, Charles Henry – 1.2.5.4, 1.2.5.5, 2.1.5.4.
CROTHERS, Thomas Dickson – 6.1.1.2.
CROW, Earl Pickett – 2.5.3.4, 2.5.3.5.
CROWTHER, Jonathan – 2.1.1.10, 2.3.2.2.
CUBIE, David Livingstone – 2.5.7.7, 2.5.7.8.
CUMBERLAND, Albert George – 2.7.4.1.
CUMBERS, Frank Henry – 1.1.2.2, 4.4.2.13*.
CUMING, Geoffrey John – 2.3.5.3*, 2.9.1.4*, 4.1.2.24*.
CUMMINGS, Arthur Dagg – 1.1.2.3.
CUNNINGHAM, Valentine David – 3.5.1.1.
CURNOCK, Nehemiah – 2.2.14.9*.
CURRIE, Robert – 1.2.1.6, 1.2.1.7, 3.1.2.1.
CUSHMAN, Robert Earl – 2.4.2.15*, 2.5.1.8, 2.5.3.6.
CUSTER, Watson Stanley – 2.5.4.1.

DAKIN, Donald Hubert – 3.5.1.2.
DALE, James – 2.2.16.14*, 2.6.5.1, 2.6.5.2.
DALLIMORE, Arnold Arthur – 2.3.11.5.
DAMM, Ulrich F. – 2.4.5.3.
DANIEL, Wilborn Harrison – 3.4.1.3.
DARBY, James Carter – 2.5.7.9.
DAVEY, Cyril James – 1.2.1.8, 1.4.4.2, 1.4.4.3, 2.3.2.3, 4.2.24.2, 7.5.2.1, 7.5.2.2.
DAVIE, Donald – 2.6.6.9.
DAVIES, Daniel Horton Marlais – 2.4.5.4, 2.6.3.3, 3.2.3.2.
DAVIES, Edward Tegla – 1.2.1.16.
DAVIES, Rupert Eric – 1.2.1.9, 1.2.3.2*, 1.2.4.3*, 1.2.5.6*, 1.4.4.1*, 1.5.3.5*, 2.2.6.12*, 2.2.20.7*, 2.4.4.7*, 2.5.1.9, 2.6.1.2*, 2.6.1.7*, 2.6.3.5*, 2.7.2.9*, 3.1.2.10*, 3.1.2.11*, 3.1.2.15*, 3.1.2.16*, 3.2.3.3*, 4.1.2.12*, 4.1.2.17*, 4.1.2.22*, 4.2.13.1*, 4.3.1.7*, 7.1.2.2, 7.1.2.3.
DAVIES, William Rhys – 2.3.3.4, 2.9.4.4.
DAVIS, Mollie Camp – 2.3.6.3.
DAVISON, John – 5.2.3.2.
DAW, A. R. – 2.1.4.2.
DAWSON, Joseph – 4.2.15.1, 4.2.21.1.
DEAN, William Walter – 2.6.8.1, 4.3.5.1.
DEARING, Trevor – 2.6.3.4.
DECANVER, H. C. *pseud.* – 2.9.2.2.
DENYER, Allen Stewart – 2.6.5.3.
DESCHNER, John William – 2.5.4.2.

EDWARDS, Michael Stone – 3.1.3.5, 3.1.3.6, 3.4.1.4, 4.2.12.2, 4.2.12.3, 4.2.23.1, 4.2.23.2, 4.6.2.1, 6.5.6.1.
EHRENSTROM, Nils – 7.1.1.3*.
EICKEN, Erich von – 2.5.5.5.
ELLINGWORTH, Paul – 2.6.6.10.
ELLIOTT, Charles Middleton – 2.8.2.9, 4.1.3.3.
ELLIS, Martin – 1.3.5.3.
ELLIS, Miriam – 1.3.5.3.
ELTIS, David – 4.5.1.2*.
ELTZHOLTZ, Carl Frederik – 2.2.9.5.
ENGEMAN, Thomas Sledge – 4.5.1.5.
ENGLAND, Martha Winburn – 2.2.16.5, 2.8.5.5.
ENGLISH, John Cammel – 2.4.6.4, 2.4.6.5, 2.4.7.4, 2.4.8.3, 2.5.1.13, 2.5.1.14, 2.6.2.7, 2.7.2.7.
ENTWISLE, Joseph – 4.2.27.6.
ETHERIDGE, John Wesley – 2.3.2.5, 4.2.8.3.
ETHRIDGE, Willie Snow – 2.2.18.9.
EVANS, Charles – 2.2.1.5.
EVANS, Eifion – 2.3.5.1.
EVANS, John – 2.2.6.13.
EVANS, Richard William – 2.1.3.1.
EVANS, William Abraham – 4.1.4.3.
EVERETT, James – 2.1.2.7, 2.1.2.8, 4.2.8.4.

FARNDALE, William Edward – 5.1.2.5, 5.2.2.5.
FAULKNER, Harold Underwood – 3.4.1.5.
FAULKNER, John Alfred – 2.4.4.3.
FEATHER, Howard Rodney – 3.4.4.2.
FENNELL, William O. – 4.2.25.2.
FERGUSON, Duncan S. – 2.4.2.8.
FIELD, Clive Douglas – 1.1.1.5, 1.2.1.12, 2.3.3.5, 3.1.2.3, 3.1.3.7.
FINDLATER, John – 2.5.7.10.
FINDLAY, George Gillanders – 4.2.17.1, 4.4.6.1, 4.4.6.2.
FINDLAY, George Hindson – 2.6.4.7, 2.6.6.11, 2.6.6.12.
FINDLAY, Mary Grace – 4.4.6.1.
FITCHETT, William Henry – 2.2.6.14.
FLACHSMEIER, Horst Reinhold – 2.8.2.10.
FLANAGAN, James – 5.2.4.2.
FLEMING, Richard Lee – 2.6.2.8.
FLEW, Robert Newton – 2.5.7.11, 2.6.6.13.
FLINT, Charles Wesley – 2.2.20.3.
FOREMAN, Henry – 3.4.3.1.
FORKEL, Frederick William – 2.8.2.11.
FORSAITH, Peter S. – 2.3.3.6, 2.3.3.7.
FORTNEY, Edward L. – 1.1.1.6.
FOWLER, Edith Henrietta – 4.2.28.4.
FOWLER, James Wiley – 2.2.7.4.
FRANCIS, David Noel – 2.7.3.2*, 3.3.2.1*.

HOCKING, Silas Kitto – 6.3.7.2.
HODGEN, Margaret Trabue – 2.5.2.6.
HODGES, Herbert Arthur – 2.5.5.6.
HODGSON, Elsie Marjorie – 2.2.16.8, 2.6.6.14, 2.6.6.15.
HOFFMAN, Thomas G. – 2.8.2.13.
HOLDSWORTH, William West – 4.4.6.2.
HOLIFIELD, Elmer Brooks – 4.3.1.3.
HOLLAND, Bernard George – 2.2.9.7, 2.2.10.6, 2.6.2.14, 3.2.2.2, 4.3.2.1, 4.3.2.2.
HOLLAND, Lynwood Mathis – 2.8.1.16, 2.8.1.17.
HOLMES, David – 2.2.6.20.
HOLYOAKE, George Jacob – 4.2.23.3.
HOOKER, Morna Dorothy – 5.4.1.2.
HOOLE, Elijah – 2.9.2.5.
HOON, Paul Waitman – 2.5.1.18.
HORN, Pamela R. – 3.4.1.13, 5.2.7.2.
HORN, Wilhelm – 2.8.5.8.
HORNBY, George Goodall – 1.2.1.16, 6.3.9.1.
HORNE, John T. – 6.5.3.1.
HORNER, John Pennock – 3.1.3.10.
HORSLEY, Lee – 1.2.1.7.
HOSMAN, Glenn Burton – 2.8.1.18.
HOUGHTON, Edward – 2.2.16.9, 2.6.4.11.
HOVEY, Rosa – 4.5.3.10.
HOWARD, Wilbert Francis – 2.2.13.3, 5.2.9.2*.
HOWARTH, David Heighton – 4.2.6.2, 4.2.6.3, 4.4.5.5.
HOWELL, David – 5.1.4.1.
HOWELL, Ronald F. – 2.8.1.17.
HOWKINS, Alun – 5.5.1.3.
HOWORTH, Franklin – 6.5.7.3.
HOYLE, Arthur – 4.2.27.16.
HUBERY, Douglas Stanley – 1.5.3.3.
HUGHES, Dorothea Price – 4.2.10.1, 4.6.1.1.
HUGHES, Henry Trevor – 2.4.6.8.
HUGHES, Hugh Joshua – 2.3.5.2.
HUGHES, John Thomas – 6.3.1.4.
HUGHES, Leo – 2.9.2.6.
HULL, James Ernest – 2.3.6.5.
HULME, Samuel – 6.1.1.1, 6.1.6.3, 6.1.6.4.
HUMPHREYS, Thomas Jones – 4.1.4.4.
HUMPHRIES, Albert Lewis – 5.4.1.4*.
HUNT, Raymond Fletcher – 2.8.3.5.
HUNTER, Frederick – 2.3.9.8, 2.4.6.9, 2.4.6.10, 2.6.3.8, 2.6.3.9, 2.9.3.2.
HURD, F. H. – 5.2.1.3.
HURLEY, Michael – 2.6.2.17*, 2.9.6.1*, 4.6.2.3*.
HURST, John Fletcher – 1.2.1.18.
HUSTON, Robert – 4.1.6.4, 4.2.27.13.
HUTCHINSON, Francis Ernest – 2.4.6.11.

Joy, Donald Marvin – 2.5.1.20.
Joy, James Richard – 2.2.11.5.
Judson, Sandra – 2.2.5.4.

Källstad, Thorvald – 2.2.7.9, 2.4.2.12.
Kamm, Otto Friedrich – 2.8.5.9.
Kapp, John Ruse – 2.8.1.25.
Keddie, Henrietta – see Tytler, Sarah *pseud.*
Keefer, Luke L. – 2.4.3.4, 2.4.3.5.
Keller, Rosemary Skinner – 2.2.3.2*, 2.2.18.10*, 2.3.6.3*, 2.7.3.5*.
Kellett, Norman Lawrence – 2.5.6.3.
Kellogg, Amherst W. – 1.2.1.20.
Kelly, Charles Henry – 4.2.27.17.
Kelly, Hugh – 6.5.1.1.
Kelynack, William Sydney – 2.3.1.4.
Kemnitz, Thomas Milton – 4.2.23.5.
Kendall, Charles – 5.2.6.7.
Kendall, Holliday Bickerstaffe – 5.1.2.7, 5.1.2.8, 5.1.2.9.
Kent, John Henry Somerset – 2.8.1.26, 3.1.2.4, 3.1.2.5, 3.3.4.3, 4.1.2.11,
    4.1.2.12, 4.2.5.2, 4.2.10.2, 4.4.2.9, 7.1.1.3.
Kenyon, Edith C. – 2.2.6.22.
Ker, R. Alan – 4.1.6.7.
Ker, Robert Ernest – 1.3.5.5.
Kilham, Alexander – 6.1.5.3.
Kim, Seung Lak – 2.5.6.4.
King, Charles Harold – 2.3.11.12.
King, William McGuire – 4.2.10.3.
Kingdon, Robert Maccune – 2.8.2.17.
Kinghorn, Kenneth Cain – 2.3.3.8.
Kinsman, Richard – 6.2.2.10.
Kirby, Gilbert Walter – 2.3.6.6.
Kirk, John – 2.2.3.6.
Kirkham, Donald Henry – 2.8.1.27, 2.9.2.7.
Kirsop, Joseph – 6.3.1.5.
Kishida, Yuki – 2.8.2.18, 2.8.2.19.
Kissack, Reginald – 1.3.2.1.
Klapas, Janina Alina – 3.1.3.11.
Knickerbocker, Waldo Emerson – 2.4.1.5, 2.4.1.6.
Knight, Helen Cross – 2.3.6.7.
Knight, John Allan – 2.3.3.9, 2.5.1.21.
Knox, Robert Buick – 2.3.5.3.
Knox, Ronald Arbuthnott – 2.5.1.22.
Koepp, Wilhelm – 2.5.7.15*.
Koerber, Charles J. – 2.5.6.5.
Koss, Stephen Edward – 3.4.1.14, 4.5.1.14.

La Gorce, Agnès de – 2.2.6.23, 2.8.1.28.
Lambert, David Willoughby – 4.4.5.7.

MacArthur, Kathleen Walker – 2.8.2.20.
McCarthy, Daryl – 2.4.2.14.
McConnell, Francis John – 2.2.5.6, 2.2.6.28.
McCormick, Kelley Steve – 2.4.3.6.
McCrea, Alexander – 4.1.6.6*.
M'Cullagh, Henry Hays – 4.2.27.19.
M'Cullagh, Thomas – 2.2.5.7, 4.2.21.2, 4.2.28.11.
McCulloh, Gerald O. – 2.7.2.21*.
Macdonald, Frederic William – 2.3.3.12, 4.2.14.1, 4.2.14.2, 4.2.21.3.
McDonald, Hugh Dermot – 2.4.1.8.
Macdonald, James – 4.2.3.1.
McEldowney, James Edward – 2.4.1.9.
McEllhenney, John Galen – 2.8.5.10.
Macfarlane, David Laing – 1.2.4.2.
McGonigle, Herbert – 2.5.6.6.
McGovern, Terrence Xavier – 2.8.5.11.
McIntosh, Lawrence Dennis – 2.2.5.8, 2.2.9.9, 2.4.1.10.
McKechnie, Colin Campbell – 5.2.2.1.
Mackenzie, Peter Donald – 2.6.8.2.
McKeon, Francis James – 5.1.2.10.
Mackintosh, Harold Vincent – 7.2.3.1.
McLachlan, Herbert John – 6.5.2.1, 6.5.2.2, 6.5.7.4.
McLellan, Nathaniel Johnston – 3.4.1.15.
McNeill, John Thomas – 2.2.9.10.
McNulty, Frank John – 2.8.2.21.
MacPherson, James – 5.1.2.13, 5.2.5.1.
McQuaid, Ina Debord – 2.8.3.6.
McTyeire, Holland Nimmons – 2.1.1.19.
Maddox, Randy Lynn – 2.5.3.16.
Madron, Thomas William – 2.8.1.31, 2.8.2.22, 2.8.2.23, 2.8.2.24.
Malekin, Peter – 2.3.9.10.
Malins, Joseph – 4.2.27.20.
Mallinson, Joel – 4.1.3.11.
Mallinson, William – 6.3.8.1.
Manifold, Orrin Avery – 2.5.7.18.
Mankin, Kenneth – 1.3.5.6.
Manning, Bernard Lord – 2.6.4.12.
Mantle, John Gregory – 4.2.10.4.
Margull, Hans Jochen – 2.3.3.19*.
Marlow, Joyce *pseud.* – 4.5.1.15.
Marquardt, Manfred – 2.5.5.7, 2.8.2.25.
Marquis, James Wilson – 3.4.1.16.
Marshall, Ian Howard – 2.5.7.19.
Marshall, Madeleine Forell – 2.6.4.13.
Marshall, Ronald – 4.5.3.12.
Marshall, Ronald Philip – 2.4.5.10.
Martin, Hugh – 1.3.3.1*.
Martin, Roger Harry – 4.4.6.4.

Moss, Reginald – 2.1.2.13.
Moss, Richard Waddy – 4.1.2.13, 4.2.20.1.
Moulton, Harold Keeling – 4.2.16.1.
Moulton, Wilfrid Johnson – 2.5.7.21.
Moulton, William Fiddian – 4.2.16.2, 4.2.17.2, 4.4.5.8.
Mounfield, Arthur – 6.5.1.3*.
Muelder, Walter George – 7.1.1.3*.
Mullen, Wilbur H. – 2.4.2.16, 2.5.1.27.
Mumford, Norman William – 2.6.1.11, 3.2.2.3, 3.2.2.4.
Munson, James Edward Bradbury – 3.4.1.18.
Murray, Harold – 4.2.26.1.
Murray, James – 6.5.1.2.
Murray, Nancy Uhlar – 4.1.2.14.
Mussman, Robert Byron – 2.5.7.22.
Myers, James – 5.1.3.5.
Myers, Lucia – 2.3.6.10.
Myles, William – 2.1.1.20, 2.3.4.4.

Naglee, David Ingersoll – 2.6.2.15.
Nagler, Arthur Wilford – 2.4.5.11.
Nausner, Helmut – 2.5.7.23.
Neff, Blake J. – 2.5.7.24.
New, Alfred Henry – 2.3.6.11.
Newell, Roy Norman – 7.2.2.1.
Newman, Leslie Arthur – 2.4.8.6.
Newnes, T. M. – 4.2.8.8.
Newton, John – 2.3.4.5.
Newton, John Anthony – 2.2.3.7, 2.2.3.8, 2.4.7.7, 2.4.7.8, 2.5.1.28, 2.5.7.25,
    2.9.3.3, 7.2.2.2.
Nicholson, Roy Stephen – 2.5.7.26, 2.5.7.27, 2.6.5.9, 2.9.3.4.
Nightingale, Joseph – 2.1.1.21.
Noll, Mark Allan – 2.5.6.7, 2.6.6.17.
Norman, David Douglas Robert – 2.5.4.3.
Noro, Yoshio – 2.2.6.33, 2.5.7.28.
North, Eric McCoy – 2.8.2.27.
Norwood, Frederick Abbott – 1.1.1.10, 1.1.1.13, 1.1.1.14.
Nottingham, Elizabeth Kristine – 2.2.7.12.
Nuelsen, John Louis – 2.2.16.10. 2.3.3.15, 2.7.2.14.
Nuttall, Geoffrey Fillingham – 2.3.5.5, 2.9.5.5, 5.1.2.12.
Nygren, Ellis Herbert – 2.7.2.15, 2.7.2.16.
Obelkevich, James – 3.1.3.15.
Oberman, Heiko Augustinus – 2.4.2.20*.
O'bryan, William – 6.2.2.4.
Odom, Stephen Allan – 7.3.1.1.
Ollerhead, Peter Edward – 3.1.3.16.
Ong, Walter Jackson – 2.1.1.22.
Orcibal, Jean – 2.4.4.6, 2.4.4.7.
Orr, James Edwin – 3.3.4.4.

PORTER, Laurence E. – 2.3.7.5.
POTTER, Sarah Caroline – 4.4.6.8.
POTTER, William – 5.2.6.9.
PRINCE, John Wesley – 2.8.3.8.
PRIOR, Jacob Hunt – 6.2.2.10.
PRITCHARD, Frank Cyril – 1.5.3.5, 1.5.3.6, 4.5.3.15, 4.5.3.16.
PRITCHARD, James – 5.2.6.10, 5.2.6.11.
PROBERT, John Charles Cripps – 1.2.2.6, 1.3.4.6, 1.4.3.3, 5.1.3.9.
PROSSER, David Samuel – 5.2.1.1.
PURCELL, William Ernest – 7.2.2.4.
PYKE, Richard – 6.2.2.5, 6.2.2.6, 6.2.5.4, 6.2.7.1, 6.2.7.2, 6.2.7.3.

QUEEN, Louise L. – 2.2.3.2*, 2.2.18.10*, 2.3.6.3*.

RACK, Henry Derman – 1.1.1.15, 1.2.1.22, 2.8.4.13, 4.1.2.16, 4.1.2.17, 4.3.5.3.
RADFORD, G. Elizabeth – 7.2.2.5.
RAIMO, John William – 2.1.2.14.
RAKESTRAW, Robert Vincent – 2.5.3.18.
RAMAGE, Ian – 2.2.10.8.
RANDOLPH, Jerry Ralph – 2.2.8.7.
RATLEDGE, Wilbert Harold – 4.5.2.4.
RATTENBURY, John Ernest – 2.1.1.23, 2.2.9.11, 2.6.2.18, 2.6.5.6.
RAWLINSON, Arthur – 4.1.3.15.
RAYMOND, Allan – 2.8.1.33.
REDFERN, William – 3.1.2.7.
REILLY, William – 4.2.19.2.
REIST, Irwin W. – 2.5.3.19, 2.5.3.20, 2.6.2.19.
RENSHAW, John Rutherford – 2.5.4.4.
RICE, Robert Jay – 3.3.4.5.
RICHARDS, Edgar – 4.4.2.12.
RICHARDS, Glyn – 4.3.1.4.
RICHARDS, Thomas – 2.3.5.10*.
RICHARDSON, Sidney Yearsley – 5.5.1.4.
RICHARDSON, W. F. – 1.2.2.7.
RIGG, James Harrison – 2.6.1.12, 4.2.5.4, 4.2.22.1.
RITSON, Joseph – 5.1.2.14.
RIVERS, Isabel – 2.2.12.11, 2.7.2.18.
ROBBINS, Peggy – 2.2.8.8.
ROBERTS, Gomer Morgan – 2.3.5.6.
ROBERTS, Griffith Thomas – 1.2.3.2, 2.1.3.3, 2.3.5.7, 2.3.5.8.
ROBERTS, John Price – 4.2.10.5.
ROBINS, Matthew – 6.2.2.10.
ROBSON, William J. – 5.1.3.12*.
ROGAL, Samuel J. – 2.1.2.15, 2.1.4.6, 2.2.3.9, 2.2.4.8, 2.2.4.9, 2.2.5.12,
    2.2.11.6, 2.2.11.7, 2.2.11.8, 2.2.12.12, 2.2.13.6, 2.2.17.10, 2.2.17.11,
    2.2.19.5, 2.4.2.19, 2.6.4.15, 2.6.4.16, 2.6.5.7, 2.8.1.34, 2.8.2.29, 2.8.2.30,
    2.8.3.9, 2.8.4.14, 3.1.1.1.
ROGERS, Charles Allen – 2.2.17.12, 2.4.6.14, 2.5.3.21.

SELLERS, Ian – 3.1.2.8, 3.1.3.18, 4.3.1.6.

SEMMEL, Bernard – 2.1.1.13*, 2.1.1.24.

SEMMENS, Bernard L. – 4.1.2.18.

SEYMOUR, Aaron Crossley Hobart – 2.3.6.12.

SHARP, John Alfred – 1.1.1.17.

SHARPLEY, Arthur Edward – 4.2.27.25.

SHAW, A. Mary – 6.2.7.4.

SHAW, George – 5.2.6.13.

SHAW, Thomas – 1.1.2.14*, 1.2.2.8, 2.7.4.3, 6.2.2.7, 6.2.2.8.

SHEARD, Michael Rowland – 3.3.4.6, 5.1.3.10, 5.1.3.11.

SHEILS, William J. – 2.8.4.13*, 4.3.1.1*.

SHELTON, Raymond Larry – 2.4.2.22.

SHEPHERD, Thomas Boswell – 2.6.4.17, 2.8.5.12, 2.8.5.13, 3.5.1.5.

SHERMER, Robert Charles – 2.5.3.23.

SHERRIFF, Collin Bedford – 2.3.11.15.

SHERWIN, Oscar – **2.2.17.14.**

SHIMIZU, Mitsuo – 2.4.8.7.

SHIPLEY, David Clark – 2.3.3.16, 2.5.3.24, 2.7.2.21.

SHREWSBURY, John Vincent Brainerd – 4.2.27.26.

SIL, Narasingha Prosad – 2.8.1.35.

SIMON, John Smith – 2.1.1.25, 2.2.6.36, 2.2.6.37, 2.2.6.38, 2.2.6.39, 2.2.6.40, 2.2.10.9, 2.2.15.6, 2.4.2.23, 2.7.1.2, 2.7.2.22, 4.1.2.19, 4.5.1.17, 5.1.2.16, 6.1.1.6, 6.2.2.9, 6.3.1.6, 6.3.1.7, 6.3.1.8, 6.3.1.9, 6.3.1.10, 6.3.1.11.

SIMPSON, John – 5.2.2.6.

SIMPSON, William John Sparrow – 2.9.4.7.

SKINNER, John William – 4.5.3.19.

SLAATTE, Howard Alexander – 2.3.3.17, 2.5.1.38.

SLATER, A. P. L. – 4.5.3.20.

SLUGG, Josiah Thomas – 4.5.3.21.

SMART, Henry Thomas – 4.2.9.2, 4.2.9.3.

SMITH, Alfred Owen – 4.2.27.23*.

SMITH, Benjamin – 2.1.2.18.

SMITH, George – 4.1.2.20.

SMITH, Harmon Lee – 2.5.5.9.

SMITH, Henry – 6.1.4.2, 6.3.10.1, 6.4.1.2*.

SMITH, James Weldon – 2.5.3.25.

SMITH, Mary Ann – 4.2.8.9, 4.2.27.27.

SMITH, Neil Gregor – 2.2.11.9.

SMITH, Samuel – 5.1.2.17.

SMITH, Timothy Lawrence – 2.2.15.7, 2.4.2.24, 2.5.6.10, 2.5.7.35, 2.5.7.36, 2.6.5.9.

SMITH, Warren Thomas – 2.2.8.10, 2.9.5.7.

SMITH, William – 4.1.6.8.

SNOW, Michael Lawrence – 2.9.2.11.

SNYDER, Howard Albert – 2.6.1.15, 2.6.1.16.

SOMMER, Carl Ernst – 2.3.3.18, 2.3.3.19, 2.4.4.9.

SOMMER, E. F. – 2.2.5.13.

SOMMER, Johann Wilhelm Ernst – **2.8.2.32.**

TENNEY, Mary Alice – 2.2.14.8.

THOMAS, Antony Charles – 4.5.3.24.

THOMAS, David Hubert – 4.5.3.25.

THOMAS, Edward – 6.1.6.6.

THOMAS, Hilah Frances – 2.2.3.2*, 2.2.18.10*, 2.3.6.3*, 2.7.3.5*.

THOMAS, Hugh – 1.4.4.3.

THOMAS, John A. – 7.3.3.3.

THOMAS, Wilhelm – 2.5.7.39.

THOMPSON, Claude H. – 2.3.3.21.

THOMPSON, David Decamp – 2.8.2.33.

THOMPSON, Douglas Weddell – 7.2.2.7.

THOMPSON, Edgar Wesley – 2.2.7.13, 2.7.2.23, 2.7.2.24, 2.7.2.25.

THOMPSON, Edward Palmer – 3.4.1.22.

THOMPSON, John Day – 5.1.2.18.

THOMPSON, Richard Walker – 2.3.8.3.

THOMPSON, Rosalie Budgett – 4.2.27.29.

THOMSON, Arthur Alexander – 7.2.3.1*.

THORBURN, Donald Burns – 3.5.1.6.

THORNE, James – 6.2.2.10, 6.2.5.5.

THORNE, John – 6.2.5.6.

THORNE, Roger Frank Sidney – 1.1.1.20, 6.2.3.2.

THORNE, Samuel Ley – 6.2.5.7, 6.2.5.8, 6.2.5.9.

TICE, Frank – 1.2.2.10.

TIDBALL, Derek John – 3.3.4.7.

TODD, Janet – 2.6.4.13.

TODD, John Murray – 2.4.4.11.

TONKS, William C. – 5.1.3.13.

TOWLSON, Clifford William – 2.4.5.18, 4.5.3.29*.

TOWNS, Elmer L. – 2.8.3.11.

TOWNSEND, James A. – 2.5.6.13.

TOWNSEND, Michael Jonathan – 2.6.4.18.

TOWNSEND, William John – 1.1.1.22*, 1.2.5.5*, 2.1.1.3*, 2.1.1.12*, 2.2.6.7*, 2.6.4.23*, 3.3.5.1*, 4.1.2.9*, 4.1.2.13*, 5.1.2.9*, 6.1.1.3*, 6.1.5.4, 6.1.6.7, 6.4.1.3.

TRAVIS, James – 5.2.6.14.

TREFFRY, Richard – 4.2.3.2.

TREFFRY, William – 6.4.1.2*.

TRIPP, David Howard – 1.3.4.7, 3.2.2.5, 7.3.2.2.

TSOUMAS, George J. – 2.7.2.26, 2.7.2.27.

TUCKER, Robert Leonard – 2.9.4.8.

TUCKWELL, Miriam – see ELLIS, Miriam.

TURNER, Bryan Stanley – 1.5.1.1, 7.1.2.4.

TURNER, George Allen – 2.4.2.25.

TURNER, John Munsey – 1.6.1.1, 2.5.1.40, 3.1.2.10, 3.1.2.11, 3.4.1.23, 4.6.2.4, 5.1.2.19.

TURRELL, Walter John – 2.8.4.20.

TUTTLE, Robert Gregory – 2.2.6.43, 2.4.4.12.

TYERMAN, Luke – 2.2.2.2, 2.2.6.44, 2.3.3.22, 2.3.7.6, 2.3.11.16.

WARNER, Wellman Joel – 2.8.2.34.

WATKINS, Owen Spencer – 4.4.5.12.

WATMOUGH, Abraham – 2.1.2.23.

WATSON, Aaron – 5.2.10.2.

WATSON, David Lowes – 2.5.4.6, 2.6.8.4.

WATSON, F. E. – 4.5.3.27.

WATSON, John Richard – 2.7.2.18*.

WATSON, Kathleen – 3.5.1.7.

WATSON, Philip Saville – 2.4.2.26, 2.5.7.43.

WATSON, Richard – 2.2.6.48.

WEARMOUTH, Robert Featherstone – 2.1.1.30, 2.7.1.4, 3.1.2.13, 3.1.2.14, 3.4.1.24, 3.4.1.25, 3.4.1.26.

WEATHERHEAD, Andrew Kingsley – 7.2.2.9.

WEDGWOOD, Julia – 2.1.1.31.

WEINSTEIN, Alfred Abraham – 2.8.4.21.

WEISSBACH, Jürgen – 2.5.1.42.

WELCH, Barbara Ann – 2.6.4.20.

WELCH, Charles Edwin – 2.1.1.32.

WELLER, John Christopher – 3.1.3.20.

WELLS, Raymond James – 4.2.8.10.

WERNER, Julia Stewart – 5.1.2.21.

WESLEY, Charles – 2.2.4.11, 2.2.20.11, 2.2.20.12, 2.6.4.21, 2.6.4.22, 2.8.1.38.

WESLEY, John – 2.1.3.4, 2.2.4.11, 2.2.6.49, 2.2.12.15, 2.2.13.8, 2.2.13.9, 2.2.13.10, 2.2.14.9, 2.2.15.8, 2.2.15.9, 2.2.16.13, 2.2.16.14, 2.3.3.23, 2.6.3.13, 2.6.4.22, 2.8.4.22, 2.9.6.1.

WESLEYAN PREACHER, A – 4.2.8.11, 4.2.18.2.

WEST, Nathaniel – 2.5.4.7.

WEST, Robert Athow – 4.2.1.4.

WEST, William Morris Schumm – 2.9.5.8.

WESTBROOK, Francis Brotherton – 1.3.5.7, 2.6.7.6.

WHALING, Frank – 2.2.4.11*.

WHITE, James Floyd – 2.6.3.13*.

WHITED, Harold Vaughn – 2.2.15.10.

WHITEFIELD, George – 2.3.11.17.

WHITEHEAD, John – 2.2.6.5, 2.2.6.50.

WHITELEY, David – 3.3.2.3*.

WHITEMAN, Anne – 4.4.2.15*.

WHITNEY, Arthur Percy – 2.9.1.5, 4.5.1.20.

WIGGINS, James Bryan – 2.3.3.24, 2.3.3.25.

WILBERFORCE, David L. – 2.4.1.12.

WILCOXON, C. D. – 2.8.4.23.

WILDER, Franklin – 2.2.2.3, 2.2.3.11, 2.2.20.13, 2.8.4.24.

WILDER, James Simpson – 2.7.3.11.

WILKES, Arthur – 5.1.2.22.

WILKINSON, John F. – 2.1.2.24.

WILKINSON, John Thomas – 3.1.2.15, 3.1.2.16, 5.2.2.8, 5.2.2.9, 5.2.3.5, 5.2.3.6, 5.2.9.1*, 5.2.9.4.

WILKINSON, Thomas Gordon – 3.4.3.4.

YOUNG, John – 6.3.8.3.
YOUNG, Kenneth – 3.1.2.17.

ZEHRER, Karl – 2.4.5.21.

Index of Documents and Source Material

This index is designed as a guide to the main contents of the collection of documents and source material. It does not cover editorial matter or incidental references to persons and places. Reference is normally to Wesleyanism unless otherwise indicated.